Basic Standard Deduction An

Filing Status	Standard Deduction Amount	
	2013	2014
Single	$ 6,100	$ 6,200
Married, filing jointly	12,200	12,400
Surviving spouse	12,200	12,400
Head of household	8,950	9,100
Married, filing separately	6,100	6,200

Amount of Each Additional Standard Deduction

Filing Status	2013	2014
Single	$1,500	$1,550
Married, filing jointly	1,200	1,200
Surviving spouse	1,200	1,200
Head of household	1,500	1,550
Married, filing separately	1,200	1,200

Personal and Dependency Exemption

2013	2014
$3,900	$3,950

Income Tax Rates—Corporations

Taxable Income	Tax Rate
Not over $50,000	15%
Over $50,000 but not over $75,000	25%
Over $75,000 but not over $100,000	34%
Over $100,000 but not over $335,000	39%*
Over $335,000 but not over $10,000,000	34%
Over $10,000,000 but not over $15,000,000	35%
Over $15,000,000 but not over $18,333,333	38%**
Over $18,333,333	35%

*Five percent of this rate represents a phaseout of the benefits of the lower tax rates on the first $75,000 of taxable income.
**Three percent of this rate represents a phaseout of the benefits of the lower tax rate (34% rather than 35%) on the first $10 million of taxable income.

THOMSON REUTERS
CHECKPOINT®

3 Simple Ways CHECKPOINT® Helps You Make Sense of All Those Taxes.

- Find what you are looking for quickly and easily online with Checkpoint

- A comprehensive collection of primary tax law, cases and rulings, along with analytical insight you simply can't find anywhere else

- Checkpoint has built-in productivity tools such as calculators to make research more efficient – a resource more tax pros use than any other

Titles that include Checkpoint Student Edition

- **Hoffman/Smith,** *South-Western Federal Taxation: Individual Income Taxes, 2015 Edition*

- **Hoffman/Raabe/Maloney/Young/Smith,** *South-Western Federal Taxation: Corporations, Partnerships, Estates & Trusts, 2015 Edition*

- **Hoffman/Maloney/Raabe/Young,** *South-Western Federal Taxation: Comprehensive Volume, 2015 Edition*

- **Smith/Raabe/Maloney/Young,** *South-Western Federal Taxation: Essentials of Taxation: Individuals and Business Entities, 2015 Edition*

- **Murphy/Higgins,** *Concepts in Federal Taxation, 2015 Edition*

IMPORTANT INFORMATION

The purchase of this textbook includes access to Thomson Reuters Checkpoint Student Edition for a 6-month duration.

To log in visit **http://checkpoint.thomsonreuters.com**
You will be asked to supply a User ID and Password. Please use the following:

USER ID: CEN14-2888

PASSWORD: CEN14-2888

PLEASE NOTE: If you have purchased a used copy of this text, the User ID and Password may have already been used. A new User ID and Password may be obtained by purchasing a new copy of this text.

 THOMSON REUTERS

ISBN-13: 978-1-285-43891-7 • ISBN-10: 1-285-43891-4

"★★★★★"
CPA Practice Advisor
2004, 2005, 2006, 2007, 2008, 2009, 2010, 2011, 2012, 2013

For technical support please visit
www.cengage.com/support

SOUTH-WESTERN
FEDERAL TAXATION

ESSENTIALS OF TAXATION: INDIVIDUALS AND BUSINESS ENTITIES

2015 *EDITION*

GENERAL EDITORS

James E. Smith
Ph.D., CPA
College of William and Mary

William A. Raabe
Ph.D., CPA
University of Wisconsin-Whitewater

David M. Maloney
Ph.D., CPA
University of Virginia

James C. Young
Ph.D., CPA
Northern Illinois University

CENGAGE
Learning®

Australia • Brazil • Japan • Korea • Mexico • Singapore • Spain • United Kingdom • United States

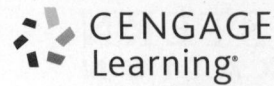

South-Western Federal Taxation: Essentials of Taxation: Individuals and Business Entities, 2015 Edition

James E. Smith, William A. Raabe, David M. Maloney, James C. Young

Product Director: Rob Dewey

Senior Product Manager: Sharon Oblinger

Associate Content Developer: Tristann Jones

Product Assistant: A.J. Smiley

Marketing Director: Natalie King

Associate Marketing Manager:
    Courtney Doyle Chambers

Senior Marketing Coordinator: Eileen Corcoran

Media Developer: Lysa Kosins

Content Digitization Project Manager:
    Nikkita Kendrick

Manufacturing Planner: Doug Wilke

Senior Content Project Manager: Tim Bailey

Production Service: Cenveo Publisher Services

Senior Art Director: Michelle Kunkler

Cover and Internal Designer: Kim Torbeck/
    Imbue Design

Cover Image: © Dennis Flaherty/Getty Images, Inc.

Intellectual Property:

    Analyst: Christina Ciaramella

    Project Manager: Amber Hosea

Unless otherwise noted, all items © Cengage Learning.

All tax forms within the text are: Source: Internal Revenue Service.

Student Edition ISBN 13: 978-1-285-43980-8
Student Edition ISBN 10: 1-285-43980-5
Student Edition with CD ISBN 13: 978-1-285-43974-7
Student Edition with CD ISBN 10: 1-285-43974-0

ISSN: 1544-3590
2015 Annual Edition

Cengage Learning
200 First Stamford Place, 4th Floor
Stamford, CT 06902
USA

Cengage Learning is a leading provider of customized learning solutions with office locations around the globe, including Singapore, the United Kingdom, Australia, Mexico, Brazil, and Japan. Locate your local office at: **www.cengage.com/global**

Cengage Learning products are represented in Canada by Nelson Education, Ltd.

To learn more about Cengage Learning Solutions, visit **www.cengage.com**

Purchase any of our products at your local college store or at our preferred online store **www.cengagebrain.com**

Authors for the South-Western Federal Taxation Series

James H. Boyd
Ph.D., CPA
Arizona State University

Steven C. Dilley
J.D., Ph.D., CPA
Michigan State University

Mark B. Persellin
Ph.D., CPA, CFP®
St. Mary's University

Debra L. Sanders
Ph.D., CPA
Washington State University, Vancouver

D. Larry Crumbley
Ph.D., CPA
Louisiana State University

William H. Hoffman, Jr.
J.D., Ph.D., CPA
University of Houston

Boyd C. Randall
J.D., Ph.D.
Brigham Young University

W. Eugene Seago
J.D., Ph.D., CPA
Virginia Polytechnic Institute and State University

Preface

Committed to Educational Success

South-Western Federal Taxation (SWFT) is the most trusted and best-selling series in college taxation. We are focused exclusively on providing the most useful, comprehensive, and up-to-date tax texts, online study aids, tax preparation tools, and research tools to help instructors and students succeed in their tax courses and beyond.

SWFT is a comprehensive package of teaching and learning materials, significantly enhanced each edition to meet instructor and student needs and to add overall value to learning taxation.

Essentials of Taxation: Individuals and Business Entities, 2015 Edition provides a dynamic learning experience inside and outside of the classroom. Built with resources and tools that have been identified as the most important, our complete learning system provides options for students to achieve success.

Essentials of Taxation: Individuals and Business Entities, 2015 Edition provides accessible, comprehensive, and authoritative coverage of the relevant tax code and regulations as they pertain to the individual taxpayer, as well as coverage of all major developments in Federal Taxation.

Formerly titled *Taxation of Business Entities*, this text is an ideal fit for programs that offer only one course in taxation. After conducting extensive market research on how the text was actually being used, the table of contents was revised for the 2015 Edition to provide for greater integration of tax concepts that are relevant to the individual taxpayer. In addition, the text now follows how instructors normally teach taxation, covering individual taxation first, and then corporate and other business entity taxation. The **Tax Planning Framework** available throughout the text helps users fit tax planning strategies into an innovative pedagogical framework, making this text perfect for introductory taxation courses.

In revising the 2015 Edition, we focused on:

- **Accessibility. Clarity. Substance.** The text authors and editors made this their mantra as they revised the 2015 edition. Coverage has been streamlined to make it more accessible to students. Difficult concepts have been clarified, all without losing the substance that makes up the *South-Western Federal Taxation* series.

- **CengageNOW as a complete learning system.** Cengage understands that digital learning solutions are central to the classroom. Through sustained research, we continually refine our learning solutions in CengageNOW to meet evolving student and instructor needs. CengageNOW fulfills learning and course management needs by offering a personalized study plan, video lectures, auto-graded homework, auto-graded tests, and a full eBook with features and advantages that address common challenges.

Leadership, Innovation, and Service in the Ever-Changing Tax Law Environment

LEADERSHIP

South-Western Federal Taxation leads the market in the number of instructors and students using its resources. And it leads the way in its *authoritative and comprehensive coverage* of the latest taxation practices and legislation presented in a student-accessible manner.

INNOVATION

South-Western Federal Taxation offers students and instructors the *broadest and most innovative* selection of learning and teaching solutions available:

- **CengageNOW™** is a powerful course management and online homework and learning tool that provides robust control and customization for instructors, coupled with a unique learning process for students. Together, CengageNOW's features combine to meet individual, class, departmental, and school outcomes. More than 500,000 students use CengageNOW every year!
- **Checkpoint® Student Edition** from Thomson Reuters offers career-bound students use of *true professional tax research software* to build familiarity with the Tax Code and its various administrative and judicial interpretations.*
- **H&R Block®** facilitates tax preparation practice using one of the industry's most popular tax preparation software packages.

Each of these innovative *South-Western Federal Taxation* assets helps students learn and retain with customized homework help and feedback while introducing them to the professional tools that will make them successful in their future careers.

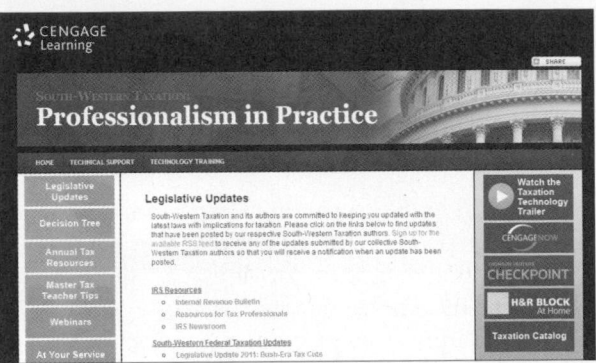

DEDICATED, ONGOING SERVICE FOR INSTRUCTORS

The South-Western Taxation Community website at **www.cengage.com/community/tax** is a *one-stop destination* for instructors' complete teaching and support needs. In addition to the Legislative Updates page shown above, instructors can access a host of other instructional materials, technology demos, annual resources, support, and training.

- Sign up for **The South-Western Taxation Annual Resources Program** and indicate which textbook you use. Upon registration, we promise to send your textbook and instructor resources automatically as they are published. This convenient service will save you time!
- **Legislative Updates** are regularly available by visiting the Community Site or simply by subscribing to our RSS feed that will link out to the newly posted updates.
- View demonstrations of the **technology products** offered with the series.
- Find **Technical Support and Training** when and how you need it.

Learning Tools and Features to Help Students Make the Connection

*S*outh-Western Federal Taxation's Essentials of Taxation: Individuals and Business Entities, 2015 Edition includes *enhanced learning features* designed to take students beyond the usual textbook experience to a deeper understanding of the real application of tax concepts and tax law.

*Not available with the Professional Editions of South-Western Federal Taxation.

SEEING THE BIG PICTURE

Taxation comes alive at the start of each chapter. **The Big Picture: Tax Solutions for the Real World** is a glimpse into the lives, families, careers, and tax situations of typical business or individual filers. Each Big Picture case asks students to apply what they will learn in the upcoming chapter to develop the best tax solution to these real-life dilemmas.

At least four examples per chapter tie back to the Big Picture. This helps eliminate confusion for students by providing a more consistent application of the data and providing a tax story that spans the whole chapter.

Finally, to solidify student comprehension, each chapter concludes with a **Refocus on the Big Picture** summary and tax planning scenario. These scenarios apply the concepts and topics from the chapter in a reasonable and professional way.

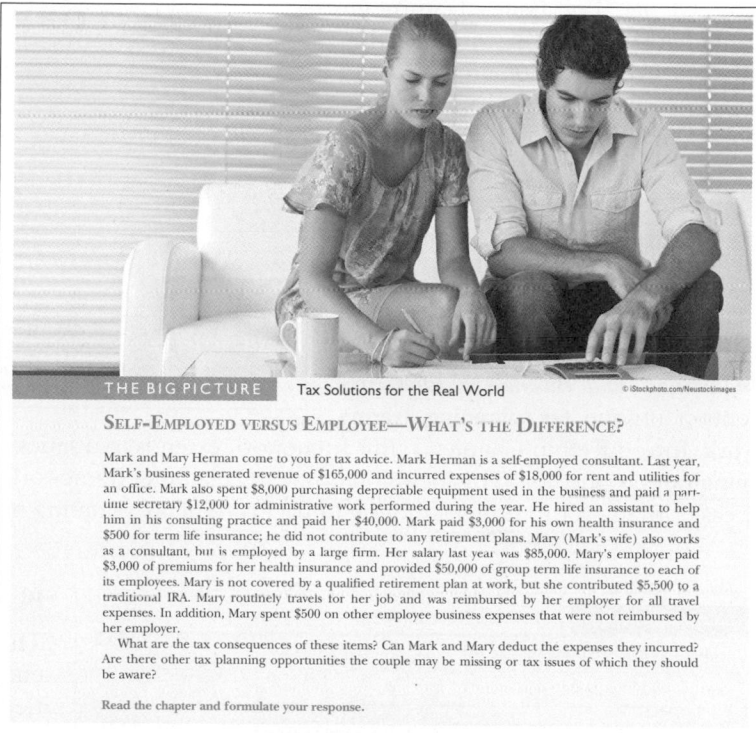

THE BIG PICTURE   Tax Solutions for the Real World   © iStockphoto.com/Neustockimages

SELF-EMPLOYED VERSUS EMPLOYEE—WHAT'S THE DIFFERENCE?

Mark and Mary Herman come to you for tax advice. Mark Herman is a self-employed consultant. Last year, Mark's business generated revenue of $165,000 and incurred expenses of $18,000 for rent and utilities for an office. Mark also spent $8,000 purchasing depreciable equipment used in the business and paid a part-time secretary $12,000 for administrative work performed during the year. He hired an assistant to help him in his consulting practice and paid her $40,000. Mark paid $3,000 for his own health insurance and $500 for term life insurance; he did not contribute to any retirement plans. Mary (Mark's wife) also works as a consultant, but is employed by a large firm. Her salary last year was $85,000. Mary's employer paid $3,000 of premiums for her health insurance and provided $50,000 of group term life insurance to each of its employees. Mary is not covered by a qualified retirement plan at work, but she contributed $5,500 to a traditional IRA. Mary routinely travels for her job and was reimbursed by her employer for all travel expenses. In addition, Mary spent $500 on other employee business expenses that were not reimbursed by her employer.

What are the tax consequences of these items? Can Mark and Mary deduct the expenses they incurred? Are there other tax planning opportunities the couple may be missing or tax issues of which they should be aware?

Read the chapter and formulate your response.

MAKING THE CONNECTION

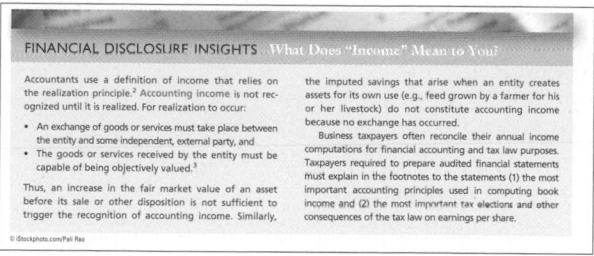

FINANCIAL DISCLOSURE INSIGHTS   What Does "Income" Mean to You?

Accountants use a definition of income that relies on the realization principle.[2] Accounting income is not recognized until it is realized. For realization to occur:

- An exchange of goods or services must take place between the entity and some independent, external party, and
- The goods or services received by the entity must be capable of being objectively valued.[3]

Thus, an increase in the fair market value of an asset before its sale or other disposition is not sufficient to trigger the recognition of accounting income. Similarly,

the imputed savings that arise when an entity creates assets for its own use (e.g., feed grown by a farmer for his or her livestock) do not constitute accounting income because no exchange has occurred.

Business taxpayers often reconcile their annual income computations for financial accounting and tax law purposes. Taxpayers required to prepare audited financial statements must explain in the footnotes to the statements (1) the most important accounting principles used in computing book income and (2) the most important tax elections and other consequences of the tax law on earnings per share.

© iStockphoto.com/Pali Rao

BRIDGE DISCIPLINE BOXES AND END-OF-CHAPTER QUESTIONS

Bridge Discipline Boxes throughout the text present material and concepts from other disciplines such as economics, financial accounting, and finance. They help to bridge the gap between taxation issues and issues raised in other business courses. **Bridge Discipline Questions,** in the end-of-chapter material, help test these concepts and give students the chance to apply concepts they've learned in the Bridge Discipline boxes.

FINANCIAL DISCLOSURE INSIGHTS

Tax professionals need to understand how taxes affect the income statement and balance sheet. **Financial Disclosure Insights,** appearing throughout the text, use current data about existing taxpayers to highlight book-tax reporting differences, effective tax rates, and trends in reporting conventions. Financial Disclosure Insights help students integrate their financial accounting knowledge with the results of state and Federal tax law. Financial Disclosure Insights help make SWFT's coverage of the role of tax data on financial statements the best in the business.

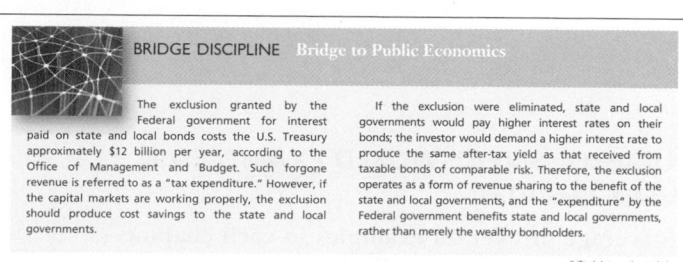

BRIDGE DISCIPLINE   Bridge to Public Economics

The exclusion granted by the Federal government for interest paid on state and local bonds costs the U.S. Treasury approximately $12 billion per year, according to the Office of Management and Budget. Such forgone revenue is referred to as a "tax expenditure." However, if the capital markets are working properly, the exclusion should produce cost savings to the state and local governments.

If the exclusion were eliminated, state and local governments would pay higher interest rates on their bonds; the investor would demand a higher interest rate to produce the same after-tax yield as that received from taxable bonds of comparable risk. Therefore, the exclusion operates as a form of revenue sharing to the benefit of the state and local governments, and the "expenditure" by the Federal government benefits state and local governments, rather than merely the wealthy bondholders.

© iStockphoto.com/enot-poloskun

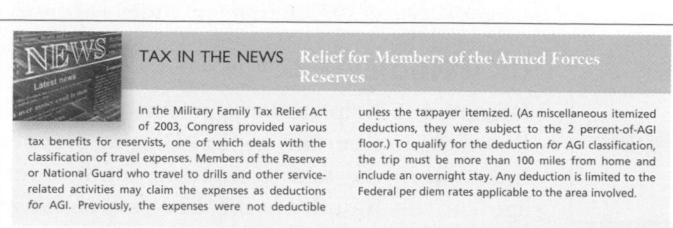

NEWS Latest news   TAX IN THE NEWS   Relief for Members of the Armed Forces Reserves

In the Military Family Tax Relief Act of 2003, Congress provided various tax benefits for reservists, one of which deals with the classification of travel expenses. Members of the Reserves or National Guard who travel to drills and other service-related activities may claim the expenses as deductions for AGI. Previously, the expenses were not deductible

unless the taxpayer itemized. (As miscellaneous itemized deductions, they were subject to the 2 percent-of-AGI floor.) To qualify for the deduction for AGI classification, the trip must be more than 100 miles from home and include an overnight stay. Any deduction is limited to the Federal per diem rates applicable to the area involved.

© iStockphoto.com/Andrey Prokhorov

TAX IN THE NEWS

Drawn from today's business and popular press, **Tax in the News** features enliven class discussions by presenting current issues that illustrate the chapter material and applying them to real life. These plentiful and relevant news items make tax law concepts come to life.

GLOBAL TAX ISSUES

The **Global Tax Issues** feature gives insight into the ways in which taxation is affected by international concerns and illustrates the effects of various events on tax liabilities across the globe.

Exchange for Foreign Property Yields Recognized Recapture Gain

Tangible personal property used in a trade or business may be the subject of a like-kind exchange, and the postponed gain is most likely postponed § 1245 gain. However, tangible personal property used predominantly within the United States cannot be exchanged tax-free for tangible personal property used predominantly outside the United States. Thus, such an exchange would cause recognized gain, and as long as the fair market value of the property given up does not exceed its original cost, all of the gain is § 1245 depreciation recapture gain.

Global Tax Issues

© iStockphoto.com/Andrey Prokhorov

TAX PLANNING FRAMEWORK

To demonstrate the relevance of tax planning for business and individual taxpayers, *Essentials of Taxation: Individuals and Business Entities* presents a unique **tax planning framework**. Introduced in Chapter 1, this framework extends to a series of **Planning Strategies** incorporated throughout the remainder of the text. The inclusion of the tax planning framework, and the planning strategies in each chapter, makes it easier than ever to understand the impact careful tax planning has in today's world.

FIGURE 1.3	General Framework for Income Tax Planning	
Tax Formula	**Tax Planning Strategy**	**Tax Planning Examples**
Income and exclusions	➤ Avoid income recognition.	Compensate employees with nontaxable fringe benefits (see Example 19).
	➤ Postpone recognition of income to achieve tax deferral.	Postpone sale of assets (see Example 20).

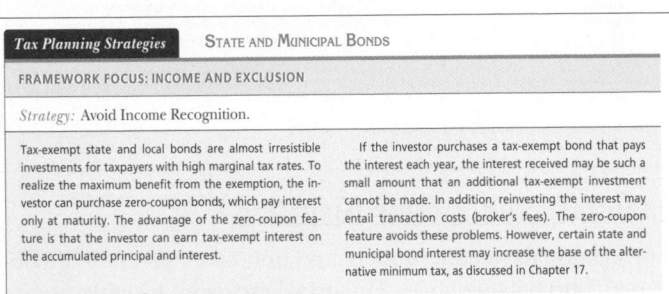

Tax Planning Strategies   STATE AND MUNICIPAL BONDS

FRAMEWORK FOCUS: INCOME AND EXCLUSION

Strategy: Avoid Income Recognition.

Tax-exempt state and local bonds are almost irresistible investments for taxpayers with high marginal tax rates. To realize the maximum benefit from the exemption, the investor can purchase zero-coupon bonds, which pay interest only at maturity. The advantage of the zero-coupon feature is that the investor can earn tax-exempt interest on the accumulated principal and interest.

If the investor purchases a tax-exempt bond that pays the interest each year, the interest received may be such a small amount that an additional tax-exempt investment cannot be made. In addition, reinvesting the interest may entail transaction costs (broker's fees). The zero-coupon feature avoids these problems. However, certain state and municipal bond interest may increase the base of the alternative minimum tax, as discussed in Chapter 17.

PLANNING STRATEGIES

The tax planning framework extends to subsequent chapters as **Tax Planning Strategies boxes** that are tied to the topical coverage of the chapters. Planning Strategies often contain examples to further illustrate the concept for students.

Because some tax planning strategies do not fit neatly into the framework, the text also provides tax planning strategies called **Thinking Outside the Framework**.

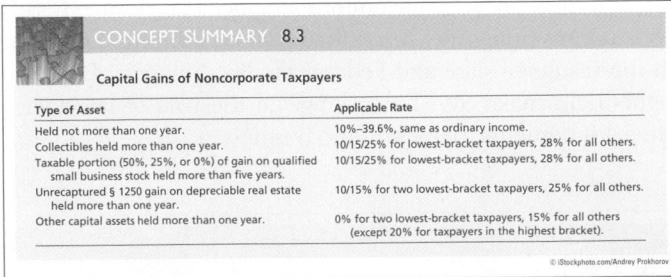

CONCEPT SUMMARY 8.3

Capital Gains of Noncorporate Taxpayers

Type of Asset	Applicable Rate
Held not more than one year.	10%–39.6%, same as ordinary income.
Collectibles held more than one year.	10/15/25% for lowest-bracket taxpayers, 28% for all others.
Taxable portion (50%, 25%, or 0%) of gain on qualified small business stock held more than five years.	10/15/25% for lowest-bracket taxpayers, 28% for all others.
Unrecaptured § 1250 gain on depreciable real estate held more than one year.	10/15% for two lowest-bracket taxpayers, 25% for all others.
Other capital assets held more than one year.	0% for two lowest-bracket taxpayers, 15% for all others (except 20% for taxpayers in the highest bracket).

© iStockphoto.com/Andrey Prokhorov

CONCEPT SUMMARIES

These exhibits within sections of the chapters help students by organizing and summarizing the key concepts in the text using lists, tables, and other pedagogical tools.

NUMEROUS REAL-WORLD EXAMPLES IN EVERY CHAPTER

An **average of over 40 examples in each chapter** use realistic situations to illustrate the complexities of the tax law and allow students to integrate chapter concepts with illustrations and examples.

Example 6

Isabella gives a song she composed to her son. Her son sells the song to a music publisher for $5,000. Her son has a $5,000 ordinary gain from the sale of an ordinary asset unless he elects to treat the gain as a capital gain. If he inherits the song from Isabella, his basis for the song is its fair market value at Isabella's death. In this situation, the song is a capital asset because the son's basis is not related to Isabella's basis for the song (i.e., the song was not a *lifetime* gift).

DIGGING DEEPER

Designed to help students go further in their knowledge of certain topics, **Digging Deeper** links within the text to more in-depth coverage can be found on the book's website at **www.cengage.brain.com**.

In-depth coverage can be found on this book's companion website: **www.cengagebrain.com** | Digging Deeper

© tuulijumala/Shutterstock.com

A Complete Learning System—CengageNOW

CengageNOW for Taxation takes students from motivation to mastery. Built on principles of learning, designed and created hand-in-hand with educators, Cengage Learning digital solutions focus on engagement, taking students through levels of application, analysis, and critical thinking with depth and context unmatched in the market.

CengageNOW elevates thinking by providing superior content designed with the entire student workflow in mind. Students learn more efficiently with the variety of engaging assessment and learning tools. For instructors, CengageNOW provides ultimate control and customization and a clear view into student performance that allows for the opportunity to tailor the learning experience to improve outcomes.

MOTIVATION

Many instructors find that students come to class unmotivated and unprepared. To help with engagement and preparedness, CengageNOW for SWFT offers the following features:

- **"Tell Me More" videos provide a summary of the chapter at a glance.** These videos will help students become familiar with the key terms and concepts presented in each chapter, prior to class lectures.

- **"Tax Drills" test students on key concepts and applications.** With 3 to 5 questions per learning objective, these "quick-hit" questions help students prepare for class lectures or review prior to an exam.

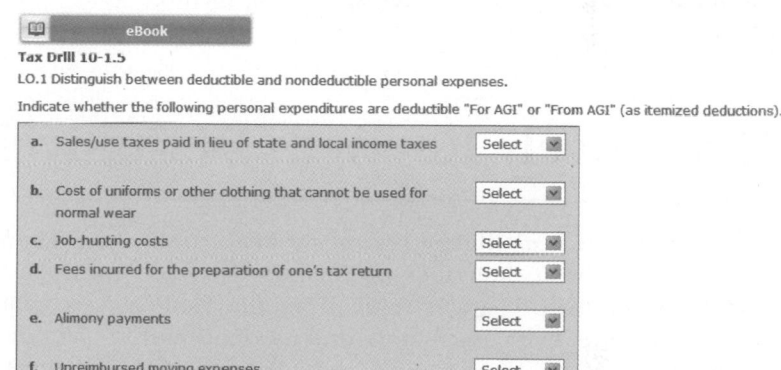

APPLICATION

Students need to learn problem-solving behavior and skills in order to complete taxation problems on their own. However, as students try to work through homework problems, sometimes they become stuck and need guidance. To help reinforce concepts and keep students on the right track, CengageNOW for SWFT offers the following:

- **End-of-chapter homework from the text** is expanded and enhanced to follow the workflow a professional would use to solve various client scenarios. These enhancements better engage students and encourage them to think like tax professionals.

- **Algorithmic versions** of end-of-chapter homework are available for at least 15 problems per chapter.

- **Detailed feedback for each homework question.** Homework questions include enhanced, immediate feedback so students can learn as they go. Levels of feedback include an option for "check my work" prior to submission of an assignment. Then, after submitting an assignment, students receive even more extensive feedback explaining why their answers were incorrect. Instructors can decide how much feedback their students receive and when, including the full solution, if they wish.

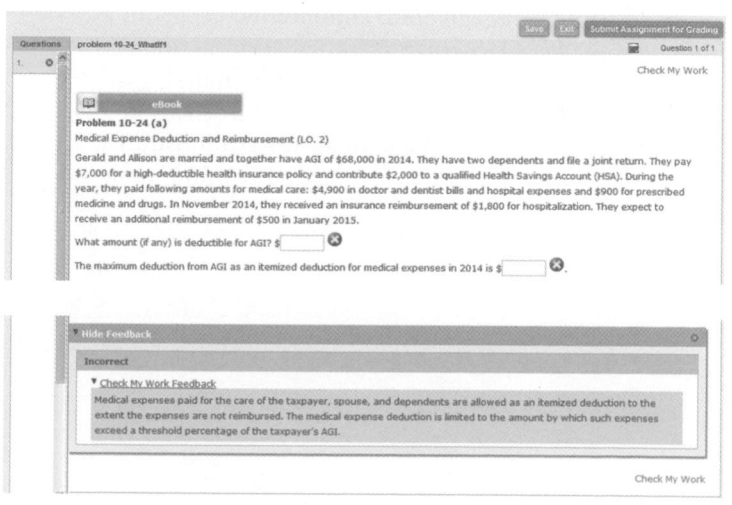

- **"Show Me How" videos walk students step-by-step through the process of solving a problem** from the end-of-chapter material. These videos focus on the more difficult problems that tie multiple learning objectives together.

- Built-in **Test Bank** for online assessment.

- For students needing additional support, CengageNOW's **Personalized Study Plan** is complete with pre-tests and post-tests, an eBook, practice quizzes, and more.

MASTERY

Finally, students need to make the leap from memorizing concepts to actual critical thinking. They need to be able to connect multiple topics and master the material. To help students grasp the big picture of taxation and achieve the end goal of mastery, CengageNOW for SWFT offers the following:

- **"What If" versions of problems** provide students with additional opportunities to practice key taxation concepts and scenarios. These alternate versions allow students to work the same problem multiple times with changing tax attributes. This encourages deeper understanding of the material because students are challenged to use their prior knowledge of the tax situation and critically think through the new attributes to determine how the outcome will change.

CengageNOW Instant Access Code ISBN: 978-1-285-44281-5

Text + CengageNOW Bundle ISBN: 978-1-305-25036-9

Extensively Revised. Definitively Up to Date.

Each year the *South-Western Federal Taxation* series is updated with thousands of changes to each text. Some of these changes result from the feedback we receive from instructors and students in the form of reviews, focus groups, web surveys, and personal e-mail correspondence to our authors and team members. Other changes come from our careful analysis of the evolving tax environment. **We make sure that every tax law change relevant to the introductory taxation course was considered, summarized, and fully integrated into the revision of text and supplementary materials.**

The *South-Western Federal Taxation* community website (**www.cengage.com/community/tax**) offers immediate access to current information as soon as it is available. Instructors and students may log on and learn about the most recent tax information—including the Code and Regulations, administrative interpretations, new court rulings, and other newsworthy items.

The *South-Western Federal Taxation* authors have made every effort to keep specific chapters up to date and accurate. All chapters of *Essentials of Taxation: Individuals and Business Entities* contain the following general changes for the 2015 Edition.

- Revised numerous materials as the result of changes caused by indexing of statutory amounts.
- Revised Problem Materials.
- Updated Tax in the News items with coverage of recent events.
- Updated Chapter Outlines to provide an overview of the material and to make it easier to locate specific topics.
- Revised Financial Disclosure Insights and Global Tax Issues as to current developments.
- Streamlined chapter content (where applicable) to clarify material and make it easier for students to understand.

Chapter 1
- Updated materials concerning the computation of estate, gift, and Social Security taxes.
- Updated statistics about taxpayers at which income levels pay how much Federal income tax. Incorporated the additional taxes to support the health care system in this analysis.
- Updated statistics about national taxes on gasoline and cigarette consumption.
- Updated statistics about Federal budget receipts and tax collections, and about Tax Freedom Day.
- Added a Digging Deeper item about local taxes.
- Updated statistics as to individual and business tax expenditures.
- Revised materials as to the Federal and state income taxation of same-sex marriages.

Chapter 2
- Replaced Big Picture materials and discussions.
- Updated statistics as to annual Federal tax expenditures and the volume of the U.S. tax laws.
- Added a Tax in the News item about Abraham Lincoln's tax payments.
- Added a Digging Deeper item about Tax Court decisions.
- Clarified the facts of the case study illustrating how the tax research process works.
- Updated the listing of commercial income tax services and professional tax journals.
- Updated material about the placement of tax research cases on the CPA examination.

Chapter 3
- Streamlined the chapter introductory material.
- Added comments about the importance of tax items in the SEC material weakness and restatement process.
- Revised comments as to the financial reporting effects of goodwill impairment write-downs.
- Streamlined comments about the effective tax rates of certain U.S. multinational corporations.
- Updated statistics as to items included in Schedule UTP reporting.
- Reorganized materials concerning valuation allowances and their computation.
- Streamlined discussion of financial accounting for tax uncertainties.

Chapter 4
- Revised the facts and taxpayer identities for The Big Picture material.
- Streamlined the chapter introductory discussions.
- Clarified the introductory material as to original issue discount income.
- Streamlined the material concerning income from advance payments for services.
- Updated statistics as to Form 1040 types of reported gross income.
- Updated materials as to the tax rates applicable to dividend income and long-term capital gains.
- Updated the materials concerning income from debt forgiveness on a principal residence, due to a law change.

Chapter 5
- Modified the facts in The Big Picture scenario to make it more realistic.
- Updated the discussion to reflect changes generated by annual indexation and phaseouts.
- Rearranged material on disallowed losses in dealings between related parties to clarify how these situations arise.
- Revised and clarified text and examples throughout the chapter.
- Reorganized depreciation materials—focusing on MACRS and splitting this discussion into a section on the basic rules (including personal property, mid-quarter convention, straight-line election, and real property) followed by a section on special rules (including bonus depreciation, the § 179 expense election, listed property, farm property, leasehold improvements, and the alternative depreciation system).

Chapter 6
- Revised and clarified text and examples throughout the chapter.
- Amplified and clarified the "Tax Shelter Problem."
- Revised and simplified the coverage of the material participation requirements.
- Condensed the discussion of rental activities that are not treated as rental property for purposes of the passive loss rules.
- Added a Tax in the News item concerning the difficulty encountered by a full-time employee qualifying as a real estate professional.

Chapter 7
- Revised and clarified text and examples throughout the chapter.
- Eliminated redundancy of the Recovery of Capital Doctrine coverage, as it was included with other materials in the chapter.
- Updated Tax in the News item related to cost basis reporting.
- Simplified discussion of basis adjustments for gift taxes paid given the rarity of the adjustment.
- Updated Tax in the News item related to the use of eminent domain for nonpublic projects.
- Revised and clarified Concept Summary that lists the replacement property that qualifies to defer recognition of gain.
- Clarified and simplified the material on avoiding gain on the disposition of a "principal residence."

Chapter 8
- Revised and clarified text and examples throughout the chapter.
- Revised Concept Summary 8.4 and linked the summary to chapter materials.
- Reduced the coverage of § 1250 depreciation recapture due to its limited application.
- Added a new Tax in the News item on the cost segregation of buildings.

Chapter 9 (formerly first half of Chapter 16)
- Added a new Big Picture scenario to accompany the discussion in the chapter.

- Updated materials to reflect inflation indexation.
- Revised and clarified text and examples throughout the chapter.
- Added information on filing requirements for same-sex marriages.
- Distinguished between same-sex marriages and domestic partnerships and civil unions.

Chapter 10 (formerly second half of Chapter 16)
- Modified the factual pattern of The Big Picture example in order to clarify the key issues involved.
- Clarified the tax differences between property settlements, alimony, and child support.
- Made necessary adjustments for annual indexation required by tax law.
- Clarified the discussion relating to capital expenditures incurred for medical purposes.
- Reorganized and expanded the discussion of the limitation on the deduction for investment interest.
- Revised and clarified text and examples throughout the chapter.

Chapter 11 (formerly Chapter 17)
- Revised and clarified text and examples throughout the chapter.
- Updated feature boxes throughout the chapter for currency.
- Added new Tax in the News item about working-from-home trends.
- Updated Tax in the News item about the tax gap.
- Revised the Social Security coverage (both as an employee and as a self-employed taxpayer) to reflect the increase in the statutory ceiling from $113,700 in 2013 to $117,000 in 2014.
- Clarified that the income from a hobby and the related deductions are reported separately on the tax return.

Chapter 12 (formerly Chapter 9)
- Updated text and problem materials to reflect indexation.
- Further clarified the tax differences in the tax treatment of individual and corporate taxpayers.
- Enhanced The Big Picture examples to make them more realistic.
- Added clarity to the text discussion and revised and combined various illustrative examples.

Chapter 13 (formerly Chapter 10)
- Updated statistics as to the amount of annual corporate distributions and the entities that make the distributions.
- Clarified material as to what makes up a constructive dividend, especially concerning shareholder loans.
- Revised planning strategies concerning stock redemptions.

Chapter 14 (formerly Chapter 11)
- Updated materials about partners/members of pass-through entities, the businesses that they operate, and their profitability.
- Added comments about the breadth of the use of pass-through entities in the U.S. economy.

- Revised materials about filing requirements for the Form 1065.
- Reorganized Concept Summary materials and placement.
- Clarified terminology as to the initial costs of an entity.
- Clarified rules as to the at-risk limitation on pass-through losses.

Chapter 15 (formerly Chapter 12)
- Updated statistics about S corporations, the business that they operate, and their shareholders.
- Clarified materials about who can be an S shareholder.
- Updated requirements for an S corporation to file a Schedule M–3.
- Updated materials about the self-employment income of S shareholders.

Chapter 16 (formerly Chapter 13)
- Updated statistics concerning the size of the U.S. and international economies, exports and imports from the U.S., and overseas investments by U.S. persons.
- Updated statistics as to the combined income tax rates of various countries, including the U.S.
- Expanded materials about how FATCA affects overseas investors and financial institutions.
- Added a discussion about how to measure income repatriations to the U.S. by domestic entities.
- Updated statistics about the use of the foreign tax credit and about the tax returns of non-U.S. persons who generate U.S. taxable income.
- Updated statistics about the tax collections of the U.S. states.
- Streamlined materials about the states' income taxation of telecommuting income.
- Added a Digging Deeper item about income tax apportionment.
- Added a discussion about the ethics of granting local tax incentives to attract new business to an area.

Chapter 17 (formerly Chapter 14)
- Revised and clarified text and examples throughout the chapter.
- Updated feature boxes throughout the chapter for currency.
- Updated Tax in the News item about "nonpayers" due to tax credits.
- Revised AMT calculations for the individual taxpayer to reflect the increase in the statutory amount subject to the 26 percent rate from $175,000 to $182,500 for 2014.
- Discussed the statutory change that has resulted in the AMT calculations now being subject to indexing.

Chapter 18 (formerly Chapter 15)
- Revised and clarified text and examples throughout the chapter.
- Updated feature boxes throughout the chapter for currency.
- Updated text to incorporate the indexation attributable to inflation.

TAX LAW OUTLOOK

From your SWFT Series Editors:
Federal budget deficits and concerns about debt levels and limitations will keep income tax issues at the forefront of Congressional discussions throughout 2014 and 2015. Revenue raisers of all sorts will be considered as Federal budgets are crafted, including those to support the retirement and health care systems. Federal tax treatments of income from overseas sources also may be reviewed. While a comprehensive "tax reform" bill is not likely, there will be serious consideration of various proposals throughout the year involving broad-based tax changes. Expect added pressure to be placed on Congress to extend tax provisions that expired at the end of 2013. Many of the tax provisions that expired in 2013 could be extended to 2014 on a retroactive basis.

Congress may consider Federal corporate tax law changes during 2014–2015, including a decrease in the top tax rate and a move toward a territorial system in taxing income from overseas sources. Tax deferrals for unrepatriated global profits also may receive Congressional attention. State and local governments also have budget problems, and they are looking for new revenue sources, including an adoption of the unitary concept and a broadening of the income and sales/use tax bases.

As these pending issues are resolved, SWFT will keep our readers apprised of the changes. You can find legislative updates at **www.cengage.com/community/tax**.

Supplements Support Students and Instructors

*S*WFT *2015: Essentials of Taxation: Individuals and Business Entities* provides a complete *teaching and learning experience* inside and outside of the classroom. Built around the areas students and instructors have identified as the most important, our integrated supplements package offers more flexibility than ever before to suit the way instructors teach and students learn.

ONLINE AND DIGITAL RESOURCES FOR STUDENTS

CengageNOW is a powerful course management and online homework tool that provides robust instructor control and customization to optimize the student learning experience and meet desired outcomes.

CengageNOW Instant Access Code ISBN:
978-1-285-44281-5

Text + CengageNOW Bundle ISBN:
978-1-305-25036-9

THOMSON REUTERS
CHECKPOINT®

Checkpoint® Student Edition from Thomson Reuters is the leading online tax research database used by professionals. There are three simple ways Checkpoint helps introduce students to tax research:
- Intuitive web-based design makes it fast and simple to find what you need.
- Checkpoint provides a comprehensive collection of primary tax law, cases, and rulings along with analytical insight you simply can't find anywhere else.
- Checkpoint has built-in productivity tools such as calculators to make research more efficient—a resource more tax pros use than any other.

Six months' access to Checkpoint Student Edition (after activation) is packaged automatically with every NEW copy of the textbook.*

*Checkpoint® Student Edition is not available with the Professional Editions of South-Western Federal Taxation texts. For all other editions, all NEW printed copies of the textbook are automatically packaged with Checkpoint Student Edition and H&R Block® tax software. If students purchase the eBook, they will not automatically receive access to Checkpoint Student Edition and H&R Block software. They must purchase the tax media pack offering both of these products. The ISBN is 978-1-285-44270-9 and can be purchased at **www.cengagebrain.com**.

TAX SOFTWARE

More than software: Put the experience of H&R Block tax professionals on your side.

- A step-by-step interview guides you through a customized process.
- Accurate calculations and 100% satisfaction—guaranteed.
- Worry-free Audit Support™ and tax advice from an H&R Block tax professional.

H&R Block® is offered with each NEW copy of the textbook—at no additional cost to students!*

CENGAGE**brain**.com

Students save time and money. Students can use **CengageBrain.com** to select this textbook and access Cengage Learning content, empowering them to choose the most suitable format and giving them a better chance of success in the course. Buy printed materials, eBooks, and digital resources directly through Cengage Learning and save at **CengageBrain.com**.

Online Student Resources

Students can go to **www.cengagebrain.com** for free resources to help them study as well as the opportunity to purchase additional study aids. These valuable free study resources will help students earn a better grade:

- Interactive quizzes are short and auto-graded to help students brush up on important chapter topics.
- Flashcards use chapter terms and definitions to aid students in learning tax terminology for each chapter.
- Online glossary for each chapter provides terms and definitions from the text in alphabetical order for easy reference.
- Learning objectives can be downloaded for each chapter to help keep students on track.
- Tax Tips for the Recent Graduate introduce the college graduate to some common tax considerations that could be beneficial in reducing the dreaded "tax bite."
- Tax Updates provide the most recent tax information and major changes to the tax law.
- Tax tables used in the textbook are downloadable for reference.

PRINTED RESOURCES FOR STUDENTS

Looseleaf Edition (978-1-285-44280-8)

This version provides all the pages of the text in an unbound, three-hole punched format for portability and ease of use. H&R Block® is included with every NEW textbook as well as Checkpoint® Student Edition from Thomson Reuters.*

COMPREHENSIVE SUPPLEMENTS SUPPORT INSTRUCTORS' NEEDS

CengageNOW is a powerful course management and online homework tool that provides robust instructor control and customization to optimize the student learning experience and meet desired outcomes. In addition to the features and benefits mentioned earlier for students, CengageNOW includes these features for instructors:

- **Learning Outcomes Reporting** and the ability to analyze student work from the gradebook. Each exercise and problem is tagged by topic, learning objective, level of difficulty, estimated completion time, and business program standards to allow greater guidance in developing assessments and evaluating student progress.
- **Built-in Test Bank for online assessment**. The test bank files have been imported into CengageNOW so that they may be used as additional homework or tests.

Solutions Manual (978-1-305-08661-6)

Written by the South-Western Federal Taxation editors and authors, the Solutions Manual features solutions arranged in accordance with the sequence of chapter material. A matrix labels the problems by topical coverage; denotes which problems are new, modified, or unchanged from the prior edition. This matrix also references the prior edition's problem number for the unchanged and modified problems.

Solutions to all homework items are tagged with their Estimated Time to Complete, Level of Difficulty, and Learning Objective(s), as well as the AACSB's and AICPA's core competencies—giving instructors more control than ever in selecting homework to match the topics covered. **Available in print and on Instructor Companion Website at http://login .cengage.com.**

Instructor's Guide with Lecture Notes

Prepared by Peter Westort (University of Wisconsin, Oshkosh), the Instructor's Guide contains resources designed to streamline and maximize the effectiveness of your course preparation. The Instructor's Guide contains lecture notes for each chapter, Big Picture integration, and solutions to Research Problems. Lecture notes present an outline the instructor can use in classroom presentation. **Available on Instructor Companion Website at http://login.cengage.com.**

*Checkpoint® Student Edition is not available with the Professional Editions of South-Western Federal Taxation.

PowerPoint® Lectures

Prepared by Donald R. Trippeer (SUNY College at Oneonta), the Instructor PowerPoint Lectures contain more than 30 slides per chapter, including outlines, concept definitions, alternate figures, and key points. **Available on Instructor Companion Website at http://login.cengage.com.**

Test Bank

Written by the *South-Western Federal Taxation* editors and authors, the Test Bank contains approximately 2,200 items and solutions arranged in accordance with the sequence of chapter matcrial. To help the instructor create an exam, a matrix labels the questions by topical coverage—reflecting which are new or modified from the prior edition.

Each test item is tagged with its Estimated Time to Complete, Level of Difficulty, and Learning Objective(s), as well as the AACSB's and AICPA's core competencies—for easier instructor planning and test item selection. For the 2015 edition, the Test Bank will be available in Cengage's new test generator software, Cognero.

Cengage Learning Testing Powered by Cognero is a flexible, online system that allows you to:
- author, edit, and manage test bank content from multiple Cengage Learning solutions
- create multiple test versions in an instant
- deliver tests from your LMS, your classroom, or wherever you want
- Create tests from school, home, the coffee shop—anywhere with Internet access. (No special installs or downloads needed.)

Test Bank files in Word format, along with versions to import into your LMS, available on Instructor Companion Website. Cognero Test Banks available via Single Sign-on account at http://login.cengage.com.

For the 2015 Edition, all course materials are posted online at Cengage.com. Instructors should visit **Cengage.com** and select this textbook to access the online Instructor Resources.
- Solutions Manual
- Instructor's Guide
- Additional Test Bank items and solutions
- Solutions to Tax Return Problems
- PowerPoint Lectures

There will no longer be an Instructor's Resource CD to accompany the SWFT series, as all materials are available via the Instructor Companion Website.

Custom Solutions

Cengage Learning Custom Solutions develops personalized solutions to meet your taxation education needs. Consider the following for your adoption of *South-Western Federal Taxation 2015 Edition*:
- Remove chapters you do not cover or rearrange their order to create a streamlined and efficient text.
- Add your own material to cover new topics or information.
- Add relevance by including sections from Smith's *Internal Revenue Code and Regulations,* Sawyers/Raabe/Whittenburg/Gill's *Federal Tax Research,* or your state's tax laws and regulations.

Acknowledgments

South-Western Federal Taxation continually polls adopters and non-adopters in a variety of ways. We are grateful to these individuals whose comments helped us in the development of the *South-Western Federal Taxation* texts:

Deborah S. Adkins, *Nperspective, LLC*
Amy An, *University of Iowa*
Susan E. Anderson, *Elon University*
Henry M. Anding, *Woodbury University*

Jennifer A. Bagwell, *Ohio University*
George Barbi, *Lanier Technical College*
Terry W. Bechtel, *Texas A&M University-Texarkana*
Chris Becker, *LeMoyne College*
John G. Bell
Tamara Berges, *UCLA*
Ellen Best, *University of North Georgia*
Tim Biggart, *Berry College*
Rachel Birkey, *Illinois State University*
Chris E. Bjornson, *Indiana University Southeast*

Patrick M. Borja, *Citrus College / California State University, Los Angeles*
Dianne H. Boseman, *Nash Community College*
Cathalene Bowler, *University of Northern Iowa*
Darryl L. Brown, *Illinois Wesleyan University*
Timothy G. Bryan, *University of Southern Indiana*
Robert S. Burdette, *Salt Lake Community College*
Lisa Busto, *William Rainey Harper College*

Julia M. Camp, *Providence College*

Al Case, *Southern Oregon University*

Machiavelli W. Chao, *Merage School of Business University of California, Irvine*

Eric Chen, *University of Saint Joseph*

James Milton Christianson, *Southwestern University and Austin Community College*

Ann Burstein Cohen, *University at Buffalo, The State University of New York*

Ciril Cohen, *Fairleigh Dickinson University*

Dixon H. Cooper, *University of Arkansas*

Rick L. Crosser, *Metropolitan State University of Denver*

Susan E.M. Davis, *South University*

Dwight E. Denman, *Newman University*

James M. DeSimpelare, *Ross School of Business at the University of Michigan*

John Dexter, *Northwood University*

Michael P. Donohoe, *University of Illinois at Urbana Champaign*

Deborah A. Doonan, *Johnson & Wales University*

Monique O. Durant, *Central Connecticut State University*

Wayne L. Edmunds, *Virginia Commonwealth University*

Dr. Rafi Efrat, *California State University, Northridge*

Elizabeth C. Ekmekjian, *William Paterson University*

Charles R. Enis, *The Pennsylvania State University*

Frank J. Faber

A. Anthony Falgiani, *University of South Carolina, Beaufort*

Jason Fiske, *Thomas Jefferson School of Law*

John Forsythe, *Eagle Gate College*

Alexander L. Frazin, *University of Redlands*

Carl J. Gabrini, *College of Coastal Georgia*

Kenneth W. Gaines, *East-West University, Chicago, Illinois*

Carolyn Galantine, *Pepperdine University*

Stephen C. Gara, *Drake University*

Sheri Geddes, *Hope College*

Alexander Gelardi, *University of St. Thomas*

Daniel J. Gibbons, *Waubonsee Community College*

Martie Gillen, *University of Florida*

Charles Gnizak, *Fort Hays State University*

Prof. J. David Golub, *Northeastern University*

George G. Goodrich, *John Carroll University*

Dr. Marina Grau, *Houston Community College – Houston TX*

Vicki Greshik, *University of Jamestown College*

Jeffrey S. Haig, *Santa Monica College*

Marcye S. Hampton, *University of Central Florida*

Mary Ann Hofmann, *Appalachian State University*

Susanne Holloway, *Salisbury University*

Susan A. Honig, *Herbert H. Lehman College*

Christopher R. Hoyt, *University of Missouri (Kansas City) School of Law*

Marsha M. Huber, *Youngstown State University*

Carol Hughes, *Asheville-Buncombe Technical Community College*

Dr. Helen Hurwitz, *Saint Louis University*

Richard R. Hutaff, *Wingate University*

Zite Hutton, *Western Washington University*

Debra M. Johnson, *Montana State University Billings*

Brad Van Kalsbeek, *University of Sioux Falls*

John E. Karayan, *Woodbury University*

Cynthia Khanlarian, *Concord University*

Bob Kilpatrick, *Northern Arizona University*

Gordon Klein, *Lecturer, UCLA Anderson School*

Taylor S. Klett, *Sam Houston State University*

Aaron P. Knape, *Peru State College*

Ausher M. B. Kofsky, *Western New England University*

Emil Koren, *Saint Leo University*

Timothy R. Koski, *Middle Tennessee State University*

Sandra Kranz, *Bemidji State University*

Jack Lachman, *Brooklyn COLLEGE-CUNY*

Richard S. Leaman, *University of Denver*

Gene Levitt, *Mayville State University*

Stephanie Lewis, *The Ohio State University*

Teresa Lightner, *University of North Texas*

Sara Linton, *Roosevelt University*

Jane Livingstone, *Western Carolina University*

Mabel Machin, *Florida Institute of Technology*

Maria Alaina Mackin, *ECPI University*

Anne M. Magro, *George Mason University*

Richard B. Malamud, *California State University, Dominguez Hills*

Harold J. Manasa, *Winthrop University*

Barry R. Marks, *University of Houston-Clear Lake*

Anthony Masino, *East Tennessee State University*

Bruce W. McClain, *Cleveland State University*

Allison M. McLeod, *University of North Texas*

Meredith A. Menden, *Southern New Hampshire University*

John G. Miller, *Skyline College*

Lisa Nash, *CPA, MA, Vincennes University*

Mary E. Netzler, *Eastern Florida State College*

Joseph Malino Nicassio, *Westmoreland County Community College*

Mark R. Nixon, *Bentley University*

Garth Novack, *Pantheon Heavy Industries & Foundry*

Claude R. Oakley, *DeVry University, Georgia*

Al Oddo, *Niagara University*

Sandra Owen, *Indiana University – Bloomington*

Vivian J. Paige, *Old Dominion University*

Carolyn Payne, *University of La Verne*

Nichole L Pendleton, *Friends University*

Mark Persellin, *St. Mary's University*

Chuck Pier, *Angelo State University*

Lincoln M. Pinto, *DeVry University*

Sonja Pippin, *University of Nevada – Reno*

Steve Platau, *The University of Tampa*

Walfyette Powell, *Strayer University*

John S. Repsis, *University of Texas at Arlington*

John D. Rice, *Trinity University*

Jennifer Hardwick Robinson, *Trident Technical College*

Shani N. Robinson, *Sam Houston State University*

Ray Rodriguez, *Murray State University*

Richard L. Russell, *Jackson State University*

Robert L. Salyer, *Northern Kentucky University*

Rhoda Sautner, *University of Mary*

Dr. Bunney L. Schmidt, *Keiser University*

Eric D. Schwartz, *LaRoche College*

Tony L. Scott, *Norwalk Community College*

Randy Serrett, *University of Houston – Downtown*

Paul Shoemaker, *University of Nebraska – Lincoln*

Kimberly Sipes, *Kentucky State University*

Georgi Smatrakalev, *Florida Atlantic University*

Leslie S. Sobol, *California State University Northridge*

Marc Spiegel, *University of California, Irvine*

Jason W. Stanfield, *Purdue University*

George Starbuck, *McMurry University*

Teresa Stephenson, *University of Wyoming*

Beth Stetson, *Oklahoma City University*

Frances A. Stott, *Bowling Green State University*

Todd S. Stowe, *Southwest Florida College*

Martin Stub, *DeVry University*

Kent Swift, *University of Montana*

Robert L. Taylor, *Lees-McRae College*

Francis C. Thomas, *Richard Stockton College of New Jersey*

Randall R. Thomas, *Upper Iowa University*

Ronald R. Tidd, *Central Washington University*

James P. Trebby, *Marquette University*

Donald R. Trippeer, *State University of New York College at Oneonta*

James M. Turner, *Georgia Institute of Technology*

Anthony W. Varnon, *Southeast Missouri State University*

Adria Palacios Vasquez, *Texas A&M University – Kingsville*

Terri Walsh, *Seminole State College of Florida*

Marie Wang

Natasha R. Ware, *Southeastern University*

Sarah Webber, *University of Dayton*

Bill Weispfenning, *University of Jamestown (ND)*

Andrew Whitehair

Kent Williams, *Indiana Wesleyan University*

Candace Witherspoon, *Valdosta State University*

Sheila Woods, *DeVry University*

Special Thanks

We are grateful to **James C. Young** (Northern Illinois University) for providing us with his inflation adjustments, which are available prior to the release of the official amounts by the IRS. We also thank **Gregory A. Carnes** (University of North Alabama), **Annette Nellen** (San Jose State University), and **Kristina Zvinakis** (The University of Texas at Austin) for their work as chapter authors. Further thanks go to Annette Nellen who also served as editor for several chapters.

In addition, many thanks to the faculty members who have diligently worked through the problems and test questions to ensure the accuracy of the *South-Western Federal Taxation* homework, solutions manuals, test banks, comprehensive tax form problems, and practice sets. Their comments and corrections helped us focus on clarity as well as accuracy and tax law currency. They are **Sandra A. Augustine**, Hilbert College; **Chris E. Bjornson**, Indiana University Southeast; **Bradrick M. Cripe**, Northern Illinois University; **Eileen Eichler**, Farmingdale State College; **Elizabeth C. Ekmekjian**, William Paterson University; **Stephen C. Gara**, Drake University; **Mary Ann Hofmann**, Appalachian State University; **Debra M. Johnson**, Montana State University, Billings; **Timothy R. Koski**, Middle Tennessee State University; **Sandra J. Kranz**, Bemidji State University; **Stephanie Lewis**, The Ohio State University; **Joan M. Miller**, William Paterson University; **Randall Rinke**, Mercyhurst University – North East Campus; **Ray Rodriguez**, Southern Illinois University, Carbondale; **Lucia N. Smeal**, Georgia State University; **Eric Smith**, Weber State University; **Jason W. Stanfield**, Purdue University; **George R. Starbuck**, McMurry University; **Kent Swift**, University of Montana; **Ralph B. Tower**, Wake Forest University; **Donald R. Trippeer**, State University of New York College at Oneonta; **Raymond Wacker**, Southern Illinois University, Carbondale; **Sarah Webber**, University of Dayton; **Michael Weissenfluh**, Tillamook Bay Community College; **Marvin J. Williams**, University of Houston, Downtown; **Scott A. Yetmar**, Cleveland State University. We are grateful for their efforts.

We are also grateful for the assistance of **Bonnie Hoffman**, CPA who conducted a manuscript review. We also wish to thank Thomson Reuters for its permission to use Checkpoint with the text.

James E. Smith / William R. Raabe / David M. Maloney / James C. Young

2015 *EDITION*

The South-Western Federal Taxation Series

To find out more about these books, go to www.cengagebrain.com.

INDIVIDUAL INCOME TAXES, 2015 EDITION

(HOFFMAN, SMITH, Editors) provides accessible, comprehensive, and authoritative coverage of the relevant tax code and regulations as they pertain to the individual taxpayer, as well as coverage of all major developments in Federal taxation.

(ISBN 978-1-285-43884-9)

CORPORATIONS, PARTNERSHIPS, ESTATES & TRUSTS, 2015 EDITION

(HOFFMAN, RAABE, MALONEY, YOUNG, SMITH, Editors) covers tax concepts as they affect corporations, partnerships, estates, and trusts. The authors provide accessible, comprehensive, and authoritative coverage of relevant tax code and regulations, as well as all major developments in Federal income taxation. This market-leading text is intended for students who have had a previous course in tax. The text includes **Chapter 14, "Taxes on the Financial Statements."**

(ISBN 978-1-285-43829-0)

COMPREHENSIVE VOLUME, 2015 EDITION

(HOFFMAN, MALONEY, RAABE, YOUNG, Editors) Combining the number one individual tax text with the number one corporations text, *Comprehensive Volume, 2015 Edition* is a true winner. An edited version of the first two *South-Western Federal Taxation* textbooks, this book is ideal for undergraduate or graduate levels. This text works for either a one-semester course in which an instructor wants to integrate coverage of individual and corporate taxation or for a two-semester sequence in which the use of only one book is desired.

(ISBN 978-1-285-43963-1)

ESSENTIALS OF TAXATION: INDIVIDUALS AND BUSINESS ENTITIES, 2015 EDITION

(SMITH, RAABE, MALONEY, YOUNG, Editors) emphasizes tax planning and the multidisciplinary aspects of taxation. Formerly titled *Taxation of Business Entities*, this text is designed with the AICPA Model Tax Curriculum in mind, presenting the introductory Federal taxation course from a business entity perspective. Its **Tax Planning Framework** helps users fit tax planning strategies into an innovative pedagogical framework. The text is an ideal fit for programs that offer only one course in taxation where users need to be exposed to individual taxation, as well as corporate and other business entity taxation. This text assumes no prior course in taxation has been taken.

(ISBN 978-1-285-43974-7)

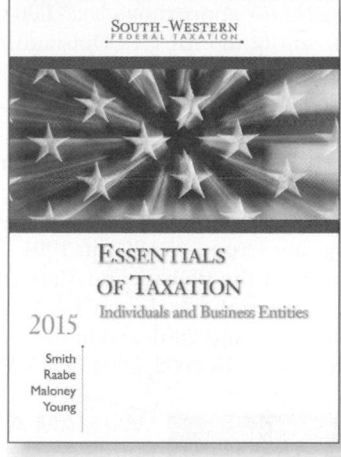

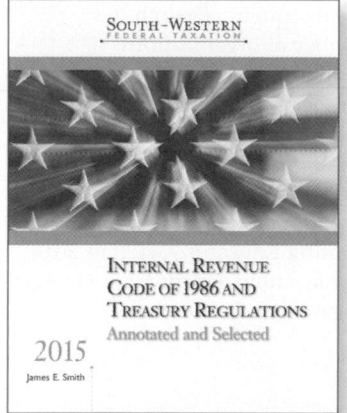

INTERNAL REVENUE CODE OF 1986 AND TREASURY REGULATIONS: *Annotated and Selected, 2015 Edition*

(JAMES E. SMITH) An ideal alternative to the traditional, bulky, and expensive multivolume set of code and regulations, this single-volume reference provides a useful selection of code and regulations sections and clear annotations in the form of editorial summaries that explain, analyze, and cross-reference topics to help students fully understand the intricacies of the tax code. The text is a perfect supplement for any *South-Western Federal Taxation* text as well as an excellent primary text for a Federal taxation course that stresses a code and regulations approach.

2015 Edition coming in July 2014 (ISBN 978-1-285-44149-8)

FEDERAL TAX RESEARCH, 10E

(SAWYERS, RAABE, WHITTENBURG, AND GILL) *Federal Tax Research*, Tenth Edition, offers hands-on tax research analysis and fully covers computer-oriented tax research tools. The tenth edition offers a new chapter on Financial Accounting Research that, when combined with their study of tax research, will equip students with the valuable research skills they need to be marketable to future employers. Also included in this edition is coverage on international tax research, an expanded review of tax ethics, and many new real-life cases to help foster a true understanding of federal tax law.

(ISBN 978-1-285-43939-6)

About the Editors

JAMES E. SMITH is the John S. Quinn Professor of Accounting at the College of William and Mary. He has been a member of the Accounting Faculty for over 30 years. He received his Ph.D. degree from the University of Arizona. Professor Smith has served as a discussion leader for Continuing Professional Education programs for the AICPA, Federal Tax Workshops, and various state CPA societies. He has conducted programs in more than 40 states for approximately 25,000 CPAs. He has been the recipient of the AICPA's Outstanding Discussion Leader Award and the American Taxation Association/Arthur Andersen Teaching Innovation Award. Among his other awards are the Virginia Society of CPAs' Outstanding Accounting Educator Award and the James Madison University's Outstanding Accounting Educator Award. He was the President of the Administrators of Accounting Programs Group (AAPG) in 1991–1992. He was the faculty adviser for the William and Mary teams that received first place in the Andersen Tax Challenge in 1994, 1995, 1997, 2000, and 2001 and in the Deloitte Tax Case Study Competition in 2002, 2004, 2005, 2006, 2008, and 2011.

WILLIAM A. RAABE is the Distinguished Professor of Accounting in the College of Business and Economics of the University of Wisconsin—Whitewater. A graduate of Carroll University (Wisconsin) and the University of Illinois, Dr. Raabe's teaching and research interests include international and multistate taxation, technology in tax education, personal financial planning, and the economic impact of sports teams and fine arts groups. Professor Raabe also writes *Federal Tax Research* and the PricewaterhouseCoopers Tax Case Studies. He has written extensively about book-tax differences in financial reporting. Dr. Raabe has been a visiting tax faculty member for a number of public accounting firms, bar associations, and CPA societies. He has received numerous teaching awards, including the Accounting Educator of the Year award from the Wisconsin Institute of CPAs. He has been the faculty adviser for student teams in the Deloitte Tax Case Competition (national finalists at three different schools) and the PricewaterhouseCoopers Extreme Tax policy competition (national finalist). For more information about Dr. Raabe, visit **BillRaabeTax.com** and BillRaabeTax on YouTube and Twitter.

DAVID M. MALONEY, Ph.D., CPA, is the Carman G. Blough Professor of Accounting Emeritus at the University of Virginia's McIntire School of Commerce. He completed his undergraduate work at the University of Richmond and his graduate work at the University of Illinois at Urbana-Champaign. Upon joining the Virginia faculty in January 1984, Professor Maloney taught Federal taxation in the graduate and undergraduate programs and was a recipient of major research grants from the Ernst & Young and KPMG Foundations. In addition, some of his published work appears in numerous professional journals, including *Journal of Taxation, The Tax Adviser, Tax Notes, Corporate Taxation, Accounting Horizons, Journal of Taxation of Investments,* and *Journal of Accountancy.*

JAMES C. YOUNG is the Crowe Horwath Professor of Accountancy at Northern Illinois University. A graduate of Ferris State University (B.S.) and Michigan State University (M.B.A. and Ph.D.), Jim's research focuses on taxpayer responses to the income tax using archival data. His dissertation received the PricewaterhouseCoopers/American Taxation Association Dissertation Award, and his subsequent research has received funding from a number of organizations, including the Ernst & Young Foundation Tax Research Grant Program. His work has been published in a variety of academic and professional journals, including the *National Tax Journal, The Journal of the American Taxation Association,* and *Tax Notes.* Jim is a Northern Illinois University Presidential Teaching Professor, received the Illinois CPA Society Distinguished Accounting Educator Award in 2012, and has received outstanding teaching awards from George Mason University and Michigan State University.

Brief Contents

Part 5: Business Entities

Part 6: Special Business Topics

Contents

Part 2: Structure of the Federal Income Tax

Part 3: Property Transactions

CHAPTER 7
PROPERTY TRANSACTIONS: BASIS, GAIN AND LOSS, AND NONTAXABLE EXCHANGES

Part 5: Business Entities

xxx   Contents

APPENDIXES

part 1

THE WORLD OF TAXATION

Dennis Flaherty/Photographer's Choice/Getty Images

Part 1 provides an introduction to taxation in the United States. Various taxes imposed by Federal, state, and local governments are discussed. A unique tax planning framework is developed that is applied throughout the book in developing tax planning strategies for business entities and for individual taxpayers. This tax planning framework serves as a unifying theme throughout the book. The role of the IRS and the courts in the evolution of the Federal tax system is presented. The tax research process, including the relevance of the legislative, administrative, and judicial sources of the tax law, is discussed. Part 1 concludes with a chapter on accounting for income taxes, as a bridge to courses that the student already has taken.

Introduction to Taxation

LEARNING OBJECTIVES: *After completing Chapter 1, you should be able to:*

LO.1 **Review and illustrate the components of a tax.**

LO.2 **Identify the various taxes affecting business enterprises.**

LO.3 **Describe the basic tax formula for individuals and taxable business entities.**

LO.4 **State and explain the relationship between business entities and their owners.**

LO.5 **Recognize tax planning opportunities and apply a general framework for tax planning.**

LO.6 **Recognize the economic, social, equity, and political considerations that underlie the tax law.**

LO.7 **Describe the role played by the IRS and the courts in the evolution of the Federal tax system.**

CHAPTER OUTLINE

TAX TALK *How many people were taxed, who was taxed, and what was taxed tell more about a society than anything else.* —CHARLES ADAMS

A TYPICAL TAX YEAR FOR A MODERN FAMILY

Travis and Betty Carter are married and live in a state that imposes both a sales tax and an income tax. They have two children, April (age 17) and Martin (age 18). Travis is a mining engineer who specializes in land reclamation. After several years with a mining corporation, Travis established a consulting practice that involves a considerable amount of travel.

Betty is a registered nurse who, until recently, was a homemaker. In November of this year, she decided to reenter the job market and accepted a position with a medical clinic.

The Carters live only a few blocks from Ernest and Mary Walker, Betty Carter's parents. The Walkers are retired and live on interest, dividends, and Social Security benefits.

Various developments occurring during the year with possible tax ramifications are summarized below.

- The ad valorem property taxes on the Carters' residence are increased, while those on the Walkers' residence are lowered.
- When Travis registers an automobile purchased last year in another state, he is forced to pay a sales tax to his home state.
- As an anniversary present, the Carters gave the Walkers a recreational vehicle (RV).
- When Travis made a consulting trip to Chicago, the client withheld Illinois state income tax from the payment made to Travis for his services.
- Travis employs his children to draft blueprints and prepare scale models for use in his work. Both April and Martin have had training in drafting and topography.
- Early in the year, the Carters are audited by the state on an income tax return filed several years ago. Later in the year, they are audited by the IRS on a Form 1040 they filed for the same year. In each case, a tax deficiency and interest were assessed.
- The Walkers are audited by the IRS. Unlike the Carters, they did not have to deal with a revenue agent, but settled the matter by mail.

Explain these developments and resolve the issues raised.

Read the chapter and formulate your response.

axes have a pervasive impact on our lives. They affect every individual in the United States from birth to death, and even beyond death (through taxation of an individual's estate). Taxes likewise affect every business from formation of the business entity to its operations, distribution of profits to owners, and ultimate disposition or liquidation.

Despite the wide-ranging impact of taxes, most studies of the tax law overemphasize the provisions applying to individual taxpayers and ignore much of the tax law relevant to business. That approach fails to address the role of taxes in *business decisions*, and it fails to provide the broad knowledge base necessary to succeed in today's business environment. This text adopts a more balanced approach; it introduces the tax laws that apply to individuals, and those rules applicable to all business entities, and it surveys the tax rules specific to each type of taxpayer. It also recognizes that both tax and nontax considerations are important in personal and business affairs.

1-1 THE STRUCTURE OF TAXES

LO.1

Review and illustrate the components of a tax.

Most taxes have two components: a tax rate and a tax base (such as income, wages, value, or sales price). Tax liability is computed by multiplying these two components. Taxes vary by the structure of their rates and by the base subject to tax.

1-1a Tax Rates

Tax rates can be progressive, proportional, or regressive. A tax rate is *progressive* if it increases as the tax base increases. The Federal income tax is structured so as to be progressive. For example, the Federal income tax rates for corporations range from 15 to 39 percent. These rates increase with increases in taxable income.

Example 1

Refer to the corporate Tax Rate Schedule inside the front cover of this text. If Abel Corporation records taxable income of $5,000, its income tax is $750 and its average tax rate is 15% ($750/$5,000, or the ratio of tax liability to the tax base). If, however, Abel's taxable income is $200,000, its income tax is $61,250 [$22,250 + .39($200,000 − $100,000)] and its average tax rate is 30.63% ($61,250/$200,000). The tax is progressive because the average tax rate increases with increases in the tax base (income).

A tax is *proportional* if the rate of tax is constant, regardless of the size of the tax base. State retail **sales taxes** are proportional. Proportional tax rates also underlie the various "flat tax" proposals recently in the news.[1]

Example 2

Bob purchases an automobile for $6,000. If the sales tax on automobiles is 7% in Bob's state, he will pay a $420 tax. Alternatively, if Bob pays $20,000 for a car, his sales tax will be $1,400 (still 7% of the sales price). Because the average tax rate does not change with the tax base (sales price), the sales tax is proportional.

Finally, *regressive* tax rates decrease as the tax base increases. Federal **employment taxes**, such as FICA and FUTA, are regressive. When the tax base and the taxpayer's ability to pay generally are positively correlated (i.e., when they move in the same direction), many tax pundits view regressive tax rates as unfair. This is because the tax burden decreases as a *percentage* of the taxpayer's ability to pay.

---

[1]Flat tax proposals call for a new tax with one low proportional rate (usually between 15% and 20%). Such a tax would have a very broad base, taxing almost all forms of income with few deductions. To avoid taxing the poor, large personal exemptions would be provided (e.g., $50,000 for a family of four).

TAX FACT Carrying the Tax Burden

Data from the IRS indicate that the progressive nature of the Federal income tax, accelerated by laws passed under Presidents Bush I and Clinton, remains largely intact for U.S. individuals, even after the broad tax cuts issued under President Bush II.

Annual median adjusted gross income (defining the upper and lower one-half of citizens) is about $35,000. Income of about $390,000 puts a taxpayer in the top 1 percent of filers, and effective Federal taxes for the top 10 percent of earners have increased faster than their incomes. The following table shows the share of taxes paid by various income categories.

Income Category	Share of Total Income (%)	Share of Federal Income Taxes Paid (%)
Top 1%	18	35
Top 5%	34	56
Bottom 50%	11	3

Additional observations include the following.

- Individuals earning less than $45,000 per year likely pay zero Federal income tax, and their payroll and gasoline taxes may be partly rebated through the earned income credit as well.
- When considering income, sales, payroll, property, and other taxes that are levied by U.S. governmental bodies of all sizes, taxpayers at nearly all income levels pay about 30 percent of their income in taxes.
- As new taxes kick in that are designated to pay for the Obamacare system, the degree of progressivity of the Federal income tax will increase even further.
- The 400 individual Forms 1040 with the highest taxable income pay only about a 20 percent average Federal income tax rate, due chiefly to tax incentives that apply to investment income.

© iStockphoto.com/Pali Rao

Example 3

In 2014, the combined Social Security and Medicare tax rate levied on the wages of employees is 7.65% up to a maximum of $117,000 and 1.45% on all wages over $117,000. Sarah earns a salary of $30,000. She pays FICA taxes of $2,295, an average tax rate of 7.65%. Alternatively, if Sarah earns $150,000, she pays $9,429 [(.0765 × $117,000) + .0145 × ($150,000 − $117,000)], an average tax rate of 6.29%.

Once the FICA base exceeds the maximum amount subject to the Social Security part of FICA, the FICA tax becomes regressive because the average tax rate decreases as the tax base increases.

Under all three tax rate structures, the *amount* of taxes due increases as the tax base increases. The structure of tax rates only affects the *rate* of increase (i.e., progressive taxes increase at an increasing rate, proportional taxes increase at a constant rate, and regressive taxes increase at a decreasing rate).

1-1b Tax Bases

Most taxes are levied on one of four kinds of tax bases.

- Transactions (including sales or purchases of goods and services and transfers of wealth).
- Property or wealth (including ownership of specific kinds of property).
- Privileges and rights (including the ability to do business as a corporation, the right to work in a certain profession, and the ability to move goods between countries).
- Income on a gross or net-of-expenses basis.

Because the Federal income tax usually has the most significant influence on business decisions, it is the principal focus of this text. Other taxes can play an important role, however, so it is important to have at least some familiarity with them. The next section introduces many of the taxes imposed on individuals and businesses in the United States.

Digging Deeper | In-depth coverage can be found on this book's companion website: **www.cengagebrain.com**

1-1c Incidence of Taxation

The degree to which various segments of society share the total tax burden is difficult to assess. Assumptions must be made concerning who absorbs the burden of paying the tax. For example, because dividend payments to shareholders are not deductible by a corporation and generally are taxable to shareholders, the same income is subject to a form of double taxation. Concern over double taxation is valid to the extent that corporations are *not* able to shift the corporate tax to the consumer through higher prices and lower wages. Many research studies have shown a high degree of shifting of the corporate income tax (i.e., so that it is borne by the ultimate purchasers of goods).

The progressiveness of the Federal income tax rate structure for individuals has varied over the years. In 1986, for example, there were 15 rates, ranging from 0 to 50 percent. These later were reduced to two rates of 15 and 28 percent. Currently, there are seven rates ranging from 10 to 39.6 percent.

1-2 TYPES OF TAXES

LO.2

Identify the various taxes affecting business enterprises.

After taxes on income, the various transaction taxes usually play the most important role in business (and personal) contexts. In many countries, transaction taxes are even more important than income taxes. There are three types of transaction taxes: sales and certain **excise taxes**, employment taxes, and taxes on the transfer of wealth.

1-2a Taxes on the Production and Sale of Goods

Sales tax and some excise taxes are imposed on the production, sale, or consumption of commodities or the use of services. Excise taxes and general sales taxes differ by the breadth of their bases. An excise tax base is limited to a specific kind of good or service, while a general sales tax is broad-based (e.g., it might be levied on all retail sales). All levels of government impose excise taxes, while state and local governments make heavy use of the general sales tax.

Federal Excise Taxes

Together with customs duties, excise taxes served as the principal source of revenue for the United States during its first 150 years of existence. Since World War II, the role of excise taxes in the Federal government's fund-raising efforts has steadily declined, falling from about 30 to 40 percent of revenues just prior to the war to about 4 percent now. During this time, the Federal government came to rely upon income and employment taxes as its principal sources of funds.

Despite the decreasing contribution of excise taxes to the Federal coffers, they continue to have a significant impact on specific industries. Currently, trucks, trailers, tires, liquor, tobacco, firearms, certain sporting equipment, and air travel all are subject to Federal excise taxes. In the past, the sale and manufacture of a variety of other goods, including furs, jewelry, boats, luxury automobiles, and theater tickets, have been taxed. Excise taxes extend beyond sales transactions. They are also levied on privileges and rights, as discussed below.

The bases used for Federal excise taxes are as diverse as the goods that are taxed. Fuels are taxed by the gallon, vaccines by the dose, telephone service and air travel by the price paid for the service, water travel by the passenger, coal by the ton extracted or by the sales price, insurance by the premiums paid, and the gas guzzler tax by the mileage rating on the automobile produced. Some of these taxes are levied on producers, some on resellers, and some on consumers. In almost every circumstance, the tax rate structure is proportional.

With the exception of Federal excise taxes on alcohol, tobacco, and firearms, Federal excise taxes are due at least quarterly, when the Federal excise tax return (Form 720) is filed.

State Excise Taxes

Many states levy excise taxes on the same items taxed by the Federal government. For example, most states have excise taxes on gasoline, liquor, and tobacco. However, the tax on specific goods can vary dramatically among states. Compare New York's $4.35 tax on each pack of 20 cigarettes to Georgia's $.37 tax. These differences at the state level provide ample incentive for smuggling between states and for state-line enterprises specializing in taxed goods.[2]

Other goods and services subject to state and local excise taxes include admission to amusement facilities; hotel occupancy; rental of other facilities; and sales of playing cards, oleomargarine products, and prepared foods. Most states impose a tax on transfers of property that require recording of documents (such as real estate sales and sales of stock and securities).

Local Excise Taxes

Over the last few years, two types of excise taxes imposed at the local level have become increasingly popular. These are the hotel occupancy tax and the rental car "surcharge." Because they tax the visitor who cannot vote, they are a political windfall and serve as a means of financing special projects that generate civic pride (e.g., convention centers, state-of-the-art sports arenas).

General Sales Tax

The broad-based general sales tax is a major source of revenue for most state and local governments. It is used in all but five states (Alaska, Delaware, Montana, New Hampshire, and Oregon). While specific rules vary from state to state, the sales tax typically employs a proportional tax rate and includes retail sales of tangible personal property (and occasionally personal services) in the base. Some states exempt medicine and food from the base, and sometimes tax rates vary with the good being sold (e.g., the sales tax rate for automobiles may differ from the rate on other goods). The sales tax is collected by the retailer and then paid to the state government.

Local general sales taxes, over and above those levied by the state, are common. It is not unusual to find taxpayers living in the same state who pay different general rates of sales taxes due to the location of their purchases.

For various reasons, some jurisdictions suspend the application of a general sales tax. The prevalent justification for these sales tax holidays involves the purchase of back-to-school items. Granted by approximately 20 states, the exemption typically is available in early August and covers modest expenditures for clothing and school supplies. Some states have used sales tax holidays to encourage the purchase of energy-conserving appliances (e.g., Maryland, Missouri, and Texas) and hurricane preparedness items (e.g., Louisiana and Virginia).

Use Taxes

One obvious approach to avoiding state and local sales taxes is to purchase goods in a state that has little or no sales tax and then transport the goods back to one's home state. **Use taxes** exist to prevent this tax reduction ploy. The use tax is a value-based tax, usually imposed at the same rate as the sales tax, on the use, consumption, or storage of tangible property. Every state that imposes a general sales tax levied on the consumer also applies a use tax.

---

[2]Some excise taxes are referred to as "sin" taxes (because goods such as liquor and tobacco are subject to the tax). Although it is commonly believed that these taxes are imposed for the purpose of discouraging consumption, evidence frequently fails to show this effect. Because demand for alcohol products and gasoline tends to be relatively inelastic (insensitive to price), the increase in price caused by excise taxes has little to do with rates of consumption.

Global Tax Issues

Why Is Gasoline Expensive? It Depends on Where You Live

In recent years, increases in the cost of gasoline and fuel oil have sometimes aroused such a furor in the United States that supplies have been released from the national oil reserve. Whether such tactics reduce prices more than temporarily seems doubtful. But in the United States, unlike other countries, the price of gasoline largely is attributable to the cost of crude oil. In January 2014, the average price per gallon of gasoline in the United States was about $3.15.

In other countries, the real culprit is the amount of tax imposed. Consider the following situations.

Country	Price per Gallon (U.S. $)
United Kingdom	7.87
Japan	7.15
Russia	3.80
Saudi Arabia	0.45
Venezuela	0.06

While other factors may contribute to the various gasoline prices, the primary factor is the amount of tax charged in those countries. For example, in the United Kingdom, approximately 60 percent of the cost of gasoline is attributable to taxes.

THE BIG PICTURE

Example 4

Return to the facts of *The Big Picture* on p. 1-1. The payment Travis made when he registered the car is probably a use tax. When the car was purchased in another state, likely no (or a lesser) sales tax was levied. The current payment makes up for the amount of sales tax he would have paid had the car been purchased in his home state.

The use tax is difficult to enforce for many purchases; therefore, the purchaser often does not pay it. Most of the states are taking steps to curtail this loss of revenue.

Value Added Tax

The value added tax (VAT) is a variation of a sales tax; it is levied at each stage of production on the value added by the producer. VAT is in widespread use in many countries around the world (most notably in the European Union and in Canada). The tax typically serves as a major source of revenue for governments that use it.[3]

Example 5

Farmer Brown sells wheat to a flour mill for $100. If the wheat cost $65 for Brown to produce and if the VAT rate is 10%, then Brown will owe a VAT of $3.50 [.10($100 − $65)]. If the mill sells the flour for $200 to a baker and if it cost the mill $120 to make the flour (including the cost of Brown's wheat), then it will pay a VAT of $8 [.10($200 − $120)]. If the baker sells the bread he makes from the flour for $400 and if it cost the baker $280 to make the bread, then he will pay a VAT of $12 [.10($400 − $280)]. The consumer who buys the bread will not pay any VAT directly. It is likely, however, that some or all of the total VAT paid of $23.50 ($3.50 + $8 + $12) will be paid by the consumer in the form of higher prices for the bread.

---

[3]Some proposals to reduce the Federal government's reliance on the employment and income taxes have focused on VAT as an alternative tax system.

1-2b Employment Taxes

Both Federal and state governments tax the salaries and wages paid to employees. On the Federal side, employment taxes represent a major source of funds. For example, the FICA tax accounts for more than one-third of revenues in the Federal budget, second only to the income tax in its contribution.

The Federal government imposes two kinds of employment tax. The Federal Insurance Contributions Act (FICA) imposes a tax on self-employed individuals, employees, and employers. The proceeds of the tax are used to finance Social Security and Medicare benefits. The Federal Unemployment Tax Act (FUTA) imposes a tax on employers only. The FUTA tax provides funds to state unemployment benefit programs. Most state employment taxes are similar to the FUTA tax, with proceeds used to finance state unemployment benefit payments.

FICA Taxes

The FICA tax has two components: old age, survivors, and disability insurance payments (commonly referred to as Social Security) and Medicare health insurance payments. For 2014, the Social Security tax rate is 6.2 percent for the employee and 6.2 percent for the employer, and the Medicare tax rate is 1.45 percent for both the employer and the employee. The maximum base for the Social Security tax is $117,000 for 2014. There is no ceiling on the base amount for the Medicare tax. The employer withholds the FICA tax from an employee's wages.

Payments usually are made through weekly or monthly electronic payments or deposits to a Federal depository. Employers must also file Form 941, Employer's Quarterly Federal Tax Return, by the end of the first month following each quarter of the calendar year (e.g., by July 31 for the quarter ending on June 30) and pay any remaining amount of employment taxes due for the previous quarter. Failure to pay can result in large and sometimes ruinous penalties.

FICA tax is not assessed on all wages paid. For example, wages paid to children under the age of 18 who are employed in a parent's trade or business are exempt from the tax.

THE BIG PICTURE

Example 6

Return to the facts of *The Big Picture* on p. 1-1. Presuming that April and Martin perform meaningful services for Travis (which the facts seem to imply), they are legitimate employees. April is not subject to Social Security tax because she is under the age of 18. However, Martin is 18, and Travis needs to pay and collect FICA taxes for him.

Furthermore, recall that Betty Carter now is working and likewise is subject to the Social Security and Medicare taxes. Travis, as an independent contractor, is subject to self-employment tax, discussed in the next section.

An additional .9 percent Medicare tax is imposed on earned income (including self-employment income) *above* $200,000 (single filers) or $250,000 (married filing jointly). Unlike the Social Security tax of 6.2 percent and the regular Medicare portion of 1.45 percent, an employer does not match the employees' .9 percent additional Medicare tax.

Similarly, an additional 3.8 percent Medicare tax is assessed on the investment income of individuals whose modified adjusted gross income exceeds $200,000 or $250,000, as above. For this purpose, investment income includes interest, dividends, net capital gains, and income for similar portfolio items.

THE BIG PICTURE

Example 7

Return to the facts of *The Big Picture* on p. 1-1. The combined income of Travis and Betty Carter may be large enough to trigger one or both of the additional Medicare taxes. The marginal tax rate[4] of "upper income" taxpayers like the Carters is higher than that of other individuals because of these taxes. Congress has designated these taxes as part of the payment for Federal health care costs. The application of these taxes may affect Betty's decision to re-enter the workforce.

Self-Employment Tax

Self-employed individuals also pay into the FICA system in the form of a self-employment (SE) tax (determined on Schedule SE, filed with Form 1040, U.S. Individual Income Tax Return). Self-employed individuals are required to pay both the employer and the employee portion of the FICA taxes. Therefore, the 2014 SE tax rate is 15.3 percent on self-employment income up to $117,000 and 2.9 percent on all additional self-employment income. Self-employed individuals deduct half of the SE tax—the amount normally deductible by an employer as a business expense. Self-employment income is discussed in more detail in Chapter 11.

Unemployment Taxes

For 2014, FUTA applies at a rate of 6.0 percent on the first $7,000 of covered wages paid during the year to each employee. As with FICA, this represents a regressive rate structure. The Federal government allows a credit for unemployment tax paid (or allowed under a merit rating system)[5] to the state. The credit cannot exceed 5.4 percent of the covered wages. Thus, the amount required to be paid to the IRS could be as low as .6 percent (6.0% − 5.4%).

FUTA and state unemployment taxes differ from FICA in that the tax is imposed only on the employer. A few states, however, levy a special tax on employees to provide disability benefits or supplemental unemployment compensation, or both.

Employers file Form 940, Employer's Annual Federal Employment Tax Return, to determine the amount of Federal unemployment taxes due in a given year. The return is due on or before January 31 of the following year. Most states also require unemployment tax returns to be filed with quarterly estimated payments.

1-2c Taxes at Death

The transfer of property upon the death of the owner may be a taxable event. If the tax is imposed on the transferor at death, it is called an **estate tax**. If it taxes the recipient of the property, it is termed an **inheritance tax**. As is typical of other types of transaction taxes, the value of the property transferred provides the base for determining the amount of the tax at death.

---

[4]A taxpayer's *marginal tax rate* (or *marginal tax bracket*) is the rate that would be paid on an additional dollar of taxable income.

[5]States follow a policy of reducing unemployment tax on employers with stable employment. Thus, an employer with no employee turnover might face state unemployment tax rates as low as .1% or, in some cases, zero. This *merit rating system* explicitly accounts for the savings generated by steady employment.

The Federal government imposes an estate tax. A few state governments, however, levy their own additional inheritance taxes, estate taxes, or both.

> **Example 8**
>
> At the time of her death, Wilma lived in a state that imposes an inheritance tax but not an estate tax. Mary, one of Wilma's heirs, lives in the same state. Wilma's estate is subject to the Federal estate tax, and Mary is subject to the state inheritance tax.

The Federal Estate Tax

Never designed to generate a large amount of revenue, the Federal estate tax was intended to prevent large concentrations of wealth from being kept within a family for many generations. Whether this objective has been accomplished is debatable, because estate taxes can be substantially reduced (or deferred for decades) through careful tax planning activities.

Determination of the estate tax base begins with the *gross estate*, which includes property the decedent owned at the time of death. It also includes property interests, such as life insurance proceeds paid to the estate or to a beneficiary other than the estate if the deceased-insured had any ownership rights in the policy. Most property included in the gross estate is valued at fair market value as of the date of death.

Deductions from the gross estate in arriving at the *taxable estate* include funeral and administration expenses, certain taxes, debts of the decedent, and transfers to charitable organizations. A *marital deduction* is available for amounts passing to a surviving spouse (a widow or widower).

> **Example 9**
>
> When Luis died, he owned $10 million in various securities, real estate, and personal effects. Under his will, Luis paid $1 million to the local art museum and $2 million to his surviving wife Angelina. Luis's executor computes a Federal estate tax on the $7 million taxable estate.

Once the taxable estate has been determined and certain taxable gifts have been added to it, one must determine a tentative tax liability. The tentative liability is reduced by a variety of credits to arrive at the amount due.

In most cases, the first $5 million of a U.S. decedent's estate effectively is excluded from the estate tax, with a maximum 40 percent tax rate on any excess. Spouses can share a $10 million estate tax exclusion. The $5 million and $10 million amounts are indexed for inflation.[6]

State Taxes at Death

States usually levy an inheritance tax, an estate tax, or both. The two forms of tax differ according to whether the liability is imposed on the heirs or on the estate.

Characteristically, an inheritance tax divides the heirs into classes based on their relationship to the decedent. The more closely related the heir, the lower the rates imposed and the greater the exemption allowed. Some states completely exempt amounts passing to a surviving spouse from taxation.

1-2d Gift Tax

Like estate and inheritance taxes, the Federal **gift tax** is an excise tax levied on the right to transfer property. In this case, however, the tax is imposed on transfers made during the owner's life rather than at death. A gift tax applies only to transfers that are not supported by full and adequate consideration (i.e., gifts).

> **Example 10**
>
> Carl sells property worth $20,000 to his daughter for $1,000. Although property worth $20,000 has been transferred, only $19,000 represents a gift, because this is the portion not supported by full and adequate consideration.

---

[6]For 2014, the indexed exemption amount for each individual is $5.34 million, and spouses share a $10.68 million Federal estate tax exclusion.

The Federal gift tax is intended to complement the estate tax. The gift tax base is the sum of all taxable gifts made *during one's lifetime.* Gifts are valued at the fair market value of the property on the date of the gift. To compute the tax due in a year, the tax rate schedule is applied to the sum of all lifetime taxable gifts. The resulting tax is then reduced by gift taxes paid in prior years.

The Federal gift tax and the Federal estate tax are *unified.*[7] The transfer of assets by a decedent at death effectively is treated as a final gift under the tax law. Thus, the $5 million exclusion (as indexed) and the 40 percent top tax rate for the estate tax also is available to calculate the tax liability generated by lifetime gifts. If the exclusion is exhausted during one's lifetime against taxable gifts, it is not available to reduce the estate tax liability. The same tax rate schedule applies to both lifetime gifts and the estate tax.

Example 11

Before his death, Ben makes $5 million of taxable gifts. Ignore indexing of the exemption amounts. Because the unified transfer tax exclusion was used up during his life to offset the tax due on these gifts, no further amount is left to reduce Ben's estate tax liability.

Annual taxable gifts are determined by reducing the fair market value of gifts given by an *annual exclusion* of $14,000 per donee. A married couple can elect *gift splitting,* which enables them to transfer twice the annual exclusion ($28,000) per donee per year.

Taxable gifts are reduced by deductions for gifts to charity and to one's spouse (the *marital deduction*). Gifts for medical and educational purposes may be exempt from the gift tax as well.

Example 12

Marco made the following gifts: $500,000 to his wife Irena, $100,000 to their daughter Anita, and $100,000 to the San Mateo Church.

The marital and charitable deductions offset the gifts to Irena and the church. The $14,000 per donee annual exclusion reduces the taxable gift to Anita. Another $14,000 of the taxable gift could be eliminated if Irena agrees to a gift-splitting election.

Example 13

On December 31, 2014, Vera gives $14,000 to each of her four married children, their spouses, and her eight grandchildren. On January 3, 2015, she repeats the procedure.

Due to the annual exclusion, Vera has *not* made a taxable gift, although she transferred $224,000 [$14,000 × 16 (the number of donees)] in each of the years, for a total of $448,000.

If Vera had been married, she could have given twice as much ($896,000) by electing gift splitting with her husband.

Unlike death, the timing of which usually is involuntary, the making of a gift is a voluntary parting of ownership. Thus, the ownership of a business or a plot of land can be transferred gradually without incurring drastic and immediate tax consequences.

1-2e Property Taxes

A property tax can be a tax on the ownership of property or a tax on wealth, depending on the base used. Any measurable characteristic of the property being taxed can be used as a base (e.g., weight, size, number, or value). Most property taxes in the United States are taxes on wealth; they use value as a base. These value-based property taxes are known as **ad valorem taxes.** Property taxes generally are administered by state and local governments, where they serve as a significant source of revenue.

[7]§§ 2010 and 2505.

TAX IN THE NEWS The Backdoor Tax Increase

Can a landowner's property taxes increase even though the tax rate has not changed? Yes, if the assessed value of the property is increased! Known as a "backdoor tax increase," this procedure allows the taxing authority to generate additional revenue without having to secure voter approval for an increase in the tax rate.

Even more aggravating for the property owner is an increase in assessed value that is based on past market values and does not reflect the true current value. This kind of increase often occurs during periods of economic downturn (i.e., when real estate prices decline). Under these conditions, increases in assessed value are likely to cause considerable taxpayer dissatisfaction and lead to proposals for legislative relief, such as a freeze on upward property assessments.

Taxes on Realty

Property taxes on realty are used exclusively by states and their local political subdivisions such as cities, counties, and school districts. They represent a major source of revenue for local governments, but their importance at the state level is limited.

How realty is defined can have an important bearing on which assets are subject to tax. This is especially true in jurisdictions that do not impose ad valorem taxes on personalty. Realty generally includes real estate and any capital improvements that are classified as fixtures. A fixture is something so permanently attached to the real estate that its removal will cause irreparable damage. A built-in bookcase might be a fixture, whereas a movable bookcase is not. Certain items such as electrical wiring and plumbing change from personalty to realty when installed in a building.

The following are some of the characteristics of ad valorem taxes on realty.

- Property owned by the Federal government is exempt from tax. Similar immunity usually is extended to property owned by state and local governments and by certain charitable organizations.
- Some states provide for lower valuations on property dedicated to agricultural use or other special uses (e.g., wildlife sanctuaries).
- Some states partially exempt the homestead, or personal residence, portion of property from taxation.
- Lower taxes may apply to a residence owned by a taxpayer age 65 or older.
- Some jurisdictions extend immunity from tax for a specified period of time (a tax holiday) to new or relocated businesses.

THE BIG PICTURE

Example 14

Return to the facts of *The Big Picture* on p. 1-1. Why did the Walkers' taxes decrease while those of the Carters increased? A likely explanation is that one (or both) of the Walkers achieved senior citizen status. In the case of the Carters, the assessed value of their property probably increased. Perhaps they made significant home improvements (e.g., kitchen/bathroom renovation, addition of a sundeck).

Taxes on Personalty

Personalty includes all assets that are not realty. It may be helpful to distinguish between the classification of an asset (realty or personalty) and the use to which it

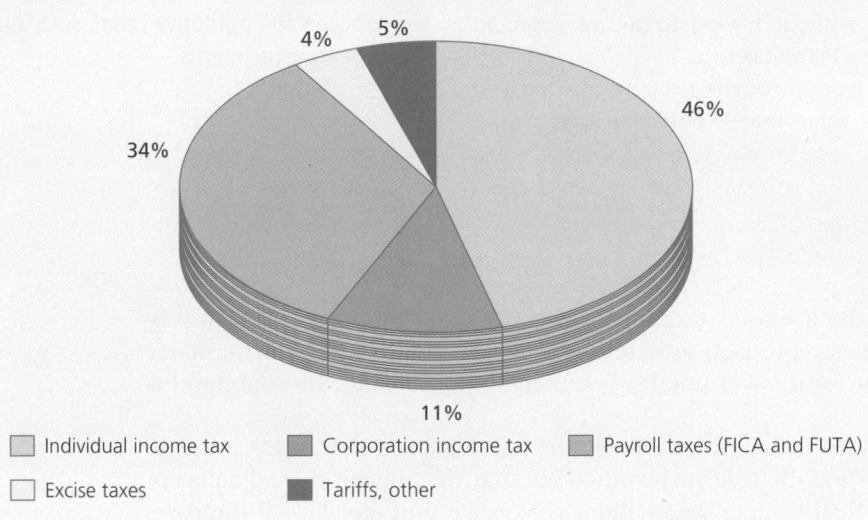

TAX FACT   A Profile of Tax Collections

Federal budget receipts as scheduled for fiscal 2014 indicate a dependence by the government on payroll and individual income taxes. Corporate income tax collections likely are far below what the general public might estimate.

Federal Tax Collections

- 46% — Individual income tax
- 11% — Corporation income tax
- 34% — Payroll taxes (FICA and FUTA)
- 4% — Excise taxes
- 5% — Tariffs, other

is put. Realty and personalty can be either business-use or personal-use property. Examples include a residence (personal-use realty), an office building (business-use realty), surgical instruments (business-use personalty), and casual clothing (personal-use personalty).

Personalty can also be classified as tangible property or intangible property. For property tax purposes, intangible personalty includes stocks, bonds, and various other securities (e.g., bank shares).

The following generalizations may be made concerning the property taxes on personalty.

- Particularly with personalty devoted to personal use (e.g., jewelry, household furnishings), taxpayer compliance ranges from poor to zero. Some jurisdictions do not even attempt to enforce the tax on these items. For automobiles devoted to personal use, many jurisdictions have converted from value as the tax base to a tax based on the weight of the vehicle. Some jurisdictions also consider the vehicle's age (e.g., automobiles six years or older are not subject to the ad valorem tax because they are presumed to have little value).
- For personalty devoted to business use (e.g., inventories, trucks, machinery, equipment), taxpayer compliance and enforcement procedures are notably better.
- Some jurisdictions impose an ad valorem property tax on intangibles.

Digging Deeper   2   In-depth coverage can be found on this book's companion website: **www.cengagebrain.com**

1-2f Taxes on Privileges and Rights

Taxes on privileges and rights are usually considered excise taxes. The most important of these taxes are reviewed here.

TAX FACT   What Is the U.S. Tax Burden?

One popular measure of the burden of taxes in the U.S. economy is the Tax Foundation's "Tax Freedom Day." This statistic is a determination of the day upon which an individual has completed the entire year's obligation to governmental units (i.e., if all earnings were paid as taxes to this point, annual taxes would be paid up and one would now begin to "work for his or her own account").

Being "free from taxes" may bring about a feeling of relief, but in reality, tax burdens vary greatly from state to state. And as the U.S. economy has evolved and develops a more complex tax structure, adding emphasis on income and sales/use taxes and reducing the relative reliance on tariffs and excise taxes, year-to-year comparisons become difficult. Nonetheless, as a rough measure of the presence of government in our lives, Tax Freedom Day carries some importance.

If one is in need of consolation, Tax Freedom Day in Canada was June 10, 2013.

Year	Tax Freedom Day
1902	1/31
1930	2/12
1945	4/4
1960	4/15
1970	4/26
1990	5/1
1999	5/11
2000	5/3
2010	4/12
2013	4/18

© iStockphoto.com/Pali Rao

Federal Customs Duties

Customs duties or tariffs can be characterized as a tax on the right to move goods across national borders. These taxes, together with selective excise taxes, provided most of the revenues needed by the Federal government during the nineteenth century. For example, tariffs and excise taxes alone paid off the national debt in 1835 and enabled the U.S. Treasury to pay a surplus of $28 million to the states. Today, however, customs duties account for only 1 percent of revenues in the Federal budget.

In recent years, tariffs have acted more as an instrument for carrying out protectionist policies than as a means of generating revenue. Thus, a particular U.S. industry might be saved from economic disaster, so the argument goes, by placing customs duties on the importation of foreign goods that can be sold at lower prices. Protectionists contend that the tariff therefore neutralizes the competitive edge held by the producer of the foreign goods.[8]

Protectionist policies seem more appropriate for less-developed countries whose industrial capacity has not yet matured. In a world where a developed country should have everything to gain by encouraging international free trade, such policies may be of dubious value because tariffs often lead to retaliatory action on the part of the nation or nations affected.

Franchise Taxes and Occupational Taxes

A franchise tax is a tax on the privilege of doing business in a state or local jurisdiction. Typically, the tax is imposed by states on corporations, but the tax base varies from state to state. While some states use a measure of corporate net income as part of the base, most states base the tax on the capitalization of the corporation (with or without certain long-term debt).

Closely akin to the franchise tax are occupational taxes applicable to various trades or businesses, such as a liquor store license, a taxicab permit, or a fee to practice a profession such as law, medicine, or accounting. Most of these are not significant revenue producers and fall more into the category of licenses than

---

[8]The North American Free Trade Agreement (NAFTA) substantially reduces the tariffs on trade between Canada, Mexico, and the United States.

taxes. The revenue derived is used to defray the cost incurred by the jurisdiction to regulate the business or profession for the public good.

THE BIG PICTURE

Example 15

Return to the facts of *The Big Picture* on p. 1-1. Although the facts do not mention the matter, both Travis and Betty will almost certainly pay occupational fees—Travis for engineering and Betty for nursing.

Severance Taxes

Severance taxes are based on the extraction of natural resources (e.g., oil, gas, iron ore, and coal). They are an important source of revenue for many states; Alaska does not levy either a state-level income or sales/use tax, because the collections from its severance taxes are so large.

1-2g Income Taxes

Income taxes are levied by the Federal government, most states, and some local governments. In recent years, the trend in the United States has been to place greater reliance on this method of taxation while other countries are relying more heavily on transactions taxes such as the VAT.

Income taxes generally are imposed on individuals, corporations, and certain fiduciaries (estates and trusts). Most jurisdictions attempt to ensure the collection of income taxes by requiring certain pay-as-you-go procedures, including withholding requirements for employees and estimated tax prepayments for all taxpayers.

The Structure of the Federal Income Tax

LO.3

Describe the basic tax formula for individuals and taxable business entities.

Although some variations exist, the basic Federal income tax formula is similar for all taxable entities. This formula is shown in Figure 1.1.

The income tax is based on the doctrine known as *legislative grace*: all income is subject to tax and no deductions are allowed unless specifically provided for in the law. Some types of income are excluded on the basis of various economic, social, equity, and political considerations. Examples of such exclusions from the income tax base include gifts, inheritances, life insurance proceeds received by reason of death, and interest income from state and local bonds.

All entities are allowed to deduct business expenses from gross income, but a number of limitations and exceptions are applied. A variety of credits against the tax are also allowed, again on the basis of economic, social, equity, or political goals of Congress.

Income tax rates for all entities are progressive. The corporate rates range from 15 percent on the lowest level of taxable income to 35 percent on the highest level. Individual rates range from 10 percent to 39.6 percent. Estates and trusts are also subject to income taxation, with rates ranging from 15 percent to 39.6 percent. Additional Medicare taxes (discussed previously) apply on top of these rates for certain upper-income taxpayers.

Partnerships, qualifying small business corporations, and some limited liability companies are not taxable entities, but must file information returns. Owners of these business entities then are taxed on the net taxable income of the enterprise, proportionate to their holdings.

For individuals, deductions are separated into two categories—deductions *for* adjusted gross income (AGI) and deductions *from* AGI. Generally, deductions *for* AGI are related to business activities, while deductions *from* AGI often are personal in nature (e.g., medical expenses, mortgage interest and property taxes on a personal residence, charitable contributions, and personal casualty losses) or are related to investment activities. Deductions *from* AGI take the form of *itemized deductions* and personal and dependency exemptions. Individuals may take a *standard deduction* (a specified amount based on filing status) rather than itemize actual deductions. An overview of the individual income tax formula is provided in Figure 1.2.

FIGURE 1.1	Basic Formula for Federal Income Tax

Income (broadly conceived)	$xxx,xxx
Less: Exclusions (income that is not subject to tax)	(xx,xxx)
Gross income (income that is subject to tax)	$xxx,xxx
Less: Deductions	(xx,xxx)
Taxable income	$xxx,xxx
Federal income tax on taxable income (see Tax Rate Schedules inside front cover of text)	$ xx,xxx
Less: Tax credits (including Federal income tax withheld and other prepayments of Federal income taxes)	(x,xxx)
Tax owed (or refund)	$ xxx

In-depth coverage can be found on this book's companion website: **www.cengagebrain.com**    **3**   Digging Deeper

State Income Taxes

Most states (except Alaska, Florida, Nevada, South Dakota, Texas, Washington, and Wyoming) impose a traditional income tax on individuals. Tennessee and New Hampshire tax only certain dividend and interest income. Most states also impose either a corporate income tax or a franchise tax based in part on corporate income. The following additional points can be made about state income taxes.

- State income tax usually relies on Federal income tax laws to some degree— the states use Federal taxable income as a base, with a few adjustments (e.g., a few allow a deduction for Federal income taxes paid and sometimes an exclusion on interest income earned on Federal securities).
- For individuals, a few states impose a flat rate on Federal AGI.
- Several states piggyback directly on the Federal income tax system by using the Federal income tax liability as a tax base.

FIGURE 1.2	Federal Income Tax Formula for Individuals

Income (broadly conceived)	$xx,xxx
Less: Exclusions (income that is not subject to tax)	(x,xxx)
Gross income (income that is subject to tax)	$xx,xxx
Less: Certain business and investment deductions (usually referred to as deductions *for* adjusted gross income)	(x,xxx)
Adjusted gross income	$xx,xxx
Less: The greater of certain personal and employee deductions (usually referred to as *itemized deductions*)	
or	
The standard deduction (including any *additional* standard deduction)	(x,xxx)
Less: Personal and dependency exemptions	(x,xxx)
Taxable income	$xx,xxx
Federal income tax on taxable income (see Tax Rate Schedules inside front cover of text)	$ x,xxx
Less: Tax credits (including Federal income tax withheld and other prepayments of Federal income taxes)	(xxx)
Tax owed (or refund)	$ xxx

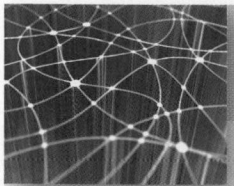

BRIDGE DISCIPLINE   Bridge to Political Science and Sociology

The tax law and its effects on citizens and businesses of the United States are included in many other academic disciplines. Tax burdens are part of American fiction, family studies, and minority issues, as well as economics, finance, and management courses.

In the Bridge feature found in most chapters of this text, we relate the concerns of other disciplines to a more specific review of tax law, as presented here. With the topical knowledge obtained in this text, the reader can better understand the issues raised by other disciplines, sometimes to support beliefs held by others and sometimes to refute them.

For instance, the structure of the U.S. tax system raises many issues of equity and fairness. Politicians and journalists discuss these issues freely, often without the requisite tax knowledge to draw proper conclusions.

- Should the property tax on real estate be used to finance the local public education system? Why should elderly taxpayers with grown children or parents who send their children to private schools continue to pay for public schools through these taxes?
- Would the lack of a charitable contribution deduction impair the ability of charities to raise operating and capital funds?
- Does a regressive sales/use tax fall harder on individuals of color?
- Is the tax law "friendly" to marriage and families with children?
- How should the tax law be used to encourage investments in "green" energy products? In improving access speeds for the Internet?

© iStockphoto.com/enot-poloskun

- Most states also require withholding of state income tax from salaries and wages and estimated payments by corporations and self-employed individuals.
- Most states have their own set of rates, exemptions, and credits.
- Many states also allow a credit for taxes paid to other states.
- Virtually all state income tax returns provide checkoff boxes for donations to various causes. Many are dedicated to medical research and wildlife programs, but special projects are not uncommon. For example, Oklahoma uses a checkoff to retire the debt incurred for its capitol dome addition, while a Wisconsin checkoff financed part of the renovations of Lambeau Field (home of the Green Bay Packers). These checkoff boxes have been criticized as adding complexity to the returns and misleading taxpayers.

Local Income Taxes

Cities imposing an income tax include Baltimore, Cincinnati, Cleveland, Columbus, Denver, Detroit, Kansas City (MO), New York, Philadelphia, San Francisco, and St. Louis, among others. City income taxes usually apply to anyone who earns income in a city. They are designed to collect contributions for government services from those who live in the suburbs but work in the city as well as from local residents.

Digging Deeper   4      In-depth coverage can be found on this book's companion website: **www.cengagebrain.com**

1-3 INCOME TAXATION OF BUSINESS ENTITIES

LO.4

State and explain the relationship between business entities and their owners.

1-3a Proprietorships

The simplest form of business entity is a **proprietorship**, which is not a separate taxable entity. Instead, the proprietor reports the net profit of the business on his or her own individual tax return.

© tuulijumala/Shutterstock.com

FINANCIAL DISCLOSURE INSIGHTS *What Do You Mean by "Income" Anyway?*

Most business taxpayers keep at least "two sets of books," in that they report one amount of "income" for financial accounting purposes and another amount of "taxable income" as required by various taxing jurisdictions—the definition that will be used throughout this book. In fact, "income" might be defined in many different ways, depending on the recipient of the income reports of the enterprise. For instance, a business entity might prepare markedly different income reports for lenders, employee unions, managers in operating divisions, and international agencies.

Financial accounting income guidance is provided for U.S. businesses by the **Financial Accounting Standards Board (FASB)**, using the accumulated **Generally Accepted Accounting Principles (GAAP)** for the reporting period. When an entity conducts business outside the United States, the **International Financial Reporting Standards (IFRS)** of the **International Accounting Standards Board (IASB)** also may apply.

Throughout this book, we point out some of the effects that Federal income tax provisions can have on the taxpayer's financial accounting results for the tax year. The vast majority of an entity's business transactions receive identical treatment under GAAP, IFRS, and the Federal tax law. But when the applicable provisions differ, "income" can be reported as different amounts—accounting professionals often refer to these as "book-tax differences."

A tax professional must be able to identify and explain the various constructs of "income" so that the business entity's operating results will be accurately reflected in its stock price, loan covenants, and cash-flow demands.

Individuals who own proprietorships often have specific tax goals with regard to their financial interactions with the business. Because a proprietorship is, by definition, owned by an individual, the individual has great flexibility in structuring the entity's transactions in a way that will minimize his or her marginal income tax rate (or, in some cases, the marginal income tax rates of the family unit).

A proprietorship itself is not a taxpaying entity. The owner of the proprietorship reports the income and deductions of the business on a Schedule C (Profit or Loss from Business) and the net profit (or loss) of the proprietorship on his or her Form 1040 (U.S. Individual Income Tax Return). Specific issues related to the taxation of sole proprietorships are presented in detail in Chapter 11.

1-3b Corporations

Some corporations pay tax on corporate taxable income, while others pay no tax at the corporate level. Corporations that are separate taxable entities are referred to as **C corporations**, because they are governed by Subchapter C of the Internal Revenue Code. Corporations that meet certain requirements and pay no tax at the corporate level are referred to as **S corporations**, because they are governed by Subchapter S of the Code. S corporations are discussed in detail in Chapter 15. C corporations are addressed in Chapters 12 and 13.

A C corporation is required to file a tax return (Form 1120) and is subject to the Federal income tax. The shareholders then pay income tax on the dividends they receive when the corporation distributes its profits. Thus, the profits of the corporation can be seen as subject to double taxation, first at the corporate level and then at the shareholder level.

Joseph is the president and sole shareholder of Falcon Corporation. Falcon's taxable income is $100,000, and its tax liability is $22,250. If Joseph has the corporation pay all of its after-tax income to him as a dividend, he will receive $77,750 and pay Federal income tax on that amount as an individual taxpayer. Falcon's $100,000 income has been subjected to Federal income tax twice.

Example 16

1-3c Partnerships

A partnership is not a separate taxable entity. The partnership is required to file a tax return (Form 1065) on which it summarizes the financial results of the business. Each partner then reports his or her share of the net income or loss and other special items that were reported on the partnership return.

Example 17

Cameron and Connor form a partnership in which they are equal partners. The partnership reports a $100,000 net profit on its tax return, but is not subject to the Federal income tax. Cameron and Connor each report $50,000 net income from the partnership on their separate individual income tax returns.

1-3d S Corporations

An S corporation is treated like a C corporation for all nontax purposes. Shareholders have limited liability, shares are freely transferable, the entity uses centralized management (vested in the board of directors), and there can be an unlimited continuity of life (i.e., the corporation continues to exist after the withdrawal or death of a shareholder).

With regard to tax factors, however, an S corporation is more like a partnership. The S corporation is not subject to the Federal *income tax*. Like a partnership, it does file a tax return (Form 1120S), but the shareholders report their share of net income or loss and other special items on their own tax returns.

Example 18

Kay and Dawn form a corporation and elect to treat it as an S corporation. Kay owns 60% of the stock of the corporation, and Dawn owns 40%. The S corporation reports a $100,000 net profit on its tax return, but is not subject to the income tax. Kay reports $60,000 net income from the S corporation on her individual income tax return, and Dawn reports $40,000 on her tax return.

1-3e Limited Liability Companies and Limited Liability Partnerships

Limited liability companies (LLCs) and limited liability partnerships (LLPs) offer limited liability and some (but not all) of the other nontax features of corporations. Both forms usually are treated as partnerships for tax purposes.

The S corporation, limited liability company, and partnership forms of organization, which are referred to as *flow-through* entities, avoid the double taxation problem associated with the C corporation.

1-3f Dealings between Individuals and Entities

Many of the provisions in the tax law deal with the relationships between owners and the business entities they own. The following are some of the major interactions between owners and business entities.

- Owners put assets into a business when they establish a business entity (e.g., a proprietorship, partnership, or corporation).
- Owners take assets out of the business during its existence in the form of salary, dividends, withdrawals, redemptions of stock, etc.
- Through their entities, owner-employees set up retirement plans for themselves, including IRAs, Keogh plans, and qualified pension plans.
- Owners dispose of all or part of a business entity.

Every major transaction that occurs between an owner and a business entity has important tax ramifications. The following are a few of the many tax issues that arise.

FINANCIAL DISCLOSURE INSIGHTS   Book-Tax Differences

"Income" is defined differently for Federal income tax and financial accounting purposes. Financial accounting income (FAI) is designed to indicate the profitability of the business entity for the reporting period, in a fair and understandable way, to shareholders, creditors, and other parties who are interested in the results. Taxable income is a device used by Congress to raise revenue; stimulate or stabilize the economy; and accomplish other economic, social, and political goals in an equitable manner. In general, FAI recognizes *revenue* and *expenses*, while taxable income includes *gross income* and *deductions*.

The taxable income of a business taxpayer is not identical to FAI to the extent that *temporary* and *permanent* book-tax differences exist. Broadly, book-tax differences result when:

- Tax benefits are accelerated or deferred relative to their recognition for book purposes, for example, when cost recovery deductions are claimed earlier than depreciation expenses are allowed.
- Tax benefits are not recognized at all for book purposes; for example, there is no book expense item corresponding to the domestic production activities deduction.

As a result of temporary book-tax differences, income tax payable (the amount due on the tax return, referred to by many tax professionals as the "cash tax") is not equal to the income tax expense on the book income statement. The income statement reflects the full income tax burden for the FAI of the reporting period, under the GAAP matching principle, but it is broken into the components *current income tax expense* and *deferred income tax expense*.

When a tax benefit is delayed for book purposes, such as for accelerated cost recovery deductions, a deferred tax liability is created on the entity's balance sheet. Taxable income will be greater than FAI in a subsequent year.

When a tax benefit is delayed for tax purposes, such as when a bad debt allowance is used for accounts receivable but is not permissible on the tax return, a deferred tax asset is created on the balance sheet. Taxable income will be less than FAI in a subsequent year.

Permanent book-tax differences, such as the exclusion for interest income from a state bond, do not affect the balance sheet. But because FAI and taxable income differ in this amount, the effective tax rate of the taxpayer is higher or lower than might be expected. The financial statement footnotes reconcile the statutory and effective tax rates of the entity, in dollar and/or percentage amounts.

The balance sheet accounts for deferred taxes can be sizable. For instance, in most years, Citigroup's deferred tax assets make up about one-third of its tangible equity capital.

- How to avoid taxation at both the owner level and the entity level (i.e., the multiple taxation problem).
- How to get assets into the business with the least adverse tax consequences.
- How to get assets out of the business with the least adverse tax consequences.
- How to dispose of the business entity with the least adverse tax consequences.

When addressing these (and other) tax issues, a common set of tax planning tools can be applied. These tax planning fundamentals are introduced in the next section.

In-depth coverage can be found on this book's companion website: **www.cengagebrain.com**   5   Digging Deeper

1-4 TAX PLANNING FUNDAMENTALS

1-4a Overview of Tax Planning and Ethics

Taxpayers generally attempt to minimize their tax liabilities, and it is perfectly acceptable to do so using legal means. It is a long-standing principle that taxpayers have no obligation to pay more than their fair share of taxes. The now-classic words

LO.5

Recognize tax planning opportunities and apply a general framework for tax planning.

of Judge Learned Hand in *Commissioner v. Newman* reflect the true values a taxpayer should have.

> Over and over again courts have said that there is nothing sinister in so arranging one's affairs as to keep taxes as low as possible. Everybody does so, rich or poor; and all do right, for nobody owes any public duty to pay more than the law demands; taxes are enforced exactions, not voluntary contributions. To demand more in the name of morals is mere cant.[9]

Tax Planning: Avoidance Versus Evasion

Minimizing taxes legally is referred to as **tax avoidance**. On the other hand, some taxpayers attempt to *evade* income taxes through illegal actions. There is a major distinction between tax avoidance and **tax evasion**. Although eliminating or reducing taxes is also a goal of tax evasion, the term *evasion* implies the use of subterfuge and fraud as a means to this end. Tax avoidance is legal, while tax evasion subjects the taxpayer to numerous civil and criminal penalties, including prison sentences.

Clients expect tax practitioners to provide advice to help them minimize their tax costs. This part of the tax practitioner's practice is referred to as *tax planning*. To structure a sound tax minimization plan, a practitioner must have a thorough knowledge of the tax law. Tax planning skill is based on knowledge of tax saving provisions in the tax law, as well as provisions that contain costly pitfalls for the unwary.

Thorough study of the remainder of this text will provide a solid base of the knowledge required to recognize opportunities and avoid pitfalls. Tax planning requires the practitioner to have in mind both a framework for planning and an understanding of the tax planning implications of a client's situation.

The Ethics of Tax Planning

Tax planning (avoidance) is a fully ethical activity by the taxpayer and the tax professional, but tax evasion (fraud) is not. The tax adviser's actions are limited by the codes of conduct of various professional organizations, such as the American Institute of CPAs or the pertinent state bar association.

Other formal restrictions and directives concerning the conduct of the tax professional can be found in two broad forms.

* Penalties and interest may apply to the taxpayer when a tax liability is understated. Examples include penalties for filing a tax return after its due date, understating gross income amounts, and underpaying withholding or estimated taxes that are due.
* Sanctions are used for tax preparers who disregard the tax law. The Treasury issues a regulation known as *Circular 230* to provide guidance to tax return preparers. Tax penalties also apply when the tax preparer fails to sign a tax return that he or she has worked on or takes an improper filing position on a tax return.

Digging Deeper   **6**   In-depth coverage can be found on this book's companion website: **www.cengagebrain.com**

★ Tax Planning Framework

1-4b A General Framework for Income Tax Planning

The primary goal of tax planning is to design a transaction so as to minimize its tax costs, while meeting the other nontax objectives of the client. Generally, this means that the client attempts to maximize the present value of its after-tax income and assets. Selecting a specific form of transaction solely for the sake of tax minimization often leads to a poor business decision. Effective tax planning requires careful consideration of the nontax issues involved in addition to the tax consequences.

[9]47–1 USTC ¶9175, 35 AFTR 857, 159 F.2d 848 (CA–2, 1947).

FIGURE 1.3	General Framework for Income Tax Planning

Tax Formula	Tax Planning Strategy	Tax Planning Examples
Income and exclusions	➤ **Avoid income recognition.**	Compensate employees with nontaxable fringe benefits (see Example 19).
	➤ **Postpone recognition of income to achieve tax deferral.**	Postpone sale of assets (see Example 20).
− Deductions	➤ **Maximize deductible amounts.**	Invest in stock of another corporation (see Example 21).
	➤ **Accelerate recognition of deductions to achieve tax deferral.**	Elect to deduct charitable contribution in year of pledge rather than in year of payment (see Example 22).
= Taxable income		
× Tax rate	➤ **Shift net income from high-bracket years to low-bracket years.**	Postpone recognition of income to a low-bracket year (see Example 23).
		Postpone recognition of deductions to a high-bracket year (see Example 24).
	➤ **Shift net income from high-bracket taxpayers to low-bracket taxpayers.**	Pay children to work in the family business (see Example 25).
	➤ **Shift net income from high-tax jurisdictions to low-tax jurisdictions.**	Establish subsidiary operations in countries with low tax rates (see Examples 26 and 27).
	➤ **Control the character of income and deductions.**	Hold assets long enough to qualify for long-term capital gain rates before selling them (see Example 28).
		Invest in small business stock to obtain ordinary loss treatment under § 1244 (see Example 29).
	➤ **Avoid double taxation.**	Operate as a flow-through entity rather than a C corporation (see Example 30).
		Maximize deductible expenses paid by a C corporation to a shareholder/employee (see Example 31).
= Federal income tax		
− Tax credits	➤ **Maximize tax credits.**	Hire employees who qualify the business for the work opportunity tax credit (see Example 33).
= Tax owed (or refund)		

Careful analysis of the tax formula (refer to Figure 1.1) reveals a series of tax minimization strategies. Through creative tax planning that also takes into consideration a client's nontax concerns, each component of the tax formula can be managed in a way that will help to minimize the client's tax liability. The General Framework for Income Tax Planning in Figure 1.3 lists each element in the income tax formula, develops tax planning strategies designed to minimize taxes, and provides brief summaries of specific examples of tax planning. The framework is followed by a discussion of the tax planning strategies, along with detailed examples of how the strategies can be applied. In Chapters 4 through 18 of this book, these strategies and their tax formula components provide the framework for Tax Planning Strategies features.

1-4c Tax Minimization Strategies Related to Income

★ **Framework Focus: Income**

➤ *Tax Planning Strategy*

➤ *Avoid Income Recognition.* Section 61(a) defines gross income as "all income from whatever source derived." However, the Code contains provisions that allow various types of income to be excluded from the tax base. Numerous exclusions are available for individuals, but very few are available for corporations. However, a corporation can provide excludible income for its owners at no tax cost to the corporation.

Example 19

The average employee of Penguin Corporation is a 25% bracket taxpayer. In negotiations with the employees' union, Penguin proposes that it will increase the amount it spends on nontaxable fringe benefits by an average of $3,000 per employee in lieu of granting a $3,000 average salary increase. The average employee will be better off by $750 if the union accepts Penguin's offer.

	Salary Increase	Fringe Benefit Increase
Value of compensation received	$3,000	$3,000
Tax on employee's compensation	(750)	(–0–)
After-tax increase in compensation	$2,250	$3,000

Although the average employee receives a $750 benefit, there is no tax cost to Penguin because both fringe benefits and salaries are deductible by the corporation.

> *Tax Planning Strategy*

> ➤ *Postpone Recognition of Income to Achieve Tax Deferral.* The tax law requires that both income and expenses be reported in the proper tax year. If not for this requirement, taxpayers could freely shift income and expenses from year to year to take advantage of tax rate differentials or could defer tax liabilities indefinitely. Although various rules limit the shifting of income and deductions across time periods, some opportunities still exist.

Example 20

In 2006, Turquoise Corporation acquired land for investment purposes at a cost of $500,000. In November 2014, Turquoise is negotiating to sell the land to Aqua Corporation for $800,000. Aqua insists that the transaction be completed in 2014, but Turquoise wants to delay the sale until 2015 to defer the tax on the gain. In an effort to compromise, Turquoise agrees to sell the land in November 2014 and asks Aqua to pay for the land in two installments, $400,000 in December 2014 and $400,000 in January 2015. This enables Turquoise to use the installment method for recognizing the gain, under which Turquoise will report $150,000 of the gain in 2014 and the remaining $150,000 in 2015.

By electing the installment method, Turquoise defers the payment of tax on $150,000 of the gain for one year. If the marginal tax rate for Turquoise is 35%, this tax deferral strategy provides $52,500 ($150,000 $\times$ 35%) to be invested or used in the business for another year.

★ **Framework Focus:
Deductions**

> *Tax Planning Strategy*

1-4d Tax Minimization Strategies Related to Deductions

> ➤ *Maximize Deductible Amounts.* A corporation that owns stock in another corporation is eligible for a *dividends received deduction (DRD)*. The DRD is equal to a specified percentage of the dividends received. The percentage is based on the amount of stock that the investor corporation owns in the investee corporation.

- 70 percent deduction for ownership of less than 20 percent.
- 80 percent deduction for ownership of 20 percent or more but less than 80 percent.
- 100 percent deduction for ownership of 80 percent or more.

Example 21

Falcon Corporation invests in bonds of Sparrow Corporation and receives interest of $20,000. Red Hawk Corporation acquires 15% of the stock of Pheasant Corporation and receives a $20,000 dividend. Falcon's taxable income is increased by $20,000 of interest received. Red Hawk's income is increased by $20,000 in dividend income, but it is allowed a $14,000 dividends received deduction, thus increasing taxable income by only $6,000.

Example 21 demonstrates the *tax* advantage of dividend income versus interest income. However, it is also important to consider *nontax* factors. Is the investment in bonds safer than the investment in stock? Does the potential growth in the value of stock outweigh the possible risk of investing in stock versus bonds?

TAX FACT   The Rewards of Tax Planning

Federal tax law does not fall equally on all taxpayers. Congress has allowed numerous tax incentives by which the taxpayer can manage long-term tax liabilities, when applying sound and ethical tax planning techniques. Here are some observations about the context in which the tax professional works with the taxpayer.

- The Federal income tax law provides over $1.2 trillion in credits, exemptions, exclusions, and deductions. The average individual reduces his or her tax liability by about $4,000 when these tax reductions are claimed.
- The most popular important Federal tax incentives for individuals include the following.

Tax Provision	Estimated Revenue Loss ($B)
Exclusions, deductions for health care costs	248
Exclusions for retirement plan income	170
Earned income, child credits	118
Deduction for home mortgage interest	70
Low tax rates on capital gains	43
Deduction for gifts to charity	39

- The most important tax incentives for corporate taxpayers include the following. Corporations claim about 10 percent of all tax expenditures.

Tax Provision	Estimated Revenue Loss ($B)
Accelerated depreciation deductions	59
Deferral of overseas income not repatriated	53
Credit, deduction for research activities	11
Deduction for domestic manufacturing profits	26
Credit for providing low-income housing	7

> *Accelerate Recognition of Deductions to Achieve Tax Deferral.* Both corporate and noncorporate taxpayers may deduct charitable contributions if the recipient is a qualified charitable organization. Generally, a deduction is allowed only for the year in which the payment is made. However, an important exception is available for *accrual basis corporations.* They may claim the deduction in the year *preceding* payment if two requirements are met. First, the contribution must be authorized by the board of directors by the end of that year. Second, the contribution must be paid on or before the fifteenth day of the third month of the next year.

> *Tax Planning Strategy*

Example 22

Blue, Inc., a calendar year, accrual basis corporation, wants to make a $10,000 donation to the Atlanta Symphony Association (a qualified charitable organization), but does not have adequate funds to make the contribution in 2014. On December 28, 2014, Blue's board of directors *authorizes* a $10,000 contribution to the Association. The donation is made on March 14, 2015. Because Blue is an accrual basis corporation, it may claim the $10,000 donation as a deduction for tax year 2014, even though payment is not made until 2015.

Blue was able to take advantage of a tax provision and reduce 2014 taxable income by $10,000. If Blue is in the 35% marginal bracket, the corporation defers payment of $3,500 in Federal income tax. The $3,500 can be invested or used in the business for another tax year.

1-4e Tax Minimization Strategies Related to Tax Rates

★ **Framework Focus: Tax Rates**

> *Tax Planning Strategy*

> *Shift Net Income from High-Bracket Years to Low-Bracket Years.* One objective of shifting income is to defer the payment of income tax (refer to Example 20). A second time-shifting strategy is to shift *net* income from high-tax to low-tax years.

This can be accomplished by shifting income from high-bracket years to low-bracket years or by shifting deductions from low-bracket years to high-bracket years.

Example 23

Egret Corporation, a calendar year taxpayer, is in the 34% bracket in 2014, but expects to be in the 25% bracket in 2015. The corporation, which is negotiating a $10,000 service contract with a client, decides to wait until 2015 to sign the contract and perform the services. The client is indifferent as to when the contract is completed. Thus, Egret saves $900 in income tax by deferring the service contract income to 2015, when it will be taxed at the 25% rate instead of the current 34% rate.

In this case, the income-shifting strategy is used to accomplish two tax planning objectives. First, shifting the income defers the payment of income tax from 2014 to 2015. Second, the shifting strategy results in the income being taxed at a rate of 25% rather than 34%.

Example 24

Macaw Corporation has been sued for $125,000 damages by a customer, and the parties decided to settle out of court for $100,000. Macaw expects to be in the 25% bracket in 2014 and the 35% bracket in 2015. Macaw will save $10,000 in income tax if it finalizes the agreement in January 2015 rather than December 2014 [$100,000 × (35% − 25%)].

➤ *Tax Planning Strategy*

➤ *Shift Net Income from High-Bracket Taxpayers to Low-Bracket Taxpayers.* Individual income tax rates range from 10 to 35 percent (39.6 percent for certain high-income taxpayers). Although several provisions in the tax law prevent shifting income from high-bracket taxpayers to low-bracket taxpayers, many opportunities to do so remain. Business entities can be effective vehicles for shifting income to low-bracket taxpayers.

Example 25

Bill Gregory is the president and sole shareholder of Grayhawk, Inc., an S corporation. He projects that Grayhawk will earn $400,000 this year. Bill is taxed on this income at a 35% marginal rate. Bill and his wife have four teenage children, all of whom are dependents. The Gregorys record no other taxable income; they file a joint return.

Bill employs the children as part-time workers throughout the year and pays them $11,000 each. This reduces Bill's income from Grayhawk by $44,000 and reduces his Federal income tax by $15,400 ($44,000 × 35%).

The salaries paid to the children will be subject to their lower Federal income tax rates. The salaries also might be exempt from the FICA and other payroll taxes; so the family unit's total tax liability has been reduced by shifting taxable income to the children.

➤ *Tax Planning Strategy*

➤ *Shift Net Income from High-Tax Jurisdictions to Low-Tax Jurisdictions.* A choice of the state or country where income is earned (or where a deduction is incurred) can have a large effect on an entity's overall tax liability. Hence, shifting income from high-tax jurisdictions to low-tax jurisdictions or shifting deductions from low-tax jurisdictions to high-tax jurisdictions is an important tax planning strategy.

Example 26

Gold International owns a sales subsidiary in Texas and a manufacturing subsidiary in Ireland (which imposes a 15% tax rate on certain types of business income). The Irish subsidiary makes drill presses and sells them for $4 million to the Texas subsidiary, which then modifies them and offers them for sale to businesses in the United States for $8.4 million. The cost of manufacturing and modifying each drill press is $3 million.

Of the $5.4 million of profit earned, $1 million is attributable to the Irish corporation (which is subject to a 15% tax rate), and $4.4 million is attributable to the U.S. corporation (which is subject to a 34% tax rate). Gold's total tax liability is $1,646,000 [($1,000,000 × 15%) + ($4,400,000 × 34%)].

Example 27

Assume the same facts as in the previous example, except that $5 million of the profit is attributable to the Irish corporation and $400,000 is attributable to the U.S. corporation. In this case, Gold's total tax liability is $886,000 [($5,000,000 × 15%) + ($400,000 × 34%)]. Thus, by altering the amount of work done in each of the two subsidiaries and the amount of income generated by each, Gold's tax liability is decreased by $760,000 ($1,646,000 − $886,000).

TAX FACT The U.S. Federal Income Tax

The Federal income tax is pervasive throughout our lives, but how much do we know about where it came from and how it works?

- The current version of the Internal Revenue Code has surpassed its 100th birthday; it was first effective on March 1, 1913.
- A temporary Federal income tax was used to finance the Civil War and the Spanish-American War. The current Federal tax code was adopted after Britain, Germany, France, and other countries in Europe had adopted similar taxing systems.
- The first Form 1040 was four pages long.
- The tax return became Form 1040 because that was the next number sequentially in issued Federal forms.

- The first Form 1040 was due on March 1, 1914. The unextended due date became March 15 for 1919, and April 15 for 1955.
- Taxes largely are paid today using a withholding system, a creation made necessary to pay for World War II. But at first, no money was sent with the return. A field auditor checked every return and sent a bill to the taxpayer by June 1, payable by June 30.
- The tax code is about 4 million words long. The IRS estimates that it annually takes more than 7 billion hours to comply with the tax law.
- Of all the Forms 1040 filed, only about 60 percent of them have a positive tax liability. Of the 58 million returns with a zero or negative tax liability, about 91 percent of them reported adjusted gross income under $40,000.

© iStockphoto.com/Pali Rao

➤ *Control the Character of Income and Deductions.* For various policy reasons, Congress has chosen to treat certain categories of income and losses more favorably than others. For instance, the provisions that apply to most individuals and tax long-term capital gains at a maximum rate of 20 percent, compared to a top 39.6 percent rate on ordinary income, were enacted to encourage individuals to make long-term investments of capital in the economy.

➤ *Tax Planning Strategy*

Example 28

Lisa is the proprietor of Designer Enterprises. Because a proprietorship is a flow-through entity, Lisa reports all of Designer's transactions on her individual income tax return. On October 9, 2014, Lisa invested $25,000 of Designer's excess cash in Lavender Corporation stock. On October 1, 2015, the stock was worth $35,000.

Lisa's marginal tax rate is 33% for ordinary income and 15% for long-term capital gain. She has decided to sell the stock and use the cash to increase Designer's inventory. She must hold the stock until October 10, 2015, for the gain to qualify as long term (held more than a year). If Lisa sells the stock before October 10, 2015, the gain is taxed as short term and she pays 33% tax on the gain. If she sells the stock after October 9, 2015, the gain is long term and she will pay 15% tax on the gain.

To encourage investment in small businesses, Congress enacted the § 1244 provisions, which provide favorable Federal income tax treatment of losses incurred on the sale of qualifying small business stock. Generally, losses on the sale of stock are treated as capital losses. Individuals with capital losses in excess of capital gains are permitted to deduct only $3,000 of such losses against ordinary income in a tax year. To make small business stock more attractive as an investment, § 1244 allows up to $50,000 ($100,000 if married filing jointly) of losses on such stock to be treated as ordinary losses, thus exempting the § 1244 losses from being offset against capital gains and then from the $3,000 limit that would otherwise apply to any excess capital losses.

Example 29

Roberto invested $80,000 in Mauve Corporation stock. He sold the stock this year for $40,000. He has no other capital asset transactions and does not expect to have any in future years. If the Mauve stock qualifies as § 1244 stock, Roberto may deduct the entire $40,000 as an ordinary loss. If the stock does not qualify as § 1244 stock, Roberto may deduct only $3,000 as a capital loss in the current tax year. He carries the remaining loss of $37,000 forward. In future years, the loss will continue to be subject to the annual $3,000 limitation unless there are offsetting capital gains.

➤ *Tax Planning Strategy*

➤ *Avoid Double Taxation.* The owners of a corporation can choose between two entity forms. A C corporation, also referred to as a regular corporation, is a taxable entity that pays tax on corporate profits. Shareholders also pay tax on dividends received from a C corporation, resulting in what is commonly referred to as *double taxation* (refer to Example 16). Note, however, as discussed in Chapter 4, that the dividends may be eligible for a beneficial tax rate.

Shareholders can avoid double taxation by electing that a corporate entity become an S corporation. Unlike a C corporation, an S corporation is not a taxable entity. Instead, the profits and losses of the S corporation flow through to the shareholders and are reported on their tax returns (see Chapter 15).

Example 30

Chickadee, Inc., a C corporation with net income of $100,000, pays Carl, its sole shareholder, a $77,750 dividend. Chickadee must pay corporate income tax of $22,250 on the net income of $100,000, and Carl must pay tax on the $77,750 dividend. Sparrow, Inc., an S corporation, also earns $100,000. Sparrow is not a taxable entity, so it pays no income tax on the $100,000 net income. Sam, who is the sole shareholder of Sparrow, includes $100,000 in computing his taxable income.

Other entity choices can be used to avoid double taxation, including partnerships and limited liability companies. Partnerships and limited liability companies, like S corporations, are flow-through entities rather than taxable entities (see Chapter 14).

Choosing to operate as a **flow-through entity** is not the only way to avoid double taxation. Double taxation can be avoided or minimized by having the corporation make payments, such as salaries, rent, and interest to the shareholders.

Example 31

Walt is the president and sole shareholder of Meadowlark, Inc., a C corporation. Meadowlark's taxable income before any payment to Walt is $600,000. Walt, a skilled manager, is primarily responsible for the profitability of the corporation. If Meadowlark pays Walt a dividend of $400,000, the corporation must pay Federal income tax on $600,000 and Walt must include the $400,000 dividend in gross income. However, if Meadowlark pays Walt a salary of $400,000, the salary is deductible and the corporation has only $200,000 of taxable income. Walt must include the $400,000 salary in gross income.

In either case, Walt includes $400,000 in gross income (the dividends may be eligible for a beneficial tax rate). Meadowlark, on the other hand, reports $400,000 less taxable income if the payment to Walt is a salary payment rather than a dividend payment.

★ **Framework Focus: Credits**

➤ *Tax Planning Strategy*

1-4f Tax Minimization Strategies Related to Credits

➤ *Maximize Tax Credits.* Congress uses the tax credit provisions of the Internal Revenue Code liberally in implementing tax policy. It is important to understand the difference between a credit and a deduction, both of which reduce a taxpayer's tax liability. A deduction reduces taxable income, which results in a reduction of the tax paid. The tax benefit of the deduction depends on the amount of the qualifying expenditure and the taxpayer's tax rate. A tax credit reduces the tax liability dollar for dollar and is not affected by the taxpayer's tax rate.

Example 32

Oriole Corporation, which is in the 25% marginal bracket, has a $6,000 deduction for expenditures made to repair a machine. The deduction reduces taxable income by $6,000 and results in a tax liability reduction of $1,500 ($6,000 deduction × 25% marginal rate).

Oriole also incurred expenditures of $6,000 to rehabilitate a building, which qualifies the corporation for a tax credit of $600 ($6,000 rehabilitation expenditures × 10% rate for the credit). The rehabilitation expenditures credit results in a $600 reduction of Oriole's tax liability. In addition, Oriole's depreciable basis for the building increases by $5,400 ($6,000 expenditures − $600 credit).

One example of the use of credits to influence taxpayer behavior is the work opportunity tax credit, which was enacted to encourage employers to hire employees from several targeted and economically disadvantaged groups, including high-risk youths, summer youth employees, and military veterans. The employee is certified to be a member of a qualifying targeted group. The work opportunity tax credit is 40 percent of the first $6,000 of wages paid during the first 12 months of employment. For long-term family assistance recipients, the credit is even greater.

> **Example 33**
>
> Robin Corporation hired a high-risk youth for four months at a cost of $6,000. Robin qualifies for the work opportunity tax credit and is allowed a credit of $2,400 ($6,000 wages × 40% credit rate) and a wage deduction of $3,600 ($6,000 wages − $2,400 credit). Robin is a 34% bracket taxpayer. The $3,600 deduction reduces Robin's income tax by $1,224 ($3,600 × 34%). The total tax saving thus is $3,624 ($1,224 from the deduction + $2,400 from the credit).
>
> If the employee does not qualify Robin for the work opportunity tax credit, Robin is allowed a deduction of $6,000, which results in a tax saving of $2,040 ($6,000 × 34%). Thus, hiring an employee who qualifies Robin for the work opportunity tax credit saves an additional $1,584 in tax ($3,624 − $2,040).

1-4g Thinking Outside the Framework

Although the General Framework for Income Tax Planning in Figure 1.3 is broad and covers most tax planning strategies, some strategies fall outside the framework. In addition, other planning ideas can supplement the strategies in the framework. Some of these ideas are discussed below.

Determining the Tax Burden

To engage in effective tax planning, one must be able to identify the relevant tax rate that will be applied to a transaction. There are at least three kinds of tax rates to consider in making a financial decision. A taxpayer's *marginal* tax rate is paid on an additional dollar of taxable income. Referring to the corporate income tax rate schedule on the inside front cover of this text, a C corporation's marginal tax rate on its first dollar of income is 15 percent. Similarly, the marginal tax rate faced by a corporation with $100,001 of income is 39 percent.

The *average* tax rate is the ratio of taxes paid to the tax base. Thus, a corporation with $100,000 of taxable income is subject to an average tax rate of 22.25 percent ($22,250 in tax divided by $100,000 in taxable income).

A third kind of tax rate computation, the *effective* tax rate, can be seen as either (1) the ratio of taxes paid to financial net income before tax or (2) the sum of currently payable and deferred tax expense divided by the book net income before tax. Of these approaches to determining a taxpayer's tax rate, the marginal tax rate is most appropriate for tax planning purposes.

> **Example 34**
>
> Azure Corporation reports taxable income of $80,000. Azure also received $10,000 of tax-free interest income from municipal bonds. Using the corporate tax rate schedule on the inside front cover of this text, one can determine that the company's tax liability is $15,450.
>
> If Azure were to earn an additional dollar in taxable income, it would pay an extra $.34 in tax. Thus, the company's marginal tax rate is 34%. Azure's average tax rate is the ratio of taxes paid to book income, or 19.3% ($15,450/$80,000). Finally, the company has an effective rate of tax of 17.2% ($15,450/$90,000), the ratio of taxes paid to book net income before tax (here, the sum of taxable income and tax-free income).

The actual tax paid may not always be apparent. For example, the amount of taxes paid should include both current taxes and the present value of future taxes generated by a transaction. Present value and future value tables are included in Appendix F of this text.

Example 35

Magenta Corporation is a publishing company that specializes in electronic media. It is a new corporation that was formed on January 1, 2013. During that year, it generated a net operating loss (NOL) of $300,000. The NOL can be carried forward to offset future years' taxable income and thereby reduce Magenta's future tax liabilities. Magenta expects to earn $100,000 of income each year over the next four years. The NOL should completely offset the company's taxable income for the first three of these years.

At the beginning of 2014, Magenta must decide whether to invest in a project that will earn an additional $40,000 of taxable income during 2014 or in a project that will generate $36,000 of tax-free income. The company's president reasons that because the company has an NOL carryforward, the applicable tax rate is 0%, so the taxable project should be chosen.

The president's reasoning is incorrect, because an additional $40,000 of income now will result in $40,000 of taxable income in 2016 (because there will be $40,000 less NOL available in that year).

	2014	2015	2016	2017
Alternative 1 (tax-free investment)				
Pre-NOL taxable income	$ 100,000	$ 100,000	$ 100,000	$100,000
NOL carryforward (from 2013)	(300,000)	(200,000)	(100,000)	–0–
Taxable income	$ –0–	$ –0–	$ –0–	$100,000
Alternative 2 (taxable investment)				
Pre-NOL taxable income	$ 140,000	$ 100,000	$ 100,000	$100,000
NOL carryforward (from 2013)	(300,000)	(160,000)	(60,000)	–0–
Taxable income	$ –0–	$ –0–	$ 40,000	$100,000

The tax cost of the $40,000 project equals the discounted value of the tax due for 2016. Assuming a 10% after-tax internal rate of return and a 15% corporate tax rate, the present value of taxes deferred for three years is $4,508 and the discounted tax rate is 11.27%. Thus, the after-tax proceeds on the taxable project are $35,492, or $508 *less* than the $36,000 earnings on the tax-free project.

1-5 UNDERSTANDING THE FEDERAL TAX LAW

LO.6

Recognize the economic, social, equity, and political considerations that underlie the tax law.

The Federal tax law is a mosaic of statutory laws, administrative pronouncements, and court decisions. Anyone who has attempted to work with these provisions would admit to their complexity. For the person who has to trudge through a mass of rules to find the solution to a tax problem, it may be of some consolation to know that the law's complexity generally can be explained. Whether sound or not, there are reasons for the formulation of every rule. Recognizing these reasons, therefore, is an important step toward understanding the Federal tax law.

1-5a Revenue Needs

The foundation of the income tax system is the raising of revenue to cover the cost of government operations. Ideally, annual outlays should not exceed anticipated revenues, thereby leading to a balanced budget with no resulting deficit. Many states have achieved this objective by passing laws or constitutional amendments precluding deficit spending.

The U.S. Constitution allows deficit spending, and politicians often find it hard to resist the temptation to spend more than the tax system collects currently. Congress uses several approaches to reduce a tax bill's net revenue loss. When tax

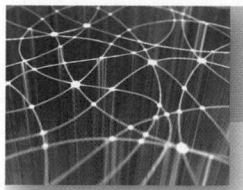

BRIDGE DISCIPLINE Bridge to Political Science, Economics, Health Care

When the tax law is used to accomplish goals other than revenue collection, fiscal "winners" and "losers" can be created. The distribution is not equal across income levels for Federal tax expenditures and other Federal benefits. For this purpose, "Federal benefits" include retirement, health care, and poverty reduction programs that trigger payments to individuals.

"Federal tax breaks" usually do not involve an appropriation and payment by Congress. Instead, they represent tax reductions from individuals' exemptions, the standard deduction, itemized deductions (e.g., for payments of home mortgage interest), and lower tax rates on investment income.

Federal Benefits Received

Income Quintile	$ Received per Family Unit	% of Total Benefits Received	$B in Benefits Received
Lowest (#1)	18,007	33	666
2	17,755	27	551
3	13,003	17	349
4	10,780	12	246
Highest (#5)	10,087	10	203

Federal Tax Breaks Received

Income Quintile	$ Received per Family Unit	% of Total Benefits Received	$B in Benefits Received
Lowest (#1)	1,110	4	40
2	2,149	7	74
3	2,757	8	91
4	5,021	14	152
Highest (#5)	24,693	67	723

reductions are involved, the full impact of the legislation can be phased in over a period of years. Or as an alternative, the tax reduction can be limited to a period of years. When the period expires, Congress can then renew or not renew the provision in light of budget considerations.

1-5b Economic Considerations

Using the tax system in an effort to accomplish economic objectives has become increasingly popular in recent years. Generally, proponents of this approach use tax legislation to promote measures designed to help control the economy or encourage certain economic activities and businesses.

Encouragement of Certain Activities

Without passing judgment on the wisdom of any such choices, it is clear that the tax law encourages certain types of economic activity or segments of the economy. For example, the favorable treatment (immediate deduction) allowed research and development expenditures can be explained by the desire to foster technological progress.

Similarly, Congress has used depreciation deductions as a means of encouraging investment in business capital. Theoretically, shorter asset lives and accelerated methods should encourage additional investment in depreciable property acquired for business use. Conversely, longer asset lives and the required use of the straight-line method of depreciation dampen the tax incentive for capital outlays.

Part of the tax law addresses the global energy crisis—in terms of both our reliance on foreign oil and the need to ease the problem of global warming.

Global Tax Issues

© iStockphoto.com/Andrey Prokhorov

Outsourcing of Tax Return Preparation

The use of foreign nationals to carry out certain job assignments for U.S. businesses is an increasingly popular practice. Outsourcing such activities as telemarketing to India, for example, usually produces the same satisfactory result but at a much lower cost.

Now outsourcing also is being applied to the preparation of tax returns. Not only can this practice be expected to continue, but it probably will increase in volume. Outsourcing tax return preparation does not violate Federal law, and the practice is compatible with accounting ethical guidelines as long as three safeguards are followed: First, the practitioner must make sure that client confidentiality is maintained. Second, the practitioner must verify the accuracy of the work that has been outsourced. Third, the practitioner must gain the consent of clients when any offshore third-party contractor is used to provide professional services.

Tax professionals justify tax preparation outsourcing as a means of conserving time and effort that can be applied toward more meaningful tax planning on behalf of their clients.

Sources: Reg. § 301.7216–2(c)(2); AICPA Ethics Ruling No. 1 (under Rule 301), see **www.aicpa.org/Research/standards/CodeofConduct/Pages/et_391.aspx**.

Ecological considerations justify a tax provision that permits a more rapid expensing of the costs of installing pollution control facilities. Measures such as these that aid in maintaining a clean air environment and conserving energy resources also can be justified under social considerations.

Is it wise to stimulate U.S. exports of goods and services? Considering the pressing and continuing problem of a deficit in the U.S. balance of payments, the answer should be clear. In an international setting, Congress has deemed it advisable to establish incentives for U.S. citizens who accept employment overseas.

Is saving desirable for the economy? Saving leads to capital formation and thereby makes funds available to finance home construction and industrial expansion. The tax law encourages saving by according preferential treatment to private retirement plans. Not only are deductions allowed for contributions to certain retirement plans and Individual Retirement Accounts (IRAs), but income on the contributions might not be taxed until withdrawn.

Encouragement of Certain Industries

A sound agricultural base is necessary for a well-balanced national economy. Undoubtedly, this explains why farmers are accorded special treatment under the Federal income tax system. Among the benefits available to farmers are the election to expense rather than capitalize certain soil and water conservation expenditures and fertilizers and the election to defer the recognition of gain on the receipt of crop insurance proceeds.

To stimulate the manufacturing industry, Congress enacted the domestic production activities deduction. The provision creates a tax benefit in the form of a deduction for profits derived from manufacturing activities conducted within the United States. By restricting the deduction to manufacturing income attributable to wages reportable to the IRS, new U.S. jobs will result and the outsourcing of labor is discouraged. Thus, the tax system is used to encourage both domestic manufacturing and job growth.

Encouragement of Small Business

It seems that in the United States, a consensus exists that what is good for small business is good for the economy as a whole. This assumption has led to a definite bias in the tax law favoring small business. Several income tax provisions can be explained by the desire to benefit small business, including the low marginal tax rates applied to the first dollars of the entity's income.

1-5c Social Considerations

Some provisions of the Federal tax law, particularly those dealing with the income tax of individuals, can be explained by a desire to encourage certain social results.

- Certain benefits provided to employees through accident and health insurance plans financed by employers are nontaxable to employees. Encouraging such plans is considered socially desirable because they provide medical benefits in the event of an employee's illness or injury.
- A contribution made by an employer to a qualified pension or profit sharing plan for an employee may receive special treatment. The contribution and any income it generates are not taxed to the employee until the funds are distributed. Such an arrangement also benefits the employer by allowing a tax deduction when the contribution is made to the qualified plan. Various types of retirement plans are encouraged to supplement the subsistence income level the employee otherwise would obtain under the Social Security system.
- A deduction is allowed for contributions to qualified charitable organizations. The deduction attempts to shift some of the financial and administrative burden of socially desirable programs from the public (government) to the private (citizens) sector.
- Various tax credits, deductions, and exclusions are designed to encourage taxpayers to obtain or extend their level of education.
- A tax credit is allowed for amounts spent to furnish care for certain minor or disabled dependents to enable the taxpayer to seek or maintain gainful employment.
- A tax deduction is denied for certain expenditures deemed to be contrary to public policy. This disallowance extends to items such as fines, penalties, illegal kickbacks, bribes to government officials, and gambling losses in excess of gains. Social considerations dictate that the tax law should not encourage these activities by permitting a deduction.

1-5d Equity Considerations

The concept of equity is relative. Reasonable persons can, and often do, disagree about what is fair or unfair. In the tax area, moreover, equity is most often tied to a particular taxpayer's personal situation. To illustrate, compare the tax positions of those who rent their personal residences with those who own their homes. Renters may not take a Federal income tax deduction for the rent they pay. For homeowners, however, a large portion of the house payments they make may qualify for the Federal mortgage interest and property tax deductions. Although renters may have difficulty understanding this difference in tax treatment, the encouragement of home ownership can be justified on both economic and social grounds.

In many other parts of the law, however, equity concerns are evident. The concept of equity appears in tax provisions that alleviate the effect of multiple taxation and postpone the recognition of gain when the taxpayer lacks the ability or wherewithal to pay the tax. Provisions that mitigate the effect of the application of the annual accounting period concept also reflect equity considerations.

Alleviating the Effect of Multiple Taxation

The income earned by a taxpayer may be subject to taxes imposed by different taxing authorities. If, for example, the taxpayer is a resident of New York City, income might be subject to Federal, state of New York, and city of New York income taxes. To compensate for this apparent inequity, the Federal tax law allows a taxpayer to claim a deduction for state and local income taxes.

The deduction does not, however, neutralize the effect of multiple taxation because the benefit derived depends on the taxpayer's Federal income tax rate. Only a 100% rate tax credit, rather than a deduction, would completely eliminate the effects of multiple taxation on the same income. Equity considerations also can explain the Federal tax treatment of certain income from non-U.S. sources.

The Wherewithal to Pay Concept

The wherewithal to pay concept recognizes the inequity of taxing a transaction when the taxpayer lacks the means to pay the tax. The wherewithal to pay concept underlies a provision in the tax law dealing with the treatment of gain resulting from an involuntary conversion. An involuntary conversion occurs when property is destroyed by casualty or taken by a public authority through condemnation. If gain results from the conversion, it need not be recognized if the taxpayer replaces the property within a specified time period. The replacement property must be similar or related in service or use to that involuntarily converted.

Example 36

Ron, a rancher, has some pasture land that is condemned by the state for use as a game preserve. The condemned pasture land cost Ron $120,000, but the state pays him $150,000 (its fair market value). Shortly thereafter, Ron buys more pasture land for $150,000.

Ron has a realized gain of $30,000 [$150,000 (condemnation award) − $120,000 (cost of land)]. It would be inequitable to require Ron to pay a tax on this gain for two reasons. First, without disposing of the property acquired (the new land), Ron would be hard-pressed to pay the tax. Second, his economic position has not changed.

What if Ron reinvests only $140,000 of the award in new pasture land? Now Ron recognizes a $10,000 taxable gain in the current year. Instead of ending up with only replacement property, Ron now holds land and $10,000 in cash.

Mitigating the Effect of the Annual Accounting Period Concept

Federal income tax returns are due for every tax year of the taxpayer. The application of this annual accounting period concept can lead to dissimilar tax treatment for taxpayers who are, from a long-range standpoint, in the same economic position.

Example 37

José and Alicia, both sole proprietors, experienced the following results during the indicated tax years.

| Year | Profit (or Loss) | |
	José	Alicia
2013	$50,000	$150,000
2014	60,000	60,000
2015	60,000	(40,000)

Although José and Alicia have the same profit of $170,000 over the period from 2013 through 2015, the annual accounting period concept places Alicia at a disadvantage for tax purposes. However, the net operating loss deduction generated in 2015 offers Alicia some relief by allowing her to carry back some or all of her 2015 loss to the earlier profitable years (in this case, 2013). Thus, with an NOL carryback, Alicia can obtain an immediate refund for some of the taxes she paid on the $150,000 profit reported for 2013.

1-5e Political Considerations

A large segment of the Federal tax law is made up of statutory provisions. Because these statutes are enacted by Congress, is it any surprise that political considerations influence tax law?

Special Interest Legislation

Certain provisions of the tax law can largely be explained by the political influence some groups have had on Congress. For example, is there any other realistic reason that prepaid subscription and dues income is not taxed until earned, while prepaid rents are taxed to the landlord in the year received?

Special interest legislation is not necessarily to be condemned if it can be justified on economic, social, or some other utilitarian grounds. In most cases, however, it is objectionable in that it adds further complexity to an already cluttered tax law. At any rate, it is an inevitable product of our political system.

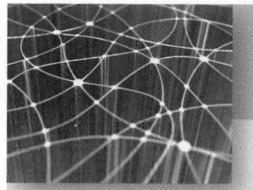

BRIDGE DISCIPLINE   Bridge to Political Science and Sociology

The country's wrestling with the issue of same-sex marriage has important tax ramifications. One recent study noted that if all committed same-sex couples were to be legally married under state laws (perhaps 600,000 filers), any income tax revenue increase would be offset many times over by the additional Social Security and Medicare claims from one member of the couple against the other's accounts.

But this issue is still working its way through the statehouses and courthouses. For instance, same-sex marriage is allowed in perhaps one-half of the U.S. states. On an income tax return for a state in which same-sex marriage is not recognized, but a Federal joint return has been filed by the married couple, how are various income and deduction items to be recomputed?

State-Federal law conflicts have affected citizens at other times in U.S. history.

- A few states allowed voting by women before the U.S. Constitution adopted the rule.
- "Nevada divorces" were not recognized by the home states of all couples. As recently as 1940, charges of bigamy were brought against those with Nevada divorces who remarried outside Nevada.
- A few states now recognize same-sex marriages performed in other jurisdictions, including those performed outside the United States.

Who would have thought that the important tax question "Are you married?" could become so difficult to answer?

State and Local Government Influences

State law has had an influence in shaping our present Federal tax law. One example of this effect is the evolution of Federal tax law in response to states with community property systems. The states with community property systems are Louisiana, Texas, New Mexico, Arizona, California, Washington, Idaho, Nevada, and Wisconsin. Spouses in Alaska can elect community property treatment. The rest of the states are common law jurisdictions.

The difference between common law and community property systems centers around the property rights possessed by married persons. In a common law system, each spouse owns whatever he or she earns. Under a community property system, one-half of the earnings of each spouse is considered owned by the other spouse.

Example 38

Al and Fran are husband and wife, and their only income is the $80,000 annual salary Al receives. If they live in New Jersey (a common law state), the $80,000 salary belongs to Al. If, however, they live in Arizona (a community property state), the $80,000 is divided equally, in terms of ownership, between Al and Fran.

At one time, the tax position of the residents of community property states was so advantageous that many common law states adopted community property systems. Needless to say, the political pressure placed on Congress to correct the disparity in tax treatment was considerable. To a large extent, this was accomplished in 1948 when the law extended many of the community property tax advantages to residents of common law jurisdictions.

The major advantage extended was the provision allowing married taxpayers to file joint returns and compute the tax liability as if one-half of the income had been earned by each spouse. This result is automatic in a community property state because half of the income earned by one spouse belongs to the other spouse. The income-splitting benefits of a joint return are incorporated as part of the tax rates applicable to married taxpayers. A similar motivation can be seen for the gift-splitting provisions of the Federal gift tax and the marital deduction of the Federal estate and gift taxes.

TAX FACT   The Costs of Complexity

A tax system that is designed to accomplish so many, sometimes contradictory, goals is bound to be a complex animal. According to the Tax Foundation, the current system may actually be so complex as to be self-defeating.

By one estimate, the cost of compliance with Federal tax laws exceeds $425 billion per year. Roughly, this means that compliance costs act as an additional tax of about 30 cents for every tax dollar collected. This amount exceeds the annual costs of compensation for all of the workers at Walmart, UPS, IBM, McDonald's, and Citigroup combined.

For this study, the following items were counted as costs of tax compliance.

- The value of taxpayers' time spent record keeping, filing, planning, and otherwise complying with the tax laws.
- Tax collection costs (chiefly wages and benefits) of IRS employees.
- Expenditures made to professional tax preparers, consultants, and other preparers.

© iStockphoto.com/Pali Rao

1-5f Influence of the Internal Revenue Service

LO.7

Describe the role played by the IRS and the courts in the evolution of the Federal tax system.

The influence of the IRS on tax law is apparent in many areas beyond its role in issuing the administrative pronouncements that make up a considerable portion of our tax law. The IRS has been instrumental in securing the passage of much legislation designed to curtail the most flagrant tax avoidance practices (to "close tax loopholes"). In addition, the IRS has sought and obtained legislation to make its own job easier (to attain administrative feasibility).

Closing Perceived Tax Loopholes

Certain tax provisions are intended to prevent a loophole from being used to avoid the tax consequences intended by Congress. Working within the letter of existing law, taxpayers and their advisers devise techniques that accomplish indirectly what cannot be accomplished directly. As a consequence, legislation is enacted to close the loopholes that taxpayers have located and exploited. Some tax law can be explained in this fashion and is discussed in the chapters to follow.

Administrative Feasibility

Some tax law is justified on the grounds that it simplifies the task of the IRS in collecting the revenue and administering the law. With regard to collecting the revenue, the IRS long ago realized the importance of placing taxpayers on a pay-as-you-go basis. Elaborate withholding procedures apply to wages, and accrual basis taxpayers often must pay taxes on prepaid income in the year received and not when earned. The approach may be contrary to generally accepted accounting principles, but it is consistent with the wherewithal to pay concept.

Of considerable aid to the IRS in collecting revenue are the numerous provisions that impose interest and penalties on taxpayers for noncompliance with the tax law. Provisions such as the penalties for failure to pay a tax or to file a return that is due, the negligence penalty for intentional disregard of Federal tax rules and regulations, and various penalties for civil and criminal fraud serve as deterrents to taxpayer noncompliance.

One of the keys to an effective administration of our tax system is the audit process conducted by the IRS. To carry out this function, the IRS is aided by provisions that reduce the chance of taxpayer error or manipulation and therefore reduce the audit effort that is necessary. An increase in the amount of the standard deduction, for example, reduces the number of individual taxpayers who will choose the alternative of itemizing their personal deductions. With fewer deductions to check, the audit function is simplified.

In-depth coverage can be found on this book's companion website: **www.cengagebrain.com** **7**   Digging Deeper

1-5g Influence of the Courts

In addition to interpreting statutory provisions and the administrative pronouncements issued by the IRS, the Federal courts have influenced tax law in two other respects. First, the courts have formulated certain judicial concepts that serve as guides in the application of various tax provisions. Second, certain key decisions have led to changes in the Internal Revenue Code.

Judicial Concepts Relating to Tax

Particularly in dealings between related parties, the courts test transactions by looking to whether the taxpayers acted in an arm's length manner. The question to be asked is: Would unrelated parties have handled the transaction in the same way?

Example 39

Rex, the sole shareholder of Silver Corporation, leases property to the corporation for a yearly rent of $6,000. To test whether the corporation should be allowed a rent deduction for this amount, the IRS and the courts will apply the arm's length concept. Would Silver have paid $6,000 a year in rent if it had leased the same property from an unrelated party (rather than from Rex)?

Suppose it is determined that an unrelated third party would have charged an annual rent for the property of only $5,000. Under these circumstances, Silver deducts only $5,000. The other $1,000 it paid for the use of the property represents a nondeductible dividend. Accordingly, Rex is treated as having received rent income of $5,000 and dividend income of $1,000.

Judicial Influence on Statutory Provisions

Some court decisions have been of such consequence that Congress has incorporated them into statutory tax law. For example, many years ago, the courts found that stock dividends distributed to the shareholders of a corporation were not taxable as income. This result largely was accepted by Congress, and a provision in the tax statutes now addresses the issue.

On occasion, however, Congress has reacted negatively to judicial interpretations of the tax law.

Example 40

Nora leases unimproved real estate to Wade for 20 years. At a cost of $400,000, Wade erects a building on the land. The building is worth $150,000 when the lease terminates and Nora takes possession of the property. Does Nora have any gross income either when the improvements are made or when the lease terminates? In a landmark decision, a court held that Nora must recognize income of $150,000 upon the termination of the lease.

Congress believed that the result reached in Example 40 was inequitable in that it was not consistent with the wherewithal to pay concept. Consequently, the tax law was amended to provide that a landlord does not recognize any income either when the improvements are made (unless made in lieu of rent) or when the lease terminates.

1-6 Summary

Tax laws are pervasive in today's global economy. Individuals and businesses must contend with complex rules in planning their personal and professional activities. Taxes can fall on income, wealth, asset transfers, consumer expenditures, and other events.

Tax planning is a means by which to manage the amount and timing of tax liabilities to accomplish one's long-term objectives. The conduct of tax practitioners is regulated by professional associations, lawmakers, and the taxing agencies.

Taxing systems are designed to provide revenues for governments to accomplish the common goals of citizens. In addition to its necessary revenue-raising objective, the Federal tax law has developed in response to several other factors.

- *Economic considerations.* Tax provisions can help to regulate the economy and encourage certain activities and types of businesses.
- *Social considerations.* Some tax provisions are designed to encourage (or discourage) socially desirable (or undesirable) practices.
- *Equity considerations.* Tax provisions can alleviate the effect of multiple taxation, recognize the wherewithal to pay concept, and mitigate the effect of the annual accounting period concept.
- *Political considerations.* Tax provisions can represent special interest legislation and reflect the effect of state and local law.
- *Influence of the IRS.* Many tax provisions are intended to aid the IRS in the collection of revenue and the administration of the tax law.
- *Influence of the courts.* Court decisions have established a body of judicial concepts relating to tax law and have, on occasion, led Congress to enact statutory provisions to either clarify or negate their effect.

REFOCUS ON THE BIG PICTURE

A TYPICAL TAX YEAR FOR A MODERN FAMILY

The explanation given for the difference in the ad valorem property taxes—the Carters' increase and the Walkers' decrease—seems reasonable. It is not likely that the Carters' increase was due to a *general* upward assessment in valuation, as the Walkers' taxes on their residence (located nearby) dropped. More business use of the Carters' residence (presuming that Travis conducts his consulting practice from his home) might be responsible for the increase, but capital improvements appear to be a more likely cause.

The imposition of the use tax when Travis registered the new automobile illustrates one of the means by which a state can preclude the avoidance of its sales tax (see Example 4).

When gifts between family members are material in amount (e.g., an RV) and exceed the annual exclusion, a gift tax return needs to be filed. Even though no gift tax may be due because of the availability of the $5 ($5.34 indexed amount) million exclusion, the filing of a return starts the running of the statute of limitations.

The imposition of the "jock tax" on nonathletes is unusual but not improper. The Carters must recognize that some of their income is subject to income taxes in two states and take advantage of whatever relief is available to mitigate the result.

What If?

Because of the double audit (i.e., both state and Federal) and the deficiency assessed, the Carters need to make sure that future returns do not contain similar errors. As the text suggests, taxpayers with prior deficiencies are among those whose returns may be selected for audit.

© Corbis/SuperStock

Suggested Readings

Jill Lepore, "Tax Time: Why We Pay," *The New Yorker*, November 26, 2012.

Mark Robyn, Micah Cohen, and Joseph Henchman, "Sales Tax Holidays: Politically Expedient but Poor Tax Policy," July 24, 2013 working paper, **www.taxfoundation.org**.

Joseph J. Thorndike, "The Tenacity of Tax Complexity," December 2001 working paper, **www.taxhistory.org**.

"What the Federal Tax System Is Costing You—Tax Compliance Facts," 2007 working paper, **www.fairtax.org**.

Key Terms

Ad valorem taxes, 1-10

C corporations, 1-17

Deferred tax asset, 1-19

Deferred tax liability, 1-19

Effective tax rate, 1-19

Employment taxes, 1-2

Estate tax, 1-8

Excise taxes, 1-4

FICA tax, 1-7

Financial Accounting Standards Board (FASB), 1-17

Flow-through entity, 1-26

Franchise tax, 1-13

FUTA tax, 1-7

Generally Accepted Accounting Principles (GAAP), 1-17

Gift tax, 1-9

Inheritance tax, 1-8

International Accounting Standards Board (IASB), 1-17

International Financial Reporting Standards (IFRS), 1-17

Occupational taxes, 1-13

Personalty, 1-11

Proprietorship, 1-16

Realty, 1-11

S corporations, 1-17

Sales taxes, 1-2

Tax avoidance, 1-20

Tax evasion, 1-20

Use taxes, 1-5

Value added tax (VAT), 1-6

Wherewithal to pay, 1-32

Problems

1. **LO.1, 2, 5** James Corporation believes that it will have a better distribution location for its product if it relocates the corporation to another state. What considerations (both tax and nontax) should James weigh before making a decision on whether to make the move?   *Issue ID*

2. **LO.1** Distinguish between taxes that are *proportional* and those that are *progressive*.

3. **LO.2** Several years ago, Ethan purchased the former parsonage of St. James Church to use as a personal residence. To date, Ethan has not received any ad valorem property tax bills from either the city or the county tax authorities.   *Issue ID*
   a. What is a reasonable explanation for this oversight?
   b. What should Ethan do?

4. **LO.1, 6** In terms of Adam Smith's canon of economy, how does the Federal income tax fare?   *Critical Thinking*

5. **LO.2** Jim, a resident of Washington (which imposes a general sales tax), goes to Oregon (which does not impose a general sales tax) to purchase his automobile. Will Jim successfully avoid the Washington sales tax? Explain.

6. **LO.2** What is the difference between an excise tax and a general sales tax?
   a. Do all states impose a general sales tax?
   b. Does the Federal government impose a general sales tax?

7. **LO.2** How much property can Herman, a widower, give to his four married children, their spouses, and eight grandchildren over a period of 10 years without making a taxable gift? Show your computations.

8. **LO.2** Once its new facilities are finished, the Church of the Good Samaritan moves from downtown Madison City to the suburbs. Instead of disposing of the old location,   *Issue ID*

the church leases it to a former mayor of Madison City, who converts the church building and its parking lot into a high-end restaurant. Comment on any tax ramifications of this arrangement.

Ethics and Equity

9. **LO.2** The Toth family lives in a residence that they have owned for several years. They purchased the residence from St. Matthew's Catholic Church, which had used the house as a rectory for its priest. To the Toths' surprise, since they purchased the residence, they have not received any ad valorem property tax bills from either the city or the county. Is there a plausible explanation for this? Explain. What, if anything, should the Toths do about the property tax matter?

Issue ID

10. **LO.2** The Irontown Independent School District wants to sell a parcel of unimproved land that it does not need. Its three best offers are as follows: from the State Department of Public Safety (DPS), $4.3 million; from Trinity Lutheran Church, $4.2 million; and from Baker Motors, $3.9 million. DPS would use the property for a new state highway patrol barracks, Trinity would start a church school, and Baker would open a car dealership. As the financial adviser for the school district, which offer would you prefer? Why?

Issue ID

11. **LO.2** Eileen, a resident of Wyoming, goes to Montana to purchase her new automobile. She does this because Wyoming imposes a sales tax while Montana does not. Has Eileen successfully avoided the Wyoming sales tax? Explain.

12. **LO.2** Due to the economic downturn, many states are encountering reduced tax revenues—particularly from property and sales taxes. Several states with large mineral resources (e.g., Alaska and oil, Wyoming and coal), however, are making up the shortfall with another type of tax. Explain.

13. **LO.2** The Grays live in Clay County, which is adjacent to Jackson County. Although the retail stores in both counties are comparable, the Grays usually drive a few extra miles to shop in Jackson County. As to why the Grays might do this, consider the following:
    a. Clay County is in a different state than Jackson County.
    b. Clay County and Jackson County are in the same state.

Issue ID

14. **LO.2** Sophia lives several blocks from her parents in the same residential subdivision. Sophia is surprised to learn that her ad valorem property taxes for the year were raised, while those of her parents were lowered. What is a possible explanation for the difference?

Issue ID

15. **LO.2** During a social event, Muriel and Earl are discussing the home computer each recently purchased. Although the computers are identical makes and models, Muriel is surprised to learn that she paid a sales tax while Earl did not. Comment as to why this could happen.

16. **LO.3** In arriving at taxable income, how does the Federal income tax imposed on corporations differ from that imposed on individuals?

Decision Making

Communications

17. **LO.4, 5** Marco and Cynthia have decided to go into business together. They will operate a burrito delivery business. They expect to have a loss in the first and second years of the business and subsequently expect to make a substantial profit.

   Marco and Cynthia are concerned about potential liability if a customer ever gets sick after eating one of their products. They have called your office and asked for advice about whether they should run their business as a partnership or as a corporation. Write a letter to Cynthia Clay, at 1206 Seventh Avenue, Fort Worth, TX 76101, describing the alternative forms of business they can select. In your letter, explain what form or forms of business you recommend and why.

Decision Making

18. **LO.4, 5** Ashley runs a small business in Boulder, Colorado, that makes snow skis. She expects the business to grow substantially over the next three years. Because she is concerned about product liability and is planning to take the company public in 2014, she is currently considering incorporating the business. Financial data are as follows.

	2013	2014	2015
Sales revenue	$150,000	$320,000	$600,000
Tax-free interest income	5,000	8,000	15,000
Deductible cash expenses	30,000	58,000	95,000
Tax depreciation	25,000	20,000	40,000

Ashley expects her combined Federal and state marginal income tax rate to be 35% over the next three years before any profits from the business are considered. Her after-tax cost of capital is 12%.

a. Compute the present value of the future cash flows for 2013 to 2015 assuming that Ashley incorporates the business and pays all after-tax income as dividends (for Ashley's dividends that qualify for the 15% rate).

b. Compute the present value of the future cash flows for 2013 to 2015 assuming that Ashley continues to operate the business as a sole proprietorship.

c. Should Ashley incorporate the business this year? Why or why not?

19. **LO.3, 5** Palmer, Inc., has a net operating loss carryforward of $100,000. If Palmer continues its business with no changes, it will have $50,000 of taxable income (before the NOL) in both 2014 and 2015. If Palmer decides to invest in a new product line instead, it expects to have taxable income of $70,000 in 2014 and $50,000 in 2015. What marginal tax rate does the new product line face in 2014 and in 2015?

20. **LO.3, 5** Mauve Supplies, Inc., reports total income of $120,000. The corporation's taxable income is $105,000. What are Mauve's marginal, average, and effective tax rates?

21. **LO.2** Franklin County is in dire financial straits and is considering a number of sources for additional revenue. Evaluate the following possibilities in terms of anticipated taxpayer compliance.

    Issue ID

a. A property tax on business inventories.

b. A tax on intangibles (i.e., stocks and bonds) held as investments.

c. A property tax on boats used for recreational purposes.

22. **LO.5** Mason owns and operates a pharmacy as a sole proprietor. He manages to compete with the national chains because of the personalized service he provides to his customers. Mason also maintains a large and varied assortment of medical equipment and supplies (e.g., wheelchairs, walkers, and bath aids).

    Ethics and Equity

Mason uses the cash method of accounting, and he immediately deducts all purchases of goods for resale. He sees no need to keep inventory accounts, as it "all washes out" over time—last year's ending inventory becoming this year's beginning inventory. Thus, any misstatement of income in one year is offset in the following year.

Comment on Mason's rationalization and the propriety of his approach.

23. **LO.6** The Benson CPA firm is considering utilizing an offshore service provider to prepare many of its tax returns. In this regard, what ethical considerations must Benson take into account?

    Ethics and Equity

24. **LO.6** Discuss the probable justification for each of the following provisions of the tax law.

a. A tax credit allowed for electricity produced from renewable sources.

b. A tax credit allowed for the purchase of a motor vehicle that operates on alternative energy sources (e.g., nonfossil fuels).

c. A deduction for state and local income taxes.

d. The deduction for personal casualty losses that is subject to computational limitations.

e. Favorable treatment accorded to research and development expenditures.

f. A deduction allowed for income resulting from U.S. production (manufacturing) activities.

g. The deduction allowed for contributions to qualified charitable organizations.

h. An election that allows certain corporations to avoid the corporate income tax and pass losses through to their shareholders.

25. **LO.6** Discuss the probable justification for each of the following aspects of the tax law.

a. A tax credit is allowed for amounts spent to furnish care for minor children while the parent works.

b. Deductions for interest on home mortgage and property taxes on one's personal residence.

c. The income splitting benefits of filing a joint return.

d. Gambling losses in excess of gambling gains.

e. Net operating losses of a current year can be carried back to profitable years.

f. A taxpayer who sells property on an installment basis can recognize gain on the sale over the period the payments are received.

g. The exclusion from Federal tax of certain interest income from state and local bonds.

h. Prepaid income is taxed to the recipient in the year it is received and not in the year it is earned.

Critical Thinking

26. **LO.2** Contrast a value added tax (VAT) with a national sales tax in terms of anticipated taxpayer compliance.

Critical Thinking
Communications

27. **LO.2** Go to **www.taxfoundation.org**, and determine Tax Freedom Day for your state for 1950, 1960, 1970, 1980, 1990, 2000, and 2010. Report your results as a line graph.

Critical Thinking
Communications

28. Although the Federal income tax law is complex, most individual taxpayers are able to complete their tax returns without outside assistance. Gather data as to the accuracy of this statement. Summarize your comments in an e-mail to your instructor.

Ethics and Equity

29. President Franklin D. Roosevelt once said, "I am wholly unable to figure out the amount of tax," and wrote to the Federal Commissioner of Revenue, "may I ask that [the agency] let me know the amount of the balance due."

When a friend of FDR was ordered to pay $420,000 in tax penalties, the President called the Commissioner within earshot of reporters and told him to cut the penalties to $3,000. One listener, journalist David Brinkley, recalled years later: "Nobody seemed to think it was news or very interesting." Evaluate the President's comments and actions.

Critical Thinking
Communications

30. In no more than five PowerPoint slides, discuss the means by which the IRS selects individual income tax returns for audit.

31. **LO.5** Mia owns a warehouse that has a cost basis to her of $80,000. The city condemns the warehouse to make room for a new fire station. It pays Mia $400,000 for the property, its agreed-to fair market value.

Shortly after the condemnation, Mia purchases another warehouse as a replacement. What is her recognized gain if the new property costs:
a. $280,000?
b. $444,000?
c. $80,000?
d. Explain the justification for deferring the recognition of gain on the involuntary conversion.

BRIDGE DISCIPLINE

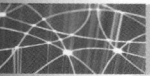

1. Discuss with respect to the Federal policy for reducing poverty:
   a. The individual income tax.
   b. The Social Security tax.

Communications

2. Prepare a two-page paper titled "How I Would Apply Federal Income Tax Law to Encourage the Availability of Universal Broadband in This Community" to submit to your economics professor.

Communications

3. Prepare an outline for a 10-minute speech to give to your government class. The speech is titled "If You Don't Pay Federal Taxes, You Can't Vote."

4. When taxes are "too high," taxpayers start to cheat on their taxes and dangerous consequences can result. Evaluate this statement. Give at least two examples to illustrate your conclusions.

Communications

5. In no more than six PowerPoint slides, summarize your comments for a debate with other business students on the topic "Resolved: The U.S. Should Adopt a Value Added Tax (VAT)."

6. LO.6 Some tax rules can be justified on multiple grounds (e.g., economic or social). In this connection, comment on the possible justification for the rules governing the following.
   a. Pension plans.
   b. Education.
   c. Home ownership.

Working with the Tax Law

LEARNING OBJECTIVES: *After completing Chapter 2, you should be able to:*

LO.1 **Describe the statutory, administrative, and judicial sources of the tax law and the purpose of each source.**

LO.2 **Locate and work with the tax law and understand the tax research process.**

LO.3 **Communicate the results of the tax research process in a client letter and a tax file memorandum.**

LO.4 **Employ a strategy of how best to use a computer when performing tax research and in taking the CPA exam.**

CHAPTER OUTLINE

TAX TALK *The less people know about how sausages and laws are made, the better they'll sleep at night.* —OTTO VON BISMARCK

Dennis Flaherty/Photographer's Choice/Getty Images

THE BIG PICTURE   Tax Solutions for the Real World

RESEARCHING TAX QUESTIONS

Early in December, Fred and Megan Samuels review their financial and tax situation with their son, Sam, and daughter-in-law, Dana. Sam and Dana live with Fred and Megan. Fred and Megan are in the 28% tax bracket. Both Sam and Dana are age 21.

Sam, a student at a nearby university, owns some publicly traded stock that he inherited from his grandmother. A current sale would result in approximately $8,000 of gross income ($19,000 amount realized − $11,000 adjusted basis).

At this point, Fred and Megan provide about 55% of Sam and Dana's support. Although neither is now employed, Sam has earned $960 and Dana has earned $900. The problem: Should the stock be sold, and would the sale prohibit Fred and Megan from claiming Sam and Dana as dependents? Would the stock sale result in a tax liability for Sam and Dana?

Read the chapter and formulate your responses.

F ederal tax law is a mixture of statutory provisions, administrative pronouncements, and court decisions. Anyone who has attempted to work with this body
of knowledge is familiar with its complexity. Tax research provides the vehicle
by which one makes sense out of this complexity.

2-1 TAX LAW SOURCES

LO.1

Describe the statutory, administrative, and judicial sources of the tax law and the purpose of each source.

Understanding taxation requires a mastery of the sources of the *rules of tax law.*
These sources include not only legislative provisions in the form of the Internal
Revenue Code but also congressional Committee Reports, Treasury Department
Regulations, other Treasury Department pronouncements, and court decisions.
Thus, the *primary sources* of tax information include pronouncements from all three
branches of government: legislative, executive, and judicial.

In addition to being able to locate and interpret the sources of the tax law, a tax professional must understand the relative weight of authority within these sources. The
tax law is of little significance, however, until it is applied to a set of facts and circumstances. This chapter, therefore, both introduces the statutory, administrative, and judicial sources of the tax law *and* explains how the law is applied to business and
individual transactions. It also explains how to apply research techniques effectively.

Tax research is necessary because the application of the law to a specific situation sometimes is not clear. As complicated as the Internal Revenue Code is, it cannot clearly address every conceivable situation. Accordingly, the tax professional
must search other sources (such as administrative rulings and judicial decisions) to
determine the most likely tax treatment of a transaction.

The tax research process can yield widely differing results for similar fact patterns. One of the goals of tax research is to discover which facts and which legal
rules are most relevant in determining the ultimate tax consequences. Working
with such knowledge, a tax professional then can advise the client about the tax
consequences of several possible courses of action. Tax research, in other words, is
of critical importance not only in properly characterizing completed events but also
in planning proposed transactions.

2-1a Statutory Sources of the Tax Law

Statutory sources of law include the Constitution (Article I, Sections 7, 8, and 10),
tax treaties (agreements between countries to mitigate the double taxation of taxpayers subject to the tax laws of those countries), and the Internal Revenue Code.
The Constitution grants Congress the power to impose and collect taxes, and it
authorizes the creation of treaties with other countries. The Internal Revenue
Code is the statutory basis for arriving at solutions to all tax questions.

Origin of the Internal Revenue Code

Before 1939, the statutory provisions relating to taxation were contained in the
individual revenue acts enacted by Congress every year or two. The inconvenience
and confusion that resulted from dealing with many separate acts led Congress to
codify all of the Federal tax laws in 1939. Known as the Internal Revenue Code of
1939, this codification arranged all Federal tax provisions in a logical sequence and
placed them in a separate part of the Federal statutes. A further rearrangement
took place in 1954 and resulted in the Internal Revenue Code of 1954, which continued in effect until it was replaced by the Internal Revenue Code of 1986.[1]

Statutory amendments to the tax law are integrated into the existing Code.
Thus, subsequent tax legislation, such as the Patient Protection and Affordable
Care Act of 2010 and the American Taxpayer Relief Act of 2012, became part of
the Internal Revenue Code of 1986.

[1]Aside from changes due to a large tax act, the organization of the Internal
Revenue Code of 1986 is not substantively different from the organization
of the 1954 Code. In contrast, the numbering scheme of sections in the
1939 Code differs from that used in the 1954 Code.

TAX FACT   Scope of the U.S. Tax System

Although it started out in 1913 as a tax on only the uppermost-income individuals, the tax system today is pervasive in our lives.

- In the typical tax year, the IRS receives about 20 million Forms 1040EZ and about 40 million Forms 1040A.
- The typical Form 1040 requires 7.25 hours to gather records and assemble the return, and 6.25 hours to prepare the form and attachments. The estimated cost of complying with tax rules is $425 billion per year.

- The Internal Revenue Code is about 4 million words (9,000 pages) long, and the Regulations require another 8 million words (165,000 pages). Combined, these documents are 12 times the length of Shakespeare's combined works and 15 times the length of the King James Bible.
- In filing Federal income tax returns, a majority of all individual taxpayers at every income level employ a professional tax preparer.

© iStockphoto.com/Pali Rao

The Legislative Process

Federal tax legislation generally originates in the House of Representatives, where it first is considered by the House Ways and Means Committee. It is also possible for tax bills to originate in the Senate if they are attached as riders to other legislative proposals. If acceptable to the committee, the proposed bill is referred to the entire House of Representatives for approval or disapproval. Approved bills are sent to the Senate, where they initially are considered by the Senate Finance Committee.

The next step is referral from the Senate Finance Committee to the entire Senate. Assuming no disagreement between the House and Senate, passage by the Senate means referral to the President for approval or veto. If the bill is approved or if the President's veto is overridden, the bill becomes law and part of the Internal Revenue Code.

When the Senate version of the bill differs from that passed by the House, the Conference Committee, which includes members of both the House Ways and Means Committee and the Senate Finance Committee, is called upon to resolve the differences. House and Senate versions of major tax bills frequently differ. One reason bills often are changed in the Senate is that each senator has considerable latitude to make amendments when the Senate as a whole is voting on a bill referred to it by the Senate Finance Committee. In contrast, the entire House of Representatives either accepts or rejects what is proposed by the House Ways and Means Committee, and changes from the floor are rare.

The deliberations of the Conference Committee usually produce a compromise between the two versions, which is then voted on by both the House and the Senate. If both bodies accept the revised bill, it is referred to the President for approval or veto. The typical legislative process dealing with tax bills is summarized in Figure 2.1.

The role of the Conference Committee indicates the importance of compromise in the legislative process. As an example of the practical effect of the compromise process, consider what happened with amendments to the first-time homebuyer credit in the American Recovery and Reinvestment Tax Act of 2009 (see Figure 2.2 on p. 2-5).

Referrals from the House Ways and Means Committee, the Senate Finance Committee, and the Conference Committee usually are accompanied by *Committee Reports*. These Committee Reports often explain the provisions of the proposed legislation and are a valuable source for ascertaining the *intent of Congress*. What Congress had in mind when it considered and enacted tax legislation is the key to interpreting legislation. Because Regulations interpreting new legislation

| FIGURE 2.1 | Legislative Process for Tax Bills |

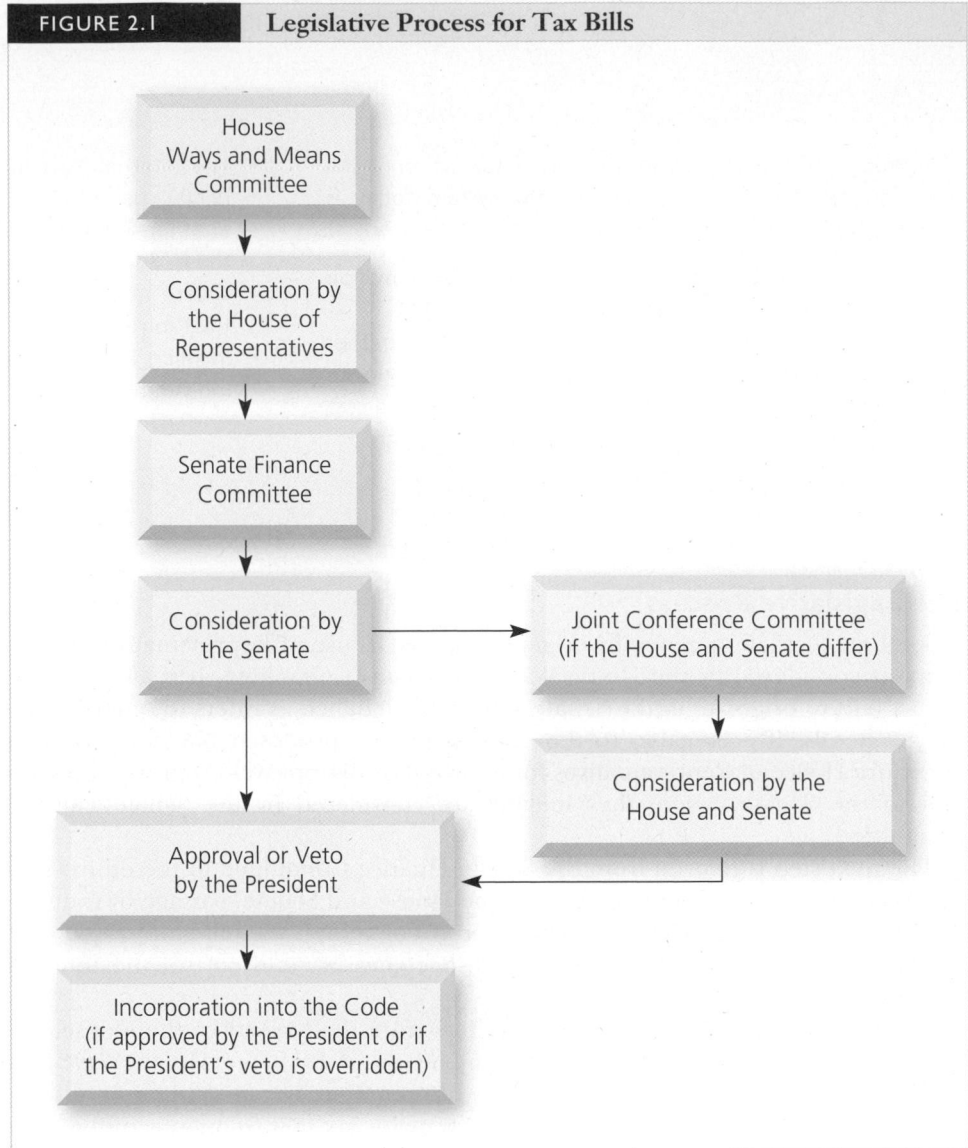

normally are not issued immediately after a statute is enacted, taxpayers and the courts look to Committee Reports to determine congressional intent.

Arrangement of the Code

The Internal Revenue Code is found in Title 26 of the U.S. Code. Here is a partial table of contents.

> Subtitle A. Income Taxes
> > Chapter 1. Normal Taxes and Surtaxes
> > > Subchapter A. Determination of Tax Liability
> > > > Part I. Tax on Individuals
> > > > > Sections 1–5
> > > > Part II. Tax on Corporations
> > > > > Sections 11–12

In referring to a provision of the Code, the tax professional usually cites the Section number. In referring to § 2(a) (dealing with the status of a surviving

| FIGURE 2.2 | Example of Compromise in the Conference Committee |

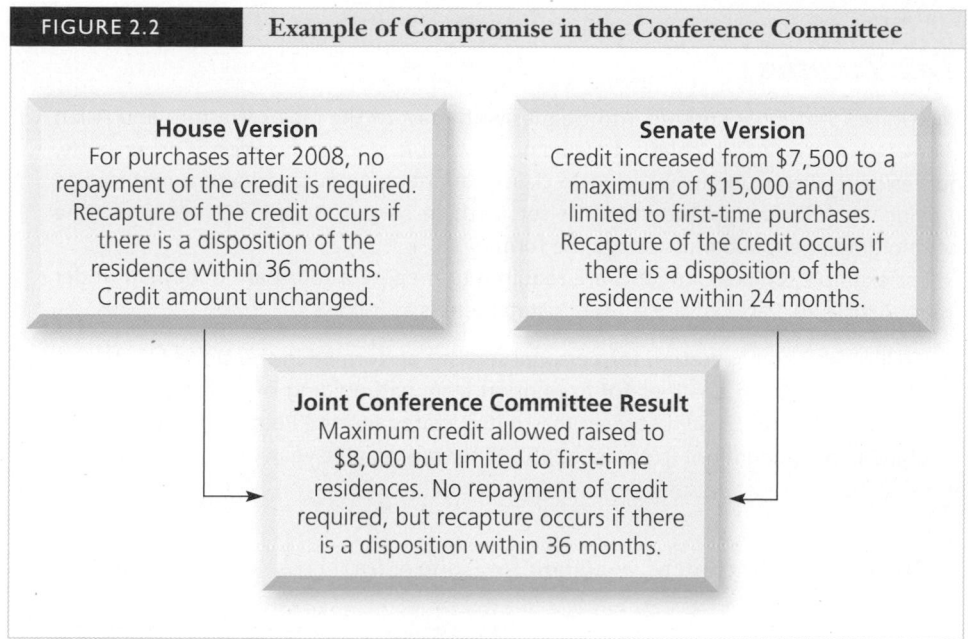

House Version
For purchases after 2008, no repayment of the credit is required. Recapture of the credit occurs if there is a disposition of the residence within 36 months. Credit amount unchanged.

Senate Version
Credit increased from $7,500 to a maximum of $15,000 and not limited to first-time purchases. Recapture of the credit occurs if there is a disposition of the residence within 24 months.

Joint Conference Committee Result
Maximum credit allowed raised to $8,000 but limited to first-time residences. No repayment of credit required, but recapture occurs if there is a disposition within 36 months.

spouse), for example, it is unnecessary to include Subtitle A, Chapter 1, Subchapter A, and Part I. Merely mentioning § 2(a) suffices because the Section numbers run consecutively and do not begin again with each new Subtitle, Chapter, Subchapter, or Part. Not all Code Section numbers are used, however. Part I ends with § 5, and Part II starts with § 11 (at present, there are no §§ 6, 7, 8, 9, and 10).[2]

Tax practitioners commonly refer to certain areas of income tax law by Subchapter designation. Some of the more common Subchapter designations include Subchapter C ("Corporate Distributions and Adjustments"), Subchapter K ("Partners and Partnerships"), and Subchapter S ("Tax Treatment of S Corporations and Their Shareholders"). Particularly in the last situation, it is more convenient to describe the effect of the applicable Code provisions (§§ 1361–1379) as "Subchapter S" than as the "Tax Treatment of S Corporations and Their Shareholders."

Citing the Code

Code Sections often are broken down into subparts.[3] Section 2(a)(1)(A) serves as an example.

§ 2 (a) (1) (A)

→ Abbreviation for "Section"
→ Section number
→ Subsection number[4]
→ Paragraph designation
→ Subparagraph designation

[2]When the Code was drafted, Section numbers were intentionally omitted so that later changes could be incorporated into the Code without disrupting its organization. When Congress does not leave enough space, subsequent Code Sections are given A, B, C, etc., designations. A good example is the treatment of §§ 280A through 280H.

[3]Some Code Sections do not have subparts. See, for example, §§ 211 and 241.

[4]Some Code Sections omit the subsection designation and use, instead, the paragraph designation as the first subpart. See, for example, §§ 212(1) and 1222(1).

Global Tax Issues

© iStockphoto.com/Andrey Prokhorov

Tax Treaties

The United States has entered into treaties with most of the major Western and Asian countries of the world, chiefly to eliminate possible double taxation. For example, nonresident alien students wanting to claim exemption from taxation are required to provide an information statement as set forth in several Revenue Procedures. The withholding agent also must certify the form.

For example, Chinese students are required to prepare a four-part statement under treaty Article 20. Part 3 of the student's statement is as follows.

I will receive compensation for personal services performed in the United States. This compensation qualifies for exemption from withholding of Federal income tax under the tax treaty between the United States and the People's Republic of China in an amount not in excess of $5,000 for any taxable year.

Broken down by content, a citation for Code § 2(a)(1)(A) appears as follows.

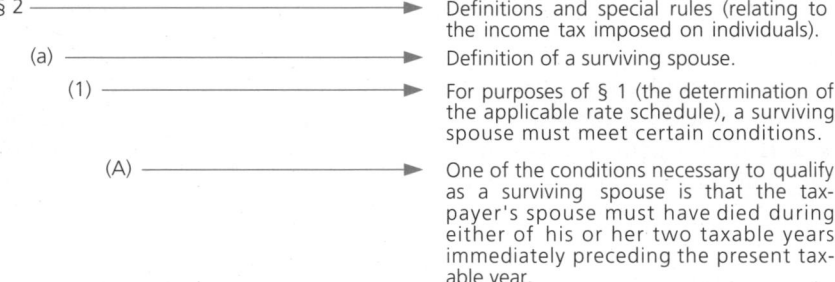

Throughout the text, references to the Code Sections are in the form given on the previous page. The symbols "§" and "§§" are used in place of "Section" and "Sections," respectively. The following table illustrates the format used in the text.

Complete Reference	Text Reference
Section 2(a)(1)(A) of the Internal Revenue Code of 1986	§ 2(a)(1)(A)
Sections 1 and 2 of the Internal Revenue Code of 1986	§§ 1 and 2
Section 2 of the Internal Revenue Code of 1954	§ 2 of the Internal Revenue Code of 1954
Section 12(d) of the Internal Revenue Code of 1939[5]	§ 12(d) of the Internal Revenue Code of 1939

Effect of Treaties

The United States signs certain tax treaties (sometimes called tax conventions) with foreign countries to render mutual assistance in tax enforcement and to avoid double taxation. These treaties affect transactions involving U.S. persons and entities operating or investing in a foreign country, as well as persons and entities of a foreign country operating or investing in the United States. Although these bilateral agreements are not codified in any one source, they are published at **www.irs.gov**, as well as in various commercial tax services.

Neither a tax law nor a tax treaty automatically takes precedence. When there is a direct conflict, the most recent item prevails. With certain exceptions, a taxpayer must disclose on the tax return any filing position for which a treaty overrides a tax law.[6] There is a $1,000 per *failure to disclose* penalty for individuals and a $10,000 per failure to disclose penalty for C corporations.[7]

---

[5]Section 12(d) of the Internal Revenue Code of 1939 is the predecessor to § 2 of the Internal Revenue Codes of 1954 and 1986.

[6]§ 7852(d).
[7]§ 6712(a).

TAX IN THE NEWS   Origin of the April 15 Tax Day

April 15 has not always been the tax return due date in the United States. Congress originally established March 1 as the due date of personal income tax returns. This date selection was apparently based upon the effective date of the Sixteenth Amendment, February 3, 1913. After a few years, taxpayers requested more time to complete the returns, so March 15 was adopted as the filing deadline.

To give taxpayers even more time to deal with the complexity of the tax laws, the Internal Revenue Code of 1954 changed the deadline to April 15.

Source: Joseph J. Thorndike, "Why Is Tax Day April 15?" *Tax Notes,* April 16, 2012.

© iStockphoto.com/Andrey Prokhorov

2-1b Administrative Sources of the Tax Law

The administrative sources of the Federal tax law can be grouped as follows: Treasury Department Regulations, Revenue Rulings and Revenue Procedures, and various other administrative pronouncements (see Exhibit 2.1). All are issued by either the U.S. Treasury Department or the IRS.

Treasury Department Regulations

Regulations are issued by the U.S. Treasury Department under authority granted by Congress.[8] Usually interpretive by nature, they provide taxpayers with considerable guidance on the meaning and application of the Code and often include examples. Regulations carry considerable authority as the official interpretation of tax statutes. They are an important resource to consider in complying with the tax law.

Treasury Regulations are arranged in the same sequence as the Code. A number is added at the beginning, however, to indicate the type of tax or other matter to which they relate. For example, the prefix 1 designates the Regulations under the income tax law. Thus, the Regulations under Code § 2 would be cited as Reg. § 1.2, with subparts added for further identification. The numbering pattern of these subparts often has no correlation with the Code subsections. The prefix 20 designates estate tax Regulations, 25 addresses gift tax Regulations, 31 relates to employment taxes, and 301 refers to procedure and administration. This list is not all-inclusive. Reg. § 1.351–1(a)(2) is an example of such a citation.

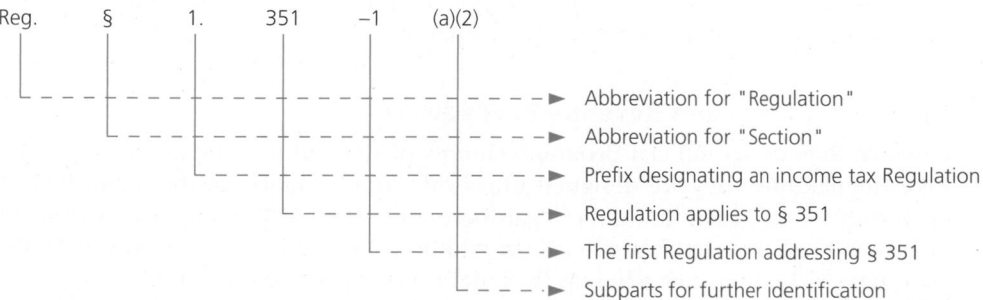

New Regulations and changes in existing Regulations usually are issued in proposed form before they are finalized. The interval between the proposal of a Regulation and its finalization permits taxpayers and other interested parties to comment on the propriety of the proposal. These comments usually are provided in writing, but oral comments can be offered at hearings held by the IRS on the Regulations in question pursuant to a public notice. This practice of notice-and-comment is a major distinction between Regulations and other forms of Treasury guidance such as Revenue Rulings, Revenue Procedures, and the like.

[8]§ 7805.

EXHIBIT 2.1 Administrative Sources

Source	Location	Authority***
Regulations	*Federal Register** *Internal Revenue Bulletin*	Force and effect of law. May be cited as precedent.
Temporary Regulations	*Federal Register** *Internal Revenue Bulletin* .	May be cited as a precedent.
Proposed Regulations	*Federal Register** *Internal Revenue Bulletin*	Preview of final Regulations. Not yet a precedent.
Revenue Rulings Revenue Procedures Treasury Decisions Actions on Decisions	*Internal Revenue Bulletin***	IRS interpretation only. Weak precedent.
Determination Letters Technical Advice Memoranda	Tax Analysts' *Tax Notes* RIA's *Internal Memoranda of the IRS* CCH's *IRS Position Reporter*	IRS interpretation only. Weak precedent.
Letter Rulings	Research Institute of America and Commerce Clearing House tax services**	Applicable only to taxpayer addressed. May not be cited as precedent.

*Final, Temporary, and Proposed Regulations are published in soft-cover form and online by several publishers.
**Revenue Rulings, Revenue Procedures, and letter rulings also are published online by several publishers.
***Each of these sources may be substantial authority for purposes of the accuracy-related penalty in § 6662.

Proposed Regulations under Code § 2, for example, are cited as Prop.Reg. § 1.2. The Tax Court indicates that Proposed Regulations carry little weight in the litigation process.[9]

The Treasury Department issues **Temporary Regulations** relating to matters where immediate guidance is important. These Regulations are issued without the comment period required for Proposed Regulations. Temporary Regulations have the same authoritative value as final Regulations and may be cited as precedents. However, Temporary Regulations also are issued as Proposed Regulations and automatically expire within three years after the date of their issuance.[10]

Proposed, Temporary, and **Final Regulations** are published in the *Federal Register*, the *Internal Revenue Bulletin*, and major tax services.

Regulations may also be classified as *legislative, interpretive,* or *procedural.* This classification scheme is discussed later in the chapter.

Revenue Rulings and Revenue Procedures

Revenue Rulings are official pronouncements of the National Office of the IRS.[11] Like Regulations, they are designed to provide interpretation of the tax law. However, they do not carry the same legal force and effect as Regulations and usually deal with more restricted problems. In addition, Regulations are approved by the Secretary of the Treasury, whereas Revenue Rulings generally are not.

Both Revenue Rulings and Revenue Procedures serve an important function in providing *guidance* to IRS personnel and taxpayers in handling routine tax matters. Revenue Rulings and Revenue Procedures generally apply retroactively and may be revoked or modified by subsequent rulings or procedures, Regulations, legislation, or court decisions.

Revenue Rulings typically provide one or more examples of how the IRS would apply a law to specific fact situations. Revenue Rulings may arise from technical advice memoranda of the IRS, court decisions, suggestions from tax practitioner

[9]*F. W. Woolworth Co.,* 54 T.C. 1233 (1970); *Harris M. Miller,* 70 T.C. 448
(1978); and *James O. Tomerlin Trust,* 87 T.C. 876 (1986).

[10]§ 7805(e).
[11]§ 7805(a).

groups, and various tax publications. A Revenue Ruling also may arise from a specific taxpayer's request for a letter ruling. If the IRS believes that a taxpayer's request for a letter ruling deserves official publication due to its widespread effect, the letter ruling is converted into a Revenue Ruling and issued for the information and guidance of taxpayers, tax practitioners, and IRS personnel. Names, identifying descriptions, and money amounts are changed to conceal the identity of the requesting taxpayer.

Revenue Procedures are issued in the same manner as Revenue Rulings, but deal with the internal management practices and procedures of the IRS. Familiarity with these procedures increases taxpayer compliance and helps make the administration of the tax laws more efficient. The failure of a taxpayer to follow a Revenue Procedure can result in unnecessary delay or, in a discretionary situation, can cause the IRS to decline to act on behalf of the taxpayer.

Some recent Revenue Procedures dealt with the following matters.

- Revised procedures for issuing determination letters on the qualified status of employee pension plans.
- Provided a list of areas in which rulings will not be issued.
- Provided procedures for requesting a filing date extension when electing S corporation status.
- Provided inflation-adjusted amounts for various Code provisions.

Revenue Rulings and Revenue Procedures are published weekly by the U.S. Government in the *Internal Revenue Bulletin* (I.R.B.).

The proper form for citing Revenue Rulings is as follows. Revenue Procedures are cited in the same manner, except that "Rev.Proc." is substituted for "Rev.Rul."

Rev.Rul. 2014–3, 2014–2 I.R.B. 259.

Explanation: Revenue Ruling Number 3, beginning at page 259 of the 2nd weekly issue of the *Internal Revenue Bulletin* for 2014.

Revenue Rulings and other tax resources may be found in the *Tax Almanac*, a free online resource at **www.taxalmanac.org**.[12]

Letter Rulings

Letter rulings are issued for a fee upon a taxpayer's request. They describe how the IRS will treat a *proposed* transaction for tax purposes. Letter rulings can be useful to taxpayers who want to be certain of how a transaction will be taxed before proceeding with it. Letter rulings allow taxpayers to avoid unexpected tax costs.

The procedure for requesting a ruling can be quite cumbersome, although it sometimes is the most effective way to carry out tax planning. The IRS limits the issuance of letter rulings to restricted, pre-announced areas of taxation; it generally will not rule on situations that are fact-intensive. Thus, a ruling may not be obtained on many of the problems that are particularly troublesome to taxpayers.[13]

The IRS makes letter rulings available for public inspection after identifying details are deleted.[14] Published digests of private letter rulings are found in RIA's *Private Letter Rulings*, BNA's *Daily Tax Reports*, and Tax Analysts' *Tax Notes*. *IRS Letter Rulings Reports* (published by Commerce Clearing House) contains both digests and full texts of all letter rulings. *Letter Ruling Review* (published by Tax Analysts), a monthly publication, selects and discusses the most important of the approximately 40 letter rulings issued each week. In addition, computerized databases of letter rulings are available through several commercial publishers.

---

[12]Commercial sources for Revenue Rulings and Revenue Procedures are available, usually requiring a subscription fee. Older Revenue Rulings and Revenue Procedures are often cited as being published in the *Cumulative Bulletin* (C.B.) rather than the *Internal Revenue Bulletin* (I.R.B.).

[13]The first *Internal Revenue Bulletin* issued each year contains a list of areas in which the IRS will not issue advance rulings. This list may be modified throughout the year. See, for example, Rev.Proc. 2014–1, 2014–1 I.R.B. 1.

[14]§ 6110.

TAX IN THE NEWS   Did Honest Abe Have to Pay Taxes?

When Congress passed a comprehensive income tax in 1862 to pay for the Civil War, the lawmakers included themselves as taxpayers. However, the tax did not apply to President Abraham Lincoln and Federal judges.

Although some observers insisted that the President was excluded from the tax, Lincoln apparently made voluntary payments to the Treasury equal to the taxes he might have owed. Whether or not the payments were voluntary, $92 per month was withheld from his paycheck.

Eventually, the Treasury refunded $3,556 to Lincoln's estate in 1872.

Source: J. J. Thorndike, "Abraham Lincoln Paid Income Taxes—But He Didn't Have To," *Tax Notes,* July 8, 2013.

Letter rulings are issued multidigit file numbers that indicate the year and week of issuance as well as the number of the ruling during that week. Consider, for example, Ltr.Rul. 201314038, which determines that income derived by a master limited partnership from processing natural gas into dimethyl ether is qualified income for a real estate investment trust.

2013	14	038
Year 2013	14th week of issuance	38th ruling issued during the 14th week

Other Administrative Pronouncements

Treasury Decisions (TDs) are issued by the Treasury Department to promulgate new Regulations, amend or otherwise change existing Regulations, or announce the position of the Government on selected court decisions. Like Revenue Rulings and Revenue Procedures, TDs are published in the *Internal Revenue Bulletin.*

The IRS publishes other administrative communications in the *Internal Revenue Bulletin,* such as Announcements, Notices, Proposed Regulations, Termination of Exempt Organization Status, Practitioner Disciplinary Actions, and Prohibited Transaction Exemptions.

Like letter rulings, **determination letters** are issued at the request of taxpayers and provide guidance on the application of the tax law. They differ from letter rulings in that the issuing source is an IRS executive, rather than the National Office of the IRS. Further, determination letters usually involve *completed* (as opposed to proposed) transactions. Determination letters are not published regularly, and they are released officially only to the party making the request.

Example 1

The shareholders of Red Corporation and Green Corporation want assurance that the consolidation of their corporations into Blue Corporation will be a nontaxable reorganization. The proper approach is to ask the National Office of the IRS to issue a letter ruling concerning the income tax effect of the proposed transaction.

Example 2

Chris operates a barbershop in which he employs eight barbers. To comply with the rules governing income tax and payroll tax withholdings, Chris wants to know whether the barbers working for him are employees or independent contractors. The proper procedure is to request a determination letter on their status from the IRS.

The National Office of the IRS releases **Technical Advice Memoranda (TAMs)** weekly. TAMs resemble letter rulings in that they give the IRS's determination of an issue. Letter rulings, however, are responses to requests by taxpayers, whereas TAMs are issued by the National Office of the IRS in response to questions raised by IRS field personnel during audits. TAMs deal with completed rather than proposed transactions and often are requested for questions relating to exempt organizations and employee plans.[15]

In-depth coverage can be found on this book's companion website: **www.cengagebrain.com** | Digging Deeper

2-1c Judicial Sources of the Tax Law

After a taxpayer has exhausted some or all of the remedies available within the IRS (no satisfactory settlement has been reached at the agent level or at the Appeals Division level), a dispute can be taken to the Federal courts. The dispute first is considered by a **court of original jurisdiction** (known as a trial court), with any appeal (either by the taxpayer or the IRS) taken to the appropriate appellate court. In most situations, the taxpayer has a choice of four trial courts: a **District Court**, the **Court of Federal Claims**, the **Tax Court**, or the **Small Cases Division** of the Tax Court. The court system for Federal tax litigation is illustrated in Figure 2.3.

The broken line between the Tax Court and the Small Cases Division indicates that there is no appeal from the Small Cases Division, by either party to the case. Decisions from the Small Cases Division have no precedential value. Some of these cases are found on the U.S. Tax Court website. They may not be relied upon by other taxpayers, or even by the taxpayer itself in subsequent years. The jurisdiction of the Small Cases Division is limited to cases involving tax, interest, and penalty amounts of $50,000 or less.

In-depth coverage can be found on this book's companion website: **www.cengagebrain.com** 2 | Digging Deeper

Knowledge of several terms is important in understanding court decisions. The plaintiff is the party requesting action in a court, and the defendant is the party against whom the suit is brought. Sometimes a court uses the terms *petitioner* and *respondent*. In general, *petitioner* is a synonym for *plaintiff*, and *respondent* is a synonym for *defendant*. At the trial court level, a taxpayer usually is the plaintiff (or petitioner), and the government is the defendant (or respondent). If the taxpayer wins and the Government appeals as the new petitioner (or appellant), the taxpayer now is the respondent.

Trial Courts

The differences among the various trial courts (courts of original jurisdiction) can be summarized as follows.

- *Number of courts.* There is only one Court of Federal Claims and only one Tax Court, but there are many District Courts. The taxpayer does not select the District Court that will hear the dispute, but must sue in the one that has jurisdiction where the taxpayer resides.
- *Number of judges.* A case tried in a District Court is heard before only 1 judge. The Court of Federal Claims has 16 judges, and the Tax Court has 19 regular judges. The entire Tax Court, however, reviews a case (the case is heard *en banc*), thereby taking on a more compelling authority, when important or novel tax issues are involved. Most cases, though, are heard and decided by only 1 of the 19 regular judges.

---

[15]Determination letters and technical advice memoranda may constitute substantial authority for purposes of the § 6662 accuracy-related penalty. Notice 90–20, 1990–1 C.B. 328.

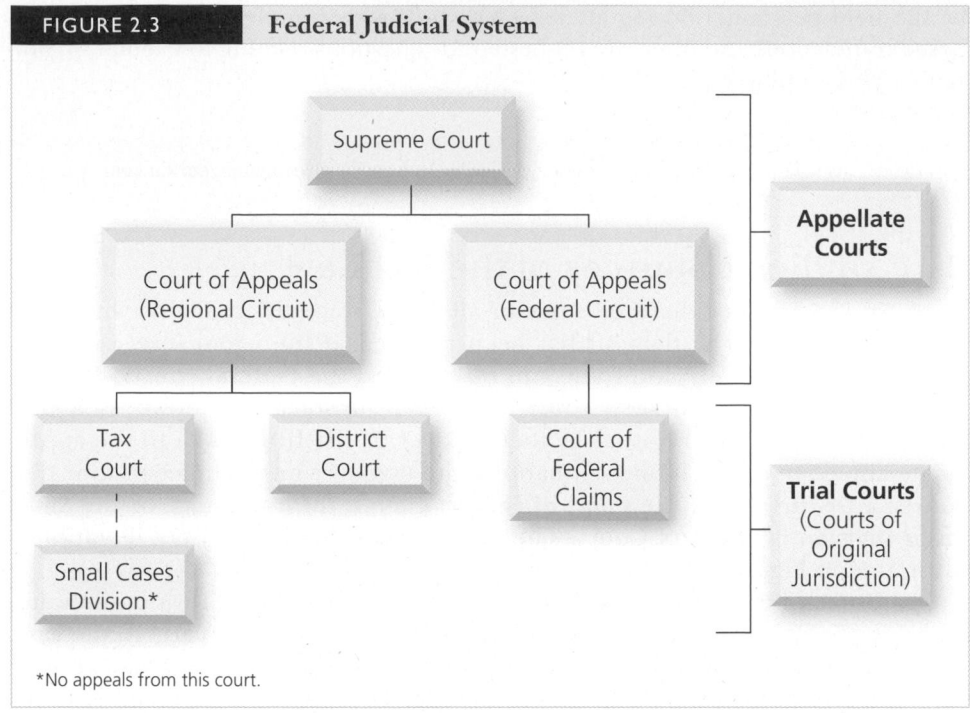

FIGURE 2.3   **Federal Judicial System**

*No appeals from this court.

- *Location.* The Court of Federal Claims meets most often in Washington, D.C., while a District Court meets at a prescribed seat for the particular district. Each state has at least one District Court, and many of the populous states have more than one. Choosing the District Court usually minimizes the inconvenience and expense of traveling for the taxpayer and his or her counsel. The Tax Court is based in Washington, D.C., but various judges travel to different parts of the country and hear cases at predetermined locations and dates. This procedure eases the distance problem for the taxpayer, but it can mean a delay before the case comes to trial.
- *Jurisdiction of the Court of Federal Claims.* The Court of Federal Claims has jurisdiction over any claim against the United States that is based upon the Constitution, any Act of Congress, or any Regulation of an executive department. Thus, the Court of Federal Claims hears nontax litigation as well as tax cases.
- *Jurisdiction of the Tax Court and District Courts.* The Tax Court hears only tax cases and is the most frequently used forum for tax cases. The District Courts hear a wide variety of nontax cases, including drug crimes and other Federal violations, as well as tax cases. For this reason, some people suggest that the Tax Court has more expertise in tax matters.
- *Jury trial.* The only court in which a taxpayer can obtain a jury trial is a District Court. Juries can decide only questions of fact and not questions of law. If a jury trial is not elected, the judge decides all issues. A District Court decision applies only in the district in which the court has jurisdiction.
- *Payment of deficiency.* Before the Court of Federal Claims or a District Court can have jurisdiction, the taxpayer must pay the tax deficiency assessed by the IRS and then sue for a refund. If the taxpayer wins (assuming no successful appeal by the Government), the tax paid plus appropriate interest is recovered. Jurisdiction in the Tax Court, however, usually is obtained without first paying the assessed tax deficiency.

CONCEPT SUMMARY 2.1

Federal Judicial System: Trial Courts

Issue	Tax Court	District Court	Court of Federal Claims
Number of judges per court	19	1 per case	16
Payment of deficiency before trial	No	Yes	Yes
Jury trial available	No	Yes	No
Types of dispute	Tax cases only	Mostly criminal and civil issues	Claims against the United States
Jurisdiction	Nationwide	Location of taxpayer	Nationwide
IRS acquiescence policy	Yes	Yes	Yes
Appeal is to	U.S. Court of Appeals	U.S. Court of Appeals	Court of Appeals for the Federal Circuit

- *Appeals.* Appeals from a District Court or a Tax Court decision go to the Court of Appeals for the circuit in which the taxpayer resides. Appeals from the Court of Federal Claims go to the Court of Appeals for the Federal Circuit. Few Tax Court cases are appealed, and when appeals are made, most are filed by the taxpayer rather than the IRS.
- *Bankruptcy.* When a taxpayer files a bankruptcy petition, the IRS, like other creditors, is prevented from taking action against the taxpayer. Sometimes a bankruptcy court settles a tax claim.

For a summary of several attributes of the Federal trial courts, see Concept Summary 2.1.

Appellate Courts

The losing party can appeal a trial court decision to a **Circuit Court of Appeals**. The 11 geographic circuits, the circuit for the District of Columbia, and the Federal Circuit[16] are shown in Figure 2.4.

Process and Outcomes If the government loses at the trial court level (District Court, Tax Court, or Court of Federal Claims), it need not (and frequently does not) appeal. The fact that an appeal is not made, however, does not indicate that the IRS agrees with the result and will not litigate similar issues in the future. The IRS may decide not to appeal for a number of reasons. First, its current litigation load may be heavy. As a consequence, the IRS may decide that available personnel should be assigned to other more important cases. Second, the IRS may not appeal for strategic reasons. For example, the taxpayer may be in a sympathetic position, or the facts may be particularly strong in his or her favor. In that event, the IRS may wait for a weaker case to test the legal issues involved. Third, if the appeal is from a District Court or the Tax Court, the Court of Appeals of jurisdiction could have some bearing on whether the IRS decides to pursue an appeal. Based on past experience and precedent, the IRS may conclude that the chance for success on a particular issue might be more promising in another Court of Appeals. If so, the IRS will wait for a similar case to arise in a different jurisdiction.

The role of appellate courts is limited to a review of the record of the case that was compiled by the trial courts. Thus, the appellate process usually involves a determination of whether the trial court applied the proper law in arriving at its decision, rather than a consideration of the trial court's factual findings.

---

[16]The Court of Appeals for the Federal Circuit hears decisions appealed from the Court of Federal Claims.

FIGURE 2.4   The Federal District Courts and Circuit Courts of Appeals

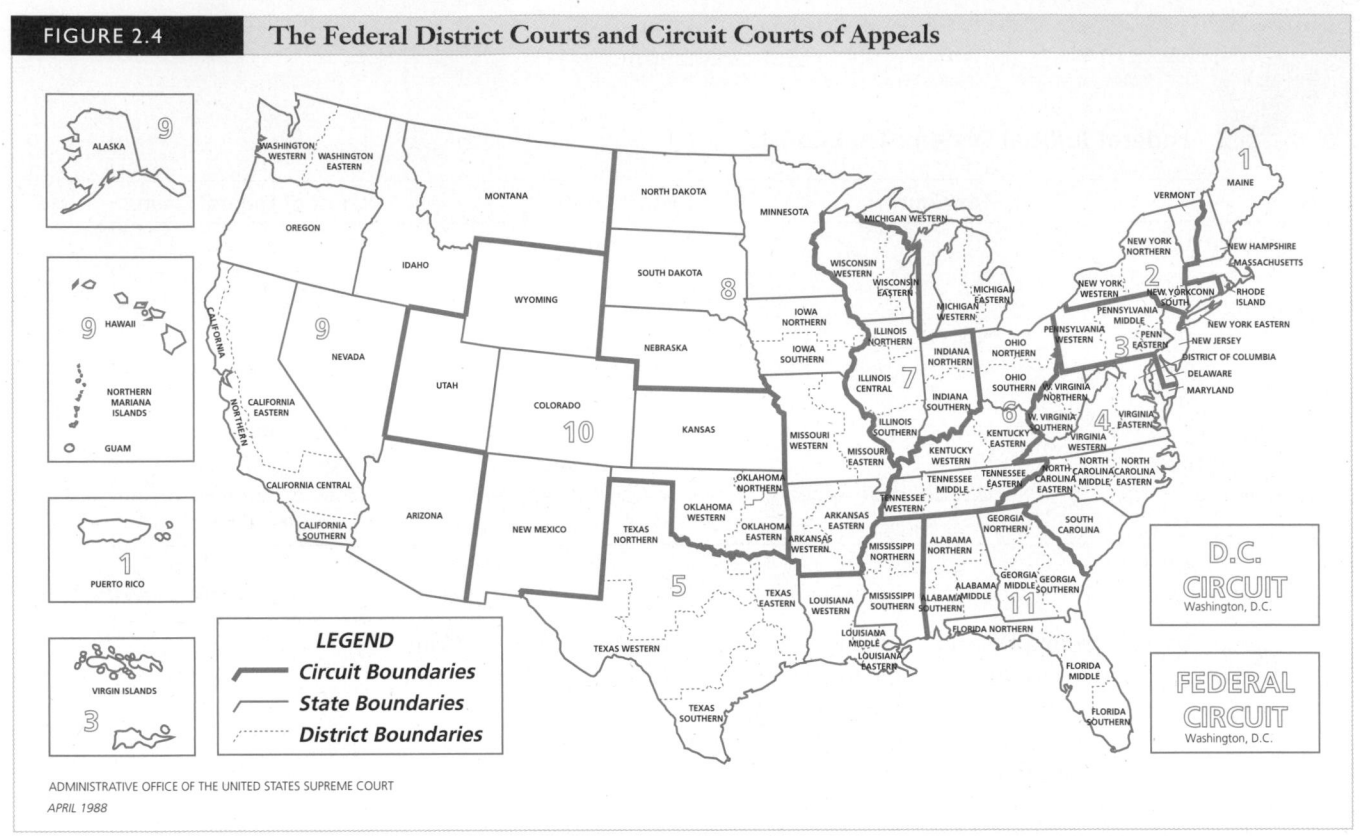

ADMINISTRATIVE OFFICE OF THE UNITED STATES SUPREME COURT
APRIL 1988

An appeal can have any of a number of possible outcomes. The appellate court may let stand (affirm) or overturn (reverse) the lower court's finding, or it may send the case back for further consideration (remand). When many issues are involved, a mixed result is not unusual. Thus, the lower court may be affirmed (*aff'd.*) on Issue A and reversed (*rev'd.*) on Issue B, while Issue C is remanded (*rem'd.*) for additional fact finding.

When more than one judge is involved in the decision-making process, disagreements are not uncommon. In addition to the majority view, one or more judges may concur (agree with the result reached but not with some or all of the reasoning) or dissent (disagree with the result). In any one case, the majority view controls. But concurring and dissenting views can influence other courts or, at some subsequent date when the composition of the court has changed, even when involving the same court.

Other Rules and Strategies The Federal Circuit at the appellate level provides a taxpayer with an alternative forum to the Court of Appeals of his or her home circuit. When a particular circuit has issued an adverse decision for a case that is similar in facts, the taxpayer may prefer the Court of Federal Claims, because any appeal will be to the Court of Appeals for the Federal Circuit.

District Courts, the Tax Court, and the Court of Federal Claims must abide by the **precedents** set by the Court of Appeals of their jurisdiction. A particular Court of Appeals need not follow the decisions of another Court of Appeals. All courts, however, must follow decisions of the **Supreme Court**.

This pattern of appellate precedents raises an issue for the Tax Court. Because the Tax Court is a national court, it decides cases from all parts of the country. Appeals from its decisions, however, go to all of the Courts of Appeals except the Court of Appeals for the Federal Circuit. Accordingly, identical Tax Court cases might be appealed to different circuits with different results. As a result of *Golsen*,[17]

---

[17] *Jack E. Golsen*, 54 T.C. 742 (1970).

the Tax Court will not follow its own precedents in a subsequent case if the Court of Appeals with jurisdiction over the taxpayer in question has previously reversed the Tax Court on the specific issue at hand.

Example 3

Emily lives in Texas and sues in the Tax Court on Issue A. The Fifth Circuit Court of Appeals is the appellate court with jurisdiction. The Fifth Circuit already has decided, in a case involving similar facts but a different taxpayer, that Issue A should be resolved against the Government. Although the Tax Court maintains that the Fifth Circuit is wrong, under its *Golsen* policy, it will render judgment for Emily.

Shortly thereafter, in a comparable case, Rashad, a resident of New York, sues in the Tax Court on Issue A. The Second Circuit Court of Appeals, the appellate court with jurisdiction in New York, never has expressed itself on Issue A. Presuming that the Tax Court has not reconsidered its position on Issue A, it will decide against Rashad. Thus, it is possible for two taxpayers suing in the same court to end up with opposite results merely because they live in different parts of the country.

Appeal to the Supreme Court is not automatic. It must be applied for via a **Writ of Certiorari**. If the Court agrees to hear the case, it will grant the Writ (*Cert. granted*). Most often, it declines to hear the case (*Cert. denied*). In fact, the Supreme Court rarely hears tax cases. The Court usually grants certiorari to resolve a conflict among the Courts of Appeals (e.g., two or more appellate courts have opposing positions on a particular issue) or where the tax issue is extremely important. The granting of a *Writ of Certiorari* indicates that at least four of the nine members of the Supreme Court believe that the issue is of sufficient importance to be heard by the full Court.

Judicial Citations

Court decisions are an important source of tax law. The ability to locate a case and to cite it is a must in working with the tax law. Judicial citations usually follow a standard pattern: case name, volume number, reporter series, page or paragraph number, court (where necessary), and year of decision.

Judicial Citations—The Tax Court The Tax Court issues two types of decisions: Regular and Memorandum. The Chief Judge decides whether the opinion is issued as a Regular or Memorandum decision. The distinction between the two involves both substance and form. In terms of substance, *Memorandum* decisions deal with situations necessitating only the application of already established principles of law. *Regular* decisions involve novel issues of the tax law which have not previously been resolved by the court. In actual practice, however, this distinction is not always so clear. Be that as it may, both Regular and Memorandum decisions represent the position of the Tax Court and, as such, can be relied on by others.

Regular and Memorandum decisions issued by the Tax Court also differ in form. Memorandum decisions are not published officially, while Regular decisions are published by the U.S. Government in a series called *Tax Court of the United States Reports* (T.C.). Each volume of these *Reports* covers a six-month period (January 1 through June 30 and July 1 through December 31) and is given a succeeding volume number. But there is usually a time lag between the date a decision is rendered and the date it appears in official form. A temporary citation often is used, to help the researcher locate a recent Regular decision. Consider, for example, the temporary and permanent citations for *Rachel George*, a decision filed on December 19, 2012.

Temporary Citation	{ *Rachel George*, 139 T.C. ___, No. 19 (2012).
	Explanation: Page number left blank because not yet known.
Permanent Citation	{ *Rachel George*, 139 T.C. 508 (2012).
	Explanation: Page number now available.

The temporary citation tells us that the case ultimately will appear in Volume 139 of the *Tax Court of the United States Reports*. Until this volume becomes available to the general public, however, the page number is left blank. Instead, the temporary citation identifies the case as being the 19th Regular decision issued by the Tax Court since Volume 138 ended. With this information, the decision easily can be located at the Tax Court website, or in the Tax Court services published by Commerce Clearing House (CCH) and Research Institute of America (RIA). Once Volume 139 is released, the permanent citation is substituted, and the number of the case is dropped. Regular decisions and Memorandum decisions are published and searchable at **www.ustaxcourt.gov**.

Before 1943, the Tax Court was called the Board of Tax Appeals, and its decisions were published as the *United States Board of Tax Appeals Reports* (B.T.A.). These 47 volumes cover the period from 1924 to 1942. For example, the citation *Karl Pauli*, 11 B.T.A. 784 (1928) refers to the 11th volume of the *Board of Tax Appeals Reports*, page 784, issued in 1928.

If the IRS loses a decision, it may indicate whether it agrees or disagrees with the results reached by the court by publishing an **acquiescence** ("A" or "*Acq.*") or **nonacquiescence** ("NA" or "*Nonacq.*"), respectively. The acquiescence program is used where guidance is helpful, regardless of the court that issued the opinion. The acquiescence or nonacquiescence is published in the *Internal Revenue Bulletin* and the *Cumulative Bulletin* as an *Action on Decision*. The IRS can revoke an acquiescence retroactively.

Digging Deeper   **4**      In-depth coverage can be found on this book's companion website: **www.cengagebrain.com**

As noted earlier, Memorandum decisions are found at **www.ustaxcourt.gov**. Memorandum decisions also are published by CCH and RIA. Consider, for example, the three different ways that the *Nick R. Hughes* case can be cited.

> *Nick R. Hughes*, T.C.Memo. 2009–94.
> The 94th Memorandum decision issued by the Tax Court in 2009.

> *Nick R. Hughes*, 97 TCM 1488 (2009).
> Page 1488 of Volume 97 of the CCH *Tax Court Memorandum Decisions*.

> *Nick R. Hughes*, RIA T.C.Memo. ¶2009,094.
> Paragraph 2009,094 of the RIA *T.C. Memorandum Decisions*.

The second citation requires a parenthetical reference to the year in which the case was published. The other two citations do not need this reference, as the publication date is included elsewhere in the citation.

U.S. Tax Court Summary Opinions relate to decisions of the Tax Court's Small Cases Division. These opinions are published commercially, and on the U.S. Tax Court website, with the warning that they may not be treated as precedent for any other case. For example, *Martin Toombs*, filed on June 25, 2013, is cited as follows.

> *Martin Toombs*, T.C. Summary Opinion 2013–51.

Judicial Citations—The District Courts, Court of Federal Claims, and Courts of Appeals
District Court, Court of Federal Claims, and Court of Appeals decisions dealing with Federal tax matters are reported in both the *U.S. Tax Cases* (USTC) and the *American Federal Tax Reports* (AFTR) series.

District Court decisions, dealing with *both* tax and nontax issues, are also published in the *Federal Supplement Series* (F.Supp.). Volume 999, published in 1998, was the last volume of the Federal Supplement Series. The *Federal Supplement Second*

Series (F.Supp.2d) now is used. A District Court case can be cited in three different forms.

Turner v. U.S., 2004–1 USTC ¶60,478 (D.Ct. N.Tex.).

Explanation: Reported in the first volume of the *U.S. Tax Cases* (USTC) for calendar year 2004 (2004–1) and located at paragraph 60,478 (¶60,478).

Turner v. U.S., 93 AFTR 2d 2004–686 (D.Ct. N.Tex.).

Explanation: Reported in the 93rd volume of the second series of the *American Federal Tax Reports* (AFTR 2d) beginning on page 686.

Turner v. U.S., 306 F.Supp.2d 668 (D.Ct. N.Tex., 2004).

Explanation: Reported in the 306th volume of the *Federal Supplement Second Series* (F.Supp.2d) beginning on page 668. The date reference is needed, as it is not found elsewhere in the citation.

In all of the preceding citations, the names of both of the parties to the case are listed. This is a common practice in virtually all legal citations, with the name of the plaintiff or petitioner listed first. But in a Tax Court citation, because all such cases are brought by the taxpayer, no reference to the government is needed (i.e., "*v. Commissioner*" is omitted).

Decisions of the Courts of Appeals are published in the USTCs, the AFTRs, and the *Federal Second Series* (F.2d). Volume 999, published in 1993, was the last volume of the *Federal Second Series*. The *Federal Third Series* (F.3d) now is used. Decisions of the Court of Federal Claims are published in the USTCs, the AFTRs, and the *Claims Court Reporter* (abbreviated as Cl.Ct.).

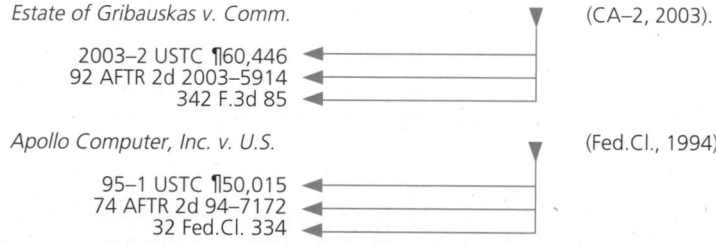

Gribauskas is a decision rendered by the Second Circuit Court of Appeals in 2003 (CA–2, 2003), while *Apollo Computer, Inc.* was issued by the Court of Federal Claims in 1994 (Fed.Cl., 1994), but not published in the USTC until 1995.

In-depth coverage can be found on this book's companion website: **www.cengagebrain.com**  **5** | Digging Deeper

---

Judicial Citations—The Supreme Court Like all other Federal tax decisions (except those rendered by the Tax Court), Supreme Court decisions dealing with Federal tax matters are published by CCH in the USTCs and by RIA in the AFTRs. The U.S. Government Printing Office publishes all Supreme Court decisions in the *United States Supreme Court Reports* (U.S.). Such decisions also are found in the *Supreme Court Reporter* (S.Ct.) and the *United States Reports, Lawyer's Edition* (L.Ed.).

The parenthetical reference (USSC, 1969) identifies the decision as having been rendered by the U.S. Supreme Court in 1969. In this text, the citations of Supreme Court decisions are limited to the USTC, AFTR, and S.Ct. versions.

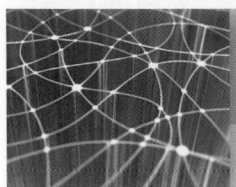

Sources of the Federal tax law reflect the general construct of the Federal government. The legislative branch issues the statutory tax law sources. The executive branch controls the administrative sources of the tax law, for the most part using the Department of the Treasury. The judicial branch issues various court decisions interpreting the tax law.

But the "checks and balances" called for by the U.S. Constitution are not so apparent in the implementation of the Federal tax law. Congressional committees often bury tax proposals that deserve greater disclosure and examination as sources of both revenue and public action. The "revenue neutrality" requirements that apply to many of the actions of Congress are avoided easily by applying "emergency" status to revenue and appropriation proposals. As a result, revenue-related language often is attached to numerous and diverse bills that are difficult for tax professionals to track.

Access to the judicial sources of the Federal tax law is prohibitively expensive for most taxpayers. And although the tendency to settle most litigation outside the court system may be cost-effective for all parties, it inhibits the abilities of tax researchers to identify trends in the evolution of the law. Further, the Supreme Court grants certiorari for tax cases so few times each year that the judicial system effectively includes only one trial court and then one appellate opportunity for the taxpayer.

Finally, the political process dictates that wide swings in enforcement initiatives and budgets will occur from year to year. Taxpayers must be able to predict how the law will be administered as they craft and execute their tax plans, but that becomes especially difficult when personnel turnover is common in the IRS and other tax-related agencies.

Federal tax law is a product of the rest of the governing process as it was designed long ago, but its current operations often make it a creature unto itself.

2-2 WORKING WITH THE TAX LAW—TAX RESEARCH

LO.2

Locate and work with the tax law and understand the tax research process.

Tax research is undertaken to determine the best available solution to a situation that has tax consequences. In the case of a completed transaction, the objective of the research is to determine the tax result of what has already taken place. For example, is the expenditure incurred by the taxpayer deductible or not deductible for tax purposes? When dealing with proposed transactions, tax research is concerned with the determination of possible alternative tax consequences to facilitate effective tax planning.

Tax research involves the following procedures.

- Identifying and refining the problem.
- Locating the appropriate tax law sources.
- Assessing the tax law sources.
- Arriving at the solution or at alternative solutions while giving due consideration to nontax factors.
- Effectively communicating the solution to the taxpayer or the taxpayer's representative.
- Following up on the solution (where appropriate) in light of new developments.

This process is depicted schematically in Figure 2.5. The broken lines indicate steps of particular interest when tax research is directed toward proposed, rather than completed, transactions.

2-2a Identifying the Problem

Problem identification starts with a compilation of the relevant facts involved. In this regard, *all* of the facts that may have a bearing on the problem must be gathered, as any omission could modify the solution reached. To illustrate, consider what appears to be a very simple problem.

FIGURE 2.5   **Tax Research Process**

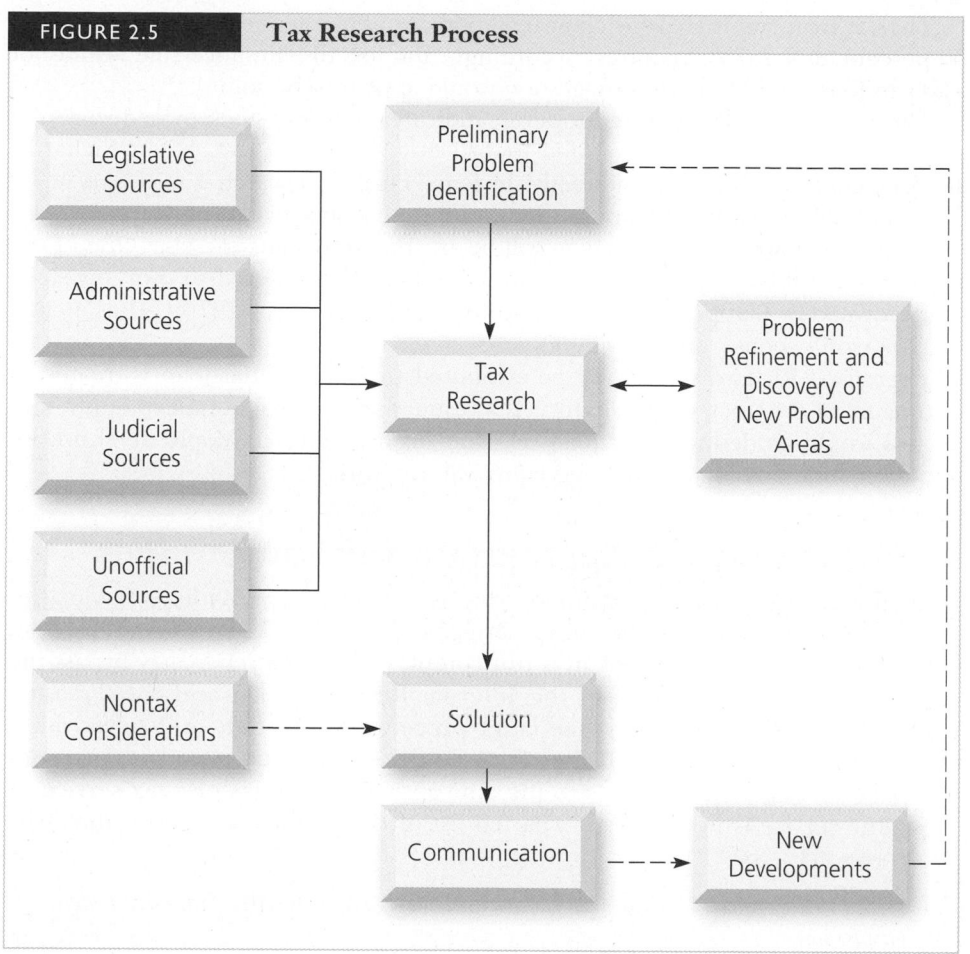

In reviewing their tax and financial situation, Joan and Richard, a married couple, notice that Joan's investment in Airways stock has declined from its purchase price of $8,000 to a current market value of $5,500. Joan wants to sell this stock now and claim the $2,500 loss ($5,500 value − $8,000 cost) as a deduction this year. Richard, however, believes that Airways will yet prosper and does not want to part with the stock. Their daughter Margaret suggests that they sell the Airways stock to Maple, Inc., a corporation owned equally by Joan and Richard. That way, they can claim the deduction this year but still hold the stock through their corporation. Will this suggestion work?

Example 4

2-2b Refining the Problem

Joan and Richard in Example 4 face three choices.

1. Sell the Airways stock through their regular investment broker and get a deduction in the current year (Joan's plan).
2. Continue to hold the Airways stock (Richard's plan).
3. Sell the Airways stock to a corporation owned 50–50 by Joan and Richard (Margaret's suggestion).

The tax consequences of plans (1) and (2) are clear, but the question that Joan and Richard want to resolve is whether plan (3) will work as anticipated. Refining the problem further, can shareholders deduct a loss from the sale of an asset to a corporation that they control? Section 267(a)(1) indicates that losses from the sale of property between persons specified in § 267(b) are not deductible. This subsection lists 12 different relationships, including in § 267(b)(2): "an individual and a corporation more than 50 percent in value of the outstanding stock of which is owned, directly or indirectly, by or for such individual."

Thus, if Joan and Richard each own 50 percent of Maple, neither owns *more than* 50 percent, as § 267(b) requires. Accordingly, the loss disallowance rule would not apply to Joan, and Margaret's suggestion would appear to be sound.

The language of the statute, however, indicates that any stock owned *directly or indirectly* by an individual is counted toward the 50 percent test. Might Richard's stock be considered owned "indirectly" by Joan? Further research is necessary.

Section 267(c) contains rules for determining "constructive ownership of stock," or when stock owned by one person will be attributed to someone else. One of the rules in this subsection declares that an individual is considered to own any stock that is owned by that person's *family*, and family is defined in § 267(c)(4) as including a person's spouse, among others.

Therefore, Richard's stock will be attributed to Joan, so that Joan is treated as owning all of the stock of Maple, Inc. As a result, § 267(a) would indeed apply, and no loss would be deductible if Joan sells the Airways stock to Maple. In short, we must conclude that Margaret's suggestion will not work.

2-2c Locating the Appropriate Tax Law Sources

Once the problem is clearly defined, what is the next step? While it is a matter of individual judgment, most tax research begins with a keyword search of an online tax service. If the problem is not complex, the researcher may bypass the tax service and turn directly to the Internal Revenue Code and the Treasury Regulations. For the beginner, the latter procedure saves time and solves many of the more basic problems. If the researcher does not have a personal copy of the Code or Regulations, access to the appropriate volume(s) of a tax service or an online service is necessary.[18] A partial list of the major tax services and their publishers are:

CCH IntelliConnect, Commerce Clearing House. Includes the *Standard Federal Tax Reporter.*

RIA Checkpoint, Research Institute of America. Includes the *United States Tax Reporter* and the *Federal Tax Coordinator.*

ATX/Kleinrock *Tax Expert*, CCH/Wolters Kluwer.

Tax Management Portfolios, Bloomberg BNA.

Westlaw services. Includes access to *Tax Management Portfolios* and *Federal Tax Coordinator.*

TaxCenter, LexisNexis, primary law sources and various materials taken from CCH, Kleinrock, and Bloomberg BNA.

Federal Research Library, Tax Analysts (a nonprofit organization), primary law sources including treaties, with newsletters and commentaries.

Digging Deeper 6  In-depth coverage can be found on this book's companion website: **www.cengagebrain.com**

Working with Tax Services

In this text, it is not feasible to explain the use of any particular tax service—this ability can be obtained with further study and professional experience. However, several important observations about the use of tax services cannot be overemphasized. First, always check for current developments. Online tax services are updated several times a day, and tax newsletters often feature highlights of recent tax law

---

[18]Several of the major tax services publish paperback editions of the Code and Treasury Regulations that can be purchased at modest prices. These editions are usually revised twice each year. For an annotated and abridged version of the Code and Regulations that is published annually, see James E. Smith, *South-Western Federal Taxation: Internal Revenue Code of 1986 and Treasury Regulations: Annotated and Selected* (Cengage/South-Western, 2015).

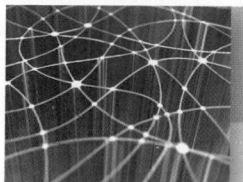

BRIDGE DISCIPLINE   Bridge to Business Law

U.S. income tax laws change daily by the action of Congress, tax administrators, and the courts. This process matches the three-branch structure of the rest of the government, with the legislative, executive, and judicial branches each having a say in making tax law. But this distinction among the functions of government is perhaps less clear when it involves the tax law.

- Presidential vetoes of tax legislation are rare.
- The Tax Court is a creation of the Congress in the Internal Revenue Code, not of the U.S. Constitution.
- The cost of tax litigation and the time it takes for a case to work its way through the judicial system render the courts unavailable to most taxpayers.

Under the U.S. Constitution, legislation involving government revenues must start in the House of Representatives. This provision likely was included so that the public would have greater control over those who want greater access to their pocketbooks. Several recent pieces of tax legislation, though, have been initiated as bills in the Senate. And during the years of the deepest Federal deficits, all bills introduced in both houses of Congress are required to be "revenue-neutral" (i.e., they must include provisions by which the legislation's new programs will be paid for). In both houses, this has resulted in amendments to the Internal Revenue Code being attached to legislation involving clean air and water standards, child care programs, and product import and export limitations.

In a few cases, the courts considered a taxpayer challenge to the way this tax legislation was crafted. But so far the courts have failed to overturn any tax provisions solely because they were initiated in the Senate. The courts' rationale for this seemingly unconstitutional position is that (1) the House and its committees heard a full discussion of the proposal and (2) too much time has passed since adoption of the legislation to easily unwind it and undertake a refund procedure.

developments. Second, there is no substitute for the original source. Do not base a conclusion solely on a tax service's commentary. If a Code Section, Regulation, or case is vital to the research, read it.

Tax Commentary

Various tax publications are another source of relevant information. The use of tax editorial commentary in these publications often can shorten the research time needed to resolve a tax issue. If an article or a posting is relevant to the issue at hand, it may provide the references needed to locate the primary sources of the tax law that apply (e.g., citations to judicial decisions, Regulations, and other IRS pronouncements). Thus, the researcher obtains a "running start" in arriving at a solution to the problem.

The following are some of the more useful tax publications.

Journal of Taxation
Journal of International Taxation
Practical Tax Strategies
Estate Planning
Corporate Taxation
Business Entities
Taxation of Exempts
Real Estate Taxation
ria.thomsonreuters.com/journals

The Tax Executive
www.tei.org

The Tax Adviser
aicpa.org/pubs/taxadv

The Tax Lawyer
www.law.georgetown.edu/journals/tax

The ATA Journal of Legal Tax Research
aaahq.org/ata/_atamenu/
atapubjltr.html

Trusts and Estates
trustsandestates.com

Journal of Passthrough Entities
TAXES—The Tax Magazine
tax.cchgroup.com/books

Tax Notes
taxanalysts.com

2-2d Assessing Tax Law Sources

Once a source has been located, the next step is to assess it in light of the problem at hand. Proper assessment involves careful interpretation of the tax law and consideration of its relevance and significance.

Interpreting the Internal Revenue Code

The language of the Code often is difficult to comprehend fully. Contrary to many people's suspicions, the Code is not written deliberately to confuse its readers. Nevertheless, it often has that effect. The Code is intended to apply to more than 300 million citizens, most of whom are willing to exploit any linguistic imprecision to their benefit—to find a "loophole," in popular parlance. Moreover, many of the Code's provisions are limitations or restrictions involving two or more variables. Expressing such concepts algebraically would be more direct; using words to accomplish this task instead is often quite cumbersome.

Nevertheless, the Code is the governing law, the only source of tax law (other than treaties) that has received the actual approval of Congress and the President. Accordingly, it is usually the first source to be consulted, and often it is the only source needed.

Assessing the Significance of a Treasury Regulation

Treasury Regulations are the official interpretation of the Code and are entitled to great deference. Occasionally, however, a court will invalidate a Regulation or a portion thereof on the grounds that the Regulation is contrary to the intent of Congress. Usually, courts do not question the validity of Regulations because of the belief that "the first administrative interpretation of a provision as it appears in a new act often expresses the general understanding of the times or the actual understanding of those who played an important part when the statute was drafted."[19]

Keep in mind the following observations when assessing the significance of a Regulation.

- IRS agents *must* give the Code and any related Regulations equal weight when dealing with taxpayers and their representatives.
- Proposed Regulations provide a preview of future final Regulations, but they are not binding on the IRS or taxpayers.
- In a challenge, the burden of proof is on the taxpayer to show that a Regulation varies from the language of the statute and has no support in the Committee Reports.
- Final Regulations can be classified as procedural, interpretive, or legislative. **Procedural Regulations** neither establish tax laws nor attempt to explain tax laws. Procedural Regulations often include procedural instructions, indicating information that taxpayers should provide the IRS, as well as information about the internal management and conduct of the IRS itself.
- **Interpretive Regulations** rephrase and elaborate what Congress stated in the Committee Reports that were issued when the tax legislation was enacted. If the language has gone through the public notice and comment procedures discussed earlier in the chapter, interpretive Regulations are *hard and solid* and almost impossible to overturn unless they do not clearly reflect the intent of Congress.
- In some Code Sections, Congress has given the *Treasury Secretary or a delegate* the specific authority to prescribe Regulations to carry out the details of administration or to otherwise create rules not included in the Code. Under such circumstances, Congress effectively is delegating its legislative powers to the Treasury Department. Regulations issued pursuant to this type of authority possess the force and effect of law and often are called **Legislative Regulations** [e.g., see § 385(a)].

---

[19]*Augustus v. Comm.*, 41–1 USTC ¶9255, 26 AFTR 612, 118 F.2d 38 (CA–6, 1941).

In-depth coverage can be found on this book's companion website: **www.cengagebrain.com** **7** | Digging Deeper

Assessing the Significance of Other Administrative Sources of the Tax Law

Revenue Rulings issued by the IRS carry much less weight than Treasury Department Regulations. Revenue Rulings are important, however, in that they reflect the position of the IRS on tax matters. In any dispute with the IRS on the interpretation of tax law, taxpayers should expect agents to follow the results reached in applicable Revenue Rulings. It is not unusual, however, for courts to overturn Revenue Rulings as incorrect applications of the law to the facts presented.

THE BIG PICTURE

Example 5

Return to the facts of *The Big Picture* on p. 2-1. Tax law involving the sale of investment assets is found largely in the Internal Revenue Code. The Samuels family will find incontrovertible law for these transactions in the Code.

Rules concerning dependency exemptions chiefly are found in Regulations, Revenue Rulings, and instructions to IRS forms. With respect to these tax law sources, the authority of each is less than that of the Code, and the Regulations carry much more weight than the form instructions.

Assessing the Significance of Judicial Sources of the Tax Law

The judicial process as it relates to the formulation of tax law has been described. How much reliance can be placed on a particular decision depends upon the following factors.

- *The level of the court.* A decision rendered by a trial court (e.g., a District Court) carries less weight than one issued by an appellate court (e.g., the Fifth Circuit Court of Appeals). Until Congress changes the Code, decisions by the U.S. Supreme Court represent the last word on any tax issue.
- *The legal residence of the taxpayer.* If, for example, a taxpayer lives in Texas, a decision of the Fifth Circuit Court of Appeals means more than one rendered by the Second Circuit Court of Appeals. This is the case because any appeal from a District Court or the Tax Court would be to the Fifth Circuit and not to the Second Circuit.
- *The type of decision.* A Tax Court Regular decision carries more weight than a Memorandum decision; the Tax Court does not consider Memorandum decisions to have precedential value.[20]
- *The weight of the decision.* A decision that is supported by cases from other courts carries more weight than a decision that is not supported by other cases.
- *Subsequent events.* Was the decision affirmed or overruled on appeal?

In connection with the last two factors, a citator is helpful to tax research.[21] A **citator** provides the history of a case, including the authority relied on (e.g., other judicial decisions) in reaching the result. Reviewing the references listed in the citator discloses whether the decision was appealed and, if so, with what result (e.g., affirmed, reversed, remanded). It also reveals other cases with the same or similar issues and how they were decided. Thus, a citator reflects on the validity of a case and may lead to other relevant judicial material. If one plans to rely on a judicial decision to any significant degree, "running" the case through a citator is imperative.

---

[20]*Severino R. Nico, Jr.*, 67 T.C. 647 (1977).

[21]The major citators are published by CCH, RIA, WESTLAW, and Shepard's Citations, Inc.

THE BIG PICTURE

Example 6

Return to the facts of *The Big Picture* on p. 2-1. Assume that on the Samuels's joint return a dependency exemption is claimed for both Sam and Dana. The IRS challenges these exemptions after an audit. The likelihood of a successful challenge to the IRS's position in this dispute will turn on several factors.

- Was an appellate court ruling in their favor issued by the Federal circuit in which they live? If so, that decision is controlling law. If not and the Samuels's circuit has not ruled to the contrary on the issue but another circuit has ruled in their favor, the taxpayers could use the decision as support for their side of the argument.
- Assume a Revenue Ruling also is found that supports the taxpayers' claim of the exemptions. But how long ago were the Revenue Ruling and appellate decision issued? A legal precedent generally is stronger if it was issued more recently.
- If the Samuels's circuit has ruled favorably, have other courts discussed the appellate court holding? Were those discussions favorable or unfavorable to the Samuels's position? The more courts that follow a holding and cite it favorably, the stronger the legal precedent of the holding. Information of this sort can be found by reviewing the case history of the decision or by consulting a citator.

Understanding Judicial Opinions

Reading judicial opinions can be more productive if certain conventions of usage are understood. Some courts, including the Tax Court, apply the terms *petitioner* and *respondent* to the plaintiff and defendant, respectively, particularly when the case does not involve an appellate proceeding. Appellate courts often use the terms *appellant* and *appellee* instead.

It is also important to distinguish between a court's final determination, or *holding*, and passing comments made in the course of its opinion. These latter remarks, examples, and analogies, often collectively termed *dicta*, are not part of the court's conclusion and do not have precedential value. Nevertheless, they often facilitate one's understanding of the court's reasoning and can enable a tax adviser to better predict how the court might resolve some future tax case.

Digging Deeper   8   In-depth coverage can be found on this book's companion website: **www.cengagebrain.com**

Assessing the Significance of Other Sources

Primary sources of tax law include the Constitution, legislative history materials (e.g., Committee Reports), statutes, treaties, Treasury Regulations, IRS pronouncements, and judicial decisions. In general, the IRS regards only primary sources as substantial authority. However, reference to *secondary materials* such as tax publications, treatises, legal opinions, and written determinations may be useful. In general, secondary sources do not constitute tax authority.

Although the statement that the IRS regards only primary sources as substantial authority is generally true, there is one exception. Substantial authority *for purposes of* the accuracy-related penalty in § 6662 includes a number of secondary materials (e.g., letter rulings).[22] "Authority" does not include conclusions reached in treatises, textbooks and Web postings by tax commentators, and written opinions rendered for compensation by tax professionals.

A letter ruling or determination letter can be relied upon *only* by the taxpayer to whom it is issued, except as noted previously with respect to the accuracy-related penalty.

---

[22]Reg. § 1.6661–3(b)(2).

TAX IN THE NEWS   Baseball and Tax Research

An analogy based on the philosophy of Sandy Koufax, a great pitcher for the Los Angeles Dodgers in the early 1960s, may be appropriate for a tax researcher. Koufax is one of only some 21 baseball players to pitch a perfect game. He said that whenever he started a game, he tried to pitch a perfect game. If he was not successful, he tried for a no-hitter and then a shutout (no runs), and if he failed at all of these, he tried to win the game.

In researching a tax problem, the researcher tries first to find a Code Section, a tax treaty, or a committee report to support his or her position. If not successful in doing this, the researcher tries to find a Regulation, then a Revenue Ruling, and then a court decision (in this order). If no primary authority can be found, the researcher looks for a Bluebook passage, a letter ruling, a learned book or article, or a comment from a tax service.

© iStockphoto.com/Andrey Prokhorov

In-depth coverage can be found on this book's companion website: **www.cengagebrain.com**   **9**   Digging Deeper

2-2e Arriving at the Solution or at Alternative Solutions

Example 4 raises the question of whether taxpayers would be denied a loss deduction from the sale of stock to a corporation that they own. The solution depends, in part, on the relationship of the corporation's shareholders to each other. Because Richard and Joan are married to each other, § 267(c)(2) attributes Richard's stock to Joan in applying the "more than 50 percent" test of § 267(b)(2). Accordingly, Joan and Maple, Inc., are considered related parties under § 267(a), and a sale between them does not produce a deductible loss. If Richard and Joan were not related to each other, the constructive stock ownership rules would not apply and a loss could be deducted on a sale by Joan to Maple.

If Maple, Inc., were a *partnership* instead of a corporation, § 267 would not apply.[23] However, a different Code Section, namely § 707, produces the same result: no deduction is allowed for the loss from a sale between a "more than 50 percent" partner and the partnership. This additional research prevents the couple from erroneously selling their Airways stock to a partnership in hopes of obtaining a loss deduction from the sale. Accordingly, Joan still must sell the Airways stock to an unrelated party to deduct the loss.

Because Richard still wants to own Airways stock, he might consider purchasing new Airways Co. stock to replace the stock that Joan sells to the unrelated party. Additional research reveals that for the loss on the sale to be deductible, the "wash sale" rule requires that more than 30 days elapse between the purchase of the new stock and the sale of the old stock.[24] This rule applies to purchases and sales of *substantially identical stock or securities*. As a result, to deduct the loss on the Airways stock, Richard either must wait more than 30 days after Joan sells the shares to buy new Airways stock or acquire stock in a different company at any time. This new company can even be in the same general business as Airways.[25]

2-2f Communicating Tax Research

Once the problem has been researched adequately, a memorandum, a letter, or a speech setting forth the result may need to be prepared. The form the communication takes could depend on a number of considerations. For example, does an employer or instructor recommend a particular procedure or format for tax research memos? Is the memo to be given directly to the client, or will it first go to

LO.3

Communicate the results of the tax research process in a client letter and a tax file memorandum.

---

[23]Reg. § 1.267(b)–1(b)(1).
[24]§ 1091.

[25]Rev.Rul. 59–44, 1959–1 C.B. 205.

the preparer's employer? If the communication is a speech, who is the audience? How long should one speak?[26] Whatever form it takes, a good research communication should contain the following elements.

- A clear statement of the issue.
- In more complex situations, a short review of the fact pattern that raises the issue.
- A review of the pertinent tax law sources (e.g., Code, Regulations, Revenue Rulings, and judicial authority).
- Any assumptions made in arriving at the solution.
- The solution recommended and the logic or reasoning supporting it.
- The references consulted in the research process.

A memo to the tax file is a collection of thoughts resulting from a current tax research project. It is shared with others who have access to the memo files so that they do not need to duplicate the current work at a later date. The file memo is written by a tax professional, to be read by another tax professional, so it features citations in good form to the Code, Regulations, and other sources of the law, often hyperlinking directly to the underlying document. A file memo is organized so as to list the pertinent facts, open tax issues, a brief conclusion, and a discussion of the research findings and underlying tax logic. A file memo seldom exceeds two pages in length.

A letter to the client is written to convey the results of a research engagement and to identify the next steps for the taxpayer to consider. Because most clients have little knowledge or experience in working with tax source documents, citations typically are not used. If the recipient of the letter is a tax executive or other colleague, a more technical approach might be taken in the letter. The letter typically does not exceed a page or two, and it sometimes is supplemented with an attached spreadsheet or chart. It includes various social graces and any needed regulatory language.

Illustrations of the memo for the tax file and the client letter associated with Example 4 appear in Figures 2.6 and 2.7.

2-2g Follow-Up Procedures

Because tax research may involve a proposed (as opposed to a completed) transaction, a change in the tax law (legislative, administrative, or judicial) could alter the original conclusion. Additional research may be necessary to test the solution in light of current developments (refer to the broken lines at the right in Figure 2.5).

LO.4

Employ a strategy of how best to use a computer when performing tax research and in taking the CPA exam.

2-2h Online Tax Research

Computer-based tax research tools dominate the tax practice. Electronic tax resources allow the tax library to reflect the tax law's dynamic and daily changes. Nevertheless, using a computer to locate tax law sources cannot substitute for developing and maintaining a thorough knowledge of the tax law or for careful analysis when addressing tax research issues.

Most computerized services allow a user to retrieve documents in order of relevance, or in the order listed by database sources. Although this can be useful, just because a document is placed high on the relevance list does not mean it is valid law. Reading the primary sources, validating their authority, and checking the citator are essential in reaching a correct answer.

---

[26]See W. A. Raabe and G. E. Whittenburg, "Talking Tax: How to Make a Tax Presentation," *The Tax Adviser*, March 1997, pp. 179–182.

FIGURE 2.6	Tax File Memorandum

August 26, 2014

TAX FILE MEMORANDUM

FROM   Gillian J. Jones

SUBJECT Joan and Richard Taxpayer
             Engagement

Today I talked with Joan concerning her August 14, 2014 letter requesting tax assistance. Joan wants to know if she can sell some stock in Airways Co. to Maple, Inc., and deduct the $2,500 loss realized.

FACTS Maple, Inc., is owned 50% by Richard and 50% by Joan. Richard wants to continue holding Airways stock in anticipation of a rebound in its value, but Joan wants to sell her shares and deduct the realized loss. They have asked about a proposed sale of this stock to Maple.

ISSUE Can shareholders deduct a loss on the sale of an asset to a corporation, all of whose stock they own?

CONCLUSION Joan should *not* sell the Airways stock to Maple, if the couple wants to deduct the realized loss in the current tax year. Instead, Joan should sell this stock to a third party. Then the couple should either acquire new Airways stock more than 30 days before or after the date of sale, or acquire stock of a similar company.

ANALYSIS Section 267(a) provides that no loss is deductible on a sale or exchange between certain related parties. One of these relationships involves a corporation and a shareholder who owns "more than 50 percent" of that corporation's stock [see § 267(b)(2)]. Although Richard owns only 50% of Maple, Inc., his wife, Joan, owns the other 50%. The constructive ownership rule of § 267(c)(2) attributes stock held by family members, and a spouse is part of a taxpayer's family for this purpose, according to § 267(c)(4). Consequently, Richard's stock is attributed to Joan, who is then treated as owning 100% of Maple, Inc. The related-party disallowance rule then applies to the loss from Joan's selling the Airways stock to Maple. Accordingly, Joan must sell this stock to an unrelated party to make the realized loss deductible.

Because Richard wants to retain an investment in Airways, he can purchase replacement stock either before or after Joan sells the original Airways stock. Section 1091(a), however, requires that more than 30 days elapse between the purchase and the sale, or the sale and the purchase, as the case may be. Moreover, for this purpose, an option to buy the stock is treated as equivalent to the stock itself. As a result, Richard must wait more than 30 days between transactions and cannot utilize stock options in the interim to minimize his stock price exposure.

A final alternative might be to replace the Airways stock with securities of a comparable company in the same industry. Although no two companies are exactly alike, there may be another company whose management philosophy, marketing strategy, and financial data are sufficiently similar to Airways to provide an equivalent return on investment. Under this alternative, Richard could acquire the new company's shares immediately, without waiting the 30 days mandated by § 1091(a). Despite the two companies' investment similarity, they would not be treated as "substantially identical" for this purpose (see Rev.Rul. 59–44, 1959–1 C.B. 205), and the Airways realized loss could be recognized.

Using Electronic Tax Services

Usually, tax professionals use one of the following strategies when performing computer-based tax research.

- *Search* various databases using keywords that are likely to be found in the underlying documents, as written by Congress, the judiciary, or administrative sources.
- *Link* to tax documents for which all or part of the proper citation is known.
- *Browse* the tax databases, examining various tables of contents and indexes in a traditional manner or using cross-references in the documents to jump from one tax law source to another.

Virtually all of the major commercial tax publishers and most of the primary sources of the law itself, such as the Supreme Court and some of the Courts of Appeals, provide tax material in a variety of electronic formats.

Online Commercial Services

Online tax research systems allow practitioners to obtain virtually instantaneous use of tax law sources by accessing databases via the Internet. Some online services may employ price-per-search cost structures, which can be as much as $200 per hour. Thus, unless a practitioner who is subject to this pricing structure can pass along related costs to clients or others, online searching generally is limited to the

FIGURE 2.7	Client Letter

Smith, Raabe, Maloney, & Young, CPAs
5191 Natorp Boulevard
Mason, OH 45040

August 30, 2014

Mr. and Ms. Richard Taxpayer
111 Tragg Boulevard
Williamsburg, Virginia 23185

Dear Joan and Richard:

It was good to see you last week at our firm's golf outing. I'm glad that your children are doing so well in college and that our work to build up their education funds was so effective in providing the needed cash flow!

I am responding to your request to review your family's financial and tax situation. Our conclusions are based upon the facts as outlined in your August 14 letter. Any change in the facts may affect our conclusions.

Joan owns stock in Airways Co. that has declined in value, but Richard would like to retain this stock in anticipation of a rebound in its value. You have proposed a sale of this stock at its current market value to Maple, Inc., a corporation owned 50–50 by the two of you. Such a sale, however, would not permit the loss to be deducted.

A better approach would be to sell the Airways stock to a third party before year-end and repurchase this stock in the market. Please understand that the loss will not be deductible unless more than 30 days elapse between the sale and the repurchase of the stock. You can either sell the old stock first and then buy the new stock or buy the new stock first and then sell the old stock. However, it is essential that more than 30 days elapse between the sale and purchase transactions. Using options during this 30-day period is ineffective and will prevent the loss from being deducted in the current taxable year.

If the 30-day requirement is unacceptable, you might consider replacing the Airways stock with securities of some other company, perhaps even a company in the same general business as Airways. In that situation, your loss on the Airways stock can be deducted without regard to when you buy the new stock.

Let's meet to discuss this some more—and to allow me to show you our new office. Please e-mail me if I can clarify any of these points or if you have more information for me to consider. My work on this engagement is regulated by Treasury Circular 230.

Sincerely yours,

Gillian J. Jones, CPA
Partner

most important issues and to the researchers with the most experience and training in search techniques.

Other Web Sources

The Internet provides a wealth of tax information in several popular forms, sometimes at no direct cost to the researcher. Using current browser software and an Internet connection, the tax professional can access information provided around the world that can aid in the research process.

- *The Web* provides access to a number of sites maintained by accounting and consulting firms, publishers, tax academics and libraries, and governmental bodies. The best sites offer links to other sites and direct contact to the site providers. Exhibit 2.2 lists some of the websites that may be most useful to tax researchers and their Internet addresses as of press date.
- *Blogs and newsletters* provide a means by which information related to the tax law can be exchanged among taxpayers, tax professionals, and others who subscribe to the group's services. The tax professional can read the exchanges among other members and offer replies and suggestions to inquiries as desired. Discussions address the interpretation and application of existing law, analysis of proposals and new pronouncements, and reviews of tax software.

EXHIBIT 2.2	Tax-Related Websites	
Website	**Web Address at Press Date**	**Description**
Internal Revenue Service	**irs.gov**	News releases, downloadable forms and instructions, tables, Circular 230, and e-mail.
Tax Analysts	**taxanalysts.com**	Policy-oriented readings on tax laws and proposals to change it, moderated bulletins on various tax subjects.
Tax Sites Directory	**taxsites.com**	References and links to tax sites on the Internet, including state and Federal tax sites, academic and professional pages, tax forms, and software.
Tax laws online	**law.cornell.edu/cfr**	Treasury Regulations.
	law.cornell.edu/uscode	Internal Revenue Code.
	uscode.house.gov/search/criteria.shtml	
Motley Fool Tax Page	**fool.com/taxes**	Articles and links to tax sites on the Internet.
Commercial tax publishers	For example, **cch.com**	Information about products and services available by subscription and newsletter excerpts.
Accounting firms and professional organizations	For example, the AICPA's page is at **aicpa.org**, Ernst & Young is at **ey.com**, and KPMG is at **kpmg.com**	Tax planning newsletters, descriptions of services offered and career opportunities, and exchange of data with clients and subscribers.
Cengage Learning South-Western	**cengagebrain.com**	Informational updates, newsletters, support materials for students and adopters, and continuing education.

Note: Web addresses change frequently.

While tax information on the Internet is plentiful, public domain information never should be relied upon without referring to other, more reliable sources. Always remember that anyone can set up a website and that quality control can be difficult for the tax professional to ascertain.

In many situations, solutions to research problems benefit from or require the use of various electronic tax research tools. A competent tax professional must become familiar and proficient with these tools and be able to use them effectively to meet the expectations of clients and the necessities of work in the modern world.[27]

2-3 TAX RESEARCH ON THE CPA EXAMINATION

The CPA examination is computer-based, and it emphasizes information technology and general business knowledge. The 14-hour exam has four sections, and taxation is included in the 3-hour Regulation section, which covers these topics.

- Federal tax procedures and accounting issues.
- Federal taxation of property transactions.
- Federal taxation—individuals.
- Federal taxation—entities.

Each exam section includes multiple-choice questions and case studies called simulations. About 60 multiple-choice tax questions appear in the Regulation

---

[27]For a more detailed discussion of the use of electronic tax research in a tax practice, see W. A. Raabe, G. E. Whittenburg, D. L. Sanders, and R. B. Sawyers, *South-Western Federal Tax Research*, 10th ed. (Cengage Learning/South-Western, 2015).

FINANCIAL DISCLOSURE INSIGHTS   Where Does GAAP Come From?

As this chapter has described, the tax law is developed by many entities, including Congress, the legislators of other countries, the courts, and the IRS. Accounting principles also have many sources. Consequently, in reconciling the tax and financial accounting reporting of a transaction, the tax professional will need to know the hierarchy of authority of accounting principles—in particular, the level of importance to assign to a specific GAAP document. The diagram below presents the sources of GAAP arranged in a general order of authority from highest to lowest.[28]

Professional research is conducted to find and analyze the sources of accounting reporting standards, in much the same way a tax professional conducts research concerning an open tax question. In fact, many of the publishers that provide tax research materials also can be used to find GAAP and IFRS documents. These include Research Institute of America (RIA) and Commerce Clearing House (CCH). The Financial Accounting Standards Board (FASB) also makes its standards and interpretations available by subscription.

Highest Authority
- Financial Accounting Standards and Interpretations of the FASB.
- Pronouncements of bodies that preceded the FASB, such as the Accounting Principles Board (APB).

- FASB Technical Bulletins.
- Audit and Accounting Guides, prepared by the American Institute of CPAs (AICPA) and cleared by the FASB.
- Practice Bulletins, prepared by the American Institute of CPAs (AICPA) and cleared by the FASB.

- Interpretation Guides of the FASB Staff.
- Accounting Interpretations of the AICPA.
- IASB Accounting Standards.
- FASB Concepts Standards.
- Widely accepted accounting practices, professional journals, accounting textbooks, and treatises.

section of the exam. All written communications tasks are placed in the Business Environment and Concepts section of the exam.

Simulations are small case studies designed to test a candidate's tax knowledge and skills using real-life work-related situations. Simulations include a four-function pop-up calculator, a blank spreadsheet with some elementary functionality, and authoritative literature for the candidate to research in completing the tax case study simulations (e.g., Internal Revenue Code, Regulations, IRS publications, and Federal tax forms). Examples of such simulations follow.

Example 7

The tax *citation type* simulation requires the candidate to research the Internal Revenue Code and enter a Code Section and subsection citation. For example, Amber Company is considering using the simplified dollar-value method of pricing its inventory for purposes of the LIFO method that is available to certain small businesses. What Internal Revenue Code Section is the relevant authority to which you should turn to determine whether the taxpayer is eligible to use this method? To be successful, the candidate needs to find § 474.

---

[28]See Chapter 10 of Raabe, et al., cited in footnote 27, for a discussion of strategies and techniques used in conducting research with financial accounting resources.

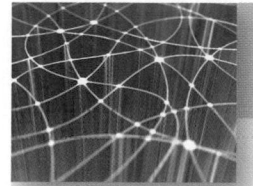

BRIDGE DISCIPLINE   Bridge to Regulation and Oversight

The interests of the public are represented by Federal, state, and local governments, as they oversee the various economic transactions carried out by individuals and businesses. Control of the financial sector is assigned to the Treasury and the Securities and Exchange Commission, among other agencies.

Most citizens assume that attorneys and CPAs hold broad high-level skills in working with the tax laws. But the nature of today's economy dictates that professionals working in law and accounting instead develop narrower specialties that clients will find valuable in the marketplace. Only a subset of CPAs and attorneys practice regularly with the tax law, but all such professionals must hold and maintain broad-based skills in taxation.

Tax law is the subject of only one of the sections of the CPA exam, and only a portion of those questions relate to specific provisions of the tax law. The exam also tests the candidate's research and communication skills, and because it is administered with computer software, the candidate must have some technological facility as well.

The depth and variety of the skills that are required of an effective tax professional almost certainly are not measured well by the CPA or bar examinations. The integrity of the taxing system may be at risk when one can attain credible professional certification with only entry-level skills. It is likely that several further levels of specialty certifications, and rigorous, lifelong skill improvement, should be required of tax professionals.

Example 8

A *tax form completion* simulation requires the candidate to fill out a portion of a tax form. For example, Red is a limited liability company (LLC). Complete the income section of the Form 1065 for Red Company using the values found and calculated on previous tabs along with the following data.

Ordinary income from other partnerships	$ 5,200
Net gain (loss) from Form 4797	2,400
Management fee income	12,000

The candidate is provided with page 1 of Form 1065 on which to record the appropriate amounts.

Candidates can learn more about the CPA examination at **www.cpa-exam.org**. This online tutorial site reviews the exam's format, navigation functions, and tools. A 30- to 60-minute sample exam will familiarize a candidate with the types of questions on the examination.

REFOCUS ON THE BIG PICTURE

RESEARCHING TAX QUESTIONS

Finding the various legislative, administrative, and judicial sources of tax law dealing with a specific issue and interpreting and assessing their relative importance is a difficult process. While Revenue Rulings are important in that they reflect the position of the IRS on specific tax issues, they do not carry as much weight as Treasury Department Regulations or the Internal Revenue Code. It is not unusual for a court to disagree with the findings of the IRS. However, the reliance that can be placed on the court decision depends on a number of factors, including the level of the court, the legal residence of the taxpayer, and the similarity of the case to the taxpayer's situation. An appellate court decision carries significant weight, particularly if it comes from the taxpayer's own circuit.

What If?

What if your research turns up a Tax Court case that supports the IRS's argument that the income is taxable? In this situation, the tax researcher should look carefully at the weight of the decision and any subsequent events that might have transpired. Is the decision supported by cases from other courts? Was the Tax Court decision appealed?

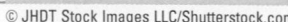

Suggested Readings

Sheldon I. Banoff and Richard M. Lipton, Editors' Shop Talk, "Is Wikipedia Good Authority in the Tax Court?" *Journal of Taxation*, April 2007.

"Can Treasury and the IRS Write Rules in 'Plain' Langauge?" *Journal of Taxation*, December 2010.

Alexandra Defelice, "Tax Research Comes in Many Flavors," *Accounting Today*, April 2009, **tinyurl.com/tax-research-flavors**.

T. S. Rose and J. Temares, "Tax Research Tips to Solve Tax Problems," *CPA Magazine*, **tinyurl.com/tax-research-tips**.

G. E. Whittenburg, M. Flatley, and W. A. Raabe, "Improving Accountants' Writing Skills," *National Public Accountant*, November 1998.

Key Terms

Acquiescence, 2-16

Circuit Court of Appeals, 2-13

Citator, 2-23

Court of Federal Claims, 2-11

Court of original jurisdiction, 2-11

Determination letters, 2-10

District Court, 2-11

Final Regulations, 2-8

Interpretive Regulations, 2-22

Legislative Regulations, 2-22

Letter rulings, 2-9

Nonacquiescence, 2-16

Precedents, 2-14

Procedural Regulations, 2-22

Proposed Regulations, 2-8

Revenue Procedures, 2-9

Revenue Rulings, 2-8

Small Cases Division, 2-11

Supreme Court, 2-14

Tax Court, 2-11

Technical Advice Memoranda (TAMs), 2-10

Temporary Regulations, 2-8

Writ of Certiorari, 2-15

Problems

1. **LO.1** What precedents must each of these courts follow?
   a. U.S. Tax Court.
   b. U.S. Court of Federal Claims.
   c. U.S. District Court.

Communications

2. **LO.1, 3** Butch Bishop operates a small international firm named Tile, Inc. A new treaty between the United States and Spain conflicts with a Section of the Internal Revenue Code. Butch asks you for advice. If he follows the treaty position, does he need to disclose this on this year's tax return? If he is required to disclose, are there any penalties for failure to disclose? Prepare a letter in which you respond to Butch. Tile's address is 100 International Drive, Tampa, FL 33620.

3. **LO.1** What is the function of the Joint Conference Committee of the House Ways and Means Committee and the Senate Finance Committee?

4. **LO.1** Distinguish between the following.
   a. Treasury Regulations and Revenue Rulings.
   b. Revenue Rulings and Revenue Procedures.
   c. Revenue Rulings and letter rulings.
   d. Letter rulings and determination letters.

5. **LO.1, 2** Rank the following items from the lowest to the highest authority in the Federal tax law system.
   a. Interpretive Regulation.
   b. Legislative Regulation.
   c. Letter ruling.
   d. Revenue Ruling.
   e. Internal Revenue Code.
   f. Proposed Regulation.

6. **LO.1** Explain how tax Regulations are arranged. How would the following Regulations be cited?
   a. Final Regulations under § 152.
   b. Proposed Regulations under § 274.
   c. Temporary Regulations under § 163.

7. **LO.1** Interpret each of the following citations.
   a. Temp.Reg. § 1.956–2T.
   b. Rev.Rul. 2012–15, 2012–23 I.R.B. 975.
   c. Ltr.Rul. 200204051.

8. **LO.1** Which of the following would be considered advantages of the Small Cases Division of the Tax Court?
   a. Appeal to the Tax Court is possible.
   b. A hearing of a deficiency of $65,000 is considered on a timely basis.
   c. Taxpayer can handle the litigation without using an attorney or a certified public accountant.
   d. Taxpayer can use Small Cases Division decisions for precedential value.
   e. The hearing is conducted informally.
   f. Travel time probably will be reduced.

9. **LO.1** List an advantage and a disadvantage of using the U.S. Court of Federal Claims as the trial court for Federal tax litigation.

10. **LO.1, 3** Eddy Falls is considering litigating a tax deficiency of approximately $229,030 in the court system. He asks you to provide him with a short description of his litigation alternatives, indicating the advantages and disadvantages of each. Prepare your response to Eddy in the form of a letter. His address is 200 Mesa Drive, Tucson, AZ 85714.

   Communications

11. **LO.1** A taxpayer lives in Michigan. In a controversy with the IRS, the taxpayer loses at the trial court level. Describe the appeal procedure for each of the following trial courts.
    a. Small Cases Division of the Tax Court.
    b. Tax Court.
    c. District Court.
    d. Court of Federal Claims.

12. **LO.1** The U.S. Government loses a tax case in the U.S. Tax Court and does not appeal the result. What does the failure to appeal signify?

13. **LO.1** For the Tax Court, District Court, and the Court of Federal Claims, indicate the following.
    a. Number of regular judges per court.
    b. Availability of a jury trial.
    c. Whether the deficiency must be paid before the trial.

14. **LO.1** A taxpayer living in the following states would appeal a decision of the U.S District Court to which Court of Appeals?
    a. Wyoming.
    b. Nebraska.
    c. Idaho.
    d. Louisiana.
    e. Illinois.

15. **LO.1** What is meant by the term *petitioner*?

    Critical Thinking

16. **LO.1, 2** In assessing the validity of a prior court decision, discuss the significance of the following on the taxpayer's issue.
    a. The decision was rendered by the U.S. District Court of Wyoming. Taxpayer lives in Wyoming.
    b. The decision was rendered by the Court of Federal Claims. Taxpayer lives in Wyoming.
    c. The decision was rendered by the Second Circuit Court of Appeals. Taxpayer lives in California.
    d. The decision was rendered by the Supreme Court.
    e. The decision was rendered by the Tax Court. The IRS has acquiesced in the result.
    f. Same as (e), except that the IRS has nonacquiesced in the result.

17. **LO.1** What is the difference between a Regular decision, a Memorandum decision, and a Summary Opinion of the Tax Court?

18. **LO.1** Explain the following abbreviations.

    a. CA–2.
    b. Fed.Cl.
    c. *aff'd.*
    d. *rev'd.*
    e. *rem'd.*
    f. *Cert. denied.*
    g. *acq.*
    h. B.T.A.
    i. USTC.
    j. AFTR.
    k. F.3d.
    l. F.Supp.
    m. USSC.
    n. S.Ct.
    o. D.Ct.

19. **LO.2** Referring to the citation only, determine which tax law source issued these documents.

    a. 716 F.2d 693 (CA–9, 1983).
    b. 92 T.C 400 (1998).
    c. 70 U.S. 224 (1935).
    d. 3 B.T.A. 1042 (1926).
    e. T.C.Memo. 1957–169.
    f. 50 AFTR 2d 92–6000 (Cl.Ct., 1992).
    g. Ltr.Rul. 9046036.
    h. 111 F.Supp.2d 1294 (S.D. N. Y., 2000).
    i. 98–50, 1998–1 C.B. 10.

20. **LO.2** Interpret each of the following citations.

    a. 14 T.C. 74 (1950).
    b. 592 F.2d 1251 (CA–5, 1979).
    c. 95–1 USTC ¶ 50,104 (CA–6, 1995).
    d. 75 AFTR 2d 95–110 (CA–6, 1995).
    e. 223 F.Supp. 663 (W.D. Tex., 1963).

21. **LO.2** Where can one locate a published decision of the U.S. Court of Federal Claims?

22. **LO.2** Which of the following items can probably be found in the *Internal Revenue Bulletin*?

    a. Action on Decision.
    b. Small Cases Division of the Tax Court decision.
    c. Letter ruling.
    d. Revenue Procedure.
    e. Final Regulation.
    f. Court of Appeals decision.
    g. Acquiescences to Tax Court decisions.
    h. U.S. Circuit Court of Appeals decision.

23. **LO.2** Answer the following questions based upon this citation: *United Draperies, Inc. v. Comm.*, 340 F.2d 936 (CA–7, 1964), *aff'g* 41 T.C. 457 (1963), *cert. denied* 382 U.S. 813 (1965).

    a. In which court did this decision first appear?
    b. Did the appellate court uphold the trial court?
    c. Who was the plaintiff?
    d. Did the Supreme Court uphold the appellate court decision?

Issue ID

24. **LO.2, 4** For her tax class, Yvonne is preparing a research paper discussing the tax aspects of child support payments. Explain to Yvonne how she can research the provisions on this topic.

25. **LO.1, 2** Tom, an individual taxpayer, has been audited by the IRS and, as a result, has been assessed a substantial deficiency (which has not yet been paid) in additional income taxes. In preparing his defense, Tom advances the following possibilities.

    a. Although a resident of Kentucky, Tom plans to sue in a U.S. District Court in Oregon that appears to be more favorably inclined toward taxpayers.
    b. If (a) is not possible, Tom plans to take his case to a Kentucky state court where an uncle is the presiding judge.
    c. Because Tom has found a B.T.A. decision that seems to help his case, he plans to rely on it under alternative (a) or (b).
    d. If he loses at the trial court level, Tom plans to appeal either to the U.S. Court of Federal Claims or to the U.S. Second Circuit Court of Appeals because he has relatives in both Washington, D.C., and New York. Staying with these relatives could save Tom lodging expense while his appeal is being heard by the court selected.
    e. Whether or not Tom wins at the trial court or appeals court level, he feels certain of success on an appeal to the U.S. Supreme Court.

    Evaluate Tom's notions concerning the judicial process as it applies to Federal income tax controversies.

26. **LO.1** Using the legend provided, classify each of the following statements (more than one answer per statement may be appropriate).

Legend

D = Applies to the District Court
T = Applies to the Tax Court
C = Applies to the Court of Federal Claims
A = Applies to the Circuit Court of Appeals
U = Applies to the Supreme Court
N = Applies to none of the above

---

   a. Decides only Federal tax matters.
   b. Decisions are reported in the F.3d Series.
   c. Decisions are reported in the USTCs.
   d. Decisions are reported in the AFTRs.
   e. Appeal is by *Writ of Certiorari*.
   f. Court meets most often in Washington, D.C.
   g. Offers the choice of a jury trial.
   h. Is a trial court.
   i. Is an appellate court.
   j. Allows appeal to the Court of Appeals for the Federal Circuit and bypasses the taxpayer's own Circuit Court of Appeals.
   k. Has a Small Cases Division.
   l. Is the only trial court where the taxpayer does not have to first pay the tax assessed by the IRS.

27. **LO.1, 2** Using the legend provided, classify each of the following citations as to the type of court.

Legend

D = District Court
T = Tax Court
C = Court of Federal Claims
A = Circuit Court of Appeals
U = Supreme Court
N = None of the above

---

   a. Rev.Rul. 2009–34, 2009–42 I.R.B. 502.
   b. *Joseph R. Bolker*, 81 T.C. 782 (1983).
   c. *Magneson*, 753 F.2d 1490 (CA–9, 1985).
   d. *Lucas v. Ox Fibre Brush Co.*, 281 U.S. 115 (1930).
   e. *Ashtabula Bow Socket Co.*, 2 B.T.A. 306 (1925).
   f. *BB&T Corp.*, 97 AFTR 2d 2006–873 (D.Ct. Mid.N.Car., 2006).
   g. *Choate Construction Co.*, T.C.Memo. 1997–495.
   h. Ltr.Rul. 200940021.
   i. *John and Rochelle Ray*, T.C. Summary Opinion 2006–110.

28. **LO.1, 2** Using the legend provided, classify each of the following tax sources.

Legend

P = Primary tax source
S = Secondary tax source
B = Both
N = Neither

---

   a. Sixteenth Amendment to the U.S. Constitution.
   b. Tax treaty between the United States and India.
   c. Revenue Procedure.
   d. Chief Counsel Advice (issued 2009).
   e. U.S. District Court decision.
   f. *Yale Law Journal* article.
   g. Temporary Regulations (issued 2013).
   h. U.S. Tax Court Memorandum decision.
   i. Small Cases Division of the U.S. Tax Court decision.
   j. House Ways and Means Committee report.

29. **LO.1** In which Subchapter of the Internal Revenue Code would one find information about corporate distributions?
   a. Subchapter S.
   b. Subchapter C.
   c. Subchapter P.
   d. Subchapter K.
   e. Subchapter M.

30. **LO.1, 2** To locate an IRS Revenue Procedure that was issued during the past week, which source would you consult?
   a. *Federal Register.*
   b. *Internal Revenue Bulletin.*
   c. Internal Revenue Code.
   d. Some other source. Identify it.

31. **LO.1, 2** In the citation *Schuster's Express, Inc.*, 66 T.C. 588 (1976), *aff'd* 562 F.2d 39 (CA–2, 1977), *nonacq.*, to what do the 66, 39, and *nonacq.* refer?

32. **LO.1** Is there an automatic right to appeal to the U.S. Supreme Court? If so, what is the process?

Ethics and Equity

33. **LO.2** An accountant friend of yours tells you that he "almost never" does any tax research because he believes that "research usually reveals that some tax planning idea has already been thought up and shot down." Besides, he points out, most tax returns are never audited by the IRS. Can a tax adviser who is dedicated to reducing his client's tax liability justify the effort to engage in tax research? Do professional ethics *demand* such efforts? Which approach would a client probably prefer?

Communications

34. **LO.1, 4** Go to the U.S. Tax Court website.
   a. What different types of cases can be found on the site?
   b. What is a Summary Opinion? Find one.
   c. What is a Memorandum decision? Find one.
   d. Find the court's Rules of Practice and Procedures.
   e. Is the site user-friendly? E-mail suggested improvements to the site's webmaster.

Critical Thinking

35. **LO.2, 3** Locate the following Code provisions, and give a brief description of each in an e-mail to your instructor.

Communications

   a. § 61(a)(13).
   b. § 643(a)(2).
   c. § 2503(g)(2)(A).

BRIDGE DISCIPLINE

1. Comment on these statements.
   a. The tax law is created and administered in the same way as other Federal provisions.
   b. Most taxpayers find it too expensive and time-consuming to sue the government in a tax dispute.

2. Using the title "The Federal Taxing System Operates Outside the U.S. Constitution," write a two-page paper to submit in your Government Policy course. Do not address "tax protester" issues (e.g., that the income tax is unconstitutional or that one's taxes should be measured using only the gold standard). Instead, concentrate on how Federal tax law is made and interpreted, and how the process measures up to other governmental standards.

   Communications

3. Develop an outline from which you will deliver a 10-minute talk to the local Chamber of Commerce, with the title "Regulation of the Tax Profession in the 21st Century." Use no more than four PowerPoint slides for your talk, and discuss what the business community now needs with respect to oversight of a stable, yet productive, revenue-raising system. Include administrative developments of the last two years in your research.

   Communications

4. A friend of yours, who is a philosophy major, has overheard the conversation described in Problem 33 and declares that all tax research is "immoral." She says that tax research enables people with substantial assets to shift the burden of financing public expenditures to those who "get up every morning, go to work, play by the rules, and pay their bills." How do you respond?

   Ethics and Equity

Research Problems

Note: Solutions to Research Problems can be prepared by using the **Checkpoint®** **Student Edition** online research product, which is available to accompany this text. It is also possible to prepare solutions to the Research Problems by using tax research materials found in a standard tax library.

THOMSON REUTERS
CHECKPOINT®

Research Problem 1. Locate the following items, and e-mail to your professor a brief summary of the results.
   a. *Charles Y. Choi*, T.C. Memo. 2002–183.
   b. Ltr.Rul. 200231003.
   c. Action on Decision, 2000–004, May 10, 2000.

   Communications

Research Problem 2. Locate the following Code citations, and give a brief topical description of each.
   a. § 708(a).
   b. § 1371(a).
   c. § 2503(a).

Research Problem 3. Locate the following Regulations, and give a brief topical description of each. Summarize your comments in an e-mail to your instructor.
   a. Reg. § 1.170A–4A(b)(2)(ii)(C).
   b. Reg. § 1.672(b)–1.
   c. Reg. § 20.2031–7(f).

   Communications

Research Problem 4. Describe the material that is found in Subtitle E of the Code. Would you expect these provisions not to be addressed anywhere else in the Code? Explain.

Research Problem 5. Determine the missing data in these court decisions and rulings.
   a. *Higgins v. Comm.*, 312 U.S._____ (1941).
   b. *Talen v. U.S.*, 355 F.Supp.2d 22 (D.Ct. D.C., _____).
   c. Rev.Rul. 2008–18, 2008–13 I.R.B._____.
   d. *Pahl v. Comm.*, 150 F.3d 1124 (CA–9, _____).
   e. *Veterinary Surgical Consultants PC*, 117 T.C._____(2001).
   f. *Yeagle Drywall Co.*, T.C. Memo. 2001_____.

Research Problem 6. Locate the following Tax Court case: *Thomas J. Green, Jr.,* 59 T.C. 456 (1972). Briefly describe the issue in the case and explain what the Tax Court said about using IRS publications to support a research conclusion.

Research Problem 7. Can a Tax Court Small Cases decision be treated as a precedent by other taxpayers? Explain.

Partial list of research aids:
§ 7463(b).
Maria Antionette Walton Mitchell, T.C. Summary Opinion 2004–160.

Research Problem 8. Find *Kathryn Bernal,* 120 T.C. 102 (2003), and answer the following questions.
  a. What was the docket number?
  b. When was the dispute filed?
  c. Who is the respondent?
  d. Who was the attorney for the taxpayers?
  e. Who was the judge who wrote the opinion?
  f. What was the disposition of the dispute?

Decision Making

Communications

Research Problem 9. This year, Frank lived with and supported Daisy, an unrelated 20-year-old woman to whom he was not married. Frank lives in a state that has a statute that makes cohabitation a misdemeanor for a man and a woman who are not married to each other. May Frank claim Daisy as a dependent, assuming that he meets all of the applicable tests to claim the exemption? Should Frank and Daisy move to another state? Describe your research path in a PowerPoint presentation for your classmates.

Partial list of research aids:
§ 152(f)(3).
John T. Untermann, 38 T.C. 93 (1962).

Internet Activity

Use the tax resources of the Internet to address the following questions. Do not restrict your search to the Web, but include a review of newsgroups and general reference materials, practitioner sites and resources, primary sources of the tax law, chat rooms and discussion groups, and other opportunities.

Research Problem 10. Go to **www.legalbitstream.com** and find the case in which Mark Spitz, the Olympic gold medalist, is the petitioner. Answer the following questions.
  a. What tax years are at issue in the case?
  b. In what year was the case decided?
  c. What tax issues were involved? Did the court decide in favor of Spitz or the IRS?
  d. Were any penalties imposed on the taxpayer? Why or why not?

Communications

Research Problem 11. Find tax research documents for the following on the Internet. Send one citation for each item to your instructor in an e-mail.
  a. The U.S. Supreme Court, a Circuit Court of Appeals, the Internal Revenue Service, and final Regulations.
  b. Sources of proposed Federal tax legislation.
  c. A collection of tax rules for your state.

Communications

Research Problem 12. Find three blogs related to tax practice. On one PowerPoint slide, list the URLs for each blog and the general topical areas addressed at each. Send your slide to the others in your course.

Communications

Research Problem 13. Find one instance of each of the following using a nonsubscription site on the Web or an online library at your school. In an e-mail to your professor, give a full citation for the document and describe how you found it.
  a. Letter Ruling.
  b. Action on Decision.
  c. IRS Notice.
  d. Revenue Ruling.
  e. Revenue Procedure.
  f. Code Section.
  g. Tax Regulation.
  h. Tax treaty.
  i. Tax Court Summary Opinion.
  j. Tax Court Regular decision.

Taxes on the Financial Statements

LEARNING OBJECTIVES: *After completing Chapter 3, you should be able to:*

LO.1 Enumerate the differences between book and tax methods of computing income tax expense.

LO.2 Compute a corporation's book income tax expense.

LO.3 Describe the purpose of the valuation allowance.

LO.4 Interpret the disclosure information contained in the financial statements.

LO.5 Identify the **GAAP** treatment concerning tax uncertainties and unrepatriated foreign earnings.

LO.6 Use financial statement income tax information to benchmark a company's tax position.

CHAPTER OUTLINE

TAX TALK *Truth is, figuring out how much tax a company actually pays is impossible.... Tax disclosure is just inscrutable.* —ROBERT WILLENS

THE BIG PICTURE   Tax Solutions for the Real World

© Pukhov Konstantin/Shutterstock.com

TAXES ON THE FINANCIAL STATEMENTS

Raymond Jones, the CEO of Arctic Corporation, would like some help reconciling the amount of income tax expense on Arctic's financial statements with the amount of income tax reported on the company's corporate income tax return for its first year of operations. Mr. Jones does not understand why he can't simply multiply the financial statement income by the company's 35 percent marginal tax rate to get the financial tax expense. While the financial statements show book income before tax of $25 million, the reported Federal tax expense is only $7.7 million. In addition, the corporate tax return reports taxable income of $19 million and Federal income taxes payable of only $6.65 million.

Without knowing the specifics of the company's financial statements, does Arctic's situation look reasonable? Why is Arctic's financial tax expense not equal to $8.75 million ($25 million × 35%)? What causes the $1.05 million difference between the taxes shown on the financial statements and the taxes due on the tax return?

Read the chapter and formulate your response.

The ultimate result of the many tax planning ideas, advice, and compliance efforts provided by tax professionals to their clients is captured in a simple summary number—income tax expense. A U.S. corporation's tax expense is reported in its annual Federal tax return, its financial statements, and other regulatory filings and is often the starting point for state and local tax returns. As it turns out, however, deriving a corporation's income tax expense is not so simple.

A corporation may report millions of dollars in tax expense in its financial statements and yet pay virtually nothing to the U.S., state, or foreign governments. Alternatively, a corporation may pay substantial amounts to the U.S., state, and foreign governments and report very little income tax expense in its financial statements. Why do such differences exist? Which income tax expense is the "correct" number? How can data regarding a corporation's income tax expense provide valuable information for the corporation, its competitors, and tax professionals assisting in the planning function? This chapter addresses these questions.

3-1 BOOK-TAX DIFFERENCES

LO.1

Enumerate the differences between book and tax methods of computing income tax expense.

A significant difference may exist between a corporation's Federal income tax liability as reported on its Form 1120 (tax) and the corporation's income tax expense as reported on its financial statements (book) prepared using **generally accepted accounting principles (GAAP)**. This book-tax difference is caused by any or all of the following.

* Differences in reporting entities included in the calculation.
* Different definition of taxes included in the income tax expense amount.
* Different accounting methods.

A corporation's activities are captured in its accounting records, producing general ledger results. At the end of the year, these records are summarized to produce a trial balance. Adjustments to these accounting data may be necessary to produce both the corporation's financial statements and its corporate income tax return. These book and tax adjustments rarely match. Different entities may be included in the reports, and the book and tax rules can be quite different. For instance, GAAP includes a materiality principle, under which some items can be ignored if they are insignificant in amount. The tax law includes no similar materiality threshold: all items are material in computing taxable income.

On a tax return, Schedule M–1 or M–3 reconciles the differences between an entity's book income and its taxable income. See Figure 3.1.

3-1a Different Reporting Entities

A corporate group must consolidate all U.S. and foreign subsidiaries within a single financial statement for book purposes when the parent corporation controls more than 50 percent of the voting power of those subsidiaries.[1] In cases where the parent corporation owns between 20 and 50 percent of another corporation, the parent uses the **equity method** to account for the earnings of the subsidiary. Under the equity method, the parent currently records its share of the subsidiary's income or loss for the year.[2] Corporations that own less than 20 percent of other corporations typically use the *cost method* to account for income from these investments and include income only when actual dividends are received.

---

[1] *Consolidation*, ASC Topic 810 (formerly *Consolidation of All Majority Owned Subsidiaries*, Statement of Financial Accounting Standards No. 94). Certain adjustments are made to reduce book income for the after-tax income related to minority shareholders.

[2] *Investments—Equity Method and Joint Ventures*, ASC Topic 323 (formerly *The Equity Method of Accounting for Investments in Common Stock*, Accounting Principles Board Opinion No. 18).

TAX IN THE NEWS The Watchdog Is Watching

A recent report by the SEC listed the watchdog agency's areas of focus with respect to the financial statements of publicly traded corporations as they pertain to issues in accounting for income taxes. Inquiries and comment letters from the SEC can be anticipated in these areas. The most important of the focus areas include the following.

- Realizability of deferred tax assets—how positive and negative evidence supporting the deferrals is assessed by the taxpayer.
- Uncertain tax positions—whether ASC 740-10 (FIN 48) disclosures are comprehensive and complete.

- Foreign earnings—whether sufficient information is provided concerning the reinvestments of overseas earnings and their effects on the effective tax rate.
- Intraperiod allocation—how the tax accounts reflect transactions involving continuing operations and income from other sources.

Income tax matters remain the accounting area most frequently identified as a material weakness for large entities, and income taxes always rank among the ten most frequent restatement issues.

The Edgar database is a good place to follow trends in the agency's information requests and the taxpayer's responses.

© iStockphoto.com/Andrey Prokhorov

FIGURE 3.1 **Flow of Accounting Data**

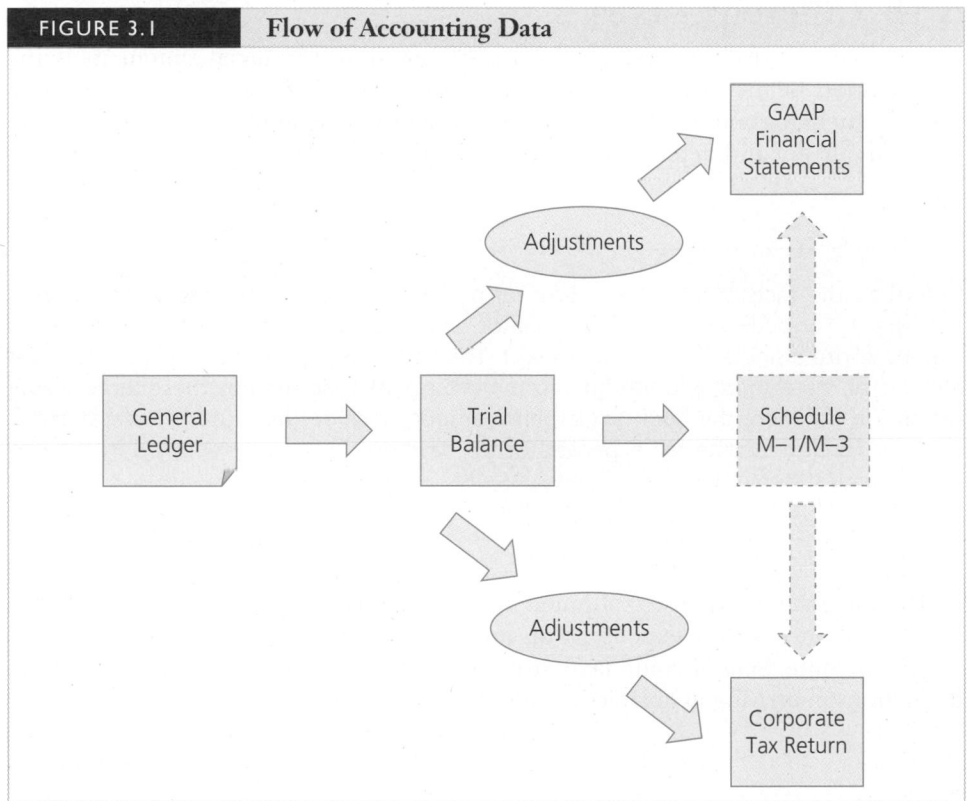

THE BIG PICTURE

Example 1

Return to the facts of *The Big Picture* on p. 3-1. Arctic Corporation owns 100% of Gator, Inc., a domestic corporation; 100% of Hurricane, Ltd., a foreign corporation; and 40% of Beach, Inc., a domestic corporation. Arctic's combined financial statement includes its own net income and the net income of both Gator and Hurricane. In addition, Arctic's financial statement includes its 40% share of Beach's net income. Arctic's financial statement includes the income of these subsidiaries regardless of whether Arctic receives any actual profit distributions from its subsidiaries.

For Federal income tax purposes, a U.S. corporation may elect to include any *domestic* subsidiaries that are 80 percent or more owned in its consolidated U.S. tax return.[3] On the other hand, the income of non-U.S. subsidiaries and less than 80 percent owned domestic subsidiaries is not included in the consolidated tax return.

THE BIG PICTURE

Example 2

Return to the facts of *The Big Picture* on p. 3-1. Also assume the facts presented in Example 1. If Arctic elects to include Gator as part of its consolidated Federal income tax return, Arctic's return includes its own taxable income and the taxable income generated by Gator. Hurricane's taxable income is not included in the consolidated return because it is a non-U.S. corporation. Beach, although a domestic corporation, cannot be consolidated with Arctic because Arctic owns only 40% of the stock. Income from Hurricane and Beach will be included in Arctic's U.S. taxable income only when Arctic receives actual or constructive dividends.

3-1b Different Taxes

The income tax expense reported on a corporation's financial statement is the combination of the entity's Federal, state, local, and foreign income taxes. This number includes both current and deferred tax expense amounts. The distinction between current and deferred income taxes is discussed later in this chapter.

THE BIG PICTURE

Example 3

Return to the facts of *The Big Picture* on p. 3-1. Also assume the facts presented in Example 1. For book purposes, Arctic, Gator, and Hurricane combine their income and expenses into a single financial statement. The book tax expense for the year includes all Federal, state, local, and foreign income taxes paid or accrued by these three corporations. In addition, the book tax expense amount includes any future Federal, state, local, or foreign income tax expenses (or tax savings) on income reported in the current income statement.

The income tax expense computed on the Federal income tax return is only the U.S. *Federal* income tax expense. This amount is based on the U.S. corporation's taxable income. State income taxes are reported on the Federal tax return, but as deductions in arriving at taxable income.

THE BIG PICTURE

Example 4

Return to the facts of *The Big Picture* on p. 3-1. Also assume the facts presented in Examples 1 and 2. Arctic and Gator file a consolidated Federal tax return. The tax expense reported on the Form 1120 is only the U.S. Federal income tax expense for the consolidated taxable income of Arctic and Gator. This tax expense does not include the income taxes that Arctic and its subsidiaries paid to state, local, or foreign governments.

---

[3]§§ 1501–1504. An election to consolidate an 80% or more owned subsidiary generally can be changed only with the permission of the IRS.

3-1c Different Methods

Many differences exist between book and tax accounting methods. Some are simply **temporary differences**, with income and expenses appearing in both the financial statement and the tax return, but in different periods (i.e., a timing difference). Others are **permanent differences**, with items appearing in the financial statement or the tax return, but not both.

Examples of temporary differences include the following.

- *Depreciation on fixed assets.* Taxpayers may use an accelerated depreciation method under the modified accelerated cost recovery system (MACRS) rules but a straight-line method for book purposes. Even if identical methods are used, the period over which the asset is depreciated may differ between book and tax.
- *Compensation-related expenses.* Generally, the tax law does not allow for the use of estimates or reserves, as is common under GAAP. For example, under GAAP, corporations accrue the future expenses related to providing postretirement benefits other than pensions (e.g., health insurance coverage). However, these expenses are deductible for tax purposes only when paid.
- *Accrued income and expenses.* Although most income and expense items are recognized for tax and book purposes in the same period, a number of items potentially appear in different periods. For example, warranty expenses are accrued for book purposes but are not deductible for tax purposes until incurred. Inventory write-offs are accrued for book but are not deductible for tax until incurred. On the income side, different methods regarding the timing of income recognition may create temporary differences. For instance, GAAP recognizes income and loss when the *fair value* of most investment assets changes during the year, while tax rules recognize such realized gain or loss only upon a sale or other taxable disposition of the asset.
- *Net operating losses.* Operating losses from one tax year may be used to offset taxable income in another tax year. Thus, the losses incurred in one year for book purposes may be used as a deduction for tax purposes in a different year. No such loss carryovers are used under GAAP.
- *Intangible assets.* Goodwill and some other intangibles are not amortizable for book purposes. However, GAAP requires an annual determination of whether the intangible asset has suffered a reduction in value (i.e., impairment).[4] If an intangible has suffered an impairment, a current expense is required to reduce the asset's book value to the lower level. For tax purposes, certain intangibles can be amortized over 15 years.[5]

Examples of permanent differences include the following.

- *Nontaxable income.* A common example is municipal bond interest, which is income for book purposes but is not taxable.
- *Nondeductible expenses.* For example, the disallowed portion of meals and entertainment expense and certain penalties are not deductible for tax purposes, but they are expensed in arriving at book income.[6]
- *Special tax deductions.* GAAP does not allow expenses for certain income tax deductions, such as the domestic production activities deduction (DPAD) and the dividends-received deduction.
- *Tax credits.* Credits such as the research activities credit reduce Federal income tax liability but have no corresponding book treatment.

---

[4]*Intangibles—Goodwill and Other*, ASC Topic 350 (formerly *Goodwill and Other Intangible Assets*, Statement of Financial Accounting Standards No. 142).

[5]§ 197.

[6]Federal income tax liabilities are another example of this type of permanent book-tax difference.

FINANCIAL DISCLOSURE INSIGHTS   Supersized Goodwill

When a balance sheet includes an asset value for goodwill, the company's total valuation is seen to exceed the aggregate value of its physical assets, such as cash and equipment. Goodwill typically is created as the result of the takeover of a target entity in an acquisition transaction.

GAAP rules concerning goodwill and its impairment evolved in a context of stable market values and managed income. But when goodwill gets to be so large that it is a major asset in itself, are GAAP impairment write-downs sure to follow?

An impairment write-down often is an indication that an acquiror overpaid for the target entity in a takeover transaction. Thus, conglomerates that grow by a series of acquisitions may be doubly exposed to goodwill write-downs. Accordingly, goodwill and its impairment can become an outsized element of the financial statements for many companies.

Some analysts believe that they can anticipate future impairment write-downs simply by reviewing the relative size of goodwill on the balance sheet. If such a write-down fails to materialize, the analyst may take an optimistic view for the future of the company, if not for the economy as a whole. In a recent year, the following data concerning recorded goodwill were reported.

Company	Goodwill as a % of Total Value
Frontier Communications	165.7
Republic Services	108.8
Time Warner	80.8
Kraft Foods	54.3
Dow Chemical	34.2
Dr Pepper Snapple Group	32.2
Starbucks Corporation	0.8
Netflix	0.0

Digging Deeper | In-depth coverage can be found on this book's companion website: **www.cengagebrain.com**

Example 5

Wise, Inc., reported the following results for the current year.

Book income (before tax)	$ 685,000
Tax depreciation in excess of book	(125,000)
Nondeductible warranty expense	65,000
Municipal bond interest income	(35,000)
Taxable income (Form 1120)	$ 590,000

Wise reports net income before tax of $685,000 on its financial statement but must adjust this amount for differences between book and tax income.

Tax depreciation in excess of book is a tax deduction not deducted for book purposes, and warranty expense is deductible for book purposes but not yet deductible for tax. Both of these items are temporary differences, because they eventually reverse (with book depreciation eventually exceeding tax depreciation and the warranty expense ultimately deducted for tax when incurred).

The municipal bond interest is a permanent difference because this income will never be subject to tax.

3-1d Tax Return Disclosures

Book-tax differences are reported in the Federal income tax returns of most business entities.

Figure 3.2 contains the **Schedule M–1** from Form 1120, the corporate income tax return. The purpose of Schedule M–1 is to reconcile book income to the

FIGURE 3.2 | Schedule M–1

Schedule M-1	**Reconciliation of Income (Loss) per Books With Income per Return**

Note: Schedule M-3 required instead of Schedule M-1 if total assets are $10 million or more—see instructions

1	Net income (loss) per books		7	Income recorded on books this year not included on this return (itemize): Tax-exempt interest $
2	Federal income tax per books			
3	Excess of capital losses over capital gains .			
4	Income subject to tax not recorded on books this year (itemize):		8	Deductions on this return not charged against book income this year (itemize):
5	Expenses recorded on books this year not deducted on this return (itemize):		a	Depreciation . . $
			b	Charitable contributions $
a	Depreciation . . . . $			
b	Charitable contributions . $			
c	Travel and entertainment . . $		9	Add lines 7 and 8 . . . . . .
6	Add lines 1 through 5		10	Income (page 1, line 28)—line 6 less line 9

taxable income as reported on the tax return. Line 1 is the net income or loss per books, and line 2 adds back the book tax expense to get back to book income before tax.[7] The remainder of Schedule M–1 contains adjustments for both temporary and permanent differences, until arriving at taxable income on line 10.[8]

Schedule M–3 is required for a consolidated tax group with total year-end assets of $10 million or more. Other corporations voluntarily may file a Schedule M–3. Appendix B of this text includes a copy of the Schedule M–3.

The Schedule M–3 provides the IRS with more detailed information than is provided in the Schedule M–1. A more specific "book income" starting point is used, with the taxpayer identifying the source of the book net income amount by answering a series of questions in Part I. Detail then is provided on differences due to the income or loss from foreign entities, along with data about eliminated intercompany transactions.

The listing of potential book-tax differences is significantly more comprehensive than that in the Schedule M–1, with income items reported in Part II and deduction items reported in Part III. Unlike the Schedule M–1, Schedule M–3 requires identification of whether a book-tax difference is temporary or permanent.

Schedule M–1 or M–3 is typically the starting point for IRS audits of corporations. Identifying large differences between book and taxable income may offer the IRS auditor insights into tax saving strategies (some perhaps questionable) employed by the taxpayer. See Chapter 12 for additional discussion of the Schedules M–1 and M–3. Concept Summary 3.1 summarizes the book-tax differences in arriving at income tax expense.

Uncertain Tax Positions

The IRS requires that large corporations list the tax return positions they have taken that may not be fully supported by the law. Schedule UTP ("uncertain tax positions") is added to the Form 1120 for all corporations with assets of at least $10 million.

---

[7]Line 1, "Net income (loss) per books," is not defined in the instructions to the form, and corporations can use various starting points in the Schedule M–1 (e.g., only the book income from U.S. members of the group). The Schedule M–3 is more specific in defining book income.

[8]Form 1120, page 1, line 28 represents corporate taxable income before subtracting the net operating loss and dividends-received deductions.

CONCEPT SUMMARY 3.1

Income Reporting: Book versus Tax

Financial Statement	U.S. Federal Income Tax Return
Reporting entities	**Reporting entities**
• 50% or more owned domestic and foreign subsidiaries *must* be consolidated.	• 80% or more owned domestic subsidiaries *may* be consolidated.
• Share of income from 20 to 50% owned domestic and foreign corporations included in current income.	• Share of income from other corporations reported only when actual or constructive dividends are received.
Income tax expense	**Income tax expense**
• Federal income taxes.	• Federal income taxes.
• State income taxes.	• Current only.
• Local income taxes.	
• Foreign income taxes.	
• Current and deferred.	
Methods	**Methods**
• Temporary differences.	• Temporary differences.
• Permanent differences.	• Permanent differences.
• Income tax note reconciliation.	• Schedule M–1 or M–3 reconciliation.

© iStockphoto.com/Andrey Prokhorov

Some tax professionals worry that the Schedule UTP alerts the IRS to specific items that will be most vulnerable to audit adjustments. Because tax returns are confidential documents, though, the public does not have access to a corporation's Schedule UTP.

Disclosures on the Schedule UTP include an enumeration of tax return positions for the current and prior tax years where:

- The taxpayer or a related party recorded a reserve against the Federal income tax expense on its audited financial statements, and
- The taxpayer did not record a tax reserve based on its analysis of expected litigation. This means that in the taxpayer's view, the probability of settling the item with the IRS is less than 50 percent and that the taxpayer determines that it is more likely than not (a greater than 50 percent likelihood) to prevail on the merits of the issue in litigation.

Disclosures are not required for items that are immaterial under GAAP rules, or for which the filing position is sufficiently certain that no financial accounting reserve is required.

The IRS maintains that it will limit releases of the Schedule UTP to other taxing jurisdictions, and that it will not use Schedule UTP data to usurp the attorney-client and tax practitioner privileges of confidentiality or the work-product doctrine. Taxpayers are not required to disclose the amounts of any reserves or the precise nature of the tax planning technique that led to the reserve for the filing position.

The Schedule UTP represents an increased level of information exchange between the IRS and the taxpayer, focusing on filing-year disclosures rather than audit-year items. The IRS admits that it is directing its audit efforts toward large business entities, and it says that its compliance activities will be both more efficient and more effective as a result.

TAX FACT   The World of Schedule UTP

Some observations can be made about the Schedules UTP that large corporations file with the IRS.

Number of taxpayers filing a Schedule UTP for the tax year	About 2,500
Average number of tax positions reported on the Schedule UTP	2 per return
Percentage of uncertain positions that involved international tax issues	25%, most of which involved transfer pricing computations
Percentage of Schedules UTP that were filed by taxpayers in New York, Texas, and California	30%
Percentage of Schedules UTP that were attached to returns prepared by the Big Four accounting firms	40%
Three most commonly encountered tax issues disclosed on Schedules UTP	(1) Research credit
	(2) Transfer pricing
	(3) Business deductions *vs.* capitalization

© iStockphoto.com/Pali Rao

3-2 INCOME TAXES IN THE FINANCIAL STATEMENTS

3-2a GAAP Principles

As pointed out earlier, a corporation's financial statements are prepared in accordance with GAAP. The purpose and objectives of these statements are quite different from the objective of the corporation's income tax return.

The **ASC 740 (SFAS 109)** approach produces a total income tax expense (also called the **income tax provision**) for the income currently reported on a corporation's combined financial statement.[9] This approach follows the matching principle, where all of the expenses related to earning income are reported in the same period as the income without regard to when the expenses are actually paid.

LO.2

Compute a corporation's book income tax expense.

Example 6

PanCo, Inc., earns $100,000 in book income before tax and is subject to a 35% marginal Federal income tax rate. PanCo records a single temporary difference. Tax depreciation exceeds book depreciation by $20,000. Accordingly, PanCo's taxable income is $80,000 ($100,000 − $20,000 additional tax deduction).

On its income tax return, PanCo reports total Federal tax expense of $28,000 ($80,000 × 35%). On its financial statement, PanCo reports a total tax expense of $35,000 ($100,000 × 35%). This $7,000 book-tax difference is the difference between the book and tax basis of the depreciable asset times the current corporate tax rate ($7,000 = $20,000 × 35%).

Although PanCo did not actually pay the $7,000 this year, in future years when the book-tax depreciation difference reverses, the $7,000 eventually is paid. Hence, the *future* income tax expense related to the current book income is reported in the current year.

---

[9]*Income Taxes*, ASC Topic 740 (formerly *Accounting for Income Taxes*, Statement of Financial Accounting Standards No. 109).

FINANCIAL DISCLOSURE INSIGHTS   The Book-Tax Income Gap

The corporate financial scandals of Enron and others have heightened interest in whether corporations are making appropriate disclosures (i.e., transparency) and in whether they are shouldering their fair share of the tax burden. In some years, the gap between book income and taxable income seems to be growing.

According to one study, 115 companies in the Standard and Poor's stock index incurred a Federal and state income tax rate of less than 20 percent. In fact, the rate for 39 of those companies was less than 10 percent.

At least 30 of the Fortune 500 companies paid zero or negative Federal corporate income taxes over a recent three-year period. These companies included General Electric, American Electric Power, Boeing, and PG&E. Pepco Holdings reported an effective Federal income tax rate of *negative* 57.6 percent!

The firms maintained that they had paid all of their required tax liabilities, and that a poor economy and effective income tax planning had resulted in their zero or negative effective tax rates.

Corporations further maintain that the large differences in book and tax income are a function of the different rules and objectives of GAAP for financial statements and the Internal Revenue Code for tax returns.

Low effective tax rates often are traceable to one or more of the following.

- Use of NOL carryovers.
- Large investments in depreciable assets.
- Use of state, local, federal, and international tax incentives (e.g., to encourage new companies and targeted industries such as high-tech, energy, and domestic manufacturing).
- Use of temporary tax provisions (e.g., stimulus, anti-recession, or other rules designed to stimulate the economy via tax cuts).
- Negotiations and settlements with revenue agencies.[10]
- Application of tax planning techniques.

The total book tax expense under ASC 740 (SFAS 109) is made up of both current and deferred components. The **current tax expense** theoretically represents the taxes actually payable to (or refund receivable from) the governmental authorities for the current period.

One might think of this amount as the actual check the taxpayer writes to the government (or refund received) for the current year. Keep in mind, though, that the current portion of the book income tax expense rarely matches the taxpayer's actual tax liability. Numerous items may lead to differences between actual current tax payments and the reported current tax expense. Figure 3.3 summarizes the computation of a corporation's current tax expense.

The deferred component of the book tax expense is called the **deferred tax expense** or **deferred tax benefit**. This component represents the future tax cost (or

FIGURE 3.3	Current Tax Expense*
	Pretax book income
±	Schedule M–1/M–3 adjustments
	Taxable income before NOLs
−	NOL carryforwards
	Taxable income
×	Applicable tax rate
	Current tax expense (provision) before tax credits
−	Tax credits
	Current tax expense (tax provision)

*Simplified calculation.

[10]For instance, AstraZeneca recently reduced its effective tax rate after settling an audit with U.S. and U.K. tax authorities about its transfer pricing policies (see Chapter 16). The taxpayer's liability after the settlement was less than the tax reserve it had set aside on its GAAP statements with respect to the audit.

Accounting for Income Taxes in International Standards

The FASB and the International Accounting Standards Board (IASB) have worked to move the GAAP and IFRS treatment of income taxes closer together in light of the proposed convergence of GAAP and IFRS. Both ASC 740 (SFAS 109) and IAS 12 (the IFRS guidance for income taxes) are based on a balance sheet approach.

Nevertheless, several significant differences exist between the two standards. These include the thresholds for recognition and approach to valuation allowances, the treatment of foreign subsidiaries and undistributed earnings, and the measurement of uncertain tax positions.[11]

Global Tax Issues

© iStockphoto.com/Andrey Prokhorov

savings) connected with income reported in the current-period financial statement. Deferred tax expense or benefit is created as a result of temporary differences. More technically, ASC 740 (SFAS 109) adopts a balance sheet approach to measuring deferred taxes. Under this approach, the deferred tax expense or benefit is the change from one year to the next in the net deferred tax liability or deferred tax asset.

A deferred tax liability is the expected future tax liability related to current income (measured using enacted tax rates and rules). A deferred tax liability is created in the following situations.

- An item is deductible for tax in the current period but is not expensed for book until some future period.
- Income is includible currently for book purposes but is not includible in taxable income until a future period.

In essence, a deferred tax liability is created when the book basis of an asset exceeds its tax basis (the opposite results in a deferred tax asset).

Example 7

PJ Enterprises earns net income before depreciation of $500,000 in 2014 and $600,000 in 2015. PJ uses a single depreciable asset acquired in 2014 for $80,000. For tax purposes, PJ may deduct $60,000 in depreciation expense for the first year and $20,000 in depreciation expense for the second year (i.e., it uses an accelerated method). For book purposes, assume that PJ depreciates the asset on a straight-line basis over two years ($40,000 depreciation expense per year).

2014	Book	Tax
Income before depreciation	$500,000	$500,000
Depreciation	(40,000)	(60,000)
Income after depreciation	$460,000	$440,000
Corporate tax rate	× 35%	× 35%
Income tax expense/payable	$161,000	$154,000
Current tax expense	$154,000	
Deferred tax expense	$ 7,000	
Starting adjusted basis in depreciable asset	$ 80,000	$ 80,000
Ending adjusted basis in depreciable asset	(40,000)	(20,000)
Change in adjusted basis	$ 40,000	$ 60,000
Book-tax balance sheet difference	↘ $20,000 ↙	
Corporate tax rate	× 35%	
Deferred tax liability	$ 7,000	

In this example, it is easy to "back into" the deferred tax expense amount of $7,000 by simply taking the difference between the tax payable per the tax return ($154,000) and the book tax expense ($161,000). This method is referred to as the "APB 11" approach, as it applies to the method used before ASC 740 (SFAS 109). This method may provide a quick check on the calculation in simple cases, but it is not always correct. The deferred tax expense is based on the difference between the book and tax asset basis numbers ($20,000) at the enacted corporate tax rate (35%).

2015	Book	Tax
Income before depreciation	$600,000	$600,000
Depreciation	(40,000)	(20,000)
Income after depreciation	$560,000	$580,000
Corporate tax rate	× 35%	× 35%
Income tax expense/payable	$196,000	$203,000
Current tax expense	$203,000	
Deferred tax expense	($ 7,000)	
Starting adjusted basis in depreciable asset	$ 40,000	$ 20,000
Ending adjusted basis in depreciable asset	(–0–)	(–0–)
Change in adjusted basis	$ 40,000	$ 20,000
Book-tax balance sheet difference	($20,000)	
Corporate tax rate	× 35%	
Deferred tax liability	($ 7,000)	

In the next tax year, the book-tax difference in the asset basis reverses, with a resulting reverse in the deferred tax liability account.

Example 8

Continue with the facts in Example 7. The following journal entries record the book tax expense (provision) for each year. The book total tax expense combines the current amount (income tax payable) and the future amount (deferred tax liability).

2014 Journal Entry
Income tax expense (provision) $161,000
   Income tax payable $154,000
   Deferred tax liability   7,000
2015 Journal Entry
Income tax expense (provision) $196,000
Deferred tax liability   7,000
   Income tax payable $203,000

At the end of 2014, the balance sheet reflects a net deferred tax liability of $7,000. At the end of 2015, the balance sheet contains no deferred tax liability because the temporary difference that created the deferred tax liability has reversed itself.

A deferred tax asset is the expected future tax benefit related to current book income (measured using enacted tax rates and rules). A deferred tax asset is created in the following situations.

- An expense is claimed for book purposes in the current period but is not deductible for tax until some future period.
- Income is includible in taxable income currently but is not recorded as book income until a future period.

MollCo, Inc., earns net income before warranty expense of $400,000 in 2014 and $450,000 in 2015. In 2014, MollCo deducts $30,000 in warranty expense for book purposes related to expected warranty repairs. This warranty expense is not deductible for tax purposes until actually incurred. Assume that the $30,000 warranty expense is paid in 2015, and that this is MollCo's only temporary difference.

Example 9

2014

	Book	Tax
Income before warranty expense	$400,000	$400,000
Warranty expense	(30,000)	—
Income after warranty expense	$370,000	$400,000
Corporate tax rate	× 35%	× 35%
Income tax expense/payable	$129,500	$140,000
Current tax expense	$140,000	
Deferred tax expense	($ 10,500)	
Basis in warranty expense payable	$ 30,000	$ —0—
Book-tax balance sheet difference		($30,000)
Corporate tax rate		× 35%
Deferred tax asset		($10,500)

Once again, it is easy to "back into" the deferred tax expense amount of $10,500 simply by taking the difference between the tax payable per the tax return ($140,000) and the book tax expense ($129,500). However, the correct computation of the deferred tax expense is based on the difference between the book and tax basis in the warranty expense payable ($30,000) at the corporate tax rate (35%).

2015

	Book	Tax
Income before warranty expense	$450,000	$450,000
Warranty expense	—	(30,000)
Income after depreciation	$450,000	$420,000
Corporate tax rate	× 35%	× 35%
Income tax expense/payable	$157,500	$147,000
Current tax expense	$147,000	
Deferred tax expense	$ 10,500	
Basis in warranty expense payable	$ —0—	$ 30,000
Book-tax balance sheet difference		$30,000
Corporate tax rate		× 35%
Deferred tax asset		$10,500

In the next tax year, the book-tax difference in the warranty expense payable reverses, with a resulting elimination of the deferred tax asset account.

FINANCIAL DISCLOSURE INSIGHTS   Tax Losses and the Deferred Tax Asset

Although a current-year net operating loss (NOL) represents a failure of an entity's business model to some, others see it as an immediate tax refund. But when an NOL hits the balance sheet as a deferred tax asset, the story is not over. The NOL creates or increases a deferred tax asset that may or may not be used in future financial accounting reporting periods. The key question for a financial analyst is whether the entity will generate enough net revenue in future years to create a positive tax liability that can be offset by the NOL carryover amount.

For every reporting period, the managers of a business entity holding a loss carryforward must assess whether the loss is likely to be used to create cash flow in the future, as it offsets operating or other profits from future years. When it is more likely than not that a loss carryforward *will not be realized*, GAAP requires that a valuation allowance be created to reduce the deferred tax asset to a lower amount, that which is expected to be realized in the future. The valuation allowance is a contra-asset account (like accumulated depreciation on a fixed asset) against the deferred tax asset.

The IFRS rules do not allow for a valuation allowance. Under IAS 12, a deferred tax asset is recorded only when it is "probable" (a higher standard than GAAP's "more likely than not") that the deferred tax amount will be realized, and then only to the extent of that probable amount. Thus, no offsetting valuation allowance is needed.

© iStockphoto.com/Pali Rao

Example 10

Continue with the facts in Example 9. The following journal entries record the book tax expense (provision) for each year. Notice that the book total tax expense combines the current amount (income tax payable) and the future amount (deferred tax asset).

2014 Journal Entry

Income tax expense (provision)	$129,500	
Deferred tax asset	10,500	
Income tax payable		$140,000

2015 Journal Entry

Income tax expense (provision)	$157,500	
Deferred tax asset		$ 10,500
Income tax payable		147,000

At the end of 2014, the balance sheet reflects a net deferred tax asset of $10,500. At the end of 2015, the balance sheet contains no deferred tax asset because the temporary difference that created the deferred tax asset has reversed.

Deferred tax assets and liabilities are reported on the balance sheet just as any other asset or liability would be. However, the interpretation of these assets and liabilities is quite different. Typically, an asset is "good" because it represents a claim on something of value, and a liability is "bad" because it represents a future claim against the corporation's assets. In the case of deferred tax assets and liabilities, the interpretation is reversed. Deferred tax liabilities are "good" because they represent an amount that may be paid to the government in the future.

In essence, deferred tax liabilities are like an interest-free loan from the government with a due date perhaps many years in the future. Deferred tax assets, on the other hand, are future tax benefits and thus are similar to a receivable from the government that may not be received until many years in the future.

3-2b Valuation Allowance

LO.3

Describe the purpose of the valuation allowance.

Much of GAAP is based on the conservatism principle. That is, accounting rules are designed to provide assurance that assets are not overstated and liabilities are not understated. Current recognition of deferred tax liabilities does not require significant professional judgment because future tax liabilities always are expected to be settled. However, under ASC 740 (SFAS 109), deferred tax assets are recognized only when it is probable that the future tax benefits will be realized.

Warren, Inc., reported book income before tax of $2 million in 2014. Warren's taxable income also is $2 million (i.e., there are no temporary or permanent differences). Warren reports a current U.S. income tax liability for 2014 of $700,000 before tax credits ($2 million × 35%). During 2014, Warren paid $100,000 in foreign income taxes that it is not able to use as a credit on its 2014 tax return because of the foreign tax credit (FTC) limitation (see Chapter 16). Warren's auditors believe it is more likely than not that Warren will be able to use the $100,000 in FTCs within the next 10 years before they expire. Consequently, the future tax benefit of the FTCs is accounted for in the current-year book tax expense as a $100,000 future tax benefit.

| Example 11 |

The current and deferred tax expense are calculated as follows.

	Book	Tax
Income tax expense/payable	$600,000	$700,000
Current tax expense	$700,000	
Deferred tax expense (benefit)	($100,000)	

Warren records the following journal entry for the book income tax expense and deferred tax asset related to the expected use of the FTCs.

Income tax expense (provision)	$600,000	
Deferred tax asset	100,000	
Income tax payable		$700,000

Because Warren is able to record the benefit of the future FTCs, its effective tax rate is 30% ($600,000 tax expense/$2 million book income before tax).

When a deferred tax asset does not meet the *more likely than not* threshold for recognition, ASC 740 (SFAS 109) requires that a **valuation allowance** be created. The valuation allowance is a contra-asset account that offsets all or a portion of the deferred tax asset.

Assume that the auditors in Example 11 believe that Warren will be able to use only $40,000 of the FTCs, with the remaining $60,000 expiring. In this case, the future tax benefit recognized currently should be only $40,000 rather than the full $100,000. To implement this reduction in the deferred tax asset, Warren must record a valuation allowance of $60,000, resulting in a book tax expense of $660,000.

| Example 12 |

	Book	Tax
Income tax expense/payable	$660,000	$700,000
Current tax expense	$700,000	
Deferred tax expense (benefit)	($ 40,000)	

Warren records the following journal entry for the book income tax expense and deferred tax asset related to the expected use of the FTCs.

Income tax expense (provision)	$660,000	
Deferred tax asset	100,000	
Valuation allowance		$ 60,000
Income tax payable		700,000

Warren reduces the deferred tax asset by $60,000, which increases its effective tax rate to 33% ($660,000 tax expense/$2 million book income before tax), compared with the 30% effective tax rate in Example 11.

To determine whether a valuation allowance is required, both positive and negative evidence must be evaluated. Negative evidence (i.e., evidence suggesting that the deferred tax asset will not be realized) includes the following.

- History of losses.
- Expected future losses.
- Short carryback/carryforward periods.
- History of tax credits expiring unused.

Positive evidence (i.e., support for realizing the current benefit of future tax savings) includes the following.

- Strong earnings history.
- Existing contracts.
- Unrealized appreciation in assets.
- Sales backlog of profitable orders.

The valuation allowance is examined for appropriateness each year. The allowance may be increased or decreased in subsequent reporting periods if facts and circumstances change.

Tax Planning Strategies   RELEASING VALUATION ALLOWANCES

FRAMEWORK FOCUS: DEDUCTIONS

Strategy: Maximize Deductible Amounts.

When a corporation records a valuation allowance, it loses the ability to recognize the benefit of future tax savings in the current period. However, all is not lost if the taxpayer can demonstrate that facts and circumstances have changed. For example, if a taxpayer generates a net operating loss (NOL), it records a deferred tax asset for the future tax savings related to using the NOL. However, if the evidence suggests that it is more likely than not that the NOL will expire unused, a valuation allowance must be recorded. To reduce this valuation allowance, the taxpayer must demonstrate that there will be future taxable income sufficient to absorb the NOL within the carryforward period. Sources of future taxable income include reversals of temporary differences that will produce future taxable income and other sources of future profits. Taxpayers also may demonstrate that the adoption of new tax planning strategies will allow the use of deferred tax assets.

For example, assume that Warren, Inc., from Example 12, adopts new planning strategies in 2015 that will allow it ultimately to use all $100,000 of its FTC carryforward. Warren earns $2.3 million in book income before tax and reports $2.3 million in taxable income in 2015 (i.e., no permanent or temporary differences). The current tax expense is $805,000 ($2.3 million × 35%).

Based on new evidence (implementation of tax planning strategies), the auditors determine that the entire $100,000 in FTCs will be used in the future before expiration. Accordingly, the $60,000 valuation allowance from 2014 is "released," and the tax benefit of this release affects the 2015 financial results as follows.

	Book	Tax
Income tax expense/payable	$745,000	$805,000
Current tax expense	$805,000	
Deferred tax expense	($ 60,000)	

Warren makes the following journal entry to record the book income tax expense and valuation allowance release related to the expected use of the FTCs.

Income tax expense (provision)	$745,000	
Valuation allowance	60,000	
Income tax payable		$805,000

Warren's effective tax rate for 2015 is 32.4 percent ($745,000/$2.3 million). Without the valuation allowance release, Warren's effective tax rate would have been 35 percent ($805,000/$2.3 million). This tax rate benefit is realized even though the $100,000 in FTC carryforwards have yet to be used in Warren's tax return.

FINANCIAL DISCLOSURE INSIGHTS   Valuation Allowances for NOLs

Financial analysts use the valuation allowance system to help them determine an entity's expected future cash flows. Some critics of the GAAP rules for valuation allowances maintain that the process allows management to manipulate profits and earnings per share in an arbitrary fashion.

Only a few of the largest business entities, supported by going-concern assumptions and access to worldwide debt and equity capital, need to record a sizable valuation allowance. But valuation allowances also often are found in the financial reports of smaller entities and those in volatile industries, whose future profitability is likely to present questions.

In a recent reporting year, for instance, the following telecommunications businesses reported a valuation allowance related to expectations that their NOLs (for Federal and/or state taxing jurisdictions) would expire unused.

	Deferred Tax Assets ($ in 000's)	Valuation Allowance ($ in 000's)
Verizon	$10,750	$2,700
Bell South	2,100	1,100
AT&T	11,400	1,050
SBC Communications	3,900	150

Establishing a valuation allowance does not affect the entity's internal cash balances, but it might have an effect on the stock price. Valuation allowances can be "released" by management when evidence develops that the carryforwards are more likely to be used in the future, for example, if profitability improves and appears to be sustainable. For instance, the homebuilder Toll Brothers created a large valuation allowance when the real estate market collapsed, but it will release the allowance when housing prices stabilize and increase.

© iStockphoto.com/Pali Rao

THE BIG PICTURE

Example 13

Return to the facts of *The Big Picture* on p. 3-1. Arctic Corporation has recorded a $3 million deferred tax asset for an NOL carryforward. The deferred tax asset has been offset by a $1 million valuation allowance, due to doubts over the levels of future sales and profitability.

But this year, Arctic completed improvements to its inventory management system that are likely to increase the contribution margin of every product that Arctic sells. In addition, two of Arctic's largest customers have secured financing that will relieve the financial difficulties that have restricted them. In fact, Arctic just received purchase orders from those customers that will increase unit sales by 20% over the next 18 months. As a result, Arctic's auditors now support a release of $200,000 of the valuation allowance in the current quarter.

In-depth coverage can be found on this book's companion website: **www.cengagebrain.com**   **2**   Digging Deeper

3-2c Tax Disclosures in the Financial Statements

As illustrated earlier, any temporary differences create deferred tax liabilities or deferred tax assets, and these amounts appear in the corporation's balance sheet.

LO.4

Interpret the disclosure information contained in the financial statements.

The Balance Sheet

As with any asset or liability, these accounts are classified as either current or non-current, based on the assets or liabilities that created the temporary difference. If

© tuulijumala/Shutterstock.com

TAX FACT   Effective Tax Rates for Selected Fortune 100 Companies

Here are some recent provisions for income taxes (state, federal, and international) made by selected major corporations, as a percentage of their book income before taxes. Recall that the top statutory Federal tax rate is 35%. State and local taxes generally add another 5 percentage points to that rate.

Aetna	34.9%
Apple	24.2
Boeing	34.0
Chevron	43.2
Citigroup	0.3

Disney	33.3%
ExxonMobil	44.0
Ford	28.8
General Electric	14.4
Google	19.4
IBM	24.2
JPMorgan Chase	24.6
Pfizer	21.2
United Health Group	35.9
Wal-Mart	32.6
Yahoo!	20.7

the deferred tax liability or asset is not related to any asset, then the classification is based on the expected reversal period.

Example 14

JenCo, Inc., holds a deferred tax liability generated because tax depreciation exceeds book depreciation on manufacturing equipment. Because the equipment is a noncurrent asset, the deferred tax liability also is noncurrent. JenCo also reports a deferred tax asset related to bad debt expenses deductible for book purposes but not yet deductible for tax purposes. Because the bad debt expense is related to accounts receivable, a current asset, the associated deferred tax asset is classified as current.

If JenCo incurs an NOL, a deferred tax asset is created, because of the future tax benefit provided by the NOL deduction. The NOL is not related to any specific asset or liability. Accordingly, the deferred tax asset is classified based on when the corporation expects to use the NOL. If the expected use is more than one year in the future, the deferred tax asset is classified as noncurrent.

A corporation may hold both deferred tax assets and liabilities, current and noncurrent. The corporation reports the *net* current deferred tax assets or liabilities and the *net* noncurrent deferred tax assets or liabilities.

THE BIG PICTURE

Example 15

Return to the facts of *The Big Picture* on p. 3-1. Arctic Corporation holds the following deferred tax asset and liability accounts for the current year.

Current deferred tax assets	$50,000
Current deferred tax liabilities	72,000
Noncurrent deferred tax assets	93,000
Noncurrent deferred tax liabilities	28,000

On its balance sheet, Arctic reports a $22,000 current net deferred tax liability ($72,000 − $50,000) and a $65,000 noncurrent net deferred tax asset ($93,000 − $28,000).

The Income Statement

In its income statement, a corporation reports a total income tax expense that consists of both the current tax expense (or benefit) and the deferred tax expense (or benefit). The tax expense is allocated among income from continuing operations, discontinued operations, extraordinary items, prior-period adjustments, and the cumulative effect of accounting changes. Additional disclosures are required for the tax expense allocated to income from continuing operations (e.g., current versus deferred, benefits of NOL deductions, and changes in valuation allowances).

Financial Statement Footnotes

The income tax note contains a wealth of information, including the following.

- Breakdown of income between domestic and foreign.
- Detailed analysis of the provision for income tax expense.
- Detailed analysis of deferred tax assets and liabilities.
- Effective tax rate reconciliation (dollar amount or percentage).
- Information on use of ASC 740-30 (APB 23) for the earnings of foreign subsidiaries.
- Discussion of significant tax matters.

Rate Reconciliation

The purpose of the rate reconciliation is to demonstrate how a corporation's actual book effective tax rate relates to its "hypothetical tax rate" as if the book income were taxed at the U.S. corporate rate of 35 percent. Although similar to Schedule M–1 or M–3, the tax note rate reconciliation generally reports only differences triggered by permanent differences. As discussed in the benchmarking section later in this chapter, an analysis of the rate reconciliation can provide substantial indicators as to the tax planning strategies adopted (or not adopted) by a company.

The steps in determining a corporation's income tax expense for book purposes are summarized in Concept Summary 3.2.

CONCEPT SUMMARY 3.2

Steps in Determining the Book Tax Expense

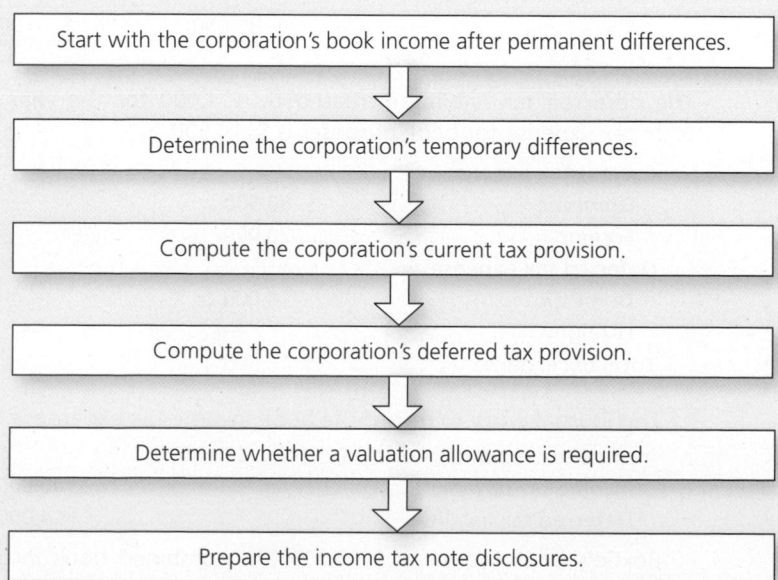

Start with the corporation's book income after permanent differences.

↓

Determine the corporation's temporary differences.

↓

Compute the corporation's current tax provision.

↓

Compute the corporation's deferred tax provision.

↓

Determine whether a valuation allowance is required.

↓

Prepare the income tax note disclosures.

Illustrations

Example 16

BoxCo, Inc., a domestic corporation, owns 100% of PaperCo, Ltd., an Irish corporation. The U.S. corporate tax rate is 35%, and the Irish rate is 10%. As discussed later in the chapter, BoxCo reports book but not taxable income for PaperCo's overseas profits, under ASC 740-30 (APB 23). Book income, permanent and temporary differences, and current tax expense are computed as follows.

	BoxCo	PaperCo
Book income before tax	$300,000	$200,000
Permanent differences		
Meals and entertainment expense	20,000	—
Municipal bond interest income	(50,000)	—
Book income after permanent differences	$270,000	$200,000
Temporary differences		
Tax > book depreciation	(50,000)	—
Book > tax bad debt expense	10,000	—
Taxable income	$230,000	$200,000
Tax rate	× 35%	× 10%
Current tax expense	$ 80,500	$ 20,000

Assume that the beginning-of-the-year difference between book and tax basis in the depreciable assets is $150,000, and that the beginning-of-the-year difference between book and tax basis in the bad debt expense is $50,000. Thus, the beginning-of-the-year deferred tax liability is $35,000 [($150,000 − $50,000) × 35%]. To determine the deferred tax expense (benefit) for the current year, the change in the balance sheet amounts for these temporary differences from the beginning to the end of the year must be determined and then multiplied by the appropriate tax rate.

Temporary Differences	Beginning of Year	Change	End of Year
Depreciation	$150,000	$ 50,000	$200,000
Bad debts	(50,000)	(10,000)	(60,000)
Total temporary differences	$100,000	$ 40,000	$140,000
Tax rate	× 35%	× 35%	× 35%
	$ 35,000	$ 14,000	$ 49,000

The deferred tax liability increased by $14,000 for the year. Consequently, BoxCo's total tax expense for book purposes is $114,500.

Current tax expense	
Domestic	$ 80,500
Foreign	20,000
Deferred tax expense	
Domestic	14,000
Foreign	—
Total tax expense	$114,500

The journal entry to record the book income tax expense is constructed as follows.

Income tax expense (provision)	$114,500	
Income tax payable		$100,500
Deferred tax liability		14,000

BoxCo's book income is $500,000 (the combined book income of both BoxCo and PaperCo). The effective tax rate reconciliation is based on this book income, with the dollar amounts in the table representing the tax expense (benefit) related to the item and the percentage representing the tax expense (benefit) as a percentage of book income. For example, the municipal bond interest of $50,000 reduces tax liability by $17,500 ($50,000 × 35%). This $17,500 as a percentage of the $500,000 book income is 3.5%.

	Effective Tax Rate Reconciliation	
	$	%
Hypothetical tax at U.S. rate	$175,000	35.0
Disallowed meals and entertainment expense	7,000	1.4
Municipal bond interest	(17,500)	(3.5)
Foreign income taxed at less than U.S. rate	(50,000)*	(10.0)
Income tax expense (provision)	$114,500	22.9

*$200,000 × (35% − 10%)

Only permanent differences appear in the rate reconciliation. Temporary differences do not affect the *total* book income tax expense; they simply affect the amount of the tax expense that is current versus deferred.

Example 17

Assume the same facts as Example 16, except that a new income tax law is enacted before the end of the current year that will increase the U.S. corporate tax rate to 40% beginning next year. In this case, multiply the year-end total temporary differences of $140,000 by 40% rather than 35%. This results in an increase in the deferred tax liability of $21,000.

Temporary Differences	Beginning of Year	End of Year	Effect of Rate Change
Depreciation	$150,000	$200,000	
Bad debts	(50,000)	(60,000)	
Total temporary differences	$100,000	$140,000	
Tax rate	× 35%	× 40%	
Deferred tax liability	$ 35,000	$ 56,000	$21,000

The current-year deferred tax liability is a function of both the change in temporary differences at the enacted rate ($40,000 × 40%) and the additional 5% tax on the beginning temporary differences [$100,000 × (40% − 35%)]. This example illustrates the need for the "balance sheet" approach of ASC 740 (SFAS 109). Use of the APB 11 shortcut method would have produced the wrong answer with these facts.

TAX FACT Effective Tax Rates Examined

A U.S. Government Accountability Office (GAO) study examined the tax returns of profitable U.S. corporations with at least $10 million in revenues for a recent tax year; the data came from an analysis of corporate Schedules M–3. Some of the most interesting findings from the study include the following.

- The effective tax rate for these entities was 12.6 percent of worldwide income. Including income tax obligations to state, local, and non-U.S. governments, the effective tax rate became 16.9 percent. The statutory Federal tax rate for these entities was 35 percent.
- The 16.9 percent effective tax rate compares to a rate averaging about 20 percent in prior years.

- The net pretax profits for these entities for the year totaled $1.4 trillion.
- Some of the largest reported book-tax differences included:
  - Interest deductions that were deferred for tax purposes.
  - Cost recovery deductions that were accelerated.
  - Retirement plan contributions that were accelerated.
  - Tax deductions for current non-U.S. income that were allowed.

Source: www.gao.gov/assets/660/654957.pdf.

Example 18

LibbyCo, Inc., is a U.S. corporation that operates retail outlets selling eyeglasses. During the current year, LibbyCo reported pretax book income of $1,800. LibbyCo's U.S. corporate tax rate is 34%. It reports no NOLs, credits, or foreign or state income taxes. The entity is not subject to the alternative minimum tax.

LibbyCo's year-end tax and book balance sheet is summarized below, before accounting for tax deferrals. The statement highlights the book-tax basis differences for all assets and liabilities.

	Tax Debit/(Credit)	Book Debit/(Credit)	Difference
Assets			
Cash	$ 2,000	$ 2,000	$ −0−
Accounts receivable	5,400	5,400	−0−
Buildings	400,000	400,000	−0−
Accumulated depreciation	(315,000)	(330,000)	15,000
Furniture & fixtures	100,000	100,000	−0−
Accumulated depreciation	(70,000)	(45,000)	(25,000)
Total assets	$122,400	$132,400	($ 10,000)
Liabilities			
Accrued vacation pay	$ −0−	($ 25,000)	$ 25,000
Note payable	(16,400)	(16,400)	−0−
Total liabilities	($ 16,400)	($ 41,400)	$ 25,000
Stockholders' Equity			
Paid-in capital	($ 6,000)	($ 6,000)	
Retained earnings	(100,000)	(85,000)	
Total liabilities and stockholders' equity	($122,400)	($132,400)	

The difference between the book and tax basis of these assets and liabilities is the cumulative difference from all prior years. These differences are *not* the Schedule M–1 or M–3 differences. To determine the temporary differences for the current year and any associated deferred tax liability or deferred tax asset, these differences are compared with the basis differences at the beginning of the year.

Assume the following beginning-of-the-year book-tax differences. The end-of-the-year differences are calculated above. The differences are classified based on whether they produce a future tax benefit (*deductible temporary differences*) or a future tax cost (*taxable temporary differences*).

	Beginning of Year	Current-Year Difference	End of Year
Deductible Temporary Differences			
Buildings—accumulated depreciation	$10,000	$ 5,000	$15,000
Accrued vacation pay	17,000	8,000	25,000
Subtotal	$27,000	$13,000	$40,000
Applicable tax rate	× 34%		× 34%
Gross deferred tax asset	$ 9,180		$13,600
	↘	✓	
Change in deferred tax asset		$ 4,420	
Taxable Temporary Differences			
Furniture & fixtures—accumulated depreciation	($22,000)	($ 3,000)	($25,000)
Subtotal	($22,000)	($ 3,000)	($25,000)
Applicable tax rate	× 34%		× 34%
Gross deferred tax liability	($ 7,480)		($ 8,500)
	↘	✓	
Change in deferred tax liability		($ 1,020)	
Net deferred tax asset / (deferred tax liability)	$ 1,700	$ 3,400	$ 5,100

The journal entry to record the deferred tax asset is constructed as follows.

Deferred tax asset	$3,400	
Income tax expense		$3,400

In addition to the temporary differences identified above, LibbyCo reported two permanent differences between book and taxable income. It earned $1,400 in tax-exempt municipal bond interest, and it incurred $2,000 in nondeductible meals and entertainment expense. With this information, the current tax expense is determined as follows.

Pretax book income	$ 1,800
Book-tax adjustments	
Permanent items	
Tax-exempt income	(1,400)
Nondeductible meals and entertainment	2,000
Temporary differences	
Building depreciation	5,000
Accrued vacation pay	8,000
Furniture & fixtures depreciation	(3,000)
Taxable income	$12,400
Current tax expense (34%)	$ 4,216

The building depreciation for book purposes exceeds tax depreciation, the furniture and fixtures depreciation for tax purposes exceeds book depreciation, and the accrued vacation pay is deductible for book purposes but is not yet deductible for tax. These current-year temporary differences, combined with the two permanent items, also constitute the Schedule M–3 differences.

The journal entry to record the current tax expense is constructed as follows.

Income tax expense	$4,216	
Current income tax payable		$4,216

Assuming that no valuation allowance is required, the effect of these entries on the income statement is as follows. The current-year change in the deferred tax asset allows the book tax expense to be reduced by $3,400, producing a total book tax expense of $816 ($4,216 − $3,400).

Net income before tax	$1,800
Provision for income tax expense	(816)
Net income after tax	$ 984

The income tax footnote rate reconciliation is presented as follows.

Tax on book income at statutory rate	$ 612	34.00%
Tax-exempt income	(476)	(26.44)%
Nondeductible meals and entertainment	680	37.77%
Provision for income tax expense	$ 816	45.33%

With these facts, the shortcut APB 11 method illustrated below produces the same results as the ASC 740 (SFAS 109) method. The two methods would produce different results had there been changes to LibbyCo's applicable tax rate from the prior year, or if a valuation allowance had been required.

Pretax book income	$ 1,800
Permanent items	
Tax-exempt income	(1,400)
Nondeductible meals and entertainment	2,000
Book equivalent to taxable income	$ 2,400
Statutory tax rate	× 34%
Total book tax expense	$ 816

Tax Planning Strategies	TAX SAVINGS ARE NOT ALWAYS CREATED EQUAL

FRAMEWORK FOCUS: THINKING OUTSIDE THE FRAMEWORK

Many different types of tax planning strategies can produce tax savings. Yet, even when planning ideas produce identical current cash-flow effects, some ideas may have an edge. CEOs and CFOs of public companies are focused on the bottom line—the company's net income after tax and related earnings per share. A CFO is likely to be just as interested in an idea's effect on the company's bottom line income as on the cash tax savings.

For example, consider two tax planning ideas that each produce $700,000 of current tax savings. The first idea generates its $700,000 in tax savings by increasing tax depreciation relative to book depreciation by $2 million ($700,000 = $2 million × 35%). The second idea produces

research activities tax credits of $700,000, thus reducing current-year tax by $700,000.

Idea 1 produces its current tax savings via a temporary difference. Accordingly, the book tax expense will not reflect the $700,000 in tax savings. Instead, this $700,000 simply moves from the current tax category to the deferred tax category. Even if the book-tax difference is not expected to reverse in the next 30 years (effectively generating "permanent" savings), the book tax expense does not reflect this savings.

In contrast, idea 2 produces its current tax savings via a permanent difference. Thus, the book tax expense also declines by $700,000. This item is a reconciling item in the income tax note rate reconciliation.

3-2d Special Issues

Financial Accounting for Tax Uncertainties

LO.5

Identify the GAAP treatment concerning tax uncertainties and unrepatriated foreign earnings.

Companies take positions in their tax returns that may not ultimately survive the scrutiny of the IRS or other tax authorities. If a taxpayer loses the benefit of a favorable tax position after a future audit, there may be an unfavorable effect on the company's financial statement tax expense in that future year. The additional tax cost will become part of the current tax expense, yet the income that this tax is related to would have been reported in the initial year. This result can wreak havoc with a company's effective tax rate.

To avoid such an increase in effective tax rate, companies may record a book reserve (or "cushion") for the uncertain tax position in the initial year. That is, rather than book the entire tax benefit (and thus reduce tax expense in the current year), the company may book only a portion (or none) of the tax benefit. If the company later loses the actual tax benefit upon audit, to the extent the additional tax imposed is charged against the reserve, the additional tax does not affect the future-year tax expense. If the company's tax position is not challenged in the future (or the company successfully defends any challenge), the reserve can be released. This release reduces the current tax expense in the future (release) year, and it lowers the company's effective tax rate in that year.

To add more structure to the accounting for tax reserves, the FASB released an interpretation, "Accounting for Uncertainty in Income Taxes" [**ASC 740-10 (FIN 48)**]. The approach required under this interpretation results in significantly more disclosure about uncertain tax positions by companies.

When ASC 740-10 (FIN 48) applies, uncertain tax positions effectively are defined as those material items not fully certain by the taxpayer to be sustainable upon a later review based on technical merits. Such tax positions result in a permanent reduction of income taxes payable, a deferral of income taxes otherwise currently payable to future years, or a change in the expected realizability of deferred tax assets.

Application of the ASC 740-10 (FIN 48) rules essentially is a two-step process—recognition and measurement. These steps are illustrated in Concept Summary 3.3.

First, a tax benefit from an uncertain tax position may be *recognized* in the financial statements only if it is more likely than not (a greater than 50 percent likelihood) that the position would be sustained on its technical merits. In this regard, audit or detection risk cannot be considered. This first step determines whether any of the tax benefit is recognized.

CONCEPT SUMMARY 3.3

Disclosures Under ASC 740-10 (FIN 48)

RECOGNITION	MEASUREMENT	FINANCIAL STATEMENT DISCLOSURE
Regarding the uncertain tax position, is it *more likely than not* that the tax benefit will be recognized?	Determine the recognized amount of the tax benefit.	Reassess for every reporting period.

If the more likely than not standard is failed, no financial statement disclosure is required. If the uncertain tax position meets the more likely than not threshold, the second step is to determine the amount of the tax benefit to report.

Measurement of the amount of the tax benefit to be disclosed then occurs. This computation is based on the probabilities associated with the position not being challenged, or with it being challenged using a negotiated settlement or litigation.

The recognition and measurement of uncertain tax positions is reassessed at each reporting date. ASC 740-10 (FIN 48) requires a reconciliation of the beginning and ending balances of the unrecognized tax benefits and a discussion of potential changes in these unrecognized tax benefits that might occur over the next 12 months.

Earnings of Foreign Subsidiaries

As discussed earlier, a corporate group's financial statements include both domestic and foreign controlled subsidiaries. However, foreign corporations, even those controlled by U.S. shareholders, are not part of a U.S. consolidated tax return. Consequently, U.S. taxpayers can achieve deferral of current U.S. taxes on foreign income if they operate their overseas activities through foreign subsidiary corporations in jurisdictions with lower tax rates than those of the United States (see Chapter 16). Although the *actual* U.S. taxes on foreign corporations' profits are deferred, the reported effective tax rate for financial statement purposes may not reflect this deferral, because ASC 740 (SFAS 109) requires that a corporate group report both current and deferred income tax expense.

Example 19

USCo, a domestic corporation, operates a manufacturing facility in Singapore through a Singapore corporation. Assume that the U.S. tax rate is 35% and that the Singapore tax rate is 6%. For the current year, USCo earns $600,000 in taxable income. The Singapore corporation earns $400,000 in taxable income from its operations, pays $24,000 in taxes to Singapore, and makes no distributions to its U.S. parent. The Singapore corporation is not taxed in the United States because it is not a U.S. person, and it conducts no activities in the United States.

USCo is not taxed on the Singapore profits because it has not received any distributions of these profits. Accordingly, USCo has achieved deferral and reduced its worldwide cash tax costs.

However, for financial statement purposes, the USCo group includes the $400,000 in Singapore profits in its net income. It reports both the Singapore tax and any *potential* U.S. tax (after allowable FTCs) as its total tax expense.

U.S. Tax Return		Potential U.S. Tax on Non-U.S. Income	
Income	$600,000	Income	$400,000
Tax rate	× 35%	Tax rate	× 35%
U.S. tax	$210,000	Total tax	$140,000
		Foreign tax credit	(24,000)
		Net U.S. tax	$116,000

Consequently, the total tax expense for financial statement purposes is $350,000. Keep in mind that the actual deferred tax liability is determined by multiplying the difference in the book and tax basis of the foreign subsidiary by the U.S. tax rate. A book-tax difference exists because the tax basis in the subsidiary is the original cost, but the book basis has increased under the equity method of accounting by the equity in the subsidiary's earnings.

Current U.S. tax	$210,000
Current foreign tax	24,000
Deferred U.S. tax	116,000
Total tax expense	$350,000

The financial statement effective tax rate on USCo's global income is 35% ($350,000 total tax expense/$1,000,000 net income). Thus, although USCo paid only $234,000 in taxes, its after-tax book income does not reflect the savings generated from operating in Singapore, a low-tax country.

FINANCIAL DISCLOSURE INSIGHTS   Corporate Tax Rate Cuts: Be Careful What You Wish For

Many lawmakers, businesses, and think tanks are calling for a reform to the U.S. corporate income tax, including a cut in the top tax rate from the current 35 percent to perhaps 25 percent—a reduction in the top rate of almost 30 percent. The lower rate would match that used by most other developed countries, and a rate cut might make U.S. entities more competitive in the global marketplace. A rate cut would be paid for by repealing various deductions and credits that corporations use to reduce their average and effective tax rates.

But for those corporations that hold deferred tax assets (e.g., NOL and credit carryforwards), the corresponding GAAP results might not be so attractive. Deferred tax assets (DTAs) would be written down for book purposes (because lower tax rates will apply in the future, the deferred deductions and credits will produce lower tax savings). Such write-downs of the DTAs thus would reduce current book income—perhaps by dramatic amounts. That cannot be good for stock prices and executive bonuses.

A corporation's specific DTAs are not publicly disclosed, but a 30 percent cut in the U.S. corporate income tax rates would, on average, trigger a 30 percent DTA write-down. Could the GAAP consequences of a corporate income tax rate reduction be so negative as to move businesses to block the cut itself?

ASC 740-30 (APB 23) provides an exception to ASC 740 (SFAS 109) for income from foreign subsidiaries.[12] If a corporation documents that it is **permanently reinvesting** the earnings of its foreign subsidiaries outside the United States, the corporation does not record as an expense any future U.S. income tax the corporation may pay on such earnings.

USCo, in Example 19, uses ASC 740-30 (APB 23) to avoid reporting the $116,000 in deferred taxes. Because USCo plans to reinvest its Singapore earnings indefinitely outside the United States, it is not required to include the deferred U.S. taxes as part of its total tax expense. USCo's total financial statement income remains $1 million, but its total tax expense is only $234,000 (the taxes currently paid to the United States and Singapore). The resulting financial statement effective tax rate is 23.4% ($234,000/$1,000,000), and the USCo group's after-tax book income reflects the Singapore tax savings.	**Example 20**

Using ASC 740-30 (APB 23) is not an "all or nothing" decision. It can be adopted in some years and not others. Even within a year, it may be used for only a portion of foreign subsidiary earnings.

THE BIG PICTURE

Example 21

Return to the facts of *The Big Picture* on p. 3-1. Recall from Example 1 that Arctic Corporation has a wholly owned foreign subsidiary, Hurricane, Ltd. Assume that Arctic also owns 100% of another foreign corporation, Typhoon, Ltd. Arctic can choose to apply ASC 740-30 (APB 23) to both of its foreign subsidiaries in year 1 and to only Hurricane in year 2. In year 3, Arctic can choose to use ASC 740-30 (APB 23) for 40% of Hurricane's earnings and 80% of Typhoon's earnings.

ASC 740-30 (APB 23) is a major issue only when the foreign subsidiary is taxed at rates below the applicable U.S. tax rate. Otherwise, there is no potential for tax deferral.

An assertion by management that foreign earnings will remain overseas indefinitely converts a temporary book-tax difference into a permanent difference. This can result in a significant decrease in the entity's book effective tax rate.

Raven is a U.S. corporation that is subject to a 35% U.S. income tax rate. Its 100% owned subsidiary Cuervo operates in Despina, a country that does not levy an income tax. Cuervo makes no distributions to Raven during the tax year. Raven's book-tax differences and effective tax rate are computed as follows. If Raven's management asserts that Cuervo's profits are to be permanently invested in Despina, the book effective tax rate decreases by about one-third.	**Example 22**

	Cuervo Earnings Are "Permanently Reinvested" in Despina ($ in 000's)	Cuervo Earnings Are *Not* "Permanently Reinvested" in Despina ($ in 000's)
Pretax U.S. book income	$100,000	$100,000
Pretax Despina book income	50,000	50,000
Total pretax book income	$150,000	$150,000
Temporary book-tax difference: Despina earnings		(50,000)
Permanent book-tax difference: Despina earnings	(50,000)	
Taxable income	$100,000	$100,000
U.S. income tax	$ 35,000	$ 35,000
Deferred income tax expense		17,500
Total income tax expense	$ 35,000	$ 52,500
GAAP effective tax rate	23.3%	35.0%

---

[12]Formerly *Opinion No. 23—Accounting for Income Taxes—Special Areas,* Accounting Principles Board.

<table>
<tr><td colspan="2">Tax Planning Strategies</td><td colspan="2">REDUCING EFFECTIVE TAX RATES WITH ASC 740-30 (APB 23) CAN BACKFIRE</td></tr>
</table>

FRAMEWORK FOCUS: DEDUCTIONS

Strategy: **Maximize Deductible Amounts.**

Because ASC 740-30 (APB 23) allows for higher reported book earnings (no deferred U.S. tax expense is recorded), its use may be reflected in higher stock prices and increased shareholder wealth. Many U.S. multinationals with foreign subsidiaries use ASC 740-30 (APB 23) to avoid reporting U.S. deferred taxes on foreign earnings.

The "permanent reinvestment" exception should not be employed unless the corporation truly expects to keep its foreign earnings outside the United States. Using ASC 740-30 (APB 23) and then repatriating foreign profits after all can cause extreme spikes in a corporation's effective tax rate.

Example 23

USCo, a domestic corporation, owns 100% of Shamrock, Ltd., an Irish corporation. The U.S. tax rate is 35%, and the Irish tax rate is 10%. In 2014, USCo earns $100,000 in taxable income and pays $35,000 to the United States. Shamrock earns $400,000 in taxable income and pays $40,000 in taxes to Ireland. Shamrock makes no distributions to its U.S. parent and is not taxed in the United States because it is not a U.S. person and has no activities in the United States.

USCo is not taxed on the Irish profits because it has not received any distributions of these profits. Furthermore, USCo uses ASC 740-30 (APB 23) to avoid recording any deferred U.S. income tax expense on its financial statements. Accordingly, USCo has achieved deferral and reduced its worldwide cash tax costs and book income tax expense.

USCo's total tax expense for financial statement purposes is $75,000.

Current U.S. tax	$35,000
Current foreign tax	40,000
Total tax expense	$75,000

The financial statement effective tax rate on USCo's global income is 15% ($75,000 total tax expense/$500,000 net income). Thus, the USCo group has achieved higher after-tax book income and earnings per share.

In 2015, USCo earns $200,000 in taxable income and pays $70,000 to the United States. Shamrock breaks even for the year and pays no taxes to Ireland. At the same time, USCo decides that Shamrock should pay it a dividend of $360,000.

U.S. Tax Return	
U.S. income	$200,000
Foreign dividend*	400,000
Taxable income	$600,000
Tax rate	× 35%
	$210,000
FTC	(40,000)
Net U.S. tax	$170,000

*The total gross income is the $360,000 cash dividend grossed up by the $40,000 potential FTC (see Chapter 16).

For book purposes, USCo reports only $200,000 in net income (the $400,000 in Irish income was included in book income in 2014 and is not included again). The 2015 total tax expense for financial statement purposes is $170,000.

Current U.S. tax	$170,000
Current foreign tax	–0–
Total tax expense	$170,000

The financial statement effective tax rate on USCo's global income is 85% ($170,000 total tax expense/$200,000 net income). This extremely high effective rate is caused by the mismatching of the Irish income (reported in 2014) and the U.S. taxes on the Irish income (reported in 2015). ∎

3-2e Summary

The tax department of a business often is charged with constructing the entity's tax strategies (*tax planning*) and filing all required tax returns (*tax compliance*) while preparing for subsequent audit and litigation activity (*tax controversy*). Tax professionals often work closely with those who prepare the entity's financial statements, especially concerning the tax footnote, tax deferral accounts, and tax rate reconciliations. Professional tax and accounting research underlies all of this work.

The efforts of a modern tax department are depicted in Figure 3.4. Tax professionals must be proficient in all of the indicated areas, so that they can meet the demands placed upon the entity by shareholders, regulators, and taxing agencies.

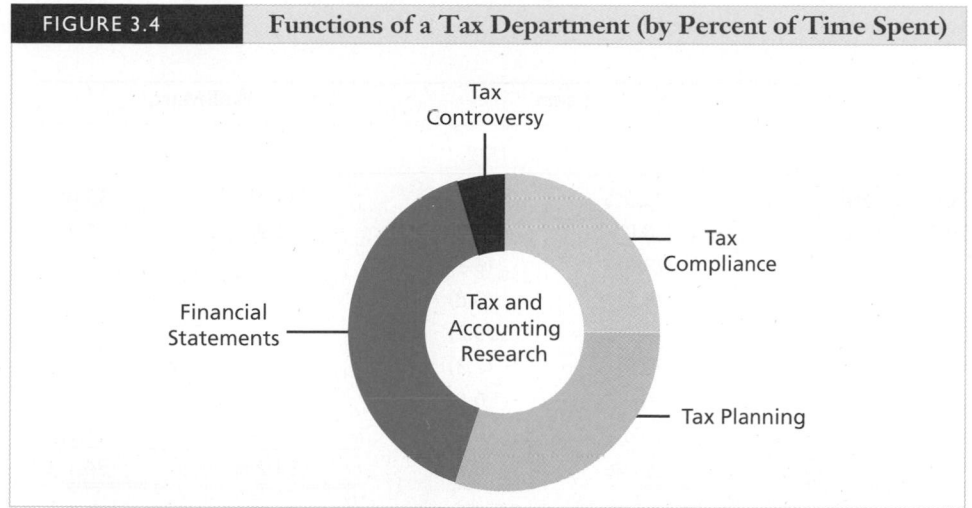

FIGURE 3.4	Functions of a Tax Department (by Percent of Time Spent)

3-3 BENCHMARKING

An entity's income tax expense amount may appear to be of little interest to anyone beyond the taxpayer that makes the payment and the government agencies that collect it. The tax year is over, the transactions are completed, and the final costs have been tallied. Still, this historical tax information may prove valuable. A company's income tax expense is one of the single largest expense items on its income statement, and understanding the components of this expense is a critical activity for the tax professional.

Consider a typical baseball game. Two teams meet, interact following a specific set of rules, and ultimately complete the game, generating a final score. Of course, the final score is of immediate interest to the teams and the fans, but once the game is over, the score and associated statistics (runs, hits, and errors) are relegated to the history books. Yet, these statistics still can be quite useful. A team coach may use the game statistics to evaluate the strengths and weaknesses of the players to assist in improving performance. Other teams may use the statistics to develop strategies for upcoming games. Players can use the statistics to "benchmark" themselves against their own performance in prior games or against players on other teams. In short, there is a wealth of information in these historical data.

A taxpayer's reported income tax expense likewise is a valuable source of information for the company, its tax advisers, and its competitors. The reported information provides clues about a company's operational and tax planning strategies.

Companies may benchmark their tax situation to other years' results or to other companies in the same industry. The starting point for a **benchmarking** exercise usually is the data from the income tax note rate reconciliation.

3-3a Dynamic Benchmarking

Table 3.1 shows the tax rate reconciliation information from the income tax notes for two recent years of Sears Holding Corporation (Sears) and Wal-Mart Stores, Inc. (Wal-Mart). Both companies are listed on the New York Stock Exchange, are in the same industry, and operate both inside and outside the United States. Although the income and tax expense amounts of both companies are quite different in magnitude, the tax amounts are converted to percentage of income numbers for comparability purposes. In year 1, Sears reported an effective tax rate that was 12 percentage points higher than Wal-Mart's rate. In year 2, Sears's effective tax rate was 4.9 points below Wal-Mart's rate. What factors created these differences? Rate reconciliation information can provide clues.

Sears reported a higher effective tax rate in year 1 because its state and local income tax burden was higher, and because it suffered a goodwill impairment (the goodwill write-off is not tax deductible). These increase items were offset by

LO.6

Use financial statement income tax information to benchmark a company's tax position.

| TABLE 3.1 | Tax Rate Reconciliation for Sears and Wal-Mart |

	Sears		Wal-Mart	
	Year 2	Year 1	Year 2	Year 1
Hypothetical tax (benefit) at U.S. Federal rate	35.0%	35.0%	35.0%	35.0%
State and local income taxes, net of Federal benefit	6.0	7.2	1.9	1.7
Tax credits	(3.0)	(6.3)		
Resolution of income tax matters	(6.2)	(6.8)		
Basis difference in domestic subsidiary	—	(30.2)		
Non-U.S. income taxed at different rates	(0.9)	(2.3)	(1.7)	(1.6)
Nondeductible goodwill	—	50.0		
Other	(1.6)	(0.4)	(1.0)	(1.0)
	29.3%	46.2%	34.2%	34.1%
Book income before tax (in millions)	$420.0	$184.0	$20,898.0	$20,158.0

reductions caused by certain basis differences in a domestic subsidiary, larger benefits from tax credits, and a larger benefit from a favorable resolution of tax matters.

When comparing effective tax rates, it is important to consider which components of the effective tax rate produce one-time effects, and which will be observed permanently. For example, for year 2, the effective tax rates of both companies were more similar (Sears was about 5 percentage points lower than Wal-Mart). In particular, without the large effects of nondeductible goodwill and the domestic subsidiary basis difference, Sears approaches the effective tax rate of Wal-Mart.

Consequently, it appears that there are no long-term structural differences in the tax burdens faced by the two companies. This is not surprising, given that both companies are incorporated in the United States, perform in the same industry, and operate in many of the same jurisdictions.

However, items such as the nondeductible goodwill difference do indicate that there may be potential fundamental differences in how Sears's management deals with growth via expansion rather than acquisitions. It is acquired goodwill rather than the homegrown sort that faces potential impairment. The Sears example shows that the results of past and current strategic decisions eventually may show up in the income tax footnote.

3-3b Refining the Analysis

In addition to comparing effective tax rates, companies can compare levels of deferred tax assets and liabilities.

Example 24

Akiko Enterprises reports a net deferred tax liability of $280,000. Erde, Inc., a company in the same industry, reports a net deferred tax liability of $860,000. The presence of deferred tax liabilities on the balance sheet indicates that both companies are benefiting from deferring actual tax payments (essentially, an interest-free loan from the government).

At first glance, it may appear that Erde is doing better in this regard. However, what if Akiko holds total assets of $2.6 million and Erde's assets total $19.2 million? This information indicates that Akiko has 10.8% ($280,000/$2.6 million) of its total assets "financed" with an interest-free loan from the government, while Erde has only 4.5% ($860,000/$19.2 million) of its assets "financed" with its deferred tax liabilities.

A company may do a more refined benchmarking analysis by examining each component of its deferred tax assets and liabilities as a percentage of total assets. For example, an observer can examine how the deferred tax assets or liabilities related to property, plant, and equipment compare with those of its competitors.

BRIDGE DISCIPLINE Bridge to Financial Analysis

Financial analysts perform an important function for the capital markets in their detailed analyses of companies. The analyst combs through the financial reports and other information about a company to produce an informed opinion on how a company is performing. Analysts' earnings forecasts often constitute an important metric to examine when making decisions about investing in companies.

An experienced financial analyst typically will have a good handle on interpreting financial statement information.

However, even experienced analysts often will "punt" when it comes to interpreting the tax information contained in a financial statement, preferring to look at net income before taxes (or even EBITDA, earnings before interest, taxes, depreciation, and amortization).

A great deal of useful information about a business is contained in its tax footnote, and analysts might have an edge if they work at understanding the mysteries of taxes in the financial statements.

The nature of the components of deferred tax liabilities and deferred tax assets becomes quite important in a benchmarking analysis.

Example 25

LinCo reports total book income before taxes of $10 million and a total tax expense of $3.2 million, producing a 32% effective tax rate. TuckCo also reports book income before taxes of $10 million. TuckCo's total tax expense is $3.1 million, producing an effective tax rate of 31%. At first glance, it appears that both companies are similar with regard to effective tax rates. The total tax expense divided between current and deferred is as follows (in millions).

	LinCo	TuckCo
Current tax expense	$ 4.1	$ 4.2
Deferred tax benefit	(0.9)	(1.1)
Total tax expense	$ 3.2	$ 3.1

Again, it appears that both companies have created deferred tax assets in the current year that are expected to produce tax savings in the future. Knowing the nature of the underlying deferred tax assets will add greatly to one's interpretation of the effective tax rates.

The deferred tax asset generating LinCo's $900,000 expected future tax savings is the use of an NOL. The deferred tax asset generating TuckCo's expected future tax savings is generated by different book and tax methods in accounting for warranty expense. This additional information reveals that LinCo previously has incurred losses, and it is critical that it earn future taxable income in order to use the NOL.

This is quite different from TuckCo's situation, which reveals only that common differences in accounting methods exist. Although the tax positions of LinCo and TuckCo seem very similar on the surface, a closer look reveals a striking difference.

Example 26

WageCo and SalaryCo operate in the same industry, and they both report a 38% effective tax rate. Their book income and current, deferred, and total tax expense were reported as follows.

	WageCo	SalaryCo
Book income before tax	$1,500,000	$2,300,000
Current tax expense	$ 980,000	$ 24,000
Deferred tax expense (benefit)	(410,000)	850,000
Total tax expense	$ 570,000	$ 874,000
Effective tax rate	38%	38%

WageCo's total tax expense is highly dependent on the current recognition of future tax savings of $410,000. SalaryCo appears to be deferring a substantial portion of its tax expense to future years. Although both companies report a 38% effective tax rate, the details indicate that the two companies face very different tax situations.

3-3c Sustaining the Tax Rate

It is important in benchmarking exercises to remove the effect of one-time items in comparing sustainable effective tax rates across time or companies. Examples of one-time items include restructuring costs, legal settlements, and IRS or other tax liability settlements. A one-time item may seem beneficial or detrimental to a company's effective tax rate. But the very nature of such an item implies that it has little to do with the company's long-term sustainable tax costs.

Example 27

MetalCo and IronCo operate in the same industry, and they report the following tax rate reconciliations in their tax footnotes.

	MetalCo	IronCo
Hypothetical tax at U.S. rate	35.0%	35.0%
State and local taxes	2.2	2.1
Foreign income taxed at less than U.S. rate	(6.2)	(6.1)
Tax Court settlement on disputed tax issue	(18.6)	—
Effective tax rate	12.4%	31.0%

Although it appears that MetalCo has a significantly lower effective tax rate (12.4%) than IronCo (31.0%), removing MetalCo's one-time item related to the court settlement indicates that both companies may operate under a 31% effective tax rate (12.4% + 18.6% = 31%).

3-3d Uses of Benchmarking Analysis

Benchmarking is part science and part art. A useful analysis requires both an accountant's knowledge of how the underlying financial statements are constructed, including arriving at the appropriate tax expense, and a detective's sense of where to look and what questions to ask. Concept Summary 3.4 summarizes the most typical uses of benchmarking in an analysis of an entity's financial results.

CONCEPT SUMMARY 3.4

Benchmarking Analysis

A benchmarking analysis can be helpful in comparing the tax positions of two or more business entities. One might consider the following aspects of the taxpayers' financial disclosures in this regard. This list is not all-inclusive; benchmarking also includes the judgment and experience of the parties conducting the analysis.

- Compare the effective tax rates of the entities.
- Explain the differences in effective rates. Are these differences sustainable over time?
- Apply the analysis to both the tax dollars involved and the underlying net assets of the entities.
- Discount (but do not ignore) any one-time tax benefits/detriments that are observed.

REFOCUS ON THE BIG PICTURE

Raymond Jones should understand that the tax expense reported on the company's financial statements and the tax payable on the company's income tax returns often differ as a result of differences in the reporting entities used in the calculation and the different accounting methods used for book purposes and tax purposes. The use of different accounting methods may result in both temporary and permanent differences in financial statement income and taxable income. Examples of permanent differences include nontaxable income such as municipal bond interest and tax credits. Temporary differences include depreciation differences and other amounts that are affected by the timing of a deduction or an inclusion, but they ultimately result in the same amount being reflected in the financial statements and income tax returns.

Permanent differences such as municipal bond interest cause Arctic's book income to be greater than its taxable income. In calculating the tax expense shown on the financial statements, Arctic's book income must be adjusted for these permanent differences. This results in an effective tax rate for financial statement purposes (30.8 percent) that is below the top U.S. statutory corporate income tax rate of 35 percent.

In this case, Arctic's income tax expense of $7.7 million is higher than the current Federal income tax payable. This results from timing differences and creates a $1.05 million deferred tax liability that is reported on the company's balance sheet. Unlike other liabilities, deferred tax liabilities are "good" in the sense that they represent an amount that may be paid to the government in the future rather than today.

What If?

Mr. Jones is concerned about a newspaper article that said that companies reporting less tax on their tax returns than on their financial statements were cheating the IRS. Is this an accurate assessment?

While differences in income taxes payable to the IRS and financial tax expense can result from aggressive and illegal tax shelters, differences also result from different methods of accounting that are required for financial statement reporting using GAAP and tax laws enacted by Congress.

TAXES ON THE FINANCIAL STATEMENTS

© Pukhov Konstantin/Shutterstock.com

Suggested Readings

Cheryl Anderson, "Creating Value in the Corporate Tax Function Through Benchmarking," *AICPA Tax Adviser*, September 2008.

Jerald D. August, "The Uncertain State of Uncertain Tax Positions," *Journal of Corporate Taxation*, November/December 2011.

J. O. Everett, C. J. Hennig, and W. A. Raabe, *Schedule M–3 Compliance*, 2nd ed., Commerce Clearing House, 2008.

J. Richard Harvey, "Schedule UTP—Why So Few Disclosures?" *Tax Notes*, April 1, 2013.

C. J. Hennig, W. A. Raabe, and J. O. Everett, "FIN 48 Compliance," *AICPA Tax Adviser*, January 2008.

Key Terms

ASC 740 (SFAS 109), 3-9	Deferred tax benefit, 3-10	Permanently reinvesting, 3-26
ASC 740-10 (FIN 48), 3-24	Deferred tax expense, 3-10	Rate reconciliation, 3-19
ASC 740-30 (APB 23), 3-26	Deferred tax liability, 3-11	Schedule M–1, 3-6
Balance sheet approach, 3-11	Equity method, 3-2	Schedule M–3, 3-7
Benchmarking, 3-29	Generally accepted accounting	Temporary differences, 3-5
Conservatism principle, 3-14	principles (GAAP), 3-2	Valuation allowance, 3-15
Current tax expense, 3-10	Income tax provision, 3-9	
Deferred tax asset, 3-11	Permanent differences, 3-5	

Problems

Ethics and Equity

1. **LO.1** Evaluate the following statement: For most business entities, book income differs from taxable income because "income" has different meanings for the users of the data in the income computation.

2. **LO.1** Parent, a domestic corporation, owns 100% of Block, a foreign corporation, and Chip, a domestic corporation. Parent also owns 45% of Trial, a domestic corporation. Parent receives no distributions from any of these corporations. Which of these entities' net income is included in Parent's income statement for current-year financial reporting purposes?

3. **LO.1** Parent, a domestic corporation, owns 100% of Block, a foreign corporation, and Chip, a domestic corporation. Parent also owns 45% of Trial, a domestic corporation. Parent receives no distributions from any of these corporations. Which of these entities' taxable income is included in Parent's current-year Form 1120, U.S. income tax return? Parent consolidates all eligible subsidiaries.

Communications

4. **LO.1** Marcellus Jackson, the CFO of Mac, Inc., notices that the tax liability reported on Mac's tax return is less than the tax expense reported on Mac's financial statements. Provide a letter to Jackson outlining why these two tax expense numbers differ. Mac's address is 482 Linden Road, Paris, KY 40362.

Issue ID

5. **LO.1** Define the terms *temporary difference* and *permanent difference* as they pertain to the financial reporting of income tax expenses. Describe how these two book-tax differences affect the gap between book and taxable income. How are permanent and temporary differences alike? How are they different?

Communications

6. **LO.1** In no more than three PowerPoint slides, list several commonly encountered temporary and permanent book-tax differences. The slides will be used in your presentation next week to your school's Future CPAs Club.

7. **LO.1** Indicate whether the following items create temporary or permanent differences.
   a. Book depreciation in excess of tax depreciation.
   b. Tax depreciation in excess of book depreciation.
   c. Increase in the allowance for doubtful accounts.
   d. Increase in the reserve for warranty settlements.
   e. Municipal bond interest income.
   f. Federal income tax.

8. **LO.2** Indicate whether the following book-tax differences produce deferred tax assets, deferred tax liabilities, or neither. Consider each item independently.
   a. Book depreciation in excess of tax depreciation.
   b. Tax depreciation in excess of book depreciation.
   c. Increase in the allowance for doubtful accounts.
   d. Increase in the reserve for warranty settlements.
   e. Energy tax credits.
   f. A current-year NOL.

9. **LO.2, 4** Indicate whether the following temporary differences produce current or non-current deferred tax assets or deferred tax liabilities (considered independently).
   a. Book depreciation in excess of tax depreciation.
   b. Tax depreciation in excess of book depreciation.
   c. Increase in the allowance for doubtful accounts.
   d. Increase in the reserve for warranty settlements.
   e. Write-down for impairment of book goodwill.
   f. A current-year NOL.

10. **LO.1** Evaluate the following statement: The primary purpose of the Schedule M–1 and Schedule M–3 is to help the IRS craft its audits of the taxpayer. (Hint: Focus on the primary reason the IRS wants to see this information.)

11. **LO.2** Cramer, a stock analyst, wants to understand how the income tax expense reported in financial statements affects stock prices. Briefly describe the objective of ASC 740 (SFAS 109) with regard to reporting income tax expense.

12. **LO.2** Prance, Inc., earns pretax book net income of $800,000 in 2014. Prance acquires a depreciable asset in 2014, and first-year tax depreciation exceeds book depreciation by $80,000. Prance reports no other temporary or permanent book-tax differences. Assuming that the pertinent U.S. tax rate is 35%, compute Prance's total income tax expense, current income tax expense, and deferred income tax expense.

13. **LO.2** Using the facts of Problem 12, determine the 2014 end-of-year balance in Prance's deferred tax asset and deferred tax liability balance sheet accounts.

14. **LO.2** Prance, in Problem 12, reports $600,000 of pretax book net income in 2015. Prance's book depreciation exceeds tax depreciation in this year by $20,000. Prance reports no other temporary or permanent book-tax differences. Assuming that the pertinent U.S. tax rate is 35%, compute Prance's total income tax expense, current income tax expense, and deferred income tax expense.

15. **LO.2** Using the facts of Problem 14, determine the 2015 end-of-year balance in Prance's deferred tax asset and deferred tax liability balance sheet accounts.

16. **LO.2** Mini, Inc., earns pretax book net income of $750,000 in 2014. Mini deducted $20,000 in bad debt expense for book purposes. This expense is not yet deductible for tax purposes. Mini records no other temporary or permanent differences. Assuming that the U.S. tax rate is 35%, compute Mini's total income tax expense, current income tax expense, and deferred income tax expense.

17. **LO.2** Using the facts of Problem 16, determine the 2014 end-of-year balance in Mini's deferred tax asset and deferred tax liability balance sheet accounts.

18. **LO.2** Mini, in Problem 16, reports $800,000 of pretax book net income in 2015. Mini did not deduct any bad debt expense for book purposes but did deduct $15,000 in bad debt expense for tax purposes. Mini records no other temporary or permanent differences. Assuming that the U.S. tax rate is 35%, compute Mini's total income tax expense, current income tax expense, and deferred income tax expense.

19. **LO.2** Using the facts of Problem 18, determine the 2015 end-of-year balance in Mini's deferred tax asset and deferred tax liability balance sheet accounts.

20. **LO.3** What is a valuation allowance? Why is such a book account created? Be specific.

21. **LO.3** Cortel, Inc., hopes to report a total book tax expense of $90,000 in the current year. This $90,000 expense consists of $160,000 in current tax expense and a $70,000 tax benefit related to the expected future use of an NOL by Cortel. If the auditors determine that a valuation allowance of $30,000 must be placed against Cortel's deferred tax assets, what is Cortel's total book tax expense?

22. **LO.3** You saw on the online Business News Channel that YoungCo has "released one-third of its valuation allowances because of an upbeat forecast for sales of its tablet computers over the next 30 months." What effect does such a release likely have on YoungCo's current-year book effective tax rate? Be specific.

Critical Thinking   23. **LO.1** Lily Enterprises acquires another corporation. This acquisition created $30 million of goodwill for both book and tax purposes. The $30 million in goodwill is amortized over 15 years for tax purposes but is not deductible for book purposes unless impaired. Will this book-tax difference create a permanent or temporary book-tax difference for Lily?

Decision Making   24. **LO.6** Jill is the CFO of PorTech, Inc. PorTech's tax advisers have recommended two tax planning ideas that will each provide $5 million of current-year cash tax savings. One idea is based on a timing difference and is expected to reverse in full 10 years in the future. The other idea creates a permanent difference that never will reverse.

Communications

Determine whether these ideas will allow PorTech to reduce its reported book income tax expense for the current year. Illustrate in a table or timeline your preference for one planning strategy over the other. Which idea will you recommend to Jill?

Communications   25. **LO.1, 5** Sam Taggart, the CEO of Skate, Inc., has reviewed Skate's tax return and its financial statement. He notices that both the Schedule M–3 and the rate reconciliation in the income tax note provide a reconciliation of tax information. However, he sees very little correspondence between the two schedules. Outline the differences between these two schedules in a letter to Sam. Skate's address is 499 Lucerne Avenue, Ocala, FL 34482.

Decision Making   26. **LO.4** RadioCo, a domestic corporation, owns 100% of TVCo, a manufacturing facility in Ireland. TVCo has no operations or activities in the United States. The U.S. tax rate is 35%, and the Irish tax rate is 15%. For the current year, RadioCo earns $200,000 in taxable income from its U.S. operations. TVCo earns $800,000 in taxable income from its operations, pays $120,000 in taxes to Ireland, and makes no distributions to RadioCo.

a. Determine RadioCo's effective tax rate for book purposes with and without the permanent reinvestment assumption of ASC 740-30 (APB 23).

b. Under what conditions should RadioCo adopt ASC 740-30 (APB 23) for TVCo's earnings?

Issue ID   27. **LO.4** Underwood, the CFO of TechCo, Inc., has used ASC 740-30 (APB 23) to avoid reporting any U.S. deferred tax expense on $50 million of the earnings of TechCo's foreign subsidiaries. All of these subsidiaries operate in countries with lower tax rates than in the United States. Underwood wants to bring to the United States $10 million in profits from these foreign subsidiaries in the form of dividends. How will this profit repatriation affect TechCo's book effective tax rate?

Issue ID   28. **LO.4** Jaime, the CFO of BuildCo, Inc., has used ASC 740-30 (APB 23) to avoid reporting any U.S. deferred tax expense on $100 million of the earnings of BuildCo's foreign subsidiaries. All of these subsidiaries operate in countries with higher tax rates than the ones that apply under U.S. law. Jaime wants to bring home $30 million in profits from these foreign subsidiaries in the form of dividends. How will this profit repatriation affect BuildCo's book effective tax rate?

29. **LO.6** RoofCo reports total book income before taxes of $20 million and a total tax expense of $8 million. FloorCo reports book income before taxes of $30 million and a total tax expense of $12 million. The companies' breakdown between current and deferred tax expense (benefit) is as follows.

	RoofCo	FloorCo
Current tax expense	$10.0	$13.0
Deferred tax benefit	(2.0)	(1.0)
Total tax expense	$ 8.0	$12.0

RoofCo's deferred tax benefit is from a deferred tax asset created because of differences in book and tax depreciation methods for equipment. FloorCo's deferred tax benefit is created by the expected future use of an NOL. Compare and contrast these two companies' effective tax rates. How are they similar? How are they different?

30. **LO.6** LawnCo and TreeCo operate in the same industry, and both report a 30% effective tax rate. Their book income and current, deferred, and total tax expense are reported below.

Communications

	LawnCo	TreeCo
Book income before tax	$500,000	$650,000
Current tax expense	$200,000	$ 20,000
Deferred tax expense (benefit)	(50,000)	175,000
Total tax expense	$150,000	$195,000
Effective tax rate	30%	30%

ShrubCo is a competitor of both of these companies. Prepare a letter to Laura Collins, VP-Taxation of ShrubCo, outlining your analysis of the other two companies' effective tax rates, using only the preceding information. ShrubCo's address is 9979 West Third Street, Peru, IN 46970.

31. **LO.6** HippCo and HoppCo operate in the same industry and report the following tax rate reconciliations in their tax footnotes. Compare and contrast the effective tax rates of these two companies.

	HippCo	HoppCo
Hypothetical tax at U.S. rate	35.0%	35.0%
State and local taxes	2.7	3.9
Foreign income taxed at less than U.S. rate	(12.5)	(7.8)
Tax Court settlement on disputed tax issue	6.0	—
Effective tax rate	31.2%	31.1%

32. **LO.6** In the current year, Dickinson, Inc., reports an effective tax rate of 36%, and Badger, Inc., reports an effective tax rate of 21%. Both companies are domestic and operate in the same industry. Your initial examination of the financial statements of the two companies indicates that Badger apparently is doing a better job with its tax planning, explaining the difference in effective tax rates. Consequently, all else being equal, you decide to invest in Badger.

Ethics and Equity

In a subsequent year, it comes to light that Badger had used some very aggressive tax planning techniques to reduce its reported tax expense. After an examination by the IRS, Badger loses the tax benefits and reports a very large tax expense in that year. Over this multiple-year period, it turns out that Dickinson had the lower effective tax rate after all.

Do you believe Badger was ethical in not fully disclosing the aggressiveness of its tax positions in its current financial statements? How does ASC 740-10 (FIN 48) affect Badger's disclosure requirement? Does ASC 740-10 (FIN 48) still leave room for ethical decision making by management in determining how to report uncertain tax positions? Explain.

33. **LO.2** Phillips, Inc., a cash basis C corporation, completes $100,000 in sales for year 1, but only $75,000 of this amount is collected during year 1. The remaining $25,000 from these sales is collected promptly during the first quarter of year 2. The applicable income tax rate for year 1 and thereafter is 30%. Compute Phillips's year 1 current and deferred income tax expense.

34. **LO.2** Continue with the results of Problem 33. Prepare the GAAP journal entries for Phillips's year 1 income tax expense.

35. **LO.2** Britton, Inc., an accrual basis C corporation, sells widgets on credit. Its book and taxable income for year 1 totals $60,000 before accounting for bad debts. Britton's book allowance for uncollectible accounts increased for year 1 by $10,000, but none of the entity's bad debts received a specific write-off for tax purposes. The applicable income tax rate for year 1 and thereafter is 30%. Compute Britton's year 1 current and deferred income tax expense.

36. **LO.2** Continue with the results of Problem 35. Prepare the GAAP journal entries for Britton's year 1 income tax expense.

37. **LO.2** Rubio, Inc., an accrual basis C corporation, reports the following amounts for the tax year. The applicable income tax rate is 30%. Compute Rubio's taxable income.

Book income, including the items below	$80,000
Increase in book allowance for anticipated warranty costs	5,000
Interest income from City of Westerville bonds	10,000
Bribes paid to Federal inspectors	17,000

38. **LO.2** Continue with the results of Problem 37. Determine Rubio's income tax expense and GAAP income for the year.

39. **LO.2** Willingham, Inc., an accrual basis C corporation, reports pretax book income of $1.6 million. At the beginning of the tax year, Willingham reported no deferred tax accounts on its balance sheet. It is subject to a 35% U.S. income tax rate in the current year and for the foreseeable future.

    Willingham's book-tax differences include the following. Compute the entity's current and deferred income tax expense for the year.

Addition to the book reserve for uncollectible receivables (no specific write-offs occurred)	$4,000,000
Tax depreciation in excess of book	3,000,000
Book gain from installment sale of nonbusiness asset, deferred for tax	2,000,000
Interest income from school district bonds	200,000

40. **LO.2** Continue with the results of Problem 39. Prepare the GAAP journal entries for Willingham's income tax expense.

41. **LO.2** Relix, Inc., is a domestic corporation with the following balance sheet for book and tax purposes at the end of the year. Based on this information, determine Relix's net deferred tax asset or net deferred tax liability at year-end. Assume a 34% corporate tax rate and no valuation allowance.

	Tax Debit/(Credit)	Book Debit/(Credit)
Assets		
Cash	$ 500	$ 500
Accounts receivable	8,000	8,000
Buildings	750,000	750,000
Accumulated depreciation	(450,000)	(380,000)
Furniture & fixtures	70,000	70,000
Accumulated depreciation	(46,000)	(38,000)
Total assets	$ 332,500	$ 410,500
Liabilities		
Accrued litigation expense	$ –0–	($ 50,000)
Note payable	(78,000)	(78,000)
Total liabilities	($ 78,000)	($ 128,000)
Stockholders' Equity		
Paid-in capital	($ 10,000)	($ 10,000)
Retained earnings	(244,500)	(272,500)
Total liabilities and stockholders' equity	($ 332,500)	($ 410,500)

42. **LO.2** Based on the facts and results of Problem 41 and the beginning-of-the-year book-tax basis differences listed below, determine the change in Relix's deferred tax assets for the current year.

	Beginning of Year
Accrued litigation expense	$34,000
Subtotal	$34,000
Applicable tax rate	× 34%
Gross deferred tax asset	$11,560

43. **LO.2** Based on the facts and results of Problem 41 and the beginning-of-the-year book-tax basis differences listed below, determine the change in Relix's deferred tax liabilities for the current year.

	Beginning of Year
Building—accumulated depreciation	($57,000)
Furniture & fixtures—accumulated depreciation	(4,200)
Subtotal	($61,200)
Applicable tax rate	× 34%
Gross deferred tax liability	($20,808)

44. **LO.2** Based on the facts and results of Problems 41–43, determine Relix's change in net deferred tax asset or net deferred tax liability for the current year. Provide the journal entry to record this amount.

45. **LO.2** In addition to the temporary differences identified in Problems 41–44, Relix reported two permanent differences between book and taxable income. It earned $2,375 in tax-exempt municipal bond interest, and it incurred $780 in nondeductible meals and entertainment expense. Relix's book income before tax is $4,800. With this additional information, calculate Relix's current tax expense.

46. **LO.2** Provide the journal entry to record Relix's current tax expense as determined in Problem 45.

47. **LO.2** Based on the facts and results of Problems 41–46, calculate Relix's total provision for income tax expense reported in its financial statements and its book net income after tax.

48. **LO.2** Based on the facts and results of Problems 41–47, provide the income tax footnote rate reconciliation for Relix.

49. **LO.2** Kantner, Inc., is a domestic corporation with the following balance sheet for book and tax purposes at the end of the year. Based on this information, determine Kantner's net deferred tax asset or net deferred tax liability at year-end. Assume a 34% corporate tax rate and no valuation allowance.

	Tax Debit/(Credit)	Book Debit/(Credit)
Assets		
Cash	$ 1,000	$ 1,000
Accounts receivable	9,000	9,000
Buildings	850,000	850,000
Accumulated depreciation	(700,000)	(620,000)
Furniture & fixtures	40,000	40,000
Accumulated depreciation	(10,000)	(8,000)
Total assets	$ 190,000	$ 272,000
Liabilities		
Accrued warranty expense	$ –0–	($ 40,000)
Note payable	(16,000)	(16,000)
Total liabilities	($ 16,000)	($ 56,000)
Stockholders' Equity		
Paid-in capital	($ 50,000)	($ 50,000)
Retained earnings	(124,000)	(166,000)
Total liabilities and stockholders' equity	($ 190,000)	($ 272,000)

50. **LO.2** Based on the facts and results of Problem 49 and the beginning-of-the-year book-tax basis differences listed below, determine the change in Kantner's deferred tax assets for the current year.

	Beginning of Year
Accrued warranty expense	$30,000
Subtotal	$30,000
Applicable tax rate	× 34%
Gross deferred tax asset	$10,200

51. **LO.2** Based on the facts and results of Problem 49 and the beginning-of-the-year book-tax basis differences listed below, determine the change in Kantner's deferred tax liabilities for the current year.

	Beginning of Year
Building—accumulated depreciation	($62,000)
Furniture & fixtures—accumulated depreciation	(400)
Subtotal	($62,400)
Applicable tax rate	× 34%
Gross deferred tax liability	($21,216)

52. **LO.2** Based on the facts and results of Problems 49–51, determine Kantner's change in net deferred tax asset or net deferred tax liability for the current year. Provide the journal entry to record this amount.

53. **LO.2** In addition to the temporary differences identified in Problems 49–52, Kantner reported two permanent book-tax differences. It earned $7,800 in tax-exempt municipal bond interest, and it reported $850 in nondeductible meals and entertainment expense. Kantner's book income before tax is $50,000. With this additional information, calculate Kantner's current tax expense.

54. **LO.2** Provide the journal entry to record Kantner's current tax expense as determined in Problem 53.

55. **LO.2** Based on the facts and results of Problems 49–54, calculate Kantner's total provision for income tax expense reported on its financial statement and its book net income after tax.

56. **LO.2** Based on the facts and results of Problems 49–55, provide the income tax footnote rate reconciliation for Kantner.

BRIDGE DISCIPLINE

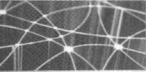

1. Using publicly available resources, locate summary financial information for two companies in the same industry. Compare and contrast the following items across the two companies: debt-to-equity ratio, return on assets, return on equity, inventory turnover ratio, and effective tax rate.

Communications

2. Using publicly available information, locate news or other items reporting financial analysts' forecasts or other information regarding two different companies. Determine whether the analyst appears to use tax information in the report. For example, does the analyst use pretax or after-tax earnings in the analysis? Draft an e-mail to your instructor describing your findings.

Communications

3. Using the annual reports or 10-Ks of two different public companies in the same industry, locate information regarding the compensation paid to their executives. Prepare a table comparing the compensation levels (cash and noncash) of top executives across the two companies, and send the table to your instructor. Illustrate the relationship between executive compensation and company performance by comparing the compensation to other company information such as net income.

Research Problems

Internet Activity

Use the tax resources of the Internet to address the following questions. Do not restrict your search to the Web, but include a review of newsgroups and general reference materials, practitioner sites and resources, primary sources of the tax law, chat rooms and discussion groups, and other opportunities.

Research Problem 1. Locate the web page of Citizens for Tax Justice. Find the report "Corporate Taxpayers and Corporate Tax Dodgers, 2008-10." In no more than four PowerPoint slides for your classmates, summarize the following.   Communications

- Methodology, motivation, and background of the study.
- Five notable companies, their book income and their effective Federal income tax rates, and where those rates are zero or negative.
- Five industries, their effective tax rates, and the dollar amounts of the tax subsidies they receive.
- Five notable companies, their effective domestic effective Federal income tax rate, and the effective tax rate on their overseas profits.

Research Problem 2. Locate the most recent financial statements of two companies in the same industry using the companies' websites or the SEC's website (**www.sec.gov**). Perform a benchmarking analysis of the two companies' effective tax rates, components of the effective tax rate reconciliation, levels of deferred tax assets and liabilities, and other relevant data. Summarize this information in an e-mail to your instructor.   Communications

Research Problem 3. In May 2013, the Government Accountability Office (GAO) released Report 13-520, *Corporate Income Tax: Effective Tax Rates Can Differ Significantly from the Statutory Rate.* In an e-mail to your instructor, answer the following questions.   Communications

- What was the average effective tax rate (ETR) of the corporations included in the GAO study?
- How is ETR calculated in the study? How does this compare to the ETR reported in companies' financial statements?
- The study was based on information from 2010. Were there any temporary tax provisions in effect in 2010 that may have reduced the average ETR, as calculated in the report, relative to what might have been calculated for 2009 or 2012? What impact, if any, does this have on the interpretation of the study's results? Would these temporary tax provisions have had the same effect on the ETRs reported in companies' financial statements for 2010? Why or why not?

Research Problem 4. Schedule M–1 and Schedule M–3 of Form 1120 provide a reconciliation of book income to taxable income. Locate the instructions for both of these schedules at the IRS website (**www.irs.gov**). Review the definition of book income for purposes of the two schedules. Identify three specific items included in the Schedule M–3 determination of book income. Discuss why these items are useful in determining a corporation's appropriate book income to use in the reconciliation. Send your comments as an e-mail to your instructor.   Communications

Research Problem 5. Locate articles or other discussions regarding the key differences between ASC 740 (SFAS 109) and International Accounting Standard No. 12 (related to income taxes). Summarize these key differences in an e-mail to your instructor. Make certain you have found the most current information for this comparison. Provide the URL for each of your sources.   Communications

Research Problem 6. Locate the financial statements of three different companies that report information in the income tax footnote regarding uncertain tax positions under ASC 740-10 (FIN 48). Create a schedule that compares and contrasts the changes in uncertain tax positions reported by the three companies. E-mail the schedule to your instructor.   Communications

Communications   **Research Problem 7.** Locate the financial statements of three different companies. Review the income tax footnote information on deferred tax assets (DTAs) and deferred tax liabilities (DTLs). Create a schedule that compares and contrasts the end-of-the year amounts of DTAs and DTLs, including any valuation allowances. E-mail the schedule to your instructor.

Research Problem 8. Using publicly available resources, locate summary financial information for two companies in the same industry. Compare and contrast the following items across the two companies: debt-to-equity ratio, return on assets, shareholder yield, return on equity, inventory turnover ratio, and effective tax rate. In your comparison, include the Federal, state/local, and international effective rates for the entities. Summarize in one paragraph the key reasons why the effective tax rates are similar (or different).

Communications   **Research Problem 9.** Locate the financial statements of two different companies in two different industries that appear to have very different state and local tax burdens based on the rate reconciliation contained in the income tax footnote. Describe the difference in state and local effective rates, and provide your thoughts on why the industry may be a factor in the differing state and local average tax rates. E-mail this discussion to your instructor.

Communications   **Research Problem 10.** Using publicly available resources, locate news or other items reporting financial analysts' forecasts or other information regarding two different companies. Determine whether the analyst appears to use tax information in the report. For example, does the analyst use EBITDA, pretax, or after-tax earnings in the analysis? Send an e-mail to your instructor describing your findings.

part 2

STRUCTURE OF THE FEDERAL INCOME TAX

CHAPTER **4**   **Gross Income**

CHAPTER **5**   **Business Deductions**

CHAPTER **6**   **Losses and Loss Limitations**

Part 2 introduces the components of the basic tax model. The gross income component, including the effect of exclusions, the accounting period, and the accounting method, is presented. This presentation is followed by an analysis of business deductions, including deductions that are allowed, deductions that are disallowed, and the effect of the accounting period and the accounting method on the timing of deductions. Included in the presentation are the deduction for charitable contributions, research and experimental expenditures, domestic production activities, interest and taxes, cost recovery, amortization, and depletion. Part 2 concludes with a discussion of losses. Included are coverage on bad debts, casualty and theft losses, net operating losses, the tax shelter issue, the at-risk limitations, and the passive activity loss limitations.

4 Gross Income

LEARNING OBJECTIVES: *After completing Chapter 4, you should be able to:*

LO.1 **Explain the concepts of gross income and realization and distinguish between the economic, accounting, and tax concepts of gross income.**

LO.2 **State and explain when the cash, accrual, and hybrid methods of accounting are used and how they are applied.**

LO.3 **Identify who should pay the tax on an item of income.**

LO.4 **Review and illustrate that statutory authority is required to exclude an item from gross income.**

LO.5 **Apply the tax provisions on loans made at below-market interest rates.**

LO.6 **Determine the extent to which receipts can be excluded under the tax benefit rule.**

LO.7 **Review and apply the tax provision that excludes interest on state and local government obligations from gross income.**

LO.8 **Use the tax rules concerning the exclusion of leasehold improvements from gross income.**

LO.9 **Determine the extent to which life insurance proceeds are excluded from gross income.**

LO.10 **Describe the circumstances under which income must be reported from the discharge of indebtedness.**

LO.11 **Describe the general tax consequences of property transactions.**

CHAPTER OUTLINE

TAX TALK *The first nine pages of the Internal Revenue Code define income. The remaining 1,100 pages spin the web of exceptions and preferences.* —WARREN G. MAGNUSON

Dennis Flaherty/Photographer's Choice/Getty Images

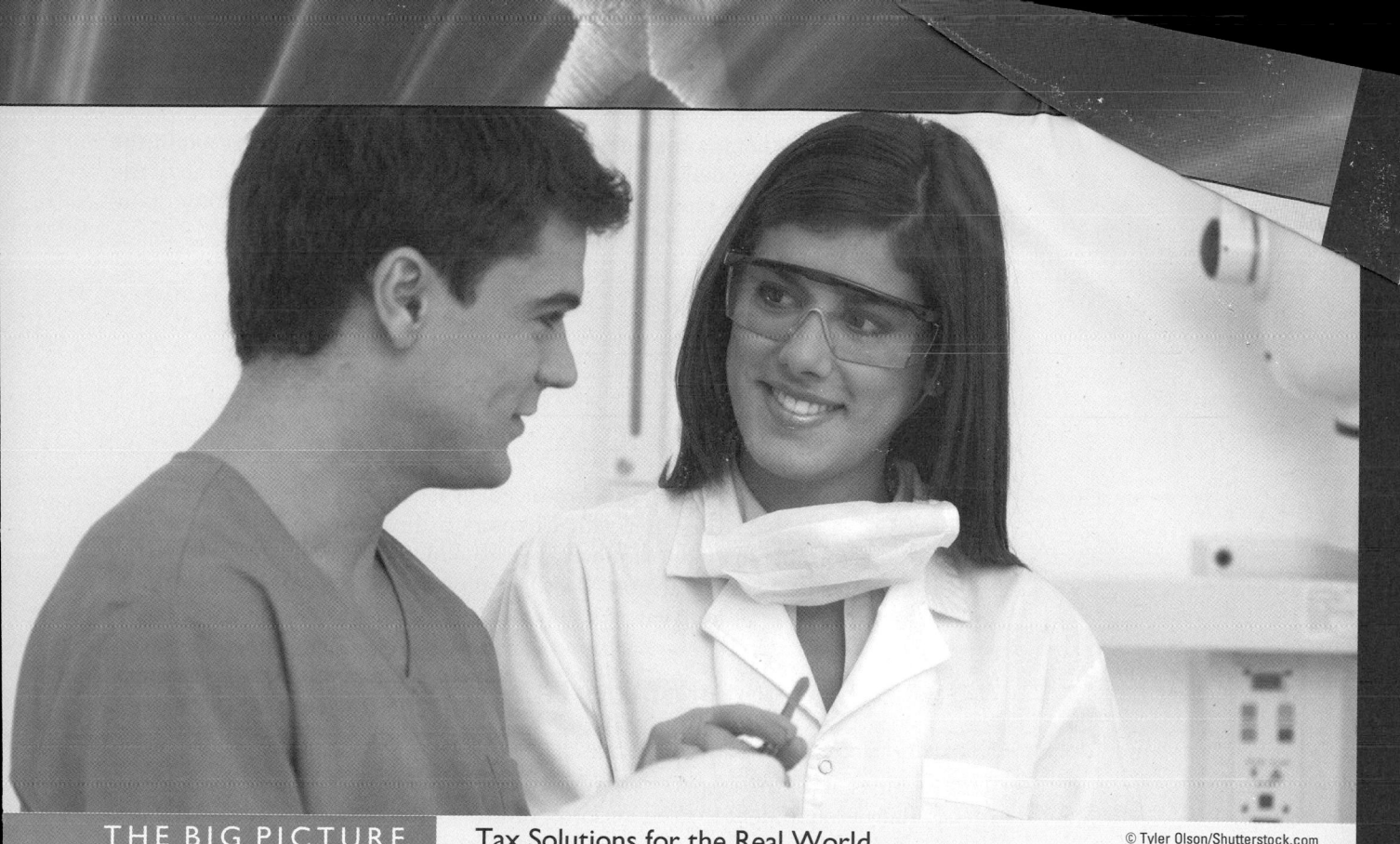

THE BIG PICTURE　　Tax Solutions for the Real World

JUST WHAT IS INCLUDED IN GROSS INCOME?

At the beginning of the year, Dr. Cliff Payne, age 27, opens his new dental practice as a qualified personal service corporation. For his new business, he selects a December 31 year-end and the accrual method of accounting. During the year, Dr. Payne billed patients and insurance companies for $385,000 of dental services. At the end of the year, $52,000 of this amount has not been collected. Dr. Payne earns $500 interest on a money market account held at the local bank and another $500 interest on an investment in bonds issued by the Whitehall School District.

Dr. Payne's salary from his corporation is $10,000 per month. However, he did not cash his December payroll check until January. To help provide funds to invest in the new business, Dr. Payne's parents loaned him $150,000 and did not charge him any interest. He also owns stock that has increased in value from $7,000 at the beginning of the year to more than $25,000 at the end of the year.

Although Dr. Payne took several accounting classes in college, he would like your help in calculating the correct amounts of his gross income and the gross income of the corporation.

Read the chapter and formulate your response.

The first step in computing an income tax liability is the determination of the amount of income that is subject to tax. In completing that step, some of the following questions must be answered. We will address these and other concerns in this chapter.

- *What:* What is income?
- *When:* In which tax period is the income recognized?
- *Who:* Who is taxed on the income?

4-1 THE TAX FORMULA

The basic income tax formula was introduced in Chapter 1 and summarized in Figure 1.1. This chapter, together with Chapters 5 through 8, examines the elements of this formula in detail. However, before embarking on a detailed study of the income tax, a brief introduction of each component of the tax formula, which follows, is provided as an overview.

4-1a Components of the Tax Formula

Income (Broadly Conceived)

This includes all of the taxpayer's income, both taxable and nontaxable. Although it essentially is equivalent to gross receipts, it does not include a return of capital or borrowed funds.

Exclusions

For various reasons, Congress has chosen to exclude certain types of income from the income tax base. The principal income exclusions that apply to all entities (e.g., life insurance proceeds received by reason of death of the insured and state and local bond interest) are discussed later in this chapter, while exclusions that are unique to individuals are addressed in Chapters 9 through 11.

Gross Income

Section 61 of the Internal Revenue Code provides the following definition of gross income.

> Except as otherwise provided in this subtitle, gross income means all income from whatever source derived.

This language is based on the Sixteenth Amendment to the Constitution. The "except as otherwise provided" phrase refers to exclusions.

Supreme Court decisions have made it clear that *all* sources of income are subject to tax unless Congress specifically excludes the type of income received.

> The starting point in all cases dealing with the question of the scope of what is included in "gross income" begins with the basic premise that the purpose of Congress was to use the full measure of its taxing power.[1]

---

[1] *James v. U.S.,* 61-1 USTC ¶9449, 7 AFTR 2d 1361, 81 S.Ct. 1052 (USSC, 1961).

From "All Sources" Is a Broad Definition

When § 61 refers to "income from whatever source derived," the taxing authorities are reaching far beyond the borders of the United States. Although one interpretation of "source" in this context is type of income (e.g., wages, interest, etc.), a broader interpretation revolves around the place where the income is generated. In this context, citizens and residents of the United States are subject to taxation on income earned from sources both inside and outside the country. This "worldwide income" tax base can cause potential double taxation problems, with other countries also taxing income earned within their borders, but mechanisms such as the foreign tax credit can alleviate these tax burdens.

Recently, some U.S. corporations have relocated to other countries to avoid the higher U.S. tax rates on income earned abroad.

Global Tax Issues

© iStockphoto.com/Andrey Prokhorov

While it is clear that income is to be broadly construed, the statutory law fails to provide a satisfactory definition of the term and lists only a small set of items that are specifically included in income, including:

- Compensation for services.
- Business income.
- Gains from sales and other disposition of property.
- Interest.
- Dividends.
- Rents and royalties.
- Certain income arising from discharge of indebtedness.
- Income from partnerships.

Deductions

Generally, all ordinary and necessary trade or business expenses are deductible by taxpaying entities. Such expenses include the cost of goods sold, salaries, wages, operating expenses (such as rent and utilities), research and development expenditures, interest, taxes, depreciation, amortization, and depletion.

As noted in Chapter 1, individuals can use two categories of deductions—deductions *for* AGI and deductions *from* AGI. In addition, individuals are unique among taxpaying entities in that they are permitted to deduct a variety of personal expenses (i.e., expenses unrelated to business or investment), they are allowed a standard deduction if this amount exceeds the deductible personal expenses, and they can claim a deduction for personal and dependency exemptions.

Determining the Tax

Taxable income is determined by subtracting deductions (after any applicable limitations) from gross income. The tax rates (located on the inside front cover of this text) then are applied to determine the tax. Finally, tax prepayments (such as Federal income tax withholding on salaries and estimated tax payments) and a wide variety of credits are subtracted from the tax to determine the amount due to the Federal government or the refund due to the taxpayer.

4-2 GROSS INCOME—WHAT IS IT?

4-2a Economic and Accounting Concepts of Income

As noted above, Congress failed to provide in the Code a clear definition of income. Instead, it was left to the judicial and administrative branches of government to determine the meaning of the term. As the income tax law developed, two

LO.1

Explain the concepts of gross income and realization and distinguish between the economic, accounting, and tax concepts of gross income.

FINANCIAL DISCLOSURE INSIGHTS What Does "Income" Mean to You?

Accountants use a definition of income that relies on the realization principle.[2] **Accounting income** is not recognized until it is realized. For realization to occur:

- An exchange of goods or services must take place between the entity and some independent, external party, and
- The goods or services received by the entity must be capable of being objectively valued.[3]

Thus, an increase in the fair market value of an asset before its sale or other disposition is not sufficient to trigger the recognition of accounting income. Similarly, the imputed savings that arise when an entity creates assets for its own use (e.g., feed grown by a farmer for his or her livestock) do not constitute accounting income because no exchange has occurred.

Business taxpayers often reconcile their annual income computations for financial accounting and tax law purposes. Taxpayers required to prepare audited financial statements must explain in the footnotes to the statements (1) the most important accounting principles used in computing book income and (2) the most important tax elections and other consequences of the tax law on earnings per share.

competing models of income were considered by these agencies: economic income and accounting income.

The term **income** is used in the Code but is defined very broadly. Early in the history of our tax laws, the courts were required to interpret "the commonly understood meaning of the term which must have been in the minds of the people when they adopted the Sixteenth Amendment."[4]

Economists measure income (**economic income**) by determining the change (increase or decrease) in the fair market value of the entity's assets (net of liabilities) from the beginning to the end of the year. This focus on change in *net worth* as a measure of income (or loss) requires no disposition of assets. For *individual* taxpayers, one then adds the value of the year's personal consumption of goods and services (e.g., food, the rental value of owner-occupied housing, etc.).[5]

Example 1

Helen's economic income is calculated by comparing her net worth at the end of the year (December 31) with her net worth at the beginning of the year (January 1) and adding her personal consumption.

Fair market value of Helen's assets on December 31	$220,000	
Less liabilities on December 31	(40,000)	
Net worth on December 31		$ 180,000
Fair market value of Helen's assets on January 1	$200,000	
Less liabilities on January 1	(80,000)	
Net worth on January 1		(120,000)
Increase in net worth		$ 60,000
Consumption		
Food, clothing, and other personal expenditures	$ 25,000	
Imputed rental value of the home Helen owns and occupies	12,000	
Total consumption		37,000
Economic income		$ 97,000

The tax law relies to some extent on net worth as a measure of income.[6] Potentially, anything that increases net worth is income, and anything that decreases net worth is deductible (if permitted by statute). Thus, *windfall income* such as buried

[2]See the American Accounting Association Committee Report on the "Realization Concept," *The Accounting Review* (April 1965): 312–322.

[3]Valuation is carried out in the local currency of the reporting entity.

[4]*Merchants Loan and Trust Co. v. Smietanka*, 1 USTC ¶42, 3 AFTR 3102, 41 S.Ct. 386 (USSC, 1921).

[5]See Henry C. Simons, *Personal Income Taxation* (Chicago: University of Chicago Press, 1933), Chapters 2–3.

[6]*Comm. v. Glenshaw Glass Co.*, 55–1 USTC ¶9308, 47 AFTR 162, 348 U.S. 426 (USSC, 1955).

treasure found in one's backyard is taxable, under the theory that net worth has increased.[7] Likewise, a lender does *not* recognize gross income on receipt of loan principal repayments. The lender's investment simply changes from a loan receivable to cash, so net worth does not change.

Because the strict application of a tax based on economic income would require taxpayers to determine the value of their assets annually, compliance would be burdensome. Controversies between taxpayers and the IRS inevitably would arise under an economic approach to income determination because of the subjective nature of valuation in many circumstances. In addition, using market values to determine income for tax purposes could result in liquidity problems. That is, a taxpayer's assets could increase in value but not be easily converted into the cash needed to pay the resulting tax (e.g., increases in the value of commercial real estate).[8] Thus, the IRS, Congress, and the courts have rejected broad application of the economic income concept as impractical.

THE BIG PICTURE

Example 2

Return to the facts of *The Big Picture* on p. 4-1. Dr. Payne's portfolio has increased in value by more than 250% during the tax year, and that additional value constitutes economic income to him. But the Federal income tax law does not include the value increase in Dr. Payne's gross income, even though the taxpayer could convert some of those gains to cash through, say, a margin loan from his broker.

4-2b Comparison of the Accounting and Tax Concepts of Income

Although income tax rules frequently parallel financial accounting measurement concepts, differences do exist. Of major significance, for example, is the fact that unearned (prepaid) income received by an accrual basis taxpayer often is taxed in the year of receipt. For financial accounting purposes, such prepayments are not treated as income until earned. Because of this and other differences, many corporations report financial accounting income that is substantially different from the amounts reported for tax purposes.

The Supreme Court provided an explanation for some of the variations between accounting and taxable income in a decision involving inventory and bad debt adjustments.

> The primary goal of financial accounting is to provide useful information to management, shareholders, creditors, and others properly interested; the major responsibility of the accountant is to protect these parties from being misled. The primary goal of the income tax system, in contrast, is the equitable collection of revenue.... Consistently with its goals and responsibilities, financial accounting has as its foundation the principle of conservatism, with its corollary that "possible errors in measurement [should] be in the direction of understatement rather than overstatement of net income and net assets." In view of the Treasury's markedly different goals and responsibilities, understatement of income is not destined to be its guiding light....
>
> Financial accounting, in short, is hospitable to estimates, probabilities, and reasonable certainties; the tax law, with its mandate to preserve the revenue, can give no quarter to uncertainty.[9]

---

[7]*Cesarini v. U.S.*, 69–1 USTC ¶9270, 23 AFTR 2d 69–997, 296 F.Supp. 3 (D.Ct. N.Oh., 1969), *aff'd* 70–2 USTC ¶9509, 26 AFTR 2d 70–5107, 428 F.2d 812 (CA–6, 1970); Rev.Rul. 61, 1953–1 C.B. 17.

[8]In Chapter 1, this was identified as a justification of the wherewithal to pay concept.

[9]*Thor Power Tool Co. v. Comm.*, 79–1 USTC ¶9139, 43 AFTR 2d 79–362, 99 S.Ct. 773 (USSC, 1979).

4-2c Form of Receipt

Gross income is not limited to cash received. "It includes income realized in any form, whether in money, property, or services. Income may be realized [and recognized], therefore, in the form of services, meals, accommodations, stock or other property, as well as in cash."[10]

Example 3	Ostrich Corporation allows Cameron, an employee, to use a company car for his vacation. Cameron realizes income equal to the rental value of the car for the time and mileage.

Example 4	Donna is a CPA specializing in individual tax return preparation. Her neighbor, Jill, is a dentist. Each year, Donna prepares Jill's tax return in exchange for two dental checkups. Jill and Donna both have gross income equal to the fair market value of the services they provide.

4-3 YEAR OF INCLUSION

4-3a Taxable Year

The annual accounting period or **taxable year** is a basic component of our tax system. Generally, an entity must use the *calendar year* to report its income. However, a *fiscal year* (a period of 12 months ending on the last day of any month other than December) can be elected if the taxpayer maintains adequate books and records.[11] This fiscal year option generally is not available to partnerships, S corporations, and personal service corporations.

Determining the tax year in which the income is recognized is important in determining the tax consequences of the income.

- With a progressive tax rate system, a taxpayer's marginal tax rate can change from year to year.
- Congress may change the tax rates.
- The relevant rates may change because of a change in the entity's status (e.g., a proprietorship may incorporate).
- Several provisions in the Code require computations using the taxpayer's income for the year (e.g., the charitable contribution deduction).
- The taxpayer wants to reduce the present value of any tax that is owed. In this regard, income recognition in a later year is preferred; the longer payment of the tax can be postponed, the lower the present value of the tax.

4-3b Accounting Methods

LO.2

State and explain when the cash, accrual, and hybrid methods of accounting are used and how they are applied.

The year in which an item of income is subject to tax often depends upon the **accounting method** the taxpayer employs. The three primary methods of accounting are (1) the cash receipts and disbursements method, (2) the accrual method, and (3) the hybrid method. Most individuals use the cash receipts and disbursements method of accounting, while most larger businesses use the accrual method. Because the Regulations require the accrual method for determining purchases and sales when inventory is an income-producing factor,[12] some businesses employ a hybrid method that is a combination of the cash and accrual methods.

In addition to these overall accounting methods, a taxpayer may choose to spread the gain from an installment sale of property over the collection period by using the *installment method* of income recognition. Contractors may either spread profits from contracts over the period in which the work is done (the *percentage of*

---

[10]Reg. § 1.61–1(a).

[11]§ 441; Reg. § 1.441–1(c)(2).

[12]Reg. § 1.446–1(c)(2)(i).

completion method) or defer all profit until the year in which the project is completed (the *completed contract method*) in limited circumstances.[13]

The IRS can prescribe the accounting method to be used by the taxpayer. The IRS holds broad powers to determine whether an accounting method *clearly reflects income*.

> If no method of accounting has been regularly used by the taxpayer, or if the method used does not clearly reflect income, the computation of taxable income shall be made under such method as, in the opinion of the Secretary ... does clearly reflect income.[14]

Cash Receipts Method

Under the cash receipts method, property or services received are included in the taxpayer's gross income in the year of actual or constructive receipt by the taxpayer or agent, regardless of whether the income was earned in that year.[15] The income received need not be reduced to cash in the same year. All that is necessary for income recognition is that property or services received be measurable by a fair market value.[16] Thus, a cash basis taxpayer that receives a note in payment for services has income in the year of receipt equal to the fair market value of the note. However, a creditor's mere promise to pay (e.g., an account receivable), with no supporting note, usually is not considered to have a fair market value.[17] Thus, the cash basis taxpayer defers income recognition until the account receivable is collected.

Finch & Thrush, a CPA firm, uses the cash receipts method of accounting. In 2014, the firm performs an audit for Orange Corporation and bills the client for $5,000, which is collected in 2015. In 2014, the firm also performs an audit for Blue Corporation. Because of Blue's precarious financial position, Finch & Thrush requires Blue to issue an $8,000 secured negotiable note in payment of the fee. The note has a fair market value of $6,000. The firm collects $8,000 on the note in 2015. Finch & Thrush reports the following gross income for the two years.

Example 5

	2014	2015
Fair market value of note received from Blue	$6,000	
Cash received		
From Orange on account receivable		$ 5,000
From Blue on note receivable		8,000
Less: Recovery of capital	–0–	(6,000)
Total gross income	$6,000	$ 7,000

---

[13]§§ 453 and 460.

[14]§ 446(b).

[15]*Julia A. Strauss*, 2 B.T.A. 598 (1925). The doctrine of *constructive receipt* holds that if income is unqualifiedly available although not physically in the taxpayer's possession, it is subject to the income tax. An example is accrued interest on a savings account. Under the doctrine of constructive receipt, the interest is taxed to a depositor in the year available, rather than the year actually withdrawn. The fact that the depositor uses the cash basis of accounting for tax purposes is irrelevant. Reg. § 1.451–2.

[16]Reg. §§ 1.446–1(a)(3) and (c)(1)(i).

[17]*Bedell v. Comm.*, 1 USTC ¶359, 7 AFTR 8469, 30 F.2d 622 (CA–2, 1929).

Generally, a cash basis taxpayer recognizes gross income when a check is received in payment for goods or services rendered in a business setting. This is true even if the taxpayer receives the check after banking hours. But if the person paying with the check requests that the check not be cashed until a subsequent date, the cash basis income is deferred until the date the check can be cashed.[18]

Certain taxpayers are not permitted to use the cash method of accounting regardless of whether inventories are material. Specifically, the accrual basis must be used to report the income earned by (1) corporations (other than S corporations), (2) partnerships with a corporate partner (other than an S corporation), and (3) tax shelters.[19] A number of other businesses still can use the cash method.

- A farming business.
- A qualified personal service corporation (e.g., a corporation performing services in health, law, engineering, architecture, accounting, actuarial science, performing arts, or consulting).
- Any entity that is not a tax shelter whose average annual gross receipts for the most recent three-year period are $5 million or less.[20]

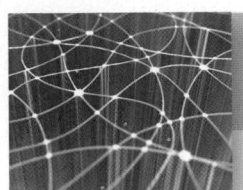

BRIDGE DISCIPLINE Bridge to Economics and Finance

Nontaxable Economic Benefits

Home ownership is the prime example of economic income from capital that is not subject to tax. If the taxpayer uses his or her capital to purchase investments but pays rent on a personal residence, the taxpayer pays tax on the income from the investments but cannot deduct the rent payment.

However, if the taxpayer purchases a personal residence instead of the investments, he or she removes the investment income from the tax return but incurs no other form of gross income. A homeowner "pays rent to himself," but such rent is not subject to income tax. Thus, the homeowner has substituted nontaxable for taxable income.

Tax Deferral

Because deferred taxes are tantamount to interest-free loans from the government, the deferral of taxes is a worthy goal of the tax planner. However, the tax planner also must consider the tax rates for the years the income is shifted from and to. For example, a one-year deferral of income from a year in which the taxpayer's tax rate was 28 percent to a year in which the tax rate will be 35 percent would not be advisable if the taxpayer expects to

earn less than a 7 percent after-tax return on the deferred tax dollars.

The taxpayer often can defer the recognition of income from appreciated property by postponing the event triggering realization (e.g., the final closing on a sale or exchange of property). If the taxpayer needs cash, obtaining a loan by using the appreciated property as collateral may be the least costly alternative. When the taxpayer anticipates reinvesting the proceeds, a sale may be inadvisable.

Example 6

Ira owns 100 shares of Pigeon Company common stock with a cost of $20,000 and a fair market value of $50,000. Although the stock's value has increased substantially in the past three years, Ira thinks the growth cycle for the stock is over. If he sells the Pigeon stock, Ira will invest the proceeds from the sale in other common stock. Assuming that Ira's marginal tax rate on the sale is 20%, he keeps only $44,000 [$50,000 − .20($50,000 − $20,000)] to reinvest. The alternative investment must substantially outperform Pigeon in the future for the sale to be beneficial. ■

---

[18]*Charles F. Kahler*, 18 T.C. 31 (1952); *Bright v. U.S.*, 91–1 USTC ¶50,142, 67 AFTR 2d 91–673, 926 F.2d 383 (CA–5, 1991).

[19]§ 448(a).

[20]§ 448(b)(3).

Tax Planning Strategies — CASH RECEIPTS METHOD

FRAMEWORK FOCUS: INCOME

Strategy: Postpone Recognition of Income to Achieve Tax Deferral.

FRAMEWORK FOCUS: TAX RATE

Strategy: Shift Net Income from High-Bracket Years to Low-Bracket Years.

The timing of income from services often can be controlled through the cash method of accounting. The usual lag between billings and collections (e.g., December's billings collected in January) can result in a deferral of some income until the last year of operations. For example, before rendering services, a corporate officer approaching retirement may contract with the corporation to defer a portion of his or her compensation to the lower tax bracket retirement years.

Accrual Method

Under the **accrual method**, an item generally is included in gross income for the year in which it is earned, regardless of when the income is collected. The income is earned when (1) all the events have occurred that fix the right to receive the income and (2) the amount to be received can be determined with reasonable accuracy.[21]

Generally, the taxpayer's rights to the income accrue when title to property passes to the buyer or the services are performed for the customer or client.[22] If the rights to the income have accrued but are subject to a potential refund claim (e.g., under a product warranty), the income is reported in the year of sale and a deduction is allowed in subsequent years when actual claims accrue.[23]

Where the taxpayer's rights to the income are being contested (e.g., when a contractor fails to meet specifications), gross income is recognized only when payment has been received.[24] If the payment is received before the dispute is settled, however, the court-made **claim of right doctrine** requires the taxpayer to recognize the income in the year of receipt.[25]

If Finch & Thrush in Example 5 uses the accrual basis of accounting, it recognizes $13,000 ($8,000 + $5,000) income in 2014, the year its rights to the income accrue.

Example 7

Tangerine Construction, Inc., completes construction of a building in 2014 and presents a bill to the customer. The customer refuses to pay the bill and claims that Tangerine has not met specifications. A settlement with the customer is not reached until 2015. No income accrues to Tangerine until 2015. Alternatively, if the customer pays for the work and then files suit for damages, Tangerine cannot defer the income recognition; it is taxable in 2014.

Hybrid Method

The accrual method is used to determine sales and cost of goods sold. To simplify record keeping, some taxpayers account for inventory using the accrual method and use the cash method for all other income and expense items. This approach, called the **hybrid method**, is used primarily by small businesses when inventory is a material income-producing factor.

---

[21] Reg. § 1.451–1(a).

[22] *Lucas v. North Texas Lumber Co.*, 2 USTC ¶484, 8 AFTR 10276, 50 S.Ct. 184 (USSC, 1930).

[23] *Brown v. Helvering*, 4 USTC ¶1222, 13 AFTR 851, 54 S.Ct. 356 (USSC, 1933).

[24] *Burnet v. Sanford and Brooks*, 2 USTC ¶636, 9 AFTR 603, 51 S.Ct. 150 (USSC, 1931).

[25] *North American Oil Consolidated Co. v. Burnet*, 3 USTC ¶943, 11 AFTR 16, 52 S.Ct. 613 (USSC, 1932).

4-3c Special Rules for Cash Basis Taxpayers

Constructive Receipt

Income that has not actually been received by the taxpayer is taxed as though it had been received—the income is constructively received—under the following conditions.

- The amount is made readily available to the taxpayer.
- The taxpayer's actual receipt is not subject to substantial limitations or restrictions.[26]

The rationale for the **constructive receipt** doctrine is that if the income is available, the taxpayer should not be allowed unilaterally to postpone income recognition. For instance, a taxpayer is not permitted to defer income for December services by refusing to accept payment until January.

| Example 8 | Rob, a physician, conducts his medical practice as a sole proprietorship. Rob is also a member of a barter club. In 2014, Rob provided medical care for other club members and earned 3,000 points. Each point entitles him to $1 in goods and services sold by other members of the club; the points can be used at any time. In 2015, Rob exchanged his points for a new high-definition TV. Rob recognizes $3,000 gross income in 2014, when the 3,000 points were credited to his account.[27] |

| Example 9 | On December 31, an employer issued a bonus check to an employee but asked her to hold it for a few days until the company could make deposits to cover the check. The income was not constructively received on December 31 because the issuer did not have sufficient funds in its account to pay the debt.[28] |

| Example 10 | Mauve, Inc., an S corporation, owned interest coupons that matured on December 31. The coupons can be converted to cash at any bank at maturity. Thus, the income was constructively received on December 31, even though Mauve failed to cash in the coupons until the following year.[29] |

| Example 11 | Flamingo Company mails dividend checks on December 31. The checks will not be received by the shareholders until January. The shareholders do not realize gross income until January.[30] |

The constructive receipt doctrine does not reach income the taxpayer is not yet entitled to receive, even though the taxpayer could have contracted to receive the income at an earlier date.

| Example 12 | Murphy offers to pay Peach Corporation (a cash basis taxpayer) $100,000 for land in December 2014. Peach Corporation refuses, but offers to sell the land to Murphy on January 1, 2015, when the corporation will be in a lower tax bracket. If Murphy accepts Peach's offer, the gain is taxed to Peach in 2015, when the sale is completed.[31] |

Digging Deeper | In-depth coverage can be found on this book's companion website: **www.cengagebrain.com**

---

[26]Reg. § 1.451–2(a).
[27]Rev.Rul. 80–52, 1980–1 C.B. 100.
[28]*L. M. Fischer*, 14 T.C. 792 (1950).
[29]Reg. § 1.451–2(b).

[30]Reg. § 1.451–2(b).
[31]*Cowden v. Comm.*, 61–1 USTC ¶9382, 7 AFTR 2d 1160, 289 F.2d 20 (CA–5, 1961).

TAX IN THE NEWS Congress Rescues Lottery Winners from Constructive Receipt Problems

Under the general rules of constructive receipt, a lottery winner who elected to receive the winnings in installments could face horrendous tax problems. If the winner had the right to receive the entire amount but elected to be paid in installments, tax could be due on the present value of the amounts to be received in the future as well as the amount received currently. Frequently, the winner made the election without being aware of the tax consequences.

To protect poorly advised, or unadvised, lottery winners, Congress changed the tax law so that the constructive receipt doctrine does not apply to "qualified prizes," a term crafted specifically to address the lottery and prize-winner's situation. Thus, lottery winnings can be received in installments and included in gross income as the installments are received.

Original Issue Discount

Lenders frequently make loans that require a payment at maturity of more than the amount of the original loan. The difference between the amount due at maturity and the amount of the original loan is actually interest but is referred to as **original issue discount**. In these circumstances, the Code requires the original issue discount to be reported when it is earned, regardless of the taxpayer's accounting method.[32] The *interest earned* is calculated by the effective interest rate method.

Example 13

On January 1, 2014, Blue and White, a cash basis partnership, pays $92,456 for a 24-month certificate of deposit. The certificate is priced to yield 4% (the effective interest rate) with interest compounded annually. No interest is paid until maturity, when Blue and White receives $100,000.

The partnership's gross income from the certificate is $7,544 ($100,000 − $92,456). Blue and White calculates income earned each year as follows.

2014 (.04 × $92,456) =	$3,698
2015 [.04($92,456 + $3,698)] =	3,846
	$7,544

The original issue discount rules do not apply to U.S. savings bonds or to obligations with a maturity date of one year or less from the date of issue.[33]

Amounts Received under an Obligation to Repay

The receipt of funds with an obligation to repay that amount in the future is the essence of borrowing. The taxpayer's assets and liabilities increase by the same amount, so no income is realized when the borrowed funds are received.

Example 14

A landlord receives a damage deposit from a tenant. The landlord does not recognize income until the deposit is forfeited because the landlord has an obligation to repay the deposit if no damage occurs.[34] However, if the deposit is in fact a prepayment of rent, it is taxed in the year of receipt.

---

[32]§§ 1272(a)(3) and 1273(a).
[33]§ 1272(a)(2).

[34]*John Mantell*, 17 T.C. 1143 (1952).

4-3d Special Rules for Accrual Basis Taxpayers

Prepaid Income

For financial reporting purposes, advance payments received from customers are reflected as prepaid income and as a liability of the seller. For tax purposes, however, the prepaid income often is taxed in the year of receipt.

Example 15

In December 2014, Jared's sole proprietorship pays its January 2015 rent of $1,000. Jared's calendar-year, accrual basis landlord includes the $1,000 in 2014 gross income for tax purposes, although $1,000 unearned rent income is reported as a liability on the landlord's financial accounting balance sheet for December 31, 2014.

Deferral of Advance Payments for Goods

Generally, an accrual basis taxpayer can elect to defer recognition of income from advance payments for goods if the method of accounting for the sale is the same for tax and financial reporting purposes.[35]

Example 16

Brown Company ships goods only after payment for the goods has been received. In December 2014, Brown receives $10,000 for goods that are not shipped until January 2015. Brown can elect to report the income in 2015 for tax purposes, assuming that the company reports the income in 2015 for financial reporting purposes.

Deferral of Advance Payments for Services

When payments are received for services that will be performed in a later tax year, an accrual basis taxpayer can defer for one year the recognition of income for the services that will be performed later.[36]

Advance payments for prepaid rent or prepaid interest, however, always are taxed in the year of receipt.

Example 17

Yellow Corporation, an accrual basis calendar-year taxpayer, sells its computer consulting services under 12-month, 24-month, and 36-month contracts. The corporation provides services to each customer every month. On May 1, 2014, Yellow sold the following contracts.

Length of Contract	Total Proceeds
12 months	$3,000
24 months	4,800
36 months	7,200

Yellow may defer until 2015 all of the income that will be earned after 2014.

Length of Contract	Income Recorded in 2014	Income Recorded in 2015
12 months	$2,000 ($3,000 × 8/12)	$1,000 ($3,000 × 4/12)
24 months	1,600 ($4,800 × 8/24)	3,200 ($4,800 × 16/24)
36 months	1,600 ($7,200 × 8/36)	5,600 ($7,200 × 28/36)

[35]Reg. § 1.451–5(b). See Reg. § 1.451–5(c) for exceptions to this deferral opportunity.

[36]Rev.Proc. 2004–34, 2004–1 C.B. 991.

Tax Planning Strategies PREPAID INCOME

FRAMEWORK FOCUS: INCOME

Strategy: Postpone Recognition of Income to Achieve Tax Deferral.

The accrual basis taxpayer who receives advance payments from customers should structure the transactions using the rules discussed previously to avoid a payment of tax on income before the time the income is actually earned.

In addition, both cash and accrual basis taxpayers sometimes can defer income by stipulating that the payments are deposits rather than prepaid income. For example, a tax-savvy landlord might consider requiring an equivalent damage deposit rather than prepayment of the last month's rent.

4-4 INCOME SOURCES

4-4a Personal Services

It is a well-established principle of taxation that income from personal services must be included in the gross income of the person who performs the services. This principle was first established in a Supreme Court decision, *Lucas v. Earl.*[37] Mr. Earl entered into a binding agreement with his wife under which Mrs. Earl was to receive one-half of Mr. Earl's salary. Justice Holmes used the celebrated fruit and tree metaphor to explain that the fruit (income) must be attributed to the tree from which it came (Mr. Earl's services). A mere assignment of income to another party does not shift the liability for the tax.

LO.3

Identify who should pay the tax on an item of income.

Services of an Employee

Services performed by an employee for the employer's customers are considered performed by the employer. Thus, the employer is taxed on the income from the services provided to the customer, and the employee is taxed on any compensation received from the employer.[38]

THE BIG PICTURE

Example 18

Return to the facts of *The Big Picture* on p. 4-1. Dr. Payne has entered into an employment contract with his corporation and receives a salary. All patients contract to receive their dental services from the corporation, and those services are provided through the corporation's employee, Dr. Payne.

Thus, the corporation earned the income from patients' services and must include the patients' fees in its gross income. Dr. Payne includes his salary in his own gross income. The corporation claims a deduction for the reasonable salary paid to Dr. Payne.

In-depth coverage can be found on this book's companion website: **www.cengagebrain.com** **2** Digging Deeper

---

[37] 2 USTC ¶496, 8 AFTR 10287, 50 S.Ct. 241 (USSC, 1930).

[38] *Sargent v. Comm.*, 91–1 USTC ¶50,168, 67 AFTR 2d 91–718, 929 F.2d 1252 (CA–8, 1991).

TAX IN THE NEWS   The General Welfare Exception

The broad concept of gross income and the government's role in promoting the general welfare sometimes are in conflict. For example, if the government makes payments to persons based on their need, it does not make sense for the government to extract a tax from those same individuals and thus reduce the relief it intended to confer.

Therefore, the courts and the IRS have created the "general welfare exception," which excludes from gross income certain types of governmental payments that otherwise might be taxable under the broad gross income concept. To qualify for this exception, the payments must be:

- Made from a governmental welfare fund.
- Based on need.
- Not made as a payment for services.

The exception has been applied to a wide range of government payments,[39] including Federal grants to rebuild homes destroyed by Superstorm Sandy, and to make mortgage payments for persons suffering severe hardship. It also applies to grants by state governments to motivate the purchase of appliances with an Energy Star rating.

4-4b Income from Property

Income earned from property (e.g., interest, dividends, rent) is included in the gross income of the owner of the property. If a shareholder clips interest coupons from bonds shortly before the interest payment date and transfers the coupons to his or her solely owned corporation, the interest still is taxed to the shareholder.

Often income-producing property is transferred after income from the property has accrued but before the income is recognized under the transferor's method of accounting. The IRS and the courts have developed rules to allocate the income between the transferor and the transferee. These allocation rules are addressed below. Other allocation rules address income in community property states.

Digging Deeper 3   In-depth coverage can be found on this book's companion website: **www.cengagebrain.com**

Interest

According to the tax law, interest accrues daily. Therefore, the interest for the period that includes the date of an asset transfer is allocated between the transferor and the transferee based on the number of days during the period that each owned the property.

Example 19

Floyd, a cash basis taxpayer, gives his son, Seth, corporate bonds with a face amount of $12,000 and a 5% stated annual interest rate. The interest is payable on the last day of each quarter. Floyd makes the gift to Seth on February 28. Floyd recognizes $100 interest income at the time of the gift ($12,000 × 5% × 3/12 interest for the quarter × 2/3 months in the quarter earned before the gift).

For the transferor, the timing of the recognition of gross income from the property depends upon the pertinent accounting method and the manner in which the property was transferred. In the case of a gift of income-producing property, the donor's share of the accrued income is recognized at the time it would have been recognized had the donor continued to own the property.[40] If the transfer is a sale, however, the transferor recognizes the accrued income at the time of the sale, because the accrued amount is included in the sales proceeds.

---

[39]For example, see Rev.Rul. 2009–19, I.R.B. No. 28, 111; Notice 2011–14, 2011–11, I.R.B. 544.

[40]Rev.Rul. 72–312, 1972–1 C.B. 22.

TAX FACT   How Much and What Type of Income?

Of the 145 million individual income tax returns filed for the 2011 tax year, 82 percent included wage or salary income, and about 40 percent included some amount of interest income. But except for these two categories, no other type of income was found in even a quarter of the returns filed. Sales of business assets were found on fewer than one-half percent of the returns, and about 6 percent of the returns included flow-through income or loss from partnerships and S corporations. Capital gains showed up on about a quarter of the returns, but only when distributions from mutual fund investments were included.

© iStockphoto.com/Pali Rao

Example 20

Mia purchased a corporate bond at its face amount on January 1 for $10,000. The bond paid 5% interest each December 31. On March 31, Mia sold the bond for $10,600. Mia recognizes $125 interest income, accrued as of the date of the sale (5% × $10,000 × 3/12 months before the sale). She also recognizes a $475 capital gain from the sale of the bond, computed as follows.

Amount received from sale	$ 10,600
Accrued interest income already recognized	(125)
Selling price of bond, less interest	$ 10,475
Less cost of the bond	(10,000)
Capital gain recognized on sale	$ 475

Dividends

A corporation is taxed on its earnings, and the shareholders are taxed on the dividends paid to them from the corporation's after-tax earnings.

Partial relief from the double taxation of dividends has been provided in that *qualified dividends* are taxed at the same marginal rate that is applicable to a net capital gain.[41] Distributions that are not qualified dividends are taxed at the rates that apply to ordinary income.

Tax Rate That Applies to the Taxpayer's Ordinary Income	Tax Rate That Applies to Dividend Income
0, 10, or 15%	0%
25, 28, 33, or 35%	15%
39.6%	20%

A holding period requirement must be satisfied for the lower tax rates to apply: the stock that paid the dividend must have been held for more than 60 days during the 121-day period beginning 60 days before the ex-dividend date.[42] The purpose of this requirement is to prevent the taxpayer from buying the stock shortly before the dividend is paid, receiving the dividend, and then selling the stock at a short-term capital loss after the stock goes ex-dividend. A stock's price often declines after the stock goes ex-dividend.

Because the beneficial tax rate is intended to mitigate double taxation, only certain dividends are eligible for the beneficial treatment. Excluded are certain dividends from non-U.S. corporations, dividends from tax-exempt entities, and dividends that do not satisfy the holding period requirement.

[41]§ 1(h)(11). Qualified dividends are not treated as capital gains in the gains and losses netting process; thus, they are *not* reduced by capital losses. Qualified dividend income merely is taxed at the rates that would apply to the taxpayer if he or she had an excess of net long-term capital gain over net short-term capital loss.

[42]The ex-dividend date is the date before the record date on which the corporation finalizes the list of shareholders who will receive the dividends.

© iStockphoto.com/Andrey Prokhorov

Global Tax Issues

Which Foreign Dividends Get the Discounted Rate?

A dividend from a non-U.S. corporation is eligible for qualified dividend status only if one of the following requirements is met: (1) the foreign corporation's stock is traded on an established U.S. securities market or (2) the foreign corporation is eligible for the benefits of a comprehensive income tax treaty or information-sharing agreement between its country of incorporation and the United States.[43]

Example 21

Green Corporation pays a dividend of $1.50 on each share of its common stock. Madison and Daniel, two unrelated shareholders, each own 1,000 shares of the stock. Consequently, each receives a dividend of $1,500 (1,000 shares × $1.50). Assume that Daniel satisfies the 60/120-day holding period rule, but Madison does not.

The $1,500 that Daniel receives is subject to the lower rates on qualified dividends. The $1,500 that Madison receives, however, is not. Because Madison did not comply with the holding period rule, her dividend is not a *qualified dividend* and is taxed at ordinary income rates.

Example 22

Assume that both Madison and Daniel in Example 21 are in the 35% Federal income tax bracket. Consequently, Madison pays a tax of $525 (35% × $1,500) on her dividend, while Daniel pays a tax of $225 (15% × $1,500) on his. The $300 saving that Daniel enjoys underscores the advantages of receiving a qualified dividend.

Unlike interest, dividends do not accrue on a daily basis because the declaration of a dividend is at the discretion of the corporation's board of directors. Generally, dividends are taxed to the person who is entitled to receive them—the shareholder of record as of the corporation's record date.[44] Thus, if a taxpayer sells stock after a dividend has been declared but before the record date, the dividend generally is taxed to the purchaser.

If a donor makes a gift of stock to someone (e.g., a family member) after the declaration date but before the record date, the donor does not shift the dividend income to the donee. The *fruit* has ripened sufficiently as of the declaration date to tax the dividend income to the donor of the stock.[45]

Digging Deeper 4   In-depth coverage can be found on this book's companion website: **www.cengagebrain.com**

Example 23

On June 20, the board of directors of Black Corporation declares a $10 per share dividend. The dividend is payable on June 30 to shareholders of record on June 25. As of June 20, Kathleen owns 200 shares of Black stock. On June 21, Kathleen sells 100 of the shares to Jon for their fair market value and gives 100 of the shares to Andrew (her son). Both Jon and Andrew are shareholders of record as of June 25.

Jon (the purchaser) is taxed on $1,000 because he is entitled to receive the dividend. However, Kathleen (the donor) is taxed on the $1,000 received by Andrew (the donee) because the gift was made after the declaration date but before the record date of the dividend.

---

[43]§§ 1(h)(11)(C)(i), (ii).

[44]Reg. § 1.61–9(c). The record date is the cutoff for determining the shareholders who are entitled to receive the dividend.

[45]M. G. Anton, 34 T.C. 842 (1960).

© tuulijumala/Shutterstock.com

TAX FACT Business Income and Loss

Sole proprietors reporting net business income or loss on Form 1040 constitute almost 16 percent of all returns filed. About 9 percent of all Forms 1040 show income from rentals or farming operations. And more than 1 percent of individuals report winnings from gambling activities!

© iStockphoto.com/Pali Rao

Tax Planning Strategies TECHNIQUES FOR REDUCING GROSS INCOME

FRAMEWORK FOCUS: INCOME

Strategy: Postpone Recognition of Income to Achieve Tax Deferral.

Because no tax is due until a gain has been recognized, the law favors investments that yield appreciation rather than annual income.

Example 24

Vera can buy a low-rated corporate bond or an acre of land for $10,000. The bond pays $1,000 of interest (10%) each year, and Vera expects the land to increase in value 10% each year for the next 10 years. She is in the 40% (combined Federal and state) tax bracket for ordinary income and 26% for qualifying capital gains. If the bond would mature or the land would be sold in 10 years and Vera would reinvest the interest at a 10% before-tax return, she would accumulate the following amount at the end of 10 years.

		Bond	Land
Original investment		$10,000	$10,000
Annual income	$1,000		
Less tax	(400)		
	$ 600		
Compound amount reinvested for 10 years at 6% after-tax	×13.18	7,908	
Future value		$17,908	
Compound amount, 10 years at 10%			× 2.59
			$25,900
Less tax on sale: 26%($25,900 − $10,000)			(4,134)
Future value			$21,766

Therefore, the value of the deferral that results from investing in the land rather than in the bond is $3,858 ($21,766 − $17,908). ■

4-4c Income Received by an Agent

Income received by the taxpayer's agent is considered to be received by the taxpayer. A cash basis principal must recognize the income at the time it is received by the agent.[46]

Example 25

Longhorn, Inc., a cash basis corporation, delivers cattle to the auction barn in late December. The auctioneer, acting as the corporation's agent, sells the cattle and collects the proceeds in December. The auctioneer does not pay Longhorn until the following January. Longhorn includes the sales proceeds in its gross income in the year the auctioneer received the funds.

4-5 SPECIFIC ITEMS OF GROSS INCOME

The all-inclusive principles of gross income determination as applied by the IRS and the courts have, on occasion, been expanded or modified by Congress through legislation. This legislation generally provides more specific rules for determining gross income from certain sources. Most of these special rules appear in §§ 71–90 of the Code.

LO.4

Review and illustrate that statutory authority is required to exclude an item from gross income.

---

[46]Rev.Rul. 79–379, 1979–2 C.B. 204.

FINANCIAL DISCLOSURE INSIGHTS   Loans to Executives Prohibited

Interest-free loans have become a popular form of compensation for executives. Several examples of multimillion-dollar loans have come to light as a result of recent bankruptcies by large corporations. The board of directors often justifies the loans as necessary to enable the executive to be able to purchase a residence or to buy stock in the company.

Loans by publicly held corporations to their executives generally are prohibited by Federal law. The Sarbanes-Oxley provisions generally prohibit loans by corporations to their executives. However, an exception permits corporate loans to finance the acquisition of a personal residence for an executive.

© iStockphoto.com/Pali Rao

In addition to provisions describing how specific sources of gross income are to be taxed, several specific rules *exclude* items from gross income. Authority for excluding specific items is provided in §§ 101–150 and in various other provisions in the Code.

Many statutory exclusions are unique to *individual taxpayers* (e.g., gifts and inheritances,[47] scholarships,[48] and a variety of fringe benefits paid to *employees*). These exclusions are discussed in Chapters 9 through 11. Other exclusions are broader and apply to all entities. These exclusions include interest on state and local bonds (§ 103), life insurance proceeds received by reason of death of the insured (§ 101), the fair market value of leasehold improvements received by the lessor when a lease is terminated (§ 109),[49] and income from discharge of indebtedness (§ 108). Some of the broadly applied statutory rules describing inclusions and exclusions are discussed next.

4-5a   Imputed Interest on Below-Market Loans

LO.5

Apply the tax provisions on loans made at below-market interest rates.

As discussed earlier in the chapter, generally, no income is recognized unless it is realized. Realization usually occurs when the taxpayer performs services or sells goods, thus becoming entitled to a payment from the other party. It follows that no income is realized if the goods or services are provided at no charge. Under this prior-law interpretation of the realization requirement, interest-free loans were used to shift income between taxpayers.

Example 26

Brown Corporation is in the 35% tax bracket and has $400,000 in a money market account earning 5% interest. Jack is the sole shareholder of Brown. He is in the 15% tax bracket and has no investment income. In view of the difference in tax rates, Jack believes that it would be better for him to receive and pay tax on the earnings from Brown's $400,000 investment. Jack does not want to receive the $400,000 from Brown as a dividend because that would trigger a tax.

Under prior law, Jack could receive the money market account from Brown in exchange for a $400,000 non-interest-bearing note, payable on Brown's demand. As a result, Jack would receive the $20,000 annual earnings on the money market account, and the combined taxes of Brown and Jack would be decreased every year by $4,000.

Decrease in Brown's tax (.05 × $400,000) × .35	($7,000)
Increase in Jack's tax (.05 × $400,000) × .15	3,000
Overall decrease in tax liability	($4,000)

The Code no longer allows this income-shifting result. Brown Corporation in the preceding example is deemed to have received an interest payment from Jack even though no interest was actually paid.[50] This payment of imputed interest is taxable to Brown. Jack may be able to deduct the imaginary interest payment on

---

[47]§ 102.
[48]§ 117.

[49]If the tenant made the improvements in lieu of rent payments, the value of the improvements is not eligible for exclusion.
[50]§ 7872(a)(1).

his return as investment interest if he itemizes deductions. Brown then is deemed to return the interest to Jack in the form of a taxable dividend.

Imputed interest is calculated using rates the Federal government pays on new borrowings and is compounded semiannually. The Federal rates are adjusted monthly and are published by the IRS.[51] There are three Federal rates: short-term (not over three years and including demand loans), mid-term (over three years but not over nine years), and long-term (over nine years).

If interest is charged on the loan but is less than the Federal rate, the imputed interest is the difference between the amount that would have been charged at the Federal rate and the amount actually charged.

Example 27

Assume that the Federal rate applicable to the loan in the preceding example is 3.5% through June 30 and 4% from July 1 through December 31. Brown Corporation made the loan on January 1, and the loan is still outstanding on December 31. Brown recognizes interest income of $15,140, and Jack reports interest expense of $15,140. Brown is deemed to have paid a $15,140 dividend to Jack.

Interest Calculations	
January 1 to June 30 (.035 × $400,000) (½ year)	$ 7,000
July 1 to December 31 [.04($400,000 + $7,000)] (½ year)	8,140
	$15,140

If Brown had charged 3% interest under the terms of the note, compounded annually, the deemed interest amount would have been $3,140.

Interest at the Federal rate	$ 15,140
Less interest actually charged (.03 × $400,000)	(12,000)
Imputed interest	$ 3,140

The imputed interest rules apply to the following types of below-market loans.[52]

1. Gift loans (made out of love, respect, or generosity).
2. Compensation-related loans (employer loans to employees).
3. Corporation-shareholder loans (a corporation's loans to its shareholders, as in Example 26).

The effects of these loans on the borrower and lender are summarized in Concept Summary 4.1.

CONCEPT SUMMARY 4.1

Effect of Certain Below-Market Loans on the Lender and Borrower

Type of Loan		Lender	Borrower
Gift	Step 1	Interest income	Interest expense
	Step 2	Gift made*	Gift received
Compensation related	Step 1	Interest income	Interest expense
	Step 2	Compensation expense	Compensation income
Corporation to shareholder	Step 1	Interest income	Interest expense
	Step 2	Dividend paid	Dividend income

*The gift may be subject to the Federal gift tax (refer to Chapter 1).

---

[51]§§ 7872(b)(2) and (f)(2).

[52]§ 7872(c). Additional situations exist where these rules apply. See, e.g., §§ 7872(c)(1)(D), (E).

Exceptions and Limitations

No interest is imputed on total outstanding *compensation-related loans* or *corporation-shareholder loans* of $10,000 or less unless the purpose of the loan is tax avoidance.[53] This vague tax avoidance standard exposes practically all compensation-related and corporation-shareholder loans to possible imputed interest problems. Nevertheless, the $10,000 exception should apply when an employee's borrowing was necessitated by personal needs (e.g., to meet unexpected expenses) rather than tax considerations.

Similarly, no interest is imputed on outstanding *gift loans* of $10,000 or less between individuals, unless the loan proceeds are used to purchase income-producing property.[54] This exemption eliminates from these complex provisions immaterial amounts that do not result in sizable shifts of income.

On loans of $100,000 or less between individuals, the imputed interest cannot exceed the borrower's net investment income for the year (gross income from all investments less the related expenses).[55] Through the gift loan provision, the imputed interest rules are designed to prevent high-income individuals from shifting income to relatives in a lower marginal bracket. This shifting of investment income is considered to occur only to the extent that the borrower also recognizes net investment income. Thus, the income imputed to the lender is limited to the borrower's net investment income.

THE BIG PICTURE

Example 28

Return to the facts of *The Big Picture* on p. 4-1. Dr. Payne's loan from his parents likely is a *gift loan*, as his parents are not shareholders in the personal service corporation. Imputed interest must be computed annually with regard to this loan by both Dr. Payne and his parents, as the principal amount of the loan exceeds $100,000 and the loan proceeds were invested in an income-producing asset.

If the borrower's net investment income for the year does not exceed $1,000, no interest is imputed on loans of $100,000 or less. However, this exemption does not apply if a principal purpose of a loan is tax avoidance. In such a case, interest is imputed, and the imputed interest is not limited to the borrower's net investment income.[56]

These exceptions to the imputed interest rules are summarized in Concept Summary 4.2.

CONCEPT SUMMARY 4.2

Exceptions to the Imputed Interest Rules for Below-Market Loans

Exception	Eligible Loans	Ineligible Loans and Limitations
De minimis—aggregate loans of $10,000 or less	Gift loans	Proceeds used to purchase income-producing assets.
	Employer-employee	Principal purpose is tax avoidance.
	Corporation-shareholder	Principal purpose is tax avoidance.
Aggregate loans of $100,000 or less	Gift loans between individuals	Principal purpose is tax avoidance. For all other loans, interest is imputed to the extent of the borrower's net investment income if it exceeds $1,000.

---

[53]§ 7872(c)(3).
[54]§ 7872(c)(2).

[55]§ 7872(d). The $100,000 provision applies only to gift loans.
[56]§ 7872(d)(1)(B).

TAX IN THE NEWS State Taxation of Other States' Interest

Like many other states, Kentucky exempts from taxation interest earned on its own state bonds, but it taxes its own residents on interest income received from bonds issued by other states. A married couple residing in Kentucky challenged the law as unconstitutionally discriminating against interstate commerce by treating Kentucky bonds more favorably than the bonds issued by other states. The U.S. Supreme Court ruled in favor of Kentucky, thus permitting the state (and the 36 other states with similar laws) to tax the out-of-state bond interest while exempting Kentucky bond interest.

Many taxpayers invest in mutual funds that purchase bonds issued by several states. Although the interest from all of the state bonds generally is exempt from Federal income tax, the investor may owe state income tax to the state of residence on the interest received on the bonds of other states. Thus, a bond-oriented mutual fund must inform the investor of the amount of interest income earned from the bonds issued by the various states.

Source: *Department of Revenue of Kentucky v. Davis*, 128 S.Ct. 1801, 553 U.S. 328 (USSC, 2008).

© iStockphoto.com/Andrey Prokhorov

Example 29

Vicki made interest-free gift loans as follows.

Borrower	Amount	Borrower's Net Investment Income	Purpose
Susan	$ 8,000	$–0–	Education
Dan	9,000	500	Purchase of stock
Bonnie	25,000	–0–	Purchase of a business
Olaf	120,000	–0–	Purchase of a residence

Tax avoidance is not a principal purpose of any of the loans. The loan to Susan is not subject to the imputed interest rules because the $10,000 exception applies. The $10,000 exception does not apply to the loan to Dan because the proceeds were used to purchase income-producing assets. However, under the $100,000 exception, the imputed interest is limited to Dan's investment income ($500). Because the $1,000 exception also applies to this loan, no interest is imputed.

No interest is imputed on the loan to Bonnie because the $100,000 exception applies. None of the exceptions apply to the loan to Olaf because the loan was for more than $100,000.

4-5b Tax Benefit Rule

LO.6

Determine the extent to which receipts can be excluded under the tax benefit rule.

Generally, if a taxpayer obtains a deduction for an item in one year and in a later year recovers all or a portion of the prior deduction, the recovery is included in gross income in the year received.[57]

Example 30

MegaCorp deducted as a loss a $1,000 receivable from a customer when it appeared the amount would never be collected. The following year, the customer paid $800 on the receivable. MegaCorp reports the $800 as gross income in the year it is received.

However, the **tax benefit rule** limits income recognition when a deduction does not yield a tax benefit in the year it is taken. If the taxpayer in Example 30 reported no tax liability in the year of the deduction, the $800 receipt would be excluded from gross income in the year of the recovery.

---

[57]§ 111(a).

Example 31

Before deducting a $1,000 loss from an uncollectible business receivable, Tulip Company reported taxable income of $200. The business bad debt deduction yields only a $200 tax benefit (assuming no loss carryback is made). That is, taxable income is reduced by only $200 (to zero) as a result of the bad debt deduction. Therefore, if the customer makes a payment on the previously deducted receivable in the following year, only the first $200 is a taxable recovery of a prior deduction. Any additional amount collected is nontaxable because only $200 of the loss yielded a reduction in taxable income (i.e., a tax benefit).

4-5c Interest on Certain State and Local Government Obligations

LO.7

Review and apply the tax provision that excludes interest on state and local government obligations from gross income.

At the time the Sixteenth Amendment was ratified by the states, there was some question as to whether the Federal government possessed the constitutional authority to tax interest on state and local government obligations. Taxing such interest was thought to violate the doctrine of intergovernmental immunity because the tax would impair the ability of state and local governments to finance their operations.[58] Thus, interest on state and local government obligations was specifically exempted from Federal income taxation.[59] However, the Supreme Court has concluded that there is no constitutional prohibition against levying a nondiscriminatory Federal income tax on state and local government obligations.[60] Nevertheless, the statutory exclusion still exists.

The current exempt status applies solely to state and local government bonds. Thus, income received from the accrual of interest on a condemnation award or an overpayment of state tax is fully taxable.[61] Nor does the exemption apply to gains on the sale of tax-exempt securities.

Example 32

Macaw Corporation purchases State of Virginia bonds for $10,000 on July 1, 2014. The bonds pay $400 interest each June 30 and December 31. On March 31, 2015, Macaw sells the bonds for $10,500 plus $200 of accrued interest. Macaw recognizes a $500 taxable gain ($10,500 − $10,000), but the $200 accrued interest is exempt from taxation.

Digging Deeper   5   In-depth coverage can be found on this book's companion website: **www.cengagebrain.com**

The interest exclusion reduces the cost of borrowing for state and local governments. A taxpayer with a 35 percent marginal tax rate requires only a 5.2 percent yield on a tax-exempt bond to obtain the same after-tax income as a taxable bond paying 8 percent interest [$5.2\% \div (1 - .35) = 8\%$].

Although the Internal Revenue Code excludes from Federal gross income the interest on state and local government bonds, the interest on U.S. government bonds is not excluded from the Federal tax base. Congress has decided, however, that if the Federal government is not to tax state and local bond interest, the state and local governments are prohibited from taxing interest on U.S. government bonds.[62] While this parity between the Federal and state and local governments

---

[58]*Pollock v. Farmer's Loan & Trust Co.*, 3 AFTR 2602, 15 S.Ct. 912 (USSC, 1895).

[59]§ 103(a).

[60]*South Carolina v. Baker III*, 88–1 USTC ¶9284, 61 AFTR 2d 88–995, 108 S.Ct. 1355 (USSC, 1988).

[61]*Kieselbach v. Comm.*, 43–1 USTC ¶9220, 30 AFTR 370, 63 S.Ct. 303 (USSC, 1943); *U.S. Trust Co. of New York v. Anderson*, 3 USTC ¶1125, 12 AFTR 836, 65 F.2d 575 (CA–2, 1933).

[62]31 U.S.C.A. § 742.

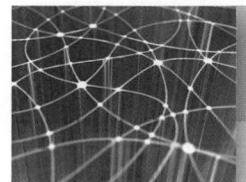

BRIDGE DISCIPLINE   Bridge to Public Economics

The exclusion granted by the Federal government for interest paid on state and local bonds costs the U.S. Treasury approximately $12 billion per year, according to the Office of Management and Budget. Such forgone revenue is referred to as a "tax expenditure." However, if the capital markets are working properly, the exclusion should produce cost savings to the state and local governments.

If the exclusion were eliminated, state and local governments would pay higher interest rates on their bonds; the investor would demand a higher interest rate to produce the same after-tax yield as that received from taxable bonds of comparable risk. Therefore, the exclusion operates as a form of revenue sharing to the benefit of the state and local governments, and the "expenditure" by the Federal government benefits state and local governments, rather than merely the wealthy bondholders.

exists with regard to taxing each others' obligations, the states are free to tax another's obligations. Thus, some states exempt the interest on the bonds they issue, but tax the interest on bonds issued by other states.

THE BIG PICTURE

Example 33

Return to the facts of *The Big Picture* on p. 4-1. Dr. Payne includes in gross income the $500 of interest income from the bank's money market account, but not the $500 that is earned on the Whitehall School District bonds.

Tax Planning Strategies   STATE AND MUNICIPAL BONDS

FRAMEWORK FOCUS: INCOME AND EXCLUSION

Strategy: Avoid Income Recognition.

Tax-exempt state and local bonds are almost irresistible investments for taxpayers with high marginal tax rates. To realize the maximum benefit from the exemption, the investor can purchase zero-coupon bonds, which pay interest only at maturity. The advantage of the zero-coupon feature is that the investor can earn tax-exempt interest on the accumulated principal and interest.

If the investor purchases a tax-exempt bond that pays the interest each year, the interest received may be such a small amount that an additional tax-exempt investment cannot be made. In addition, reinvesting the interest may entail transaction costs (broker's fees). The zero-coupon feature avoids these problems. However, certain state and municipal bond interest may increase the base of the alternative minimum tax, as discussed in Chapter 17.

4-5d Improvements on Leased Property

When a real property lease expires, the landlord regains control of both the real property and any improvements to the property (e.g., buildings and landscaping) made by the tenant during the term of the lease. Any improvements made to the leased property are excluded from the landlord's gross income unless the improvement is made to the property in lieu of rent.[63]

LO.8

Use the tax rules concerning the exclusion of leasehold improvements from gross income.

---

[63]§ 109.

TAX IN THE NEWS   Corporate-Owned Life Insurance May Not Yield Corporate Benefits

Many corporations purchase insurance policies on the lives of key employees (employees who are extremely important to the company's success, such as the CEO and CFO). The corporation is the beneficiary, and the insurance proceeds are excluded from the corporation's gross income under § 101.

Before changes in the tax laws some time ago, corporations could deduct the interest on loans to purchase the insurance policies. Many large corporations took advantage of these rules and purchased insurance policies not only on key employees but also on their rank-and-file employees (frequently referred to as "janitor's insurance"), with the corporation as the beneficiary.

In recent years, some heirs of deceased employees who were covered by such janitor's insurance have successfully sued the insurance companies and the employers to recover the insurance proceeds, on the theory that the employer did not have an "insurable interest." Such an interest is required under the laws of most states to prevent individuals from "gambling" on the lives of people in whom they otherwise have no financial interest.

The next chapter in this judicial saga will determine whether the heirs who collect the insurance proceeds in this way are "beneficiaries" under § 101.

© iStockphoto.com/Andrey Prokhorov

Example 34

Mahogany Corporation leases office space to Zink and Silver, Attorneys-at-Law. When the law firm took possession of the office space, it added wall partitions, a wireless computer network, and a variety of other improvements to the space. The improvements were not made in lieu of rent payments to Mahogany. When the lease expires and Mahogany regains possession of the space, the value of the improvements is excluded from Mahogany's gross income.

4-5e Life Insurance Proceeds

General Rule

LO.9

Determine the extent to which life insurance proceeds are excluded from gross income.

Life insurance proceeds paid to the beneficiary because of the death of the insured are exempt from income tax.[64] Congress chose to exempt life insurance proceeds from gross income for several reasons, including the following.

- For family members, life insurance proceeds serve much the same purpose as a nontaxable inheritance.
- In a business context (as well as in a family situation), life insurance proceeds replace an economic loss suffered by the beneficiary.

Thus, Congress concluded that, in general, making life insurance proceeds exempt from income tax was a good policy.

Example 35

Sparrow Corporation purchased an insurance policy on the life of its CEO and named itself as the beneficiary. Sparrow paid $24,000 in premiums. When the company's CEO died, Sparrow collected the insurance proceeds of $60,000. The $60,000 is excluded from Sparrow's gross income.

Exceptions to Exclusion Treatment

The income tax exclusion applies only when the insurance proceeds are received because of the death of the insured. If the owner cancels the policy and receives the cash surrender value, he or she must recognize gain to the extent of the excess of the amount received over the cost of the policy.[65]

---

[64]*Estate of D. R. Daly*, 3 B.T.A. 1042 (1926).

[65]*Landfield Finance Co. v. U.S.*, 69–2 USTC ¶9680, 24 AFTR 2d 69–5744, 418 F.2d 172 (CA–7, 1969).

Another exception to exclusion treatment applies if the policy is transferred after the insurance company issues it. If the policy is transferred for valuable consideration, the insurance proceeds are includible in the gross income of the transferee to the extent the proceeds received exceed the amount paid for the policy by the transferee plus any subsequent premiums paid.

> **Example 36**
>
> Platinum Corporation pays premiums of $5,000 for an insurance policy with a face amount of $12,000 on the life of Beth, an officer of the corporation. Subsequently, Platinum sells the policy to Beth's husband, Jamal, for $5,500. On Beth's death, Jamal receives the proceeds of $12,000. Jamal excludes from gross income $5,500 plus any premiums he paid subsequent to the transfer. The remainder of the proceeds constitutes gross income to Jamal, as he acquired the policy for cash consideration.

The Code, however, provides several major exceptions to the consideration rule.[66] These exceptions permit exclusion treatment for transfers to the following parties. The first three exceptions facilitate the use of insurance contracts to fund **buy-sell agreements**.

1. A partner of the insured.
2. A partnership in which the insured is a partner.
3. A corporation in which the insured is an officer or shareholder.
4. A transferee whose basis in the policy is determined by reference to the transferor's basis, such as a gift or a transfer due to a divorce.
5. The insured party under the policy.

> **Example 37**
>
> Rick and Sam are equal partners who have a buy-sell agreement that allows either partner to purchase the interest of a deceased partner for $500,000. Neither partner has sufficient cash to buy the other partner's interest, but each has a life insurance policy on his own life in the amount of $500,000. Rick and Sam could exchange their policies (usually at little or no taxable gain), and upon the death of either partner, the surviving partner could collect tax-free insurance proceeds. The proceeds then could be used to purchase the decedent's interest in the partnership.

Investment earnings arising from the reinvestment of life insurance proceeds generally are subject to income tax. For example, the beneficiary may elect to collect the insurance proceeds in installments that include taxable interest income. The interest portion of each installment is included in gross income.

In-depth coverage can be found on this book's companion website: **www.cengagebrain.com** **6** | Digging Deeper

---

Tax Planning Strategies   LIFE INSURANCE

FRAMEWORK FOCUS: INCOME AND EXCLUSION

Strategy: Avoid Income Recognition.

Life insurance is a tax-favored investment. The annual increase in the cash surrender value of the policy is not taxable because it is subject to substantial restrictions (no income has been actually or constructively received). By borrowing on the policy's cash surrender value, the owner can receive the policy's increase in value in cash without recognizing income.

---

[66]§ 101(a)(2).

4-5f Income from Discharge of Indebtedness

LO.10

Describe the circumstances under which income must be reported from the discharge of indebtedness.

Gross income is generated when appreciated property is used to pay a debt or when the creditor cancels debt. If appreciated property is used to pay a debt, the transaction is treated as a sale of the appreciated property, followed by payment of the debt.[67] Foreclosure by a creditor is also treated as a sale or exchange of the property.[68]

Example 38

Juan owed the State Bank $100,000 on an unsecured note. Juan satisfied the note by transferring to the bank common stock with a basis of $60,000 and a fair market value of $100,000. Juan recognizes a $40,000 gain on the transfer.

Juan also owed the bank $50,000 on a note secured by land. When Juan's basis in the land was $20,000 and the land's fair market value was $50,000, the bank foreclosed on the loan and took title to the land. Juan recognizes a $30,000 gain on the foreclosure.

A creditor may cancel debt to ensure the viability of the debtor. In such cases, the debtor's net worth is increased by the amount of debt forgiven. Generally, the debtor recognizes gross income equal to the amount of debt canceled.[69]

Example 39

Brown Corporation is unable to meet the mortgage payments on its factory building. Both the corporation and the mortgage holder are aware of the depressed market for industrial property in the area. Foreclosure would only result in the creditor's obtaining unsellable property.

To improve Brown's financial position and thus improve its chances of obtaining the additional credit necessary for survival from other lenders, the creditor agrees to forgive all amounts past due and to reduce the principal amount of the mortgage. Brown's net worth is increased by the amount of past due debt that was forgiven *plus* the reduction in the mortgage balance.

Example 40

A corporation issues bonds with a face value of $500,000. Subsequently, the corporation repurchases the bonds in the market for $150,000. It has effectively canceled its $500,000 debt with a $150,000 payment, so it recognizes $350,000 in gross income.[70]

Example 41

Keri borrowed $60,000 from National Bank to purchase a warehouse. Keri agreed to make monthly principal and interest payments for 15 years. The interest rate on the note was 3%.

When the balance on the note had been reduced through monthly payments to $48,000, the bank offered to accept $45,000 in full settlement of the note. The bank made the offer because interest rates had increased to 4.5%. Keri accepted the bank's offer. As a result, she recognizes $3,000 ($48,000 − $45,000) gross income.[71]

A discharge of indebtedness generally increases the taxpayer's gross income, but the reduction in debt is excluded in each of the following situations.[72]

1. Creditors' gifts.
2. Discharges under Federal bankruptcy law.
3. Discharges that occur when the debtor is insolvent.
4. Discharge of the farm debt of a solvent taxpayer.
5. Discharge of **qualified real property business indebtedness**.
6. A seller's cancellation of a buyer's indebtedness.
7. A shareholder's cancellation of a corporation's indebtedness.
8. Forgiveness of certain loans to students.
9. Discharge of indebtedness on the taxpayer's principal residence that occurs after 2006 and before 2014, and is the result of the financial condition of the debtor.

---

[67]Reg. § 1.1001–2(a).

[68]*Estate of Delman v. Comm.*, 73 T.C. 15 (1979).

[69]§ 61(a)(12).

[70]See *U.S. v. Kirby Lumber Co.*, 2 USTC ¶814, 10 AFTR 458, 52 S.Ct. 4 (USSC, 1931).

[71]Rev.Rul. 82–202, 1982–1 C.B. 35.

[72]§§ 108 and 1017.

Creditors' Gifts

If the creditor reduces the debt as an act of *love, respect, or generosity*, the debtor has simply received a nontaxable gift (situation 1). Such motivations generally arise only on loans between friends or family members. Rarely will a gift be found to have occurred in a business context. A businessperson may settle a debt for less than the amount due, but only as a matter of business expediency (e.g., high collection costs or disputes as to contract terms) rather than generosity.[73]

Insolvency and Bankruptcy

Cancellation of indebtedness income is excluded when the debtor is insolvent (i.e., the debtor's liabilities exceed the fair market value of the assets) or when the cancellation of debt results from a bankruptcy proceeding (situations 2 and 3). The insolvency exclusion is limited to the amount of insolvency. The tax law permits this exclusion to avoid imposing undue hardship on the debtor (wherewithal to pay) and the debtor's limited resources.

The law imposes a cost for the insolvency and bankruptcy exclusion. More specifically, the debtor must decrease certain tax benefits (capital loss carryforwards, net operating loss carryforwards, some tax credits, and suspended passive losses)[74] by the amount of income excluded. In addition, if the amount of excluded income exceeds these tax benefits, the debtor must then reduce the basis in assets.[75] Thus, excluded cancellation of indebtedness income either accelerates recognition of future income (by reducing tax benefit carryforwards) or is deferred until the debtor's assets are sold (or depreciated).

Before any debt cancellation, Maroon Corporation has assets with a fair market value of $500,000 and liabilities of $600,000. A creditor agrees to cancel $125,000 of liabilities. Maroon excludes $100,000 of the debt cancellation income (the amount of insolvency) and is taxed on $25,000. Maroon also reduces any tax benefits and the basis of its assets by $100,000 (the excluded income).	**Example 42**

Qualified Real Property Indebtedness

Taxpayers (other than C corporations) can elect to exclude income from cancellation of indebtedness if the canceled debt is secured by real property used in a trade or business (situation 5). The debt must have been used to acquire or improve real property in a trade or business to qualify for the exclusion.[76]

The amount of the exclusion is limited to the *lesser of* (1) the excess of the debt over the fair market value of the real property or (2) the adjusted basis of all depreciable real property held. In addition, the basis of all depreciable real property held by the debtor is reduced by the excluded amount.

Blue, Inc., owns a warehouse worth $5 million, with a $3 million basis. The warehouse is subject to a $7 million mortgage that was incurred in connection with the acquisition of the warehouse. In lieu of foreclosure, the lender decides that it will reduce the mortgage to $4.5 million. Blue may elect to exclude $2 million from gross income ($7 million – $5 million). If Blue makes the election, it reduces the aggregate basis of its depreciable realty by $2 million. If the basis of the warehouse had been $1 million, and the warehouse was the only piece of depreciable realty that Blue owned, only $1 million of the debt cancellation income would be excluded.	**Example 43**

---

[73]*Comm. v. Jacobson*, 49–1 USTC ¶9133, 37 AFTR 516, 69 S.Ct. 358 (USSC, 1949).

[74]See Chapter 6 for a discussion of net operating loss carryforwards and suspended passive losses. Chapter 8 discusses capital loss carryforwards. Chapter 17 discusses tax credits.

[75]§ 108(b).

[76]§ 108(a)(1)(D).

Seller Cancellation

When a seller of property cancels debt previously incurred by a buyer in a purchase transaction, the cancellation generally does not trigger gross income to the buyer (situation 6). Instead, the reduction in debt is considered to be a reduction in the purchase price of the asset. Consequently, the basis of the asset is reduced in the hands of the buyer.[77]

Example 44

Snipe, Inc., purchases a truck from Sparrow Autos for $10,000 in cash and a $25,000 note payable. Two days after the purchase, Sparrow announces a sale on the same model truck, with a sales price of $28,000. Snipe contacts Sparrow and asks to be given the sales price on the truck. Sparrow complies by canceling $7,000 of the note payable. The $7,000 is excluded from Snipe's gross income, and the basis of the truck to Snipe is $28,000.

Shareholder Cancellation

If a shareholder cancels the corporation's indebtedness to him or her (situation 7) and receives nothing in return, the cancellation usually is considered a contribution of capital to the corporation by the shareholder. Thus, the corporation recognizes no gross income. Instead, its paid-in capital is increased, and its liabilities are decreased by the same amount.[78]

Digging Deeper   7   🔍   In-depth coverage can be found on this book's companion website: **www.cengagebrain.com**

© tuulijumala/Shutterstock.com

Student Loans

Many states make loans to students on the condition that the loan will be forgiven if the student practices a profession in the state upon completing his or her studies. The amount of the loan that is forgiven (situation 8) is excluded from gross income.[79]

4-5g Gains and Losses from Property Transactions

General Rules

LO.11

Describe the general tax consequences of property transactions.

When property is sold or otherwise disposed of, gain or loss may result. Such gain or loss has an effect on the gross income of the party making the sale or other disposition when the gain or loss is *realized* and *recognized* for tax purposes. The concept of realized gain or loss is expressed as follows.

$$\begin{array}{c} \text{Amount realized} \\ \text{from the sale} \end{array} - \begin{array}{c} \text{Adjusted basis of} \\ \text{the property} \end{array} = \begin{array}{c} \text{Realized gain} \\ \text{(or loss)} \end{array}$$

The *amount realized* is the selling price of the property less any costs of disposition (e.g., brokerage commissions) incurred by the seller. The *adjusted basis* of the property is determined as follows.

Cost (or other original basis) at date of acquisition[80]
Add: Capital additions
Subtract: Depreciation (if appropriate) and other capital recoveries (see Chapter 5)
Equals: Adjusted basis at date of sale or other disposition

---

[77]§ 108(e)(5).
[78]§ 108(e)(6).
[79]§ 108(f).

[80]Cost usually means purchase price plus expenses related to the acquisition of the property and incurred by the purchaser (e.g., brokerage commissions). For the basis of property acquired by gift or inheritance and other basis rules, see Chapter 7.

Without realized gain or loss, generally, there can be no recognized (taxable) gain or loss. All realized gains are recognized unless some specific part of the tax law provides otherwise. Realized losses may or may not be recognized (deductible) for tax purposes, depending on the circumstances involved. For example, losses realized from the disposition of personal-use property (property held by individuals and not used for business or investment purposes) are not recognized.

> During the current year, Ted sells his sailboat (adjusted basis of $4,000) for $5,500. Ted also sells one of his personal automobiles (adjusted basis of $8,000) for $5,000. Ted's realized gain of $1,500 from the sale of the sailboat is recognized. The $3,000 realized loss on the sale of the automobile, however, is not recognized. Thus, the gain is taxable, but the loss is not deductible.

Example 45

Once it has been determined that the disposition of property results in a recognized gain or loss, the next step is to classify the gain or loss as capital or ordinary. Although ordinary gain is fully taxable and ordinary loss is fully deductible, the same is not true for capital gains and capital losses.

Capital Gains and Losses

Gains and losses from the disposition of capital assets receive special tax treatment. Capital assets are defined in the Code as any property held by the taxpayer *other than* property listed in § 1221. The list in § 1221 includes, among other things, inventory, accounts receivable, and depreciable property or real estate used in a business. The sale or exchange of assets in these categories usually results in ordinary income or loss treatment (see Chapter 8). The sale of any other asset generally creates a capital gain or loss.

> Cardinal, Inc., owns a pizza parlor. During the current year, Cardinal sells an automobile. The automobile, which had been used as a pizza delivery car for three years, was sold at a loss of $1,000. Because this automobile was a depreciable asset used in its business, Cardinal reports an ordinary loss of $1,000, rather than a capital loss. Cardinal also sold securities held for investment during the current year. The securities were sold for a gain of $800. The securities are capital assets. Therefore, Cardinal has a capital gain of $800.

Example 46

Computing the Net Capital Gain/Loss To ascertain the appropriate tax treatment of capital gains and losses, a netting process first is applied.

1. Capital gains and losses are classified as:
   a. short term, if the sold asset was held for one year or less, or
   b. long term, if the sold asset was held for more than one year.
2. Capital gains and losses then are netted within these two classifications. Specifically, short-term capital losses (STCL) are offset against short-term capital gains (STCG), resulting in either a net short-term capital loss (NSTCL) or a net short-term capital gain (NSTCG).
3. Similarly, long-term capital losses (LTCL) are offset against long-term capital gains (LTCG), resulting in either a net long-term capital gain (NLTCG) or a net long-term capital loss (NLTCL).
4. If the resulting amounts are of opposite signs (i.e., there remains a gain and a loss), those amounts are netted against each other. This produces the taxpayer's net capital gain or loss for the tax year. It is entirely long- or short-term, as dictated by the number that was larger in steps 2 and 3.

Example 47

Colin is subject to a 35% marginal tax rate and reports the following capital transactions from asset sales during the year.

Penguin Corporation stock (held for 7 months)	$ 1,000
Owl Corporation stock (held for 9 months)	(3,000)
Flamingo Corporation bonds (held for 14 months)	2,000
Land (held for 3 years)	4,000

SHORT TERM: The Penguin gain of $1,000 is offset by the Owl loss of $3,000. This results in a $2,000 NSTCL.

LONG TERM: Netting the results of the sales of the bonds and the land, a $6,000 NLTCG is computed.

CONTINUE NETTING: Because there remains a gain and a loss, net these amounts against each other. A $4,000 net long-term capital gain results.

Taxing the Net Capital Gain/Loss Individuals and corporations are taxed differently on their net capital gains and losses. An individual's *net capital gain* is subject to the following *maximum* tax rates.[81]

	Maximum Rate[82]
Short-term gains	39.6%
Long-term gains	20%

A corporation's net capital gain does not receive any beneficial tax treatment. It is taxed as ordinary business income.

The net capital losses of individuals can be used to offset up to $3,000 of ordinary income each year. Any remaining capital loss is carried forward indefinitely until it is exhausted.

Corporations may deduct capital losses only to the extent of capital gains. Capital losses of corporations in excess of capital gains may not be deducted against ordinary income. A corporation's unused capital losses can be carried back three years and then carried forward five years to offset capital gains in those years.[83]

Example 48

Jones records a short-term capital loss of $5,000 during 2015 and no capital gains. If Jones is an individual, she can deduct $3,000 of this amount as an ordinary loss. The remaining $2,000 loss is carried forward to 2016 and thereafter, until it is fully deducted against ordinary income or netted against other capital gains and losses.

If Jones is a C corporation, none of the capital loss is deductible in 2015. All of the $5,000 loss is carried back and offset sequentially against capital gains in 2012, 2013, and 2014 (generating an immediate tax refund). Any remaining capital loss is carried forward and offset against capital gains in tax years 2016 to 2020.

Digging Deeper   8   In-depth coverage can be found on this book's companion website: **www.cengagebrain.com**

---

[81]§ 1(h).

[82]Certain assets, such as collectibles (e.g., art, antiques, stamps, etc.) and some real estate, receive special treatment. When the 15% or 20% long-term capital gains tax rate otherwise applies, the collectibles gain is taxed

at a maximum rate of 28%, and certain real estate gains are taxed at a maximum tax rate of 25%. See Chapter 8.

[83]§§ 1211 and 1212.

REFOCUS ON THE BIG PICTURE

JUST WHAT IS INCLUDED IN GROSS INCOME?

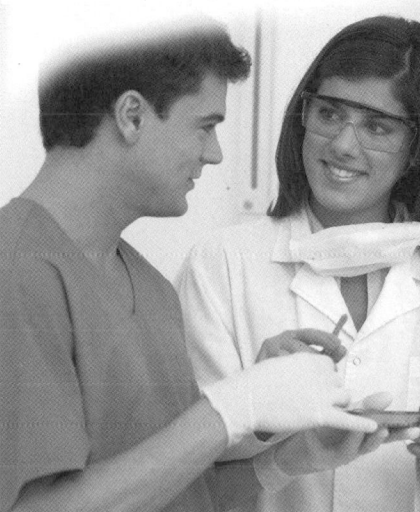

Using the accrual method of accounting, the gross income recognized by Cliff Payne's corporation is $385,500. This includes the entire $385,000 of revenue earned from providing services to patients during the year and the $500 of interest income earned on the money market account. The $500 of school district bond interest is excluded from gross income.

Dr. Payne's own gross income includes $120,000 of salary earned during the year. Even though Cliff did not cash his December paycheck until January, he is considered to have constructively received the income because it was readily available to him. Dr. Payne may be able to reduce his taxable income in the amount of the imputed interest expense on the below-market loan from his parents. The increase in value on his stock does not result in gross income until he sells the stock and realizes a gain or loss.

What If?

Rather than electing the accrual method, what if Dr. Payne had chosen to use the cash method of accounting for his business? Using the cash method is acceptable for certain personal service corporations. While using the cash method would reduce the company's gross income from $385,000 to $333,000 ($385,000 amount billed less $52,000 still to be received), this is only part of the picture. Using the cash method also might result in some of the corporation's expenses not being deducted until they are paid in a future year.

© Tyler Olson/Shutterstock.com

Suggested Readings

Sheldon I. Banoff and Richard M. Lipton, "Tax Consequences of Recovering 'Mislaid Property,'" *Journal of Taxation*, July 2012.

Thomas Dalton, Richard E. Custin, and Linda L. Barkacs, "Debt Cancellation in the Age of Mortgage Foreclosures," *Journal of Real Estate Taxation*, 2011 Second Quarter.

"Delay in Cashing Not Delay in Taxing," *Practical Tax Strategies*, September 2005.

C. J. Langstraat and W. G. Prascher, "Cancellation of Debt Income Exclusions for Individuals: Good and Bad News," *Practical Tax Strategies*, July 2010.

Key Terms

Accounting income, 4-4	Constructive receipt, 4-10	Original issue discount, 4-11
Accounting method, 4-6	Economic income, 4-4	Qualified real property business
Accrual method, 4-9	Fruit and tree metaphor, 4-13	indebtedness, 4-26
Assignment of income, 4-13	Gross income, 4-2	Tax benefit rule, 4-21
Buy-sell agreements, 4-25	Hybrid method, 4-9	Taxable year, 4-6
Cash receipts method, 4-7	Income, 4-4	
Claim of right doctrine, 4-9	Life insurance proceeds, 4-24	

Problems

1. **LO.1** Howard buys wrecked cars and stores them on his property. Recently, he purchased a 1990 Ford Taurus for $400. If he can sell all of the usable parts, his total proceeds from the Taurus will be over $2,500. As of the end of the year, he has sold only the radio for $75, and he does not know how many, if any, of the remaining parts will ever be sold. What are Howard's income recognition issues?

2. **LO.1** Determine the taxpayer's current-year (1) economic income and (2) gross income for tax purposes from the following events.
   a. Sam's employment contract as chief executive of a large corporation was terminated, and he was paid $500,000 not to work for a competitor of the corporation for five years.
   b. Elliot, a 6-year-old child, was paid $5,000 for appearing in a television commercial. His parents put the funds in a savings account for the child's education.
   c. Valerie found a suitcase that contained $100,000. She could not determine who the owner was.
   d. Winn purchased a lottery ticket for $5 and won $750,000 from it.
   e. Larry spent $1,000 to raise vegetables that he and his family consumed. The cost of the vegetables in a store would have been $2,400.
   f. Dawn purchased an automobile for $1,500 that was worth $3,500. The seller was in desperate need of cash.

3. **LO.1** The roof of your corporation's office building recently suffered some damage as the result of a storm. You, the president of the corporation, are negotiating with a carpenter who has quoted two prices for the repair work: $600 if you pay in cash ("folding money") and $700 if you pay by check. The carpenter observes that the IRS can more readily discover his receipt of a check. Thus, he hints that he will report the receipt of the check (but not the cash).

   The carpenter holds another full-time job and will do the work after hours and on the weekend. He comments that he should be allowed to keep all he earns after regular working hours. Evaluate what you should do.

4. **LO.1** Dolly is a college student who works as a part-time server in a restaurant. Her usual tip is 20% of the price of the meal. A customer ordered a piece of pie and said that he would appreciate prompt service. Dolly fulfilled the customer's request. The customer's bill was $8, but the customer left a $100 bill on the table and did not ask for a receipt. Dolly gave the cashier $8 and pocketed the $100 bill.

   Dolly concludes that the customer thought that he had left a $10 bill, although the customer did not return to correct the apparent mistake. The customer had commented about how much he appreciated Dolly's prompt service. Dolly thinks that a $2 tip would be sufficient and that the other $98 is like "found money." How much should Dolly include in her gross income?

5. **LO.2** Determine Amos's gross income in each of the following cases.
   a. In the current year, Amos purchased an automobile for $25,000. As part of the transaction, Amos received a $1,500 rebate from the manufacturer.
   b. Amos sold his business. In addition to the selling price of the stock, he received $50,000 for a covenant not to compete—an agreement that he will not compete directly with his former business for five years.
   c. Amos owned some land he held as an investment. As a result of a change in the zoning rules, the property increased in value by $20,000.

6. **LO.2** The Bluejay Apartments, a new development, is in the process of structuring its lease agreements. The company would like to set the damage deposits high enough that tenants will keep the apartments in good condition. The company actually is more concerned about such damage than about tenants not paying their rent.
   a. Discuss the tax effects of the following alternatives.

   - $500 damage deposit and $500 rent for the final month of the lease.
   - $1,000 rent for the final two months of the lease and no damage deposit.
   - $1,000 damage deposit with no rent prepayment.

   b. Which option do you recommend? Why?

7. **LO.2, 11** Julie is considering three alternative investments of $10,000. Julie is in the 28% marginal tax bracket for ordinary income and 15% for qualifying capital gains in all tax years. The selected investment will be liquidated at the end of five years. The alternatives are:

Decision Making

- A taxable corporate bond yielding 5% before tax and the interest reinvested at 5% before tax.
- A tax-favored bond that will have a maturity value of $12,200 (a 4% pretax rate of return).
- Land that will increase in value.

The gain on the land will be classified and taxed as a long-term capital gain. The interest from the bonds is taxed as ordinary income: the interest from the corporate bond as it is earned annually, but that from the tax-favored bond is recognized only upon redemption. How much must the land increase in value to yield a greater after-tax return than either of the bonds?

The compound amount of $1 and compound value of $1 annuity payments at the end of five years are given as:

Interest Rate	Future Value, $1 Compounded for 5 Years	Future Value, 5-Year Annuity of $1 Each
5%	$1.28	$5.53
4%	1.22	5.42
3.6%	1.19	5.37

8. **LO.1** Determine the taxpayer's gross income for tax purposes in each of the following situations.
   a. Deb, a cash basis taxpayer, traded a corporate bond with accrued interest of $300 for corporate stock with a fair market value of $12,000 at the time of the exchange. Deb's cost of the bond was $10,000. The value of the stock had decreased to $11,000 by the end of the year.
   b. Deb needed $10,000 to make a down payment on her house. She instructed her broker to sell some stock to raise the $10,000. Deb's cost of the stock was $3,000. Based on her broker's advice, instead of selling the stock, she borrowed the $10,000 using the stock as collateral for the debt.
   c. Deb's boss gave her two tickets to the Rabid Rabbits rock concert because Deb met her sales quota. At the time Deb received the tickets, each ticket had a face price of $200 and was selling on eBay for $300 each. On the date of the concert, the tickets were selling for $250 each. Deb and her son attended the concert.

9. **LO.2** Al is a medical doctor who conducts his practice as a sole proprietor. During 2014, he received cash of $280,000 for medical services. Of the amount collected, $40,000 was for services provided in 2013. At the end of 2014, Al held accounts receivable of $60,000, all for services rendered in 2014. In addition, at the end of the year, Al received $12,000 as an advance payment from a health maintenance organization (HMO) for services to be rendered in 2015. Compute Al's gross income for 2014:
   a. Using the cash basis of accounting.
   b. Using the accrual basis of accounting.

10. **LO.2** Selma operates a contractor's supply store. She maintains her books using the cash method. At the end of the year, her accountant computes her accrual basis income that is used on her tax return. For 2014, Selma had cash receipts of $1.4 million, which included $200,000 collected on accounts receivable from 2013 sales. It also included the proceeds of a $100,000 bank loan. At the end of 2014, she had $250,000 in accounts receivable from customers, all from 2014 sales.
   a. Compute Selma's accrual basis gross receipts for 2014.
   b. Selma paid cash for all of the purchases. The total amount paid for merchandise in 2014 was $1.3 million. At the end of 2013, she had merchandise on hand with a cost of $150,000. At the end of 2014, the cost of merchandise on hand was $300,000. Compute Selma's gross income from merchandise sales for 2014.

Communications

11. **LO.2** Trip Garage, Inc. (459 Ellis Avenue, Harrisburg, PA 17111), is an accrual basis taxpayer that repairs automobiles. In late December 2014, the company repaired Samuel Mosley's car and charged him $1,000. Samuel did not think the problem had been fixed, so he refused to pay; thus, Trip refused to release the automobile.

In early January 2015, Trip made a few adjustments under the hood; Trip then convinced Samuel that the automobile was working properly. At that time, Samuel agreed to pay only $900 because he did not have the use of the car for a week. Trip said "fine," accepted the $900, and released the automobile to Samuel.

An IRS agent thinks Trip, as an accrual basis taxpayer, should report $1,000 of income in 2014, when the work was done, and then deduct a $100 business loss in 2015. Prepare a memo to Susan Apple, the treasurer of Trip, with your recommended treatment for the disputed income.

Ethics and Equity

12. **LO.1, 4** Each Saturday morning, Ted makes the rounds of the local yard sales. He has developed a keen eye for bargains, but he cannot use all of the items he thinks are "real bargains." Ted has found a way to share the benefits of his talent with others. If Ted spots something priced at $40 that he knows is worth $100, for example, he will buy it and list it on eBay for $70.

Ted does not include his gain in his gross income because he reasons that he is performing a valuable service for others (both the original sellers and the future buyers) and sacrificing profit he could receive. "Besides," according to Ted, "the IRS does not know about these transactions." Should Ted's ethical standards depend on his perception of his own generosity and the risk that his income-producing activities will be discovered by the IRS? Discuss.

Ethics and Equity

13. **LO.2** Accounting students understand that the accrual method of accounting is superior to the cash method for measuring the income and expenses from an ongoing business for financial reporting purposes. Thus, CPAs advise their clients to use the accrual method of accounting. Yet, CPA firms generally use the cash method to prepare their own tax returns. Are the CPAs being hypocritical? Explain.

14. **LO.2** Drake Appliance Company, an accrual basis taxpayer, sells home appliances and service contracts. Determine the effects of each of the following transactions on the company's 2014 gross income assuming that the company uses any available options to defer its taxes.
   a. In December 2013, the company received a $1,200 advance payment from a customer for an appliance that Drake had special ordered from the manufacturer. The appliance did not arrive from the manufacturer until January 2014, and Drake immediately delivered it to the customer. The sale was reported in 2014 for financial accounting purposes.
   b. In October 2014, the company sold a 6-month service contract for $240. The company also sold a 36-month service contract for $1,260 in July 2014.
   c. On December 31, 2014, the company sold an appliance for $1,200. The company received $500 cash and a note from the customer for $700 and $260 interest, to be paid at the rate of $40 a month for 24 months. Because of the customer's poor credit record, the fair market value of the note was only $600. The cost of the appliance was $750.

Ethics and Equity

15. **LO.2** Dr. Randolph, a cash basis taxpayer, knows that he will be in a lower marginal tax bracket next year. To take advantage of the expected decrease in his tax rate, Dr. Randolph instructs his office manager to delay filing the medical insurance claims for services performed in November and December until January of the following year. This will ensure that the receipts will not be included in his current gross income. Is Dr. Randolph abusing the cash method of accounting rules? Why or why not?

Decision Making

Communications

16. **LO.2** Your client is a new partnership, ARP Associates, which is an engineering consulting firm. Generally, ARP bills clients for services at the end of each month. Client billings are about $50,000 each month. On average, it takes 45 days to collect the receivables. ARP's expenses are primarily for salary and rent. Salaries are paid on the last day of each month, and rent is paid on the first day of each month.

The partnership has a line of credit with a bank, which requires monthly financial statements. These must be prepared using the accrual method. ARP's managing partner, Amanda Sims, has suggested that the firm also use the accrual method for tax purposes and thus reduce accounting fees by $600.

The partners are in the 35% (combined Federal and state) marginal tax bracket. Write a letter to your client explaining why you believe it would be worthwhile for ARP to file its tax return on the cash basis even though its financial statements are prepared on the accrual basis. ARP's address is 100 James Tower, Denver, CO 80208.

17. **LO.3** Alva received dividends on her stocks as follows.

Amur Corporation (a French corporation whose stock is traded on an established U.S. securities market)	$60,000
Blaze, Inc., a Delaware corporation	40,000
Grape, Inc., a Virginia corporation	22,000

a. Alva purchased the Grape stock three years ago, and she purchased the Amur stock two years ago. She purchased the Blaze stock 18 days before it went ex-dividend and sold it 20 days later at a $5,000 loss. Alva reported no other capital gains and losses for the year. She is in the 35% marginal tax bracket. Compute Alva's tax on her dividend income.

b. Alva's daughter, Veda, who is age 25 and who is not Alva's dependent, reported taxable income of $10,000, which included $1,000 of dividends on Grape stock. Veda purchased the stock two years ago. Compute Veda's tax liability on the dividends.

18. **LO.4, 5** Roy decides to buy a personal residence, and he goes to the bank for a $150,000 loan. The bank tells Roy that he can borrow the funds at 4% if his father will guarantee the debt. Roy's father, Hal, owns a $150,000 CD currently yielding 3.5%. The Federal rate is 3%. Hal agrees to either of the following.

Decision Making

- Roy borrows from the bank with Hal's guarantee provided to the bank.
- Cash in the CD (with no penalty) and lend Roy the funds at 2% interest.

Hal is in the 33% marginal tax bracket. Roy, whose only source of income is his salary, is in the 15% marginal tax bracket. The interest that Roy pays on the mortgage will be deductible by him. Which option will maximize the family's after-tax wealth?

19. **LO.5** Brad is the president of the Yellow Corporation. He and other members of his family control the corporation. Brad has a temporary need for $50,000, and the corporation has excess cash. He could borrow the money from a bank at 9%, and Yellow is earning 6% on its temporary investments. Yellow has made loans to other employees on several occasions. Therefore, Brad is considering borrowing $50,000 from the corporation. He will repay the loan principal in two years plus interest at 5%. Identify the relevant tax issues for Brad and Yellow Corporation.

Issue ID

20. **LO.5** Ridge is a generous individual. During the year, he made interest-free loans to various family members when the Federal interest rate was 3%. What are the Federal tax consequences of the following loans by Ridge?
a. On June 30, Ridge loaned $12,000 to his cousin, Jim, to buy a used truck. Jim's only source of income was his wages on various construction jobs during the year.
b. On August 1, Ridge loaned $8,000 to his niece, Sonja. The loan was meant to enable her to pay her college tuition. Sonja reported $1,200 interest income from CDs that her parents had given her.
c. On September 1, Ridge loaned $25,000 to his brother, Al, to start a business. Al reported only $220 of dividends and interest for the year.
d. On September 30, Ridge loaned $150,000 to his mother so that she could enter a nursing home. His mother's only income was $9,000 in Social Security benefits and $500 interest income received.

21. **LO.5** Indicate whether the imputed interest rules apply in the following situations.
a. Mike loaned his sister $90,000 to buy a new home. Mike did not charge interest on the loan. The Federal rate was 5%. Mike's sister had $900 of investment income for the year.
b. Sam's employer maintains an emergency loan fund for its employees. During the year, Sam's wife was very ill, and he incurred unusually large medical expenses. He borrowed $8,500 from his employer's emergency loan fund for six months. The Federal rate was 5.5%. Sam and his wife had no investment income for the year.

c. Jody borrowed $25,000 from her controlled corporation for six months. She used the funds to pay her daughter's college tuition. The corporation charged Jody 4% interest. The Federal rate was 5%. Jody had $3,500 of investment income for the year.

d. Kait loaned her son, Jake, $60,000 for six months. Jake used the $60,000 to pay off college loans. The Federal rate was 5%, and Kait did not charge Jake any interest. Jake had dividend and interest income of $2,100 for the tax year.

22. **LO.5** Vito is the sole shareholder of Vito, Inc. The corporation also employs him. On June 30, 2014, Vito borrowed $8,000 from Vito, Inc., and on July 1, 2015, he borrowed an additional $10,000. Both loans were due on demand. No interest was charged on the loans, and the Federal interest rate was 4% for all relevant dates.

    Vito used the money to purchase a boat. Elsewhere on his return, Vito recognized $2,500 of investment income. Determine the tax consequences to Vito and Vito, Inc., if:

    a. The loans are considered employer-employee loans.

    b. The loans are considered corporation-shareholder loans.

23. **LO.6** How does the tax benefit rule apply in the following cases?

    a. In 2012, the Orange Furniture Store, an accrual method taxpayer, sold furniture on credit for $1,000 to Sammy. Orange's cost of the furniture was $600. In 2013, Orange took a bad debt deduction for the $1,000 because Sammy would not pay his bill.

       In 2014, Sammy inherited some money and paid Orange the $1,000 he owed. Orange was in the 35% marginal tax bracket in 2012, the 15% marginal tax bracket in 2013, and the 35% marginal tax bracket in 2014.

    b. In 2013, Barb, a cash basis taxpayer, was in an accident and incurred $8,000 in medical expenses, which she claimed as an itemized deduction for medical expenses. Because of a limitation, though, the expense reduced her taxable income by only $3,000. In 2014, Barb successfully sued the person who caused the physical injury and collected $8,000 to reimburse her for the cost of her medical expenses. Barb was in the 15% marginal tax bracket in both 2013 and 2014.

24. **LO.7** Determine Hazel's Federal gross income from the following receipts for the year.

Gain on sale of Augusta County bonds	$800
Interest on U.S. government savings bonds	400
Interest on state income tax refund	200
Interest on Augusta County bonds	700

Decision Making   25. **LO.7** Tammy, a resident of Virginia, is considering whether to purchase a North Carolina bond that yields 4.6% before tax. She is in the 35% Federal marginal tax bracket and the 5% state marginal tax bracket.

    Tammy is aware that State of Virginia bonds of comparable risk are yielding 4.5%. Virginia bonds are exempt from Virginia tax, but the North Carolina bond interest is taxable in Virginia.

    Which of the two options will provide the greater after-tax return to Tammy? Tammy can deduct all state taxes paid on her Federal income tax return.

Decision Making   26. **LO.7** Tonya, a Virginia resident, inherited a $100,000 State of Virginia bond this year. Her marginal Federal income tax rate is 35%, and her marginal state tax rate is 5%. The Virginia bond pays 3.3% interest, which is not subject to Virginia income tax. Alternatively, Tonya can purchase a corporate bond of comparable risk that will yield 5.2% or a U.S. government bond that pays 4.6% interest. Tonya does not itemize her deductions. Which investment provides the greatest after-tax yield?

Decision Making   27. **LO.9** The Egret Company has a 40% combined Federal and state marginal tax rate. Egret's board estimates that, if its current president should die, the company would incur $200,000 in costs to find a suitable replacement. In addition, profits on various projects the president is responsible for would likely decrease by $300,000. The president has recommended that Egret purchase a $500,000 life insurance policy. How much insurance should the company carry on the life of its president to compensate for the after-tax loss that would result from the president's death? Assume that the $200,000 costs of finding a president are deductible and the lost profits would have been taxable.

28. **LO.9** Ray and Carin are partners in an accounting firm. The partners have entered into an arm's length agreement requiring Ray to purchase Carin's partnership interest from Carin's estate if she dies before Ray. The price is set at 120% of the book value of Carin's partnership interest at the time of her death.

    Ray purchased an insurance policy on Carin's life to fund this agreement. After Ray had paid $45,000 in premiums, Carin was killed in an automobile accident, and Ray collected $800,000 of life insurance proceeds. Ray used the life insurance proceeds to purchase Carin's partnership interest.

    What amount should Ray include in his gross income from receiving the life insurance proceeds?

29. **LO.9** Laura recently was diagnosed with cancer and has begun chemotherapy treatments. A cancer specialist has given Laura less than one year to live. She has incurred sizable medical bills and other general living expenses and is in need of cash. Therefore, Laura is considering selling stock that cost her $35,000 in 2005 and now has a fair market value of $50,000. This amount would be sufficient to pay her medical bills.

    Critical Thinking

    Decision Making

    However, she has read about a company (VitalBenefits.com) that would purchase her life insurance policy for $50,000. To date, Laura has paid $30,000 in premiums on the policy.
    a. Considering only the Federal income tax effects, would selling the stock or selling the life insurance policy result in more beneficial tax treatment?
    b. Assume that Laura is a dependent child and that her mother owns the stock and the life insurance policy, which is on the mother's life. Which of the alternative means of raising the cash would result in more beneficial tax treatment?

30. **LO.10** Vic, who was experiencing financial difficulties, was able to adjust his debts as follows. Determine the Federal income tax consequences to Vic.
    a. Vic is an attorney. Vic owed his uncle $25,000. The uncle told Vic that if he serves as the executor of the uncle's estate, Vic's debt will be canceled in the uncle's will.
    b. Vic borrowed $80,000 from First Bank. The debt was secured by land that Vic purchased for $100,000. Vic was unable to pay, and the bank foreclosed when the liability was $80,000, which was also the fair market value of the property.
    c. The Land Company, which had sold land to Vic for $80,000, reduced the mortgage on the land by $12,000.

31. **LO.10** Harry purchased equipment for his business and gave the seller cash and a note due in two years. Carrie also purchased business equipment, but financed the transaction with a bank loan. Because both Harry and Carrie were having financial difficulties, the creditors reduced the balance due on each mortgage by $50,000. What are the Federal income tax effects of the debt adjustments experienced by Harry and Carrie?

32. **LO.11** During the year, Olivia recorded the following transactions involving capital assets.

Gain on the sale of unimproved land (held as an investment for 4 years)	$ 4,000
Loss on the sale of a camper (purchased 2 years ago and used for family vacations)	(5,000)
Loss on the sale of IBM stock (purchased 9 months ago as an investment)	(1,000)
Gain on the sale of a fishing boat and trailer (acquired 11 months ago at an auction and used for recreational purposes)	2,000

    a. If Olivia is in the 33% bracket, how much Federal income tax results?
    b. If Olivia is in the 15% bracket, how much Federal income tax results?

33. **LO.11** Andy reported the following gains and losses from the sale of capital assets.

    Critical Thinking

Loss on Pigeon Corporation stock (held 9 months)	($14,000)
Gain on painting (held for 2 years as an investment)	5,000
Gain on unimproved land (held for 3 years as an investment)	3,000

    a. If Andy is in the 35% tax bracket, determine the Federal income tax consequences of these transactions.
    b. What if Andy is in the 15% tax bracket?
    c. What if Andy is a C corporation in the 35% tax bracket?

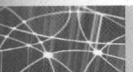

Critical Thinking   34. **LO.11** Liz and Doug were divorced on July 1 of the current year after 10 years of marriage. Their current year's income received before the divorce included:

Doug's salary	$41,000
Liz's salary	55,000
Rent on apartments purchased by Liz 15 years ago	8,000
Dividends on stock Doug inherited from his mother 4 years ago	1,900
Interest on a savings account in Liz's name funded with her salary	2,400

Allocate the income to Liz and Doug assuming that they live in:
a. California.
b. Texas.

BRIDGE DISCIPLINE

1. Find the audited financial statements of a major U.S. corporation.
   a. Summarize its most important financial accounting policies.
   b. Describe two elements of the Federal income tax law that significantly affected the corporation's earnings per share for the operating year.

Communications   2. For the same corporation, summarize three key tax accounting applications, and point out how they differ from book income principles. Summarize your findings, and present them to your classmates in no more than five PowerPoint slides.

3. The exclusion of state and local bond interest from Federal income tax often is criticized as creating a tax haven for the wealthy. Critics, however, often fail to take into account the effect of market forces. In recent months, the long-term tax-exempt interest rate has been 3.5%, while the long-term taxable rate for bonds of comparable risk was approximately 4.7%. On the other hand, state and local governments do enjoy a savings in interest costs because of the tax-favored status of their bonds.

   To date, Congress has concluded that the benefits gained by the states and municipalities and their residents, such as the access to capital and the creation of jobs to construct and maintain critical infrastructure, outweigh any damages to our progressive income tax system. Do you agree with the proponents of the exclusion? Why or why not?

Critical Thinking   4. In a two-page paper, separately evaluate each of the following alternative proposals for taxing the income from property.

Communications   a. All assets would be valued at the end of the year, any increase in value that occurred during the year would be included in gross income, and any decrease in value would be deductible from gross income.
      b. No gain or loss would be recognized until the taxpayer sold or exchanged the property.
      c. Increases or decreases in the value of property traded on a national exchange (e.g., the New York Stock Exchange) would be reflected in gross income for the years in which the changes in value occur. For all other assets, no gain or loss would be recognized until the owner disposes of the property.

Communications   5. Various Federal stimulus provisions were designed to assist state and local governments in borrowing funds, leveraging the gross income exclusion for such bond interest so that such jurisdictions would have increased access to funds. One of the justifications for these provisions was that state and local governments cannot run budget deficits and cannot "print money," so the recent recession put them in a difficult cash-flow position.

   Audits of the use of these borrowed funds showed that some of the bond proceeds were used by the jurisdictions to participate in "public-private partnerships," where government funds were used to assist private entities in expanding in or relocating to the jurisdiction. Specifically, bond proceeds were found to have been used to provide targeted road-building and utility-construction projects to benefit large commercial entities.

   Is this an appropriate use of the gross income exclusion for state and local bond interest? Summarize your comments in an e-mail to your instructor.

Research Problems

Note: Solutions to Research Problems can be prepared by using the **Checkpoint®
Student Edition** online research product, which is available to accompany this text. It is
also possible to prepare solutions to the Research Problems by using tax research materials found in a standard tax library.

THOMSON REUTERS

CHECKPOINT®

Research Problem 1. Tranquility Funeral Home, Inc., your client, is an accrual basis taxpayer that sells "pre-need" funeral contracts. Under these contracts, the customer pays in advance for goods and services to be provided at the contract beneficiary's death. These payments are refundable at the contract purchaser's request, pursuant to state law, at any time until the goods and services are furnished. Tranquility, consistent with its financial accounting reporting, includes the payments in income for the year the funeral service is provided.

Communications

An IRS agent insists that the contract payments constitute prepaid income subject to tax in the year of receipt. Your client believes the amounts involved are tax-deferred customer deposits.

Write a letter to Tranquility that contains your tax advice about how the issue should be resolved. The client's address is 400 Rock Street, Memphis, TN 38152.

Research Problem 2. Clint, your client, owns a life insurance policy on his own life. He has paid $6,800 in premiums, and the cash surrender value of the policy is $30,000. Clint borrowed $30,000 from the insurance company, using the cash surrender value as collateral. He is considering canceling the policy in payment of the loan. Clint would like to know the Federal income tax consequences of canceling his policy. Summarize your findings in a brief research memo.

Communications

Research Problem 3. Your client, New Shoes Ltd., is a retailer that often issues store gift (debit) cards to customers in lieu of a cash refund. You recall that the IRS issued a revenue procedure that provided that the prepaid income rules in Revenue Procedure 2004–34 could be applied to the income from the gift cards. Locate a more recent revenue procedure that authorizes the deferral of gross income from gift cards. Outline the key points of this document, and send the outline to your instructor.

Communications

Research Problem 4. Kristina soon will graduate from law school with more than $40,000 in student loans. She would like to work as a public defender, but the pay for such a position is not enough to allow her to meet her living expenses and repay the student loans. Kristina's law school offers a "debt forgiveness program" for graduates who enter public service, including working as a public defender. Under the program, the school will pay off the student's debt, but the graduate will owe an equal amount to the program. However, if the graduate remains in public service for at least four years, the debt is forgiven.

Kristina would like to know the Federal income tax consequences to her if she decides to utilize this program.

Use the tax resources of the Internet to address the following questions. Do not restrict your search to the Web, but include a review of newsgroups and general reference materials, practitioner sites and resources, primary sources of the tax law, chat rooms and discussion groups, and other opportunities.

Internet Activity

Research Problem 5. Construct a chart for your state and four of its neighboring states. Provide "Yes/No" entries for each state in the following categories. Send the chart to your classmates by e-mail.

Communications

- Does the state exclude interest income from U.S. Treasury bonds?
- Does the state exclude interest income from Fannie Mae bonds?
- Does the state exclude interest income from bonds issued by governments in its own state?
- Does the state exclude interest income from bonds issued by governments in other states?

Communications   **Research Problem 6.** Determine the applicable Federal interest rate as of today for purposes of § 7872 below-market loans. In an e-mail to your professor, describe how the rate is determined and how you discovered the pertinent rules.

Research Problem 7. Go to the web page for a securities broker or mutual fund. Use a "calculator" provided there to indicate the following.

Taxable Interest Rate	Your Marginal Tax Rate	Break-Even Exempt Interest Rate
5%	35%	?
5%	15%	?
8%	28%	?
8%	33%	?

Communications   **Research Problem 8.** Lottery winnings are taxable for Federal income tax purposes. What many lottery hopefuls forget, though, is that lottery winnings are also taxable in many states. Search the Internet to determine if lottery winnings are taxable for California residents. For residents of your own state.

5 Business Deductions

LEARNING OBJECTIVES: *After completing Chapter 5, you should be able to:*

LO.1 Articulate the meaning and application of the ordinary, necessary, and reasonableness requirements for the deduction of business expenses.

LO.2 Describe the cash and accrual methods of accounting for business deductions.

LO.3 Apply a variety of Internal Revenue Code deduction disallowance provisions.

LO.4 Recognize the limitations applicable to the charitable contribution deduction for corporations.

LO.5 State and apply the alternative tax treatments for research and experimental expenditures and understand several other common business deductions.

LO.6 Determine the amount of cost recovery under MACRS and apply the § 179 expensing election and the deduction limitations on listed property and automobiles when making the MACRS calculation.

LO.7 Identify intangible assets that are eligible for amortization and calculate the amount of the deduction.

LO.8 Determine the amount of depletion expense and recognize the alternative tax treatments for intangible drilling and development costs.

CHAPTER OUTLINE

TAX TALK *Last year I had difficulty with my income tax. I tried to take my analyst off as a business deduction. The Government said it was entertainment. We compromised finally and made it a religious contribution.* —WOODY ALLEN

© moodboard/Jupiter Images

CALCULATING DEDUCTIBLE EXPENSES

Michael Forney reports the following expense information from the financial reporting system associated with his small engine service and repair business. Mr. Forney operates his business as a C corporation with a December 31 year-end, uses the accrual method of accounting, and has $330,500 of gross income.

Forney owns 80 percent of the corporation's stock, while his wife, Kathleen, and his mother, Terry, each own 10 percent of the stock. Michael is a full-time employee at his business, and his mother helps out with the books for about two hours a week. At this time, Kathleen does not work at the business.

Salaries and wages (including Michael's salary of $55,000 and Terry's salary of $3,000)	$150,000
Building rent	24,000
Depreciation of machinery, equipment, and office furnishings*	2,500
Insurance (coverage for machinery, equipment, and office furnishings)	12,000
Utilities	12,000
Taxes and licenses	6,000
Fine paid to city	2,500
Advertising	3,000
Interest expense on loan to buy new machinery	6,000
Charitable contributions	3,000
Political contributions	2,000

*$25,000 of new machinery and equipment were purchased in January 2014. The financial reporting system depreciation is based on straight-line depreciation over 10 years. The MACRS cost recovery period for tax purposes is 7 years.

Michael would like to know the amount of his deductible expenses for tax purposes.

Michael would also like your advice on another matter. Because his business has been very profitable over the years, it has built up large cash reserves, and its cash flow continues to be strong. Even with the high levels of cash in the business, it has never paid any dividends to the shareholders. For next year, he is considering paying himself a salary of $140,000 and his mother a salary of $30,000. This would give them more cash to spend for planned vacations and home improvements.

Finally, during the year, Michael purchased another personal residence for $300,000 and converted his original residence to rental property; Michael purchased his original residence for $250,000 five years ago and it has a current market value of $180,000. He also purchased a condo during the year for $170,000 near his business, which he will rent to tenants. He would like to know the tax implications, if any, of these transactions.

Read the chapter and formulate your response.

T he tax law has an all-inclusive definition of income; that is, income from whatever source derived is includible in gross income. Income cannot be excluded
unless there is a specific statement to that effect in the Internal Revenue Code.
Conversely, deductions are disallowed unless a specific provision in the tax law
permits them. The inclusive definition of income and the exclusive definition of
deductions may not seem fair to taxpayers, but it is the structure of the law. This
chapter discusses many of the common business deductions encountered by taxpayers that are specified in the Code.

5-1 OVERVIEW OF BUSINESS DEDUCTIONS

LO.1

Articulate the meaning and application of the ordinary, necessary, and reasonableness requirements for the deduction of business expenses.

As just noted, an income tax deduction is not allowed under Federal law unless
Congress creates a specific provision allowing it. For businesses, trade or business
deductions are allowed by statute, but only if they are both *ordinary and necessary*
and *reasonable* in amount.

5-1a Ordinary and Necessary Requirement

Section 162(a) permits a deduction for all ordinary and necessary expenses paid or
incurred in carrying on a trade or business. To understand the scope of this provision, it is critical to understand the meanings of the terms *ordinary* and *necessary*.

Neither ordinary nor necessary is defined in the Code or Regulations. However,
the courts have had to deal with these terms on numerous occasions and have held
that an expense is necessary if a prudent businessperson would incur the same
expense and the expense is expected to be appropriate and helpful in the taxpayer's business.[1] But as Example 1 shows, no deduction will be allowed unless the
expense is also ordinary.

Example 1

Pat purchased a business that had just been adjudged bankrupt. Because the business
had a poor financial rating, Pat wanted to restore its financial reputation. Consequently, he paid off some of the debts owed by the former owners that had been cancelled by the bankruptcy court. Because Pat had no legal obligation to make these
payments, the U.S. Supreme Court found he has trying to generate goodwill. Although
the payments were necessary (i.e., appropriate and helpful), they were *not* ordinary
and their deduction *was not* allowed.[2]

An expense is ordinary if it is normal, usual, or customary in the type of business
conducted by the taxpayer and is not capital in nature.[3] However, an expense need
not be recurring to be deductible as ordinary. For example, a business may be in a
situation that is a very rare occurrence and incur an expense. If other businesses in
a similar situation are likely to incur a similar expense, then the expense can be ordinary, even though it is not recurring.

Example 2

Zebra Corporation engaged in a mail-order business. The post office judged that
Zebra's advertisements were false and misleading. Under a fraud order, the post office
stamped "fraudulent" on all letters addressed to Zebra's business and returned them
to the senders. Zebra spent $30,000 on legal fees in an unsuccessful attempt to force
the post office to stop. The legal fees (although not recurring) were ordinary business
expenses because they were normal, usual, or customary under the circumstances.[4]

5-1b Reasonableness Requirement

Although § 162 is intended to allow taxpayers to deduct a broad range of trade or
business expenses, the Code applies a reasonableness requirement solely to salaries

---

[1] *Welch v. Helvering*, 3 USTC ¶1164, 12 AFTR 1456, 54 S.Ct. 8 (USSC, 1933).

[2] *Welch v. Helvering*, cited in footnote 1. But compare *Dunn and McCarthy, Inc. v. Comm.*, 43–2 USTC ¶9688, 31 AFTR 1043, 139 F.2d 242 (CA–2, 1943) where a deduction was allowed. In *Dunn*, most of the creditors were unpaid creditor-employees. As they continued to work for the new owner,

repaying their loans was maintaining *existing* goodwill—not creating *new* goodwill.

[3] *Deputy v. DuPont*, 40–1 USTC ¶9161, 23 AFTR 808, 60 S.Ct. 363 (USSC, 1940).

[4] *Comm. v. Heininger*, 44–1 USTC ¶9109, 31 AFTR 783, 64 S.Ct. 249 (USSC, 1943).

and other compensation for services.[5] However, the courts have held that for *any* business expense to be ordinary and necessary, it must also be reasonable in amount.[6]

What constitutes reasonableness is a question of fact.[7] If an expense is unreasonable, the excess amount is not allowed as a deduction. The question of reasonableness usually arises with respect to closely held corporations with no separation of ownership and management.

Transactions between shareholders and a closely held corporation may result in the disallowance of deductions for excessive salaries, rent, and other expenses paid by the corporation to the shareholders. The courts will view an unusually large salary in light of all relevant circumstances and may find that the salary is reasonable despite its size. If excessive payments for salaries, rent, and other expenses are closely related to the percentage of stock owned by the recipients, the payments are generally treated as dividends.[8] Because dividends are not deductible by the corporation, the disallowance results in an increase in corporate taxable income. Deductions for reasonable salaries will not be disallowed solely because the corporation has paid insubstantial portions of its earnings as dividends to its shareholders.

THE BIG PICTURE

Example 3

Return to the facts of *The Big Picture* on p. 5-1. The small engine service and repair business, a closely held C corporation, is owned by Michael Forney, his wife, Kathleen, and his mother, Terry. The company has been highly profitable for several years and has never paid dividends. Michael is the key employee of the business, while his mother plays a very minor role. Assume that their current salaries of $55,000 and $3,000 are comparable to what they could earn at similar companies for the work they do.

If Mr. Forney's plan to more than double his salary and increase his mother's salary by tenfold is implemented, the amounts in excess of their current salaries may be deemed unreasonable; if that is the case, the excess would be disallowed as deductible salary. The disallowed amounts would then be treated as dividends rather than salary income to Michael and Terry. Salaries are deductible by the corporation, but dividends are not. Note, however, that the shareholders may benefit from this reclassification. Salaries would be taxed at ordinary income rates and are subject to payroll taxes. However, dividend income would be taxed at long-term capital rates if qualified (see Chapter 13).

Tax Planning Strategies   UNREASONABLE COMPENSATION

FRAMEWORK FOCUS: TAX RATE

Strategy: Avoid Double Taxation.

In substantiating the reasonableness of a shareholder-employee's compensation, an internal comparison test is sometimes useful. If it can be shown that nonshareholder-employees and shareholder-employees in comparable positions receive comparable compensation, it is indicative that compensation is not unreasonable.

Another possibility is to demonstrate that the shareholder-employee has been underpaid in prior years. For example, the shareholder-employee may have agreed to take a less-than-adequate salary during the unprofitable formative years of the business. He or she would

expect the "postponed" compensation to be paid in later, more profitable years. The agreement should be documented, if possible, in the corporate minutes.

Keep in mind that in testing for reasonableness, the total pay package must be considered. Compensation includes all fringe benefits or perquisites, such as contributions by the corporation to a qualified pension plan, regardless of when the funds are available to the employee.

For additional discussion of the meaning of reasonable compensation, see Chapter 13.

---

[5]§ 162(a)(1).

[6]*Comm. v. Lincoln Electric Co.,* 49–2 USTC ¶9388, 38 AFTR 411, 176 F.2d 815 (CA–6, 1949).

[7]*Kennedy, Jr. v. Comm.,* 82–1 USTC ¶9186, 49 AFTR 2d 82–628, 671 F.2d 167 (CA–6, 1982), *rev'g* 72 T.C. 793 (1979).

[8]Reg. § 1.162–8.

EXHIBIT 5.1	Partial List of Business Deductions
Advertising	Pension and profit sharing plans
Bad debts	Rent or lease payments
Commissions and fees	Repairs and maintenance
Depletion	Salaries and wages
Depreciation	Supplies
Employee benefit programs	Taxes and licenses
Insurance	Travel and transportation
Interest	Utilities

Common Business Deductions

The language of § 162 is broad enough to permit the deduction of many different types of ordinary and necessary business expenses. Some of the more common deductions are listed in Exhibit 5.1.

5-2 TIMING OF EXPENSE RECOGNITION

LO.2

Describe the cash and accrual methods of accounting for business deductions.

A taxpayer's accounting method is a major factor in determining taxable income. The method used determines *when* an item is includible in income and *when* an item is deductible on the tax return. Usually, the taxpayer's regular method of record keeping is used for income tax purposes.[9] The taxing authorities require that the method used clearly reflect income and that items be handled consistently.[10] The most common methods of accounting are the cash method and the accrual method. If a taxpayer owns multiple businesses, it may be possible to use the cash method for some and the accrual method for others.

Throughout the portions of the Code dealing with deductions, the phrase *paid or incurred* is used. A cash basis taxpayer is allowed a deduction only in the year an expense is *paid*. An accrual basis taxpayer is allowed a deduction in the year in which the liability for the expense is *incurred* (becomes certain).

5-2a Cash Method Requirements

The expenses of cash basis taxpayers are deductible only when they are actually paid with cash or other property. Promising to pay or issuing a note does not satisfy the actually paid requirement.[11] However, the payment can be made with borrowed funds. Thus, taxpayers are allowed to claim the deduction at the time they charge expenses on credit cards. They are deemed to have simultaneously borrowed money from the credit card issuer and constructively paid the expenses.[12]

Although the cash basis taxpayer must have actually or constructively paid the expense, payment does not ensure a current deduction. The Regulations require capitalization of any expenditure that creates an asset having a useful life that extends substantially beyond the end of the tax year.[13] Thus, cash basis and accrual basis taxpayers cannot take a current deduction for capital expenditures except through amortization, depletion, or depreciation over the tax life of the asset.

Example 4

Redbird, Inc., a calendar year and cash basis taxpayer, rents property from Bluejay, Inc. On July 1, 2014, Redbird pays $24,000 rent for the 24 months ending June 30, 2016. The prepaid rent extends 18 months after the close of the tax year—substantially beyond the year of payment. Therefore, Redbird must capitalize the prepaid rent and amortize the expense on a monthly basis. Redbird's deduction for 2014 is $6,000.

---

[9]§ 446(a).

[10]§§ 446(b) and (e); Reg. § 1.446–1(a)(2).

[11]*Page v. Rhode Island Trust Co., Exr.*, 37–1 USTC ¶9138, 19 AFTR 105, 88 F.2d 192 (CA–1, 1937).

[12]Rev.Rul. 78–39, 1978–1 C.B. 73. See also Rev.Rul. 80–335, 1980–2 C.B. 170, which applies to pay-by-phone arrangements.

[13]Reg. § 1.461–1(a).

Tax Planning Strategies TIME VALUE OF TAX DEDUCTIONS

FRAMEWORK FOCUS: DEDUCTIONS

Strategy: Accelerate Recognition of Deductions to Achieve Tax Deferral.

Cash basis taxpayers often have the ability to make early payments for their expenses at the end of the tax year. This may permit the payments to be deducted in the year of payment instead of in the following tax year. In view of the time value of money, a tax deduction this year may be worth more than the same deduction next year. Before employing this strategy, the taxpayer must consider what next year's expected income and tax rates will be and whether a cash-flow problem may develop from early payments. Thus, a variety of considerations must be taken into account when planning the timing of tax deductions.

In-depth coverage can be found on this book's companion website: **www.cengagebrain.com**   I   Digging Deeper

5-2b Accrual Method Requirements

The period in which an accrual basis taxpayer can deduct an expense is determined by applying the *all events test* and the *economic performance test*. That is, a deduction cannot be claimed until (1) all of the events have occurred to create the taxpayer's liability and (2) the amount of the liability can be determined with reasonable accuracy. Once these requirements are satisfied, the deduction is permitted only if economic performance has occurred. The economic performance test is met only when the service, property, or use of property giving rise to the liability is actually performed for, provided to, or used by the taxpayer.[14]

Example 5

Robin, Inc., an entertainment business, sponsored a jazz festival in a rented auditorium at City College. Robin is responsible for cleaning up after the festival, which took place on December 22, 2014, and reinstalling the auditorium seats. Because the college is closed over the Christmas holidays, the company hired by Robin to perform the work did not begin these activities until January 2, 2015. Robin cannot deduct its $1,200 labor cost until 2015, when the services are performed.

In-depth coverage can be found on this book's companion website: **www.cengagebrain.com**   2   Digging Deeper

As illustrated in Examples 6 and 7, an exception to the economic performance requirement allows some *recurring* items to be deducted if certain conditions are met.[15]

Example 6

Towhee Company, an accrual basis, calendar year taxpayer, entered into a monthly maintenance contract during the year. Towhee makes a monthly accrual at the end of every month for this service and pays the fee sometime between the first and fifteenth of the following month when services are performed. The December 2014 accrual is deductible in 2014 even though the service is performed on January 12, 2015.

Example 7

Tanager, Inc., an accrual basis, calendar year taxpayer, shipped merchandise sold on December 30, 2014, via Greyhound Van Lines on January 2, 2015, and paid the freight charges at that time. Because Tanager reported the sale of the merchandise in 2014, the shipping charge should also be deductible in 2014. This procedure results in a better matching of income and expenses.

---

[14]§ 461(h).   [15]§ 461(h)(3)(A).

Reserves for estimated expenses (frequently employed for financial accounting purposes) generally are not allowed for tax purposes because the economic performance test cannot be satisfied.

Example 8

Oriole Airlines is required by Federal law to test its engines after 3,000 flying hours. Aircraft cannot return to flight until the tests have been conducted. An unrelated aircraft maintenance company does all of the company's tests for $1,500 per engine.

For financial reporting purposes, the company accrues an expense based upon $.50 per hour of flight and credits an allowance account. The actual amounts paid for maintenance are offset against the allowance account.

For tax purposes, the economic performance test is not satisfied until the work has been done. Therefore, the reserve method cannot be used for tax purposes.

5-3 DISALLOWANCE POSSIBILITIES

LO.3

Apply a variety of Internal Revenue Code deduction disallowance provisions.

While most ordinary and necessary business expenses are deductible, the tax law contains provisions that disallow a deduction for certain expenditures. The most frequently encountered disallowance provisions are discussed next.

5-3a Public Policy Limitations

Certain disallowance provisions are a codification or extension of prior court decisions. For example, after the courts denied deductions for payments considered to be in violation of public policy, the tax law was changed to provide specific authority for the disallowance of these deductions.

Justification for Denying Deductions

The courts developed the principle that a payment in violation of public policy is not a necessary expense and is not deductible.[16] Although a bribe or fine may be helpful, and may even contribute to the profitability of an activity, allowing a deduction for such expenses would be contrary to public policy. A deduction would, in effect, represent an indirect governmental subsidy for taxpayer wrongdoing.

Under legislation enacted based on this principle, the following deductions are disallowed for specific types of expenditures that are considered contrary to public policy:

* Bribes and kickbacks illegal under either Federal or state law, including those associated with Medicare or Medicaid.
* Two-thirds of the treble damage payments made to claimants resulting from violation of antitrust law.[17]
* Fines and penalties paid to a government for violation of law.

THE BIG PICTURE

Example 9

Refer to the facts of *The Big Picture* on p. 5-1. Michael Forney had not instituted proper procedures for disposing of used motor oil and other engine fluids from his business. During the current tax year, he was fined $2,500 by the city. Mr. Forney believes the fine should be deducted as an ordinary business expense. However, because the fine was due to a violation of public policy, the $2,500 is not deductible.

Digging Deeper **3** In-depth coverage can be found on this book's companion website: **www.cengagebrain.com**

---

[16]*Tank Truck Rentals, Inc. v. Comm.*, 58–1 USTC ¶9366, 1 AFTR 2d 1154, 78 S.Ct. 507 (USSC, 1958). [17]§§ 162(c), (f), and (g).

Legal Expenses Incurred in Defense of Civil or Criminal Penalties

To deduct legal expenses as trade or business expenses, the taxpayer must be able to show that the origin and character of the claim are directly related to a trade or business. Personal legal expenses are not deductible. Thus, legal fees incurred in connection with a criminal defense are deductible only if the crime is associated with the taxpayer's trade or business.[18]

Debra, a majority shareholder and chief financial officer of Blue Corporation, incurs legal expenses in connection with her defense in a criminal indictment for evasion of Blue's income taxes. Debra may deduct her legal expenses because she is deemed to be in the trade or business of being an executive. The legal action impairs her ability to conduct this business activity.[19]	**Example 10**

Expenses Related to an Illegal Business

The usual expenses of operating an illegal business (e.g., a gambling operation) are deductible.[20] While allowing deductions for illegal activity may seem inappropriate, recall that the law taxes net income from a business operation, not gross revenue. However, § 162 disallows a deduction for fines, bribes to public officials, illegal kickbacks, and other illegal payments without regard to whether these payments are part of a legal or illegal business.

Grizzly, Inc., owns and operates a restaurant. In addition, Grizzly operates an illegal gambling establishment out of the restaurant's back room. In connection with the illegal gambling activity, Grizzly has the following expenses during the year:	**Example 11**

Rent	$ 60,000
Payoffs to police	40,000
Depreciation on equipment	100,000
Wages	140,000
Interest	30,000
Criminal fines	50,000
Illegal kickbacks	10,000
Total	$430,000

All of the usual expenses (rent, depreciation, wages, and interest) are deductible; payoffs, fines, and kickbacks are not deductible. Of the $430,000 spent, $330,000 is deductible and $100,000 is not.

An exception applies to expenses incurred in illegal trafficking in drugs.[21] Drug dealers are not allowed a deduction for ordinary and necessary business expenses incurred in their business. In arriving at gross income from the business, however, dealers may reduce total sales by the cost of goods sold.[22]

5-3b Political Contributions and Lobbying Activities

Political Contributions

Generally, no business deduction is permitted for direct or indirect payments for political purposes.[23] Historically, the government has been reluctant to extend favorable tax treatment to political expenditures by businesses. Allowing deductions might encourage abuses and enable businesses to have undue influence on the political process.

[18]*Comm. v. Tellier*, 66–1 USTC ¶9319, 17 AFTR 2d 633, 86 S.Ct. 1118 (USSC, 1966).

[19]Rev.Rul. 68–662, 1968–2 C.B. 69.

[20]*Comm. v. Sullivan*, 58–1 USTC ¶9368, 1 AFTR 2d 1158, 78 S.Ct. 512 (USSC, 1958).

[21]§ 280E.

[22]Reg. § 1.61–3(a). Gross income is defined as sales minus cost of goods sold. Thus, while § 280E prohibits any deductions for drug dealers, it does not modify the normal definition of gross income.

[23]§ 276.

Global Tax Issues

Enforcement of Foreign Anti-Bribery Laws

The Foreign Corrupt Practices Act (FCPA) is intended to punish taxpayers who make illegal payments to foreign officials to obtain economic advantages. Not only are such payments (usually improperly recorded as business expenses) nondeductible for income tax purposes, but serious and consistent violations can lead to the imposition of fines. Severe consequences can result from violating the bribery provisions of the FCPA, as Ralph Lauren recently discovered.

Ralph Lauren Corporation is known for its high-quality and expensive merchandise. To remove some of the bureaucratic hurdles that could significantly delay the time it takes to get merchandise into Argentina, Ralph Lauren employees had been providing dresses, perfume, and cash to Argentine customs officials. The bribes, which occurred over a five-year period, were labeled as "loading and delivery expenses" to disguise them. An internal investigation at Ralph Lauren uncovered this illegal activity, and company officials reported the crimes to the Department of Justice and the Securities and Exchange Commission. The company was required to pay over $1.5 million in penalties due to violation of the FCPA. Note that companies spend large amounts of money to conduct investigations such as the one performed by Ralph Lauren to ensure compliance with the FCPA.

While the Ralph Lauren managers in Argentina were willing to violate the law to attempt to increase their business sales, the efforts had little success. Besides resulting in large penalties for Ralph Lauren (which are not deductible), the company decided to leave the Argentina market in 2012 due to economic and currency issues.

Source: Based on Chad Bray, "Perfume, Dresses and Cash in Ralph Lauren Bribe Case," *Wall Street Journal,* April 23, 2013, pp. B1 and B2.

THE BIG PICTURE

Example 12

Refer to the facts of *The Big Picture* on p. 5-1. Michael Forney had made political contributions to the State Senate campaigns of Tom Smith and Virginia White. Mr. Forney made these contributions to encourage these candidates to support a new bill that is beneficial to the state's small businesses. Therefore, he assumed that these would be deductible business expenses. However, political contributions are not deductible, so he will receive no tax benefit from them.

Lobbying Expenditures

The Code places severe restrictions on the deductibility of expenses incurred in connection with lobbying activities.[24] These provisions deny deductions for expenditures incurred in connection with attempting to influence:

- State or Federal legislation and
- The actions of certain high-ranking public officials.

The disallowance also applies to a pro rata portion of the membership dues of trade associations and other groups that are involved in lobbying activities. There are three exceptions to the disallowance provisions. First, an exception is provided for influencing *local* legislation (e.g., city and county governments). Second, the disallowance provision does not apply to activities devoted solely to *monitoring* legislation. Third, a *de minimis* exception allows the deduction of up to $2,000 of annual

---

[24]§ 162(e).

in-house expenditures if the expenditures are not otherwise disallowed under the provisions discussed above. In-house lobbying expenditures do not include expenses paid to professional lobbyists or any portion of dues used by associations for lobbying. If in-house expenditures exceed $2,000, none of the in-house expenditures can be deducted.

Example 13

Egret Company pays a $10,000 annual membership fee to the Free Trade Group, a trade association for plumbing wholesalers. The trade association estimates that 70% of its dues are allocated to lobbying activities. Thus, Egret's deduction is limited to $3,000 ($10,000 × 30%), the amount not associated with lobbying activities.

5-3c Excessive Executive Compensation

The Code contains a *millionaires' provision* that applies to compensation paid by *publicly held* corporations.[25] The provision does not limit the amount of compensation that can be *paid* to an employee. Instead, it limits the amount the employer can *deduct* for the compensation of a covered executive to $1 million annually. Covered employees as defined by the SEC are the principal executive officer (PEO), the principal financial officer (PFO), and the three other most highly compensated executives. Employee compensation for this purpose *excludes* the following:

- Commissions based on individual performance.
- Certain performance-based compensation tied to company performance using a formula approved by a board of directors compensation committee (composed solely of two or more outside directors) and by shareholder vote. The performance attainment must be certified by this compensation committee.
- Payments to tax-qualified retirement plans.
- Payments that are excludible from the employee's gross income (e.g., certain fringe benefits).

5-3d Disallowance of Deductions for Capital Expenditures

The Code specifically disallows a deduction for "any amount paid out for new buildings or for permanent improvements or betterments made to increase the value of any property or estate."[26] The Regulations further define capital expenditures to include expenditures that add to the value or prolong the life of property or adapt the property to a new or different use.[27] Incidental repairs and maintenance of the property are not capital expenditures and can be deducted as ordinary and necessary business expenses. Repairing a roof is a deductible expense, but replacing a roof is a capital expenditure subject to depreciation deductions over a prescribed period. The tune-up of a delivery truck is an expense; a complete overhaul probably is a capital expenditure. Adding new gravel to a gravel parking lot is a repair, but paving the parking lot is a capital expenditure because this is doing more than restoring the asset to its original condition.

New temporary Regulations take effect January 1, 2014, which provide additional guidance on whether expenditures to acquire, produce, or improve tangible property must be capitalized or deducted.[28]

Capitalization versus Expense

When an expenditure is capitalized rather than expensed, the deduction is at best deferred and at worst lost forever. Although an immediate tax benefit for a large cash expenditure is lost, the cost may be deductible in increments over a longer period of time as the asset is depreciated, amortized, or depleted.

---

[25]§ 162(m).
[26]§ 263(a)(1).

[27]Reg. § 1.263(a)–1(b).
[28]Reg. § 1.263(a)–1T(a).

TAX IN THE NEWS   Do Deduction Limits Affect Executive Compensation?

Only $1 million of compensation can be deducted for the CEO, CFO, and three other highest-compensated executives of publicly traded companies. However, as noted on the previous page, this limitation does not apply to performance-based compensation. One interesting issue is whether this exception is broad enough to allow publicly traded companies to pay substantial compensation to executives and still receive a tax deduction. The answer is clearly yes.

For example, in 2012 the CEO of eBay received base salary of $970,353, which is just under the $1 million limitation. However, he received bonuses and stock incentives of over $28.5 million, which are deductible under the performance-based exception. The CEO of Textron had salary of exactly $1 million, and performance-based compensation was over $10 million. The biggest payday was for Robert Iger, CEO of Walt Disney, who had salary of $2.5 million and performance-based compensation of almost $34 million.

Of 170 S&P 500 CEO salaries that were analyzed by *USA TODAY*, only two had a base salary greater than $2 million, and many had a base salary at or very close to $1 million. This indicates that the $1 million limit does have an influence on the base salary of CEOs. However, because of the performance-based exception, this tax law appears to have had very little impact on the escalation of executive salaries.

Source: Based on Matt Krantz and Barbara Hansen, "CEO Pay Rockets As Economy, Stocks Recover," *USA TODAY*, April 1, 2013, www.usatoday.com/story/money/business/2013/03/27/ceo-pay-executive-compensation-2012/2006203/.

If the expenditure is for a tangible asset that has an ascertainable life, it is capitalized and may be deducted as depreciation over the life of the asset or as a cost recovery allowance over its depreciable life. (Depreciation and cost recovery allowances are discussed later in this chapter.) Land is not subject to depreciation (or cost recovery) because it does not have an ascertainable life.

Example 14

Buffalo Corporation purchases an old but usable apartment building and land located in an apartment-zoned area. Buffalo pays $500,000 for the property and immediately has the building demolished at a cost of $100,000. The $500,000 purchase price and the $100,000 demolition costs must be capitalized, and the tax basis of the land is $600,000. Because land is a nondepreciable asset, no deduction is allowed.

5-3e Investigation of a Business

Investigation expenses are paid or incurred to determine the feasibility of entering a new business or expanding an existing business. They include costs such as travel, engineering and architectural surveys, marketing reports, and various legal and accounting services. How such expenses are treated for tax purposes depends on a number of variables, including the following:

- The current business, if any, of the taxpayer.
- The nature of the business being investigated.
- Whether the acquisition actually takes place.

If the taxpayer is in a business that is the same as or similar to that being investigated, all investigation expenses are deductible in the year paid or incurred. The tax result is the same whether or not the taxpayer acquires the business being investigated.[29]

---

[29] *York v. Comm.*, 58–2 USTC ¶9952, 2 AFTR 2d 6178, 261 F.2d 421 (CA–4, 1958).

Example 15

Return to the facts of *The Big Picture* on p. 5-1. Michael Forney believes that his mechanical and business skills can be used to turn around other small engine businesses whose revenues have been declining. He investigates Southside Small Engine Services, LLC, a nearby competitor that is for sale. Expenses paid to consultants and accountants as part of this investigation totaled $6,000. He determined that Southside Small Engine Services would not be a good investment, so he did not buy it.

The $6,000 spent to investigate this business is deductible as a business expense because Mr. Forney is already in the small engine service and repair business. Investigating new business opportunities in one's current trade or business is an ordinary and necessary business expense.

When the taxpayer is not in a business that is the same as or similar to the one being investigated, the tax result depends on whether the new business is acquired. If the business is not acquired, all investigation expenses generally are nondeductible.[30]

Example 16

Lynn, president and sole shareholder of Marmot Corporation, incurs expenses when traveling from Rochester, New York, to California to investigate the feasibility of acquiring several auto care centers. Marmot is in the residential siding business. If no acquisition takes place, Marmot may not deduct any of the expenses.

If the taxpayer is not in a business that is the same as or similar to the one being investigated and actually acquires the new business, the expenses must be capitalized as **startup expenditures**. Startup expenditures are not deductible under § 162 because they are incurred *before* a business begins rather than in the course of operating a trade or business. The first $5,000 of the expenses is immediately deducted. Any excess of expenses is amortized over a period of 180 months (15 years). In arriving at the $5,000 immediate deduction allowed, a dollar-for-dollar reduction must be made for those expenses in excess of $50,000.[31] An election can be made by the taxpayer to not deduct or amortize any portion of the startup costs. In that case, this intangible asset will remain on the balance sheet until the business is sold.

Example 17

Tina, a sole proprietor, owns and operates 10 restaurants located in various cities throughout the Southeast. She travels to Atlanta to discuss the acquisition of an auto dealership. In addition, she incurs legal and accounting costs associated with the potential acquisition. After incurring total investigation costs of $52,000, she acquires the auto dealership on October 1, 2014.

Tina may immediately deduct $3,000 [$5,000 − ($52,000 − $50,000)] and amortize the balance of $49,000 ($52,000 − $3,000) over a period of 180 months. For calendar year 2014, therefore, Tina can deduct $3,817 [$3,000 + ($49,000 × 3/180)].

In-depth coverage can be found on this book's companion website: **www.cengagebrain.com**

 4 Digging Deeper

5-3f Transactions between Related Parties

The Code places restrictions on the recognition of gains and losses from **related-party transactions**. Without these restrictions, relationships created by birth, marriage, and business would provide endless possibilities for engaging in financial transactions that produce tax savings with no real economic substance or change. For example, to create an artificial loss, a corporation could sell investment property to its sole shareholder at a loss and deduct the loss on the corporate return.

[30]Rev.Rul. 57–418, 1957–2 C.B. 143; *Morton Frank*, 20 T.C. 511 (1953); and *Dwight A. Ward*, 20 T.C. 332 (1953).

[31]§ 195(b).

The shareholder could then hold the asset indefinitely. Although title to the property has changed, there has been no real economic loss if the shareholder and corporation are considered an economic unit. A complex set of laws has been designed to eliminate such possibilities.

Relationships and Constructive Ownership

Before reviewing the tax consequences of related party transactions, it is important to know the individuals and business entities that are considered to be related parties. *Related parties* include the following:

- Brothers and sisters (whether whole, half, or adopted), spouse, ancestors (parents and grandparents), and lineal descendants (children and grandchildren) of the taxpayer.
- A corporation owned more than 50 percent (directly or indirectly) by the taxpayer.
- Two corporations that are members of a controlled group.
- A series of other complex relationships between trusts, corporations, and individual taxpayers.

Constructive ownership provisions are applied to determine whether the taxpayers are related. Under these provisions, stock owned by certain relatives or related entities is *deemed* to be owned by the taxpayer for purposes of applying the loss and expense deduction disallowance provisions. For example, a taxpayer is deemed to own not only his or her stock but also the stock owned by his or her lineal descendants, ancestors, brothers and sisters or half-brothers and half-sisters, and spouse.

Example 18	The stock of Sparrow Corporation is owned 20% by Ted, 30% by Ted's father, 30% by Ted's mother, and 20% by Ted's sister. On July 1 of the current year, Ted loaned $10,000 to Sparrow Corporation at 6% annual interest, principal and interest payable on demand. For tax purposes, Sparrow uses the accrual basis and Ted uses the cash basis. Both report on a calendar year basis.

Through constructive ownership, Ted is deemed also to own the 80% held by his parents and sister. Thus, he actually and constructively owns 100% of Sparrow. As discussed on the next page, if the corporation accrues the interest within the taxable year, no deduction can be taken until payment is made to Ted.

Losses

The Code provides for the disallowance of any losses from sales or exchanges of property directly or indirectly between related parties.[32] A right of offset is created equal to the disallowed loss. When the property is subsequently sold to an unrelated party, any gain recognized is reduced by the right of offset. However, the right of offset cannot create or increase a loss. Any right of offset not used by the related-party buyer to offset some or all of the recognized gain on a subsequent sale or exchange to an unrelated party is permanently lost.

THE BIG PICTURE

Example 19

Return to the facts of *The Big Picture* on p. 5-1. Assume that Michael Forney, the 80% shareholder in his small engine service and repair business, sells a stock investment in his personal portfolio with a basis of $10,000 to his corporation for its fair market value of $8,000. Michael's $2,000 loss from the sale of the stock is disallowed because the sale is to a related party. The disallowed loss creates a $2,000 right of offset.

Michael's business sells the stock several years later for $11,000. However, only $1,000 of gain ($11,000 selling price − $8,000 basis − $2,000 right of offset) is taxable to the business upon the subsequent sale.

---

[32]§ 267(a)(1).

Assume the same facts as Example 19, except that the corporation sells the stock for $9,000 to an unrelated party. The corporation's gain of $1,000 ($9,000 selling price − $8,000 basis) is not recognized because of the right of offset of $2,000 from Michael's sale.

The offset may result in only a partial tax benefit upon the subsequent sale (as in this case). If Michael originally had sold the stock to an unrelated party rather than to his corporation, he could have recognized a $2,000 loss. However, aggregating the effect to Michael and his corporation, they can benefit from only $1,000 of loss.

Unpaid Expenses and Interest

The law prevents related taxpayers from engaging in tax avoidance schemes where one related taxpayer uses the accrual method of accounting and the other uses the cash basis. The accrual basis allows the deduction of expenses when incurred, while the cash method requires that income be reported when received. In the absence of restrictions, an accrual basis, closely held corporation, for example, could borrow funds from a cash basis individual shareholder. At the end of the year, the corporation would accrue and deduct the interest expense, but the cash basis lender would not recognize interest income because no interest had been paid. Section 267 specifically defers the accrual of an interest deduction until the lender is required to include the interest in income; that is, when it is actually received by the cash basis taxpayer. This matching provision also applies to other expenses, such as salaries and bonuses. While this provision applies to related parties as previously defined, note that it also applies to transactions between any partner (shareholder) and a partnership (S corporation), regardless of the ownership interest held by the partner or shareholder.

The deduction deferral provision does not apply if both of the related taxpayers use the accrual method or both use the cash method. Likewise, it does not apply if the related party reporting income uses the accrual method and the related party taking the deduction uses the cash method.

5-3g Lack of Adequate Substantiation

The tax law is built on a voluntary compliance system. Taxpayers file their tax returns, report income and take deductions to which they are entitled, and pay their taxes through withholding or estimated tax payments during the year. The taxpayer has the burden of proof for substantiating expenses deducted on the returns and must retain adequate records. Upon audit, the IRS can disallow any undocumented or unsubstantiated deductions. These requirements have resulted in numerous conflicts between taxpayers and the IRS.

For example, in the case of charitable contributions, Congress has enacted stringent substantiation requirements. One of these requires all cash contributions to be supported by receipts (e.g., canceled checks).[33] Single donations of $250 or more of cash and/or property value require an acknowledgment from the charity. Substantial donations of property (i.e., $500 or more in fair market value) necessitate the filing of Form 8283 and may have to be supported by appraisals (see Chapter 10 for further details).

5-3h Expenses and Interest Related to Tax-Exempt Income

Certain income, such as interest on municipal bonds, is tax-exempt.[34] The law also allows the taxpayer to deduct expenses incurred for the production of income.[35] However, the law does not permit a taxpayer to profit at the expense of the government by excluding interest income and deducting any related interest expense.[36]

---

[33]Rev.Proc. 92–71, 1992–2 C.B. 437, addresses circumstances where checks are not returned by a financial institution or where electronic transfers are made.

[34]§ 103.
[35]§ 212.
[36]§ 265.

Example 21

Oriole, Inc., a corporation in the 35% bracket, purchased $100,000 of 6% municipal bonds. At the same time, Oriole used the bonds as collateral on a bank loan of $100,000 at 8% interest. A positive cash flow would result from the tax benefit as follows:

Cash paid out on loan	($8,000)
Cash received from bonds	6,000
Net negative cash flow	($2,000)

Had the deduction of $8,000 been allowed for interest expense, this would have resulted in a tax benefit of $2,800 (35% × $8,000). In that case, a positive cash flow of $800 ($6,000 + $2,800 − $8,000) would have resulted.

To eliminate the possibility illustrated in the preceding example, the Code specifically disallows a deduction for the expenses of producing tax-exempt income. Interest on any indebtedness incurred or continued to purchase or carry tax-exempt obligations also is disallowed.

Example 22

In January of the current year, Crane Corporation borrowed $100,000 at 8% interest. Crane used the loan proceeds to purchase 5,000 shares of stock in White Corporation. In July, Crane sold the stock for $120,000 and reinvested the proceeds in City of Denver bonds, the income from which is tax-exempt. Assuming that the $100,000 loan remained outstanding throughout the entire year, Crane cannot deduct the interest attributable to the period when it held the bonds.

Judicial Interpretations

It is often difficult to show a direct relationship between borrowings and investments in tax-exempt securities. Suppose, for example, a taxpayer borrows money, adds it to existing funds, buys inventory and stocks, and later sells the inventory and buys municipal bonds. A series of transactions such as these can completely obscure any connection between the loan and the tax-exempt investment. One solution would be to disallow interest on any debt to the extent that the taxpayer holds any tax-exempt securities. The law was not intended to go to such extremes. As a result, judicial interpretations have tried to be reasonable in disallowing interest deductions.[37]

Digging Deeper 5    In-depth coverage can be found on this book's companion website: **www.cengagebrain.com**

5-4 CHARITABLE CONTRIBUTIONS

LO.4

Recognize the limitations applicable to the charitable contribution deduction for corporations.

Corporations and individuals are allowed to deduct contributions made to qualified domestic charitable organizations.[38] Qualified organizations include:[39]

*   A state or possession of the United States or any subdivisions thereof.
*   A corporation, trust, or community chest, fund, or foundation that is situated in the United States and is organized and operated exclusively for religious, charitable, scientific, literary, or educational purposes or for the prevention of cruelty to children or animals.

Digging Deeper 6    In-depth coverage can be found on this book's companion website: **www.cengagebrain.com**

Generally, a deduction for a charitable contribution will be allowed only for the year in which the payment is made. However, an *accrual basis corporation* may claim the deduction in the year preceding payment if two requirements are met. First, the contribution must be *authorized* by the board of directors by the end of that

---

[37]See, for example, *The Wisconsin Cheeseman, Inc. v. U.S.*, 68–1 USTC ¶9145, 21 AFTR 2d 383, 388 F.2d 420 (CA–7, 1968).

[38]§ 170.

[39]§ 170(c).

year. Second, it must be *paid* on or before the fifteenth day of the third month of the following year.

On December 29, 2014, Blue Company, a calendar year, accrual basis partnership, authorizes a $5,000 donation to the Atlanta Symphony Association (a qualified charitable organization). The donation is made on March 12, 2015. Because Blue Company is a partnership, the contribution can be deducted only in 2015.[40] However, if Blue Company is a corporation and the December 29, 2014 authorization was made by its board of directors, Blue may claim the $5,000 donation as a deduction for calendar year 2014.	**Example 23**

5-4a Property Contributions

The amount that can be deducted for a noncash charitable contribution depends on the type of property contributed. Property must be identified as capital gain property or ordinary income property. **Capital gain property** is property that, if sold, would result in long-term capital gain or § 1231 gain for the taxpayer. Such property generally must be a capital asset and must be held for the long-term holding period (more than one year). **Ordinary income property** is property that, if sold, would result in ordinary income for the taxpayer. Examples of ordinary income property include inventory and capital assets held short term (one year or less). Refer to Chapter 4 for a brief introduction to the distinction between capital and ordinary assets.

The deduction for a charitable contribution of capital gain property is generally measured by the property's *fair market value.*

During the current year, Mallard Corporation donates a parcel of land (a capital asset) to Oakland Community College. Mallard acquired the land five years ago for $60,000, and the fair market value on the date of the contribution is $100,000. The corporation's charitable contribution deduction (subject to a percentage limitation discussed later) is measured by the asset's fair market value of $100,000, even though the $40,000 of appreciation on the land has never been included in Mallard's income.	**Example 24**

In two situations, a charitable contribution of capital gain property is measured by the basis of the property, rather than fair market value. If a corporation contributes *tangible personal property* and the charitable organization puts the property to an *unrelated use*, the appreciation on the property is not deductible. Unrelated use is defined as use that is not related to the purpose or function that qualifies the organization for exempt status.

White Corporation donates a painting worth $200,000 to Western States Art Museum (a qualified charity), which exhibits the painting. White had acquired the painting in 2000 for $90,000. Because the museum put the painting to a related use, White is allowed to deduct $200,000, the fair market value of the painting.	**Example 25**

Assume the same facts as in the previous example, except that White Corporation donates the painting to the American Cancer Society, which sells the painting and deposits the $200,000 proceeds in the organization's general fund. White's deduction is limited to the $90,000 basis because it contributed tangible personal property that was put to an unrelated use by the charitable organization.	**Example 26**

The deduction for charitable contributions of capital gain property to certain private nonoperating foundations (defined in §§ 4942 and 509) is also limited to the basis of the property.

As a general rule, the deduction for a contribution of ordinary income property is limited to the *basis* of the property. On certain contributions of inventory by *corporations*, however, the amount of the deduction is equal to the lesser of (1) the sum of the property's basis plus 50 percent of the appreciation on the property or

---

[40]Each partner will report an allocable portion of the charitable contribution deduction as of December 31, 2015 (the end of the partnership's tax year). See Chapter 14.

TAX FACT   What Ten Percent Ceiling?

Just how generous is corporate America? Based on recent data, of the approximate $1.022 trillion of corporate income subject to tax, contributions and gifts totaled about $16.32 billion. In other words, only about 1.597 percent of the average corporation's taxable income goes to charity.

Source: 2010 Corporation Returns—Returns of Active Corporations; Table 2—Balance Sheet, Income Statement, and Selected Other Items by Size of Total Assets; 2013.

(2) twice the property's basis. The following contributions of inventory qualify for this increased contribution amount.

- A contribution of property to a charitable organization for use that is related to the organization's exempt function and such use is solely for the care of the ill, needy, or infants.
- A contribution of tangible personal research property constructed by the corporation to a qualified educational or scientific organization that uses the property for research or experimentation or for research training. (The property must be contributed within two years from the date of its construction by the donor, and its original use must begin with the donee.)[41]

Example 27

Lark Corporation, a clothing retailer, donates children's clothing to the Salvation Army to be used to attire homeless children. Lark's basis in the clothes is $2,000, and the fair market value (the sales price to customers) is $3,000. Lark's deduction is $2,500 [$2,000 basis + 50% × ($3,000 − $2,000)].

If, instead, the fair market value of the clothes is $7,000, Lark's deduction is $4,000 (2 × $2,000 basis).

5-4b Limitations Imposed on Charitable Contribution Deductions

Both corporations and individuals are subject to percentage limitations on the charitable contribution deduction.[42] The complex limitations for individual taxpayers are covered in Chapter 10.

For any tax year, a corporate taxpayer's contribution deduction is limited to 10 percent of taxable income. For this purpose, taxable income is computed without regard to the charitable contribution deduction, any net operating loss carryback or capital loss carryback, the dividends received deduction, and the domestic production activities deduction. Any contributions in excess of the 10 percent limitation may be carried forward to the five succeeding tax years. Any carryforward must be added to subsequent contributions and will be subject to the 10 percent limitation. In applying this limitation, the current year's contributions must be deducted first, with carryover amounts from previous years deducted in order of time.[43]

Example 28

During 2014, Orange Corporation (a calendar year taxpayer) had the following income and expenses.

Income from operations	$140,000
Expenses from operations	110,000
Dividends received	10,000
Charitable contributions made in May 2014	6,000

---

[41]These conditions are set forth in §§ 170(e)(3) and (4).

[42]The percentage limitations applicable to individuals and corporations are set forth in § 170(b).

[43]The carryover rules relating to all taxpayers are in § 170(d).

For purposes of the 10% limitation only, Orange Corporation's taxable income is $40,000 ($140,000 − $110,000 + $10,000). Consequently, the allowable charitable contribution deduction for 2014 is $4,000 (10% × $40,000). The $2,000 unused portion of the contribution can be carried forward to 2015, 2016, 2017, 2018, and 2019 (in that order) until exhausted.

Example 29

Assume the same facts as in the previous example. In 2015, Orange Corporation has taxable income (for purposes of the 10% limitation) of $50,000 and makes a charitable contribution of $4,500. The maximum deduction allowed for 2015 is $5,000 (10% × $50,000). The entire 2015 contribution of $4,500 and $500 of the 2014 charitable contribution carryforward are currently deductible. The remaining $1,500 of the 2014 carryforward may be carried over to 2016 (and later years, if necessary).

5-5 RESEARCH AND EXPERIMENTAL EXPENDITURES

Section 174 covers the treatment of **research and experimental expenditures**. The Regulations define research and experimental expenditures as follows:

> all such costs incident to the development of an experimental or pilot model, a plant process, a product, a formula, an invention, or similar property, and the improvement of already existing property of the type mentioned. The term does not include expenditures such as those for the ordinary testing or inspection of materials or products for quality control or those for efficiency surveys, management studies, consumer surveys, advertising, or promotions.[44]

LO.5

State and apply the alternative tax treatments for research and experimental expenditures and understand several other common business deductions.

The law permits *three alternatives* for handling research and experimental expenditures.

- Deduct in the year paid or incurred.
- Defer and amortize.
- Capitalize.

If the costs are capitalized, a deduction is not available until the research project is abandoned or is deemed worthless. Because many products resulting from research projects do not have a definite and limited useful life, a taxpayer should ordinarily elect to write off (deduct) the expenditures immediately or to defer and amortize them. It is generally preferable to elect an immediate write-off of the research expenditures because of the time value of the tax savings related to the deduction.

The law also provides for a research activities credit. The credit amounts to 20 percent of certain research and experimental expenditures.[45]

5-5a Expense Method

A taxpayer can elect to deduct all of the research and experimental expenditures incurred in the current year and all subsequent years. The consent of the IRS is not required if the method is adopted for the first taxable year in which such expenditures were paid or incurred. Once the election is made, the taxpayer must continue to deduct all qualifying expenditures unless a request for a change is made to, and approved by, the IRS. In certain instances, a taxpayer may incur research and experimental expenditures before actually engaging in any trade or business activity. In such instances, the Supreme Court has applied a liberal standard of deductibility and permitted a deduction in the year of incurrence.[46]

---

[44]Reg. § 1.174–2(a)(1).

[45]§ 41. See Chapter 17 for a more detailed discussion of the research activities credit. Congress is expected to extend this credit, which expired on December 31, 2013.

[46]*Snow v. Comm.*, 74–1 USTC ¶9432, 33 AFTR 2d 74–1251, 94 S.Ct. 1876 (USSC, 1974).

5-5b Deferral and Amortization Method

Alternatively, research and experimental expenditures may be deferred and amortized if the taxpayer makes an election.[47] Under the election, research and experimental expenditures are amortized ratably over a period of not less than 60 months. A deduction is allowed beginning with the month in which the taxpayer first realizes benefits from the research and experimental expenditures. The election is binding, and a change requires permission from the IRS.

Example 30

Gold Corporation decides to develop a new line of adhesives. The project begins in 2014. Gold incurs the following expenses in 2014 and 2015 in connection with the project.

	2014	2015
Salaries	$25,000	$18,000
Materials	8,000	2,000
Depreciation on machinery	6,500	5,700

The benefits from the project will be realized starting in March 2016. If Gold Corporation elects a 60-month deferral and amortization period, there is no deduction prior to March 2016, the month benefits from the project begin to be realized. The deduction for 2016 is $10,867, computed as follows:

Salaries ($25,000 + $18,000)	$43,000
Materials ($8,000 + $2,000)	10,000
Depreciation ($6,500 + $5,700)	12,200
Total	$65,200
$65,200 × (10 months/60 months)	$10,867

The option to treat research and experimental expenditures as a deferred expense is usually employed when a company does not have sufficient income to offset the research and experimental expenses. Rather than create net operating loss carryovers that might not be utilized because of the 20-year limitation on such carryovers, the deferral and amortization method may be used. The deferral of research and experimental expenditures should also be considered if the taxpayer expects higher tax rates in the future.

5-6 OTHER EXPENSE RULES

In addition to the provisions related to charitable contributions and research and experimental expenditures, a variety of other expenses are subject to special rules and limitations. Some of these rules are noted briefly in the paragraphs that follow.

5-6a Interest Expense

Generally, corporations are not limited in the amount of interest expense they may deduct. However, the deductibility of expenses (including interest) from certain activities may be limited.[48] In contrast, individuals generally may not deduct interest expense on loans used for personal purposes. However, if the loan is secured by the taxpayer's personal residence, the related interest may be deductible. Furthermore, individuals may deduct interest expense associated with investments to the extent of net investment income and interest on qualified student loans.[49]

Because the deductibility of interest expense associated with certain activities is limited, the IRS provides rules for allocating interest expense among activities. Under these rules, interest is allocated in the same manner as the debt with respect to which the interest is paid, and debt is allocated by tracing disbursements of the

---

[47]§ 174(b)(2).

[48]See, for example, the discussion of the passive activity limits in Chapter 6.

[49]See Chapter 10 for a more detailed discussion of the deductibility of interest by individuals.

debt proceeds to specific expenditures. The interest tracing rules are complex and depend on whether loan proceeds are commingled with other cash and the length of time the loan proceeds are held before they are spent.

5-6b Taxes

As with interest expense, tax payments in a business or investment context are generally deductible. However, most Federal taxes are not deductible. Individuals may also deduct tax payments, subject to limitations (discussed in Chapter 10). One unique problem associated with determining the deductibility of taxes relates to real estate taxes paid during a year when the real estate is sold.

Real estate taxes for the entire year are apportioned between the buyer and seller based on the number of days the property was held by each during the real property tax year. This apportionment is required whether the tax is paid by the buyer or the seller or is prorated according to the purchase agreement. The apportionment determines who is entitled to deduct the real estate taxes in the year of sale. The required apportionment prevents the shifting of the deduction for real estate taxes from buyer to seller, or vice versa. In making the apportionment, the assessment date and the lien date are disregarded. The date of sale counts as a day the property is owned by the buyer.

> **Example 31**
> A county's real property tax year runs from January 1 to December 31. Nuthatch Corporation, the owner on January 1 of real property located in the county, sells the real property to Crane, Inc., on June 30. Crane owns the real property from June 30 through December 31. The tax for the real property tax year, January 1 through December 31, is $3,650. Assuming that this is not a leap year, the portion of the real property tax treated as imposed upon Nuthatch, the seller, is $1,800 [(180/365) × $3,650, January 1 through June 29], and $1,850 [(185/365) × $3,650, June 30 through December 31] of the tax is treated as imposed upon Crane, the purchaser.

If the actual real estate taxes are not prorated between the buyer and seller as part of the purchase agreement, adjustments are required. The adjustments are necessary to determine the amount realized by the seller and the adjusted basis of the property to the buyer. If the buyer pays the entire amount of the tax, it effectively has paid the seller's portion of the real estate tax and has therefore paid more for the property than the actual purchase price. Thus, the amount of real estate tax that is apportioned to the seller (for Federal income tax purposes) and paid by the buyer is added to the buyer's adjusted basis. The seller must increase the amount realized on the sale by the same amount.

> **Example 32**
> Seth sells real estate on October 3 for $400,000. The buyer, Winslow Company, pays the real estate taxes of $3,650 for the calendar year, which is the real estate property tax year. Assuming that this is not a leap year, $2,750 (for 275 days) is apportioned to and is deductible by the seller, Seth, and $900 (for 90 days) of the taxes is deductible by Winslow. The buyer has paid Seth's real estate taxes of $2,750 and has therefore paid $402,750 for the property. Winslow's basis is increased to $402,750, and the amount realized by Seth from the sale is increased to $402,750.

The opposite result occurs if the seller (rather than the buyer) pays the real estate taxes. In this case, the seller reduces the amount realized from the sale by the amount that has been apportioned to the buyer. The buyer is required to reduce his or her adjusted basis by a corresponding amount.

> **Example 33**
> Silver Corporation sells real estate to Butch for $400,000 on October 3. While Silver held the property, it paid the real estate taxes of $3,650 for the calendar year, which is the real estate property tax year. Although Silver paid the entire $3,650 of real estate taxes, $900 of that amount is apportioned to Butch, based on the number of days he owned the property, and is therefore deductible by him. The effect is that the buyer, Butch, has paid only $399,100 ($400,000 − $900) for the property. The amount realized by Silver, the seller, is reduced by $900, and Butch reduces his basis in the property to $399,100.

5-6c Domestic Production Activities Deduction

A number of years ago, Congress replaced certain tax provisions that our world trading partners regarded as allowing unfair advantage to U.S. exports. As part of these changes, Congress created a deduction based on the income from U.S. manufacturing activities (designated as *production activities*). The **domestic production activities deduction (DPAD)** is contained in § 199. Form 8903 is used to report the calculation of the domestic production activities deduction.

Calculation of the Domestic Production Activities Deduction

The DPAD is based on the following formula:[50]

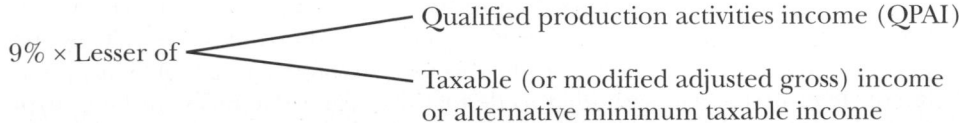

$$9\% \times \text{Lesser of} \begin{cases} \text{Qualified production activities income (QPAI)} \\ \text{Taxable (or modified adjusted gross) income} \\ \text{or alternative minimum taxable income} \end{cases}$$

For this computation, taxable income is determined without regard to the DPAD. In the case of an individual (a sole proprietorship or an owner of a flow-through entity), **modified adjusted gross income** is substituted for taxable income.[51]

The taxable income limitation is determined after the application of any net operating loss (NOL) deduction for the tax year (NOLs are explained in Chapter 6). Thus, a company with an NOL carryforward for a tax year is ineligible for the DPAD if the carryforward eliminates current taxable income. Further, a taxpayer that has an NOL carryback may lose part or all of the DPAD benefit for that year. As taxable income is reduced by the NOL carryback, there is a corresponding reduction in the DPAD. If qualified production activities income (QPAI) cannot be used in a particular year due to the taxable income limitation (see the preceding formula), it is lost forever. (The calculation of QPAI is explained in the next section.)

Example 34	Opal, Inc., manufactures and sells costume jewelry. It also sells costume jewelry purchased from other manufacturers. During 2014, Opal had a *profit* of $200,000 (QPAI) from the sale of its own manufactured jewelry and a *loss* of $50,000 from the sale of the purchased jewelry. Based on this information, Opal's QPAI is $200,000 and its taxable income is $150,000 ($200,000 − $50,000). Opal's DPAD becomes $13,500 [9% of the lesser of $200,000 (QPAI) or $150,000 (taxable income)].

Example 35	Assume the same facts as in the previous example, except that Opal also has an NOL carryover from 2013 of $300,000. As taxable income for 2014 is zero ($200,000 − $50,000 − $300,000), there is no DPAD.

Another important limitation is that the amount of the DPAD cannot exceed 50 percent of certain **W–2 wages** paid by the taxpayer during the tax year.[52] If no W–2 wages are paid, no DPAD will be allowed. So, part of the rationale behind this limitation is to preserve U.S. manufacturing jobs and discourage their outsourcing.

An employer's W–2 wages include the sum of the aggregate amount of wages and elective deferrals required to be included on the W–2 wage statements for certain employees during the employer's taxable year. Elective deferrals include those amounts deferred under § 457 plans and Roth IRA contributions. An employer previously included wages paid to all workers during a tax year and not just the wages of the employees engaged in qualified production activities. However, as a result of a recent statutory change, an employer is permitted to include only those W–2 wages paid to employees engaged in qualified production activities.

---

[50]§ 199(a).

[51]§ 199(d)(2). Generally, modified AGI is AGI prior to the effect of § 199.

[52]§ 199(b).

In 2014, Red, Inc., a calendar year taxpayer, has QPAI of $2 million and taxable income of $2.1 million. Because Red outsources much of its work to independent contractors, its W–2 wage base, which for Red is related entirely to production activities, is $80,000. Although Red's DPAD normally would be $180,000 [9% of the lesser of $2 million (QPAI) or $2.1 million (taxable income)], it is limited to $40,000 [50% of $80,000 (W–2 wages)].	**Example 36**

Assume the same facts as in the previous example, except that Red also pays salaries of $50,000 related to its *nonproduction* activities. Because these wages are not paid to employees engaged in production activities, the wage limitation on the DPAD remains at $40,000 [50% of $80,000 ($80,000 + $0)].	**Example 37**

Calculation of Qualified Production Activities Income

Qualified production activities income (QPAI) is the excess of domestic production gross receipts (DPGR) over the sum of:

- The cost of goods sold allocated to such receipts.
- Other deductions, expenses, or losses directly allocated to such receipts.
- The ratable portion of deductions, expenses, and losses not directly allocable to such receipts or another class of income.[53]

QPAI is determined on an item-by-item basis—not on a division-by-division or a transaction-by-transaction basis. Because all items must be netted in the calculation, the final QPAI amount can be either positive or negative. The effect of the netting rule is to preclude taxpayers from selecting only profitable product lines or profitable transactions when calculating QPAI.

A taxpayer manufactures pants and shirts with the following QPAI results: $5 for one pair of pants and a negative $2 for one shirt. Because the two items are netted, the QPAI amount that controls is $3 ($5 − $2).	**Example 38**

Five specific categories of DPGR qualify for the DPAD.[54]

- The lease, license, sale, exchange, or other disposition of qualified production property (QPP) that was manufactured, produced, grown, or extracted (MPGE) in the United States.
- Qualified films largely created in the United States.
- The production of electricity, natural gas, or potable water.
- Construction (but not self-construction) performed in the United States.
- Engineering and architectural services for domestic construction.

The sale of food and beverages prepared by a taxpayer at a retail establishment and the transmission or distribution of electricity, natural gas, or potable water are specifically excluded from the definition of DPGR.

Eligible Taxpayers

The deduction is available to a variety of taxpayers, including individuals, partnerships, S corporations, C corporations, cooperatives, estates, and trusts. For a pass-through entity (e.g., partnerships and S corporations), the deduction flows through to the owners. In the case of a sole proprietor, a deduction *for* AGI results and is claimed on Form 1040, line 35 on page 1.

---

[53]§ 199(c).   [54]§ 199(c)(4).

TAX FACT   Cost Recovery by Any Other Name

Of the more than $943.5 billion of corporate cost recovery deductions claimed in a recent tax year, the three most familiar types of these asset-related tax incentives were reported as shown in the table to the right.

	Percentage of Total Deductions Claimed
Amortization	20.40
Cost recovery or depreciation	77.14
Depletion	2.46
	100.00

Source: 2010 Corporation Returns—Returns of Active Corporations; Table 2—Balance Sheet, Income Statement and Selected Other Items by Size of Total Assets, 2013.

5-7 COST RECOVERY ALLOWANCES

LO.6

Determine the amount of cost recovery under MACRS and apply the § 179 expensing election and the deduction limitations on listed property and automobiles when making the MACRS calculation.

5-7a Overview

Taxpayers may "write off" (deduct) the cost of certain assets that are used in a trade or business or held for the production of income. A write-off may take the form of a *cost recovery allowance* (depreciation under prior law), depletion, or amortization. Tangible assets, other than natural resources, are written off through cost recovery allowances. Natural resources, such as oil, gas, coal, and timber, are *depleted*. Intangible assets, such as copyrights and patents, are *amortized*. Generally, no write-off is allowed for an asset that does not have a determinable useful life.

The tax rules for writing off the cost of business assets differ from the accounting rules. Several methods are available for determining depreciation for accounting purposes, including the straight-line, declining-balance, and sum-of-the-years' digits methods. Historically, *depreciation* for tax purposes was computed using variations of these accounting methods. Congress completely overhauled the **depreciation** rules in 1981 by creating the **accelerated cost recovery system (ACRS)**, which shortened depreciable lives and allowed accelerated depreciation methods. In 1986, Congress made substantial modifications to ACRS, which resulted in the **modified accelerated cost recovery system (MACRS)**. Tax professionals use the terms depreciation and **cost recovery** interchangably.

The statutory changes that have taken place since 1980 have widened the gap that exists between the accounting and tax versions of depreciation. The tax rules that existed prior to 1981 were much more compatible with generally accepted accounting principles. This chapter focuses on the MACRS rules because they cover current acquisitions (i.e., after 1986).

5-7b Depreciation and Cost Recovery

Nature of Property

Property includes both realty (real property) and personalty (personal property). *Realty* generally includes land and buildings permanently affixed to the land. *Personalty* is defined as any asset that is not realty. Personalty includes furniture, machinery, equipment, and many other types of assets. Do not confuse personalty (or personal property) with personal-use property. Personal-use property is any property (realty or personalty) that is held for personal use rather than for use in a trade or business or an income-producing activity. Cost recovery deductions are not allowed for personal-use assets.

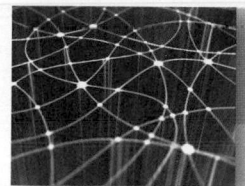

BRIDGE DISCIPLINE   Bridge to Finance

For many business entities, success in producing goods for sale is dependent on the efficient use of fixed assets, such as machinery and equipment. An important question for such businesses to resolve is how they should gain access to the required complement of fixed assets: that is, whether the assets should be purchased or leased. To answer this question, the taxpayer must determine which alternative is more cost-effective. Critical to this assessment is quantifying the after-tax cost (including the associated tax benefits) of each option.

Purchasing productive assets for business use often necessitates an immediate cash outflow. However, the tax savings resulting from the available depreciation expense deductions mitigate the impact of that outflow by reducing the taxpayer's taxable income and the income tax paid for the year. Consequently, the tax savings from the depreciation calculation associated with the purchase of an asset reduce the after-tax cost of employing the asset. The analysis can be refined further by evaluating the tax savings from the depreciation deductions in present value terms by quantifying the tax savings from the depreciation expense over the life of the asset. The asset's purchase also can be financed with debt.

Taxpayers who lease rather than buy an asset benefit by not giving up the use of funds that otherwise would have gone to purchase the asset. Lessees also forgo the opportunity to claim depreciation deductions; however, they reduce the cost of the leasing option by claiming the lease expense as a deduction against their tax base.

In summary, both realty and personality can be either business-use/income-producing property or personal-use property. Examples include:

- a residence (realty that is personal use),
- an office building (realty that is business use),
- a dump truck (personalty that is business use), and
- common wearing apparel (personalty that is personal use).

It is imperative that this distinction between the classification of an asset (realty or personalty) and the use to which the asset is put (business or personal) be understood.

Assets used in a trade or business or for the production of income (e.g., an automobile that the taxpayer rents to third parties) are eligible for cost recovery if they are subject to wear and tear, decay or decline from natural causes, or obsolescence. Assets that do not decline in value on a predictable basis or that do not have a determinable useful life (e.g., land, stock, and antiques) are not eligible for cost recovery.

Placed in Service Requirement

The key date for the commencement of depreciation is the date an asset is placed in service. This date, and not the purchase date of an asset, is the relevant date. This distinction is particularly important for an asset that is purchased near the end of the tax year, but not placed in service until after the beginning of the following tax year.

Cost Recovery Allowed or Allowable

The basis of cost recovery property is reduced by the cost recovery *allowed*, and by not less than the *allowable* amount. The allowed cost recovery is the cost recovery actually deducted, whereas the allowable cost recovery is the amount that could have been taken under the applicable cost recovery method. If the taxpayer does not claim any cost recovery on property during a particular year, the basis of the property still is reduced by the amount of cost recovery that should have been deducted (the *allowable* cost recovery).

Example 39

On March 15, 2014, Heron, Inc., purchased a copier, to use in its business, for $10,000. The copier is 5-year property, and Heron elected to use the straight-line method of cost recovery. Heron made the election because its business was new, and Heron reasoned that in the first few years of the business, a large cost recovery deduction was not needed.

Because the business was doing poorly, Heron did not even claim any cost recovery deductions in years 3 and 4. In years 5 and 6, Heron deducted the proper amount of cost recovery. Therefore, the allowed cost recovery (cost recovery actually deducted) and the allowable cost recovery are computed as follows:[55]

	Cost Recovery Allowed	Cost Recovery Allowable
Year 1	$1,000	$ 1,000
Year 2	2,000	2,000
Year 3	–0–	2,000
Year 4	–0–	2,000
Year 5	2,000	2,000
Year 6	1,000	1,000
Totals	$6,000	$10,000

The adjusted basis of the copier at the end of year 6 is $0 ($10,000 cost – $10,000 *allowable* cost recovery). If Heron sells the copier for $800 in year 7, it will recognize an $800 gain ($800 amount realized – $0 adjusted basis).

Cost Recovery Basis for Personal-Use Assets Converted to Business or Income-Producing Use

If personal-use assets are converted to business or income-producing use, the basis for cost recovery and for loss is the lower of the adjusted basis or the fair market value at the time the property was converted. As a result of this basis rule, losses that occurred while the property was personal-use property are not recognized for tax purposes through the cost recovery of the property.

THE BIG PICTURE

Example 40

Return to the facts of *The Big Picture* on p. 5-1. Five years ago, Michael Forney purchased a personal residence for $250,000. In the current year, with the housing market down, Michael found an attractively priced larger home that he acquired for his personal residence. Because of the downturn in the housing market, however, he was not able to sell his original residence and recover his purchase price of $250,000. The residence was appraised at $180,000.

Instead of continuing to try to sell the original residence, he converted it to rental property. The basis for cost recovery of the rental property is $180,000 because the fair market value is less than the adjusted basis. The $70,000 decline in value is deemed to be personal (because it occurred while the property was held for Michael's personal use) and therefore nondeductible.

5-7c Modified Accelerated Cost Recovery System (MACRS)

MACRS provides separate cost recovery periods and methods for realty (real property) and personalty (personal property). Cost recovery allowances for real

---

[55]The cost recovery allowances are based on the half-year convention, which allows a half-year's cost recovery in the first and last years of the recovery period.

EXHIBIT 5.2	Cost Recovery Periods: MACRS Personalty

Class	Examples
3-year	Tractor units for use over-the-road Any horse that is not a racehorse and is more than 12 years old at the time it is placed in service Special tools used in the manufacturing of motor vehicles, such as dies, fixtures, molds, and patterns
5-year	Automobiles and taxis Light and heavy general-purpose trucks Calculators and copiers Computers and peripheral equipment
7-year	Office furniture, fixtures, and equipment Agricultural machinery and equipment
10-year	Vessels, barges, tugs, and similar water transportation equipment Assets used for petroleum refining or for the manufacture of grain and grain mill products, sugar and sugar products, or vegetable oils and vegetable oil products Single-purpose agricultural or horticultural structures
15-year	Land improvements Assets used for industrial steam and electric generation and/or distribution systems Assets used in the manufacture of cement
20-year	Farm buildings except single-purpose agricultural and horticultural structures Water utilities

property, other than land, are based on recovery lives specified in the law. The IRS provides tables that specify cost recovery allowances for personalty and for realty. Concept Summary 5.1 provides an overview of the various conventions that apply under MACRS.

5-7d Cost Recovery for Personal Property

MACRS provides that the cost recovery basis of eligible personalty (and certain realty) is recovered over 3, 5, 7, 10, 15, or 20 years.[56] Examples of property in the different cost recovery categories are shown in Exhibit 5.2.[57]

Accelerated depreciation is allowed for these six MACRS classes of property. The appropriate computational methods and conventions are built into the tables; so in general, it is not necessary to perform any calculations. To determine the amount of the cost recovery allowance, simply identify the asset by class and go to the appropriate table.[58] The MACRS percentages for personalty are shown in Table 5.1 (MACRS tables are located at the end of the chapter prior to the problem materials).

Taxpayers may *elect* the straight-line method to compute cost recovery allowances for each of these classes of property. Certain property is not eligible for accelerated cost recovery and must be depreciated under an alternative depreciation system (ADS). Both the straight-line election and ADS are discussed later in the chapter.

MACRS views personal property as placed in service in the middle of the asset's first year and allows a half-year of cost recovery in the year of acquisition and in the final year of cost recovery (the **half-year convention**).[59] Thus, for example, the statutory

[56]Property is classified by recovery period under MACRS based on asset depreciation range (ADR) midpoint lives provided by the IRS. Rev.Proc. 87–56, 1987–2 C.B. 674 is the source for the ADR midpoint lives.

[57]§ 168(e).
[58]§ 168(b).
[59]§ 168(d)(4)(A).

CONCEPT SUMMARY 5.1

Statutory Percentage Method under MACRS

	Personal Property	Real Property*
Convention	Half-year or mid-quarter	Mid-month
Cost recovery deduction in the year of disposition	Half-year for year of disposition or half-quarter for quarter of disposition	Half-month for month of disposition

*Straight-line method must be used.

© iStockphoto.com/Andrey Prokhorov

recovery period for property with a life of three years begins in the middle of the year the asset is placed in service and ends three years later. In practical terms, this means that the actual write-offs are claimed over 4, 6, 8, 11, 16, and 21 tax years. MACRS also allows for a half-year of cost recovery in the year of disposition or retirement.

Example 41

Robin Corporation acquires a 5-year class asset on April 10, 2014, for $30,000. Robin's cost recovery deduction for 2014 is computed as follows:

MACRS calculation based on Table 5.1 ($30,000 × .20) $6,000

Example 42

Assume the same facts as in the previous example. Robin disposes of the asset on March 5, 2016. Robin's cost recovery deduction for 2016 is $2,880 [$30,000 × 1/2 × .192 (Table 5.1)].

Mid-Quarter Convention

The half-year convention arises from the simplifying presumption that assets generally will be acquired evenly throughout the tax year. However, Congress was concerned that taxpayers might override that presumption by placing large amounts of property in service during the last quarter of the taxable year (and, by doing so, receive a half-year's depreciation on those large, fourth-quarter acquisitions).

To inhibit this behavior, Congress added the **mid-quarter convention** that applies if more than 40 percent of the value of property other than eligible real estate[60] is placed in service during the last quarter of the year.[61] Under the convention, property acquisitions are grouped by the quarter they were acquired for cost recovery purposes. Acquisitions during the first quarter are allowed 10.5 months (three and one-half quarters) of cost recovery; the second quarter, 7.5 months (two and one-half quarters); the third quarter, 4.5 months (one and one-half quarters); and the fourth quarter, 1.5 months. The percentages are shown in Table 5.2.

Example 43

Silver Corporation puts into service the following new 5-year class property in 2014.

Acquisition Dates	Cost
February 15	$ 200,000
July 10	400,000
December 5	600,000
Total	$1,200,000

Under the statutory percentage method, Silver's cost recovery allowances for the first two years are computed as follows. Because more than 40% ($600,000/$1,200,000 = 50%) of the acquisitions are in the last quarter, the mid-quarter convention applies.

---

[60]See Cost Recovery for Real Estate on the following page for a discussion of eligible real estate.

[61]§ 168(d)(3).

2014

	Mid-Quarter Convention Depreciation (Table 5.2)		Total Depreciation
February 15	$200,000 × .35	=	$ 70,000
July 10	$400,000 × .15	=	60,000
December 5	$600,000 × .05	=	30,000
Total			$160,000

2015

	Mid-Quarter Convention Depreciation (Table 5.2)		Total Depreciation
February 15	$200,000 × .26	=	$ 52,000
July 10	$400,000 × .34	=	136,000
December 5	$600,000 × .38	=	228,000
Total			$416,000

Without the mid-quarter convention, Silver's 2014 MACRS deduction would have been $240,000 [$1,200,000 × .20 (Table 5.1)]. The mid-quarter convention slows down the taxpayer's available cost recovery deductions.

When property to which the mid-quarter convention applies is disposed of, the property is treated as though it were disposed of at the midpoint of the quarter. Hence, in the quarter of disposition, cost recovery is allowed for one-half of the quarter.

Example 44

Assume the same facts as in the previous example, except that Silver Corporation sells the $400,000 asset on November 30, 2015. The cost recovery allowance for 2015 is computed as follows (Table 5.2):

February 15	$200,000 × .26	=	$ 52,000
July 10	$400,000 × .34 × (3.5/4)	=	119,000
December 5	$600,000 × .38	=	228,000
Total			$399,000

5-7e Cost Recovery for Real Estate

Under MACRS, the cost recovery period for residential rental real estate is 27.5 years, and the straight-line method is used for computing the cost recovery allowance. **Residential rental real estate** includes property where 80 percent or more of the gross rental revenues are from nontransient dwelling units (e.g., an apartment building). Hotels, motels, and similar establishments are not residential rental property. Nonresidential real estate uses a recovery period of 39 years; it also is depreciated using the straight-line method.[62]

Some items of real property are not treated as real estate for purposes of MACRS. For example, single-purpose agricultural structures are in the 10-year MACRS class. Land improvements are in the 15-year MACRS class.

All eligible real estate placed in service after June 22, 1984 (under both ACRS and MACRS) is depreciated using the **mid-month convention**.[63] Regardless of when the property is placed in service, it is deemed to have been placed in service at the middle of the month. This allows for one-half month's cost recovery for the month the property is placed in service. If the property is disposed of before the end of the recovery period, one-half month's cost recovery is permitted for the month of disposition regardless of the specific date of disposition.

---

[62]§§ 168(b), (c), and (e). A 31.5-year life is used for such property placed in service before May 13, 1993.

[63]§ 168(d)(1).

Global Tax Issues

© iStockphoto.com/Andrey Prokhorov

Classification of Property

In New Zealand, it is important for tax depreciation purposes to know the difference between a dairy shed and a fence. Dairy sheds are classified as buildings with an expected life of 25 years and a straight-line depreciation rate of 4 percent. If a fenced holding yard is built next to the shed and deemed to be part of the shed, the depreciation rate for the pipe railings and the gate are the same as for the shed. If the holding yard is deemed not to be part of the shed, the costs associated with the holding yard can be expensed.

Source: Based on "Tax Deductions Can be Tricky," *Taranaki Daily News,* July 12, 2012, p. 14.

Cost recovery is computed by multiplying the applicable rate (taken from a table) by the cost recovery basis. The MACRS real property rates are provided in Table 5.3.

Example 45

Badger Rentals, Inc., acquired a building on April 1, 1996, for $800,000. If the building is classified as residential real estate, the cost recovery deduction for 2014 is $29,088 (.03636 × $800,000). If the building is sold on October 7, 2014, the cost recovery deduction for 2014 is $23,028 [.03636 × (9.5/12) × $800,000].

   If the building is acquired on March 2, 1993, for $1 million and is classified as non-residential real estate, the cost recovery deduction for 2014 is $31,740 (.03174 × $1,000,000). If the building is sold on January 5, 2014, the cost recovery deduction for 2014 is $1,323 [.03174 × (.5/12) × $1,000,000]. (See the first two sections of Table 5.3 for the percentages.)

Example 46

Oakenwood Properties, Inc., acquired a building on November 19, 2014, for $1.2 million. If the building is classified as nonresidential real estate, the cost recovery deduction for 2014 is $3,852 (.00321 × $1,200,000). The cost recovery deduction for 2015 is $30,768 (.02564 × $1,200,000). If the building is sold on May 21, 2015, the cost recovery deduction for 2015 is $11,538 [.02564 × (4.5/12) × $1,200,000]. (See the last section of Table 5.3 for the percentages.)

5-7f Straight-Line Election

Although MACRS requires straight-line depreciation for all eligible real estate, the taxpayer may *elect* to use the straight-line method for depreciable personal property.[64] The property is depreciated using the class life (recovery period) of the asset with a half-year convention or a mid-quarter convention, whichever applies. The election is available on a class-by-class and year-by-year basis. The percentages for the straight-line election with a half-year convention appear in Table 5.4.

Example 47

Terry puts into service a new 10-year class asset on August 4, 2014, for $100,000. He elects the straight-line method of cost recovery. Terry's cost recovery deduction for 2014 is $5,000 ($100,000 × .05). His cost recovery deduction for 2015 is $10,000 ($100,000 × .10). (See Table 5.4 for the percentages.)

Example 48

Assume the same facts as in the previous example, except that Terry sells the asset on November 21, 2015. His cost recovery deduction for 2015, which is subject to the half-year convention, is $5,000 [$100,000 × .10 × ½ (Table 5.4)].

---

[64] § 168(b)(5).

FINANCIAL DISCLOSURE INSIGHTS   Tax and Book Depreciation

A common book-tax difference relates to the depreciation amounts that are reported for GAAP and Federal income tax purposes. Typically, tax depreciation deductions are accelerated; that is, they are claimed in earlier reporting periods than is the case for financial accounting purposes.

Almost every tax law change since 1980 has included depreciation provisions that accelerate the related deductions relative to the expenses allowed under GAAP. Accelerated cost recovery deductions represent a means by which the taxing jurisdiction infuses the business with cash flow created by the reduction in the year's tax liabilities.

For instance, recently, about one-quarter of General Electric's deferred tax liabilities related to depreciation differences. For Toyota's and Ford's depreciation differences, that amount was about one-third. And for the trucking firm Ryder Systems, depreciation differences accounted for all but 1 percent of the deferred tax liabilities.

© iStockphoto.com/Pali Rao

5-7g Additional First-Year Depreciation

As noted in Chapter 1, Congress uses the tax system to stimulate the economy—especially in times of recession. Such is the case with **additional first-year depreciation** (also referred to as "bonus depreciation"). In 2012 and 2013, taxpayers were allowed to take an additional 50 percent cost recovery in the year qualified property was placed in service. Although the provision was written to expire at the end of 2013, Congress may extend this provision during 2014.

Qualified property includes most *new* depreciable assets other than buildings. *New* means original or first use of the property. Property that is used but newly acquired by the taxpayer does not qualify.[65]

The additional first-year depreciation is taken in the year in which the qualifying property is placed in service. This amount may be claimed in addition to otherwise available depreciation deductions. For property placed in service in 2012 or 2013, after the additional first-year depreciation is calculated, the standard MACRS cost recovery allowance is calculated by multiplying the cost recovery basis (original cost recovery basis less additional first-year depreciation) by the percentage that reflects the applicable cost recovery method and convention.

A taxpayer may elect *not* to claim additional first-year depreciation. Examples 49 and 50 reflect the tax treatment for 2013.

		Example 49
Morgan acquires, for $50,000, and places in service a 5-year class asset on March 20, 2013. Morgan's total 2013 cost recovery deduction is:		
50% additional first-year depreciation ($50,000 × .50)	$25,000	
MACRS cost recovery [($50,000 − $25,000) × .20 (Table 5.1)]	5,000	
Total cost recovery	$30,000	

	Example 50
Assume the same facts as in the previous example. Morgan disposes of the asset on October 22, 2014. Morgan's 2014 cost recovery deduction for the asset is $4,000 [$25,000 × 1/2 year × .32 (Table 5.1)].	

5-7h Election to Expense Assets (§ 179)

Section 179 (Election to Expense Certain Depreciable Business Assets) permits a taxpayer to elect to deduct up to $25,000 in 2014 ($500,000 in 2013)[66] of the acquisition cost of *tangible personal property* used in a trade or business. Amounts that are expensed under § 179 may not be capitalized and depreciated.

---

[65]§ 168(k). The 50 percent additional first-year depreciation is allowed for qualified property placed in service after December 31, 2011 and before January 1, 2014; different rules applied between 2008 and 2011.

[66]The expense amount also was $500,000 for assets placed in service in 2012. During 2014, Congress may change the election and phaseout amounts, applying any change in the law to the entire year.

TAX IN THE NEWS   Cost Segregation

Cost segregation identifies certain assets within a commercial property that can qualify for shorter depreciation schedules than the building itself. The identified assets are classified as 5-, 7-, or 15-year property, rather than 39-year property, as part of the building. This allows for greater accelerated depreciation, which reduces taxable income and hence the tax liability.

For instance, a telecommunications system might be segregated from the building in which it is installed. This allows the system to be depreciated over 5 or 7 years, instead of 39 years.

© iStockphoto.com/Andrey Prokhorov

The **§ 179 expensing election** is an annual election that applies to the acquisition cost of property placed in service that year. The immediate expense election generally is not available for real property or for property used for the production of income.[67]

Any elected § 179 expense is taken *before* additional first-year and any other depreciation is computed. The base for calculating both any additional first-year cost recovery and the standard MACRS deduction is determined net of the § 179 expense.

Example 51

Kodiak Corporation acquires and places in service equipment (5-year class asset) on February 1, 2013, at a cost of $525,000. It elects to expense $500,000 under § 179. Kodiak also claims the 50 percent additional first-year cost recovery deduction for 2013. As a result, the total deduction for the year is calculated as follows:

§ 179 expense	$500,000
50% additional first-year depreciation [($525,000 − $500,000) × 50%]	12,500
Standard MACRS amount [($525,000 − $500,000 − $12,500) × .20]	2,500
Total cost recovery claimed	$515,000

Annual Limitations

Two additional limitations apply to the amount deductible under § 179. First, the ceiling amount on the deduction is reduced dollar for dollar when § 179 property placed in service during the taxable year exceeds a maximum amount ($200,000 in 2014; $2 million in 2013). Second, the § 179 deduction cannot exceed the taxpayer's trade or business taxable income, computed without regard to the § 179 amount.

Any § 179 deduction in excess of taxable income is carried forward to future taxable years and added to other amounts eligible for expensing. The § 179 amount eligible for expensing in a carryforward year is limited to the *lesser* of (1) the appropriate statutory dollar amount ($25,000 in 2014; $500,000 in 2013) reduced by the cost of § 179 property placed in service in excess of $200,000 in 2014 ($2 million in 2013) in the carryforward year or (2) business taxable income in the carryforward year.

Example 52

Continue with the facts of the previous example. If Congress does not extend bonus depreciation and makes no changes to the scheduled 2014 § 179 expense limitation and related phaseout amounts, Kodiak's cost recovery deduction is much different if the equipment is acquired in 2014.

§ 179 expense (assets placed in service exceed phaseout)	$ –0–
50% additional first-year depreciation (provision expired)	–0–
Standard MACRS calculation ($525,000 × .20)	105,000
	$105,000

---

[67]§§ 179(b) and (d).

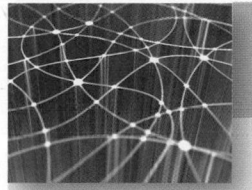

BRIDGE DISCIPLINE Bridge to Economics and the Business Cycle

Congress has passed several stimulus packages intended to stabilize and accelerate the economy. One provision increased the amount of certain fixed asset acquisition costs that could be expensed rather than depreciated. Given the still-struggling economy, however, many companies are not able to take advantage of the increased deductions because they cannot afford to purchase new assets. Businesses do not purchase assets simply to save on taxes.

Source: Based on Joyce Rosenberg, "Deduction Dilemma Hits Companies," *Telegraph Herald* (Dubuque, Iowa), November 9, 2008, p. B2.

© iStockphoto.com/enot-poloskun

Example 53

Jill owns a computer service and operates it as a sole proprietorship. In 2014, taxable income is $12,500 before considering any § 179 deduction. If Jill spends $204,000 on new equipment, her § 179 expense deduction is computed as follows:

§ 179 deduction before adjustment	$25,000
Less: Dollar limitation reduction ($204,000 − $200,000)	(4,000)
Remaining § 179 deduction	$21,000
Business income limitation	$12,500
§ 179 deduction allowed	$12,500
§ 179 deduction carryforward ($21,000 − $12,500)	$ 8,500

Effect on Basis

The basis of the property for cost recovery purposes is reduced by the § 179 amount after accounting for the current-year amount of property placed in service in excess of $200,000 in 2014 ($2 million in 2013). This adjusted amount does not reflect any business income limitation.

5-7i Business and Personal Use of Automobiles and Other Listed Property

Limits exist on MACRS deductions for automobiles and other **listed property** used for both personal and business purposes.[68] These limits would apply, for example, to an automobile used by a sole proprietor partly for business purposes and partly for personal use.

If the listed property is *predominantly* used for business, the taxpayer can use the MACRS tables to recover the cost. In cases where the property is *not predominantly* used for business, the cost is recovered using the *straight-line method.* The statutory percentage method results in a faster recovery of cost than the straight-line method. Listed property includes:[69]

- Any passenger automobile.
- Any other property used as a means of transportation.
- Any property of a type generally used for purposes of entertainment, recreation, or amusement.
- Any computer or peripheral equipment, with the exception of equipment used exclusively at a regular business establishment, including a qualifying home office.
- Any other property specified in the Regulations.

---

[68]§ 280F.

[69]§ 280F(d)(4).

© iStockphoto.com/Andrey Prokhorov

Global Tax Issues

Accelerated Depreciation for Wind Power Producers

The government of India has extended accelerated depreciation for wind power producers. Accelerated depreciation has been a major support to producers trying to achieve energy independence and freeze power costs.

Source: Based on Shreya Jai, "Government Extends Popular Accelerated Depreciation Scheme for Wind Power Producers," *The Economic Times*, March 28, 2012.

Automobiles and Other Listed Property Used Predominantly in Business

For listed property to be considered as predominantly used in business, its *business usage* must exceed 50 percent.[70] The use of listed property for production of income does not qualify as business use for purposes of the more-than-50 percent test. However, both production-of-income and business-use percentages are used to compute the cost recovery deduction.

Example 54

On September 1, 2014, Emma acquires and places in service listed 5-year recovery property. The property cost $10,000. Emma does not claim any available additional first-year cost recovery.

If Emma uses the property 40% for business and 25% for the production of income, the property is not considered as predominantly used for business. The asset cost is recovered using the straight-line method. Emma's cost recovery allowance for the year is $650 ($10,000 × .10 × .65).

If, however, Emma uses the property 60% for business and 25% for the production of income, the property is considered as used predominantly for business. Therefore, she may use the MACRS tables. Emma's cost recovery allowance for the year is $1,700 ($10,000 × .20 × .85).

In determining the percentage of business usage for listed property, a mileage-based percentage is used for automobiles. For other listed property, one employs the most appropriate unit of time (e.g., hours) for which the property actually is used (rather than its availablility for use).[71]

Limits on Cost Recovery for Automobiles

The law places special limitations on cost recovery deductions for *passenger automobiles*.[72] These statutory dollar limits were imposed on passenger automobiles because of the belief that the tax system was being used to underwrite automobiles whose cost and luxury features far exceeded what was needed for the taxpayer's business use.

The following "luxury auto" depreciation limits apply.[73]

Date Placed in Service	First Year	Second Year	Third Year	Fourth and Later Years
2012–2013*	$3,160	$5,100	$3,050	$1,875
2010–2011	$3,060	$4,900	$2,950	$1,775
2009	$2,960	$4,800	$2,850	$1,775

*Because the 2014 indexed amounts were not available at the time of this writing, the 2013 amounts are used in the Examples and Problem Materials.

[70]§ 280F(b)(3).
[71]Reg. § 1.280F–6T(e).
[72]§ 280F(d)(5).

[73]§ 280F(a)(1); Rev.Proc. 2013-21, 2013–12 I.R.B.660.

For an automobile placed in service prior to 2009, the limitation for subsequent years' cost recovery is based on the limits for the year the automobile was placed in service.[74] If a new passenger automobile otherwise qualifies for additional first-year depreciation, the *luxury auto* limitation increases by $8,000 for aquisitions made in 2013 (i.e., to $11,160).

There are also separate cost recovery limitations for trucks and vans and for electric automobiles. Because these limitations are applied in the same manner as those imposed on passenger automobiles, these additional limitations are not discussed further in this chapter.

The luxury auto limits are imposed before any percentage reduction for personal use. In addition, the limitation in the first year includes any amount the taxpayer elects to expense under § 179.[75] If the passenger automobile is used partly for personal use, the personal-use percentage is ignored for the purpose of determining the unrecovered cost available for deduction in later years.

Example 55

On July 1, 2014, Dan acquires and places in service a new automobile that cost $40,000. He does not elect § 179 expensing and he elects not to take any available additional first-year depreciation. The car is used 80% for business and 20% for personal purposes in each tax year. Dan chooses the MACRS 200% declining-balance method of cost recovery (the auto is a 5-year asset). The depreciation computation for 2014 through 2019 is summarized in the table below. The cost recovery allowed is the lesser of the MACRS amount or the recovery limitation.

Year	MACRS Amount	Recovery Limitation	Depreciation Allowed
2014	$6,400 ($40,000 × 20% × 80%)	$2,528 ($3,160 × 80%)	$2,528
2015	$10,240 ($40,000 × 32% × 80%)	$4,080 ($5,100 × 80%)	$4,080
2016	$6,144 ($40,000 × 19.2% × 80%)	$2,440 ($3,050 × 80%)	$2,440
2017	$3,686 ($40,000 × 11.52% × 80%)	$1,500 ($1,875 × 80%)	$1,500
2018	$3,686 ($40,000 × 11.52% × 80%)	$1,500 ($1,875 × 80%)	$1,500
2019	$1,843 ($40,000 × 5.76% × 80%)	$1,500 ($1,875 × 80%)	$1,500

If Dan continues to use the car after 2019, his cost recovery is limited to the lesser of the recoverable basis or the recovery limitation (i.e., $1,875 × business-use percentage). For this purpose, the recoverable basis is computed as if the full cost recovery limitation was allowed, even if the full deduction was not claimed. Thus, the recoverable basis as of January 1, 2020, is $23,065 ($40,000 − $3,160 − $5,100 − $3,050 − $1,875 − $1,875 − $1,875).

If Dan placed the car in service in 2013 and took additional first-year cost recovery, the MACRS amount would have been $16,000 ($40,000 × 80% × 50%). However, the deduction would have been limited to $8,928 [($8,000 + $3,160) × 80%].

The cost recovery limitations are maximum amounts. If the regular MACRS calculation produces a lesser amount of cost recovery, the lesser amount is used.

Example 56

On April 2, 2014, Gail places in service a pre-owned automobile that cost $10,000. The car is always used 70% for business and 30% for personal use. Therefore, the cost recovery allowance for 2014 is $1,400 ($10,000 × .20 × 70%), and not $2,212 (the $3,160 passenger auto maximum × 70%).

---

[74]Cost recovery limitations for years prior to 2009 are found in IRS Publication 463.

[75]§ 280F(d)(1).

The luxury auto limitations apply *only* to passenger automobiles and not to other listed property.

Limitation for SUVs

A $25,000 limit applies to the § 179 deduction when the luxury auto limits do not apply. The limit is in effect for sport utility vehicles (SUVs) with an unloaded gross vehicle weight (GVW) rating of more than 6,000 pounds and not more than 14,000 pounds.[76]

Example 57

During 2013, Jay acquires and places in service a new SUV that cost $70,000 and has a GVW of 8,000 pounds. Jay uses the vehicle 100% of the time for business purposes. The total deduction for 2013 with respect to the SUV is computed as follows:

§ 179 expense, as limited	$25,000
50% additional first-year depreciation [($70,000 − $25,000) × 50%]	22,500
Standard MACRS amount [($70,000 − $25,000 − $22,500) × .20]	4,500
Total cost recovery claimed	$52,000

Automobiles and Other Listed Property Not Used Predominantly in Business

For automobiles and other listed property not used predominantly in business in the year of acquisition (i.e., 50 percent or less), the straight-line method under the alternative depreciation system is required (see Section 5-7l).[77] Under this system, the straight-line recovery period for automobiles is five years. However, the cost recovery allowance for any passenger automobile cannot exceed the luxury auto amount.

The straight-line method is used even if, at some later date, the business usage of the property increases to more than 50 percent. In that case, the amount of cost recovery reflects the increase in business usage.

Change from Predominantly Business Use

If the business-use percentage of listed property falls to 50 percent or less after the year the property is placed in service, the property is subject to *cost recovery recapture*. The amount required to be recaptured and included in the taxpayer's return as ordinary income is the excess cost recovery. *Excess cost recovery* is the excess of the cost recovery deduction taken in prior years using the statutory percentage method over the amount that would have been allowed if the straight-line method had been used since the property was placed in service.[78]

After the business usage of the listed property drops below the more-than-50 percent level, the straight-line method must be used for the remaining life of the property.

Leased Automobiles

A taxpayer who leases a passenger automobile for business purposes reports an *inclusion amount* in gross income. The inclusion amount is computed from an IRS table for each taxable year for which the taxpayer leases the automobile. The purpose of this provision is to prevent taxpayers from circumventing the luxury auto and other limitations by leasing, instead of purchasing, an automobile.

The inclusion amount is based on the fair market value of the automobile; it is prorated for the number of days the auto is used during the taxable year. The prorated dollar amount then is multiplied by the business and income-producing usage percentage.[79] The taxpayer deducts the lease payments, multiplied by the

[76]§ 179(b)(6).
[77]§ 280F(b)(1).
[78]§ 280F(b)(2).
[79]Reg. § 1.280F–7(a).

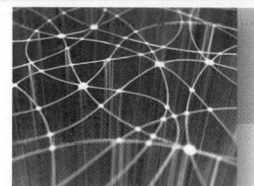

BRIDGE DISCIPLINE Bridge to Finance and Economics

A new car, on average, loses a much larger portion of its value during the first five years through economic depreciation than it loses during later years. Depreciation accounts for about 35 percent of the ownership costs of a car during this five-year period.

Leasing a car will not eliminate the problem because the monthly lease payments are determined, in part, by the projected value of the car at the end of the lease. Because a new car loses its value faster in the earlier years, the shorter the lease, the higher the economic cost of depreciation.

business and income-producing usage percentage. In effect, the taxpayer's annual deduction for the lease payment is reduced by the inclusion amount.

Example 58

On April 1, 2014, Jim leases and places in service a passenger automobile worth $52,400. The lease is to be for a period of five years. During the taxable years 2014 and 2015, Jim uses the automobile 70% for business and 30% for personal use.

Assuming that the dollar amounts from the IRS table for 2014 and 2015 are $20 and $43, respectively, Jim includes in gross income:

2014: $20 × (275/365) × .70 = $11
2015: $43 × (365/365) × .70 = $30

In each year, Jim still can deduct 70% of the lease payments made, related to his business use of the auto.

Substantiation Requirements

Listed property is subject to the substantiation requirements of § 274. This means that the taxpayer must prove for any business usage the amount of expense or use, the time and place of use, the business purpose for the use, and the business relationship to the taxpayer of persons using the property.

Substantiation requires adequate records or sufficient evidence corroborating the taxpayer's statement. However, these substantiation requirements do not apply to vehicles that, by reason of their nature, are not likely to be used more than a *de minimis* amount for personal purposes.[80]

5-7j Farm Property

A farming business is defined as the trade or business of farming, which includes operating a nursery or sod farm and the raising or harvesting of trees bearing fruit, nuts, or other crops, or ornamental trees.[81] When tangible personal property is used in a farming business, the cost of the asset generally is recovered under MACRS using the 150 percent declining-balance method.[82] However, the MACRS straight-line method is required for any tree or vine bearing fruits or nuts.[83]

In general, the cost of real property used in the farming business is recovered over the usual recovery periods (27.5 years and 39 years) using the straight-line method. Exhibit 5.3 shows examples of cost recovery periods for some typical farming assets.

Special rules are used if the uniform capitalization rules apply to the farming business.[84] Under the uniform capitalization rules, the costs of property produced or acquired for resale must be capitalized.

---

[80]§§ 274(d) and (i).
[81]§ 263A(e)(4).
[82]§ 168(b)(2)(B).

[83]§§ 168(b)(3)(E) and 168(e)(3)(D)(ii).
[84]§ 263A(d)(3)(A).

EXHIBIT 5.3	Cost Recovery Periods for Farming Assets	

	Recovery Period in Years	
Assets	**MACRS**	**ADS**
Agricultural structures (single purpose)	10	15
Cattle (dairy or breeding)	5	7
Farm buildings	20	25
Farm machinery and equipment	7	10
Fences (agricultural)	7	10
Horticultural structures (single purpose)	10	15
Trees or vines bearing fruit or nuts	10	20
Truck (heavy-duty, unloaded weight 13,000 pounds or more)	5	6
Truck (actual weight less than 13,000 pounds)	5	5

Alternatively, a farmer can elect to not have the uniform capitalization rules apply. In this case, the alternative depreciation system (ADS) straight-line method must be used (see Section 5-7l). Section 179 expensing can be used even when the ADS is in effect.[85]

Example 59

Redberry Farms, Inc., purchased new farm equipment on July 10, 2014, for $80,000. If Redberry does not elect to expense any of the cost under § 179, its cost recovery deduction for 2014 is $8,568 [(.1071 × $80,000) (Table 5.5)].

Example 60

Assume the same facts as in the previous example, except that Redberry Farms, Inc., has made an election not to have the uniform capitalization rules apply. Redberry's 2014 cost recovery deduction is $4,000 [(.05 × $80,000) (Table 5.6)].

5-7k Leasehold Improvement Property

When the lessor is the owner of leasehold improvement property, the cost recovery period is the statutorily prescribed life. The recovery period for residential rental real estate is 27.5 years, and the recovery period for nonresidential real estate is 39 years. For these real property leasehold improvements, the straight-line method is used. If the improvement is tangible personal property, the shorter MACRS lives and accelerated methods are used.

When lessor-owned leasehold improvements are disposed of or abandoned by the lessor because of the termination of the lease, the property is treated as disposed of by the lessor; hence, a loss can be deducted relative to any unrecovered basis.[86]

Example 61

On April 7, 2014, Mary signed a 10-year lease with Teal Company on a building to be used for her business. The lease period begins on May 1, 2014, and ends on April 30, 2024. Prior to the signing of the lease, Teal paid $300,000 to have a unique storefront added to the building. Teal's cost recovery deduction for 2014 for the addition is $4,815 [(.01605 × $300,000) (Table 5.3)].

Example 62

Assume the same facts as in the previous example. Teal's cost recovery deduction for 2024 is $2,244 {[.02564 × (3.5/12) × $300,000] (Table 5.3)}. At the end of the lease, Teal Company must remove the unique storefront so that it can lease the building to other

[85]Reg. § 1.263A–4(d)(4)(ii).   [86]§ 163(i)(8)(B).

tenants. Teal's loss as a result of the termination of the lease and removal of the unique storefront is computed as follows:

Cost	$300,000
Less: Cost recovery	
2014 (see Example 61)	(4,815)
2015–2023 (.02564 × $300,000 × 9 years)	(69,228)
2024 (.02564 × $300,000 × 3.5/12 months)	(2,244)
Loss (unrecovered cost)	$223,713

The costs of improvements made to leased property and owned by the lessee are recovered in accordance with the general cost recovery rules. This means that the cost recovery period is determined without regard to the lease term. Any unrecovered basis in the leasehold improvement property not retained by the lessee is deducted in the year the lease is terminated.

5-71 Alternative Depreciation System (ADS)

The **alternative depreciation system (ADS)** must be used in lieu of MACRS:[87]

- To calculate the portion of depreciation treated as an alternative minimum tax (AMT) adjustment (see Chapter 17).[88]
- To compute depreciation allowances for property:
  - Used predominantly outside the United States.
  - Leased or otherwise used by a tax-exempt entity.
  - Financed with the proceeds of tax-exempt bonds.
  - Imported from foreign countries that maintain discriminatory trade practices or otherwise engage in discriminatory acts.
- To compute depreciation allowances as part of earnings and profits (see Chapter 13).

Tables 5.5, 5.6, and 5.7 provide cost recovery rates under the ADS method. Generally, personal property is depreciated under the ADS using the appropriate asset class life (e.g., 5- or 7-year) and the 150 percent declining-balance method. ADS uses straight-line depreciation for all realty, over a 40-year class life.

5-8 AMORTIZATION

Taxpayers can claim an **amortization** deduction on certain intangible assets. The amount of the deduction is determined by amortizing the adjusted basis of such intangibles ratably over a 15-year period beginning in the month in which the intangible is acquired.[89]

An *amortizable § 197 intangible* is any § 197 intangible acquired after August 10, 1993, and held in connection with the conduct of a trade or business or for the production of income. Section 197 intangibles include goodwill and going-concern value, franchises, trademarks, and trade names. Covenants not to compete, copyrights, and patents also are included if they are acquired in connection with the acquisition of a business. Generally, self-created intangibles are not § 197 intangibles.

The 15-year amortization period applies regardless of the actual useful life of an amortizable § 197 intangible. No other depreciation or amortization deduction is permitted with respect to any amortizable § 197 intangible except those permitted under the 15-year amortization rules.

LO.7

Identify intangible assets that are eligible for amortization and calculate the amount of the deduction.

---

[87]§ 168(g).
[88]This AMT adjustment applies for real and personal property placed in service before 1999. However, it continues to apply for personal property placed in service after 1998 if the taxpayer uses the 200% declining-balance method for regular income tax purposes. See Chapter 17.
[89]§ 197(a).

Example 63	On June 1, Sally purchased and began operating the Falcon Café. Of the purchase price, $90,000 is allocated to goodwill. The year's § 197 amortization deduction is $3,500 [($90,000 ÷ 15) × (7/12)].

Tax Planning Strategies   STRUCTURING THE SALE OF A BUSINESS

FRAMEWORK FOCUS: TAX RATE

Strategy: Control the Character of Income and Deductions.

On the sale of a sole proprietorship where the sales price exceeds the fair market value of the tangible assets and stated intangible assets, a planning opportunity may exist for both the seller and the buyer.

The seller's preference is for the excess amount to be allocated to *goodwill* because goodwill is a capital asset whose sale may result in favorably taxed long-term capital gain. Amounts received for a *covenant not to compete,* however, produce ordinary income, which is not subject to favorable long-term capital gain rates.

Because a covenant and goodwill both are amortized over a statutory 15-year period, the tax results of a covenant not to compete versus goodwill are the same for the *buyer.* However, the buyer should recognize that an allocation to goodwill rather than a covenant may provide a tax benefit to the seller. Therefore, the buyer, in negotiating the purchase price, should factor in the tax benefit to the seller of having the excess amount labeled goodwill rather than a covenant not to compete. Of course, if the non-competition aspects of a covenant are important to the buyer, a portion of the excess amount can be assigned to a covenant.

5-9 DEPLETION

LO.8

Determine the amount of depletion expense and recognize the alternative tax treatments for intangible drilling and development costs.

Natural resources (e.g., oil, gas, coal, gravel, and timber) are subject to depletion, which can be seen as a form of depreciation applicable to natural resources. Land generally cannot be depleted.

The owner of an interest in the natural resource is entitled to deduct depletion. An owner is one who has an economic interest in the property.[90] An economic interest requires the acquisition of an interest in the resource in place and the receipt of income from the extraction or severance of that resource. Although all natural resources are subject to depletion, oil and gas wells are used as an example in the following paragraphs to illustrate the related costs and issues.

In developing an oil or gas well, the producer typically makes four types of expenditures:

- Natural resource costs.
- Intangible drilling and development costs.
- Tangible asset costs.
- Operating costs.

Natural resources are physically limited, and the costs to acquire them (e.g., oil under the ground) are, therefore, recovered through depletion. Costs incurred in making the property ready for drilling, such as the cost of labor in clearing the property, erecting derricks, and drilling the hole, are intangible drilling and development costs (IDCs). These costs generally have no salvage value and are a lost cost if the well is not productive (dry).

Costs for tangible assets such as tools, pipes, and engines are capital in nature. These costs must be capitalized and recovered through depreciation (cost recovery). Costs incurred after the well is producing are operating costs. These costs

---

[90]Reg. § 1.611–1(b).

include expenditures for items such as labor, fuel, and supplies. Operating costs are deductible when incurred (on the accrual basis) or when paid (on the cash basis).

The expenditures for depreciable assets and operating costs pose no unusual problems for producers of natural resources. The tax treatment of depletable costs and intangible drilling and development costs is quite a different matter.

5-9a Intangible Drilling and Development Costs (IDCs)

Intangible drilling and development costs can be handled in one of two ways at the option of the taxpayer. They can be either charged off as an expense in the year in which they are incurred or capitalized and written off through depletion. The taxpayer makes the election in the first year such expenditures are incurred, either by taking a deduction on the return or by adding them to the depletable basis.

Once made, the election is binding on both the taxpayer and the IRS for all such expenditures in the future. If the taxpayer fails to elect to expense IDCs, on the original timely filed return for the first year in which such expenditures are incurred, an irrevocable election to capitalize them has been made.

As a general rule, it is more advantageous to expense IDCs. The obvious benefit of an immediate write-off (as opposed to a deferred write-off through depletion) is not the only advantage. Because a taxpayer can use percentage depletion, which is calculated without reference to basis, the IDCs may be completely lost as a deduction if they are capitalized.

5-9b Depletion Methods

There are two methods of calculating depletion. *Cost depletion* can be used on any wasting asset (and is the only method allowed for timber). *Percentage depletion* is subject to a number of limitations, particularly for oil and gas deposits. Depletion should be calculated both ways, and the method that results in the larger deduction should be used. The choice between cost depletion and percentage depletion is an annual decision; the taxpayer can use cost depletion in one year and percentage depletion in the following year.

Cost Depletion

Cost depletion is determined by using the adjusted basis of the asset.[91] The basis is divided by the estimated recoverable units of the asset (e.g., barrels and tons) to arrive at the depletion per unit. This amount then is multiplied by the number of units sold (not the units produced) during the year to arrive at the cost depletion allowed. Cost depletion, therefore, resembles the units-of-production method of calculating depreciation.

> **Example 64**
>
> On January 1, 2014, Pablo purchases the rights to a mineral interest for $1 million. At that time, the remaining recoverable units in the mineral interest are estimated to be 200,000. The depletion per unit is $5 [$1,000,000 (adjusted basis) ÷ 200,000 (estimated recoverable units)].
>
> If 60,000 units are mined and 25,000 are sold, the cost depletion is $125,000 [$5 (depletion per unit) × 25,000 (units sold)].

If the taxpayer later discovers that the original estimate was incorrect, the depletion per unit for future calculations is redetermined, using the revised estimate.[92]

---

[91]§ 612.   [92]§ 611(a).

Example 65

Assume the same facts as in the previous example. In 2015, Pablo realizes that an incorrect estimate was made. The remaining recoverable units now are determined to be 400,000. Based on this new information, the revised depletion per unit is $2.1875 [$875,000 (adjusted basis) ÷ 400,000 (estimated recoverable units)]. The adjusted basis is the original cost ($1,000,000) reduced by the depletion claimed in 2014 ($125,000).

If 30,000 units are sold in 2015, the depletion for the year is $65,625 [$2.1875 (depletion per unit) × 30,000 (units sold)].

Percentage Depletion

Percentage depletion (also referred to as statutory depletion) uses a specified percentage provided by the Code. The percentage varies according to the type of mineral interest involved. A sample of these percentages is shown in Exhibit 5.4. The rate is applied to the gross income from the property, but in no event may percentage depletion exceed 50 percent of the taxable income from the property before the allowance for depletion.[93]

Example 66

CarrolCo reports gross income of $100,000 and other property-related expenses of $60,000 and uses a depletion rate of 22%. CarrollCo's depletion allowance is determined as follows:

Gross income	$100,000
Less: Other expenses	(60,000)
Taxable income before depletion	$ 40,000
Depletion allowance [the lesser of $22,000 (22% × $100,000) or $20,000 (50% × $40,000)]	(20,000)
Taxable income after depletion	$ 20,000

The adjusted basis of CarrollCo's property is reduced by $20,000, the depletion deduction allowed. If the other expenses had been only $55,000, the full $22,000 could have been deducted, and the adjusted basis would have been reduced by $22,000.

Note that percentage depletion is based on a percentage of the gross income from the property and makes no reference to cost. Thus, when percentage depletion is used, it is possible to claim aggregate depletion deductions that exceed the original cost of the property. If percentage depletion is used, however, the adjusted basis of the property (for computing cost depletion in a future tax year) is reduced by the amount of percentage depletion taken until the adjusted basis reaches zero.

EXHIBIT 5.4	**Sample of Percentage Depletion Rates**
22% Depletion	
Cobalt	Sulfur
Lead	Tin
15% Depletion	
Copper	Oil and gas
Gold	Silver
10% Depletion	
Coal	Perlite
5% Depletion	
Gravel	Sand

---

[93]§ 613(a). Special rules apply for certain oil and gas wells (e.g., the 50% ceiling is replaced with a 100% ceiling, and the percentage depletion may not exceed 65% of the taxpayer's taxable income from all sources before the allowance for depletion). § 613A.

FRAMEWORK FOCUS: DEDUCTIONS

Strategy: Maximize Deductible Amounts.

As long as the basis of a depletable asset remains above zero, cost depletion or percentage depletion, whichever method the taxpayer elects, is used. When the basis of the asset is exhausted, percentage depletion still can be taken.

Example 67

Warbler Company reports the following related to its sulfur mine:

Remaining depletable basis	$ 11,000
Gross income (10,000 units)	100,000

Expenses (other than depletion)	$30,000
Percentage depletion rate	22%

Because cost depletion is limited to the remaining depletable basis of $11,000, Warbler would choose percentage depletion of $22,000 [lesser of ($100,000 × 22%) or ($70,000 × 50%)]. The basis in the mine then becomes zero.

In future years, however, Warbler can continue to use percentage depletion; percentage depletion is computed without reference to the remaining asset basis. ∎

5-10 COST RECOVERY TABLES

Summary of Cost Recovery Tables

Table 5.1   MACRS statutory percentage table for personalty.
Applicable depreciation methods: 200 or 150 percent declining-balance switching to straight-line.
Applicable recovery periods: 3, 5, 7, 10, 15, 20 years.
Applicable convention: half-year.

Table 5.2   MACRS statutory percentage table for personalty.
Applicable depreciation method: 200 percent declining-balance switching to straight-line.
Applicable recovery periods: 3, 5, 7 years.
Applicable convention: mid-quarter.

Table 5.3   MACRS straight-line table for realty.
Applicable depreciation method: straight-line.
Applicable recovery periods: 27.5, 31.5, 39 years.
Applicable convention: mid-month.

Table 5.4   MACRS optional straight-line table for personalty.
Applicable depreciation method: straight-line.
Applicable recovery periods: 3, 5, 7, 10, 15, 20 years.
Applicable convention: half-year.

Table 5.5   ADS for Alternative Minimum Tax: 150 percent declining-balance table for personalty.
Applicable depreciation method: 150 percent declining-balance switching to straight-line.
Applicable recovery periods: 3, 5, 7, 9.5, 10, 12 years.
Applicable convention: half-year.

Table 5.6   ADS straight-line table for personalty.
Applicable depreciation method: straight-line.
Applicable recovery periods: 5, 10, 12 years.
Applicable convention: half-year.

Table 5.7   ADS straight-line table for realty.
Applicable depreciation method: straight-line.
Applicable recovery period: 40 years.
Applicable convention: mid-month.

TABLE 5.1	MACRS Accelerated Depreciation for Personal Property Assuming Half-Year Convention

For Property Placed in Service after December 31, 1986

Recovery Year	3-Year (200% DB)	5-Year (200% DB)	7-Year (200% DB)	10-Year (200% DB)	15-Year (150% DB)	20-Year (150% DB)
1	33.33	20.00	14.29	10.00	5.00	3.750
2	44.45	32.00	24.49	18.00	9.50	7.219
3	14.81*	19.20	17.49	14.40	8.55	6.677
4	7.41	11.52*	12.49	11.52	7.70	6.177
5		11.52	8.93*	9.22	6.93	5.713
6		5.76	8.92	7.37	6.23	5.285
7			8.93	6.55*	5.90*	4.888
8			4.46	6.55	5.90	4.522
9				6.56	5.91	4.462*
10				6.55	5.90	4.461
11				3.28	5.91	4.462
12					5.90	4.461
13					5.91	4.462
14					5.90	4.461
15					5.91	4.462
16					2.95	4.461
17						4.462
18						4.461
19						4.462
20						4.461
21						2.231

*Switchover to straight-line depreciation.

TABLE 5.2	MACRS Accelerated Depreciation for Personal Property Assuming Mid-Quarter Convention

For Property Placed in Service after December 31, 1986 (Partial Table*)

	3-Year			
Recovery Year	First Quarter	Second Quarter	Third Quarter	Fourth Quarter
1	58.33	41.67	25.00	8.33
2	27.78	38.89	50.00	61.11
	5-Year			
Recovery Year	First Quarter	Second Quarter	Third Quarter	Fourth Quarter
1	35.00	25.00	15.00	5.00
2	26.00	30.00	34.00	38.00
	7-Year			
Recovery Year	First Quarter	Second Quarter	Third Quarter	Fourth Quarter
1	25.00	17.85	10.71	3.57
2	21.43	23.47	25.51	27.55

*The figures in this table are taken from the official tables that appear in Rev.Proc. 87–57, 1987–2 C.B. 687. Because of their length, the complete tables are not presented.

TABLE 5.3	MACRS Straight-Line Depreciation for Real Property Assuming Mid-Month Convention*

For Property Placed in Service after December 31, 1986: 27.5-Year Residential Real Property

Recovery Year(s)	The Applicable Percentage Is (Use the Column for the Month in the First Year the Property Is Placed in Service):											
	1	2	3	4	5	6	7	8	9	10	11	12
1	3.485	3.182	2.879	2.576	2.273	1.970	1.667	1.364	1.061	0.758	0.455	0.152
2–18	3.636	3.636	3.636	3.636	3.636	3.636	3.636	3.636	3.636	3.636	3.636	3.636
19–27	3.637	3.637	3.637	3.637	3.637	3.637	3.637	3.637	3.637	3.637	3.637	3.637
28	1.970	2.273	2.576	2.879	3.182	3.485	3.636	3.636	3.636	3.636	3.636	3.636
29	0.000	0.000	0.000	0.000	0.000	0.000	0.152	0.455	0.758	1.061	1.364	1.667

For Property Placed in Service after December 31, 1986, and before May 13, 1993: 31.5-Year Nonresidential Real Property

Recovery Year(s)	The Applicable Percentage Is (Use the Column for the Month in the First Year the Property Is Placed in Service):											
	1	2	3	4	5	6	7	8	9	10	11	12
1	3.042	2.778	2.513	2.249	1.984	1.720	1.455	1.190	0.926	0.661	0.397	0.132
2–19	3.175	3.175	3.175	3.175	3.175	3.175	3.175	3.175	3.175	3.175	3.175	3.175
20–31	3.174	3.174	3.174	3.174	3.174	3.174	3.174	3.174	3.174	3.174	3.174	3.174
32	1.720	1.984	2.249	2.513	2.778	3.042	3.175	3.175	3.175	3.175	3.175	3.175
33	0.000	0.000	0.000	0.000	0.000	0.000	0.132	0.397	0.661	0.926	1.190	1.455

For Property Placed in Service after May 12, 1993: 39-Year Nonresidential Real Property

Recovery Year(s)	The Applicable Percentage Is (Use the Column for the Month in the First Year the Property Is Placed in Service):											
	1	2	3	4	5	6	7	8	9	10	11	12
1	2.461	2.247	2.033	1.819	1.605	1.391	1.177	0.963	0.749	0.535	0.321	0.107
2–39	2.564	2.564	2.564	2.564	2.564	2.564	2.564	2.564	2.564	2.564	2.564	2.564
40	0.107	0.321	0.535	0.749	0.963	1.177	1.391	1.605	1.819	2.033	2.247	2.461

*The official tables contain a separate row for each year. For ease of presentation, certain years are grouped in these tables. In some instances, this will produce a difference of .001 for the last digit when compared with the official tables.

TABLE 5.4	MACRS Straight-Line Depreciation for Personal Property Assuming Half-Year Convention*

For Property Placed in Service after December 31, 1986

MACRS Class	% First Recovery Year	Other Recovery Years		Last Recovery Year	
		Years	%	Year	%
3-year	16.67	2–3	33.33	4	16.67
5-year	10.00	2–5	20.00	6	10.00
7-year	7.14	2–7	14.29	8	7.14
10-year	5.00	2–10	10.00	11	5.00
15-year	3.33	2–15	6.67	16	3.33
20-year	2.50	2–20	5.00	21	2.50

*The official table contains a separate row for each year. For ease of presentation, certain years are grouped in this table. In some instances, this will produce a difference of .01 for the last digit when compared with the official table.

TABLE 5.5	ADS for Alternative Minimum Tax: 150% Declining-Balance for Personal Property Assuming Half-Year Convention

For Property Placed in Service after December 31, 1986 (Partial Table*)

Recovery Year	3-Year 150%	5-Year 150%	7-Year 150%	9.5-Year 150%	10-Year 150%	12-Year 150%
1	25.00	15.00	10.71	7.89	7.50	6.25
2	37.50	25.50	19.13	14.54	13.88	11.72
3	25.00**	17.85	15.03	12.25	11.79	10.25
4	12.50	16.66**	12.25**	10.31	10.02	8.97
5		16.66	12.25	9.17**	8.74**	7.85
6		8.33	12.25	9.17	8.74	7.33**
7			12.25	9.17	8.74	7.33
8			6.13	9.17	8.74	7.33
9				9.17	8.74	7.33
10				9.16	8.74	7.33
11					4.37	7.32
12						7.33
13						3.66

*The figures in this table are taken from the official table that appears in Rev.Proc. 87–57, 1987–2 C.B. 687. Because of its length, the complete table is not presented.
**Switchover to straight-line depreciation.

TABLE 5.6	ADS Straight-Line for Personal Property Assuming Half-Year Convention

For Property Placed in Service after December 31, 1986 (Partial Table*)

Recovery Year	5-Year Class	10-Year Class	12-Year Class
1	10.00	5.00	4.17
2	20.00	10.00	8.33
3	20.00	10.00	8.33
4	20.00	10.00	8.33
5	20.00	10.00	8.33
6	10.00	10.00	8.33
7		10.00	8.34
8		10.00	8.33
9		10.00	8.34
10		10.00	8.33
11		5.00	8.34
12			8.33
13			4.17

*The figures in this table are taken from the official table that appears in Rev.Proc. 87–57, 1987–2 C.B. 687. Because of its length, the complete table is not presented. The tables for the mid-quarter convention also appear in Rev.Proc. 87–57.

| TABLE 5.7 | | ADS Straight-Line for Real Property Assuming Mid-Month Convention | | | | | | | | | | | |

For Property Placed in Service after December 31, 1986

Recovery Year(s)	Month Placed in Service											
	1	2	3	4	5	6	7	8	9	10	11	12
1	2.396	2.188	1.979	1.771	1.563	1.354	1.146	0.938	0.729	0.521	0.313	0.104
2–40	2.500	2.500	2.500	2.500	2.500	2.500	2.500	2.500	2.500	2.500	2.500	2.500
41	0.104	0.312	0.521	0.729	0.937	1.146	1.354	1.562	1.771	1.979	2.187	2.396

REFOCUS ON THE BIG PICTURE

CALCULATING DEDUCTIBLE EXPENSES

In general, the expenses incurred in Michael Forney's small engine service and repair business are deductible as long as they are ordinary and necessary expenses. In addition, the salaries and wages paid must be reasonable. However, his plan to increase salaries radically next year for himself and his mother probably should not be pursued, because most or all of the increase could be considered unreasonable. Charitable contributions generally are limited to 10 percent of taxable income before the charitable contribution deduction, and political contributions and the fine are not deductible.

Michael can elect to expense the costs of the machinery and equipment under the provisions of § 179. For 2014, the § 179 deduction is limited to $25,000 and cannot exceed the taxable income derived from the business (before the § 179 deduction). In this case, the entire purchase price of $25,000 is deductible.

Gross income	$ 330,500
Less: Salaries and wages	(150,000)
Building rent	(24,000)
§ 179 deduction	(25,000)
Insurance	(12,000)
Utilities	(12,000)
Taxes and licenses	(6,000)
Advertising	(3,000)
Interest expense	(6,000)
Taxable income before the charitable contribution deduction	$ 92,500
Less: Charitable contributions (limited to 10% of taxable income)	(3,000)
Taxable income	$ 89,500

Michael also will be able to deduct depreciation on the house he converted from personal use to rental use and on the rental condo he purchased.

What If?

Instead assume that Mr. Forney purchased and placed in service in 2014 $37,000 of new machinery and equipment of the type that qualifies for the § 179 deduction. In addition, Michael thinks that he can justify increasing his salary to $125,500 because of special expertise he developed recently, which will increase total salaries and wages to $220,500. Michael still can elect to expense $25,000 of the cost of the machinery and equipment under § 179. The remaining $12,000 of basis can be depreciated using the MACRS rules. For 7-year property, the first-year depreciation deduction is 14.29 percent or $1,715; assume that Michael decides not to claim any available additional first-year depreciation. As a result of the increased salary and MACRS deductions, the charitable contribution deduction now is limited to $2,029. The remainder ($971) is carried over to the next tax year.

CONTINUED

Gross income	$ 330,500
Less: Salaries and wages	(220,500)
Building rent	(24,000)
§ 179 deduction	(25,000)
MACRS depreciation	(1,715)
Insurance	(12,000)
Utilities	(12,000)
Taxes and licenses	(6,000)
Advertising	(3,000)
Interest expense	(6,000)
Taxable income before the charitable contribution deduction	$ 20,285
Less: Charitable contributions (limited to 10% of taxable income)	(2,029)
Taxable income	$ 18,256

Suggested Readings

Susan E. Anderson, "Key Aspects of the New Tangible Property Regulations," *The Tax Adviser*, January 2013.

Wilton B. Hyman, "Finding Breaks for Business in the American Taxpayer Relief Act of 2012," *Business Entities*, July/August 2013.

Robert W. Jamison and Christopher W. Hesse, "Controlled Groups and the Sec. 179 Election for S Corporations," *The Tax Adviser*, November 2013.

Kreig D. Mitchell, "The R&D Tax Credit for Start-Up Companies," *Practical Tax Strategies*, February 2012.

Debra T. Sinclair and Britton A. McKay, "Excess Compensation and the Independent Investor Test," *Practical Tax Strategies*, April 2013.

David M. Wooldridge, Ronald A. Levitt, Gregory P. Rhodes, and Nathan Vinson, "Proving the Value of a Charitable Donation May Be the Least of Your Problems," *Journal of Taxation*, August 2011.

Key Terms

1. **LO.2** Duck, an accrual basis corporation, sponsored a rock concert on December 29, 2014. Gross receipts were $300,000. The following expenses were incurred and paid as indicated:

Expense		Payment Date
Rental of coliseum	$ 25,000	December 21, 2014
Cost of goods sold:		
Food	30,000	December 30, 2014
Souvenirs	60,000	December 30, 2014
Performers	100,000	January 5, 2015
Cleaning of coliseum	10,000	February 1, 2015

   Because the coliseum was not scheduled to be used again until January 15, the company with which Duck had contracted did not perform the cleanup until January 8–10, 2015.
   Calculate Duck's net income from the concert for tax purposes for 2014.

2. **LO.3** Ted, an agent for Waxwing Corporation, which is an airline manufacturer, is negotiating a sale with a representative of the U.S. government and with a representative of a developing country. Waxwing has sufficient capacity to handle only one of the orders. Both orders will have the same contract price. Ted believes that if Waxwing authorizes a $500,000 payment to the representative of the foreign country, he can guarantee the sale. He is not sure that he can obtain the same result with the U.S. government. Identify the relevant tax issues for Waxwing.

   Issue ID

3. **LO.3** Linda operates an illegal gambling operation and incurs the following expenses. Which of these expenses can reduce her taxable income?
   a. Bribes paid to city employees.
   b. Salaries to employees.
   c. Security cameras.
   d. Kickbacks to police.
   e. Rent on an office.
   f. Depreciation on office furniture and equipment.
   g. Tenant's casualty insurance.
   h. Utilities.

4. **LO.3** Cardinal Corporation is a trucking firm that operates in the Mid-Atlantic states. One of Cardinal's major customers frequently ships goods between Charlotte and Baltimore. Occasionally, the customer sends last-minute shipments that are outbound for Europe on a freighter sailing from Baltimore. To satisfy the delivery schedule in these cases, Cardinal's drivers must substantially exceed the speed limit. Cardinal pays for any related speeding tickets. During the past year, two drivers had their licenses suspended for 30 days each for driving at such excessive speeds. Cardinal continues to pay each driver's salary during the suspension periods.

   Ethics and Equity

   Cardinal believes that it is necessary to conduct its business in this manner if it is to be profitable, maintain the support of the drivers, and maintain the goodwill of customers. Evaluate Cardinal's business practices.

5. **LO.3** Quail Corporation anticipates that being positively perceived by the individual who is elected mayor will be beneficial for business. Therefore, Quail contributes to the campaigns of both the Democratic and Republican candidates. The Republican candidate is elected mayor. Can Quail deduct any of the political contributions it made? Explain.

6. **LO.3** Melissa, the owner of a sole proprietorship, does not provide health insurance for her 20 employees. She plans to spend $1,500 lobbying in opposition to legislation that would require her to provide such insurance. Discuss the tax advantages and disadvantages of paying the $1,500 to a professional lobbyist rather than spending the $1,500 on in-house lobbying expenditures.

Issue ID

7. **LO.3** Ella owns 60% of the stock of Peach, Inc. The stock has declined in value since she purchased it five years ago. She is going to sell 5% of the stock to a relative. Ella is also going to make a gift of 10% of the stock to another relative. Identify the relevant tax issues for Ella.

8. **LO.3** Jarret owns City of Charleston bonds with an adjusted basis of $190,000. During the year, he receives interest payments of $3,800. Jarret partially financed the purchase of the bonds by borrowing $100,000 at 5% interest. Jarret's interest payments on the loan this year are $4,900, and his principal payments are $1,100.
   a. Should Jarret report any interest income this year? Explain.
   b. Can Jarret deduct any interest expense this year? Explain.

9. **LO.3** Nancy, the owner of a very successful hotel chain in the Southeast, is exploring the possibility of expanding the chain into a city in the Northeast. She incurs $35,000 of expenses associated with this investigation. Based on the regulatory environment for hotels in the city, she decides not to expand. During the year, she also investigates opening a restaurant that will be part of a national restaurant chain. Her expenses for this are $53,000. The restaurant begins operations on September 1. Determine the amount Nancy can deduct in the current year for investigating these two businesses.

Decision Making

Communications

10. **LO.3** Brittany Callihan sold stock (basis of $184,000) to her son, Ridge, for $160,000, the fair market value.
   a. What are the tax consequences to Brittany?
   b. What are the tax consequences to Ridge if he later sells the stock for $190,000? For $152,000? For $174,000?
   c. Write a letter to Brittany in which you inform her of the tax consequences if she sells the stock to Ridge for $160,000. Explain how a sales transaction could be structured that would produce better tax consequences for her. Brittany's address is 32 Country Lane, Lawrence, KS 66045.

11. **LO.3** For each of the following independent transactions, calculate the recognized gain or loss to the seller and the adjusted basis to the buyer.
   a. Bonnie sells Parchment, Inc. stock (adjusted basis $17,000) to Phillip, her brother, for its fair market value of $12,000.
   b. Amos sells land (adjusted basis $85,000) to his nephew, Boyd, for its fair market value of $70,000.
   c. Susan sells a tax-exempt bond (adjusted basis $20,000) to her wholly owned corporation for its fair market value of $19,000.
   d. Ron sells a business truck (adjusted basis $20,000) that he uses in his sole proprietorship to his cousin, Agnes, for its fair market value of $18,500.
   e. Martha sells her partnership interest (adjusted basis $175,000) in Pearl Partnership to her adult daughter, Kim, for $220,000.

Decision Making

12. **LO.4** In 2014, Gray Corporation, a calendar year C corporation, holds a $75,000 charitable contribution carryover from a gift made in 2009. Gray is contemplating a gift of land to a qualified charity in either 2014 or 2015. Gray purchased the land as an investment five years ago for $100,000 (current fair market value is $250,000).

Before considering any charitable deduction, Gray projects taxable income of $1 million for 2014 and $1.2 million for 2015. Should Gray make the gift of the land to charity in 2014 or in 2015? Provide support for your answer.

Decision Making

Communications

13. **LO.4** Dan Simms is the president and sole shareholder of Simms Corporation, 1121 Madison Street, Seattle, WA 98121. Dan plans for the corporation to make a charitable contribution to the University of Washington, a qualified public charity. He will have the corporation donate Jaybird Corporation stock, held for five years, with a basis of $11,000 and a fair market value of $25,000. Dan projects a $310,000 net profit for Simms Corporation in 2014 and a $100,000 net profit in 2015. Dan calls you on December 12, 2014, and asks whether Simms should make the contribution in 2014 or 2015. Write a letter advising Dan about the timing of the contribution.

14. **LO.5** Blue Corporation, a manufacturing company, decided to develop a new line of merchandise. The project began in 2014. Blue had the following expenses in connection with the project.

	2014	2015
Salaries	$500,000	$600,000
Materials	90,000	70,000
Insurance	8,000	11,000
Utilities	6,000	8,000
Cost of inspection of materials for quality control	7,000	6,000
Promotion expenses	11,000	18,000
Advertising	–0–	20,000
Equipment depreciation	15,000	14,000
Cost of market survey	8,000	–0–

The new product will be introduced for sale beginning in July 2016. Determine the amount of the deduction for research and experimental expenditures for 2014, 2015, and 2016 if:
   a. Blue Corporation elects to expense the research and experimental expenditures.
   b. Blue Corporation elects to amortize the research and experimental expenditures over 60 months.

15. **LO.5** Sarah Ham, operating as a sole proprietor, manufactures printers in the United States. For 2014, the proprietorship has QPAI of $400,000. Sarah's modified AGI was $350,000. The W–2 wages paid by the proprietorship to employees engaged in the qualified domestic production activity were $60,000. Calculate Sarah's DPAD for 2014.

16. **LO.5** In 2014, Rose, Inc., has QPAI of $4 million and taxable income of $3 million. Rose pays independent contractors $500,000. Rose's W–2 wages are $600,000, but only $400,000 of the wages are paid to employees engaged in qualified domestic production activities.   *Decision Making*
   a. Calculate the DPAD for Rose, Inc., for 2014.
   b. What suggestions could you make to enable Rose to increase its DPAD?

17. **LO.6** On November 4, 2012, Blue Company acquired an asset (27.5-year residential real property) for $200,000 for use in its business. In 2012 and 2013, respectively, Blue took $642 and $5,128 of cost recovery. These amounts were incorrect; Blue applied the wrong percentages (i.e., those for 39-year rather than 27.5-year property). Blue should have taken $910 and $7,272 of cost recovery in 2012 and 2013, respectively. On January 1, 2014, the asset was sold for $180,000. Calculate the gain or loss on the sale of the asset in 2014.

18. **LO.6** Juan, a sole proprietor, acquires a new 5-year class asset on March 14, 2014, for $200,000. This is the only asset Juan acquired during the year. He does not elect immediate expensing under § 179. Juan does not claim any available additional first-year depreciation. On July 15, 2015, Juan sells the asset.
   a. Determine Juan's cost recovery for 2014.
   b. Determine Juan's cost recovery for 2015.

19. **LO.6** Debra acquired the following new assets during 2014.

Date	Asset	Cost
April 11	Furniture	$40,000
July 28	Trucks	40,000
November 3	Computers	70,000

Determine Debra's cost recovery deductions for the current year. Debra does not elect immediate expensing under § 179. She does not claim any available additional first-year depreciation.

20. **LO.6** On May 5, 2014, Christy purchased and placed in service a hotel. The hotel cost $10.8 million. Calculate Christy's cost recovery deductions for 2014 and for 2024.

21. **LO.6** Janice acquired an apartment building on June 4, 2014, for $1.6 million. The value of the land is $300,000. Janice sold the apartment building on November 29, 2020.
    a. Determine Janice's cost recovery deduction for 2014.
    b. Determine Janice's cost recovery deduction for 2020.

22. **LO.6** During March 2014, Sam constructed new agricultural fences on his farm. The cost of the fencing was $80,000. Sam does not elect immediate expensing under § 179 and he does not claim any available additional first-year depreciation. However, an election not to have the uniform capitalization rules apply is in effect. Compute Sam's cost recovery deduction for 2014. Sam wants to maximize his cost recovery deductions.

Critical Thinking

23. **LO.6** On January 1, 2006, Jim leased a building to be used in his business as an office building. The lease will terminate on December 31, 2014. On February 2, 2008, Jim made a capital improvement to the exterior of the building. The cost of the leasehold improvement to Jim was $80,000. Jim has no legal rights in the capital improvement after the termination of the lease. Determine Jim's 2014 loss deduction for unrecovered costs, if any, with respect to the leasehold improvement as a result of the termination of the lease.

Decision Making

24. **LO.6** Lori, who is single, purchased 5-year class property for $31,000 and 7-year class property for $42,000 on May 20, 2014. Lori expects the taxable income derived from her business (without regard to the amount expensed under § 179) to be about $100,000. Lori wants to elect immediate § 179 expensing, but she doesn't know which asset she should expense under § 179. Lori does not claim any available additional first-year depreciation.
    a. Determine Lori's total deduction if the § 179 expense is first taken with respect to the 5-year class asset.
    b. Determine Lori's total deduction if the § 179 expense is first taken with respect to the 7-year class asset.
    c. What is your advice to Lori?

25. **LO.6** Olga is the proprietor of a small business. In 2014, the business's income, before consideration of any cost recovery or § 179 deduction, is $104,000.

    Olga spends $40,000 on new 7-year class assets and elects to take the § 179 deduction on them. She does not claim any available additional first-year depreciation. Olga's cost recovery deduction for 2014, except for the cost recovery with respect to the new 7-year assets, is $86,000. Determine Olga's total cost recovery for 2014 with respect to the 7-year class assets and the amount of any § 179 carryforward.

26. **LO.6** On June 5, 2013, Dan purchased and placed in service a 7-year class asset costing $550,000. Determine the maximum deductions that Dan can claim with respect to this asset in 2013 and 2014.

Communications

27. **LO.6** John Johnson is considering acquiring an automobile at the beginning of 2014 that he will use 100% of the time as a taxi. The purchase price of the automobile is $35,000. John has heard of cost recovery limits on automobiles and wants to know the maximum amount of the $35,000 he can deduct in the first year.

    Write a letter to John in which you present your calculations. Also prepare a memo for the tax files, summarizing your analysis. John's address is 100 Morningside, Clinton, MS 39058.

28. **LO.6** On October 15, 2014, Jon purchased and placed in service a used car. The purchase price was $25,000. This was the only business-use asset Jon acquired in 2014. He used the car 80% of the time for business and 20% for personal use. Jon used the MACRS statutory percentage method. Calculate the total deduction Jon may take for 2014 with respect to the car.

29. **LO.6** On June 5, 2013, Leo purchased and placed in service a new car that cost $20,000. The business-use percentage for the car is always 100%. Leo claims any available additional first-year depreciation. Compute Leo's cost recovery deduction for 2013 and 2014.

30. **LO.6** On May 28, 2014, Mary purchased and placed in service a new $20,000 car. The car was used 60% for business, 20% for production of income, and 20% for personal use in 2014. In 2015, the usage changed to 40% for business, 30% for production of income, and 30% for personal use. Mary did not elect immediate expensing under § 179. She did not claim any available additional first-year depreciation. Compute Mary's cost recovery deduction and any cost recovery recapture in 2015.

Critical Thinking

31. **LO.6** In 2014, Muhammad purchased a new computer for $16,000. The computer is used 100% for business. Muhammad did not make a § 179 election with respect to the computer. He does not claim any available additional first-year depreciation. If Muhammad uses the MACRS statutory percentage method, determine his cost recovery deduction for 2014 for computing taxable income and for computing his alternative minimum tax.

32. **LO.6** Jamie purchased $100,000 of new office furniture for her business in June of the current year. Jamie understands that if she elects to use ADS to compute her regular income tax, there will be no difference between the cost recovery for computing the regular income tax and the AMT. Jamie wants to know the *regular* income tax cost, after three years, of using ADS rather than MACRS. Assume that Jamie does not elect § 179 limited expensing and that her marginal tax rate is 28%. She does not claim any available additional first-year depreciation.

Decision Making

33. **LO.7** Mike Saxon is negotiating the purchase of a business. The final purchase price has been agreed upon, but the allocation of the purchase price to the assets is still being discussed. Appraisals on a warehouse range from $1,200,000 to $1,500,000. If a value of $1,200,000 is used for the warehouse, the remainder of the purchase price, $800,000, will be allocated to goodwill. If $1,500,000 is allocated to the warehouse, goodwill will be $500,000.

    Mike wants to know what effect each alternative will have on cost recovery and amortization during the first year. Under the agreement, Mike will take over the business on January 1 of next year. Write a letter to Mike in which you present your calculations and recommendation. Also prepare a memo for the tax files. Mike's address is 200 Rolling Hills Drive, Shavertown, PA 18708.

Decision Making

Communications

34. **LO.8** Sam Jones owns a granite stone quarry. When he acquired the land, Sam allocated $800,000 of the purchase price to the quarry's recoverable mineral reserves, which were estimated at 10 million tons of granite stone. Based on these estimates, the cost depletion was $.08 per ton. In April of the current year, Sam received a letter from the State Department of Highways notifying him that part of his property was being condemned so that state could build a new road. At that time, the recoverable mineral reserves had an adjusted basis of $600,000 and 7.5 million tons of granite rock. Sam estimates that the land being condemned contains about 2 million tons of granite. Therefore, for the current year, Sam has computed his cost depletion at $.11 per ton [$600,000/(7,500,000 − 2,000,000)]. Evaluate the appropriateness of what Sam is doing.

Ethics and Equity

35. **LO.8** Wes acquired a mineral interest during the year for $10 million. A geological survey estimated that 250,000 tons of the mineral remained in the deposit. During the year, 80,000 tons were mined, and 45,000 tons were sold for $12 million. Other related expenses amounted to $5 million. Assuming that the mineral depletion rate is 22%, calculate Wes's lowest taxable income, after any depletion deductions.

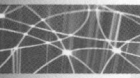

BRIDGE DISCIPLINE

Decision Making

1. Sparrow Corporation is considering the acquisition of an asset for use in its business over the next five years. However, Sparrow must decide whether it would be better served by leasing the asset or buying it. An appropriate asset could be purchased for $15,000, and it would qualify as a three-year asset under the MACRS classification. Assume that the election to expense assets under § 179 is not available, that any available additional first-year depreciation is not claimed, and that the asset is not expected to have a salvage value at the end of its use by Sparrow. Alternatively, Sparrow could lease the asset for a $3,625 annual cost over the five-year period. If Sparrow is in the 34% tax bracket, would you recommend that Sparrow buy or lease the asset? In your calculations, assume that 10% is an appropriate discount factor.

Decision Making

2. Lark Corporation is considering the acquisition of an asset for use in its business over the next five years. However, Lark must decide whether it would be better served by leasing the asset or buying it. An appropriate asset could be purchased for $15,000, and it would qualify as a three-year asset under the MACRS classification. Assume that the election to expense assets under § 179 is made, but any available additional first-year depreciation is not claimed, and that the asset is not expected to have a salvage value at the end of its use by Lark. Alternatively, Lark could lease the asset for a $3,625 annual cost over the five-year period. If Lark is in the 34% tax bracket, would you recommend that Lark buy or lease the asset? In your calculations, assume that 10% is an appropriate discount factor.

3. Wayside Fruit Company is a sole proprietorship owned by Neil Stephenson. The company's records reflect the following:

Sales revenue	$185,000
Operating expenses	125,000
Depreciation expense for book	13,000
Cost recovery allowance for tax	17,500
Loss on the sale of delivery truck to Neil's brother	5,000
Amount paid to fruit inspector to overlook below-standard fruit shipped to various vendors	3,000

Compute the net income before tax for book purposes and the amount of taxable income for Wayside Fruit Company.

Research Problems

THOMSON REUTERS
CHECKPOINT®

Note: Solutions to Research Problems can be prepared by using the **Checkpoint®** **Student Edition** online research product, which is available to accompany this text. It is also possible to prepare solutions to the Research Problems by using tax research materials found in a standard tax library.

Research Problem 1. In early 2012, Walter Hodges began investigating the real estate market with the intention of acquiring real estate for investment or rental. He had not previously been involved in any real estate rental or investment ventures.

Walter started marketing his business via business cards, flyers, and word of mouth in spring 2012. At the same time, he completed a business plan for buying, remodeling, and renting property.

In October 2012, Walter paid $25,000 for training classes designed to provide real estate investment skills. He obtained a loan for his business of $45,000 from the U.S. Small Business Administration in November 2012. During the same month, he obtained an employer ID number from the IRS. In December 2012, he opened a checking account and obtained a credit card in the name of the business.

Walter attempted to purchase several properties during the last half of 2012, but he was unsuccessful until he acquired property on December 30, 2012. He listed the property for rent in early January 2013 and was successful in renting it in March 2013.

On his Form 1040 for 2012, Walter prepared a Schedule C on which he showed a business loss of $29,000. He included the cost of the training classes, automobile expenses, meals and entertainment, computer and software expenses, and supplies.

Walter asked a friend, who is a CPA, to review his Schedule C calculations. His friend suggested that Walter should not be able to deduct the $29,000 on his 2012 return as he did not believe that Walter was in a trade or business during 2012. Evaluate whether Walter's trade or business activity began in 2012 or 2013.

Research Problem 2. Gray Chemical Company manufactured pesticides that were toxic. Over the course of several years, the toxic waste contaminated the air and water around the company's plant. Several employees suffered toxic poisoning, and the Environmental Protection Agency cited the company for violations. In court, the judge found Gray guilty and imposed fines of $15 million. The company voluntarily set up a charitable fund for the purpose of bettering the environment and funded it with $8 million. The company incurred legal expenses in setting up the foundation and defending itself in court. The court reduced the fine from $15 million to $7 million.

Communications

Gray deducted the $8 million paid to the foundation and the legal expenses incurred. The IRS disallowed both deductions on the grounds that the payment was, in fact, a fine and in violation of public policy.

Gray's president, Ted Jones, has contacted you regarding the deductibility of the $7 million fine, the $8 million payment to the foundation, and the legal fees. Write a letter to Mr. Jones that contains your advice, and prepare a memo for the tax files. Gray's address is 200 Lincoln Center, Omaha, NE 68182.

Partial list of research aids:
§§ 162(a) and (f).
Reg. § 1.162–21(b).

Research Problem 3. In 2010, Jed James began planting a vineyard. The costs of the land preparation, labor, rootstock, and planting were capitalized. The land preparation costs do not include any nondepreciable land costs. In 2014, when the plants became viable, Jed placed the vineyard in service. Jed wants to know whether he can claim a deduction under § 179 on his 2014 income tax return for the costs incurred in 2010 with respect to planting the vineyard.

Research Problem 4. Juan owns a business that acquires exotic automobiles that are high-tech, state-of-the-art vehicles with unique design features or equipment. The exotic automobiles are not licensed, nor are they set up to be used on the road. Rather, the cars are used exclusively for car shows or related promotional photography. With respect to the exotic automobiles, can Juan take a cost recovery deduction on his Federal income tax return? Prepare an outline for your classmates addressing this issue.

Communications

Partial list of research aids:
Bruce Selig, 70 TCM 1125, T.C.Memo. 1995–519.

Research Problem 5. Your client, Dave's Sport Shop, sells sports equipment and clothing in three retail outlets in New York City. Earlier this year, the CFO decided that keeping track of inventory using a combination of QuickBooks and Excel was not an efficient way to manage the stores' inventories. So Dave's purchased an inventory management system for $9,000 that allowed the entity to keep track of inventory, as well as automate ordering and purchasing, without replacing QuickBooks for its accounting function.

Communications

The CFO would like to know whether the cost of the inventory management program can be expensed in the year of purchase. Write a letter to the CFO, Cassandra Martin, that addresses the tax treatment of purchased software. Cassandra's mailing address is 867 Broadway, New York, NY 10003.

**Internet
Activity**

Use the tax resources of the Internet to address the following questions. Do not restrict your search to the Web, but include a review of newsgroups and general reference materials, practitioner sites and resources, primary sources of the tax law, chat rooms and discussion groups, and other opportunities.

Research Problem 6. Many states that have corporate income taxes "piggyback" onto the Federal corporate income tax calculation. In other words, these states' corporate income tax calculations incorporate many of the Federal calculations and deductions to make both compliance and verification of tax liability easier. However, some state legislatures were concerned that the domestic production activities deduction, if allowed for state tax purposes, would result in significant revenue losses. Determine whether states with corporate income taxes allow or disallow the domestic production activities deduction in the calculation of the state's corporate income tax liability.

Communications

Research Problem 7. Changes to depreciation systems often are discussed by policymakers and observers of the tax system. In no more than three PowerPoint slides, outline the terms and policy objectives of one of the changes currently proposed by the Treasury, a member of Congress, or a tax policy think tank.

Losses and Loss Limitations

LEARNING OBJECTIVES: *After completing Chapter 6, you should be able to:*

LO.1 **Determine the amount, classification, and timing of the bad debt deduction.**

LO.2 **State and illustrate the tax treatment of worthless securities, including § 1244 stock.**

LO.3 **Identify a casualty and determine the amount, classification, and timing of casualty and theft losses.**

LO.4 **Describe the impact of the net operating loss carryback and carryover provisions on previous and subsequent years' taxable income.**

LO.5 **Explain the tax shelter problem and the reasons for at-risk and passive loss limitations.**

LO.6 **Describe how the at-risk limitation and the passive loss rules limit deductions for losses and identify taxpayers subject to these restrictions.**

LO.7 **Discuss the definitions of activity, material participation, and rental activity under the passive loss rules.**

LO.8 **Determine the relationship between the at-risk and passive loss limitations.**

LO.9 **Recognize the special treatment available to real estate activities.**

LO.10 **Determine the consequences of the disposition of passive activities.**

CHAPTER OUTLINE

TAX TALK *The income tax has made more liars out of the American people than golf has. Even when you make a tax form out on the level, you don't know when it's through if you are a crook or a martyr.* —WILL ROGERS

THE BIG PICTURE   Tax Solutions for the Real World

© G. Baden/Corbis

RECEIVING TAX BENEFITS FROM LOSSES

Robyn, an unmarried cash basis taxpayer, is nearing the end of a year that she would like to forget. Several years ago, she loaned a friend, Jamil, $25,000 to enable him to start a business. Jamil had made scheduled payments of $7,000 (including $1,000 of interest) when he suddenly died in January. At the time of his death, he was insolvent, and Robyn's attempts to collect the debt were fruitless.

Last year, Robyn invested $60,000 by purchasing stock in Owl Corporation, a closely held small business corporation started by her brother. However, the company declared bankruptcy in May of this year, and Robyn was notified by the bankruptcy trustee that she can expect to receive nothing from the company.

Robyn has owned and operated a bookstore as a sole proprietorship for the past 10 years. The bookstore has been profitable and produced annual taxable income of approximately $75,000. However, due to the downturn in the economy, the business lost $180,000 this year.

In September, a tornado caused a large oak tree to blow over onto Robyn's house. The cost of removing the tree and making repairs to the house was $32,000. Robyn received a check for $25,000 from her insurance company. Her adjusted basis for the house was $280,000.

Finally, Robyn invested $20,000 for a 10 percent interest in a limited partnership that owns and operates orange groves in Florida. Due to a hard freeze that damaged much of the fruit, the partnership lost $200,000 and allocated $20,000 of ordinary loss to Robyn.

Robyn comes to you for tax advice and would like to know the tax ramifications of each of the events and transactions listed above.

Read the chapter and formulate your response.

hapter 5 introduced rules governing the deductibility of trade or business expenses. This chapter extends the notion of deductibility to losses occurring in the course of business operations. In particular, special rules concerning the tax treatment of bad debts, casualty losses, and operating losses are reviewed. In addition, tax shelters and the rules that limit their usefulness as tax avoidance devices are discussed.

6-1 BAD DEBTS

LO.1

Determine the amount, classification, and timing of the bad debt deduction.

If a taxpayer lends money or purchases a debt instrument and the debt is not repaid, a **bad debt** deduction is allowed. Similarly, if an accrual basis taxpayer sells goods or provides services on credit and the account receivable subsequently becomes worthless, a bad debt deduction is permitted.[1] No deduction is allowed, however, for a bad debt arising from the sale of a product or service when the taxpayer is on the cash basis because no income is reported until the cash has been collected. Permitting a bad debt deduction for a cash basis taxpayer would amount to a double deduction because the expenses of the product or service rendered are deducted when payments are made to suppliers and to employees or when the sale is made.

Example 1

Ella, an individual, is a sole proprietor. She operates a business named Executive Accounting and Tax Services. Last year, Pat hired Ella to help him with the accounting for his small business. Ella also prepared the S corporation income tax return for the business and Pat's personal income tax return. Ella billed Pat $8,000 for the services she performed. Pat has never paid the bill, his business no longer exists, and his whereabouts are unknown.

If Ella is an accrual basis taxpayer, she includes the $8,000 in income when the services are performed. When she determines that Pat's account will not be collected, she deducts the $8,000 as a bad debt.

If Ella is a cash basis taxpayer, she does not include the $8,000 in income until payment is received. When she determines that Pat's account will not be collected, she cannot deduct the $8,000 as a bad debt expense because it was never recognized as income.

THE BIG PICTURE

Example 2

Return to the facts of *The Big Picture* on p. 6-1. Because Robyn is a cash basis taxpayer, she cannot take as a bad debt deduction any unpaid accrued interest on the loan to her friend, Jamil, because it was never recognized as income.

6-1a Specific Charge-Off Method

Most taxpayers are required to use the **specific charge-off method** when accounting for bad debts. However, some financial institutions are permitted to use an alternative **reserve method** for computing bad debt deductions.

A taxpayer using the specific charge-off method may claim a deduction when a specific *business* debt becomes either partially or wholly worthless or when a specific *nonbusiness* debt becomes wholly worthless.[2] For a business debt, the taxpayer must satisfy the IRS that the debt is partially worthless and must demonstrate the amount of worthlessness. If a business debt previously deducted as partially worthless becomes totally worthless in a future year, only the remainder not previously deducted can be deducted in the future year.

---

[1]Reg. § 1.166–1(e).

[2]§ 166(a).

TAX IN THE NEWS   Impact of Funding Cuts on Skilled Nursing Facilities

A so-called "bad debt" provision contained in the Middle Class Tax Relief Act of 2012 is having a negative impact on skilled nursing facilities (SNFs). An analysis shows that Medicare funding cuts to SNFs in the states of Florida, Ohio, Illinois, Pennsylvania, North Carolina, Louisiana, Indiana, Tennessee, Georgia, and New Jersey will reduce payments by a least $3 billion over the period 2012–2021. It has been pointed out that the term *bad debt* is a complete misnomer. The Federal government prevents SNFs from collecting as much as 90 percent of SNF debts from state Medicaid agencies. The bad debt is more accurately described as "uncollectible debt" as mandated by Federal law.

Source: Based on "New Avalere Health Analysis Details State Impact of 'Bad Debt' SNF Medicare Funding Cuts," *PR Newswire Association LLC*, April, 3, 2012.

In the case of total worthlessness, a deduction is allowed for the entire amount in the year that the debt becomes worthless. The amount of the deduction depends on the taxpayer's basis in the bad debt. If the debt arose from the sale of services or products and the face amount was previously included in income, that amount is deductible. If the taxpayer purchased the debt, the deduction equals the amount the taxpayer paid for the debt instrument.

Determining when a bad debt becomes worthless can be a difficult task. Legal proceedings need not be initiated against the debtor when the surrounding facts indicate that such action will not result in collection.

> In 2012, Partridge Company lent $1,000 to Kay, who agreed to repay the loan in two years. In 2014, Kay disappeared after the note became delinquent. If a reasonable investigation by Partridge indicates that Kay cannot be found or that a suit against Kay would not result in collection, Partridge can deduct the $1,000 in 2014.

Example 3

Bankruptcy is generally an indication of at least partial worthlessness of a debt. Bankruptcy may create worthlessness before the settlement date. If this is the case, the deduction may be taken in the year of worthlessness.

> In Example 3, assume that Kay filed for personal bankruptcy in 2013 and that the debt is a business debt. At that time, Partridge learned that unsecured creditors (including Partridge) were ultimately expected to receive 20 cents on the dollar. In 2014, settlement is made, and Partridge receives only $150. Partridge should deduct $800 ($1,000 loan − $200 expected settlement) in 2013 and $50 in 2014 ($200 balance − $150 proceeds).

Example 4

TAX FACT   Just How Good Is Your Credit?

To be successful, a business must generate sales among customers who are willing and able to pay their obligations. Nonetheless, if a sale is made and it is determined that the related account receivable is uncollectible, an accrual method business is allowed to claim a bad debt deduction. Recently, corporations claimed bad debt deductions of approximately $316 billion against business receipts of about $23.06 trillion.

Source: 2010 Corporation Returns—Returns of Active Corporations; Table 2—Balance Sheet, Income Statement, and Selected Other Items, by Size of Total Assets; 2013.

CONCEPT SUMMARY 6.1

The Tax Treatment of Bad Debts Using the Specific Charge-Off Method

	Business Bad Debts	Nonbusiness Bad Debts
Timing of deduction	A deduction is allowed when the debt becomes either partially or wholly worthless.	A deduction is allowed *only* when the debt becomes wholly worthless.
Character of deduction	The bad debt may be deducted as an ordinary loss.	The bad debt is classified as a short-term capital loss, subject to the $3,000 capital loss limitation for individuals.
Recovery of amounts previously deducted	If the account recovered was written off during the current tax year, the write-off entry is reversed. If the account was written off in a previous tax year, income is created subject to the tax benefit rule.	If the account recovered was written off during the current tax year, the write-off entry is reversed. If the account was written off in a previous tax year, income is created subject to the tax benefit rule.

If a receivable is written off (deducted) as uncollectible and is subsequently collected during the same tax year, the write-off entry is reversed. If a receivable has been written off (deducted) as uncollectible, collection in a later tax year may result in income being recognized. Income will result if the deduction yielded a tax benefit in the year it was taken (the tax benefit rule).

See Concept Summary 6.1.

6-1b Business versus Nonbusiness Bad Debts

The nature of a debt depends upon whether the lender is engaged in the business of lending money or whether there is a proximate relationship between the creation of the debt and the *lender's* trade or business. Where either of these conditions is true, a bad debt is classified as a **business bad debt**. If these conditions are not met, a bad debt is classified as a **nonbusiness bad debt**. The use to which the borrowed funds are put is of no consequence when making this classification decision.

THE BIG PICTURE

Example 5

Return to the facts of *The Big Picture* on p. 6-1. Robyn loaned her friend, Jamil, $25,000. Jamil used the money to start a business, which subsequently failed. When Jamil died after having made principal payments of $6,000 on the loan, he was insolvent. Even though the proceeds of the loan were used in a business, the loan is a nonbusiness bad debt because the business was Jamil's, not Robyn's.

Example 6

Horace operates a sole proprietorship that sells premium electronic equipment. Horace uses the accrual method to account for sales of the electronic equipment. During the year, he sold $4,000 of equipment to Herbie on credit. Later that year, the account receivable becomes worthless. The loan is a business bad debt, because the debt was related to Horace's business.

Generally, nonbusiness bad debts are incurred only by individuals. It is assumed that any loans made by a corporation are related to its trade or business. Therefore, any bad debts resulting from loans made by a corporation are automatically business bad debts.

Selling Bad Debts

The Russian Unicredit Bank has decided to begin selling some of its bad debt portfolio to reduce the amount of bad debts the bank is carrying on its books. The debts that will be sold are the loans that are overdue by two to three years.

Source: Based on "Russian Banks to Sell Bad Debt to Collectors," *Interfax-America, Inc.*, May 5, 2012.

Global Tax Issues

© iStockphoto.com/Andrey Prokhorov

The distinction between a business bad debt and a nonbusiness bad debt is important. A business bad debt is deductible as an ordinary loss in the year incurred, whereas a nonbusiness bad debt is always treated as a short-term capital loss. Thus, regardless of the age of a nonbusiness bad debt, the deduction may be of limited benefit due to the $3,000 capital loss limitation for individuals (refer to the discussion in Chapter 4).

6-1c Loans between Related Parties

Loans between related parties raise the issue of whether the transaction was a *bona fide* loan or some other type of transfer, such as a gift, a disguised dividend payment, or a contribution to capital. The Regulations state that a bona fide debt arises from a debtor-creditor relationship based on a valid and enforceable obligation to pay a fixed or determinable sum of money. Thus, individual circumstances must be examined to determine whether advances between related parties are loans. Some considerations are these:

- Was a note properly executed?
- Was there a reasonable rate of interest?
- Was collateral provided?
- What collection efforts were made?
- What was the intent of the parties?

Example 7

Ted, who is the sole shareholder of Penguin Corporation, lends the corporation $10,000 so that it can continue business operations. The note specifies a 2% interest rate and is payable on demand. Penguin has shown losses in each year of its five-year existence. The corporation also has liabilities greatly in excess of its assets. It is likely that Ted's transfer to the corporation would be treated as a contribution to capital rather than a liability. Consequently, no bad debt deduction would be allowed upon default by Penguin.

In-depth coverage can be found on this book's companion website: **www.cengagebrain.com**

 | Digging Deeper

6-2 WORTHLESS SECURITIES

A loss is allowed for securities that become *completely* worthless during the year (**worthless securities**).[3] Such securities are shares of stock, bonds, notes, or other evidence of indebtedness issued by a corporation or government. The losses generated are treated as capital losses (refer to Chapter 4) deemed to have occurred on

LO.2

State and illustrate the tax treatment of worthless securities, including § 1244 stock.

[3] § 165(g).

the *last day* of the tax year. By treating losses as having occurred on the last day of the tax year, a loss that would otherwise have been classified as short term (if the date of worthlessness were used) may be classified as long term.

THE BIG PICTURE

Example 8

Return to the facts of *The Big Picture* on p. 6-1. Assume that Robyn is a calendar year taxpayer. She owned stock in Owl Corporation that she acquired as an investment on October 1, 2013, at a cost of $60,000. On May 31, 2014, the stock became worthless when the company declared bankruptcy. Because the stock is deemed to have become worthless as of December 31, 2014, Robyn has a capital loss from an asset held for 15 months (a long-term capital loss). Alternatively, if the stock is § 1244 small business stock (see the following section), she has a $50,000 ordinary loss and a $10,000 long-term capital loss.

6-2a Small Business Stock (§ 1244)

The general rule is that shareholders receive capital loss treatment for losses from the sale or exchange of corporate stock. As noted in Chapter 4, the deductibility of capital losses is limited. However, it is possible to avoid capital loss limitations if the loss is sustained on **small business stock (§ 1244 stock)**. Such a loss could arise from a sale of the stock or from the stock becoming worthless. Only *individuals*[4] who acquired the stock *from* the issuing corporation are eligible to receive ordinary loss treatment under § 1244. The ordinary loss treatment is limited to $50,000 ($100,000 for married individuals filing jointly) per year. Losses on § 1244 stock in excess of the statutory limits are treated as capital losses.

The issuing corporation must meet certain requirements for the loss on § 1244 stock to be treated as an *ordinary*—rather than a capital—loss. The principal requirement is that the total capitalization of the corporation is limited to a maximum of $1 million. This capital limit includes all money and other property received by the corporation for stock and all capital contributions made to the corporation. The $1 million test is made at the time the stock is issued. There are no requirements regarding the kind of stock issued. Section 1244 stock can be either common or preferred.

Section 1244 applies only to losses. If § 1244 stock is sold at a gain, the provision does not apply and the gain is capital gain (which, for individuals, may be subject to preferential tax treatment, as discussed in Chapter 4).

Example 9

Iris, a single individual, was looking for an investment that would give some diversification to her stock portfolio. A friend suggested that she acquire some stock in Eagle Corporation, a new startup company. On July 1, 2012, Iris purchased 100 shares of Eagle Corporation for $100,000. At the time Iris acquired her stock from Eagle Corporation, the corporation had $700,000 of paid-in capital. Hence, the stock qualified as § 1244 stock. On June 20, 2014, Iris sold all of her Eagle stock to Michael for $20,000. Because the Eagle stock is § 1244 stock, Iris has $50,000 of ordinary loss and $30,000 of long-term capital loss.

If Michael were to sell the stock later for $8,000 in a taxable transaction, the $12,000 loss would not qualify for ordinary loss treatment under §1244 because Eagle Corporation had not issued the stock to him.

---

[4]The term *individuals* for this purpose does not include a trust or an estate (but could include a partnership or an LLC).

Tax Planning Strategies	MAXIMIZING THE BENEFITS OF § 1244

FRAMEWORK FOCUS: TAX RATE

Strategy: Control the Character of Income and Deductions.

Because § 1244 limits the amount of loss classified as ordinary loss on a yearly basis, a taxpayer might maximize the benefits of § 1244 by selling the stock in more than one taxable year.

Example 10

Mitch, a single individual, purchased small business stock in 2012 for $150,000 (150 shares at $1,000 per share). On December 20, 2014, the stock is worth $60,000 (150 shares at $400 per share). Mitch wants to sell the stock at this time. He earns a salary of $80,000 a year, has no other capital transactions, and does not expect any in the future. If Mitch sells all of the small business stock in 2014, his recognized loss will be $90,000 ($60,000 selling price −

$150,000 cost). The loss will be characterized as a $50,000 ordinary loss and a $40,000 long-term capital loss. In computing taxable income for 2014, Mitch could deduct the $50,000 ordinary loss but could deduct only $3,000 of the capital loss (assuming that he has no capital gains). The remainder of the capital loss could be carried over and used in future years subject to the capital loss limitations.

Alternatively, if Mitch sells 82 shares in 2014, he will recognize an ordinary loss of $49,200 [82 × ($400 − $1,000)]. If Mitch then sells the remainder of the shares in 2015, he will recognize an ordinary loss of $40,800 [68 × ($400 − $1,000)], successfully avoiding the capital loss limitation. Mitch could deduct the $49,200 ordinary loss in computing 2014 taxable income and the $40,800 ordinary loss in computing 2015 taxable income. ∎

6-3 CASUALTY AND THEFT LOSSES

Losses on business property are deductible, whether attributable to casualty, theft, or some other cause (e.g., rust, termite damage). While all *business* property losses are generally deductible, the amount and timing of casualty and theft losses are determined using special rules. Furthermore, for individual taxpayers, who may deduct casualty losses on personal-use (nonbusiness) property as well as on business and investment property (held in partnerships and S corporations or in an individual capacity), a set of special limitations applies. Casualty gains are also afforded special consideration in the tax law.

LO.3

Identify a casualty and determine the amount, classification, and timing of casualty and theft losses.

6-3a Definition of Casualty

The term *casualty* generally includes *fire, storm, shipwreck,* and *theft.* In addition, losses from *other casualties* are deductible. Such losses generally include any loss resulting from an event that is (1) identifiable; (2) damaging to property; and (3) sudden, unexpected, and unusual in nature. The term also includes accidental loss of property provided the loss qualifies under the same rules as any other casualty.

A *sudden event* is an event that is swift and precipitous and not gradual or progressive. An *unexpected event* is one that is ordinarily unanticipated and occurs without the intent of the taxpayer who suffers the loss. An *unusual event* is an event that is extraordinary and nonrecurring and does not commonly occur during the activity in which the taxpayer was engaged when the destruction occurred.[5] Examples include hurricanes, tornadoes, floods, storms, shipwrecks, fires, sonic booms, vandalism, and mine cave-ins. A taxpayer also can take a deduction for a casualty loss from an automobile accident if the accident is not attributable to the taxpayer's willful act or willful negligence. Weather that causes damage (e.g., drought) must be unusual and severe for the particular region to qualify as a casualty. Furthermore, damage must be to the *taxpayer's* property to be deductible.

---

[5]Rev.Rul. 72–592, 1972–2 C.B. 101.

Events That Are Not Casualties

Not all acts of God are treated as casualty losses for income tax purposes. Because a casualty must be sudden, unexpected, and unusual, progressive deterioration (such as erosion due to wind or rain) is not a casualty because it does not meet the suddenness test.

An example of an event that generally does not qualify as a casualty is insect damage. When termites caused damage over a period of several years, some courts have disallowed a casualty loss deduction.[6] On the other hand, some courts have held that termite damage over periods of up to 15 months after infestation constituted a sudden event and was, therefore, deductible as a casualty loss.[7] Despite the existence of some judicial support for the deductibility of termite damage as a casualty loss, the current position of the IRS is that termite damage is not deductible.[8]

Other examples of events that are not casualties are losses resulting from a decline in value rather than an actual loss of the property. For example, a taxpayer was allowed a loss for the actual flood damage to his property but not for the decline in market value due to the property being flood-prone.[9] Similarly, a decline in value of an office building due to fire damage to nearby buildings is not deductible as a casualty.

6-3b Definition of Theft

Theft includes, but is not necessarily limited to, larceny, embezzlement, and robbery.[10] Theft does not include misplaced items.[11]

Theft losses are treated like other casualty losses, but the *timing* of recognition of the loss differs. A theft loss is deducted in the *year of discovery*, not the year of the theft (unless, of course, the discovery occurs in the same year as the theft). If in the year of the discovery a claim exists (e.g., against an insurance company) and there is a reasonable expectation of recovering the adjusted basis of the asset from the insurance company, no deduction is permitted.[12] If in the year of settlement the recovery is less than the asset's adjusted basis, a deduction may be available. If the recovery is greater than the asset's adjusted basis, *casualty gain* may be recognized.

Example 11	Sakura, Inc., owned a computer that was stolen from its offices in December 2013. The theft was discovered on June 3, 2014, and the corporation filed a claim with its insurance company that was settled on January 30, 2015. Assuming that there is a reasonable expectation of full recovery, no deduction is allowed in 2014. A deduction may be available in 2015 if the actual insurance proceeds are less than the adjusted basis of the asset. (Loss measurement rules are discussed later in this chapter.)

6-3c When to Deduct Casualty Losses

General Rule

Generally, a casualty loss is deducted in the year the loss occurs. However, no casualty loss is permitted if a reimbursement claim with a reasonable *prospect of full recovery* exists.[13] If the taxpayer has a partial claim, only part of the loss can be claimed in the year of the casualty and the remainder is deducted in the year the claim is settled.

Example 12	Fuchsia Corporation's new warehouse was completely destroyed by fire in 2014. Its cost and fair market value were $250,000. Fuchsia's only claim against the insurance company was on a $70,000 policy and was not settled by year-end. The following year, 2015, Fuchsia settled with the insurance company for $60,000. Fuchsia is entitled to a $180,000 deduction in 2014 and a $10,000 deduction in 2015.

---

[6]*Fay v. Helvering*, 41–2 USTC ¶9494, 27 AFTR 432, 120 F.2d 253 (CA–2, 1941); *U.S. v. Rogers*, 41–1 USTC ¶9442, 27 AFTR 423, 120 F.2d 244 (CA–9, 1941).

[7]*Rosenberg v. Comm.*, 52–2 USTC ¶9377, 42 AFTR 303, 198 F.2d 46 (CA–8, 1952); *Shopmaker v. U.S.*, 54–1 USTC ¶9195, 45 AFTR 758, 119 F.Supp. 705 (D.Ct. Mo., 1953).

[8]Rev.Rul. 63–232, 1963–2 C.B. 97.

[9]*S. L. Solomon*, 39 TCM 1282, T.C.Memo. 1980–87.

[10]Reg. § 1.165–8(d).

[11]*Mary Francis Allen*, 16 T.C. 163 (1951).

[12]Reg. §§ 1.165–1(d)(2) and 1.165–8(a)(2).

[13]Reg. § 1.165–1(d)(2)(i).

Tax Planning Strategies

DOCUMENTATION OF RELATED-TAXPAYER LOANS, CASUALTY LOSSES, AND THEFT LOSSES

FRAMEWORK FOCUS: DEDUCTIONS

Strategy: Maximize Deductible Amounts.

Because the validity of loans between related taxpayers might be questioned, adequate documentation is needed to substantiate a bad debt deduction if the loan subsequently becomes worthless. Documentation should include proper execution of the note (legal form) and the establishment of a bona fide purpose for the loan. In addition, it is desirable to stipulate a reasonable rate of interest and a fixed maturity date.

Because a theft loss deduction is not permitted for misplaced items, a police report and evidence of the value of the property (e.g., appraisals, pictures of the property, and purchase receipts) are necessary to document a theft.

Similar documentation of the value of property should be provided to support a casualty loss deduction because the amount of loss is measured, in part, by the decline in fair market value of the property.

Casualty loss deductions must be reported on Form 4684.

If a taxpayer receives reimbursement for a casualty loss sustained and deducted in a previous year, an amended return is not filed for that year. Instead, the taxpayer must include the reimbursement in gross income on the return for the year in which it is received to the extent the previous deduction resulted in a tax benefit (refer to Chapter 4).

Example 13

Golden Hawk, Inc., had a deductible casualty loss of $15,000 on its 2013 tax return. Golden Hawk's taxable income for 2013 was $60,000 after deducting the $15,000 loss. In June 2014, the corporation is reimbursed $13,000 for the prior year's casualty loss. Golden Hawk includes the entire $13,000 in gross income for 2014 because the deduction in 2013 produced a tax benefit.

Disaster Area Losses

An exception to the general rule for the time of deduction is allowed for **disaster area losses**, which are casualties or disaster-related business losses sustained in an area designated as a disaster area by the President of the United States.[14] In such cases, the taxpayer may *elect* to treat the loss as having occurred in the taxable year immediately *preceding* the taxable year in which the disaster actually occurred. The rationale for this exception is to provide immediate relief to disaster victims in the form of accelerated tax benefits.

If the due date, plus extensions, for the prior year's return has not passed, a taxpayer makes the election to claim the disaster area loss on the prior year's tax return. If a disaster area is designated after the prior year's return has been filed, it is necessary to file either an amended return or a refund claim. In any case, the taxpayer must show clearly that such an election is being made.

THE BIG PICTURE

Example 14

Return to the facts of *The Big Picture* on p. 6-1. On September 28, 2014, Robyn's personal residence was damaged when a tornado caused an oak tree to fall on the house. The amount of her uninsured casualty loss was $7,000 ($32,000 − $25,000 insurance recovery). Because of the extent of the damage in the area, the President of the United States designated the area a disaster area. Because Robyn's loss is a disaster area loss, she may elect to file an amended return for 2013 and take the loss in that year. If Robyn elects this course of action, the amount of the loss will be reduced first by $100 (the materiality amount in 2013) and then by 10% of her 2013 AGI. If Robyn forgoes the election, she may take the loss on her 2014 income tax return. The amount of the loss will be reduced first by $100 (the materiality amount in 2014) and then by 10% of her 2014 AGI.

---

[14]§ 165(h).

6-3d Measuring the Amount of Loss

Amount of Loss

The rules for determining the amount of a loss depend in part on whether business, investment, or personal-use (nonbusiness) property was involved. Another factor that must be considered is whether the property was partially or completely destroyed.

If business property or investment property (e.g., rental property) is *completely destroyed*, the loss is equal to the adjusted basis[15] (typically cost less depreciation) of the property at the time of destruction.

A different measurement rule applies for *partial destruction* of business and investment property and for *partial* or *complete destruction* of personal-use property held by individuals. In these situations, the loss is the *lesser* of:

- The adjusted basis of the property, or
- The difference between the fair market value of the property before the event and the fair market value immediately after the event.

Example 15

Wynd and Rain, a law firm, owned an airplane that was used only for business purposes. The airplane was damaged in an accident. On the date of the accident, the fair market value of the plane was $52,000, and its adjusted basis was $32,000. After the accident, the plane was appraised at $24,000. The law firm's loss deduction is $28,000 (the lesser of the adjusted basis or the decrease in fair market value). If instead the airplane had been completely destroyed in the accident, the loss deduction would have been $32,000 (the adjusted basis of the airplane).

Any insurance recovery reduces the loss for business, investment, and personal-use losses. In fact, a taxpayer may realize a gain if the insurance proceeds exceed the adjusted basis of the property. Chapter 8 discusses the treatment of net gains and losses on business property and income-producing property.

A special rule on insurance recovery applies to *personal-use property*. In particular, individuals are not permitted to deduct a casualty loss for damage to insured personal-use property unless an insurance claim is filed. This rule applies, whether the insurance provides partial or full reimbursement for the loss.[16]

Generally, an appraisal before and after the casualty is needed to measure the amount of loss. However, the *cost of repairs* to the damaged property generally is acceptable as a method of establishing the loss in value.[17]

Digging Deeper   2   In-depth coverage can be found on this book's companion website: **www.cengagebrain.com**

Multiple Losses

When multiple casualty losses occur during the year, the amount of each loss is computed separately. The rules for computing loss deductions where multiple losses have occurred are illustrated in Example 16.

---

[15]See Chapter 7 for a detailed discussion of basis rules.
[16]§ 165(h)(5)(E).
[17]Reg. § 1.165–7(a)(2)(ii).

Example 16

During the year, Swan Enterprises had the following business casualty losses:

| | | **Fair Market Value of the Asset** | | |
Asset	Adjusted Basis	Before the Casualty	After the Casualty	Insurance Recovery
A	$900	$600	$–0–	$400
B	300	800	250	150

The following losses are allowed:

- Asset A: $500. The complete destruction of a business asset results in a deduction of the adjusted basis of the property (reduced by any insurance recovery), regardless of the asset's fair market value.
- Asset B: $150. The partial destruction of a business asset results in a deduction equal to the lesser of the adjusted basis ($300) or the decline in value ($550), reduced by any insurance recovery ($150).

6-3e Casualty and Theft Losses of Individuals

Recall from Chapter 4 that the individual income tax formula distinguishes between deductions *for* AGI and deductions *from* AGI. Casualty and theft losses incurred by an individual in connection with a business or with rental and royalty activities are deductible *for* AGI and are limited only by the rules previously discussed.[18] Losses from most other investment activities and personal-use losses are generally deducted *from* AGI. Investment casualty and theft losses (e.g., the theft of a security) are classified as other miscellaneous itemized deductions (not subject to a 2 percent-of-AGI floor as explained in Chapter 10). Casualty and theft losses of personal-use property are subject to special limitations discussed next.

Personal-Use Property

In addition to the valuation rules discussed previously, casualty and theft loss deductions from personal-use property must be reduced by a $100 *per event* floor and a 10 percent-of-AGI *aggregate* floor.[19] The $100 floor applies separately to each casualty or theft and applies to the entire loss from each casualty or theft (e.g., if a storm damages both a taxpayer's residence and automobile, only $100 is subtracted from the total amount of the loss). All personal-use losses incurred during the year are then added together, and the total is reduced by 10 percent of the taxpayer's AGI. The resulting amount is the taxpayer's itemized deduction for personal-use casualty and theft losses.

Example 17

Rocky, who had AGI of $30,000, was involved in a motorcycle accident in 2014. His motorcycle, which was used only for personal use and had a fair market value of $12,000 and an adjusted basis of $9,000, was completely destroyed. He received $5,000 from his insurance company. Rocky's casualty loss deduction is $900 [$9,000 basis − $5,000 insurance recovery − $100 floor − $3,000 (.10 × $30,000 AGI)]. The $900 casualty loss is an itemized deduction (*from* AGI).

Where there are both casualty and theft gains and losses from personal-use property, special netting rules apply. Generally, if casualty and theft gains exceed losses during the year, the gains and losses are treated as capital gains and losses. Alternatively, if losses exceed gains, the casualty and theft gains (and losses to the extent of gains) are treated as ordinary gains and losses. Any excess losses are deductible as personal-use casualty and theft losses.

See Concept Summary 6.2 for a review of the tax treatment of casualty gains and losses.

---

[18]§ 62(a)(1).   [19]§§ 165(c)(3) and (h).

CONCEPT SUMMARY 6.2

Casualty Gains and Losses

	Business-Use or Income-Producing Property	Personal-Use Property
Event creating the loss	Any event.	Casualty or theft.
Amount	The lesser of the decline in fair market value or the adjusted basis, but always the adjusted basis if the property is totally destroyed.	The lesser of the decline in fair market value or the adjusted basis.
Insurance	Insurance proceeds received reduce the amount of the loss.	Insurance proceeds received (or for which there is an unfiled claim) reduce the amount of the loss.
$100 floor	Not applicable.	Applicable per event.
Gains and losses	Gains and losses are netted (see detailed discussion in Chapter 8).	Personal casualty and theft gains and losses are netted.
Gains exceeding losses		The gains and losses are treated as gains and losses from the sale of capital assets.
Losses exceeding gains		The gains—and the losses to the extent of gains—are treated as ordinary items in computing AGI. The losses in excess of gains, to the extent that they exceed 10% of AGI, are itemized deductions (*from* AGI).

© iStockphoto.com/Andrey Prokhorov

Digging Deeper   3   In-depth coverage can be found on this book's companion website: **www.cengagebrain.com**

6-4 NET OPERATING LOSSES

LO.4

Describe the impact of the net operating loss carryback and carryover provisions on previous and subsequent years' taxable income.

6-4a Introduction

The requirement that every taxpayer file an annual income tax return (whether on a calendar year or a fiscal year) can lead to inequities for taxpayers who experience uneven income over a series of years. These inequities result from the application of progressive tax rates to taxable income determined on an annual basis.

TAX FACT   The Utility of the NOL Deduction

Recently, corporations claimed net operating loss deductions of approximately $162.2 billion against business receipts of about $23.06 trillion.

Source: 2010 Corporation Returns—Returns of Active Corporations; Table 2—Balance Sheet, Income Statement, and Selected Other Items, by Size of Total Assets and Table 20—Tax Items: Number of Returns by Selected Types of Tax, Dividend Items, Net Income or Deficit, Statutory Special Deductions, Income Subject to Tax, Taxes, Credits, and Payments, by Selected Sectors; 2013.

FINANCIAL DISCLOSURE INSIGHTS   Tax Losses and the Deferred Tax Asset

To some people, a current-year net operating loss (NOL) represents a failure of an entity's business model, but others see it as an immediate tax refund. But when an NOL hits the balance sheet as a deferred tax asset, the story is not over. The NOL creates or increases a deferred tax asset that may or may not be used in future financial accounting reporting periods: the key question for a financial analyst is whether the entity will generate enough net revenue in future years that can be offset by the NOL carryover amount.

When a business entity holds a loss carryforward, for every reporting period, its management must assess whether the loss is likely to be used to create cash flow in the future, as the loss carryforward offsets operating or other profits from future years. When it is more likely than not that a loss carryforward *will not be realized*, GAAP requires that a valuation allowance be created to reduce the deferred tax asset to a lower amount that is expected to be realized in the future. The valuation allowance is a contra-asset account (like accumulated depreciation on a fixed asset) against the deferred tax asset.

A valuation allowance against an NOL carryforward might be created when there is doubt as to the level of the entity's future net profits. The valuation allowance is reduced or eliminated, though, when it appears that the NOL will be fully realized due to any of the following:

- Future years' net income from operations or other activities.
- New product orders or contracts for a business.
- The reversal of other temporary book-tax differences.
- An effective use of tax planning strategies.

Evidence that a loss carryforward might not be realized in the future includes the following:

- A series of operating losses in previous years for the reporting entity.
- A history of the entity's tax losses expiring unused.
- Open transactions, such as lawsuits and regulatory challenges, that might reduce the business's future profits.

The current version of IFRS does not allow for a valuation allowance. Under IAS 12, a deferred tax asset is recorded only when it is "probable" (a higher standard than GAAP's "more likely than not") that the deferred tax amount will be realized, and then only to the extent of that probable amount. Thus, no offsetting valuation allowance is needed.

© iStockphoto.com/Pali Rao

Example 18

Orange, Inc., realizes the following taxable income or loss over a five-year period: year 1, $50,000; year 2, ($30,000); year 3, $100,000; year 4, ($200,000); and year 5, $380,000. Blue Corporation has taxable income of $60,000 every year. Note that both corporations have total taxable income of $300,000 over the five-year period. Assume that there is no provision for carryback or carryover of net operating losses. Orange and Blue would have the following five-year tax liabilities:

Year	Orange's Tax	Blue's Tax
1	$ 7,500	$10,000
2	–0–	10,000
3	22,250	10,000
4	–0–	10,000
5	129,200	10,000
	$158,950	$50,000

Note: The computation of tax is made without regard to any NOL benefit. Rates applicable to 2014 are used to compute the tax.

Even though Orange and Blue realized the same total taxable income ($300,000) over the five-year period, Orange would have to pay taxes of $158,950, while Blue would pay taxes of only $50,000.

To provide partial relief from this inequitable tax treatment, a deduction is allowed for **net operating losses (NOLs)**.[20] This provision permits an NOL for any

---
[20]§ 172.

TAX IN THE NEWS   Using NOLs

Solyndra, once the poster child of the Obama administration's stimulus program, filed for bankruptcy still owing taxpayers $528 million from the stimulus payments the company received from the Federal government. Solyndra is now preparing to restructure under a plan that might allow Argonaut Ventures and Madrone Capital Partners to use Solyndra's NOLs to reduce hundreds of millions of dollars in future income taxes.

Source: Based on Jim McElhatton, "Solyndra Investors Could Reap Tax Windfall," *McClatchy-Tribune Information Services*, August 28, 2012.

one year to offset taxable income in other years. The NOL provision provides relief only for losses from the operation of a trade or business or from casualty and theft.

Only C corporations and individuals are permitted an NOL deduction because losses of partnerships and S corporations pass through to their owners. For C corporations, the NOL equals any negative taxable income for the year, with an adjustment for the dividends received deduction (see Chapter 12). In addition, deductions for prior-year NOLs are not allowed when determining a current-year NOL.

NOLs of individuals are computed by adding back to negative taxable income the excess of nonbusiness deductions (deductions not attributable to, or derived from, a taxpayer's trade or business, such as the standard deduction, charitable contributions, and alimony payments) over nonbusiness income (income not attributable to, or derived from, a taxpayer's trade or business, such as dividends and alimony received), personal and dependency exemptions, and any net capital loss deducted in calculating taxable income. Business deductions that are allowed for determining the NOL include moving expenses; losses on rental property; loss on the sale of small business stock; part of the self-employment tax (refer to Chapter 1); and losses from a sole proprietorship, a partnership, or an S corporation.

6-4b Carryback and Carryover Periods

General Rules

A current-year NOL is usually carried back and deducted against income over the two preceding tax years.[21] It is carried back first to the second year before the loss year and then to the year immediately preceding the loss year (until it fully offsets income). If the loss is not completely used against income in the carryback period, it is carried forward for 20 years following the loss year. NOLs that are not used within the 20-year carryforward period are lost. Thus, an NOL sustained in 2014 is used first in 2012 and then 2013. Then the loss is carried forward and offsets income in 2015 through 2034.

When an NOL is carried back, the taxpayer requests an immediate refund of prior years' taxes by filing an amended return for the previous two years. When an NOL is carried forward, the current return shows an NOL deduction for the prior year's loss. Thus, a struggling business with an NOL can receive rapid cash-flow assistance.

NOLs from Multiple Tax Years

When the taxpayer has NOLs in two or more years, the earliest year's loss is used first. Later years' losses can then be used until they offset income or are lost. Thus,

---

[21]A three-year carryback period is available for any portion of an individual's NOL resulting from a casualty or theft loss. The three-year carryback rule also applies to NOLs that are attributable to presidentially declared disaster areas that are incurred by a small business. For purposes of this provision, a small business is a business whose average annual gross receipts for a three-year period are $5 million or less. See § 172(b)(1)(F).

one year's return could show NOL carryovers from two or more years. Each loss is computed and applied separately.

Election to Forgo Carryback

A taxpayer can *irrevocably elect* not to carry back an NOL. The election is made on a corporate tax return (Form 1120) by checking the appropriate box. Individuals can make the election by attaching a statement to their tax return. If the election is made, the loss can *only* be carried forward for 20 years. This election may be desirable in circumstances where marginal tax rates in future years are expected to exceed rates in prior years.

6-5 THE TAX SHELTER PROBLEM

Before Congress enacted legislation to reduce their effectiveness, **tax shelters** provided a popular way to avoid or defer taxes, as they could generate losses and other benefits to offset income from other sources. Because of the tax avoidance potential of many tax shelters, they were attractive to wealthy taxpayers with high marginal tax rates. Many tax shelters merely provided an opportunity for "investors" to buy deductions and credits in ventures that were not expected to generate a profit, even in the long run.

Although it may seem odd that a taxpayer would intentionally invest in an activity that was designed to produce losses, there is a logical explanation. The typical tax shelter operated as a partnership and relied heavily on nonrecourse financing.[22] Accelerated depreciation and interest expense deductions generated large losses in the early years of the activity. At the very least, the tax shelter deductions deferred the recognition of any net income from the venture until the activity was sold. In the best of situations, the investor could realize additional tax savings by offsetting other income (e.g., salary, interest, dividends) with losses flowing from the tax shelter. Ultimately, the sale of the investment would result in *tax-favored* capital gain. The following example illustrates what was possible *before* Congress enacted legislation to curb tax shelter abuses.

LO.5

Explain the tax shelter problem and the reasons for at-risk and passive loss limitations.

> Bob, who earned a salary of $400,000 as a business executive and dividend income of $15,000, invested $20,000 for a 10% interest in a cattle-breeding tax shelter. He did not participate in the operation of the business. Through the use of $800,000 of nonrecourse financing and available cash of $200,000, the partnership acquired a herd of an exotic breed of cattle costing $1 million. Depreciation, interest, and other deductions related to the activity resulted in a loss of $400,000, of which Bob's share was $40,000. Bob was allowed to deduct the $40,000 loss even though he had invested and stood to lose only $20,000 if the investment became worthless. The net effect of the $40,000 deduction from the partnership was that a portion of Bob's salary and dividend income was "sheltered," and as a result, he was required to calculate his tax liability on only $375,000 of income [$415,000 (salary and dividends) − $40,000 (deduction)] rather than $415,000. If this deduction were available under current law and if Bob was in a combined Federal and state income tax bracket of 40%, a tax savings of $16,000 ($40,000 × 40%) would be generated in the first year alone!

Example 19

A review of Example 19 shows that the taxpayer took a two-for-one write-off ($40,000 deduction, $20,000 amount invested). In the heyday of these types of tax shelters, promoters often promised tax deductions for the investor well in excess of the amount invested.

---

[22]Nonrecourse debt is an obligation for which the borrower is not personally liable. An example of nonrecourse debt is a liability on real estate acquired by a partnership without the partnership or any of the partners assuming any liability for the mortgage. The acquired property generally is pledged as collateral for the loan.

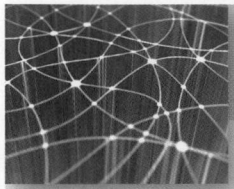

An overarching requirement to maximizing wealth is to reduce the present value cost of taxation. One way to reduce the cost of taxation in present value terms is to defer the payment of a tax into the future for as long as possible. This can be accomplished by reducing the taxpayer's tax base (i.e., taxable income) either by deferring the recognition of income or by accelerating the timing of deductions. As a result, to the extent that the tax cost associated with an investment alternative is reduced, the after-tax benefit from that investment and the investor's wealth position are enhanced.

For example, a common attribute of many tax-advantaged investments is the availability of tax losses that investors may claim on their own income tax returns.

Many times, these tax losses are the result of investment-level deductions, such as interest and depreciation expenses, that are bunched in the early years of the life of the investment rather than being due to economic woes of the investment itself.

Through the at-risk limitations and the passive loss rules, the tax law works to scale back the ability of taxpayers to claim tax losses flowing from certain investments. These limitations have a direct impact on *when* investors can claim loss deductions flowing from affected investments. The typical result of these provisions is that the loss deductions are deferred. Therefore, when evaluating competing investment alternatives, taxpayers must address the impact of these tax limitations in projecting the after-tax benefits that can be expected to follow.

The first major provision aimed at tax shelters is the **at-risk limitation**. Its objective is to limit a taxpayer's deductions to the amount that the taxpayer could actually lose from the investment (the amount "at risk") if it becomes worthless. Thus, in Example 19, the at-risk rule limits Bob's loss to $20,000—the amount at risk.

The second major attack on tax shelters came with the passage of the **passive loss** rules. The passive loss rules require the taxpayer to segregate all income and losses into three categories: active, portfolio, and passive. (These categories are defined in Section 6-7.) In general, the passive loss limits *disallow* the deduction of passive losses *against active or portfolio income* even when the taxpayer is at risk to the extent of the loss. In general, passive losses can only offset passive income.

Thus, in Example 19, the passive loss rules disallow a current deduction for any of the loss. The loss from the tax shelter is a passive loss because Bob does not materially participate in the activity. Therefore, the $20,000 loss that is allowed under the at-risk rules is disallowed under the passive loss rules because Bob does not report any passive income for the year—he reports only active and portfolio income. Consequently, Bob's current-year income must reflect his nonpassive income of $415,000. As explained later in the chapter, the disallowed $20,000 passive loss is suspended and may be deducted in a future year under certain conditions.

The following two sections explore the nature of the at-risk limits and the passive activity loss rules and their impact on investors. Congress intentionally structured these rules so that investors evaluating potential investments must consider mainly the *economics* of the venture instead of the *tax benefits* or tax avoidance possibilities that an investment may generate.

6-6 AT-RISK LIMITATIONS

LO.6

Describe how the at-risk limitation and the passive loss rules limit deductions for losses and identify taxpayers subject to these restrictions.

The at-risk provisions limit the deductibility of losses from business and income-producing activities. These provisions, which apply to individuals and closely held corporations, are designed to prevent taxpayers from deducting losses in excess of their actual economic investment in an activity. In the case of an S corporation or a partnership, the at-risk limits apply at the owner level. Under the at-risk rules, a taxpayer's deductible loss from an activity for any taxable year is limited to the amount the taxpayer has at risk at the end of the taxable year (i.e., the amount the taxpayer could actually lose in the activity).

While the amount at risk generally vacillates over time, the initial amount considered at risk consists of the following:[23]

- The amount of cash and the adjusted basis of property contributed to the activity by the taxpayer.
- Amounts borrowed for use in the activity for which the taxpayer is personally liable.
- The adjusted basis of property pledged as security that is not used in the activity.

This amount generally is increased each year by the taxpayer's share of income and is decreased by the taxpayer's share of losses and withdrawals from the activity. In addition, because *general partners* are jointly and severally liable for recourse debts of the partnership, their at-risk amounts are increased when the partnership increases its debt and are decreased when the partnership reduces its debt. However, a taxpayer generally is not considered at risk with respect to borrowed amounts if either of the following is true:

- The taxpayer is not personally liable for repayment of the debt (e.g., non-recourse debt).
- The lender has an interest (other than as a creditor) in the activity.

An important exception provides that in the case of an activity involving the holding of real property, a taxpayer is considered at risk for his or her share of any *qualified nonrecourse financing* that is secured by real property used in the activity.[24]

Subject to the passive activity rules discussed later in the chapter, a taxpayer may deduct a loss as long as the at-risk amount is positive. However, once the at-risk amount is exhausted, any remaining loss cannot be deducted until a later year. Any losses disallowed for any given taxable year by the at-risk rules may be deducted in the first succeeding year in which the rules do not prevent the deduction—that is, when there is, and to the extent of, a positive at-risk amount.

> **Example 20**
>
> In 2014, Sue invests $40,000 in an oil partnership. The partnership incurs a first-year net loss, of which $60,000 is her share. Assume that Sue's interest in the partnership is subject to the at-risk limits but is not subject to the passive loss limits. Because Sue has only $40,000 of capital at risk, she cannot deduct more than $40,000 against her other income and must reduce her at-risk amount to zero ($40,000 at-risk amount − $40,000 loss deducted). The nondeductible loss of $20,000 ($60,000 loss generated − $40,000 loss allowed) can be carried over to 2015.
>
> In 2015, Sue has taxable income of $15,000 from the oil partnership and invests an additional $10,000 in the venture. Her at-risk amount is now $25,000 ($0 beginning balance + $15,000 taxable income + $10,000 additional investment). This enables Sue to deduct the $20,000 carryover loss and requires her to reduce her at-risk amount to $5,000 ($25,000 at-risk amount − $20,000 carryover loss allowed).

Complicating the at-risk rule is the fact that previously allowed losses must be recaptured as income to the extent the at-risk amount is reduced below zero.[25] This rule applies in situations such as those when the amount at risk is reduced below zero by distributions to the taxpayer or when the status of indebtedness changes from recourse to nonrecourse.

Calculation of at-risk amount is reviewed in Table 6.1.

---

[23]§ 465(b)(1).
[24]Section 465(b)(6) defines qualified nonrecourse financing.

[25]§ 465(e).

TABLE 6.1	Calculation of At-Risk Amount

Increases to a taxpayer's at-risk amount:	Decreases to a taxpayer's at-risk amount:
• Cash and the adjusted basis of property contributed to the activity. • Amounts borrowed for use in the activity for which the taxpayer is personally liable. • The adjusted basis of property pledged as security that is not used in the activity. • Taxpayer's share of amounts borrowed for use in the activity that are qualified nonrecourse financing. • Taxpayer's share of the activity's income.	• Withdrawals from the activity. • Taxpayer's share of the activity's deductible loss. • Taxpayer's share of any reductions of debt for which recourse against the taxpayer exists or any reductions of qualified nonrecourse debt.

6-7 PASSIVE LOSS LIMITS

This section identifies and explains a number of key issues that are pertinent when applying the passive loss limits.

- The limits apply only to passive losses incurred by certain types of taxpayers.
- Losses are limited under these rules only if they are generated by a passive activity.
- Special rules exist for interests in real estate activities.
- Benefits may arise when a disposition of a passive activity occurs.

6-7a Classification and Impact of Passive Income and Loss

The passive loss rules operate by requiring taxpayers to classify their income and losses into various categories. Then the rules limit the extent to which losses in the passive category can be used to offset income in the other categories.

Classification

The passive loss rules require income and loss to be classified into one of three categories: *active, portfolio,* or *passive.* **Active income** includes the following:

- Wages, salary, commissions, bonuses, and other payments for services rendered by the taxpayer.
- Profit from a trade or business in which the taxpayer is a material participant.

Portfolio income includes the following:

- Interest, dividends, annuities, and royalties not derived in the ordinary course of a trade or business.
- Gain or loss from the disposition of property that produces portfolio income or is held for investment purposes.

Section 469 provides that passive income or loss arises from activities that are treated as passive, which include:

- Any trade or business or income-producing activity in which the taxpayer does not materially participate.
- Subject to certain exceptions, all rental activities, whether or not the taxpayer materially participates.

Although the Code defines rental activities as passive activities, several exceptions allow losses from certain real estate rental activities to offset nonpassive (active or portfolio) income. These exceptions are discussed under Special Rules for Real Estate later in the chapter.

General Impact

Losses or expenses generated by passive activities can only be deducted to the extent of income from passive activities. Any excess may not be used to offset income from active or portfolio income. Instead, any unused passive losses are suspended and carried forward to future years to offset passive income generated in those years. Otherwise, suspended losses may be used only when a taxpayer disposes of his or her entire interest in an activity. In that event, all current and suspended losses related to the activity may offset active and portfolio income.

THE BIG PICTURE

Example 21

Return to the facts of *The Big Picture* on p. 6-1. Recall that Robyn invested $20,000 in the Florida orange grove limited partnership, which produced an allocable $20,000 loss for her this year. Assume that Robyn earns a salary of $100,000 along with $12,000 in dividends and interest from various portfolio investments. Because her at-risk basis in the partnership is $20,000, the current $20,000 loss is not limited by the at-risk rules. However, because the loss is a passive loss, it is not deductible against her other income. The loss is suspended and is carried over to the future. If Robyn has passive income from this investment or from other passive investments in the future, she can offset the suspended loss against that passive income. If she does not have passive income to offset this suspended loss in the future, she will be allowed to offset the loss against other types of income when she eventually disposes of her investment in the passive activity.

Impact of Suspended Losses

The actual economic gain or loss from a passive investment (including any suspended losses) can be determined when a taxpayer disposes of his or her entire interest in the investment. As a result, under the passive loss rules, upon a fully taxable disposition, any overall loss realized from the taxpayer's activity is recognized and can be offset against passive, active, and portfolio income.

A fully taxable disposition generally involves a sale of the property to a third party at arm's length and thus, presumably, for a price equal to the property's fair market value. As presented in the following example, a gain recognized upon the transfer of an interest in a passive activity generally is treated as passive and is first offset by the suspended losses from that activity.

Example 22

Rex sells an apartment building, a passive activity, with an adjusted basis of $100,000 for $180,000. In addition, he has suspended passive losses of $60,000 associated with the building. His total gain, $80,000, and his taxable gain, $20,000, are calculated as follows:

Net sales price	$ 180,000
Less: Adjusted basis	(100,000)
Total gain	$ 80,000
Less: Suspended losses	(60,000)
Taxable gain (passive)	$ 20,000

If current and suspended losses of the passive activity exceed the gain realized from the sale or if the sale results in a realized loss, the amount of

- any loss from the activity for the tax year (including losses suspended in the activity disposed of)

in excess of

- net income or gain for the tax year from all passive activities (without regard to the activity disposed of) is treated as a loss that is not from a passive activity. In computing the loss from the activity for the year of disposition, any gain or loss recognized is included in the calculation.

Example 23

Dean sells an apartment building, a passive activity, with an adjusted basis of $100,000 for $150,000. In addition, he has current and suspended passive losses of $60,000 associated with the building and has no other passive activities. His total gain of $50,000 and his deductible loss of $10,000 are calculated as follows:

Net sales price	$ 150,000
Less: Adjusted basis	(100,000)
Total gain	$ 50,000
Less: Suspended losses	(60,000)
Deductible loss (not passive)	($ 10,000)

The $10,000 loss can be deducted against Dean's active and portfolio income. Even if the building is sold for a loss (i.e., the adjusted basis exceeds the sales price), the total loss, including the suspended losses, is deductible as a nonpassive loss.

Carryovers of Suspended Losses

The preceding examples assumed that the taxpayer had an interest in only one passive activity; as a result, the suspended loss was related exclusively to the activity that was disposed of. However, taxpayers often own more than one passive activity, in which case any suspended losses must be allocated among those passive activities. The allocation to an activity is made by multiplying the disallowed passive activity loss from all activities using the following fraction:

$$\frac{\text{Loss from one passive activity}}{\text{Sum of losses for taxable year from all passive activities having losses}}$$

Example 24

Diego has investments in three passive activities with the following income and losses for 2013:

Activity A	($30,000)
Activity B	(20,000)
Activity C	25,000
Net passive loss	($25,000)
Net passive loss allocated to:	
Activity A [$25,000 × ($30,000/$50,000)]	($15,000)
Activity B [$25,000 × ($20,000/$50,000)]	(10,000)
Total suspended losses	($25,000)

Suspended losses are carried over indefinitely and are offset in the future against any passive income from the activities to which they relate.[26]

Example 25

Assume that the facts are the same as in the preceding example and that Activity A produces $10,000 of income in 2014. Of the suspended loss of $15,000 from 2013 for Activity A, $10,000 is offset against the income from this activity. If Diego sells Activity A in early 2015, the remaining $5,000 suspended loss is used to determine his final gain or loss.

Passive Credits

Credits (such as the low-income housing credit and rehabilitation credit—discussed in Chapter 17) that arise from passive activities are limited in much the same way as passive losses. Passive credits can be utilized only against regular tax attributable to passive income,[27] which is calculated by comparing the tax on all income (including passive income) with the tax on income excluding passive income.

Example 26

Sam owes $50,000 of tax, disregarding net passive income, and $80,000 of tax, considering both net passive and other taxable income (disregarding the credits in both cases). The amount of tax attributable to the passive income is $30,000.

In the preceding example, Sam can claim a maximum of $30,000 of passive activity credits; the excess credits are carried over. These passive activity credits can be used only against the *regular* tax attributable to passive income. If a taxpayer has a net loss from passive activities during a given year, no credits can be used.

Carryovers of Passive Credits

Tax credits attributable to passive activities can be carried forward indefinitely, much like suspended passive losses. Unlike passive losses, however, passive credits are lost forever when the activity is disposed of in a taxable transaction where loss is recognized. Credits are allowed on dispositions only when there is sufficient tax on passive income to absorb them.

Example 27

Alicia sells a passive activity for a gain of $10,000. The activity had suspended losses of $40,000 and suspended credits of $15,000. The $10,000 gain is offset by $10,000 of the suspended losses, and the remaining $30,000 of suspended losses is deductible against Alicia's active and portfolio income. The suspended credits are lost forever because the sale of the activity did not generate any tax after the effect of the suspended losses was considered.

Example 28

If Alicia in the preceding example had realized a $100,000 gain on the sale of the passive activity, the suspended credits could have been used to the extent of the regular tax attributable to the net passive income.

Gain on sale	$100,000
Less: Suspended losses	(40,000)
Net gain	$ 60,000

If the tax attributable to the net gain of $60,000 is $15,000 or more, the entire $15,000 of suspended credits can be used. If the tax attributable to the gain is less than $15,000, the excess of the suspended credits over the tax attributable to the gain is lost forever.

When a taxpayer has sufficient regular tax liability from passive activities to trigger the use of suspended credits, the credits lose their character as passive credits. They are reclassified as regular tax credits and made subject to the same limits as other credits (see Chapter 17).

Passive Activity Changes to Active

If a formerly passive activity becomes active, suspended losses are allowed to the extent of income from the now active business.[28] If any of the suspended loss remains, it continues to be treated as a loss from a passive activity. The excess suspended loss can be deducted against passive income or carried over to the next tax year and deducted to the extent of income from the now active business in the succeeding year(s).

[27]§ 469(d)(2).　　　[28]§ 469(f).

TAX IN THE NEWS   If You Can't Trust Your Tax Preparer, Who Can You Trust?

Many taxpayers choose to remain ignorant of the tax law because they assume that by paying a "professional" to complete their returns, they have shifted all responsibility to someone else. But they do so at their own risk. Failure to have at least a general understanding of the tax rules that apply to one's return can be a big mistake and can lead to various tax penalties.

One such taxpayer invested in several partnerships that engaged in horse activities in California. Being fully employed in New York, he did not participate in the partnerships' activities and had no knowledge of their business operations. When he received the tax information from the partnerships about his investments, he simply turned over the statements to his tax preparer, who included the information on the return filed. Essentially, the tax return reflected the taxpayer's losses from the horse activities even though they are disallowed under the passive loss rules.

When the IRS discovered the error, the taxpayer pleaded ignorance and blamed the tax preparer. The taxpayer claimed that he had been "duped by a charlatan" and pleaded for mercy. The Tax Court showed no compassion and held that he owed additional taxes, interest, and penalties (*Ralph P. Cunningham,* 98 TCM 143, T.C.Memo. 2009–194). Perhaps the result would have been different if the taxpayer had had a better understanding of the tax law in general and the passive activity rules in particular. Reliance on a tax preparer is not an excuse for blindly signing a tax return without understanding its content.

Example 29

Rebecca has owned an interest in a passive activity for several years, which has produced losses of $80,000 during that period. Because she did not have passive income from other sources, she could not deduct any of the activity's passive losses. In the current year, she becomes a material participant in the activity and her share of the business profits total $25,000. As a result, she may use $25,000 of the suspended passive loss to offset the current business profits. Rebecca's remaining suspended passive loss from the activity is $55,000 ($80,000 − $25,000), which is carried over to future years.

6-7b Taxpayers Subject to the Passive Loss Rules

The passive loss rules apply to individuals, estates, trusts, personal service corporations, and closely held C corporations.[29] Passive income or loss from investments in partnerships or S corporations (see Chapters 14 and 15) flows through to the owners, and the passive loss rules are applied at the owner level. Consequently, it is necessary to understand how the passive activity rules apply to both entities *and* their owners (including individual taxpayers).

Personal Service Corporations

Application of the passive loss limitations to personal service corporations is intended to prevent taxpayers from sheltering personal service income by creating personal service corporations and acquiring passive activities at the corporate level.

Example 30

Two tax accountants who earn an aggregate of $200,000 a year in their individual practices agree to work together in a newly formed personal service corporation. Shortly after its formation, the corporation invests in a passive activity that produces a $200,000 loss during the year. Because the passive loss rules apply to personal service corporations, the corporation may not deduct the $200,000 passive loss against the $200,000 of active income.

---

[29]§ 469(a).

Determination of whether a corporation is a **personal service corporation** is based on rather broad definitions. A personal service corporation is a regular (or C) corporation that meets both of the following conditions:

- The principal activity is the performance of personal services.
- Such services are substantially performed by owner-employees.

Generally, personal service corporations include those in the fields of health, law, engineering, architecture, accounting, actuarial science, performing arts, and consulting.[30]

In-depth coverage can be found on this book's companion website: **www.cengagebrain.com** **4** Digging Deeper

Closely Held C Corporations

Application of the passive loss rules to closely held (nonpersonal service) C corporations is also intended to prevent individuals from incorporating to avoid the passive loss limitations. A corporation is classified as a **closely held C corporation** if at any time during the taxable year, more than 50 percent of the value of its outstanding stock is owned, directly or indirectly, by or for five or fewer individuals. Closely held C corporations (other than personal service corporations) may use passive losses to offset *active* income but *not portfolio* income.

> Silver Corporation, a closely held (nonpersonal service) C corporation, has a $500,000 passive loss from a rental activity, $400,000 of active income, and $100,000 of portfolio income. The corporation may offset $400,000 of the $500,000 passive loss against the $400,000 of active business income but may not offset the remainder against the $100,000 of portfolio income. Thus, $100,000 of the passive loss is suspended ($500,000 passive loss − $400,000 offset against active income).

Example 31

Application of the passive loss limitations to closely held C corporations prevents shareholders from transferring their portfolio investments to such corporations to offset passive losses against portfolio income.

6-7c Working with the Definition of Passive Activities

Identifying what constitutes an activity is a necessary first step in applying the passive loss limitation. The rules used to delineate an activity state that in general a taxpayer can treat one or more trade or business activities or rental activities as a single activity if those activities form an *appropriate economic unit* for measuring gain or loss. The Regulations provide guidelines for identifying appropriate economic units.[31] These guidelines are designed to prevent taxpayers from arbitrarily combining different businesses in an attempt to circumvent the passive loss limitation. For example, combining a profitable active business and a passive business generating losses into one activity would allow the taxpayer to offset passive losses against active income.

LO.7

Discuss the definitions of activity, material participation, and rental activity under the passive loss rules.

In-depth coverage can be found on this book's companion website: **www.cengagebrain.com** **5** Digging Deeper

To determine which ventures form an appropriate economic unit, all of the relevant facts and circumstances must be considered. However, special rules restrict the grouping of rental and nonrental activities.[32] The following example, adapted from the Regulations, illustrates the application of the activity grouping rules.[33]

---

[30]§ 448(d)(2)(A).
[31]Reg. § 1.469–4.

[32]Reg. § 1.469–4(d).
[33]Reg. § 1.469–4(c)(3).

Example 32

George owns a men's clothing store and an Internet café in Chicago. He also owns a men's clothing store and an Internet café in Milwaukee. Reasonable methods of applying the facts and circumstances test may result in any of the following groupings:

- All four businesses may be grouped into a single activity because of common ownership and control.
- The clothing stores may be grouped into an activity, and the Internet cafés may be grouped into an activity.
- The Chicago businesses may be grouped into an activity, and the Milwaukee businesses may be grouped into an activity.
- Each of the four businesses may be treated as a separate activity.

Once a set of activities has been grouped by the taxpayer using the above rules, the grouping cannot be changed unless a material change in the facts and circumstances occurs or the original grouping was clearly inappropriate. In addition, the Regulations also grant the IRS the right to regroup activities when one of the primary purposes of the taxpayer's grouping is to avoid the passive loss limitation and the grouping fails to reflect an appropriate economic unit.[34]

6-7d Material Participation

As indicated previously, if a taxpayer materially participates in a nonrental trade or business activity, any loss from that activity is treated as an active loss that can offset active or portfolio income. (Participation is defined later in the chapter.) If a taxpayer does not materially participate, however, the loss is treated as a passive loss, which can only offset passive income. Therefore, controlling whether a particular activity is treated as active or passive is an important part of the tax strategy of a taxpayer who owns an interest in one or more businesses. Consider the following examples.

Example 33

Cameron, a corporate executive, earns a salary of $600,000 per year. In addition, he owns a separate business in which he participates. The business produces a loss of $100,000 during the year. If Cameron materially participates in the business, the $100,000 loss is an active loss that may offset his active income from his corporate employer. If he does not materially participate, the loss is passive and is suspended. Cameron may use the suspended loss in the future only when he has passive income or disposes of the activity.

Example 34

Connor, an attorney, earns $350,000 a year in his law practice. In addition, he owns interests in two activities, A and B, in which he participates. Activity A, in which he does not *materially* participate, produces a loss of $50,000. Connor has not yet met the material participation standard, described below, for Activity B, which produces income of $80,000. However, he can meet the material participation standard if he spends an additional 50 hours in Activity B during the year. Should Connor attempt to meet the material participation standard for Activity B? If he continues working in Activity B and becomes a material participant, the $80,000 of income from the activity is active and the $50,000 passive loss from Activity A must be suspended. A more favorable tax strategy is for Connor *not to meet* the material participation standard for Activity B, thus making the income from that activity passive. This enables him to offset the $50,000 passive loss from Activity A against most of the passive income from Activity B.

It is possible to devise numerous scenarios in which the taxpayer could control the tax outcome by increasing or decreasing participation in different activities. Examples 33 and 34 demonstrate two of the possibilities. The conclusion reached in most analyses of this type is that taxpayers will benefit by having profitable activities classified as passive so that any passive losses can be used to offset that passive

---

[34]Reg. § 1.469–4(f).

TABLE 6.2	Tests to Determine Material Participation

Tests Based on Current Participation

1. The individual participates in the activity for more than 500 hours during the year.
2. The individual's participation in the activity for the taxable year constitutes substantially all of the participation in the activity of all individuals (including nonowner employees) for the year.
3. The individual participates in the activity for more than 100 hours during the year, and this participation is not less than that participation of any other individual (including nonowner employees) for the year.
4. The activity is a significant participation activity (where the person's participation *exceeds* 100 hours during the year), and the aggregate of all significant participation activities during the year is more than 500 hours.

Tests Based on Prior Participation

5. The individual materially participated in the activity for any 5 taxable years during the 10 taxable years that immediately precede the current taxable year.
6. The activity is a personal service activity, and the individual materially participated in the activity for any three preceding taxable years.

Test Based on Facts and Circumstances

7. Based on all of the facts and circumstances, the individual participates in the activity on a regular, continuous, and substantial basis during the year.

income. If the activity produces a loss, however, the taxpayer will benefit if it is classified as active so that the loss is not subject to the passive loss limitations.

Temporary Regulations[35] provide seven tests (listed in Table 6.2) that are intended to help taxpayers determine when material participation is achieved.

| In-depth coverage can be found on this book's companion website: **www.cengagebrain.com** | **6** | Digging Deeper |

Participation Defined

Participation generally includes any work done by an individual in an activity that he or she owns. Participation does not include work if it is of a type not customarily done by owners *and* if one of its principal purposes is to avoid the disallowance of passive losses or credits. Also, work done in an individual's capacity as an investor (e.g., reviewing financial reports in a nonmanagerial capacity) is not counted in applying the material participation tests. However, participation by an owner's spouse counts as participation by the owner.[36]

Example 35

Tom, who is a partner in a CPA firm, owns a computer store that operated at a loss during the year. To offset this loss against the income from his CPA practice, Tom would like to avoid having the computer business classified as a passive activity. During the year, he worked 480 hours in the business in management and selling activities and 30 hours doing janitorial chores. In addition, Tom's wife participated 40 hours as a salesperson. It is likely that Tom's 480 hours of participation in management and selling activities will count as participation in work customarily done by owners, but the 30 hours spent doing janitorial chores will not. However, the 40 hours of participation by his wife will count. Assuming none of the participation's principal purposes is to avoid the allowance of passive losses or credits, Tom will qualify as a material participant under the more-than-500-hour rule (480 + 40 = 520).

---

[35]Temp.Reg. § 1.469–5T(a).   [36]§ 469(h)(5) and Temp.Reg. § 1.469–5T(f)(3).

TAX IN THE NEWS Caution Is Needed in the Classification of Owners in LLCs and LLPs as Material Participants

When the passive loss rules were enacted in the mid-1980s, LLCs and LLPs had not developed as entity forms that could be used to operate businesses. But as their popularity increased, the impact of the passive loss rules on owners became a matter of conflict between taxpayers and the IRS.

In general, § 469(h)(2) states that limited partners are treated as not materially participating and, as a consequence, are subject to the passive loss restrictions. Similarly, the IRS treated owners who had limited liability protection in other business forms (i.e., LLCs and LLPs) in like fashion. In other words, the only way an LLC member or an LLP partner could be considered a material participant was by meeting the requirements under Test 1, 5, or 6 in Table 6.2.

In recent years, numerous courts have assigned material participation status to owners in LLCs and LLPs (over the objections of the IRS) based on the rights to participate in the management of their businesses. Ultimately, the IRS reversed its position with the release of Prop.Reg. § 1.469–5. The new holding eliminates limited liability as the determinant of material participation status and makes the status dependent on an investor's general involvement in the business.

Nonetheless, the new rules remain tentative until the Proposed Regulations (or some variation thereof) become final. In the meantime, owners of LLCs and LLPs should operate with caution.

Limited Partners

A *limited* partner is a partner whose liability to third-party creditors of the partnership is limited to the amount the partner has invested in the partnership. Such a partnership must have at least one *general* partner, who is fully liable in an individual capacity for the debts of the partnership to third parties. Generally, a *limited partner* is not considered a material participant unless he or she qualifies under Test 1, 5, or 6 as shown in Table 6.2. However, a *general partner* may qualify as a material participant by meeting any of the seven tests. If a general partner also owns a limited interest in the same limited partnership, all interests are treated as a general interest.[37]

Corporations

Personal service corporations and closely held C corporations cannot directly participate in an activity. However, a corporation is deemed to materially participate if its owners materially participate in an activity of the corporation. Together, the participating owners must own directly or indirectly more than 50 percent of the value of the outstanding stock of the corporation.[38] Alternatively, a closely held C corporation may be deemed to materially participate in an activity if, during the entire year, it has at least one full-time employee actively managing the business and at least three full-time nonowner employees working for the business. In addition, the corporation's trade or business expenses must exceed the gross income from that business by 15 percent for the year.[39]

6-7e Rental Activities

Subject to certain exceptions, all rental activities are to be treated as passive activities.[40] A rental activity is defined as any activity where payments are received principally for the use of tangible (real or personal) property.[41] Importantly, an activity that is classified as a rental activity is subject to the passive activity loss rules even if the taxpayer involved is a material participant.

---

[37]§ 469(h)(2) and Temp.Reg. § 1.469–5T(e)(3)(ii).
[38]Temp.Reg. § 1.469–1T(g)(3)(i)(A).
[39]Temp.Reg. § 1.469–1T(g)(3)(i)(B).

[40]§ 469(c)(2).
[41]§ 469(j)(8).

TAX IN THE NEWS   The Passive Loss Rules Are a Trap for the Novice Landlord

Most sophisticated investors are well aware of the passive loss rules. Such investors are not surprised when the rules apply and have learned how to minimize their negative effect.

The real damage caused by the passive loss rules often falls on taxpayers who have never heard of them and hold passive activities "on the side" only as secondary ventures. Suppose, for example, that Taylor just inherited her aunt's furnished residence. Rather than sell the house in a depressed market, she is attracted by the regular cash flow provided by rent income. Although Taylor knows to expect a tax benefit from the paper loss that may result from rental property, does she know about the passive loss limitations? Unlike the professional, most novice landlords are surprised by these rules on an after-the-fact basis.

Example 36

Sarah owns a fleet of automobiles that are held for rent, and she spends an average of 60 hours a week in the activity. Assuming that her automobile business is classified as a rental activity, it is automatically subject to the passive activity rules even though Sarah spends more than 500 hours a year in its operation.

Temporary Regulations, however, provide exceptions for certain situations where activities involving rentals of real and personal property are *not* to be *treated* as rental activities.[42] Activities covered by any of the exceptions provided by the Temporary Regulations are not *automatically* treated as passive activities because they would not be classified as rental activities. Instead, the activities are subject to the material participation tests shown in Table 6.2.

In-depth coverage can be found on this book's companion website: **www.cengagebrain.com**   **7** | Digging Deeper

Example 37

Dan owns a bicycle rental business at a nearby resort. Because the average period of customer use is seven days or less, Dan's business is not treated as a rental activity.

This exception is based on the presumption that a person who rents property for seven days or less is generally required to provide significant services to the customer. Providing such services supports a conclusion that the person is engaged in a service business rather than a rental business.

The fact that Dan's business in the previous example is not treated as a rental activity does not necessarily mean that it is classified as a nonpassive activity. Instead, the business is treated as a trade or business activity subject to the material participation standards listed in Table 6.2. If Dan is a material participant, the business is treated as active. If he is not a material participant, it is treated as a passive activity. For additional discussion of the rental exceptions, see IRS Publication 925 (*Passive Activity and At-Risk Rules*).

The general rules relating to passive activity losses are reviewed in Concept Summary 6.3.

6-7f Interaction of At-Risk and Passive Loss Limits

The determination of whether a loss is suspended under the passive loss rules is made *after* application of the at-risk rules, as well as other provisions relating to the measurement of taxable income. A loss that is not allowed for the year because the taxpayer is not at risk with respect to it is suspended under the at-risk provisions, not under the passive loss rules. Further, a taxpayer's at-risk basis is reduced by the

LO.8

Determine the relationship between the at-risk and passive loss limitations.

---

[42]Temp.Reg. § 1.469–1T(e)(3).

CONCEPT SUMMARY 6.3

Passive Activity Loss Rules: Key Issues and Answers

What is the fundamental passive activity rule?	Passive activity losses may be deducted only against passive activity income and gains. Losses not allowed are suspended and used in future years.
Who is subject to the passive activity rules?	Individuals. Estates. Trusts. Personal service corporations. Closely held C corporations.
What is a passive activity?	Trade or business or income-producing activity in which the taxpayer does not materially participate during the year, or rental activities, subject to certain exceptions, regardless of the taxpayer's level of participation.
What is an activity?	One or more trades or businesses or rental activities that comprise an appropriate economic unit.
How is an appropriate economic unit determined?	Based on a reasonable application of the relevant facts and circumstances.
What is material participation?	In general, the taxpayer participates on a regular, continuous, and substantial basis. More specifically, when the taxpayer meets the conditions of one of the seven tests provided in the Regulations.
What is a rental activity?	In general, an activity where payments are received for the use of tangible property. Special rules apply to rental real estate.

© iStockphoto.com/Andrey Prokhorov

losses (but not below zero) even if the deductions are not currently usable because of the passive loss rules. The following examples illustrate these points.

Example 38

Jack's adjusted basis in a passive activity is $10,000 at the beginning of 2013. His loss from the activity in 2013 is $4,000. Because Jack has no passive activity income, the $4,000 cannot be deducted. At year-end, Jack has an adjusted basis and an at-risk amount of $6,000 in the activity and a suspended passive loss of $4,000.

Example 39

Jack in the preceding example has a loss of $9,000 in the activity in 2014. Because the $9,000 exceeds his at-risk amount ($6,000) by $3,000, that $3,000 loss is disallowed by the at-risk rules. If Jack has no passive activity income, the remaining $6,000 is suspended under the passive activity rules. At year-end, he has:

- A $3,000 loss suspended under the at-risk rules.
- $10,000 of suspended passive losses ($4,000 from 2013 and $6,000 from 2014).
- An adjusted basis and at-risk amount in the activity of zero.

Example 40

Jack in Example 39 realizes $1,000 of passive income from the activity in 2015. Because the $1,000 increases his at-risk amount, $1,000 of the $3,000 unused loss from 2014 is reclassified as a passive loss. If he has no other passive income, the $1,000 income is offset by $1,000 of suspended passive losses. At the end of 2015, Jack has:

- No taxable passive income.
- $2,000 ($3,000 − $1,000) of unused losses under the at-risk rules.
- $10,000 of (reclassified) suspended passive losses ($10,000 + $1,000 of reclassified unused at-risk losses − $1,000 of passive losses offset against passive income).
- An adjusted basis and an at-risk amount in the activity of zero.

Example 41

In 2016, Jack has no gain or loss from the activity in Example 40. He contributes $5,000 more to the passive activity. Because the $5,000 contribution increases his at-risk amount, the $2,000 of losses suspended under the at-risk rules is reclassified as passive. Jack gets no passive loss deduction in 2016. At year-end, he has:

- No suspended losses under the at-risk rules.
- $12,000 of suspended passive losses ($10,000 + $2,000 of reclassified suspended at-risk losses).
- An adjusted basis and an at-risk amount of $3,000 ($5,000 additional investment − $2,000 of reclassified losses).

6-7g Special Rules for Real Estate

The passive loss rules contain two exceptions related to real estate activities. These exceptions allow all or part of real estate rental losses to offset active or portfolio income even though the activity otherwise is defined as a passive activity.

LO.9

Recognize the special treatment available to real estate activities.

Real Estate Professionals

The first exception allows certain real estate professionals to avoid passive loss treatment for losses from real estate rental activities.[43] To qualify for nonpassive treatment, a taxpayer must satisfy both of the following requirements:

- More than half of the personal services that the taxpayer performs in trades or businesses are performed in real property trades or businesses in which the taxpayer materially participates.
- The taxpayer performs more than 750 hours of services in these real property trades or businesses as a material participant.

Taxpayers who do not satisfy the above requirements must continue to treat losses from real estate rental activities as passive losses.

Example 42

During the current year, Della performs personal service activities as follows: 900 hours as a personal financial planner, 550 hours in a real estate development business, and 600 hours in a real estate rental activity. Any loss Della incurs in either real estate activity will not be subject to the passive loss rules. Being a nonrental business, the real estate development business is deemed active under the more-than-500-hour rule. The real estate rental activity is active because more than 50% of her personal services are devoted to real property trades or businesses (i.e., the development and rental businesses) and her material participation in those real estate activities exceeds 750 hours. Thus, any losses from either real estate activity can offset active and portfolio income.

As discussed earlier, a spouse's work is taken into consideration in satisfying the material participation requirement. However, the hours worked by a spouse are not taken into account when ascertaining whether a taxpayer has worked for more than 750 hours in real property trades or businesses during a year. Services performed by an employee are not treated as being related to a real estate trade or business unless the employee performing the services owns more than a 5 percent interest in the employer. In addition, a closely held C corporation may also qualify for the passive loss relief if more than 50 percent of its gross receipts for the year are derived from real property trades or businesses in which it materially participates.[44]

---

[43]§ 469(c)(7).

[44]§ 469(c)(7)(B) and Reg. § 1.469–9.

TAX IN THE NEWS   Full-Time Employees May Face Difficulty Showing Real Estate Professional Status

To qualify as a real estate professional, a taxpayer must devote more than 50 percent of his or her personal services to real property trades or businesses. This requirement typically would make it very difficult for a person with a full-time job to qualify for this status because the efforts as an employee likely would comprise the bulk of the taxpayer's labor.

If you were a judge, how reasonable would a taxpayer's assertion be that he worked more time on his real estate properties than his full-time, 40-hour-a-week job? One taxpayer, who faced such a challenge before the Tax Court (*Mohammad Hassanipour* 105 TCM 1542, T.C. Memo. 2013–88), was unable to convince the judge. Consequently, he was required to pay additional taxes

and penalties—over $45,000—for inappropriately claiming deductions as a real estate professional.

Essentially, the taxpayer reported that he worked 1,936 hours for his employer and was not able to persuade the judge that he spent more than this working on his real estate properties. In the end, the Tax Court stated that the taxpayer's testimony was undermined by "his questionable claims about the contemporaneous calendar, and by the vagueness and inherent improbability of his estimates."

A basic premise of tax compliance illustrated by the case is that a taxpayer should never claim a deduction unless it can be supported with adequate and convincing documentation.

Rental Real Estate Deduction

The second exception is more significant in that it is not restricted to real estate professionals. This exception allows individuals to deduct up to $25,000 of losses from real estate rental activities against active and portfolio income.[45] The potential annual $25,000 deduction is reduced by 50 percent of the taxpayer's adjusted gross income (AGI) in excess of $100,000. Thus, the entire deduction is phased out at $150,000. If married individuals file separately, the $25,000 deduction is reduced to zero unless they lived apart for the entire year, in which case the loss amount is $12,500 each and the phaseout begins at $50,000.

To qualify for the $25,000 exception, a taxpayer must meet both of the following requirements:[46]

- *Actively participate* in the real estate rental activity.
- Own 10 percent or more (in value) of all interests in the activity during the entire taxable year (or shorter period during which the taxpayer held an interest in the activity).

The difference between *active participation* and *material participation* is that the former can be satisfied without regular, continuous, and substantial involvement in operations as long as the taxpayer participates in making management decisions in a significant and bona fide sense. In this context, relevant management decisions include decisions such as approving new tenants, deciding on rental terms, and approving capital or repair expenditures.

The $25,000 allowance is available after all active participation rental losses and gains are netted and applied to other passive income. If a taxpayer has a real estate rental loss in excess of the amount that can be deducted under the real estate rental exception, that excess is treated as a passive loss.

Example 43

Brad, who has $90,000 of AGI before considering rental activities, has $85,000 of losses from a real estate rental activity in which he actively participates. He also actively participates in another real estate rental activity from which he has $25,000 of income. He has other passive income of $36,000. Of the net rental loss of $60,000 ($85,000 − $25,000), $36,000 is absorbed by the passive income, leaving $24,000 that can be deducted against active or portfolio income because of the availability of the $25,000 allowance.

---

[45]§ 469(i).   [46]§ 469(i)(6).

The $25,000 offset allowance is an aggregate of both deductions and credits in deduction equivalents. The deduction equivalent of a passive activity credit is the amount of deductions that reduces the tax liability for the taxable year by an amount equal to the credit.[47] A taxpayer with $5,000 of credits and a marginal tax rate of 25 percent would have a deduction equivalent of $20,000 ($5,000/25%).

If total deductions and deduction equivalents exceed $25,000, the taxpayer must allocate the benefit on a pro rata basis. First, the allowance must be allocated among the losses (including real estate rental activity losses suspended in prior years) and then to credits.

Kevin is an active participant in a real estate rental activity that produces $8,000 of income, $26,000 of deductions, and $1,500 of credits. Kevin, whose marginal tax rate is 25%, may deduct the net passive loss of $18,000 ($8,000 − $26,000). After deducting the loss, he has an available deduction equivalent of $7,000 ($25,000 − $18,000 passive loss). Therefore, the maximum amount of credits he may claim is $1,750 ($7,000 × 25%). Because the actual credits are less than this amount, Kevin may claim the entire $1,500 credit.	**Example 44**

Kelly, whose marginal tax rate is 25%, actively participates in three separate real estate rental activities. The relevant tax results for each activity are as follows:

Example 45

- Activity A: $20,000 of losses.
- Activity B: $10,000 of losses.
- Activity C: $4,200 of credits.

Kelly's deduction equivalent from the credits is $16,800 ($4,200/25%). Therefore, the total passive deductions and deduction equivalents are $46,800 ($20,000 + $10,000 + $16,800), which exceeds the maximum allowable amount of $25,000. Consequently, Kelly must allocate pro rata first from among losses and then from among credits. Deductions from losses are limited as follows:

- Activity A: $25,000 × [$20,000/($20,000 + $10,000)] = $16,667.
- Activity B: $25,000 × [$10,000/($20,000 + $10,000)] = $8,333.

Because the amount of passive deductions exceeds the $25,000 maximum, the deduction balance of $5,000 and passive credits of $4,200 must be carried forward. Kelly's suspended losses and credits by activity are as follows:

		Activity		
	Total	**A**	**B**	**C**
Allocated losses	$ 30,000	$ 20,000	$10,000	$ –0–
Allocated credits	4,200	–0–	–0–	4,200
Utilized losses	(25,000)	(16,667)	(8,333)	–0–
Suspended losses	5,000	3,333	1,667	–0–
Suspended credits	4,200	–0–	–0–	4,200

---

[47]§ 469(j)(5).

6-7h Disposition of Passive Activities

LO.10

Determine the consequences of the disposition of passive activities.

Recall from an earlier discussion that if a taxpayer disposes of an entire interest in a passive activity, any suspended losses (and in certain cases, suspended credits) may be utilized when calculating the final economic gain or loss on the investment. In addition, if a loss ultimately results, that loss can offset other types of income. However, the consequences may differ if the activity is disposed of in a transaction that is not fully taxable. The following sections discuss the treatment of suspended passive losses in two such dispositions.

Disposition of a Passive Activity at Death

When a transfer of a taxpayer's interest occurs because of the taxpayer's death, suspended losses are allowed (to the decedent) to the extent they exceed the amount, if any, of the allowed step-up in basis.[48] Suspended losses that are equal to or less than the amount of the basis increase are, however, lost. The losses allowed generally are reported on the final return of the deceased taxpayer.

Example 46

Alyson dies with passive activity property having an adjusted basis of $40,000, suspended losses of $10,000, and a fair market value at the date of her death of $75,000. The increase (i.e., step-up) in basis (see Chapter 7) is $35,000 (fair market value at date of death in excess of adjusted basis). None of the $10,000 suspended loss is deductible on Alyson's final return or by the beneficiary. The suspended losses ($10,000) are lost because they do not exceed the step-up in basis ($35,000).

Example 47

Assume the same facts as in the previous example except that the property's fair market value at the date of Alyson's death is $47,000. Because the step-up in basis is only $7,000 ($47,000 − $40,000), the suspended losses allowed are limited to $3,000 ($10,000 suspended loss at time of death − $7,000 increase in basis). The $3,000 loss available to Alyson is reported on her final income tax return.

Disposition of a Passive Activity by Gift

In a disposition of a taxpayer's interest in a passive activity by gift, the suspended losses are added to the basis of the property.[49]

As such, the suspended losses become permanently nondeductible to both the donor and the donee. Nonetheless, a tax *benefit* may be available to the donee for another reason. Due to the increase in the property's basis, greater depreciation deductions can result and there will be less gain (or more loss) on a subsequent sale of the property. The side benefits of increased basis do not materialize if the recipient is a charity, as such organizations generally are not subject to income taxation.

Example 48

Carlton makes a gift to Yolanda of passive activity property having an adjusted basis of $40,000, suspended losses of $10,000, and a fair market value at the date of the gift of $100,000. Carlton cannot deduct the suspended losses in the year of the disposition. However, the suspended losses of $10,000 transfer with the property and are added to the adjusted basis of the property, thus becoming $50,000 in Yolanda's hands. Assuming Yolanda is able to sell the property for $105,000 soon after she receives the gift, her taxable gain would be $55,000 ($105,000 − $50,000), which reflects the benefit from the increased basis.

---

[48]§ 469(g)(2).   [49]§ 469(j)(6).

| *Tax Planning Strategies* | UTILIZING PASSIVE LOSSES |

FRAMEWORK FOCUS: TAX RATE

Strategy: Control the Character of Income and Deductions.

Perhaps the biggest challenge individuals face with the passive loss rules is to recognize the potential impact of the rules and then to structure their affairs to minimize this impact. Taxpayers who have passive activity losses (PALs) should adopt a strategy of generating passive activity income that can be sheltered by existing passive losses. One approach is to buy an interest in a passive activity that is generating income (referred to as a passive income generator, or PIG). Then the PAL can offset income from the PIG. From a tax perspective, it would be foolish to buy a loss-generating passive activity unless one has passive income to shelter or the activity is rental real estate that can qualify for the $25,000 exception or the exception available to real estate professionals.

If a taxpayer does invest in an activity that produces losses subject to the passive loss rules, the following strategies may help minimize the loss of current deductions:

- If money is borrowed to finance the purchase of a passive activity, the associated interest expense is generally treated as part of any passive loss. Consequently, by using more available (i.e., not borrowed) cash to purchase the passive investment, the investor will need less debt and will incur less interest expense. By incurring less interest expense, a possible suspended passive loss deduction is reduced.

- If the investor does not have sufficient cash readily available for the larger down payment, it can be obtained by borrowing against the equity in his or her personal residence. The interest expense on such debt will be deductible under the qualified residence interest provisions (see Chapter 10) and will not be subject to the passive loss limitations. Thus, the taxpayer avoids the passive loss limitation and secures a currently deductible interest expense.

As explained earlier, unusable passive losses often accumulate and provide no current tax benefit because the taxpayer has no passive income. When the taxpayer disposes of the entire interest in a passive activity, however, any suspended losses from that activity are used to reduce the taxable gain. If any taxable gain still remains, it can be offset by losses from other passive activities. As a result, the taxpayer should carefully select the year in which to dispose of a passive activity. It is to the taxpayer's advantage to wait until sufficient passive losses have accumulated to offset any gain recognized on the asset's disposition.

Example 49

Bill, a calendar year taxpayer, owns interests in two passive activities: Activity A, which he plans to sell in December of this year at a gain of $100,000, and Activity B, which he plans to keep indefinitely. Current and suspended losses associated with Activity B total $60,000, and Bill expects losses from the activity to be $40,000 next year. If Bill sells Activity A this year, the $100,000 gain can be offset by the current and suspended losses of $60,000 from Activity B, producing a net taxable gain of $40,000. However, if Bill delays the sale of Activity A until January of next year, the $100,000 gain will be fully offset by the $100,000 of losses generated by Activity B ($60,000 current and prior losses + $40,000 next year's loss). Consequently, by postponing the sale by one month, he could avoid recognizing $40,000 of gain that would otherwise result. ■

Taxpayers with passive losses should consider the level of their involvement in all other trades or businesses in which they have an interest. If they show that they do not materially participate in a profitable activity, the activity becomes a passive activity. Current and suspended passive losses then could shelter any income generated by the profitable business. Family partnerships in which certain members do not materially participate would qualify. The silent partner in any general partnership engaged in a trade or business would also qualify.

Example 50

Gail has an investment in a limited partnership that produces annual passive losses of approximately $25,000. She also owns a newly acquired interest in a convenience store where she works. Her share of the store's income is $35,000. If she works enough to be classified as a material participant, her $35,000 share of income is treated as active income. This results in $35,000 being subject to tax every year, while her $25,000 loss is suspended. However, if Gail reduces her involvement at the store so that she is not a material participant, the $35,000 of income receives passive treatment. Consequently, the $35,000 of income can be offset by the $25,000 passive loss, resulting in only $10,000 being subject to tax. Thus, by reducing her involvement, Gail ensures that the income from the profitable trade or business receives passive treatment and can then be used to absorb passive losses from other passive activities. ■

The passive loss rules can have a dramatic effect on a taxpayer's ability to claim passive losses currently. As a result, it is important to keep accurate records of all sources of income and losses, particularly any suspended passive losses and credits and the activities to which they relate, so that their potential tax benefit will not be lost.

REFOCUS ON THE BIG PICTURE

RECEIVING TAX BENEFITS FROM LOSSES

While Robyn's circumstances were unfortunate, the good news is that she will be able to receive some tax benefits from the losses.

- *Bad debt.* Based on the facts provided, it appears that Robyn's loan to her friend, Jamil, was a bona fide nonbusiness bad debt. The amount of the loss deduction is the unpaid principal balance of $19,000 ($25,000 − $6,000). As a nonbusiness bad debt, the loss is classified as a short-term capital loss (see Example 5).
- *Loss from stock investment.* Likewise, the $60,000 loss on the Owl Corporation stock investment is deductible. If Robyn purchased the stock directly from the company, the stock may qualify as small business stock under § 1244. If this is the case, the first $50,000 of the loss is an ordinary loss and the remaining $10,000 loss is treated as a long-term capital loss. If the stock is not § 1244 stock, the entire $60,000 loss is treated as a long-term capital loss (see Example 8).
- *Loss from bookstore.* The $180,000 loss from the bookstore is reported on Schedule C of Robyn's Form 1040. It is an ordinary loss and qualifies for net operating loss (NOL) treatment if she does not have enough other income this year against which the loss could be offset. Any NOL can be carried back or carried forward to produce refunds of taxes paid from prior years or to reduce taxes owed on income earned in the future.
- *Casualty loss.* The loss from the damage to Robyn's personal residence is a personal casualty loss. Using the cost of repairs method, the amount of the casualty loss is $7,000 ($32,000 loss − $25,000 insurance recovery). However, this amount must be reduced by the statutory amount of $100 and 10 percent of AGI (see Example 14).
- *Passive activity loss.* The $20,000 loss on the limited partnership is not deductible currently due to the passive loss limitation. However, the loss can be carried forward and utilized in the future to offset any passive income generated from the venture (see Example 21).

What If?

What if instead of operating orange groves the partnership owns and rents apartments to college students and Robyn actively participates in the venture? In this case, Robyn may qualify for a $20,000 ordinary loss deduction under the rental real estate exception.

© G. Baden/Corbis

Suggested Readings

James A. Beavers, "Expense Does Not Qualify as Compensation but Does Qualify as Theft Loss," *The Tax Adviser,* June 2011.

Todd D. Keator, "Rental Real Estate and the Net Investment Income Tax," *Journal of Taxation,* August 2013.

Matthew A. Melone, "Applying the Medicare Surtax to Passive Activities Under the Proposed Regulations," *Practical Tax Strategies,* March 2013.

Daniel Rowe, "Activity Grouping: The Impact of Recent Developments," *The Tax Adviser,* February 2013.

David A. Thornton, "Deducting Losses on Worthless Investment Securities," *The Tax Adviser,* September 2012.

Key Terms

Active income, 6-18

At-risk limitation, 6-16

Bad debt, 6-2

Business bad debt, 6-4

Casualty losses, 6-8

Closely held C corporation, 6-23

Disaster area losses, 6-9

Material participation, 6-25

Net operating losses (NOLs), 6-13

Nonbusiness bad debt, 6-4

Passive loss, 6-16

Personal service corporation, 6-23

Portfolio income, 6-18

Rental activity, 6-26

Reserve method, 6-2

Significant participation activity, 6-25

Small business stock (§ 1244 stock), 6-6

Specific charge-off method, 6-2

Tax shelters, 6-15

Theft losses, 6-8

Valuation allowance, 6-13

Worthless securities, 6-5

Problems

1. **LO.1** Several years ago, Loon Finance Company, which is in the lending business, loaned Sara $30,000 to purchase an automobile to be used for personal purposes. In August of the current year, Sara filed for bankruptcy, and Loon was notified that it could not expect to receive more than $4,000. As of the end of the current year, Loon has received $1,000. Loon has contacted you about the possibility of taking a bad debt deduction for the current year.

   Write a letter to Loon Finance Company that contains your advice as to whether it can claim a bad debt deduction for the current year. Also prepare a memo for the tax files. Loon's address is 100 Tyler Lane, Erie, PA 16563.

   Communications

2. **LO.1** Monty loaned his friend Ned $20,000 three years ago. Ned signed a note and made payments on the loan. Last year, when the remaining balance was $11,000, Ned filed for bankruptcy and notified Monty that he would be unable to pay the balance on the loan. Monty treated the $11,000 as a nonbusiness bad debt. Last year, Monty had capital gains of $4,000 and taxable income of $20,000. During the current year, Ned paid Monty $10,000 in satisfaction of the debt. Determine Monty's tax treatment for the $10,000 received in the current year.

3. **LO.2** Many years ago, Jack purchased 400 shares of Canary stock. During the current year, the stock became worthless. It was determined that the company "went under" because several corporate officers embezzled a large amount of company funds. Identify the relevant tax issues for Jack.

   Issue ID

4. **LO.1** Jake and Mary Snow are residents of the state of New York. They are cash basis taxpayers and file a joint return for the calendar year. Jake is a licensed master plumber. Two years ago, Jake entered into a contract with New York City to perform plumbing services. During the current year, Jake was declared to be in breach of the contract, and he ceased performing plumbing services. Jake received a Form W–2 that reported $50,000 for wages paid. He also maintains that the city has not paid him $35,000 for work he performed. Jake is considering claiming a $35,000 business bad debt on his tax return. Evaluate Jake's plan.

   Ethics and Equity

5. **LO.1, 2** Mable and Jack file a joint return. For the current year, they had the following items:

Salaries	$120,000
Loss on sale of § 1244 stock acquired two years ago	105,000
Gain on sale of § 1244 stock acquired six months ago	20,000
Nonbusiness bad debt	19,000

   Determine the impact of the above items on Mable and Jack's income for the current year.

6. **LO.2** Mary, a single taxpayer, purchased 10,000 shares of § 1244 stock several years ago at a cost of $20 per share. In November of the current year, Mary receives an offer to sell the stock for $12 per share. She has the option of either selling all of the stock now or

   Decision Making

selling half of the stock now and half of the stock in January of next year. Mary's salary is $80,000 for the current year, and it will be $90,000 next year. Mary has long-term capital gains of $8,000 for the current year and will have $10,000 next year. If Mary's goal is to minimize her AGI for the two years, determine whether she should sell all of her stock this year or half of her stock this year and half next year.

Critical Thinking

Communications

7. **LO.2** Paul Sanders, a married taxpayer who files a joint return with his wife, acquired stock in a corporation that qualified as a small business corporation under § 1244. The stock cost $30,000 and was acquired three years ago. A few months after he acquired the stock, he gave it to his brother, Mike Sanders. The stock was worth $30,000 on the date of the gift. Mike, who is married and files a joint return with his wife, sells the stock for $10,000 in the current tax year. You represent Mike, who asks you whether he can take a loss deduction on the sale of the stock. If so, how will the loss be treated for tax purposes? Prepare a letter to your client and a memo for the files. Mike's address is 2600 Riverview Drive, Cape Girardeau, MO 63701.

Decision Making

8. **LO.3** Olaf lives in the state of Minnesota. A tornado hit the area and damaged his home and automobile. Applicable information is as follows:

Item	Adjusted Basis	FMV before	FMV after	Insurance Proceeds
Home	$350,000	$500,000	$100,000	$280,000
Auto	60,000	40,000	10,000	20,000

Because of the extensive damage caused by the tornado, the President designated the area a disaster area.

Olaf and his wife, Anna, always file a joint return. Their return for last year shows AGI of $180,000 and taxable income of $140,000. For the current year, their return shows AGI of $300,000 and taxable income (exclusive of the casualty loss deduction) of $215,000.

Determine the amount of Olaf and Anna's loss and the year in which they should take the loss.

Issue ID

9. **LO.3** In 2011, John opened an investment account with Randy Hansen, who held himself out to the public as an investment adviser and securities broker. John contributed $200,000 to the account in 2011. John provided Randy with a power of attorney to use the $200,000 to purchase and sell securities on John's behalf. John instructed Randy to reinvest any gains and income earned. In 2011, 2012, and 2013, John received statements of the amount of income earned by his account and included these amounts in his gross income for these years. In 2014, it was discovered that Randy's purported investment advisory and brokerage activity was in fact a fraudulent investment arrangement known as a Ponzi scheme. In reality, John's account balance was zero, the money having been used by Randy in his scheme. Identify the relevant tax issues for John.

Decision Making

Communications

10. **LO.3** On November 1 of the current year, Sam Smith dropped off to sleep while driving home from a business trip. Luckily, he was only slightly injured in the resulting accident, but the company car that he was driving was damaged significantly.

Sam is an employee of Snipe Industries. The corporation purchased the car new two years ago for $40,000. The automobile had a fair market value of $30,000 before the accident and $12,000 after the accident. The car was covered by an insurance policy that had a $3,000 deductible clause. The corporation is afraid that the policy will be canceled if it makes a claim for the damages. Therefore, Snipe is considering not filing a claim. The company believes that the casualty loss deduction will help mitigate the loss of the insurance reimbursement. The corporation's taxable income for the current year is $25,000.

Write a letter to Snipe Industries that contains your advice regarding the filing of an insurance claim for reimbursement for the damages to the company's car. Snipe Industries' address is 450 Colonel's Way, Warrensburg, MO 64093.

11. **LO.4** Mary, a single taxpayer with two dependent children, has the following items of income and expense during 2014:

Gross receipts from business	$144,000
Business expenses	180,000
Alimony received	22,000
Interest income	3,000
Itemized deductions (no casualty or theft)	24,000

Critical Thinking

a. Determine Mary's taxable income for 2014.
b. Determine Mary's NOL for 2014.

12. **LO.6** In 2013, Fred invested $50,000 in a general partnership. Fred's interest is not considered to be a passive activity. If his share of the partnership losses is $35,000 in 2013 and $25,000 in 2014, how much can he deduct in each year?

13. **LO.6** In the current year, Bill Parker (54 Oak Drive, St. Paul, MN 55164) is considering making an investment of $60,000 in Best Choice Partnership. The prospectus provided by Bill's broker indicates that the partnership investment is not a passive activity and that Bill's share of the entity's loss in the current year will likely be $40,000, while his share of the partnership loss next year will probably be $25,000. Write a letter to Bill in which you indicate how the losses would be treated for tax purposes in the current year and the following year.

Communications

14. **LO.6, 7, 8** In the current year, David and Debbie Wayland, both successful physicians, made a cash investment for a limited partnership interest in a California berry farm. In addition to the cash obtained from the investors, management borrowed a substantial sum to purchase assets necessary for the farm's operations. The Waylands' investment adviser told them that their share of the tax loss in the first year alone would be in excess of their initial cash investment. This would be followed by several more years of losses. They feel confident that their interest in the berry farm is a sound investment. Identify the tax issues facing the Waylands.

Issue ID

15. **LO.6** A number of years ago, Kay acquired an interest in a partnership in which she is not a material participant. Kay's basis in her partnership interest at the beginning of 2013 is $40,000. Kay's share of the partnership loss is $35,000 in 2013, while her share of the partnership income is $15,000 in 2014. How much may Kay deduct in 2013 and 2014, assuming she owns no other passive activities?

16. **LO.5, 6** Ray acquired an activity several years ago, and in the current year, it generates a loss of $50,000. Ray has AGI of $140,000 before considering the loss from the activity. If the activity is a bakery and Ray is not a material participant, what is his AGI?

17. **LO.6** Jorge owns two passive investments, Activity A and Activity B. He plans to dispose of Activity A in the current year or next year. Juanita has offered to buy Activity A this year for an amount that would produce a taxable passive gain to Jorge of $115,000. However, if the sale, for whatever reason, is not made to Juanita, Jorge believes that he could find a buyer who would pay about $7,000 less than Juanita. Passive losses and gains generated (and expected to be generated) by Activity B follow:

Decision Making

Two years ago	($35,000)
Last year	(35,000)
This year	(8,000)
Next year	(30,000)
Future years	Minimal profits

All of Activity B's losses are suspended. Should Jorge close the sale of Activity A with Juanita this year, or should he wait until next year and sell to another buyer? Jorge is in the 28% tax bracket.

18. **LO.6** Sarah has investments in four passive activity partnerships purchased several years ago. Last year, the income and losses were as follows:

Activity	Income (Loss)
A	$ 30,000
B	(30,000)
C	(15,000)
D	(5,000)

In the current year, she sold her interest in Activity D for a $10,000 gain. Activity D, which had been profitable until last year, had a current loss of $1,500. How will the sale of Activity D affect Sarah's taxable income in the current year?

19. **LO.6** Leon sells his interest in a passive activity for $100,000. Determine the tax effect of the sale based on each of the following independent facts:
    a. Adjusted basis in this investment is $35,000. Losses from prior years that were not deductible due to the passive loss restrictions total $40,000.
    b. Adjusted basis in this investment is $75,000. Losses from prior years that were not deductible due to the passive loss restrictions total $40,000.
    c. Adjusted basis in this investment is $75,000. Losses from prior years that were not deductible due to the passive loss restrictions total $40,000. In addition, suspended credits total $10,000.

20. **LO.6** Ash, Inc., a closely held personal service corporation, has $100,000 of passive losses. In addition, Ash has $80,000 of active business income and $20,000 of portfolio income. How much of the passive loss may Ash use to offset the other types of income?

21. **LO.6** In the current year, White, Inc., earns $400,000 from operations and receives $36,000 in dividends and interest from various portfolio investments. White also pays $150,000 to acquire a 20% interest in a passive activity that produces a $200,000 loss.
    a. Assuming that White is a personal service corporation, how will these transactions affect its taxable income?
    b. Same as (a), except that White is closely held but not a personal service corporation.

22. **LO.7** John, an engineer, operates a separate business that he acquired eight years ago. If he participates 85 hours in the business and it incurs a loss of $34,000, under what circumstances can John claim an active loss?

Issue ID

23. **LO.7** Rene retired from public accounting after a long and successful career of 45 years. As part of her retirement package, she continues to share in the profits and losses of the firm, albeit at a lower rate than when she was working full-time. Because Rene wants to stay busy during her retirement years, she has invested and works in a local hardware business, operated as a partnership. Unfortunately, the business has recently gone through a slump and has not been generating profits. Identify relevant tax issues for Rene.

Decision Making

Communications

24. **LO.6, 8** Kristin Graf (123 Baskerville Mill Road, Jamison, PA 18929) is trying to decide how to invest a $10,000 inheritance. One option is to make an additional investment in Rocky Road Excursions in which she has an at-risk basis of $0, suspended losses under the at-risk rules of $7,000, and suspended passive losses of $1,000. If Kristin makes this investment, her share of the expected profits this year will be $8,000. If her investment stays the same, her share of profits from Rocky Road Excursions will be $1,000. Another option is to invest $10,000 as a limited partner in the Ragged Mountain Winery; this investment will produce passive income of $9,000. Write a letter to Kristin to review the tax consequences of each alternative. Kristin is in the 28% tax bracket.

Decision Making

25. **LO.8** The end of the year is approaching, and Maxine has begun to focus on ways of minimizing her income tax liability. Several years ago, she purchased an investment in Teal Limited Partnership, which is subject to the at-risk and the passive activity loss rules. (Last year, Maxine sold a different investment that was subject to these rules and that produced passive income.) She believes that her investment in Teal has good long-term economic prospects. However, it has been generating tax losses for several years in a row. In fact, when she was discussing last year's income tax return with her tax accountant, he said that unless "things change" with respect to her investments, she would not be able to deduct losses this year.

a. What was the accountant referring to in his comment?

b. You learn that Maxine's current at-risk basis in her investment is $1,000 and that her share of the current loss is expected to be $13,000. Based on these facts, how will her loss be treated?

c. After reviewing her situation, Maxine's financial adviser suggests that she invest at least an additional $12,000 in Teal to ensure a full loss deduction in the current year. How do you react to his suggestion?

d. What would you suggest Maxine consider as she attempts to maximize her current-year deductible loss?

26. **LO.8** A number of years ago, Lee acquired a 20% interest in the BlueSky Partnership for $60,000. The partnership was profitable through 2013, and Lee's amount at risk in the partnership interest was $120,000 at the beginning of 2014. BlueSky incurred a loss of $400,000 in 2014 and reported income of $200,000 in 2015. Assuming that Lee is not a material participant, how much of his loss from BlueSky Partnership is deductible in 2014 and 2015? Consider the at-risk and passive loss rules, and assume Lee owns no other investments.

27. **LO.6** Grace acquired an activity four years ago. The loss from the activity is $50,000 in the current year (at-risk basis of $40,000 as of the beginning of the year). Without considering the loss from the activity, she has gross income of $140,000. If the activity is a convenience store and Grace is a material participant, what is the effect of the activity on her taxable income?

28. **LO.5, 6, 8** Jonathan, a physician, earns $200,000 from his practice. He also receives $18,000 in dividends and interest from various portfolio investments. During the year, he pays $45,000 to acquire a 20% interest in a partnership that produces a $300,000 loss. Compute Jonathan's AGI assuming that:

a. He does not participate in the operations of the partnership.

b. He is a material participant in the operations of the partnership.

29. **LO.5, 6, 8** Five years ago, Gerald invested $150,000 in a passive activity, his sole investment venture. On January 1, 2013, his amount at risk in the activity was $30,000. His shares of the income and losses were as follows:

Year	Income (Loss)
2013	($40,000)
2014	(30,000)
2015	50,000

Gerald holds no suspended at-risk or passive losses at the beginning of 2013. How much can Gerald deduct in 2013 and 2014? What is his taxable income from the activity in 2015? Consider the at-risk rules as well as the passive loss rules.

30. **LO.9** Several years ago Benny Jackson (125 Hill Street, Charleston, WV 25311) acquired an apartment building that currently generates a loss of $60,000. Benny's AGI is $130,000 before considering the loss. The apartment building is in an exclusive part of the city, and Benny is an active participant. Write a letter to Benny explaining what effect the loss will have on his AGI.

Communications

31. **LO.5, 6, 7** You have just met with Scott Myers (603 Pittsfield Drive, Champaign, IL 61821), a successful full-time real estate developer and investor. During your meeting, you discussed his tax situation because you are starting to prepare his current Federal income tax return. During your meeting, Scott mentioned that he and his wife, Susan, went to great lengths to maximize their participation in an apartment complex that they own and manage. In particular, Scott included the following activities in the 540 hours of participation for the current year:

Ethics and Equity

Communications

- Time spent thinking about the rentals.
- Time spent by Susan on weekdays visiting the apartment complex to oversee operations of the buildings (i.e., in a management role).
- Time spent by both Scott and Susan on weekends visiting the apartment complex to assess operations. Scott and Susan always visited the complex together on weekends, and both counted their hours (i.e., one hour at the complex was two hours of participation).

- Time spent on weekends driving around the community looking for other potential rental properties to purchase. Again, both Scott's hours and Susan's hours were counted, even when they drove together.

After reviewing Scott's records, you note that the apartment complex generated a significant loss this year. Prepare a letter to Scott describing your position on the deductibility of the loss.

Decision Making   32. **LO.6, 9** Bonnie and Jake (ages 35 and 36, respectively) are married with no dependents and live in Montana (not a community property state). Because Jake has large medical expenses, they seek your advice about filing separately to save taxes. Their income and expenses for 2014 are as follows:

Bonnie's salary	$ 42,500
Jake's salary	26,000
Interest income (joint)	1,500
Rental loss from actively managed rental property	(23,000)
Jake's unreimbursed medical expenses	8,500
All other itemized deductions:*	
Bonnie	9,000
Jake	3,400

*None subject to limitations.

Determine whether Bonnie and Jake should file jointly or separately for 2014.

33. **LO.9** During the current year, Gene, a CPA, performs services as follows: 1,800 hours in his tax practice and 50 hours in an apartment leasing operation in which he has a 15% interest. Because of his oversight duties, Gene is considered to be an active participant. He expects that his share of the loss realized from the apartment leasing operation will be $30,000 and that his tax practice will show a profit of approximately $80,000. Gene is single and has no other income. Discuss the character and treatment of the income and losses generated by these activities.

34. **LO.9** Ida, who has AGI of $80,000 before considering rental activities, is active in three separate real estate rental activities. Ida has a marginal tax rate of 28%. She has $12,000 of losses from Activity A, $18,000 of losses from Activity B, and income of $10,000 from Activity C. She also has $2,100 of tax credits from Activity A. Calculate the deductions and credits that she is allowed and the suspended losses and credits.

35. **LO.9** Ella has $105,000 of losses from a real estate rental activity in which she actively participates. She has other rent income of $25,000 and other passive income of $32,000. How much rental loss can Ella deduct against active and portfolio income (ignoring the at-risk rules)? Does she have any suspended losses to carry over? Explain.

Ethics and Equity   36. **LO.5, 6, 10** Lucien dies in the current year owning a limited partnership interest in a partnership that owns and operates an apartment complex. Associated with Lucien's interest is a $10,000 suspended passive activity loss that he had not been able to claim. Ron, the executor of Lucien's estate, learns from the partnership's general partner that she is not aware of any recent qualified appraisals or sales that would help determine the fair market value of the limited partnership interest. Ron thinks that the cost of hiring a qualified appraiser to determine the value of the interest is not necessary because Lucien's estate is not large enough to be subject to the Federal estate tax. Lucien's records reflect a basis of $65,000 for the partnership interest immediately before his death.

The partnership's bookkeeper has a "gut feeling" that the partnership interest is worth anywhere between $65,000 and $80,000. This is good news to Ron. Based on her "guesstimate," Ron sets the value of the interest at $65,000.

What is Ron trying to accomplish in setting this valuation? What ethical issues arise?

37. **LO.5, 6, 10** In the current year, Abe gives an interest in a passive activity to his daughter, Andrea. The value of the interest at the date of the gift is $25,000, and its adjusted basis to Abe is $13,000. During the time that Abe owned the investment, losses of $3,000 could not be deducted because of the passive loss limitations. What is the tax treatment of the suspended passive activity losses to Abe and Andrea?

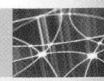

BRIDGE DISCIPLINE

1. Marketplace, Inc., has recognized over time that a certain percentage of its customer accounts receivable will not be collected. To ensure the appropriate matching of revenues and expenditures in its financial reports, Marketplace uses the reserve method for bad debts. Records show the following pertaining to its treatment of bad debts.

Beginning allowance for bad debts	$120,000
Ending allowance for bad debts	123,000
Bad debts written off during the year	33,000

    a. What was the bad debt expense for financial accounting purposes during the year?
    b. What was the bad debt expense for income tax purposes during the year?
    c. Assuming that the before-tax net income for financial accounting purposes was $545,000, what is the taxable income for the year if the treatment of bad debts is the only book-tax difference?

2. Heather wants to invest $40,000 in a relatively safe venture and has discovered two alternatives that would produce the following ordinary income and loss over the next three years:

    Decision Making

Year	Alternative 1 Income (Loss)	Alternative 2 Income (Loss)
1	($20,000)	($48,000)
2	(28,000)	32,000
3	72,000	40,000

    She is interested in the after-tax effects of these alternatives over a three-year horizon. Assume that:

    • Heather's investment portfolio produces sufficient passive income to offset any potential passive loss that may arise from these alternatives.
    • Heather's marginal tax rate is 25%, and her cost of capital is 6% (the present value factors are .9434, .8900, and .8396).
    • Each investment alternative possesses equal growth potential and comparable financial risk.
    • In the loss years for each alternative, there is no cash flow from or to the investment (i.e., the loss is due to depreciation), while in those years when the income is positive, cash flows to Heather equal the amount of the income.

    Based on these facts, compute the present value of these two investment alternatives and determine which option Heather should choose.

3. Emily has $100,000 that she wants to invest and is considering the following two options:

    Decision Making

    • Option A: Investment in Redbird Mutual Fund, which is expected to produce interest income of $8,000 per year.
    • Option B: Investment in Cardinal Limited Partnership (buys, sells, and operates wine vineyards). Emily's share of the partnership's ordinary income and loss over the next three years would be as follows:

Year	Income (Loss)
1	($ 8,000)
2	(2,000)
3	34,000

    Emily is interested in the after-tax effects of these alternatives over a three-year horizon. Assume that Emily's investment portfolio produces ample passive income to offset any passive losses that may be generated. Her cost of capital is 8% (the present value factors are .92593, .85734, and .79383), and she is in the 28% tax bracket. The two investment alternatives possess equal growth potential and comparable financial risk. Based on these facts, compute the present value of these two investment alternatives and determine which option Emily should choose.

Research Problems

THOMSON REUTERS

CHECKPOINT®

Note: Solutions to Research Problems can be prepared by using the **Checkpoint®** **Student Edition** online research product, which is available to accompany this text. It is also possible to prepare solutions to the Research Problems by using tax research materials found in a standard tax library.

Research Problem 1. Esther owns a large home on the East Coast. Her home is surrounded by large, mature oak trees that significantly increase the value of her home. In August 2013, a hurricane damaged many of the trees surrounding her home. In September 2013, Esther engaged a local arborist to evaluate and treat the trees, but five of the largest trees were seriously weakened by the storm. These trees died from disease in 2014. Esther has ascertained that the amount of the casualty loss from the death of the five trees is $25,000; however, she is uncertain in which year to deduct this loss. Discuss whether the casualty loss should be deducted in the calculation of Esther's 2013 or 2014 taxable income.

Research Problem 2. Five years ago Bridget decided to purchase a limited partnership interest in a fast-food restaurant conveniently located near the campus of Southeast State University. The general partner of the restaurant venture promised her that the investment would prove to be a winner. During the process of capitalizing the business, $2 million was borrowed from Northside Bank; however, each of the partners was required to pledge as collateral personal assets to satisfy the bank loan in the event the restaurant defaulted. Bridget pledged shares of publicly traded stock (worth $200,000, basis of $75,000) to satisfy the bank's requirement.

The restaurant did a good business until just recently, when flagrant health code violations were discovered and widely publicized by the media. As a result, business has declined to a point where the restaurant's continued existence is doubtful. In addition, the $2 million loan is now due for payment. Because the restaurant cannot pay, the bank has called for the collateral provided by the partners to be used to satisfy the debt. Bridget sells the pledged stock for $200,000 and forwards the proceeds to the bank. Bridget believes that her share of the restaurant's current and suspended passive losses can offset the $125,000 gain from the stock sale. As a result, after netting the passive losses against the gain, none of the gain is subject to tax.

How do you react to Bridget's position?

Communications

Research Problem 3. David Drayer (2632 Holkham Drive, Lewisburg, PA 17837) is the lead partner in a local accounting firm whose practice consists of tax consulting and compliance. The firm also serves clients by providing write-up and payroll processing services. As his firm has grown, David has developed various ways to build its business.

David and his wife, Judy, created DJ Partnership to purchase an office building where David moved his practice. Because the building is larger than what the practice currently needs, space is rented to other tax practitioners. In addition to providing office space, the partnership offers professional and administrative services on an exclusive basis to the tenants. These services include secretarial support, a telephone answering service, tax professionals available for special projects, access to a tax research library, computer hardware technology, and miscellaneous administrative support. DJ Partnership considers its primary activity to be providing professional and administrative services to its tenants rather than being a lessor.

Because of the attractiveness of the services offered to its tenants, the building is fully leased. In the first year, Judy works full-time at the partnership and David commits about 550 hours to its operations. For the first year, the partnership incurs a tax loss of $60,000. Without considering the impact of the loss, David and Judy's AGI is $175,000. Write a letter to David in which you advise him on the deductibility of the $60,000 loss for Federal income tax purposes. Because David is a tax professional, your letter can include technical language and references to tax law sources.

Partial list of research aids:
Reg. § 1.469–1T(e)(3)(ii).

Use the tax resources of the Internet to address the following questions. Do not restrict your search to the Web, but include a review of newsgroups and general reference materials, practitioner sites and resources, primary sources of the tax law, chat rooms and discussion groups, and other opportunities.

Internet Activity

Research Problem 4. Find a newspaper article that discusses tax planning for casualty losses when a disaster area designation is made. Does the article convey the pertinent tax rules correctly? Then list all of the locations identified by the President as Federal disaster areas in the last two years.

Research Problem 5. Investment advisers and tax professionals are continuously striving to create sophisticated transactions and investment vehicles (i.e., tax-advantaged investments) that are designed to provide economic benefits to investors by reducing their taxes. These professionals might like to patent such schemes. Identify whether patenting a tax shelter is a legal possibility.

Research Problem 6. In a recent Tax Court decision, a taxpayer argued that he met the 750-hour requirement for materially participating in his rental real estate activities. The taxpayer, James Moss, asserted that because the time he spent "on call" related to his rental properties, the hours should be included in the 750-hour calculation. Moss claimed that whenever he was not at his regular job, he was on call because he could have been called to deal with a problem at the rental properties at any time.

Go to the U.S. Tax Court website (**www.ustaxcourt.gov**) and find the Moss decision. What did the Tax Court conclude about including "on-call" hours in the 750-hour requirement?

part 3

PROPERTY TRANSACTIONS

Part 3 presents the tax treatment of sales, exchanges, and other dispositions of property. Included are the determination of the realized gain or loss, recognized gain or loss, and the classification of the recognized gain or loss as capital or ordinary. The topic of basis is evaluated both in terms of its effect on the calculation of the gain or loss and in terms of the determination of the basis of any contemporaneous or related subsequent acquisitions of property.

Dennis Flaherty/Photographer's Choice/Getty Images

CHAPTER

7

Property Transactions: Basis, Gain and Loss, and Nontaxable Exchanges

LEARNING OBJECTIVES: *After completing Chapter 7, you should be able to:*

LO.1 **State and explain the computation of realized gain or loss on property dispositions.**

LO.2 **Distinguish between realized and recognized gain or loss.**

LO.3 **Review and illustrate how basis is determined for various methods of asset acquisition.**

LO.4 **Describe various loss disallowance provisions.**

LO.5 **Apply the nonrecognition provisions and basis determination rules for like-kind exchanges.**

LO.6 **Explain the nonrecognition provisions available on the involuntary conversion of property.**

LO.7 **Identify other nonrecognition provisions contained in the Code.**

TAX TALK *To base all of your decisions on tax consequences is not necessarily to maintain the proper balance and perspective on what you are doing.* —BARBER CONABLE

© iStockphoto.com/Nikki Bidgood

CALCULATING BASIS AND RECOGNIZED GAIN FOR PROPERTY TRANSACTIONS

Alice owns land that she received from her father 10 years ago as a gift. The land was purchased by her father in 1991 for $2,000 and was worth $10,000 at the time of the gift. Alice's father did not owe gift taxes upon making the transfer. The property is currently worth about $50,000. Alice is considering selling the land and purchasing a piece of undeveloped property in the mountains.

Alice also owns 500 shares of AppleCo stock, 300 of which were acquired as an inheritance when her grandfather died in 1996. Alice's grandfather paid $12,000 for the shares, and the shares were worth $30,000 at the time of his death. The other 200 shares of AppleCo were purchased by Alice two months ago for $28,000. The stock is currently worth $120 per share, and Alice is considering selling the shares.

In addition, Alice owns a house that she inherited from her grandmother two years ago. Her grandmother lived in the house for over 50 years. Alice has many fond memories associated with the house because she spent many summer vacations there, and she has been reluctant to sell the house. However, a developer has recently purchased several homes in the area and has offered Alice $600,000 for the property. Based on the estate tax return, the fair market value of the house at the date of her grandmother's death was $475,000. According to her grandmother's attorney, her grandmother's basis for the house was $275,000. Alice is considering selling the house. She expects any selling expenses to be minimal because she already has identified a buyer for the property.

The building Alice used in her business was destroyed by a fire on October 5, 2014. Fortunately, the building (adjusted basis of $50,000) was insured and on November 17, 2014, she receives an insurance reimbursement of $100,000 for the loss. Alice intends to invest $80,000 in a new building and use the other $20,000 of insurance proceeds to pay off credit card debt.

Alice has come to you for tax advice with respect to the property she owns. What is the recognized gain or loss for the land, stock, and house if they are sold? What tax consequences arise with respect to the involuntary conversion of her business building? Can Alice avoid paying taxes on any of the sales? Alice's objectives are to minimize the recognition of any realized gain and to maximize the recognition of any realized loss.

Read the chapter and formulate your response.

T his chapter and the following chapter are concerned with the income tax consequences of property transactions, including the sale or other disposition of property. Specifically, the next questions considered pertain to the sale or other disposition of property:

- Is there a realized gain or loss?
- If so, is that gain or loss recognized for tax purposes?
- If that gain or loss is recognized, is it ordinary or capital?
- What is the basis of any replacement property that is acquired?

This chapter discusses the determination of realized and recognized gain or loss and the basis of property. The next chapter covers the classification of recognized gain or loss as ordinary or capital.

For the most part, the rules discussed in Chapters 7 and 8 apply to all types of taxpayers. Individuals, partnerships, closely held corporations, limited liability companies, and publicly held corporations all own assets for use in business activities or as investments in entities that themselves conduct business activities. Individuals, however, are unique among taxpayers because they also own assets that are used in daily life and have no significant business or investment component. Because of that possibility, some property transaction concepts apply somewhat differently to individual taxpayers depending upon how a person uses the specific asset in question. Nevertheless, the material that follows pertains to taxpayers generally except where otherwise noted.

7-1 DETERMINATION OF GAIN OR LOSS

7-1a Realized Gain or Loss

LO.1

State and explain the computation of realized gain or loss on property dispositions.

For tax purposes, gain or loss is the difference between the *amount realized* from the sale or other disposition of property and the property's *adjusted basis* on the date of disposition. If the amount realized exceeds the property's adjusted basis, the result is a **realized gain**. Conversely, if the property's adjusted basis exceeds the amount realized, the result is a **realized loss**.[1]

Example 1	Lavender, Inc., sells Swan Corporation stock with an adjusted basis of $3,000 for $5,000. Lavender's realized gain is $2,000. If Lavender had sold the stock for $2,000, it would have had a realized loss of $1,000.

Sale or Other Disposition

The term *sale or other disposition* is defined broadly to include virtually any disposition of property. Thus, trade-ins, casualties, condemnations, thefts, and bond retirements are all treated as dispositions of property. The most common disposition of property is a sale or an exchange. Usually, the key factor in determining whether a disposition has taken place is whether an identifiable event has occurred[2] as opposed to a mere fluctuation in the value of the property.[3]

Example 2	Heron & Associates owns Tan Corporation stock that cost $3,000. The stock has appreciated in value by $2,000 since Heron purchased it. Heron has no realized gain because mere fluctuation in value is not a disposition or an identifiable event for tax purposes. Nor would Heron have a realized loss had the stock declined in value.

---

[1]§ 1001(a) and Reg. § 1.1001–1(a).
[2]Reg. § 1.1001–1(c)(1).

[3]*Lynch v. Turrish*, 1 USTC ¶18, 3 AFTR 2986, 38 S.Ct. 537 (USSC, 1918).

Amount Realized

The **amount realized** from a sale or other disposition of property is the sum of any money received plus the fair market value of other property received. The amount realized also includes any real property taxes treated as imposed on the seller that are actually paid by the buyer.[4] The reason for including these taxes in the amount realized is that by paying the taxes, the purchaser is, in effect, paying an additional amount to the seller for the property.

The amount realized also includes any liability on the property disposed of, such as a mortgage debt, if the buyer assumes the mortgage or the property is sold subject to the mortgage.[5] The amount of the liability is included in the amount realized, even if the debt is nonrecourse and even if the amount of the debt is greater than the fair market value of the mortgaged property.[6]

Bunting & Co. sells property to Orange, Inc., for $50,000 cash. There is a $20,000 mortgage on the property. Bunting's amount realized from the sale is $70,000 if Orange assumes the mortgage or takes the property subject to the mortgage.	**Example 3**

The **fair market value** of property received in a sale or other disposition has been defined by the courts as the price at which the property will change hands between a willing seller and a willing buyer when neither is compelled to sell or buy.[7] Fair market value is determined by considering the relevant factors in each case.[8] An expert appraiser is often required to evaluate these factors in arriving at fair market value. When the fair market value of the property received cannot be determined, the value of the property given up by the taxpayer may be used.[9]

In calculating the amount realized, selling expenses (such as advertising, commissions, and legal fees) relating to the disposition are deducted. The amount realized is the net amount the taxpayer received directly or indirectly, in the form of cash or anything else of value, from the disposition of the property.

Adjusted Basis

The **adjusted basis** of property disposed of is the property's original basis adjusted to the date of disposition.[10] Original basis is the cost or other basis of the property on the date the property is acquired by the taxpayer. Considerations involving original basis are discussed later in this chapter. *Capital additions* increase and *recoveries of capital* decrease the original basis so that on the date of disposition, the adjusted basis reflects the unrecovered cost or other basis of the property.[11] Adjusted basis is determined as follows:

  Cost (or other adjusted basis) on date of acquisition
  + Capital additions
  − Capital recoveries
  = Adjusted basis on date of disposition

Capital Additions

Capital additions include the cost of capital improvements and betterments made to the property by the taxpayer. These expenditures are distinguishable from expenditures for the ordinary repair and maintenance of the property, which are neither capitalized nor added to the original basis (refer to Chapter 5). The latter

---

[4]§ 1001(b) and Reg. § 1.1001–1(b).
[5]*Crane v. Comm.*, 47–1 USTC ¶9217, 35 AFTR 776, 67 S.Ct. 1047 (USSC, 1947). Although a legal distinction exists between the direct assumption of a mortgage and the taking of property subject to a mortgage, the tax consequences in calculating the amount realized are the same.
[6]*Comm. v. Tufts*, 83–1 USTC ¶9328, 51 AFTR 2d 83–1132, 103 S.Ct. 1826 (USSC, 1983).

[7]*Comm. v. Marshman*, 60–2 USTC ¶9484, 5 AFTR 2d 1528, 279 F.2d 27 (CA–6, 1960).
[8]*O'Malley v. Ames*, 52–1 USTC ¶9361, 42 AFTR 19, 197 F.2d 256 (CA–8, 1952).
[9]*U.S. v. Davis*, 62–2 USTC ¶9509, 9 AFTR 2d 1625, 82 S.Ct. 1190 (USSC, 1962).
[10]§ 1011(a) and Reg. § 1.1011–1.
[11]§ 1016(a) and Reg. § 1.1016–1.

expenditures are deductible in the current taxable year if they are related to business or income-producing property. Amounts representing real property taxes treated as imposed on the seller but paid or assumed by the buyer are part of the cost of the property.[12] Any liability on property that is assumed by the buyer is also included in the buyer's original basis of the property. The same rule applies if property is acquired subject to a liability. In a similar fashion, amortization of the discount on bonds increases the adjusted basis of the bonds.[13]

Example 4

Bluebird Corporation purchased some manufacturing equipment for $25,000. Whether Bluebird uses $25,000 from the business's cash account to pay for this equipment or uses $5,000 from that account and borrows the remaining $20,000, the basis of this equipment will be the same—namely, $25,000. Moreover, it does not matter whether Bluebird borrowed the $20,000 from the equipment's manufacturer, from a local bank, or from any other lender.

Capital Recoveries

Capital recoveries decrease the adjusted basis of property. The prominent types of capital recoveries are discussed below.

Depreciation and Cost Recovery Allowances. The original basis of depreciable property is reduced by the annual depreciation charges (or cost recovery allowances) while the property is held by the taxpayer. The amount of depreciation that is subtracted from the original basis is the greater of the *allowed* or *allowable* depreciation calculated on an annual basis.[14] In most circumstances, the allowed and allowable depreciation amounts are the same (refer to Chapter 5).

Casualties and Thefts. A casualty or theft may result in the reduction of the adjusted basis of property.[15] The adjusted basis is reduced by the amount of the deductible loss. In addition, the adjusted basis is reduced by the amount of insurance proceeds received. However, the receipt of insurance proceeds may result in a recognized gain rather than a deductible loss. The gain increases the adjusted basis of the property.[16]

Example 5

An insured truck owned by Falcon Corporation is destroyed in an accident. At the time of the accident, the adjusted basis was $8,000, and the fair market value was $6,500. Falcon receives insurance proceeds of $6,500. The amount of the casualty loss is $1,500 ($6,500 insurance proceeds − $8,000 adjusted basis). The truck's adjusted basis becomes $0 ($8,000 pre-accident adjusted basis, reduced by the $1,500 casualty loss and the $6,500 of insurance proceeds received).

Example 6

Osprey, Inc., owned an insured truck that was destroyed in an accident. At the time of the accident, the adjusted basis and fair market value of the truck were $6,500 and $8,000, respectively. Osprey receives insurance proceeds of $8,000. The amount of the casualty *gain* is $1,500 ($8,000 insurance proceeds − $6,500 adjusted basis). The truck's adjusted basis is increased by the $1,500 casualty gain and is reduced by the $8,000 of insurance proceeds received ($6,500 basis before casualty + $1,500 casualty gain − $8,000 insurance proceeds = $0 ending adjusted basis).

Certain Corporate Distributions. A corporate distribution to a shareholder that is not taxable is treated as a return of capital, and it reduces the basis of the shareholder's stock in the corporation.[17] Once the basis of the stock is reduced to zero, the amount of any subsequent distributions is a capital gain if the stock in the hands of the shareholder is a capital asset. See Chapter 13.

---

[12]Reg. §§ 1.1001–1(b)(2) and 1.1012–1(b). Refer to Chapter 5 for a discussion of this subject.

[13]See Chapter 4 for a discussion of bond discount and the related amortization.

[14]§ 1016(a)(2) and Reg. § 1.1016–3(a)(1)(i).

[15]Refer to Chapter 6 for the discussion of casualties and thefts.

[16]Reg. § 1.1016–6(a).

[17]§ 1016(a)(4) and Reg. § 1.1016–5(a).

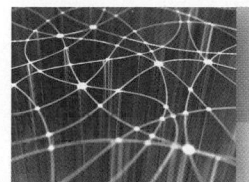

BRIDGE DISCIPLINE   Bridge to Financial Accounting

Certain property transactions discussed later in this chapter are treated differently for tax purposes than for financial accounting purposes. For example, the category of transactions generally referred to as "nontaxable exchanges," such as like-kind exchanges and involuntary conversions, gives taxpayers the opportunity to defer the recognition of gain on the disposition of property in qualifying transactions. The gains or losses deferred under tax law, however, are not deferred for financial reporting purposes. Instead, the actual gain or loss realized is reflected in the entity's financial reports.

Identifying and calculating the book-tax differences that arise from *taxable* dispositions of certain other property may not be so easy. For example, as discussed in

Chapter 5, cost recovery (i.e., depreciation) rules provided by the tax law specify various ways in which an asset's cost may be recovered over time. These methods often differ from the methods used to depreciate an asset for book purposes. Consequently, the annual book-tax differences in these depreciation expense calculations are noted in the financial reports. But in addition, these cumulative differences, as reflected in the accumulated depreciation account, will also produce a book-tax difference on the asset's disposition. That is, because an asset's accumulated depreciation may differ for book and tax purposes, its adjusted basis will also differ. Consequently, when the asset is sold, the amount of gain or loss for book purposes will differ from that recognized for tax purposes.

© iStockphoto.com/enot-poloskun

Amortizable Bond Premium. The basis in a bond purchased at a premium is reduced by the amortizable portion of the bond premium.[18] Investors in taxable bonds may *elect* to amortize the bond premium.[19] The amount of the amortized premium on taxable bonds is allowed as an interest deduction. Therefore, the election enables the taxpayer to take an annual interest deduction to offset ordinary income in exchange for a larger capital gain or smaller capital loss on the disposition of the bond (due to the basis reduction).

In-depth coverage can be found on this book's companion website: **www.cengagebrain.com**    | Digging Deeper

In contrast to the treatment of taxable bonds, the premium on tax-exempt bonds *must* be amortized, and no interest deduction is permitted. Furthermore, the basis of tax-exempt bonds is reduced even though the amortization is not allowed as a deduction. No amortization deduction is permitted on tax-exempt bonds because the interest income is exempt from tax, and the amortization of the bond premium merely represents an adjustment of the effective amount of such income.

Navy, Inc., purchases Eagle Corporation taxable bonds with a face value of $100,000 for $110,000, thus paying a premium of $10,000. The annual interest rate is 7%, and the bonds mature 10 years from the date of purchase. The annual interest income is $7,000 (7% × $100,000). If Navy elects to amortize the bond premium, the $10,000 premium is deducted over the 10-year period. Navy's basis for the bonds is reduced each year by the amount of the amortization deduction. If the bonds were tax-exempt, amortization of the bond premium and the basis adjustment would be mandatory and no deduction would be allowed for the amortization.

Example 7

Easements. An easement is the legal right to use another's land for a special purpose. Historically, easements were commonly used to obtain rights-of-way for utility lines, roads, and pipelines. In recent years, grants of conservation easements have

---

[18]§ 1016(a)(5) and Reg. § 1.1016–5(b). The accounting treatment of bond premium amortization is the same as for tax purposes. The amortization results in a decrease in the bond investment account.

[19]§ 171(c).

TAX IN THE NEWS   A Hard Way to Avoid the Disallowance of a Loss

One of the results of the bursting of the housing bubble has been to create "accidental landlords." These owners intended to sell but were unable to find a buyer for the "right price." Because of continuing low housing values in certain parts of the country, they have decided to rent their homes for the time being. By doing so, they hope the fair market value will increase so that a later sale will generate greater revenue, thereby avoiding any loss. Moreover, a loss on the sale of a personal residence is not deductible for Federal income tax purposes.

But such accidental landlords should be aware of the potential negative consequences that could result, including:

- The damage caused by unruly tenants.
- The legal responsibilities involved in being a landlord.

- The maintenance and repair costs associated with renting property.
- Other unforeseen headaches.

Perhaps the worst scenario is that the house does not increase in value and the homeowner eventually sells at a price that is the same as or less than what could have been obtained originally. The only positive result of this situation is that any loss that occurs after the conversion to rental property is now deductible for tax purposes. Note that the loss that occurred prior to conversion to rental property is still nondeductible.

Source: Based on "Accidental Landlords," *Wall Street Journal,* December 12, 2011, p. R7; "Accidental Landlords: The Next Real Estate Nightmare or Effective Housing Solution?" *Forbes,* May 29, 2012.

become a popular means of obtaining charitable contribution deductions and reducing the value of real estate for transfer tax (i.e., estate and gift) purposes. Likewise, scenic easements are used to reduce the value of land as assessed for ad valorem property tax purposes.

If the taxpayer does not retain any right to the use of the land, all of the basis is assigned to the easement. However, if the use of the land is only partially restricted, an allocation of some of the basis to the easement is appropriate.

LO.2

Distinguish between realized and recognized gain or loss.

7-1b Recognized Gain or Loss

Recognized gain is the amount of the realized gain that is included in the taxpayer's gross income.[20] A **recognized loss**, on the other hand, is the amount of a realized loss that is deductible for tax purposes.[21] As a general rule, the entire amount of a realized gain or loss is recognized when it is realized.[22]

Concept Summary 7.1 summarizes the realized gain or loss and recognized gain or loss concepts.

7-1c Nonrecognition of Gain or Loss

In certain cases, a realized gain or loss is not recognized upon the sale or other disposition of property. One such case involves nontaxable exchanges, which are covered later in this chapter. In addition, realized losses from the sale or exchange of property between certain related parties are not recognized.[23]

Dispositions of Personal-Use Assets

For individual taxpayers, special rules apply to *personal-use* assets (i.e., assets such as a residence or an automobile that are not used in any business or investment activity). A loss from the sale, exchange, or condemnation of such assets is not recognized for tax purposes. An exception exists for casualty or theft losses from personal-use assets (refer to Chapter 6). In contrast, any gain realized from the disposition of personal-use assets is generally taxable.

---

[20]§ 61(a)(3) and Reg. § 1.61–6(a).
[21]§ 165(a) and Reg. § 1.165–1(a).

[22]§ 1001(c) and Reg. § 1.1002–1(a).
[23]§ 267(a)(1).

CONCEPT SUMMARY 7.1

Recognized Gain or Loss

© iStockphoto.com/Andrey Prokhorov

> **Example 8**
>
> Freda sells an automobile, which she has held exclusively for personal use, for $6,000. The adjusted basis of the automobile is $5,000. Freda has a realized and recognized gain of $1,000. If she sold this automobile for $4,500, she would have a realized loss of $500, but the loss would not be recognized for tax purposes.

In-depth coverage can be found on this book's companion website: **www.cengagebrain.com**   **2** **Digging Deeper**

7-2 BASIS CONSIDERATIONS

7-2a Determination of Cost Basis

As noted earlier, the basis of property is generally the property's cost. Cost is the amount paid for the property in cash or other property.[24] This general rule follows logically from the recovery of capital doctrine; that is, the cost or other basis of property is to be recovered tax-free by the taxpayer.

A *bargain purchase* of property is an exception to the general rule for determining basis. A bargain purchase may result when an employer transfers property to an employee at less than the property's fair market value (as compensation for services) or when a corporation transfers property to a shareholder at less than the property's fair market value (a dividend). These transfers create taxable income for the purchaser equal to the difference between fair market value and purchase price. The basis of property acquired in a bargain purchase is the property's fair market value.[25] If the basis of the property were not increased by the bargain amount, the taxpayer would be taxed on this amount again at disposition.

LO.3

Review and illustrate how basis is determined for various methods of asset acquisition.

---

[24]§ 1012 and Reg. § 1.1012–1(a).

[25]Reg. §§ 1.61–2(d)(2)(i) and 1.301–1(j). See the discussion in Chapter 11 of the circumstances under which what appears to be a taxable bargain purchase is an excludible qualified employee discount.

| **Example 9** | Wade buys land from his employer for $10,000. The fair market value of the land is $15,000. Wade must include the $5,000 difference between the cost and the fair market value of the land in his gross income. The bargain element represents additional compensation to Wade. His basis for the land is $15,000, the land's fair market value. |

Identification Problems

Sometimes, it can be difficult to determine the cost of an asset being sold. This problem is frequently encountered in sales of corporate stock, because a taxpayer may purchase separate lots of a company's stock on different dates and at different prices. When the stock is sold, if the taxpayer cannot identify the specific shares being sold (specific identification), the stock sold is determined on a first-in, first-out (FIFO) basis. Thus, the holding period and cost of the stock sold are determined by referring to the purchase date and cost of the first lot of stock acquired.[26] But if the stock being sold can be adequately identified, then the basis and holding period of the specific stock sold are used in determining the nature and amount of gain or loss.[27] Thus, to avoid FIFO treatment when the sold securities are held by a broker, it is often necessary to provide specific instructions and receive written confirmation of the securities being sold.

| **Example 10** | Pelican, Inc., purchases 100 shares of Olive Corporation stock on July 1, 2012, for $5,000 ($50 a share) and another 100 shares of Olive stock on July 1, 2013, for $6,000 ($60 a share). Pelican sells 50 shares of the stock on January 2, 2014. The cost of the stock sold, assuming that Pelican cannot adequately identify the shares, is $50 a share (from shares purchased on July 1, 2012), or $2,500. This is the cost Pelican will compare with the amount realized in determining the gain or loss from the sale. |

Allocation Problems

When a taxpayer acquires *several assets in a lump-sum purchase*, the total cost must be allocated among the individual assets.[28] Allocation is necessary for several reasons:

- Some of the assets acquired may be depreciable (e.g., buildings), while others may not be (e.g., land).
- Only a portion of the assets acquired may be sold.
- Some of the assets may be capital or depreciable assets that receive special tax treatment upon subsequent sale or other disposition.

The lump-sum cost is allocated on the basis of the fair market values of the individual assets acquired.

| **Example 11** | Magenta Corporation purchases a building and land for $800,000. Because of the depressed nature of the industry in which the seller was operating, Magenta was able to negotiate a very favorable purchase price. Appraisals of the individual assets indicate that the fair market value of the building is $600,000 and that of the land is $400,000. Magenta's basis for the building is $480,000 [($600,000/$1,000,000) × $800,000], and its basis for the land is $320,000 [($400,000/$1,000,000) × $800,000]. |

If a business is purchased and **goodwill** is involved, a special allocation applies. Initially, the purchase price is assigned to the assets, excluding goodwill, to the extent of their total fair market value. This assigned amount is allocated among the assets on the basis of the fair market value of the individual assets acquired. Goodwill is then assigned the residual amount of the purchase price. The resultant allocation is applicable to both the buyer and the seller.[29]

---

[26]*Kluger Associates, Inc.*, 69 T.C. 925 (1978).
[27]Reg. § 1.1012–1(c)(1).
[28]Reg. § 1.61–6(a).

[29]§ 1060. The classification of the seller's recognized gain associated with the goodwill is discussed in Chapter 8.

TAX IN THE NEWS Brokers Provide Cost Basis Data to Taxpayers (and the IRS)

Brokers and others in similar enterprises are now required to provide investors with an annual report on the cost basis of their stocks sold during the year (to be included on Form 1099–B and reported to the IRS). The new reporting rules, part of the Emergency Economic Stabilization Act of 2008, are being phased in over several years: banks and brokers were required to begin tracking and reporting the cost basis of stocks purchased in 2011 or later years and held in taxable accounts [so, for example, IRAs or § 401(k) accounts are not covered]. Mutual funds, dividend reinvestment plans, and certain exchange-traded funds are subject to the rules if purchased on or after January 1, 2012. Debt instruments, options, and other securities are covered if purchased on or after January 1, 2013.

According to the legislation, the primary reason for the requirement is to enable taxpayers to use the correct basis in calculating the gain or loss on the sale of the stock. In the simplest situation in which only a single lot of the stock was purchased, the taxpayer still may not have this information available when the stock is sold—perhaps many years later. Even if the investor maintains good records, nontaxable stock dividends, stock splits, and spin-offs may create confusion and result in unreliable data being used to determine the basis. For the investor who has multiple purchases of a stock, the likelihood of making an incorrect determination of cost basis is even greater.

A secondary reason for the reporting requirement is to generate more revenue for the Treasury. The government believes that taxpayers are knowingly underreporting capital gains on the sale of securities. The Treasury believes that it will collect an additional $6 billion to $9 billion per year as a result of this requirement. Tax professionals will also benefit by providing consulting related to the requirements—some estimate the related compliance costs will exceed $500 million per year.

As a result of these requirements, the primary burden for determining cost basis is placed on the broker. As a practical matter, however, the ultimate responsibility for reporting the information correctly remains on the taxpayer (and his or her tax adviser).

Sources: Based on "Cost Basis Reporting: Why Corporate Issuers (and Not Just Brokers) Should Care," *A&M Tax Advisor Weekly*, **www.taxand.com**, July 14, 2011; Laura Saunders, "When Your Broker 'Outs' You," *Wall Street Journal*, March 2, 2013, p. D3; Tara Siegel Bernard, "New Tax Laws Take Guesswork Out of Investment Tax Liability," *New York Times*, March 15, 2013.

Example 12

Roadrunner, Inc., sells its business to Coyote Corporation. The two companies agree that the values of the specific assets are as follows:

Marketable securities	$ 5,000
Inventory	35,000
Building	500,000
Land	200,000

After negotiations, Roadrunner and Coyote agree on a sales price of $1 million. Applying the residual method, the residual purchase price is allocated to goodwill, resulting in the following basis of assets to Coyote Corporation:

Marketable securities	$ 5,000
Inventory	35,000
Building	500,000
Land	200,000
Goodwill	260,000

In the case of *nontaxable stock dividends*, the allocation depends on whether the dividend is a common stock dividend on common stock or a preferred stock dividend on common stock. If the stock dividend is common on common, the cost of the original common shares is allocated to the total shares owned after the dividend.[30]

---

[30]§§ 305(a) and 307(a). The holding period of the new shares includes the holding period of the old shares. § 1223(5) and Reg. § 1.1223–1(e). See Chapter 8 for a discussion of the importance of the holding period.

Example 13

Yellow, Inc., owns 100 shares of Sparrow Corporation common stock for which it paid $1,100. Yellow receives a 10% common stock dividend, giving it a new total of 110 shares. Before the stock dividend, Yellow's basis was $11 per share ($1,100 ÷ 100 shares). The basis of each share after the stock dividend is $10 ($1,100 ÷ 110 shares).

If the nontaxable stock dividend is preferred stock on common, the cost of the original common shares is allocated between the common and preferred shares on the basis of their relative fair market values on the date of distribution.[31]

Example 14

Brown Company owns 100 shares of Cardinal Corporation common stock for which it paid $1,000. Brown receives a nontaxable stock dividend of 50 shares of preferred stock on the Cardinal common stock. The fair market values on the date of distribution of the preferred stock dividend are $30 a share for common stock and $40 a share for preferred stock.

Fair market value of common ($30 × 100 shares)	$3,000
Fair market value of preferred ($40 × 50 shares)	2,000
	$5,000
Basis of common: 3/5 × $1,000	$ 600
Basis of preferred: 2/5 × $1,000	$ 400

The basis per share for the common stock is $6 ($600/100 shares). The basis per share for the preferred stock is $8 ($400/50 shares).

7-2b Gift Basis

Although business entities can neither make nor receive gratuitous transfers, ownership interests in such entities are frequently the subject of lifetime and testamentary gifts. Partnership interests, stock in closely or publicly held corporations, and other assets are regularly passed from one generation of owners to another for a variety of family and business reasons. Special basis rules apply to such transfers.

When a taxpayer receives property as a gift, there is no cost to the donee (recipient). Thus, under the cost basis provision, the donee's basis would be zero. With a zero basis, if the donee sold the property, the entire amount realized would be treated as taxable gain. Instead, the Code[32] assigns a basis to the property received that depends upon the following:

- The date of the gift.
- The basis of the property to the donor.
- The fair market value of the property.
- The amount of the gift tax paid, if any.

Gift Basis Rules If No Gift Tax Is Paid

If a property's fair market value on the date of the gift exceeds the donor's basis in the property, the donor's basis carries over to the new owner.[33] This basis is called a *carryover basis* and is used in determining the donee's gain or loss.

THE BIG PICTURE

Example 15

Return to the facts of *The Big Picture* on p. 7-1. Alice's father purchased the land in 1991 for $2,000. He gave the land to Alice 10 years ago, when the fair market value was $10,000. No gift tax was paid on the transfer. Alice is considering selling the land, which is currently worth $50,000. If she sells the property for $50,000, Alice will have a realized gain of $48,000 ($50,000 amount realized − $2,000 basis in the land).

---

[31]Reg. § 1.307–1(a).

[32]§ 1015(a).

[33]§ 1015(a) and Reg. § 1.1015–1(a)(1). See Reg. § 1.1015–1(a)(3) for cases in which the facts necessary to determine the donor's adjusted basis are

unknown. See Example 19 for the effect of depreciation deductions by the donee.

If the property's fair market value on the date of the gift is *lower* than the donor's basis in the property, the donee's basis cannot be determined until the donee disposes of the property. For the purpose of determining *gain*, the donor's basis will carry over, as in the preceding example. But for determining *loss*, the property's basis will be its fair market value when the gift was made.

THE BIG PICTURE

Example 16

Return to the facts of *The Big Picture* on p. 7-1. Instead, assume that Alice's father had purchased the land in 1991 for $12,000. He gave the land to Alice 10 years ago, when the fair market value was $10,000. No gift tax was paid on the transfer. If Alice sells the property for $50,000, she has a realized gain of $38,000 ($50,000 amount realized − $12,000 basis in the land). However, if the property has declined in value because of the discovery of contaminants on the property and Alice is able to sell the land for only $8,000, she will realize a loss of $2,000 ($8,000 amount realized − $10,000 basis in the land).

Note that this loss basis rule prevents the donee from receiving a tax benefit from a decline in value that occurred while the donor held the property. Therefore, in the preceding example, Alice has a loss of only $2,000 rather than a loss of $4,000. The $2,000 difference represents the decline in value that occurred while Alice's father held the property. Ironically, however, a donee might be subject to income tax on the appreciation that occurred while the donor held the property, as illustrated in Example 15.

In any case, the operation of this dual basis rule produces a curious anomaly: if the sales proceeds fall *between* the donor's adjusted basis and the property's fair market value at the date of gift, no gain or loss is recognized.

THE BIG PICTURE

Example 17

Return to the facts of *The Big Picture* on p. 7-1. Instead, assume that Alice's father had purchased the land in 1991 for $12,000. He gave the land to Alice 10 years ago, when the fair market value was $10,000. No gift tax was paid on the transfer. Now Alice plans to sell the property for $11,000. To calculate gain, she would use a basis of $12,000, her father's basis. But when a $12,000 basis is compared with the $11,000 sales proceeds, a *loss* is produced. Yet in determining loss, Alice must use the property's fair market value at the date of gift—namely, $10,000. When a $10,000 basis is compared to sales proceeds of $11,000, a *gain* is produced. Accordingly, no gain or loss is recognized on this transaction.

Adjustment for Gift Tax

Because of the size of the unified estate and gift tax exemption ($5.34 million in 2014), basis adjustments for gift taxes paid are rare. If, however, gift taxes are paid by the donor, the portion of the gift tax paid that is related to any appreciation is taken into account in determining the donee's gain basis.[34]

For *gifts made before 1977*, the full amount of the gift tax paid is added to the donor's basis, with basis capped at the donor's fair market value at the date of the gift.

---

[34]§ 1015(d)(6) and Reg. § 1.1015–5(c)(2). Examples illustrating these rules can be found in Reg. § 1.1015–5(c)(5) and IRS Publication 551 (*Basis of Assets*), p. 9.

Tax Planning Strategies	GIFT PLANNING

FRAMEWORK FOCUS: TAX RATE

Strategy: Shift Net Income from High-Bracket Taxpayers to Low-Bracket Taxpayers.

FRAMEWORK FOCUS: DEDUCTIONS

Strategy: Maximize Deductible Amounts.

Gifts of *appreciated property* can produce tax savings if the donee is in a lower tax bracket than the donor. The carry-over basis rule effectively shifts the tax on the property's appreciation to the new owner, even if all of the appreciation arose while the property was owned by the donor.

On the other hand, donors should generally avoid making gifts of property that are worth less than the donor's adjusted basis (loss property). The operation of the basis rule for losses may result in either (1) a realized loss that is not deductible by either the donor or the donee or (2) reduced tax benefits when the loss is recognized by a donee facing lower marginal tax rates. Unless the property is expected to rebound in value before it is sold, a donor would be better advised to sell the property that has declined in value, deduct the resulting loss, and then transfer the proceeds to the prospective donee.

Holding Period

The **holding period** for property acquired by gift begins on the date the donor acquired the property,[35] unless the special circumstance requiring use of the property's fair market value at the date of gift applies. If so, the holding period starts on the date of the gift.[36] The significance of the holding period for capital assets is discussed in Chapter 8.

The following example summarizes the basis and holding period rules for gift property.

Example 18

Jill acquired 100 shares of Wren Corporation stock on December 30, 2011, for $40,000. On January 3 of this year, when the stock has a fair market value of $38,000, Jill gives it to Dennis and pays gift tax of $4,000. The basis is not increased by a portion of the gift tax paid because the property has not appreciated in value at the time of the gift. Therefore, Dennis's basis for determining gain is $40,000. Dennis's basis for determining loss is $38,000 (fair market value), because the fair market value on the date of the gift is less than the donor's adjusted basis.

- If Dennis sells the stock for $45,000, he has a recognized gain of $5,000. The holding period for determining whether the capital gain is short-term or long-term begins on December 30, 2011, the date Jill acquired the property.
- If Dennis sells the stock for $36,000, he has a recognized loss of $2,000. The holding period for determining whether the capital loss is short-term or long-term begins on January 3 of this year, the date of the gift.
- If Dennis sells the property for $39,000, no gain or loss is recognized because the amount realized is between the property's fair market value when given ($38,000) and the donor's adjusted basis of $40,000.

Basis for Depreciation

The basis for depreciation on depreciable gift property is the donee's basis for determining gain.[37] This rule is applicable even if the donee later sells the property at a loss and uses the property's fair market value at the date of gift in calculating the amount of the realized loss.

---

[35]§ 1223(2) and Reg. § 1.1223–1(b).
[36]Rev.Rul. 59–86, 1959–1 C.B. 209.

[37]§ 1011 and Reg. §§ 1.1011–1 and 1.167(g)–1.

> **Example 19**
>
> Vito gave a machine to Tina earlier this year. At that time, the adjusted basis was $32,000 (cost of $40,000 − accumulated depreciation of $8,000), and the fair market value was $26,000. No gift tax was due. Tina's basis for determining gain is $32,000, and her loss basis is $26,000. During this year, Tina deducts depreciation (cost recovery) of $6,400 ($32,000 × 20%). (Refer to Chapter 5 for the cost recovery tables.) At the end of this year, Tina's basis determinations are calculated as follows:
>
> | | Gain Basis | Loss Basis |
> | --- | --- | --- |
> | Donor's basis or fair market value | $32,000 | $26,000 |
> | Depreciation | (6,400) | (6,400) |
> | | $25,600 | $19,600 |

7-2c Property Acquired from a Decedent

General Rules

The basis of property acquired from a decedent is generally the property's fair market value at the date of death (referred to as the *primary valuation amount*).[38] The property's basis is the fair market value six months after the date of death if the executor or administrator of the estate *elects* the alternate valuation date for estate tax purposes. This amount is referred to as the *alternate valuation amount*.

In-depth coverage can be found on this book's companion website: **www.cengagebrain.com**   3   Digging Deeper

> **Example 20**
>
> Linda and various other family members inherited stock in a closely held corporation from Linda's father, who died earlier this year. At the date of death, her father's adjusted basis for the stock Linda inherited was $35,000. The stock's fair market value at the date of death was $50,000. The alternate valuation date was not elected. Linda's basis for income tax purposes is $50,000. This is commonly referred to as a *stepped-up basis*. If, instead, the stock's fair market value at the date of death was $20,000, Linda's basis would be $20,000. This is commonly referred to as a *stepped-down basis*.

THE BIG PICTURE

> **Example 21**
>
> Return to the facts of *The Big Picture* on p. 7-1. Alice owns 500 shares of AppleCo stock, 300 of which were inherited from her grandfather. Her grandfather's cost basis in the stock was $12,000 (i.e., its purchase price), but the shares were worth $30,000 at the time of his death. Alice purchased the other 200 shares for $28,000. Therefore, the basis in her 500 AppleCo shares is $58,000: the 300 shares received as an inheritance take a stepped-up basis of $30,000, and the 200 shares purchased take a cost basis of $28,000.

No estate tax return must be filed for estates below a threshold amount (refer to Chapter 1). In such cases, the alternate valuation date and amount are not available. Even if an estate tax return is filed and the executor elects the alternate valuation date, the six-months-after-death date is available only for property that the

---

[38]§ 1014(a) and § 1022.

executor has not distributed before this date. For any property distributed or otherwise disposed of by the executor during the six-month period preceding the alternate valuation date, the adjusted basis to the beneficiary will equal the fair market value on the date of distribution or other disposition.[39]

The alternate valuation date can be elected *only if*, as a result of the election, *both* the value of the gross estate and the estate tax liability are lower than they would have been if the primary valuation date had been used. This provision prevents the alternate valuation election from being used to increase the basis of the property to the beneficiary for income tax purposes without simultaneously increasing the estate tax liability (because of estate tax deductions or credits).[40]

Example 22	Nancy inherited investment real estate from her father, who died earlier this year. Her father's adjusted basis for the property at the date of death was $650,000. The property's fair market value was $5,750,000 at the date of death and $5,760,000 six months after death. The alternate valuation date cannot be elected because the value of the gross estate has increased during the six-month period. Nancy's basis for income tax purposes is $5,750,000.

Example 23	Assume the same facts as in Example 22, except that the property's fair market value six months after death was $5,745,000. If the executor elects the alternate valuation date, Nancy's basis for income tax purposes is $5,745,000.

Example 24	Assume the same facts as in Example 23, except that the property is distributed four months after the date of the decedent's death. At the distribution date, the property's fair market value is $5,747,500. Because the executor elected the alternate valuation date, Nancy's basis for income tax purposes is $5,747,500.

Digging Deeper   4   In-depth coverage can be found on this book's companion website: **www.cengagebrain.com**

Tax Planning Strategies   PROPERTY FROM A DECEDENT

FRAMEWORK FOCUS: INCOME

Strategy: Avoid Income Recognition.

FRAMEWORK FOCUS: DEDUCTIONS

Strategy: Maximize Deductible Amounts.

If a taxpayer *retains appreciated property* until death, the property's basis will be "stepped up" to its fair market value at that time. Thus, no income tax will be paid on the property's appreciation by either the former owner (the decedent) or the new owner (the heir).

On the other hand, *depreciated property should be sold* prior to death. Otherwise, the property's basis in the heir's hands will be its declined fair market value, and neither the decedent nor the heir will be able to deduct the loss that occurred while the property was owned by the decedent.

Holding Period of Property Acquired from a Decedent

The holding period of property acquired from a decedent is *deemed to be long-term* (held for the required long-term holding period). This provision applies regardless of whether the property is disposed of at a gain or at a loss.[41]

[39] § 2032(a)(1) and Rev.Rul. 56–60, 1956–1 C.B. 443.
[40] § 2032(c).
[41] § 1223(11).

7-2d Disallowed Losses

Related Taxpayers

Section 267 provides that realized losses from sales or exchanges of property between certain related parties are not recognized. This loss disallowance provision applies to several types of related-party transactions.[42] The most common involve (1) members of a family and (2) an individual and a corporation in which the individual owns, directly or indirectly, more than 50 percent in value of the corporation's outstanding stock. Section 707 provides a similar loss disallowance provision where the related parties are a partner and a partnership in which the partner owns, directly or indirectly, more than 50 percent of the capital interests or profits interests in the partnership. Neither provision, however, prevents the recognition of *gains* between related parties. The rules governing the relationships covered by § 267 were discussed in Chapter 5.

If income-producing or business property is transferred to a related party and a loss is disallowed, the basis of the property to the recipient is the property's cost to the transferee. However, if a subsequent sale or other disposition of the property by the original transferee results in a realized gain, the amount of gain is reduced by the loss that was previously disallowed. This *right of offset* is not applicable if the original sale involved the sale of a personal-use asset (e.g., a personal residence). Furthermore, the right of offset is available only to the original transferee (the related-party buyer). See Example 19 and Example 20 in Chapter 5.

LO.4

Describe various loss disallowance provisions.

In-depth coverage can be found on this book's companion website: **www.cengagebrain.com**  **5** Digging Deeper

Wash Sales

Section 1091 stipulates that in certain cases, a realized loss on the sale or exchange of stock or securities is not recognized. Specifically, if a taxpayer sells or exchanges stock or securities and within 30 days before *or* after the date of the sale or exchange acquires *substantially identical* stock or securities, any loss realized from the sale or exchange is not recognized because the transaction is a **wash sale**.[43] The term *acquire* means acquire by purchase or in a taxable exchange and includes an option to purchase substantially identical securities. *Substantially identical* means the same in all important particulars. Corporate bonds and preferred stock normally are not considered substantially identical to a corporation's common stock. However, if the bonds and preferred stock are convertible into common stock, they may be considered substantially identical under certain circumstances.[44] Attempts to avoid the application of the wash sale rules by having a related taxpayer repurchase the securities have been unsuccessful.[45] The wash sale provisions do *not* apply to gains.

Recognition of the loss is disallowed because the taxpayer is considered to be in substantially the same economic position after the sale and repurchase as before. This disallowance rule does not apply to taxpayers engaged in the business of buying and selling securities.[46] Investors, however, are not allowed to create losses through wash sales to offset income for tax purposes.

A realized loss that is not recognized is added to the *basis* of the substantially identical stock or securities whose acquisition resulted in the nonrecognition of loss.[47] In other words, the basis of the replacement stock or securities is increased by the amount of the unrecognized loss. If the loss were not added to the basis of the newly acquired stock or securities, the taxpayer would never recover the entire

[42]§ 267(b).
[43]§ 1091(a) and Reg. §§ 1.1091–1(a) and (f).
[44]Rev.Rul. 56–406, 1956–2 C.B. 523.
[45]*McWilliams v. Comm.*, 47–1 USTC ¶9289, 35 AFTR 1184, 67 S.Ct. 1477 (USSC, 1947).
[46]Reg. § 1.1091–1(a).
[47]§ 1091(d) and Reg. § 1.1091–2(a).

basis of the old stock or securities. As a result, the wash sale rule operates to *defer* the recognition of the taxpayer's loss.

Example 25

Oriole Manufacturing Company sold 50 shares of Green Corporation stock (adjusted basis of $10,000) for $8,000. Ten days later, Oriole purchased 50 shares of the same stock for $7,000. Oriole's realized loss of $2,000 ($8,000 amount realized − $10,000 adjusted basis) is not recognized because it resulted from a wash sale. Oriole's basis in the newly acquired stock is $9,000 ($7,000 purchase price + $2,000 unrecognized loss from the wash sale).

The basis of the new stock or securities includes the unrecovered portion of the basis of the formerly held stock or securities. Therefore, the *holding period* of the new stock or securities begins on the date of acquisition of the old stock or securities.[48]

A taxpayer may acquire fewer shares than the number sold in a wash sale. In this case, the loss from the sale is prorated between recognized and unrecognized loss on the basis of the ratio of the number of shares acquired to the number of shares sold.[49]

Tax Planning Strategies AVOIDING WASH SALES

FRAMEWORK FOCUS: DEDUCTIONS

Strategy: Maximize Deductible Amounts.

The wash sale restriction can be avoided by replacing the sold security with a *similar* but not "substantially identical" security. For example, if IBM common stock is sold to claim an unrealized loss, the taxpayer could immediately acquire Intel common stock without triggering the wash sale rule.

Nontax considerations must also come into play, however, because IBM and Intel are two different companies with different investment prospects. Although both securities will be affected by many of the same factors, they will also be subject to different factors that may be even more significant than the ones they share.

7-2e Conversion of Property from Personal Use to Business or Income-Producing Use

As discussed previously, losses from the sale of personal-use assets are not recognized for tax purposes, but losses from the sale of business and income-producing assets are deductible. Can a taxpayer convert a personal-use asset that has declined in value to business or income-producing use and then sell the asset to recognize a business or income-producing loss? The tax law prevents this practice by specifying that the *basis for determining loss* on personal-use assets converted to business or income-producing use is the *lower* of the property's adjusted basis or its fair market value on the date of conversion.[50] The *gain basis* for converted property is the property's adjusted basis on the date of conversion, regardless of whether the property's use is business, income-producing, or personal in nature.

Example 26

Diane's personal residence has an adjusted basis of $175,000 and a fair market value of $160,000. When she converts the personal residence to residential rental property on January 1, her basis for determining loss is $160,000 (lower of $175,000 adjusted basis and fair market value of $160,000). The $15,000 decline in value is a personal loss and can never be recognized for tax purposes. Diane's basis for determining gain is $175,000.

---

[48]§ 1223(4) and Reg. § 1.1223–1(d).
[49]§ 1091(b) and Reg. § 1.1091–1(c).

[50]Reg. § 1.165–9(b)(2).

The basis for determining loss is also the *basis for depreciating* the converted property.[51] This is an exception to the general rule that the basis for depreciation is the basis for determining gain (e.g., property received by gift). This exception prevents the taxpayer from recovering a personal loss indirectly through depreciation of the higher original basis. Once property is converted, both its basis for loss and its basis for gain are adjusted for depreciation deductions from the date of conversion to the date of disposition.

Assume the same facts as in Example 26. The MACRS cost recovery deduction for the current year is $5,576 ($160,000 × 3.485%). Thus, at the end of the current year, Diane's adjusted basis for gain for the rental property is $169,424 ($175,000 − $5,576), and her adjusted basis for loss is $154,424 ($160,000 − $5,576).	**Example 27**

In-depth coverage can be found on this book's companion website: **www.cengagebrain.com**   **6, 7**   Digging Deeper

7-2f Summary of Basis Adjustments

Some of the more common items that either increase or decrease the basis of an asset appear in Concept Summary 7.2.

In discussing the topic of basis, a number of specific techniques for determining basis have been presented. Although the various techniques are responsive to and mandated by transactions occurring in the marketplace, they possess enough common characteristics to be categorized as follows:

- The basis of the asset may be determined by its cost.
- The basis of the asset may be determined by the basis of another asset.
- The basis of the asset may be determined by its fair market value.
- The basis of the asset may be determined by the basis of the asset in the hands of another taxpayer.

7-3 GENERAL CONCEPT OF A NONTAXABLE EXCHANGE

A taxpayer who is going to replace a productive asset (e.g., machinery) used in a trade or business may structure the transaction as a sale of the old asset and the purchase of a new asset. When this approach is used, any realized gain or loss on the sale of the old asset is recognized. The basis of the new asset is its cost. Alternatively, the taxpayer may be able to trade the old asset for the new asset. This exchange of assets may produce beneficial tax consequences as a nontaxable exchange.

The tax law recognizes that nontaxable exchanges result in a change in the *form* but not the *substance* of a taxpayer's relative economic position. The replacement property received in the exchange is viewed as essentially a continuation of the old investment.[52] Additional justification for nontaxable treatment is that this type of transaction does not provide the taxpayer with the wherewithal to pay the tax on any realized gain.

The nonrecognition provisions for nontaxable exchanges do not apply to realized losses from the sale or exchange of personal-use assets. Such losses are never recognized (i.e., they are disallowed) because they are personal in nature.

In contrast, in a **nontaxable exchange**, recognition of gains or losses is *postponed* (i.e., deferred) until the new property received in the nontaxable exchange is subsequently disposed of in a taxable transaction. This is accomplished by assigning a carryover basis to the replacement property.

---

[51]Reg. § 1.167(g)–1.   [52]Reg. § 1.1002–1(c).

CONCEPT SUMMARY 7.2

Adjustments to Basis

Item	Effect	Refer to Chapter	Explanation
Amortization of bond discount.	Increase	7	Amortization is mandatory for certain taxable bonds and elective for tax-exempt bonds.
Amortization of bond premium.	Decrease	7	Amortization is mandatory for tax-exempt bonds and elective for taxable bonds.
Amortization of covenant not to compete.	Decrease	5	Covenant must be for a definite and limited time period. The amortization period is a statutory period of 15 years.
Amortization of intangibles.	Decrease	5	Intangibles are amortized over a 15-year period.
Bad debts.	Decrease	6	Most taxpayers must use the specific charge-off method.
Capital additions.	Increase	7	Certain items, at the taxpayer's election, can be capitalized or deducted.
Casualty.	Decrease	7	For a casualty loss, the amount of the adjustment is the sum of the deductible loss and the insurance proceeds received. For a casualty gain, the amount of the adjustment is the insurance proceeds received reduced by the recognized gain.
Condemnation.	Decrease	7	See casualty explanation.
Cost recovery.	Decrease	5	Section 168 is applicable to tangible assets placed in service after 1980 whose useful life is expressed in terms of years.
Depletion.	Decrease	5	Use the greater of cost or percentage depletion. Percentage depletion can be deducted even when the basis is zero.
Depreciation.	Decrease	5	Section 167 is applicable to tangible assets placed in service before 1981 and to tangible assets not depreciated in terms of years.
Easement.	Decrease	7	If the taxpayer does not retain any use of the land, all of the basis is allocable to the easement transaction. However, if only part of the land is affected by the easement, only part of the basis is allocable to the easement transaction.
Improvements by lessee to lessor's property.	Increase	4	Adjustment occurs only if the lessor is required to include the fair market value of the improvements in gross income under § 109.
Imputed interest.	Decrease		Amount deducted is not part of the cost of the asset.
Inventory: lower of cost or market.	Decrease		Not available if the LIFO method is used.
Limited expensing under § 179.	Decrease	5	Occurs only if the taxpayer elects § 179 treatment.
Medical capital expenditure deducted as a medical expense.	Decrease	10	Adjustment is the amount of the deduction (the effect on basis is to increase it by the amount of the capital expenditure net of the deduction).
Real estate taxes: apportionment between the buyer and seller.	Increase or decrease	5	To the extent the buyer pays the seller's pro rata share, the buyer's basis is increased. To the extent the seller pays the buyer's pro rata share, the buyer's basis is decreased.
Rebate from manufacturer.	Decrease		Because the rebate is treated as an adjustment to the purchase price, it is not included in the buyer's gross income.
Stock dividend.	Decrease	7	Adjustment occurs only if the stock dividend is nontaxable. While the basis per share decreases, the total stock basis does not change.
Stock rights.	Decrease	13	Adjustment to stock basis occurs only for nontaxable stock rights and only if the fair market value of the rights is at least 15% of the fair market value of the stock, or if less than 15%, the taxpayer elects to allocate the basis between the stock and the rights.
Theft.	Decrease	6	See casualty explanation.

> Starling Management Company completes a *nontaxable exchange* of property with an adjusted basis of $10,000 and a fair market value of $12,000 for property with a fair market value of $12,000. Starling has a realized gain of $2,000 ($12,000 amount realized − $10,000 adjusted basis). Its recognized gain is $0. Starling's basis in the replacement property is a carryover basis of $10,000. Assume that the replacement property is nondepreciable and that Starling subsequently sells it for $12,000. The realized and recognized gain will be the $2,000 gain that was postponed (deferred) in the nontaxable transaction. If the replacement property is depreciable, the carryover basis of $10,000 is used in calculating depreciation.

Example 28

In some nontaxable exchanges, only some of the property involved in the transaction qualifies for nonrecognition treatment. If the taxpayer receives cash or other nonqualifying property, part or all of the realized gain from the exchange is recognized. In these situations, gain is recognized because the taxpayer has changed or improved its relative economic position and has the wherewithal to pay income tax to the extent of cash or other property received.

It is important to distinguish between a nontaxable disposition (or nonrecognition transaction, as the term is used in the statute) and a tax-free transaction. As previously mentioned, the term *nontaxable* refers to postponement of recognition via some version of carryover basis. In a *tax-free* transaction, the nonrecognition is permanent (e.g., see the discussion later in this chapter of the exclusion of gain from the sale of a principal residence).

Either way, nontaxable and tax-free transactions must be understood as exceptions to the Code's general rule that gains and losses are recognized when they are realized. These exceptions have their own sets of requirements, limitations, and restrictions, all of which must be satisfied for a transaction to be characterized as nontaxable or tax-free. Otherwise, the general rule of recognition applies to the gain or loss at hand.

7-4 LIKE-KIND EXCHANGES—§ 1031

Section 1031 provides for nontaxable exchange treatment if the following requirements are satisfied:[53]

- The form of the transaction is an exchange.
- Both the property transferred and the property received are held either for productive use in a trade or business or for investment.
- The property is like-kind property.

Qualifying **like-kind exchanges** include exchanges of business for business, business for investment, investment for business, and investment for investment property. Property held for personal use does not qualify under the like-kind exchange provisions. Thus, the purpose for which the property is held by the taxpayer in question is critical. For example, if Janet uses a small truck in her trade or business, it may qualify for like-kind treatment, but if she uses this truck as her personal-use vehicle, it is ineligible for nonrecognition treatment under § 1031.

Some assets are excluded from like-kind treatment by statute. These excluded assets include a taxpayer's inventory or "stock in trade," as well as most forms of investment other than real estate. Thus, stocks, bonds, partnership interests (whether general or limited), and other securities, even though held for investment, do not qualify for like-kind exchange treatment.

The nonrecognition provision for like-kind exchanges is *mandatory* rather than elective. A taxpayer who wants to recognize a realized gain or loss will have to structure the transaction in a form that does not satisfy the statutory requirements for a like-kind exchange.

LO.5

Apply the nonrecognition provisions and basis determination rules for like-kind exchanges.

---

[53]§ 1031(a) and Reg. § 1.1031(a)–1(a).

© tuulijumala/Shutterstock.com

Tax Planning Strategies   LIKE-KIND EXCHANGES

FRAMEWORK FOCUS: DEDUCTIONS

Strategy: **Maximize Deductible Amounts.**

Because nonrecognition of gain or loss is mandatory in like-kind exchanges, a taxpayer must affirmatively *avoid such exchanges* if nonrecognition treatment is not desired. If an asset is worth less than its adjusted basis, a *loss would result* from its disposition. Accordingly, the taxpayer should sell this property outright to ensure the deductibility of the loss, assuming it would otherwise be deductible.

Even if *disposition would result in a gain*, a taxpayer might want to recognize this gain in the current taxable year. If so, a like-kind exchange should be avoided. Circumstances suggesting this strategy include:

- Unused capital loss carryovers, especially if the taxpayer is a corporation for which such carryovers are limited in duration (see Chapters 4 and 8).
- Unused net operating loss carryovers (see Chapter 6).
- Unused general business credit carryovers (see Chapter 17).
- Suspended or current passive activity losses (see Chapter 6).

7-4a Like-Kind Property

The term *like-kind* is explained in the Regulations as follows: "The words 'like-kind' refer to the nature or character of the property and not to its grade or quality. One kind or class of property may not … be exchanged for property of a different kind or class."[54] The Regulations go on to explain that although real estate can be exchanged only for other real estate, the definition of real estate is quite broad. *Real estate* (or realty) includes principally rental buildings, office and store buildings, manufacturing plants, warehouses, and land. It is immaterial whether real estate is improved or unimproved. Thus, unimproved land can be exchanged for an apartment house. On the other hand, real property located in the United States exchanged for foreign real property (and vice versa) does not qualify as like-kind property. A similar provision applies to exchanges of foreign and domestic personalty.

In any case, real estate cannot be exchanged in a like-kind transaction for personalty. *Personalty* includes tangible assets other than real estate, such as machinery, equipment, trucks, automobiles, furniture, and fixtures. Thus, an exchange of a machine (personalty) for a small office building (realty) is not a like-kind exchange. Finally, the Code mandates that livestock of different sexes are not like-kind property.

Example 29

Pheasant, Inc., made the following exchanges during the taxable year:

a. Inventory for a machine used in business.
b. Land held for investment for a building used in business.
c. Stock held for investment for equipment used in business.
d. A light-duty business truck for a light-duty business truck.
e. Livestock for livestock of a different sex.
f. Land held for investment in New York for land held for investment in London.

Exchanges (b), investment real property for business real property, and (d), business personalty for business personalty, qualify as exchanges of like-kind property. The other exchanges do not qualify because they involve (a), inventory; (c), stock; (e), livestock of different sexes; and (f), U.S. and foreign real estate.

 Digging Deeper   8   In-depth coverage can be found on this book's companion website: **www.cengagebrain.com**

---

[54]Reg. § 1.1031(a)–1(b).

TAX FACT Classic Tax Planning Strategy Ignored

In an environment of increasing tax rates, taxpayers may be wise to consider *avoiding* the like-kind exchange rules. For example, in certain situations, the beneficial result of tax deferral of realized gain could be more than offset by future tax rate increases. Some real estate investors in the highest tax brackets who followed this approach, particularly with respect to undeveloped land, planned wisely. They were willing to accept taxation at 15 percent to avoid the possibility of future taxation at a much higher rate (which turned out to be 20 percent for certain high-income taxpayers). Although turning down a tax deferral may sound like a strange strategy, it fits the notion of "pay a tax today to avoid a higher tax tomorrow."

Special Rule for Depreciable Tangible Personal Property

The Regulations dealing with § 1031 like-kind exchanges provide greater specificity when determining whether depreciable tangible personalty is of a like kind. Such property held for productive use in a business is of like kind only if the exchanged property is within the same *general business asset class* (as specified by the IRS in Rev.Proc. 87–57 or as subsequently modified) or the same *product class* (as specified by the Department of Commerce). Property included in a general business asset class is evaluated exclusively under the Revenue Procedure, rather than under the product class system.

The following are examples of general business asset classes:

- Office furniture, fixtures, and equipment.
- Information systems (computers and peripheral equipment).
- Airplanes.
- Automobiles and taxis.
- Buses.
- Light general-purpose trucks.
- Heavy general-purpose trucks.

These Regulations narrow the range of depreciable tangible personalty subject to § 1031 like-kind exchange treatment. For example, the exchange of office equipment for a computer does not qualify as an exchange of like-kind property. Even though both assets are depreciable tangible personalty, they are not like-kind property because they are in different general business asset classes. Accordingly, any realized *gain or loss* on the office equipment would be recognized currently.

In-depth coverage can be found on this book's companion website: **www.cengagebrain.com**   9   Digging Deeper

7-4b Exchange Requirement

The transaction must generally involve a direct exchange of property to qualify as a like-kind exchange. The sale of old property and the purchase of new property, even though like kind, is not an exchange. However, the Code does provide a limited procedure for real estate to be exchanged for qualifying property that is acquired subsequent to the exchange.[55]

Of course, the taxpayer may want to avoid nontaxable exchange treatment. Recognition of gain gives the taxpayer a higher basis for depreciation. To the extent that such gains would, if recognized, either receive favorable capital gain treatment

---
[55]§ 1031(a)(3).

or be passive activity income that could be offset by passive activity losses, it might be preferable to avoid the nonrecognition provisions through an indirect exchange transaction. For example, a taxpayer may sell property to one company, recognize the gain, and subsequently purchase similar property from another company. The taxpayer may also want to avoid nontaxable exchange treatment so that a realized loss can be recognized.

| Digging Deeper | 10 🔍 | In-depth coverage can be found on this book's companion website: **www.cengagebrain.com** |

© tuulijumala/Shutterstock.com

7-4c Boot

If the taxpayer in a like-kind exchange gives or receives some property that is not like-kind property, recognition may occur. Property that is not like-kind property, including cash, is often referred to as **boot**. Although the term *boot* does not appear in the Code, tax practitioners commonly use it rather than saying "property that does not qualify as like-kind property."

The *receipt* of boot will trigger recognition of gain if there is realized gain. The amount of the recognized gain is the *lesser* of the boot received or the realized gain (realized gain serves as the ceiling on recognition).

| **Example 30** | Blue, Inc., and White Corporation exchange machinery, and the exchange qualifies as like kind under § 1031. Because Blue's machinery (adjusted basis of $20,000) is worth $24,000 and White's machine has a fair market value of $19,000, White also gives Blue cash of $5,000. Blue's recognized gain is $4,000, the lesser of the realized gain of $4,000 ($24,000 amount realized − $20,000 adjusted basis) or the fair market value of the boot received of $5,000. |

| **Example 31** | Assume the same facts as in the preceding example, except that White's machine is worth $21,000 (not $19,000). Under these circumstances, White gives Blue cash of $3,000 to make up the difference. Blue's recognized gain is $3,000, the lesser of the realized gain of $4,000 ($24,000 amount realized − $20,000 adjusted basis) or the fair market value of the boot received of $3,000. |

The receipt of boot does not result in recognition if there is realized loss.

| **Example 32** | Assume the same facts as in Example 30, except that the adjusted basis of Blue's machine is $30,000. Blue's realized loss is $6,000 ($24,000 amount realized − $30,000 adjusted basis). The receipt of the boot of $5,000 does not trigger recognition of Blue's loss. |

The *giving* of boot does not trigger recognition if the boot consists solely of cash.

| **Example 33** | Flicker, Inc., and Gadwall Corporation exchange equipment in a like-kind exchange. Flicker receives equipment with a fair market value of $75,000 and transfers equipment worth $63,000 (adjusted basis of $45,000) and cash of $12,000. Flicker's realized gain is $18,000 ($75,000 amount realized − $45,000 adjusted basis of equipment transferred − $12,000 cash), none of which is recognized. |

If, however, the boot given is appreciated or depreciated property, gain or loss is recognized to the extent of the difference between the adjusted basis and the fair market value of the boot. For this purpose, *appreciated or depreciated property* is property with an adjusted basis that differs from fair market value.

| **Example 34** | Assume the same facts as in the preceding example, except that Flicker transfers equipment worth $30,000 (adjusted basis of $36,000) and boot worth $45,000 (adjusted basis of $27,000). Flicker's net gain on this exchange is $12,000 [$75,000 amount realized less adjusted basis of $63,000 ($36,000 + $27,000)].   But |

Flicker is transferring two pieces of property: equipment (like-kind property) with a built-in realized loss of $6,000 ($30,000 fair market value less $36,000 adjusted basis) and non-like-kind property (boot) with a built-in realized gain of $18,000 ($45,000 fair market value less $27,000 adjusted basis).

In this case, the $6,000 realized loss on the like-kind property is *deferred* (not recognized) and the $18,000 realized gain on the non-like-kind property is recognized. In other words, the realized loss on the like-kind property *cannot* be used to offset the realized gain on the boot given up as part of the transaction.

7-4d Basis and Holding Period of Property Received

If an exchange does not qualify as nontaxable under § 1031, gain or loss is recognized and the basis of property received in the exchange is the property's fair market value. If the exchange qualifies for nonrecognition, the basis of property received must be adjusted to reflect any postponed (deferred) gain or loss. The *basis of like-kind property* received in the exchange is the property's fair market value less postponed gain or plus postponed loss. The *basis* of any *boot* received is the boot's fair market value.

Example 35

Vireo Property Management Company exchanges a building (used in its business) with an adjusted basis of $300,000 and a fair market value of $380,000 for land with a fair market value of $380,000. The land is to be held as an investment. The exchange qualifies as like kind (an exchange of business real property for investment real property). Thus, the basis of the land is $300,000 (the land's fair market value of $380,000 less the $80,000 postponed gain on the building). If the land is later sold for its fair market value of $380,000, the $80,000 postponed gain is recognized.

Example 36

Assume the same facts as in the preceding example, except that the building has an adjusted basis of $480,000 and a fair market value of only $380,000. The basis in the newly acquired land is $480,000 (fair market value of $380,000 plus the $100,000 postponed loss on the building). If the land is later sold for its fair market value of $380,000, the $100,000 postponed loss is recognized.

The Code provides an alternative approach for determining the basis of like-kind property received:

Adjusted basis of like-kind property surrendered
+ Adjusted basis of boot given
+ Gain recognized
− Fair market value of boot received
− Loss recognized
= *Basis of like-kind property received*

This approach accords with the recovery of capital doctrine. That is, the unrecovered cost or other basis is increased by additional cost (boot given) or decreased by cost recovered (boot received). Any gain recognized is included in the basis of the new property. The taxpayer has been taxed on this amount and is now entitled to recover it tax-free. Any loss recognized is deducted from the basis of the new property because the taxpayer has already received a tax benefit on that amount.

The holding period of the property surrendered in the exchange carries over and *tacks on* to the holding period of the like-kind property received.[56] This rule

[56] § 1223(1) and Reg. § 1.1223–1(a). For like-kind exchanges after March 1, 1954, the tacked-on holding period applies only if the like-kind property surrendered was either a capital asset or § 1231 property.

derives from the basic concept that the new property is a continuation of the old investment. The boot received has a new holding period (from the date of exchange) rather than a carryover holding period.

Depreciation recapture potential carries over to the property received in a like-kind exchange.[57] See Chapter 8 for a discussion of this topic.

Digging Deeper   II    In-depth coverage can be found on this book's companion website: **www.cengagebrain.com**

If the taxpayer either assumes a liability or takes property subject to a liability, the amount of the liability is treated as boot given. For the taxpayer whose liability is assumed or whose property is taken subject to the liability, the amount of the liability is treated as boot received. The following example illustrates the effect of such a liability. In addition, the example illustrates the tax consequences for both parties involved in the like-kind exchange.

Example 37

Jaeger & Company and Lark Enterprises, Inc., exchange real estate investments. Jaeger gives up property with an adjusted basis of $250,000 (fair market value of $400,000) that is subject to a mortgage of $75,000 (assumed by Lark). In return for this property, Jaeger receives property with a fair market value of $300,000 (Lark's adjusted basis in the property is $200,000) and cash of $25,000. Jaeger's and Lark's realized and recognized gains and their basis in the like-kind property received are computed as follows:[58]

	Jaeger	Lark
Amount realized:		
Like-kind property received	$ 300,000	$ 400,000
Boot received:		
Cash	25,000	
Mortgage assumed	75,000	
	$ 400,000	$ 400,000
Adjusted basis:		
Like-kind property given	(250,000)	(200,000)
Boot given:		
Cash		(25,000)
Mortgage assumed		(75,000)
Realized gain	$ 150,000	$ 100,000
Recognized gain	100,000*	–0–**
Deferred gain	$ 50,000	$ 100,000
Basis of property transferred:		
Like-kind property	$ 250,000	$ 200,000
Cash		25,000
Mortgage assumed		75,000
	$ 250,000	$ 300,000
Plus: Gain recognized	100,000	
Less: Boot received	(100,000)	
Basis of new property	$ 250,000	$ 300,000

* Lesser of boot received ($25,000 cash + $75,000 mortgage assumed = $100,000) or gain realized ($150,000).

** No boot received. Therefore, no gain is recognized.

---

[57]Reg. §§ 1.1245–2(a)(4) and 1.1250–2(d)(1).

[58]Example (2) of Reg. § 1.1031(d)–2 illustrates a special situation in which both the buyer and the seller transfer liabilities that are assumed by the other party or both parties acquire property that is subject to a liability.

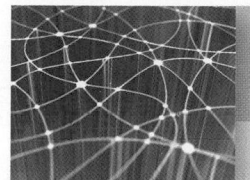

BRIDGE DISCIPLINE Bridge to Economics

One can assert that the "tax variable" is neutralized in nontaxable exchanges when taxable gains or losses do not arise. Neutralizing potential tax consequences can have a positive result given that tax costs tend to dampen economic activity. For example, in a like-kind exchange, a taxpayer can exchange one asset for another asset of like kind without having to recognize a gain or pay a tax. The justification for the tax deferral is that the taxpayer is viewed as having an equivalent economic investment after the transaction as before the transaction. But the tax-neutral result changes when the taxpayer receives property that is not "like kind" because the taxpayer's economic standing has changed.

If, for example, the taxpayer receives investment land *and* cash in exchange for investment land, her ownership in the land given up has, at least in part, been converted to cash, and to that degree, her investment has substantively changed. That is, the taxpayer's economic investment has changed from an ownership exclusively in land to ownership in land *and* cash. Alternatively, if the taxpayer gives up her investment in land for corporate stock in a high-tech venture, the nature of her investment also would substantively change as a result of the transaction. These differences in the taxpayer's economic position after the transaction lead to the transactions being taxed.

7-5 INVOLUNTARY CONVERSIONS—§ 1033

Section 1033 provides that a taxpayer who suffers an involuntary conversion of property may postpone recognition of *gain* realized from the conversion. The objective of this provision is to provide relief to the taxpayer who has suffered hardship and does not have the wherewithal to pay the tax on any gain realized from the conversion. Postponement of realized gain is permitted to the extent that the taxpayer *reinvests* the amount realized from the conversion in replacement property. If the amount reinvested in replacement property is *less than* the amount realized, realized gain *is recognized* to the extent of the deficiency.

By its terms, § 1033 generally is *elective*. A taxpayer need not postpone recognition of gain, even if replacement property is acquired. In essence, a taxpayer has three options:

- Reinvest the proceeds and elect § 1033's nonrecognition of gain.
- Reinvest the proceeds and not elect § 1033, thereby triggering recognition of realized gain under the usual rules applicable to property transactions.
- Not reinvest the proceeds and recognize the realized gain accordingly.

If a *loss* occurs on an involuntary conversion, § 1033 does not apply and the general rules for loss recognition are effective. See Chapter 6 for the discussion of the deduction of losses.

LO.6

Explain the nonrecognition provisions available on the involuntary conversion of property.

7-5a Involuntary Conversion Defined

An **involuntary conversion** results from the destruction (complete or partial), theft, seizure, requisition or condemnation, or sale or exchange under threat or imminence of requisition or condemnation of the taxpayer's property.[59] This description includes fires (other than arson),[60] tornadoes, hurricanes, earthquakes, floods, and other natural disasters. In these circumstances, *gain* can result from insurance proceeds received in an amount that exceeds the taxpayer's historical cost of the property, especially if depreciation deductions have lowered the property's adjusted basis.

For requisitions and condemnations, the amount realized includes the compensation paid by the public authority acquiring the taxpayer's property. To prove the existence of a threat or imminence of condemnation, the taxpayer must obtain

---

[59]§ 1033(a) and Reg. §§ 1.1033(a)–1(a) and –2(a).   [60]Rev.Rul. 82–74, 1982–1 C.B. 110.

confirmation that there has been a decision to acquire the property for public use. In addition, the taxpayer must have reasonable grounds to believe the property will be taken.[61] The property does not have to be sold to the authority threatening to condemn it to qualify for § 1033 postponement. If the taxpayer satisfies the confirmation and reasonable grounds requirements, he or she can sell the property to another party.[62] Likewise, the sale of property to a condemning authority by a taxpayer who acquired the property from its former owner with the knowledge that the property was under threat of condemnation also qualifies as an involuntary conversion under § 1033.[63]

Tax Planning Strategies   RECOGNIZING INVOLUNTARY CONVERSION GAINS

FRAMEWORK FOCUS: TAX RATE

Strategy: Shift Net Income from High-Bracket Years to Low-Bracket Years.

FRAMEWORK FOCUS: DEDUCTIONS

Strategy: Maximize Deductible Amounts.

Sometimes, a taxpayer may prefer to *recognize a gain from an involuntary conversion* and will choose not to elect §1033, even though replacement property is acquired. Circumstances suggesting this strategy would include:

- The taxpayer realized the gain in a low-bracket tax year, quite possibly because of the events that caused the involuntary conversion, such as a flood and its aftermath that seriously disrupted the business.
- The taxpayer has an expiring net operating loss carryover that can offset most, if not all, of the gain from the involuntary conversion.

- The replacement property is depreciable, and the taxpayer would prefer an unreduced basis for this asset to maximize depreciation deductions in future years.

Nontax considerations might also come into play, perhaps suggesting that the property not be replaced at all. Even before the event that produced the involuntary conversion, the taxpayer might have been wanting to downsize the business or terminate it outright. In any case, the taxpayer might prefer to recognize the gain, pay the tax involved, and thereby free up the remaining proceeds for other uses—business, investment, or even personal—especially if the gain is small compared to the amount of proceeds received.

Digging Deeper   12   In-depth coverage can be found on this book's companion website: **www.cengagebrain.com**

7-5b Replacement Property

The requirements for replacement property under the involuntary conversion rules generally are more restrictive than those for like-kind property under § 1031. The basic requirement is that the replacement property be similar or related in service or use to the involuntarily converted property.[64]

Different interpretations of the phrase *similar or related in service or use* apply depending on whether the involuntarily converted property is held by an *owner-user* or by an *owner-investor* (e.g., lessor). For an owner-investor, the *taxpayer use test* applies, and for an owner-user, the *functional use test* applies. Furthermore, a special test applies in the case of involuntary conversions that result from condemnations.

Functional Use Test

Under this test, a taxpayer's use of the replacement property and of the involuntarily converted property must be the same. Replacing a manufacturing plant with a

---

[61]Rev.Rul. 63–221, 1963–2 C.B. 332, and *Joseph P. Balistrieri*, 38 TCM 526, T.C.Memo. 1979–115.

[62]Rev.Rul. 81–180, 1981–2 C.B. 161.

[63]Rev.Rul. 81–181, 1981–2 C.B. 162.

[64]§ 1033(a) and Reg. § 1.1033(a)–1.

© tuulijumala/Shutterstock.com

TAX IN THE NEWS The Fight Goes On

Boxing fans know that a boxer can be knocked down and then get up off the canvas and win. It appears that this is what happened to a property owner in California named Community Youth Athletic Center (CYAC). CYAC owned and operated a gym (including a boxing ring) that it made available to at-risk kids. The local governmental authority (National City) approved a condo project that would allow a developer to acquire and demolish CYAC's gym. Under the now classic U.S. Supreme Court decision in *Kelo v. City of New London*, the power of eminent domain is available if used for the purpose of economic improvement. Without any change since *Kelo*, therefore, CYAC would lose its gym through a condemnation proceeding.

Because of the potential widespread effect on private property rights of *Kelo*, many states have enacted restrictions on the use of condemnations. In California, blight can be a justification, but only if there is "specific and quantifiable" evidence of such blight and it cannot be removed without the use of eminent domain. Although National City had asserted that the CYAC gym was in a blighted area, the California Superior Court found no such "specific and quantifiable" evidence. Thus, unlike *Kelo*, where the property owner was knocked out, in *CYAC v. National City*, the public authority was the loser.

Source: Based on "Property Rights Knockout," *Wall Street Journal*, May 2, 2011, p. A14.

© iStockphoto.com/Andrey Prokhorov

wholesale grocery warehouse does not meet this test. Instead, the plant must be replaced with another facility of similar functional use.

Taxpayer Use Test

The taxpayer use test for owner-investors provides the taxpayer with more flexibility in terms of what qualifies as replacement property than does the functional use test for owner-users. Essentially, the properties must be used by the taxpayer (the owner-investor) in similar endeavors. For example, rental property held by an owner-investor qualifies if replaced by other rental property, regardless of the type of rental property involved. The test is met when an investor replaces a manufacturing plant with a wholesale grocery warehouse if both properties are held for the production of rental income.[65] The replacement of a rental residence with a personal residence does not meet the test.[66]

Special Rule for Condemnations

In addition to the functional and taxpayer use tests, the Code provides a special rule for business or investment real property *that is condemned*. This rule applies the broad like-kind classification for real estate to such circumstances. Accordingly, improved real property can be replaced with unimproved real property.

The rules concerning the nature of replacement property are illustrated in Concept Summary 7.3.

7-5c Time Limitation on Replacement

The taxpayer normally has a two-year period after the close of the taxable year in which gain is realized from an involuntary conversion to replace the property.[67] This rule affords as much as three years from the date of realization of gain to replace the property if the realization of gain took place on the first day of the taxable year.[68]

---

[65]*Loco Realty Co. v. Comm.*, 62–2 USTC ¶9657, 10 AFTR 2d 5359, 306 F.2d 207 (CA–8, 1962).

[66]Rev.Rul. 70–466, 1970–2 C.B. 165.

[67]§§ 1033(a)(2)(B) and (g)(4) and Reg. § 1.1033(a)–2(c)(3).

[68]A taxpayer can apply for an extension of this time period anytime before its expiration [Reg. § 1.1033(a)–2(c)(3)]. Also, the period for filing the application for extension can be extended if a taxpayer shows reasonable cause.

CONCEPT SUMMARY 7.3

Involuntary Conversions: Replacement Property Tests

Type of Property and User	Taxpayer Use Test	Functional Use Test	Special Rule for Condemnations*
An investor's rented shopping mall is destroyed by fire; the mall may be replaced with other rental properties (e.g., an apartment building).	X		
A manufacturing plant is destroyed by fire; replacement property must consist of another manufacturing plant that is functionally the same as the property converted.		X	
Personal residence of a taxpayer is condemned by a local government authority; replacement property must consist of another personal residence.		X	
Land used by a manufacturing company is condemned by a local government authority.			X
Apartment and land held by an investor are sold due to the threat or imminence of condemnation.			X

* Applies the same test as in the case of like-kind exchanges.

© iStockphoto.com/Andrey Prokhorov

Example 38

Magpie, Inc.'s building is destroyed by fire on December 16, 2013. The adjusted basis is $325,000. Magpie receives $400,000 from the insurance company on January 10, 2014. The company is a calendar year taxpayer. The latest date for replacement is December 31, 2016 (the end of the taxable year in which realized gain occurred plus two years). The critical date is not the date the involuntary conversion occurred, but rather the date of gain realization (when the insurance proceeds are received).

In the case of a condemnation of real property used in a trade or business or held for investment, the Code substitutes a three-year period for the normal two-year period. In this case, a taxpayer might have as many as four years from the date of realization of gain to replace the property.

Example 39

Assume the same facts as in the preceding example, except that Magpie's building is condemned. On November 1, 2013, Magpie receives notification of the future condemnation, which occurs on December 16, 2013. The condemnation proceeds are received on January 10, 2014. The latest date for replacement is December 31, 2017 (the end of the taxable year in which realized gain occurred plus three years).

The *earliest date* for replacement typically is the date the involuntary conversion occurs. However, if the property is condemned, it is possible to replace the condemned property before this date. In this case, the earliest date is the date of the threat or imminence of requisition or condemnation of the property. The purpose of this provision is to enable the taxpayer to make an orderly replacement of the condemned property.

7-5d Nonrecognition of Gain

Nonrecognition of gain can be either mandatory or elective, depending on whether the conversion is direct (into replacement property) or indirect (into money).

Direct Conversion

If the conversion is directly into replacement property rather than into money, nonrecognition of realized gain is *mandatory*. In this case, the basis of the replacement property is the same as the adjusted basis of the converted property. Direct conversion is rare in practice and usually involves condemnations.

Example 40

Oak, Inc.'s property, with an adjusted basis of $20,000, is condemned by the state. Oak receives property with a fair market value of $50,000 as compensation for the property taken. Because the nonrecognition of realized gain is mandatory for direct conversions, Oak's realized gain of $30,000 is not recognized and the basis of the replacement property is $20,000 (adjusted basis of the condemned property).

Conversion into Money

If the conversion is into money, the realized gain is recognized only to the extent the amount realized from the involuntary conversion exceeds the cost of the qualifying replacement property.[69] This is the usual case, and nonrecognition (postponement) is *elective*. If the election is not made, the realized gain is recognized.

The basis of the replacement property is the property's cost less any postponed (deferred) gain.[70] If the election to postpone gain is made, the holding period of the replacement property includes the holding period of the converted property.

Section 1033 applies *only to gains* and *not to losses*. Losses from involuntary conversions are recognized if the property is held for business or income-producing purposes. Personal casualty losses are recognized, but condemnation losses related to personal use assets (e.g., a personal residence) are neither recognized nor postponed.

THE BIG PICTURE

Example 41

Return to the facts of *The Big Picture* on p. 7-1. Alice's building (used in her trade or business), with an adjusted basis of $50,000, is destroyed by a fire on October 5, 2014. Alice is a calendar year taxpayer. On November 17, 2014, she receives an insurance reimbursement of $100,000 for the loss. Alice invests $80,000 in a new building and uses the other $20,000 of insurance proceeds to pay off credit card debt.

- Alice has until December 31, 2016, to make the new investment and qualify for the nonrecognition election.
- Alice's realized gain is $50,000 ($100,000 insurance proceeds received − $50,000 adjusted basis of old building).
- Assuming that the replacement property qualifies as similar or related in service or use, Alice's recognized gain is $20,000. She reinvested $20,000 less than the insurance proceeds received ($100,000 proceeds − $80,000 reinvested). Therefore, her realized gain is recognized to that extent.
- Alice's basis in the new building is $50,000. This is the building's cost of $80,000 less the postponed gain of $30,000 (realized gain of $50,000 − recognized gain of $20,000).

THE BIG PICTURE

Example 42

Return to the facts of *The Big Picture* on p. 7-1. Assume the same facts as in the previous example, except that Alice receives only $45,000 of insurance proceeds. She has a realized and recognized loss of $5,000. The basis of the new building is the building's cost of $80,000.

---

[69]§ 1033(a)(2)(A) and Reg. § 1.1033(a)–2(c)(1).　　　[70]§ 1033(b).

7-6 OTHER NONRECOGNITION PROVISIONS

Several additional nonrecognition provisions are treated briefly in the remainder of this chapter.

7-6a Transfer of Assets to Business Entity—§§ 351 and 721

Taxpayers can transfer assets to corporations in exchange for stock without recognizing gain or loss on the transfer according to § 351. See Chapter 12 for the applicable restrictions and corresponding basis adjustments for the stock acquired. A similar provision (§ 721) allows the nontaxable transfer of assets to a partnership in exchange for an interest in that partnership. See Chapter 14 for a description of § 721.

7-6b Exchange of Stock for Property—§ 1032

Under § 1032, a corporation does not recognize gain or loss on the receipt of money or other property in exchange for its stock (including treasury stock). In other words, a corporation does not recognize gain or loss when it deals in its own stock. This provision accords with the accounting treatment of such transactions. See Chapter 12 for additional discussion.

7-6c Certain Exchanges of Insurance Policies—§ 1035

Under § 1035, no gain or loss is recognized from the exchange of certain insurance contracts or policies. The rules relating to exchanges not solely in kind (i.e., with boot) and the basis of the property acquired are the same as under § 1031. Exchanges qualifying for nonrecognition include the following:

- The exchange of life insurance contracts.
- The exchange of a life insurance contract for an endowment or annuity contract.
- The exchange of an endowment contract for another endowment contract that provides for regular payments beginning at a date not later than the date payments would have begun under the contract exchanged.
- The exchange of an endowment contract for an annuity contract.
- The exchange of annuity contracts.

7-6d Exchange of Stock for Stock of the Same Corporation—§ 1036

Section 1036 provides that a shareholder does not recognize gain or loss on the exchange of common stock solely for common stock in the same corporation or from the exchange of preferred stock for preferred stock in the same corporation. Exchanges between individual shareholders as well as between a shareholder and the corporation are included under this nonrecognition provision. The rules relating to exchanges not solely in kind and the basis of the property acquired are the same as under § 1031. For example, a nonrecognition exchange occurs when common stock with different rights, such as voting for nonvoting, is exchanged. A shareholder usually recognizes gain or loss from the exchange of common for preferred or preferred for common even though the stock exchanged is in the same corporation.

7-6e Rollovers into Specialized Small Business Investment Companies—§ 1044

Section 1044 provides a postponement opportunity associated with the sale of publicly traded securities. If the amount realized is reinvested in the common stock or partnership interest of a specialized small business investment company (SSBIC), the realized gain is not recognized. Gain will be recognized, however, to the extent of any amount not reinvested. To qualify, the taxpayer must reinvest the proceeds within 60 days of the date of sale.

7-6f Sale of a Principal Residence—§ 121

Section 121 allows individual taxpayers to exclude gain from the sale of a *principal residence*. This provision applies to the first $250,000 of realized gain, or $500,000 on certain joint returns. For this purpose, the residence must have been owned and used by the taxpayer as the primary residence for at least two of the five years preceding the date of sale. In addition, the exclusion is not available for sales occurring within two years of its last use. This exclusion can be prorated, however, if a taxpayer failed to meet one or more of these time period requirements due to a change in his or her place of employment or health. Moreover, a surviving spouse counts the ownership and usage periods of the decedent spouse in meeting the two-year test. This provision applies only to gains; losses on residences, like those of other personal-use assets, are not recognized for tax purposes.

In-depth coverage can be found on this book's companion website: **www.cengagebrain.com** 13, 14, 15 | Digging Deeper

7-6g Transfers of Property between Spouses or Incident to Divorce—§ 1041

Section 1041 provides for nontaxable exchange treatment on property transfers *between spouses during marriage*. The basis to the recipient spouse is a carryover basis.

Section 1041 also provides that transfers of property *between spouses or former spouses incident to divorce* are nontaxable transactions. Therefore, the basis to the recipient is a carryover basis. To be treated as incident to the divorce, the transfer must be related to the cessation of marriage or must occur within one year after the date on which the marriage ceases.

REFOCUS ON THE BIG PICTURE

CALCULATING BASIS AND RECOGNIZED GAIN FOR PROPERTY TRANSACTIONS

Alice's basis in the land acquired as a gift is a carryover basis of $2,000. If Alice sells the land outright, she will realize and recognize a gain of $48,000. However, if she replaces the property with other real property, she should be able to qualify for favorable like-kind exchange treatment under § 1031 and defer the gain on the property disposition. However, if Alice receives any cash from the exchange, realized gain would be recognized to the extent of the cash (boot) received.

Alice's basis in the 300 shares of stock received as an inheritance is the property's $30,000 fair market value at the date of death. If Alice sells the 300 shares, she will realize and recognize a $6,000 gain [$36,000 sales price (300 shares × $120) − $30,000 basis].

Alice's basis in the 200 shares of stock purchased is her purchase price of $28,000. Those shares are currently worth $24,000 (200 shares × $120). Consequently, if she sells those shares, she will realize and recognize a $4,000 loss.

You advise Alice that her basis in the house is its $475,000 fair market value on the date of her grandmother's death. If Alice sells the house for $600,000, her realized and recognized gain would be $125,000.

Regarding the fire-related involuntary conversion of Alice's business building, a $50,000 realized gain occurs upon the receipt of the $100,000 of insurance proceeds. Because she intends to invest only $80,000 of the insurance proceeds in a qualifying property, Alice's recognized gain is $20,000. She reinvested $20,000 less than the insurance proceeds received ($100,000 proceeds − $80,000 reinvested). Therefore, her realized gain is recognized to that extent (see Example 41).

CONTINUED

© iStockphoto.com/Nikki Bidgood

What If?

Alice is leaning toward selling the house. However, she knows that her grandmother would not want her to have to pay income taxes on the sale. Alice asks whether there is any way she could avoid paying taxes on the sale.

You inform Alice of the exclusion provision under § 121. Alice can qualify for this exclusion of up to $250,000 of realized gain if she owns and occupies the house as her principal residence for at least two of the five years prior to a sale.

From a tax planning perspective, what could Alice have done so that none of the $50,000 of realized gain in Example 41 from the involuntary conversion was recognized? To have full postponement of the $50,000 realized gain, Alice would have had to reinvest all of the $100,000 of insurance proceeds received in another qualified building. Under this circumstance, the basis of the replacement building would have been $50,000 ($100,000 cost of replacement building – $50,000 deferred gain).

Suggested Readings

Michael E. Bauer, Dale S. Collinson, and Deanna J. Flores, "Final Cost-Basis-Reporting Regs. on Debt Instruments, Options, and Securities Futures Contracts," *Corporate Taxation*, July/August 2013.

James R. Hamill, "Preserving the Residence Sale Exclusion for Mixed Use Property," *Practical Tax Strategies*, June 2013.

Katherine M. Hetherington and Timothy R. Hurley, "Selling Principal Residence When Debt Exceeds Fair Market Value," *Practical Tax Strategies*, February 2013.

Christian J. Kenefick, "What Is a $10 Gold Coin Worth? Basis, FMV, and Realization Issues Abound," *Journal of Taxation*, February 2013.

Jay A. Soled, Leonard Goodman, and Anthony Pochesci, "Penalty Exposure for Incorrect Tax Basis Reporting on Information Returns," *Journal of Taxation*, August 2013.

Louis S. Weller, "IRS Muddies the Like-Kind Waters in Guidance Considering State Law Classification," *Journal of Taxation*, January 2013.

Key Terms

Adjusted basis, 7-3	Holding period, 7-12	Realized loss, 7-2
Amount realized, 7-3	Involuntary conversion, 7-25	Recognized gain, 7-6
Boot, 7-22	Like-kind exchanges, 7-19	Recognized loss, 7-6
Fair market value, 7-3	Nontaxable exchange, 7-17	Wash sale, 7-15
Goodwill, 7-8	Realized gain, 7-2	

Problems

1. **LO.1** If a taxpayer sells property for cash, the amount realized consists of the net proceeds from the sale. For each of the following, indicate the effect on the amount realized:
   a. The property is sold on credit.
   b. A mortgage on the property is assumed by the buyer.
   c. A mortgage on the property of the buyer is assumed by the seller.
   d. The buyer acquires the property subject to a mortgage of the seller.
   e. Stock that has a basis to the purchaser of $6,000 and a fair market value of $10,000 is received by the seller as part of the consideration.

2. **LO.1, 2** Meg owns a personal residence that she inherited from her mother five years   *Ethics and Equity*
ago. For estate tax purposes, the house was valued at $625,000. (Her mother's adjusted
basis was $400,000.) Meg has been offered $500,000 for the inherited house.

   Meg also owns another house that she purchased in a resort community. She wants to sell
the inherited house and move to the resort community. Her brother advises Meg that losses
on the sale of personal use assets are not deductible but that losses on the sale of rental property are deductible. He suggests that she rent the inherited house to the prospective buyer,
with the option to buy it for $500,000 at the end of the one-year rental period. By doing so,
she will be able to claim a deduction for the loss. The loss on the sale would be $125,000,
reduced by the amount of depreciation deducted on the rental house. If necessary, Meg's
brother can arrange for an appraisal to reflect that the house is currently worth $625,000.

   Meg follows her brother's advice and takes a deduction for the loss when she sells the
house in one year. Has Meg acted appropriately? Explain.

3. **LO.1, 2** Pam owns a personal-use boat that has a fair market value of $35,000 and an
adjusted basis of $45,000. Pam's AGI is $100,000. Calculate the realized and recognized
gain or loss if:
   a. Pam sells the boat for $35,000.
   b. Pam exchanges the boat for another boat worth $35,000.
   c. The boat is stolen and Pam receives insurance proceeds of $35,000.
   d. Would your answer in (a) change if the fair market value and the selling price of the
      boat were $48,000?

4. **LO.1, 2** Yancy's personal residence is condemned as part of an urban renewal project.
His adjusted basis for the residence is $480,000. He receives condemnation proceeds of
$460,000 and invests the proceeds in stocks and bonds.
   a. Calculate Yancy's realized and recognized gain or loss.
   b. If the condemnation proceeds are $505,000, what are Yancy's realized and recog-
      nized gain or loss?
   c. What are Yancy's realized and recognized gain or loss in (a) if the house was rental
      property?

5. **LO.1, 2, 3** Finch, Inc., purchases 1,000 shares of Bluebird Corporation stock on October 3, 2014, for $300,000. On December 12, 2014, Finch purchases an additional 750
shares of Bluebird stock for $210,000. According to market quotations, Bluebird stock is
selling for $285 per share on December 31, 2014. Finch sells 500 shares of Bluebird
stock on March 1, 2015, for $162,500.
   a. What is the adjusted basis of Finch's Bluebird stock on December 31, 2014?
   b. What is Finch's recognized gain or loss from the sale of Bluebird stock on March 1,
      2015, assuming the shares sold are from the shares purchased on December 12, 2014?
   c. What is Finch's recognized gain or loss from the sale of Bluebird stock on March 1,
      2015, assuming Finch cannot adequately identify the shares sold?

6. **LO.2, 3** Rod Clooney purchases Agnes Mitchell's sole proprietorship for $990,000 on   *Communications*
August 15, 2014. The assets of the business are as follows:

Asset	Agnes's Adjusted Basis	FMV
Accounts receivable	$ 70,000	$ 70,000
Inventory	90,000	100,000
Equipment	150,000	160,000
Furniture and fixtures	95,000	130,000
Building	190,000	250,000
Land	25,000	75,000
Total	$620,000	$785,000

Rod and Agnes agree that $50,000 of the purchase price is for Agnes's five-year covenant
not to compete.
   a. Calculate Agnes's realized and recognized gain.
   b. Determine Rod's basis for each of the assets.
   c. Write a letter to Rod informing him of the tax consequences of the purchase. His
      address is 300 Riverview Drive, Delaware, OH 43015.

7. **LO.I, 2, 3** Roberto has received various gifts over the years. He has decided to dispose of the following assets he received as gifts:
   a. In 1951, he received land worth $32,000. The donor's adjusted basis was $35,000. Roberto sells the land for $95,000 in 2014.
   b. In 1956, he received stock in Gold Company. The donor's adjusted basis was $19,000. The fair market value on the date of the gift was $34,000. Roberto sells the stock for $40,000 in 2014.
   c. In 1962, he received land worth $15,000. The donor's adjusted basis was $20,000. Roberto sells the land for $9,000 in 2014.
   d. In 2003, he received stock worth $30,000. The donor's adjusted basis was $42,000. Roberto sells the stock for $38,000 in 2014.

   What is the recognized gain or loss from each of the preceding transactions? Assume for each of the gift transactions that no gift tax was paid.

Ethics and Equity

8. **LO.3** Holly owns stock with an adjusted basis of $2,500 and fair market value of $9,500. Holly expects the stock to continue to appreciate. Alice, Holly's best friend, recently had surgery for cancer. Alice's physicians have told her that her life expectancy is between six months and one and a half years. One day at lunch, the two friends were discussing their tax situations (both believe they pay too much), when Alice mentioned that she had read a newspaper article about a tax planning opportunity that might be suitable for Holly. Holly would make a gift of the appreciated stock to Alice. In her will, Alice would bequeath the stock back to Holly. Because Alice is confident she will live longer than a year, the basis of the stock to Holly would be the fair market value on the date of Alice's death. Alice would "feel good" because she had helped Holly "beat the tax system." You are Holly's tax adviser. How will you respond to Alice's proposal? Would your response change if the stock were a painting that Alice could enjoy for her remaining days? Explain.

9. **LO.I, 2, 3** Nicky receives a car from Sam as a gift. Sam paid $48,000 for the car. He had used it for business purposes and had deducted $10,000 for depreciation up to the time he gave the car to Nicky. The fair market value of the car is $33,000.
   a. Assuming that Nicky uses the car for business purposes, what is her basis for depreciation?
   b. Assume that Nicky deducts depreciation of $6,500 and then sells the car for $32,500. What is her recognized gain or loss?
   c. Assume that Nicky deducts depreciation of $6,500 and then sells the car for $20,000. What is her recognized gain or loss?

10. **LO.3** Margo receives a gift of real estate with an adjusted basis of $175,000 and a fair market value of $100,000. The donor paid gift tax of $15,000 on the transfer. If Margo later sells the property for $110,000, what is her recognized gain or loss?

Issue ID

11. **LO.3** Simon owns stock that has declined in value since acquired. He has decided either to give the stock to his nephew, Fred, or to sell it and give Fred the proceeds. If Fred receives the stock, he will sell it to obtain the proceeds. Simon is in the 15% tax bracket, while Fred's bracket is 25%. In either case, the holding period for the stock will be short-term. Identify the tax issues relevant to Simon in deciding whether to give the stock or the sale proceeds to Fred.

12. **LO.3** On September 18, 2014, Gerald received land and a building from Frank as a gift. Frank's adjusted basis and the fair market value at the date of the gift are as follows:

Asset	Adjusted Basis	FMV
Land	$100,000	$212,000
Building	80,000	100,000

No gift tax was paid on the transfer.
   a. Determine Gerald's adjusted basis for the land and building.
   b. Assume instead that the fair market value of the land was $87,000 and that of the building was $65,000. Determine Gerald's adjusted basis for the land and building.

13. **LO.3** As sole heir, Dazie receives all of Mary's property (adjusted basis of $1,400,000 and fair market value of $3,820,000). Six months after Mary's death in 2014, the fair market value is $3,835,000.
    a. Can the executor of Mary's estate elect the alternate valuation date and amount? Explain.
    b. What is Dazie's basis for the property?
    c. Assume instead that the fair market value six months after Mary's death is $3.8 million. Respond to (a) and (b).

14. **LO.3** Dan bought a hotel for $2,600,000 in January 2010. In May 2014, he died and left the hotel to Ed. While Dan owned the hotel, he deducted $289,000 of cost recovery. The fair market value in May 2014 was $2,800,000. The fair market value six months later was $2,850,000.
    a. What is the basis of the property to Ed?
    b. What is the basis of the property to Ed if the fair market value six months later was $2,500,000 (not $2,850,000) and the objective of the executor was to minimize the estate tax liability?

15. **LO.4** Sheila sells land to Elane, her sister, for the fair market value of $40,000. Six months later when the land is worth $45,000, Elane gives it to Jacob, her son. (No gift tax resulted.) Shortly thereafter, Jacob sells the land for $48,000.
    a. Assuming that Sheila's adjusted basis for the land is $24,000, what are Sheila's and Jacob's recognized gain or loss on the sales?
    b. Assuming that Sheila's adjusted basis for the land is $60,000, what are Sheila's and Jacob's recognized gain or loss on the sales?

16. **LO.1, 2, 3, 4** Tyneka inherited 1,000 shares of Aqua, Inc. stock from Joe. Joe's basis was $35,000, and the fair market value on July 1, 2014 (the date of death), was $45,000. The shares were distributed to Tyneka on July 15, 2014. Tyneka sold the stock on July 30, 2015, for $33,000. After giving the matter more thought, she decides that Aqua is a good investment and purchases 1,000 shares for $30,000 on August 20, 2015.
    a. What is Tyneka's basis for the 1,000 shares purchased on August 20, 2015?
    b. Could Tyneka have obtained different tax consequences in (a) if she had sold the 1,000 shares on December 27, 2014, and purchased the 1,000 shares on January 5, 2015? Explain.

Decision Making

17. **LO.1, 2, 4** Abby's home had a basis of $360,000 ($160,000 attributable to the land) and a fair market value of $340,000 ($155,000 attributable to the land) when she converted 70% of it to business use by opening a bed-and-breakfast. Four years after the conversion, Abby sells the home for $500,000 ($165,000 attributable to the land).
    a. Calculate Abby's basis for gain, loss, and cost recovery for the portion of her personal residence that was converted to business use.
    b. Calculate the cost recovery deducted by Abby during the four-year period of business use assuming that the bed-and-breakfast is opened on January 1 of year 1 and the house is sold on December 31 of year 4.
    c. What is Abby's recognized gain or loss on the sale of the business-use portion?

18. **LO.4** Surendra's personal residence originally cost $340,000 (ignore land). After living in the house for five years, he converts it to rental property. At the date of conversion, the fair market value of the house is $320,000. As to the rental property, calculate Surendra's basis for:
    a. Loss.
    b. Depreciation.
    c. Gain.
    d. Could Surendra have obtained better tax results if he had sold his personal residence for $320,000 and then purchased another house for $320,000 to hold as rental property? Explain.

Critical Thinking

Decision Making

19. **LO.5** Sue exchanges a sport utility vehicle (adjusted basis of $16,000; fair market value of $19,500) for cash of $2,000 and a pickup truck (fair market value of $17,500). Both vehicles are for business use. Sue believes that her basis for the truck is $17,500. In calculating her basis, what has Sue failed to consider?

Issue ID

20. **LO.6** A warehouse owned by M&S (a partnership) and used in its business (i.e., to store inventory) is being condemned by the city to provide a right-of-way for a highway. The warehouse has appreciated by $180,000 based on an estimate of fair market value. In the negotiations, the city is offering $35,000 less than what M&S believes the property is worth. Alan, a real estate broker, has offered to purchase the property for $20,000 more than the city's offer. The partnership plans to invest the proceeds it will receive in an office building it will lease to various tenants.

a. Identify the relevant tax issues for M&S.

b. Would the answer in (a) change if M&S's warehouse was property being held for investment rather than being used in its business? Explain.

Decision Making

Communications

21. **LO.5** Tanya Fletcher owns undeveloped land (adjusted basis of $80,000 and fair market value of $92,000) on the East Coast. On January 4, 2014, she exchanges it with Martin (an unrelated party) for undeveloped land on the West Coast and $3,000 cash. Martin has an adjusted basis of $72,000 for his land, and its fair market value is $89,000. As the real estate market on the East Coast is thriving, on September 1, 2015, Martin sells the land he acquired for $120,000.

a. What are Tanya's recognized gain or loss and adjusted basis for the West Coast land on January 4, 2014?

b. What are Martin's recognized gain or loss and adjusted basis for the East Coast land on January 4, 2014?

c. What is Martin's recognized gain or loss from the September 1, 2015 sale?

d. What effect does Martin's 2015 sale have on Tanya?

e. Write a letter to Tanya advising her of the tax consequences of this exchange. Her address is The Corral, El Paso, TX 79968.

22. **LO.5** Starling Corporation exchanges a yellow bus (used in its business) for Robin Corporation's gray bus and some garage equipment (used in its business). The assets have the following characteristics:

	Adjusted Basis	Fair Market Value
Yellow bus	$6,000	$15,000
Gray bus	3,000	11,000
Equipment	2,000	4,000

a. What are Starling's recognized gain or loss and basis for the gray bus and garage equipment?

b. What are Robin's recognized gain or loss and basis for the yellow bus?

23. **LO.5** Maple Company owns a machine (adjusted basis of $90,000; fair market value of $125,000) that it uses in its business. Maple exchanges it for another machine (worth $100,000) and stock (worth $25,000). Determine Maple's:

a. Realized and recognized gain or loss on the exchange.

b. Basis in the new machine.

c. Basis in the stock Maple received.

Issue ID

24. **LO.5** Tulip, Inc., would like to dispose of some land it acquired four years ago because the land will not continue to appreciate. Its value has increased by $50,000 over the four-year period. The company also intends to sell stock that has declined in value by $50,000 during the six months since its purchase. Tulip has four offers to acquire the stock and land:

Buyer 1:   Exchange land.

Buyer 2:   Purchase land for cash.

Buyer 3:   Exchange stock.

Buyer 4:   Purchase stock for cash.

Identify the tax issues relevant to Tulip in disposing of this land and stock.

25. **LO.5** What is the basis of the new property in each of the following exchanges?

a. Apartment building held for investment (adjusted basis of $145,000) for office building to be held for investment (fair market value of $225,000).

b. Land and building used as a barbershop (adjusted basis of $190,000) for land and building used as a grocery store (fair market value of $350,000).

    c. Office building (adjusted basis of $45,000) for bulldozer (fair market value of $42,000), both held for business use.

    d. IBM common stock (adjusted basis of $20,000) for ExxonMobil common stock (fair market value of $28,000).

    e. Rental house (adjusted basis of $90,000) for mountain cabin to be held for personal use (fair market value of $225,000).

    f. General partnership interest (adjusted basis of $400,000) for a limited partnership interest (fair market value of $580,000).

26. **LO.1, 2, 5** Rose Company owns Machine A (adjusted basis of $12,000 and fair market value of $15,000), which it uses in its business. Rose sells Machine A for $15,000 to Aubry (a dealer) and then purchases Machine B for $15,000 from Joan (also a dealer). Machine B would normally qualify as like-kind property.

    a. What are Rose Company's realized and recognized gain on the sale of Machine A?

    b. What is Rose's basis for Machine B?

    c. What factors would motivate Rose to sell Machine A and purchase Machine B rather than exchange one machine for the other?

    d. Assume that the adjusted basis of Machine A is $15,000 and the fair market value of both machines is $12,000. Respond to (a) through (c).

27. **LO.5** Cardinal Properties, Inc., exchanges real estate used in its business along with stock for real estate to be held for investment. The stock transferred has an adjusted basis of $45,000 and a fair market value of $50,000. The real estate transferred has an adjusted basis of $85,000 and a fair market value of $190,000. The real estate acquired has a fair market value of $240,000.

    a. What is Cardinal's realized gain or loss?

    b. Its recognized gain or loss?

    c. The basis of the newly acquired real estate?

28. **LO.5** Tom and Frank are brothers. Each owns investment property in the other's hometown. To make their lives easier, they decide to legally exchange the investment properties. Under the terms of the exchange, Frank will transfer realty (adjusted basis of $52,000; fair market value of $80,000) and Tom will exchange realty (adjusted basis of $60,000; fair market value of $92,000). Tom's property is subject to a mortgage of $12,000 that will be assumed by Frank.

Decision Making

    a. What are Frank's and Tom's recognized gains?

    b. What are their adjusted bases?

    c. As an alternative, Frank has proposed that rather than assuming the mortgage, he will transfer cash of $12,000 to Tom. Tom would use the cash to pay off the mortgage. Advise Tom on whether this alternative would be beneficial to him from a tax perspective.

29. **LO.5** Determine the realized, recognized, and postponed gain or loss and the new basis for each of the following like-kind exchanges:

	Adjusted Basis of Old Asset	Boot Given	Fair Market Value of New Asset	Boot Received
a.	$ 7,000	$ –0–	$12,000	$4,000
b.	14,000	2,000	15,000	–0–
c.	3,000	7,000	8,000	500
d.	15,000	–0–	29,000	–0–
e.	10,000	–0–	11,000	1,000
f.	17,000	–0–	14,000	–0–

30. **LO.5** Turquoise Realty Company owns an apartment house that has an adjusted basis of $760,000 but is subject to a mortgage of $192,000. Turquoise transfers the apartment house to Dove, Inc., and receives from Dove $120,000 in cash and an office building with a fair market value of $780,000 at the time of the exchange. Dove assumes the $192,000 mortgage on the apartment house.

    a. What is Turquoise's realized gain or loss?

    b. What is its recognized gain or loss?

    c. What is the basis of the newly acquired office building?

31. **LO.6** Howard's roadside vegetable stand (adjusted basis of $275,000) is destroyed by a tractor-trailer accident. He receives insurance proceeds of $240,000 ($300,000 fair market value less $60,000 coinsurance). Howard immediately uses the proceeds plus additional cash of $45,000 to build another roadside vegetable stand at the same location. What are the tax consequences to Howard?

32. **LO.6** For each of the following involuntary conversions, indicate whether the property acquired qualifies as replacement property, the recognized gain, and the basis for the property acquired.

    a. A warehouse is destroyed by a tornado. The space in the warehouse was rented to various tenants. The adjusted basis was $470,000. The owner of the warehouse uses all of the insurance proceeds of $700,000 to build a shopping mall in a neighboring community where no property has been damaged by tornadoes. The shopping mall is rented to various tenants.

    b. A warehouse is destroyed by fire. The adjusted basis is $300,000. Because of economic conditions in the area, the owner decides not to rebuild the warehouse. Instead, it uses all of the insurance proceeds of $400,000 to build a warehouse in another state.

    c. Ridge's personal residence is condemned as part of a local government project to widen the highway from two lanes to four lanes. The adjusted basis is $170,000. Ridge uses all of the condemnation proceeds of $200,000 to purchase another personal residence.

    d. Swallow Fashions, Inc., owns a building that is destroyed by a hurricane. The adjusted basis is $250,000. Because of an economic downturn in the area caused by the closing of a military base, Swallow decides to rent space for its retail outlet rather than replace the building. It uses all of the insurance proceeds of $300,000 to buy a four-unit apartment building in another city. A realtor in that city will handle the rental of the apartments.

    e. Susan and Rick's personal residence is destroyed by a tornado. They had owned it for 15 months. The adjusted basis was $170,000. Because they would like to travel, they decide not to acquire a replacement residence. Instead, they invest all of the insurance proceeds of $200,000 in a duplex, which they rent to tenants.

    f. Ellen and Harry's personal residence (adjusted basis of $245,000) is destroyed in a flood. They had owned it for 18 months. Of the insurance proceeds of $350,000, they reinvest $342,000 in a replacement residence four months later.

Ethics and Equity   33. **LO.6** The city of Richmond is going to condemn some buildings to build a park. Steve's principal residence is among those to be condemned. His adjusted basis for the house and land is $120,000. The appraised value of the house and land is $104,000. Steve is unaware of the future condemnation proceedings, but would like his family to move to a better neighborhood. Therefore, when Ross, a realtor, mentions that he may have a corporate client who would like to purchase the property for $130,000, Steve is ecstatic and indicates a willingness to sell.

Ross is having second thoughts about his conversation with Steve. The potential corporate purchaser is a company owned by Ross and his wife. Ross is aware of the future condemnation proceedings. He considers himself a skilled negotiator and thinks that he can negotiate a $260,000 price for the house. Ross is considering telling Steve that the corporate client has changed its mind. Ross would then indicate that he has learned the city will be condemning several buildings to create a park, but has not yet established the prices it will pay for the condemned property. He would also tell Steve that because he believes he can get more from the city than Steve would obtain, he is willing to gamble and purchase the property now from Steve for $130,000.

Ross will point out several benefits available to Steve. These include (1) not having to deal with the city, (2) receiving an amount that exceeds both the appraised value and the original purchase cost of the home, and (3) receiving the money now. While admitting that he could reap a substantial profit, Ross would emphasize that he would also be taking on substantial risks. In addition, Ross would explain that when he sells the property to the city, he will defer the taxes by reinvesting the sales proceeds (due to involuntary conversion).

Should Ross make a new proposal to Steve based on his second thoughts? How do you think Steve will respond?

34. **LO.6** Edith's warehouse (adjusted basis of $450,000) is destroyed by a hurricane in October 2014. Edith, a calendar year taxpayer, receives insurance proceeds of $525,000 in January 2015. Calculate Edith's realized gain or loss, recognized gain or loss, and basis for the replacement property if she:
    a. Acquires a new warehouse for $550,000 in January 2015.
    b. Acquires a new warehouse for $500,000 in January 2015.
    c. Does not acquire replacement property.

35. **LO.6** Parkview, Inc.'s warehouse, which has an adjusted basis of $380,000 and a fair market value of $490,000, is condemned by an agency of the Federal government to make way for a highway interchange. The initial condemnation offer is $425,000. After substantial negotiations, the agency agrees to transfer to Parkview a surplus warehouse that it believes is worth $490,000. Parkview is a calendar year taxpayer. The condemnation and related asset transfer occurred during September 2014.
    a. What are the recognized gain or loss and the basis of the replacement warehouse if Parkview's objective is to recognize as much gain as possible?
    b. Advise Parkview regarding what it needs to do by what date to achieve its objective.

Decision Making

36. **LO.6** What are the *maximum* postponed gain or loss and the basis for the replacement property for the following involuntary conversions?

	Property	Type of Conversion	Amount Realized	Adjusted Basis	Amount Reinvested
a.	Drugstore (business)	Condemned	$160,000	$120,000	$100,000
b.	Apartments (investment)	Casualty	100,000	120,000	200,000
c.	Grocery store (business)	Casualty	400,000	300,000	350,000
d.	Residence (personal)	Casualty	16,000	18,000	17,000
e.	Vacant lot (investment)	Condemned	240,000	160,000	240,000
f.	Residence (personal)	Casualty	20,000	18,000	19,000
g.	Residence (personal)	Condemned	18,000	20,000	26,000
h.	Apartments (investment)	Condemned	150,000	100,000	200,000

37. **LO.7** Wesley, who is single, listed his personal residence with a real estate agent on March 3, 2014, at a price of $390,000. He rejected several offers in the $350,000 range during the summer. Finally, on August 16, 2014, he and the purchaser signed a contract to sell for $363,000. The sale (i.e., closing) took place on September 7, 2014. The closing statement showed the following disbursements:

Critical Thinking

Real estate agent's commission	$ 21,780
Appraisal fee	600
Exterminator's certificate	300
Recording fees	800
Mortgage to First Bank	305,000
Cash to seller	34,520

Wesley's adjusted basis for the house is $200,000. He owned and occupied the house for seven years. On October 1, 2014, Wesley purchases another residence for $325,000.
    a. Calculate Wesley's recognized gain on the sale.
    b. What is Wesley's adjusted basis for the new residence?
    c. Assume instead that the selling price is $800,000. What is Wesley's recognized gain? His adjusted basis for the new residence?

38. **LO.7** Roby and James have been married for nine years. Roby sells Plum, Inc. stock that she has owned for four years to James for its fair market value of $180,000. Her adjusted basis is $200,000.
    a. Calculate Roby's recognized gain or recognized loss.
    b. Calculate James's adjusted basis for the stock.
    c. How would the tax consequences in (a) and (b) differ if Roby had made a gift of the stock to James? Which form of the transaction would you recommend?

Critical Thinking

Decision Making

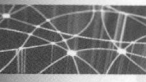

BRIDGE DISCIPLINE

1. In April of the current year, Blue Corporation purchased an asset to be used in its manu-facturing operations for $100,000. Blue's management expects the asset to ratably pro-vide valuable services in the production process for eight years and have a salvage value of $12,000. The asset is a five-year asset for tax purposes. Blue has adopted the half-year convention for book purposes in the year of acquisition and disposition; Blue uses MACRS for tax purposes.
   a. Compute the depreciation expense in the year of acquisition for book and tax purposes.
   b. Identify the book-tax difference related to the depreciation expense in the year of acquisition.

2. Refer to the facts in the preceding problem. Assume that Blue Corporation disposes of the manufacturing asset at the beginning of year 7 for $40,000. Compute the amount of gain or loss recognized for book and tax purposes. What is the book-tax difference in the year of disposition?

3. Identify whether the taxpayer's economic position has changed in the following exchanges such that they are subject to current taxation. That is, identify whether the fol-lowing qualify as like-kind exchanges under § 1031.
   a. Improved for unimproved real estate.
   b. Vending machine (used in business) for inventory.
   c. Rental house for personal residence.
   d. Business equipment for securities.
   e. Warehouse for office building (both used for business).
   f. Truck for computer (both used in business).
   g. Rental house for land (both held for investment).
   h. Ten shares of stock in Blue Corporation for 10 shares of stock in Red Corporation.
   i. Office furniture for office equipment (both used in business).
   j. Unimproved land in Jackson, Mississippi, for unimproved land in Toledo, Spain.
   k. General partnership interest for a general partnership interest.

Research Problems

Note: Solutions to Research Problems can be prepared by using the **Checkpoint®** **Student Edition** online research product, which is available to accompany this text. It is also possible to prepare solutions to the Research Problems by using tax research mate-rials found in a standard tax library.

Communications

Research Problem 1. Ruth Ames died on January 10, 2014. In filing the estate tax return, her executor, Melvin Sims, elects the primary valuation date and amount (fair market value on the date of death). On March 12, 2014, Melvin invests $30,000 of cash that Ruth had in her money market account in acquiring 1,000 shares of Orange, Inc. ($30 per share). On January 10, 2014, Orange was selling for $29 per share. The stock is distrib-uted to a beneficiary, Annette Rust, on June 1, 2014, when it is selling for $33 per share. Melvin wants you to determine the amount at which the Orange shares should appear on the estate tax return and the amount of Annette's adjusted basis for the stock. Write a let-ter to Melvin in which you respond to his inquiry and prepare a memo for the tax files. His address is 100 Center Lane, Miami, FL 33124.

Research Problem 2. Terry owns real estate with an adjusted basis of $600,000 and a fair mar-ket value of $1.1 million. The amount of the nonrecourse mortgage on the property is $2.5 million. Because of substantial past and projected future losses associated with the real estate development (occupancy rate of only 37% after three years), Terry deeds the property to the creditor.
   a. What are the tax consequences to Terry?
   b. Assume that the data are the same, except that the fair market value of the property is $2,525,000. Therefore, when Terry deeds the property to the creditor, she also receives $25,000 from the creditor. What are the tax consequences to Terry?

Research Problem 3. Ted and Marvin Brown purchased an apartment building in 2003 as equal tenants in common. After a hectic decade of co-ownership, the brothers decided that their business association should be terminated. This led to the sale of the apartment building and a division of the proceeds.

Critical Thinking

The realized gain on the sale of the apartment building for each brother was $350,000. Ted recognized gain on his share and used the net proceeds to invest in stock. Marvin wanted to defer any recognized gain, so he worked with a realtor to identify property that would be eligible for § 1031 like-kind exchange treatment. After one prospect failed, the realtor identified a single-family home on Lake Tahoe that was currently being rented by the owner. Marvin agreed with the choice and acquired the single-family house using the proceeds from the apartment building. Because the single-family house qualified as like-kind property, Marvin deferred all of his realized gain.

After attempting to rent the property for eight months without success, Marvin concluded that he could not continue to make the mortgage payments on his primary residence and this rental property. To ease his financial liquidity problem, Marvin sold his principal residence for a realized gain of $190,000 and moved into the Lake Tahoe house. He reported no recognized gain on the sale of his principal residence as the sale qualified for § 121 exclusion treatment.

The IRS issued a deficiency notice to Marvin associated with the sale of the apartment building. The position of the IRS was that Marvin did not hold the single-family residence for investment purposes as required by § 1031. Instead, his intention was personal—to use it as a replacement for his current residence that he planned on selling.

Who should prevail?

Use the tax resources of the Internet to address the following questions. Do not restrict your search to the Web, but include a review of newsgroups and general reference materials, practitioner sites and resources, primary sources of the tax law, chat rooms and discussion groups, and other opportunities.

 Internet Activity

Research Problem 4. Many see the "step-up in basis at death" rule of § 1014 as an expensive tax loophole enjoyed by the wealthy. Find the latest estimates of the revenue loss to the Treasury that is attributable to this rule.

a. How does Canada's tax law determine the basis of property acquired from a decedent?

b. Send an e-mail to a member of the House Ways and Means Committee expressing a preference for the preservation of the current § 1014 rule or the modifications made to it by the Tax Relief Reconciliation Act of 2001 and the Tax Relief Act of 2010.

Research Problem 5. Find two newspaper stories about transactions to which you believe the involuntary conversion rules could apply. Do not limit your search to individual taxpayers.

Research Problem 6. In general, the 45-day identification period and the 180-day exchange period for like-kind exchanges cannot be extended. Does this rule change if the like-kind property or the taxpayer involved in the exchange is located in a Presidentially declared disaster area? Use the IRS's website (**www.irs.gov**) to find the answer.

CHAPTER

8 Property Transactions: Capital Gains and Losses, Section 1231, and Recapture Provisions

LEARNING OBJECTIVES: *After completing Chapter 8, you should be able to:*

LO.1 **Discuss the general scheme of taxation for capital gains and losses and distinguish capital assets from ordinary assets.**

LO.2 **State and explain the relevance of a sale or exchange to classification as a capital gain or loss.**

LO.3 **Determine the applicable holding period for a capital asset.**

LO.4 **Describe the tax treatment of capital gains and losses for noncorporate taxpayers.**

LO.5 **Describe the tax treatment of capital gains and losses for corporate taxpayers.**

LO.6 **Distinguish § 1231 assets from ordinary and capital assets and calculate § 1231 gain or loss.**

LO.7 **Determine when recapture provisions apply and derive their effects.**

CHAPTER OUTLINE

TAX TALK *Governments likely to confiscate wealth are unlikely to find much wealth to confiscate in the long run.* —THOMAS SOWELL

Dennis Flaherty/Photographer's Choice/Getty Images

THE BIG PICTURE   Tax Solutions for the Real World

CAPITAL GAINS AND LOSSES, § 1231 GAINS AND LOSSES, AND RECAPTURE

Alice owns land that she received from her father 10 years ago as a gift. The land was purchased by her father in 1990 for $2,000 and was worth $10,000 at the time of the gift. The property is currently worth about $50,000. If Alice sells the land, you previously determined in Chapter 7 that she would have a taxable gain of $48,000.

Alice also owns 500 shares of Purple Company stock, 300 of which were acquired as an inheritance when Alice's grandfather died in 1995. Alice's grandfather paid $12,000 for the Purple shares, and they were worth $30,000 at the time of his death. If Alice sells those shares for $120 each, you previously determined that she would have a $6,000 taxable gain. The other 200 shares were purchased by Alice two months ago for $28,000. If Alice sells those shares for $120 each, you determined that she would have a recognized loss of $4,000.

Nine months ago, Alice purchased 100 shares of Eagle Company stock for $5,000. Also on the same day, Alice invested $50,000 in a 50 percent interest in a patent that Kathy, a former college roommate who is an unemployed inventor, had obtained for a special battery she had developed to power "green" cars. To date, Kathy has been unable to market the battery to an auto manufacturer or supplier, but she has high hopes of doing so given the current price of gasoline. In addition, Alice purchased a franchise from Orange, Inc., for $100,000.

Alice also owns a house that she inherited from her grandmother two years ago. Based on the estate tax return, the fair market value of the house at the date of her grandmother's death was $475,000, and Alice will recognize a $125,000 gain on the sale of the property.

Finally Alice's new husband, Jeff, sold depreciable equipment used in his sole proprietorship. The business purchased the equipment for $50,000 and deducted $35,000 of depreciation before selling it for $60,000.

Now Alice would like to know more about the gains and losses and the tax liability she and her husband can expect from these transactions.

Read the chapter and formulate your response.

Since the earliest days of the Federal income tax, **capital assets** have received special treatment upon their disposition. Gains from these assets have historically received *preferential treatment* in the form of either partial exclusion of gain, lower rates, or a maximum tax rate. Losses from capital assets, however, have historically received less desirable treatment than losses from other assets. Further, because a taxpayer has complete control over the timing of dispositions, the Code imposes limitations on when capital losses can be deducted to prevent taxpayers from manipulating their tax liability excessively.

During World War II, capital asset treatment was extended to other assets. These assets are now called "§ 1231 assets" after the Code Section that prescribes their special treatment. Several years after World War II ended, Congress believed that this special treatment was no longer entirely warranted. Instead of repealing § 1231, however, Congress left that section in place but eroded many—but not all—of its benefits through *recapture provisions* in § 1245 and § 1250. Together, these Code Sections constitute one of the most complicated areas of tax law affecting both individual taxpayers and business entities.

As already intimated, one concern is that taxpayers can time the realization of gains and losses by choosing when or even whether to sell the asset in question. If Lark Enterprises, Inc., owns stock with a basis of $20 per share and a current value of $80 per share, it does not pay tax on the $60 gain until it chooses to dispose of this stock in a taxable transaction. And for the most part, Lark has complete control over that decision. When it does dispose of the stock, however, its $60 gain is taxable in full, even though this gain may have accrued over many years. To mitigate the impact of this *bunching* of income in a single year and to offset the effect of inflation over the period of Lark's ownership of the stock, preferential treatment is prescribed for this **capital gain**.

The nature of this preferential treatment is discussed later in this chapter, but the essential point for now is that preferential treatment is confined to the excess of net long-term capital gains over net short-term **capital losses**. In addition, the tax law requires taxpayers to separate their capital asset transactions from their transactions involving noncapital assets. It further requires taxpayers to separate their long-term (i.e., more than one year) transactions from their short-term (i.e., one year or less) transactions. Moreover, certain types of capital assets (principally real estate and "collectibles") receive specific treatment apart from the rates generally applicable to capital assets.

8-1 GENERAL SCHEME OF TAXATION

LO.1

Discuss the general scheme of taxation for capital gains and losses and distinguish capital assets from ordinary assets.

Recognized gains and losses must be properly classified. Proper classification depends upon three characteristics.

- The tax status of the property, including the specific type of asset.
- The manner of the property's disposition.
- The holding period of the property.

The three possible tax statuses are capital asset, § 1231 asset, and ordinary asset. Property disposition may be by sale, exchange, casualty, theft, or condemnation. The two relevant holding periods are one year or less (short-term) and more than one year (long-term).

8-2 CAPITAL ASSETS

Investments comprise the most typical category of capital assets and include corporate stocks and bonds, mutual funds, partnership interests, government securities, and vacant land. These assets can be held by any type of taxpayer—individuals; partnerships; limited liability companies; and corporations, whether closely held or publicly held. In addition, individuals own certain capital assets that are part of their daily life, such as residences, automobiles, furniture, and artwork. The classification of these *personal-use* assets as capital assets is relevant only when their disposition produces a recognized gain. Losses from the disposition of personal-use assets are not recognized for tax purposes, as explained in the preceding chapter. For businesses, goodwill is often the only capital asset.

In-depth coverage can be found on this book's companion website: **www.cengagebrain.com**

 | Digging Deeper

8-2a Definition of a Capital Asset (§ 1221)

Capital assets are not directly defined in the Code. Instead, § 1221(a) defines what is *not* a capital asset. A capital asset is property held by the taxpayer that is *not* any of the following.

- Inventory or property held primarily for sale to customers in the ordinary course of a business. The Supreme Court, in *Malat v. Riddell*,[1] defined *primarily* as meaning "of first importance or principally."
- Accounts and notes receivable acquired from the sale of inventory or acquired for services rendered in the ordinary course of business.
- Depreciable property or real estate used in a business.
- Certain copyrights; literary, musical, or artistic compositions; or letters, memoranda, or similar property held by (1) a taxpayer whose efforts created the property; (2) in the case of a letter, memorandum, or similar property, a taxpayer for whom it was produced; or (3) a taxpayer who received the property as a lifetime gift from someone described in (1) or (2). When a sale or exchange involves musical compositions or copyrights in musical works either (1) created by the taxpayer's personal efforts or (2) having a basis determined by reference to the basis in the hands of a taxpayer whose personal efforts created the compositions or copyrights, the taxpayer may elect to treat the sale or exchange as the disposition of a capital asset.[2]
- U.S. government publications that are (1) received by a taxpayer from the U.S. government other than by purchase at the price at which they are offered for sale to the public or (2) held by a taxpayer who received the publication as a lifetime gift from someone described in (1).
- Supplies of a type regularly used or consumed in the ordinary course of a business.

Inventory

What constitutes inventory is determined by reference to the taxpayer's business.

Green Company buys and sells used automobiles. Its automobiles are inventory. Therefore, Green's gains from the sale of the cars are ordinary income.	**Example 1**

Soong sells her personal-use automobile at a $500 gain. The automobile is a personal-use asset and, therefore, a capital asset. Soong's gain is a capital gain.	**Example 2**

No asset is inherently capital or ordinary. If Soong in Example 2 sells her capital asset automobile to Green Company in Example 1, that very same automobile loses its capital asset status, because it is inventory to Green Company. Similar transformations can occur if, for example, an art dealer sells a painting (inventory, *not* a capital asset) to a private collector (now a capital asset). Whether an asset is capital or ordinary, therefore, depends entirely on the relationship of *that asset* to the taxpayer who sold it. This classification dilemma is but one feature of capital asset treatment that makes this area so confusing and perennially complicated.

---

[1] 66–1 USTC ¶9317, 17 AFTR 2d 604, 86 S.Ct. 1030 (USSC, 1966).   [2] § 1221(b)(3).

TAX IN THE NEWS   Certainty over Capital Gain Rates

During the fall of 2012, President Obama proposed legislation that, starting in 2013, would increase capital gain rates on many high-income taxpayers. The proposed rates were not as favorable as the rates that applied to 2011 and 2012 tax returns of individual taxpayers.

Ultimately, tax legislation was enacted early in 2013 that included higher capital gain rates for certain high-income individuals but it retained the lower tax rates on long-term capital gains for other taxpayers. The current rates are discussed later in this chapter.

Accounts and Notes Receivable

Collection of an accrual basis account receivable usually does not result in a gain or loss because the amount collected equals the receivable's basis. The *sale* of an account or note receivable may generate a gain or loss, however, because it will probably be sold for more or less than its basis. That gain or loss will be ordinary because the receivable is not a capital asset. A cash basis account receivable has no basis; so sale of such a receivable generates a gain, and that gain is ordinary income. Collection of a cash basis receivable also generates ordinary income.

Example 3

Oriole Company, an accrual basis taxpayer, has accounts receivable of $100,000. Gross income of $100,000 was recorded, and a $100,000 basis was established when the receivable was created. Because Oriole needs working capital, it sells the receivables for $83,000 to a financial institution. Accordingly, it has a $17,000 ordinary loss.

If Oriole is a cash basis taxpayer, it has $83,000 of ordinary income because it would not have recorded any income earlier and the receivable would have no tax basis.

Business Fixed Assets

Depreciable personal property and real estate (both depreciable and nondepreciable) used by a business are not capital assets. Thus, *business fixed assets* are not capital assets. Business fixed assets can sometimes be treated as capital assets pursuant to § 1231, however, as discussed later in this chapter.

Copyrights and Creative Works

Generally, the person whose efforts led to the copyright or creative work has an ordinary asset, not a capital asset. This rule makes the creator comparable to a taxpayer whose customary activity (salary, business profits) is taxed as ordinary income. *Creative works* include the works of authors, composers, and artists. Also, the person for whom a letter, a memorandum, or another similar property was created has an ordinary asset. Finally, a person receiving a copyright, creative work, a letter, a memorandum, or similar property by lifetime gift from the creator or the person for whom the work was created also has an ordinary asset. Note the exception mentioned earlier that permits the taxpayer to elect to treat the sale or exchange of a musical composition or a copyright of a musical work as the disposition of a capital asset.

Example 4

Wanda is a part-time music composer. A music publisher purchases one of her songs for $5,000. Wanda has a $5,000 ordinary gain from the sale of an ordinary asset unless she elects to treat the gain as a capital gain.

Example 5

Ed received a letter from the President of the United States in 1994. In the current year, Ed sells the letter to a collector for $300. Ed has a $300 ordinary gain from the sale of an ordinary asset (because the letter was created for Ed).

Example 6

Isabella gives a song she composed to her son. Her son sells the song to a music publisher for $5,000. Her son has a $5,000 ordinary gain from the sale of an ordinary asset unless he elects to treat the gain as a capital gain. If he inherits the song from Isabella, his basis for the song is its fair market value at Isabella's death. In this situation, the song is a capital asset because the son's basis is not related to Isabella's basis for the song (i.e., the song was not a *lifetime* gift).

U.S. Government Publications

U.S. government publications received from the U.S. government (or its agencies) for a reduced price (i.e., below that at which it is available to the general public) are not capital assets. This prevents a taxpayer from later donating the publications to charity and claiming a charitable contribution deduction equal to the fair market value of the publications. A charitable contribution of a capital asset generally yields a deduction equal to the asset's fair market value. If such property is received by gift from the original purchaser, the property is not a capital asset to the donee. (For a more comprehensive explanation of charitable contributions of property, refer to Chapter 5.)

In-depth coverage can be found on this book's companion website: **www.cengagebrain.com** **2** | Digging Deeper

8-2b Statutory Expansions

Because of the uncertainty often associated with capital asset status, Congress has occasionally enacted Code Sections to clarify the definition in particular circumstances. These statutory expansions of the capital asset definition are discussed in this section.

Dealers in Securities

As a general rule, securities (stocks, bonds, and other financial instruments) held by a dealer are considered to be inventory and are, therefore, not subject to capital gain or loss treatment. A *dealer in securities* is a merchant (e.g., a brokerage firm) that regularly engages in the purchase and resale of securities to customers. However, under the following circumstances, a dealer will have capital gain or capital loss. If a dealer clearly identifies certain securities as held for investment purposes by the close of business on the acquisition date, gain from the securities' sale will be capital gain. The gain will be ordinary if the dealer ceases to hold the securities for investment prior to the sale. Losses are capital losses if at any time the securities have been clearly identified by the dealer as held for investment.[3]

In-depth coverage can be found on this book's companion website: **www.cengagebrain.com** **3** | Digging Deeper

Real Property Subdivided for Sale (§ 1237)

Substantial real property development activities may result in the owner being considered a dealer for tax purposes. If so, income from the sale of real estate property lots will be treated as the sale of inventory and therefore will be taxed as ordinary income. However, § 1237 allows real estate investors to claim capital gain treatment

---

[3]§§ 1236(a) and (b) and Reg. §§ 1.1236–1(a) and (b).

TAX IN THE NEWS   Losses on Home Mortgages

Banks and other financial institutions have taken huge financial accounting write-downs on securities that consist of "bundles" of home mortgages. If the financial institution held these securities as investments, they were capital assets. If the financial institution held these securities as inventory, they were ordinary assets. However, writing them down for financial accounting purposes does not mean the institution actually disposed of the securities. Therefore, the loss in value of the securities is not recognized for tax purposes until the securities are transferred in a sale or exchange.

if they engage *only* in *limited* development activities. To be eligible for § 1237 treatment, the following requirements must be met.

- The taxpayer is not a corporation.
- The taxpayer is not a real estate dealer.
- No substantial improvements have been made to the lots sold. *Substantial* generally means more than a 10 percent increase in the value of a lot. Shopping centers and other commercial or residential buildings are considered substantial, while filling, draining, leveling, and clearing operations are not.
- The taxpayer has held the lots sold for at least 5 years, except for inherited property. The substantial improvements test is less stringent if the property is held at least 10 years.

If the preceding requirements are met, all gain is capital gain until the taxable year in which the *sixth* lot is sold. Sales of contiguous lots to a single buyer in the same transaction count as the sale of one lot. Beginning with the taxable year in which the *sixth* lot is sold, 5 percent of the revenue from lot sales is potential ordinary income. That potential ordinary income is offset by any selling expenses from the lot sales. Practically, sales commissions often are at least 5 percent of the sales price, so usually none of the gain is treated as ordinary income.

Section 1237 does not apply to losses. A loss from the sale of subdivided real property is ordinary loss unless the property qualifies as a capital asset under § 1221. The following example illustrates the application of § 1237.

Example 7

Ahmed owns a large tract of land and subdivides it for sale. Assume that Ahmed meets all of the requirements of § 1237 and during the tax year sells the first 10 lots to 10 different buyers for $10,000 each. Ahmed's basis in each lot sold is $3,000, and he incurs total selling expenses of $4,000 on the sales. Ahmed's gain is computed as follows.

Selling price (10 × $10,000)	$100,000	
Less: Selling expenses	(4,000)	
Amount realized		$ 96,000
Basis (10 × $3,000)		(30,000)
Realized and recognized gain		$ 66,000
Classification of recognized gain:		
Ordinary income		
Five percent of selling price (5% × $100,000)	$ 5,000	
Less: Selling expenses	(4,000)	
Ordinary gain		1,000
Capital gain		$ 65,000

8-3 SALE OR EXCHANGE

Recognition of capital gain or loss usually requires a **sale or exchange** of a capital asset. The Code uses the term *sale or exchange*, but does not define it. Generally, a property sale involves the receipt of money by the seller and/or the assumption by the purchaser of the seller's liabilities. An exchange involves the transfer of property for other property. Thus, an involuntary conversion (casualty, theft, or condemnation) is not a sale or exchange. In several situations, the determination of whether or when a sale or exchange has taken place has been clarified by the enactment of Code Sections that specifically provide for sale or exchange treatment. These situations are discussed below.

Recognized gains or losses from the cancellation, lapse, expiration, or any other termination of a right or obligation with respect to personal property (other than stock) that is or would be a capital asset in the hands of the taxpayer are capital gains or losses.[4] See the discussion under Options (below) for more details.

LO.2

State and explain the relevance of a sale or exchange to classification as a capital gain or loss.

8-3a Worthless Securities and § 1244 Stock

Occasionally, securities such as stocks and bonds may become worthless due to the insolvency of their issuer. If the security is a capital asset, the loss is deemed to have occurred as the result of a sale or exchange on the *last day* of the tax year.[5] This last-day rule may have the effect of converting a short-term capital loss into a long-term capital loss. (See Capital Losses later in this chapter.) Worthless securities are discussed in Chapter 6.

Section 1244 allows an *ordinary* deduction on disposition of stock at a loss. The stock must be that of a small business corporation, and the ordinary deduction is limited to $50,000 ($100,000 for married individuals filing jointly) per year.

8-3b Retirement of Corporate Obligations

A debt obligation (e.g., a bond or note payable) may have a tax basis different from its redemption value because it may have been acquired at a premium or discount. Consequently, the collection of the redemption value may result in a loss or a gain. Generally, the collection of a debt obligation is *treated* as a sale or exchange.[6] Therefore, any loss or gain is capital because a sale or exchange has taken place.

In-depth coverage can be found on this book's companion website: **www.cengagebrain.com** 🔍 **4** | Digging Deeper

---

Osprey, Inc., purchases $1,000 of Golden Eagle Corporation bonds for $1,020 in the open market. If the bonds are held to maturity and the bond premium is not amortized, the $20 difference between Osprey's collection of the $1,000 redemption value and its cost of $1,020 is treated as capital loss. | **Example 8**

8-3c Options

Frequently, a potential buyer of property wants to defer a final purchase decision, but wants to control the sale and/or the sale price in the meantime. **Options** are used to achieve such control. The potential purchaser (grantee) pays the property owner (grantor) for an option on the property. The grantee then becomes the option holder. An option, which usually sets the price at which a grantee can buy the property, expires after a specified period of time.

---

[4]§ 1234A.
[5]§ 165(g)(1).

[6]§ 1271.

© tuulijumala/Shutterstock.com

TAX IN THE NEWS   Bankruptcy and Worthless Stock

During 2009, General Motors went into bankruptcy, was reorganized, and emerged from bankruptcy. However, the common shareholders of the General Motors that went into bankruptcy were not the common shareholders of the General Motors that emerged from bankruptcy. The original common shareholders lost their entire investment because their stock became worthless. The holding period of their stock ended for tax purposes on December 31, 2009,

because of the worthless stock rules. They had a capital loss equal to whatever their basis was for the worthless shares. The debtors of General Motors accepted common shares in the General Motors that emerged from bankruptcy. Generally, the exchange of debt for common shares in a bankruptcy reorganization is not a taxable transaction, and the basis of the debt becomes the basis for the shares.

Sale of an Option

In addition to exercising an option or letting it expire, a grantee can often arrange for its sale or exchange. Such a sale or exchange generally results in capital gain or loss if the option property is (or would be) a capital asset to the grantee.[7]

Example 9	Robin & Associates wants to buy some vacant land for investment purposes, but cannot afford the full purchase price. Instead, Robin & Associates (grantee) pays the landowner (grantor) $3,000 for an option to buy the land for $100,000 anytime in the next two years. The option is a capital asset to Robin because if the firm actually purchased the land (the option property), the land would be a capital asset. Three months after purchasing the option, Robin sells it for $7,000. The firm has a $4,000 ($7,000 − $3,000) capital gain on this sale.

Failure to Exercise Options

If an option holder (grantee) fails to exercise the option, the lapse of the option is considered a sale or exchange on the option expiration date. Thus, the resulting loss is a capital loss if the property subject to the option is (or would be) a capital asset in the hands of the grantee.

The grantor of an option on *stocks, securities, commodities, or commodity futures* receives short-term capital gain treatment upon the expiration of the option.[8] For example, an individual investor who owns stock (a capital asset) may sell a call option, entitling the buyer of the option to acquire the stock at a specified price higher than the stock's value at the date the option is granted. The writer of the call (the grantor) receives a premium for writing the option. If the price of the stock does not increase during the option period, the option will expire unexercised. Upon the expiration of the option, the grantor must recognize a short-term capital gain equal to the premium received (whereas the grantee recognizes a loss, the character of which depends on the underlying asset). These provisions do not apply to options held for sale to customers (the inventory of a securities dealer).

Options on property *other than* stocks, securities, commodities, or commodity futures result in ordinary income to the grantor when the option expires. For instance, the landowner in the preceding example would have ordinary income of $3,000 if Robin (the grantee) had allowed the option to expire.

---

[7] § 1234(a) and Reg. § 1.1234–1(a)(1).

[8] § 1234(b)(1).

CONCEPT SUMMARY 8.1

Options

	Effect on	
Event	**Grantor**	**Grantee**
Option is granted.	Receives value and has a contract obligation (a liability).	Pays value and has a contract right (an asset).
Option expires.	Has a short-term capital gain if the option property is stocks, securities, commodities, or commodity futures. Otherwise, gain is ordinary income.	Has a loss (capital loss if option property would have been a capital asset for the grantee).
Option is exercised.	Amount received for option increases proceeds from sale of the option property.	Amount paid for option becomes part of the basis of the option property purchased.
Option is sold or exchanged by grantee.	Result depends upon whether option later expires or is exercised (see above).	Could have gain or loss (capital gain or loss if option property would have been a capital asset for the grantee).

Exercise of Options by Grantee

If an option is exercised, the amount paid for the option is added to the optioned property's selling price. This increases the gain (or reduces the loss) to the grantor resulting from the sale of the property. The grantor's gain or loss is capital or ordinary depending on the tax status of the property. The grantee adds the cost of the option to the basis of the property purchased.

THE BIG PICTURE

Example 10

Return to the facts of *The Big Picture* on p. 8-1. On February 1, 2014, Alice purchases 100 shares of Eagle Company stock for $5,000. On April 1, 2014, she writes a call option on the stock, giving the grantee the right to buy the stock for $6,000 during the following six-month period. Alice (the grantor) receives a call premium of $500 for writing the call.

- If the call is exercised by the grantee on August 1, 2014, Alice has $1,500 ($6,000 + $500 − $5,000) of short-term capital gain from the sale of the stock. The grantee has a $6,500 ($500 option premium + $6,000 purchase price) basis for the stock.
- Investors sometimes get nervous and want to "lock in" gains or losses. Assume that Alice decides to sell her stock prior to exercise for $6,000 and enters into a closing transaction by purchasing a call on 100 shares of Eagle Company stock for $5,000. Because the Eagle stock is selling for $6,000, Alice must pay a call premium of $1,000. She recognizes a $500 short-term capital loss [$500 (call premium received) − $1,000 (call premium paid)] on the closing transaction. On the actual sale of the Eagle stock, Alice has a short-term capital gain of $1,000 [$6,000 (selling price) − $5,000 (cost)]. The grantee is not affected by Alice's closing transaction. The original option is still in existence, and the grantee's tax consequences depend on what action the grantee takes—exercising the option, letting the option expire, or selling the option.
- Assume that the original option expired unexercised. Alice has a $500 short-term capital gain equal to the call premium received for writing the option. This gain is not recognized until the option expires. The grantee has a loss from expiration of the option. The nature of the loss will depend upon whether the option was a capital asset or an ordinary asset.

8-3d Patents

Transfer of a **patent** is treated as the sale or exchange of a long-term capital asset when *all substantial rights* to the patent (or an undivided interest that includes all such rights) are transferred by a *holder*.[9] The transferor/holder may receive payment in virtually any form. Lump-sum or periodic payments are most common. The amount of the payments may also be contingent on the transferee/purchaser's productivity, use, or disposition of the patent. If the transfer meets these requirements, any gain or loss is *automatically a long-term* capital gain or loss. Whether the asset was a capital asset for the transferor, whether a sale or exchange occurred, and how long the transferor held the patent are all irrelevant. Example 11 illustrates the special treatment for patents.

This special long-term capital gain or loss treatment for patents is intended to encourage technological development and scientific progress. In contrast, books, songs, and artists' works may be copyrighted, but copyrights and the assets they represent are not capital assets. Thus, the disposition of these assets by their creators usually results in ordinary gain or loss.

Substantial Rights

To receive favorable capital gain treatment, all *substantial rights* to the patent (or an undivided interest in it) must be transferred. All substantial rights to a patent means all rights that are valuable at the time the patent rights (or an undivided interest in the patent) are transferred. All substantial rights have not been transferred when the transfer is limited geographically within the issuing country or when the transfer is for a period less than the remaining legal life of the patent. The circumstances of the entire transaction, rather than merely the language used in the transfer instrument, are to be considered in deciding whether all substantial rights have been transferred.[10]

THE BIG PICTURE

Example 11

Return to the facts of *The Big Picture* on p. 8-1. Kathy transfers her rights in the battery patent to the Green Battery Company in exchange for a lump-sum payment of $1 million plus $.50 for each battery sold. Assuming that Kathy has transferred all substantial rights, the question of whether the transfer is a sale or exchange of a capital asset is not relevant. Kathy automatically has a long-term capital gain from both the lump-sum payment received and the per battery royalty to the extent that those proceeds exceed her basis for the patent. Kathy also had an automatic long-term capital gain when she sold 50% of her rights in the patent to Alice, because Kathy transferred an undivided interest that included all substantial rights in the patent.

Whether Alice gets long-term capital gain treatment on a transfer to Green Battery will depend on whether she is a holder (see the following discussion and Example 12).

Holder Defined

The *holder* of a patent must be an *individual* and is usually the invention's creator. A holder may also be an individual who purchases the patent rights from the creator before the patented invention has been reduced to practice. However, the creator's employer and certain parties related to the creator do not qualify as holders. Thus, in the common situation where an employer has all rights to an employee's inventions, the employer is not eligible for long-term capital gain treatment. More than likely, the employer will have an ordinary asset because the patent was developed as part of its business.

[9]§ 1235.   [10]Reg. § 1.1235–2(b)(1).

Continuing with the facts of Example 11, Kathy is clearly a holder of the patent because she is the inventor and was not an employee when she invented the battery. When Alice purchased a 50% interest in the patent nine months ago, she became a holder if the patent had not yet been reduced to practice. Because batteries were apparently not being manufactured at the time of the purchase, the patent had not been reduced to practice.

Consequently, Alice is also a holder, and she has an automatic long-term capital gain or loss when she transfers all substantial rights in her interest in the patent to Green Battery Company. Alice's basis for her share of the patent is $50,000, and the proceeds from the transfer of her share of the patent are $1 million plus $.50 for each battery sold. Thus, Alice will have a long-term capital gain even though she has not held her interest in the patent for more than one year.

8-3e Franchises, Trademarks, and Trade Names (§ 1253)

A mode of operation, a widely recognized brand name (trade name), and a widely known business symbol (trademark) are all valuable assets. These assets may be licensed (commonly known as *franchising*) by their owner for use by other businesses. Many fast-food restaurants (such as McDonald's and Taco Bell) are franchises. The franchisee usually pays the owner (franchisor) an initial fee plus a contingent fee. The contingent fee is often based upon the franchisee's sales volume.

For Federal income tax purposes, a **franchise** is an agreement that gives the franchisee the right to distribute, sell, or provide goods, services, or facilities within a specified area.[11] A franchise transfer includes the grant of a franchise, a transfer by one franchisee to another person, or the renewal of a franchise.

Section 1253 provides that a transfer of a franchise, trademark, or trade name is *not* a sale or exchange of a capital asset when the transferor retains any significant power, right, or continuing interest in the property transferred.

In-depth coverage can be found on this book's companion website: **www.cengagebrain.com**   5 Digging Deeper

Significant Power, Right, or Continuing Interest

Significant powers, rights, or continuing interests include control over assignment of the franchise, trademark, or trade name, as well as the quality of the transferee's products or services. The following rights also are included.

- Right to require the transferee to sell or advertise *only* the transferor's products or services.
- Right to require the transferee to purchase substantially all supplies and equipment from the transferor.
- Right to receive substantial contingent payments.
- Right to terminate the franchise, trademark, or trade name at will.

In the unusual case where no significant power, right, or continuing interest is retained by the transferor, a sale or exchange may occur, and capital gain or loss treatment may be available. For capital gain or loss treatment to be available, the asset transferred must still qualify as a capital asset.

---

[11]§ 1253(b)(1).

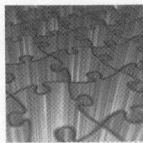

CONCEPT SUMMARY 8.2

Franchises

Event	Effect on	
	Franchisor	**Franchisee**
Franchisor Retains Significant Powers and Rights		
Noncontingent payment	Ordinary income.	Capitalized and amortized over 15 years as an ordinary deduction; if franchise is sold, amortization is subject to recapture under § 1245.
Contingent payment	Ordinary income.	Ordinary deduction.
Franchisor Does *Not* Retain Significant Powers and Rights		
Noncontingent payment	Ordinary income if franchise rights are an ordinary asset; capital gain if franchise rights are a capital asset (unlikely).	Capitalized and amortized over 15 years as an ordinary deduction; if the franchise is sold, amortization is subject to recapture under § 1245.
Contingent payment	Ordinary income.	Ordinary deduction.

THE BIG PICTURE

Example 13

Return to the facts of *The Big Picture* on p. 8-1. Alice sells for $101,000 to Mauve, Inc., the franchise purchased from Orange, Inc., nine months ago. The $101,000 received by Alice is not contingent, and all significant powers, rights, and continuing interests are transferred. The $1,000 gain ($101,000 proceeds − $100,000 adjusted basis) is a short-term capital gain because Alice has held the franchise for only nine months.

Noncontingent Payments

When the transferor retains a significant power, right, or continuing interest, the transferee's noncontingent payments to the transferor are ordinary income to the transferor. The franchisee capitalizes the payments and amortizes them over 15 years. If the franchise is sold, amortization is subject to recapture under § 1245, as discussed later in this chapter.

Example 14

Grey Company signs a 10-year franchise agreement with DOH Donuts. Grey (the franchisee) makes payments of $3,000 per year for the first 8 years of the franchise agreement—a total of $24,000. Grey cannot deduct $3,000 per year as the payments are made. Instead, Grey must amortize the $24,000 total over 15 years. Thus, Grey may deduct $1,600 per year for each of the 15 years of the amortization period.

The same result would occur if Grey had made a $24,000 lump-sum payment at the beginning of the franchise period. Assuming that DOH Donuts (the franchisor) retains significant powers, rights, or a continuing interest, it will have ordinary income when it receives the payments from Grey.

Contingent Payments

The contingent franchise payments are ordinary income for the franchisor and an ordinary deduction for the franchisee when the transferor retains a significant power, right, or continuing interest.

Example 15

TAK, a spicy chicken franchisor, transfers an eight-year franchise to Egret Corporation. TAK retains a significant power, right, or continuing interest. Egret, the franchisee, agrees to pay TAK 15% of sales. This contingent payment is ordinary income to TAK and a business deduction for Egret as the payments are made.

8-3f Lease Cancellation Payments

The tax treatment of payments received for canceling a lease depends on whether the recipient of the payments is the lessor or the lessee and whether the lease is a capital asset.

Lessee Treatment

Lease cancellation payments received by a lessee (the tenant) are treated as an exchange.[12] Thus, these payments are capital gains if the lease is a capital asset. Generally, a lessee's lease is a capital asset if the property (either personalty or realty) is used for the lessee's personal use (e.g., his or her residence). A lease held one year or less is an ordinary income asset if the property is used in the lessee's trade or business.[13]

Merganser, Inc., owns an apartment building that it is going to convert into an office building. Vicki is one of the apartment tenants who receives $1,000 from Merganser to cancel the lease. Vicki has a capital gain of $1,000 (which is long-term or short-term depending upon how long she has held the lease). Merganser has an ordinary deduction of $1,000.

Example 16

Lessor Treatment

Payments received by a lessor (the landlord) for a lease cancellation are always ordinary income because they are considered to be in lieu of rental payments.[14]

Finch & Company owns an apartment building near a university campus. Hui-Fen is one of the tenants. Hui-Fen is graduating early and offers Finch $800 to cancel the apartment lease. Finch accepts the offer. Finch has ordinary income of $800. Hui-Fen has a nondeductible payment because the apartment was personal-use property.

Example 17

8-4 HOLDING PERIOD

Property must be held more than one year to qualify for long-term capital gain or loss treatment.[15] Property not held for the required long-term period results in short-term capital gain or loss. To compute the holding period, start counting on the day after the property was acquired and include the day of disposition.

LO.3

Determine the applicable holding period for a capital asset.

THE BIG PICTURE

Example 18

Return to the facts of *The Big Picture* on p. 8-1. Assume that Alice purchased the 200 shares of Purple stock on January 15, 2013. If she sells them on January 16, 2014, Alice's holding period is more than one year. If instead Alice sells the stock on January 15, 2014, the holding period is exactly one year and the gain or loss is short-term.

To be held for more than one year, a capital asset acquired on the last day of any month must not be disposed of until on or after the first day of the thirteenth succeeding month.[16]

Example 19

Purple, Inc., purchases a capital asset on March 31, 2013. If Purple sells the asset on March 31, 2014, the holding period is one year and Purple will have a short-term capital gain or loss. If Purple sells the asset on April 1, 2014, the holding period is more than one year and it will have a long-term capital gain or loss.

---

[12]§ 1241 and Reg. § 1.1241–1(a).
[13]Reg. § 1.1221–1(b) and PLR 200045019. If the lease was held for more than one year before cancellation, it is a § 1231 asset.
[14]Reg. § 1.61–8(b).

[15]§ 1222(3).
[16]Rev.Rul. 66–7, 1966–1 C.B. 188.

Global Tax Issues

Trading ADRs on U.S. Stock Exchanges

Many non-U.S. companies now have subsidiaries that were formerly U.S. companies. For instance, Chrysler Corporation is a subsidiary of Fiat. Shares in such non-U.S. companies generally cannot be traded directly on U.S. stock exchanges. Instead, the offshore companies issue instruments called American Depository Receipts (ADRs) that can be traded on U.S. stock exchanges. Purchases and sales of ADRs are treated for tax purposes as though the ADRs were shares in the corporation that issued them.

8-4a Special Holding Period Rules

There are several special holding period rules.[17] The application of these rules varies depending upon the type of asset involved and how it was acquired.

Nontaxable Exchanges

The holding period of property received in a like-kind exchange (and certain other qualified nontaxable exchanges) includes the holding period of the former asset if the property that was exchanged was either a capital asset or a § 1231 asset.

Example 20

Red Manufacturing Corporation exchanges some vacant real estate it owns (a capital asset) for land closer to its factory. The transaction is a like-kind exchange, so the holding period of the new land includes the holding period of the old land.

Example 21

A lightning strike destroyed Vireo Company's generator (a § 1231 asset) in March. Vireo uses all of the insurance proceeds it received to acquire a comparable generator. The holding period of the new generator includes the holding period of the old generator because this is a nontaxable involuntary conversion.

Nontaxable Transactions Involving Carryover of Another Taxpayer's Basis

If a transaction is nontaxable and the former owner's basis carries over to the present owner, the former owner's holding period is included in (tacked on to) the present owner's holding period. See the discussion of nontaxable transactions in Chapter 7.

Example 22

Kareem acquired 100 shares of Robin Corporation stock for $1,000 on December 31, 2010. He transferred the shares by gift to Megan on December 31, 2013, when the stock was worth $2,000. Kareem's basis of $1,000 becomes the basis for determining gain or loss on a subsequent sale by Megan. Megan's holding period begins with the date the stock was acquired by Kareem.

Example 23

Assume the same facts as in the preceding example, except that the fair market value of the shares was only $800 on the date of the gift. If Megan sells the stock for a loss, its value on the date of the gift is her basis. Accordingly, the tacked-on holding period rule does not apply, and Megan's holding period begins with the date of the gift. So if she sells the shares for $500 on April 1, 2014, Megan has a $300 recognized capital loss and the holding period is from December 31, 2013, to April 1, 2014. Therefore, the loss is short-term.

Disallowed Loss Transactions

Under several Code provisions, realized losses are disallowed. When a loss is disallowed, there is no carryover of holding period. Losses can be disallowed under § 267 (sale or exchange between related taxpayers) and § 262 (sale or exchange of

---

[17]§ 1223.

personal-use assets) as well as other Code Sections. Taxpayers who acquire property in a disallowed loss transaction begin a new holding period and have a basis equal to the purchase price.

Janet sells her personal automobile at a loss. She may not deduct the loss because it arises from the sale of personal-use property. Janet purchases a replacement automobile for more than the selling price of her former automobile. Janet has a basis equal to the cost of the replacement automobile, and her holding period begins when she acquires the replacement automobile.	**Example 24**

Inherited Property

The holding period for inherited property is treated as long term no matter how long the property is actually held by the heir. The holding period of the decedent or the decedent's estate is not relevant to the heir's holding period.

Shonda inherits Blue Company stock from her father, who died in 2014. She receives the stock on April 1, 2014, and sells it on November 1, 2014. Even though Shonda did not hold the stock for more than one year, she receives long-term capital gain or loss treatment on the sale.	**Example 25**

8-4b Short Sales

A **short sale** occurs when a taxpayer sells borrowed property and repays the lender with substantially identical property either held on the date of the sale or purchased after the sale. Short sales typically involve corporate stock. The seller's objective is to make a profit in anticipation of a decline in the stock's price. If the price declines, the seller in a short sale recognizes a profit equal to the difference between the sales price of the borrowed stock and the price paid for its replacement.

Section 1233 provides that a short sale gain or loss is a capital gain or loss to the extent the short sale property constitutes a capital asset of the taxpayer. This gain or loss is not recognized until the short sale is closed. Generally, the holding period of the short sale property is determined by how long the property used to close the short sale was held.

On January 4, Green & Associates sold short 100 shares of Osprey Corporation for $1,500. Green closed the transaction on July 28 of the same year by purchasing 100 shares of Osprey for $1,000 and delivering them to the broker from whom the securities were borrowed. Because this stock was held less than one year (actually less than a day), Green's gain ($1,500 sale price − $1,000 cost) is short-term.	**Example 26**

Assume the same facts as in the preceding example, except that the January 4 short sale was not closed until January 28 of the *following* year. The result is the same, because the stock was acquired and used to close the transaction on the same day; that is, it was not held more than a year.	**Example 27**

If a taxpayer owns securities that are "substantially identical" to those sold short, § 1259 subjects the short sale to potential *constructive sale treatment*, and the taxpayer recognizes gain (but not loss) as of that date. If the taxpayer has not closed the short sale by delivering the short sale securities to the broker from whom the securities were borrowed before January 31 of the year following the short sale, the short sale is deemed to have closed on the short sale date. The holding period in such circumstances is determined by how long the securities in question were held.

Assume the same facts as in Example 26, except that Green & Associates owned 100 shares of Osprey Corporation when it sold short 100 shares on January 4. Green does not close the short sale before January 31 of the following year. Green must recognize any gain on its 100 shares of Osprey as of January 4 of the current year. If Green owned those shares more than one year as of that date, the gain is long-term.	**Example 28**

Tax Planning Strategies   TIMING CAPITAL GAINS

FRAMEWORK FOCUS: INCOME AND EXCLUSIONS

Strategy: Postpone Recognition of Income to Achieve Tax Deferral.

FRAMEWORK FOCUS: DEDUCTIONS

Strategy: Maximize Deductible Amounts.

Taxpayers have considerable control over the timing of their capital gains through the mechanism of realization. Accordingly, a taxpayer might want to defer recognizing a large capital gain in a year with *substantial itemized deductions*, such as large personal casualty losses or miscellaneous itemized deductions. In so doing, the taxpayer minimizes the loss of such deductions due to AGI limitations. See additional discussion in Chapter 10.

Nontax considerations, of course, often dictate when assets are sold. If a particular stock is peaking in popularity, selling it might be a wise investment strategy, even if the taxpayer's current tax situation is not optimal.

Similarly, if a taxpayer needs cash to start a business, purchase a home, or pay for a child's education or medical costs, the capital asset might need to be sold at a time when investment *and* tax considerations counsel otherwise. In these circumstances, however, a taxpayer might choose to *borrow* the money required and use the capital asset as collateral for the loan, rather than sell the asset. A loan does not trigger tax consequences, and the taxpayer can continue to hold the asset until a more opportune time—albeit at the cost of paying interest, which may be nondeductible.

Digging Deeper   6   In-depth coverage can be found on this book's companion website: **www.cengagebrain.com**

8-5 TAX TREATMENT OF CAPITAL GAINS AND LOSSES OF NONCORPORATE TAXPAYERS

LO.4

Describe the tax treatment of capital gains and losses for noncorporate taxpayers.

This section discusses how capital gains and losses are taxed to noncorporate taxpayers; that is, individuals, noncorporate partners, trusts, and estates. The rules applicable to corporations are considered in the following section of this chapter.

8-5a Capital Gains

Gains from the sale or exchange of capital assets are taxed at various rates, depending upon the holding period, the taxpayer's regular tax rate, and the type of asset involved.

Short-Term Gains

Gains on capital assets held one year or less are taxed as *ordinary income*. Accordingly, the applicable tax rates vary from 10 percent to 39.6 percent. Although short-term capital gains receive no preferential tax treatment compared to ordinary income, they do have one advantage: they can absorb capital losses without limit. As discussed later in this section, *capital losses* are deducted first against capital gains (without limit) and then against ordinary income, but only up to $3,000 per year.[18] Thus, someone with a large capital loss will find short-term capital gains attractive, even though such gains do not qualify for lower tax rates.

Long-Term Gains

Gains on capital assets held more than one year are classified as *long-term* gains and are eligible for a special 20 percent tax rate (for taxpayers in the 39.6 percent bracket), 15 percent tax rate (for taxpayers in the 25, 28, 33, or 35 percent tax bracket), or 0 percent rate (for taxpayers in the 10 or 15 percent tax bracket). The benefit of these long-term capital gain tax rates, therefore, is as follows.

---

[18]§ 1211(b).

Beneficial Tax Rates

Tax Rates		Differential (Percentage Points)
Ordinary Income	Capital Gain	
10%	0%	10
15	0	15
25	15	10
28	15	13
33	15	18
35	15	20
39.6	20	19.6

Tax Planning Strategies GIFTS OF APPRECIATED SECURITIES

FRAMEWORK FOCUS: TAX RATE

Strategy: Shift Net Income from High-Bracket Taxpayers to Low-Bracket Taxpayers.

Persons with appreciated securities that have been held over one year may reduce the tax due on their sale by giving the securities to someone (often a child) who is in the *lowest tax bracket*. The donor's holding period carries over, along with his or her basis, and the donee's lower tax rate applies when the securities are sold. As a result, the gain could be taxed at the donee's 0 percent, rather than the donor's 15 or 20 percent. The donee should be at least age 19 (or 24 in the case of a full-time student) by year-end, however, or the *kiddie tax* will nullify most of the tax advantage being sought. The kiddie tax subjects the gain to the parents' tax rate. See Chapter 9.

Such gifts usually bear no gift tax due to the annual $14,000 exclusion. But the property received after payment of the tax belongs to the donee. It is not available to the donor, nor may it be used to pay a parent's essential support obligations. Moreover, these assets may affect a child's eligibility for need-based financial aid when applying to college.

In point of fact, relatively few capital gains are realized by persons in the 10 or 15 percent tax bracket. In addition, there are relatively few taxpayers who are in the highest income tax bracket and subject to the 20 percent rate. Thus, the tax rate that generally applies to long-term capital gains is 15 percent.

TAX FACT Individual Returns Reporting Capital Gains

The number of individual income tax returns including net capital gain in AGI for a number of years is shown in the table at the right. Based on the most recent data, about 142.9 million individual returns were filed and about 14.9 percent of those returns reported capital gain income. During the stock market boom of the late 1990s, though, this percentage was higher. Nonetheless, after the turn of the century, reduced capital gain tax rates likely contributed to higher dollar amounts of net capital gains than ever. In addition, with the significant stock market rebound continuing in 2010 following the depths of the Great Recession, the net capital gains reported increased by 57.4 percent compared to the previous year!

Year	Number of Returns (in Millions)
1975	5.8
1980	7.0
1985	10.0
1990	9.2
1995	14.8
2000	22.7
2003	22.9
2008	23.7
2009	20.3
2010	21.3

Source: Based on Justin Bryan, "Individual Income Tax Returns, 2010," *SOI Bulletin*, Fall 2012, Figure B.

Global Tax Issues

Capital Gain Treatment in the United States and Other Countries

Few other countries apply an alternative tax rate or other incentive to long-term capital gains. Instead, those gains are taxed in the same manner as other income. Consequently, even though the U.S. system of identifying and taxing capital assets is complex, it may be preferable because of the lower tax rates and because the lower rates are available to taxpayers in all tax brackets.

There are two major exceptions, however, to this general treatment. The first exception relates to so-called *28% property*, which consists of the following items.

- **Collectibles** (works of art, rugs, antiques, gems, coins, stamps, and alcoholic beverages) held more than one year.[19]
- The taxable portion of the gain on sales of *qualified small business stock* (see the end of this section).

These assets are labeled *28% property*, because the gains they produce are taxed at 28 percent. But this 28 percent rate is a *maximum* rate, so a taxpayer in a lower tax bracket would pay at that rate. As a result, the benefit of the applicable tax rates for gains on 28% property is as follows.

Ordinary Income Tax Rates	Applicable Tax Rates	Differential (Percentage Points)
10%	10%	None
15	15	None
25	25	None
28	28	None
33	28	5
35	28	7
39.6	28	11.6

Note that gains on 28% property receive preferential tax treatment only when realized by taxpayers in the top three tax brackets.

The second major exception involves depreciable real estate that has been held more than one year. Some—but not all—of the gain attributable to depreciation deductions on apartments, office buildings, shopping centers, and warehouses is taxable at 25 percent rather than 0, 15, or 20 percent. The amount that is taxed in this manner depends upon how much depreciation is "recaptured" as ordinary income under § 1250, as explained later in this chapter. Accordingly, these gains are called *unrecaptured § 1250 gain*. In any case, the 25 percent rate is a *maximum* rate; so the benefit of the applicable tax rates for gains from the sale of depreciable real estate is as follows.

Ordinary Income Tax Rates	Applicable Tax Rates	Differential (Percentage Points)
10%	10%	None
15	15	None
25	25	None
28	25	3
33	25	8
35	25	10
39.6	25	14.6

---

[19]§ 408(m) and Reg. § 1.408–10(b).

CONCEPT SUMMARY 8.3

Capital Gains of Noncorporate Taxpayers

Type of Asset	Applicable Rate
Held not more than one year.	10%–39.6%, same as ordinary income.
Collectibles held more than one year.	10/15/25% for lowest-bracket taxpayers, 28% for all others.
Taxable portion (50%, 25%, or 0%) of gain on qualified small business stock held more than five years.	10/15/25% for lowest-bracket taxpayers, 28% for all others.
Unrecaptured § 1250 gain on depreciable real estate held more than one year.	10/15% for two lowest-bracket taxpayers, 25% for all others.
Other capital assets held more than one year.	0% for two lowest-bracket taxpayers, 15% for all others (except 20% for taxpayers in the highest bracket).

8-5b Capital Losses

As explained previously, capital gains can be classified into four general categories.

- Short term—taxed as ordinary income.
- 28% property—taxed at no more than 28 percent.
- Unrecaptured § 1250 gain—taxed at no more than 25 percent.
- Regular long term—taxed at 0 percent, 15 percent, or 20 percent.

A taxpayer can also have losses from capital assets in *three* of these four categories. The *unrecaptured* § 1250 *gain* category applies only to gain.

8-5c Capital Gain and Loss Netting Process

When both gains and losses occur in the year, they must be netted against each other in the following order.

Step 1. Group all gains and losses into short-term, 28% property, unrecaptured § 1250, and regular long-term categories.

Step 2. Net the gains and losses within each category to obtain net short-term, 28% property, unrecaptured § 1250, and regular long-term gain or loss.

Step 3. Offset the net 28% property and unrecaptured § 1250 amounts if they are of opposite sign. Add them if they have the same sign. Then offset the resulting amount against the regular net long-term amount if they are of opposite sign, or add the amounts if they have the same sign.

Step 4. Offset the result of step 3 with the net short-term gain *or loss* from step 2 if they are of opposite sign.

These netting rules offset net short-term capital loss against the *highest-taxed gain first.* Consequently, if there is a net short-term capital loss, it first offsets any net 28% property gain, any remaining loss offsets unrecaptured § 1250 gain, and then any remaining loss offsets regular long-term gain.

If the result of step 4 is *only* a short-term capital gain, the taxpayer is not eligible for a reduced tax rate. If the result of step 4 is a loss, a **net capital loss** exists and the taxpayer may be eligible for a *capital loss deduction* (discussed later in this chapter). If there was no offsetting in step 4 because the short-term and step 3 results were both gains *or* if the result of the offsetting is a 28% property, an unrecaptured § 1250 property, and/or a regular long-term gain, a **net capital gain** exists and the taxpayer may be eligible for a reduced tax rate. The net capital gain may consist of regular *long-term gain, unrecaptured § 1250 gain,* and/or *28% property gain.* Each of these gains may be taxed at a different rate.

Example 29

Joe is in the 35% Federal income tax bracket. He is taxed as follows.

Ordinary income	35%
Unrecaptured § 1250 gain	25%
28% gain	28%
Short-term capital gain	35%
Other long-term capital gain	15%

Example 30

This example shows how a *net long-term capital loss* is applied.

Step	Short-Term	28% Gain	Unrecaptured § 1250 Gain	Regular Long-Term	Comment
1	$ 3,000	$ 1,000		$ 3,000	
				(8,000)	
2	$ 3,000	$ 1,000		($ 5,000)	
3		(1,000)	→	1,000	Netted because of opposite sign.
		$ –0–		($ 4,000)	
4	(3,000)	→	→	3,000	The net short-term gain is netted against the net regular long-term loss, and the remaining loss is eligible for the capital loss deduction.
	$ –0–			($ 1,000)	

Example 31

This example shows how *net short-term* and *regular long-term capital losses* are applied.

Step	Short-Term	28% Gain	Unrecaptured § 1250 Gain	Regular Long-Term	Comment
1	$ 3,000	$15,000	$4,000	$ 3,000	
	(5,000)	(7,000)		(8,000)	
2	($ 2,000)	$ 8,000	$4,000	($ 5,000)	
3		(5,000)	←	5,000	Net regular long-term loss is netted against 28% gain first.
		$ 3,000		$ –0–	
4	2,000 →	(2,000)			Short-term loss is netted against 28% gain next.
	$ –0–	$ 1,000	$4,000		
		Net 28% gain	Net 25% gain		

If a net loss remains after applying these rules for offsetting losses, a noncorporate taxpayer may deduct up to $3,000 of that loss against ordinary income.[20] Losses in excess of $3,000 are carried over to future years where they are applied first against capital gains and then deducted up to $3,000 per year. Capital loss carryovers expire, however, when the taxpayer dies.

---

[20]§ 1211(b)(1). Married persons filing separate returns are limited to a $1,500 deduction per tax year.

TAX FACT   Detrimental Tax Treatment for Capital Losses

A corporate taxpayer cannot deduct a net capital loss against ordinary income. It can carry the loss back three years and forward five years in search of capital gains. An individual taxpayer can deduct a maximum of $3,000 of net capital loss against ordinary income in the current tax year. Any excess can be carried forward indefinitely in search of capital gains. After capital gains are exhausted in each carryforward year, a maximum of $3,000 of the remaining net capital loss can be deducted against ordinary income.

The number of individual income tax returns with a net capital loss in AGI is shown at the right. These numbers increased in the early 2000s, due to drops in stock prices, but modest decreases followed until 2008. With the significant stock market declines in 2008, the number of tax returns showing a net capital loss increased by 63.5 percent over the previous year. In 2010, however, reported capital losses slowed and the number of returns showing capital losses decreased by 5.4 percent as compared with losses in 2009. This is not surprising given the turnaround that was seen in the stock market in 2010.

Year	Number of Returns (in Millions)
1975	2.5
1980	2.0
1985	2.7
1990	5.0
1995	5.1
2000	6.9
2003	12.8
2008	12.4
2009	13.5
2010	12.8

Source: Based on Justin Bryan, "Individual Income Tax Returns, 2010," *SOI Bulletin*, Fall 2012, Figure C.

Example 32

James incurred a $10,000 loss on his only capital asset transaction in 2014. If he has no other capital asset transactions from that point on, his $10,000 loss is deducted as follows.

Year	Deduction
2014	$3,000
2015	3,000
2016	3,000
2017	1,000

Example 33

Assume the same facts as in the preceding example, except that James realizes a capital gain of $4,500 in 2016. At that time, his remaining capital loss carryover is $4,000 ($10,000 − $6,000 deducted previously). Because his capital gain in 2016 (i.e., $4,500) exceeds this loss carryforward, James can deduct the entire $4,000 against that year's capital gain.

Example 34

Assume the same facts as in Example 32, except that James died in late 2015. His remaining capital loss carryforward of $4,000 ($10,000 − $6,000 deducted in 2014 and 2015) expires unused.

When a taxpayer's capital loss exceeds $3,000 and derives from more than one category, it is used in the following order: first, short-term; then, 28% property; then, unrecaptured § 1250 property; and finally, regular long-term. Unused losses are carried forward as follows: short-term losses carry forward as short-term losses, and long-term losses carry forward as long-term losses.

Tax Planning Strategies   MATCHING GAINS WITH LOSSES

FRAMEWORK FOCUS: INCOME AND EXCLUSIONS

Strategy: Avoid Income Recognition.

A taxpayer who has already realized a large capital gain may want to *match this gain* with an *offsetting capital loss*. Doing so will shelter the capital gain from taxation and will also free up an asset that has declined in value. Without the capital gain, after all, the taxpayer might hesitate to sell a loss asset, because the resulting capital loss may be deductible only in $3,000 annual increments.

Similarly, a taxpayer with a large realized capital loss might use the occasion to sell some appreciated assets. Doing so would enable the taxpayer to use the capital loss immediately and at the same time realize the benefit of the asset appreciation at little or no tax cost.

On the other hand, matching capital losses and long-term capital gains means that the taxpayer utilizes the capital loss against income that would otherwise qualify for a preferential tax rate of 0, 15, or 20 percent. If the taxpayer's ordinary income is taxed at a higher rate, he or she might prefer to deduct the loss against that higher taxed income, even on a schedule of $3,000 per year. However, the *time value of money* must be considered; a current-year deduction at 0, 15, or 20 percent might be worth more than a series of annual deductions at higher rates spread over several years.

Nontax considerations, such as investment prospects for the assets in question, are also important. Future investment prospects are often unknowable or at least highly speculative, while tax effects can be determined with relative certainty—which explains some of the late December selling activity in publicly traded securities and mutual funds.

Example 35

Nancy incurs a long-term capital loss of $8,500 this year, of which $3,000 is deducted against her ordinary income. The remaining $5,500 ($8,500 loss − $3,000 deducted) carries forward as a long-term capital loss.

Digging Deeper   7   In-depth coverage can be found on this book's companion website: **www.cengagebrain.com**

8-5d Small Business Stock

A special 50 percent *exclusion* is available to noncorporate taxpayers who derive capital gains from the sale or exchange of **qualified small business stock**.[21] Thus, half of the gain is excluded from the taxpayer's gross income, and the other half is subjected to a maximum tax rate of 28 percent, as noted earlier. However, as part of the tax legislation in 2009, the exclusion temporarily increased to 75 percent for qualified small business stock acquired after February 17, 2009. And from subsequent legislation, the exclusion increased to 100 percent for qualified stock acquired after September 27, 2010, and before 2014. Thus, the effective tax rate on gains from such stock is 14 percent (28% × 50%), 7 percent (28% × 25%), or 0 percent (28% × 0%), respectively. However, beginning in 2014, the exclusion amount reverted to 50 percent of the gain.

Example 36

Yolanda realized a $100,000 gain on the sale of qualified small business stock that she acquired in 2004. Yolanda is subject to the 33% marginal tax rate without considering this gain. So $50,000 of this gain is excluded from her gross income, and the other $50,000 is taxed at a maximum tax rate of 28%. Thus, Yolanda owes income tax of $14,000 ($50,000 × 28%), an effective tax rate of 14% on the entire $100,000 capital gain.

This treatment is more favorable than the capital gain tax treatment explained previously. Accordingly, Congress imposed additional restrictions to ensure that the gains receiving this treatment were derived in the circumstances Congress intended to promote. These restrictions include the following.

---

[21]§ 1202(a).

- The stock must have been newly issued *after* August 10, 1993.
- The taxpayer must have held the stock *more than five years.*
- The issuing corporation must use at least 80 percent of its assets, determined by their value, in the *active conduct* of a trade or business.
- When the stock was issued, the issuing corporation's assets must not have exceeded $50 million, at adjusted basis, including the proceeds of the stock issuance.
- The corporation does not engage in banking, financing, insurance, investing, leasing, farming, mineral extraction, hotel or motel operations, restaurant operations, or any business whose principal asset is the *reputation or skill* of its employees (such as accounting, architecture, health, law, engineering, or financial services).

Even if each of these requirements is met, the amount of gain eligible for the exclusion is limited to the *greater* of 10 times the taxpayer's basis in the stock or $10 million per taxpayer per company,[22] computed on an aggregate basis.

Example 37

Vanita purchased $100,000 of qualified small business stock when it was first issued in October 2000. This year, she sells the stock for $4 million. Her gain is $3.9 million ($4,000,000 − $100,000). Although this amount exceeds 10 times her basis ($100,000 × 10 = $1,000,000), it is *less* than $10 million; so the entire $3.9 million gain is eligible for the 50% exclusion.

Transactions that fail to satisfy *any one* of the applicable requirements are taxed as capital gains (and losses) realized by noncorporate taxpayers generally.

Gains are also eligible for *nonrecognition* treatment if the sale proceeds are invested in other qualified small business stock within 60 days.[23] To the extent that the sale proceeds are not so invested, gain is recognized, but the exclusion still applies. To be eligible for this treatment, the stock sold must have been held more than six months.

Example 38

Assume the same facts as in the preceding example, except that Vanita sold her stock in January 2015 and used $3.5 million of the sale proceeds to purchase other qualified small business stock one month later. Vanita's gain is recognized to the extent that the sale proceeds were not reinvested—namely, $500,000 ($4,000,000 sale proceeds − $3,500,000 reinvested). The 50% exclusion will apply, however, to this amount.

In-depth coverage can be found on this book's companion website: **www.cengagebrain.com** **8** | Digging Deeper

8-6 TAX TREATMENT OF CAPITAL GAINS AND LOSSES OF CORPORATE TAXPAYERS

The treatment of a corporation's net capital gain or loss differs dramatically from the rules for noncorporate taxpayers discussed in the preceding section. Briefly, the differences are as follows.

LO.5

Describe the tax treatment of capital gains and losses for corporate taxpayers.

- Capital gains are taxed at the ordinary income tax rates.[24]
- Capital losses offset only capital gains. No deduction of capital losses is permitted against ordinary taxable income.
- There is a three-year carryback and a five-year carryforward period for net capital losses.[25] Capital loss carrybacks and carryforwards are always treated as short-term, regardless of their original nature.

---

[22]For married persons filing separately, the limitation is $5 million.
[23]§ 1045(a).

[24]§ 1201. The alternative tax rate of 35% produces no beneficial results.
[25]§ 1212(a)(1).

TAX FACT   Capital Gains for the Wealthy?

Economists and other observers of society often accuse the Code of favoring those with higher levels of income and wealth, despite a fairly substantial progressivity in the Federal income tax rate structure. The claim is that the wealthy are the primary owners of capital assets and that capital gains and dividends from those assets are

subject to highly favorable tax treatment. Current tax return data may confirm those assertions.

Source: Based on Justin Bryan, "Individual Income Tax Returns, 2010," *SOI Bulletin*, Fall 2012, Figure F.

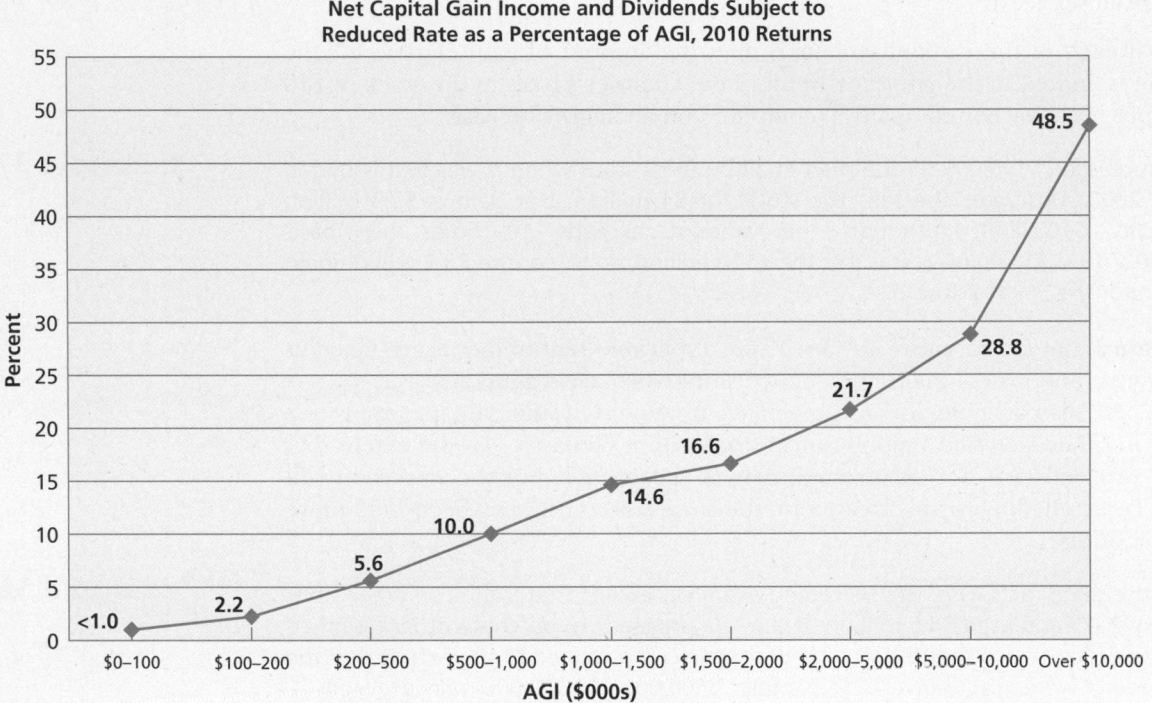

Net Capital Gain Income and Dividends Subject to Reduced Rate as a Percentage of AGI, 2010 Returns

---

Example 39

Sparrow Corporation has a $15,000 long-term capital loss for the current year and $57,000 of ordinary taxable income. Sparrow may not offset the $15,000 long-term capital loss against its ordinary income by taking a capital loss deduction. The $15,000 long-term capital loss becomes a $15,000 short-term capital loss for carryback and carryforward purposes. This amount may offset capital gains in the three-year carryback period or, if not absorbed there, offset capital gains in the five-year carryforward period. Any amount remaining after this carryforward period expires is permanently lost.

8-7 SECTION 1231 ASSETS

LO.6

Distinguish § 1231 assets from ordinary and capital assets and calculate § 1231 gain or loss.

Businesses own many assets that are used in the business rather than held for resale. In financial accounting, such assets are known as "fixed assets." For example, a foundry's 30,000-pound stamping machine is a fixed asset. It is also a depreciable asset. The building housing the foundry is another fixed asset. The remainder of this chapter largely deals with how to *classify* the gains and losses from the disposition of fixed assets. Chapter 5 discussed how to depreciate such assets. Chapter 7 discussed how to determine the adjusted basis and the amount of gain or loss from their disposition.

8-7a Relationship to Capital Assets

At first glance, the *classification of fixed assets* ought to be straightforward. Section 1221(a)(2) specifically excludes from the capital asset definition any property that is depreciable or that is real estate "used in a trade or business." Accordingly, the foundry's stamping machine and the building housing the foundry described earlier are not capital assets. Therefore, one would expect gains to be taxed as ordinary income and losses to be deductible as ordinary losses. Since World War II, however, certain business assets have received more favorable treatment.

Section 1231 provides that business assets held for more than one year can receive the best of both worlds: capital gain treatment on gains and ordinary loss treatment on losses. More specifically, this provision requires that gains and losses from **§ 1231 property** be aggregated at the end of the taxable year; the *net result* is then classified as capital gain if a net gain is produced, or as ordinary loss if a net loss is produced. As a result, a particular disposition's character as capital or ordinary is not determined until the taxable year has concluded and all of the taxpayer's **§ 1231 gains and losses** are tabulated.

Brown & Co. sells a building at a $5,000 gain and equipment at a $3,000 loss. Both properties were § 1231 assets because they were used in Brown's trade or business and held for more than one year. Brown's net gain is $2,000, and that net gain may be treated as a long-term capital gain under § 1231.	**Example 40**

Chickadee, Inc., sells equipment at a $10,000 loss and business land at a $2,000 gain. Both properties were held for more than one year and, therefore, are § 1231 assets. Chickadee's net loss is $8,000, and that net § 1231 loss is an ordinary loss.	**Example 41**

In-depth coverage can be found on this book's companion website: **www.cengagebrain.com**   9 | Digging Deeper

8-7b Property Included

Section 1231 property includes the following.

- Depreciable or real property used in business (principally machinery and equipment, buildings, and land).
- Property held for the production of income if it has been involuntarily converted.
- Timber, coal, or domestic iron ore to which § 631 applies.
- Livestock held for draft, breeding, dairy, or sporting purposes.
- Unharvested crops on land used in business.
- Certain *purchased* intangible assets (such as patents and goodwill) that are eligible for amortization.

In-depth coverage can be found on this book's companion website: **www.cengagebrain.com**  10, 11 | Digging Deeper

8-7c Property Excluded

Section 1231 property generally does *not* include the following.

- Property not held more than one year. Livestock must be held at least 12 months (24 months in some cases). Unharvested crops do not have to be held for more than one year, but the land must be so held.
- Property not put to a personal use, where casualty losses exceed casualty gains for the taxable year. If a taxpayer has a net casualty loss, the casualty gains and losses are treated as ordinary gains and losses.
- Inventory and property held primarily for sale to customers.
- Copyrights; literary, musical, or artistic compositions, etc.; and certain U.S. government publications.
- Accounts receivable and notes receivable arising in the ordinary course of the trade or business.

TAX IN THE NEWS   Loss from Cattle Rustling

A newspaper in "cattle country" reported that rustlers had stolen 20 head of prime milk cows from a local ranch. The rancher never recovered the cows. According to the article, the rancher had no insurance on the cows and was upset because he had no way of recovering his loss. A CPA might advise the rancher that he could be entitled to a special "theft loss" for tax purposes because the theft loss rules apply to § 1231 assets such as cattle held for 24 months or more.

8-7d Casualty or Theft and Nonpersonal-Use Capital Assets

When § 1231 assets are disposed of by casualty or theft, a special netting rule is applied. For simplicity, the term *casualty* is used to mean both casualty and theft dispositions. First, the casualty gains and losses from § 1231 assets *and* the casualty gains and losses from **long-term nonpersonal-use capital assets** are determined. For business entities, virtually any capital asset is a nonpersonal-use capital asset, because partnerships, limited liability companies, and corporations are incapable of using assets *personally*. This classification, therefore, is most significant to individual taxpayers who might use certain capital assets as part of their daily life.

Once the casualty gains and losses from § 1231 assets and nonpersonal-use capital assets are determined, they are netted together. If the result is a *net gain*, the net gain is treated as § 1231 gain, but if the result is a *net loss*, the net loss is deducted outside § 1231. Thus, whether these casualties get § 1231 treatment depends on the results of the casualty netting process.

Casualties and thefts are *involuntary conversions*, it should be recalled, and gains from such conversions need not be recognized if the proceeds are timely reinvested in similar property. Thus, the netting process described previously would not consider any casualty and theft gains that are being deferred because insurance proceeds were reinvested according to the requirements of § 1033 (see Chapter 7). Section 1231, in other words, has no effect on whether a *realized* gain or loss is recognized. Instead, § 1231 merely dictates how a *recognized* gain will be classified.

This special netting process for casualties and thefts does not apply to *condemnation* gains and losses. As a result, if a § 1231 asset is disposed of by condemnation, any resulting gain or loss will get § 1231 treatment.

8-7e General Procedure for § 1231 Computation

The tax treatment of § 1231 gains and losses depends on the results of a rather complex *netting* procedure. The steps in this netting procedure are as follows.

Step 1: Casualty Netting

Net all recognized long-term gains and losses from casualties of § 1231 assets and nonpersonal-use capital assets. This casualty netting is beneficial because if there is a net gain, the gain may receive long-term capital gain treatment. If there is a net loss, it receives ordinary loss treatment.

a. If the casualty gains exceed the casualty losses, add the net gain to the other § 1231 gains for the taxable year.
b. If the casualty losses exceed the casualty gains, exclude all casualty losses and gains from further § 1231 computation. The casualty gains are ordinary income, and the casualty losses are deductible. For individual taxpayers, the casualty losses must be classified further. For individual taxpayers, § 1231 asset casualty losses are deductible *for* AGI, while other casualty losses are deductible *from* AGI (see Chapter 10).

Step 2: § 1231 Netting

After adding any net casualty gain from step 1a on the previous page to the other § 1231 gains and losses (including *recognized* § 1231 asset condemnation gains and losses), net all § 1231 gains and losses.

a. If the gains exceed the losses, the net gain is offset by the "lookback" nonrecaptured § 1231 losses (see step 3).
b. If the losses exceed the gains, the net loss is deducted against ordinary income. For individual taxpayers only, the gains are ordinary income, the § 1231 asset losses are deductible *for* AGI, and the other casualty losses are deductible *from* AGI.

CONCEPT SUMMARY 8.4

Section 1231 Netting Procedure (Discussed in Section 8-7e)

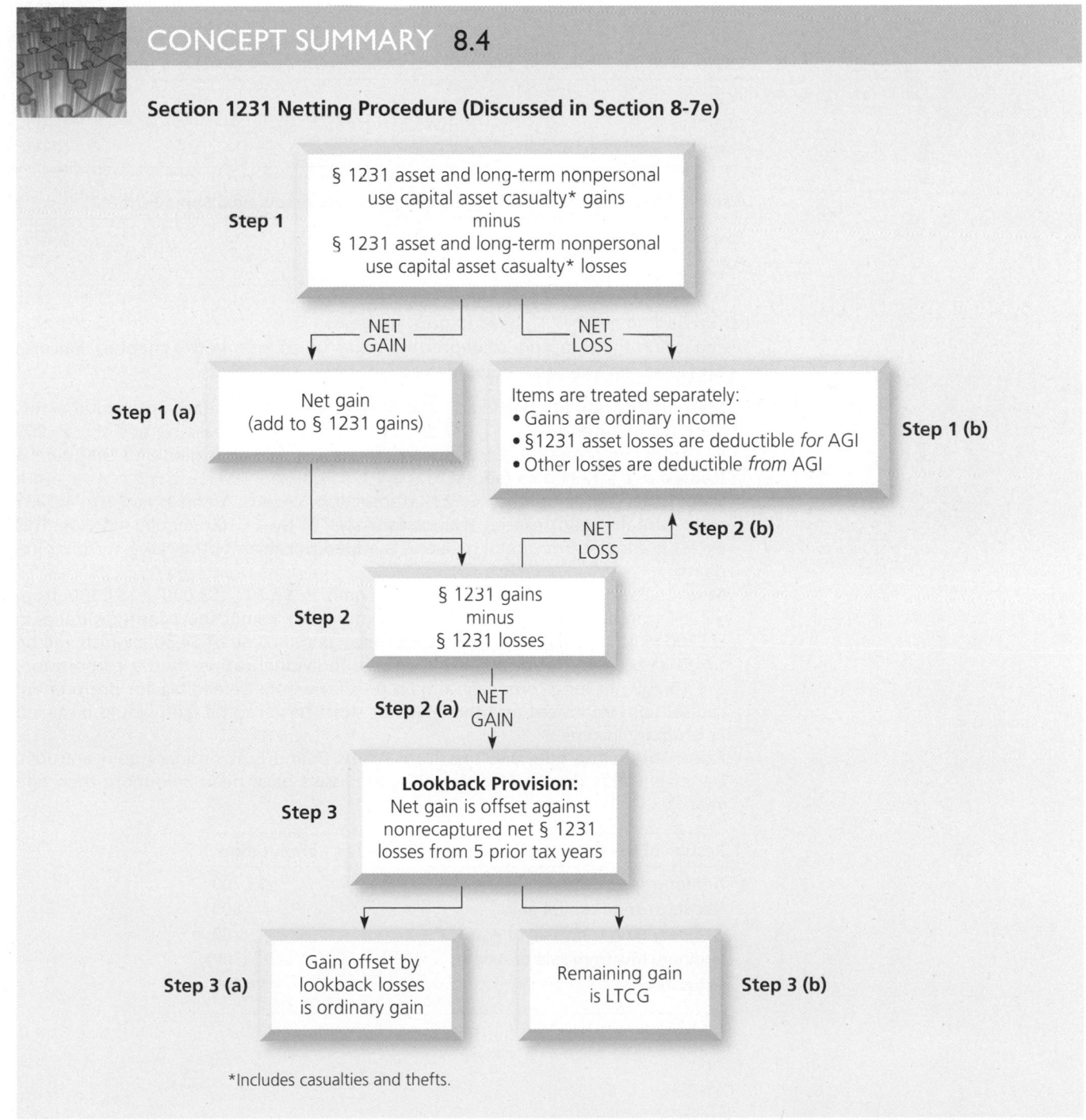

Step 1
§ 1231 asset and long-term nonpersonal use capital asset casualty* gains
minus
§ 1231 asset and long-term nonpersonal use capital asset casualty* losses

NET GAIN

NET LOSS

Step 1 (a)
Net gain
(add to § 1231 gains)

Step 1 (b)
Items are treated separately:
• Gains are ordinary income
• §1231 asset losses are deductible *for* AGI
• Other losses are deductible *from* AGI

NET LOSS   **Step 2 (b)**

Step 2
§ 1231 gains
minus
§ 1231 losses

Step 2 (a) NET GAIN

Step 3
Lookback Provision:
Net gain is offset against nonrecaptured net § 1231 losses from 5 prior tax years

Step 3 (a)
Gain offset by lookback losses is ordinary gain

Step 3 (b)
Remaining gain is LTCG

*Includes casualties and thefts.

Example 42

Falcon Management, Inc., recognized the following gains and losses this year.

Capital Gains and Losses	
Long-term capital gain	$3,000
Long-term capital loss	(400)
Short-term capital gain	1,000
Short-term capital loss	(200)

Casualties	
Gain from insurance recovery on fire loss to building, owned five years	$ 1,200
Loss from theft of computer (uninsured), owned two years	(1,000)

§ 1231 Gains and Losses from Sale of Depreciable Business Assets Held Long Term	
Asset A	$ 300
Asset B	1,100
Asset C	(500)

Gains and Losses from Sale of Depreciable Business Assets Held Short Term	
Asset D	$ 200
Asset E	(300)

Falcon had no net § 1231 losses in prior tax years.

Disregarding the recapture of depreciation (discussed later in this chapter), Falcon's gains and losses receive the following tax treatment.

- **Step 1:** The casualty netting of the § 1231 and nonpersonal-use capital assets contains two items—the $1,200 gain from the business building and the $1,000 loss from the computer. Consequently, there is a $200 net gain and that gain is treated as a § 1231 gain (added to the § 1231 gains).
- **Step 1 (a):** The gains from § 1231 transactions (Assets A and B and the § 1231 asset casualty gain) exceed the losses (Asset C) by $1,100 ($1,600 − $500). This excess is a long-term capital gain and is added to Falcon's other long-term capital gains.
- **Step 2:** Falcon's net long-term capital gain is $3,700 ($3,000 + $1,100 from § 1231 transactions − $400 long-term capital loss). Its net short-term capital gain is $800 ($1,000 − $200). The result is capital gain income of $4,500, which will be taxed at ordinary rates. If Falcon were an individual rather than a corporation, the $3,700 net long-term capital gain portion would be eligible for preferential capital gain treatment and the $800 net short-term capital gain would be taxed as ordinary income.
- Falcon treats the gain and loss from Assets D and E as ordinary gain and loss, because § 1231 does not apply unless the assets have been held more than one year.[26]

Results of the Gains and Losses on Falcon's Tax Computation	
Net long-term capital gain	$3,700
Net short-term capital gain	800
Ordinary gain from sale of Asset D	200
Ordinary loss from sale of Asset E	(300)
Gross income	$4,400

Assume the same facts as in the preceding example, except that the loss from Asset C was $1,700 instead of $500.

Example 43

- The treatment of the casualty gains and losses is the same.
- **Step 1 (b):** The losses from § 1231 transactions now exceed the gains by $100 ($1,700 − $1,600). As a result, the net loss is deducted in full as an ordinary loss.
- Capital gain income is $3,400 ($2,600 long-term + $800 short-term).

Results of the Gains and Losses on Falcon's Tax Computation	
Net long-term capital gain	$2,600
Net short-term capital gain	800
Net ordinary loss on Assets A, B, and C and § 1231 casualty gain	(100)
Ordinary gain from sale of Asset D	200
Ordinary loss from sale of Asset E	(300)
Gross income	$3,200

Step 3: § 1231 Lookback Provision

The net § 1231 gain from step 2a on p. 8-27 is offset by the nonrecaptured net § 1231 losses for the five preceding taxable years.[27] For transactions in 2014, the lookback years are 2009, 2010, 2011, 2012, and 2013.

a. To the extent of the nonrecaptured net § 1231 loss, the current-year net § 1231 gain is ordinary income. The *nonrecaptured* net § 1231 losses are losses that have not already been used to offset net § 1231 gains.

b. Only the net § 1231 gain exceeding this net § 1231 loss carryforward is given long-term capital gain treatment. The **§ 1231 lookback** provision reduces the taxpayer's ability to gain a tax advantage by "timing" sales artificially.

Komodo Manufacturing Corporation sold used equipment and some business real estate during 2014 for a net § 1231 gain of $25,000. During 2013, Komodo had no § 1231 transactions, but in 2012, it had a net § 1231 loss of $17,000. This loss causes $17,000 of the 2014 gain to be classified as ordinary income. The remaining 2014 gain of $8,000 ($25,000 of § 1231 gain − $17,000 nonrecaptured loss) is § 1231 gain.

Example 44

Assume the same facts as in the preceding example, except that Komodo had a net § 1231 loss of $37,000 in 2012 and a net § 1231 gain of $10,000 in 2013.

Example 45

- The 2012 net § 1231 loss of $37,000 would cause the net § 1231 gain of $10,000 in 2013 to be classified as ordinary income, and $27,000 ($37,000 loss − $10,000 recaptured) would carry over to 2014.
- The remaining nonrecaptured § 1231 loss of $27,000 from 2012 completely offsets the § 1231 gain of $25,000 from 2014, making that entire gain ordinary income.
- The remaining nonrecaptured § 1231 loss from 2012 is $2,000 ($27,000 carried to 2014 − $25,000 recaptured). This recapture potential carries over to 2015.

8-8 SECTION 1245 RECAPTURE

As explained earlier, when Congress determined that § 1231 was unduly generous, it chose to *recapture* some of § 1231's benefits rather than repeal that section altogether. This recapture phenomenon applies exclusively to the gain side of § 1231; the ordinary loss feature applicable to § 1231 property is not affected by the Code's recapture provisions. In essence, recapture takes part—often all—of the gain from the sale or exchange of a § 1231 asset and classifies it as *ordinary income* before the netting process of § 1231 begins. Accordingly, recaptured gain is computed *first*, without considering the other § 1231 transactions that occurred during the taxable year. This section discusses the § 1245 recapture rules, and the next section discusses the § 1250 recapture rules.

LO.7

Determine when recapture provisions apply and derive their effects.

---

[27]§ 1231(c).

Section 1245 requires taxpayers to treat all gain as ordinary gain unless the property is sold for more than its original cost. This result is accomplished by requiring that all gain be treated as ordinary gain to the extent of the depreciation taken on the property disposed of. Section 1231 gain results only if the property is disposed of for more than its original cost. The excess of the sales price over the original cost is § 1231 gain. Section 1245 applies primarily to personalty such as machinery, trucks, and office furniture.

THE BIG PICTURE

Example 46

Return to the facts of *The Big Picture* on p. 8-1. Recall that Alice's husband, Jeff, had purchased depreciable equipment for use in his business for $50,000 and deducted $35,000 of depreciation. If Jeff sold the equipment for $45,000, his gain would have been $30,000 [$45,000 amount realized − $15,000 adjusted basis ($50,000 cost − $35,000 depreciation taken)]. Section 1245 treats as ordinary income (not as § 1231 gain) any gain to the extent of depreciation taken. In this example, the entire $30,000 gain would be ordinary income.

THE BIG PICTURE

Example 47

Continuing with the facts of Example 46, if instead, Jeff sold the equipment for $60,000, he would have a gain of $45,000 ($60,000 amount realized − $15,000 adjusted basis). The § 1245 gain would be $35,000 (equal to the depreciation taken), and the remaining gain of $10,000 (equal to the excess of the sales price over the original cost) would be § 1231 gain.

THE BIG PICTURE

Example 48

Continue with the facts of Example 46, except that Jeff sold the equipment for $8,000 instead of $45,000. Jeff would have a loss of $7,000 ($8,000 amount realized − $15,000 adjusted basis). Because there is a loss, there is no depreciation recapture. All of the loss is § 1231 loss.

Section 1245 recapture applies to the portion of *recognized* gain from the sale or other disposition of § 1245 property that represents depreciation, including § 167 depreciation, § 168 cost recovery, § 179 immediate expensing, § 168(k) additional first-year depreciation, and § 197 amortization. Section 1245 merely *classifies* gain as ordinary income; it does not cause gain to be recognized. Thus, in Example 46, Jeff recaptures as ordinary income only the $30,000 of actual gain, not the entire $35,000 of depreciation taken. In other words, § 1245 recaptures the *lower* of the depreciation taken or the gain recognized.

The method of depreciation (e.g., accelerated or straight-line) does not matter. All depreciation taken is potentially subject to recapture. Thus, § 1245 recapture is often referred to as *full recapture.* Any remaining gain after subtracting the amount recaptured as ordinary income will usually be § 1231 gain. The remaining gain is casualty gain, however, if the asset is disposed of in a casualty event. For example, if the equipment in Example 47 had been disposed of by casualty and the $60,000 received had been an insurance recovery, Jeff would still have a gain of $45,000, and $35,000 of that gain would still be recaptured by § 1245 as ordinary gain. The other $10,000 of gain, however, would be casualty gain.

If § 1245 property is disposed of in a transaction other than a sale, exchange, or involuntary conversion, the maximum amount recaptured is the excess of the property's fair market value over its adjusted basis. See the discussion under Exceptions to §§ 1245 and 1250 later in this chapter.

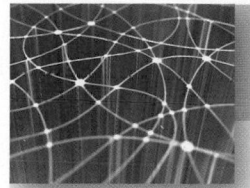

BRIDGE DISCIPLINE Bridge to Financial Accounting

The essence of much of the tax code is to create definitions that discriminate among certain types of income or expenditures so that special tax treatment can be afforded to one of the definitional groups. For instance, municipal bond interest might be favored over corporate bond interest income, long-term capital gains over short-term capital gains or ordinary income, and processing fees to bribes. In each case, the former generally allows a reduction of taxable income or the tax liability and helps the taxpayer meet its goal of maximizing the available after-tax income that it generates.

Maximizing net income also is a goal of financial accounting, at least from the viewpoint of current and potential shareholders. In the long run, stock prices may advance solely because of the positive earnings that the corporation generates relative to the rest of the capital markets. The greater the net earnings, the greater the increase in stock price and private wealth.

But financial accounting makes far fewer distinctions when classifying the reporting entity's revenues and expenses. Most of the tax code's definitions and distinctions are politically or economically motivated means designed to reduce the effective tax rate of the taxpayer, perhaps without affecting its nominal rate.

The preferential treatment of long-term capital gains is one of the most long-lived of these tax fictions. The "best of both worlds" § 1231 treatment is over 65 years old itself. Whereas the gain or loss generated by the sale of a business or investment asset is merely included in the body of the income statement of the reporting entity, § 1221 and § 1231 can reduce the taxpayer's effective tax rate and § 1245 and § 1250 can increase it.

Differences in classification of income and deductions created solely by the tax code constitute most of the items to be reconciled in the Schedule M–1 or M–3 of the C corporation, S corporation, partnership, and limited liability entity. Many of these items must be reported as permanent or temporary differences in the Deferred Tax Liability account regulated by ASC 740 (SFAS 109).

8-8a Section 1245 Property

Generally, **§ 1245 property** includes all depreciable personal property (e.g., machinery and equipment), including livestock. Buildings and their structural components usually are not § 1245 property. The following property is *also* subject to § 1245 treatment.

- Amortizable personal property such as goodwill, patents, copyrights, and leaseholds of § 1245 property.
- Professional baseball and football player contracts.
- Expensed costs to remove architectural and transportation barriers that restrict the handicapped and/or elderly.
- Section 179 immediately expensed depreciable tangible personal property.
- Certain depreciable tangible real property (other than buildings and their structural components) employed as an integral part of certain activities such as manufacturing and production. For example, a natural gas storage tank where the gas is used in the manufacturing process is § 1245 property.
- Pollution control facilities, railroad grading and tunnel bores, on-the-job training facilities, and child care facilities on which amortization is taken.
- Single-purpose agricultural and horticultural structures and petroleum storage facilities (e.g., a greenhouse or silo).

8-8b Observations on § 1245

- In most instances, the total depreciation taken will exceed the recognized gain. Therefore, the disposition of § 1245 property usually results in ordinary income rather than § 1231 gain (refer to Example 46).
- Recapture applies to the total amount of depreciation allowed or allowable regardless of the depreciation method used (i.e., full recapture).

TAX IN THE NEWS   Recapture and Casualty Loss

A fire completely destroyed an abandoned rental motor home. The local newspaper reported that the fire was "suspicious," meaning that it may have been deliberately set. The owner of the property was a local travel company with rental motor homes. The taxpayer, according to the newspaper article, had a $60,000 tax basis for the destroyed motor home and it was uninsured. The motor home was a § 1231 asset destroyed in a casualty event. There would be no § 1245 depreciation recapture because the motor home was disposed of at a loss—§ 1245 depreciation recapture only recaptures *gains*. Instead, the $60,000 loss is a *casualty loss*, not a *§ 1231 loss*, because it was disposed of by casualty, not by sale.

- Recapture applies regardless of the holding period of the property. Of course, the entire recognized gain would be ordinary income if the property was not held more than one year, because then § 1231 would not apply.
- Section 1245 does not apply to losses, which receive § 1231 treatment.
- Gains from the disposition of § 1245 assets may also be treated as passive activity gains (refer to Chapter 6).

Example 49

Upon sale of some business equipment held for five years, Pink Corporation recognized a $7,500 loss. All of the $20,000 § 1245 depreciation recapture potential for the asset disappears as a result of the disposition. The transaction receives § 1231 loss treatment, and none of Pink's cost recovery deductions are recaptured into ordinary income for this asset.

Tax Planning Strategies   DEPRECIATION RECAPTURE AND § 179

FRAMEWORK FOCUS: DEDUCTIONS

Strategy: Accelerate Recognition of Deductions to Achieve Tax Deferral.

Section 1245 recapture applies to all types of depreciation, including § 179 *immediate expensing*. Expensing under § 179, however, is elective and entirely within the discretion of the taxpayer. Choosing this option accelerates depreciation on the affected property but increases the potential recapture as well. Therefore, if a taxpayer anticipates that an asset will generate a gain when it is sold and that such sale will occur in the early years of the asset's life, the taxpayer might decide to forgo electing the additional depreciation under § 179.

On the other hand, electing § 179 remains attractive if little or no gain is anticipated upon an asset's disposition. After all, § 1245 recapture applies only to the extent gain is actually realized. Moreover, even if a substantial gain is anticipated upon an asset's disposition, the *time value of money* might suggest that § 179 be elected if the disposition is expected to be many years away. In any case, the taxpayer can usually control when an asset is sold or exchanged and can thereby extend the time before the taxes saved by electing § 179 must be returned as § 1245 recapture.

8-9 SECTION 1250 RECAPTURE

Some depreciable property that is not subject to § 1245 recapture faces a separate recapture computation mechanism in § 1250. For the most part, § 1250 applies to *depreciable real property* (principally buildings and their structural components), such as apartments, office buildings, factories, stores, and warehouses. Intangible real property, such as leaseholds of **§ 1250 property**, also is included.

TAX IN THE NEWS   Building or Tangible Personal Property?

Many taxpayers have "cost-segregated" their buildings. This means that an engineering study is done to determine whether some of a building's cost can be segregated into tangible personal property (generally a 5-year or 7-year MACRS life with accelerated depreciation) rather than real property (a 27.5-year or 39-year MACRS life with straight-line depreciation). The faster depreciation for the tangible personal property yields significant tax savings.

However, there is a downside. When the property is sold, the tangible personal property gains are taxable as ordinary income due to § 1245 depreciation recapture, whereas the gain from the sale of the building is not subject to recapture, is a § 1231 gain, and may receive long-term capital gain treatment.

© iStockphoto.com/Andrey Prokhorov

Section 1250 recapture is less onerous than § 1245 recapture. Section 1250 recaptures only a property's *additional depreciation*, which is the excess of the depreciation actually deducted over the amount that would have been allowed under the straight-line method of depreciation. For this reason, § 1250 recapture is often referred to as *partial recapture*, in contrast to § 1245's full recapture.

Because § 1250 recaptures only the excess over straight-line depreciation, the concept does not apply to properties that were depreciated using the straight-line method (unless they were held for one year or less). Real property placed in service *after 1986* can only be depreciated using the straight-line method, so there is *no § 1250 recapture* upon the disposition of such properties that are held for longer than one year. Finally, § 1250 does not affect the § 1231 treatment of realized losses.

> **Example 50**
>
> Sanjay Enterprises, Ltd., acquires a residential rental building on January 1, 2013, for $300,000. It receives an offer of $450,000 for the building and sells it on December 23, 2014.
>
> - Sanjay takes $20,909 [($300,000 × .03485) + ($300,000 × .03636 × $^{11.5}/_{12}$) = $20,909] of total depreciation for 2013 and 2014. The adjusted basis of the property is $279,091 ($300,000 − $20,909).
> - Sanjay's recognized gain is $170,909 ($450,000 − $279,091).
> - All of the gain is § 1231 gain.

Concept Summary 8.5 compares and contrasts the § 1245 and § 1250 depreciation recapture rules.

8-9a Unrecaptured § 1250 Gain (Real Estate 25% Gain)

As noted previously in the chapter, *noncorporate taxpayers* pay tax at a maximum rate of 25 percent on their **unrecaptured § 1250 gain**. This gain represents that part of the gain on § 1250 property that is attributable to depreciation that was not recaptured by § 1250.

The procedure for computing this amount involves three distinct steps.

Step 1. Determine the part of the recognized gain that is attributable to *depreciation deductions* claimed in prior years.

Step 2. Apply § 1250 to determine the portion of the gain calculated in step 1 that is recaptured as ordinary income (if any).

Step 3. Subtract the gain recaptured under § 1250 (step 2) from the gain derived in step 1. This amount is the *unrecaptured § 1250 gain*.

CONCEPT SUMMARY 8.5

Comparison of § 1245 and § 1250 Depreciation Recapture

	§ 1245	§ 1250
Property affected	All depreciable personal property, including items such as § 179 expense and § 197 amortization of intangibles such as goodwill, patents, and copyrights.	Nonresidential real property acquired after 1969 and before 1981, on which accelerated depreciation was taken.
		Residential rental real property acquired after 1975 and before 1987, on which accelerated depreciation was taken.
		Additional first-year depreciation [§ 168(k)] exceeding straight-line depreciation taken on leasehold improvements, qualified restaurant property, and qualified retail property.
		Immediate expense deduction [§ 179(f)] exceeding straight-line depreciation taken on leasehold improvements, qualified restaurant property, and qualified retail improvement property.
Depreciation recaptured	Potentially all depreciation taken. If the selling price is greater than or equal to the original cost, all depreciation is recaptured. If the selling price is between the adjusted basis and the original cost, only some depreciation is recaptured.	Normally, there is no depreciation recapture, but in the special situations listed above, there can be § 1250 depreciation recapture of additional depreciation (the excess of accelerated depreciation over straight-line depreciation). All depreciation taken if property disposed of in first year.
Limit on recapture	Lower of depreciation taken or gain recognized.	Lower of additional depreciation or gain recognized.
Treatment of gain exceeding recapture gain	Usually § 1231 gain.	Usually § 1231 gain.
Treatment of loss	No depreciation recapture; loss is usually § 1231 loss.	No depreciation recapture; loss is usually § 1231 loss.

Recall that for property placed in service after 1986, § 1250 generally does not apply, because such property is depreciated using the straight-line method under MACRS. As a result, *all* of the gain attributable to depreciation on such assets is unrecaptured § 1250 gain.

Example 51

Linda placed two apartment buildings in service at a cost of $100,000 each. On each building, she claimed depreciation deductions of $78,000. Thus, her adjusted basis for each building is $22,000 ($100,000 cost − $78,000 depreciation deducted). Because the buildings were depreciated using the straight-line method, there is no § 1250 recapture. She now sells these buildings for $96,000 and $110,000, respectively, and computes her gain as follows.

	Building A	Building B
Amount realized	$ 96,000	$110,000
Adjusted basis	(22,000)	(22,000)
Recognized gain	$ 74,000	$ 88,000
Depreciation recaptured by § 1250	(–0–)	(–0–)
Remaining gain	$ 74,000	$ 88,000
Unrecaptured § 1250 gain	(74,000)	(78,000)
§ 1231 gain	None	$ 10,000

8-9b Additional Recapture for Corporations

Although depreciation recapture is generally the same for all taxpayers, corporations that sell depreciable real estate face an additional amount of depreciation recapture. Section 291(a)(1) requires recapture of 20 percent of the excess of the amount that would be recaptured under § 1245 over the amount actually recaptured under § 1250.

Example 52

Red Corporation purchases nonresidential real property on May 1, 1999, for $800,000. Straight-line depreciation is taken in the amount of $316,239 before the property is sold on October 8, 2014, for $1.2 million.

First, determine the recognized gain:

Sales price		$1,200,000
Less: Adjusted basis—		
Cost of property	$ 800,000	
Less: Cost recovery	(316,239)	(483,761)
Recognized gain		$ 716,239

Second, determine the § 1245 recapture potential. This is the lesser of $716,239 (recognized gain) or $316,239 (cost recovery claimed).

Third, determine the normal § 1250 recapture amount:

Cost recovery taken	$ 316,239
Less: Straight-line cost recovery	(316,239)
§ 1250 ordinary income	$ –0–

Fourth, because the taxpayer is a corporation, determine the additional § 291 amount:

§ 1245 recapture potential	$ 316,239
Less: § 1250 recapture amount	(–0–)
Excess § 1245 recapture potential	$ 316,239
Apply § 291 percentage	× 20%
Additional ordinary income under § 291	$ 63,248

Red Corporation's recognized gain of $716,239 is accounted for as follows:

Ordinary income under § 1250	$ –0–
Ordinary income under § 291	63,248
§ 1231 gain	652,991
Total recognized gain	$ 716,239

8-10 EXCEPTIONS TO §§ 1245 AND 1250

Recapture under §§ 1245 and 1250 does not apply to the following transactions.

8-10a Gifts

Depreciation recapture potential carries over to the donee.[28]

---

[28]§§ 1245(b)(1) and 1250(d)(1) and Reg. §§ 1.1245–4(a)(1) and 1.1250–3(a)(1).

Tax Planning Strategies   SELLING DEPRECIABLE REAL ESTATE

FRAMEWORK FOCUS: DEDUCTIONS

Strategy: Maximize Deductible Amounts.

FRAMEWORK FOCUS: TAX RATE

Strategy: Control the Character of Income and Deductions.

A building depreciated on an accelerated method eventually generates annual allowances that are smaller than the amount the straight-line method would have produced. Beyond that "cross-over" point, the *cumulative* amount of "additional depreciation" is reduced every year the asset is used. Doing so effectively converts gain for an individual taxpayer that would otherwise be subject to § 1250 recapture into "unrecaptured § 1250 gain," enabling the taxpayer to save the difference between the applicable tax rate on ordinary income and 25 percent.

Continuing to use the building, however, brings forth an array of important *nontax considerations*. Each year a building is used subjects it to additional maintenance expenses to keep it in operating condition. Moreover, a building's appeal to current and prospective tenants tends to decline over time as newer structures appear offering more modern amenities, such as wireless high-speed Internet access, and other conveniences. Finally, local real estate developments might produce lower resale prices that offset much, if not all, of the tax advantage obtained by holding the property for the additional time.

Example 53

Wade gives his daughter, Helen, § 1245 property with an adjusted basis of $1,000. The amount of recapture potential is $700. Helen uses the property in her business and claims further depreciation of $100 before selling it for $1,900. Helen's recognized gain is $1,000 [$1,900 amount realized − $900 adjusted basis ($1,000 carryover basis − $100 depreciation taken by Helen)], of which $800 is recaptured as ordinary income ($100 depreciation taken by Helen + $700 recapture potential carried over from Wade). The remaining gain of $200 is § 1231 gain. Even if Helen had used the property for personal purposes, the $700 recapture potential would have carried over.

8-10b Death

Although not an attractive tax planning approach, death eliminates all recapture potential.[29] Depreciation recapture potential does not carry over from a decedent to an estate or an heir.

Example 54

Assume the same facts as in the preceding example, except that Helen receives the property as a result of Wade's death. The $700 recapture potential from Wade is extinguished at his death. Helen has a basis in the property equal to its fair market value (assume $1,700) at Wade's death. She will have a $300 gain when the property is sold because the selling price ($1,900) exceeds the property's adjusted basis of $1,600 ($1,700 basis to Helen − $100 depreciation) by $300. Because of § 1245, Helen has ordinary income of $100. The remaining gain of $200 is § 1231 gain.

8-10c Charitable Transfers

Depreciation recapture potential reduces the amount of any charitable contribution deduction.[30]

---

[29]§§ 1245(b)(2) and 1250(d)(2).

[30]§ 170(e)(1)(A) and Reg. § 1.170A–4(b)(1). In certain circumstances, § 1231 gain also reduces the amount of the charitable contribution. See § 170(e)(1)(B).

Exchange for Foreign Property Yields Recognized Recapture Gain

Tangible personal property used in a trade or business may be the subject of a like-kind exchange, and the postponed gain is most likely postponed § 1245 gain. However, tangible personal property used predominantly within the United States cannot be exchanged tax-free for tangible personal property used predominantly outside the United States. Thus, such an exchange would cause recognized gain, and as long as the fair market value of the property given up does not exceed its original cost, all of the gain is § 1245 depreciation recapture gain.

Global Tax Issues

© iStockphoto.com/Andrey Prokhorov

Bullfinch Corporation donates to a museum § 1245 property with a fair market value of $10,000 and an adjusted basis of $7,000. Depreciation recapture potential is $2,000 (the amount of recapture that would occur if the property were sold). The company's charitable contribution deduction (subject to the limitations discussed in Chapter 5) is $8,000 ($10,000 fair market value − $2,000 recapture potential).

Example 55

8-10d Certain Nontaxable Transactions

In certain transactions, the transferor's adjusted basis for the property carries over to the transferee. Then depreciation recapture potential also carries over to the transferee.[31] Included in this category are transfers of property pursuant to the following.

- Nontaxable incorporations under § 351 (see Chapter 12).
- Certain liquidations of subsidiary corporations under § 332 (see Chapter 13).
- Nontaxable contributions to a partnership under § 721 (see Chapter 14).
- Nontaxable corporate reorganizations.

Gain may be recognized in these transactions if boot is received. If gain is recognized, it is treated as ordinary income to the extent of the recapture potential or the recognized gain, whichever is lower.[32]

8-10e Like-Kind Exchanges and Involuntary Conversions

As explained in Chapter 7, realized gain is recognized to the extent of boot received in a like-kind exchange. Realized gain is also recognized to the extent the proceeds from an involuntary conversion are not reinvested in similar property. Such recognized gain is subject to recapture as ordinary income under §§ 1245 and 1250. Any remaining recapture potential carries over to the property received in the exchange.

Crane Corporation exchanges § 1245 property with an adjusted basis of $300 for § 1245 property with a fair market value of $6,000 plus $1,000 cash (boot). The exchange qualifies as a like-kind exchange under § 1031. Crane's realized gain is $6,700 ($7,000 amount realized − $300 adjusted basis of property).

Because Crane received boot of $1,000, it recognizes gain to this extent. Assuming that the recapture potential is $7,500, Crane recognizes § 1245 gain of $1,000. The remaining recapture potential of $6,500 carries over to the like-kind property received.

Example 56

---

[31]§§ 1245(b)(3) and 1250(d)(3). Reg. §§ 1.1245–2(a)(4) and (c)(2), 1.1245–4(c), 1.1250–2(d)(1) and (3).

[32]§§ 1245(b)(3) and 1250(d)(3) and Reg. §§ 1.1245–4(c) and 1.1250–3(c).

| Digging Deeper | 12 | In-depth coverage can be found on this book's companion website: **www.cengagebrain.com** |

8-11 Reporting Procedures

Noncapital gains and losses are reported on Form 4797, Sales of Business Property. Before Form 4797 is filled out, however, Form 4684, Casualties and Thefts, Part B, must be completed to determine whether any casualties will enter into the § 1231 computation procedure. Recall that recognized gains from § 1231 asset casualties may be recaptured by § 1245 or § 1250. These gains do not appear on Form 4684. The § 1231 gains and nonpersonal-use long-term capital gains are netted against § 1231 and nonpersonal-use long-term capital losses on Form 4684 to determine whether there is a net gain to transfer to Form 4797, Part I.

| Digging Deeper | 13 | In-depth coverage can be found on this book's companion website: **www.cengagebrain.com** |

Tax Planning Strategies   TIMING OF RECAPTURE

FRAMEWORK FOCUS: TAX RATE

Strategy: Shift Net Income from High-Bracket Years to Low-Bracket Years.
Shift Net Income from High-Bracket Taxpayers to Low-Bracket Taxpayers.

Because recapture is usually not triggered until the property is sold or disposed of, it may be possible to plan for recapture in low-bracket or loss years. If a taxpayer has net operating loss carryovers that are about to expire, the recognition of ordinary income from recapture may be advisable to absorb the loss carryovers.

Example 57

Angel Corporation has a $15,000 net operating loss carryover that will expire this year. It owns a machine that it plans to sell in the early part of next year. The expected gain of $17,000 from the sale of the machine will be recaptured as ordinary income under § 1245. Angel sells the machine before the end of this year and offsets $15,000 of the ordinary income by the net operating loss carryover. ∎

It is also possible to postpone recapture or to shift the burden of recapture to others. For example, recapture is avoided upon the disposition of a § 1231 asset if the taxpayer replaces the property by entering into a like-kind exchange. In this instance, recapture potential is merely carried over to the newly acquired property (refer to Example 56).

Recapture can be shifted to others through the gratuitous transfer of § 1245 or § 1250 property to family members. A subsequent sale of such property by the donee will trigger recapture to the donee rather than the donor (refer to Example 53). This technique is advisable when the donee is in a lower income tax bracket than the donor.

8-12 Summary

The lower tax rates afforded long-term capital gains present numerous definitional and computational challenges. Most of these rules are found in court decisions and Regulations rather than in the Code. The tax professional needs to use good software to analyze all of the possibilities that are available.

CAPITAL GAINS
AND LOSSES,
§ 1231 GAINS
AND LOSSES, AND
RECAPTURE

The land, stock, franchise, and home owned by Alice are all capital assets and will produce capital gain or loss when sold. Accordingly, Alice will have a long-term capital gain of $48,000 from the sale of the land, a long-term capital gain of $6,000 from the sale of 300 shares of inherited stock, a short-term capital loss of $4,000 from the sale of the other 200 shares of stock, a short-term capital gain of $1,000 from the sale of the franchise, and a $125,000 long-term capital gain from the sale of the house. The treatment given to the Eagle stock will depend on the nature of its disposition (see Example 10).

For the patent, because Alice is a "holder" of the patent, it will qualify for the beneficial capital gain rate regardless of the holding period if the patent should produce income in excess of her $50,000 investment. However, if Alice loses money on the investment, she will be able to deduct only $3,000 of the loss per year against her ordinary income (assuming that there are no offsetting capital gains in the year of a sale).

The depreciable property owned by Alice's husband is § 1231 property. The $45,000 gain from the sale of the property ($60,000 amount realized − $15,000 basis) is subject to depreciation recapture under § 1245. Accordingly, the first $35,000 of the gain (up to the amount of depreciation taken on the property) is taxed as ordinary income. The remaining $10,000 is § 1231 gain and is given long-term capital gain treatment.

As a result of these transactions where the amount of gain or loss is determined, Alice and her husband have a net long-term capital gain of $189,000 ($48,000 + $6,000 + $125,000 + $10,000) and a net short-term capital loss of $3,000 ($1,000 gain − $4,000 loss). The long-term capital gain and short-term capital loss are netted, so the final result is a net capital gain of $186,000, which is taxed at the 15 or 20 percent tax rate. Alice and her husband also report $35,000 of ordinary income on their joint income tax return because of the depreciation recapture provisions.

What If?

What if the depreciable business property was worth only $10,000 when it was sold? In this case, there is no depreciation recapture, and the $5,000 loss is deductible as an ordinary loss under § 1231.

© Monkey Business Images/Shutterstock.com

Suggested Readings

Tom Crice, "The Perils of Winning: Settlement Payments, Trade Secrets, and Taxes," *Practical Tax Strategies*, September 2012.

"LLC Members Received Capital Gains Income from Sale of LLC's Assets," *Practical Tax Strategies*, October 2012.

Nancy B. Nichols, William M. Vandenburgh, and Luis Betancourt, "Taxing Implications of Exchange Traded Funds," *Practical Tax Strategies*, September 2010.

Patrick J. Smith, Francois Hechinger, John M. Nuckolls, "Capital Gain Exclusion on Small Business Stock," *The Tax Adviser*, May 2011.

James G. S. Yang, Wing W. Poon, and Beixin Betsy Lin, "Tax Planning Strategies Under the American Taxpayer Relief Act of 2012," *Practical Tax Strategies*, July 2013.

Key Terms

Capital assets, 8-2

Capital gain, 8-2

Capital losses, 8-2

Collectibles, 8-18

Franchise, 8-11

Holding period, 8-13

Lessee, 8-13

Lessor, 8-13

Long-term nonpersonal-use capital assets, 8-26

Net capital gain, 8-19

Net capital loss, 8-19

Options, 8-7

Patent, 8-10

Qualified small business stock, 8-22

Sale or exchange, 8-7

Section 1231 gains and losses, 8-25

Section 1231 lookback, 8-29

Section 1231 property, 8-25

Section 1245 property, 8-31

Section 1245 recapture, 8-30

Section 1250 property, 8-32

Section 1250 recapture, 8-33

Short sale, 8-15

Unrecaptured § 1250 gain, 8-33

Problems

Issue ID

1. **LO.1** An individual taxpayer sells some used assets at a garage sale. Why are none of the proceeds taxable in most situations?

Issue ID

2. **LO.1** Alison owns a painting that she received as a gift from her aunt 10 years ago. The aunt created the painting. Alison has displayed the painting in her home and has never attempted to sell it. Recently, a visitor noticed the painting and offered Alison $5,000 for it. If Alison decides to sell the painting, what tax issues does she face?

3. **LO.1** During the year, Eugene had the four property transactions summarized below. Eugene is a collector of antique glassware and occasionally sells a piece to get funds to buy another. What are the amount and nature of the gain or loss from each of these transactions?

Property	Date Acquired	Date Sold	Adjusted Basis	Sales Price
Antique vase	06/18/03	05/23/14	$37,000	$42,000
Blue Growth Fund (100 shares)	12/23/05	11/22/14	22,000	38,000
Orange bonds	02/12/06	04/11/14	34,000	42,000*
Green stock (100 shares)	02/14/14	11/23/14	11,000	13,000

*The sales price included $750 of accrued interest income.

Decision Making

4. **LO.1** Rennie owns a video game arcade. He buys vintage video games from estates, often at much less than the retail value of the property. He usually installs the vintage video games in a special section of his video game arcade that appeals to players of "classic" video games. Recently, Rennie sold a classic video game that a customer "just had to have." Rennie paid $11,250 for it, owned it for 14 months, and sold it for $18,000. Rennie had suspected that this particular classic video game would be of interest to collectors; so he had it refurbished, put it on display in his video arcade, and listed it for sale on the Internet. No customers in the arcade had played it other than those testing it before considering it for purchase. Rennie would like the gain on the sale of the classic video game to be a long-term capital gain. Did he achieve that objective? Why or why not?

5. **LO.1** George is the owner of numerous classic automobiles. His intention is to hold the automobiles until they increase in value and then sell them. He rents the automobiles for use in various events (e.g., antique automobile shows) while he is holding them. In 2014, he sold a classic automobile for $1.5 million. He had held the automobile for five years, and it had a tax basis of $750,000. Was the automobile a capital asset? Why or why not?

Communications

6. **LO.1** Hyacinth, Inc., is a dealer in securities. The firm has spotted a fast-rising company and would like to buy and hold its stock for investment. The stock is currently selling for $2 per share, and Hyacinth thinks it will climb to $40 a share within two years. How can Hyacinth ensure that any gain it realizes will be taxed as long-term capital gain? Draft a

letter responding to Hyacinth's inquiry. The firm's address is 200 Catamon Drive, Great Falls, MT 59406.

7. **LO.1** Eagle Partners meets all of the requirements of § 1237 (subdivided realty). In 2014, Eagle Partners begins selling lots and sells four separate lots to four different purchasers. Eagle Partners also sells two contiguous lots to another purchaser. The sales price of each lot is $30,000. The partnership's basis for each lot is $15,000. Selling expenses are $500 per lot.
    a. What are the realized and recognized gain?
    b. Explain the nature of the gain (i.e., ordinary income or capital gain).
    c. Would your answers change if, instead, the lots sold to the fifth purchaser were not contiguous? If so, how?

8. **LO.1, 2** Benny purchased $400,000 of Peach Corporation face value bonds for $320,000 on November 13, 2013. The bonds had been issued with $80,000 of original issue discount because Peach was in financial difficulty in 2013. On December 3, 2014, Benny sold the bonds for $283,000 after amortizing $1,000 of the original issue discount. What are the nature and amount of Benny's gain or loss? *Critical Thinking*

9. **LO.2** Carla was the owner of vacant land that she was holding for investment. She paid $2 million for the land in 2012. Raymond was an investor in vacant land. He thought Carla's land might be the site of an exit ramp from a new freeway. Raymond gave Carla $836,000 for an option on her land in 2013. The option was good for two years and gave Raymond the ability to purchase Carla's land for $4,765,000. The freeway was not approved by the government, and Raymond's option expired in 2014. Does Carla have $836,000 of long-term capital gain upon the expiration of the option? Explain.

10. **LO.2, 3, 4** Mac, an inventor, obtained a patent on a chemical process to clean old aluminum siding so that it can be easily repainted. Mac has a $50,000 tax basis in the patent. Mac does not have the capital to begin manufacturing and selling this product, so he has done nothing with the patent since obtaining it two years ago. *Decision Making*

    Now a group of individuals has approached him and offered two alternatives. Under one alternative, they will pay Mac $600,000 (payable evenly over the next 15 years) for the exclusive right to manufacture and sell the product. Under the other, they will form a business and contribute capital to it to begin manufacturing and selling the product; Mac will receive 20% of the company's shares of stock in exchange for all of his patent rights. Discuss which alternative is better for Mac.

11. **LO.2** Blue Corporation and Fuchsia Corporation are engaged in a contract negotiation over the use of Blue's trademarked name, DateSiteForSeniors. For a one-time payment of $45,000, Blue licensed Fuchsia to use the name DateSiteForSeniors, and the license requires that Fuchsia pay Blue a royalty every time a new customer signs up on Fuchsia's website. Blue is a developer of "website ideas" that it then licenses to other companies such as Fuchsia. Did Fuchsia purchase a franchise right from Blue, or did Fuchsia purchase the name DateSiteForSeniors from Blue?

12. **LO.2** Freys, Inc., sells a 12-year franchise to Red Company. The franchise contains many restrictions on how Red may operate its store. For instance, Red cannot use less than Grade 10 Idaho potatoes; must fry the potatoes at a constant 410 degrees; must dress store personnel in Freys-approved uniforms; and must have a Freys sign that meets detailed specifications on size, color, and construction. When the franchise contract is signed, Red makes a noncontingent $160,000 payment to Freys. During the same year, Red pays Freys $300,000—14% of Red's sales. How does Freys treat each of these payments? How does Red treat each of the payments?

13. **LO.3** Maria held vacant land that qualified as an investment asset. She purchased the vacant land on April 10, 2010. She exchanged the vacant land for a rental house in a qualifying like-kind exchange on January 22, 2014. Maria was going to hold the house for several years and then sell it. However, she got an "offer she could not refuse" and sold it on November 22, 2014, for a substantial gain. What was Maria's holding period for the house?

14. **LO.3** Thrasher Corporation sells short 100 shares of ARC stock at $20 per share on January 15, 2014. It buys 200 shares of ARC stock on April 1, 2014, at $25 per share. *Critical Thinking*

On May 2, 2014, Thrasher closes the short sale by delivering 100 of the shares purchased on April 1.

a. What are the amount and nature of Thrasher's loss upon closing the short sale?
b. When does the holding period for the remaining 100 shares begin?
c. If Thrasher sells (at $27 per share) the remaining 100 shares on January 20, 2015, what will be the nature of its gain or loss?

Communications

15. **LO.1, 3, 4** Elaine Case (single with no dependents) has the following transactions in 2014:

AGI (exclusive of capital gains and losses)	$240,000
Long-term capital gain	22,000
Long-term capital loss	(8,000)
Short-term capital gain	19,000
Short-term capital loss	(23,000)

What is Elaine's net capital gain or loss? Draft a letter to Elaine describing how the net capital gain or loss will be treated on her tax return. Assume that Elaine's income from other sources puts her in the 39.6% bracket. Elaine's address is 300 Ireland Avenue, Shepherdstown, WV 25443.

Decision Making

16. **LO.4** Sally has taxable income of $160,000 as of November 30 of this year. She wants to sell a Rodin sculpture that has appreciated $90,000 since she purchased it six years ago, but she does not want to pay more than $15,000 of additional tax on the transaction. Sally also owns various stocks, some of which are currently worth less than their basis. How can she achieve her desired result?

17. **LO.5** Platinum, Inc., has determined its taxable income as $215,000 before considering the results of its capital gain or loss transactions. Platinum has a short-term capital loss of $24,000, a long-term capital loss of $38,000, and a short-term capital gain of $39,000. What is Platinum's taxable income? What (if any) are the amount and nature of its capital loss carryover?

Ethics and Equity

18. **LO.1, 4** The taxpayer is an antiques collector and is going to sell an antique purchased many years ago for a large gain. The facts and circumstances indicate that the taxpayer might be classified as a dealer rather than an investor in antiques. The taxpayer will save $40,000 in taxes if the gain is treated as long-term capital gain rather than as ordinary income. The taxpayer is considering the following options as ways to ensure the $40,000 tax savings.

- Give the antique to his daughter, who is an investment banker, to sell.
- Merely assume that he has held the antique as an investment.
- Exchange the antique in a like-kind exchange for another antique he wants.

One of the tax preparers the taxpayer has contacted has said that he would be willing to prepare the return under the second option. Would you? Why or why not? Evaluate the other options.

Communications

19. **LO.1, 4** In 2014, Bertha Jarow (head of household with three dependents) had a $28,000 loss from the sale of a personal residence. She also purchased from an individual inventor for $7,000 (and resold in two months for $18,000) a patent on a rubber bonding process. The patent had not yet been reduced to practice. Bertha purchased the patent as an investment. In addition, she had the following capital gains and losses from stock transactions:

Long-term capital loss	($ 6,000)
Long-term capital loss carryover from 2013	(12,000)
Short-term capital gain	21,000
Short-term capital loss	(7,000)

What is Bertha's net capital gain or loss? Draft a letter to Bertha explaining the tax treatment of all of these transactions. Assume that Bertha's income from other sources puts her in the 28% bracket. Bertha's address is 1120 West Street, Ashland, OR 97520.

Issue ID

20. **LO.1, 3, 4** Bridgette is known as the "doll lady." She started collecting dolls as a child, always received one or more dolls as gifts on her birthday, never sold any dolls, and eventually owned 600 dolls. She is retiring and moving to a small apartment and has decided to sell her collection. She lists the dolls on an Internet auction site and, to her great surprise, receives an offer from another doll collector of $45,000 for the entire

collection. Bridgette sells the entire collection, except for five dolls she purchased during the last year. She had owned all of the dolls sold for more than a year. What tax factors should Bridgette consider in deciding how to report the sale?

21. **LO.1, 2, 4** Two years ago, Harriet Company (an unincorporated entity) developed a process for preserving doughnuts that gives the doughnuts a much longer shelf life. The process is not patented or copyrighted, and only Harriet knows how it works. A conglomerate has approached Harriet with an offer to purchase the formula for the process. Specifically, the offer allows Harriet to choose between the following. Which option should Harriet accept?

    Critical Thinking

    Decision Making

    • $650,000 cash for the formula and a 10-year covenant not to compete, paying Harriet $65,000 per year for 10 years.
    • $650,000 cash for a 10-year covenant not to compete, and an annual $65,000 royalty for the formula, payable for 10 years.

22. **LO.6** A sculpture that Tulip & Co. held for investment was destroyed in a flood. The sculpture was insured, and Tulip had a $60,000 gain from this casualty. It also had a $17,000 loss from an uninsured antique vase that was destroyed by the flood. The vase was also held for investment. Tulip had no other property transactions during the year and has no nonrecaptured § 1231 losses from prior years. Both the sculpture and the vase had been held for more than one year when the flood occurred. Compute Tulip's net gain or loss, and identify how it would be treated. Write a letter to Tulip explaining the nature of the gain or loss. Tulip's address is 2367 Meridian Road, Hannibal, MO 63401.

    Communications

23. **LO.6, 7** Sissie owns two items of business equipment. They were both purchased in 2010 for $100,000, both have a seven-year recovery period, and both have an adjusted basis of $37,490. Sissie is considering selling these assets in 2014. One of them is worth $60,000, and the other is worth $23,000. Because both items were used in her business, Sissie simply assumes that the loss on one will be offset against the gain from the other and that the net gain or loss will increase or reduce her business income. Is she correct? Explain.

    Issue ID

24. **LO.6** Harold, a CPA, has a new client who recently moved to town. Harold prepares the client's current-year tax return, which shows a net § 1231 gain. Harold calls the client to request copies of the returns for the preceding five years to determine if there are any § 1231 lookback losses. The client says that the returns are "still buried in the moving mess somewhere" and cannot be found. The client also says that he does not remember any § 1231 net losses on the prior year returns. What should Harold do? Justify your answer.

    Ethics and Equity

25. **LO.6** Geranium, Inc., has the following net § 1231 results for each of the years shown. What is the nature of the net gain in 2013 and 2014?

Tax Year	Net § 1231 Loss	Net § 1231 Gain
2009	$18,000	
2010	33,000	
2011	42,000	
2012		$41,000
2013		30,000
2014		41,000

26. **LO.6** Delphinium Company owns two parcels of land (§ 1231 assets). One parcel can be sold at a loss of $60,000, and the other parcel can be sold at a gain of $70,000. The company has no nonrecaptured § 1231 losses from prior years. The parcels could be sold at any time because potential purchasers are abundant. The company has a $35,000 short-term capital loss carryover from a prior tax year and no capital assets that could be sold to generate long-term capital gains. Both land parcels have been held more than one year. What should Delphinium do based upon these facts? (Assume that tax rates are constant and ignore the present value of future cash flows.)

    Decision Making

27. **LO.6, 7** Siena Industries (a sole proprietorship) sold three § 1231 assets on October 10, 2014. Data on these property dispositions are as follows.

Asset	Cost	Acquired	Depreciation	Sold for
Rack	$100,000	10/10/10	$62,000	$85,000
Forklift	35,000	10/16/11	23,000	5,000
Bin	87,000	03/12/13	34,000	60,000

a. Determine the amount and the character of the recognized gain or loss from the disposition of each asset in 2014.

b. Assuming that Siena has no nonrecaptured net § 1231 losses from prior years, how much of the recognized gains are treated as long-term capital gains?

Communications

28. **LO.6, 7** On December 1, 2012, Lavender Manufacturing Company (a corporation) purchased another company's assets, including a patent. The patent was used in Lavender's manufacturing operations; $49,500 was allocated to the patent, and it was amortized at the rate of $275 per month. On July 30, 2014, Lavender sold the patent for $95,000. Twenty months of amortization had been taken on the patent. What are the amount and nature of the gain Lavender recognizes on the disposition of the patent? Write a letter to Lavender discussing the treatment of the gain. Lavender's address is 6734 Grover Street, Boothbay Harbor, ME 04538. The letter should be addressed to Bill Cubit, Controller.

29. **LO.6, 7** Larry is the sole proprietor of a trampoline shop. During 2014, the following transactions occurred.

- Unimproved land adjacent to the store was condemned by the city on February 1. The condemnation proceeds were $15,000. The land, acquired in 1985, had an allocable basis of $40,000. Larry has additional parking across the street and plans to use the condemnation proceeds to build his inventory.
- A truck used to deliver trampolines was sold on January 2 for $3,500. The truck was purchased on January 2, 2010, for $6,000. On the date of sale, the adjusted basis was zero.
- Larry sold an antique rowing machine at an auction. Net proceeds were $4,900. The rowing machine was purchased as used equipment 17 years ago for $5,200 and is fully depreciated.
- Larry sold an apartment building for $300,000 on September 1. The rental property was purchased on September 1, 2011, for $150,000 and was being depreciated over a 27.5-year life using the straight-line method. At the date of sale, the adjusted basis was $124,783.
- Larry's personal yacht was stolen on September 5. The yacht had been purchased in August at a cost of $25,000. The fair market value immediately preceding the theft was $19,600. Larry was insured for 50% of the original cost, and he received $12,500 on December 1.
- Larry sold a Buick on May 1 for $9,600. The vehicle had been used exclusively for personal purposes. It was purchased on September 1, 2010, for $20,800.
- Larry's trampoline stretching machine (owned two years) was stolen on May 5, but the business's insurance company will not pay any of the machine's value because Larry failed to pay the insurance premium. The machine had a fair market value of $8,000 and an adjusted basis of $6,000 at the time of theft.
- Larry had AGI of $102,000 from sources other than those described above.
- Larry has no nonrecaptured § 1231 lookback losses.

a. For each transaction, what are the amount and nature of recognized gain or loss?

b. What is Larry's 2014 AGI?

Critical Thinking

30. **LO.6, 7** A business building on which straight-line depreciation of $13,000 was taken is sold on the installment basis for $100,000 with $20,000 down and four yearly installments of $20,000 plus interest. The adjusted basis for the building is $35,000 at the time of the sale. The building had been held for more than 12 months. What are the amount and nature of the recognized gain?

31. **LO.7** Nicholas owns business equipment with a $155,000 adjusted basis; he paid $200,000 for the equipment, and it is currently worth $173,000. Nicholas dies suddenly, and his son Alvin inherits the property. What is Alvin's basis for the property? What happens to the § 1245 depreciation recapture potential?

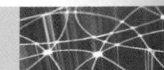

BRIDGE DISCIPLINE

1. Using an online research service, find the audited financial statements of a major U.S. corporation.
   a. List some of the items that the corporation reports as having different treatment for tax and financial accounting purposes. These items often are mentioned in the footnotes to the statements.
   b. List two or more such items that seem to increase the taxpayer's after-tax income and two or more that seem to decrease it.

Research Problems

THOMSON REUTERS

CHECKPOINT®

Note: Solutions to Research Problems can be prepared by using the **Checkpoint®** **Student Edition** online research product, which is available to accompany this text. It is also possible to prepare solutions to the Research Problems by using tax research materials found in a standard tax library.

Research Problem 1. Clyde had worked for many years as the chief executive of Red Industries, Inc., and had been a major shareholder. Clyde and the company had a falling out, and Clyde was terminated. Clyde and Red executed a document under which Clyde's stock in Red would be redeemed and Clyde would agree not to compete against Red in its geographic service area. After extensive negotiations between the parties, Clyde agreed to surrender his Red stock in exchange for $600,000. Clyde's basis in his shares was $143,000, and he had held the shares for 17 years. The agreement made no explicit allocation of any of the $600,000 to Clyde's agreement not to compete against Red. How should Clyde treat the $600,000 payment on his 2014 tax return?

Research Problem 2. Ali owns 100 shares of Brown Corporation stock. He purchased the stock at five different times and at five different prices per share as indicated.

Decision Making

Share Block	Number of Shares	Per Share Price	Purchase Date
A	10	$60	10/10/1997
B	20	20	08/11/1998
C	15	15	10/24/1999
D	35	30	04/23/2000
E	20	25	07/28/2001

On April 28, 2014, Ali will sell 40 shares of Brown stock for $40 per share. All of Ali's shares are held by his stockbroker. The broker's records track when the shares were purchased. May Ali designate the shares he sells? If so, which shares should he sell? Assume that Ali wants to maximize his gain because he has a capital loss carryforward.

Research Problem 3. Siva Nathaniel owns various plots of land in Fulton County, Georgia. He acquired the land at various times during the last 20 years. About every fourth year, Siva subdivides into lots one of the properties he owns. He then has water, sewer, natural gas, and electricity hookups put in each lot and paves new streets. Siva has always treated his sales of such lots as sales of capital assets. His previous tax returns were prepared by an accountant whose practice you recently purchased. Has the proper tax treatment been used on the prior tax returns? Explain.

Partial list of research aids:
§§ 1221 and 1237.
Jesse W. and Betty J. English, 65 TCM 2160, T.C.Memo. 1993–111.

Research Problem 4. Clean Corporation runs a chain of dry cleaners. Borax is used heavily in Clean's dry cleaning process and has been in short supply several times in the past. Several years ago, Clean Corporation bought a controlling interest in Dig Corporation—a borax mining concern—to ensure Clean of a continuous supply of borax if another

Communications

shortage developed. Clean has just sold the stock at a loss because Dig is in financial straits and because Clean has obtained an alternative source of borax. What is the nature of Clean's loss on the disposition of the Dig Corporation stock? Write a letter to the controller, Salvio Guitterez, that contains your advice, and prepare a memo for the tax files. The mailing address of Clean Corporation is 4455 Whitman Way, San Mateo, CA 94404.

Research Problem 5. Walter is both a real estate developer and the owner and manager of residential rental real estate. Walter is retiring and is going to sell both the land he is holding for future development and the rental properties he owns. Straight-line depreciation was used to depreciate the rental real estate. The rental properties will be sold at a substantial loss, and the development property will be sold at a substantial gain. What is the nature of these gains and losses?

Partial list of research aids:
§§ 1221 and 1231.
Zane R. Tollis, 65 TCM 1951, T.C.Memo. 1993–63.

Research Problem 6. An individual cash basis taxpayer sells rental real estate on the installment basis. The gain from the disposition is $45,000: $30,000 potential 25% gain and $15,000 potential 0%/15%/20% gain. In what sequence are these gains recognized on the installment sale?

Internet Activity

Use the tax resources of the Internet to address the following questions. Do not restrict your search to the Web, but include a review of newsgroups and general reference materials, practitioner sites and resources, primary sources of the tax law, chat rooms and discussion groups, and other opportunities.

Research Problem 7. Find a website, other than the IRS website, that discusses the taxation of short sales of securities. Discuss short sales with a classmate.

Research Problem 8. Perform a Google search to find information about capital gains tax rates worldwide (and across U.S. states). Try searching for: "capital gains rate by country (state)". What jurisdiction has the highest capital gains tax rate? What U.S. states have high capital gains tax rates?

Research Problem 9. Find a state website that has tax forms and instructions for the state. Call that state "X." Find a discussion in those sources that reveals whether state X taxes gains from the sale of real estate that is located in state Y when the taxpayer is an individual and a full-time resident of state X.

part 4

TAXATION OF INDIVIDUALS

Part 4 focuses on the numerous tax concepts that are designed to apply specifically to the individual taxpayer. The individual provisions complement the tax concepts and principles that have been discussed earlier in this text in applying the basic tax model to compute a Federal income tax liability.

Individuals as the Taxpayer

LEARNING OBJECTIVES: *After completing Chapter 9, you should be able to:*

LO.1 **Recognize and apply the components of the Federal income tax formula for individuals.**

LO.2 **Explain the standard deduction and evaluate its choice in arriving at taxable income.**

LO.3 **Apply the rules for arriving at personal exemptions.**

LO.4 **Explain the rules for determining dependency exemptions.**

LO.5 **List the filing requirements and choose the proper filing status.**

LO.6 **Demonstrate the proper procedures for determining the tax liability.**

LO.7 **Identify and report kiddie tax situations.**

CHAPTER OUTLINE

TAX TALK *I'm proud of paying taxes in the United States. The only thing is—I could be just as proud for half the money.* —ARTHUR GODFREY

A DIVIDED HOUSEHOLD

Polly maintains a household in which she lives with her unemployed husband (Nick), stepdaughter (Paige), and a family friend (Maude). She provides more than one-half of the support for both Paige and Maude. Maude was fatally injured in an automobile accident in February, and Polly paid for her hospitalization and funeral expenses. Paige, an accomplished gymnast, graduated from high school last year. Paige has a part-time job but spends most of her time training and looking for an athletic scholarship to the "right" college. In March, Nick left for parts unknown and has not been seen or heard from since. Polly was more surprised than distressed over Nick's unexpected departure.

    Based on these facts, what are Polly's income tax concerns for the current year?

Read the chapter and formulate your response.

The individual income tax accounts for approximately 32 percent of Federal budget receipts, compared with approximately 7 percent for the corporate income tax. The tax laws affecting individuals have become increasingly complex in recent years as the government adds new laws to protect or increase this important source of revenue. Taxpayers respond to each new tax act with techniques to exploit loopholes, and the government responds with loophole-closing provisions, making the individual income tax law even more complex.[1]

9-1 THE INDIVIDUAL TAX FORMULA

LO.1

Recognize and apply the components of the Federal income tax formula for individuals.

Individuals are subject to Federal income tax based on taxable income. This chapter explains how taxable income and the income tax of an individual taxpayer are determined. To compute taxable income, it is necessary to understand the tax formula in Figure 9.1.

Although this formula is rather simple, determining an individual's taxable income can be quite complex because of the numerous provisions that govern the determination of gross income and allowable deductions.

After taxable income is computed, the appropriate rates must be applied. This requires a determination of the individual's filing status because different rates apply for single taxpayers, married taxpayers, and heads of household. The individual tax rate structure is progressive, with rates for 2014 ranging from 10 percent to 39.6 percent.[2] For comparison, the lowest rate structure, which was in effect from 1913 to 1915, ranged from 1 to 7 percent, and the highest, in effect during 1944 to 1945, ranged from 23 to 94 percent.

Once the individual's tax has been computed, prepayments and credits are subtracted to determine whether the taxpayer owes additional tax or is entitled to a refund.

9-1a Components of the Tax Formula

Before the application of the tax formula is illustrated, a brief discussion of each of its components is helpful.

Income (Broadly Conceived)

In the tax formula, "income" is broadly conceived and includes all of the taxpayer's income, both taxable and nontaxable. Although it is essentially equivalent to gross receipts, it does not include a return of capital or receipt of borrowed funds. Nor does gross income include unrealized appreciation in the value of a taxpayer's assets.

Example 1

Dan decides to quit renting and buy a new house. Consequently, the owner of the apartment building returns to Dan the $600 damage deposit he previously made. To make a down payment on the house, Dan sells stock for $20,000 (original cost of $8,000) and borrows $150,000 from a bank. Only the $12,000 gain from the sale of the stock is income to Dan. The $600 damage deposit and the $8,000 cost of the stock are a return of capital. The $150,000 bank loan is not income as Dan has an obligation to repay that amount.

Exclusions

For various reasons, Congress has chosen to exclude certain types of income from the income tax base. The principal income exclusions are listed in Exhibit 9.1. The exclusions most commonly encountered by individual taxpayers (employee fringe benefits) are discussed in detail in Chapter 11.

[1]Refer to the discussion of tax complexity in Chapter 1.

[2]The current Tax Rate Schedules that apply to individuals are shown on the inside front cover of the text.

TAX FACT The Government's Interest in Our Work

How many days does the typical American work just to pay Federal, state, and local taxes? According to the Tax Foundation, the answer is 108 days, and that day arrived on April 18 in 2013. However, the required effort also depends on where the individual lives. In high-tax jurisdictions such as

Connecticut and New York, people need to work until May 13 and May 6, respectively, while in Mississippi and Louisiana, taxpayers are required to work only until March 29.

_____

Source: Tax Foundation, 2013.

FIGURE 9.1	Individual Income Tax Formula	
Income (broadly conceived)		$xx,xxx
Less: Exclusions		(x,xxx)
Gross income		$xx,xxx
Less: Deductions *for* adjusted gross income		(x,xxx)
Adjusted gross income (AGI)		$xx,xxx
Less: The greater of—		
Total itemized deductions *or*		
Standard deduction		(x,xxx)
Less: Personal and dependency exemptions		(x,xxx)
Taxable income		$xx,xxx
Tax on taxable income (see Tax Tables or Tax Rate Schedules)		$ x,xxx
Less: Tax credits (including income taxes withheld and prepaid)		(xxx)
Tax due (or refund)		$ xxx

EXHIBIT 9.1	Partial List of Exclusions from Gross Income

Accident and health insurance proceeds

Annuity payments (to the extent proceeds represent a recovery of the taxpayer's investment)

Child support payments

Damages for personal injury or sickness

Fringe benefits of employees:

- Educational assistance payments provided by employer
- Employer-provided accident and health insurance
- Group term life insurance (for coverage up to $50,000)
- Meals and lodging (if furnished for convenience of employer)
- Tuition reductions for employees of educational institutions
- Miscellaneous benefits

Gains from sale of principal residence (subject to statutory ceiling)

Gifts and inheritances received

Interest from state and local bonds

Life insurance paid upon death of insured

Scholarship grants (to a limited extent)

Social Security benefits (to a limited extent)

Workers' compensation benefits

EXHIBIT 9.2	Partial List of Gross Income Items
Alimony	Jury duty fees
Bargain purchase from employer	Partnership income
Bonuses	Pensions
Breach of contract damages	Prizes (with some exceptions)
Business income	Professional fees
Commissions	Punitive damages
Compensation for services	Rents
Debts forgiven (with some exceptions)	Rewards
Dividends	Royalties
Embezzled funds	Salaries
Farm income	Severance pay
Fees	Strike and lockout benefits
Gains from illegal activities	Tips and gratuities
Gains from sale of property	Treasure trove (found property)
Gambling winnings	Wages
Hobby income	
Interest	

Gross Income

The Internal Revenue Code defines gross income broadly as "except as otherwise provided ..., all income from whatever source derived."[3] The "except as otherwise provided" refers to exclusions. Gross income includes, but is not limited to, the items in Exhibit 9.2.

Example 2

Beth received the following amounts during the year:

Salary	$30,000
Interest on savings account	900
Gift from her aunt	10,000
Prize won in state lottery	1,000
Alimony from ex-husband	12,000
Child support from ex-husband	6,000
Damages for injury in auto accident	25,000
Ten $50 bills in an unmarked envelope found in an airport lounge (airport authorities could not locate anyone who claimed ownership)	500
Federal income tax refund for last year's tax overpayment	120
Increase in the value of stock held for investment	5,000

Review Exhibits 9.1 and 9.2 to determine the amount Beth must include in the computation of taxable income and the amount she may exclude. Then check your answer in footnote 4.[4]

Deductions *for* Adjusted Gross Income

Individual taxpayers have two categories of deductions: (1) deductions *for* adjusted gross income (deductions to arrive at adjusted gross income) and (2) deductions

---

[3]§ 61(a).

[4]Beth must include $44,400 in computing taxable income ($30,000 salary + $900 interest + $1,000 lottery prize + $12,000 alimony + $500 found property). She can exclude $41,000 ($10,000 gift from aunt + $6,000 child support + $25,000 damages). The $120 Federal income tax refund is excluded because it represents an adjustment (i.e., overpayment) of a nondeductible expenditure made in the previous year. The unrealized gain of $5,000 on the stock held for investment is not included in gross income. Such gain will be included in gross income only when it is realized upon disposition of the stock.

from adjusted gross income. Deductions *for* adjusted gross income (AGI) include the following:[5]

- Ordinary and necessary expenses incurred in a trade or business.
- Part of the self-employment tax paid.
- Alimony paid.
- Certain payments to traditional Individual Retirement Accounts and Health Savings Accounts.
- Moving expenses.
- The capital loss deduction (limited to $3,000).

The effect on AGI of deductions *for* AGI is illustrated below.

			Example 3

Mason, age 45, earned a salary of $78,000 in the current year. He contributed $4,000 to his traditional Individual Retirement Account (IRA), sold stock held as an investment for a short-term capital loss of $2,000, and paid $4,600 in alimony to his ex-wife. His AGI is determined as follows:

Gross income		
Salary		$ 78,000
Less: Deductions *for* AGI		
IRA contribution	$4,000	
Capital loss	2,000	
Alimony paid	4,600	(10,600)
AGI		$ 67,400

Deductions *from* Adjusted Gross Income

As a general rule, personal expenditures are disallowed as deductions in arriving at taxable income. However, Congress allows specified personal expenses as deductions *from* AGI (commonly referred to as **itemized deductions**). Itemized deductions are discussed in Chapter 10.

AGI is an important subtotal that serves as the basis for computing percentage limitations on certain itemized deductions such as medical expenses, charitable contributions, and certain casualty losses. For example, medical expenses are deductible only to the extent they exceed 10 percent (or 7.5 percent) of AGI, and charitable contribution deductions may not exceed 50 percent of AGI. These limitations might be described as a percentage *floor* under the medical expense deduction and a 50 percent *ceiling* on the charitable contribution deduction.

Example 4

Assume the same facts as in Example 3 except that Mason also had unreimbursed medical expenses of $8,000. Medical expenses may be included in his itemized deductions to the extent they exceed 10% of AGI. In computing his itemized deductions, Mason may include medical expenses of $1,260 [$8,000 medical expenses − $6,740 (10% × $67,400 AGI)].

Trade or business expenses, which are deductions *for* AGI, must be incurred in connection with a trade or business. Nonbusiness expenses, on the other hand, are expenses incurred in connection with an income-producing activity that does not qualify as a trade or business. Such expenses are itemized deductions.

Example 5

Leo is the owner and operator of a video game arcade. All allowable expenses that he incurs in connection with the arcade business are deductions *for* AGI. In addition, Leo paid medical expenses, mortgage interest, state income tax, and charitable contributions. These personal expenses are allowable as itemized deductions.

[5]See § 62 for a comprehensive list of items that are deductible *for* AGI. Deductions *for* AGI are sometimes known as *above-the-line* deductions because on the tax return, they are taken before the "line" designating AGI.

Global Tax Issues

Citizenship Is Not Tax-Free

Gross income from "whatever source derived" includes income from both U.S. and foreign sources. This approach to taxation, where the government taxes its citizens and residents on their worldwide income regardless of where earned, is referred to as a *global* system. Income earned by U.S. citizens outside the United States can be subject to additional taxes, however, because all countries maintain the right to tax income earned within their borders. Consequently, the U.S. tax law includes various mechanisms to alleviate the double taxation that arises when income is subject to tax in multiple jurisdictions. These mechanisms include the foreign tax deduction, the foreign tax credit, the foreign earned income exclusion for U.S. citizens and residents working abroad, and various tax treaty provisions.

Many industrialized countries use variants of the global system. An alternative approach is the *territorial* system, where a government taxes only the income earned within its borders. Hong Kong and Guatemala, for example, use a territorial approach.

Standard Deduction

In lieu of claiming itemized deductions, taxpayers will use the **standard deduction**. As discussed later in the chapter, the standard deduction varies depending on filing status, age, and blindness. The standard deduction is adjusted (i.e., indexed) each year for inflation.

Personal and Dependency Exemptions

Exemptions are allowed for the taxpayer, the taxpayer's spouse, and each dependent of the taxpayer. Like the standard deduction, personal and dependency exemptions (discussed later) are adjusted each year for inflation. The exemption amount for 2014 is $3,950 (up from $3,900 in 2013).

Taxable Income

The determination of taxable income is illustrated in Example 6.

Example 6

Grace, age 25, is single and has her disabled and dependent mother living with her. This qualifies Grace for head-of-household filing status and a standard deduction of $9,100 in 2014. In 2014, Grace earned a $42,000 salary as a high school teacher. Her other income consisted of $1,000 interest on a certificate of deposit (CD) and $500 of nontaxable interest on municipal bonds she had received as a graduation gift in 2010. During 2014, she sustained a deductible capital loss of $1,000. Her itemized deductions are $9,500. Grace's taxable income for the year is computed as follows:

Income (broadly conceived)		
Salary		$42,000
Interest on a CD		1,000
Interest on municipal bonds		500
Total income		$43,500
Less: Exclusion—		
Interest on municipal bonds		(500)
Gross income		$43,000
Less: Deduction *for* adjusted gross income—capital loss		(1,000)
Adjusted gross income (AGI)		$42,000
Less: The *greater* of—		
Total itemized deductions	$9,500	
or the standard deduction for head of household	9,100	(9,500)
Less: Personal and dependency exemptions (2 × $3,950)		(7,900)
Taxable income		$24,600

Note that the exclusion of $500 (i.e., interest from municipal bonds) is subtracted in determining gross income. The loss of $1,000 from a property transaction is classified as a deduction *for* AGI. Grace chose to itemize her deductions *from* AGI as they exceed the standard deduction (see Table 9.1 for the derivation of the $9,100 amount). Grace's income tax is determined later in this chapter in Example 36.

9-2 STANDARD DEDUCTION

A major component of the tax formula is the standard deduction. The effect of the standard deduction is to exempt part of a taxpayer's income from Federal income tax liability. In the past, Congress has attempted to set the tax-free amount represented by the standard deduction approximately equal to an estimated poverty level,[6] but it has not always been consistent in doing so.

LO.2

Explain the standard deduction and evaluate its choice in arriving at taxable income.

9-2a Basic and Additional Standard Deduction

The standard deduction is the sum of two components: the *basic* standard deduction and the *additional* standard deduction.[7] Table 9.1 lists the basic standard deduction allowed for taxpayers in each filing status. All taxpayers allowed a *full* standard deduction are entitled to the applicable amount listed in Table 9.1. The standard deduction amounts are subject to adjustment for inflation each year.

Certain taxpayers are not allowed to claim *any* standard deduction, and the standard deduction is *limited* for others. These provisions are discussed later in the chapter.

A taxpayer who is age 65 or over *or* blind in 2014 qualifies for an *additional standard deduction* of $1,200 or $1,550, depending on filing status (see amounts in Table 9.2).Two additional standard deductions are allowed for a taxpayer who is age 65 or over *and* blind. The additional standard deduction provisions also apply for a qualifying spouse who is age 65 or over or blind, but a taxpayer may not claim an additional standard deduction for a dependent.

TABLE 9.1	Basic Standard Deduction Amounts	
	Standard Deduction Amount	
Filing Status	**2013**	**2014**
Single	$ 6,100	$ 6,200
Married, filing jointly	12,200	12,400
Surviving spouse	12,200	12,400
Head of household	8,950	9,100
Married, filing separately	6,100	6,200

TABLE 9.2	Amount of Each Additional Standard Deduction	
Filing Status	**2013**	**2014**
Single	$1,500	$1,550
Married, filing jointly	1,200	1,200
Surviving spouse	1,200	1,200
Head of household	1,500	1,550
Married, filing separately	1,200	1,200

[6]S.Rep. No. 92–437, 92nd Cong., 1st Sess., 1971, p. 54. Another purpose of the standard deduction was discussed in Chapter 1 under Influence of the Internal Revenue Service—Administrative Feasibility. The size of the standard deduction has a direct bearing on the number of taxpayers who are in a position to itemize deductions. Reducing the number of taxpayers who itemize also reduces the audit effort required from the IRS.

[7]§ 63(c)(1).

To determine whether to itemize, the taxpayer compares the *total* standard deduction (the sum of the basic standard deduction and any additional standard deductions) with total itemized deductions. Taxpayers are allowed to deduct the *greater* of itemized deductions or the standard deduction. The choice is elective. Undoubtedly, some taxpayers claim the standard deduction because they do not want to bother completing the Schedule A required for itemizing deductions *from* AGI. Likewise, the choice is an annual one, and a taxpayer is not bound by what was done on returns filed for past years. For example, many taxpayers who have previously claimed the standard deduction will switch to itemizing after purchasing a home (because of the mortgage interest and property tax deductions). In other circumstances, the reverse could be true—the taxpayer will switch from itemizing to taking the standard deduction. As illustrated in the next example, age can make a difference.

Example 7

Prior to 2014, Sara, who is single, had always chosen to itemize. In 2014, however, she reaches age 65. Her itemized deductions for 2014 are $6,500, but her total standard deduction is $7,750 [$6,200 (basic standard deduction) + $1,550 (additional standard deduction)]. Sara should compute her taxable income for 2014 using the standard deduction ($7,750) because it exceeds her itemized deductions ($6,500).

Digging Deeper | In-depth coverage can be found on this book's companion website: **www.cengagebrain.com**

9-2b Special Limitations on the Standard Deduction for Dependents

Special rules apply to the standard deduction and personal exemption of an individual who can be claimed as a dependent on another person's tax return.

When filing his or her own tax return, a *dependent's* basic standard deduction in 2014 is limited to the greater of $1,000 or the sum of the individual's earned income for the year plus $350.[8] However, if the sum of the individual's earned income plus $350 exceeds the normal standard deduction, the standard deduction is limited to the appropriate amount shown in Table 9.1. These limitations apply only to the basic standard deduction. A dependent who is 65 or over or blind or both is also allowed the additional standard deduction amount on his or her own return (refer to Table 9.2). These provisions are illustrated in Examples 8 through 11.

Example 8

Susan, who is 17 years old and single, is claimed as a dependent on her parents' tax return. During 2014, she received $1,200 of interest (unearned income) on a savings account. She also earned $400 from a part-time job. When Susan files her own tax return, her standard deduction is $1,000 (the greater of $1,000 or the sum of earned income of $400 plus $350).

Example 9

Assume the same facts as in Example 8, except that Susan is 67 years old and is claimed as a dependent on her son's tax return. In this case, when Susan files her own tax return, her standard deduction is $2,550 [$1,000 (the greater of $1,000 or the sum of earned income of $400 plus $350) + $1,550 (the additional standard deduction allowed because Susan is age 65 or over)].

Example 10

Peggy, who is 16 years old and single, earned $700 from a summer job and had no unearned income during 2014. She is claimed as a dependent on her parents' tax return. Her standard deduction is $1,050 (the greater of $1,000 or the sum of earned income of $700 plus $350).

[8]§ 63(c)(5). Both the $1,000 amount and the $350 amount are subject to adjustment for inflation each year. In 2013, the amounts were $1,000 and $350; in 2012, the amounts were $950 and $300.

Example 11

Jack, who is 20 years old, single, and a full-time college student, is claimed as a dependent on his parents' tax return. He worked as a musician during the summer of 2014, earning $6,400. Jack's standard deduction is $6,200 (the greater of $1,000 or the sum of earned income of $6,400 plus $350, but limited to the $6,200 standard deduction for a single taxpayer).

9-3 PERSONAL EXEMPTIONS

The use of exemptions in the tax system is based in part on the idea that a taxpayer with a small amount of income should be exempt from income taxation. An exemption frees a specified amount of income from tax ($3,950 in 2014 and $3,900 in 2013). The exemption amount is adjusted (i.e., indexed) annually for inflation.

Exemptions that are allowed for the taxpayer and spouse are designated as **personal exemptions**. Those exemptions allowed for the care and maintenance of other persons are called dependency exemptions and are discussed in the next section.

An individual cannot claim a personal exemption if he or she is claimed as a dependent by another.

LO.3

Apply the rules for arriving at personal exemptions.

Example 12

Assume the same facts as in Example 11. On his own income tax return,[9] Jack's taxable income is determined as follows:

Gross income	$ 6,400
Less: Standard deduction	(6,200)
Personal exemption	(–0–)
Taxable income	$ 200

Note that Jack is not allowed a personal exemption because he is claimed as a dependent by his parents.

When a husband and wife file a joint return, they may claim two personal exemptions. However, when separate returns are filed, a married taxpayer cannot claim an exemption for his or her spouse *unless* the spouse has no gross income and is not claimed as the dependent of another taxpayer.[10]

The determination of marital status generally is made at the end of the taxable year, except when a spouse dies during the year. Spouses who enter into a legal separation under a decree of divorce or separate maintenance before the end of the year are considered to be unmarried at the end of the taxable year.

The amount of the exemption is not reduced due to the taxpayer's death. The same rule applies to dependency exemptions. As long as an individual qualified as a dependent at the time of death, the full amount of the exemption can be claimed.

9-4 DEPENDENCY EXEMPTIONS

As is the case with personal exemptions, a taxpayer is permitted to claim an exemption of $3,950 in 2014 ($3,900 in 2013) for each person who qualifies as a dependent. A **dependency exemption** is available for either a qualifying child or a qualifying relative and must not run afoul of certain other rules (i.e., joint return or nonresident alien prohibitions).

LO.4

Explain the rules for determining dependency exemptions.

---

[9]As noted on p. 9-17, Jack's situation is such that he will be required to file an income tax return.

[10]§ 151(b).

9-4a Qualifying Child

In the interest of uniformity, Congress has tried to establish a uniform definition of a qualifying child. The qualifying child definition applies to the following tax provisions:

- Dependency exemption.
- Head-of-household filing status.
- Earned income tax credit.
- Child tax credit.
- Credit for child and dependent care expenses.

A **qualifying child** must meet the relationship, abode, age, and support tests.[11] For dependency exemption purposes, a qualifying child must also satisfy the joint return test and the citizenship or residency test.

Relationship Test

The relationship test includes a taxpayer's child (son or daughter), adopted child, stepchild, eligible foster child, brother, sister, half brother, half sister, stepbrother, stepsister, or a *descendant* of any of these parties (e.g., grandchild, nephew, and niece). Note that *ancestors* of any of these parties (e.g., uncles and aunts) and in-laws (e.g., son-in-law and brother-in-law) *are not included*.

An adopted child includes a child lawfully placed with the taxpayer for legal adoption even though the adoption is not final. An eligible foster child is a child who is placed with the taxpayer by an authorized placement agency or by a judgment decree or other order of any court of competent jurisdiction.

Abode Test

A qualifying child must live with the taxpayer for more than half of the year. For this purpose, temporary absences (e.g., school, vacation, medical care, military service, detention in a juvenile facility) are disregarded. Special rules apply in the case of certain kidnapped children.[12]

Age Test

A qualifying child must be under age 19 or under age 24 in the case of a student. A student is a child who, during any part of five months of the year, is enrolled full-time at a school or government-sponsored on-farm training course.[13] Also, an individual cannot be older than the taxpayer claiming him or her as a qualifying child (e.g., a brother cannot claim his older sister as a qualifying child). The age test does not apply to a child who is disabled during any part of the year.[14]

THE BIG PICTURE

Example 13

Return to the facts of *The Big Picture* on p. 9-1. Does Paige meet the requirements of a qualifying child as to Polly? Paige satisfies the relationship and abode tests, but the answer to the age test remains unclear. Because she is not a full-time student or disabled, she must be under 19 to meet the age test. Unfortunately, the facts given do not provide Paige's age.

Support Test

To be a qualifying child, the individual must not be self-supporting (i.e., provide more than one-half of his or her own support). In the case of a child who is a full-time student, scholarships are not considered to be support.[15]

---

[11]§ 152(c).
[12]§ 152(f)(6).
[13]§ 152(f)(2).

[14]Within the meaning of § 22(e)(3) for purposes of the credit for the elderly or disabled.
[15]§ 152(f)(5).

TABLE 9.3	Tiebreaker Rules for Claiming Qualifying Child
Persons Eligible to Claim Exemption	**Person Prevailing**
One of the persons is the parent.	Parent
Both persons are the parents, and the child lives longer with one parent.	Parent with the longer period of residence
Both persons are the parents, and the child lives with each the same period of time.	Parent with the higher adjusted gross income (AGI)
None of the persons are the parent.	Person with highest AGI

Example 14

Shawn, age 23, is a full-time student and lives with his parents and an older cousin. During 2014, Shawn receives his support from the following sources: 30% from a part-time job, 30% from a scholarship, 20% from his parents, and 20% from the cousin. Shawn is not self-supporting and can be claimed by his parents as a dependent even though his parents only contribute 20% of his support. (Note: Shawn cannot be a qualifying child as to his cousin due to the relationship test.)

Tiebreaker Rules

In some situations, a child may be a qualifying child to more than one person. In this event, the tax law specifies which person has priority in claiming the dependency exemption.[16] Called "tiebreaker rules," these rules are summarized in Table 9.3.

In-depth coverage can be found on this book's companion website: **www.cengagebrain.com** 2 | Digging Deeper

9-4b Qualifying Relative

Besides the category of a qualifying child, there is a second category of dependency exemption designated as the **qualifying relative**.

A qualifying relative must meet the relationship, gross income, and support tests.[17] As in the case of the qualifying child category, qualifying relative status also requires that the joint return and nonresident alien restrictions be avoided (see Other Rules for Dependency Exemptions later in the chapter).

Relationship Test

The relationship test for a qualifying relative is more expansive than for a qualifying child. Also included are the following relatives:

- Lineal ascendants (e.g., parents and grandparents).
- Collateral ascendants (e.g., uncles and aunts).
- Certain in-laws (e.g., son-, daughter-, father-, mother-, brother-, and sister-in-law).[18]

Children who do not satisfy the qualifying child definition may meet the qualifying relative criteria.

Example 15

Inez provides more than half of the support of her son, age 20, who is neither disabled nor a full-time student. The son is not a qualifying child due to the age test, but is a qualifying relative if the gross income test is met. Consequently, Inez may claim a dependency exemption for her son.

---

[16]§ 152(c)(4).
[17]§ 152(d).

[18]Once established by marriage, in-law status continues to exist and survives divorce.

The relationship test also includes unrelated parties who live with the taxpayer all year (i.e., are members of the household). Member-of-the-household status is not available for anyone whose relationship with the taxpayer violates local law or anyone who was a spouse during any part of the year.[19] However, an ex-spouse can qualify as a member of the household in a year following the divorce.

As the relationship test indicates, the category designation of "qualifying relative" is somewhat misleading. As just noted, persons other than relatives can qualify as dependents. Furthermore, not all relatives will qualify—notice the absence of the "cousin" grouping.

THE BIG PICTURE

Example 16

Return to the facts of *The Big Picture* on p. 9-1. Although Maude is unrelated to Polly, she qualifies as Polly's dependent by being a member of the household. Because Maude is a dependent, Polly can also claim the medical expenses she paid on Maude's behalf. The funeral expenses are not deductible. Although Maude lived for only two months, the full amount of the dependency exemption is allowed and does not have to be apportioned.

Gross Income Test

A dependent's gross income must be *less* than the exemption amount—$3,950 in 2014 and $3,900 in 2013. Gross income is determined by the income that is taxable. In the case of scholarships, for example, include the taxable portion (e.g., amounts received for room and board) and exclude the nontaxable portion (e.g., amounts received for books and tuition). See the discussion of scholarships in Chapter 10.

Example 17

Elsie provides more than half of the support of her son, Tom, who does not live with her. Tom, age 26, is a full-time student in medical school, earns $3,000 from a part-time job, and receives a $12,000 scholarship covering his tuition. Elsie may claim Tom as a dependent because he meets the gross income test and is a qualifying relative. (Note: Tom is not a qualifying child due to either the abode or the age test.)

Example 18

Aaron provides more than half of the support of his widowed aunt, Myrtle, who does not live with him. Myrtle's income for the year is as follows: dividend income of $1,100, earnings from pet sitting of $1,200, nontaxable Social Security benefits of $6,000, and nontaxable interest from City of Milwaukee bonds of $8,000. Because Myrtle's gross income is only $2,300 ($1,100 + $1,200), she meets the gross income test and can be claimed as Aaron's dependent.

THE BIG PICTURE

Example 19

Return to the facts of *The Big Picture* on p. 9-1. Assuming that Paige is not a qualifying child (see Example 13), can she be a qualifying relative for dependency exemption purposes? She meets the relationship and support tests, but what about the gross income test? If her income from her part-time job is less than $3,950, she does qualify and can be claimed by Polly as a dependent.

Support Test

Over one-half of the support of the qualifying relative must be furnished by the taxpayer. Support includes food, shelter, clothing, toys, medical and dental care, and

---

[19]§§ 152(d)(2)(H) and (f)(3).

education. However, a scholarship (both taxable and nontaxable portions) received by a student is not included for purposes of determining whether the taxpayer furnished more than half of the child's support.

Hal contributed $3,400 (consisting of food, clothing, and medical care) toward the support of his nephew, Sam, who lives with him. Sam earned $1,300 from a part-time job and received $2,000 from a student loan to attend a local university. Assuming that the other dependency tests are met, Hal can claim Sam as a dependent because Hal has contributed more than half of Sam's support.	**Example 20**

If an individual does not spend funds that have been received from any source, the unspent amounts are not counted for purposes of the support test.

Emily contributed $3,000 to her father's support during the year. In addition, her father received $2,400 in Social Security benefits, $200 of interest, and wages of $600. Her father deposited the Social Security benefits, interest, and wages in his own savings account and did not use any of the funds for his support. Thus, the Social Security benefits, interest, and wages are not considered to be support provided by Emily's father. Emily may claim her father as a dependent if the other tests are met.	**Example 21**

An individual's own funds, however, must be taken into account if applied toward support. In this regard, the source of the funds so used is immaterial.

Frank contributes $8,000 toward his parents' total support of $20,000. The parents, who do not live with Frank, obtain the other $12,000 from savings and a home equity loan on their residence. Although the parents have no income, their use of savings and borrowed funds are counted as part of their support. Because Frank does not satisfy the support test, he cannot claim his parents as dependents.	**Example 22**

Capital expenditures for items such as furniture, appliances, and automobiles are included for purposes of the support test if the item does, in fact, constitute support.

Norm purchased a television set costing $950 and gave it to his mother, who lives with him. The television set was placed in the mother's bedroom and was used exclusively by her. Norm should include the cost of the television set in determining the support of his mother.	**Example 23**

Multiple Support Agreements An exception to the support test involves a **multiple support agreement**. A multiple support agreement permits one of a group of taxpayers who furnish support for a qualifying relative to claim a dependency exemption for that individual even if no one person provides more than 50 percent of the support.[20] The group together must provide more than 50 percent of the support. Any person who contributed *more than 10 percent* of the support is entitled to claim the exemption if each person in the group who contributed more than 10 percent files a written consent. This provision frequently enables one of the children of aged dependent parents to claim an exemption when none of the children meets the 50 percent support test.

Each person who is a party to the multiple support agreement must meet all other requirements (except the support requirement) for claiming the exemption. A person who does not meet the relationship or member-of-the-household test, for instance, cannot claim the dependency exemption under a multiple support agreement. It does not matter if he or she contributes more than 10 percent of the individual's support.

---

[20]§ 152(d)(3).

Example 24

Wanda, who resides with her son, Adam, received $12,000 from various sources during the year. This constituted her entire support for the year. She received support from the following individuals:

	Amount	Percentage of Total
Adam, a son	$ 5,760	48
Bob, a son	1,200	10
Carol, a daughter	3,600	30
Diane, a friend	1,440	12
	$12,000	100

If Adam and Carol file a multiple support agreement, either may claim the dependency exemption for Wanda. Bob may not claim Wanda because he did not contribute *more than 10%* of her support. Bob's consent is not required for Adam and Carol to file a multiple support agreement. Diane does not meet the relationship or member-of-the-household test and cannot be a party to the agreement. The decision as to who claims Wanda rests with Adam and Carol. It is possible for Carol to claim Wanda, even though Adam furnished more of Wanda's support.

Digging Deeper   **3**   In-depth coverage can be found on this book's companion website: **www.cengagebrain.com**

Tax Planning Strategies   MULTIPLE SUPPORT AGREEMENTS AND THE MEDICAL EXPENSE DEDUCTION

FRAMEWORK FOCUS: DEDUCTIONS

Strategy: Maximize Deductible Amounts.

Generally, medical expenses are deductible only if they are paid on behalf of the taxpayer, his or her spouse, and their dependents.[21] Because deductibility may rest on dependency status, planning is important in arranging multiple support agreements.

Example 25

During the year, Suzanne will be supported by her two sons (Gary and Alan) and her daughter (Maria). Each will furnish approximately one-third of the required support. If the parties decide that the dependency exemption should be claimed by Maria under a multiple support agreement, any medical expenses incurred by Suzanne should be paid by Maria. ∎

In planning a multiple support agreement, take into account which of the parties is most likely to exceed the 10 percent (7.5 percent if at least 65) limitation. In Example 25, for instance, Maria might be a poor choice if she and her family do not expect to incur many medical expenses of their own.

Children of Divorced or Separated Parents Another exception to the support test applies when parents with children are divorced or separated under a decree of separate maintenance. For unmarried parents, living apart (for the last six months of the year) will suffice. Special rules apply if the parents meet the following conditions:

- They would have been entitled to the dependency exemption(s) had they been married and filed a joint return.
- They have custody (either jointly or singly) of the child (or children) for more than half of the year.

---

[21]See the discussion of medical expenses in Chapter 10.

Under the general rule, the parent having custody of the child (children) for the greater part of the year (i.e., the custodial parent) is entitled to the dependency exemption(s). The general rule does not apply if a multiple support agreement is in effect. It also does not apply if the custodial parent issues a waiver in favor of the noncustodial parent.[22]

In-depth coverage can be found on this book's companion website: **www.cengagebrain.com**   **4** | Digging Deeper

9-4c Other Rules for Dependency Exemptions

In addition to fitting into either the qualifying child or the qualifying relative category, a dependent must meet the joint return and the citizenship or residency tests.

Joint Return Test

If a dependent is married, the supporting taxpayer (e.g., the parent of a married child) generally is not permitted a dependency exemption if the married individual files a joint return with his or her spouse.[23] The joint return rule does not apply, however, if the following conditions are met:

- The reason for filing is to claim a refund for tax withheld.
- No tax liability would exist for either spouse on separate returns.
- Neither spouse is required to file a return.

Example 26

Paul provides over half of the support of his son, Quinn. He also provides over half of the support of Vera, who is Quinn's wife. During the year, both Quinn and Vera had part-time jobs. To recover the taxes withheld, they file a joint return. If Quinn and Vera have income low enough that they are not *required* to file a return, Paul is allowed to claim both as dependents.

Tax Planning Strategies   PROBLEMS WITH A JOINT RETURN

FRAMEWORK FOCUS: DEDUCTIONS

Strategy: Maximize Deductible Amounts.

A married person who files a joint return generally cannot be claimed as a dependent by another taxpayer. If a joint return has been filed, the damage may be undone if separate returns are substituted on a timely basis (on or before the due date of the return).

Example 27

While preparing a client's 2013 income tax return on April 2, 2014, a tax practitioner discovered that the client's daughter had filed a joint return with her husband in late January 2014. Presuming that the daughter otherwise qualifies as the client's dependent, the exemption is not lost if she and her husband file separate returns on or before April 15, 2014. ∎

Citizenship or Residency Test

To be a dependent, the individual must be a U.S. citizen, a U.S. resident, or a resident of Canada or Mexico for some part of the calendar year in which the taxpayer's tax year begins.[24]

---

[22]See Reg. § 1.152–4T and §§ 152(e)(2) and (5).   [24]§ 152(b)(3).
[23]§ 152(b)(2).

CONCEPT SUMMARY 9.1

Tests for Dependency Exemption

Category	
Qualifying Child	**Qualifying Relative**
Relationship[1]	Support
Abode	Relationship[2] or member of household
Age	Gross income
Support	Joint return[3]
Joint return[3]	Citizenship or residency[3]
Citizenship or residency[3]	

[1] Children and their descendants, and siblings and stepsiblings and their descendants.
[2] Children and their descendants, siblings and their children, parents and their ascendants, uncles and aunts, stepparents and stepsiblings, and certain in-laws.
[3] The joint return rules and the citizenship or residency rules are the same for each category.

9-4d Comparison of Categories for Dependency Exemptions

Concept Summary 9.1 sets forth the tests for the two categories of dependency exemptions. In contrasting the two categories, the following observations are in order:

- As to the relationship tests, the qualifying relative category is considerably more expansive. Besides including those prescribed under the qualifying child grouping, other relatives are added. Nonrelated persons who are members of the household are also included.
- The support tests are entirely different. In the case of a qualifying child, support is not necessary. What is required is that the child not be self-supporting.
- The qualifying child category has no gross income limitation, whereas the qualifying relative category has no age restriction.

9-4e Phaseout of Exemptions

Several provisions of the tax law are intended to increase the tax liability of more affluent taxpayers who might otherwise enjoy some benefit from having some of their taxable income subject to the lower income tax brackets (e.g., 10 percent, 15 percent, 25 percent). One such provision phases out certain itemized deductions and is discussed in Chapter 10. Another provision phases out personal and dependency exemptions.[25] The exemption phaseout occurs as AGI exceeds specified threshold amounts (indexed annually for inflation). The phaseout begins when AGI exceeds the following:

Filing Status	2013	2014
Married, filing jointly	$300,000	$305,050
Head of household	275,000	279,650
Single	250,000	254,200
Married, filing separately	150,000	152,525

Exemptions are phased out by 2 percent for each $2,500 (or fraction thereof) by which the taxpayer's AGI exceeds the threshold amounts. For a married taxpayer

---

[25]§ 151(d)(3); this provision did not apply in 2010, 2011, or 2012.

filing separately, the phaseout is 2 percent for each $1,250 (or fraction thereof). The allowable exemption amount can be determined with the following steps:

1. AGI − threshold amount = excess amount.
2. Excess amount ÷ $2,500 = reduction factor [rounded up to the next whole number (e.g., 18.1 = 19)] × 2 = phaseout percentage.
3. Phaseout percentage (from step 2) × exemption amount = phaseout amount.
4. Exemption amount − phaseout amount = allowable exemption deduction.

Example 28

Brad files as a single individual in 2014. His AGI is $286,850. He is entitled to one personal exemption. Brad's allowable exemption amount is determined as follows:

1. $286,850 − $254,200 = $32,650 excess amount.
2. [($32,650 ÷ $2,500) = 13.06; rounded to 14]; 14 × 2 = 28% (phaseout percentage).
3. 28% × $3,950 = $1,106 phaseout amount.
4. $3,950 − $1,106 = $2,844 allowable exemption deduction.

9-5 TAX DETERMINATION—FILING CONSIDERATIONS

LO.5

List the filing requirements and choose the proper filing status.

Once taxable income has been ascertained, a two step process is used in determining income tax due (or refund available). First, certain procedural matters must be resolved. Second, the tax has to be computed and adjusted for available tax credits—see Figure 9.1 and the tax formula. This section deals with the procedural aspects—designated as filing considerations. The next section covers the computation procedures.

Under the category of filing considerations, the following questions need to be resolved:

- Is the taxpayer required to file an income tax return?
- If so, which form should be used?
- When and how should the return be filed?
- What is the taxpayer's filing status?

9-5a Filing Requirements

General Rules

An individual must file a tax return if certain minimum amounts of gross income have been received. The general rule is that a tax return is required for every individual who has gross income that equals or exceeds the sum of the exemption amount plus the applicable standard deduction.[26] For example, a single taxpayer under age 65 must file a tax return in 2014 if gross income equals or exceeds $10,150 ($3,950 exemption plus $6,200 standard deduction).[27]

In-depth coverage can be found on this book's companion website: **www.cengagebrain.com**      **5**   Digging Deeper

---

The additional standard deduction for being age 65 or older is considered in determining the gross income filing requirements. For example, the 2014 filing requirement for a single taxpayer age 65 or older is $11,700 ($6,200 basic standard deduction + $1,550 additional standard deduction + $3,950 exemption).

A self-employed individual with net earnings of $400 or more from a business or profession must file a tax return regardless of the amount of gross income.

---

[26]Because the exemption and standard deduction amounts are subject to an annual inflation adjustment, the gross income amounts for determining whether a tax return must be filed normally change each year.

[27]§ 6012(a)(1).

TAX IN THE NEWS   How to Subtly Pluck the Chicken

No government likes to admit that it is enacting new taxes or even raising the rates on existing taxes. Needless to say, this is particularly true of the U.S. Congress. But there are more subtle ways to raise revenue (or to curtail revenue loss). The most popular way is to use a so-called *stealth tax*. A stealth tax is not really a tax at all. Instead, it is a means of depriving higher-income taxpayers of the benefits of certain tax provisions thought to be available to all.

The heart and soul of the stealth tax is the phaseout approach. Thus, as income increases, the tax benefit thought to be derived from a particular relief provision decreases. Because the phaseout usually is gradual and not drastic, many affected taxpayers are unaware of what has happened.

The tax law is rampant with phaseouts. One of the most prominent phaseouts limits the deductibility of personal and dependency exemptions (which was discussed earlier in this chapter). In addition, here are some other examples of these stealth taxes, each of which is discussed in Chapter 10:

- Child tax credit.
- Social Security benefits.
- Interest deduction on student loans.
- Itemized deductions.
- Education tax credits.
- Earned income credit.

© iStockphoto.com/Andrey Prokhorov

Even though an individual has gross income below the filing level amounts and therefore does not owe any tax, he or she must file a return to obtain a tax refund of amounts withheld. A return is also necessary to obtain the benefits of the earned income credit (see Chapter 10) allowed to taxpayers with little or no tax liability.

Filing Requirements for Dependents

Computation of the gross income filing requirement for an individual who can be claimed as a dependent on another person's tax return is subject to more complex rules. For example, such an individual must file a return if he or she has earned income only and gross income that is more than the total standard deduction (including any additional standard deduction) the individual is allowed for the year.

Digging Deeper   **6**   In-depth coverage can be found on this book's companion website: **www.cengagebrain.com**

Selecting the Proper Form

Although a variety of forms are available to individual taxpayers, the use of some of these forms is restricted. For example, Form 1040–EZ cannot be used if:

- Taxpayer claims any dependents,
- Taxpayer (or spouse) is 65 or older or blind, or
- Taxable income is $100,000 or more.

Taxpayers who want to itemize deductions *from* AGI cannot use Form 1040–A, but must file Form 1040 (the so-called long form).

The E-File Approach

In addition to traditional paper returns, the e-file program is an increasingly popular alternative. Here, the required tax information is transmitted to the IRS electronically either directly from the taxpayer (i.e., an "e-file online return") or indirectly through an electronic return originator (ERO). EROs are tax professionals who have been accepted into the electronic filing program by the IRS. Such parties hold themselves out to the general public as "authorized IRS e-file providers." Providers often are the preparers of the return as well.

TAX FACT **What Form of Tax Compliance Is Right for You?**

Based on recent projections from the IRS, when preparing about 152 million individual income tax returns expected to be filed in 2015, taxpayers will be using relatively fewer paper Forms 1040, 1040A, and 1040–EZ. As a result, the IRS expects the level of electronically filed returns to be at or near an all-time high.

	Percentage
Paper individual returns	15
Electronically filed individual returns	85
	100

Source: Fiscal Year Return Projections for the United States: 2013–2020, IRS, Document 6292, Spring 2013 Update, Table 1.

Through prearrangement with the IRS, approximately 15 software providers offer free e-filing services. These services generally are available only to taxpayers who have AGI of $57,000 or below. A list of these providers and their eligibility requirements can be obtained through the IRS website.

The e-file approach has two major advantages. First, compliance with the format required by the IRS eliminates many errors that would otherwise occur. Second, the time required for processing a refund usually is reduced to three weeks or less.

When and Where to File

Tax returns of individuals are due on or before the fifteenth day of the fourth month following the close of the tax year. For the calendar year taxpayer, the usual filing date is on or before April 15 of the following year.[28] When the due date falls on a Saturday, Sunday, or legal holiday, the last day for filing falls on the next business day.

If a taxpayer is unable to file the return by the specified due date, a six-month extension of time can be obtained by filing Form 4868 (Application for Automatic Extension of Time to File U.S. Individual Income Tax Return).[29]

Although obtaining an extension excuses a taxpayer from a penalty for failure to file, it does not insulate against the penalty for failure to pay. If more tax is owed, the filing of Form 4868 should be accompanied by an additional remittance to cover the balance due. The return should be sent or delivered to the Regional Service Center listed in the instructions for each type of return or contained in software applications.[30]

Mode of Payment

Usually, payment is made by check. However, the IRS has approved the use of MasterCard, American Express, Discover, and Visa to pay Federal taxes through a card service provider. The use of a credit card or debit card to pay taxes will result in a charge against the cardholder by the credit card company and service provider.

9-5b Filing Status

The amount of tax will vary considerably depending on which Tax Rate Schedule is used. This is illustrated in the following example.

---

[28]§ 6072(a).

[29]Reg. § 1.6081–4. See also *Your Federal Income Tax* (IRS Publication 17).

[30]The Regional Service Centers and the geographic area each covers can also be found at **www.irs.gov/file**.

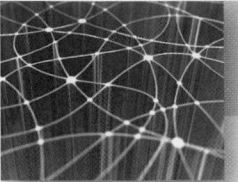

BRIDGE DISCIPLINE   Bridge to Equity or Fairness

Much has been made in the press and in political circles over the years concerning the so-called marriage penalty tax. This marriage penalty refers to the additional income tax that married couples pay over and above the aggregate amount two single individuals would pay with equal amounts of income. The marriage penalty arose because of the nature of the income tax rate structure that applies to individual taxpayers.

Relevant policy and ethical issues related to this dilemma are:

• Should the income tax system contain a bias against marriage?

• Should the income tax system require two people of economic means equal to that of two other people to pay a different amount of income taxes?
• Should the income tax system encourage two individuals to cohabit outside the commitment of marriage?

Long aware of the inequity of the marriage penalty, Congress reduced the effect of the problem with tax legislation in 2003. These changes were made permanent by the American Taxpayer Relief Act of 2012. Consequently, the standard deduction available to married filers is 200 percent of that applicable to single persons. Furthermore, the 15 percent bracket for joint filers equals 200 percent of the size of that applicable to single filers.

© iStockphoto.com/enot-poloskun

Example 29

The following amounts of tax are computed using the 2014 Tax Rate Schedules for a taxpayer (or taxpayers in the case of a joint return) with $60,000 of taxable income (see Appendix A).

Filing Status	Amount of Tax
Single	$10,856
Married, filing joint return	8,093
Married, filing separate return	10,856
Head of household	9,413

Besides the effect from the tax rates that will apply, filing status also has an impact on the amount of the standard deduction that is allowed—see Tables 9.1 and 9.2 earlier in the chapter.

Single Taxpayers

A taxpayer who is unmarried or separated from his or her spouse by a decree of divorce or separate maintenance and does not qualify for another filing status must use the rates for single taxpayers. Marital status is determined as of the last day of the tax year, except when a spouse dies during the year. In that case, marital status is determined as of the date of death.

Married Individuals

The joint return was originally enacted to establish equity between married taxpayers in common law states and those in community property states. Before the joint return rates were enacted, taxpayers in community property states were in an advantageous position relative to taxpayers in common law states because they could split their income.

Taxpayers in common law states did not have this income-splitting option, so their taxable income was subject to higher marginal rates. This inconsistency in treatment was remedied by the joint return provisions. The progressive rates in the joint return Tax Rate Schedule are constructed based on the assumption that income is earned equally by the two spouses.

Same-sex couples that are legally married in a state or jurisdiction that recognizes same-sex marriages will be treated as married for Federal tax purposes (no matter where they live). According to the IRS, registered domestic partners are not "spouses" under Federal law. Therefore, they cannot file Federal tax returns using married filing jointly or married filing separately status. The same rule applies to same-sex partners in civil unions.[31]

If married individuals elect to file separate returns, each reports only his or her own income, exemptions, deductions, and credits, and each must use the Tax Rate Schedule applicable to married taxpayers filing separately. It is generally advantageous for married individuals to file a joint return because the combined amount of tax is lower. However, special circumstances (e.g., significant medical expenses incurred by one spouse subject to the 10 percent limitation) may warrant the election to file separate returns. It may be necessary to compute the tax under both assumptions to determine the most advantageous filing status. Filing a joint return carries the potential disadvantage of joint and several liability. This means that the IRS can pursue the collection of the tax due for that year against either spouse.

Marriage Penalty When Congress enacted the rate structure available to those filing joint returns, it generally favored married taxpayers. In certain situations, however, the parties would incur less tax if they were not married and filed separate returns. The additional tax that a joint return caused, commonly called the **marriage penalty**, usually developed when *both* spouses had large taxable incomes.

In-depth coverage can be found on this book's companion website: **www.cengagebrain.com** **7** | Digging Deeper

---

Surviving Spouse The joint return rates also apply for two years following the death of one spouse if the surviving spouse maintains a household for a dependent child. The child must be a son, stepson, daughter, or stepdaughter who qualifies as a dependent of the taxpayer. This is referred to as **surviving spouse** status.[32]

Head of Household

Unmarried individuals who maintain a household for a dependent (or dependents) are generally entitled to use the **head-of-household** rates.[33] The tax liability using the head-of-household rates falls between the liability using the joint return Tax Rate Schedule and the liability using the Tax Rate Schedule for single taxpayers.

To qualify for head-of-household rates, a taxpayer must pay more than half the cost of maintaining a household as his or her home. The household must also be the principal home of a dependent. Except for temporary absences (e.g., school, hospitalization), the dependent must live in the taxpayer's household for over half the year.

THE BIG PICTURE

Example 30

Return to the facts of *The Big Picture* on p. 9-1. Assuming that Polly can be treated as single (i.e., not married), can Maude qualify Polly for head-of-household filing status? The answer is no. Even though Maude can be claimed as Polly's dependent (see Example 16), she does not meet the relationship test.

In-depth coverage can be found on this book's companion website: **www.cengagebrain.com** **8** | Digging Deeper

---

[31]Rev.Rul. 2013–17, 2013–38 I.R.B. 201 and *U.S. v. Windsor*, 2013–2 USTC ¶50,400, 111 AFTR 2d 2013–2385, 133 S.Ct. 2675; **www.irs.gov/uac/ Answers-to-Frequently-Asked-Questions-for-Registered-Domestic-Partners-and-Individuals-in-Civil-Unions**.

[32]§ 2(a). The IRS label for surviving spouse status is "qualifying widow(er) with dependent child."

[33]§ 2(b).

Global Tax Issues

© iStockphoto.com/Andrey Prokhorov

Filing a Joint Return

John Garth is a U.S. citizen and resident, but he spends a lot of time in London, where his employer sends him on frequent assignments. John is married to Victoria, a citizen and resident of the United Kingdom.

Can John and Victoria file a joint return for U.S. Federal income tax purposes? Although § 6013(a)(1) specifically precludes the filing of a joint return if one spouse is a nonresident alien, another Code provision permits an exception. Under § 6013(g), the parties can elect to treat the nonqualifying spouse as a "resident" of the United States. This election would allow John and Victoria to file jointly.

But should John and Victoria make this election? If Victoria has considerable income of her own (from non-U.S. sources), the election could be ill-advised. As a nonresident alien, Victoria's non-U.S. source income *would not* be subject to the U.S. income tax. If she is treated as a U.S. resident, however, her non-U.S. source income *will be subject to U.S. tax.* Under the U.S. global approach to taxation, all income (regardless of where earned) of anyone who is a *resident* or *citizen* of the United States is subject to tax.

Abandoned Spouse Rules

Congress has enacted provisions that allow married taxpayers, commonly referred to as abandoned spouses, to file as a head of household if the following conditions are satisfied:

- The taxpayer does not file a joint return.
- The taxpayer paid more than one-half the cost of maintaining his or her home for the tax year.
- The taxpayer's spouse did not live in the home during the last six months of the tax year.
- The home was the principal residence of the taxpayer's son, daughter, stepson, stepdaughter, foster child, or adopted child for more than half the year, and the child can be claimed as a dependent.

The resulting tax burden using the relatively favorable head-of-household status is lower than when using the married filing separately rate schedule.

THE BIG PICTURE

Example 31

Return to the facts of *The Big Picture* on p. 9-1. Can Polly qualify as an abandoned spouse? Yes, if she can claim Paige as a dependent—either as a qualifying child (see Example 13) or as a qualifying relative (see Example 19). If so, Polly can use head-of-household filing status. If not, her filing status is married person filing separately.

9-6 TAX DETERMINATION—COMPUTATION PROCEDURES

LO.6

Demonstrate the proper procedures for determining the tax liability.

The computation of income tax due (or refund) involves applying the proper set of tax rates to taxable income and then adjusting for available credits. In certain cases, however, the application of the kiddie tax will cause a modification of the means by which the tax is determined.

9-6a Tax Table Method

The tax liability is computed using either the Tax Table method or the Tax Rate Schedule method. Most taxpayers compute their tax using the **Tax Table**. Eligible

TABLE 9.4		2014 Tax Rate Schedule for Single Taxpayers	
If Taxable Income Is			
Over	**But Not Over**	**The Tax Is:**	**Of the Amount Over**
$ –0–	$ 9,075	10%	$ –0–
9,075	36,900	$ 907.50 + 15%	9,075
36,900	89,350	5,081.25 + 25%	36,900
89,350	186,350	18,193.75 + 28%	89,350
186,350	405,100	45,353.75 + 33%	186,350
405,100	406,750	117,541.25 + 35%	405,100
406,750		118,118.75 + 39.6%	406,750

taxpayers compute taxable income (as shown in Figure 9.1) and *must* determine their tax by reference to the Tax Table.

In-depth coverage can be found on this book's companion website: **www.cengagebrain.com**   **9**   Digging Deeper

Although the Tax Table is derived from the Tax Rate Schedules (discussed next), the tax calculated using the two methods may vary slightly. This variation occurs because the tax for a particular income range in the Tax Table is based on the midpoint amount.

> **Example 32**
>
> Linda is single and has taxable income of $30,000 for calendar year 2013. To determine Linda's tax using the Tax Table (see Appendix A),[34] find the $30,000 to $30,050 income line. The tax of $4,058 is actually the tax the Tax Rate Schedule for 2013 would yield on taxable income of $30,025 (i.e., the midpoint amount between $30,000 and $30,050).

9-6b Tax Rate Schedule Method

The 2014 rate schedule for single taxpayers is reproduced in Table 9.4.[35] This schedule is used to illustrate the tax computations in Examples 33 and 34.

> **Example 33**
>
> Pat is single and had $5,870 of taxable income in 2014. His tax is $587 ($5,870 × 10%).

Several terms are used to describe tax rates. The rates in the Tax Rate Schedules are often referred to as *statutory* (or nominal) rates. The *marginal* rate is the highest rate that is applied in the tax computation for a particular taxpayer. In Example 33, the statutory rate and the marginal rate are both 10 percent.

> **Example 34**
>
> Chris is single and had taxable income of $90,000 in 2014. Her tax is $18,375.75 [$18,193.75 + 28%($90,000 − $89,350)].

The *average* rate is equal to the tax liability divided by taxable income. In Example 34, Chris has statutory rates of 10 percent, 15 percent, 25 percent, and 28 percent and a marginal rate of 28 percent. Chris's average rate is 20.4 percent ($18,375.75 tax liability ÷ $90,000 taxable income).

---

[34]The 2014 Tax Table was not available from the IRS at the date of publication of this text. The Tax Table for 2013 is located at **www.irs.gov** and is used to illustrate this computation.

[35]Individual tax rates are found in § 1.

A tax is *progressive* (or graduated) if a higher rate of tax applies as the tax base increases. The progressive nature of the Federal income tax on individuals is illustrated by computing the tax in Example 34 utilizing each rate bracket.

Tax on first $9,075 at 10%	$ 907.50
Tax on $36,900 − $9,075 at 15%	4,173.75
Tax on $89,350 − $36,900 at 25%	13,112.50
Tax on $90,000 − $89,350 at 28%	182.00
Total tax on taxable income of $90,000	$18,375.75

A special computation limits the effective tax rate on qualified dividends (see Chapter 4) and net long-term capital gains (see Chapter 8).

Tax Planning Strategies   SHIFTING INCOME AND DEDUCTIONS ACROSS TIME

FRAMEWORK FOCUS: TAX RATE

Strategy: Shift Net Income from High-Bracket Years to Low-Bracket Years.

It is natural for taxpayers to be concerned about the tax rates that apply to them. How does a tax practitioner communicate information about rates to clients? There are several possibilities. For example, a taxpayer who is in the 15 percent bracket this year and expects to be in the 28 percent bracket next year should, if possible, defer payment of deductible expenses until next year to maximize the tax benefit of the deduction.

A note of caution is in order with respect to shifting income and expenses between years. Congress has recognized the tax planning possibilities of such shifting and has enacted many provisions to limit a taxpayer's ability to do so. Some of these limitations on the shifting of income and deductions are discussed in Chapters 4 through 6.

9-6c Computation of Net Taxes Payable or Refund Due

The pay-as-you-go feature of the Federal income tax system requires payment of all or part of the taxpayer's income tax liability during the year. These payments take the form of Federal income tax withheld by employers or estimated tax paid by the taxpayer or both.[36] The payments are applied against the tax from the Tax Table or Tax Rate Schedules to determine whether the taxpayer will get a refund or pay additional tax.

Employers are required to withhold income tax on compensation paid to their employees and to pay this tax to the government. The employer notifies the employee of the amount of income tax withheld on Form W–2 (Wage and Tax Statement). The employee should receive this form by January 31 after the year in which the income tax is withheld.

If taxpayers receive income that is not subject to withholding or income from which insufficient tax is withheld, they may have to pay estimated tax. These individuals must file Form 1040–ES (Estimated Tax for Individuals) and pay in quarterly installments the income tax and self-employment tax estimated to be due.

The income tax from the Tax Table or the Tax Rate Schedules also is reduced by the individual's tax credits. There is an important distinction between tax credits and tax deductions. Tax credits (including tax withheld) reduce the tax liability dollar for dollar. Tax deductions reduce taxable income on which the tax liability is based.

---

[36]See § 3402 for withholding and § 6654 for estimated payments.

TAX IN THE NEWS   Same-Sex Couples Face a Tax Filing Nightmare

In *U.S. v. Windsor*, the Supreme Court struck down portions of the Defense of Marriage Act. Specifically, this decision invalidated a Federal definition of marriage as between one man and one woman. Recent guidance from the IRS (Rev.Rul. 2013–17) provides that a same-sex couple possessing a marriage license from any U.S. state will be considered married for Federal income tax purposes (no matter where they live). However, this interpretation of marriage does not extend to "domestic partnerships" or "civil unions." Couples in these relationships are still regarded as *single* by the IRS.

As far as income taxes are concerned, have these new rules resolved the prior difficulties of same-sex couples? The answer depends on where they live and whether such location imposes an income tax. Consider the following possibilities as to residence.

1. No state or local income taxes imposed.
2. State and local income taxes imposed and jurisdiction recognizes same-sex marriages.
3. State and local income taxes imposed but jurisdiction does not recognize same-sex marriages.

Category (1) was never a problem and category (2) has largely been resolved. Thus, the filing status used for state and local purposes (e.g., married filing jointly) will also be available for Federal purposes. Category (3), moreover, continues to yield divergent results. For example, married persons for Federal purposes are "single" under state law.

For persons who are in a domestic partnership or civil union, a different inconsistency comes about. They could be treated as married for state purposes but single in terms of Federal tax law.

Example 35

Gail is a taxpayer in the 25% tax bracket. As a result of incurring $1,000 in child care, she is entitled to a $200 credit for child and dependent care expenses ($1,000 child care expenses × 20% credit rate). She also contributed $1,000 to the American Cancer Society and included this amount in her itemized deductions. The credit for child and dependent care expenses results in a $200 reduction of Gail's tax liability for the year. The contribution to the American Cancer Society reduces taxable income by $1,000 and results in a $250 reduction in Gail's tax liability ($1,000 reduction in taxable income × 25% tax rate).

Selected tax credits for individuals are discussed in Chapter 10. Following are some of the more common credits available to individuals:

- Child tax credit.
- Credit for child and dependent care expenses.
- Earned income credit.

The computation of net taxes payable or refund due can be illustrated by returning to the facts of Example 6.

Example 36

Grace is single and has her disabled and dependent mother living with her. Recall that Example 6 established that Grace has taxable income of $24,600. Further assume that she has the following income tax withheld, $2,500; estimated tax payments, $600; and a credit for dependent care expenses, $200. Grace's net tax payable (refund due) is computed as follows:

Income tax (from 2014 Tax Rate Schedule for head of household)		$3,043 (rounded)
Less: Tax credits and prepayments—		
Credit for dependent care expenses	$ 200	
Income tax withheld	2,500	
Estimated tax payments	600	(3,300)
Net taxes payable (refund due if negative)		($ 257)

TAX FACT   The Tightening Tax Squeeze

How has the total tax burden changed over time? Many Americans would likely assert that more of their income than ever goes just to pay taxes. The Tax Foundation contends that such assertion is correct. It reports that the percentage of income claimed by Federal, state, and local taxes has increased from 5.9 percent in 1900 to 29.4 percent in 2013.

_____

Source: Tax Foundation, 2013.

9-6d Kiddie Tax—Unearned Income of Children Taxed at Parents' Rate

LO.7

Identify and report kiddie tax situations.

Most individuals compute taxable income using the tax formula shown in Figure 9.1. Special provisions govern the computation of taxable income and the tax liability for certain children who have **unearned income** in excess of specified amounts.

Recall that individuals who are claimed as dependents by other taxpayers cannot claim an exemption on their own return. This prevents parents from shifting the tax on investment income (such as interest and dividends) to a child by transferring ownership of the assets producing the income. Without this provision, the child would pay no tax on the income to the extent it was sheltered by the child's exemption and standard deduction amounts.

Current tax law also reduces or eliminates the possibility of saving taxes by shifting income from parents to children by taxing the net unearned income of these children as if it were the parents' income. Unearned income includes income such as taxable interest, dividends, capital gains, rents, royalties, pension and annuity income, and income (other than earned income) received as the beneficiary of a trust.

This provision, commonly referred to as the **kiddie tax**, applies to any child who is under age 19 (or under age 24 if a full-time student) and has unearned income of more than $2,000 (in 2014 or 2013).[37] The kiddie tax does not apply if the child has earned income that exceeds half of his or her support, if the child is married and files a joint return, or if both parents are deceased.

Net Unearned Income

In 2014, net unearned income of a dependent child is computed as follows:

>   Unearned income
>   Less: $1,000
>   Less: The *greater* of
> $1,000 of the standard deduction *or*
>   The amount of allowable itemized deductions directly connected with the production of the unearned income
>   Equals: Net unearned income

If net unearned income is zero (or negative), the child's tax is computed without using the parents' rate. If the amount of net unearned income (regardless of source) is positive, the net unearned income will be taxed at the parents' rate. The child's remaining taxable income (known as nonparental source income) is taxed at the

[37]§ 1(g)(2).

child's rate. The $1,000 amounts in the preceding formula are subject to adjustment for inflation each year.

In-depth coverage can be found on this book's companion website: **www.cengagebrain.com** 10 | Digging Deeper

Election to Report Certain Unearned Income on Parents' Return

If a child who is subject to the kiddie tax is required to file a tax return and meets all of the following requirements, the parents may elect to report the child's unearned income that exceeds $2,000 on the parents' own tax return.

- Gross income is from interest and dividends only.
- Gross income is more than $1,000 but less than $10,000.
- No estimated tax has been paid in the name and Social Security number of the child, and the child is not subject to backup withholding.

If the parental election is made, the child is treated as having no gross income and is not required to file a tax return. In this case, Form 8814 (Parents' Election to Report Child's Interest and Dividends) must be filed as part of the parents' tax return.

The parent(s) must also pay an additional tax equal to the smaller of $100 or 10 percent of the child's gross income over $1,000. Parents who have substantial itemized deductions based on AGI may find that making the parental election increases total taxes for the family unit. Taxes should be calculated both with and without the parental election to determine the appropriate choice.

Tax Planning Strategies | INCOME OF CERTAIN CHILDREN

FRAMEWORK FOCUS: TAX RATE

Strategy: Shift Net Income from High-Bracket Taxpayers to Low-Bracket Taxpayers.

Taxpayers can use several strategies to avoid or minimize the effect of the rules that tax the unearned income of certain children at the parents' rate. With the cutoff age being 19 (under 24 for full-time students), many children are vulnerable to the application of the kiddie tax. Parents should consider giving a younger child assets that defer the inclusion in gross income until the child reaches a non-vulnerable age. For example, U.S. government Series EE savings bonds can be used to defer income until the bonds are cashed in.

Growth stocks typically pay little in the way of dividends. However, the unrealized appreciation on an astute investment may more than offset the lack of dividends. The child can hold the growth stock until he or she reaches a safe age. If the stock is sold then at a profit, the profit is taxed at the child's low rates.

Taxpayers in a position to do so can employ their children in their business and pay them a reasonable wage for the work they actually perform (e.g., light office help such as filing). The child's earned income is sheltered by the standard deduction, and the parents' business is allowed a deduction for the wages. The kiddie tax rules have no effect on earned income, even if it is earned from the parents' business.

REFOCUS ON THE BIG PICTURE

A DIVIDED HOUSEHOLD

© Michael DeFreitas Caribbean/Alamy

Of major concern to Polly is her filing status. If she qualifies as an abandoned spouse, she is entitled to file as head of household. If not, she is considered to be a married person filing separately. Moreover, to be an abandoned spouse, Polly must be able to claim Paige as a dependent. To be a dependent, Paige must meet the requirements of a qualifying child or a qualifying relative.

For qualifying child purposes, Paige must meet either the age (i.e., under age 19) or the full-time student (under age 24) test. (A disabled child exception seems highly unlikely.) Because Paige currently is not a full-time student, is she under age 19? If so, she is a qualifying child (see Example 13). If Paige is not a qualifying child, is she a qualifying relative? Here, the answer depends on meeting the gross income test (see Example 19). How much did Paige earn from her part-time job? If her earnings are under $3,950, she satisfies the gross income test. Thus, if Paige can be claimed as a dependent under either the qualifying child or the qualifying relative category, Polly is an abandoned spouse entitled to head-of-household filing status (see Example 31). If not, she is a married person filing separately.

Maude can be claimed as Polly's dependent because she is a member of the household. It does not matter that she died in February, and the dependency exemption amount need not be apportioned and is allowed in full. Because Maude is her dependent, Polly can claim the medical expenses she paid on Maude's behalf. The funeral expenses, however, are not deductible (see Example 16).

Does Maude qualify Polly for head-of-household filing status? No—although she is a dependent, Maude does not meet the relationship test (see Example 30).

What If?

Assume that Nick left for parts unknown in August (not March). Now Polly cannot qualify as an abandoned spouse. Her spouse lived in the home during part of the last six months of the year. Consequently, Polly is treated as married and cannot qualify for head-of-household filing status. She must file as a married person filing separately. The change in when Nick left will not affect the dependency issue regarding Paige, however.

Suggested Readings

Reed W. Easton, "Tax Planning Opportunities for Nontraditional Families after *Windsor*," *Practical Tax Strategies*, September 2013.

Jeffrey L. Hamm, "The IRS Gives 'Innocent Spouses' More Time," *Practical Tax Strategies*, September 2012.

Andrew Lafond and Bruce A. Leauby, "Help Wanted: Hire Your Kids for Tax Savings," *Practical Tax Strategies*, October 2013.

M. Jill Lockwood, Britton McKay, and Michael Wiggins, "Tax Planning for Divorce: Avoiding the Pitfalls," *Practical Tax Strategies*, September 2012.

James G. S. Yang, Wing W. Poon, and Beixin Betsy Lin, "Tax Planning Strategies Under the American Taxpayer Relief Act of 2012," *Practical Tax Strategies*, July 2013.

Key Terms

Dependency exemption, 9-9

E-file, 9-18

Head-of-household, 9-21

Itemized deductions, 9-5

Kiddie tax, 9-26

Marriage penalty, 9-21

Multiple support agreement, 9-13

Personal exemptions, 9-9

Qualifying child, 9-10

Qualifying relative, 9-11

Standard deduction, 9-6

Surviving spouse, 9-21

Tax Table, 9-22

Unearned income, 9-26

Problems

1. **LO.1** Rearrange the following items to show the correct formula for arriving at *taxable income* of individuals under the Federal income tax:
   a. Deductions *for* AGI.
   b. Income (broadly conceived).
   c. Taxable income.
   d. Adjusted gross income.
   e. Personal and dependency exemptions.
   f. Gross income.
   g. Exclusions.
   h. The greater of the standard deduction or itemized deductions.

2. **LO.1** Which of the following items are *inclusions* in gross income?
   a. During the year, stock the taxpayer purchased as an investment doubled in value.
   b. Amount an off-duty motorcycle police officer received for escorting a funeral procession.
   c. While his mother was in the hospital, the taxpayer sold her jewelry and gave the money to his girlfriend.
   d. Child support payments received.
   e. A damage deposit the taxpayer recovered when he vacated the apartment he had rented.
   f. Interest received by the taxpayer on an investment in general purpose bonds issued by IBM.
   g. Amounts received by the taxpayer, a baseball "Hall of Famer," for autographing sports equipment (e.g., balls and gloves).
   h. Tips received by a bartender from patrons. (Taxpayer is paid a regular salary by the cocktail lounge that employs him.)
   i. Taxpayer sells his Super Bowl tickets for three times what he paid for them.
   j. Taxpayer receives a new BMW from his grandmother when he passes the CPA exam.

3. **LO.1** Which of the following items are *exclusions* from gross income?
   a. Alimony payments received.
   b. Damages award received by the taxpayer for personal physical injury—none were for punitive damages.
   c. A new golf cart won in a church raffle.
   d. Amount collected on a loan previously made to a college friend.
   e. Insurance proceeds paid to the taxpayer on the death of her uncle—she was the designated beneficiary under the policy.
   f. Interest income on City of Chicago bonds.
   g. Jury duty fees.
   h. Stolen funds the taxpayer had collected for a local food bank drive.
   i. Reward paid by the IRS for information provided that led to the conviction of the taxpayer's former employer for tax evasion.
   j. An envelope containing $8,000 found (and unclaimed) by the taxpayer in a bus station.

Decision Making

4. **LO.1** In late 2014, the Polks come to you for tax advice. They are considering selling some stock investments for a loss and making a contribution to a traditional IRA. In reviewing their situation, you note that they have large medical expenses and a casualty loss, neither of which is covered by insurance. What advice would you give the Polks?

5. **LO.1, 2, 3, 4** Compute the taxable income for 2014 in each of the following independent situations:
   a. Drew and Meg, ages 40 and 41, respectively, are married and file a joint return. In addition to four dependent children, they have AGI of $65,000 and itemized deductions of $15,000.
   b. Sybil, age 40, is single and supports her dependent parents, who live with her, as well as her grandfather, who is in a nursing home. She has AGI of $80,000 and itemized deductions of $8,000.
   c. Scott, age 49, is a surviving spouse. His household includes two unmarried stepsons who qualify as his dependents. He has AGI of $75,000 and itemized deductions of $10,100.
   d. Amelia, age 33, is an abandoned spouse who maintains a household for her three dependent children. She has AGI of $58,000 and itemized deductions of $9,500.
   e. Dale, age 42, is divorced but maintains the home in which he and his daughter, Jill, live. Jill is single and qualifies as Dale's dependent. Dale has AGI of $64,000 and itemized deductions of $9,900.

6. **LO.1, 2, 3, 4** Compute the taxable income for 2014 for Emily on the basis of the following information. Her filing status is single.

Salary	$85,000
Interest income from bonds issued by Xerox	1,100
Alimony payments received	6,000
Contribution to traditional IRA	5,500
Gift from parents	25,000
Short-term capital gain from stock investment	2,000
Amount lost in football office pool (sports gambling is against the law where Emily lives)	500
Number of potential dependents (two cousins, who live in Canada)	?
Age	40

7. **LO.1, 2, 3, 4** Compute the taxable income for 2014 for Aiden on the basis of the following information. Aiden is married but has not seen or heard from his wife since 2012.

Salary	$ 80,000
Interest on bonds issued by the City of Boston	3,000
Interest on CD issued by Wells Fargo Bank	2,000
Cash dividend received on Chevron common stock	2,200
Life insurance proceeds paid on death of aunt (Aiden was the designated beneficiary of the policy)	200,000
Inheritance received upon death of aunt	100,000
Jackson (a cousin) repaid a loan Aiden made to him in 2008 (no interest was provided for)	5,000
Itemized deductions (state income tax, property taxes on residence, interest on home mortgage, and charitable contributions)	9,400
Number of dependents (children, ages 17 and 18, and mother-in-law, age 70)	3
Age	43

Issue ID

8. **LO.2** In choosing between the standard deduction and itemizing deductions *from* AGI, what effect, if any, does each of the following have?
   a. The age of the taxpayer(s).
   b. The health (i.e., physical condition) of the taxpayer.
   c. Whether taxpayers rent or own their residence.
   d. Taxpayer's filing status (e.g., single, married, filing jointly).
   e. Whether married taxpayers decide to file separate returns.
   f. The taxpayer's uninsured personal residence was recently destroyed by fire.
   g. The number of personal and dependency exemptions the taxpayer can claim.

9. **LO.2** Sam and Abby are dependents of their parents, and each has income of $2,100 for the year. Sam's standard deduction for the year is $1,000, while Abby's is $2,450. As their income is the same, what causes the difference in the amount of the standard deduction?

Issue ID

10. **LO.2** Determine the amount of the standard deduction allowed for 2014 in the following independent situations. In each case, assume that the taxpayer is claimed as another person's dependent.
    a. Curtis, age 18, has income as follows: $700 interest from a certificate of deposit and $6,000 from repairing cars.
    b. Mattie, age 18, has income as follows: $600 cash dividends from a stock investment and $4,700 from handling a paper route.
    c. Mel, age 16, has income as follows: $800 interest on a bank savings account and $700 for painting a neighbor's fence.
    d. Lucy, age 15, has income as follows: $400 cash dividends from a stock investment and $500 from grooming pets.
    e. Sarah, age 67 and a widow, has income as follows: $500 from a bank savings account and $3,200 from babysitting.

11. **LO.2** Each year, Tom and Cindy Bates normally have itemized deductions of $10,000, including a $4,000 pledge payment to their church. Upon the advice of a friend, they do the following: in early January 2013, they pay their pledge for 2012; during 2013, they pay the pledge for 2013; and in late December 2013, they prepay their pledge for 2014.
    a. Explain what the Bateses are trying to accomplish.
    b. What will be the tax saving if their marginal tax bracket is 25% for all three years? (Assume that the standard deduction amounts for 2013 and 2014 are the same.)
    c. Write a letter to Tom and Cindy Bates (8212 Bridle Court, Reston, VA 20194) summarizing your analysis.

Decision Making

Communications

12. **LO.4** Using the legend provided below, classify each statement as to the taxpayer for dependency exemption purposes.

Legend
QC = Could be a qualifying child
QR = Could be a qualifying relative
B = Could satisfy the definition of *both* a qualifying child *and* a qualifying relative
N = Could not satisfy the definition of *either* a qualifying child *or* a qualifying relative

    a. Taxpayer's son has gross income of $7,000.
    b. Taxpayer's niece has gross income of $3,000.
    c. Taxpayer's uncle lives with him.
    d. Taxpayer's daughter is age 25 and disabled.
    e. Taxpayer's daughter is age 18, has gross income of $8,000, and does not live with him.
    f. Taxpayer's cousin does not live with her.
    g. Taxpayer's brother does not live with her.
    h. Taxpayer's sister has dropped out of school, is age 17, and lives with him.
    i. Taxpayer's older nephew is age 23 and a full-time student.
    j. Taxpayer's grandson lives with her and has gross income of $7,000.

13. **LO.3, 4** For tax year 2014, determine the number of personal and dependency exemptions in each of the following independent situations:
    a. Leo and Amanda (ages 48 and 46, respectively) are husband and wife and furnish more than 50% of the support of their two children, Elton (age 18) and Trista (age 24). During the year, Elton earns $4,500 providing transportation for elderly persons with disabilities, and Trista receives a $5,000 scholarship for tuition at the law school she attends.
    b. Audry (age 45) was divorced this year. She maintains a household in which she, her ex-husband (Clint), and his mother (Olive) live and furnishes more than 50% of their support. Olive is age 91 and blind.
    c. Crystal, age 45, furnishes more than 50% of the support of her married son, Andy (age 18), and his wife, Paige (age 19), who live with her. During the year, Andy earned $8,000 from a part-time job. All parties live in Iowa (a common law state).

d. Assume the same facts as in (c), except that all parties live in Washington (a community property state).

14. **LO.3, 4** Sam and Elizabeth Jefferson file a joint return and have three children—all of whom qualify as dependents. If the Jeffersons have AGI of $327,000, what is their allowable deduction for personal and dependency exemptions for 2014?

15. **LO.4** Wesley and Myrtle (ages 90 and 88, respectively) live in an assisted care facility and for 2013 and 2014 received their support from the following sources:

	Percentage of Support
Social Security benefits	16%
Son	20
Niece	29
Cousin	12
Brother	11
Family friend (not related)	12

a. Which persons are eligible to claim the dependency exemptions under a multiple support agreement?
b. Must Wesley and Myrtle be claimed by the same person(s) for both 2013 and 2014? Explain.
c. Who, if anyone, can claim their medical expenses?

Critical Thinking

16. **LO.2, 7** Taylor, age 18, is claimed as a dependent by her parents. For 2014, she has the following income: $4,000 of wages from a summer job, $1,800 of interest from a money market account, and $2,000 of interest from City of Boston bonds.
a. What is Taylor's taxable income for 2014?
b. What is Taylor's tax for 2014? [Her parents file a joint return and have taxable income of $130,000 (no dividends or capital gains).]

Issue ID

Decision Making

17. **LO.4** Walter and Nancy provide 60% of the support of their daughter (age 18) and son-in-law (age 22). The son-in-law (John) is a full-time student at a local university, while the daughter (Irene) holds various part-time jobs from which she earns $11,000. Walter and Nancy engage you to prepare their tax return for 2014. During a meeting with them in late March 2015, you learn that John and Irene have filed a joint return. What tax advice would you give based on the following assumptions:
a. All parties live in Louisiana (a community property state).
b. All parties live in New Jersey (a common law state).

18. **LO.1, 4, 6** Charlotte (age 40) is a surviving spouse and provides all of the support of her four minor children who live with her. She also maintains the household in which her parents live and furnished 60% of their support. Besides interest on City of Miami bonds in the amount of $6,500, Charlotte's father received $2,400 from a part-time job. Charlotte has a salary of $80,000, a short-term capital loss of $2,000, a cash prize of $4,000 from a church raffle, and itemized deductions of $10,500. Using the Tax Rate Schedules, compute the 2014 tax liability for Charlotte.

19. **LO.1, 2, 3, 4, 5, 6** Morgan (age 45) is single and provides more than 50% of the support of Rosalyn (a family friend), Flo (a niece, age 18), and Jerold (a nephew, age 18). Both Rosalyn and Flo live with Morgan, but Jerold (a French citizen) lives in Canada. Morgan earns a salary of $95,000, contributes $5,000 to a traditional IRA, and receives sales proceeds of $15,000 for an RV that cost $60,000 and was used for vacations. She has $8,200 in itemized deductions. Using the Tax Rate Schedules, compute the 2014 tax liability for Morgan.

Ethics and Equity

20. **LO.5** Bob and Carol have been in and out of marital counseling for the past few years. Early in 2014, they decide to separate. However, because they are barely able to get by on their current incomes, they cannot afford separate housing or the legal costs of a divorce. So, Bob moves out of their house in March and takes up residence in their detached garage (which has an enclosed workshop and bathroom). Carol stays in the house with their two children and pays more than half of the costs of maintaining their residence. Bob does not enter the house for the remainder of the year. Can Carol qualify as an abandoned spouse?

21. **LO.5** Which of the following individuals are required to file a tax return for 2014? Should any of these individuals file a return even if filing is not required? Why or why not?

   a. Patricia, age 19, is a self-employed single individual with gross income of $5,200 from an unincorporated business. Business expenses amounted to $4,900.

   b. Mike is single and is 67 years old. His gross income from wages was $10,800.

   c. Ronald is a dependent child under age 19 who received $6,500 in wages from a part-time job.

   d. Sam is married and files a joint return with his spouse, Lana. Both Sam and Lana are 67 years old. Their combined gross income was $22,750.

   e. Quinn, age 20, is a full-time college student who is claimed as a dependent by his parents. For 2014, Quinn has taxable interest and dividends of $2,500.

Critical Thinking

22. **LO.5, 6** Roy and Brandi are engaged and plan to get married. During 2014, Roy is a full-time student and earns $9,000 from a part-time job. With this income, student loans, savings, and nontaxable scholarships, he is self-supporting. For the year, Brandi is employed and has wages of $61,000. How much income tax, if any, can Brandi save if she and Roy marry in 2014 and file a joint return?

Decision Making

23. **LO.1, 3, 7** Paige, age 17, is claimed as a dependent on her parents' 2014 return, on which they report taxable income of $120,000 (no qualified dividends or capital gains). Paige earned $3,900 pet sitting and $4,000 in interest on a savings account. What are Paige's taxable income and tax liability for 2014?

Critical Thinking

24. **LO.1, 3, 7** Terri, age 16, is claimed as a dependent on her parents' 2014 return. During the year, Terri earned $5,000 in interest income and $3,000 from part-time jobs.

   a. What is Terri's taxable income?

   b. How much of Terri's income is taxed at her rate? At her parents' rate?

   c. Can the parental election be made? Why or why not?

Critical Thinking

Comprehensive Tax Return Problems

1. Lance H. and Wanda B. Dean are married and live at 431 Yucca Drive, Santa Fe, NM 87501. Lance works for the convention bureau of the local Chamber of Commerce, while Wanda is employed part-time as a paralegal for a law firm.

   During 2013, the Deans had the following receipts:

Tax Return Problem

TAX SOFTWARE

Salaries ($60,000 for Lance, $41,000 for Wanda)		$101,000
Interest income		
City of Albuquerque general purpose bonds	$1,000	
Ford Motor Company bonds	1,100	
Ally Bank certificate of deposit	400	2,500
Child support payments from John Allen		7,200
Annual gifts from parents		26,000
Settlement from Roadrunner Touring Company		90,000
Lottery winnings		600
Federal income tax refund (for tax year 2012)		400

   Wanda was previously married to John Allen. When they divorced several years ago, Wanda was awarded custody of their two children, Penny and Kyle. (Note: Wanda has never issued a Form 8332 waiver.) Under the divorce decree, John was obligated to pay alimony and child support—the alimony payments were to terminate if Wanda remarried.

   In July, while going to lunch in downtown Santa Fe, Wanda was injured by a tour bus. As the driver was clearly at fault, the owner of the bus, Roadrunner Touring Company, paid her medical expenses (including a one-week stay in a hospital). To avoid a lawsuit, Roadrunner also transferred $90,000 to her in settlement of the personal injuries she sustained.

The Deans had the following expenditures for 2013:

Medical expenses (not covered by insurance)		$7,200
Taxes—		
Property taxes on personal residence	$3,600	
State of New Mexico income tax (includes amount withheld from wages during 2013)	4,200	7,800
Interest on home mortgage		6,000
Paid church pledge		3,600
Life insurance premiums (policy on Lance's life)		1,200
Contribution to traditional IRA (on Wanda's behalf)		5,000
Traffic fines		300
Contribution to the reelection campaign fund of the mayor of Santa Fe		500
Funeral expenses for Wayne Boyle		6,300

The life insurance policy was taken out by Lance several years ago and designates Wanda as the beneficiary. As a part-time employee, Wanda is excluded from coverage under her employer's pension plan. Consequently, she provides for her own retirement with a traditional IRA obtained at a local trust company. Because the mayor is a member of the local Chamber of Commerce, Lance felt compelled to make the political contribution.

The Deans' household includes the following, for whom they provide more than half of the support:

	Social Security Number*	Birth Date
Lance Dean (age 42)	123-45-6786	12/16/1971
Wanda Dean (age 40)	123-45-6787	08/08/1973
Penny Allen (age 19)	123-45-6788	10/09/1994
Kyle Allen (age 17)	123-45-6789	05/03/1996
Wayne Boyle (age 75)	123-45-6785	06/15/1938

*In the interest of privacy and to protect against taxpayer identification misuse, Social Security numbers used throughout the textbook have been replaced with fictitious numbers.

Penny graduated from high school on May 9, 2013, and is undecided about college. During 2013, she earned $8,500 (placed in a savings account) playing a harp in the lobby of a local hotel. Wayne is Wanda's widower father, who died on January 20, 2013. For the past few years, Wayne qualified as a dependent of the Deans.

Federal income tax withheld is $5,200 (Lance) and $3,100 (Wanda). The proper amount of Social Security and Medicare tax was withheld.

Determine the Federal income tax for 2013 for the Deans on a joint return by completing the appropriate forms. They do not want to contribute to the Presidential Election Campaign Fund. If an overpayment results, it is to be refunded to them. Suggested software: H&R BLOCK Tax Software.

Tax Return Problem

Decision Making

Communications

TAX SOFTWARE

2. Logan B. Taylor is a widower whose wife, Sara, died on June 6, 2011. He lives at 4680 Dogwood Lane, Springfield, MO 65801. He is employed as a paralegal by a local law firm. During 2013, he had the following receipts:

Salary		$ 80,000
Interest income—		
Money market account at Omni Bank	$ 300	
Savings account at Boone State Bank	1,100	
City of Springfield general purpose bonds	3,000	4,400
Inheritance from Daniel		60,000
Life insurance proceeds		200,000
Amount from sale of St. Louis lot		80,000
Proceeds from estate sale		9,000
Federal income tax refund (for 2012 tax overpayment)		700

Logan inherited securities worth $60,000 from his uncle, Daniel, who died in 2013. Logan also was the designated beneficiary of an insurance policy on Daniel's life with a maturity value of $200,000. The lot in St. Louis was purchased on May 2, 2008, for $85,000 and held as an investment. As the neighborhood has deteriorated, Logan decided to cut his losses and sold the lot on January 5, 2013, for $80,000. The estate sale consisted largely of items belonging to Sara and Daniel (e.g., camper, boat, furniture, and fishing and hunting equipment). Logan estimates that the property sold originally cost at least twice the $9,000 he received and has declined or stayed the same in value since Sara and Daniel died.

Logan's expenditures for 2013 include the following:

Medical expenses (including $10,500 for dental)		$11,500
Taxes—		
State of Missouri income tax (includes withholdings during 2013)	$3,200	
Property taxes on personal residence	4,500	7,700
Interest on home mortgage		4,600
Contribution to church (paid pledges for 2013 and 2014)		4,800

Logan and his dependents are covered by his employer's health insurance policy. However, he is subject to a deductible, and dental care is not included. The $10,500 dental charge was for Helen's implants. Helen is Logan's widowed mother, who lives with him (see below). Logan normally pledges $2,400 ($200 per month) each year to his church. On December 5, 2013, upon the advice of his pastor, he prepaid his pledge for 2014.

Logan's household, all of whom he supports, includes the following:

	Social Security Number	Birth Date
Logan Taylor (age 48)	123-45-6787	08/30/1965
Helen Taylor (age 70)	123-45-6780	01/13/1943
Asher Taylor (age 23)	123-45-6783	07/18/1990
Mia Taylor (age 22)	123-45-6784	02/16/1991

Helen receives a modest Social Security benefit. Asher, a son, is a full-time student in dental school and earns $4,500 as a part-time dental assistant. Mia, a daughter, does not work and is engaged to be married.

Part 1—Tax Computation

Using the appropriate forms and schedules, compute Logan's income tax for 2013. Federal income tax of $5,500 was withheld from his wages. If Logan has any overpayment on his income tax, he wants the refund sent to him. Assume that the proper amounts of Social Security and Medicare taxes were withheld. Logan does not want to contribute to the Presidential Election Campaign Fund. Suggested software: H&R BLOCK Tax Software.

Part 2—Follow-Up Advice

In early 2014, the following take place:

- Helen decides she wants to live with one of her daughters and moves to Arizona.
- Asher graduates from dental school and joins an existing practice in St. Louis.
- Mia marries, and she and her husband move in with his parents.
- Using the insurance proceeds he received on Daniel's death, Logan pays off the mortgage on his personal residence.

Logan believes these events may have an effect on his tax position for 2014. Therefore, he requests your advice.

Write a letter to Logan explaining in general terms the changes that will occur for tax purposes. Assume that Logan's salary and other factors not mentioned (e.g., property and state income taxes) will remain the same. Use the Tax Rate Schedules in projecting Logan's tax for 2014.

Research Problems

Note: Solutions to Research Problems can be prepared by using the **Checkpoint®** **Student Edition** online research product, which is available to accompany this text. It is also possible to prepare solutions to the Research Problems by using tax research materials found in a standard tax library.

Communications

Research Problem 1. Kathy and Brett Ouray married in 1996. They began to experience marital difficulties in 2010 and, in the current year, although they are not legally separated, consider themselves completely estranged. They have contemplated getting a divorce. However, because of financial concerns and because they both want to remain involved in the lives of their three sons, they have not yet filed for divorce. In addition, their financial difficulties have meant that Kathy and Brett cannot afford to live in separate residences. So although they consider themselves emotionally estranged, they and their three sons all reside in a single-family home in Chicago, Illinois.

Although Brett earns significantly more than Kathy, both contribute financially to maintaining their home and supporting their teenage sons. In one of their few and brief conversations this year, they determined that Brett had contributed far more than Kathy to the maintenance of their home and the support of their sons. Thus, Brett has decided that for the current tax year, they will file separate Federal income tax returns and that he will claim head-of-household filing status. While they live under the same roof, Brett believes that he and Kathy should maintain separate households. Given this fact and the fact that he provides significantly more for the support of his and Kathy's sons, he believes he is eligible for head-of-household filing status. Advise Brett on which filing status is most appropriate for him in the current year.

Research Problem 2. Tom and Sandy were divorced on July 7, 2012. Under the divorce decree, Sandy received full custody of their three children, and Tom was awarded the dependency exemptions for them. After the trial was over, Tom had Sandy sign a Form 8332 (Release/Revocation of Release of Claim to Exemption for Child by Custodial Parent), releasing her rights to the dependency exemptions for the next five years. In early April 2014, Sandy realizes the tax costs of losing the deduction for the dependency exemptions. Besides contacting Tom, who is already delinquent in his child support payments, does she have any way out? Explain.

Internet
Activity

Use the tax resources of the Internet to address the following questions. Do not restrict your search to the Web, but include a review of newsgroups and general reference materials, practitioner sites and resources, primary sources of the tax law, chat rooms and discussion groups, and other opportunities.

Research Problem 3. Locate IRS Form 2120 (at **www.irs.gov**) and answer the following questions.
a. Who must sign the form?
b. Who must file the form?
c. Can it be used for someone who is not related to the taxpayer? Explain.

Research Problem 4. What purpose is served by Form 8857? Read the directions to the form and see IRS Publication 971 for additional information.

Research Problem 5. A nonresident alien earns money in the United States that is subject to Federal income tax. What guidance does the IRS provide about what tax form needs to be used and when it should be filed? In terms of the proper filing date, does it matter whether the earnings were subject to income tax withholding? Explain.

Research Problem 6. When taxpayers pay their income taxes by means of a credit or debit card, they are charged "convenience fees" by the issuer of the card. Are these fees deductible for income tax purposes? Explain. See the instructions for Schedule A(Form 1040), line 23.

10

Individuals: Income, Deductions, and Credits

CHAPTER OUTLINE

TAX TALK *A tax loophole is something that benefits the other guy. If it benefits you, it is tax reform.* —RUSSELL B. LONG

© wavebreakmedia ltd/Shutterstock.com

THE TAX IMPLICATIONS OF LIFE!

Donna and David Steele, ages 35 and 37, respectively, recently married and have come to you for tax advice. They have several questions about their tax situation. Both are employed, and they expect to have combined wages from all sources of $70,000 during the year.

    During the year, Donna was an intern with a CPA firm, working in the compliance area. She was paid well enough for her work as an intern that she was able to save some money for school. The CPA firm was so pleased with Donna's work that at the conclusion of her internship, she was given a bonus of $1,500 more than the firm had agreed to pay her. The extra amount was intended to help with her graduate school expenses in the masters of accounting program at State University. Because of her excellent academic record, the university awarded Donna a graduate assistantship that waived her tuition of $6,000 per semester and paid her $400 per month. In exchange, Donna was required to teach a principles of accounting course during each semester. She used the $400 per month for books and incidental fees. Donna also paid $400 of interest during the year on student loans still outstanding from her undergraduate years.

    Donna and David also received a wedding gift of $10,000 from her grandmother, and the couple earned $250 of interest on a savings account they opened with the money. David sold stock for $1,000 that was purchased two years ago for $5,000.

    Late in the year, Donna was crossing a street in the pedestrian crosswalk when a delivery van struck her. The driver of the truck had a blood alcohol level of .12. She suffered a severe injury to her right arm that required her to miss work for a month or so. The delivery company's insurance company settled the case by paying damages as follows:

Compensatory damages:	
Medical expenses	$ 30,000
Injury to Donna's right arm	100,000
Pain and suffering	50,000
Loss of income	10,000
Legal fees	25,000
Punitive damages	160,000
	$375,000

This is David's second marriage, and he pays alimony to his ex-wife. He has custody of his 15-year-old son, Stephen, who lives with Donna and David for nine months each year. The Steeles rent their home, paid $3,500 of state income taxes, paid an $812 motor vehicle registration tax on their personal car, incurred additional medical expenses of $25,000, and made $2,500 of charitable contributions.

Without calculating Donna and David's tax liability, what are the tax implications of the transactions noted above? Are there other tax deductions or credits for which they may qualify or other tax issues about which they should be made aware?

Read the chapter and formulate your response.

This chapter focuses on the computation of taxable income for individual taxpayers. Recall that taxable income is the base on which the tax liability is calculated. In the simplest of terms, taxable income is determined by reducing *gross income* by allowable *tax deductions*. Prior chapters provided discussions where the meanings of these terms were explored in a general sense. However, this chapter describes special rules that apply to individual taxpayers, with respect to both income and deduction items. Finally, the chapter concludes by discussing key individual tax credits that may further reduce an individual's tax liability.

10-1 OVERVIEW OF INCOME PROVISIONS APPLICABLE TO INDIVIDUALS

LO.1

Identify specific income inclusions and exclusions applicable to individuals.

As indicated in Chapter 9, the definition of gross income is broad enough to include almost all receipts of money, property, or services. However, the tax law provides for exclusion of many types of income.[1] The following income provisions, which apply to all taxpayers (including individuals), were discussed in Chapter 4:

* Interest from state and local bonds.
* Life insurance paid on death of the insured.
* Imputed interest on below-market loans.
* Income from discharge of indebtedness.
* Income included under the tax benefit rule.

Most *exclusions* available only to individuals are for *fringe benefits* received by *employees* (refer to Exhibit 9.1 in Chapter 9). Fringe benefits are discussed in Chapter 11. Other specific inclusions and exclusions for individuals are discussed next.

10-2 SPECIFIC INCLUSIONS APPLICABLE TO INDIVIDUALS

As discussed earlier, the general principles of gross income determination have occasionally yielded results that Congress found unacceptable. Thus, Congress has provided more specific rules for determining the amount of gross income from certain sources. Some of these special rules appear in §§ 71–90 of the Code. The following provisions applicable to individuals are covered in this chapter:

* Alimony and separate maintenance payments.
* Prizes and awards.
* Unemployment compensation.
* Social Security benefits.

[1]See §§ 101–140.

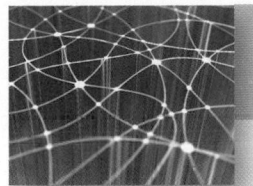

BRIDGE DISCIPLINE   Bridge to Economics and Finance

As is the case for business entities, a primary financial goal for individual taxpayers should entail maximizing the *after-tax value* of their assets over time. This approach requires not only selecting the best investment alternatives but also choosing those investments with the most favorable tax attributes. Fundamental to this notion is recognizing the key role the government plays in all economic activity through its taxing authority. As a result, an investor should consider economically sound strategies that minimize the extent to which the government can stake a claim to his or her success. For example, taxpayers can reduce the government's share of their wealth accumulations by deferring the payment of taxes until future years and by taking advantage of investment strategies for which tax incentives are available. Taxpayers should choose the investment alternatives that provide the best after-tax return over time and not necessarily the ones that lead to the least amount of taxation.

These points can be illustrated by examining two classic strategies. One of the best ways for individuals to maximize their personal wealth is to invest to the extent possible in qualified retirement savings programs [e.g., traditional Individual Retirement Accounts, § 401(k) accounts]. Not only do current additions to such accounts provide a current tax deduction, but earnings in the account are not subject to taxation until they are withdrawn, which, in most cases, is during the retirement years of the owner. Postponing the tax in these two ways reduces the present value of the tax cost, which increases the after-tax value of the investment. Another strategy involves investing in tax-free municipal bonds, which produce interest income that is free of Federal income tax. The returns from such investments, however, should be compared with the after-tax returns flowing from available taxable debt securities. For example, a relevant question is how the implicit tax (see Chapter 1) associated with a municipal bond compares with the explicit tax associated with a taxable bond.

10-2a Alimony and Separate Maintenance Payments

When a married couple divorce or become legally separated, state law generally requires a division of the property accumulated during the marriage. In addition, one spouse may have a legal obligation to support the other spouse. The Code distinguishes between the support payments (alimony or separate maintenance) and the property division in terms of the tax consequences.

Alimony and separate maintenance payments are deductible by the party making the payments and are includible in the gross income of the party receiving the payments.[2] Thus, taxation of the income is shifted from the income earner to the income beneficiary.

> Pete and Tina are divorced, and Pete is required to pay Tina $15,000 of alimony each year. Pete earns $61,000 a year. Therefore, Tina must include the $15,000 in her gross income, and Pete is allowed to deduct $15,000 from his gross income.

Example 1

Property Settlements

A transfer of property other than cash to a former spouse under a divorce decree or agreement is not a taxable event. The transferor is not entitled to a deduction and does not recognize gain or loss on the transfer. The transferee does not recognize income and takes a basis equal to the transferor's basis.[3]

> Paul transfers stock to Rosa this year as part of a divorce settlement. The cost of the stock to Paul was $12,000, and the stock's fair market value at the time of the transfer is $15,000. Rosa later sells the stock for $16,000. Paul is not required to recognize gain from the transfer of the stock to Rosa, and Rosa has a realized *and* recognized gain of $4,000 ($16,000 − $12,000) when she sells the stock.

Example 2

---

[2]§§ 71 and 215.

[3]Section 1041 was added to the Code in 1984 to repeal the rule of *U.S. v. Davis*, 62–2 USTC ¶9509, 9 AFTR 2d 1625, 82 S.Ct. 1190 (USSC, 1962).

Under the *Davis* rule, which applied to pre-1985 divorces, a property transfer incident to divorce was a taxable event.

Requirements for Alimony

To clarify whether payments are classified as support obligation (alimony) or as property of the other spouse (property settlement), Congress developed the following objective rules. Payments made under agreements and decrees are *classified as alimony* only if the following conditions are satisfied:

- The payments are in cash. (This clearly distinguishes alimony from property division.)
- The agreement or decree does not specify that the payments are not alimony. (This allows the parties to determine by agreement whether the payments will be alimony.)
- The payor and payee are not members of the same household at the time the payments are made. (This ensures the payments are for maintaining two households.)
- There is no liability to make the payments for any period after the death of the payee.[4]

Digging Deeper | In-depth coverage can be found on this book's companion website: **www.cengagebrain.com**

Child Support

While alimony is taxable, a taxpayer does *not* report income from the receipt of child support payments made by his or her former spouse. This result occurs because the money is received subject to the duty to use the money for the child's benefit. The payor is not allowed to deduct the child support payments because the payments are made to satisfy the payor's legal obligation to support the child.

In many cases, it is difficult to determine whether an amount received is alimony or child support. If the amount of the payments would be reduced upon the happening of a contingency related to a child (e.g., the child attains age 21 or dies), the amount of the future reduction in the payment is deemed child support.[5]

| **Example 3** | Under the divorce agreement, Matt is required to make periodic alimony payments of $500 per month to Grace. However, when Matt and Grace's child reaches age 21, marries, or dies (whichever occurs first), the payments will be reduced to $300 per month. Child support payments are $200 each month, and alimony is $300 each month. |

10-2b Prizes and Awards

The fair market value of prizes and awards must be included in gross income.[6] Therefore, TV giveaway prizes, magazine publisher prizes, door prizes, and awards from an employer to an employee in recognition of performance are fully taxable to the recipient.

A narrow exception permits a prize or an award to be excluded from gross income if *all* of the following requirements are satisfied:

- The prize or award is received in recognition of religious, charitable, scientific, educational, artistic, literary, or civic achievement (e.g., Nobel Prize, Pulitzer Prize, or faculty teaching award).
- The recipient was selected without taking any action to enter the contest or proceeding.
- The recipient is not required to render substantial future services as a condition for receiving the prize or award.[7]
- The recipient arranges for the prize or award to be paid *directly* to a qualified governmental unit or nonprofit organization.

---

[4]See *Divorced or Separated Individuals* (IRS Publication 504) for additional information on alimony.

[5]§ 71(c)(2).

[6]§ 74.

[7]§ 74(b).

TAX IN THE NEWS   Social Security Benefits as a Source of Federal Revenue

Recipients' Social Security benefits are indexed for inflation, but the base amounts used in the formula to calculate the taxable portion of the benefits are not indexed. (For a complete discussion of this formula, see the materials associated with Digging Deeper 2.) The $25,000 and $32,000 base amounts were established in 1984. If they were indexed for inflation, these nontaxable amounts would have doubled by 2010. Thus, as income and Social Security benefits rise with inflation, taxable income increases more than the related increase in "real" benefits.

A taxpayer can avoid including prizes and awards in gross income by refusing to accept the prize or award.

Another exception is provided to allow exclusion of certain employee achievement awards in the form of tangible personal property (e.g., a gold watch). The awards must be made in recognition of length of service or safety achievement. Generally, the ceiling on the excludible amount for an employee is $400 per taxable year. However, if the award is a *qualified plan award,* the ceiling on the exclusion is $1,600 per taxable year.[8]

10-2c Unemployment Compensation

The unemployment compensation program is sponsored and operated by the states and Federal government to provide a source of income for people who have been employed and are temporarily out of work. In a series of rulings over a period of 40 years, the IRS exempted unemployment benefits from tax. These payments were considered social benefit programs for the promotion of the general welfare. After experiencing dissatisfaction with the IRS's treatment of unemployment compensation, Congress amended the Code to make the benefits taxable.[9]

10-2d Social Security Benefits

If a taxpayer's income exceeds a specified base amount, as much as 50 or 85 percent of Social Security retirement benefits must be included in gross income. The taxable amount of benefits is determined through the application of one of two complex formulas described in § 86.

In-depth coverage can be found on this book's companion website: **www.cengagebrain.com**   **2**   Digging Deeper

10-3 SPECIFIC EXCLUSIONS APPLICABLE TO INDIVIDUALS

10-3a Gifts and Inheritances

Beginning with the Income Tax Act of 1913 and continuing to the present, Congress has allowed the recipient of a gift to exclude the value of the property from gross income. The exclusion applies to gifts made during the life of the donor (*inter vivos* gifts) and transfers that take effect upon the death of the donor (bequests and inheritances).[10] However, the recipient of a gift of income-producing property is subject to tax on the income subsequently earned from the property.

[8]§§ 74(c) and 274(j).
[9]§ 85.
[10]§ 102.

TAX IN THE NEWS   Begging as a Tax-Disfavored Occupation

The Tax Court has ruled that amounts received from begging are nontaxable gifts. In a reversal of the normal roles, the beggars contended that the amounts received were earned income while the IRS argued that the taxpayers had merely received gifts. The beggars wanted the fruit of their efforts to be treated as earned income to qualify them for the

earned income credit (see discussion later in this chapter). In all cases addressing the issue, the taxpayers were incarcerated and received the money from relatives and friends who had few prospects for being repaid.

Source: *John Walter Wolf,* 78 TCM 488, T.C.Memo. 1990–320.

Also, as discussed in Chapter 1, the donor or the decedent's estate may be subject to gift or estate taxes on such transfers.

In numerous cases, "gifts" are made in a business setting. For example, a salesperson gives a purchasing agent free samples, an employee receives cash from his or her employer upon retirement, or a corporation makes payments to employees who were victims of a natural disaster. In these and similar instances, it is frequently unclear whether the payment was a gift or represents compensation for past, present, or future services.

The courts have defined a gift as "a voluntary transfer of property by one to another without adequate consideration or compensation therefrom."[11] If the payment is intended to be for services rendered, it is not a gift, even though the payment is made without legal or moral obligation and the payor receives no economic benefit from the transfer. To qualify as a gift, the payment must be made "out of affection, respect, admiration, charity or like impulses."[12] Thus, the cases on this issue have been decided on the basis of the donor's intent.[13]

In the case of cash or other property received by an employee from his or her employer, Congress has eliminated any ambiguity. Transfers from an employer to an employee cannot be excluded as a gift.[14]

THE BIG PICTURE

Example 4

Return to the facts of *The Big Picture* on p. 10-1. The $1,500 bonus paid to Donna by the CPA firm was compensation for her services rather than a gift, even though the employer had not contracted to pay this additional amount. This results because the payment was most likely not motivated by the employer's generosity, but rather was made as a result of business considerations. Even if the payment had been made out of generosity, because the payment was received from her employer, Donna could not exclude the "gift."

Digging Deeper   **3**   In-depth coverage can be found on this book's companion website: **www.cengagebrain.com**

10-3b Scholarships

General Information

Payments or benefits received by a student at an educational institution may be (1) compensation for services, (2) a gift, or (3) a scholarship. If the payments or

---

[11]*Estate of D. R. Daly,* 3 B.T.A. 1042 (1926).

[12]*Robertson v. U.S.,* 52–1 USTC ¶9343, 41 AFTR 1053, 72 S.Ct. 994 (USSC, 1952).

[13]See, for example, *Comm. v. Duberstein,* 60–2 USTC ¶9515, 5 AFTR 2d 1626, 80 S.Ct. 1190 (USSC, 1960).

[14]§ 102(c). But see § 139 for qualified disaster situations.

benefits are received as compensation for services (past or present), the fact that the recipient is a student generally does not render the amounts received nontaxable.[15] Thus, a university teaching or research assistant is generally considered an employee, and his or her stipend is taxable compensation for services rendered. On the other hand, athletic scholarships generally are nontaxable when the individual is not required to participate in the sport.[16] In general, amounts received to be used for educational purposes (other than amounts received from family members) cannot be excluded as gifts because conditions attached to the receipt of the funds mean that the payments were not made out of "detached generosity."

The **scholarship** rules are intended to provide exclusion treatment for education-related benefits that cannot qualify as gifts but are not compensation for services. According to the Regulations, "a scholarship is an amount paid or allowed to, or for the benefit of, an individual to aid such individual in the pursuit of study or research."[17] The recipient must be a candidate for a degree at an educational institution.[18]

THE BIG PICTURE

Example 5

Return to the facts of *The Big Picture* on p. 10-1. State University waives tuition for all graduate teaching assistants. The tuition waived is intended as compensation for services and is therefore included in the graduate assistants' gross income. Therefore, the $6,000 Donna received in the form of a tuition waiver each semester is compensation for her services. The $400 she received each month also is compensation for services. The fact that she used the funds for educational expenses does not change the tax treatment of the compensation.

Example 6

Terry enters a contest sponsored by a local newspaper. Each contestant is required to submit an essay on local environmental issues. The prize is one year's tuition at State University. Terry wins the contest. The newspaper has a legal obligation to Terry (as the contest winner). Thus, the benefits are not a gift. However, because the tuition payment aids Terry in pursuing her studies and is not compensation for services, the payment is a scholarship.

As an exception to the compensation for services, nonprofit educational institutions can provide qualified tuition reduction plans for their employees and the employees can exclude the tuition from their gross income. The exclusion also applies to tuition reductions granted to the employee's spouse and the employee's dependent children.[19]

A scholarship recipient may exclude from gross income the amount used for tuition and related expenses (fees, books, supplies, and equipment required for courses), provided the conditions of the grant do not require that the funds be used for other purposes.[20]

Example 7

Kelly receives a scholarship of $9,500 from State University to be used to pursue a bachelor's degree. She spends $4,000 on tuition, $3,000 on books and supplies, and $2,500 for room and board. Kelly may exclude $7,000 ($4,000 + $3,000) from gross income. The $2,500 spent for room and board is includible in Kelly's gross income.

---

[15]Reg. § 1.117–2(a). See *C. P. Bhalla*, 35 T.C. 13 (1960), for a discussion of the distinction between a scholarship and compensation. See also *Bingler v. Johnson*, 69–1 USTC ¶9348, 23 AFTR 2d 1212, 89 S.Ct. 1439 (USSC, 1969). For potential exclusion treatment, see the discussion of qualified tuition reductions in Chapter 11.

[16]Rev.Rul. 77–263, 1977–2 C.B. 47.
[17]Prop.Reg. § 117–6(c)(3)(i).
[18]§ 117(a).
[19]§ 117(d).
[20]§ 117(b).

Timing Issues

Frequently, the scholarship recipient is a cash basis taxpayer who receives the money in one tax year but pays the educational expenses in a subsequent year. The amount eligible for exclusion may not be known at the time the money is received. In that case, the transaction is held open until the educational expenses are paid.[21]

| Example 8 | In August 2014, Sanjay received $10,000 as a scholarship for the academic year 2014–2015. Sanjay's expenditures for tuition, books, and supplies were as follows: |

August–December 2014	$3,000
January–May 2015	4,500
	$7,500

Sanjay's gross income for 2015 includes $2,500 ($10,000 − $7,500) that is not excludible as a scholarship. None of the scholarship is included in his gross income in 2014.

Disguised Compensation

Some employers make scholarships available solely to the children of key employees. The tax objective of these plans is to provide a nontaxable fringe benefit to the executives by making the payment to the child in the form of an excludible scholarship. However, the IRS has ruled that the payments are generally includible by the parent-employee as compensation for services.[22]

10-3c Damages

A person who suffers harm caused by another is often entitled to **compensatory damages**. The tax consequences of the receipt of damages depend on the type of harm the taxpayer has experienced. The taxpayer may seek recovery for (1) a loss of income, (2) expenses incurred, (3) property destroyed, or (4) personal injury.

Generally, reimbursement for a loss of income is taxed in the same manner as the income replaced (see the exception under Personal Injury below). Damages that are a recovery of expenses previously deducted by the taxpayer are generally taxable under the tax benefit rule (refer to Chapter 4).

A payment for damaged or destroyed property is treated as an amount received in a sale or exchange of the property. Thus, the taxpayer has a realized gain if the damages payments received exceed the property's basis. Damages for personal injuries receive special treatment under the Code.

Personal Injury

The legal theory of personal injury damages is that the amount received is intended "to make the plaintiff [the injured party] whole as before the injury."[23] It follows that if the damages payments received were subject to tax, the after-tax amount received would be less than the actual damages incurred and the injured party would not be "whole as before the injury." With regard to personal injury damages, a distinction is made between compensatory damages and **punitive damages**.

Compensatory damages are intended to compensate the taxpayer for the damages incurred. Only those compensatory damages received on account of *physical personal injury or sickness* can be excluded from gross income.[24] Such exclusion treatment includes amounts received for loss of income associated with the physical personal injury or physical sickness. Compensatory damages awarded on account of emotional distress are not received on account of physical injury or sickness and thus cannot be excluded from gross income (except to the extent of any amount

[21]Prop.Reg. § 1.117–6(b)(2).
[22]Rev.Rul. 75–448, 1975–2 C.B. 55 and *Richard T. Armantrout*, 67 T.C. 996 (1977).
[23]*C. A. Hawkins*, 6 B.T.A. 1023(1928).
[24]§ 104(a)(2).

CONCEPT SUMMARY 10.1

Taxation of Damages

Type of Claim	Taxation of Award or Settlement
Breach of contract (generally loss of income)	Taxable.
Property damages	Recovery of cost; gain to the extent of the excess over basis. A loss is deductible for business property and investment property to the extent of basis over the amount realized. A loss may be deductible for personal-use property (see discussion of casualty losses in Chapter 6).
Personal injury	
Physical	All compensatory amounts are excluded unless previously deducted (e.g., medical expenses). Amounts received as punitive damages are included in gross income.
Nonphysical	Compensatory damages and punitive damages are included in gross income.

© iStockphoto.com/Andrey Prokhorov

received for medical care). Likewise, any amounts received for age discrimination or injury to one's reputation cannot be excluded.

Punitive damages are amounts the party that caused the harm must pay to the victim as punishment for outrageous conduct. Punitive damages are not intended to compensate the victim, but rather to punish the party that caused the harm. Thus, it follows that amounts received as punitive damages may actually place the victim in a better economic position than before the harm was experienced. Thus, punitive damages are included in gross income.

These rules are set forth in Concept Summary 10.1.

Return to the facts of *The Big Picture* on p. 10-1. The damages Donna received were awarded as a result of a physical personal injury. Therefore, all of the compensatory damages can be excluded. Note that even the compensation for the loss of income of $10,000 can be excluded. The punitive damages Donna received, however, must be included in her gross income.

10-3d Workers' Compensation

State workers' compensation laws require the employer to pay fixed amounts for specific job-related injuries. The state laws were enacted so that the employee will not have to go through the ordeal of a lawsuit (and possibly not collect damages because of some defense available to the employer) to recover the damages. Although the payments are intended, in part, to compensate for a loss of future income, Congress has specifically exempted workers' compensation benefits from inclusion in gross income.[25]

10-3e Accident and Health Insurance Benefits

The income tax treatment of **accident and health insurance benefits** depends on whether the policy providing the benefits was purchased by the taxpayer or the taxpayer's

---

[25]§ 104(a)(1).

employer. Benefits collected under an accident and health insurance policy purchased by the taxpayer are excludible even though the payments are a substitute for income.[26]

Example 10

Bonnie purchases a medical and disability insurance policy. The insurance company pays Bonnie $1,000 per week to replace wages she loses while in the hospital. Although the payments serve as a substitute for income, the amounts received are tax-exempt benefits collected under Bonnie's insurance policy.

A different set of rules applies if the accident and health insurance protection was purchased by the individual's employer, as discussed in Chapter 11.

10-3f Educational Savings Bonds

The cost of a college education has risen dramatically during the past several decades. According to U.S. Department of Education estimates, the cost of attending a publicly supported university for four years now commonly exceeds $60,000. For a private university, the cost often exceeds $200,000. Consequently, Congress has attempted to assist low- to middle-income parents in saving for their children's college education.

One of the ways that Congress assists such families is through an interest income exclusion on **educational savings bonds**.[27] The interest on U.S. government Series EE savings bonds may be excluded from gross income if the bond proceeds are used to pay qualified higher education expenses. The exclusion applies only if both of the following requirements are satisfied:

- The savings bonds are issued after December 31, 1989.
- The savings bonds are issued to an individual who is at least 24 years old at the time of issuance.

The redemption proceeds must be used to pay qualified higher education expenses. Qualified higher education expenses consist of tuition and fees paid to an eligible educational institution for the taxpayer, spouse, or dependent. In calculating qualified higher education expenses, the tuition and fees paid are reduced by excludible scholarships and veterans' benefits received. If the redemption proceeds (both principal and interest) exceed the qualified higher education expenses, only a pro rata portion of the interest will qualify for exclusion treatment.

Example 11

Tracy's redemption proceeds from qualified savings bonds during the taxable year are $6,000 (principal of $4,000 and interest of $2,000). Tracy's qualified higher education expenses are $5,000. Because the redemption proceeds exceed the qualified higher education expenses, only $1,667 [($5,000/$6,000) × $2,000] of the interest is excludible.

The exclusion is limited by the application of the wherewithal to pay concept. That is, once the *modified AGI (MAGI)* exceeds a threshold amount, the phaseout of the exclusion begins. The threshold amounts are adjusted for inflation each year. For 2014, the phaseout begins at $76,000 ($113,950 on a joint return).[28] The phaseout is completed when MAGI exceeds the threshold amount by more than $15,000 ($30,000 on a joint return). The otherwise excludible interest is reduced by the amount calculated as follows:

$$\frac{MAGI - \$76,000}{\$15,000} \times \frac{\text{Excludible interest}}{\text{before phaseout}} = \frac{\text{Reduction in}}{\text{excludible interest}}$$

On a joint return, $113,950 is substituted for $76,000 (in 2014), and $30,000 is substituted for $15,000.

---

[26]§ 104(a)(3).
[27]§ 135.

[28]The indexed amounts for 2013 were $74,700 and $112,050.

Assume the same facts as in Example 11, except that Tracy's MAGI for 2014 is $81,300. Tracy is single. The phaseout results in Tracy's interest exclusion being reduced by $589 $\{[(\$81,300 - \$76,000)/\$15,000] \times \$1,667\}$. Therefore, Tracy's exclusion is $1,078 ($1,667 − $589).	**Example 12**

10-4 ITEMIZED DEDUCTIONS

Taxpayers are allowed to deduct specified expenditures as itemized deductions. Itemized deductions, which are reported on Schedule A, can be classified as follows:

- Expenses that are purely *personal* in nature.
- Expenses incurred by *employees* in connection with their employment activities.
- Expenses related to (1) the *production or collection of income* and (2) the *management of property* held for the production of income.[29]

Expenses in the third category, sometimes referred to as *nonbusiness expenses*, differ from trade or business expenses (discussed previously). Trade or business expenses, which are deductions *for* AGI, must be incurred in connection with a trade or business. Nonbusiness expenses, on the other hand, are expenses incurred in connection with an income-producing activity that does not qualify as a trade or business. If the nonbusiness expense is incurred in connection with rent or royalty property, it is classified as a deduction *for* AGI. Otherwise, it is classified as a deduction *from* AGI. Itemized deductions include, but are not limited to, the expenses listed in Exhibit 10.1.

Allowable itemized deductions are deductible *from* AGI in arriving at taxable income if the taxpayer elects to itemize. The election to itemize is appropriate when total itemized deductions exceed the standard deduction based on the taxpayer's filing status (see Chapter 9). The more important itemized deductions are discussed next.

LO.2

Determine an individual's allowable itemized deductions.

EXHIBIT 10.1	Partial List of Itemized Deductions

Personal Expenditures
Medical expenses in excess of 10% (7.5% if at least age 65) of AGI
State and local income taxes or sales taxes
Real estate taxes
Personal property taxes
Interest on home mortgage
Charitable contributions (limited to a maximum of 50% of AGI)
Casualty and theft losses (in excess of 10% of AGI)
Tax return preparation fee (in excess of 2% of AGI)

Expenditures Related to Employment (in Excess of 2% of AGI)
Union dues
Professional dues and subscriptions
Certain educational expenses
Unreimbursed employee business expenses

Expenditures Related to Income-Producing Activities
Investment interest (to the extent of net investment income)
Investment counsel fees (in excess of 2% of AGI)
Other investment expenses (in excess of 2% of AGI)

---

[29]Section 212 allows itemized deductions for these types of activities. However, expenses related to the production of *rental or royalty income* are deductions *for* AGI, not itemized deductions, under § 62(a)(4).

10-4a Medical Expenses

Medical expenses paid for the care of the taxpayer, spouse, and dependents are allowed as an itemized deduction to the extent the expenses are not reimbursed. The medical expense deduction is limited to the amount by which such expenses exceed a threshold percentage of the taxpayer's AGI. Beginning in 2013, the threshold percentage is 10 percent for most taxpayers. For taxpayers age 65 and older, however, the threshold is 7.5 percent of AGI until 2017, when it increases to 10 percent.[30]

THE BIG PICTURE

Example 13

Return to the facts of *The Big Picture* on p. 10-1. In addition to the medical expenses incurred associated with Donna's accident that were later reimbursed by the delivery company's insurance company, the Steeles had other qualifying medical expenses. Assuming that their AGI for the year is $200,000, they will need to itemize their deductions and have more than $20,000 ($200,000 × 10%) in unreimbursed medical expenses to receive a tax benefit from those expenses.

Medical Expenses Defined

The term *medical care* includes expenditures incurred for the "diagnosis, cure, mitigation, treatment, or prevention of disease, or for the purpose of affecting any structure or function of the body."[31] Medical expense also includes premiums paid for health care insurance, prescribed drugs and insulin, and lodging while away from home for the purpose of obtaining medical care. Examples of deductible and nondeductible medical expenses appear in Exhibit 10.2.

Cosmetic Surgery

Amounts paid for unnecessary cosmetic surgery are not deductible medical expenses. However, if cosmetic surgery is deemed necessary, it is deductible as a medical expense. Cosmetic surgery is necessary when it improves the effects of (1) a deformity arising from a congenital abnormality, (2) a personal injury, or (3) a disfiguring disease.

Nursing Home Care

The cost of care in a nursing home or home for the aged, including meals and lodging, can be included in deductible medical expenses if the primary reason for being in the home is to get medical care. If the primary reason for being there is personal, any costs for medical or nursing care can be included in deductible medical expenses, but the cost of meals and lodging must be excluded.

Capital Expenditures

When capital expenditures are incurred for medical purposes, they must be deemed medically necessary by a physician, the facility must be used primarily by the patient alone, and the expense must be reasonable. Examples of such expenditures include dust elimination systems,[32] elevators,[33] and vans specially designed for wheelchair-bound taxpayers. Other examples of expenditures that may qualify are swimming pools if the taxpayer does not have access to a neighborhood pool and air conditioners if they do not become permanent improvements (e.g., window units).[34]

Both a capital expenditure for a permanent improvement and expenditures made for the operation or maintenance of the improvement may qualify as medical

---

[30]Prior to 2013, the percentage threshold for regular income tax purposes was 7.5 percent of AGI for all taxpayers.

[31]§ 213(d).

[32]Ltr.Rul. 7948029.

[33]*Riach v. Frank*, 62–1 USTC ¶9419, 9 AFTR 2d 1263, 302 F.2d 374 (CA–9, 1962).

[34]Reg. § 1.213–1(e)(1)(iii).

EXHIBIT 10.2	Examples of Deductible and Nondeductible Medical Expenses

Deductible	Nondeductible
Medical (including dental, mental, and hospital) care	Funeral, burial, or cremation expenses
Prescription drugs and insulin	Nonprescription drugs (except insulin)
Special equipment	Bottled water
Wheelchairs	Diaper service, maternity clothes
Crutches	Programs for the general improvement of health
Artificial limbs	Weight reduction
Eyeglasses (including contact lenses)	Health spas
Hearing aids	Social activities (e.g., dancing and swimming lessons)
Transportation for medical care	Unnecessary cosmetic surgery
Medical and hospital insurance premiums	
Long-term care insurance premiums (subject to limitations)	
Cost of alcohol and drug rehabilitation	
Certain costs to stop smoking	
Weight reduction programs related to obesity	

expenses. The allowable cost of such qualified medical expenditures is deductible in the year incurred. Although depreciation is required for most other capital expenditures, it is not required for those qualifying for medical purposes.

Medical Expenses for Spouse and Dependents

In computing the medical expense deduction, a taxpayer may include medical expenses for a spouse and for a person who was a dependent at the time the expenses were paid or incurred. Of the requirements that normally apply in determining dependency status, neither the gross income nor the joint return test applies in determining dependency status for medical expense deduction purposes.

Transportation and Lodging

Payments for transportation to and from a hospital or other medical facility for medical care are deductible as medical expenses (subject to the AGI floor). These costs include bus, taxi, train, or plane fare; charges for ambulance service; and out-of-pocket expenses for the use of an automobile. A mileage allowance of 23.5 cents per mile[35] for 2014 may be used instead of actual out-of-pocket automobile expenses. Whether the taxpayer chooses to claim out-of-pocket automobile expenses or the 23.5 cents per mile automatic mileage option, related parking fees and tolls can also be deducted. Also included are transportation expenditures for someone such as a parent or nurse who must accompany the patient. The cost of meals while en route to obtain medical care is not deductible.

In-depth coverage can be found on this book's companion website: **www.cengagebrain.com**    **4** | Digging Deeper |

Health Savings Accounts

Qualifying individuals may make deductible contributions to a **Health Savings Account (HSA)**. An HSA is a qualified trust or custodial account administered by a qualified HSA trustee, which can be a bank, an insurance company, or another

---
[35]This amount is adjusted periodically. The amount was 24 cents per mile for 2013.

TAX IN THE NEWS   The President and Vice President Itemize

Approximately two-thirds of all individual taxpayers take the standard deduction each year rather than itemize. President Barack H. Obama and Vice President Joseph R. Biden are among the one-third who itemize. Both the President and the Vice President, who file joint returns with their wives, released their 2012 income tax returns to the public in 2013. Their itemized deductions, along with certain other information from their tax returns, are shown at the right.

	President Obama	Vice President Biden
Gross income	$662,076	$385,072
Adjusted gross income	$608,611	$385,072
Itemized deductions:		
Medical expenses	$ –0–	$ –0–
Taxes	63,305	28,521
Interest	45,046	26,679
Charitable contributions	150,034	7,190
Job expenses and other miscellaneous deductions	–0–	–0–
Total itemized deductions	$258,385	$ 62,390

IRS-approved trustee.[36] A taxpayer can use an HSA in conjunction with a high-deductible medical insurance policy to help reduce the overall cost of medical coverage. The high-deductible policy provides coverage for extraordinary medical expenses (in excess of the deductible), and expenses not covered by the policy can be paid with funds withdrawn tax-free from the HSA.

Example 14	Sanchez, who is married and has three dependent children, carries a high-deductible medical insurance policy with a deductible of $4,400. He establishes an HSA and contributes the maximum allowable amount to the HSA in 2014. During 2014, the Sanchez family incurs medical expenses of $7,000. The high-deductible policy covers $2,600 of the expenses ($7,000 expenses – $4,400 deductible). Sanchez may withdraw $4,400 from the HSA to pay the medical expenses not covered by the high-deductible policy.

High-Deductible Plans High-deductible policies are less expensive than low-deductible policies, so taxpayers with low medical costs can benefit from the lower premiums and use funds from the HSA to pay costs not covered by the high-deductible policy. A plan must meet two requirements to qualify as a high-deductible plan.[37]

1. The annual deductible in 2014 is not less than $1,250 for self-only coverage ($2,500 for family coverage).
2. The annual limit in 2014 on total out-of-pocket costs (excluding the premiums) under the plan does not exceed $6,350 for self-only coverage ($12,700 for family coverage).

Tax Treatment of HSA Contributions and Distributions To establish an HSA, a taxpayer contributes funds to a tax-exempt trust.[38] As illustrated in the preceding example, funds can be withdrawn from an HSA to pay medical expenses that are not covered by the high-deductible policy. The following general tax rules apply to HSAs:

1. Contributions made by the taxpayer to an HSA are deductible from gross income to arrive at AGI (deduction *for* AGI). Thus, the taxpayer does not need to itemize to take the deduction.

---

[36]§ 223.
[37]§ 223(c)(2).

[38]§ 223(d).

2. Earnings on HSAs are not subject to taxation unless distributed, in which case taxability depends on the way the funds are used.[39]

   • Distributions from HSAs are excluded from gross income if they are used to pay for medical expenses not covered by the high-deductible policy.
   • Distributions that are not used to pay for medical expenses are included in gross income and are subject to an additional 20 percent penalty if made before age 65, death, or disability. Such distributions made by reason of death or disability and distributions made after the HSA beneficiary becomes eligible for Medicare are taxed but not penalized.

HSAs have at least two other attractive features. First, an HSA is portable. Taxpayers who switch jobs can take their HSAs with them. Second, anyone under age 65 who has a high-deductible plan and is not covered by another policy that is not a high-deductible plan can establish an HSA.

Deductible Amount The annual deduction for contributions to an HSA is limited to the sum of the monthly limitations. The monthly limitation is calculated for each month the individual is an eligible individual. The monthly deduction is not allowed after the individual becomes eligible for Medicare coverage.

The amount of the monthly limitation for an individual who has self-only coverage in 2014 is one-twelfth of $3,300, while the monthly limitation for an individual who has family coverage in 2014 is one-twelfth of $6,550. These amounts are subject to annual cost-of-living adjustments.[40] An eligible taxpayer who has attained the age of 55 by the end of the tax year may make an additional annual contribution in 2014 of up to $1,000.

Liu, who is married and self-employed, carries a high-deductible medical insurance policy with family coverage and an annual deductible of $4,000. In addition, he has established an HSA. Liu's maximum annual contribution to the HSA in 2014 is $6,550.	**Example 15**

During 2014, Adam, who is self-employed, made 12 monthly payments of $1,200 for an HSA contract that provides medical insurance coverage with a $3,600 deductible. The plan covers Adam, his wife, and their two children. Of the $1,200 monthly fee, $675 was for the high-deductible policy, and $525 was deposited into an HSA. The deductible monthly contribution to the HSA is calculated as follows:	**Example 16**

Maximum annual deduction for family coverage	$6,550.00
Monthly limitation (1/12 of $6,550)	545.83

Because Adam is self-employed, he can deduct $8,100 of the amount paid for the high-deductible policy ($675 per month × 12 months) as a deduction *for* AGI (refer to Chapter 11). In addition, he can deduct the $6,300 ($525 × 12) paid to the HSA as a deduction *for* AGI. Note that the $6,300 HSA deduction does not exceed the $6,550 ceiling.

10-4b Taxes

A deduction is allowed for certain state and local taxes paid or accrued by a taxpayer.[41] The deduction was created to relieve the burden of multiple taxation upon the same source of revenue.

Deductible taxes must be distinguished from nondeductible fees. Fees for special privileges or services are not deductible as itemized deductions if personal in nature. Examples include fees for dog licenses, automobile inspections, automobile titles and registration, hunting and fishing licenses, bridge and highway tolls, drivers' licenses, parking meter deposits, and postage. These items, however, could be deductible if incurred as a business expense or for the production of income (refer

---

[39]§ 223(f).
[40]§ 223(b)(2). The annual limits were $3,250 and $6,450 in 2013.

[41]Most deductible taxes are listed in § 164, while the nondeductible items are included in § 275.

EXHIBIT 10.3	Deductible and Nondeductible Taxes

Deductible	Nondeductible
State, local, and foreign real property taxes	Federal income taxes
State and local personal property taxes	FICA taxes imposed on employees
State and local income taxes *or* sales/use taxes*	Employer FICA taxes paid on domestic household workers
Foreign income taxes	Estate, inheritance, and gift taxes
	Federal, state, and local excise taxes (e.g., gasoline, tobacco, and spirits)
	Taxes on real property to the extent such taxes are to be apportioned and treated as imposed on another taxpayer
	Special assessments for streets, sidewalks, curbing, and other similar improvements

* The sales/use tax alternative is available through 2013. Many tax professionals expect Congress to extend this provision.

to Chapter 5). Deductible and nondeductible taxes for purposes of computing itemized deductions are summarized in Exhibit 10.3.

Personal Property Taxes

Deductible personal property taxes must be *ad valorem* (assessed in relation to the value of the property). Therefore, a motor vehicle tax based on weight, model, year, or horsepower is not an ad valorem tax. In contrast, a motor vehicle tax based on the value of the car is deductible.

THE BIG PICTURE

Example 17

Return to the facts of *The Big Picture* on p. 10-1. In Donna and David Steele's state, the government imposes a motor vehicle registration tax equal to 2% of the value of the vehicle plus 40 cents per hundredweight. The Steeles own a car having a value of $20,000 and weighing 3,000 pounds. They pay an annual registration tax of $412. Of this amount, $400 (2% of $20,000) is deductible as a personal property tax if they itemize their deductions. The remaining $12, based on the weight of the car, is not deductible.

Real Estate Taxes

Real estate taxes of individuals are generally deductible. Taxes on personal-use property and investment property are deductible as itemized deductions. Taxes on business property are deductible as business expenses. Real property taxes on property that is sold during the year must be allocated between the buyer and the seller (refer to Chapter 5).

State and Local Income Taxes and Sales Taxes

The position of the IRS is that state and local *income* taxes imposed upon an individual are deductible only as itemized deductions, even if the taxpayer's sole source of income is from a business, rents, or royalties.

Cash basis taxpayers are entitled to deduct state income taxes withheld by the employer in the year the taxes are withheld. In addition, estimated state income tax payments are deductible in the year the payment is made by cash basis taxpayers even if the payments relate to a prior or subsequent year.[42] If the taxpayer overpays state income taxes because of excessive withholdings or

---

[42]Rev.Rul. 71–190, 1971–1 C.B. 70. See also Rev.Rul. 82–208, 1982–2 C.B. 58, where a deduction is not allowed when the taxpayer cannot, in good faith, reasonably determine that there is additional state income tax liability.

Deductibility of Foreign Taxes

Global Tax Issues

© iStockphoto.com/Andrey Prokhorov

Josef, a citizen of the United States who works primarily in New York, also works several months each year in Austria. He owns a residence in Austria and pays income taxes to Austria on the income he earns there. Both the property tax he pays on his Austrian residence and the income tax he pays on his Austrian income are deductible in computing U.S. taxable income. However, if Josef deducts the Austrian income tax, he may not claim the foreign tax credit with respect to this tax (see Chapters 16 and 17).

estimated tax payments, the refund received is included in gross income of the following year to the extent the deduction reduced the taxable income in the prior year.

Example 18

Leona, a cash basis, unmarried taxpayer, had $800 of state income tax withheld during 2014. Also in 2014, Leona paid $100 that was due when she filed her 2013 state income tax return in 2014 and made estimated payments of $300 on her 2014 state income tax. When Leona files her 2014 Federal income tax return in April 2015, she elects to itemize deductions, which amount to $7,500, including the $1,200 of state income tax payments and withholdings. The itemized deductions reduce her taxable income.

As a result of overpaying her 2014 state income tax, Leona receives a refund of $200 early in 2015. She will include this amount in her 2015 gross income in computing her Federal income tax. It does not matter whether Leona received a check from the state for $200 or applied the $200 toward her 2015 state income tax.

Individuals can elect to deduct either their state and local income taxes *or* their sales/use taxes paid as an itemized deduction on Schedule A of Form 1040. The annual election can reflect actual sales/use tax payments *or* an amount from an IRS table. The amount from the table may be increased by sales tax paid on the purchase of motor vehicles, boats, and other specified items. Most likely, the sales tax deduction will be elected by those living in states with no individual income tax. At the time of this writing, this deduction alternative was available through 2013. However, many tax professionals believe that Congress will extend this provision.

Tax Planning Strategies	TIMING THE PAYMENT OF DEDUCTIBLE TAXES

FRAMEWORK FOCUS: DEDUCTIONS

Strategy: Accelerate Recognition of Deductions to Achieve Tax Deferral.

It is sometimes possible to defer or accelerate the payment of certain deductible taxes, such as state income tax, real property tax, and personal property tax. For instance, the final installment of estimated state income tax is generally due after the end of a given tax year. However, accelerating the payment of the final installment could result in larger itemized deductions for the current year.

10-4c Interest

For Federal income tax purposes, interest must be divided into five categories: business interest, personal interest, interest on qualified student loans, qualified residence interest, and investment interest. Business interest is fully deductible as an ordinary and necessary expense. Currently, personal (consumer) interest is not deductible. This includes credit card interest; interest on car loans; and other types of interest. However, interest on qualified student loans, investment interest, and qualified residence (home mortgage) interest are deductible, subject to the limits discussed below.

Interest on Qualified Student Loans

Taxpayers who pay interest on a qualified student loan may be able to deduct the interest as a deduction *for* AGI. The deduction is allowable only to the extent the proceeds of the loan are used to pay qualified education expenses. The maximum annual deduction is $2,500. However, in 2014, the deduction is phased out for taxpayers with modified AGI (MAGI) between $65,000 and $80,000 ($130,000 and $160,000 on joint returns). The deduction is not available for taxpayers who are claimed as dependents or for married taxpayers filing separately.[43]

Example 19	In 2014, Curt and Rita, who are married and file a joint return, paid $3,000 of interest on a qualified student loan. Their MAGI was $137,500. Their maximum potential deduction for qualified student loan interest is $2,500, but it must be reduced by $625 as a result of the phaseout rules.

$$\$2{,}500 \text{ interest} \times (\$137{,}500 \text{ MAGI} - \$130{,}000 \text{ phaseout floor})/$$
$$\$30{,}000 \text{ phaseout range} = \$625 \text{ reduction}$$

Curt and Rita would be allowed a student loan interest deduction of $1,875 ($2,500 maximum deduction − $625 reduction = $1,875 deduction *for* AGI).

Investment Interest

Years ago, well-to-do taxpayers used the interest deduction in the tax law to create wealth. By borrowing to purchase investments that would appreciate in the future, the interest on the debt was claimed as an ordinary deduction when paid. Later, when the asset was sold at a gain, only a capital gains tax was due on the appreciation. Thus, today's interest deduction could lead to tomorrow's capital gain.

In response, Congress has limited the deductibility of **investment interest**, which is interest paid on debt borrowed for the purpose of purchasing or continuing to hold investment property. The deduction for investment interest allowed during the tax year is limited to the lesser of the investment interest paid or net investment income.[44]

Net investment income, which serves as the ceiling on the deductibility of investment interest, is the excess of investment income over investment expenses. Investment income includes gross income from interest, annuities, and royalties not derived in the ordinary course of a trade or business.

Investment expenses are those deductible expenses directly connected with the production of investment income, such as brokerage and investment counsel fees. Investment expenses do not include interest expense.

After net investment income is determined, the allowable deductible investment interest expense is calculated.

Example 20	Ethan's financial records for the year reflect the following:

Interest income from bank savings account	$10,000
Taxable annuity receipts	5,500
Investment counsel fee	1,100
Safe deposit box rental (to hold annuity documents)	200
Investment interest expense	17,000

Ethan's investment income amounts to $15,500 ($10,000 + $5,500) and investment expenses total $1,300 ($1,100 + $200). Therefore, his net investment income is $14,200 ($15,500 − $1,300). Consequently, the investment interest deduction is limited to $14,200, the lesser of investment interest paid or net investment income.

---

[43]§ 221. See § 221(b)(2)(C) for the definition of MAGI. For 2013, the MAGI threshold amounts were $60,000 and $75,000 ($125,000 and $155,000 on joint returns).

[44]§ 163(d)(1).

TAX IN THE NEWS Don't Allow the Tax Tail to Wag the Dog

Sometimes taxpayers are lulled into the belief that it is always a good idea to maximize their tax deductions. After all, higher income tax deductions reduce taxable income, which leads to a lower tax payment to Uncle Sam. However, taxpayers who follow this approach without evaluating broader economic considerations often regret their decisions.

The deduction for interest paid on home equity line debt has become very popular over the years. Home equity debt is considered "good debt" while credit card debt is considered "bad debt" because the after-tax cost of interest on home equity debt is typically much lower than interest on credit cards.

Further, not long ago when home valuations were at record highs, many taxpayers saw no measurable risk in borrowing against the equity in their homes. However, many taxpayers now regret having consumed too much of their home equity and using their home equity as a "piggy bank" to pay for expensive vacations and fancy new cars.

With the downturn in the economy and the real estate bubble having popped, a substantial percentage of homeowners find that their homes are worth less than the debt they owe on their homes. Apparently, the easy borrowing terms amid high home valuations of yesteryear were too much of an attraction to turn down. Perhaps they wish now that they hadn't tapped their home equity to finance the expensive vacation that now is but a memory. As home values have dropped, even though they have recovered some, many of these taxpayers are finding it difficult to get back on their feet.

© iStockphoto.com/Andrey Prokhorov

The amount of investment interest disallowed is carried over to future years. No limit is placed on the length of the carryover period.

In-depth coverage can be found on this book's companion website: **www.cengagebrain.com** **5** Digging Deeper

Qualified Residence Interest

Qualified residence interest is interest paid or accrued during the taxable year on indebtedness (subject to limitations) secured by any property that is a qualified residence of the taxpayer. Qualified residence interest falls into two categories: (1) interest on **acquisition indebtedness** and (2) interest on **home equity loans**. Before each of these categories is discussed, however, the term *qualified residence* must be defined.

A qualified residence includes the taxpayer's principal residence and one other residence of the taxpayer or spouse. The principal residence is one that meets the requirement for nonrecognition of gain upon sale under § 121 (see Chapter 7). The one other residence, or second residence, refers to one that is used as a residence if not rented or, if rented, meets the requirements for a personal residence under the rental of vacation home rules. A taxpayer who has more than one second residence can make the selection each year as to which one is the qualified second residence. A residence includes, in addition to a house in the ordinary sense, cooperative apartments, condominiums, and mobile homes and boats that have living quarters (sleeping accommodations and toilet and cooking facilities).

Although in most cases interest paid on a home mortgage is fully deductible, there are limitations.[45] Interest paid or accrued during the tax year on aggregate acquisition indebtedness of $1 million or less ($500,000 for married persons filing separate returns) is deductible as qualified residence interest. *Acquisition indebtedness* refers to amounts incurred in acquiring, constructing, or substantially improving a qualified residence of the taxpayer.

Qualified residence interest also includes interest on home equity loans. These loans utilize the personal residence of the taxpayer as security, typically in the form of a second mortgage. Because the funds from home equity loans can be used for personal purposes (e.g., auto purchases and medical expenses), what would otherwise have been nondeductible personal interest becomes deductible qualified

---

[45]§ 163(h)(3).

© tuuljumala/Shutterstock.com

residence interest. However, interest is deductible only on the portion of a home equity loan that does not exceed the lesser of:

- The fair market value of the residence, reduced by the acquisition indebtedness, or
- $100,000 ($50,000 for married persons filing separate returns).

Example 21   Larry owns a personal residence with a fair market value of $450,000 and an outstanding first mortgage of $420,000. Therefore, his equity in his home is $30,000 ($450,000 − $420,000). Larry issues a second mortgage on the residence and in return borrows $15,000 to purchase a new family automobile. All interest on the $435,000 of first and second mortgage debt is treated as qualified residence interest.

Example 22   Leon and Pearl, married taxpayers, took out a mortgage on their home for $200,000 in 1997. In March of the current year, when the home has a fair market value of $400,000 and they owe $195,000 on the mortgage, Leon and Pearl take out a home equity loan for $120,000. They use the funds to purchase an airplane to be used for recreational purposes. On a joint return, Leon and Pearl can deduct all of the interest on the first mortgage because it is acquisition indebtedness. Of the $120,000 home equity loan, only the interest on the first $100,000 is deductible. The interest on the remaining $20,000 is not deductible because the debt exceeds the statutory ceiling of $100,000.

Under current law, mortgage insurance premiums paid by the taxpayer on a qualified residence may be deducted (treated as qualified residence interest). However, the deduction begins to phase out for taxpayers with AGI in excess of $100,000 ($50,000 for married taxpayers filing separately). The deduction is fully phased out when AGI exceeds $109,000 ($54,500 for married taxpayers filing separately).[46]

Interest Paid for Services

Mortgage loan companies commonly charge a fee, often called a loan origination fee, for finding, placing, or processing a mortgage loan. Loan origination fees are typically nondeductible amounts included in the basis of the acquired property. Other fees, sometimes called **points** and expressed as a percentage of the loan amount, are paid to reduce the interest rate charged over the term of the loan. Essentially, the payment of points is a prepayment of interest and is considered compensation to a lender solely for the use or forbearance of money. To be deductible, points must be in the nature of interest and cannot be a form of service charge or payment for specific services.[47]

Points must be capitalized and are amortized and deductible ratably over the life of the loan. A special exception, however, permits the purchaser of a principal residence to deduct qualifying points in the year of payment.[48] The exception also covers points paid to obtain funds for home improvements.

Points paid to refinance an existing home mortgage cannot be immediately deducted, but must be capitalized and amortized as an interest deduction over the life of the new loan.[49]

Example 23   Sandra purchased her residence many years ago, obtaining a 30-year mortgage at an annual interest rate of 8%. In the current year, Sandra refinances the mortgage to reduce the interest rate to 4%. To obtain the refinancing, she has to pay points of $2,600. The $2,600, which is considered prepayment of interest, must be capitalized and amortized over the life of the mortgage.

---

[46]§§ 163(h)(3)(E)(i) and (ii). This provision expired at the end of 2013. At the time of this writing, Congress has not extended this deduction.
[47]Rev.Rul. 69–188, 1969–1 C.B. 54.
[48]§ 461(g)(2).
[49]Rev.Rul. 87–22, 1987–1 C.B. 146.

Prepayment Penalty

When a mortgage or loan is paid off in full in a lump sum before its term, the lending institution may require an additional payment of a certain percentage applied to the unpaid amount at the time of prepayment. This is known as a prepayment penalty and is considered to be interest (e.g., personal, qualified residence, investment) in the year paid. The general rules for deductibility of interest also apply to prepayment penalties.

Interest Paid to Related Parties

Nothing prevents the deduction of interest paid to a related party as long as the payment actually took place and the interest meets the requirements for deductibility. However, a special rule applies for related taxpayers when the debtor uses the accrual basis and the related creditor is on the cash basis. If this rule is applicable, interest that has been accrued but not paid at the end of the debtor's tax year is not deductible until payment is made and the income is reportable by the cash basis recipient.

Tax-Exempt Securities

The tax law provides that no deduction is allowed for interest on debt incurred to purchase or carry tax-exempt securities.[50] A major problem for the courts has been to determine what is meant by the words *to purchase or carry*. Refer to Chapter 5 for a detailed discussion of these issues.

Prepaid Interest

Accrual method reporting is imposed on cash basis taxpayers for interest prepayments that extend beyond the end of the taxable year.[51] Such payments must be allocated to the tax years to which the interest payments relate. These provisions are intended to prevent cash basis taxpayers from *manufacturing* tax deductions before the end of the year by prepaying interest.

Classification of Interest Expense

Whether interest is deductible *for* AGI or as an itemized deduction (*from* AGI) depends on whether the indebtedness has a business, investment, or personal purpose. If the indebtedness is incurred in relation to a business (other than performing services as an employee) or for the production of rent or royalty income, the interest is deductible *for* AGI. If the indebtedness is incurred for personal use, such as qualified residence interest, any deduction allowed is taken *from* AGI and is reported on Schedule A of Form 1040 if the taxpayer elects to itemize. Note, however, that interest on a student loan is deductible *for* AGI. If the taxpayer is an employee who incurs debt in relation to his or her employment, the interest is considered to be personal, or consumer, interest and is not deductible. Business expenses appear on Schedule C of Form 1040, and expenses related to rents or royalties are reported on Schedule E.

10-4d Charitable Contributions

As noted in Chapter 5, § 170 allows individuals to deduct contributions made to qualified domestic organizations. Contributions to qualified charitable organizations serve certain social welfare needs and thus relieve the government of the cost of providing these needed services to the community.

Criteria for a Gift

A **charitable contribution** is defined as a gift made to a qualified organization.[52] The major elements needed to qualify a contribution as a gift are a donative intent, the absence of consideration, and acceptance by the donee. Consequently, the

---

[50] § 265(a)(2).
[51] § 461(g)(1).

[52] § 170(c).

taxpayer has the burden of establishing that the transfer was made from motives of disinterested generosity as established by the courts.[53] This test is quite subjective and has led to problems of interpretation (refer to the discussion of gifts earlier in this chapter).

Benefit Received Rule

When a donor derives a tangible benefit from a contribution, he or she cannot deduct the value of the benefit.

Example 24	Ralph purchases a ticket at $100 for a special performance of the local symphony (a qualified charity). If the price of a ticket to a symphony concert is normally $35, Ralph is allowed only $65 as a charitable contribution. Even if Ralph does not attend the concert, his deduction is limited to $65. However, if he does not accept the ticket from the symphony, he can deduct the full $100.

An exception to this benefit rule provides for the deduction of an automatic percentage of the amount paid for the right to purchase athletic tickets from colleges and universities.[54] Under this exception, 80 percent of the amount paid to or for the benefit of the institution qualifies as a charitable contribution deduction.

Digging Deeper 6 	In-depth coverage can be found on this book's companion website: **www.cengagebrain.com**

Contribution of Services

No deduction is allowed for the value of one's services contributed to a qualified charitable organization. However, unreimbursed expenses related to the services rendered may be deductible. For example, the cost of a uniform (without general utility) that is required to be worn while performing services may be deductible, as are certain out-of-pocket transportation costs incurred for the benefit of the charity. In lieu of these out-of-pocket costs for an automobile, a standard mileage rate of 14 cents per mile is allowed.[55] Deductions are permitted for transportation, reasonable expenses for lodging, and the cost of meals while away from home that are incurred in performing the donated services. The travel expenses are not deductible if the travel involves a significant element of personal pleasure, recreation, or vacation.[56]

Nondeductible Items

In addition to the benefit received rule and the restrictions placed on the contribution of services, the following items may not be deducted as charitable contributions:

- Dues, fees, or bills paid to country clubs, lodges, fraternal orders, or similar groups.
- Cost of raffle, bingo, or lottery tickets.
- Cost of tuition.
- Value of blood given to a blood bank.
- Donations to homeowners associations.
- Gifts to individuals.
- Rental value of property used by a qualified charity.

Time of Deduction

A charitable contribution generally is deducted in the year the payment is made. This rule applies to both cash and accrual basis individuals. A contribution is ordinarily deemed to have been made on the date of delivery of the property to the donee. A contribution made by check is considered delivered on the date of mailing. Thus, a check mailed on December 31, 2014, is deductible on the taxpayer's

---

[53]*Comm. v. Duberstein*, 60–2 USTC ¶9515, 5 AFTR 2d 1626, 80 S.Ct. 1190 (USSC, 1960).

[54]§ 170(l).

[55]§ 170(i).

[56]§ 170(j).

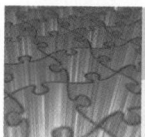

CONCEPT SUMMARY 10.2

Deductibility of Personal, Education, Investment, and Mortgage Interest

Type	Deductible	Comments
Personal (consumer) interest	No	Includes any interest that is not qualified residence interest, interest on qualified student loans, investment interest, or business interest. Examples include interest on car loans and credit card debt.
Qualified student loan interest	Yes	Deduction *for* AGI; subject to limitations.
Investment interest (*not* related to rental or royalty property)	Yes	Itemized deduction; limited to net investment income for the year; disallowed interest can be carried over to future years.
Investment interest (related to rental or royalty property)	Yes	Deduction *for* AGI; limited to net investment income for the year; disallowed interest can be carried over to future years.
Qualified residence interest on acquisition indebtedness	Yes	Deductible as an itemized deduction; limited to indebtedness of $1 million.
Qualified residence interest on home equity indebtedness	Yes	Deductible as an itemized deduction; limited to indebtedness equal to lesser of $100,000 or FMV of residence minus acquisition indebtedness.

© iStockphoto.com/Andrey Prokhorov

2014 tax return. If the contribution is charged on a credit card, the date the charge is made determines the year of deduction.

Record-Keeping Requirements

No deduction is allowed for a charitable contribution made to a qualified organization unless the taxpayer gathers (and, in some cases, supplies to the IRS) the appropriate documentation and substantiation. The specific type of documentation required depends on the amount of the contribution and whether the contribution is made in cash or noncash property.[57] In addition, special rules may apply to gifts of certain types of property (e.g., used automobiles) where Congress has noted taxpayer abuse in the past. Further, for certain gifts of noncash property, Form 8283 (Noncash Charitable Contributions) must be attached to the taxpayer's return.

The required substantiation must be obtained before the earlier of (1) the due date (including extensions) of the return for the year the contribution is claimed or (2) the date the return is filed. Failure to comply with the reporting rules may result in disallowance of the charitable contribution deduction. In addition, significant overvaluation exposes the taxpayer to stringent penalties.

Valuation Requirements

Property donated to a charity is generally valued at fair market value at the time the gift is made. The Code and Regulations give very little guidance on the measurement of the fair market value except to say, "The fair market value is the price at which the property would change hands between a willing buyer and a willing seller, neither being under any compulsion to buy or sell and both having reasonable knowledge of relevant facts."

Generally, charitable organizations do not attest to the fair market value of the donated property. Nevertheless, the taxpayer must maintain reliable written evidence as to its value.

© tuulijumala/Shutterstock.com

In-depth coverage can be found on this book's companion website: **www.cengagebrain.com**

 7 | Digging Deeper

---

[57]The specific documentation thresholds and requirements are provided in § 170(f).

Global Tax Issues

Choose the Charity Wisely

Aiko, a U.S. citizen of Japanese descent, was distressed by the damage caused by a major earthquake in Japan. She donated $100,000 to the Earthquake Victims' Relief Fund, a Japanese charitable organization that was set up to help victims of the earthquake. Kaito, also a U.S. citizen of Japanese descent, donated $100,000 to help with the relief effort. However, Kaito's contribution went to his church, which sent the proceeds of a fund drive to the Earthquake Victims' Relief Fund in Japan. Aiko's contribution is not deductible, but Kaito's is. Why? Contributions to charitable organizations are not deductible unless the organization is a U.S. charity.

Limitations on Charitable Contribution Deduction

The potential charitable contribution deduction is the total of all donations, both money and property, that qualify for the deduction. After this determination is made, the actual amount of the charitable contribution deduction that is allowed for individuals for the tax year is limited as follows:

- If the qualifying contributions for the year total 20 percent or less of AGI, they are fully deductible.
- If the qualifying contributions are more than 20 percent of AGI, the deductible amount may be limited to 20 percent, 30 percent, or 50 percent of AGI, depending on the type of property given and the type of organization to which the donation is made.
- In any case, the maximum charitable contribution deduction may not exceed 50 percent of AGI for the tax year.

To understand the complex rules for computing the amount of a charitable contribution deduction, it is necessary to understand the distinction between **capital gain property** and **ordinary income property**. These rules, which were discussed in Chapter 5, are summarized in Concept Summary 10.3.

In addition, it is necessary to understand when the 50 percent, 30 percent, and 20 percent limitations apply. If a taxpayer's contributions for the year exceed the applicable percentage limitations, the excess contributions may be carried forward and deducted during a five-year carryover period. These topics are discussed in the sections that follow.

Fifty Percent Ceiling

Contributions made to public charities may not exceed 50 percent of an individual's AGI for the year. The 50 percent ceiling on contributions applies to public charities such as churches; schools; hospitals; and Federal, state, or local governmental units. The 50 percent ceiling also applies to contributions to private operating foundations and certain private nonoperating foundations.

In the remaining discussion of charitable contributions, public charities and private foundations (both operating and nonoperating) that qualify for the 50 percent ceiling will be referred to as 50 percent organizations.

Thirty Percent Ceiling

A 30 percent ceiling applies to contributions of cash and ordinary income property to private nonoperating foundations that are not 50 percent organizations. The 30 percent ceiling also applies to contributions of appreciated capital gain property to 50 percent organizations unless the taxpayer makes a special election (see Example 26).

In the event the contributions for any one tax year involve both 50 percent and 30 percent property, the allowable deduction comes first from the 50 percent property.

CONCEPT SUMMARY 10.3

Determining the Deduction for Contributions of Property by Individuals

If the Type of Property Contributed Is:	And the Property Is Contributed to:	The Contribution Is Measured by:	But the Deduction Is Limited to:
Capital gain property	A 50% organization	Fair market value of the property	30% of AGI
Ordinary income property	A 50% organization	The basis of the property*	50% of AGI
Capital gain property (and the property is tangible personal property put to an unrelated use by the donee)	A 50% organization	The basis of the property*	50% of AGI
Capital gain property (and the reduced deduction is elected)	A 50% organization	The basis of the property	50% of AGI
Capital gain property	A private nonoperating foundation that is not a 50% organization	The basis of the property*	The lesser of: 1. 20% of AGI 2. 50% of AGI minus other contributions to 50% organizations
Ordinary income property	A private nonoperating foundation that is not a 50% organization	The basis of the property*	30% of AGI

*If the FMV of the property is less than the adjusted basis (i.e., the property has declined in value instead of appreciating), the FMV is used.

Example 25

During the year, Lisa makes the following donations to her church: cash of $2,000 and unimproved land worth $30,000. Lisa had purchased the land four years ago for $22,000 and held it as an investment. Therefore, it is capital gain property. Lisa's AGI for the year is $60,000. Disregarding percentage limitations, Lisa's potential deduction is $32,000 [$2,000 (cash) + $30,000 (fair market value of land)].

In applying the percentage limitations, however, the current deduction for the land is limited to $18,000 [30% (limitation applicable to capital gain property) × $60,000 (AGI)]. Thus, the total current deduction is $20,000 ($2,000 cash + $18,000 land). Note that the total deduction does not exceed $30,000, which is 50% of Lisa's AGI.

Under a special election, a taxpayer may choose to permanently forgo a deduction of the appreciation on capital gain property. Referred to as the reduced deduction election, this enables the taxpayer to move from the 30 percent limitation to the 50 percent limitation.

Example 26

Assume the same facts as in Example 25, except that Lisa makes the reduced deduction election. Now the deduction becomes $24,000 [$2,000 (cash) + $22,000 (basis in land)] because both donations fall under the 50% limitation. Thus, by making the election, Lisa has increased her current charitable contribution deduction by $4,000 [$24,000 − $20,000 (Example 25)].

Although the reduced deduction election appears attractive, it should be considered carefully. The election sacrifices a deduction for the appreciation on capital gain property that might eventually be allowed. Note that in Example 25, the potential deduction was $32,000, yet in Example 26, only $24,000 is allowed. The reason the potential deduction is decreased by $8,000 ($32,000 − $24,000) is that no carryover is allowed for the amount sacrificed by the election.

Twenty Percent Ceiling

A 20 percent ceiling applies to contributions of appreciated capital gain property to private nonoperating foundations that are not 50 percent organizations. Also recall from Chapter 5 that only the basis of the contributed property is allowed as a deduction.

Contribution Carryovers

Contributions that exceed the percentage limitations for the current year can be carried over for five years.[58] In the carryover process, such contributions do not lose their identity for limitation purposes. Thus, if the contribution originally involved 30 percent property, the carryover will continue to be classified as 30 percent property in the carryover year.

Example 27   Assume the same facts as in Example 25. Because only $18,000 of the $30,000 value of the land is deducted in the current year, the balance of $12,000 may be carried over to the following year. But the carryover will still be treated as capital gain property and will be subject to the 30%-of-AGI limitation.

In applying the percentage limitations, current charitable contributions must be claimed first before any carryovers can be considered. If carryovers involve more than one year, they are utilized in a first-in, first-out order.

10-4e Miscellaneous Itemized Deductions Subject to Two Percent Floor

In general, no deduction is allowed for personal, living, or family expenses.[59] However, a taxpayer may incur a number of deductible expenditures related to employment. If an employee or outside salesperson incurs unreimbursed business expenses or expenses that are reimbursed under a nonaccountable plan (see Chapter 11), including travel and transportation, the expenses are deductible as **miscellaneous itemized deductions**.[60] Certain other expenses also fall into the special category of miscellaneous itemized deductions. Some are deductible only to the extent they exceed 2 percent of the taxpayer's AGI. These miscellaneous itemized deductions include the following:

- Professional dues to membership organizations.
- Cost of uniforms or other clothing that cannot be used for normal wear.
- Fees incurred for the preparation of one's tax return or fees incurred for tax litigation before the IRS or the courts.
- Job-hunting costs.
- Fee paid for a safe deposit box used to store papers and documents relating to taxable income-producing investments.
- Investment expenses that are deductible under § 212 as discussed previously in this chapter.
- Appraisal fees to determine the amount of a casualty loss or the fair market value of donated property.
- Hobby losses up to the amount of hobby income (see Chapter 11).
- Unreimbursed employee expenses (refer to Chapter 11).

Certain employee business expenses that are reimbursed are not itemized deductions, but are deducted *for* AGI. Employee business expenses are discussed in depth in Chapter 11.

10-4f Other Miscellaneous Deductions

Certain expenses and losses do not fall into any category of itemized deductions already discussed but are nonetheless deductible. The following expenses and losses

---

[58]§ 170(d); Reg. § 1.170A–10.
[59]§ 262.

[60]Actors and performing artists who meet certain requirements are not subject to this rule. See § 62(a)(2)(B).

are deductible on Schedule A as Other Miscellaneous Deductions. These are not subject to the 2 percent-of-AGI floor.

- Gambling losses up to the amount of gambling winnings.
- Impairment-related work expenses of a handicapped person.
- Federal estate tax on income in respect of a decedent.
- Deduction for repayment of amounts under a claim of right if more than $3,000.

10-4g Overall Limitation on Certain Itemized Deductions

In the American Taxpayer Relief Act of 2012, Congress reinstated several provisions limiting tax benefits for high-income taxpayers. The limitations include the exemption phaseout (discussed in Chapter 9) and a phaseout of itemized deductions. During the 2010–2012 period, these two phaseouts did not apply. However, beginning with 2013, these phaseouts returned, and the phaseout of itemized deductions (also referred to as a *cutback adjustment*) applies to married taxpayers filing jointly whose 2014 AGI exceeds $305,050 ($254,200 for single filers).[61] Phaseouts of this type are sometimes referred to as "stealth taxes."

The limitation applies to the following frequently encountered itemized deductions:

- Taxes.
- Home mortgage interest, including points.
- Charitable contributions.
- Unreimbursed employee expenses subject to the 2 percent-of-AGI floor.
- All other expenses subject to the 2 percent-of-AGI floor.

The following are *not* subject to the limitation on itemized deductions:

- Medical expenses.
- Investment interest expense.
- Nonbusiness casualty and theft losses.
- Gambling losses.

Taxpayers subject to the limitation must reduce itemized deductions by the *lesser* of:

- 3 percent of the amount by which AGI exceeds $305,050 ($254,200 if single).
- 80 percent of itemized deductions that are affected by the limit.

The overall limitation is applied after applying all other limitations to those itemized deductions that are affected by the overall limitation. For example, other limitations apply to charitable contributions, certain meals and entertainment expenses, and certain miscellaneous itemized deductions.

Example 28

Gavin, who is single and age 45, had AGI of $275,000 for 2014. He incurred the following expenses and losses during the year:

Medical expenses before 10%-of-AGI limitation	$29,500
State and local income taxes	3,200
Real estate taxes	2,800
Home mortgage interest	7,200
Charitable contributions	2,000
Casualty loss before 10% limitation (after $100 floor)	29,000
Unreimbursed employee expenses (subject to 2%-of-AGI limitation)	5,800
Gambling losses (Gavin had $3,000 of gambling income)	7,000

[61]§ 68. The AGI thresholds are $279,650 for heads of household and $152,525 for married taxpayers filing separately. In 2013, the phaseouts applied to married taxpayers filing jointly whose AGI exceeded $300,000 ($250,000 for single taxpayers, $275,000 for heads of household, and $150,000 for married taxpayers filing separately).

Gavin's itemized deductions *before* the overall limitation are computed as follows:

Medical expenses [$29,500 − (10% × $275,000)]	$ 2,000
State and local income taxes	3,200
Real estate taxes	2,800
Home mortgage interest	7,200
Charitable contributions	2,000
Casualty loss [$29,000 − (10% × $275,000)]	1,500
Unreimbursed employee expenses [$5,800 − (2% × $275,000)]	300
Gambling losses ($7,000 loss limited to $3,000 of gambling income)	3,000
Total itemized deductions before overall limitation	$22,000

Gavin's itemized deductions subject to the overall limitation are as follows:

State and local income taxes	$ 3,200
Real estate taxes	2,800
Home mortgage interest	7,200
Charitable contributions	2,000
Unreimbursed employee expenses	300
Total	$15,500

Gavin must reduce the amount by the lesser of the following:

• 3% × ($275,000 AGI − $254,200)	$ 624
• 80% of itemized deductions subject to limitation ($15,500 × .80)	12,400

Therefore, the amount of the reduction is $624, and Gavin has $21,376 of deductible itemized deductions, computed as follows:

Deductible itemized deductions subject to overall limitation ($15,500 − $624)	$14,876
Itemized deductions not subject to overall limitation:	
Medical expenses	2,000
Casualty loss	1,500
Gambling losses	3,000
Deductible itemized deductions	$21,376

Tax Planning Strategies	EFFECTIVE UTILIZATION OF ITEMIZED DEDUCTIONS

FRAMEWORK FOCUS: DEDUCTIONS

Strategy: **Maximize Deductible Amounts.**

An individual may use the standard deduction in one year and itemize deductions in another year. Therefore, it is frequently possible to obtain maximum benefit by shifting itemized deductions from one year to another. For example, if a taxpayer's itemized deductions and the standard deduction are approximately the same for each year of a two-year period, the taxpayer should use the standard deduction in one year and shift itemized deductions (to the extent permitted by law) to the other year. The individual could, for example, prepay a church pledge for a particular year or avoid paying end-of-the-year medical expenses to shift the deduction to the following year.

10-5 INDIVIDUAL TAX CREDITS

10-5a Adoption Expenses Credit

Adoption expenses paid or incurred by a taxpayer may give rise to the **adoption expenses credit**.[62] The provision is intended to assist taxpayers who incur nonrecurring costs directly associated with the adoption process, such as adoption fees, attorney fees, court costs, social service review costs, and transportation costs.

In 2014, up to $13,190 of costs incurred to adopt an eligible child qualify for the credit. An eligible child is one who is:

- Under 18 years of age at the time of the adoption, or
- Physically or mentally incapable of taking care of himself or herself.

A taxpayer may claim the credit in the year qualifying expenses were paid or incurred if they were paid or incurred during or after the tax year in which the adoption was finalized. For qualifying expenses paid or incurred in a tax year prior to the year the adoption was finalized, the credit must be claimed in the tax year following the tax year during which the expenses are paid or incurred. A married couple must file a joint return to claim the credit.

> **Example 29**
>
> In late 2013, Sam and Martha pay $4,000 in legal fees, adoption fees, and other expenses directly related to the adoption of an infant daughter, Susan. In 2014, the year in which the adoption becomes final, they pay an additional $10,000. Sam and Martha are eligible for a $13,190 credit in 2014 (for expenses of $14,000, limited by the $13,190 ceiling, paid in 2013 and 2014).

The amount of the credit that is otherwise available is subject to phaseout for taxpayers whose AGI (modified for this purpose) exceeds $197,880 in 2014, and it is phased out completely when AGI reaches $237,880. The resulting credit is calculated by reducing the allowable credit (determined without this reduction) by the amount determined using the following formula:

$$\text{Allowable credit} \times \frac{\text{AGI} - \$197,880}{\$40,000}$$

> **Example 30**
>
> Assume the same facts as in the previous example, except that Sam and Martha's AGI is $222,880 in 2014. As a result, their available credit in 2014 is reduced from $13,190 to $4,946 {$13,190 − [$13,190 × ($25,000/$40,000)]}.

The credit is nonrefundable and is available to taxpayers only in a year in which this credit and the other nonrefundable credits do not exceed the taxpayer's tax liability. However, any unused adoption expenses credit may be carried over for up to five years, being utilized on a first-in, first-out basis.

10-5b Child Tax Credit

The **child tax credit** provision allows individual taxpayers to take a tax credit based solely on the *number* of their qualifying children. This credit is one of several "family-friendly" provisions that currently are part of our tax law. To be eligible for the credit, the child must be under age 17, must be a U.S. citizen, and must be claimed as a dependent on the taxpayer's return.

Maximum Credit and Phaseouts

Under current law, the maximum credit available is $1,000 per child.[63] The available credit is phased out for higher-income taxpayers beginning when AGI reaches

---

[62]§ 23.

[63]§ 24. The maximum credit per child is scheduled to remain at $1,000 through 2017.

$110,000 for joint filers ($55,000 for married taxpayers filing separately) and $75,000 for single taxpayers. The credit is phased out by $50 for each $1,000 (or part thereof) of AGI above the threshold amounts.[64] Because the maximum credit available to taxpayers depends on the number of qualifying children, the income level at which the credit is phased out completely also depends on the number of children qualifying for the credit.[65]

Example 31	Juanita and Alberto are married and file a joint tax return claiming their two children, ages 6 and 8, as dependents. Their AGI is $122,400. Juanita and Alberto's maximum child tax credit is $2,000 ($1,000 × 2 children). Because Juanita and Alberto's AGI is in excess of the $110,000 threshold, the maximum credit must be reduced by $50 for every $1,000 (or part thereof) above the threshold amount {$50 × [($122,400 − $110,000)/$1,000]}. Thus, the credit reduction equals $650 [$50 × 13 (rounded up from 12.4)]. Therefore, Juanita and Alberto's child tax credit is $1,350.

10-5c Credit for Child and Dependent Care Expenses

The **credit for child and dependent care expenses** mitigates the inequity felt by working taxpayers who must pay for child care services to work outside the home.[66] This credit is a specified percentage of expenses incurred to enable the taxpayer to work or to seek employment. Expenses on which the credit for child and dependent care expenses is based are subject to limitations.

Eligibility

To be eligible for the credit, an individual must have either of the following:

- A dependent under age 13.
- A dependent or spouse who is physically or mentally incapacitated and who lives with the taxpayer for more than one-half of the year.

Generally, married taxpayers must file a joint return to obtain the credit.

Eligible Employment-Related Expenses

Eligible expenses include amounts paid for household services and care of a qualifying individual that are incurred to enable the taxpayer to be employed. Child and dependent care expenses include expenses incurred in the home, such as payments for a housekeeper. Out-of-the-home expenses incurred for the care of a dependent under the age of 13 also qualify for the credit. In addition, out-of-the-home expenses incurred for an older dependent or spouse who is physically or mentally incapacitated qualify for the credit if that person regularly spends at least eight hours each day in the taxpayer's household. This makes the credit available to taxpayers who keep handicapped older children and elderly relatives in the home instead of institutionalizing them. Out-of-the-home expenses incurred for services provided by a dependent care center will qualify only if the center complies with all applicable laws and regulations of a state or unit of local government.

Child care payments to a relative are eligible for the credit unless the relative is a child (under age 19) of the taxpayer.

Earned Income Ceiling

Qualifying employment-related expenses are limited to an individual's earned income. For married taxpayers, this limitation applies to the spouse with the lesser

---

[64]AGI is modified for purposes of this calculation. The threshold amounts are *not* indexed for inflation. See §§ 24(a) and (b).
[65]The child tax credit is generally refundable to the extent of 15% of the taxpayer's earned income in excess of an inflation-adjusted amount. The American Recovery and Reinvestment Tax Act of 2009 set this amount at $3,000 for 2009 and 2010, and subsequent legislation extends this modification through 2017. Prior to ARRTA of 2009, the 2009 threshold was $12,550.
[66]§ 21.

amount of earned income. Special rules are provided for taxpayers with nonworking spouses who are disabled or are full-time students. If a nonworking spouse is physically or mentally disabled or is a full-time student, he or she is deemed to have earned income for purposes of this limitation. The deemed amount is $250 per month if there is one qualifying individual in the household or $500 per month if there are two or more qualifying individuals in the household. In the case of a student-spouse, the student's income is deemed to be earned only for the months the student is enrolled on a full-time basis at an educational institution.[67]

Calculation of the Credit

In general, the credit is equal to a percentage of unreimbursed employment-related expenses up to $3,000 for one qualifying individual and $6,000 for two or more individuals. The credit rate varies between 20 percent and 35 percent, depending on the taxpayer's AGI. The following chart shows the applicable percentage for taxpayers as AGI increases:

Adjusted Gross Income		Applicable Rate of Credit
Over	But Not Over	
$ 0	$15,000	35%
15,000	17,000	34%
17,000	19,000	33%
19,000	21,000	32%
21,000	23,000	31%
23,000	25,000	30%
25,000	27,000	29%
27,000	29,000	28%
29,000	31,000	27%
31,000	33,000	26%
33,000	35,000	25%
35,000	37,000	24%
37,000	39,000	23%
39,000	41,000	22%
41,000	43,000	21%
43,000	No limit	20%

Example 32

Nancy, who has two children under age 13, worked full-time while her spouse, Ron, attended college for 10 months during the year. Nancy earned $22,000 and incurred $6,200 of child care expenses. Ron is deemed to be fully employed and to have earned $500 for each of the 10 months (or a total of $5,000). Because Nancy and Ron have AGI of $22,000, they are allowed a credit rate of 31%. Nancy and Ron are limited to $5,000 in qualified child care expenses ($6,000 maximum expenses, limited to Ron's deemed earned income of $5,000). Therefore, they are entitled to a tax credit of $1,550 (31% × $5,000) for the year.

10-5d Education Tax Credits

Two credits, the **American Opportunity credit** and the **lifetime learning credit**,[68] are available to help qualifying low- and middle-income individuals defray the cost of higher education. The credits are available for qualifying tuition and related expenses incurred by students pursuing undergraduate or graduate degrees or

---

[67]§ 21(d).

[68]§ 25A. The HOPE scholarship credit was modified and renamed the American Opportunity tax credit by the American Recovery and Rein-

vestment Tax Act of 2009 for the 2009 and 2010 tax years. Subsequent legislation extends this credit through 2017. Without congressional intervention, the HOPE scholarship credit will return in 2018.

TAX IN THE NEWS Millions Are Wrongly Claiming Tax Credits

An estimated 2.1 million taxpayers may have received $3.2 billion in erroneous education credits, according to a report from the Treasury Inspector General for Tax Administration (TIGTA). The American Recovery and Reinvestment Act of 2009 created a refundable tax credit—the American Opportunity Tax Credit—to help taxpayers offset the cost of higher education. TIGTA found that 1.7 million taxpayers erroneously received an estimated $2.6 billion in education credits even though the Internal Revenue Service had no supporting documentation that these taxpayers had attended an eligible institution, defined as an accredited institution of higher learning. In addition, TIGTA found that almost 400,000 taxpayers received an estimated $550 million in education credits for which they were not eligible because they did not attend college for the required amount of time and/or were post-graduate students.

"Based on the results of our review, the IRS does not have effective processes to identify taxpayers who claim erroneous education credits," said J. Russell George, Treasury Inspector General for Tax Administration. "If not addressed, this could result in up to $12.8 billion in potentially erroneous refunds over four years," Mr. George added.

In a different report released in August 2013, TIGTA said that the IRS issued $11.6 billion to $13.6 billion in improper earned income tax credits in 2012, representing 21 to 25 percent of all payments in that category for the year. The numbers show an improvement of more than 15 percent compared with 2011, but they are still higher than the $11.2 billion to $13.3 billion range in 2009.

As part of their investigations, TIGTA made a number of recommendations to the IRS. In response, the IRS indicated that it has begun to take steps to increase monitoring and improve compliance.

Sources: Based on Stephen Dinan, "$3.2 Billion Wrongly Taken in Tuition Tax Credits," *Washington Times*, October 20, 2011; Bernie Becker, "Millions Are Wrongly Claiming Education Tax Credit," *The Hill*, October 20, 2011; Treasury Inspector General for Tax Administration Report 2013-40-084 (August 28, 2013).

vocational training. Books and other course materials are eligible for the American Opportunity credit (but not the lifetime learning credit).[69] Room and board are ineligible for both credits.

Maximum Credit

The American Opportunity credit permits a maximum credit of $2,500 per year (100 percent of the first $2,000 of tuition expenses plus 25 percent of the next $2,000 of tuition expenses) for the *first four years* of postsecondary education.[70] The lifetime learning credit permits a credit of 20 percent of qualifying expenses (up to $10,000 per year) incurred in a year in which the American Opportunity credit is not claimed with respect to a given student. Generally, the lifetime learning credit is used for individuals who are beyond the first four years of postsecondary education.

Eligible Individuals

Both education credits are available for qualified expenses incurred by a taxpayer, taxpayer's spouse, or taxpayer's dependent. The American Opportunity credit is available per eligible student, while the lifetime learning credit is calculated per taxpayer. To be eligible for the American Opportunity credit, a student must take at least one-half of the full-time course load for at least one academic term at a qualifying educational institution. No comparable requirement exists for the lifetime learning credit. Therefore, taxpayers who are seeking new job skills or maintaining existing skills through graduate training or continuing education are eligible for the lifetime learning credit. Taxpayers who are married must file a joint return to claim either education credit.

[69]§ 25A(i)(3).

[70]For years prior to 2009, the qualifying expense base for the HOPE scholarship credit was subject to inflation adjustment. The base was $1,200 in 2008 and $1,100 in 2007.

Income Limitations and Refundability

Both education credits are subject to income limitations.[71] In addition, the American Opportunity credit is partially refundable and may be used to offset a taxpayer's alternative minimum tax (AMT) liability (the lifetime learning credit is neither refundable nor an AMT liability offset).

The American Opportunity credit amount is phased out beginning when the taxpayer's AGI (modified for this purpose) reaches $80,000 ($160,000 for married taxpayers filing jointly).[72] The reduction is equal to the extent to which AGI exceeds $80,000 ($160,000 for married taxpayers filing jointly) as a percentage of a $10,000 phaseout range ($20,000 for married taxpayers filing jointly). As a result, the credit is completely eliminated when modified AGI reaches $90,000 ($180,000 for married taxpayers filing jointly). The entire credit allowed may be used to reduce a taxpayer's AMT liability. In addition, 40 percent of the American Opportunity credit is refundable.[73]

In 2014, the lifetime learning credit amount is phased out beginning when the taxpayer's AGI (modified for this purpose) reaches $54,000 ($108,000 for married taxpayers filing jointly). The reduction is equal to the extent to which AGI exceeds $54,000 ($108,000 for married filing jointly) as a percentage of a $10,000 ($20,000 for married filing jointly) phaseout range. The credit is completely eliminated when AGI reaches $64,000 ($128,000 for married filing jointly).

Example 33

Tom and Jennifer are married; file a joint tax return; have modified AGI of $158,000; and have two children, Lora and Sam. Tom and Jennifer paid $7,500 of tuition and $8,500 for room and board for Lora (a freshman) and $8,100 of tuition plus $7,200 for room and board for Sam (a junior). Both Lora and Sam are full-time students and are Tom and Jennifer's dependents. Lora's tuition and Sam's tuition are qualified expenses for the American Opportunity credit. For 2014, Tom and Jennifer may claim a $2,500 American Opportunity credit for both Lora's and Sam's expenses [(100% × $2,000) + (25% × $2,000)]. So, in total, they qualify for a $5,000 American Opportunity credit.

Example 34

Assume the same facts as in Example 33, except that Tom and Jennifer's modified AGI for 2014 is $172,000, instead of $158,000. Tom and Jennifer are eligible to claim a $2,000 American Opportunity credit for 2014. The potential $5,000 American Opportunity credit must be reduced because their modified AGI exceeds the $160,000 limit for married taxpayers. The percentage reduction is computed as the amount by which modified AGI exceeds the limit, expressed as a percentage of the phaseout range, or [($172,000 − $160,000)/$20,000], resulting in a 60% reduction. Therefore, the maximum available credit for 2014 is $2,000 ($5,000 × 40% allowable portion).

Restrictions on Double Tax Benefit

Taxpayers are prohibited from receiving a double tax benefit associated with qualifying educational expenses. Therefore, taxpayers who claim an education credit may not deduct the expenses, nor may they claim the credit for amounts that are otherwise excluded from gross income (e.g., scholarships and employer-paid educational assistance). However, a taxpayer may claim an education tax credit and exclude from gross income amounts distributed from a Coverdell Education Savings Account (CESA) as long as the distribution is not used for the same expenses for which the credit is claimed.

10-5e Earned Income Credit

The **earned income credit**, which has been a part of the law for many years, has been justified as a means of providing tax equity to the working poor. In addition, the credit has been designed to help offset regressive taxes, such as the gasoline

---

[71]In 2008 and prior years, the HOPE scholarship and lifetime learning credits were combined and subject to a single modified AGI limitation.

[72]These amounts are not adjusted for inflation.

[73]If the credit is claimed for a taxpayer subject to § 1(g) (the "kiddie tax"), the credit is not refundable.

tax, that impose a relatively larger burden on low-income taxpayers. Further, the credit is intended to encourage economically disadvantaged individuals to become contributing members of the workforce.[74]

Eligibility Requirements

Eligibility for the credit depends not only on whether the taxpayer meets the earned income and AGI thresholds but also on whether he or she has a qualifying child. The term *qualifying child* generally has the same meaning here as it does for purposes of determining who qualifies as a dependent.

In addition to being available for taxpayers with qualifying children, the earned income credit is also available to certain workers without children. However, this provision is available only to such taxpayers ages 25 through 64 who cannot be claimed as a dependent on another taxpayer's return.

Amount of the Credit

The earned income credit is determined by multiplying a maximum amount of earned income by the appropriate credit percentage. Generally, earned income includes employee compensation and net earnings from self-employment but excludes items such as interest, dividends, pension benefits, nontaxable employee compensation, and alimony. If a taxpayer has children, the credit percentage used in the calculation depends on the number of qualifying children. For 2009 through 2017, Congress has increased the credit percentage for families with three or more children and increased the phaseout threshold amounts for married taxpayers filing joint returns. Thus, in 2014, the maximum earned income credit is $3,305 ($9,720 × 34%) for a taxpayer with one qualifying child, $5,460 ($13,650 × 40%) for a taxpayer with two qualifying children, and $6,143 ($13,650 × 45%) for a taxpayer with three or more qualifying children. However, the maximum earned income credit is phased out completely if the taxpayer's earned income or AGI exceeds certain thresholds. To the extent the greater of earned income or AGI exceeds $23,260 in 2014 for married taxpayers filing a joint return ($17,830 for other taxpayers), the difference, multiplied by the appropriate phaseout percentage, is subtracted from the maximum earned income credit.

It is not necessary for the taxpayer to actually compute the earned income credit. To simplify the compliance process, the IRS issues an Earned Income Credit Table for determining the appropriate amount of the credit. This table and a worksheet are included in the instructions available to individual taxpayers.

REFOCUS ON THE BIG PICTURE

THE TAX IMPLICATIONS OF LIFE!

While Donna and David's wages and salaries of $70,000 are taxable, they should be aware that their employers may have provided them with a number of tax-free fringe benefits. In addition, if Donna and David paid monthly premiums for accident and health care plans or contributed to a flexible spending account, those amounts may reduce their taxable income (these items are discussed more fully in Chapter 11). The good news is that the $10,000 gift received from Donna's grandmother can be excluded from gross income. However, the $250 of interest earned on the money is taxable, as is the $1,500 bonus Donna earned at the CPA firm.

Donna's tuition waiver of $6,000 and the related payments of $400 per month are intended as a form of compensation. Therefore, she must include both of these in her gross income. However, insofar as the damages awards are concerned, all of the compensatory damages of $215,000 can be excluded from gross income because they relate to personal physical injury or sickness. However the punitive damages of $160,000 must be included in Donna's gross income.

---

[74]§ 32. This credit is subject to indexation.

Donna and David have several deductions *for* adjusted gross income. In addition to the alimony paid by David, $3,000 of the capital loss from the stock sale is deductible *for* AGI and interest on the qualified student loan is deductible *for* AGI (subject to a phaseout).

While medical expenses, state income taxes, personal property taxes, and charitable contributions are deductible *from* AGI, Donna and David should claim the standard deduction for a married couple as it appears to exceed their itemized deductions.

Donna and David will claim three personal and dependency exemptions—one for each spouse and one for David's son. They will determine their tax liability using the tax rate schedule for married couples filing a joint return.

Donna and David may be eligible for one or more tax credits, including the child tax credit and an education tax credit related to the tuition paid by Donna. If Stephen has unearned income in excess of certain thresholds, Donna and David should be made aware of the potential "kiddie" tax problem.

What If?

What if Donna and David purchase a house in the current year? What are the likely tax implications of owning a new home? If Donna and David purchase a new home, mortgage interest and property taxes paid on the home are treated as additional itemized deductions. Depending on the amount of these deductions, Donna and David's itemized deductions might then exceed the standard deduction amount, giving them a larger tax deduction and reducing their tax liability even more.

© wavebreakmedia ltd/Shutterstock.com

Suggested Readings

James A. Beavers, "No Deduction for Donating Right to Burn House," *The Tax Adviser,* September 2012.

David J. Hess and Lois D. Bryan, "Using An IRA for A Planned Charitable Gift," *Practical Tax Strategies,* March 2012.

Mark Jackson, "Unintended Consequences of the Earned Income Tax Credit," *Practical Tax Strategies,* February 2013.

M. Jill Lockwood, Britton McKay, and Michael Wiggins, "Tax Planning for Divorce: Avoiding the Pitfalls," *Practical Tax Strategies,* September 2012.

Matthew A. Melone, "Sophy's Choice: Applying the Mortgage Interest Debt Limitations," *Practical Tax Strategies,* July 2013.

Key Terms

Accident and health insurance benefits, 10-9

Acquisition indebtedness, 10-19

Adoption expenses credit, 10-29

Alimony and separate maintenance payments, 10-3

American Opportunity credit, 10-31

Capital gain property, 10-24

Charitable contribution, 10-21

Child tax credit, 10-29

Compensatory damages, 10-8

Credit for child and dependent care expenses, 10-30

Earned income credit, 10-33

Educational savings bonds, 10-10

Health Savings Account (HSA), 10-13

Home equity loans, 10-19

Investment interest, 10-18

Lifetime learning credit, 10-31

Medical expenses, 10-12

Miscellaneous itemized deductions, 10-26

Net investment income, 10-18

Ordinary income property, 10-24

Points, 10-20

Punitive damages, 10-8

Qualified residence interest, 10-19

Scholarship, 10-7

WWW **For the latest in changes to tax legislation, visit www.cengagebrain.com**

Problems

Issue ID

1. **LO.I** William and Abigail, who live in San Francisco, have been experiencing problems with their marriage. They have a 3-year-old daughter, April, who stays with William's parents during the day because both William and Abigail are employed. Abigail worked to support William while he attended medical school, and now she has been accepted by a medical school in Mexico. Abigail has decided to divorce William and attend medical school. April will stay in San Francisco because of her strong attachment to her grandparents and because they can provide her with excellent day care. Abigail knows that William will expect her to contribute to the cost of raising April. Abigail also believes that to finance her education, she must receive cash for her share of the property they accumulated during their marriage. In addition, she believes that she should receive some reimbursement for her contribution to William's support while he was in medical school. She expects the divorce proceedings to take several months. Identify the relevant tax issues for Abigail.

Decision Making

2. **LO.I** Alicia and Rafel are in the process of negotiating a divorce agreement. They both worked during the marriage and contributed an equal amount to the marital assets. They own a home with a fair market value of $400,000 (cost of $300,000) that is subject to a mortgage of $250,000. They have lived in the home for 12 years. They also have investment assets with a cost of $160,000 and a fair market value of $410,000. Thus, the net worth of the couple is $560,000 ($400,000 − $250,000 + $410,000). The holding period for the investments is longer than one year. Alicia would like to continue to live in the house. Therefore, she has proposed that she receive the residence subject to the mortgage, a net value of $150,000. In addition, she would receive $17,600 each year for the next 10 years, which has a present value (at 6% interest) of $130,000. Rafel would receive the investment assets. If Rafel accepts this plan, he must sell one-half of the investments so that he can purchase a home. Assume that you are counseling Alicia. Explain to Alicia whether the proposed agreement would be "fair" on an after-tax basis.

3. **LO.I** For each of the following, determine the amount that should be included in gross income:
   a. Peyton was selected the most valuable player in the Super Bowl. In recognition of this, he was awarded an automobile with a value of $60,000. Peyton did not need the automobile, so he asked that the title be put in his parents' names.
   b. Jacob was awarded the Nobel Peace Prize. When he was presented the check for $1.4 million, Jacob said, "I do not need the money. Give it to the United Nations to use toward the goal of world peace."
   c. Linda won the Craig County Fair beauty pageant. She received a $10,000 scholarship that paid her $6,000 for tuition and $4,000 for meals and housing for the academic year.

Critical Thinking

Decision Making

4. **LO.I** Linda and Don are married and file a joint return. In 2014, they received $12,000 in Social Security benefits and $35,000 in taxable pension benefits and interest.
   a. Compute the couple's adjusted gross income on a joint return.
   b. Don would like to know whether they should sell for $100,000 (at no gain or loss) a corporate bond that pays 8% in interest each year and use the proceeds to buy a $100,000 nontaxable State of Virginia bond that will pay $6,000 in interest each year.
   c. If Linda in (a) works part-time and earns $30,000, how much will Linda and Don's adjusted gross income increase?

5. **LO.I** Adrian was awarded an academic scholarship to State University for the 2014–2015 academic year. He received $6,500 in August and $7,200 in December 2014. Adrian had enough personal savings to pay all expenses as they came due. Adrian's expenditures for the relevant period were as follows:

Tuition, August 2014	$3,700
Tuition, January 2015	3,750
Room and board	
August–December 2014	2,800
January–May 2015	2,500
Books and educational supplies	
August–December 2014	1,000
January–May 2015	1,200

Determine the effect on Adrian's gross income for 2014 and 2015.

6. **LO.1** Leigh sued an overzealous bill collector and received the following settlement:

Damage to her automobile that the collector attempted to repossess	$ 3,300
Physical damage to her arm caused by the collector	15,000
Loss of income while her arm was healing	6,000
Punitive damages	80,000

   a. What effect does the settlement have on Leigh's gross income?
   b. Assume that Leigh also collected $25,000 of damages for slander to her personal reputation caused by the bill collector misrepresenting the facts to Leigh's employer and other creditors. Is this $25,000 included in Leigh's gross income? Explain.

7. **LO.2** Emma Doyle, age 55, is employed as a corporate attorney. For calendar year 2014, she had AGI of $100,000 and paid the following medical expenses:

Communications

Medical insurance premiums	$3,700
Doctor and dentist bills for Bob and April (Emma's parents)	6,800
Doctor and dentist bills for Emma	5,200
Prescription medicines for Emma	400
Nonprescription insulin for Emma	350

   Bob and April would qualify as Emma's dependents, except that they file a joint return. Emma's medical insurance policy does not cover them. Emma filed a claim for reimbursement of $2,800 of her own expenses with her insurance company in December 2014 and received the reimbursement in January 2015. What is Emma's maximum allowable medical expense deduction for 2014? Prepare a memo for your firm's tax files in which you document your conclusions.

8. **LO.2** Michael has always been overweight, and now he has decided to do something about it. He recently read in a news story that the IRS allows a medical expense deduction for the cost of certain weight reduction programs. He scheduled an appointment with his doctor to discuss enrolling in the clinic's weight reduction program and mentioned that he was happy that he would be able to deduct the cost. His doctor, who was familiar with the IRS's position, informed Michael that he was 10 pounds below the weight considered obese under the IRS guidelines and would not be able to take the medical expense deduction. Michael scheduled another appointment and proceeded to eat much more than usual for the next month. He returned 20 pounds heavier than at the first appointment and joked with the doctor that he now qualified for the medical expense deduction. Discuss whether Michael is justified in deducting the cost of the weight reduction program.

Ethics and Equity

9. **LO.1, 2** A local ophthalmologist's advertising campaign included a certificate for free LASIK eye surgery for the lucky winner of a drawing. Ahmad held the winning ticket, which was drawn in December 2013. Ahmad had no vision problems and was uncertain what he should do with the prize. In February 2014, Ahmad's daughter, who lives with his former wife, was diagnosed with a vision problem that could be treated with either prescription glasses or LASIK eye surgery. The divorce decree requires that Ahmad pay all medical expenses incurred for his daughter. Identify the relevant tax issues for Ahmad.

Issue ID

10. **LO.2** Paul, age 62, suffers from emphysema and severe allergies and, upon the recommendation of his physician, has a dust elimination system installed in his personal residence. In connection with the system, Paul incurs and pays the following amounts during 2014.

Doctor and hospital bills	$ 2,500
Dust elimination system	10,000
Increase in utility bills due to the system	450
Cost of certified appraisal	300

In addition, Paul pays $750 for prescribed medicines.
   The system has an estimated useful life of 20 years. The appraisal was to determine the value of Paul's residence with and without the system. The appraisal states that his residence was worth $350,000 before the system was installed and $356,000 after the

installation. Paul's AGI for the year was $50,000. How much of the medical expenses qualify for the medical expense deduction in 2014?

11. **LO.2** Norma, who uses the cash method of accounting, lives in a state that imposes an income tax. In April 2014, she files her state income tax return for 2013 and pays an additional $1,000 in state income taxes. During 2014, her withholdings for state income tax purposes amount to $7,400, and she pays estimated state income tax of $700. In April 2015, she files her state income tax return for 2014, claiming a refund of $1,800. Norma receives the refund in August 2015.

   a. Assuming that Norma itemized deductions in 2014, how much may she claim as a deduction for state income taxes on her Federal return for calendar year 2014 (filed in April 2015)?

   b. Assuming that Norma itemized deductions in 2014, how will the refund of $1,800 that she received in 2015 be treated for Federal income tax purposes?

   c. Assume that Norma itemized deductions in 2014 and that she elects to have the $1,800 refund applied toward her 2015 state income tax liability. How will the $1,800 be treated for Federal income tax purposes?

   d. Assuming that Norma did not itemize deductions in 2014, how will the refund of $1,800 received in 2015 be treated for Federal income tax purposes?

Decision Making

Communications

Critical Thinking

12. **LO.2** In 2014, Kathleen Tweardy incurs $30,000 of interest expense related to her investments. Her investment income includes $7,500 of interest, $6,000 of qualified dividends, and a $12,000 net capital gain on the sale of securities. Kathleen asks you to compute the amount of her deduction for investment interest, taking into consideration any options she might have. In addition, she wants your suggestions as to any tax planning alternatives that are available. Write a letter to her that contains your advice. Kathleen lives at 11934 Briarpatch Drive, Midlothian, VA 23113.

Critical Thinking

13. **LO.2** Helen borrowed $150,000 to acquire a parcel of land to be held for investment purposes. During 2014, she paid interest of $12,000 on the loan. She had AGI of $90,000 for the year. Other items related to Helen's investments include the following:

Investment income	$11,000
Long-term capital gain on sale of stock	3,500
Investment counsel fees	100

   Helen is unmarried and does not itemize her deductions.

   a. Determine Helen's investment interest deduction for 2014.

   b. Discuss the treatment of the portion of Helen's investment interest that is disallowed in 2014.

14. **LO.2** In 2005, Roland, who is single, purchased a personal residence for $340,000 and took out a mortgage of $200,000 on the property. In May of the current year, when the residence had a fair market value of $440,000 and Roland owed $140,000 on the mortgage, he took out a home equity loan for $220,000. He used the funds to purchase a recreational vehicle, which he uses 100% for personal use. What is the maximum amount on which Roland can deduct home equity interest?

Decision Making

Communications

15. **LO.2** Pedro contributes a painting to an art museum in October of this year. He has owned the painting for 12 years, and it is worth $130,000 at the time of the donation. Pedro's adjusted basis for the painting is $90,000, and his AGI for the year is $250,000. Pedro has asked you whether he should make the reduced deduction election for this contribution. Write a letter to Pedro Valdez at 1289 Greenway Avenue, Foster City, CA 94404, and advise him on this matter.

Decision Making

Communications

16. **LO.2** In December each year, Eleanor Young contributes 10% of her gross income to the United Way (a 50% organization). Eleanor, who is in the 28% marginal tax bracket, is considering the following alternatives for satisfying the contribution.

	Fair Market Value
(1) Cash donation	$23,000
(2) Unimproved land held for six years ($3,000 basis)	23,000
(3) Blue Corporation stock held for eight months ($8,000 basis)	23,000
(4) Gold Corporation stock held for two years ($28,000 basis)	23,000

Eleanor has asked you to help her decide which of the potential contributions listed above will be most advantageous taxwise. Evaluate the four alternatives and write a letter to Eleanor to communicate your advice to her. Her address is 2622 Bayshore Drive, Berkeley, CA 94709.

17. **LO.2** Ramon had AGI of $180,000 in 2014. He contributed stock in Charlton, Inc. (a publicly traded corporation), to the American Heart Association, a qualified charitable organization. The stock was worth $105,000 on the date it was contributed. Ramon had acquired it as an investment two years ago at a cost of $84,000.

    a. Assuming that Ramon carries over any disallowed contribution from 2014 to future years, what is the total amount he can deduct as a charitable contribution?
    b. What is the maximum amount Ramon can deduct as a charitable contribution in 2014?
    c. What factors should Ramon consider in deciding how to treat the contribution for Federal income tax purposes?
    d. Assume that Ramon dies in December 2014. What advice would you give the executor of his estate with regard to possible elections that can be made relative to the contribution?

Decision Making

18. **LO.2** Linda, age 37, who files as a single taxpayer, had AGI of $280,000 for 2014. She incurred the following expenses and losses during the year:

Medical expenses before the 10%-of-AGI limitation	$33,000
State and local income taxes	4,500
State sales tax	1,300
Real estate taxes	4,000
Home mortgage interest	5,000
Automobile loan interest	750
Credit card interest	1,000
Charitable contributions	7,000
Casualty loss before 10% limitation (after $100 floor)	34,000
Unreimbursed employee expenses subject to the 2%-of-AGI limitation	7,600

Calculate Linda's allowable itemized deductions for the year.

19. **LO.3** Ann and Bill were on the list of a local adoption agency for several years, seeking to adopt a child. Finally, in 2013, good news came their way, and an adoption seemed imminent. They paid qualified adoption expenses of $4,000 in 2013 and $11,000 in 2014. Assume that the adoption becomes final in 2014. Ann and Bill always file a joint income tax return.

    a. Determine the amount of the adoption expenses credit available to Ann and Bill assuming that their combined annual income is $100,000. In what year(s) will they benefit from the credit?
    b. Assuming that Ann and Bill's modified AGI in 2013 and 2014 is $200,000, calculate the amount of the adoption expenses credit.

20. **LO.3** Paul and Karen are married, and both are employed (Paul earns $44,000 and Karen earns $9,000 during 2014). Paul and Karen have two dependent children, both under the age of 13. So they can work, Paul and Karen pay $3,800 to various unrelated parties to care for their children while they are working. Assuming that Paul and Karen file a joint return, what, if any, is their tax credit for child and dependent care expenses?

21. **LO.3** Jim and Mary Jean are married and have two dependent children under the age of 13. Both parents are gainfully employed and during 2014 earn salaries as follows: $16,000 (Jim) and $5,200 (Mary Jean). To care for their children while they work, they pay Eleanor (Jim's mother) $5,600. Eleanor does not qualify as a dependent of Jim and Mary Jean. Assuming that Jim and Mary Jean file a joint tax return, what, if any, is their credit for child and dependent care expenses?

22. **LO.3** Bernadette, a longtime client of yours, is an architect and the president of the local Rotary chapter. To keep up to date with the latest developments in her profession, she attends continuing education seminars offered by the architecture school at State University. During 2014, Bernadette spends $2,000 on course tuition to attend such seminars. She also spends another $400 on architecture books during the year. Bernadette's son is a senior majoring in engineering at the University of the Midwest. During the 2014 calendar

Communications

year, Bernadette's son incurs the following expenses: $8,200 for tuition ($4,100 per semester) and $750 for books and course materials. Bernadette's son, whom she claims as a dependent, lives at home while attending school full-time. Bernadette is married, files a joint return, and has a combined AGI with her husband of $110,000.

a. Calculate Bernadette's education tax credit for 2014.

b. In her capacity as president of the local Rotary chapter, Bernadette has asked you to make a 30- to 45-minute speech outlining the different ways the tax law helps defray (1) the cost of higher education and (2) the cost of continuing education once someone is in the workforce. Prepare an outline of possible topics for presentation. A tentative title for your presentation is "How Can the Tax Law Help Pay for College and Continuing Professional Education?"

23. **LO.3** Briefly discuss the requirements that must be satisfied for a taxpayer to qualify for the earned income tax credit.

Ethics and Equity

24. **LO.3** For many years, Loretta Johnson, a single mother of three children, has been struggling to make ends meet by working at two jobs that pay barely the minimum wage and together provide just over $15,000. Fortunately, her housing and food costs have been partially subsidized through various government programs. In addition, she has been able to take advantage of the earned income credit, which has provided around $3,000 annually to help her with living expenses. The credit has truly made a difference in the lives of Loretta and her family by helping them keep their creditors at bay. She is proud that she has worked hard and provided for her family for many years without having to accept welfare.

Now, however, Loretta faces a problem as her children have grown up and moved out of her home. With no qualifying children in her household, she no longer qualifies for the earned income credit. Although she will continue working at her two jobs, such a significant loss to her household budget cuts into her ability to be self-reliant. As a survival strategy and as a way of keeping the earned income credit, Loretta arranges to have one of her grandchildren live with her for just over six months every year. This enables a significant percentage of her household budget to be secure. How do you react to Loretta's strategy?

Critical Thinking

Decision Making

25. **LO.3** Joyce, a widow, lives in an apartment with her two minor children (ages 8 and 10), whom she supports. Joyce earns $33,000 during 2014. She uses the standard deduction.

a. Calculate the amount, if any, of Joyce's earned income credit.

b. During the year, Joyce is offered a new job that has greater future potential than her current job. If she accepts the job offer, her earnings for the year will be $39,000; however, she is afraid she will not qualify for as much of the earned income credit. Using after-tax cash-flow calculations, determine whether Joyce should accept the new job offer.

Comprehensive Tax Return Problems

Tax Return Problem

Decision Making

TAX SOFTWARE

1. Alice J. and Bruce M. Byrd are married taxpayers who file a joint return. Their Social Security numbers are 123-45-6789 and 111-11-1111, respectively. Alice's birthday is September 21, 1966, and Bruce's is June 27, 1965. They live at 473 Revere Avenue, Lowell, MA 01850. Alice is the office manager for Lowell Dental Clinic, 433 Broad Street, Lowell, MA 01850 (employer identification number 98-765432). Bruce is the manager of a Super Burgers fast-food outlet owned and operated by Plymouth Corporation, 1247 Central Avenue, Hauppauge, NY 11788 (employer identification number 11-1111111).

The following information is shown on their Wage and Tax Statements (Form W–2) for 2013.

Line	Description	Alice	Bruce
1	Wages, tips, other compensation	$58,000	$62,100
2	Federal income tax withheld	4,500	6,300
3	Social Security wages	58,000	62,100
4	Social Security tax withheld	3,596	3,850
5	Medicare wages and tips	58,000	62,100
6	Medicare tax withheld	841	900
15	State	Massachusetts	Massachusetts
16	State wages, tips, etc.	58,000	62,100
17	State income tax withheld	2,950	3,100

The Byrds provide over half of the support of their two children, Cynthia (born January 25, 1989, Social Security number 123-45-6788) and John (born February 7, 1993, Social Security number 123-45-6786). Both children are full-time students and live with the Byrds except when they are away at college. Cynthia earned $4,200 from a summer internship in 2013, and John earned $3,800 from a part-time job.

During 2013, the Byrds furnished 60% of the total support of Bruce's widower father, Sam Byrd (born March 6, 1937, Social Security number 123-45-6787). Sam lived alone and covered the rest of his support with his Social Security benefits. Sam died in November, and Bruce, the beneficiary of a policy on Sam's life, received life insurance proceeds of $800,000 on December 28.

The Byrds had the following expenses relating to their personal residence during 2013:

Property taxes	$5,000
Qualified interest on home mortgage	8,800
Repairs to roof	5,750
Utilities	4,100
Fire and theft insurance	1,900

The following facts relate to medical expenses for 2013:

Medical insurance premiums	$4,500
Doctor bill for Sam incurred in 2012 and not paid until 2013	7,600
Operation for Sam	8,500
Prescription medicines for Sam	900
Hospital expenses for Sam	3,500
Reimbursement from insurance company, received in 2013	3,600

The medical expenses for Sam represent most of the 60% that Bruce contributed toward his father's support.

Other relevant information follows:

- When they filed their 2012 state return in 2013, the Byrds paid additional state income tax of $900.
- During 2013, Alice and Bruce attended a dinner dance sponsored by the Lowell Police Disability Association (a qualified charitable organization). The Byrds paid $300 for the tickets. The cost of comparable entertainment would normally be $50.
- The Byrds contributed $5,000 to Lowell Presbyterian Church and gave used clothing (cost of $1,200 and fair market value of $350) to the Salvation Army. All donations are supported by receipts, and the clothing is in very good condition.
- In 2013, the Byrds received interest income of $2,750, which was reported on a Form 1099–INT from Second National Bank.
- Alice's employer requires that all employees wear uniforms to work. During 2013, Alice spent $450 on new uniforms and $225 on laundry charges.
- Bruce paid $400 for an annual subscription to the *Journal of Franchise Management*.
- Neither Alice's nor Bruce's employer reimburses for employee expenses.
- The Byrds do not keep the receipts for the sales taxes they paid and had no major purchases subject to sales tax.
- Alice and Bruce paid no estimated Federal income tax. Neither Alice nor Bruce wants to designate $3 to the Presidential Election Campaign Fund.

Part 1—Tax Computation

Compute net tax payable or refund due for Alice and Bruce Byrd for 2013. If they have overpaid, they want the amount to be refunded to them. If you use tax forms for your computations, you will need Forms 1040 and 2106 and Schedules A and B. Suggested software: H&R BLOCK Tax Software.

Part 2—Tax Planning

Alice and Bruce are planning some significant changes for 2014. They have provided you with the following information and asked you to project their taxable income and tax liability for 2014.

The Byrds will invest the $800,000 of life insurance proceeds in short-term certificates of deposit (CDs) and use the interest for living expenses during 2014. They expect to earn total interest of $32,000 on the CDs.

Bruce has been promoted to regional manager, and his salary for 2014 will be $88,000. He estimates that state income tax withheld will increase by $4,000 and the Social Security tax withheld will be $5,456.

Alice, who has been diagnosed with a serious illness, will take a leave of absence from work during 2014. The estimated cost for her medical treatment is $15,400, of which $6,400 will be reimbursed by their insurance company in 2014. Their medical insurance premium will increase to $9,769.

John will graduate from college in December 2013 and will take a job in New York City in January 2014. His starting salary will be $46,000.

Assume that all of the information reported in 2013 will be the same in 2014 unless other information has been presented.

Tax Computation Problem

2. Paul and Donna Decker are married taxpayers, ages 44 and 42, respectively, who file a joint return for 2014. The Deckers live at 1121 College Avenue, Carmel, IN 46032. Paul is an assistant manager at Carmel Motor Inn, and Donna is a teacher at Carmel Elementary School. They present you with W–2 forms that reflect the following information:

	Paul	Donna
Salary	$68,000	$56,000
Federal tax withheld	6,770	6,630
State income tax withheld	900	800
FICA (Social Security and Medicare) withheld	5,202	4,284
Social Security numbers*	111-11-1111	123-45-6789

*In the interest of privacy and to protect against taxpayer identification misuse, Social Security numbers used throughout the textbook have been replaced with fictitious numbers.

Donna is the custodial parent of two children from a previous marriage who reside with the Deckers through the school year. The children, Larry and Jane Parker, reside with their father, Bob, during the summer. Relevant information for the children follows:

	Larry	Jane
Age	17	18
Social Security numbers	123-45-6788	123-45-6787
Months spent with Deckers	9	9

Under the divorce decree, Bob pays child support of $150 per month per child during the nine months the children live with the Deckers. Bob says that he spends $200 per month per child during the three summer months they reside with him. Donna and Paul can document that they provide $2,000 of support per child per year. The divorce decree is silent as to which parent can claim the exemptions for the children.

In August, Paul and Donna added a suite to their home to provide more comfortable accommodations for Hannah Snyder (Social Security number 123-45-6786), Donna's mother, who had moved in with them in February 2013 after the death of Donna's father. Not wanting to borrow money for this addition, Paul sold 300 shares of Acme Corporation stock for $50 per share on May 3, 2014, and used the proceeds of $15,000 to cover construction costs. The Deckers had purchased the stock on April 29, 2009, for $25 per share. They received dividends of $750 on the jointly owned stock a month before the sale.

Hannah, who is 66 years old, received $7,500 in Social Security benefits during the year, of which she gave the Deckers $2,000 to use toward household expenses and deposited the remainder in her personal savings account. The Deckers determine that they have spent $2,500 of their own money for food, clothing, medical expenses, and other items for Hannah. They do not know what the rental value of Hannah's suite would be, but they estimate it would be at least $300 per month.

Interest paid during the year included the following:

Home mortgage interest (paid to Carmel Federal Savings and Loan)	$7,890
Interest on an automobile loan (paid to Carmel National Bank)	1,660
Interest on Citibank Visa card	620

In July, Paul hit a submerged rock while boating. Fortunately, he was uninjured after being thrown from the boat and landing in deep water. However, the boat, which was uninsured, was destroyed. Paul had paid $25,000 for the boat in June 2013, and its value was appraised at $18,000 on the date of the accident.

The Deckers paid doctor and hospital bills of $10,700 and were reimbursed $2,000 by their insurance company. They spent $640 for prescription drugs and medicines and $5,904 for premiums on their health insurance policy. They have filed additional claims of $1,200 with their insurance company and have been told they will receive payment for that amount in January 2015. Included in the amounts paid for doctor and hospital bills were payments of $380 for Hannah and $850 for the children.

Additional information of potential tax consequence follows:

Real estate taxes paid	$3,850
Sales taxes paid (per table)	1,379
Contributions to church	1,950
Appraised value of books donated to public library	740
Paul's unreimbursed employee expenses to attend hotel management convention:	
Airfare	340
Hotel	170
Meals	95
Registration fee	340
Refund of state income tax for 2013 (the Deckers itemized on their 2013 Federal tax return)	1,520

Compute net tax payable or refund due for the Deckers for 2014. Ignore the child tax credit in your computations. If the Deckers have overpaid, the amount is to be credited toward their taxes for 2015.

BRIDGE DISCIPLINE

1. George comes to you asking for your advice. He wants to invest $10,000 either in a debt security or in an equity investment. His choices are shown below.

    *   Redbreast Corporation bond, annual coupon rate of 7.50%.
    *   City of Philadelphia general obligation bond, coupon rate of 6.00%.
    *   Blue Corporation 7.50% preferred stock (produces qualified dividend income).

    These alternatives are believed to carry comparable risk. Assuming that George is in the 35% marginal tax bracket, which investment alternative could be expected to produce the superior annual after-tax rate of return?

2. Assume the same facts as in Problem 1, except that George is a C corporation rather than an individual and is in the 34% marginal tax bracket. Which investment strategy would maximize George, Inc.'s annual return?

Research Problems

THOMSON REUTERS
CHECKPOINT®

Note: Solutions to Research Problems can be prepared by using the **Checkpoint®** **Student Edition** online research product, which is available to accompany this text. It is also possible to prepare solutions to the Research Problems by using tax research materials found in a standard tax library.

Research Problem 1. Aubrey Brown is a decorated veteran of the Vietnam War. As a result of his exposure to Agent Orange during the war, Aubrey developed lung cancer and is unable to work. He received $12,000 of Social Security disability payments in the current year. He reasons that the payments should be excluded from his gross income because the payments are compensation for the physical injury he suffered as a result of his service in the armed forces. Is Aubrey correct? Explain.

Partial list of research aids:
Rev.Rul. 77–318, 1977–2 C.B. 45.
Reimels v. Comm., 2006–1 USTC ¶50,147, 97 AFTR 2d 2006–820, 436 F.3d 344 (CA–2, 2006).

Research Problem 2. Tom and Mary Smith, whose son was found murdered in a parking garage, offered a $100,000 reward for the city police to use to obtain information leading to the arrest and conviction of the murderer. As a result of the reward, a person who had overheard the murderer telling a friend about the crime reported the conversation to the police. The murderer was arrested and convicted, and the Smiths contributed the money to the police department, which gave the reward to the informant. Can the Smiths treat the payment as an itemized deduction? Explain.

Research Problem 3. Ken and Mary Jane Blough, your neighbors, have asked you for advice after receiving correspondence in the mail from the IRS. You learn that the IRS is asking for documentation in support of the itemized deductions the Bloughs claimed on a recent tax return. The Bloughs tell you that their income in the year of question was $75,000. Because their record-keeping habits are poor, they felt justified in claiming itemized deductions equal to the amounts that represent the average claimed by other taxpayers in their income bracket. These averages are calculated and reported by the IRS annually based on actual returns filed in an earlier year. Accordingly, they claimed medical expenses of $7,102, taxes of $6,050, interest of $10,659, and charitable contributions of $2,693. What advice do you give the Bloughs?

Partial list of research aids:
Cheryl L. de Werff, T.C. Summary Opinion, 2011–29.

Internet Activity

Communications

Use the tax resources of the Internet to address the following questions. Do not restrict your search to the Web, but include a review of newsgroups and general reference materials, practitioner sites and resources, primary sources of the tax law, chat rooms and discussion groups, and other opportunities.

Research Problem 4. Go to the IRS website and download instructions and Regulations relative to educational savings bonds and qualified tuition programs. In outline format, summarize one of the key provisions in these materials.

Research Problem 5. The cutback adjustment that limits the amount of itemized deductions for some taxpayers is otherwise known as the Pease limitation. This limitation is named after former Congressman Donald Pease and was first in effect for tax years after December 31, 1990. The purpose of this limitation is to raise additional tax revenue by limiting some popular and common itemized deductions incurred by high-income taxpayers. One such deduction is the charitable contribution deduction. Search Google or a business press database to see what tax law analysts speculated the consequences would be of limiting charitable contribution deductions. Also determine whether such speculation has materialized.

CHAPTER

11

Individuals as Employees and Proprietors

LEARNING OBJECTIVES: *After completing Chapter 11, you should be able to:*

LO.1 Distinguish between employee and self-employed status.

LO.2 State and explain the exclusions from income available to employees who receive fringe benefits.

LO.3 Apply the rules for computing deductible expenses of employees, including transportation, travel, moving, education, and entertainment expenses.

LO.4 Appreciate the difference between accountable and nonaccountable employee plans and understand the

opportunities to build wealth through Individual Retirement Accounts.

LO.5 State and explain the tax provisions applicable to proprietors.

LO.6 Distinguish between business and hobby activities and apply the rules limiting the deduction of hobby losses.

CHAPTER OUTLINE

TAX TALK *The taxpayer—that's someone who works for the Federal government but doesn't have to take a civil service examination.* —RONALD REAGAN

Dennis Flaherty/Photographer's Choice/Getty Images

THE BIG PICTURE Tax Solutions for the Real World

SELF-EMPLOYED VERSUS EMPLOYEE—WHAT'S THE DIFFERENCE?

Mark and Mary Herman come to you for tax advice. Mark Herman is a self-employed consultant. Last year, Mark's business generated revenue of $165,000 and incurred expenses of $18,000 for rent and utilities for an office. Mark also spent $8,000 purchasing depreciable equipment used in the business and paid a part-time secretary $12,000 for administrative work performed during the year. He hired an assistant to help him in his consulting practice and paid her $40,000. Mark paid $3,000 for his own health insurance and $500 for term life insurance; he did not contribute to any retirement plans. Mary (Mark's wife) also works as a consultant, but is employed by a large firm. Her salary last year was $85,000. Mary's employer paid $3,000 of premiums for her health insurance and provided $50,000 of group term life insurance to each of its employees. Mary is not covered by a qualified retirement plan at work, but she contributed $5,500 to a traditional IRA. Mary routinely travels for her job and was reimbursed by her employer for all travel expenses. In addition, Mary spent $500 on other employee business expenses that were not reimbursed by her employer.

What are the tax consequences of these items? Can Mark and Mary deduct the expenses they incurred? Are there other tax planning opportunities the couple may be missing or tax issues of which they should be aware?

Read the chapter and formulate your response.

A n individual may be an employee or may be self-employed. The terms *proprietor* and *independent contractor* are both used to describe self-employed individuals. These terms are used interchangeably throughout this chapter. In many cases, it is difficult to distinguish between employees and self-employed individuals. This chapter begins with a discussion of the factors that must be considered in determining whether an individual is an employee or is self-employed. This is followed by a discussion of tax provisions applicable to employees and then by a discussion of tax provisions related to self-employed individuals.

11-1 EMPLOYEE VERSUS SELF-EMPLOYED

LO.1

Distinguish between employee and self-employed status.

When one person performs services for another, the person performing the services either is an employee or is self-employed (i.e., an **independent contractor**). Failure to recognize one's work status correctly can have serious consequences. Tax deficiencies as well as interest and penalties may result.

The determination of employment status is already controversial and can be expected to become an even greater problem in the future. As a means for achieving greater flexibility and cost control, businesses are increasingly relying on self-employed persons (i.e., independent contractors) rather than employees for many services.

The IRS is very much aware that businesses have a tendency to wrongly classify workers as self-employed rather than as employees. In some cases, misclassification is unintentional and results from difficulty in applying the complex set of rules related to employee versus independent contractor status. In other cases, misclassification may be an intentional strategy to avoid certain costs that are associated with employees. Unlike employees, self-employed persons do not have to be included in various fringe benefit programs and retirement plans. Furthermore, employers are not required to pay FICA and unemployment taxes (refer to Chapter 1) on compensation paid to independent contractors.

In terms of tax consequences, employment status also makes a great deal of difference to the worker. Allowable business expenses of self-employed taxpayers are classified as deductions *for* AGI and are reported on Schedule C (Profit or Loss from Business) of Form 1040.[1] On the other hand, unreimbursed business expenses incurred by employees are classified as itemized deductions and are deductible on Schedule A (as itemized deductions) only to the extent the sum of certain miscellaneous itemized deductions exceeds 2 percent of the taxpayer's AGI. Unreimbursed employee expenses are reported on Form 2106 (Employee Business Expenses) and Schedule A (Itemized Deductions) of Form 1040.

Employee expenses that are reimbursed under an **accountable plan** (covered later in this chapter) are also reported as deductions *for* AGI. Employee expenses that are not reimbursed under an accountable plan are treated in the same way as unreimbursed expenses—deductible *from* AGI and limited to the excess over 2 percent of AGI.[2]

11-1a Factors Considered in Classification

The pivotal issue in classifying an individual as an independent contractor or an employee is whether an employer-employee relationship exists. The IRS has created a complex *20-factor test* for determining whether a worker is an employee or an independent contractor. The courts, which have focused on a small number of these factors, generally hold that an individual is an employee if the individual or business acquiring the services:[3]

---

[1]§§ 62(a)(1) and 162(a).
[2]§ 67(a).

[3]Reg. § 31.3401(c)–(1)(b).

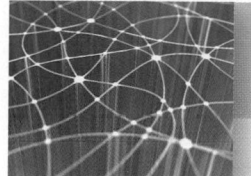

BRIDGE DISCIPLINE   Bridge to Equity or Fairness and Business Law

Max performs services for Calico, Inc. Amy performs services for Amber, Inc. They perform basically the same service. Yet, Max is classified as an employee, and Amy is classified as an independent contractor. Does such a legal classification produce equitable results in terms of the effects it has on Max and Amy?

Employee status produces a number of potential perks. Included are coverage in the employer's fringe benefits programs such as medical insurance, group term life insurance, and § 132 fringe benefits. For an employee, the current tax rate for Social Security is 6.2 percent and for Medicare, the rate is 1.45 percent (i.e., the employer is responsible for matching the employee amounts). For a self-employed person, the tax rates for Social Security and Medicare are 12.4 percent and 2.9 percent, respectively.

In distinguishing between an employee and an independent contractor, the overriding theme of common law is that the employee is subject to the will and control of the employer as to what is to be done and how it is to be done. Put in more legal terminology, an employer has the right to control and direct the individual who performs the services, not only as to the result to be accomplished by the work but also as to the details and means by which the result is accomplished. Among the factors generally considered in determining whether this right exists are the following:

- Degree of control exercised over the details of the work.
- Provision of facilities used in the work.
- Opportunity for profit or loss.
- Right to discharge.
- Whether work is part of regular business.
- Permanency of the relationship.
- Relationship that the parties believe they are creating.
- Manner of payment, by the job or by the hour.
- Skill required.
- Offering of the services to the general public rather than to one individual or entity.
- Distinct occupation or recognized trade or calling involved.
- Custom in the trade.

© iStockphoto.com/enot-poloskun

- Has the right to specify the end result and the ways and means by which that result is to be attained;
- Can exert will and control over the person providing the services with respect not only to *what* shall be done but also to *how* it shall be done;
- Has the right to discharge, without legal liability, the person performing the service;
- Furnishes tools or a place to work; and
- Bases payment on time spent rather than the task performed.

Each case is tested on its own merits, and the right to control the means and methods of accomplishment is the definitive test. Generally, physicians, lawyers, dentists, contractors, subcontractors, and others who offer services to the public are not classified as employees.

In-depth coverage can be found on this book's companion website: **www.cengagebrain.com** | Digging Deeper

THE BIG PICTURE

Example 1

Return to the facts of *The Big Picture* on p. 11-1. Mark is a consultant whose major client accounts for 60% of his billings. He does the routine consulting work at the client's request. He is paid a monthly retainer in addition to amounts charged for extra work. Mark is a self-employed individual. Even though most of his income comes from one client, he still has the right to determine *how* the end result of his work is attained.

THE BIG PICTURE

Example 2

Return to the facts of *The Big Picture* on p. 11-1. Ellen is a recent MBA graduate hired by Mark to assist him in the performance of services for the client mentioned in Example 1. Ellen is under Mark's supervision; he reviews her work and pays her an hourly fee. Ellen is Mark's employee.

Digging Deeper 2

In-depth coverage can be found on this book's companion website: **www.cengagebrain.com**

11-2 EXCLUSIONS AVAILABLE TO EMPLOYEES

LO.2

State and explain the exclusions from income available to employees who receive fringe benefits.

Several exclusions that are available to *all taxpayers* were discussed in Chapter 4; these include interest income on obligations of state and local governments, life insurance proceeds, and income from discharge of indebtedness. Other exclusions, available only to *individuals*, were discussed in Chapter 10; these exclusions include gifts and inheritances, scholarships, and compensation for injuries and sickness. Exclusions available only to *employees* are discussed next.

Tax Planning Strategies   SELF-EMPLOYED INDIVIDUALS

FRAMEWORK FOCUS: DEDUCTIONS

Strategy: Maximize Deductible Amounts.

Some taxpayers have the flexibility to be classified as either employees or self-employed individuals. Examples include real estate agents and direct sellers. These taxpayers should carefully consider all factors and not automatically assume that self-employed status is preferable.

It is advantageous to deduct one's business expenses *for* AGI and avoid the 2 percent floor for miscellaneous itemized deductions. However, a self-employed individual may incur additional expenses such as local gross receipts taxes, license fees, franchise fees, personal property taxes, and occupation taxes. Record-keeping and filing requirements can also be quite burdensome.

One of the most expensive considerations is the **self-employment tax** imposed on independent contractors and other self-employed individuals. For an employee in 2013

and 2014, for example, the Social Security tax applies at a rate of 6.2 percent on a base amount of wages of $113,700 in 2013, and $117,000 in 2014. The Medicare tax applies at a rate of 1.45 percent with no limit on the base amount.

For self-employed persons, the rate, but not the base amount, for each tax doubles. For 2013 and 2014, the Social Security rate is 12.4 percent, while the Medicare rate is 2.9 percent. Even though a deduction *for* AGI is allowed for one-half of the self-employment tax paid, an employee and a self-employed individual are not in the same tax position on equal amounts of earnings. For the applicability of these taxes to workers, see Chapter 1.

After analyzing all of these factors, taxpayers in many cases may decide that employee status is preferable to self-employed status.

11-2a Advantages of Qualified Fringe Benefits

Exclusions available only to *employees* are generally referred to as *qualified fringe benefits*. The popularity of fringe benefits is attributable to the fact that the cost of such benefits is deductible by employers and excludible by employees.

Example 3

Cardinal Corporation, which has a marginal tax rate of 35%, provides health insurance coverage to employees at a cost of $1,000 per employee. Because Cardinal can deduct the health insurance premiums paid to provide this coverage, the net cost to the corporation is $650 per employee ($1,000 cost − $350 tax savings). The employee is allowed to exclude the value of this fringe benefit, so there is no tax cost to the employee.

The average employee of Cardinal Corporation is in the 28% bracket. If Cardinal did not provide the health insurance coverage and the employee paid a $1,000 premium, the employee would have to use after-tax dollars to acquire the coverage. The employee would have to earn $1,389 to pay for the coverage [$1,389 wages − ($1,389 × 28% tax)]. The after-tax cost to the corporation of $1,389 in wages is $903 ($1,389 wages − $486 corporate tax savings). Thus, the cost of health insurance coverage is $253 less per employee ($903 − $650) because it is both deductible by the corporation and excludible by the employee.

11-2b Employer-Sponsored Accident and Health Plans

Congress encourages employers to provide employees, retired former employees, and their dependents with accident and health benefits, disability insurance, and long-term care plans. The *premiums* are deductible by the employer and are excluded from the employee's gross income.[4] Although § 105(a) provides the general rule that the employee has includible income when he or she collects the insurance *benefits*, two exceptions are provided.

Section 105(b) generally excludes payments received for medical care of the employee, spouse, and dependents. However, if the payments are for expenses that do not meet the Code's definition of medical care,[5] the amount received must be included in gross income. In addition, the taxpayer must include in gross income any amounts received for medical expenses that were deducted by the taxpayer on a prior return.

> **Example 4**
>
> Tab's employer-sponsored health insurance plan paid $4,000 for hair transplants that did not meet the Code's definition of medical care. Tab must include the $4,000 in his gross income.

Section 105(c) excludes payments for the permanent loss or the loss of the use of a member or function of the body or the permanent disfigurement of the employee, the spouse, or a dependent. However, payments that are a substitute for salary (e.g., related to the period of time absent) are included in income.

> **Example 5**
>
> Jill lost an eye in an automobile accident unrelated to her work. As a result of the accident, Jill incurred $2,000 of medical expenses, which she deducted on her return. She collected $10,000 from an accident insurance policy carried by her employer. The benefits were paid according to a schedule of amounts that varied with the part of the body injured (e.g., $10,000 for loss of an eye and $20,000 for loss of a hand). Because the payment was for loss of a *member or function of the body*, the $10,000 is excluded from Jill's gross income. Jill was absent from work for a week as a result of the accident. Her employer also provided her with insurance that reimbursed her for the loss of income due to illness or injury. Jill collected $500, which is includible in her gross income.

11-2c Medical Reimbursement Plans

As noted previously, the amounts received through the insurance coverage (insured plan benefits) are excluded from gross income under § 105. Unfortunately, because of cost considerations, the insurance companies that issue this type of policy usually require a broad coverage of employees. An alternative is to have a plan that is not funded with insurance (a self-insured arrangement). Under a self-insured plan, the employer reimburses employees directly for any medical expenses. The benefits received under a self-insured plan can be excluded from the employee's gross income if the plan does not discriminate in favor of highly compensated employees.

---

[4]§ 106, Reg. § 1.106–1, and Rev.Rul. 82–196, 1982–1 C.B. 106.   [5]See the discussion of medical care in Chapter 10.

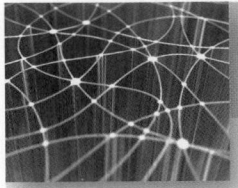
Archer **Medical Savings Accounts (MSAs)** provided an alternative means of accomplishing a medical reimbursement plan. The MSA had two parts: catastrophic insurance coverage that kicked in after the deductible had been paid and a savings account that could be tapped to pay the deductible and any uncovered medical expenses.

Later legislation created the **Health Savings Account (HSA)**, which broadened the concept of MSAs and extended it to a larger set of taxpayers.[6] See additional discussion in Chapter 10.

11-2d Long-Term Care Benefits

Generally, long-term care insurance, which covers expenses such as the cost of care in a nursing home, is treated the same as accident and health insurance benefits. Thus, the employee does not recognize income when the employer pays the premiums. This exclusion is subject to annual limits as follows:

Insured's Age before Close of Tax Year	2013	2014
40 or less	$ 360	$ 370
41 to 50	680	700
51 to 60	1,360	1,400
61 to 70	3,640	3,720
More than 70	4,550	4,660

When benefits are received from the policy, whether the employer or the individual purchased the policy, the exclusion from gross income is limited to the *greater* of the following amounts:

- $330 (indexed amount for 2014) for each day the patient receives the long-term care.
- The actual cost of the care.

The excludible amount is reduced by any amounts received from other third parties (e.g., damages received).[7]

[6]§ 223.　　　　[7]§ 7702B.

Example 6

Hazel, who suffers from Alzheimer's disease, was a patient in a nursing home for the last 30 days of 2014. While in the nursing home, she incurred total costs of $7,600. Medicare paid $3,200 of the costs. Hazel received $6,750 from her long-term care insurance policy (which paid $225 per day while she was in the facility). The amount Hazel may exclude is calculated as follows:

Greater of:		
Daily statutory amount of $330 ($330 × 30 days)	$9,900	
Actual cost of the care	7,600	$ 9,900
Less: Amount received from Medicare		(3,200)
Amount of exclusion		$ 6,700

Therefore, Hazel must include $50 ($6,750 − $6,700) of the long-term care benefits received in her gross income.

The exclusion for long-term care insurance is not available if it is provided as part of a cafeteria plan or a flexible spending plan (discussed later in this chapter).

11-2e Meals and Lodging Furnished for the Convenience of the Employer

Income can take any form, including meals and lodging. However, § 119 excludes from gross income the value of meals and lodging provided to the employee and the employee's spouse and dependents under the following conditions:[8]

- The meals and/or lodging are *furnished by the employer*, on the employer's *business premises*, for the *convenience of the employer*.
- In the case of lodging, the *employee is required* to accept the lodging as a condition of employment.

The courts have interpreted these requirements strictly, as discussed below.

Furnished by the Employer

The following two questions have been raised with regard to the *furnished by the employer* requirement:

- Who is considered an *employee*?
- What is meant by *furnished*?

For the employee issue, the IRS and some courts have reasoned that because a partner is not an employee, the exclusion does not apply to a partner. However, the Tax Court and the Fifth Circuit Court of Appeals have ruled in favor of the taxpayer on this issue.[9]

On the issue of whether meals and lodging are *furnished* by the employer, the Supreme Court held that a *cash meal allowance* was ineligible for the exclusion because the employer did not actually furnish the meals.[10] Similarly, one court denied the exclusion where the employer paid for the food and supplied the cooking facilities but the employee prepared the meal.[11]

On the Employer's Business Premises

The *on the employer's business premises* requirement, applicable to both meals and lodging, has resulted in much litigation. The Regulations define business premises as simply "the place of employment of the employee."[12] Thus, the Sixth Circuit Court of Appeals held that a residence, owned by the employer and occupied by an

---

[8]§ 119(a). The value of meals and lodging is also excluded from FICA and FUTA tax. *Rowan Companies, Inc. v. U.S.*, 81–1 USTC ¶9479, 48 AFTR 2d 81–5115, 101 S.Ct. 2288 (USSC, 1981).

[9]Rev.Rul. 80, 1953–1 C.B. 62; *Comm. v. Doak*, 56–2 USTC ¶9708, 49 AFTR 1491, 234 F.2d 704 (CA–4, 1956); but see *G. A. Papineau*, 16 T.C. 130 (1951); *Armstrong v. Phinney*, 68–1 USTC ¶9355, 21 AFTR 2d 1260, 394 F.2d 661 (CA–5, 1968).

[10]*Comm. v. Kowalski*, 77–2 USTC ¶9748, 40 AFTR 2d 6128, 98 S.Ct. 315 (USSC, 1977).

[11]*Tougher v. Comm.*, 71–1 USTC ¶9398, 27 AFTR 2d 1301, 441 F.2d 1148 (CA–9, 1971).

[12]Reg. § 1.119–1(c)(1).

employee, located two blocks from the motel that the employee managed was not part of the business premises.[13] However, the Tax Court considered an employer-owned house located across the street from the hotel that was managed by the taxpayer to be on the business premises of the employer.[14] Perhaps these two cases can be reconciled by comparing the distance from the lodging facilities to the place where the employer's business was conducted. The closer the lodging to the business operations, the more likely the convenience of the employer is served.

For the Convenience of the Employer

The *convenience of the employer* test is intended to focus on the employer's motivation for furnishing the meals and lodging rather than on the benefits received by the employee. If the employer furnishes the meals and lodging primarily to enable the employee to perform his or her duties properly, it does not matter that the employee considers these benefits to be a part of his or her compensation.

The Regulations give the following examples in which the tests for excluding meals are satisfied:[15]

- A waitress is required to eat her meals on the premises during the busy lunch and breakfast hours.
- A bank furnishes a teller meals on the premises to limit the time the employee is away from his booth during the busy hours.
- A worker is employed at a construction site in a remote part of Alaska. The employer must furnish meals and lodging due to the inaccessibility of other facilities.

If more than half of the meals provided to employees are furnished for the convenience of the employer, all such employee meals are treated as provided for the convenience of the employer. Thus, in this situation, all employees are treated the same (either all of the employees are allowed exclusion treatment or none of the employees can exclude the meals from gross income).

Example 7	Allison's Restaurant has a restaurant area and a bar. Nine employees work in the restaurant, and three work in the bar. All of the employees are provided one meal per day. In the case of the restaurant workers, the meals are provided for the convenience of the employer. The meals provided to the bar employees do not satisfy the convenience of the employer requirement. Because more than half of the employees receive their meal for the convenience of the employer, all 12 employees qualify for exclusion treatment.

Required as a Condition of Employment

The *required as a condition of employment* test applies only to lodging. If the employee's use of the housing would serve the convenience of the employer but the employee is not required to use the housing, the exclusion is not available.

Example 8	VEP, a utilities company, has all of its service personnel on 24-hour call for emergencies. The company encourages its employees to live near the plant so that they can respond quickly to emergency calls. Company-owned housing is available rent-free. Only 10 of the employees live in the company housing because it is not suitable for families. Although the company-provided housing serves the convenience of the employer, it is not required. Therefore, the employees who live in the company housing must include its value in gross income.

In addition, if the employee has the option of cash or lodging, the employer-required test is not satisfied.

Example 9	Khalid is the manager of a large apartment complex. The employer gives Khalid the option of rent-free housing (value of $9,600 per year) or an additional $7,500 per year. Khalid selects the housing option. Therefore, he must include $9,600 in gross income.

---

[13]*Comm. v. Anderson*, 67–1 USTC ¶9136, 19 AFTR 2d 318, 371 F.2d 59 (CA–6, 1966).

[14]*J. B. Lindeman*, 60 T.C. 609 (1973).

[15]Reg. § 1.119–1(f).

Other housing exclusions are available for certain employees of educational institutions, ministers of the gospel, and military personnel.

11-2f Group Term Life Insurance

For many years, the IRS did not attempt to tax the value of life insurance protection provided to an employee by the employer. Some companies took undue advantage of the exclusion by providing large amounts of insurance protection for key executives. In response, Congress enacted § 79, which created a limited exclusion for group term life insurance. Current law allows an exclusion of premiums on the first $50,000 of group term life insurance protection.

The benefits of this exclusion are available only to employees. Proprietors and partners are not considered employees. Moreover, the Regulations generally require broad-scale coverage of employees to satisfy the group requirement (e.g., shareholder-employees would not constitute a qualified group). The exclusion applies only to term insurance (protection for a period of time but with no cash surrender value) and not to ordinary life insurance (lifetime protection plus a cash surrender value that can be drawn upon before death).

As mentioned, the exclusion applies to the first $50,000 of group term life insurance protection. For each $1,000 of coverage in excess of $50,000, the employee must include the amounts indicated in Table 11.1 in gross income.[16]

In-depth coverage can be found on this book's companion website: **www.cengagebrain.com**      **3**   Digging Deeper

Example 10

Finch Corporation has a group term life insurance policy with coverage equal to the employee's annual salary. Keith, age 52, is president of the corporation and receives an annual salary of $75,000. Keith must include $69 in gross income from the insurance protection for the year.

$$[(\$75,000 - \$50,000) \div \$1,000] \times \$.23 \times 12 \text{ months} = \$69$$

If the plan discriminates in favor of certain key employees (e.g., officers), the key employees are not eligible for the exclusion. In such a case, the key employees must include in gross income the *greater* of actual premiums paid by the employer or the amount calculated from the Uniform Premiums table in Table 11.1. The other employees are still eligible for the $50,000 exclusion and continue to

TABLE 11.1	Uniform Premiums for $1,000 of Group Term Life Insurance Protection
5-Year Age Bracket	**Cost of $1,000 of Protection for a One-Month Period***
Under 25	$ .05
25–29	.06
30–34	.08
35–39	.09
40–44	.10
45–49	.15
50–54	.23
55–59	.43
60–64	.66
65–69	1.27
70 and above	2.06

*Reg. § 1.79–3, effective for coverage after June 30, 1999.

[16]Reg. § 1.79–3(d)(2).

TAX IN THE NEWS   Employee Tuition Assistance Offers Benefits to Employers Too

Some employers are reluctant to provide college tuition assistance to employees because they fear the employees may use the benefits to enhance their qualifications so that they can find a job with another employer. Recent studies, however, have consistently shown that tuition assistance programs tend to attract higher-quality employees who stay on the job longer with that employer.

Large employers are more likely to provide educational assistance. According to academic research, 85 percent of 1,000 surveyed large employers offered some form of tuition assistance. The employers see these programs as both a recruitment tool and a retention tool. More education enables the employees to enjoy upward mobility within the company, and retaining highly trained employees is becoming more important as the baby boomers start to retire and the labor market becomes more competitive.

Source: Based on Erin White, "Corporate Tuition Aid Appears to Keep Workers Loyal," *Wall Street Journal,* May 21, 2007, p. B4.

use the Uniform Premiums table to compute the income from excess insurance protection.[17]

11-2g Qualified Tuition Reduction Plans

Employees (including retired and disabled former employees) of nonprofit educational institutions are allowed to exclude a tuition waiver from gross income if the waiver is pursuant to a qualified tuition reduction plan.[18] The plan may not discriminate in favor of highly compensated employees. The exclusion applies to the employee, the employee's spouse, and the employee's dependent children. The exclusion also extends to tuition reductions granted by any nonprofit educational institution to employees of any other nonprofit educational institution (reciprocal agreements).

Example 11

ABC University allows the dependent children of XYZ University employees to attend ABC University with no tuition charge. XYZ University grants reciprocal benefits to the children of ABC University employees. The dependent children can also attend tuition-free the university where their parents are employed. Employees who take advantage of these benefits are not required to recognize gross income.

Generally, the exclusion is limited to undergraduate tuition waivers. However, in the case of teaching or research assistants, graduate tuition waivers may also qualify for exclusion treatment. According to Proposed Regulations, the exclusion is limited to the value of the benefit in excess of the employee's reasonable compensation.[19] Thus, a tuition reduction that is a substitute for cash compensation cannot be excluded.

Example 12

Susan is a graduate research assistant. She receives a $5,000 salary for 500 hours of service over a nine-month period. This pay, $10 per hour, is reasonable compensation for Susan's services. In addition, Susan receives a waiver of $6,000 for tuition. Susan may exclude the tuition waiver from gross income.

11-2h Other Specific Employee Fringe Benefits

Congress has dealt specifically with some other fringe benefits, which are summarized below.

- The employee can exclude from gross income the value of child and dependent care services paid for by the employer and incurred to enable the employee to work. The exclusion cannot exceed $5,000 per year ($2,500 if married and filing separately). For a married couple, the annual exclusion

---

[17]§ 79(d).

[18]§ 117(d).

[19]Prop.Reg. § 1.117–6(d).

TAX IN THE NEWS Providing a Feel-Good Fringe Benefit at a Low Cost

Employers can provide employees with a variety of fringe benefits that are eligible for exclusion treatment. One such benefit is the adoption expense exclusion (subject to a statutory indexed ceiling amount).

Adoption assistance programs offered by employers to employees enjoy a family-friendly image and are inexpensive to provide from a total labor force perspective. According to Hewitt Associates, a benefits consulting firm, only about .1 percent of eligible workers use the exclusion each year. Nevertheless, in the current economic environment, employers are reducing such programs as a way to cut costs. In 2009, employers offering adoption assistance programs fell to 10 percent, down from 22 percent in 2006, according to a survey of 522 employers by the Society for Human Resource Management. General Motors suspended its adoption assistance program five months before filing for bankruptcy.

International adoptions by U.S. parents have fallen 24 percent since 2004, with only 17,438 such adoptions taking place in 2008. At the same time adoption assistance programs are being cut, costs for international adoptions are increasing and now range between $15,000 and $40,000.

Source: Based on Sue Shellenbarger, "Targeting 'Feel-Good' Benefits," *Wall Street Journal,* July 8, 2009, p. D1.

cannot exceed the earned income of the spouse who has the lesser amount of earned income. For an unmarried taxpayer, the exclusion cannot exceed the taxpayer's earned income.[20]

- The value of the use of a gymnasium or other athletic facilities by employees, their spouses, and their dependent children may be excluded from an employee's gross income. The facilities must be on the employer's premises, and substantially all of the use of the facilities must be by employees and their family members.[21]

- Qualified employer-provided educational assistance (tuition, fees, books, and supplies) at the undergraduate and graduate levels is excludible from gross income. The exclusion does not cover meals, lodging, and transportation costs. In addition, it does not cover educational payments for courses involving sports, games, or hobbies. The exclusion is limited to a maximum of $5,250 annually.[22]

- The employee can exclude from gross income up to $13,190 of expenses incurred to adopt a child where the adoption expenses are paid or reimbursed by the employer under a qualified adoption assistance program.[23] The limit on the exclusion is the same even if the child has special needs (is not physically or mentally capable of caring for himself or herself). The exclusion is phased out over the AGI range from $197,880 to $237,880.

11-2i Cafeteria Plans

Generally, if an employee is offered a choice between cash and some other form of compensation, the employee is deemed to have constructively received the cash even when the noncash option is elected. Thus, the employee has gross income regardless of the option chosen.

An exception to this constructive receipt treatment is provided under the cafeteria plan rules. Under such a plan, the employee is permitted to choose between cash and nontaxable benefits (e.g., group term life insurance, health and accident protection, child care). If the employee chooses the otherwise nontaxable benefits, the cafeteria plan rules allow the benefits to be excluded from the employee's gross income.[24] **Cafeteria plans** provide tremendous flexibility in tailoring the employee

---

[20] § 129. The exclusion applies to the same types of expenses that, if paid by the employee (and not reimbursed by the employer), would be eligible for the credit for child and dependent care expenses, discussed in Chapter 10.

[21] § 132(j)(4).
[22] § 127.
[23] § 137.
[24] § 125.

TAX IN THE NEWS   Patient Protection and Affordable Care Act of 2010 Affects Flexible Spending Plans

Determining all of the tax ramifications of the 2010 health care law will take time. But already it is clear that companies will be modifying their flexible spending plans as a result of the legislation, if they haven't already done so. Beginning in 2013, the annual income exclusion under flexible benefit plans was reduced to $2,500. Also, with respect to medicines, only prescription drugs and insulin are eligible for reimbursement.

Source: Internal Revenue Code §§ 125(i) and 106(f).

pay package to fit individual needs. Some employees (usually the younger group) prefer cash, while others (usually the older group) will opt for the fringe benefit program. However, long-term care insurance cannot be part of a cafeteria plan. Thus, an employer that wants to provide long-term care benefits must provide such benefits separate from the cafeteria plan.[25]

Example 13

Hawk Corporation offers its employees (on a nondiscriminatory basis) a choice of any one or all of the following benefits:

Benefit	Cost
Group term life insurance	$ 200
Hospitalization insurance for family members	2,400
Child care payments	1,800
	$4,400

If a benefit is not selected, the employee receives cash equal to the cost of the benefit.

Kay, an employee, has a spouse who works for another employer that provides hospitalization insurance but no child care payments. Kay elects to receive the group term life insurance, the child care payments, and $2,400 of cash. Only the $2,400 must be included in Kay's gross income.

11-2j Flexible Spending Plans

Flexible spending plans (often referred to as flexible benefit plans) operate much like cafeteria plans. Under these plans, the employee accepts lower cash compensation (as much as $2,500) in return for the employer's agreement to pay certain costs the employer can pay without the employee recognizing gross income. For example, assume that the employer's health insurance policy does not cover dental expenses. The employee could estimate his or her dental expenses for the upcoming year and agree to a salary reduction equal to the estimated dental expenses. The employer then pays or reimburses the employee for the actual dental expenses incurred, up to the amount of the salary reduction. If the employee's actual dental expenses are less than the reduction in cash compensation, the employee cannot recover the difference. Hence, these plans are often referred to as *use or lose* plans. To avoid forfeiture of unpaid amounts, the IRS allows a payment until March 15 of the following year to count. As is the case for cafeteria plans, flexible spending plans cannot be used to pay long-term care insurance premiums.

11-2k General Classes of Excluded Benefits

An employer can provide a variety of economic benefits to employees. Under the all-inclusive concept of income, the benefits are taxable unless one of the provisions previously discussed specifically excludes the item from gross income. The amount of the income is the fair market value of the benefit. This reasoning can lead to results that Congress considers unacceptable, as illustrated in the following example.

[25]§ 125(f).

TAX IN THE NEWS   Employees Lose Some under "Use or Lose Plans"

Over 21 million Americans lose between $125 and $200 every year as a result of overfunding their flexible benefit accounts. If the employee overestimates the amount required to provide the flexible benefits, and thus the reduction in the employee's salary, the unused portion of the fund is forfeited to the employer. The total forfeited amounts exceed $2 billion annually. Thus, employees appear to be substantial losers under these "use-it-or-lose-it" plans. Even though employees can still be net beneficiaries from the portion of the accounts that is actually used, the employees simply are not maximizing the benefits.

Tax legislation has been proposed on several occasions recently to allow any unused amount in a flexible benefit account to be transferred to various types of employee retirement accounts or to otherwise carry over for the employee's benefit. To date, none of these proposals has been enacted.

However, in a recent Notice, the IRS announced that employers can now amend their plans to allow employees a grace period of two and one-half months. That is, the amount set aside in a calendar year plan can be used until March 15 of the following year. Employers will generally amend the plans to provide that payments made before March 15 of the current year be taken first from the beginning-of-the-year balance in the account.

Example 14

Vern is employed in New York as a ticket clerk for Trans National Airlines. Vern would like to visit his mother, who lives in Miami, Florida, but he has no money for plane tickets. Trans National has daily flights from New York to Miami that often leave with empty seats. The cost of a round-trip ticket is $500. If Trans National allows Vern to fly without charge to Miami, under the general gross income rules, Vern has income equal to the value of a ticket. Therefore, Vern must include $500 in gross income for the value of a trip to Miami.

If Trans National in Example 14 will allow employees to use resources that would otherwise be wasted, why should the tax laws interfere with the employee's decision to take advantage of the available benefit? Thus, to avoid the economic inefficiency that occurs in Example 14 and in similar situations, as well as to create uniform rules for fringe benefits, Congress established seven broad classes of nontaxable employee benefits:[26]

- No-additional-cost services.
- Qualified employee discounts.
- Working condition fringes.
- *De minimis* fringes.
- Qualified transportation fringes.
- Qualified moving expense reimbursements.
- Qualified retirement planning services.

No-Additional-Cost Services

Return to Example 14. This illustrates the reason for the no-additional-cost services type of fringe benefit. **No-additional-cost services** are excluded from an employee's gross income if all of the following conditions are satisfied:

- The employee receives services, as opposed to property.
- The employer does not incur substantial additional costs, including forgone revenue, in providing the services to the employee.
- The services must be from the same line of business in which the employee works.
- The services are offered to customers in the ordinary course of the business in which the employee works.[27]

---

[26]See, generally, § 132.   [27]Reg. § 1.132–2.

Example 15

In Example 14, although the airplane may burn slightly more fuel because Vern is aboard and Vern may receive the same meal or snacks as paying customers, the additional costs would not be substantial. Thus, the trip could qualify as a no-additional-cost service.

On the other hand, assume that Vern is given a reserved seat on a flight that is frequently full. The employer would be forgoing revenue to allow Vern to fly. This forgone revenue would be a substantial additional cost, and thus the benefit would be taxable to Vern.

Digging Deeper 4

In-depth coverage can be found on this book's companion website: **www.cengagebrain.com**

The no-additional-cost exclusion extends to the employee's spouse and dependent children and to retired and disabled former employees. In the Regulations, the IRS has conceded that partners who perform services for the partnership are employees for purposes of the exclusion.[28] However, the exclusion is not extended to highly compensated employees unless the benefit is available on a nondiscriminatory basis.

Qualified Employee Discounts

When the employer sells goods or services (other than no-additional-cost benefits just discussed) to the employee for a price that is less than the price charged regular customers, the employee ordinarily recognizes income equal to the discount. However, qualified employee discounts can be excluded from the gross income of the employee, subject to the following conditions and limitations:

- The exclusion is not available for discounted sales of real property (e.g., a house) or for personal property of the type commonly held for investment (e. g., common stocks).
- The property or services must be from the same line of business in which the employee works.
- In the case of property, the exclusion cannot exceed the gross profit component of the price to customers.
- In the case of services, the exclusion is limited to 20 percent of the customer price.[29]

Example 16

Silver Corporation, which operates a department store, sells a television set to a store employee for $300. The regular customer price is $500, and the gross profit rate is 25%. The corporation also sells the employee a service contract for $100. The regular customer price for the contract is $150. The employee must recognize income of $95, computed as follows:

Customer price for property	$ 500	
Less: Qualifying discount (25% gross profit × $500 price)	(125)	
	$ 375	
Employee price	(300)	
Excess discount recognized as income		$75
Customer price for service	$ 150	
Less: Qualifying discount (20%)	(30)	
	$ 120	
Employee price	(100)	
Excess discount recognized as income		20
Total income recognized		$95

---

[28]Reg. § 1.132–1(b).   [29]§ 132(c).

Assume the same facts as in Example 16, except that the employee is a clerk in a hotel operated by Silver Corporation. Because the line of business requirement is not met, the employee must recognize $200 of income ($500 − $300) from the discount on the television and $50 of income ($150 − $100) from the service contract.

As in the case of no-additional-cost benefits, the exclusion applies to employees, their spouses and dependent children, and retired and disabled former employees. However, the exclusion does not extend to highly compensated individuals unless the discount is available on a nondiscriminatory basis.

Working Condition Fringes

Generally, an employee may exclude the cost of property or services provided by the employer if the employee could deduct the cost of those items if he or she had actually paid for them.[30] These benefits are called **working condition fringes**.

Mitch is a certified public accountant employed by an accounting firm. The employer pays Mitch's annual dues to professional organizations. Mitch is not required to include the payment of the dues in gross income because if he had paid the dues, he would have been allowed to deduct the amount as an employee business expense (as discussed later in this chapter).

In many cases, this exclusion merely avoids reporting income and an offsetting deduction. However, in two specific situations, the working condition fringe benefit rules allow an exclusion where the expense would not be deductible if paid by the employee:

- Some automobile salespeople are allowed to exclude the value of certain personal use of company demonstrators (e.g., commuting to and from work).[31]
- The employee business expense would be eliminated by the 2 percent floor on miscellaneous itemized deductions under § 67 (refer to Chapter 10).

Unlike the other fringe benefits discussed previously, working condition fringes can be made available on a discriminatory basis and still qualify for the exclusion.

De Minimis Fringes

As the term suggests, *de minimis* **fringe benefits** are so small that accounting for them is impractical.[32] The House Report contains the following examples of *de minimis* fringes:

- The typing of a personal letter by a company secretary, occasional personal use of a company copying machine, occasional company cocktail parties or picnics for employees, occasional supper money or taxi fare for employees because of overtime work, and certain holiday gifts of property with a low fair market value are excluded.
- The value of meals consumed in a subsidized eating facility (e.g., an employees' cafeteria) operated by the employer is excluded if the facility is located on or near the employer's business premises, if revenue equals or exceeds direct operating costs, and if nondiscrimination requirements are met.

When taxpayers venture beyond the specific examples contained in the House Report and the Regulations, there is obviously room for disagreement as to what is *de minimis*. However, note that except in the case of subsidized eating facilities, *de minimis* fringe benefits can be granted in a manner that favors highly compensated employees.

In Notice 2011–72, the IRS addressed the question of whether cell phones provided by the employer could be excluded from gross income as a working

---

[30]§ 132(d).
[31]§ 132(j)(3).

[32]§ 132(e).

condition fringe benefit. Generally, the value of the cell phone can be excluded if it is provided for business reasons such as to enable the employee to be in contact with clients when the employee is away from the office. When the primary purpose test is satisfied, any personal use of the employer-provided cell phone will be excluded as a *de minimis* fringe benefit.

Qualified Transportation Fringes

The intent of the exclusion for **qualified transportation fringes** is to encourage the use of mass transit for commuting to and from work. Qualified transportation fringes encompass the following transportation benefits provided by the employer to the employee:[33]

1. Transportation in a commuter highway vehicle between the employee's residence and the place of employment.
2. A transit pass.
3. Qualified parking.
4. Qualified bicycle commuting reimbursement.

Statutory dollar limits are placed on the amount of the exclusion. Categories (1) and (2) above are combined for purposes of applying the limit. In this case, the limit on the exclusion was $125 for 2013 and is $130 for 2014. Category (3) has a separate limit. For qualified parking, the limit on the exclusion for 2014 is $250 per month ($245 in 2013). Both of these dollar limits are indexed annually for inflation.

A commuter highway vehicle is any highway vehicle with a seating capacity of at least six adults (excluding the driver). In addition, at least 80 percent of the vehicle's use must be for transporting employees between their residences and place of employment.

Qualified parking includes the following:

- Parking provided to an employee on or near the employer's business premises.
- Parking provided to an employee on or near a location from which the employee commutes to work via mass transit, in a commuter highway vehicle, or in a carpool.

The *qualified bicycle commuting reimbursement* enables an employee to exclude up to $20 per month received from an employer as reimbursement for the cost of commuting by bicycle (i.e., bicycle purchase, improvement, repair, and storage).

Qualified transportation fringes may be provided directly by the employer or may be in the form of cash reimbursements.

Example 19   Gray Corporation's offices are located in the center of a large city. The company pays for parking spaces to be used by the company officers. Steve, a vice president, receives $300 of such benefits each month. The parking space rental qualifies as a qualified transportation fringe. Of the $300 benefit received each month by Steve, $250 is excludible from gross income. The balance of $50 is included in his gross income. The same result would occur if Steve paid for the parking and was reimbursed by his employer.

Qualified Moving Expense Reimbursements

Qualified moving expenses that are reimbursed or paid by the employer are excludible from gross income. A qualified moving expense is an expense that would be deductible under § 217. See the discussion of moving expenses later in this chapter.

Qualified Retirement Planning Services

Qualified retirement planning services include any retirement planning advice or information provided by an employer who maintains a qualified retirement plan

---

[33]§ 132(f).

to an employee or the spouse.[34] Congress decided to exclude the value of such services from gross income because they are a key part of retirement income planning. Such an exclusion should motivate more employers to provide retirement planning services to their employees.

Nondiscrimination Provisions

For no-additional-cost services, qualified employee discounts, and qualified retirement planning services that are discriminatory in favor of *highly compensated employees*,[35] exclusion treatment is denied. However, any non-highly compensated employees who receive these benefits can still enjoy exclusion treatment.[36]

Dove Company's officers are allowed to purchase goods from the company at a 25% discount. All other employees are allowed only a 15% discount. The company's gross profit margin on these goods is 30%.

Example 20

Dove Company's officers are allowed to purchase goods from the company at a 25% discount. All other employees are allowed only a 15% discount. The company's gross profit margin on these goods is 30%.

Peggy, an officer in the company, purchased goods from the company for $750 when the price charged to customers was $1,000. Peggy must include $250 in gross income because the plan is discriminatory.

Mason, an employee of the company who is not an officer, purchased goods for $850 when the customer price was $1,000. Mason is not required to recognize gross income because he received a qualified employee discount.

De minimis fringe benefits (except for subsidized eating facilities) and working condition fringe benefits can be provided on a discriminatory basis. Likewise, the qualified transportation fringe and the qualified moving expense reimbursement can be provided on a discriminatory basis.

A review of employee fringe benefits is set forth in Concept Summary 11.1.

In-depth coverage can be found on this book's companion website: **www.cengagebrain.com**    **5**   Digging Deeper

11-21 Taxable Fringe Benefits

If fringe benefits cannot qualify for any of the specific exclusions or do not fit into any of the general classes of excluded benefits, the employee must recognize gross income equal to the fair market value of the benefits received. Obviously, problems are frequently encountered in determining values. To help taxpayers cope with these problems, the IRS has issued extensive Regulations addressing the valuation of personal use of an employer's automobiles and meals provided at an employer-operated eating facility.[37]

If a fringe benefit plan discriminates in favor of highly compensated employees, generally those employees are not allowed to exclude the benefits they receive that other employees do not enjoy. However, the highly compensated employees, as well as the other employees, are generally allowed to exclude the nondiscriminatory benefits.[38]

Example 21

MED Company has a medical reimbursement plan that reimburses officers for 100% of their medical expenses, but reimburses all other employees for only 80% of their medical expenses. Cliff, the president of the company, was reimbursed $1,000 during the year for medical expenses. Cliff must include $200 in gross income [(1 − .80) × $1,000 = $200]. Mike, an employee who is not an officer, received $800 (80% of his actual medical expenses) under the medical reimbursement plan. None of the $800 is includible in his gross income.

---

[34]§§ 132(a)(7) and (m).
[35]See § 414(q) for the definition of highly compensated employee.
[36]§§ 61, 132(j)(1), and 132(m)(2).
[37]Reg. § 1.61–2T(j). Generally, the income from the personal use of the employer's automobile is based on the lease value of the automobile

(what it would have cost the employee to lease the automobile). Meals are valued at 150% of the employer's direct costs (e.g., food and labor) of preparing the meals.
[38]§§ 79(d), 105(h), 127(b)(2), and 132(j)(1).

General Classes of Fringe Benefits

Benefit	Description and Examples	Coverage Allowed	Effect of Discrimination
1. No-additional-cost services	The employee takes advantage of the employer's excess capacity (e.g., free passes for airline employees).	Current, retired, and disabled employees; their spouses and dependent children; spouses of deceased employees. Partners are treated as employees.	No exclusion for highly compensated employees.
2. Qualified discounts on goods	The employee is allowed a discount no greater than the gross profit margin on goods sold to customers.	Same as (1) above.	Same as (1) above.
3. Qualified discounts on services	The employee is allowed a discount (maximum of 20%) on services the employer offers to customers.	Same as (1) above.	Same as (1) above.
4. Working condition fringes	Expenses paid by the employer that would be deductible if paid by the employee (e.g., a mechanic's tools). Also includes auto salesperson's use of a car held for sale.	Current employees, partners, directors, and independent contractors.	No effect.
5. *De minimis* items	Expenses so immaterial that accounting for them is not warranted (e.g., occasional supper money, personal use of the copy machine).	*Any recipient* of a fringe benefit.	No effect.
6. Qualified transportation fringes	Transportation benefits provided by the employer to employees, including a commute in a commuter highway vehicle, a transit pass, qualified parking, and qualified bicycle commuting.	Current employees.	No effect.
7. Qualified moving expense reimbursements	Qualified moving expenses that are paid or reimbursed by the employer. A qualified moving expense is one that would be deductible under § 217.	Current employees.	No effect.
8. Qualified retirement planning services	Qualified retirement planning services that are provided by the employer.	Current employees and spouses.	Same as (1) above.

11-2m Foreign Earned Income

A U.S. citizen is generally subject to U.S. tax on his or her income regardless of the income's geographic origin. The income may also be subject to tax in the foreign country, and thus the taxpayer would carry a double tax burden. Out of a sense of fairness and to encourage U.S. citizens to work abroad (so that exports might be increased), Congress has provided alternative forms of relief from taxes on foreign earned income. The taxpayer can elect *either* (1) to include the foreign income in his or her taxable income and then claim a credit for foreign taxes paid or (2) to exclude the foreign earnings from his or her U.S. gross income (the foreign earned income exclusion).[39] The foreign tax credit option is discussed in Chapter 17, but as is apparent from the following discussion, most taxpayers will choose the exclusion.

Foreign earned income consists of the earnings from the individual's personal services rendered in a foreign country (other than as an employee of the U.S. government). To qualify for the exclusion, the taxpayer must be either of the following:

- A bona fide resident of the foreign country (or countries).
- Present in a foreign country (or countries) for at least 330 days during any 12 consecutive months.

Example 22

Sandra's trips to and from a foreign country in connection with her work were as follows:

Arrived in Foreign Country	Arrived in United States
March 10, 2013	February 1, 2014
March 7, 2014	June 1, 2014

During the 12 consecutive months ending on March 10, 2014, Sandra was present in the foreign country for at least 330 days (365 days less 28 days in February and 7 days in March 2014). Therefore, all income earned in the foreign country through March 10, 2014, is eligible for the exclusion. The income earned from March 11, 2014, through May 31, 2014, is also eligible for the exclusion because Sandra was present in the foreign country for 330 days during the 12 consecutive months ending on May 31, 2014.

The exclusion is *limited* to an indexed amount of $99,200 for 2014 ($97,600 in 2013). For married persons, both of whom have foreign earned income, the exclusion is computed separately for each spouse. Community property rules do not apply (the community property spouse is not deemed to have earned one-half of the other spouse's foreign earned income). If all of the days in the tax year are not qualifying days, the taxpayer must compute the maximum exclusion on a daily basis ($99,200 divided by the number of days in the entire year and multiplied by the number of qualifying days).

Example 23

Keith qualifies for the foreign earned income exclusion. He was present in France for all of 2014. Keith's salary for 2014 is $100,000. Because all of the days in 2014 are qualifying days, Keith can exclude $99,200 of his $100,000 salary.

Assume instead that only 335 days were qualifying days. Then Keith's exclusion is limited to $91,047, computed as follows:

$$\$99,200 \times \frac{335 \text{ days in foreign country}}{365 \text{ days in the year}} = \$91,047$$

11-3 EMPLOYEE EXPENSES

Once the employment relationship is established, employee expenses fall into one of the following categories:

- Transportation.
- Travel.
- Moving.
- Education.
- Entertainment.
- Other.

These expenses are discussed next in the order presented. Keep in mind, however, that these expenses are not necessarily limited to employees. A deduction for business transportation, for example, is equally available to taxpayers who are self-employed.

LO.3

Apply the rules for computing deductible expenses of employees, including transportation, travel, moving, education, and entertainment expenses.

---

[39]§ 911.

TAX IN THE NEWS Turning a Saturday Leisure Day into a Business Day

The high cost of air travel together with the substantial discount allowed for a Saturday night stayover may offer travelers an opportunity to do some sightseeing or shopping on business trips. The extra meals and lodging expenses for the nonbusiness day are deductible if the cost is less than the additional cost of flying without a Saturday stay. For the employee, any reimbursement for such costs is nontaxable. Thus, the Saturday is treated as a business day even though no business activity takes place.

Source: Private Letter Ruling (Ltr.Rul.) 9237014.

11-3a Transportation Expenses

Qualified Expenditures

An employee may deduct unreimbursed employment-related **transportation expenses** as an itemized deduction *from* AGI. Transportation expenses include only the cost of transporting the employee from one place to another when the employee is not away from home in travel status. Such costs include taxi fares, automobile expenses, tolls, and parking.

Commuting Expenses

Commuting between home and one's place of employment is a personal, nondeductible expense. The fact that one employee drives 30 miles to work and another employee walks six blocks is of no significance.[40]

Example 24	Geraldo is employed by Sparrow Corporation. He drives 22 miles each way to work. The 44 miles he drives each workday are nondeductible commuting expenses.

The expenses of getting from one job to another job or from one workstation to another workstation are deductible transportation expenses rather than nondeductible commuting expenses.

Digging Deeper 6   In-depth coverage can be found on this book's companion website: **www.cengagebrain.com**

Example 25	In the current year, Cynthia holds two jobs, a full-time job with Blue Corporation and a part-time job with Wren Corporation. Cynthia customarily leaves home at 7:30 A.M. and drives 30 miles to the Blue Corporation plant, where she works until 5:00 P.M. After dinner at a nearby café, Cynthia drives 20 miles to Wren Corporation and works from 7:00 to 11:00 P.M. The distance from the second job to Cynthia's home is 40 miles. Her deduction is based on 20 miles (the distance between jobs).

Referring back to Example 25, assume that Cynthia has an office in the home that qualifies as a principal place of business. Thus, the transportation between home and various work locations is not a commuting expense. That is, any transportation from her home to and from business sites will not be disallowed as a commuting expense.

Computation of Automobile Expenses

A taxpayer has two choices in computing deductible automobile expenses. The actual operating cost, which includes depreciation (refer to Chapter 5), gas, oil,

---

[40] *Tauferner v. U.S.*, 69–1 USTC ¶9241, 23 AFTR 2d 69–1025, 407 F.2d 243 (CA–10, 1969).

repairs, licenses, and insurance, may be used. Records must be kept that detail the automobile's personal and business use. Only the percentage allocable to business transportation and travel is allowed as a deduction.

Use of the **automatic mileage method** is the second alternative. For 2014, the deduction is based on 56 cents per mile for business miles.[41] Parking fees and tolls are allowed in addition to expenses computed using the automatic mileage method.

Generally, a taxpayer may elect either method for any particular year. However, the following restrictions apply:

* The vehicle must be owned or leased by the taxpayer.
* If five or more vehicles are in use (for business purposes) at the *same* time (not alternately), a taxpayer may not use the automatic mileage method.
* Use of the automatic mileage method in the first year the auto is placed in service is considered an election not to use the MACRS method of depreciation (refer to Chapter 5).
* A taxpayer may not switch to the automatic mileage method if the MACRS statutory percentage method or the election to expense under § 179 has been used.

In-depth coverage can be found on this book's companion website: **www.cengagebrain.com** **7** Digging Deeper

11-3b Travel Expenses

Definition of Travel Expenses

An itemized deduction is allowed for *unreimbursed* **travel expenses** related to a taxpayer's employment. Travel expenses are more broadly defined in the Code than are transportation expenses. Travel expenses include transportation expenses and meals and lodging while away from home in the pursuit of a trade or business. Meals cannot be lavish or extravagant. A deduction for meals and lodging is available only if the taxpayer is away from his or her tax home. Deductible travel expenses also include reasonable laundry and incidental expenses.

In-depth coverage can be found on this book's companion website: **www.cengagebrain.com** **8** Digging Deeper

Away-from-Home Requirement

The crucial test for the deductibility of travel expenses is whether the employee is away from home overnight. "Overnight" need not be a 24-hour period, but it must be a period substantially longer than an ordinary day's work and must require rest, sleep, or a relief-from-work period.[42] A one-day business trip is not travel status, and meals and lodging for such a trip are not deductible.

Temporary Assignments

The employee must be away from home for a temporary period. If the taxpayer-employee is reassigned to a new post for an indefinite period of time, that new post becomes his or her tax home. Temporary indicates that the assignment's termination is expected within a reasonably short period of time. The position of the IRS is that the tax home is the business location, post, or station of the taxpayer. Thus, travel expenses are not deductible if a taxpayer is reassigned for an indefinite period and does not move his or her place of residence to the new location.

---

[41]Notice 2012–72, 2012–50 I.R.B. 673. For 2013, the rate was 56.5 cents.

[42]*U.S. v. Correll*, 68–1 USTC ¶9101, 20 AFTR 2d 5845, 88 S.Ct 445 (USSC, 1967); Rev.Rul. 75–168, 1975–1 C.B. 58.

Example 26

Malcolm's employer opened a branch office in San Diego. Malcolm was assigned to the new office for three months to train a new manager and to assist in setting up the new office. He tried commuting from his home in Los Angeles for a week and decided that he could not continue driving several hours a day. He rented an apartment in San Diego, where he lived during the week. He spent weekends with his wife and children at their home in Los Angeles. Malcolm's rent, meals, laundry, incidentals, and automobile expenses in San Diego are deductible. To the extent Malcolm's transportation expense related to his weekend trips home exceeds what his cost of meals and lodging would have been, the excess is personal and nondeductible.

Example 27

Assume that Malcolm in Example 26 was transferred to the new location to become the new manager permanently. His wife and children continued to live in Los Angeles until the end of the school year. Malcolm is no longer "away from home" because the assignment is not temporary. His travel expenses are not deductible.

To curtail controversy in this area, the Code specifies that a taxpayer "shall not be treated as temporarily away from home during any period of employment if such period exceeds 1 year."[43]

Digging Deeper   **9**   In-depth coverage can be found on this book's companion website: **www.cengagebrain.com**

Determining the Tax Home

Under ordinary circumstances, determining the location of a taxpayer's tax home does not present a problem. The tax home is the area in which the taxpayer derives his or her principal source of income; when the taxpayer has more than one place of employment, the tax home is based on the amount of time spent in each area.

It is possible for a taxpayer never to be away from his or her tax home. In other words, the tax home follows the taxpayer.[44] Under such circumstances, all meals and lodging remain personal and are not deductible.

Example 28

Bill is employed as a long-haul truck driver. He is single, stores his clothes and other belongings at his parents' home, and stops there for periodic visits. Most of the time, Bill is on the road, sleeping in his truck and in motels. It is likely that Bill is never in travel status, as he is not away from home. Consequently, none of his meals and lodging are deductible.

Combined Business and Pleasure Travel

To be deductible, travel expenses need not be incurred in the performance of specific job functions. Travel expenses incurred to attend a professional convention are deductible by an employee if attendance is connected with services as an employee. For example, an employee of a law firm can deduct travel expenses incurred to attend a meeting of the American Bar Association.

In order to limit the possibility of a taxpayer claiming a tax deduction for what is essentially a personal vacation, several provisions have been enacted to restrict deductions associated with combined business and pleasure trips. If the business/pleasure trip is from one point in the United States to another point in the United States (*domestic travel*), the transportation expenses are deductible only if the trip is primarily for business.[45] Meals, lodging, and other expenses are allocated between business and personal days. If the trip is primarily for pleasure, no transportation expenses qualify as a deduction.

---

[43]§ 162(a).

[44]*Moses Mitnick*, 13 T.C. 1 (1949).

[45]Reg. § 1.162–2(b)(1).

In-depth coverage can be found on this book's companion website: **www.cengagebrain.com** **10** Digging Deeper

Example 29

In the current year, Hana travels from Seattle to New York primarily for business. She spends five days conducting business and three days sightseeing and attending shows. Her plane and taxi fare amounts to $560. Her meals amount to $100 per day, and lodging and incidental expenses are $150 per day. She can deduct the transportation expenses of $560 because the trip is primarily for business (five days of business versus three days of sightseeing). Deductible meals are limited to five days and are subject to the 50% cutback (discussed later in the chapter) for a total of $250 [5 days × ($100 × 50%)], and other deductions are limited to $750 (5 days × $150). If Hana is an employee, the unreimbursed travel expenses are miscellaneous itemized deductions subject to the 2%-of-AGI floor.

When the trip is outside the United States (*foreign travel*), special rules apply.[46] Transportation expenses must be allocated between business and personal days *unless* (1) the taxpayer is away from home for seven days or less or (2) less than 25 percent of the time was for personal purposes. No allocation is required if the taxpayer has no substantial control over arrangements for the trip or the desire for a vacation is not a major factor in taking the trip. If the trip is primarily for pleasure, no transportation charges are deductible. Days devoted to travel are considered business days. Weekends, legal holidays, and intervening days are considered business days, provided that both the preceding and succeeding days were business days.

In-depth coverage can be found on this book's companion website: **www.cengagebrain.com**  **11** Digging Deeper

Example 30

In the current year, Robert takes a trip from New York to Japan primarily for business purposes. He is away from home from June 10 through June 19. He spends three days vacationing and seven days (including two travel days) conducting business. His airfare is $2,500, his meals amount to $100 per day, and lodging and incidental expenses are $160 per day. Because Robert is away from home for more than seven days and more than 25% of his time is devoted to personal purposes, only 70% (7 days business/10 days total) of the transportation is deductible. His deductions are as follows:

Transportation (70% × $2,500)		$1,750
Lodging ($160 × 7)		1,120
Meals ($100 × 7)	$ 700	
Less: 50% cutback (discussed later in this chapter)	(350)	350
Total deductions		$3,220

If Robert is gone the same period of time but spends only two days vacationing (less than 25% of the total), no allocation of transportation is required. Because the pleasure portion of the trip is less than 25% of the total, all of the airfare qualifies for the travel deduction.

The foreign convention rules do not operate to bar a deduction to an employer if the expense is *compensatory* in nature. For example, a trip to Rome won by a top salesperson is included in the gross income of the employee and is fully deductible by the employer.

---

[46]§ 274(c) and Reg. § 1.274–4. For purposes of the seven-days-or-less exception, the departure travel day is not counted.

11-3c Moving Expenses

Moving expenses are deductible for moves in connection with the commencement of work at a new principal workplace.[47] Both employees and self-employed individuals can deduct these expenses. To be eligible for a moving expense deduction, a taxpayer must meet two basic tests: distance and time.

Distance Test

To meet the distance test, the taxpayer's new job location must be at least 50 miles farther from the taxpayer's old residence than the old residence was from the former place of employment. In this regard, the location of the new residence is not relevant. This eliminates a moving expense deduction for (1) taxpayers who purchase a new home in the same general area without changing their place of employment and (2) taxpayers who accept a new job in the same area as their old job.

Example 31

Harry is permanently transferred to a new job location. As the following diagram shows, the distance from Harry's former home to his new job (80 miles) exceeds the distance from his former home to his old job (30 miles) by at least 50 miles. Harry has met the distance test for a moving expense deduction.

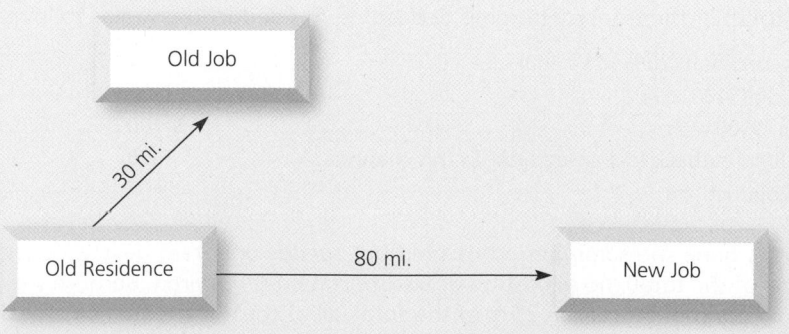

If an individual is not employed before the move, the new job must be at least 50 miles from the former residence. Thus, in Example 31, Harry's move has also met the distance test even if he was not previously employed.

Time Test

To meet the time test, an employee must be employed on a full-time basis at the new location for 39 weeks in the 12-month period following the move. If the taxpayer is a self-employed individual, he or she must work in the new location for 78 weeks

---

[47]§ 217(a).

Expatriates and the Moving Expense Deduction

Global Tax Issues

© iStockphoto.com/Andrey Prokhorov

Expatriates, U.S. persons who accept work assignments overseas, enjoy several favorable tax advantages regarding foreign moves. First, the cost of storing household goods qualifies as a moving expense. This could lead to a major tax saving because expatriates do not ship most of their household effects to the foreign location. Furthermore, the cost of storage, particularly in a climate-controlled facility, is not insignificant.

The second advantage expatriates may enjoy is an exemption from the time test. Those who return to the United States to retire are absolved from the 39-week or 78-week work requirement. Thus, the return home expenses are treated as qualified moving expenses.

Source: Internal Revenue Code § 217(i).

during the two years following the move. The first 39 weeks must be in the first 12 months. The time test is disregarded if the taxpayer dies, becomes disabled, or is discharged (other than for willful misconduct) or transferred by the employer.

In-depth coverage can be found on this book's companion website: **www.cengagebrain.com**

12 | Digging Deeper

Treatment of Moving Expenses

Qualified moving expenses include reasonable expenses of:

- Moving household goods and personal effects.
- Traveling from the former residence to the new residence.

For this purpose, traveling includes lodging, but not meals, for the taxpayer and members of the household.[48] It does not include the cost of moving servants or others who are not members of the household. The taxpayer can elect to use actual auto expenses (no depreciation is allowed) or the automatic mileage method. In this case, moving expense mileage is limited in 2014 to 23.5 cents per mile for each car. The automatic mileage rate for 2013 was 24 cents. These expenses are also limited by the reasonableness standard. For example, if a person moves from Texas to Florida via Maine and takes six weeks to do so, the transportation and lodging must be allocated between personal and moving expenses.

Example 32

Jill is transferred by her employer from the Atlanta office to the San Francisco office. In this connection, she spends the following amounts:

Cost of moving furniture	$6,800
Transportation	700
Meals	400
Lodging	900

Jill's total qualified moving expense is $8,400 ($6,800 + $700 + $900), which includes all costs listed except for the cost of meals.

The moving expense deduction is allowed regardless of whether the employee is transferred by the existing employer or is employed by a new employer. It is allowed if the employee moves to a new area and obtains employment or switches from self-employed status to employee status (and vice versa). The moving expense deduction is also allowed if an individual is unemployed before obtaining employment in a new area.

---

[48]§ 217(b).

What Is Not Included

In addition to meals while en route, the moving expense deduction does *not* include the following costs:

- New car tags and driver's licenses.
- Loss on the sale of a residence or penalty for breaking a lease.
- Forfeiture of security deposits and loss from disposing of club memberships.
- Pre-move house-hunting expenses.
- Temporary living expenses.

Digging Deeper 13 🔍   In-depth coverage can be found on this book's companion website: **www.cengagebrain.com**

Tax Planning Strategies   MOVING EXPENSES

FRAMEWORK FOCUS: DEDUCTIONS

Strategy: **Maximize Deductible Amounts.**

Persons who retire and move to a new location incur personal nondeductible moving expenses. If the retired person accepts a full-time job in the new location before moving and meets the time and distance requirements, the moving expenses are deductible.

Example 33

At the time of his retirement from the national office of a major accounting firm, Gordon had an annual salary of $480,000. He moves from New York City to Seattle to retire and accepts a full-time teaching position at a Seattle junior college at an annual salary of $22,000. If Gordon satisfies the 39-week test, his moving expenses are deductible. The disparity between the two salaries (previous and current) is of no consequence. ∎

11-3d Education Expenses

General Requirements

Employees *and* self-employed individuals can deduct expenses incurred for education as ordinary and necessary business expenses, provided the expenses are incurred to maintain or improve existing skills required in the present job. An employee can also deduct expenses incurred to meet the express requirements of the employer or the requirements imposed by law to retain his or her employment status.

Education expenses are not deductible if the education is for either of the following purposes (except as discussed under A Limited Deduction Approach, which follows):

- To meet the minimum educational standards for qualification in the taxpayer's existing job.
- To qualify the taxpayer for a new trade or business.[49]

Thus, fees incurred for professional exams (the bar exam, for example) and fees for review courses (such as a CPA review course) are not deductible.[50] If the education incidentally results in a promotion or raise, the deduction still can be taken as long as the education maintained and improved existing skills and did not qualify the person for a new trade or business. A change in duties is not always fatal to the

---

[49]Reg. §§ 1.162–5(b)(2) and (3).   [50]Reg. § 1.212–1(f) and Rev.Rul. 69–292, 1969–1 C.B. 84.

TAX IN THE NEWS   Is an MBA Degree Deductible?

Education that maintains or improves existing skills is deductible, but education that qualifies a taxpayer for a new field is not. But how do these basic rules apply to a conventional (i.e., nonspecialized) MBA degree? Does being a manager or a consultant require an MBA degree? Generally, the answer has always been that it does not. In this regard, therefore, the education does not create a new skill, so its cost should be deductible.

Several recent holdings, however, have found that an MBA degree can lead to qualifying for a new trade or business. But these holdings involved situations where the education resulted in a job change and satisfied different minimum requirements set by the employer. In one case, for example, the taxpayer moved from the position of investment analyst to become an investment banker, and the latter position required an MBA degree. Under these circumstances, the cost of the education was held to be nondeductible.

But barring a change to a job where the degree is required, the cost of an MBA degree should be deductible as merely improving existing managerial skills.

_____

Source: Daniel R. Allemeier, Jr., 90 TCM 197, T.C.Memo. 2005–207.

deduction if the new duties involve the same general work. For example, the IRS has ruled that a practicing dentist's education expenses incurred to become an orthodontist are deductible.[51]

Requirements Imposed by Law or by the Employer for Retention of Employment

Taxpayers are permitted to deduct education expenses if additional courses are required by the employer or are imposed by law. Many states require a minimum of a bachelor's degree and a specified number of additional courses to retain a teaching job. In addition, some public school systems have imposed a master's degree requirement and require teachers to make satisfactory progress toward a master's degree to keep their positions. If the required education is the minimum degree required for the job, no deduction is allowed.

Professionals (e.g., physicians, attorneys, and CPAs) may deduct expenses incurred to meet continuing professional education requirements imposed by states as a condition for retaining a license to practice.

To meet continuing professional education requirements imposed by the State Board of Public Accountancy for maintaining her CPA license, Nancy takes an auditing course sponsored by a local college. The cost of the education is deductible.	**Example 34**

In-depth coverage can be found on this book's companion website: **www.cengagebrain.com** 14   Digging Deeper

Maintaining or Improving Existing Skills

The *maintaining or improving existing skills* requirement in the Code has been difficult for both taxpayers and the courts to interpret. For example, a business executive is permitted to deduct the costs of obtaining an MBA on the grounds the advanced management education is undertaken to maintain and improve existing management skills. The executive is eligible to deduct the costs of specialized, non-degree management courses that are taken for continuing education or to maintain or improve existing skills. Expenses incurred by the executive to obtain a law

_____

[51]Rev.Rul. 74–78, 1974–1 C.B. 44.

degree are not deductible, however, because the education constitutes training for a new trade or business. The Regulations specifically deny a self-employed accountant a deduction for expenses relating to law school.[52]

Tax Planning Strategies	EDUCATION EXPENSES

FRAMEWORK FOCUS: DEDUCTIONS

Strategy: Maximize Deductible Amounts.

Education expenses are treated as nondeductible personal items unless the individual is employed or is engaged in a trade or business. A temporary leave of absence for further education is one way to ensure that the taxpayer is still treated as being engaged in a trade or business. An individual was permitted to deduct education expenses even though he resigned from his job, returned to school full time for two years, and accepted another job in the same field upon graduation. The court held that the student had merely suspended active participation in his field.[53]

If the time out of the field is too long, education expense deductions will be disallowed. For example, a teacher who left the field for four years to raise her child and curtailed her employment searches and writing activities was denied a deduction for education expenses. She was no longer actively engaged in the trade or business of being an educator.[54]

To secure the deduction, an individual should arrange his or her work situation to preserve employee or business status.

As discussed on the next page under *A Limited Deduction Approach*, a limited exception is available for taxpayers who do not meet the preceding requirements.

Classification of Specific Items

Education expenses include books, tuition, supplies, transportation (e.g., from the office to night school), and travel (e.g., meals and lodging while away from home at summer school).

Example 35

Bill, who holds a bachelor of education degree, is a secondary education teacher in the Los Angeles school system. The school board recently raised its minimum education requirement for new teachers from four years of college training to five. A grandfather clause allows teachers with only four years of college to continue to qualify if they show satisfactory progress toward a graduate degree. Bill enrolls at the University of Washington during the summer and takes three graduate courses. His unreimbursed expenses for this purpose are as follows:

Books and tuition	$2,600
Lodging while in travel status (June–August)	1,150
Meals while in travel status	800
Laundry while in travel status	220
Transportation	600

Bill has an itemized deduction as follows:

Books and tuition	$2,600
Lodging	1,150
Meals less 50% cutback (discussed later in this chapter)	400
Laundry	220
Transportation	600
	$4,970

---

[52]Reg. § 1.162–5(b)(3)(ii) Example (1).

[53]*Stephen G. Sherman*, 36 TCM 1191, T.C.Memo. 1977–301.

[54]*Brian C. Mulherin*, 42 TCM 834, T.C.Memo. 1981–454; *George A. Baist*, 56 TCM 778, T.C.Memo. 1988–554.

TABLE 11.2	Limitations for Qualified Tuition Deduction	
Filing Status	**MAGI Limit**	**Maximum Deduction Allowed**
Single	$ 65,000 ⎫	
Married	130,000 ⎭	$4,000
Single	65,001 ⎫ to ⎬ 80,000*⎭	2,000
Married	130,001 ⎫ to ⎬ 160,000*⎭	2,000

*No deduction is available if MAGI exceeds this amount.

11-3e A Limited Deduction Approach

One of the major shortcomings of the education deduction, discussed previously, is that it is unavailable for taxpayers obtaining a basic skill (i.e., to meet the minimum standards required for the taxpayer's current job). This shortcoming has been partly resolved with the **deduction for qualified tuition and related expenses**.

A deduction *for* AGI is allowed for qualified tuition and related expenses involving higher education (i.e., postsecondary). The deduction is the lesser of the qualifying amount spent or the maximum amount allowed by § 222. The maximum deductions allowed are shown in Table 11.2. Note that the limitations are based on the taxpayer's MAGI and filing status.[55] Although a phaseout is provided for, note its short and drastic effect. Only two steps are involved ($65,000/$80,000 for single and $130,000/$160,000 for married), and the benefit of § 222 *disappears completely* after the second step. Thus, a married couple with MAGI of $160,000 would lose the entire deduction if they earned an additional $1. The § 222 limitations are not indexed for inflation.

Various aspects of the higher education tuition deduction are summarized as follows:

- *Qualified tuition and related expenses* include whatever is required for enrollment at the institution. Usually, student activity fees, books, and room and board are not included.[56]
- The expense need not be employment-related, although it can be.
- The deduction is available for a taxpayer's spouse or anyone who can be claimed as a dependent and is an eligible student.
- The deduction is not available for married persons who file separate returns.[57]
- To avoid a "double benefit," the deduction must be coordinated with other education provisions (e.g., American Opportunity and lifetime learning credits as discussed in Chapter 10). Along this same line, no deduction is allowed for a taxpayer who qualifies as another's dependent.[58]
- The deduction *for* AGI classification avoids the 2 percent-of-AGI floor on miscellaneous itemized deductions. See Chapter 10.[59]

---

[55]MAGI is modified adjusted gross income as defined in § 222(b)(2). Examples of some of these modifications include the adding back to regular AGI of the foreign earned income exclusion and the domestic production activities deduction. This provision expired after December 31, 2013, but it is expected to be extended.

[56]§ 222(d)(1).
[57]§ 222(d)(4).
[58]§ 222(c).
[59]§§ 61(a)(18) and 67.

Example 36

Tina is single and a full-time employee of a CPA firm. During the current year, she attends law school at night and incurs the following expenses: $4,200 for tuition and $340 for books and supplies. Presuming that she satisfies the MAGI limitation (see Table 11.2), she can claim $4,000 as a deduction *for* AGI. If she itemizes her deductions for the year, can she claim the $540 not allowed under § 222 ($200 tuition in excess of $4,000 + $340 for books and supplies) as an education expense eligible for itemized deduction treatment? No, because obtaining a law degree leads to a new trade or business.

The deduction for qualified tuition and related expenses can be determined by completing Form 8917 (Tuition and Fees Deduction). The form should be attached to Form 1040 (or Form 1040A).

Another deduction item relating to education is the limited deduction of interest on student loans, which is covered in Chapter 10.[60]

11-3f Entertainment Expenses

Many taxpayers attempt to deduct personal entertainment expenses as business expenses. For this reason, the tax law restricts the deductibility of entertainment expenses. The Code contains strict record-keeping requirements and provides restrictive tests for the deduction of certain types of entertainment expenses.

The Fifty Percent Cutback

Only 50 percent of meal and entertainment expenses is deductible.[61] The limitation applies to employees, employers, and self-employed individuals. Although the 50 percent cutback can apply to either the employer or the employee, it will not apply twice. The cutback applies to the one who really pays (economically) for the meals or entertainment.

Digging Deeper   15    In-depth coverage can be found on this book's companion website: **www.cengagebrain.com**

Example 37

Jane, an employee of Pelican Corporation, entertains one of her clients. If Pelican Corporation does not reimburse Jane, she is subject to the cutback. If, however, Pelican Corporation reimburses Jane (or pays for the entertainment directly), Pelican suffers the cutback.

Transportation expenses are not affected by the cutback rule—only meals and entertainment expenses are reduced. The cutback also applies to taxes and tips relating to meals and entertainment. Cover charges, parking fees at an entertainment location, and room rental fees for a meal or cocktail party are also subject to the 50 percent cutback.

Digging Deeper   16    In-depth coverage can be found on this book's companion website: **www.cengagebrain.com**

Example 38

Joe pays a $30 cab fare to meet his client for dinner. The meal costs $120, and Joe leaves a $20 tip. His deduction is $100 [($120 meal costs + $20 tip) × 50% + $30 cab fare].

---

[60]§ 221.   [61]§ 274(n).

Classification of Expenses

Entertainment expenses are classified either as *directly related* to business or *associated with* business.[62] Directly related expenses are related to an actual business meeting or discussion. These expenses are distinguished from entertainment expenses that are incurred to promote goodwill, such as maintaining existing customer relations. To obtain a deduction for directly related entertainment, it is not necessary to show that actual benefit resulted from the expenditure as long as there was a reasonable expectation of benefit. To qualify as directly related, the expense should be incurred in a business setting. If there is little possibility of engaging in the active conduct of a trade or business due to the nature of the social facility, it is difficult to qualify the expenditure as directly related to business.

Expenses associated with, rather than directly related to, business entertainment must serve a specific business purpose, such as obtaining new business or continuing existing business. These expenditures qualify only if the expenses directly precede or follow a bona fide business discussion. Entertainment occurring on the same day as the business discussion is considered associated with business.

Example 39

Jerry, a manufacturer's representative, took his client to play a round of golf during the afternoon. They had dinner the same evening, during which time business was discussed. After dinner, they went to a nightclub to have drinks and listen to a jazz band. The business dinner qualifies as directly related entertainment. The golf outing and the visit to the nightclub qualify as associated with entertainment.

Tax Planning Strategies — ENTERTAINMENT EXPENSES

FRAMEWORK FOCUS: DEDUCTIONS

Strategy: Maximize Deductible Amounts.

Taxpayers should maintain detailed records of amounts, time, place, business purpose, and business relationships. A credit card receipt details the place, date, and amount of the expense. A notation made on the receipt of the names of the person(s) attending, the business relationship, and the topic of discussion should constitute sufficient documentation.[63] Failure to provide sufficient documentation could lead to disallowance of entertainment expense deductions.

Associated with or goodwill entertainment requires a business discussion to be conducted immediately before or after the entertainment. Furthermore, a business purpose must exist for the entertainment. Taxpayers should arrange for a business discussion before or after such entertainment. They also must document the business purpose, such as obtaining new business from a prospective customer.

Restrictions upon Deductibility of Business Meals

Business meals are deductible only if:[64]

- The meal is directly related to or associated with the active conduct of a trade or business,
- The expense is not lavish or extravagant under the circumstances, and
- The taxpayer (or an employee) is present at the meal.

A business meal with a business associate or customer is not deductible unless business is discussed before, during, or after the meal. This requirement does not apply to meals consumed while away from home in travel status.

[62]§ 274(a)(1)(A).
[63]*Kenneth W. Guenther*, 54 TCM 382, T.C.Memo. 1987–440.
[64]§ 274(k).

Example 40

Lacy travels to San Francisco for a business convention. She pays for dinner with three colleagues and is not reimbursed by her employer. They do not discuss business. She can deduct 50% of the cost of her meal. However, she cannot deduct the cost of her colleagues' meals.

Example 41

Lance, a party to a contract negotiation, buys dinner for other parties to the negotiation but does not attend the dinner. No deduction is allowed because Lance was not present.

Restrictions upon Deductibility of Club Dues

The Code provides that "No deduction shall be allowed … for amounts paid or incurred for membership in any club organized for business, pleasure, recreation, or other social purpose."[65] Although this prohibition seems quite broad, it does not apply to clubs whose primary purpose is public service and community volunteerism (e.g., Kiwanis, Lions, and Rotary). Although *dues* are not deductible, actual entertainment at a club may qualify.

Example 42

During the current year, Vincent spent $1,400 on business lunches at the Lakeside Country Club. The annual membership fee was $6,000, and Vincent used the facility 60% of the time for business. Presuming that the lunches meet the business meal test, Vincent may claim $700 (50% cutback × $1,400) as a deduction. None of the club dues are deductible.

Digging Deeper   17   In-depth coverage can be found on this book's companion website: **www.cengagebrain.com**

Business Gifts

Although not subject to a cutback adjustment, business gifts are deductible only to the extent of $25 per donee per year.[66] An exception is made for gifts costing $4 or less (e.g., pens with the employee's or company's name on them) or promotional materials. Such items are not treated as business gifts subject to the $25 limitation. In addition, incidental costs such as engraving of jewelry and nominal charges for gift-wrapping, mailing, and delivery are not included in the cost of the gift in applying the limitation. Gifts to superiors and employers are not deductible. The $25 limitation on business gifts cannot be circumvented by having the donor's spouse join in the gift or by making multiple gifts that include the customer's family. Records must be maintained to substantiate business gifts.

11-3g Other Employee Expenses

Office in the Home

Employees and self-employed individuals are not allowed a deduction for **office in the home expenses** unless a portion of the residence is used *exclusively and on a regular basis* as either:

- The principal place of business for any trade or business of the taxpayer.
- A place of business used by clients, patients, or customers.

Employees must meet an additional test: the use must be for the convenience of the employer rather than merely being "appropriate and helpful."[67]

The precise meaning of "principal place of business" has been the subject of considerable controversy.[68] Congress ultimately resolved the controversy by amending the Code.[69]

---

[65]§ 274(a)(3).
[66]§ 274(b)(1).
[67]§ 280A(c)(1).

[68]See the restrictive interpretation arrived at in *Comm. v. Soliman*, 93–1 USTC ¶50,014, 71 AFTR 2d 93–463, 113 S.Ct. 701 (USSC, 1993).
[69]§ 280A(c)(1) as modified by TRA of 1997.

TAX IN THE NEWS **Has the Trend Toward Working from Home Changed?**

Is the recent decision by Yahoo, Inc., to end work-from-home arrangements and require job-site presence likely to reverse the home-based work trend? That is unlikely, according to the U.S. Census Bureau. Although much depends on the industry involved, the home-based workforce keeps increasing. Driven by employers' cost savings, employees' savings in commute time, and documented productivity increases, the mutual benefits are too strong to overlook. All indicators support a continued emphasis on home-based work assignments.

Source: Based on Neil Shaw, "More Americans Working Remotely," *Wall Street Journal*, March 6, 2013, p. A4.

© iStockphoto.com/Andrey Prokhorov

The term *principal place of business* now includes a place of business that satisfies the following requirements:

- The office is used by the taxpayer to conduct administrative or management activities of a trade or business.
- There is no other fixed location of the trade or business where the taxpayer conducts these activities.

Example 43

Dr. Smith is a self-employed anesthesiologist. During the year, he spends 30 to 35 hours per week administering anesthesia and postoperative care to patients in three hospitals, none of which provides him with an office. He also spends two or three hours per day in a room in his home that he uses exclusively as an office. He does not meet patients there, but he performs a variety of tasks related to his medical practice (e.g., contacting surgeons, doing the bookkeeping, and reading medical journals). A deduction will be allowed because he uses the office in the home to conduct administrative or management activities of his trade or business and there is no other fixed location where these activities can be carried out.

The exclusive use requirement means that a specific part of the home must be used solely for business purposes. A deduction, if permitted, requires an allocation of total expenses of operating the home between business and personal use based on floor space or number of rooms.

Even if the taxpayer meets the above requirements, the allowable home office expenses cannot exceed the gross income from the business less all other business expenses attributable to the activity. That is, the home office deduction cannot create a loss. Furthermore, the home office expenses that are allowed as itemized deductions anyway (e.g., mortgage interest and real estate taxes) must be deducted first. All home office expenses of an employee are miscellaneous itemized deductions, except those (such as interest and taxes) that qualify as other personal itemized deductions. Home office expenses of a self-employed individual are trade or business expenses and are deductible *for* AGI. Any disallowed home office expenses are carried forward and used in future years subject to the same limitations.

In-depth coverage can be found on this book's companion website: **www.cengagebrain.com** 18   Digging Deeper

Example 44

Rick is a certified public accountant employed by a regional CPA firm as a tax manager. He operates a separate business in which he refinishes furniture in his home. For this business, he uses two rooms in the basement of his home exclusively and regularly. The floor space of the two rooms is 240 square feet, which constitutes 10% of the total floor space of his 2,400-square-foot residence. Gross income from the business totals

$8,000. Expenses of the business (other than home office expenses) are $6,500. Rick incurs the following home office expenses:

Real property taxes on residence	$ 4,000
Interest expense on residence	7,500
Operating expenses of residence (including homeowners insurance)	2,000
Depreciation on residence (related to 10% business use)	350

Rick's deductions are determined as follows:

Business income		$ 8,000
Less: Other business expenses		(6,500)
Net income from the business (before the office in the home deduction)		$ 1,500
Less: Allocable taxes ($4,000 × 10%)	$400	
Allocable interest ($7,500 × 10%)	750	(1,150)
		$ 350
Less: Allocable operating expenses of the residence ($2,000 × 10%)		(200)
		$ 150
Less: Allocable depreciation ($350, limited to remaining income of $150)		(150)
		$ –0–

Rick has a carryover deduction of $200 (the unused excess depreciation). Because he is self-employed, the allocable taxes and interest ($1,150), the other deductible office expenses ($200 + $150), and $6,500 of other business expenses are deductible *for* AGI.

Certain Expenses for Teachers

Recent tax legislation provides for an extension of the deduction *for* AGI for certain expenses of elementary and secondary school teachers.[70] Many teachers purchase school supplies for classroom use and are not reimbursed by their employer. Such teachers may deduct the costs they incur for books, supplies, computer equipment and related software and services, other equipment, and supplementary materials they use in the classroom. The annual statutory ceiling on the deduction *for* AGI classification is $250.

Miscellaneous Employee Expenses

Deductible miscellaneous employee expenses include special clothing and its upkeep, union dues, and professional expenses. Also deductible are professional dues, professional meetings, and employment agency fees for seeking new employment in the taxpayer's current trade or business, whether or not a new job is secured.

To be deductible, *special clothing* must be both specifically required as a condition of employment and not adaptable for regular wear. For example, a police officer's uniform is not suitable for off-duty activities. An exception is clothing used to the extent it takes the place of regular clothing (e.g., some military uniforms).

Example 45

Captain Roberts is on active duty in the U.S. Army. The cost of his regular uniforms is not deductible because such clothing is suitable for regular wear. Captain Roberts, however, spends over $1,100 to purchase "dress blues." Under military regulations, dress uniforms may be worn only during ceremonial functions (e.g., official events, parades). The $1,100 cost, to the extent it exceeds any clothing allowance, qualifies as a deduction.

---

[70]§ 62(a)(2)(D). This provision expired at the end of 2013, but it is expected to be extended.

Job Hunting

The current position of the IRS is that expenses incurred in *seeking employment* are deductible if the taxpayer is seeking employment in the same trade or business. The deduction is allowed whether or not the attempts to secure employment are successful. An unemployed taxpayer can take a deduction as long as there has been no substantial lack of continuity between the last job and the search for a new one. No deduction is allowed for persons seeking their first job or seeking employment in a new trade or business.

11-3h Classification of Employee Expenses

If employee expenses are reimbursed by the employer under an accountable plan, they are not reported by the employee at all. In effect, this result is equivalent to reporting the reimbursement as income and treating the expenses as deductions *for* AGI.[71] Alternatively, if the expenses are reimbursed under a nonaccountable plan or are not reimbursed at all, they are classified as deductions *from* AGI and can be claimed only if the taxpayer itemizes (subject to the 2 percent-of-AGI floor). Exceptions are made for moving expenses and the employment-related expenses of a qualified performing artist, where a deduction *for* AGI is allowed. Thus, the tax treatment of reimbursements under accountable and nonaccountable plans differs significantly.

LO.4

Appreciate the difference between accountable and nonaccountable employee plans and understand the opportunities to build wealth through Individual Retirement Accounts.

Accountable Plans

An accountable plan requires the employee to:

- Adequately account for (substantiate) the expenses. An employee renders an *adequate accounting* by submitting a record, with receipts and other substantiation, to the employer.[72]
- Return any excess reimbursement or allowance. An "excess reimbursement or allowance" is any amount the employee does not adequately account for as an ordinary and necessary business expense.

The law provides that no deduction is allowed for any travel, entertainment, business gift, or listed property (automobiles and computers) expenditure unless properly substantiated by adequate records. The records should contain the following information:[73]

- The amount of the expense.
- The time and place of travel or entertainment (or date of gift).
- The business purpose of the expense.
- The business relationship of the taxpayer to the person entertained (or receiving the gift).

This means that the taxpayer must maintain an account book or diary in which the above information is recorded at the time of the expenditure. Documentary evidence such as an itemized receipt is required to support any expenditure for lodging while traveling away from home and for any other expenditure of $75 or more. If a taxpayer fails to keep adequate records, each expense must be established by a written or oral statement of the exact details of the expense and by other corroborating evidence.[74]

In-depth coverage can be found on this book's companion website:**www.cengagebrain.com**   19   Digging Deeper

Bertha has travel expenses substantiated only by canceled checks. The checks establish the date, place, and amount of the expenditure. Because neither the business relationship nor the business purpose is established, the deduction is disallowed.[75]   **Example 46**

---

[71]§ 62(a)(2).
[72]Reg. § 1.162–17(b)(4).
[73]§ 274(d).

[74]Temp.Reg. § 1.274–5T(c)(3).
[75]*William T. Whitaker*, 56 TCM 47, T.C.Memo. 1988–418.

TAX IN THE NEWS   Relief for Members of the Armed Forces Reserves

In the Military Family Tax Relief Act of 2003, Congress provided various tax benefits for reservists, one of which deals with the classification of travel expenses. Members of the Reserves or National Guard who travel to drills and other service-related activities may claim the expenses as deductions *for* AGI. Previously, the expenses were not deductible unless the taxpayer itemized. (As miscellaneous itemized deductions, they were subject to the 2 percent-of-AGI floor.) To qualify for the deduction *for* AGI classification, the trip must be more than 100 miles from home and include an overnight stay. Any deduction is limited to the Federal per diem rates applicable to the area involved.

Example 47

Dwight has travel and entertainment expenses substantiated by a diary showing the time, place, and amount of the expenditure. His oral testimony provides the business relationship and business purpose; however, because he has no receipts, any expenditures of $75 or more are disallowed.[76]

Nonaccountable Plans

A nonaccountable plan is a plan in which an adequate accounting or return of excess amounts, or both, is not required. All reimbursements of expenses are reported in full as wages on the employee's Form W–2. Any allowable expenses are deductible in the same manner as unreimbursed expenses.

An employer may have an accountable plan and require employees to return excess reimbursements or allowances, but an employee may fail to follow the rules of the plan. In that case, the expenses and reimbursements are subject to nonaccountable plan treatment.

Unreimbursed Expenses

Unreimbursed employee expenses are treated in a straightforward manner. Meals and entertainment expenses are subject to the 50 percent limit. Total unreimbursed employee business expenses are usually reported as miscellaneous itemized deductions subject to the 2 percent-of-AGI floor (refer to Chapter 10). If the employee could have received, but did not seek, reimbursement for whatever reason, none of the employment-related expenses are deductible.

Tax Planning Strategies   UNREIMBURSED EMPLOYEE BUSINESS EXPENSES

FRAMEWORK FOCUS: DEDUCTIONS

Strategy: Maximize Deductible Amounts.

The 2 percent floor for unreimbursed employee business expenses offers a tax planning opportunity for married couples. If one spouse has high miscellaneous expenses subject to the floor, it may be beneficial for the couple to file separate returns. If they file jointly, the 2 percent floor is based on the adjusted gross incomes of both. Filing separately lowers the reduction to 2 percent of only one spouse's adjusted gross income.

Other provisions of the law should be considered, however. For example, filing separately could cost a couple losses of up to $25,000 from self-managed rental units under the passive activity loss rules (discussed in Chapter 6).

Another possibility is to negotiate a salary reduction with one's employer in exchange for the 100 percent reimbursement of employee expenses. The employee is better off because the 2 percent floor does not apply. The employer is better off because certain expense reimbursements are not subject to Social Security and other payroll taxes.

[76]*W. David Tyler*, 43 TCM 927, T.C.Memo. 1982–160.

In-depth coverage can be found on this book's companion website: **www.cengagebrain.com**    **20**   Digging Deeper

11-3i Contributions to Individual Retirement Accounts

Traditional IRAs

An individual can contribute to a traditional **Individual Retirement Account (IRA)** assuming the person (or spouse) receives taxable income and is under age $70\frac{1}{2}$. These contributions may be deductible, depending upon income level and access to another work-related retirement plan. For 2014, the contribution ceiling is the smaller of $5,500 (or $11,000 for spousal IRAs) or 100 percent of compensation.[77] The contribution ceiling applies to all types of IRAs (traditional deductible, traditional nondeductible, and Roth). An individual who attains the age of 50 by the end of the tax year can make an additional catch-up IRA contribution of up to $1,000 in 2014.

If the taxpayer is an active participant in a qualified plan, the traditional IRA deduction limitation is phased out *proportionately* between certain AGI ranges, as shown in Table 11.3.[78] If AGI is above the phaseout range, no IRA deduction is allowed.

AGI is calculated taking into account any passive losses and taxable Social Security benefits and ignoring any foreign income exclusion, savings bonds interest exclusion, and the IRA deduction. There is a $200 floor on the IRA deduction limitation for individuals whose AGI is not above the phaseout range.

Dan, who is single, has compensation income of $66,000 in 2014. He is an active participant in his employer's qualified retirement plan. Dan contributes $5,500 to a traditional IRA. The deductible amount is reduced from $5,500 by $3,300 because of the phaseout mechanism (see Table 11.3): $$\frac{\$6,000}{\$10,000} \times \$5,500 = \$3,300 \text{ reduction}$$ Therefore, of the $5,500 contribution, Dan can deduct only $2,200 ($5,500 − $3,300).	**Example 48**

Ben, an unmarried individual, is an active participant in his employer's qualified retirement plan in 2014. With AGI of $69,800, he would normally have an IRA deduction limit of $110 {$5,500 − [($69,800 − $60,000)/$10,000 × $5,500]}. However, because of the special floor provision, Ben is allowed a $200 IRA deduction.	**Example 49**

An individual is not considered an active participant in a qualified plan merely because the individual's spouse is an active participant in such a plan for any part of a plan year. Thus, even when filing jointly, the nonparticipating individual may take a full $5,500 deduction regardless of the participation status of his or her spouse, unless the couple has AGI above $181,000. If their AGI is above $181,000, the phaseout of the deduction begins at $181,000 and ends at $191,000 (phaseout over the $10,000 range) rather than beginning and ending at the phaseout amounts in Table 11.3.[79]

Nell is covered by a qualified employer retirement plan at work. Her husband, Nick, is not an active participant in a qualified plan. If Nell and Nick's combined AGI is $135,000, Nell cannot make a deductible IRA contribution because she exceeds the income threshold for an active participant. However, because Nick is not an active participant and their combined AGI does not exceed $181,000, he can make a fully deductible contribution of $5,500 to an IRA.	**Example 50**

---

[77]§§ 219(b)(1) and (c)(2). The limit is adjusted annually for inflation in $500 increments.

[78]§ 219(g).

[79]§ 219(g)(7).

TABLE 11.3	Phaseout of Traditional IRA Deduction of an Active Participant in 2014	

AGI Filing Status	Phaseout Begins*	Phaseout Ends
Single and head of household	$60,000	$ 70,000
Married, filing joint return	96,000	116,000
Married, filing separate return	–0–	10,000

*These amounts are indexed annually for inflation.

To the extent an individual is ineligible to make a deductible contribution to an IRA, *nondeductible contributions* can be made to separate accounts. The nondeductible contributions are subject to the same dollar limits as deductible contributions ($5,500 of earned income, $11,000 for a spousal IRA). Income in the account accumulates tax-free until distributed. Only the account earnings are taxed upon distribution because the account basis equals the contributions made by the taxpayer. A taxpayer may elect to treat deductible IRA contributions as nondeductible. If an individual has no taxable income for the year after taking into account other deductions, the election would be beneficial. The election is made on the individual's tax return for the taxable year to which the designation relates.

Roth IRAs

A Roth IRA is a *nondeductible* alternative to the traditional deductible IRA. Introduced by Congress to encourage individual savings, earnings inside a Roth IRA are not taxable, and all qualified distributions from a Roth IRA are tax-free.[80] The maximum allowable annual contribution to a Roth IRA for 2014 is the smaller of $5,500 ($11,000 for spousal IRAs) or 100 percent of the individual's compensation for the year. Contributions to a Roth IRA must be made by the due date (excluding extensions) of the taxpayer's tax return. Roth IRAs are not subject to the minimum distribution rules that apply to traditional IRAs. Contributions to a Roth IRA (unlike a traditional IRA) may continue beyond age $70\frac{1}{2}$ so long as the person generates compensation income and is not barred by the AGI limits.

A taxpayer can make tax-free withdrawals from a Roth IRA after an initial five-year holding period if any of the following requirements are satisfied:

- The distribution is made on or after the date on which the participant attains age $59\frac{1}{2}$.
- The distribution is made to a beneficiary (or the participant's estate) on or after the participant's death.
- The participant becomes disabled.
- The distribution is used to pay for qualified first-time homebuyer's expenses (statutory ceiling of $10,000).

Example 51	Edith establishes a Roth IRA at age 42 and contributes $5,000 per year for 20 years. The account is now worth $149,400, consisting of $100,000 of nondeductible contributions and $49,400 in accumulated earnings that have not been taxed. Edith may withdraw the $149,400 tax-free from the Roth IRA because she is over age 59½ and has met the five-year holding period requirement.

If the taxpayer receives a distribution from a Roth IRA and does not satisfy the aforementioned requirements, the distribution may be taxable. If the distribution represents a return of capital, it is not taxable. Conversely, if the distribution represents a payout of earnings, it is taxable. Under the ordering rules for Roth IRA

TAX FACT The Vacillating Popularity of IRAs

Individual Retirement Accounts (IRAs) became part of the tax law in 1974. The number of individual income tax returns reporting IRA contributions has varied over time, as the table at the right shows.

What probably caused the substantial decline between 1985 and 1990? Tax legislation enacted in 1986 applied the *wherewithal to pay* concept in providing for the phaseout of the IRA deduction once an AGI threshold was reached. In addition, the legislation substantially reduced tax rates for the individual taxpayer.

Year	Number of Returns (in Millions)
1975	1.2
1980	2.6
1985	16.2
1990	5.2
1995	4.3
2000	5.8
2005	4.1

Source: IRS Tax Statistics.

distributions, distributions are treated as first made from contributions (return of capital).

Example 52

Assume the same facts as in Example 51, except that Edith is only age 50 and receives a distribution of $55,000. Because her adjusted basis for the Roth IRA is $100,000 (contributions made), the distribution is tax-free and her adjusted basis is reduced to $45,000 ($100,000 − $55,000).

Roth IRAs are subject to income limits. In 2014, the maximum annual contribution of $5,500 is phased out beginning at AGI of $114,000 for single taxpayers and $181,000 for married couples who file a joint return. The phaseout range is $10,000 for married filing jointly and $15,000 for single taxpayers. For a married taxpayer filing separately, the contribution is phased out over a range beginning with AGI of $0 and ending with $10,000.

Example 53

Bev, who is single, would like to contribute $5,500 to her Roth IRA. However, her AGI in 2014 is $124,000; so her contribution is limited to $1,833 ($5,500 − $3,667) calculated as follows:

$$\frac{\$10,000}{\$15,000} \times \$5,500 = \$3,667 \text{ reduction}$$

In-depth coverage can be found on this book's companion website: **www.cengagebrain.com** 21 | Digging Deeper

Coverdell Education Savings Accounts (CESAs)

Distributions from a **Coverdell Education Savings Account (CESA)** to pay for qualified education expenses receive favorable tax treatment.[81] Qualified education expenses include tuition, fees, books, supplies, and related equipment. Room and board qualify if the student's course load is at least one-half of the full-time course load. If the CESA is used to pay the qualified education expenses of the designated beneficiary, the withdrawals are tax-free. To the extent the distributions during a tax year exceed qualified education expenses, part of the excess is treated as a return of capital (the contributions) and part is treated as a distribution of earnings under the § 72 annuity rules. Thus, the distribution is presumed to be pro rata from each category. The exclusion for the distribution of earnings part is calculated as follows:

$$\frac{\text{Qualified education expenses}}{\text{Total distributions}} \times \text{Earnings} = \text{Exclusion}$$

---
[81]§ 530.

TAX IN THE NEWS   IRA Losses from a Ponzi Scheme

The Bernard Madoff and Mark Stanford Ponzi schemes affected many taxpayers who had IRA plans with Madoff or Stanford. If a taxpayer had a traditional IRA and all contributions were deductible, the individual has a zero basis; so no loss deduction is available for the losses associated with these Ponzi schemes. If the IRA included some nondeductible contributions, a loss might be deductible if the individual withdraws the entire amount from the IRA. The miscellaneous itemized deduction, subject to the 2 percent floor, would be the difference between the basis and the amount withdrawn. Of course, there may be a 10 percent penalty tax if the withdrawal is an early withdrawal.

A taxpayer with a Roth IRA is more likely to obtain a loss deduction associated with these Ponzi schemes because Roth IRA contributions are nondeductible. The miscellaneous itemized deduction would be the amount contributed (i.e., the basis) less the value of any assets distributed to the Roth IRA owner.

Example 54

Meg receives a $2,500 distribution from her CESA. She uses $2,000 to pay for qualified education expenses. On the date of the distribution, Meg's CESA balance is $10,000, $6,000 of which represents her contributions. Because 60% ($6,000/$10,000) of her account balance represents her contributions, $1,500 ($2,500 × 60%) of the distribution is a return of capital and $1,000 ($2,500 × 40%) is a distribution of earnings. The excludible amount of the earnings is calculated as follows:

$$\frac{\$2,000}{\$2,500} \times \$1,000 = \$800$$

Thus, Meg must include $200 ($1,000 − $800) in her gross income.

The maximum amount that can be contributed annually to a CESA for a beneficiary is $2,000. A beneficiary must be an individual and cannot be a group of children or an unborn child. The contributions are not deductible. A CESA is subject to income limits. The maximum annual contribution is phased out beginning at $95,000 for single taxpayers and $190,000 for married couples who file a joint return. The phaseout range is $30,000 for married filing jointly and $15,000 for single taxpayers. Contributions cannot be made to a CESA after the date on which the designated beneficiary attains age 18. Thus, a total of up to $36,000 can be contributed for each beneficiary—$2,000 in the year of birth and in each of the 17 following years.

A 6 percent excise tax is imposed on excess contributions to a CESA. A 10 percent excise tax is imposed on any distributions that are included in gross income.

The balance in a CESA must be distributed within 30 days after the death of a beneficiary or within 30 days after a beneficiary reaches age 30. Any balance at the close of either 30-day period is considered to be distributed at such time, and the earnings portion is included in the beneficiary's gross income. Before a beneficiary reaches age 30, any balance can be rolled over tax-free into another CESA for a member of the beneficiary's family who is under age 30.

The CESA exclusion may be available in a tax year in which the beneficiary claims the American Opportunity credit or the lifetime learning credit (see Chapter 10). However, any excluded amount of the CESA distribution cannot be used for the same educational expenses for which the American Opportunity credit or the lifetime learning credit is claimed.

Contributions cannot be made to a beneficiary's CESA during any year in which contributions are made to a qualified tuition program on behalf of the same beneficiary.

11-4 INDIVIDUALS AS PROPRIETORS

11-4a The Proprietorship as a Business Entity

LO.5

State and explain the tax provisions applicable to proprietors.

A sole proprietorship is *not* a taxable entity separate from the individual who owns the proprietorship. A sole proprietor reports the results of business operations of the proprietorship on Schedule C of Form 1040. The net profit or loss from the proprietorship is then transferred from Schedule C to Form 1040, which is used by the taxpayer to determine tax liability. The proprietor reports all of the net profit or net loss from the business, regardless of the amount actually withdrawn from the proprietorship during the year.

Income and expenses of the proprietorship retain their character when reported by the proprietor. For example, ordinary income of the proprietorship is treated as ordinary income when reported by the proprietor, and capital gain of the proprietorship is treated as capital gain by the proprietor.

George is the sole proprietor of George's Record Shop. Gross income of the business in 2014 is $200,000, and operating expenses are $110,000. George also sells a capital asset held by the business for a $10,000 long-term capital gain. During 2014, he withdraws $60,000 from the business for living expenses. George reports the operating income and expenses of the business on Schedule C, resulting in net profit (ordinary income) of $90,000 ($200,000 − $110,000). Even though he withdrew only $60,000, George reports all of the $90,000 net profit from the business on Form 1040, where he computes taxable income and the tax liability for the year. He also reports a $10,000 long-term capital gain on his personal tax return (Schedule D of Form 1040).

Example 55

11-4b Income of a Proprietorship

The broad definition of gross income in § 61(a) applies equally to individuals and business entities, including proprietorships, corporations, and partnerships. Thus, it is assumed that asset inflows into a proprietorship are to be treated as income. Certain items may be excluded from gross income. Many of the exclusions available to an individual are related to the individual as an employee. Refer to Chapter 4 for a detailed discussion of gross income.

11-4c Deductions Related to a Proprietorship

Ordinary and Necessary Business Expenses

The provisions that govern business deductions also are general and not entity-specific. The § 162 requirement that trade or business expenses be *ordinary and necessary* (refer to Chapter 5) applies to proprietorships as well as corporations, partnerships, and other business entities. However, certain specific deductions are available only to self-employed taxpayers. These deductions are covered in detail below.

Health Insurance Premiums

A self-employed taxpayer may deduct 100 percent of insurance premiums paid for medical coverage as a deduction *for* AGI.[82] The deduction is allowed for premiums paid on behalf of the taxpayer, the taxpayer's spouse, and dependents of the taxpayer. The deduction is not allowed to any taxpayer who is eligible to participate in a subsidized health plan maintained by any employer of the taxpayer or of the taxpayer's spouse.

This deduction is reported in the Adjusted Gross Income section of Form 1040 rather than on Schedule C. Premiums paid for medical coverage of the *employees* of a self-employed taxpayer are deductible as business expenses on Schedule C, however.

[82]§ 162(l).

TAX IN THE NEWS   The Tax Gap Includes $58 Billion in Payroll Taxes

The "tax gap"—the difference between what taxpayers owe to the Federal government in taxes and what they pay—is approaching $400 billion annually. A significant portion of that amount consists of delinquent payroll taxes—the money withheld from employees' salaries by employers for FICA taxes (Social Security and Medicare taxes).

According to a study by the Government Accountability Office (GAO), more than 1.6 million businesses together owe in excess of $58 billion related to delinquent payroll taxes. Of that amount, $26 billion represents actual taxes owed, $18 billion is for interest, and $14 billion is for penalties. In contrast, businesses owe only $24 billion in delinquent corporate income taxes. Businesses in the construction, professional services, and health care industries have the largest payroll tax delinquencies.

Collecting payroll taxes seems to be a perennial problem. The GAO study pointed out that delinquencies today are about the same as they were a decade ago when 1.8 million businesses owed about $49 billion. Today, though, debts are more likely to be long-standing. About 500

employers owe at least 10 years' worth of taxes, and nearly 15,000 owe 5 years' worth. About half of the $58 billion owed is from 2002 or earlier. Since then, the IRS has stepped up its enforcement efforts through the use of liens and levies on businesses that fail to pay over the taxes withheld.

In July 2009, the Treasury Department released its own study of the tax gap that generally confirmed the data in the GAO study. Further, beginning in November 2009, the IRS launched a National Research Program that is conducting detailed examinations of employment tax collections. Approximately 5,000 employers will be randomly selected for audit over a three-year period. In addition to potential assessments, these audits will provide the IRS with a better understanding of overall employment tax compliance.

Sources: Based on "Businesses Owe IRS $58 Billion," *USA TODAY* (online), July 28, 2008; U.S. Department of the Treasury, "Update on Reducing the Federal Tax Gap and Improving Voluntary Compliance," July 9, 2009.

Example 56

Ellen, a sole proprietor of a restaurant, has two dependent children. During 2014, she paid health insurance premiums of $1,800 for her own coverage and $1,000 for coverage of her two children. Ellen can deduct $2,800 as a deduction *for* AGI.

Self-Employment Tax

The tax on self-employment income is levied to provide Social Security and Medicare benefits (old age, survivors, and disability insurance and hospital insurance) for self-employed individuals. Individuals with net earnings of $400 or more from self-employment are subject to the self-employment tax.[83] For 2014, the combined self-employment tax rate is 15.3 percent (12.4 percent for Social Security and 2.9 percent for Medicare). For 2014, the ceiling amount is $117,000 and for 2013, the ceiling amount is $113,700. The ceiling amount is adjusted annually for inflation.

For purposes of computing the *self-employment tax,* self-employed taxpayers are allowed a deduction from net earnings equal to one-half of the self-employment tax rate.[84] This deduction of 7.65 percent (one-half of the 15.3 percent rate) is reflected by multiplying net earnings from self-employment by 92.35 percent (100% − 7.65%), as shown in Example 57. For purposes of computing *taxable income,* an income tax deduction is allowed for part (one-half in 2013 and 2014) of the amount of self-employment tax paid.[85]

Example 57 illustrates the computation of the self-employment tax, as well as the income tax deduction for one-half of the self-employment tax paid. For income tax purposes, the amount to be reported on Schedule C is net earnings from self-employment *before* the deduction for one-half of the self-employment tax. The deduction of one-half of the self-employment tax paid is reported separately on Form 1040 as a deduction *for* AGI.

---

[83]§ 6017.
[84]§ 1402(a)(12).

[85]§ 164(f).

Example 57

Computation of the self-employment tax is determined using the steps below. The self-employment tax is determined for two taxpayers with net earnings from self-employment for 2014 as follows: Ned, $55,000 and Terry, $130,000.

Computation of Self-Employment Tax for Ned	
1. Net earnings	$55,000.00
2. Multiply line 1 by 92.35%.	$50,792.50
3. If the amount on line 2 is $117,000 or less, multiply the line 2 amount by 15.3%. This is the self-employment tax.	$ 7,771.25
4. If the amount on line 2 is more than $117,000, multiply the excess over $117,000 by 2.9% and add $17,901. This is the self-employment tax.	

Computation of Self-Employment Tax for Terry	
1. Net earnings	$130,000.00
2. Multiply line 1 by 92.35%.	$120,055.00
3. If the amount on line 2 is $117,000 or less, multiply the line 2 amount by 15.3%. This is the self-employment tax.	
4. If the amount on line 2 is more than $117,000, multiply the excess over $117,000 by 2.9% and add $17,901. This is the self-employment tax.	$ 17,989.60

For income tax purposes, Ned has net earnings from self-employment of $55,000 and a deduction *for* AGI of $3,885.63 ($7,771.25 × one-half). Terry has net earnings from self-employment of $130,000 and a deduction *for* AGI of $8,994.80 ($17,989.60 × one-half). Both taxpayers benefit from the deduction for one-half of the self-employment tax paid.

Wages of employees also are subject to Social Security and Medicare taxes. For 2013 and 2014, the combined tax rate is 15.3 percent (7.65 percent on employee and an employer match of 7.65 percent). If an individual who is self-employed also receives wages subject to the FICA tax from working as an employee of another organization, the ceiling amount of the Social Security portion on which the self-employment tax is computed is reduced. Thus, the self-employment tax may be reduced if a self-employed individual also receives Social Security wages.

Net earnings from self-employment include gross income from a trade or business less allowable trade or business deductions, the distributive share of any partnership income or loss derived from a trade or business activity, and net income from rendering personal services as an independent contractor. Gain or loss from the disposition of property (including involuntary conversions) is excluded from the computation of self-employment income unless the property involved is inventory.

11-4d Retirement Plans for Self-Employed Individuals

Self-employed individuals have several options for retirement funding. Individual Retirement Accounts (discussed earlier in this chapter) are available to both employees and self-employed individuals. Other options for self-employed individuals include, but are not limited to, H.R. 10 (Keogh) plans and SIMPLE plans, both of which are discussed next.

Keogh Plans

Self-employed individuals (e.g., partners and sole proprietors) are eligible to establish and receive qualified retirement benefits under **Keogh plans** (also known as H.R. 10 plans). Self-employed individuals who establish Keogh plans for themselves are also required to cover their *employees* under the plan.

TAX FACT   Increasing Popularity of Keogh Plans

Keogh plans are an increasingly popular retirement savings device for self-employed taxpayers. The number of individual income tax returns that included Keogh contributions is indicated at the right.

Year	Number of Returns (in Thousands)
1975	596
1980	569
1985	676
1990	824
1995	1,032
2000	1,228
2005	1,257

Source: IRS Tax Statistics.

© iStockphoto.com/Pali Rao

Keogh investments can include a variety of funding vehicles, such as mutual funds, annuities, real estate shares, certificates of deposit, debt instruments, commodities, securities, and personal properties. When an individual decides to make all investment decisions, a *self-directed retirement plan* is established. Investment in most collectibles is not allowed in a self-directed plan.

A Keogh plan may be either a *defined contribution* plan or a *defined benefit* plan. In a defined contribution plan, the amount that can be contributed each year is subject to limitations. Retirement benefits depend on the amount contributed and the amount earned by the plan. In a defined benefit plan, the amount of retirement income is fixed and is determined on the basis of the employee's compensation while working, the number of years in the plan, and age upon retirement.

A self-employed individual may annually contribute the smaller of $52,000 (in 2014) or 100 percent of earned income to a defined contribution Keogh plan.[86] If the defined contribution plan is a profit sharing plan or stock bonus plan, however, a 25 percent deduction limit applies. Under a defined benefit Keogh plan, the annual benefit is limited to the smaller of $210,000 (in 2014) or 100 percent of the average net earnings for the three highest years.[87]

Earned income refers to net earnings from self-employment.[88] Net earnings from self-employment means the gross income derived by an individual from any trade or business carried on by that individual, less appropriate deductions, plus the distributive share of income or loss from a partnership.[89] Earned income is reduced by contributions to a Keogh plan on the individual's behalf and by 50 percent of any self-employment tax.[90]

Example 58

Pat, a partner, has earned income of $150,000 in 2014 (after the deduction for one-half of self-employment tax, but before any Keogh contribution). The maximum contribution Pat may make to a defined contribution Keogh plan is $52,000, the lesser of $150,000 or $52,000.

For discrimination purposes, the 25 percent limitation on the employee contribution to a profit sharing plan or stock bonus plan is computed on the first $260,000 (in 2014) of earned income. Thus, the maximum contribution in 2014 is $52,000 ($260,000 − .25X = X; X = $208,000). Therefore, $260,000 − $208,000 = $52,000. Alternatively, this can be calculated by multiplying $260,000 by 20 percent.

---

[86]§ 415(c)(1).
[87]§ 415(b)(1). The amount is indexed annually.
[88]§ 401(c)(2).
[89]§ 1402(a).
[90]§§ 401(c)(2)(A)(v) and 164(f).

> **Example 59**
>
> Terry, a self-employed accountant, has a profit sharing plan with a contribution rate of 15% of compensation. Terry's earned income after the deduction of one-half of self-employment tax, but before the Keogh contribution, is $260,000. Terry's contribution is limited to $33,913 ($260,000 − .15X − X), because X = $226,087 and .15 × $226,087 = $33,913.

Although a Keogh plan must be established before the end of the year in question, contributions may be made up to the normal filing date for that year.

Tax Planning Strategies — IMPORTANT DATES RELATED TO IRAs AND KEOGH PLANS

FRAMEWORK FOCUS: DEDUCTIONS

Strategy: Accelerate Recognition of Deductions to Achieve Tax Deferral.

A Keogh or IRA participant may make a deductible contribution for a tax year up to the time prescribed for filing the individual's tax return for that tax year. A Keogh plan must have been *established* by the end of the *prior* tax year (e.g., December 31, 2013) to obtain a deduction on the 2013 income tax return for the contribution made in the *current* year (2014). An individual can establish an IRA during the *current* tax year (up to the normal filing date) and still receive a deduction on the prior-year income tax return for the contribution made in the *current* year.

SIMPLE Plans

Employers with 100 or fewer employees who do not maintain another qualified retirement plan may establish a *savings incentive match plan for employees* (SIMPLE plan).[91] The plan can be in the form of a § 401(k) plan or an IRA. A SIMPLE § 401(k) plan is not subject to the nondiscrimination rules that are normally applicable to § 401(k) plans.

All employees who received at least $5,000 in compensation from the employer during any two preceding years and who reasonably expect to receive at least $5,000 in compensation during the current year must be eligible to participate in the plan. The decision to participate is up to the employee. A *self-employed individual* also may participate in the plan.

The contributions made by the employee (a salary reduction approach) must be expressed as a percentage of compensation rather than as a fixed dollar amount. The SIMPLE plan must not permit the elective employee contribution for the year to exceed $12,000 (in 2014).[92] The SIMPLE elective deferral limit is increased under the catch-up provision for employees age 50 and over. The amount is $2,500 in 2014 and is indexed for inflation in $500 increments.

Generally, the employer must either match elective employee contributions up to 3 percent of the employee's compensation or provide nonmatching contributions of 2 percent of compensation for each eligible employee. Thus, for an employee under age 50, the maximum amount that may be contributed to the plan for 2014 is $19,800 [$12,000 employee contributions + $7,800 ($260,000 compensation ceiling × 3%) employer match].

No other contributions may be made to the plan other than the employee elective contribution and the required employer matching contribution (or nonmatching contribution under the 2 percent rule). All contributions are fully vested. An employer is required to make the required matching or nonmatching contributions to a SIMPLE § 401(k) plan once it is established, whereas an employer's contributions to a traditional § 401(k) plan generally may be discretionary.

An employer's deduction for contributions to a SIMPLE § 401(k) plan is limited to the greater of 25 percent of the compensation paid or accrued or the amount

---

[91]§ 408(p).   [92]For 2013, the amount also was $12,000.

the employer is required to contribute to the plan. Thus, an employer may deduct contributions to a SIMPLE § 401(k) plan in excess of 25 percent of the $260,000 salary cap. A traditional § 401(k) plan is limited to 25 percent of the total compensation of plan participants for the year (excluding age 50 catch-ups).

An employer is allowed a deduction for matching contributions only if the contributions are made by the due date (including extensions) for the employer's tax return. Contributions to a SIMPLE plan are excludible from the employee's gross income, and the SIMPLE plan is tax-exempt.

Example 60

The Mauve Company has a SIMPLE plan for its employees under which it provides nonmatching contributions of 2% of compensation for each eligible employee. The maximum amount that can be added to each participant's account in 2014 is $17,200, composed of the $12,000 employee salary reduction plus an employer contribution of $5,200 ($260,000 × 2%).

Distributions from a SIMPLE plan are taxed under the IRA rules. Tax-free rollovers can be made from one SIMPLE account to another. A SIMPLE account can be rolled over to an IRA tax-free after the expiration of a two-year period since the individual first participated in the plan. Withdrawals of contributions during the two-year period beginning on the date an employee first participates in the SIMPLE plan are subject to a 25 percent early withdrawal penalty rather than the 10 percent early withdrawal penalty that otherwise would apply.

Tax Planning Strategies   FACTORS AFFECTING RETIREMENT PLAN CHOICES

FRAMEWORK FOCUS: DEDUCTIONS

Strategy: Maximize Deductible Amounts.

An IRA might not be the best retirement plan option for many self-employed taxpayers. The maximum amount that can be deducted is $5,500 per year ($11,000 for a spousal plan), which may be too low to provide funding for an adequate level of retirement income. Other options such as Keogh plans and SIMPLE plans allow larger contributions and larger deductions. However, a self-employed individual who establishes either a Keogh or a SIMPLE plan is required to cover employees under such plans. This can result in substantial expenditures, not only for the required contributions but also for expenses of administering the plan. An advantage of an IRA is that coverage of employees is not required.

11-4e Accounting Periods and Methods

Proprietors may choose among various accounting methods, just as other business entities do (refer to Chapters 4 and 5). The cash method is commonly used by proprietorships that provide services, while the accrual or hybrid method generally is required if inventory is a material income-producing factor.

The accounting period rules for proprietorships generally are much simpler than the rules for partnerships and S corporations. Because a proprietorship is not an entity separate from the proprietor, the proprietorship must use the same tax year-end as the proprietor. This does not preclude the use of a fiscal year for a proprietorship, but most proprietorships use the calendar year.

11-4f Estimated Tax Payments

Although the following discussion largely centers on self-employed taxpayers, some of the procedures may be applicable to employed persons. In many cases, for example, employed persons may be required to pay estimated tax if they have income that is not subject to withholding (e.g., income from rentals, dividends, or interest).

Estimated Tax for Individuals

Estimated tax is the amount of tax (including alternative minimum tax and self-employment tax) an individual expects to owe for the year after subtracting tax credits and income tax withheld. Any individual who has estimated tax for the year of $1,000 or more and whose withholding does not equal or exceed the required annual payment (discussed below) must make quarterly payments.[93] Otherwise, a penalty may be assessed. No quarterly payments are required and no penalty will apply on an underpayment if the taxpayer's estimated tax is under $1,000. No penalty will apply if the taxpayer had no tax liability for the preceding tax year, the preceding tax year was a taxable year of 12 months, and the taxpayer was a citizen or resident for the entire preceding tax year. In this regard, having no tax liability is not the same as having no additional tax to pay.

The required annual payment must first be computed. This is the smaller of the following amounts:

- Ninety percent of the tax shown on the current year's return.
- One hundred percent of the tax shown on the preceding year's return (the return must cover the full 12 months of the preceding year). If the AGI on the preceding year's return exceeds $150,000 ($75,000 if married filing separately), the 100 percent requirement is increased to 110 percent.

In general, one-fourth of this required annual payment is due on April 15, June 15, and September 15 of the tax year and January 15 of the following year. Thus, the quarterly installment of the required annual payment reduced by the applicable withholding is the estimated tax to be paid. An equal part of withholding is deemed paid on each due date, even if a taxpayer's earnings fluctuate widely during the year. Payments are to be accompanied by the payment voucher from Form 1040–ES for the appropriate date.

Penalty on Underpayments

A nondeductible penalty is imposed on the amount of underpayment of estimated tax. The rate for this penalty is adjusted quarterly to reflect changes in the average prime rate.

An *underpayment* occurs when any quarterly payment (the sum of estimated tax paid and income tax withheld) is less than 25 percent of the required annual payment. The penalty is applied to the amount of the underpayment for the period of the underpayment.[94]

Example 61

Marta made the following payments of estimated tax for 2014 and had no income tax withheld:

April 15, 2014	$1,400
June 16, 2014	2,300
September 15, 2014	1,500
January 15, 2015	1,800

Marta's actual tax for 2014 is $8,000, and her tax in 2013 was $10,000. Therefore, each installment should have been at least $1,800 [($8,000 × 90%) × 25%]. Of the payment on June 16, $400 will be credited to the unpaid balance of the first quarterly installment due on April 15,[95] thereby effectively stopping the underpayment penalty for the first quarterly period. Of the remaining $1,900 payment on June 16, $100 is credited to the September 15 payment, resulting in this third quarterly payment being $200 short. Then $200 of the January 15, 2015 payment is credited to the September 15

[93]§ 6654(c)(1).
[94]§ 6654(b)(2).
[95]Payments are credited to unpaid installments in the order in which the installments are required to be paid. § 6654(b)(3).

shortfall, ending the period of underpayment for that portion due. The January 15, 2015 installment is now underpaid by $200, and a penalty will apply from January 15, 2015, to April 15, 2015 (unless paid sooner). Marta's underpayments for the periods of underpayment are as follows:

1st installment due:	$400 from April 15, 2014, to June 16, 2014
2nd installment due:	Paid in full
3rd installment due:	$200 from September 15, 2014, to January 15, 2015
4th installment due:	$200 from January 15, 2015, to April 15, 2015

If a possible underpayment of estimated tax is indicated, Form 2210 should be filed to compute the penalty due or to justify that no penalty applies.

11-5 HOBBY LOSSES

LO.6

Distinguish between business and hobby activities and apply the rules limiting the deduction of hobby losses.

Employee deductions and deductions related to a proprietorship were discussed in previous sections of this chapter. Employees are allowed to deduct certain expenditures incurred in connection with their work activities. Expenses incurred by a self-employed taxpayer are deductible only if the taxpayer can show that the activity was entered into for the purpose of making a profit.

Certain activities can have attributes that make it difficult to determine if the primary motivation for the activity is to make a profit or is for personal pleasure. Examples include raising horses and operating a farm that is also used as a weekend residence. While personal losses are not deductible, losses attributable to profit-seeking activities may be deducted and used to offset a taxpayer's other income. Activities that have both personal and profit-seeking motives are classified as hobbies, and the tax law limits the deductibility of **hobby losses**.

The income and deductions from a hobby are reported separately on the tax return. Whether deductions related to a hobby generate a tax benefit, the revenue for the hobby is always reported as other income on page 1 of Form 1040. The reporting of deductions is discussed below.

11-5a General Rules

If an individual can show that an activity has been conducted with the intent to earn a profit, losses from the activity are fully deductible. The hobby loss rules apply only if the activity is not engaged in for profit. Hobby expenses are deductible only to the extent of hobby income.[96]

The Regulations stipulate that the following nine factors should be considered in determining whether an activity is profit seeking or a hobby:[97]

- Whether the activity is conducted in a businesslike manner.
- The expertise of the taxpayers or their advisers.
- The time and effort expended.
- The expectation that the assets of the activity will appreciate in value.
- The taxpayer's previous success in conducting similar activities.
- The history of income or losses from the activity.
- The relationship of profits earned to losses incurred.
- The financial status of the taxpayer (e.g., if the taxpayer does not have substantial amounts of other income, this may indicate that the activity is engaged in for profit).
- Elements of personal pleasure or recreation in the activity.

The presence or absence of a factor is not by itself determinative of whether the activity is profit-seeking or is a hobby. Rather, the decision is a subjective one that is based on an analysis of the facts and circumstances.

---

[96]§ 183(b)(2).   [97]Reg. §§ 1.183–2(b)(1) through (9).

11-5b Presumptive Rule of § 183

The Code provides a rebuttable presumption that an activity is profit-seeking if the activity shows a profit in at least three of the previous five tax years.[98] If the activity involves horses, a profit in at least two of the previous seven tax years meets the presumptive rule. If these profitability tests are met, the activity is presumed to be a trade or business rather than a personal hobby. In this situation, the burden of proof shifts from the taxpayer to the IRS. That is, the IRS bears the burden of proving that the activity is personal rather than trade or business-related.

Example 62

Camille, an executive for a large corporation, is paid a salary of $200,000. Her husband is a collector of antiques. Several years ago, he opened an antique shop in a local shopping center. He now spends most of his time buying and selling antiques. He occasionally earns a small profit from this activity but more frequently incurs substantial losses. If the losses are business-related, they are fully deductible against Camille's salary on a joint return. The following approach should be considered in resolving this issue:

* Initially determine whether the antique activity has met the three-out-of-five-years profit test.
* If the presumption is not met, the activity may nevertheless qualify as a business if the taxpayer can show that the intent is to engage in a profit-seeking activity. It is not necessary to show actual profits.
* Attempt to fit the operation within the nine criteria prescribed in the Regulations listed above.

11-5c Determining the Amount of the Deduction

If an activity is deemed to be a hobby, the expenses are deductible only to the extent of the gross income from the hobby. These expenses must be deducted in the following order:

1. Amounts deductible under other Code Sections without regard to the nature of the activity, such as property taxes and home mortgage interest.
2. Amounts deductible under other Code Sections if the activity had been engaged in for profit, but only if those amounts do not affect adjusted basis. Examples include maintenance, utilities, and supplies.
3. Amounts that affect adjusted basis and would be deductible under other Code Sections if the activity had been engaged in for profit.[99] Examples include depreciation, amortization, and depletion.

These deductions are deductible *from* AGI as itemized deductions to the extent they exceed 2 percent of AGI.[100] If the taxpayer uses the standard deduction rather than itemizing, all hobby loss deductions are wasted.

Example 63

Jim, the vice president of an oil company, has AGI of $80,000. He decides to pursue painting in his spare time. He uses a home studio, comprising 10% of the home's square footage. During the current year, Jim incurs the following expenses:

Frames	$ 350
Art supplies	300
Fees paid to models	1,000
Expenses related to home:	
Total home property taxes	900
Total home mortgage interest	10,000
Total home maintenance and utilities	3,600
Depreciation on 10% of home used as studio	500

[98]§ 183(d).
[99]Reg. § 1.183–1(b)(1).
[100]Temp.Reg. § 1.67–1T(a)(1)(iv) and Rev.Rul. 75–14, 1975–1 C.B. 90.

During the year, Jim sold paintings for a total of $3,200. If the activity is held to be a hobby, Jim is allowed deductions as follows:

Gross income		$ 3,200
Deduct: Taxes and interest (10% of $10,900)		(1,090)
Remainder		$ 2,110
Deduct: Frames	$ 350	
Art supplies	300	
Models' fees	1,000	
Maintenance and utilities (10%)	360	(2,010)
Remainder		$ 100
Depreciation ($500, but limited to $100)		(100)
Net income		$ –0–

Jim includes the $3,200 of income in AGI, making his AGI $83,200. The taxes and interest are itemized deductions, deductible in full. Assuming that Jim has no other miscellaneous itemized deductions, the remaining expenses of $2,110 are reduced by 2% of his AGI ($1,664); so the net deduction is $446. Because the property taxes and home mortgage interest are deductible anyway, the net effect is a $2,754 ($3,200 less $446) increase in taxable income.

Example 64

If Jim's activity in Example 63 were held to be a business, he could deduct expenses totaling $3,600 *for* AGI, as shown below. All of these expenses would be trade or business expenses. His reduction in AGI would be as follows:

Gross income		$ 3,200
Deduct: Taxes and interest	$1,090	
Other business expenses	2,010	
Depreciation	500	(3,600)
Reduction in AGI		($ 400)

As in Example 63, Jim can deduct the remaining property taxes and home mortgage interest of $9,810 ($10,900 − $1,090) as itemized deductions.

REFOCUS ON THE BIG PICTURE

SELF-EMPLOYED VERSUS EMPLOYEE— WHAT'S THE DIFFERENCE?

Mark may deduct the ordinary and necessary business expenses incurred by his proprietorship. This includes the $18,000 for rent and utilities, the $12,000 paid to his secretary, and the $40,000 paid to his assistant. The $8,000 paid for equipment can be depreciated or may qualify for immediate expensing under § 179. As a self-employed taxpayer, Mark may deduct 100 percent of the $3,000 of health insurance premiums paid, but only if he is not eligible to participate in the subsidized health plan maintained by Mary's employer. On the other hand, Mark cannot deduct the premiums of $500 paid for his life insurance policy. Mark may want to consider contributing to his own IRA or establishing a Keogh plan or SIMPLE plan to allow for greater retirement contributions. Mark should be aware that in addition to paying income tax on the net income earned by his business, he will also owe self-employment tax at a combined rate of 15.3 percent in 2014 and will be able to claim an income tax deduction for half of the self-employment tax paid.

While Mary will owe income tax on her $85,000 salary, the health insurance premiums of $3,000 and group term life insurance premiums paid by her employer qualify as tax-free fringe benefits. In addition, as long as Mary is required to substantiate her travel expenses as part of an accountable plan, none of the travel-related reimbursements need to be included in Mary's gross income. Because Mary is not covered by a qualified retirement plan at work, she can also deduct the entire $5,500 contribution made to her IRA. While the $500 of employee business expenses are technically deductible, they provide a tax benefit to Mary only if they exceed 2 percent of the couple's AGI. While Mary is not subject to self-employment tax, she still incurs a 7.65 percent payroll tax in 2014 related to Social Security and Medicare. Her employer pays the other 7.65 percent.

What If?

In order to improve her skills in her current job, Mary is considering entering an MBA program at a local college. At the same time, to save money while Mary is in school, Mark is considering moving his office into a vacant room in their home. Are Mary's education expenses deductible? Can Mark deduct expenses associated with his home office? As long as the new degree is not required to meet the minimum requirements of her existing job and the degree does not qualify Mary for a new trade or business, Mary's books, tuition, and other related educational expenses are deductible as a miscellaneous itemized deduction. However, like the $500 of other employee business expenses mentioned earlier, the expenses provide a tax benefit only to the extent they exceed 2 percent of the couple's AGI. As a self-employed individual, Mark is allowed to deduct the costs of a home office as long as the office is used exclusively and on a regular basis as either the principal place of business or a place of business used by his clients and customers. Deductible expenses would include a portion of mortgage interest and property taxes paid on the home; a portion of utilities, repairs and maintenance, and other household expenses; and depreciation on the business portion of the home.

© iStockphoto.com/Neustockimages

Suggested Readings

Thomas Dalton and Shreesh Deshpande, "Quantifying the Choice Between a Roth and Traditional IRA," *Practical Tax Strategies*, September 2011.

Leonard Goodman and Jay A. Soled, "Enhanced CPA Education Restricts Graduate School Deduction," *Practical Tax Strategies*, July 2009.

David J. Hess and Lois D. Bryan, "Using an IRA for a Planned Charitable Contribution," *Practical Tax Strategies*, March 2012.

David L. Keligian, "Winning Independent Contractor Status," *Journal of Taxation*, November 2011.

Susan L. Megaard and Michael M. Megaard, "When Should the New Safe Harbor Method for Deducting Home-Office Expenses be Elected," *Journal of Taxation*, July 2013.

Ferdinand Siagian and Steven Colburn, "Working at a Temporary Job Site Can Increase Tax Deductions," *Practical Tax Strategies*, February 2010.

Key Terms

Accountable plan, 11-2

Automatic mileage method, 11-21

Cafeteria plans, 11-11

Coverdell Education Savings Account (CESA), 11-39

Deduction for qualified tuition and related expenses, 11-29

De minimis fringe benefits, 11-15

Education expenses, 11-26

Entertainment expenses, 11-30

Estimated tax, 11-47

Flexible spending plans, 11-12

Foreign earned income exclusion, 11-19

Health Savings Account (HSA), 11-6

Hobby losses, 11-48

Independent contractor, 11-2

Individual Retirement Account (IRA), 11-37

Keogh plans, 11-43

Medical Savings Accounts (MSAs), 11-6

Moving expenses, 11-24

No-additional-cost services, 11-13

Nonaccountable plan, 11-36

Office in the home expenses, 11-32

Qualified employee discounts, 11-14

Qualified transportation fringes, 11-16

Self-employment tax, 11-4

Transportation expenses, 11-20

Travel expenses, 11-21

Working condition fringes, 11-15

Problems

1. **LO.1** Mason performs services for Isabella. In determining whether Mason is an employee or an independent contractor, comment on the relevance of each of the factors listed below.
   a. Mason performs services only for Isabella and does not work for anyone else.
   b. Mason sets his own work schedule.
   c. Mason reports his job-related expenses on a Schedule C.
   d. Mason obtained his job skills from Isabella's training program.
   e. Mason performs the services at Isabella's business location.
   f. Mason is paid based on time worked rather than on task performed.

2. **LO.2** Rex, age 55, is an officer of Blue Company, which provides him with the following nondiscriminatory fringe benefits in 2014:

   • Hospitalization insurance premiums for Rex and his dependents. The cost of the coverage for Rex is $2,900 per year, and the additional cost for his dependents is $3,800 per year. The plan has a $2,000 deductible, but his employer contributed $1,500 to Rex's Health Savings Account (HSA). Rex withdrew only $800 from the HSA, and the account earned $50 of interest during the year.

   • Insurance premiums of $840 for salary continuation payments. Under the plan, Rex will receive his regular salary in the event he is unable to work due to illness. Rex collected $4,500 on the policy to replace lost wages while he was ill during the year.

   • Rex is a part-time student working on his bachelor's degree in engineering. His employer reimbursed his $5,200 tuition under a plan available to all full-time employees.

   Determine the amount Rex must include in gross income.

   Decision Making

3. **LO.2** Paul is in the 15% marginal tax bracket, and Betty is in the 35% marginal tax bracket. They each pay $6,300 in health insurance premiums for themselves and their families. Their employer has offered to provide group health insurance, but each employee would have to forgo a $7,000 salary increase. How would the change in compensation affect Paul, Betty, and the employer?

4. **LO.2** Belinda spent the last 60 days of 2014 in a nursing home. The cost of the services provided to her was $18,000 ($300 per day). Medicare paid $8,500 toward the cost of her stay. Belinda also received $5,500 of benefits under a long-term care insurance policy she purchased. What is the effect on Belinda's gross income?

5. **LO.2** Does the taxpayer recognize gross income in the following situations? Explain.
   a. Ava is a filing clerk at a large insurance company. She is permitted to leave the premises for her lunch, but she always eats in the company's cafeteria because doing so is less expensive than purchasing a comparable meal at a nearby restaurant. On average, she pays $2 for a lunch that would cost $12 at a restaurant. However, if the prices in the cafeteria were not so low and the food was not so delicious, she would probably bring her lunch at a cost of $2 per day.

b. Scott is a resident adviser (RA) in a college dormitory and is provided with lodging in the dormitory. He is not required to pay the $300 per month that a room costs other students. In addition, he is paid $100 per month.

c. Ira recently moved to accept a job. For the first month on the new job, Ira was searching for a home to purchase or rent. During this time, his employer permitted Ira to live in an apartment the company maintains for customers during the buying season. The month that Ira occupied the apartment was not during the buying season, however, and the apartment would not otherwise have been occupied.

6. **LO.2** Sally and Bill are married and file joint returns. In 2014, Bill, an accountant, has a salary of $75,000, and Sally receives a salary of $25,000 as an apartment manager. What are the tax consequences of the following benefits that Bill's and Sally's employer provide?

a. Bill receives a reimbursement of $5,000 for child care expenses. Sally and Bill have three children who are not yet school age.

b. Bill and Sally are provided a free membership at a local fitness and exercise club that allows them to attend three aerobic exercise sessions per week. The value of this type of membership is $1,600 per year.

c. Bill is provided free parking at work. The value of the parking is $1,800 per year.

d. Sally is provided with a free apartment. Living in this apartment is a condition of her employment. Similar apartments rent for $1,200 per month.

7. **LO.1, 4** Finch Construction Company provides its employees who are carpenters with all of the required tools. However, the company believes that this has led to some employees not taking care of the tools and to the mysterious disappearance of some of the tools. The company is considering requiring all of its employees to provide their own tools. Employees' salaries would be increased by $1,500 to compensate for the additional costs. Write a letter to Finch's management explaining the tax consequences of this plan to the carpenters. Finch's address is 300 Harbor Drive, Vermillion, SD 57069.

Communications

8. **LO.2** Rosa's employer has instituted a flexible benefits program. Rosa will use the plan to pay for her daughter's dental expenses and other medical expenses that are not covered by health insurance. Rosa is in the 28% marginal tax bracket and estimates that the medical and dental expenses not covered by health insurance will be within the range of $1,500 to $2,500. Her employer's plan permits her to set aside as much as $2,500 in the flexible benefits account. Rosa does not itemize her deductions.

Decision Making

a. Rosa puts $1,500 in her flexible benefits account, and her actual expenses are $2,500. What is her cost of underestimating the expenses?

b. Rosa puts $2,500 in her flexible benefits account, and her actual expenses are only $1,500. What is her cost of overestimating her expenses?

c. What is Rosa's cost of underfunding as compared to the cost of overfunding the flexible benefits account?

d. Does your answer in part (c) suggest that Rosa should fund the account closer to the low end or to the high end of her estimates?

9. **LO.2** Sparrow Corporation would like you to review its employee fringe benefits program with regard to the tax consequences of the plan for the company's president (Polly), who is also the majority shareholder.

a. The company has a qualified retirement plan. The company pays the cost of employees attending a retirement planning seminar. The employee must be within 10 years of retirement, and the cost of the seminar is $1,500 per attendee.

b. The company owns a parking garage that is used by customers, employees, and the general public. Only the general public is required to pay for parking. The charge to the general public for Polly's parking for the year would have been $3,600 (a $300 monthly rate).

c. All employees are allowed to use the company's fixed charge long-distance telephone services as long as the privilege is not abused. Although no one has kept track of the actual calls, Polly's use of the telephone had a value (what she would have paid on her personal telephone) of approximately $600.

d. The company owns a condominium at the beach, which it uses to entertain customers. Employees are allowed to use the facility without charge when the company has no scheduled events. Polly used the facility 10 days during the year. Her use had a rental value of $1,000.

e. The company is in the household moving business. Employees are allowed to ship goods without charge whenever there is excess space on a truck. Polly purchased a dining room suite for her daughter. Company trucks delivered the furniture to the daughter. Normal freight charges would have been $750.

f. The company has a storage facility for household goods. Officers are allowed a 20% discount on charges for storing their goods. All other employees are allowed a 10% discount. Polly's discounts for the year totaled $900.

10. **LO.2** Ted works for Azure Motors, an automobile dealership. All employees can buy a car at the company's cost plus 2%. The company does not charge employees the $300 dealer preparation fee that nonemployees must pay. Ted purchased an automobile for $29,580 ($29,000 + $580). The company's cost was $29,000. The price for a nonemployee would have been $33,900 ($33,600 + $300 preparation fee). What is Ted's gross income from the purchase of the automobile?

Ethics and Equity

11. **LO.2** Tom works for Roadrunner Motors, a company that manufactures automobiles. Tom purchased a new automobile from Roadrunner at the company's cost of $10,000. The retail selling price for the automobile is $15,000. Sue works for Coyote, Inc., an auto dealership, which sells the car manufactured by Roadrunner. Sue purchased an automobile identical to Tom's from Coyote. The price Sue pays is equal to Coyote's cost of the automobile ($13,500). Tom and Sue each receive a salary of $40,000 per year. Considering only the above information, do Tom and Sue have equal ability to pay income taxes for the year? Does equitable treatment occur? If not, how should the tax law be changed to produce equitable treatment?

Issue ID

12. **LO.2** Several of Egret Company's employees have asked the company to create a hiking trail that employees could use during their lunch hour. The company owns vacant land that is being held for future expansion, but would have to spend approximately $50,000 if it were to make a trail. Nonemployees would be allowed to use the facility as part of the company's effort to build strong community support. What are the relevant tax issues for the employees?

13. **LO.2** Bluebird, Inc., does not provide its employees with any tax-exempt fringe benefits. The company is considering adopting a hospital and medical benefits insurance plan that will cost approximately $9,000 per employee. To adopt this plan, the company may have to reduce salaries and/or lower future salary increases. Bluebird is in the 35% (combined Federal and state rates) bracket. Bluebird is also responsible for matching the Social Security and Medicare taxes withheld on employees' salaries (at the full 7.65% rate). The hospital and medical benefits insurance plan will not be subject to the Social Security and Medicare taxes, and the company is not eligible for the small business credit for health insurance. The employees generally fall into two marginal tax rate groups:

Income Tax	Social Security and Medicare Tax	Total
.15	.0765	.2265
.35	.0145	.3645

The company has asked you to assist in its financial planning for the hospital and medical benefits insurance plan by computing the following:

a. How much taxable compensation is the equivalent of $9,000 of exempt compensation for each of the two classes of employees?

b. What is the company's after-tax cost of the taxable compensation computed in part (a)?

c. What is the company's after-tax cost of the exempt compensation?

d. Briefly explain your conclusions from the above analysis.

14. **LO.2** George is a U.S. citizen who is employed by Hawk Enterprises, a global company. Beginning on June 1, 2014, George began working in London. He worked there until January 31, 2015, when he transferred to Paris. He worked in Paris the remainder of 2015. His salary for the first five months of 2014 was $100,000, and it was earned in the United States. His salary for the remainder of 2014 was $175,000, and it was earned in London. George's 2015 salary from Hawk was $300,000, with part being earned in London and part being earned in Paris. What is George's gross income in 2014 and 2015 (assume that the 2015 indexed amount is the same as the 2014 indexed amount)?

Critical Thinking

15. **LO.3** William is employed by an accounting firm and uses his automobile in connection with his work. During the month of October 2014, he works at the office for 4 days and

participates in the audit of a key client for 19 days. In the audit situation, William goes directly from his home to the client's office. On all other days, he drives to his employer's office. On four Saturdays in October, he drives from his home to a local university, where he attends classes in a part-time MBA program. Relevant mileage is as follows:

Home to office	12 miles
Office to audit client	13 miles
Home to audit client	14 miles
Home to university	10 miles

Using the automatic mileage method, what is William's deduction for the month?

16. **LO.3** Larry went from Cleveland to New York on business. His time was spent as follows:

Thursday	Travel
Friday	Business
Saturday and Sunday	Sightseeing
Monday and Tuesday	Business
Wednesday	Travel

During the trip, Larry incurred and paid expenses of $180 per day for lodging from Thursday night through Tuesday night and $110 per day for meals from Friday through Tuesday. Round-trip airfare was $400. Larry is a self-employed attorney who practices law in Cleveland.
  a. How much can Larry deduct for the New York trip?
  b. How will any deduction be classified?

17. **LO.3** In June of this year, Dr. and Mrs. Bret Spencer traveled to Denver to attend a three-day conference sponsored by the American Society of Implant Dentistry. Bret, a practicing oral surgeon, participated in scheduled technical sessions dealing with the latest developments in surgical procedures. On two days, Mrs. Spencer attended group meetings where various aspects of family tax planning were discussed. On the other day, she went sightseeing. Mrs. Spencer does not work for her husband, but she does their tax returns and handles the family investments. Expenses incurred in connection with the conference are summarized as follows:

Airfare (two tickets)	$2,000
Lodging (single and double occupancy are the same rate—$250 each day)	750
Meals ($200 × 3 days)*	600
Conference registration fee (includes $120 for Family Tax Planning sessions)	620
Car rental	300

*Split equally between Dr. and Mrs. Spencer.

How much, if any, of these expenses can the Spencers deduct?

18. **LO.3** On Thursday, Justin flies from Baltimore (his home office) to Cadiz (Spain). He conducts business on Friday and Tuesday; vacations on Saturday, Sunday, and Monday (a legal holiday in Spain); and returns to Baltimore on Thursday. Justin was scheduled to return home on Wednesday, but all flights were canceled due to bad weather. Therefore, he spent Wednesday watching floor shows at a local casino.
  a. For tax purposes, what portion of Justin's trip is regarded as being for business?
  b. Suppose Monday had not been a legal holiday. Would this change your answer in part (a)? Explain.
  c. Under either (a) or (b), how much of Justin's airfare qualifies as a deductible business expense?

19. **LO.3** Veronica is a key employee of Perdiz Corporation, an aerospace engineering concern located in Seattle. Perdiz would like to establish an office on the east coast of Florida and wants Veronica to be in charge of the branch. Veronica is hesitant about making the move because she fears she will have to sell her residence in Seattle at a loss. Perdiz buys the house from Veronica for $420,000, its cost to her. She has owned and occupied the house as her principal residence for eight years. One year later, Perdiz resells the property for $370,000. Nothing regarding the sale of the residence is ever reflected on Veronica's income tax returns. Needless to say, Perdiz absorbs all of Veronica's moving expenses. Do you have any qualms as to the way these matters have been handled for income tax purposes? Explain.

Ethics and Equity

20. **LO.3** Upon losing his job as a plant manager in Quincy, Massachusetts, Anthony incurs $6,200 in job search expenses. Having no success in finding new employment in the same type of work, Anthony moves to Clearwater, Florida, in 2014 and begins a charter boat business. His expenses in connection with the move are summarized below.

Penalty for breaking lease on Quincy rented residence	$2,800
Forfeiture of membership in Quincy Country Club	2,200
Packing and moving van charges	7,100
Lodging during move (3 nights)	380
Meals during move	360
Mileage (total for two automobiles)	2,400 miles

How much of these expenses may Anthony deduct?

Issue ID
21. **LO.3** Elijah is employed as a full-time high school teacher. The school district for which he works recently instituted a policy requiring all of its teachers to start working on a master's degree. Pursuant to this new rule, Elijah spent most of the summer of 2014 taking graduate courses at an out-of-town university. His expenses are as follows:

Tuition	$6,600
Books and course materials	1,500
Lodging	1,700
Meals	2,200
Laundry and dry cleaning	200
Campus parking	300

In addition, Elijah drove his personal automobile 2,200 miles in connection with the education. He uses the automatic mileage method.
   a. How much, if any, of these expenses might qualify as a deduction *for* AGI?
   b. How much, if any, of these expenses might qualify as a deduction *from* AGI?

Issue ID
22. **LO.3** In each of the following independent situations, determine how much, if any, qualifies as a deduction *for* AGI under § 222 (qualified tuition and related expenses).
   a. Lily is single and is employed as an architect. During the current year, she spent $4,100 in tuition to attend law school at night. Her MAGI is $64,000.
   b. Liam is single and is employed as a pharmacist. During the current year, he spent $2,400 ($2,100 for tuition and $300 for books) to take a course in herbal supplements at a local university. His MAGI is $81,000.
   c. Hailey is married and is employed as a bookkeeper. She spends $5,200 for tuition and $900 for books and supplies pursuing a bachelor's degree in accounting. Her MAGI is $40,000 on the separate return she files.
   d. John spends $6,500 of his savings for tuition to attend Carmine State College. John is claimed as a dependent by his parents.
   e. How much, if any, of the preceding amounts *not allowed under § 222* might otherwise qualify as a deduction *from* AGI?

23. **LO.3, 4** Elvis is a salesperson who works for Crane Sales, Inc. Typically, Elvis spends several days out of town each week. Crane provides Elvis with a travel allowance of $1,100 per month, but requires no accountability. For the current year, Elvis had the following job-related travel expenses:

Meals	$ 5,040
Lodging	10,080
Transportation	1,400

   a. What amount qualifies as a deductible travel expense?
   b. What is the classification of any such deduction?

24. **LO.3** Melanie is employed full-time as an accountant for a national hardware chain. She recently started a private consulting practice, which provides tax advice and financial planning to the general public. For this purpose, she maintains an office in her home. Expenses relating to her home are as follows:

Real property taxes	$3,600
Interest on home mortgage	3,800
Operating expenses of home	900
Depreciation allocated to 20% business use	1,500

Melanie's income from consulting is $17,000, and the related expenses are $5,000.
  a. What is Melanie's office in the home deduction?
  b. Suppose Melanie also spends $4,000 to repaint and to replace the carpet in the office. How do these additional costs change the answer to part (a)?
  c. Suppose Melanie's income from consulting is only $8,000 (not $17,000). How does this change the answer to part (a)?

25. **LO.3, 4** Charles has AGI of $94,000 during the year and the following expenses related to his employment:

Critical Thinking

Lodging while in travel status	$5,000
Meals during travel	4,000
Business transportation	6,000
Entertainment of clients	3,800
Professional dues and subscriptions	800

Charles is reimbursed $14,000 under his employer's accountable plan. What are his deductions *for* and *from* AGI?

26. **LO.4** Janet, age 29, is unmarried and is an active participant in a qualified deductible (traditional) IRA plan. Her modified AGI is $62,000 in 2014.
  a. Calculate the amount Janet can contribute to the IRA and the amount she can deduct.
  b. Assume instead that Janet is a participant in a SIMPLE IRA and that her compensation for the year is $61,000. Janet elects to contribute 4% of her compensation to the account, while her employer contributes 3%. What amount will be contributed for 2014? What amount will be vested?

27. **LO.4** Carri and Dane, ages 34 and 32, respectively, have been married for 11 years, and both are active participants in employer qualified retirement plans. Their total AGI in 2014 is $184,000, and they earn salaries of $87,000 and $95,000, respectively. What amount may Carri and Dane:
  a. Contribute to regular IRAs?
  b. Deduct for their contributions in (a)?
  c. Contribute to Roth IRAs?
  d. Deduct for their contributions in (c)?
  e. Contribute to Coverdell Education Savings Accounts for each of their three children?

28. **LO.4** Dana, age 54, has a traditional deductible IRA with an account balance of $107,600, of which $77,300 represents contributions and $30,300 represents earnings. In 2014, she converts her traditional IRA into a Roth IRA. What amount must Dana include in her gross income for 2014?

Critical Thinking

29. **LO.4** In 2014, Joyce receives a $4,000 distribution from her Coverdell Education Savings Account (CESA), which has a fair market value of $10,000. Total contributions to her CESA have been $7,000. Joyce's AGI is $25,000.
  a. Joyce uses the entire $4,000 to pay for qualified education expenses. What amount should she include in her gross income?
  b. Assume instead that Joyce uses only $2,500 of the $4,000 distribution for qualified education expenses. What amount should she include in her gross income?

30. **LO.5** In 2014, Susan's sole proprietorship earns $300,000 of self-employment net income (after the deduction for one-half of self-employment tax).
  a. Calculate the maximum amount Susan can deduct for contributions to a defined contribution Keogh plan.
  b. Suppose Susan contributes more than the allowable amount to the Keogh plan. What are the tax consequences to her?
  c. Can Susan retire and begin receiving Keogh payments at age 58 without incurring a penalty? Explain.

31. **LO.5** Harvey is a self-employed accountant with earned income from the business of $120,000 (after the deduction for one-half of his self-employment tax). He has a profit sharing plan (e.g., defined contribution Keogh plan). What is the maximum amount Harvey can contribute to his retirement plan in 2014?

Critical Thinking

32. **LO.5** In each of the following *independent* situations, determine the amount of FICA (Social Security and Medicare) the employer should withhold from the employee's 2014 salary.
   a. Harry earns a $50,000 salary, files a joint return, and claims four withholding allowances.
   b. Hazel earns a $115,000 salary, files a joint return, and claims four withholding allowances.
   c. Tracey earns a $190,000 salary, files a joint return, and claims four withholding allowances.

Critical Thinking

33. **LO.5** During 2014, Helen, the owner of a store, has the following income and expenses:

Gross profit on sales	$73,000
Income from part-time job (subject to FICA)	45,000
Business expenses (related to store)	15,000
Fire loss on store building	2,200
Dividend income	200
Long-term capital gain on the sale of a stock investment	2,000

Compute Helen's self-employment tax and allowable income tax deduction for the self-employment tax paid.

34. **LO.6** Hank is single and a doctor in a west Texas community. He owns and operates a cattle ranch, which has been profitable in only one of the last 10 years. He believes that he satisfies one-third of the nine factors that the IRS uses to determine whether an activity is profit-seeking or is a hobby. Without regard to this activity, Hank's AGI is $225,000. His only other itemized deductions are $4,000 of property taxes on his residence and $3,500 of charitable contributions. The ranch produces the following revenues and expenses in 2014:

Revenues	$31,000
Mortgage interest on barn	9,000
Property taxes on barn and land	7,500
Cattle feed	14,000
Hay	4,725
Maintenance on barn	3,000
Depreciation on barn	2,950

   a. Is Hank's cattle ranch profit-seeking, or is it a hobby? Explain the probabilities.
   b. Determine Hank's taxable income if the ranch is a hobby.
   c. Determine his taxable income if the ranch is a business.

Comprehensive Tax Return Problems

Tax Return Problem

H&R BLOCK

TAX SOFTWARE

1. Beth R. Jordan lives at 2322 Skyview Road, Mesa, AZ 85201. She is a tax accountant with Mesa Manufacturing Company, 1203 Western Avenue, Mesa, AZ 85201 (employer identification number 11-1111111). She also writes computer software programs for tax practitioners and has a part-time tax practice. Beth is single and has no dependents. Beth's birthday is July 4, 1972, and her Social Security number is 123-45-6789. She wants to contribute $3 to the Presidential Election Campaign Fund.

   The following information is shown on Beth's Wage and Tax Statement (Form W–2) for 2013.

Line	Description	Amount
1	Wages, tips, other compensation	$65,000.00
2	Federal income tax withheld	10,500.00
3	Social Security wages	65,000.00
4	Social Security tax withheld	4,030.00
5	Medicare wages and tips	65,000.00
6	Medicare tax withheld	942.50
15	State	Arizona
16	State wages, tips, etc.	65,000.00
17	State income tax withheld	1,650.00

During 2013, Beth received interest of $1,300 from Arizona Federal Savings and Loan and $400 from Arizona State Bank. Each financial institution reported the interest income on a Form 1099–INT. She received qualified dividends of $800 from Blue Corporation, $750 from Green Corporation, and $650 from Orange Corporation. Each corporation reported Beth's dividend payments on a Form 1099–DIV.

Beth received a $1,100 income tax refund from the state of Arizona on April 29, 2013. On her 2012 Federal income tax return, she reported total itemized deductions of $8,200, which included $2,200 of state income tax withheld by her employer.

Fees earned from her part-time tax practice in 2013 totaled $3,800. She paid $600 to have the tax returns processed by a computerized tax return service.

On February 8, 2013, Beth bought 500 shares of Gray Corporation common stock for $17.60 a share. On September 12, 2013, she sold the stock for $14 a share.

Beth bought a used sports utility vehicle for $6,000 on June 5, 2013. She purchased the vehicle from her brother-in-law, who was unemployed and was in need of cash. On November 2, 2013, she sold the vehicle to a friend for $6,500.

On January 2, 2013, she acquired 100 shares of Blue Corporation common stock for $30 a share. She sold the stock on December 19, 2013, for $55 a share.

During 2013, Beth received royalties of $16,000 on a software program she had written. She incurred the following expenditures in connection with her software-writing activities:

Cost of personal computer	$7,000
Cost of printer	2,000
Office furniture	3,000
Supplies	650
Fee paid to computer consultant	3,500

Beth elected to expense the maximum portion of the cost of the computer, printer, and furniture allowed under the provisions of § 179. These items were placed in service on January 15, 2013, and used 100% in her business.

Although her employer suggested that Beth attend a convention on current developments in corporate taxation, she was not reimbursed for the travel expenses of $1,420 she incurred in attending the convention. The $1,420 included $200 for the cost of meals.

During 2013, Beth paid $300 for prescription medicines and $2,875 for doctor bills and hospital bills. Medical insurance premiums were paid for her by her employer. Beth paid real property taxes of $1,766 on her home. Interest on her home mortgage was $3,845, and interest to credit card companies was $320. She contributed $30 each week to her church and $10 each week to the United Way. Professional dues and subscriptions totaled $350. Beth maintained her sales tax receipts. The total is $1,954. Beth paid estimated Federal income taxes of $1,000.

Part 1—Tax Computation

Compute the net tax payable or refund due for Beth R. Jordan for 2013. If you use tax forms for your solution, you will need Forms 1040, 2106-EZ, and 4562 and Schedules A, B, C, D, and SE. Suggested software: H&R BLOCK Tax Software.

Part 2—Tax Planning

Beth is anticipating significant changes in her life in 2014, and she has asked you to estimate her taxable income and tax liability for 2014. She just received word that she has been qualified to adopt a 2-year-old daughter. Beth expects that the adoption will be finalized in 2014 and that she will incur approximately $2,000 of adoption expenses. In addition, she expects to incur approximately $3,500 of child and dependent care expenses relating to the care of her new daughter, which will enable her to keep her job at Mesa Manufacturing Company. However, with the additional demands on her time because of her daughter, she has decided to discontinue her two part-time jobs (i.e., the part-time tax practice and her software business), and she will cease making estimated income tax payments. In your computations, assume that all other income and expenditures will remain at approximately the same levels as in 2013.

2. David R. and Ella M. Cole (ages 39 and 38, respectively) are husband and wife who live at 1820 Elk Avenue, Denver, CO 80202. David is a regional sales manager for Wren Industries, a national wholesaler of plumbing and heating supplies, and Ella is a part-time dental hygienist for a chain of dental clinics.

• David is classified by Wren as a statutory employee with compensation for 2013 (based on commissions) of $95,000. He is expected to maintain his own office and pay for all business expenses from this amount. Wren does not require him to render any accounting as to the use of these funds. It does not withhold Federal and state income taxes but does withhold and account for the payroll taxes incurred (e.g., Social Security and Medicare). David is covered by Wren's noncontributory medical plan but has chosen not to participate in its § 401(k) retirement plan.

David's employment-related expenses for 2013 are summarized below.

Airfare	$8,800
Lodging	5,000
Meals (during travel status)	4,800
Entertainment	3,600
Ground transportation (e.g., limos, rental cars, and taxis)	800
Business gifts	900
Office supplies (includes postage, overnight delivery, and copying)	1,500

The entertainment involved business meals for purchasing agents, store owners, and building contractors. The business gifts consisted of $50 gift certificates to a national restaurant. These were sent by David during the Christmas holidays to 18 of his major customers.

In addition, David drove his 2011 Ford Expedition 11,000 miles for business and 3,000 for personal use during 2013. He purchased the Expedition on August 15, 2010, and has always used the automatic (standard) mileage method for tax purposes. Parking and tolls relating to business use total $340 in 2013.

• When the Coles purchased their present residence in April 2010, they devoted 450 of the 3,000 square feet of living space to an office for David. The property cost $440,000 ($40,000 of which is attributable to the land) and has since appreciated in value. Expenses relating to the residence in 2013 (except for mortgage interest and property taxes; see below) are as follows:

Insurance	$2,600
Repairs and maintenance	900
Utilities	4,700
Painting office area; area rugs and plants (in the office)	1,800

In terms of depreciation, the Coles use the MACRS percentage tables applicable to 39-year nonresidential real property. As to depreciable property (e.g., office furniture), David tries to avoid capitalization and uses whatever method provides the fastest write-off for tax purposes.

• Ella works part-time as a substitute for whichever hygienist is ill or on vacation or when one of the clinics is particularly busy (e.g., prior to the beginning of the school year). Besides her transportation, she must provide and maintain her own uniforms. Her expenses for 2013 appear below.

Uniforms	$690
State and city occupational licenses	380
Professional journals and membership dues in the American Dental Hygiene Association	340
Correspondence study course (taken online) dealing with teeth whitening procedures	420

Ella's salary for the year is $42,000, and her Form W–2 for the year shows income tax withholdings of $4,000 (Federal) and $1,000 (state) and the proper amount of Social Security and Medicare taxes. Because Ella is a part-time employee, she is not included in her employer's medical or retirement plans.

• Besides the items already mentioned, the Coles had the following receipts during 2013.

Interest income—		
State of Colorado general purpose bonds	$2,500	
IBM bonds	800	
Wells Fargo Bank CD	1,200	$ 4,500
Federal income tax refund for year 2012		510
Life insurance proceeds paid by Eagle Assurance Corporation		200,000
Inheritance of savings account from Sarah Cole		50,000
Sales proceeds from two ATVs		9,000

For several years, the Coles's household has included David's divorced mother, Sarah, who has been claimed as their dependent. In late November 2013, Sarah unexpectedly died of coronary arrest in her sleep. Unknown to Ella and David, Sarah had a life insurance policy and a savings account (with David as the designated beneficiary of each). In 2012, the Coles purchased two ATVs for $14,000. After several near mishaps, they decided that the sport was too dangerous. In 2013, they sold the ATVs to their neighbor.

• Additional expenditures for 2013 include:

Funeral expenses for Sarah		$ 4,500
Taxes—		
Real property taxes on personal residence	$6,400	
Colorado state income tax due (paid in April 2013 for tax year 2012)	310	6,710
Mortgage interest on personal residence		6,600
Paid church pledge		2,400
Contributions to traditional IRAs for Ella and David ($5,500 + $5,500)		11,000

In 2013, the Coles made quarterly estimated tax payments of $1,400 (Federal) and $500 (state) for a total of $5,600 (Federal) and $2,000 (state).

Part 1—Tax Computation

Using the appropriate forms and schedules, compute the Coles's Federal income tax for 2013. Disregard the alternative minimum tax (AMT) and various education credits. Education credits were discussed in Chapter 10, and the AMT is discussed in Chapter 17. Relevant Social Security numbers are:

David Cole	123-45-6788
Ella Cole	123-45-6787
Sarah Cole	123-45-6799

The Coles do not want to contribute to the Presidential Election Campaign Fund. Also, they want any overpayment of tax refunded to them and *not* applied toward next year's tax liability. Suggested software: H&R BLOCK Tax Software.

Part 2—Follow-Up Advice

Ella has always wanted to pursue a career in nursing. To this end, she has earned a substantial number of college credits on a part-time basis. With Sarah no longer requiring home care, Ella believes that she can now complete her degree by attending college on a full-time basis.

David would like to know how Ella's plans will affect their income tax position. Specifically, he wants to know:

• How much Federal income tax they will save if Ella quits her job.
• Any tax benefits that might be available from the cost of the education.

Write a letter to David addressing these concerns. Note: In making your projections, assume that David's salary and expenses remain the same. Also disregard any consideration of the educational tax credits (i.e., American Opportunity and lifetime learning).

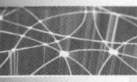

BRIDGE DISCIPLINE

1. Justin performs services for Partridge, Inc., and receives compensation of $85,000 for the year. Determine the tax consequences of Social Security and Medicare on Justin's take-home pay if:
   a. Justin is classified as an employee of Partridge.
   b. Justin is classified as an independent contractor.

2. Amanda has been an employee of Robin, Inc., for almost five years. She is a participant in Robin's defined contribution pension plan (money purchase plan). The total contributions made by Robin to the money purchase plan for Amanda are $60,000, and the balance in Amanda's account is $89,000. Amanda is considering accepting a job with a competitor of Robin's at an annual salary $7,000 higher than that received from Robin. Her boss, who is trying to convince her to stay, points out that she will not be vested in the money purchase plan until she has been employed by Robin for at least five years. In addition, she will have to start a new vesting schedule with the competitor.
   a. What is vesting? How does it affect Amanda and her decision based on the information provided?
   b. What have been the tax consequences to Amanda of Robin's annual contribution of $17,000 to its money purchase plan for her?
   c. What effect would it have on Amanda's decision if the competitor did not provide retirement benefits?

3. The Code contains provisions that are "friendly" to specific groups of taxpayers. Among these are the following:

   - Seniors.
   - Married taxpayers.
   - Employed taxpayers.
   - Taxpayers with children.
   - Self-employed individuals.

   Provide justification for the special treatment for each of the above groups, and give an example of such special treatment for each group.

Research Problems

Note: Solutions to Research Problems can be prepared by using the **Checkpoint®** **Student Edition** online research product, which is available to accompany this text. It is also possible to prepare solutions to the Research Problems by using tax research materials found in a standard tax library.

Communications

Research Problem 1. Tom Roberts, a chemical engineer, is a long-time employee of Teal Chemical Corporation. Tom's specialty is the design and construction of special-purpose chemical processing plants. Teal has decided to expand its presence in France and plans to transfer Tom to Paris on a three-year assignment. The planned foreign assignment will take Tom to age 65, Teal's normal retirement age.

Tom has been advised regarding the major income tax ramifications of working abroad. He has not, however, been told about the treatment of moving expenses. Because Teal Corporation pays its employees a substantial foreign service salary increment, it reimburses for moving expenses. In connection with the move, Tom plans to sell his residence and place most of his furniture in storage. Probabilities are good that the sale of the residence will result in a loss.
   a. Write a letter to Tom regarding the income tax treatment of his moving expenses. Tom's address is 1389 Wilson Drive, Camden, NJ 08102. Be sure to include in the discussion the move from France back to the United States.
   b. Prepare a memo for your firm's client files.

Communications

Research Problem 2. Rick Beam has been an independent sales representative for various textile manufacturers for many years. His products consist of soft goods such as tablecloths, curtains, and drapes. Rick's customers are clothing store chains, department stores, and smaller specialty stores. The employees of these companies who are responsible for purchasing merchandise are known as buyers. These companies generally prohibit their buyers from accepting gifts from manufacturers' sales representatives.

Each year, Rick gives cash gifts (never more than $25) to most of the buyers who are his customers. Generally, he cashes a large check in November and gives the money personally to the buyers around Christmas. Rick says, "This is one of the ways that I maintain my relationship with my buyers." He maintains adequate substantiation of all of the gifts.

Rick's deductions for these gifts have been disallowed by the IRS based on § 162(c)(2). Rick is confused and comes to you, a CPA, for advice.

a. Write a letter to Rick concerning his tax position on this issue. Rick's address is 948 Octavia Street, New Orleans, LA 70113.
b. Prepare a memo for your files supporting the advice you have given.

Research Problem 3. Al Hardee has been employed as a salesperson by Robin Chevrolet at its Milwaukee dealership. In early May, Al and the general manager of the office had a serious dispute over job procedures. When it became clear that the two could no longer work together amicably, Al contacted Robin's CEO regarding a possible solution. As the general manager planned to retire in five months, it was decided that Al would spend this period working at the Green Bay branch. After the manager's retirement, Al was to rejoin the Milwaukee office.

Al's residence is only a few blocks from the Milwaukee office, but it is 96 miles (one way) from the Green Bay work site. During the next five months (i.e., May to October), Al made 120 trips driving from his home in Milwaukee to the Green Bay job. His only records of his trips are a wall calendar with the workdays circled and the credit card receipts he received from gasoline purchases. The employee records of the Green Bay dealership can, however, support Al's on-the-job presence.

Upon termination of the five-month assignment and after the retirement of the general manager, Al requested a transfer back to the Milwaukee office. The CEO turned down the request on the grounds that Al was no longer needed in Milwaukee. During Al's absence and unknown to him, his position in Milwaukee had been eliminated. However, the CEO offered to make the Green Bay assignment permanent. Hurt and disgusted, Al quit and took a job with a competing Milwaukee car dealership.

On his Federal income tax return, Al claimed a deduction for employee transportation expenses, computed as follows: 120 (number of trips) × 192 (round trip mileage) × automatic mileage rate for the year. The IRS disallowed the deduction on two grounds. First, Al's job status in Green Bay was *permanent* and not *temporary*. Thus, his tax home had changed from Milwaukee to Green Bay. This, in turn, made his transportation expenses nondeductible commuting expenses. Second, even if the transportation was warranted, the expenses were not properly substantiated. Consequently, the lack of substantiation precludes any deduction.

Should Al be allowed a deduction for this transportation expense? Explain.

Partial list of research aids:
Reg. § 1.162–2(e).
Reg. § 1.274–5T(c)(3).
Rev.Rul. 99–7, 1999–1 C.B. 363.
Terisita T. Diaz, 84 TCM 148, T.C.Memo. 2002–192.
Richard M. Brockman, 85 TCM 733, T.C.Memo. 2003–3.

Research Problem 4. Herron, Inc., previously gave all of its employees a ham for Christmas. However, many of the employees do not eat ham. Therefore, Herron has decided to give each employee a coupon for $35 that can be redeemed (for food or cash) any time between December 1 and January 31 of the following year. Herron has asked you whether the coupons can be excluded from the employees' gross income as a *de minimis* fringe benefit.

Research Problem 5. You recently read an article in your school newspaper about Professor Rodney Taylor, one of your favorite professors in the religious studies department. According to the article, he and the university have been negotiating an early retirement package and have reached a stumbling block. Under the agreement, Professor Taylor is to receive a lump-sum payment equal to one year's salary in exchange for his retirement and the release of any and all rights associated with his tenure status. While recognizing that the payment would be subject to income tax, Taylor contends that the amount is not earned income and thus should not be subject to the FICA tax. The university negotiators say that they are not aware of any authority that supports Taylor's view. In fact, they have learned that other universities in the state system have been withholding amounts for FICA for years in situations involving early retirement buyout packages for high-level administrators. The university's position is that lacking the authority not to withhold for FICA and given the precedent of similar early retirement packages at other universities, it is obligated to withhold FICA from the payment. You want to come to the aid of Professor Taylor. Obviously, if the payments are considered wages subject to the FICA tax, the value of the offer to Professor Taylor will be significantly reduced. Can you find any authority for his position? Explain.

Research Problem 6. Kristina will soon graduate from law school with more than $40,000 in student loans. She would like to work as a public defender, but the pay is not enough to allow her to meet her living expenses and repay the student loans. Her law school offers a "debt forgiveness program" for graduates who enter public service, including working as a public defender. Under the program, the school will pay the student's debt, but the graduate will owe an equal amount to the program. However, if the graduate remains in public service for at least four years, the debt is forgiven. Kristina would like to know the tax consequences if she decides to utilize this program.

Internet Activity

Use the tax resources of the Internet to address the following questions. Do not restrict your search to the Web, but include a review of newsgroups and general reference materials, practitioner sites and resources, primary sources of the tax law, chat rooms and discussion groups, and other opportunities.

Research Problem 7. An employer allows its employees limited personal use of one of the corporate executive jets. Does the IRS provide any guidelines as to how much income the employee should recognize due to such use? Explain.

Research Problem 8. Sarah was contemplating making a contribution to her traditional IRA in 2013. She determined she would contribute $5,000 in December 2013, but forgot about making the contribution until she was preparing her 2013 tax return in February 2014. Use the website of any well-known IRA provider (e.g., Fidelity, Vanguard, T. Rowe Price) to determine if Sarah can make a 2013 contribution to her IRA after the tax year has ended.

part 5

BUSINESS ENTITIES

Part 5 focuses on the different types of business entities and includes a life cycle coverage of formation, operations, and termination. The specific business entities covered are the C corporation, the S corporation, the partnership, and the LLC.

CHAPTER

12

Corporations: Organization, Capital Structure, and Operating Rules

LEARNING OBJECTIVES: *After completing Chapter 12, you should be able to:*

LO.1 **Recognize major tax and nontax considerations associated with the corporate form of business.**

LO.2 **Identify the tax consequences of incorporating and transferring assets to controlled corporations.**

LO.3 **Describe the special rules that apply when a corporation assumes a shareholder's liability.**

LO.4 **Recognize the basis issues relevant to the shareholder and the corporation.**

LO.5 **Explain the tax aspects of the capital structure of a corporation.**

LO.6 **Recognize the tax differences between debt and equity investments.**

LO.7 **List and apply the tax rules unique to corporations.**

LO.8 **Compute the corporate income tax.**

LO.9 **Explain the rules unique to computing the tax of related corporations.**

LO.10 **Describe the reporting process for corporations.**

CHAPTER OUTLINE

TAX TALK *Taxes owing to the Government ... are the price that business has to pay for protection and security.* —BENJAMIN N. CARDOZO

Dennis Flaherty/Photographer's Choice/Getty Images

GROWING INTO THE CORPORATE FORM

Amber has operated her business as a sole proprietorship since it was formed 10 years ago. Now, however, she has decided to incorporate the business as Garden, Inc., because the corporate form offers several important nontax advantages, including limited liability. Also, the incorporation would enable her husband, Jimmy, to become a part owner in the business. Amber expects to transfer her business assets in exchange for her Garden stock, while Jimmy will provide accounting and legal services for his equity interest. Amber's sole proprietorship assets available for transfer to the new corporation are as follows:

	Adjusted Basis	Fair Market Value
Accounts receivable	$ –0–	$ 50,000
Building	100,000	400,000
Other assets	300,000	550,000
	$400,000	$1,000,000

Aware of the problem of double taxation associated with operating as a regular corporation, Amber is considering receiving some corporate debt at the time of the incorporation. The interest expense on the debt will then provide a deduction for Garden, Inc. Amber's main concern is whether the incorporation will be a taxable transaction. Can the transaction be structured to avoid tax?

Read the chapter and formulate your response.

B usiness operations may be conducted in a number of different forms. As with many business decisions, consideration must be given to the tax consequences of choosing a particular business entity. This chapter deals with the unique tax consequences of operating an entity as a regular corporation, including:

- Classification of the entity as a corporation.
- The tax consequences to the shareholders and the corporation upon the formation of the corporation.
- The capital structure of the corporation.
- Determination of the corporate income tax liability.
- Corporate tax filing requirements.

12-1 AN INTRODUCTION TO CORPORATE TAX

LO.1

Recognize major tax and nontax considerations associated with the corporate form of business.

Corporations are governed by Subchapter C or Subchapter S of the Internal Revenue Code. Those governed by Subchapter C are referred to as **C corporations** or **regular corporations**. Corporations governed by Subchapter S are referred to as **S corporations**.

S corporations, which generally do not pay Federal income tax, are similar to partnerships in that ordinary business income (loss) flows through to the shareholders to be reported on their separate returns. Also like partnerships, S corporations do not aggregate all income and expense items in computing ordinary business income (loss). Certain items flow through to the shareholders and retain their separate character when reported on the shareholders' returns. The S corporation ordinary business income (loss) and the separately reported items are allocated to the shareholders according to their stock ownership interests. See Chapter 15 for detailed coverage of S corporations.

12-1a Double Taxation of Corporate Income

Unlike proprietorships, partnerships, and S corporations, C corporations are subject to an entity-level Federal income tax. This results in what is known as a *double taxation* effect. A C corporation reports its income and expenses on Form 1120. The corporation computes tax on the taxable income reported on Form 1120 using the rate schedule applicable to corporations (refer to the rate schedule inside the front cover of this text). When a corporation distributes its income, the corporation's shareholders report dividend income on their own tax returns. Thus, income that has already been taxed at the corporate level is also taxed at the shareholder level. The effects of double taxation are illustrated in Examples 1 and 2.

Example 1

Lavender Corporation has taxable income of $100,000 in 2014. It pays corporate tax of $22,250 (refer to the corporate tax rate schedule on the inside front cover of this text). This leaves $77,750, all of which is distributed as a dividend to Mike, a 43-year-old single individual and the corporation's sole shareholder. Mike has no income sources other than Lavender Corporation. Mike has taxable income of $67,600 ($77,750 − $6,200 standard deduction − $3,950 personal exemption). He pays tax at the preferential rate applicable to qualified dividends received by individuals. His tax is $4,605 [($36,900 × 0%) + ($30,700 × 15%)]. The combined tax on the corporation's net profit is $26,855 ($22,250 paid by the corporation + $4,605 paid by the shareholder).

Example 2

Assume the same facts as in Example 1, except that the business is organized as a sole proprietorship. Mike reports the $100,000 profit from the business on his tax return. He has taxable income of $89,850 ($100,000 − $6,200 standard deduction − $3,950 personal exemption) and pays tax of $18,334. Therefore, operating the business as a sole proprietorship results in a tax *savings* of $8,521 in 2014 ($26,855 from Example 1 − $18,334).

Choice of Organizational Form When Operating Overseas

Global Tax Issues

© iStockphoto.com/Andrey Prokhorov

When the management of a corporation decides to expand its business by establishing a presence in a foreign market, the new business venture may take one of several organizational forms. As each form comes with its respective advantages and disadvantages, making the best choice can be difficult.

One common approach is to conduct the foreign activity as a *branch* operation of the U.S. corporation. The foreign branch is not a separate legal entity, but a division of the U.S. corporation established overseas. As a result, any gains and losses produced by the foreign unit are included in the corporation's overall financial results.

Another possibility is to organize the foreign operations as a *subsidiary* of the U.S. parent corporation. If this route is chosen, the subsidiary can be either a *domestic* subsidiary (i.e., organized in the United States) or a *foreign* subsidiary (organized under the laws of a foreign country).

One fundamental tax difference between these two approaches is that the gains and losses of a domestic subsidiary may be consolidated with the operations of the U.S. parent, while the operations of a foreign subsidiary cannot. Thus, the use of a domestic subsidiary to conduct foreign operations yields generally the same final result as the use of a branch. With both approaches, the financial statements of the U.S. parent reflect the results of its worldwide operations.

Taxation of Dividends

As noted earlier, the income of a C corporation is subject to double taxation, which stems, in part, from the fact that dividend distributions are not deductible by the corporation. Shareholders of closely held corporations frequently attempt to circumvent this disallowance by disguising a dividend distribution as some other purported transaction. One of the more common ways of disguising dividend distributions is to pay excessive compensation to shareholder-employees of a closely held corporation. The IRS scrutinizes compensation and other economic transactions (e.g., loans, leases, and sales) between shareholders and closely held corporations to ensure that payments are reasonable in amount. (See Chapter 13 for more discussion on constructive dividends.)

Double taxation also stems from the fact that dividend distributions are taxable to the shareholders. Historically, dividend income has been taxed at the same rates as ordinary income. However, to alleviate some of the double taxation effect, Congress reduced the tax rate applicable to dividend income of individuals for years after 2002. Qualified dividend income is currently taxed at the same preferential rate as long-term capital gains—15 percent (0 percent for taxpayers in the bottom two tax brackets). The American Taxpayer Relief Act of 2012 increased the maximum tax rate applied to qualified dividends from 15 percent to 20 percent for certain high-income taxpayers. The 20 percent rate applies beginning in 2013 when the taxpayer's regular tax bracket is 39.6 percent.

Beginning in 2013, § 1411 imposes a 3.8 percent Medicare surtax on a taxpayer's net investment income in excess of modified adjusted gross income of $200,000 ($250,000 if married filing jointly). Thus, for high-income taxpayers, the double taxation of dividend income is increased by this surtax.

TAX FACT   Corporations' Reporting Responsibilities

Like individuals, corporations are required to report their taxable income and other financial information to the IRS on an annual basis. The forms used depend on the type and size of the corporation. Based on projections, the IRS expects to receive approximately 6.7 million corporate income tax returns during the 2015 filing season.

Interestingly, nearly 79 percent of C and S corporations are expected to submit their returns electronically.

Type of Corporation	Form	Percentage
C Corporation	1120	26.7%
C Corporation	Others	4.9
S Corporation	1120S	68.4
		100.0%

Source: Fiscal Year Return Projections for the United States: 2013–2020, IRS, Document 6292, Spring 2013 Update, Table 1.

© iStockphoto.com/Pali Rao

12-1b Comparison of Corporations and Other Forms of Doing Business

Chapter 18 presents a detailed comparison of sole proprietorships, partnerships, S corporations, and C corporations as forms of doing business. However, it is appropriate at this point to consider some of the tax and nontax factors that favor corporations over other business entities.

Consideration of tax factors requires an examination of the corporate rate structure. The income tax rate schedule applicable to corporations is reproduced on the inside front cover of the text. As this schedule shows, the marginal tax rates for corporations range from 15 percent to 39 percent. In comparison, the marginal tax rates for individuals range from 10 percent to 35 percent (assuming the taxpayer is not a high-income taxpayer to whom the 39.6 percent rate applies). In many cases, the tax burden will be greater if a business is operated as a corporation (as in Example 1). However, the corporate form of doing business presents tax savings opportunities when the applicable corporate marginal rate is lower than the applicable individual marginal rate.

Example 3

Susanna, an individual taxpayer in the 39.6% marginal tax rate bracket, can generate $100,000 of additional taxable income in the current year. If the income is taxed to Susanna, the associated tax is $39,600 ($100,000 × 39.6%). If, however, Susanna is able to shift the income to a newly created corporation, the corporate tax is $22,250. Thus, by taking advantage of the lower corporate marginal tax rates, a tax *savings* of $17,350 ($39,600 − $22,250) is achieved.

Any attempt to take advantage of the difference between the corporate and individual marginal tax rates also must consider the double taxation effect. When the preferential rate for dividend income is considered, however, tax savings opportunities still exist.

Example 4

Assume in Example 3 that the corporation distributes all of its after-tax earnings to Susanna as a dividend. The dividend results in income tax of $15,550 [($100,000 − $22,250) × 20%] to Susanna. Thus, even when the double taxation effect is considered, the combined tax burden of $37,800 ($22,250 paid by the corporation + $15,550 paid by the shareholder) represents an income tax *savings* of $1,800 when compared to the $39,600 of tax that results when the $100,000 of income is subject to Susanna's 39.6% marginal rate.

Examples 3 and 4 ignore other tax issues that also must be considered in selecting the proper form of doing business, but they illustrate the tax savings that can be achieved by taking advantage of tax rate differentials. In addition to the 3.8 percent Medicare surtax (mentioned above), some of the other tax considerations that could affect the selection of a business form include the character of business income, the expectation of business losses, employment taxes, and state taxes.

Investment brokers and promoters often try to entice individuals to invest their disposable income in ventures designed to produce handsome returns. In most situations, the type of business entity in which the funds are invested takes the form of a "flow-through" entity, such as a limited partnership. Such investment ventures rarely operate as regular corporations.

A limited partnership is the favored investment vehicle for several reasons. One of the most significant reasons is that the investors who become limited partners are protected from exposure to unlimited liability. In addition, any operating losses of the entity (which may be expected in the venture's early years) flow through to the partners and, as a result, may provide an immediate tax benefit on the partners' returns. Another major advantage of the partnership form, in contrast to the corporate form, is that the business earnings are subject to only one level of tax—at the partner or investor level. If the investments were housed in a corporation, a tax would be levied first on the corporate earnings and then at the investor level when the corporation makes distributions to the shareholders.

Unlike other forms of business, the tax attributes of income and expense items of a C corporation do not pass through the corporate entity to the shareholders. As a result, if the business is expected to generate tax-favored income (e.g., tax-exempt income or long-term capital gains), one of the other (non-C corporation) forms of business may be desirable.

Losses of a C corporation are treated differently than losses of a proprietorship, a partnership, or an S corporation. A loss incurred by a proprietorship may be deductible by the owner, because all income and expense items are reported by the proprietor. Partnership and S corporation losses are passed through the entity and may be deductible by the partners or shareholders. C corporation losses, however, have no effect on the taxable income of the shareholders. Therefore, one of the non-C corporation forms of business may be desirable if business losses are anticipated.

> Franco plans to start a business this year. He expects that the business will incur operating losses for the first three years and then become highly profitable. Franco decides to operate as an S corporation during the loss period because the losses will flow through and be deductible on his personal return. When the business becomes profitable, he intends to switch to C corporation status.

Example 5

The net income of a proprietorship is subject to the self-employment tax, as are some partnership allocations of income to partners. In the alternative, wages paid to a shareholder-employee of a corporation (C or S) are subject to payroll taxes. The combined corporation-employee payroll tax burden should be compared with the self-employment tax associated with the proprietorship and partnership forms of business. This analysis should include the benefit of the deduction available to a corporation for payroll taxes paid, as well as the deduction available to an individual for one-half of the self-employment taxes paid.

At the entity level, state corporate income taxes and/or franchise taxes are applicable for businesses formed as corporations. Although no entity-level Federal income tax is typically assessed on S corporations, limited liability companies (LLCs), or partnerships, a few states impose a corporate income tax or franchise tax on such business forms. Consideration of state taxation when selecting a business form is particularly relevant for businesses that operate in more than one state. (See Chapter 16 for a discussion of the taxation of multistate corporations.) At the owner level, the income of sole proprietorships, S corporations, and partnerships (including most LLCs) is subject to state individual income taxation. Similarly, dividend income from corporate distributions is subject to state income taxation without any rate preference for such income.

12-1c Nontax Considerations

Nontax considerations will sometimes override tax considerations and lead to the conclusion that a business should be operated as a corporation. The following are some of the more important nontax considerations:

- Sole proprietors and general partners in partnerships face the danger of *unlimited liability*. That is, creditors of the business may file claims not only against the assets of the business but also against the *personal* assets of proprietors or general partners. State corporate law protects shareholders from claims against their personal assets for corporate debts.
- The corporate form of business can provide a vehicle for raising large amounts of capital through widespread stock ownership. Most major businesses in the United States are operated as corporations.
- Shares of stock in a corporation are freely transferable, whereas a partner's sale of his or her partnership interest is subject to approval by the other partners.
- Shareholders may come and go, but a corporation can continue to exist. Death or withdrawal of a partner, on the other hand, may terminate the existing partnership and cause financial difficulties that result in dissolution of the entity. Thus, *continuity of life* is a distinct advantage of the corporate form of doing business.
- Corporations have *centralized management*. All management responsibility is assigned to a board of directors, which appoints officers to carry out the corporation's business. Partnerships, by contrast, may have decentralized management, in which every partner has a right to participate in the organization's business decisions. **Limited partnerships**, though, may have centralized management. Centralized management is essential for the smooth operation of a widely held business.

12-1d Limited Liability Companies

The **limited liability company (LLC)** has proliferated greatly in recent years, particularly since 1988 when the IRS first ruled that it would treat qualifying LLCs as partnerships for tax purposes. All 50 states and the District of Columbia have passed laws that allow LLCs, and thousands of companies have chosen LLC status. As with a corporation, operating as an LLC allows its owners ("members") to avoid unlimited liability, which is a primary *nontax* consideration in choosing this form of business organization. The tax advantage of LLCs is that qualifying businesses may be treated as proprietorships or partnerships for tax purposes, thereby avoiding the problem of double taxation associated with regular corporations.

Some states allow an LLC to have centralized management, but not continuity of life or free transferability of interests. Other states allow LLCs to adopt any or all of the corporate characteristics of centralized management, continuity of life, and free transferability of interests. The comparison of business entities in Chapter 18 includes a discussion of LLCs.

12-1e Entity Classification

In 1996, the IRS issued its so-called **check-the-box Regulations**.[1] The Regulations enable taxpayers to choose the tax status of a business entity without regard to its corporate (or noncorporate) characteristics. These rules simplified tax administration considerably and eliminated much of the litigation that arose under prior law.

Under the check-the-box Regulations, an unincorporated entity with *more than one* owner is, by default, classified as a partnership. An unincorporated entity with *only one* owner is, by default, classified as a **disregarded entity** (or DRE). A DRE is treated as a sole proprietorship if it is owned by an individual taxpayer or as a branch or a

---

[1]Reg. §§ 301.7701–1 through –4, and –7.

division of a corporate owner. If the entity wants to use its default status, it simply files the appropriate tax return. If it wants to use a different status or change its status, it does so by "checking a box" on Form 8832. Thus, an LLC (single or multi-member) can choose to be taxed as a C corporation and, if otherwise qualifies, even elect S corporation status. See Chapter 15 for more on S corporations.

The status election is not available to entities that are incorporated under state law or to entities that are required to be taxed as corporations under Federal law (e.g., certain publicly traded partnerships). LLCs are not treated as being incorporated under state law, so they default to either partnership or DRE status. Although an LLC does not typically pay Federal income taxes, LLCs are obligated to report and pay employment and excise taxes.

In-depth coverage can be found on this book's companion website: **www.cengagebrain.com** | Digging Deeper

---

Tax Planning Strategies   RELATED GROUPS MAY UTILIZE CHECK-THE-BOX REGULATIONS

FRAMEWORK FOCUS: THINKING OUTSIDE THE FRAMEWORK

The check-the-box Regulations allow a single-owner eligible entity to be treated as a corporation or a division. Because LLCs are eligible entities, a C corporation that owns 100 percent of an LLC can treat the LLC as a division. At the same time, the parent corporation can enjoy the benefit of limited liability in the LLC operations. By electing division treatment, the income of the LLC flows directly to the parent corporation for tax purposes. Consequently, the parent corporation is able to avoid detailed and complex consolidated return Regulations and filing requirements.

12-2 ORGANIZATION OF AND TRANSFERS TO CONTROLLED CORPORATIONS

12-2a In General

Property transactions normally produce tax consequences if a gain or loss is realized. As a result, unless special provisions in the Code apply, a transfer of property to a corporation in exchange for stock is a taxable transaction. The amount of gain or loss is measured by the difference between the fair market value of the stock received and the tax basis of the property transferred.

The Code, however, permits nonrecognition of gain or loss in limited circumstances. For example, with both § 1031 (like kind exchanges—see Chapter 7) and § 351 (transfers of property to controlled corporations), gain or loss is postponed until a substantive change in the taxpayer's investment occurs (e.g., a sale of property or ownership shares to outsiders). When a taxpayer exchanges some of his or her property for other property of a like kind, § 1031 provides that gain (or loss) realized on the exchange is not recognized because a substantive change in the taxpayer's investment has not occurred. The deferral of gain or loss is accomplished by calculating a substituted basis for the like-kind property received. With this substituted basis, the realized gain or loss associated with the property given up is ultimately recognized when the property received in the exchange is sold.

In a similar fashion, § 351, which deals with transfers to *controlled corporations* (defined later in the chapter), provides that gain or loss is not recognized upon the transfer of property to a corporation in exchange for stock. For example, when a business is incorporated, the owner's economic status remains the same; only the *form* of the investment has changed. The investment in the business assets carries over to an investment in corporate stock. When only stock in the corporation is received, the shareholder is hardly in a position to pay a tax on any realized gain.

LO.2

Identify the tax consequences of incorporating and transferring assets to controlled corporations.

Thus, this approach is justified under the wherewithal to pay concept discussed in Chapter 1. As noted later, however, when the taxpayer receives property other than stock (i.e., cash or other "boot") from the corporation, some or all of the realized gain is recognized.

A further justification for the nonrecognition of gain or loss provisions under § 351 is that Congress believes tax rules should not impede the exercise of sound business judgment (e.g., choice of the corporate form of doing business).

Example 6

Ron is considering incorporating his sole proprietorship. He is concerned about his personal liability for the obligations of the business. Ron realizes that if he incorporates, he will be liable only for the debts of the business that he has personally guaranteed. If Ron incorporates his business, the following assets will be transferred to the corporation:

	Tax Basis	Fair Market Value
Cash	$ 10,000	$ 10,000
Furniture and fixtures	20,000	60,000
Land and building	240,000	300,000
	$270,000	$370,000

In exchange, Ron will receive stock in the newly formed corporation worth $370,000. Without the nonrecognition provisions of § 351, Ron would recognize a taxable gain of $100,000 ($370,000 − $270,000) on the transfer. Under § 351, however, Ron does not recognize any gain because his economic status has not changed. Ron's investment in the assets of his sole proprietorship ($270,000) carries over to his investment in the incorporated business, which is now represented by his ownership of stock in the corporation. Thus, § 351 provides for tax neutrality on the initial incorporation of Ron's sole proprietorship.

When a taxpayer participates in a like-kind exchange, gain is deferred to the extent the taxpayer receives like-kind property. However, the taxpayer must recognize some or all of the realized gain when receiving "boot" (i.e., property of an unlike kind). For example, if a taxpayer exchanges a truck used in a business for another truck to be used in the business and also receives cash, the taxpayer has the wherewithal to pay an income tax on the cash involved. Further, the taxpayer's economic status has changed to the extent of the cash (not like-kind property) received. Thus, "realized" gain on the exchange is recognized to the extent of the cash received. In like manner, if a taxpayer transfers property to a corporation and receives money or property other than stock, § 351(b) provides that gain is recognized to the extent of the lesser of the gain realized or the boot received (the amount of money and the fair market value of other property received). Gain is characterized (e.g., ordinary, capital) according to the type of asset transferred.[2] Loss on a § 351 transaction is never recognized. The nonrecognition of gain or loss is accompanied by a substituted basis in the shareholder's stock.[3]

Example 7

Abby and Bill form White Corporation. Abby transfers property with an adjusted basis of $30,000 and a fair market value of $60,000 for 50% of White's stock. Bill transfers property with an adjusted basis of $70,000 and a fair market value of $60,000 for the remaining 50% of the stock. The transfers qualify under § 351. Abby has a deferred gain of $30,000, and Bill has a deferred loss of $10,000. Both have a substituted basis in the stock of White Corporation. Abby has a basis of $30,000 in her stock, and Bill has a basis of $70,000 in his stock. Therefore, if either Abby or Bill later disposes of the White stock in a taxable transaction (e.g., a sale), this deferred gain/loss will then be fully recognized—a $30,000 gain to Abby and a $10,000 loss to Bill.

---

[2]Rev.Rul. 68–55, 1968–1 C.B. 140.   [3]§ 358(a). See the discussion preceding Example 28.

Alternatively, if Abby and Bill each had received White stock worth $50,000 and cash of $10,000, a gain would be recognized by Abby, but a loss would not be recognized by Bill. Specifically, Abby would recognize $10,000 of the $30,000 realized gain because she receives boot of $10,000, while Bill's receipt of boot would not trigger the recognition of a loss (i.e., recognition of loss never occurs in a § 351 transaction on the receipt of boot). Additional discussion of gain/loss recognition and the basis of stock received appears later in the chapter.

Section 351 is *mandatory* if a transaction satisfies the provision's requirements. There are three requirements for nonrecognition of gain or loss: (1) *property* is transferred (2) in exchange for *stock* and (3) the transferors must be in *control* of the transferee corporation immediately after the transfer. These three requirements are discussed next.

12-2b Transfer of Property

Questions have arisen concerning what constitutes **property** for purposes of § 351. The Code specifically excludes services rendered from the definition of property. With this exception, the definition of property is comprehensive. For example, along with plant and equipment, unrealized receivables held by a cash basis taxpayer and installment notes are considered property.[4] The transfer of an installment note in a transaction qualifying under § 351 is not a disposition of the installment note. Thus, gain is not recognized to the transferor. Proprietary processes and formulas as well as proprietary information in the general nature of a patentable invention also qualify as property under § 351.[5]

The rendition of services to the corporation, however, is excluded from the otherwise comprehensive definition of property. As demonstrated below, a taxpayer must report as income the fair market value of any consideration received as compensation for services because § 351 specifically excludes services from the definition of property.[6] Thus, if a taxpayer receives stock as consideration for rendering services to the corporation, the taxpayer recognizes ordinary income. In this case, the amount of income recognized by the taxpayer is equal to the fair market value of the stock received. As a consequence, the taxpayer's basis in the stock received is its fair market value.

Example 8

Ann and Bob form Brown Corporation and transfer the following consideration:

	Consideration Transferred		
	Basis to Transferor	Fair Market Value	Number of Shares Issued
From Ann:			
Personal services rendered to Brown Corporation	$ –0–	$20,000	200
From Bob:			
Installment note receivable	5,000	40,000	
Inventory	10,000	30,000	800
Proprietary process	–0–	10,000	

The value of each share in Brown Corporation is $100.[7] Ann has ordinary income of $20,000 on the transfer because services do not qualify as "property." She has a basis of $20,000 in her 200 shares of stock in Brown (i.e., Ann is treated as having bought some of the Brown stock by rendering services). Bob recognizes no gain on the transfer because all of the consideration he transferred to Brown qualifies as "property" and he has "control" of Brown after the transfer. (See the discussion concerning control on the next page.) Bob has a substituted basis of $15,000 in the Brown stock.

---

[4]*Hempt Brothers, Inc. v. U.S.*, 74–1 USTC ¶9188, 33 AFTR 2d 74–570, 490 F.2d 1172 (CA–3, 1974), and Reg. § 1.453–9(c)(2).
[5]Rev.Rul. 64–56, 1964–1 C.B. 133; Rev.Rul. 71–564, 1971–2 C.B. 179.

[6]§§ 61 and 83.
[7]The value of closely held stock normally is presumed to be equal to the value of the property transferred.

As mentioned earlier, if property is transferred to a corporation in exchange for any property other than stock, the property received constitutes boot. The boot is taxable to the transferor-shareholder to the extent of any realized gain.[8]

12-2c Stock

Generally, the term *stock* needs no clarification. It includes common stock and most preferred stock. However, the Regulations state that the term *stock* does not include stock rights and stock warrants.[9] In addition, it does not include "nonqualified preferred stock," which possesses many of the attributes of debt.[10]

Thus, any corporate debt or **securities** (i.e., long-term debt such as bonds) are treated as boot because they do not qualify as stock. Therefore, the receipt of debt in exchange for the transfer of appreciated property to a controlled corporation causes recognition of gain.

THE BIG PICTURE

Example 9

Return to the facts of *The Big Picture* on p. 12-1. Assume that the proposed transaction qualifies under § 351, but Amber decides to receive some corporate debt along with the stock. If she receives Garden stock worth $900,000 and Garden debt of $100,000 in exchange for the property transferred, Amber realizes gain of $600,000 [$1,000,000 (value of consideration received) – $400,000 (basis in the transferred property)]. However, because the transaction qualifies under § 351, only $100,000 of gain is recognized—the $100,000 of Garden debt is treated as boot. The remaining realized gain of $500,000 is deferred.

12-2d Control of the Corporation

For a transaction to qualify as nontaxable under § 351, the transferor(s) of the property must be in **control** of the corporation immediately after the exchange. That is, the person or persons transferring *property* must have at least an 80 percent stock ownership in the corporation, resulting in the entity being a controlled corporation. The property transferors must own stock possessing at least 80 percent of the total combined voting power of all classes of stock entitled to vote *and* at least 80 percent of the total *number* of shares of all other classes of stock.[11]

Control Immediately after the Transfer

Immediately after the exchange, the property transferors must control the corporation. Control can apply to a single person or to several taxpayers if they are all parties to an integrated transaction. The Regulations provide that when more than one person is involved, the exchange does not necessarily require simultaneous exchanges by two or more persons. The Regulations do, however, require that the rights of the parties (i.e., those transferring property to the corporation) be previously set out and determined. Also, the agreement to transfer property should be executed "with an expedition consistent with orderly procedure."[12]

If two or more persons transfer property to a corporation for stock, the transfers should occur close together in time and should be made in accordance with an agreement among the parties.

---

[8]§ 351(b).
[9]Reg. § 1.351–1(a)(1)(ii).
[10]§ 351(g). Examples of nonqualified preferred stock include preferred stock that is redeemable within 20 years of issuance and whose dividend rate is based on factors other than corporate performance. See also Reg. § 1.351–1(a)(1)(ii).

[11]§ 368(c). Nonqualified preferred stock is treated as stock, not boot, for purposes of this control test.
[12]Reg. § 1.351–1(a)(1).

Jack exchanges property with a basis of $60,000 and a fair market value of $100,000 for 70% of the stock of Gray Corporation. The other 30% is owned by Jane, who acquired it several years ago. The fair market value of Jack's stock is $100,000. Jack recognizes a taxable gain of $40,000 on the transfer because he does not have control immediately after the exchange and his transaction cannot be integrated with Jane's for purposes of the control requirement.

Example 10

Lana, Leo, and Lori incorporate their respective businesses by forming Green Corporation. Lana exchanges her property for 300 shares in Green on January 7, 2014. Leo exchanges his property for 400 shares in Green on January 14, 2014, and Lori exchanges her property for 300 shares in Green on March 5, 2014. The three exchanges are part of a prearranged plan, so the control requirement is met. The nonrecognition provisions of § 351 apply to all of the exchanges.

Example 11

Stock need not be issued to the property transferors in the same proportion as the relative value of the property transferred by each. However, when stock received is not proportionate to the value of the property transferred, the actual effect of the transaction must be properly characterized. For example, in such situations, one transferor may actually be making a gift to another transferor.

Ron and Shelia, father and daughter, form Oak Corporation. Ron transfers property worth $50,000 in exchange for 100 shares of stock, while Shelia transfers property worth $50,000 for 400 shares of stock. The transfers qualify under § 351 because Ron and Shelia have control of the Oak stock immediately after the transfers of property. However, the implicit gift of 150 shares by Ron to Shelia must be recognized and appropriately characterized. As such, the value of the gift might be subject to the gift tax.

Example 12

Once control has been achieved, it is not necessarily lost if, shortly after the transaction, stock received by shareholders in a § 351 exchange is sold or given to persons who are not parties to the exchange.[13]

Mark and Carl form Black Corporation. They transfer appreciated property to the corporation with each receiving 50 shares of Black stock. Shortly after the formation, Mark gives 25 shares to his son. Because Mark was not committed to making the gift, he is considered to own his original shares of Black Corporation stock and, along with Carl, to control Black Corporation "immediately after the exchange." The requirements of § 351 are met, and neither Mark nor Carl is taxed on the exchange.

Example 13

A different result might materialize if a plan for the ultimate disposition of the stock existed *before* the exchange.

Assume the same facts as in Example 13 except Mark immediately gives 25 shares to a business associate pursuant to a plan to satisfy an outstanding obligation. In this case, the formation of Black would be taxable to Mark and Carl because of their lack of control (i.e., Mark and Carl, the property transferors, would have owned only 75% of the stock).

Example 14

---
[13]*Wilgard Realty Co. v. Comm.*, 42–1 USTC ¶9452, 29 AFTR 325, 127 F.2d 514 (CA–2, 1942).

Tax Planning Strategies Ⓤtilizing § 351

FRAMEWORK FOCUS: INCOME AND EXCLUSIONS

Strategy: Avoid Income Recognition.

When using § 351, ensure that all parties transferring property (including cash) receive control of the corporation. Simultaneous transfers are not necessary, but a long period of time between transfers makes the transaction vulnerable to taxation if the transfers are not properly documented as part of a single plan. To do this, the parties should document and preserve evidence of their intentions. Also, it is helpful to have some reasonable explanation for any delay in the transfers.

To meet the requirements of § 351, mere momentary control on the part of the transferor may not suffice if loss of control is compelled by a prearranged agreement.[14]

Example 15

For many years, Todd operated a business as a sole proprietor employing Linda as manager. To dissuade Linda from quitting and going out on her own, Todd promised her a 30% interest in the business. To fulfill this promise, Todd transferred the business to newly formed Green Corporation in return for all of its stock. Immediately thereafter, Todd transfers 30% of the stock to Linda. As a consequence, he no longer meets the 80% control requirement. Section 351 probably does not apply to Todd's transfer to Green Corporation. It appears that Todd was under an obligation to relinquish control. If this preexisting obligation exists, § 351 will not be available to Todd because, as the sole property transferor, he does not have control of Green Corporation. If there is no obligation and the loss of control was voluntary on Todd's part, momentary control would suffice.[15] ■

Make sure that later transfers of property to an existing corporation satisfy the 80 percent control requirement if recognition of gain is to be avoided. Also with respect to later transfers, a transferor's interest cannot be counted if the value of stock received is relatively small compared with the value of stock already owned. Further, the primary purpose of the transfer may not be to qualify other transferors for § 351 treatment.[16]

For contributions of property by a partner to a partnership, at formation or subsequent to formation, § 721 is available to provide nonrecognition treatment. This partnership provision generally resembles § 351. However, in such situations, any partner can make a tax-deferred contribution without regard to a control test. Thus, the 80 percent control requirement, which serves as a high threshold to be met if tax deferred treatment is desired in a corporate setting, contrasts to the treatment given in partnership taxation where no such control test applies. See Chapters 14 and 18 for additional discussion.

Transfers for Property and Services

Section 351 treatment is lost if stock is transferred to persons who did not contribute property, causing those who did to lack control immediately after the exchange.

THE BIG PICTURE

Example 16

Return to the facts of *The Big Picture* on p. 12-1. Assume that Amber transfers her $1,000,000 of property to Garden, Inc., and receives 50% of its stock. Jimmy receives the other 50% of the stock for services rendered (worth $1,000,000). Both Amber and Jimmy have tax consequences from the transfers. Jimmy has ordinary income of $1,000,000 because he does not exchange property for stock. Amber has a taxable gain of $600,000 [$1,000,000 (fair market value of the stock in Garden) − $400,000 (basis in the transferred property)]. As the sole transferor of property, she receives only 50% of Garden's stock.

---

[14]Rev.Rul. 54–96, 1954–1 C.B. 111.

[15]Compare *Fahs v. Florida Machine and Foundry Co.*, 48–2 USTC ¶9329, 36 AFTR 1161, 168 F.2d 957 (CA–5, 1948), with *John C. O'Connor*, 16 TCM 213, T.C.Memo. 1957–50, *aff'd* in 58–2 USTC ¶9913, 2 AFTR 2d 6011, 260 F.2d 358 (CA–6, 1958).

[16]Reg. § 1.351–1(a)(1)(ii).

As noted earlier, a person receiving stock in exchange for services and for property transferred is taxed on the stock value related to those services but not on the stock issued for property. In addition, such a person can still be treated as a "property transferor" and in such a case, all stock received by the person transferring both property and services is counted in determining whether the transferors acquired control of the corporation.[17]

THE BIG PICTURE
Example 17

Assume the same facts as in Example 16, except that Jimmy transfers property worth $800,000 (basis of $260,000) in addition to services rendered to Garden, Inc. (valued at $200,000). Now Jimmy becomes a part of the control group. Amber and Jimmy, as property transferors, together receive 100% of the corporation's stock. Consequently, § 351 is applicable to the exchanges. Amber has no recognized gain. Jimmy does not recognize gain on the transfer of the property, but he recognizes ordinary income to the extent of the value of the shares issued for services rendered. Thus, Jimmy recognizes $200,000 of ordinary income currently.

Transfers for Services and Nominal Property

Note that to be part of the group meeting the 80 percent control test, the person contributing services must transfer property having more than a "relatively small value" compared to the value of services performed. Section 351 will not apply when a small amount of property is transferred and the primary purpose of the transfer is to qualify the transaction under § 351 for concurrent transferors.[18]

The IRS generally requires that before a transferor who receives stock for both property and services can be included in the control group, the value of the property transferred must be at least 10 percent of the value of the services provided.[19] If the value of the property transferred is less than this amount, the IRS will not issue an advance ruling that the exchange meets the requirements of § 351.

Example 18

Sara and Rick form Grouse Corporation. Sara transfers land (worth $100,000, basis of $20,000) for 50% of the stock in Grouse. Rick transfers equipment (worth $50,000, adjusted basis of $10,000) and provides services worth $50,000 for 50% of the stock. Because the value of the property Rick transfers is not small relative to the value of the services he renders, his stock in Grouse Corporation is counted in determining control for purposes of § 351; thus, the transferors own 100% of the stock in Grouse. In addition, all of Rick's stock, not just the shares received for the equipment, is counted in determining control. As a result, Sara does not recognize gain on the transfer of the land. Rick, however, must recognize income of $50,000 on the transfer of services. Even though the transfer of the equipment qualifies under § 351, his transfer of services for stock does not.

Example 19

Assume the same facts as in Example 18 except the value of Rick's property is $2,000 and the value of his services is $98,000. In this situation, the value of the property is small relative to the value of the services (and well below the 10 percent threshold provided by the IRS); therefore, Rick will not be considered a property transferor. Consequently, the control requirement is not met and the transaction is fully taxable to both Sara and Rick. None of Rick's stock is counted in determining control because the property he transfers has a nominal value in comparison to the value of the services he renders. Sara recognizes $80,000 of gain on the transfer of the land. She has a basis of $100,000 in her Grouse stock. Rick must recognize income of $98,000 on the transfer for services rendered and any realized gain or loss is recognized on the property transferred. Rick also has a $100,000 basis in his Grouse stock.

[17]Reg. § 1.351–1(a)(2), Ex. 3.
[18]Reg. § 1.351–1(a)(1)(ii).
[19]Rev.Proc. 77–37, 1977–2 C.B. 568.

Transfers to Existing Corporations

Once a corporation is in operation, § 351 also applies to any later transfers of property for stock by either new or existing shareholders.

Example 20

Sam and Beth formed Blue Corporation three years ago. Both Sam and Beth transferred appreciated property to Blue in exchange for 500 shares each in the corporation. The original transfers qualified under § 351, and neither Sam nor Beth was taxed on the exchange. In the current year, Sam transfers property (worth $100,000, adjusted basis of $5,000) for 500 additional Blue shares. Sam has a taxable gain of $95,000 on the transfer. The exchange does not qualify under § 351 because Sam does not have 80% control of Blue Corporation immediately after the transfer; he owns 1,000 shares of the 1,500 shares outstanding, or a 66⅔% interest.

If current shareholders transfer property with a small value relative to the value of stock already owned, a special rule applies (similar to the nominal property rule noted previously). In particular, if the purpose of the transfer is to qualify a transaction under § 351, the ownership of the current shareholders is not counted when determining control. Thus, in the preceding example, if Beth had contributed $200 for one share of stock at the time of Sam's contribution, Beth's ownership would not have counted toward the 80 percent control requirement and Sam would still have had a taxable exchange.

12-2e Assumption of Liabilities—§ 357

LO.3

Describe the special rules that apply when a corporation assumes a shareholder's liability.

Without a provision to the contrary, the transfer of mortgaged property to a controlled corporation could require recognition of gain by the transferor if the corporation took over the mortgage. This would be consistent with the treatment given in like-kind exchanges under § 1031. Liabilities assumed by the other party are considered the equivalent of cash and treated as boot received. Section 357(a) provides, however, that when the acquiring corporation assumes a liability in a § 351 transaction, the liability is not treated as boot received for gain recognition purposes. Nevertheless, liabilities assumed by the transferee corporation are treated as boot in determining the basis of the stock received. As a result, the basis of the stock received is reduced by the amount of the liabilities assumed by the corporation.

THE BIG PICTURE

Example 21

Return to the facts of *The Big Picture* on p. 12-1. Assume that you learn that Amber's husband, Jimmy, becomes disinterested in becoming a stockholder in Garden, Inc., and that Amber's building is subject to a liability of $70,000 that Garden assumes. Consequently, Amber receives 100% of the Garden stock and is relieved of the $70,000 liability in exchange for property with an adjusted basis of $400,000 and fair market value of $1,000,000. The exchange is tax-free under § 351 because the release of a liability is not treated as boot under § 357(a). However, the basis to Amber of the Garden stock is $330,000 [$400,000 (basis of property transferred) − $70,000 (amount of the liability assumed by Garden)].

The general rule of § 357(a) has two exceptions: (1) § 357(b) provides that if the principal purpose of the assumption of the liabilities is to avoid tax *or* if there is no bona fide business purpose behind the exchange, the liabilities are treated as boot; (2) § 357(c) provides that if the sum of the liabilities exceeds the adjusted basis of the properties transferred, the excess is taxable gain.

Does § 351 Cover the Incorporation of a Foreign Business?

Global Tax Issues

© iStockphoto.com/Andrey Prokhorov

When a taxpayer wants to incorporate a business overseas by moving assets across U.S. borders, the deferral mechanism of § 351 applies in certain situations, but not in others. In general, § 351 is available to defer gain recognition when starting up a new corporation outside the United States unless so-called tainted assets are involved. Under § 367, tainted assets, which include assets such as inventory and accounts receivable, are treated as having been sold by the taxpayer prior to the corporate formation; therefore, their transfer results in the current recognition of gain. The presence of tainted assets triggers gain because Congress does not want taxpayers to be able to shift the gain outside U.S. jurisdiction. The gain recognized is ordinary or capital depending on the nature of the asset involved.

Exception (1): Tax Avoidance or No Bona Fide Business Purpose

Unless liabilities are incurred shortly before incorporation, § 357(b) generally poses few problems. Because the liabilities transferred reduce the basis of the stock received, any realized gain merely is deferred and not completely eliminated. Any postponed gain is recognized when and if the stock is disposed of in a taxable sale or exchange.

Satisfying the bona fide business purpose is not difficult if the liabilities are incurred in connection with the transferor's normal course of conducting a trade or business. But the bona fide business purpose requirement can cause difficulty if the liability is taken out shortly before the property is transferred and the proceeds are utilized for personal purposes.[20] This type of situation is analogous to a cash distribution by the corporation, which is taxed as boot.

Example 22

Dan transfers real estate (basis of $140,000 and fair market value of $190,000) to a controlled corporation in return for stock in the corporation. Shortly before the transfer, Dan mortgages the real estate and uses the $20,000 of proceeds to meet personal obligations. Thus, along with the real estate, the mortgage is transferred to the corporation. In this case, the assumption of the mortgage lacks a bona fide business purpose. Consequently, the release of the liability is treated as boot received, and Dan has a taxable gain on the transfer of $20,000, computed as follows:[21]

Stock	$ 170,000
Release of liability—treated as boot	20,000
Total amount realized	$ 190,000
Less: Basis of real estate	(140,000)
Realized gain	$ 50,000
Recognized gain	$ 20,000

The effect of the application of § 357(b) is to taint *all* liabilities transferred, even if some are supported by a bona fide business purpose.

Example 23

Tim, an accrual basis taxpayer, incorporates his sole proprietorship. Among the liabilities transferred to the new corporation are trade accounts payable of $100,000 and a credit card bill of $5,000. Tim had used the credit card to purchase an anniversary gift for his wife. Under these circumstances, the *entire* $105,000 of liabilities is boot and triggers the recognition of gain to the extent gain is realized.

---

[20]See, for example, *Campbell, Jr. v. Wheeler*, 65–1 USTC ¶9294, 15 AFTR 2d 578, 342 F.2d 837 (CA–5, 1965).   [21]§ 351(b).

Exception (2): Liabilities in Excess of Basis

Section 357(c) states that if the amount of the liabilities assumed *exceeds* the total of the adjusted bases of the properties transferred, the excess is taxable gain. Without this provision, if liabilities exceed the basis in the property exchanged, a taxpayer would have a negative basis in the stock received in the controlled corporation.[22] Section 357(c) precludes the negative basis possibility by treating the excess over basis as gain to the transferor.

Example 24	Andre transfers land and equipment with adjusted bases of $350,000 and $50,000, respectively, to a newly formed corporation in exchange for 100% of the stock. The corporation assumes $500,000 of liabilities on the transferred land. Without § 357(c), Andre's basis in the stock of the new corporation would be negative $100,000 [$400,000 (bases of properties transferred) + $0 (gain recognized) − $0 (boot received) − $500,000 (liabilities assumed)]. Section 357(c), however, causes Andre to recognize a gain of $100,000 ($500,000 liabilities assumed − $400,000 bases of assets transferred). As a result, the stock has a zero basis in Andre's hands, determined as follows:

Bases in the properties transferred ($350,000 + $50,000)	$ 400,000
Plus: Gain recognized	100,000
Less: Boot received	(–0–)
Less: Liabilities assumed	(500,000)
Basis in the stock received	$ –0–

Thus, Andre recognizes $100,000 of gain, and a negative stock basis is avoided.

The definition of liabilities under § 357(c) excludes obligations that would have been deductible to the transferor had those obligations been paid before the transfer. Thus, accounts payable of a cash basis taxpayer that give rise to a deduction are not considered liabilities for purposes of § 357(c). In addition, they are not considered in the computation of the shareholder's stock basis.

Example 25	Tina, a cash basis taxpayer, incorporates her sole proprietorship. In return for all of the stock of the new corporation, she transfers the following items:

	Adjusted Basis	Fair Market Value
Cash	$10,000	$10,000
Unrealized accounts receivable (amounts due to Tina but not yet received by her)	–0–	40,000
Trade accounts payable	–0–	30,000
Note payable	5,000	5,000

Unrealized accounts receivable and trade accounts payable have a zero basis. Under the cash method of accounting, no income is recognized until the receivables are collected and no deduction materializes until the payables are satisfied. The note payable has a basis because it was issued for consideration received.

In this situation, the trade accounts payable are disregarded for gain recognition purposes and for the determination of Tina's stock basis. Thus, because the balance of the note payable does not exceed the basis of the assets transferred, Tina does not have a problem of liabilities in excess of basis (i.e., the note payable of $5,000 does not exceed the aggregate basis in the cash and accounts receivable of $10,000).

If §§ 357(b) and (c) both apply to the same transfer, § 357(b) dominates.[23] This could be significant because § 357(b) does not create gain on the transfer, as does § 357(c), but merely converts the liability to boot. Thus, the realized gain limitation continues to apply to § 357(b) transactions.

---

[22]*Jack L. Easson*, 33 T.C. 963 (1960), *rev'd* in 61–2 USTC ¶9654, 8 AFTR 2d 5448, 294 F.2d 653 (CA–9, 1961).   [23]§ 357(c)(2)(A).

Example 26

Chris owns land with a basis of $100,000 and a fair market value of $1 million. The land is subject to a mortgage of $300,000. One month prior to transferring the land to Robin Corporation, Chris borrows an additional $200,000 for personal purposes and gives the lender a second mortgage on the land. Therefore, upon the incorporation, Robin Corporation issues stock worth $500,000 to Chris and assumes the mortgages on the land.

Both § 357(c) and § 357(b) apply to the transfer. The mortgages on the property exceed the basis of the property. Thus, Chris has a gain of $400,000 under § 357(c). Chris borrowed $200,000 just prior to the transfer and used the loan proceeds for personal purposes. Under § 357(b), Chris has boot of $500,000 in the amount of the liabilities, which triggers $500,000 of recognized gain. Note that *all* of the liabilities are treated as boot, not just the "tainted" $200,000 liability.

	§ 357(b) Result	§ 357(c) Result
Amount realized:		
Robin Corporation stock	$ 500,000	$ 500,000
Release of mortgage on land	300,000	300,000
Release of second mortgage—personal purposes	200,000	200,000
Total amount realized	$1,000,000	$1,000,000
Basis of land	(100,000)	(100,000)
Realized gain	$ 900,000	$ 900,000
Gain recognized under § 357(b) ($300,000 + $200,000)	$ 500,000	
Gain recognized under § 357(c) [($300,000 + $200,000) − $100,000]		$ 400,000

Unfortunately for Chris, the relatively more onerous rule of § 357(b) dominates over § 357(c).

Tax Planning Strategies   **AVOIDING § 351**

FRAMEWORK FOCUS: TAX RATE

Strategy: Shift Net Income from High-Bracket Years to Low-Bracket Years.
             Control the Character of Income and Deductions.

Section 351(a) provides for the nonrecognition of gain on transfers to controlled corporations. As such, it is often regarded as a relief provision favoring taxpayers. In some situations, however, avoiding § 351(a) may produce a more advantageous tax result. The transferors might prefer to recognize gain on the transfer of property if the tax cost is low. For example, they may be in low tax brackets, or the gain may be a capital gain that could be neutralized by available capital losses. Also, recognition of gain will lead to a stepped-up basis in the transferred property in the corporation.

Another reason a particular transferor might want to avoid § 351 concerns possible loss recognition. Recall that § 351 refers to the nonrecognition of both gains and losses. Section 351(b)(2) specifically states: "No loss to such recipient shall be recognized." A transferor who wants to recognize loss has several alternatives:

- Sell the property to the corporation for its stock. The IRS could attempt to collapse the "sale," however, by taking the approach that the transfer really falls under § 351(a).[24]
- Sell the property to the corporation for other property or boot. Because the transferor receives no stock, § 351 is inapplicable.
- Transfer the property to the corporation in return for securities or nonqualified preferred stock. Recall that § 351 does not apply to a transferor who receives securities or nonqualified preferred stock. In both this and the previous alternatives, watch for the possible disallowance of the loss under the related-party rules.

Suppose loss property is to be transferred to the corporation and no loss is recognized by the transferor due to § 351(a). This could present an interesting problem in terms of assessing the economic realities involved.

---

[24]*U.S. v. Hertwig*, 68–2 USTC ¶9495, 22 AFTR 2d 5249, 398 F.2d 452 (CA–5, 1968).

Example 27

Iris and Ivan form Wren Corporation with the following investments: property by Iris (basis of $40,000 and fair market value of $50,000) and property by Ivan (basis of $60,000 and fair market value of $50,000). Each receives 50% of the Wren stock. Has Ivan acted wisely in settling for only 50% of the stock? At first, it would appear so because Iris and Ivan each invested property of the same value ($50,000). But what about tax considerations? By applying the general carryover basis rules, the corporation now has a basis of $40,000 in Iris's property and $60,000 in Ivan's property. In essence, Iris has shifted a possible $10,000 gain to the corporation while Ivan has transferred a $10,000 potential loss. Thus, an equitable allocation of the Wren stock would call for Ivan to receive a greater percentage interest than Iris would receive.

This issue is further complicated by the special basis adjustment required when a shareholder such as Ivan contributes property with a built-in loss to a corporation. (See the discussion of this basis adjustment for loss property in the next section.) In this situation, if Wren is to take a carryover basis in Ivan's property, Ivan must reduce his stock basis by the $10,000 built-in loss. This reduced stock basis, of course, could lead to a greater tax burden on Ivan when he sells the Wren stock. This may suggest additional support for Ivan having a greater percentage interest than Iris has. ■

12-2f Basis Determination and Other Issues

LO.4

Recognize the basis issues relevant to the shareholder and the corporation.

Recall that § 351(a) postpones gain or loss recognition until the taxpayer's investment changes substantively. By virtue of the basis rules described next, the postponed gain or loss is recognized when the stock is disposed of in a taxable transaction.

Basis of Stock to Shareholder

For a taxpayer transferring property to a corporation in a § 351 transaction, the basis of *stock* received in the transaction is the same as the basis the taxpayer had in the property transferred, increased by any gain recognized on the exchange of property and decreased by boot received. For basis purposes, boot received includes liabilities transferred by the shareholder to the corporation. Also note that if the shareholder receives *other property* (i.e., boot) along with the stock, it takes a basis equal to its fair market value.[25] In Figure 12.1, the reference to gain recognized does not consider any income resulting from the performance of personal services. See the discussion that follows relating to an elective stock basis reduction that may be taken when a shareholder contributes property with a net built-in loss.

Basis of Property to Corporation

The basis of property received by the corporation generally is the basis of the exchanged property in the hands of the transferor increased by the amount of any gain recognized on the transfer by the transferor-shareholder.[26]

These basis rules are illustrated in Examples 28 and 29.

FIGURE 12.1	Shareholder's Basis of Stock Received in Exchange for Property
Adjusted basis of property transferred	$xx,xxx
Plus: Gain recognized	xxx
Minus: Boot received (including any liabilities transferred)	(xxx)
Minus: Adjustment for loss property (if elected)	(xxx)
Equals: Basis of stock received	$xx,xxx

---

[25]§ 358(a). Recall from earlier discussions that the basis of stock received for services equals its fair market value.

[26]§ 362(a).

Maria and Ned form Brown Corporation. Maria transfers land (basis of $30,000 and fair market value of $70,000); Ned invests cash ($60,000). They each receive 50 shares in Brown Corporation, worth $1,200 per share, but Maria also receives $10,000 of cash from Brown. The transfers of property, the realized and recognized gain on the transfers, and the basis of the stock in Brown Corporation to Maria and Ned are as follows:

Example 28

	A	B	C	D	E	F
	Basis of Property Transferred	FMV of Stock Received	Boot Received	Realized Gain (B + C − A)	Recognized Gain (Lesser of C or D)	Basis of Stock in Brown (A − C + E)
From Maria:						
Land	$30,000	$60,000	$10,000	$40,000	$10,000	$30,000
From Ned:						
Cash	60,000	60,000	–0–	–0–	–0–	60,000

Brown Corporation has a basis of $40,000 in the land (Maria's basis of $30,000 plus her recognized gain of $10,000).

Assume the same facts as in Example 28, except that Maria's basis in the land is $68,000 (instead of $30,000). Because recognized gain cannot exceed realized gain, the transfer generates only $2,000 of gain to Maria. The realized and recognized gain and the basis of the stock in Brown Corporation to Maria are as follows:

Example 29

	A	B	C	D	E	F
	Basis of Property Transferred	FMV of Stock Received	Boot Received	Realized Gain (B + C − A)	Recognized Gain (Lesser of C or D)	Basis of Stock in Brown (A − C + E)
Land	$68,000	$60,000	$10,000	$2,000	$2,000	$60,000

Brown's basis in the land is $70,000 ($68,000 basis to Maria + $2,000 gain recognized by Maria).

Figure 12.2, which is on p. 12-21, summarizes the basis calculation for property received by a corporation. Concept Summary 12.1 shows the shareholder and corporate consequences of a transfer of property to a corporation for stock, with and without the application of § 351. The facts applicable to shareholder Maria's transfer in Example 28 are used to illustrate the differences between the transaction being tax-deferred and taxable.

Basis Adjustment for Loss Property

A corporation's basis for property received in a § 351 transaction is carried over from the shareholder. As a result, the corporation's basis has no correlation to the property's fair market value. However, in certain situations when **built-in loss property** is contributed to a corporation, the aggregate basis of the assets transferred by a shareholder exceeds their fair market value. When this built-in loss situation exists, an anti-loss duplication rule requires the basis in the loss properties to be stepped down by allocating the built-in loss proportionately among the assets.[27] This basis adjustment is necessary to prevent the parties from obtaining a double benefit from the losses involved.

---

[27]§ 362(e)(2). This adjustment is determined separately with respect to each property transferor. This adjustment also is required in the case of a contribution to capital by a shareholder.

CONCEPT SUMMARY 12.1

Tax Consequences to the Shareholders and Corporation: With and Without the Application of § 351 (Based on the Facts of Example 28)

Shareholder	With § 351			Without § 351		
	Gain/Loss Recognized	Stock Basis	Other Property Basis	Gain/Loss Recognized	Stock Basis	Other Property Basis
Maria	Realized gain recognized to extent of boot received; loss not recognized.	Substituted (see Figure 12.1).	FMV	All realized gain or loss recognized.	FMV	FMV
	$10,000	$30,000	$10,000	$40,000	$60,000	$10,000

Corporation	With § 351		Without § 351	
	Gain/Loss Recognized	Property Basis	Gain/Loss Recognized	Property Basis
Brown	No gain or loss recognized on the transfer of corporate stock for property.	Carryover (see Figure 12.2).	No gain or loss recognized on the transfer of corporate stock for property.	FMV
	$0	$40,000	$0	$70,000

Note that the benefit to Maria of deferring $30,000 of gain under § 351 comes with a cost: her stock basis is $30,000 (rather than $60,000), and the corporation's basis in the property received is $40,000 (rather than $70,000).

Example 30

In a transaction qualifying under § 351, Charles transfers the following assets to Gold Corporation in exchange for all of its stock:

	Tax Basis	Fair Market Value	Built-In Gain/(Loss)
Equipment	$100,000	$ 90,000	($10,000)
Land	200,000	230,000	30,000
Building	150,000	100,000	(50,000)
	$450,000	$420,000	($30,000)

Charles's stock basis is $450,000 [$450,000 (basis of the property transferred) + $0 (gain recognized) − $0 (boot received)]. However, Gold's basis for the loss assets transferred must be reduced by the amount of the net built-in loss ($30,000) in proportion to each asset's share of the loss.

	Unadjusted Tax Basis	Adjustment	Adjusted Tax Basis
Equipment	$100,000	($ 5,000)*	$ 95,000
Land	200,000		200,000
Building	150,000	(25,000)**	125,000
	$450,000	($ 30,000)	$420,000

*$\frac{\$10,000 \text{ (loss attributable to equipment)}}{\$60,000 \text{ (}total \text{ built-in loss)}} \times \$30,000$ (*net* built-in loss)
= $5,000 (adjustment to basis in equipment).

**$\frac{\$50,000 \text{ (loss attributable to building)}}{\$60,000 \text{ (}total \text{ built-in loss)}} \times \$30,000$ (*net* built-in loss)
= $25,000 (adjustment to basis in building).

FIGURE 12.2	Corporation's Basis in Property Received
Adjusted basis of property transferred	$xx,xxx
Plus: Gain recognized by transferor-shareholder	xxx
Minus: Adjustment for loss property (if required)	(xxx)
Equals: Basis of property to corporation	$xx,xxx

Note the end result of Example 30:

- Charles still has a built-in loss in his stock basis. Thus, if he sells the Gold Corporation stock, he will recognize a loss of $30,000 [$420,000 (selling price based on presumed value of the stock) − $450,000 (basis in the stock)].
- Gold Corporation can no longer recognize any loss on the sale of *all* of its assets [$420,000 (selling price based on value of assets) − $420,000 (adjusted basis in assets) = $0 (gain or loss)].

In the event a corporation is subject to the built-in loss adjustment, an alternative approach is available. If both the shareholder and the corporation elect, the basis reduction can be made to the shareholder's stock rather than to the corporation's property.

Example 31

Assume the same facts as in the previous example. If Charles and Gold elect, Charles can reduce his stock basis to $420,000 ($450,000 − $30,000). As a result, Gold's aggregate basis in the assets it receives is $450,000. If Charles has no intention of selling his stock, this election could be desirable as it benefits Gold by giving the corporation a higher depreciable basis in the equipment and building.

Note the end result of Example 31:

- Charles has no built-in loss. Thus, if he sells the Gold Corporation stock, he will recognize no gain or loss [$420,000 (presumed value of the stock) − $420,000 (basis in the stock)].
- Gold Corporation has a built-in loss. Thus, if it sells *all* of its assets [$420,000 (selling price based on value of assets) − $450,000 (basis in assets)], it recognizes a loss of $30,000.

Consequently, as shown in the two previous examples, the built-in loss adjustment places the loss with either the shareholder or the corporation but not both.

Stock Issued for Services Rendered

A corporation's transfer of stock for property is not a taxable exchange.[28] A transfer of shares for services is also not a taxable transaction to a corporation.[29] Can a corporation deduct as a business expense the fair market value of the stock it issues in consideration of services? Yes, unless the services are such that the payment is characterized as a capital expenditure.[30]

THE BIG PICTURE

Example 32

Return to the facts of *The Big Picture* on p. 12-1. Amber transfers her $1,000,000 of property to Garden, Inc., and receives 50% of the stock. In addition, assume that Jimmy transfers property worth $800,000 (basis of $260,000) and agrees to serve as manager of the corporation for one year (services worth $200,000) for 50% of the stock. Amber's and Jimmy's transfers qualify under § 351. Neither Amber nor Jimmy is taxed on the transfer of his or her property. However, Jimmy has income of $200,000, the value of the services he will render to Garden, Inc. Garden has a basis of $260,000 in the property it acquired from Jimmy, and it may claim a compensation expense deduction under § 162 for $200,000. Jimmy's stock basis is $460,000 [$260,000 (basis of property transferred) + $200,000 (income recognized for services rendered)].

---

[28]§ 1032.
[29]Reg. § 1.1032–1(a).

[30]Rev.Rul. 62–217, 1962–2 C.B. 59, modified by Rev.Rul. 74–503, 1974–2 C.B. 117.

Example 33

Assume in the preceding example that Jimmy receives the Garden stock as consideration for the appreciated property and for providing legal services in organizing the corporation. The value of Jimmy's legal services is $200,000. Jimmy has no gain on the transfer of the property but has income of $200,000 for the value of the services rendered. Garden, Inc., has a basis of $260,000 in the property it acquired from Jimmy and must capitalize the $200,000 as an organizational expenditure. Jimmy's stock basis is $460,000 [$260,000 (basis of property transferred) + $200,000 (income recognized for services rendered)].

Holding Period for Shareholder and Transferee Corporation

The shareholder's holding period for stock received for a capital asset or for § 1231 property includes the holding period of the property transferred to the corporation. The holding period of the property is *tacked on* to the holding period of the stock. The holding period for stock received for any other property (e.g., inventory) begins on the day after the exchange. The transferee corporation's holding period for property acquired in a § 351 transfer is the holding period of the transferor-shareholder regardless of the character of the property to the transferor. For instance, whether the property transferred is an ordinary asset (e.g., inventory), a § 1231 asset, or a capital asset, the corporation's holding period is the same as the transferor's.[31]

12-2g Recapture Considerations

In a § 351 nontaxable transfer (no boot involved) to a controlled corporation, the depreciation recapture rules do not apply.[32] Instead, any recapture potential of the property carries over to the corporation as it steps into the shoes of the transferor-shareholder for purposes of basis determination. However, to the extent gain is recognized, the recapture rules are applied.

Example 34

Paul transfers equipment (adjusted basis of $30,000, original cost of $120,000, and fair market value of $100,000) to a controlled corporation in return for stock. If Paul had sold the equipment, it would have yielded a gain of $70,000, all of which would have been recaptured as ordinary income under § 1245. If the transfer comes within § 351, Paul has no recognized gain and no depreciation to recapture. If the corporation later disposes of the equipment in a taxable transaction, it must take into account the § 1245 recapture potential originating with Paul. So, for example, if the corporation were to sell the asset shortly after incorporation for $100,000, gain recognized up to $70,000 would be given ordinary treatment because of the depreciation recapture rules.

Alternatively, if Paul had received boot of $60,000 on the transfer, all of the recognized gain would have been recaptured as ordinary income. The remaining $30,000 ($90,000 − $60,000) of recapture potential would have carried over to the corporation.

---

[31]§§ 1223(1) and (2).

[32]§§ 1245(b)(3) and 1250(d)(3).

Tax Planning Strategies	OTHER CONSIDERATIONS WHEN INCORPORATING A BUSINESS

FRAMEWORK FOCUS: TAX RATE

Strategy: Control the Character of Income and Deductions.
Shift Net Income from High-Bracket Taxpayers to Low-Bracket Taxpayers.

FRAMEWORK FOCUS: DEDUCTIONS

Strategy: Maximize Deductible Amounts.

FRAMEWORK FOCUS: INCOME AND EXCLUSIONS

Strategy: Avoid Income Recognition.

When a business is incorporated, the organizers must determine which assets and liabilities should be transferred to the corporation. A transfer of assets that produce passive income (rents, royalties, dividends, and interest) can cause the corporation to be a personal holding company in a tax year when operating income is low. Thus, the corporation could be subject to the personal holding company penalty tax (see the discussion in Chapter 13).

A transfer of the accounts payable of a cash basis taxpayer may prevent the organizer from taking a tax deduction if the accounts are paid by the corporation. Therefore, the parties should decide who will receive the greatest benefit from the deduction and then plan accordingly.

Leasing property to the corporation may be a more attractive alternative than transferring ownership. Leasing provides the taxpayer with the opportunity of withdrawing money from the corporation in a deductible form without the payment being characterized as a nondeductible dividend. If the property is donated to a family member in a lower tax bracket, the lease income can be shifted as well. If the depreciation and other deductions available in connection with the property are larger than the lease income, a high-tax-rate taxpayer could retain the property until the income exceeds the deductions.

THE BIG PICTURE

Example 35

Return to the facts of *The Big Picture* on p. 12-1. If Amber decides to retain the $50,000 of cash basis accounts receivable rather than transfer them to the newly formed Garden, Inc., she will recognize $50,000 of ordinary income upon their collection. Alternatively, if the receivables are transferred to Garden as the facts suggest, the corporation will recognize the ordinary income. However, a subsequent corporate distribution to Amber of the cash collected could be subject to double taxation as a dividend (see Chapter 13 for further discussion). Given the alternatives available, Amber needs to evaluate which approach is better for the parties involved. ■

Another way to shift income to other taxpayers is by the use of corporate debt. Shareholder debt in a corporation can be given to family members with low marginal tax rates. This technique also shifts income without a loss of control of the corporation.

12-3 CAPITAL STRUCTURE OF A CORPORATION

When forming or expanding a corporation, the transaction can be financed with capital contributions or debt proceeds, or a combination of the two. Evaluating the relative advantages and disadvantages of these two basic elements in the capital structure of a corporation can involve various considerations, including the tax aspects of each.

LO.5

Explain the tax aspects of the capital structure of a corporation.

12-3a Capital Contributions

When money or property is received in exchange for capital stock (including treasury stock), the corporation does not recognize any gain or loss.[33] Also, it does not

---

[33]§ 1032.

TAX IN THE NEWS Local and State Governments Pay to Attract New Business—But Expect Results

As a business seeks to grow and strategies shift, managers must be on the lookout for locations that will best suit their needs. Among the factors that can make a critical difference in an expansion or relocation decision is the availability of tax incentives offered by state and local governments as inducements.

But what happens when companies that have accepted these relocation incentives fail to produce? In some cases, the companies are being asked to return portions of the tax grants and incentives previously awarded.

Recently, the Arkansas Department of Economic Development has sought repayments from Hewlett-Packard because its Conway facility is smaller than that required to qualify for all of the incentives awarded in 2010. Arkansas and other jurisdictions are not shy about "clawing back" grants awarded for lack of performance.

Source: Based on Chris Hickey, "Economic Development Director Says HP Will Return Some of Incentives Package," July 10, 2013, **http://talkbusiness.net/2013/07/state-working-with-hewlett-packard-on-incentive-clawbacks/**.

include in gross income any shareholders' contributions of money or property to the capital of the corporation or through voluntary pro rata transfers. This is the case even though there is no increase in the number of outstanding shares of stock of the corporation. The payments represent an additional price paid for the shares held by the shareholders (increasing their basis) and are treated as additions to the operating capital of the corporation.[34]

Contributions by nonshareholders, such as land contributed to a corporation by a civic group or a governmental group to induce the corporation to locate in a particular community, are also excluded from the gross income of a corporation.[35] However, property that is transferred to a corporation by a nonshareholder in exchange for goods or services rendered is taxable income to the corporation.[36]

Example 36

A cable company charges its customers an initial fee to hook up to a new cable system installed in the area. These payments are used to finance the total cost of constructing the cable company's infrastructure. The customers will make monthly payments for the cable service. The initial payments are used for capital expenditures, but they represent payments for services to be rendered by the cable company. As such, they are taxable income and not contributions to capital by nonshareholders.

The basis of property received by a corporation from a shareholder as a **capital contribution** is equal to the basis of the property in the hands of the shareholder, although the basis may be subject to a downward adjustment when loss property is contributed. The basis of property transferred to a corporation by a nonshareholder as a contribution to capital is zero.

If a corporation receives *money* as a contribution to capital from a nonshareholder, a special rule applies. The basis of any property acquired with the money during a 12-month period beginning on the day the contribution was received is reduced by the amount of the contribution. The excess of money received over the cost of new property is used to reduce the basis of other property held by the corporation and is applied in the following order:

1. Depreciable property.
2. Property subject to amortization.
3. Property subject to depletion.
4. All other remaining properties.

The basis of property within each category is reduced in proportion to the relative bases of the properties.[37]

[34]§ 118 and Reg. § 1.118–1.

[35]See *Edwards v. Cuba Railroad Co.*, 1 USTC ¶139, 5 AFTR 5398, 45 S.Ct. 614 (USSC, 1925).

[36]Reg. § 1.118–1. See also *Teleservice Co. of Wyoming Valley*, 27 T.C. 722 (1957), *aff'd* in 58–1 USTC ¶9383, 1 AFTR 2d 1249, 254 F.2d 105 (CA–3, 1958), *cert. den.* 78 S.Ct. 1360 (USSC, 1958).

[37]§ 362(c); Reg. §§ 1.362–2(b) and 1.118–1.

A city donates land worth $400,000 to Cardinal Corporation as an inducement for Cardinal to locate in the city. The receipt of the land produces no taxable income to Cardinal, and the land's basis to the corporation is zero. If, in addition, the city gives the corporation $100,000 in cash, the money is not taxable income to the corporation. However, if the corporation purchases property with the $100,000 in cash within the next 12 months, the basis of the property is reduced by $100,000. Any excess cash that is retained and not used by Cardinal is handled according to the ordering rules noted previously. So, for example, if Cardinal purchases only $70,000 of property during the following year, the basis of Cardinal's other depreciable property is reduced by $30,000.

Example 37

12-3b Debt in the Capital Structure

Various tax and nontax considerations are relevant when developing the capital structure of a corporation. The relative amounts of debt and equity and their characteristics are of primary importance.

LO.6

Recognize the tax differences between debt and equity investments.

Advantages of Debt

Significant tax differences exist between debt and equity in the capital structure, and shareholders must be aware of these differences. The advantages of issuing long-term debt are numerous. Interest on debt is deductible by the corporation, while dividend payments are not. Further, the shareholders are not taxed on debt repayments unless the repayments exceed basis. An investment in stock usually cannot be withdrawn tax-free as long as a corporation has earnings and profits. Withdrawals will be deemed to be taxable dividends to the extent of earnings and profits of the distributing corporation. (The concept of earnings and profits is discussed in Chapter 13.)

Another distinction between debt and equity relates to the taxation of dividend and interest income. Dividend income on equity holdings is taxed to individual investors at the low capital gains rates, while interest income on debt is taxed at the higher ordinary income rates.

Wade transfers cash of $100,000 to a newly formed corporation for 100% of the stock. In the first year of operations, the corporation has net income of $40,000. If the corporation distributes $9,500 to Wade, the distribution is a taxable dividend with no corresponding deduction to the corporation. Assume, instead, that Wade transfers to the corporation cash of $50,000 for stock. In addition, he lends the corporation $50,000. The note is payable in equal annual installments of $5,000 and bears interest at the rate of 9%. At the end of the year, the corporation pays Wade interest of $4,500 ($50,000 × 9%) and a note repayment of $5,000. The interest payment is taxable to Wade and a deductible expense to the corporation. The $5,000 principal repayment on the loan is neither taxed to Wade nor deductible by the corporation. Based on the tax rates as noted, the after-tax impact to Wade and the corporation under each alternative is illustrated below.

Example 38

	If the Distribution Is	
	$9,500 Dividend	$5,000 Note Repayment and $4,500 Interest
*After-tax benefit to Wade**		
[$9,500 × (1 − 15%)]	$8,075	
{$5,000 + [$4,500 × (1 − 35%)]}		$7,925
*After-tax cost to corporation***		
No deduction to corporation	$9,500	
{$5,000 + [$4,500 × (1 − 35%)]}		$7,925

* Assumes that Wade's dividend income is taxed at the 15% capital gains rate and that his interest income is taxed at the 35% ordinary income rate.
** Assumes that the corporation is in the 35% marginal tax bracket.

TAX IN THE NEWS   A Careful Evaluation May Be Required to Distinguish Debt from Equity

While the tax advantages of debt over equity may be clear (i.e., interest payments on debt are deductible but dividend payments on capital contributions are not), being able to distinguish debt from equity may not be as obvious. In arm's-length, market-based transactions between unrelated parties, the debt versus equity question most likely would never arise. However, the difficulty of distinguishing debt and equity is particularly acute in situations where the parties involved are closely connected or related. To assist taxpayers in distinguishing debt financing and equity financing, the courts have developed a number of factors (noted below) to be considered in such an analysis.

In *NA General Partnership & Subsidiaries* (103 TCM 1916, T.C. Memo. 2012–172), the Tax Court evaluated the nature of advances made by a parent entity to NA General Partnership & Subsidiaries (treated as a corporation for Federal tax purposes) in light of the court-developed factors. The court noted that the substance of a transaction is controlling, and not merely its form, and that none of the factors is decisive but they should be considered in light of the facts and circumstances of the case. Based on an exhaustive evaluation of eleven factors in the taxpayer's situation, the court concluded that the advances were debt. Happily for the taxpayer, the court's decision paved the way for $932 million of payments to be treated as deductible interest rather than nondeductible dividend payments.

Reclassification of Debt as Equity (Thin Capitalization Problem)

In situations where the corporation is said to be thinly capitalized, the IRS contends that debt is an equity interest and denies the corporation the tax advantages of debt financing. **Thin capitalization** occurs when shareholder debt is high relative to shareholder equity. If a debt instrument has too many features of stock, it may be treated as a form of stock by the IRS. As a result, the principal and interest payments are considered dividends. Under § 385, the IRS has the authority to characterize corporate debt wholly as equity or as part debt and part equity. In the current environment, however, the IRS may be less inclined to raise the thin capitalization issue because the conversion of interest income to dividend income would produce a tax benefit to individual investors.

For the most part, the principles used to classify debt as equity developed in connection with closely held corporations where the holders of the debt are often shareholders. The rules have often proved inadequate for dealing with large, publicly traded corporations.

Section 385 lists several factors that *may* be used to determine whether a debtor-creditor relationship or a shareholder-corporation relationship exists. The thrust of § 385 is to authorize the Treasury to prescribe Regulations that provide more definite guidelines for determining when debt should be reclassified as equity. To date, the Treasury Department has not drafted final Regulations. Consequently, taxpayers must rely on judicial decisions to determine whether a true debtor-creditor relationship exists.

The courts have identified the following factors to be considered when classifying a security as debt or equity:

- Whether the debt instrument is in proper form. An open account advance is more easily characterized as a contribution to capital than a loan evidenced by a properly written note executed by the shareholder.[38]
- Whether the debt instrument bears a reasonable rate of interest and has a definite maturity date. When a shareholder advance does not provide for interest, the return expected is that inherent in an equity interest (e.g., a share of the profits or an increase in the value of the shares).[39] Likewise, a lender unrelated to the corporation will usually be unwilling to commit funds to the corporation for an indefinite period of time (i.e., no definite due date).

---

[38]*Estate of Mixon, Jr. v. U.S.*, 72–2 USTC ¶9537, 30 AFTR 2d 72–5094, 464 F.2d 394 (CA–5, 1972).

[39]*Slappey Drive Industrial Park v. U.S.*, 77–2 USTC ¶9696, 40 AFTR 2d 77–5940, 561 F.2d 572 (CA–5, 1977).

- Whether the debt is paid on a timely basis. A lender's failure to insist upon timely repayment (or satisfactory renegotiation) indicates that the return sought does not depend upon interest income and the repayment of principal.
- Whether payment is contingent upon earnings. A lender ordinarily will not advance funds that are likely to be repaid only if the venture is successful.
- Whether the debt is subordinated to other liabilities. Subordination tends to eliminate a significant characteristic of the creditor-debtor relationship. Creditors should have the right to share with other general creditors in the event of the corporation's dissolution or liquidation. Subordination also destroys another basic attribute of creditor status—the power to demand payment at a fixed maturity date.[40]
- Whether holdings of debt and stock are proportionate (e.g., each shareholder owns the same percentages of debt and stock). When debt and equity obligations are held in the same proportion, shareholders are, apart from tax considerations, indifferent as to whether corporate distributions are in the form of interest or dividends.
- Whether funds loaned to the corporation are used to finance initial operations or capital asset acquisitions. Funds used to finance initial operations or to acquire capital assets the corporation needs to operate are generally obtained through equity investments.
- Whether the corporation has a high ratio of shareholder debt to shareholder equity. Thin capitalization indicates that the corporation lacks reserves to pay interest and principal on debt when corporate income is insufficient to meet current needs.[41] In determining a corporation's debt-equity ratio, courts look at the relation of the debt both to the book value of the corporation's assets and to their actual fair market value.[42]

Section 385 also authorizes the Treasury to issue Regulations classifying an instrument as *wholly* debt or equity or as *part* debt and *part* equity. This flexible approach is important because some instruments cannot readily be classified either wholly as stock or wholly as debt. It may also provide an avenue for the IRS to address problems in publicly traded corporations.

12-4 CORPORATE OPERATIONS

The rules related to gross income, deductions, and losses discussed in previous chapters of this text generally apply to corporations. In a few instances, it was noted that corporations face unique limitations such as the 10 percent of taxable income limitation for charitable contributions and the limitation allowing corporate capital losses to be deductible only against capital gains. Corporations also are permitted some deductions not generally available to other entities. These special deductions and other special rules regarding the determination of the corporate income tax liability are discussed in the following pages.

LO.7

List and apply the tax rules unique to corporations.

12-4a Deductions Available Only to Corporations

Dividends Received Deduction

The purpose of the **dividends received deduction** is to mitigate multiple taxation of corporate income. Without the deduction, dividends paid between corporations could be subject to several levels of tax. For example, if Corporation A pays Corporation B a dividend and B passes the dividend on to its shareholders, the dividend

---

[40]*Fin Hay Realty Co. v. U.S.*, 68–2 USTC ¶9438, 22 AFTR 2d 5004, 398 F.2d 694 (CA-3, 1968).

[41]A court held that a debt-equity ratio of approximately 14.6:1 was not excessive. See *Tomlinson v. 1661 Corp.*, 67–1 USTC ¶9438, 19 AFTR 2d 1413, 377 F.2d 291 (CA-5, 1967). A 26:1 ratio was found acceptable in *Delta Plastics, Inc.*, 85 TCM 940, T.C.Memo. 2003–54.

[42]In *Bauer v. Comm.*, 84–2 USTC ¶9996, 55 AFTR 2d 85–433, 748 F.2d 1365 (CA-9, 1984), a debt-equity ratio of 92:1 resulted when book value was used. But the ratio ranged from 2:1 to 8:1 when equity included both paid-in capital and accumulated earnings.

is taxed at three levels: Corporation A, Corporation B, and Corporation B's shareholders. The dividends received deduction alleviates this inequity by limiting or eliminating the amount of dividend income taxable to corporations.

As the following table illustrates, the amount of the dividends received deduction depends on the percentage of ownership (voting power and value) the recipient corporate shareholder holds in a *domestic corporation* making the dividend distribution.[43]

Percentage of Ownership by Corporate Shareholder	Deduction Percentage
Less than 20%	70%
20% or more (but less than 80%)	80%
80% or more*	100%

*The payor corporation must be a member of an affiliated group with the recipient corporation.

The dividends received deduction cannot exceed the taxable income limitation. This limitation is equal to the corporation's taxable income multiplied by the percentage that corresponds with the deduction percentage. Thus, if a corporate shareholder owns less than 20 percent of the stock in the distributing corporation, the dividends received deduction is limited to 70 percent of taxable income. For this purpose, taxable income is computed without regard to the net operating loss (NOL) deduction, the domestic production activities deduction, the dividends received deduction, and any capital loss carryback. However, the taxable income limitation does not apply if the corporation has an NOL for the current taxable year.[44]

The following steps are useful in the computation of the deduction:

1. Multiply the dividends received by the deduction percentage.
2. Multiply the taxable income by the deduction percentage.
3. The deduction is limited to the lesser of step 1 or step 2, unless deducting the amount derived in step 1 results in an NOL. If it does, the amount derived in step 1 is used. This is referred to as the *NOL rule.*

Example 39

Red, White, and Blue Corporations, three unrelated calendar year corporations, report the following information for the year:

	Red Corporation	White Corporation	Blue Corporation
Gross income from operations	$ 400,000	$ 320,000	$ 260,000
Expenses from operations	(340,000)	(340,000)	(340,000)
Dividends received from domestic corporations (less than 20% ownership)	200,000	200,000	200,000
Taxable income before the dividends received deduction	$ 260,000	$ 180,000	$ 120,000

In determining the dividends received deduction, use the three-step procedure described above.

	Red	White	Blue
Step 1 (70% × $200,000)	$140,000	$140,000	$140,000
Step 2			
70% × $260,000 (taxable income)	$182,000		
70% × $180,000 (taxable income)		$126,000	
70% × $120,000 (taxable income)			$ 84,000
Step 3			
Lesser of step 1 or step 2	$140,000	$126,000	
Step 1 amount results in an NOL			$140,000

---

[43]§ 243(a). Dividends from foreign corporations generally do not qualify for a dividends received deduction. But see § 245.

[44]Further, the limitation does not apply in the case of the 100% deduction available to members of an affiliated group. § 246(b)(2).

White Corporation is subject to the 70% of taxable income limitation. It does not qualify for NOL rule treatment because subtracting $140,000 (step 1) from $180,000 (taxable income before the dividends received deduction) does not yield a negative figure. Blue Corporation qualifies under the NOL rule because subtracting $140,000 (step 1) from $120,000 (taxable income before the dividends received deduction) yields a negative figure. In summary, each corporation has a dividends received deduction for the year as follows: $140,000 for Red Corporation, $126,000 for White Corporation, and $140,000 for Blue Corporation.

No dividends received deduction is allowed unless the corporation has held the stock for more than 45 days.[45] This restriction was enacted to close a tax loophole involving dividends on stock that is held only briefly. When stock is purchased shortly before a dividend record date and soon thereafter sold ex-dividend, a capital loss corresponding to the amount of the dividend often results (ignoring other market valuation changes). If the dividends received deduction was allowed in such cases, the capital loss resulting from the stock sale would exceed the taxable portion of the related dividend income.

Example 40

On October 1, 2014, Pink Corporation declares a $1 per share dividend for shareholders of record as of November 1, 2014, and payable on December 1, 2014. Black Corporation purchases 10,000 shares of Pink stock on October 29, 2014, for $25,000 and sells those 10,000 shares ex-dividend on November 5, 2014, for $15,000. (It is assumed that there is no fluctuation in the market price of the Pink stock other than the dividend element.) The sale results in a short-term capital loss of $10,000 ($15,000 amount realized − $25,000 basis). On December 1, Black receives a $10,000 dividend from Pink. Without the holding period restriction, Black Corporation would recognize a $10,000 deduction (subject to the capital loss limitation) but only $3,000 of income [$10,000 dividend − $7,000 dividends received deduction ($10,000 × 70%)], or a $7,000 net loss. However, because Black did not hold the Pink stock for more than 45 days, no dividends received deduction is allowed.

In-depth coverage can be found on this book's companion website: **www.cengagebrain.com**   **2**   Digging Deeper

Organizational Expenditures Deduction

Expenses incurred in connection with the organization of a corporation normally are chargeable to a capital account. That they benefit the corporation during its existence seems clear. But over what period should organizational expenses be amortized? The lack of a determinable and limited estimated useful life makes such a determination difficult. Section 248 was enacted to solve this problem.

Under § 248, a corporation may *elect* to amortize **organizational expenditures** over the 180-month period beginning with the month in which the corporation begins business.[46] Organizational expenditures include:

- Legal services incident to organization (e.g., drafting the corporate charter and bylaws, minutes of organizational meetings, and terms of original stock certificates).
- Necessary accounting services.
- Expenses of temporary directors and of organizational meetings of directors or shareholders.
- Fees paid to the state of incorporation.

---

[45]The stock must be held more than 45 days during the 91-day period beginning on the date that is 45 days before the ex-dividend date (or in the case of preferred stock, more than 90 days during the 181-day period beginning on the date that is 90 days before the ex-dividend date). § 246(c).

[46]The month in which a corporation begins business may not be immediately apparent. Ordinarily, a corporation begins business when it starts the business operations for which it was organized. Reg. § 1.248–1(d). For a similar problem in the Subchapter S area, see Chapter 15.

Expenditures that *do not qualify* as organizational expenditures include those connected with issuing or selling shares of stock or other securities (e.g., commissions, professional fees, and printing costs) or with transferring assets to a corporation. These expenditures reduce the amount of capital raised and are not deductible.

The first $5,000 of organizational costs is immediately expensed, with any remaining amount of organizational costs amortized over a 180-month period. However, the $5,000 expensing amount is phased out on a dollar-for-dollar basis when these costs exceed $50,000. For example, a corporation with $52,000 of organizational costs would expense $3,000 [$5,000 − ($52,000 − $50,000)] of this amount and amortize the $49,000 balance ($52,000 − $3,000) over 180 months.

To qualify for the election, the expenditure must be *incurred* before the end of the tax year in which the corporation begins business. In this regard, the corporation's method of accounting is of no consequence. Thus, an expense incurred by a cash basis corporation in its first tax year qualifies even though the expense is not paid until a subsequent year.

A corporation is deemed to have made the election to amortize organizational expenditures for the taxable year in which it begins business. No separate statement or specific identification of the deducted amount as organizational expenditures is required. A corporation can elect to forgo the deemed election by clearly electing to capitalize organizational expenditures on a timely filed return for its first taxable year. In that case, the capitalized amount will be deductible by the corporation at such time as it ceases to do business and liquidates.

Example 41

Black Corporation, an accrual basis, calendar year taxpayer, was formed and began operations on April 1, 2014. The following expenses were incurred during its first year of operations (April 1–December 31, 2014):

Expenses of temporary directors and of organizational meetings	$15,500
Fee paid to the state of incorporation	2,000
Accounting services incident to organization	18,000
Legal services for drafting the corporate charter and bylaws	32,000
Expenses incident to the printing and sale of stock certificates	48,000

Black Corporation elects to amortize organizational costs under § 248. Because of the dollar cap (i.e., dollar-for-dollar reduction for amounts in excess of $50,000), none of the $5,000 expensing allowance is available. The monthly amortization is $375 [($15,500 + $2,000 + $18,000 + $32,000) ÷ 180 months], and $3,375 ($375 × 9 months) is deductible for tax year 2014. Note that the $48,000 of expenses incident to the printing and sale of stock certificates does not qualify for the election. These expenses cannot be deducted. Instead, they reduce the amount of the capital realized from the sale of stock.

Organizational expenditures are distinguished from *startup expenditures*.[47] Startup expenditures include various investigation expenses involved in entering a new business (e.g., travel, market surveys, financial audits, and legal fees) and operating expenses such as rent and payroll that are incurred by a corporation before it actually begins to produce any gross income. At the election of the taxpayer, such expenditures are deductible in the same manner as organizational expenditures. Thus, up to $5,000 can be immediately expensed (subject to the phaseout) and any remaining amounts amortized over a period of 180 months. The same rules that apply to the deemed election (and election to forgo the deemed election) for organizational expenditures also apply to startup expenditures.

[47]§ 195.

Tax Planning Strategies ORGANIZATIONAL EXPENDITURES

FRAMEWORK FOCUS: DEDUCTIONS

Strategy: Maximize Deductible Amounts.

To qualify for the 180-month amortization procedure of § 248, only organizational expenditures incurred in the first taxable year of the corporation can be considered. This rule could prove to be an unfortunate trap for corporations formed late in the year.

Example 42

Thrush Corporation is formed in December 2014. Qualified organizational expenditures are incurred as follows:

$62,000 in December 2014 and $30,000 in January 2015. If Thrush uses the calendar year for tax purposes, only $62,000 of the organizational expenditures qualify for amortization. ∎

A solution to the problem posed by this example may be for Thrush Corporation to adopt a fiscal year that ends on or beyond January 31. All organizational expenditures will then have been incurred before the close of the first tax year.

12-4b Determining the Corporate Income Tax Liability

Corporate Income Tax Rates

Corporate income tax rates have fluctuated over the years, with the current rate structure reflecting a significant reduction that occured in the Tax Reform Act of 1986. For example, the top statutory corporate income tax rate was reduced from 46 percent to 35 percent. Refer to the inside front cover of the text for a schedule of current corporate income tax rates. Unlike the individual income tax rate brackets, the corporate income tax brackets are *not* indexed for inflation.

LO.8

Compute the corporate income tax.

THE BIG PICTURE

Example 43

Return to the facts of *The Big Picture* on p. 12-1. Assume that Amber incorporates her business as a calendar year C corporation and that for 2014, the corporation has taxable income of $51,500. Its income tax liability is $7,875, determined as follows:

Tax on $50,000 at 15%	$7,500
Tax on $1,500 at 25%	375
Tax liability	$7,875

For taxable income in excess of $100,000, the amount of the tax is increased by the lesser of (1) 5 percent of the excess or (2) $11,750. In effect, the additional tax means a 39 percent rate for every dollar of taxable income from $100,000 to $335,000.

Example 44

Silver Corporation, a calendar year taxpayer, has taxable income of $335,000 for the current year. Its income tax liability is $113,900, determined as follows:

Tax on $100,000	$ 22,250
Tax on $235,000 × 39%	91,650
Tax liability	$113,900

Note that the tax liability of $113,900 is 34% of $335,000. Thus, due to the 39% rate (34% normal rate + 5% additional tax on taxable income between $100,000 and $335,000), the benefit of the lower rates on the first $75,000 of taxable income completely phases out at $335,000. The tax rate drops back to 34% on taxable income between $335,000 and $10 million.

Section 11(b)(2) provides that qualified **personal service corporations (PSCs)** are taxed at a flat 35 percent rate on all taxable income. Thus, PSCs do not enjoy the

TAX IN THE NEWS   Presidential Campaign Highlights Call for Corporate Tax Reform

During the 2012 presidential campaign, both candidates argued for a significant reduction in the top U.S. corporate income tax rate (currently at 35 percent). President Obama proposed lowering the top rate to 28 percent, while Governor Romney championed a top rate of 25 percent. The call for corporate tax rate reduction stems from the belief that the U.S. corporate tax system is too costly (and complex) relative to the corporate tax regimes of other countries. As evidence, proponents of corporate tax rate reduction cite the loss of U.S. jobs to foreign countries, the deferral of U.S. taxation through the use of controlled foreign corporations, and the relocation of U.S. corporations to lower-tax jurisdictions. However, achieving corporate tax rate reduction without substantively adding to the Federal budget deficit may be problematic. In a recent report on the U.S.

corporate income tax system, the Congressional Research Service reported that a reduction of the top corporate tax rate to 29.4 percent would be revenue-neutral only if all corporate tax benefits (e.g., MACRS depreciation in excess of ADS depreciation, deferral of income of controlled foreign corporations, and the domestic production activities deduction) were eliminated. Because the elimination of all corporate tax benefits is unlikely, a more realistic alternative may be a smaller rate reduction than that proposed by the presidential candidates, accompanied by the elimination of *some* corporate tax benefits.

Source: Mark P. Keightley and Molly F. Sherlock, "The Corporate Income Tax System: Overview and Options for Reform," *Congressional Research Service*, September 13, 2012.

tax savings of the 15 percent to 34 percent brackets applicable to other corporations. For this purpose, a PSC is a corporation that is substantially employee-owned. Also, it must engage in one of the following activities: health, law, engineering, architecture, accounting, actuarial science, performing arts, or consulting.

12-4c Tax Liability of Related Corporations

LO.9

Explain the rules unique to computing the tax of related corporations.

Members of a controlled group of corporations (**related corporations**) are subject to special rules for computing the income tax, the AMT exemption, and the § 179 election to expense certain depreciable assets.[48] If these restrictions did not exist, the shareholders of a corporation could gain significant tax advantages by splitting a single corporation into *multiple* corporations. The next two examples illustrate the potential *income tax* advantage of multiple corporations.

Example 45

Gray Corporation annually yields taxable income of $300,000. The corporate tax on $300,000 is $100,250, computed as follows:

Tax on $100,000	$ 22,250
Tax on $200,000 × 39%	78,000
Tax liability	$100,250

Example 46

Assume that Gray Corporation in the previous example is divided equally into four corporations. Each corporation would have taxable income of $75,000, and the tax for each (absent the special provisions for related corporations) would be computed as follows:

Tax on $50,000	$ 7,500
Tax on $25,000 × 25%	6,250
Tax liability	$13,750

The total liability for the four corporations would be $55,000 ($13,750 × 4). Consequently, the savings would be $45,250 ($100,250 − $55,000).

[48]§§ 1561(a) and 179(d)(6).

To preclude the advantages that could be gained by using multiple corporations, the tax law requires special treatment for *controlled groups* of corporations. A comparison of Examples 45 and 46 reveals that the income tax savings that could be achieved by using multiple corporations result from having more of the total taxable income taxed at lower marginal rates. To close this potential loophole, the law limits a controlled group's taxable income in the tax brackets below 35 percent to the amount the corporations in the group would have if they were one corporation. Thus, in Example 46, under the controlled corporation rules, only $12,500 (one-fourth of the first $50,000 of taxable income) for each of the four related corporations would be taxed at the 15 percent rate. The 25 percent rate would apply to the next $6,250 (one-fourth of the next $25,000) of taxable income of each corporation. This equal allocation of the $50,000 and $25,000 amounts is required unless all members of the controlled group consent to an apportionment plan providing for an unequal allocation.

Similar limitations apply to controlled groups with respect to the § 179 expense election (see Chapter 5) and to the $40,000 AMT exemption amount (see Chapter 17).

12-4d Controlled Groups

A **controlled group** of corporations includes parent-subsidiary groups, brother-sister groups, combined groups, and certain insurance companies. Parent-subsidiary controlled groups are discussed in the following section.

Parent-Subsidiary Controlled Group

A **parent-subsidiary controlled group** consists of one or more *chains* of corporations connected through stock ownership with a common parent corporation. The ownership connection can be established through either a *voting power test* or a *value test*. The voting power test requires ownership of stock possessing at least 80 percent of the total voting power of all classes of stock entitled to vote. The value test requires ownership of at least 80 percent of the total value of all shares of all classes of stock of each of the corporations, except the parent corporation, by one or more of the other corporations.[49]

Aqua Corporation owns 80% of White Corporation. Aqua and White Corporations are members of a parent-subsidiary controlled group. Aqua is the parent corporation, and White is the subsidiary.	**Example 47**

The parent-subsidiary relationship described in Example 47 is easy to recognize because Aqua Corporation is the direct owner of White Corporation. Real-world business organizations are often more complex, sometimes including numerous corporations with chains of ownership connecting them. In these complex corporate structures, determining whether the controlled group classification is appropriate becomes more difficult. The ownership requirements can be met through direct ownership (refer to Example 47) or through indirect ownership, as illustrated in the following example.

Red Corporation owns 80% of the voting stock of White Corporation, and White Corporation owns 80% of the voting stock of Blue Corporation. Red, White, and Blue Corporations constitute a controlled group in which Red is the common parent and White and Blue are subsidiaries. This parent-subsidiary relationship is diagrammed in Figure 12.3. The same result would occur if Red Corporation, rather than White Corporation, owned the Blue Corporation stock.	**Example 48**

---

[49]§ 1563(a)(1).

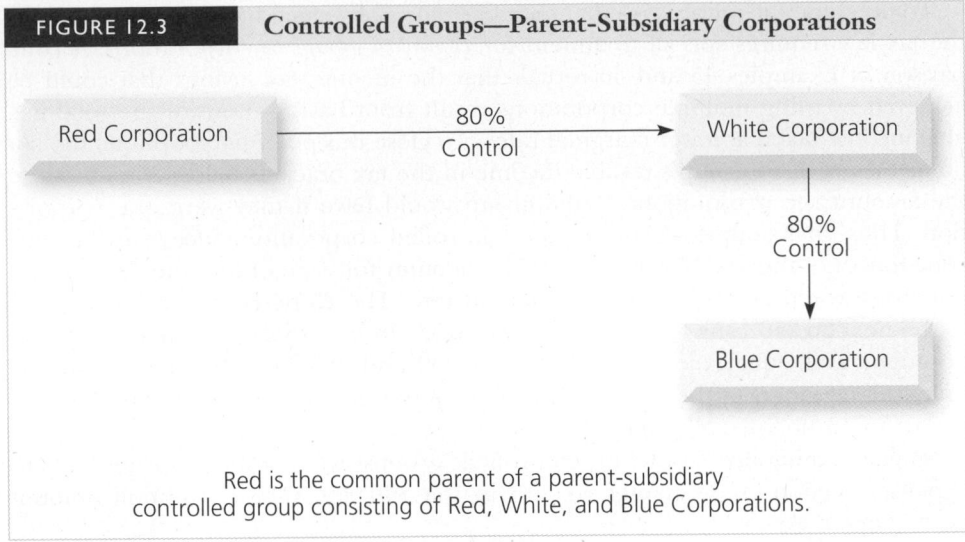

FIGURE 12.3   **Controlled Groups—Parent-Subsidiary Corporations**

Red Corporation → 80% Control → White Corporation

White Corporation → 80% Control → Blue Corporation

Red is the common parent of a parent-subsidiary controlled group consisting of Red, White, and Blue Corporations.

Digging Deeper   **3**   🔍   In-depth coverage can be found on this book's companion website: **www.cengagebrain.com**

Application of § 482

Congress has recognized that a parent corporation has the power to shift income among its subsidiaries. Likewise, shareholders who control other related groups of corporations can shift income and deductions among the related corporations.

When the true taxable income of a subsidiary or other related corporation has been understated or overstated, the IRS can reallocate the income and deductions of the related corporations under § 482. Section 482 permits the IRS to allocate gross income, deductions, and credits between any two or more organizations, trades, or businesses that are owned or controlled by the same interests. This is appropriate when the allocation is necessary to prevent avoidance of taxes or to reflect income correctly. Controlled groups of corporations, especially multi-national corporations, are particularly vulnerable to § 482.

12-5 PROCEDURAL MATTERS

LO.10

Describe the reporting process for corporations.

This section covers various aspects of the corporate income tax return, including filing requirements, estimated tax payments, and special disclosure schedules on the return.

12-5a Filing Requirements for Corporations

A corporation must file a Federal income tax return (Form 1120) whether or not it has taxable income. A corporation that was not in existence throughout an entire annual accounting period is required to file a return for the portion of the year during which it was in existence. In addition, a corporation must file a return even though it has ceased to do business if it has valuable claims for which it will bring suit. A corporation is relieved of filing income tax returns only when it ceases to do business and retains no assets.[50]

The return must be filed on or before the fifteenth day of the third month following the close of a corporation's tax year. Corporations with assets of $10 million or more generally are required to file electronically. A regular corporation, other than

---

[50]§ 6012(a)(2) and Reg. § 1.6012-2(a).

TAX FACT **Sources of Federal Government Revenues**

This pie chart shows the relative sizes of the major categories of Federal revenue for fiscal year 2013.

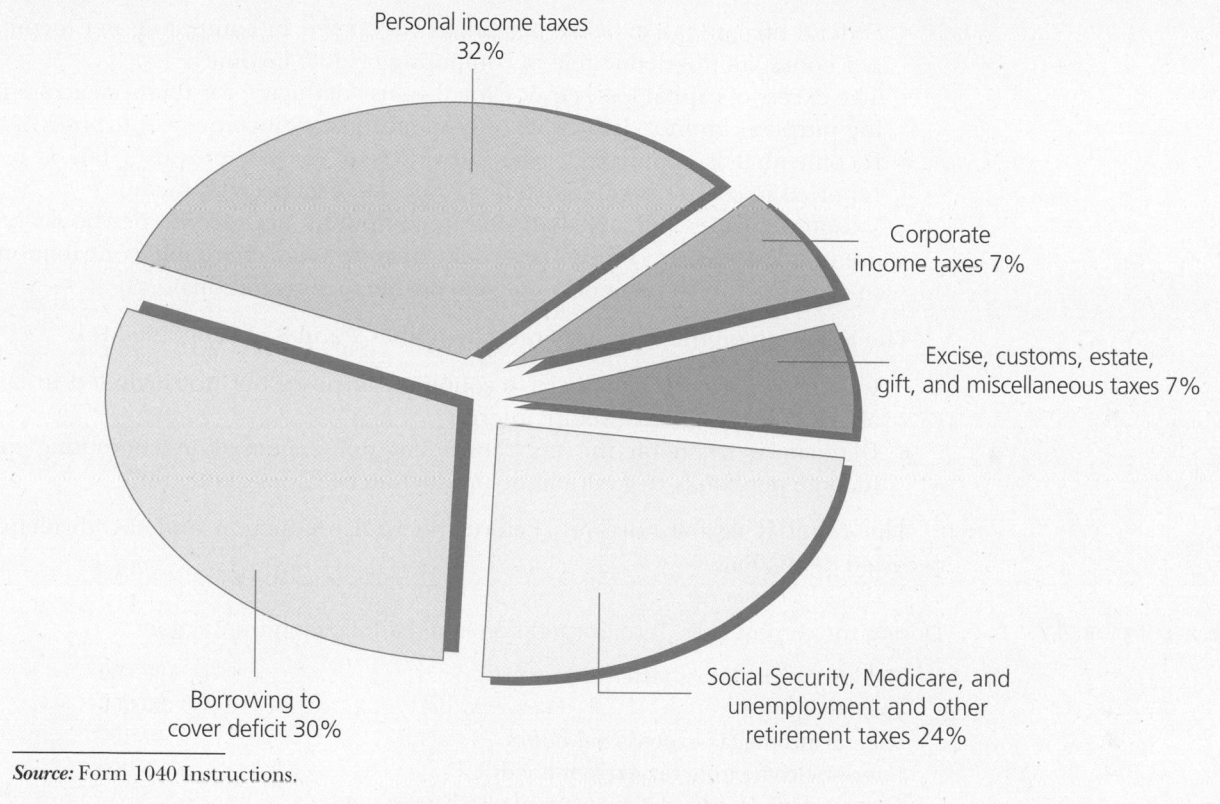

Personal income taxes
32%

Corporate
income taxes 7%

Excise, customs, estate,
gift, and miscellaneous taxes 7%

Borrowing to
cover deficit 30%

Social Security, Medicare, and
unemployment and other
retirement taxes 24%

Source: Form 1040 Instructions.

a PSC, can use either a calendar year or a fiscal year to report its taxable income. The tax year of the shareholders has no effect on the corporation's tax year.

12-5b Estimated Tax Payments

A corporation must make payments of estimated tax unless its tax liability can reasonably be expected to be less than $500. The required annual payment (which includes any estimated AMT liability) is the *lesser* of (1) 100 percent of the corporation's tax for the current year or (2) 100 percent of the tax for the preceding year (if that was a 12-month tax year, the return filed showed a tax liability, and the corporation involved is not a *large corporation*). Estimated payments can be made in four installments due on or before the fifteenth day of the fourth month, the sixth month, the ninth month, and the twelfth month of the corporate taxable year.[51] The full amount of the unpaid tax is due on the due date of the return without regard to extensions. A corporation failing to pay its required estimated tax payments will be subjected to a nondeductible penalty on the amount by which the installments are less than the tax due.

12-5c Schedule M–1—Reconciliation of Income (Loss) per Books with Income per Return

Schedule M–1 of Form 1120 is used to *reconcile* net income as computed for financial accounting purposes with taxable income reported on the corporation's income

---

[51]§ 6655. If the due date falls on a Saturday, Sunday, or legal holiday, the due date is the next business day. See § 6655(g)(2) for the definition of a *large corporation.*

tax return (commonly referred to as book-tax differences). Schedule M–1 is used by corporations with less than $10 million of total assets.

The starting point on Schedule M–1 is net income (loss) per books. Additions and subtractions are entered for items that affect financial accounting net income and taxable income differently. The following items are entered as additions (see lines 2 through 5 of Schedule M–1 on the next page):

- Federal income tax expense per books (deducted in computing net income per books but not deductible in computing taxable income).
- The excess of capital losses over capital gains (deducted for financial accounting purposes but not deductible by corporations for income tax purposes).
- Income that is reported in the current year for tax purposes but is not reported in computing net income per books (e.g., prepaid income).
- Various expenses that are deducted in computing net income per books but are not deducted in computing taxable income (e.g., charitable contributions in excess of the 10 percent ceiling applicable to corporations).

The following subtractions are entered on lines 7 and 8 of Schedule M–1:

- Income reported for financial accounting purposes but not included in taxable income (e.g., tax-exempt interest).
- Deductions taken on the tax return but not expensed in computing net income per books (e.g., domestic production activities deduction).

The result is taxable income (before the NOL deduction and the dividends received deduction).

Example 49

During the current year, Tern Corporation had the following transactions:

Net income per books (after tax)	$92,400
Taxable income	50,000
Federal income tax expense per books	7,500
Interest income from tax-exempt bonds	5,000
Interest paid on loan, the proceeds of which were used to purchase the tax-exempt bonds	500
Life insurance proceeds received as a result of the death of a key employee	50,000
Premiums paid on key employee life insurance policy	2,600
Excess of capital losses over capital gains	2,000

For book and tax purposes, Tern Corporation determines depreciation under the straight-line method. Tern's Schedule M–1 for the current year is as follows:

12-5d Schedule M–2—Analysis of Unappropriated Retained Earnings per Books

Schedule M–2 reconciles unappropriated retained earnings at the beginning of the year with unappropriated retained earnings at year-end. The beginning balance plus net income per books, as entered on line 1 of Schedule M–1, less dividend

BRIDGE DISCIPLINE Bridge to Financial Accounting

Measures of corporate income for financial reporting and income tax purposes differ because the objectives of these measures differ. Income measures for financial reporting purposes are intended to help various stakeholders have a clear view of the corporation's financial position and operational results. Income measures for Federal income tax purposes, on the other hand, must comply with the relevant provisions of the Internal Revenue Code. The tax law is intended not only to raise revenues to fund government operations but also to reflect the objectives of government fiscal policy.

As a consequence of these differing objectives, revenue and expense measurements used to determine taxable income may differ from those used in financial reporting. In most cases, differences between book and tax measurements are temporary in nature. Two such temporary differences relate to the different methods of calculating depreciation expense and the limits placed on the deductibility of net capital losses for tax purposes. Permanent differences between book and tax income, such as the dividends received deduction and the domestic production activities deduction, also may exist.

Accounting standards for reporting income tax expenses and liabilities require that the tax impact of *temporary* differences be recognized currently in the financial statements. Because many temporary differences allow a firm to postpone its tax payments to later years, the financial statements must show the amount of the expense that is paid currently and that portion that is to be paid in a later period. The portion of the taxes to be paid in a later period is shown as a liability for such future income taxes. The liability for future income taxes is referred to as a deferred income tax liability.

See Chapter 3 for a complete discussion of this topic.

© iStockphoto.com/enot-poloskun

distributions during the year equals ending retained earnings. Other sources of increases or decreases in retained earnings are also listed on Schedule M–2.

Example 50

Assume the same facts as in the preceding example. Tern Corporation's beginning balance in unappropriated retained earnings is $125,000. During the year, Tern distributed a cash dividend of $30,000 to its shareholders. Based on these further assumptions, Tern's Schedule M–2 for the current year is as follows:

Schedule M-2	Analysis of Unappropriated Retained Earnings per Books (Line 25, Schedule L)				
1	Balance at beginning of year	125,000	5	Distributions: a Cash	30,000
2	Net income (loss) per books	92,400		b Stock	
3	Other increases (itemize):			c Property	
			6	Other decreases (itemize):	
			7	Add lines 5 and 6	30,000
4	Add lines 1, 2, and 3	217,400	8	Balance at end of year (line 4 less line 7)	187,400

© www.irs.gov

In-depth coverage can be found on this book's companion website: **www.cengagebrain.com**   **4** Digging Deeper

12-5e Schedule M–3—Net Income (Loss) Reconciliation for Corporations with Total Assets of $10 Million or More

Corporate taxpayers with total assets of $10 million or more are required to report much greater detail relative to differences between income (loss) reported for financial accounting purposes and income (loss) reported for tax purposes. This expanded reconciliation of book and taxable income (loss) is reported on **Schedule M–3**. Corporations that are not required to file Schedule M–3 may do so voluntarily. Any corporation that files Schedule M–3 is not allowed to file Schedule M–1. Comparison of Schedule M–3 (see **www.irs.gov**) with Schedule M–1 (illustrated in Example 49) reveals the significantly greater disclosure requirements that apply to corporations that are required to file Schedule M–3.

Schedule M–3 is a response, at least in part, to financial reporting scandals such as Enron and WorldCom. One objective of Schedule M–3 is to create greater transparency between corporate financial statements and tax returns. Another objective

TAX IN THE NEWS   Schedule M–3 Filing Requirements Reduced by IRS Decree

The IRS has relaxed the Schedule M–3 reporting requirements for tax years ending December 31, 2014, and later. Corporations (and partnerships) with $10 million to $50 million of total assets may elect to file Schedule M–1 in lieu of Schedule M–3, parts II and III. Electing entities must still file Schedule M–3, part I

(lines 1–12). Entities with less than $10 million of assets that voluntarily file Schedule M–3 also may elect the reduced Schedule M–3 filing requirements. The new rules are intended to simplify reporting and reduce filing burdens.

Source: www.irs.gov/Businesses/Corporations/Schedule-M-3-for-Large-Business-&-International-(LB&I).

is to identify corporations that engage in aggressive tax practices by requiring that transactions that create book-tax differences be disclosed on corporate tax returns. The increase in transparency and disclosure comes at a cost, however, as the IRS estimates that, on average, almost 89 hours are needed to comply with the requirements of Schedule M–3.

Total assets for purposes of the $10 million test and the income and expense amounts required by Schedule M–3 are determined from the taxpayer's financial reports. If the taxpayer files Form 10–K with the Securities and Exchange Commission (SEC), that statement is used. If no 10–K is filed, information from another financial source is used, in the following order: certified financial statements, prepared financial statements, or the taxpayer's books and records.

Digging Deeper   5, 6   In-depth coverage can be found on this book's companion website: **www.cengagebrain.com**

12-5f Effect of Taxes on Financial Statements

Given the differences between taxable income and net income per books, what effect do these differences have on an entity's financial statements? How are income tax accruals arrived at and reported for accounting purposes? What other types of disclosures regarding present and potential tax liabilities are required to satisfy the accounting standards? Recall that these and other questions were answered and discussed at length in Chapter 3.

FINANCIAL DISCLOSURE INSIGHTS   Processing the Corporate Income Tax Return

Seldom is a Form 1120 prepared by itself. In almost every case, the taxpayer and its tax advisers start with the financial accounting records; then they modify book income directly with the book-tax differences that are known by the financial accountants and independent auditors. The tax professionals take these computations, adjust them for tax law changes, and clarify items that require detailed tax research. As the figure at the right illustrates, taxable income for the Form 1120 results from this process.

Notice that this process mirrors that of the preparation of Schedules M–1 and M–3. In preparing these schedules, book income is modified to account for various temporary and permanent book-tax differences as specified by the layout of the forms, resulting in the taxable income

amount that is used on page 1 of Form 1120. Some tax professionals maintain that given the detail required to complete Schedule M–3, the traditional structure of Form 1120 is redundant for large entities. In this regard, page 1 of Form 1120 could be eliminated—taxable income could be computed using Schedule M–3 alone.

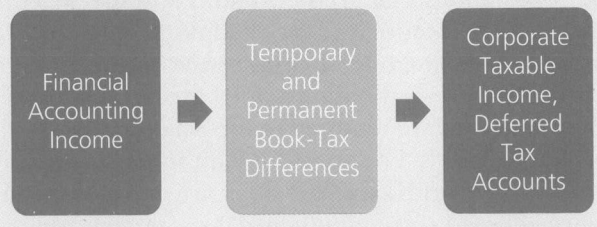

For 2013 tax returns, a corporation with total assets of $50 million or more must file Schedule UTP (Uncertain Tax Position Statement) with its Form 1120. A lower threshold of $10 million or more of assets applies for 2014 returns. In general, a corporation is required to report tax positions taken on a current or prior year's Federal income tax return and for which the corporation recorded a reserve for Federal income tax in its audited financial statements (or for which no reserve was recorded because of an expectation to litigate). Financial reporting of tax positions is discussed in Chapter 3.

12-6 SUMMARY

The evolution of the check-the-box Regulations has provided taxpayers with a simplified method for determining an entity's tax classification. Nevertheless, taxpayers should not discount the importance of choosing the appropriate form of entity. As demonstrated in this chapter and Chapter 13, a variety of tax provisions applicable to corporations do not extend to other entities. Of particular importance are the different deductions available to corporations and the corporate income tax rate structure. Corporations must also be aware of their levels of debt to avoid equity reclassification. Such reclassification causes deductible interest paid on debt to become nondeductible dividend payments. Equally important are the timing and completeness requirements of the corporate filing provisions. Failure to comply with the appropriate filing provisions may result in heavy penalties and interest.

REFOCUS ON THE BIG PICTURE

Amber, the sole property transferor, must acquire at least 80 percent of the stock issued by Garden, Inc., for the transaction to qualify for tax-deferred treatment under § 351. Otherwise, she will recognize $600,000 of taxable gain as a result of the transfer. As a corollary, Jimmy must not receive more than 20 percent of Garden's stock in exchange for services (see Example 16). Even if the requirements of § 351 are met, any debt issued by the corporation will be treated as boot and will result in at least some gain recognition to Amber (see Example 9). Therefore, Amber must evaluate the cost of recognizing gain now versus the benefit of Garden obtaining an interest deduction later.

GROWING INTO THE CORPORATE FORM

What If?

Can the § 351 transaction be modified to further reduce personal and business tax costs, both at the time of formation and in the future? Several strategies may be worth considering.

- Have Jimmy transfer some property along with the services rendered to Garden, Inc. As long as Jimmy transfers property with more than a relatively small value compared to the value of services performed, Jimmy will be considered part of the control group. This would allow Amber to own less than 80 percent of the new corporation and still have the transaction qualify under § 351.
- Instead of having Garden issue debt on formation, Amber might withhold certain assets. For example, if the building is not transferred, it can be leased to the corporation. The resulting rent payment would mitigate the double taxation problem by producing a tax deduction for Garden.
- An additional benefit results if Amber does not transfer the cash basis receivables to Garden. This approach avoids a tax at the corporate level when they are collected by the corporation and another tax on Amber when the receipts are distributed as a dividend (see Example 35).
- If Amber's sole proprietorship has any accounts payable outstanding at the time of the corporate formation, it might be wise to transfer those to Garden. The subsequent corporate payment of the liability produces a deduction that will reduce any corporate income tax.

Suggested Readings

Wei-Chih Chiang and Jianjn Du, "The Debt-Equity Debate in the *Castle Harbour* Case," *Practical Tax Strategies*, March 2013.

Janel Greiman and Thomas J. Nash, "Did Averting Fiscal Cliff Allow C Corporations to Overtake Passthroughs?," *Practical Tax Strategies*, August 2013.

William Hood, "Deducting Start-Up Costs and Organizational Costs," *Practical Tax Strategies*, April 2012.

Jeffrey L. Rubinger and Nadia E. Kruler, "Service Applies Substance Over Form Doctrine to Disallow Dividends-Received Deduction," *Journal of Taxation*, July 2013.

Michael Schlesinger, "Looming Tax Traps for Closely Held Businesses," *Practical Tax Strategies*, October 2012.

Edward J. Schnee and W. Eugene Seago, "Taxing the Transfer of Debts Between Debtors and Creditors," The *Tax Adviser*, July 2012.

Edward J. Schnee and W. Eugene Seago, "Defining Stock of Insolvent and Bankrupt Corporations," *The Tax Adviser*, September 2013.

Key Terms

Built-in loss property, 12-19

C corporations, 12-2

Capital contribution, 12-24

Check-the-box Regulations, 12-6

Control, 12-10

Controlled group, 12-33

Disregarded entity, 12-6

Dividends received deduction, 12-27

Limited liability company (LLC), 12-6

Limited partnerships, 12-6

Organizational expenditures, 12-29

Parent-subsidiary controlled group, 12-33

Personal service corporations (PSCs), 12-31

Property, 12-9

Regular corporations, 12-2

Related corporations, 12-32

S corporations, 12-2

Schedule M–1, 12-35

Schedule M–3, 12-37

Securities, 12-10

Thin capitalization, 12-26

Problems

1. **LO.1** Janice is the sole owner of Catbird Company. In the current year, Catbird had operating income of $100,000, a long-term capital gain of $15,000, and a charitable contribution of $5,000. Janice withdrew $70,000 of profit from Catbird. How should Janice report this information on her individual tax return if Catbird Company is:
   a. An LLC?
   b. An S corporation?
   c. A C corporation?

2. **LO.1** Can a sole proprietor form as a single-member limited liability company (LLC)? If so, how would such an LLC be taxed?

3. **LO.1** In the current year, Riflebird Company had operating income of $220,000, operating expenses of $175,000, and a long-term capital loss of $10,000. How do Riflebird Company and Roger, the sole owner of Riflebird, report this information on their respective Federal income tax returns for the current year under the following assumptions?
   a. Riflebird Company is a proprietorship (Roger did not make any withdrawals from the business).
   b. Riflebird Company is a C corporation (no dividends were paid during the year).

4. **LO.1** Ellie and Linda are equal owners in Otter Enterprises, a calendar year business. During the current year, Otter Enterprises has $320,000 of gross income and $210,000 of operating expenses. In addition, Otter has a long-term capital gain of $15,000 and makes distributions to Ellie and Linda of $25,000 each. Discuss the impact of this information on the taxable income of Otter, Ellie, and Linda if Otter is:
   a. A partnership.
   b. An S corporation.
   c. A C corporation.

5. **LO.1** In the current year, Azure Company has $350,000 of net operating income before deducting any compensation or other payments to its sole owner, Sasha. In addition, Azure has interest on municipal bonds of $25,000. Sasha has significant income from other sources and is in the 35% marginal tax bracket. Based on this information, determine the income tax consequences to Azure Company and to Sasha during the year for each of the following independent situations.
   a. Azure is a C corporation and pays no dividends or salary to Sasha.
   b. Azure is a C corporation and distributes $75,000 of dividends to Sasha.
   c. Azure is a C corporation and pays $75,000 of salary to Sasha.
   d. Azure is a sole proprietorship, and Sasha withdraws $0.
   e. Azure is a sole proprietorship, and Sasha withdraws $75,000.

6. **LO.2** Sarah incorporates her small business but does not transfer the machinery and equipment used by the business to the corporation. Instead, the machinery and equipment are leased to the corporation for an annual rent. What tax reasons might Sarah have for not transferring the machinery and equipment to the corporation when the business was incorporated?   Issue ID

7. **LO.2, 4** Seth, Pete, Cara, and Jen form Kingfisher Corporation with the following consideration:

	Consideration Transferred		
	Basis to Transferor	Fair Market Value	Number of Shares Issued
From Seth—			
Inventory	$30,000	$96,000	30*
From Pete—			
Equipment ($30,000 of depreciation taken by Pete in prior years)	45,000	99,000	30**
From Cara—			
Proprietary process	15,000	90,000	30
From Jen—			
Cash	30,000	30,000	10

*Seth receives $6,000 in cash in addition to the 30 shares.
**Pete receives $9,000 in cash in addition to the 30 shares.

Assume that the value of each share of Kingfisher stock is $3,000. As to these transactions, provide the following information:
   a. Seth's recognized gain or loss. Identify the nature of any such gain or loss.
   b. Seth's basis in the Kingfisher Corporation stock.
   c. Kingfisher Corporation's basis in the inventory.
   d. Pete's recognized gain or loss. Identify the nature of any such gain or loss.
   e. Pete's basis in the Kingfisher Corporation stock.
   f. Kingfisher Corporation's basis in the equipment.
   g. Cara's recognized gain or loss.
   h. Cara's basis in the Kingfisher Corporation stock.
   i. Kingfisher Corporation's basis in the proprietary process.
   j. Jen's recognized gain or loss.
   k. Jen's basis in the Kingfisher stock.

8. **LO.2, 4** Tom and Gail form Owl Corporation with the following consideration:

	Consideration Transferred		
	Basis to Transferor	Fair Market Value	Number of Shares Issued
From Tom—			
Cash	$ 50,000	$ 50,000	
Installment note	240,000	350,000	40

(continued)

	Consideration Transferred		
	Basis to Transferor	**Fair Market Value**	**Number of Shares Issued**
From Gail—			
Inventory	$ 60,000	$ 50,000	
Equipment	125,000	250,000	
Patentable invention	15,000	300,000	60

The installment note has a face amount of $350,000 and was acquired last year from the sale of land held for investment purposes (adjusted basis of $240,000). As to these transactions, provide the following information:

a. Tom's recognized gain or loss.
b. Tom's basis in the Owl Corporation stock.
c. Owl Corporation's basis in the installment note.
d. Gail's recognized gain or loss.
e. Gail's basis in the Owl Corporation stock.
f. Owl Corporation's basis in the inventory, equipment, and patentable invention.
g. How would your answers to the preceding questions change if Tom received common stock and Gail received preferred stock?
h. How would your answers change if Gail was a partnership?

Decision Making

9. **LO.2** Jane, Jon, and Clyde incorporate their respective businesses and form Starling Corporation. On March 1 of the current year, Jane exchanges her property (basis of $50,000 and value of $150,000) for 150 shares in Starling Corporation. On April 15, Jon exchanges his property (basis of $70,000 and value of $500,000) for 500 shares in Starling. On May 10, Clyde transfers his property (basis of $90,000 and value of $350,000) for 350 shares in Starling.

a. If the three exchanges are part of a prearranged plan, what gain will each of the parties recognize on the exchanges?
b. Assume that Jane and Jon exchanged their property for stock four years ago, while Clyde transfers his property for 350 shares in the current year. Clyde's transfer is not part of a prearranged plan with Jane and Jon to incorporate their businesses. What gain will Clyde recognize on the transfer?
c. Returning to the original facts, if the property that Clyde contributes has a basis of $490,000 (instead of $90,000), how might the parties otherwise structure the transaction?

Communications

10. **LO.2** Michael Robertson (1635 Maple Street, Syracuse, NY 13201) exchanges property (basis of $200,000 and fair market value of $850,000) for 75% of the stock of Red Corporation. The other 25% is owned by Sarah Mitchell, who acquired her stock several years ago. You represent Michael, who asks whether he must report gain on the transfer. Prepare a letter to Michael and a memorandum for the tax files documenting your response.

Issue ID

11. **LO.2** Dan and Patricia form Crane Corporation. Dan transfers land (worth $200,000, basis of $60,000) for 50% of the stock in Crane. Patricia transfers machinery (worth $150,000, adjusted basis of $30,000) and provides services worth ($50,000) for 50% of the stock.

a. Will the transfers qualify under § 351? Explain.
b. What are the tax consequences to Dan and Patricia?
c. What is Crane Corporation's basis in the land and the machinery?

12. **LO.2** John organized Toucan Corporation 10 years ago. He contributed property worth $1 million (basis of $200,000) for 2,000 shares of stock in Toucan (representing 100% ownership). John later gave each of his children, Julie and Rachel, 500 shares of the stock. In the current year, John transfers property worth $350,000 (basis of $170,000) to Toucan for 1,000 more of its shares. What gain, if any, will John recognize on the transfer?

13. **LO.2, 4** Ann and Bob form Robin Corporation. Ann transfers property worth $420,000 (basis of $150,000) for 70 shares in Robin Corporation. Bob receives 30 shares for property worth $165,000 (basis of $30,000) and for legal services (worth $15,000) in organizing the corporation.

a. What gain or income, if any, will the parties recognize on the transfer?

b. What basis do Ann and Bob have in the stock in Robin Corporation?
c. What is Robin Corporation's basis in the property and services it received from Ann and Bob?

14. **LO.2, 4** Assume in Problem 13 that the property Bob transfers to Robin Corporation is worth $15,000 (basis of $3,000) and that his services in organizing the corporation are worth $165,000. What are the tax consequences to Ann, Bob, and Robin Corporation?

15. **LO.2** Rhonda owns 50% of the stock of Peach Corporation. She and the other 50% shareholder, Rachel, have decided that additional contributions of capital are needed if Peach is to remain successful in its competitive industry. The two shareholders have agreed that Rhonda will contribute assets having a value of $200,000 (adjusted basis of $15,000) in exchange for additional shares of stock. After the transaction, Rhonda will hold 75% of Peach Corporation and Rachel's interest will fall to 25%.
    a. What gain is realized on the transaction? How much of the gain will be recognized?
    b. Rhonda is not satisfied with the transaction as proposed. How will the consequences change if Rachel agrees to transfer $1,000 of cash in exchange for additional stock? In this case, Rhonda would own slightly less than 75% of Peach, and Rachel's interest would be slightly more than 25%.
    c. If Rhonda still is not satisfied with the result, what should be done to avoid any gain recognition?

Decision Making

16. **LO.2, 3, 4** Adam transfers property with an adjusted basis of $50,000 (fair market value of $400,000) to Swift Corporation for 90% of the stock. The property is subject to a liability of $60,000, which Swift assumes.
    a. What is the basis of the Swift stock to Adam?
    b. What is the basis of the property to Swift Corporation?

17. **LO.2, 3, 4** Cynthia, a sole proprietor, was engaged in a service business and reported her income on the cash basis. On February 1, 2014, she incorporates her business as Dove Corporation and transfers the assets of the business to the corporation in return for all of the stock in addition to the corporation's assumption of her proprietorship's liabilities. All of the receivables and the unpaid trade payables are transferred to the newly formed corporation. The balance sheet of the corporation immediately after its formation is as follows:

Dove Corporation
Balance Sheet
February 1, 2014

Assets

	Basis to Dove	Fair Market Value
Cash	$ 80,000	$ 80,000
Accounts receivable	–0–	240,000
Equipment (cost $180,000; depreciation previously claimed $60,000)	120,000	320,000
Building (straight-line depreciation)	160,000	400,000
Land	40,000	160,000
Total	$400,000	$1,200,000

Liabilities and Stockholder's Equity

Liabilities:		
Accounts payable—trade		$ 120,000
Notes payable—bank		360,000
Stockholder's equity:		
Common stock		720,000
Total		$1,200,000

Discuss the tax consequences of the incorporation of the business to Cynthia and to Dove Corporation.

18. **LO.2, 3, 4** Allie forms Broadbill Corporation by transferring land (basis of $125,000, fair market value of $775,000), which is subject to a mortgage of $375,000. One month prior to incorporating Broadbill, Allie borrows $100,000 for personal reasons and gives the lender a second mortgage on the land. Broadbill Corporation issues stock worth $300,000 to Allie and assumes the mortgages on the land.
    a. What are the tax consequences to Allie and to Broadbill Corporation?
    b. How would the tax consequences to Allie differ if she had not borrowed the $100,000?

Decision Making

19. **LO.2, 4** Rafael transfers the following assets to Crane Corporation in exchange for all of its stock. (Assume that neither Rafael nor Crane plans to make any special tax elections at the time of incorporation.)

Assets	Rafael's Adjusted Basis	Fair Market Value
Inventory	$ 60,000	$100,000
Equipment	150,000	105,000
Shelving	80,000	65,000

    a. What is Rafael's recognized gain or loss?
    b. What is Rafael's basis in the stock?
    c. What is Crane's basis in the inventory, equipment, and shelving?
    d. If Rafael has no intentions of selling his Crane stock for at least 15 years, what action would you recommend that Rafael and Crane Corporation consider? How does this change the previous answers?

20. **LO.2, 3, 4** Kesha, a sole proprietor, is engaged in a cash basis service business. In the current year, she incorporates the business to form Kiwi Corporation. She transfers assets with a basis of $500,000 (fair market value of $1.2 million), a bank loan of $450,000 (which Kiwi assumes), and $80,000 in trade payables in return for all of Kiwi's stock. What are the tax consequences of the incorporation of the business?

Issue ID

21. **LO.2** Nancy and her daughter, Kathleen, have been working together in a cattery called "The Perfect Cat." Nancy formed the business in 1999 as a sole proprietorship, and it has been very successful. Assets have a fair market value of $450,000 and a basis of $180,000. On the advice of their tax accountant, Nancy decides to incorporate "The Perfect Cat." Because of Kathleen's participation, Nancy would like her to receive shares in the corporation. What are the relevant tax issues?

Ethics and Equity

22. **LO.2** Early in the year, Charles, Lane, and Tami form the Harrier Corporation for the express purpose of developing a shopping center. All parties are experienced contractors, and they transfer various business assets (e.g., building materials, land) to Harrier in exchange for all of its stock. Three months after it is formed, Harrier purchases two cranes from Lane for their fair market value of $400,000 by issuing four annual installment notes of $100,000 each. Because the adjusted basis of the cranes is $550,000, Lane plans to recognize a § 1231 loss of $150,000 in the year of the sale. Does Lane have any potential income tax problem with this plan? Explain.

23. **LO.2, 4** Alice and Jane form Osprey Corporation. Alice transfers property, basis of $25,000 and fair market value of $200,000, for 50 shares in Osprey Corporation. Jane transfers property, basis of $50,000 and fair market value of $165,000, and agrees to serve as manager of Osprey for one year; in return, Jane receives 50 shares in Osprey. The value of Jane's services to Osprey is $35,000.
    a. What gain or income will Alice and Jane recognize on the exchange?
    b. What basis will Osprey Corporation have in the property transferred by Alice and Jane? How should Osprey treat the value of the services that Jane renders?

24. **LO.2, 4** Assume in Problem 23 that Jane receives the 50 shares of Osprey Corporation stock in consideration for the appreciated property and for the provision of accounting services in organizing the corporation. The value of Jane's services is $35,000.
    a. What gain or income does Jane recognize?
    b. What is Osprey Corporation's basis in the property transferred by Jane? How should Osprey treat the value of the services that Jane renders?

25. **LO.2, 4** In January 2014, Wanda transferred machinery worth $200,000 (adjusted basis of $30,000) to a controlled corporation, Oriole, Inc. The transfer qualified under § 351. Wanda had deducted $165,000 of depreciation on the machinery while it was used in her proprietorship. Later in 2014, Oriole sells the machinery for $190,000. What are the tax consequences to Wanda and to Oriole on the sale of the machinery?

26. **LO.5** Red Corporation wants to set up a manufacturing facility in a midwestern state. After considerable negotiations with a small town in Ohio, Red accepts the following offer: land (fair market value of $3 million) and cash of $1 million.
    a. How much gain or income, if any, must Red Corporation recognize?
    b. What basis will Red Corporation have in the land?
    c. Within one year of the contribution, Red constructs a building for $800,000 and purchases inventory for $200,000. What basis will Red Corporation have in each of those assets?

27. **LO.6** Emily Patrick (36 Paradise Road, Northampton, MA 01060) formed Teal Corporation a number of years ago with an investment of $200,000 of cash, for which she received $20,000 in stock and $180,000 in bonds bearing interest of 8% and maturing in nine years. Several years later, Emily lent the corporation an additional $50,000 on open account. In the current year, Teal Corporation becomes insolvent and is declared bankrupt. During the corporation's existence, Emily was paid an annual salary of $60,000. Write a letter to Emily in which you explain how she should treat her losses for tax purposes.

Critical Thinking

Communications

28. **LO.7** In each of the following independent situations, determine the dividends received deduction. Assume that none of the corporate shareholders owns 20% or more of the stock in the corporations paying the dividends.

	Almond Corporation	Blond Corporation	Cherry Corporation
Income from operations	$ 700,000	$ 800,000	$ 900,000
Expenses from operations	(600,000)	(850,000)	(910,000)
Qualifying dividends	100,000	100,000	100,000

29. **LO.7** Gull Corporation, a cash method, calendar year C corporation, was formed and began business on November 1, 2014. Gull incurred the following expenses during its first year of operations (November 1, 2014–December 31, 2014):

Expenses of temporary directors and organizational meetings	$21,000
Fee paid to state of incorporation	3,000
Expenses for printing and sale of stock certificates	11,000
Legal services for drafting the corporate charter and bylaws (not paid until January 2015)	19,000

a. Assuming that Gull Corporation elects under § 248 to expense and amortize organizational expenditures, what amount may be deducted in 2014?
b. Assume the same facts as above, except that the amount paid for the legal services was $28,000 (instead of $19,000). What amount may be deducted as organizational expenditures in 2014?

30. **LO.7** Egret Corporation, a calendar year C corporation, was formed on March 7, 2014, and opened for business on July 1, 2014. After its formation but prior to opening for business, Egret incurred the following expenditures:

Accounting	$ 7,000
Advertising	14,500
Employee payroll	11,000
Rent	8,000
Utilities	1,000

What is the maximum amount of these expenditures that Egret can deduct in 2014?

31. **LO.8** In each of the following *independent* situations, determine the corporation's income tax liability. Assume that all corporations use a calendar year for tax purposes and that the tax year involved is 2014.

	Taxable Income
Purple Corporation	$ 65,000
Azul Corporation	290,000
Pink Corporation	12,350,000
Turquoise Corporation	19,000,000
Teal Corporation (a personal service corporation)	130,000

Critical Thinking

32. **LO.9** The outstanding stock in Red, Blue, and Green Corporations, each of which has only one class of stock, is owned by the following unrelated individuals:

	Corporations		
Shareholders	Red	Blue	Green
Marrin	20%	10%	30%
Murray	10%	50%	20%
Moses	50%	30%	35%

a. Determine whether Red, Blue, and Green Corporations constitute a brother-sister controlled group.

b. Assume that Murray does not own stock in any of the corporations. Would a brother-sister controlled group exist? Explain.

33. **LO.10** Emerald Corporation, a calendar year and accrual method taxpayer, provides the following information and asks you to prepare Schedule M–1 for 2014:

Net income per books (after-tax)	$257,950
Federal income tax per books	41,750
Tax-exempt interest income	15,000
Life insurance proceeds received as a result of death of corporate president	150,000
Interest on loan to purchase tax-exempt bonds	1,500
Excess of capital losses over capital gains	6,000
Premiums paid on life insurance policy on life of Emerald's president	7,800

34. **LO.10** The following information for 2014 relates to Sparrow Corporation, a calendar year, accrual method taxpayer.

Net income per books (after-tax)	$174,100
Federal income tax per books	86,600
Tax-exempt interest income	4,500
MACRS depreciation in excess of straight-line depreciation used for financial accounting purposes	7,200
Excess of capital loss over capital gains	9,400
Nondeductible meals and entertainment	5,500
Interest on loan to purchase tax-exempt bonds	1,100

Based on the above information, use Schedule M–1 of Form 1120, which is available on the IRS website, to determine Sparrow's taxable income for 2014.

Critical Thinking

35. **LO.10** In 2014, Woodpecker, Inc., a C corporation with $8.5 million in assets, deducted amortization of $40,000 on its financial statements and $55,000 on its Federal tax return. Is Woodpecker required to file Schedule M–3? If a Schedule M–3 is filed by Woodpecker, how is the difference in amortization amounts treated on that schedule?

36. **LO.10** Dove Corporation, a calendar year C corporation, had the following information for 2014:

Critical Thinking

Net income per books (after-tax)	$386,250
Taxable income	120,000
Federal income tax per books	30,050
Cash dividend distributions	150,000
Unappropriated retained earnings as of January 1, 2014	796,010

Based on the above information, use Schedule M–2 of Form 1120 (see Example 50 in the text) to determine Dove's unappropriated retained earnings balance as of December 31, 2014.

37. **LO.10** In the current year, Pelican, Inc., incurs $50,000 of nondeductible fines and penalties. Its depreciation expense is $245,000 for financial statement purposes and $310,000 for tax purposes. How is this information reported on Schedule M–3?

Critical Thinking

38. **LO.10** In January 2014, Pelican, Inc., established an allowance for uncollectible accounts (bad debt reserve) of $70,000 on its books and increased the allowance by $120,000 during the year. As a result of a client's bankruptcy, Pelican, Inc., decreased the allowance by $60,000 in November 2014. Pelican, Inc., deducted the $190,000 of increases to the allowance on its 2014 income statement, but was not allowed to deduct that amount on its tax return. On its 2014 tax return, the corporation was allowed to deduct the $60,000 actual loss sustained because of its client's bankruptcy. On its financial statements, Pelican, Inc., treated the $190,000 increase in the bad debt reserve as an expense that gave rise to a temporary difference. On its 2014 tax return, Pelican, Inc., took a $60,000 deduction for bad debt expense. How is this information reported on Schedule M–3?

Critical Thinking

Comprehensive Tax Return Problem

1. On November 1, 2005, Janet Morton and Kim Wong formed Pet Kingdom, Inc., to sell pets and pet supplies. Pertinent information regarding Pet Kingdom is summarized as follows:

Tax Return Problem

TAX SOFTWARE

- Pet Kingdom's business address is 1010 Northwest Parkway, Dallas, TX 75225; its telephone number is (214) 555-2211; and its e-mail address is petkingdom@pki.com.
- The employer identification number is 11-1111111, and the principal business activity code is 453910.
- Janet and Kim each own 50% of the common stock; Janet is president and Kim is vice president of the company. No other class of stock is authorized.
- Both Janet and Kim are full-time employees of Pet Kingdom. Janet's Social Security number is 123-45-6789, and Kim's Social Security number is 987-65-4321.
- Pet Kingdom is an accrual method, calendar year taxpayer. Inventories are determined using FIFO and the lower of cost or market method. Pet Kingdom uses the straight-line method of depreciation for book purposes and accelerated depreciation (MACRS) for tax purposes.
- During 2013, the corporation distributed cash dividends of $250,000.

Pet Kingdom's financial statements for 2013 follow.

Income Statement

Income	
Gross sales	$ 5,750,000
Sales returns and allowances	(200,000)
Net sales	$ 5,550,000
Cost of goods sold	(2,300,000)

(continued)

Income

Gross profit		$ 3,250,000
Dividends received from stock investments in less-than-20%-owned U.S. corporations		43,750
Interest income:		
State bonds	$15,000	
Certificates of deposit	20,000	35,000
Total income		$ 3,328,750

Expenses

Salaries—officers:			
Janet Morton	$262,500		
Kim Wong	262,500	$525,000	
Salaries—clerical and sales		725,000	
Taxes (state, local, and payroll)		238,000	
Repairs and maintenance		140,000	
Interest expense:			
Loan to purchase state bonds	$ 9,000		
Other business loans	207,000	216,000	
Advertising		58,000	
Rental expense		109,000	
Depreciation*		106,000	
Charitable contributions		38,000	
Employee benefit programs		60,000	
Premiums on term life insurance policies on lives of Janet Morton and Kim Wong; Pet Kingdom is the designated beneficiary		40,000	
Total expenses			(2,255,000)
Net income before taxes			$ 1,073,750
Federal income tax			(356,023)
Net income per books			$ 717,727

*Depreciation for tax purposes is $136,000. You are not provided enough detailed data to complete a Form 4562 (depreciation). If you solve this problem using H&R BLOCK Tax Software, enter the amount of depreciation on line 20 of Form 1120.

Balance Sheet

Assets	January 1, 2013	December 31, 2013
Cash	$ 1,200,000	$ 1,037,750
Trade notes and accounts receivable	2,062,500	2,147,000
Inventories	2,750,000	3,030,000
Stock investment	1,125,000	1,125,000
State bonds	375,000	375,000
Certificates of deposit	400,000	400,000
Prepaid Federal tax	–0–	3,977
Buildings and other depreciable assets	5,455,000	5,455,000
Accumulated depreciation	(606,000)	(712,000)
Land	812,500	812,500
Other assets	140,000	128,500
Total assets	$13,714,000	$13,802,727

Liabilities and Equity	January 1, 2013	December 31, 2013
Accounts payable	$ 2,284,000	$ 1,975,000
Other current liabilities	175,000	155,000
Mortgages	4,625,000	4,575,000
Capital stock	2,500,000	2,500,000
Retained earnings	4,130,000	4,597,727
Total liabilities and equity	$13,714,000	$13,802,727

During 2013, Pet Kingdom made estimated tax payments of $90,000 each quarter to the IRS. Prepare a Form 1120 for Pet Kingdom for tax year 2013. Suggested software: H&R BLOCK Tax Software.

BRIDGE DISCIPLINE

1. Charles is planning to invest $10,000 in a venture whose management is undecided as to whether it should be structured as a regular corporation or as a partnership. Charles will hold a 10% interest in the entity. Determine the treatment to Charles if the entity is a corporation and if it is a partnership. In the analysis, assume that Charles is in the 35% marginal tax bracket and that the entity, if operating as a corporation, is in the 34% marginal tax bracket. Also assume that the passive activity rules do not apply to Charles.

    a. If the entity incurs an $80,000 operating loss in year 1, what is Charles's cash outflow if the entity is a corporation? A partnership? Do not consider the 3.8% Medicare surtax in the analysis.

    b. In year 2, the entity earns operating income of $200,000 and makes no distributions to any of the owners. What is the Federal income tax burden on Charles if the investment is a corporation? A partnership?

    c. In year 3, the entity earns operating income of $200,000 and distributes all of that year's after-tax proceeds to the owners. What amount of cash is available to Charles if the entity operates as a corporation (assume that any distribution is a qualified dividend)? A partnership?

2. On your review of the books and records of Ridge Corporation, you note the following information pertaining to its tax provision:

Net income per books	$525,400
Book income tax expense	234,600
Dividends received deduction	70,000
Capital gains	50,000
Capital losses	(60,000)
MACRS depreciation	80,000
Book depreciation	65,000

    a. Calculate Ridge's taxable income and Federal income tax liability for the year.
    b. Calculate Ridge's deferred income tax liability.

Research Problems

Note: Solutions to Research Problems can be prepared by using the **Checkpoint®** **Student Edition** online research product, which is available to accompany this text. It is also possible to prepare solutions to the Research Problems by using tax research materials found in a standard tax library.

THOMSON REUTERS
CHECKPOINT®

Research Problem 1. Tim is a real estate broker who specializes in commercial real estate. Although he usually buys and sells on behalf of others, he also maintains a portfolio of property of his own. He holds this property, mainly unimproved land, either as an investment or for sale to others.

In early 2012, Irene and Al contact Tim regarding a tract of land located just outside the city limits. Tim bought the property, which is known as the Moore farm, several years ago for $600,000. At that time, no one knew that it was located on a geological fault line. Irene, a well-known architect, and Al, a building contractor, want Tim to join them in developing the property for residential use. They are aware of the fault line but believe that they can circumvent the problem by using newly developed design and construction technology. Because of the geological flaw, however, they regard the Moore farm as being worth only $450,000. Their intent is to organize a corporation to build the housing project, and each party will receive stock commensurate to the property or services contributed.

After consulting his tax adviser, Tim agrees to join the venture if certain modifications to the proposed arrangement are made. The transfer of the land would be structured as a sale to the corporation. Instead of receiving stock, Tim would receive a note from the corporation. The note would be interest-bearing and be due in five years. The maturity value of the note would be $450,000—the amount that even Tim concedes is the fair market value of the Moore farm.

What income tax consequences ensue from Tim's suggested approach? Compare this result with what would happen if Tim merely transferred the Moore farm in return for stock in the new corporation.

Communications   **Research Problem 2.** A new client, John Dobson, recently formed John's Premium Steakhouse, Inc., to operate a new restaurant. The restaurant will be a first-time business venture for John, who recently retired after 30 years of military service. John transferred cash to the corporation in exchange for 100% of its stock, and the corporation is considering leasing a building and restaurant equipment. John has asked you for guidance on the tax treatment of various expenses (e.g., licensing, training, advertising) he expects the corporation to incur during the restaurant's pre-opening period. Research the tax treatment of startup expenditures, including the point at which a business begins for purposes of determining what expenses are included. Prepare a memo for the client files describing the results of your research.

Partial list of research aids:
§ 195.
Reg. § 1.195–1.

Decision Making   **Research Problem 3.** Jonathan has owned and operated a golf driving range for a number of years. The sole proprietorship has been successful and has grown to the point where it now offers golf lessons and sponsors tournaments and other activities. Jonathan has been advised that incorporating his proprietorship would give him an opportunity to restructure the business debt and to acquire additional working capital at more favorable rates.

Based on this advice, Jonathan transfers the business assets (fair market value $1 million, adjusted basis $200,000) along with the associated debt ($325,000) to the newly formed corporation. As far as he is concerned, nothing has really changed in his relationship with the creditor bank: he still feels personally obligated to pay off the debt. In fact, before the debt is assigned to the newly formed corporation, the bank insists that Jonathan remain secondarily responsible for its payment (i.e., he guaranteed the debt). Even though the proprietorship's liabilities transferred exceed the basis of the assets transferred, Jonathan regards the transaction as tax-free because:

* Nothing has changed with his business other than its form of operation.
* A business justification exists for changing its form to that of a corporation.
* He has enjoyed no personal gain from the transaction.
* He is still obligated with respect to the debt.

Determine whether Jonathan is justified in his position. If you believe the transaction as currently planned would be taxable, identify strategies that could be used to eliminate or reduce gain recognition.

Use the tax resources of the Internet to address the following questions. Do not restrict your search to the Web, but include a review of newsgroups and general reference materials, practitioner sites and resources, primary sources of the tax law, chat rooms and discussion groups, and other opportunities.

Internet Activity

Communications

Research Problem 4. On November 21, 2013, Max Baucus, Chairman of the Senate Finance Committee, released a proposal to change several provisions related to the taxation of business income including, but not limited to, that earned by corporations. The proposal deals primarily with cost recovery and tax accounting methods. Many of the proposed changes are similar to ones contained in House Ways and Means Committee Chairman Dave Camp's small business tax reform discussion draft released earlier in the year. Locate the staff discussion draft of Chairman Baucus's proposal and prepare a PowerPoint presentation of no more than five slides highlighting the major reforms contained in the proposal.

Communications

Research Problem 5. Owners and financiers of businesses often have reasons to structure their investments as either debt or equity. Locate the July 11, 2011 report prepared by the Staff of the Joint Committee on Taxation that contains a discussion of the taxation of business debt. Summarize for your professor its conclusion on the (1) tax incentives for debt, (2) tax incentives for equity, and (3) incentives to create hybrid instruments.

Corporations: Earnings & Profits and Distributions

LEARNING OBJECTIVES: *After completing Chapter 13, you should be able to:*

LO.1 Explain the role that earnings and profits play in determining the tax treatment of distributions.

LO.2 Compute a corporation's earnings and profits (E & P).

LO.3 Apply the rules for assigning earnings and profits to distributions.

LO.4 Evaluate the tax effects of property dividends on the recipient shareholder and the corporation making the distribution.

LO.5 Identify the nature and treatment of constructive dividends.

LO.6 Distinguish between taxable and nontaxable stock dividends.

LO.7 Discuss the tax treatment of stock redemptions and corporate liquidations.

TAX TALK *The relative stability of profits after taxes is evidence that the corporation profits tax is, in effect, almost entirely shifted; the government simply uses the corporation as a tax collector.* —K. E. BOULDING

Dennis Flaherty/Photographer's Choice/Getty Images

TAXING CORPORATE DISTRIBUTIONS

Lime Corporation, an ice cream manufacturer, has had a very profitable year. To share its profits with its two shareholders, Orange Corporation and Gustavo, it distributes cash of $200,000 to Orange and real estate worth $300,000 (adjusted basis of $20,000) to Gustavo. The real estate is subject to a mortgage of $100,000, which Gustavo assumes. The distribution is made on December 31, Lime's year-end.

Lime Corporation has had both good and bad years in the past. More often than not, however, it has lost money. Despite this year's banner profits, the GAAP-based balance sheet for Lime indicates a year-end deficit in retained earnings. Consequently, the distribution of cash and land is treated as a liquidating distribution for financial reporting purposes, resulting in a reduction of Lime's paid-in capital account.

The tax consequences of the distributions to Lime Corporation and its shareholders depend on a variety of factors that are not directly related to the financial reporting treatment. Identify these factors, and explain the tax effects of the distributions to both Lime Corporation and its two shareholders.

Read the chapter and formulate your response.

Generally, a corporation cannot deduct distributions made to its shareholders. In contrast, shareholders may be required to treat distributions as fully subject to tax, a nontaxable recovery of capital, or capital gain.

Because distributions provide no deduction to the paying corporation and often require income recognition by the shareholders, a double tax seemingly results (i.e., at both the corporate and shareholder levels). Because of the possibility of a double tax when dealing with corporations, the tax treatment of distributions often raises issues such as the following.

- The availability of earnings to be distributed.
- The basis of the shareholder's stock.
- The character of the property being distributed.
- Whether the shareholder gives up ownership in return for the distribution.
- Whether the distribution is liquidating or nonliquidating.

13-1 CORPORATE DISTRIBUTIONS—OVERVIEW

LO.1

Explain the role that earnings and profits play in determining the tax treatment of distributions.

To the extent a distribution is made from corporate earnings and profits (E & P), the shareholder is deemed to receive a **dividend**, usually taxed in a preferential manner.[1] Generally, corporate distributions are presumed to be paid out of E & P (defined later in this chapter) and are treated as dividends, *unless* the parties to the transaction can show otherwise.

The portion of a corporate distribution that is not taxed as a dividend (because of insufficient E & P) is nontaxable to the extent of the shareholder's basis in the stock. The stock basis is reduced accordingly. The excess of the distribution over the shareholder's basis is treated as a gain from the sale or exchange of the stock.[2]

Example 1

At the beginning of the year, Amber Corporation (a calendar year taxpayer) holds accumulated E & P of $30,000. The corporation reports no current E & P. During the year, the corporation distributes $40,000 to its *equal* shareholders, Bob and Bonnie (i.e., each receives $20,000). Only $30,000 of the $40,000 distribution is a taxable dividend. Suppose Bob's basis in his stock is $8,000, while Bonnie's basis is $4,000. Under these conditions, Bob recognizes a taxable dividend of $15,000 and reduces the basis of his stock from $8,000 to $3,000. The $20,000 Bonnie receives from Amber Corporation is accounted for as follows.

- Taxable dividend of $15,000.
- Reduction in stock basis from $4,000 to zero.
- Taxable gain of $1,000.

13-2 EARNINGS AND PROFITS (E & P)

The notion of **earnings and profits** is similar in many respects to the financial accounting concept of retained earnings. Both are measures of the firm's accumulated capital. However, these two concepts differ in a fundamental way. The computation of retained earnings is based on financial accounting rules, while E & P is determined using rules specified in the tax law.

E & P fixes the upper limit on the amount of dividend income shareholders must recognize as a result of a distribution by the corporation. In this sense, E & P represents the corporation's economic ability to pay a dividend without impairing its capital. Thus, the effect of a specific transaction on the E & P account often can be determined by considering whether the transaction increases or decreases the corporation's capacity to pay a dividend.

---

[1]§§ 301(c)(1) and 316(a). Corporate shareholders claim a dividends received deduction. Others typically pay a tax on dividends at a maximum 15% or 20% rate.

[2]§ 301(c).

TAX FACT   Who Pays Dividends?

The vast majority of dividends paid by C corporations come from the very largest enterprises (measured by size of total assets) as reported on Forms 1120 for the latest tax year for which data are available. About 80 percent of the members of the Standard & Poor's 500 pay an annual dividend, distributing less than 40 percent of annual profits. Only about 12.5 percent of all dividend payments during a tax year are made by C corporations with less than $500 million in total assets.

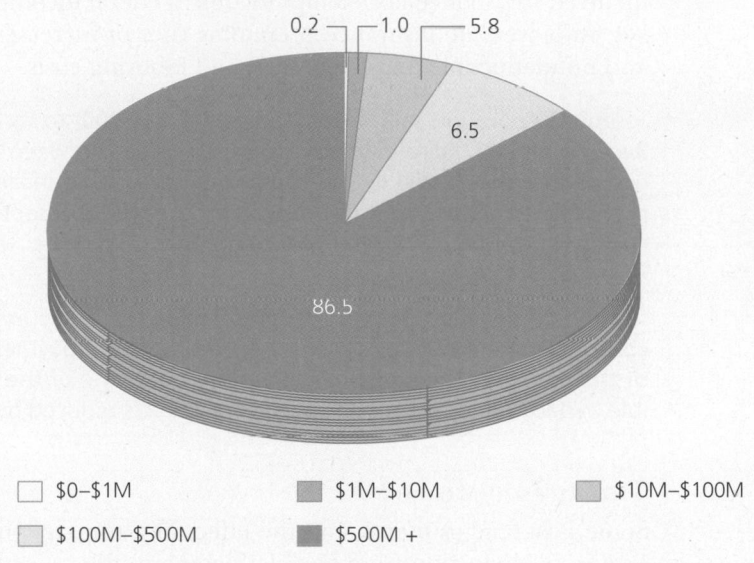

Percentage of Dividends Paid, by Size of Corporate Assets

0.2   1.0   5.8
6.5
86.5

☐ $0–$1M   ◼ $1M–$10M   ◼ $10M–$100M
☐ $100M–$500M   ◼ $500M +

© iStockphoto.com/Pali Rao

13-2a Computation of E & P

The Code does not explicitly define the term *earnings and profits*. Instead, a series of adjustments to taxable income are identified to provide a measure of the corporation's economic income.[3] In general, E & P determinations are applied in the same manner for cash and accrual basis taxpayers.

Accumulated E & P is fixed as of the beginning of the tax year, which is the sum of the undistributed earnings of the entity since the later of its incorporation date or February 28, 1913. Current E & P is that portion of E & P attributable to the current tax year's operations. It is computed by using the corporation's Federal taxable income and then applying a series of adjustments to more closely approximate the cash flow of the entity.[4]

LO.2

Compute a corporation's earnings and profits (E & P).

Additions to Taxable Income

To determine current E & P, one must add certain previously excluded income items back to taxable income. Included among these positive adjustments are interest income on municipal bonds, excluded life insurance proceeds (in excess of cash surrender value), and Federal income tax refunds from taxes paid in prior years.

In addition to excluded income items, the dividends received deduction and the domestic production activities deduction are added back to taxable income to determine E & P. Neither of these deductions decreases the corporation's assets. Instead, they are partial exclusions for specific types of income (dividend income and income from domestic production activities). Because they do not impair the corporation's ability to pay dividends, they do not reduce E & P.

---

[3]Reg. § 1.312–6(a).

[4]Section 312 describes many of the adjustments to taxable income necessary to determine E & P. Regulation § 1.312–6 addresses the effect of accounting methods on E & P.

Example 2

Eagle Corporation collects $100,000 on a key employee life insurance policy (Eagle is the owner and beneficiary of the policy). At the time the policy matured on the death of the insured employee, it possessed a cash surrender value of $30,000. None of the $100,000 is included in Eagle's taxable income, but $70,000 is added to its taxable income when computing current E & P.

Subtractions from Taxable Income

Some of the corporation's nondeductible expenditures are subtracted from taxable income to arrive at E & P. These negative adjustments include the nondeductible portion of meals and entertainment expenses; related-party losses; expenses incurred to produce tax-exempt income; Federal income taxes paid; nondeductible key employee life insurance premiums (net of increases in cash surrender value); and nondeductible fines, penalties, and lobbying costs.

Example 3

Joseph Corporation sells property (basis of $10,000) to its sole shareholder for $8,000. Because of § 267 (disallowance of losses on sales between related parties), Joseph cannot deduct the $2,000 loss in computing its taxable income. But because the overall economic effect of the transaction is a decrease in Joseph's assets by $2,000, the loss reduces current E & P for the year of the sale.

Example 4

Jacquie Corporation pays a $10,000 premium on a key employee life insurance policy covering the life of its president. As a result of the payment, the cash surrender value of the policy is increased by $7,000. Although none of the $10,000 premium is deductible by Jacquie for tax purposes, current E & P is reduced by $3,000.

Timing Adjustments

Some E & P adjustments shift the effect of a transaction from the year of its inclusion in or deduction from taxable income to the year in which it has an economic effect on the corporation. Charitable contribution carryovers, net operating loss carryovers, and capital loss carryovers all give rise to this kind of adjustment.

Example 5

During 2014, Raven Corporation makes charitable contributions, $12,000 of which cannot be deducted in arriving at its taxable income for the year because of the 10% taxable income limitation. Consequently, the $12,000 is carried forward to 2015 and fully deducted in that year. The excess charitable contribution reduces Raven's 2014 current E & P by $12,000 and increases its current E & P for 2015, when the deduction is allowed, by a like amount. The increase in 2015 E & P is necessary because the charitable contribution carryover reduces the taxable income for that year (the starting point for computing E & P) but already has been taken into account in determining 2014 current E & P.

Gains and losses from property transactions generally affect the determination of E & P only to the extent they are recognized for tax purposes. Thus, gains and losses deferred under the like-kind exchange provision and deferred involuntary conversion gains do not affect E & P until recognized. Accordingly, no timing adjustment is required for these items.

Accounting Method Adjustments

In addition to the above adjustments, accounting methods used for determining E & P are generally more conservative than those allowed for calculating taxable income. For example, the installment method is not permitted for E & P purposes even though, in some cases, it is allowed when computing taxable income. Thus, an adjustment is required for the deferred gain attributable to sales of property made during the year under the installment method. Specifically, all principal payments are treated as having been received in the year of sale.[5]

---

[5]§ 312(n)(5).

In 2014, Cardinal Corporation, a calendar year taxpayer, sells unimproved real estate (basis of $20,000) for $100,000. Under the terms of the sale, Cardinal will receive two annual payments of $50,000 beginning in 2015, each with interest of 9%. Cardinal does not elect out of the installment method.

Because Cardinal's 2014 taxable income will not reflect any of the gain from the sale, the corporation must make an $80,000 positive adjustment for that year (the deferred gain from the sale) in computing current E & P. Similarly, $40,000 negative adjustments are required in 2015 and 2016 when the deferred gain is recognized under the installment method.

Example 6

The alternative depreciation system (ADS) is used in computing E & P.[6] This method requires straight-line depreciation with a half-year convention, over a recovery period equal to the Asset Depreciation Range (ADR) midpoint life.[7] If MACRS cost recovery is used for income tax purposes, a positive or negative adjustment equal to the difference between MACRS and ADS must be made each year. Finally, no additional first-year depreciation is allowed under the ADS.[8]

Likewise, when assets are disposed of, an additional adjustment to taxable income is required to allow for the difference in gain or loss resulting from the difference in income tax basis and E & P basis.[9] The adjustments arising from depreciation are illustrated in the following example.

On January 2, 2014, White Corporation purchased equipment with an ADR midpoint life of 10 years for $30,000. The equipment was then depreciated over its 7-year MACRS class life. No § 179 or additional first-year depreciation was claimed. The asset was sold on July 2, 2016, for $27,000. For purposes of determining taxable income and E & P, cost recovery claimed on the equipment is summarized below.

Example 7

Year	Cost Recovery Computation	MACRS	ADS	Adjustment Amount
2014	$30,000 × 14.29%	$ 4,287		
	$30,000 ÷ 10-year ADR recovery period × ½ (half-year for first year of service)		$1,500	$2,787
2015	$30,000 × 24.49%	7,347		
	$30,000 ÷ 10-year ADR recovery period		3,000	4,347
2016	$30,000 × 17.49% × ½ (half-year for year of disposal)	2,624		
	$30,000 ÷ 10-year ADR recovery period × ½ (half-year for year of disposal)		1,500	1,124
	Total cost recovery	$14,258	$6,000	$8,258

Each year, White Corporation increases its taxable income by the adjustment amount indicated above to determine E & P. In addition, when computing 2016 E & P, White reduces taxable income by $8,258 to account for the excess gain recognized for income tax purposes.

	Income Tax	E & P
Amount realized	$ 27,000	$ 27,000
Adjusted basis for income tax ($30,000 cost − $14,258 MACRS)	(15,742)	
Adjusted basis for E & P ($30,000 cost − $6,000 ADS)		(24,000)
Gain on sale	$ 11,258	$ 3,000
Adjustment amount ($3,000 − $11,258)	($ 8,258)	

---

[6]§ 312(k)(3)(A).

[7]See § 168(g)(2). The ADR midpoint life for most assets is set out in Rev.Proc. 87–56, 1987–2 C.B. 674. The recovery period is 5 years for automobiles and light-duty trucks and 40 years for real property. For assets with no class life, the recovery period is 12 years.

[8]§ 168(k)(2). Under the MACRS provisions, additional first-year cost recovery is available for certain assets placed in service from 2008 through 2013. This provision likely will be extended by Congress in 2014.

[9]§ 312(f)(1).

In addition to more conservative depreciation methods, the E & P rules impose limitations on the deductibility of § 179 expense.[10] In particular, this expense is deducted over a period of five years for E & P purposes. Thus, in any year that § 179 is elected, 80 percent of the resulting expense is added back to taxable income to determine current E & P. In each of the following four years, a subtraction from taxable income equal to 20 percent of the § 179 expense is made.

The E & P rules also require specific accounting methods in various situations, making adjustments necessary when certain methods are used for income tax purposes. For example, E & P requires cost depletion rather than percentage depletion. When accounting for long-term contracts, E & P rules specify the percentage of completion method rather than the completed contract method. As the E & P determination does not allow for the amortization of organizational expenses, any such expense deducted when computing taxable income must be added back.

To account for income deferral under the LIFO inventory method, the E & P computation requires an adjustment for changes in the LIFO recapture amount (the excess of FIFO over LIFO inventory value) during the year. Increases in LIFO recapture are added to taxable income and decreases are subtracted, to the extent of prior-year increases.

E & P rules also specify that intangible drilling costs and mine exploration and development costs be amortized over a period of 60 months and 120 months, respectively.[11] For income tax purposes, however, these costs can be deducted currently.

13-2b Summary of E & P Adjustments

E & P serves as a measure of the earnings of the corporation that are available for distribution as taxable dividends to the shareholders. Current E & P is determined by making a series of adjustments to the corporation's taxable income. These adjustments are reviewed in Concept Summary 13.1.

13-2c Allocating E & P to Distributions

LO.3

Apply the rules for assigning earnings and profits to distributions.

When a positive balance exists in both the current and accumulated E & P accounts, corporate distributions are deemed to be made first from current E & P and then from accumulated E & P. When distributions exceed the amount of current E & P, it becomes necessary to allocate current and accumulated E & P to each distribution made during the year. First, dollars of current E & P are applied on a pro rata basis to each distribution. Then accumulated E & P is applied in chronological order, beginning with the earliest distribution. This allocation is important if any shareholder sells stock during the year.

Example 8

On January 1 of the current year, Black Corporation has accumulated E & P of $10,000. Current E & P for the year amounts to $30,000, earned evenly throughout the year. Megan and Matt are the sole *equal* shareholders of Black from January 1 to July 31. On August 1, Megan sells all of her stock to Helen. Black makes two distributions to shareholders during the year: $40,000 to Megan and Matt ($20,000 to each) on July 1 and $40,000 to Matt and Helen ($20,000 to each) on December 1. Current and accumulated E & P are applied to the two distributions as follows.

---

[10]§ 312(k)(3)(B).

[11]§ 312(n).

CONCEPT SUMMARY 13.1

Computing E & P

Transaction	Adjustment to Taxable Income to Determine Current E & P	
	Addition	Subtraction
Tax-exempt income	X	
Dividends received deduction	X	
Collection of proceeds from insurance policy on life of corporate officer (in excess of cash surrender value)	X	
Deferred gain on installment sale (all of the gain is added to E & P in year of sale)	X	
Future recognition of installment sale gross profit		X
Excess capital loss		X
Excess charitable contribution (over 10% limitation) in year incurred		X
Deduction of charitable contribution, NOL, or capital loss carryovers in succeeding taxable years (increase E & P because deduction reduces taxable income while E & P was reduced in a prior year)	X	
Federal income taxes paid		X
Federal income tax refund	X	
Loss on sale between related parties		X
Nondeductible fines, penalties, lobbying costs, meals, and entertainment		X
Payment of premiums on insurance policy on life of corporate officer (in excess of increase in cash surrender value of policy)		X
Realized gain (not recognized) on an involuntary conversion	No effect	
Realized gain or loss (not recognized) on a like-kind exchange	No effect	
Excess percentage depletion (only cost depletion can reduce E & P)	X	
Accelerated depreciation (E & P is reduced only by straight-line, units-of-production, or machine hours depreciation)	X	X
Additional first-year depreciation	X	
Domestic production activities deduction	X	
§ 179 expense in year elected (80%)	X	
§ 179 expense in four years following election (20% each year)		X
Increase (decrease) in LIFO recapture amount	X	X
Intangible drilling costs deducted currently (reduce E & P in future years by amortizing costs over 60 months)	X	
Mine exploration and development costs (reduce E & P in future years by amortizing costs over 120 months)	X	

	Source of Distribution		
	Current E & P	Accumulated E & P	Return of Capital
July 1 distribution ($40,000)	$15,000	$10,000	$15,000
December 1 distribution ($40,000)	15,000	–0–	25,000

Because 50% of the total distributions are made on July 1 and December 1, respectively, one-half of current E & P is assigned to each of the two distributions. Accumulated E & P is applied in chronological order, so the entire amount attaches to the July 1 distribution. The tax consequences to the shareholders follow.

	Shareholder		
	Megan	**Matt**	**Helen**
July distribution ($40,000)			
Dividend income—			
From current E & P ($15,000)	$ 7,500	$ 7,500	$ –0–
From accumulated E & P ($10,000)	5,000	5,000	–0–
Return of capital ($15,000)	7,500	7,500	–0–
December distribution ($40,000)			
Dividend income—			
From current E & P ($15,000)	–0–	7,500	7,500
From accumulated E & P ($0)	–0–	–0–	–0–
Return of capital ($25,000)	–0–	12,500	12,500
Total distribution	$20,000	$40,000	$20,000
Total dividend income	$12,500	$20,000	$ 7,500
Nontaxable return of capital (assuming sufficient basis in the stock investment)	$ 7,500	$20,000	$12,500

Because the balance in the accumulated E & P account is exhausted when it is applied to the July 1 distribution, Megan has more dividend income than Helen does, even though both receive equal distributions during the year. In addition, each shareholder's basis is reduced by the nontaxable return of capital; any excess over basis results in taxable gain.

When the tax years of the corporation and its shareholders are not the same, it may be impossible to determine the amount of current E & P on a timely basis. For example, if shareholders use a calendar year and the corporation uses a fiscal year, current E & P may not be ascertainable until after the shareholders' tax returns have been filed. To address this timing issue, the allocation rules presume that current E & P is sufficient to cover every distribution made during the year until the parties can show otherwise.

BRIDGE DISCIPLINE Bridge to Finance

Investors often have tried to read the dividend policies of a corporation as indicators of the strength of the entity: constant dividend payments indicated a stable financial structure for the corporation, while dividend increases were a predictor of good times and triggered stock price increases. Reductions in historic dividend payment patterns foreshadowed financial difficulties and often caused a quick and sizable drop in share price.

Nobel Prize winners Merton Miller, University of Chicago, and Franco Modigliani, MIT, saw things differently. They viewed dividends as a remnant of various financing sources available to the corporation: if it was cheaper to finance future growth by retaining profits and decreasing or eliminating dividend payments, so be it. The entity must reduce its cost of capital wherever

possible, and under this interpretation, a dividend decrease might indicate the internal financial strength of the corporation. Conversely, the payment of a dividend reduces the capital available to the entity, thereby forcing the entity to finance its operations and growth from some third-party source and risking future weakness if the cost of that capital increases.

Miller and Modigliani found that stock price and dividend policy were unrelated, and that changes in dividend patterns should not affect the capitalized value of the business. Even with lower tax rates on dividends, few shareholders complain that the typical growth stock rarely pays dividends. Nevertheless, shares of companies that pay dividends outperform those that don't pay dividends.

CONCEPT SUMMARY 13.2

Allocating E & P to Distributions

1. Current E & P is applied first to distributions on a pro rata basis; then accumulated E & P is applied (as necessary) in chronological order beginning with the earliest distribution. See Example 8.
2. Until the parties can show otherwise, it is presumed that current E & P covers all distributions. See Example 9.
3. When a deficit exists in accumulated E & P and a positive balance exists in current E & P, distributions are regarded as dividends to the extent of current E & P. See Example 10.
4. When a deficit exists in current E & P and a positive balance exists in accumulated E & P, the two accounts are netted at the date of distribution. If the resulting balance is zero or a deficit, the distribution is treated as a return of capital, first reducing the basis of the stock to zero, then generating taxable gain. If a positive balance results, the distribution is a dividend to the extent of the balance. Any loss in current E & P is deemed to accrue ratably throughout the year unless the corporation can show otherwise. See Example 11.

Example 9

Green Corporation uses a June 30 fiscal year for tax purposes. Carol, Green's only shareholder, uses a calendar year. On July 1, 2014, Green has a zero balance in its accumulated E & P account. For fiscal year 2014–2015, the corporation incurs a $5,000 deficit in current E & P. On August 1, 2014, Green distributed $10,000 to Carol. The distribution is dividend income to Carol and is reported when she files her income tax return for the 2014 calendar year, on or before April 15, 2015.

Because Carol cannot prove until June 30, 2015, that the corporation has a deficit for the fiscal year, she must assume that the $10,000 distribution is fully covered by current E & P. When Carol learns of the deficit, she can file an amended return for 2014 showing the $10,000 as a return of capital. Alternatively, Carol can file for an extension for her 2014 return while she awaits Green Corporation's fiscal year-end.

Additional difficulties arise when either the current or the accumulated E & P account has a deficit balance. In particular, when current E & P is positive and accumulated E & P has a deficit balance, accumulated E & P is *not* netted against current E & P. Instead, the distribution is deemed to be a taxable dividend to the extent of the positive current E & P balance.

THE BIG PICTURE

Example 10

Return to the facts of *The Big Picture* on p. 13-1. Recall that Lime Corporation had a deficit in GAAP-based retained earnings at the start of the year and banner profits during the year. Assume that these financial results translate into an $800,000 deficit in accumulated E & P at the start of the year and current E & P of $600,000. In addition, for purposes of this example, assume that there is no mortgage on the real estate.

In this case, current E & P would exceed the total cash and property distributed to the shareholders. The distributions are treated as taxable dividends; they are deemed to be paid from current E & P even though Lime still has a deficit in accumulated E & P at the end of the year.

In contrast to the previous rule, when a deficit exists in current E & P and a positive balance exists in accumulated E & P, the accounts are netted at the date of distribution. If the resulting balance is zero or negative, the distribution is a return of capital. If a positive balance results, the distribution is a dividend to the extent of the balance. Any loss in current E & P is deemed to accrue ratably throughout the year unless the parties can show otherwise.

Example 11

At the beginning of the current year, Gray Corporation (a calendar year taxpayer) has accumulated E & P of $10,000. During the year, the corporation incurs a $15,000 deficit in current E & P that accrues ratably. On July 1, Gray distributes $6,000 in cash to Hal, its sole shareholder. To determine how much of the $6,000 cash distribution represents dividend income to Hal, the balances of both accumulated and current E & P as of July 1 are determined and netted. This occurs because of the deficit in current E & P.

	Source of Distribution	
	Current E & P	Accumulated E & P
January 1		$10,000
July 1 (½ of $15,000 deficit in current E & P)	($7,500)	2,500
July 1 distribution of $6,000:		
Dividend income: $2,500		
Return of capital: $3,500		

The balance in E & P just before the July 1 distribution is $2,500. Thus, of the $6,000 distribution, $2,500 is taxed as a dividend, and $3,500 represents a return of capital.

Tax Planning Strategies   CORPORATE DISTRIBUTIONS

FRAMEWORK FOCUS: INCOME AND EXCLUSIONS

Strategy: Avoid Income Recognition.

In connection with the discussion of corporate distributions, the following points need reinforcement.

- Because E & P is the measure of dividend income, its periodic determination is essential to corporate planning. Thus, an E & P account should be established and maintained, particularly if the possibility exists that a corporate distribution might be a return of capital.
- Accumulated E & P is the sum of all past years' current E & P. Because there is no statute of limitations on the computation of E & P, the IRS can redetermine a corporation's current E & P for a tax year long since passed. Such a change affects accumulated E & P and has a direct impact on the taxability of current distributions to shareholders.
- Distributions can be planned to avoid or minimize dividend exposure.

Example 12

Flicker Corporation has accumulated E & P of $100,000 as of January 1 of the current year. During the year, it expects to generate earnings from operations of $80,000 and to sell an asset for a loss of $100,000. Thus, it anticipates a current E & P deficit of $20,000. Flicker also expects to make a cash distribution of $60,000.

A tax-effective approach is to recognize the loss as soon as possible and immediately thereafter make the cash distribution to the shareholders. Suppose these two steps take place on January 1. Because the current E & P has a deficit, the accumulated E & P account must be brought up to date (refer to Example 11). Thus, at the time of the distribution, the combined E & P balance is zero [$100,000 (beginning balance in accumulated E & P) − $100,000 (existing deficit in current E & P)], and the $60,000 distribution to the shareholders constitutes a return of capital. Current deficits are deemed to accrue pro rata throughout the year unless the parties can prove otherwise. Here they can. ■

Example 13

After several unprofitable years, Darter Corporation has a deficit in accumulated E & P of $100,000 as of January 1, 2014. Starting in 2014, Darter expects to generate annual E & P of $50,000 for the next four years and would like to distribute this amount to its shareholders. The corporation's cash position (for dividend purposes) will correspond to the current E & P generated. Compare the following possibilities.

1. On December 31 of 2014, 2015, 2016, and 2017, Darter Corporation distributes cash of $50,000.
2. On December 31 of 2015 and 2017, Darter Corporation distributes cash of $100,000.

The two alternatives are illustrated as follows.

Year	Accumulated E & P (First of Year)	Current E & P	Distribution	Amount of Dividend
Alternative 1				
2014	($100,000)	$50,000	$50,000	$50,000
2015	(100,000)	50,000	50,000	50,000
2016	(100,000)	50,000	50,000	50,000
2017	(100,000)	50,000	50,000	50,000
Alternative 2				
2014	($100,000)	$50,000	$ –0–	$ –0–
2015	(50,000)	50,000	100,000	50,000
2016	(50,000)	50,000	–0–	–0–
2017	–0–	50,000	100,000	50,000

Alternative 1 produces $200,000 of dividend income because each $50,000 distribution is fully paid from current E & P.

Alternative 2, however, produces only $100,000 of dividend income to the shareholders. The remaining $100,000 is a return of capital. Why?

At the time Darter made its first distribution of $100,000 on December 31, 2015, it had a deficit of $50,000 in accumulated E & P (the original deficit of $100,000 is reduced by the $50,000 of current E & P from 2014). Consequently, the $100,000 distribution yields a $50,000 dividend (the current E & P for 2015), and $50,000 is treated as a return of capital. As of January 1, 2016, Darter's accumulated E & P now has a deficit balance of $50,000, because a distribution cannot increase a deficit in E & P. Adding the remaining $50,000 of current E & P from 2016, the balance as of January 1, 2017, is zero. Thus, the second distribution of $100,000 made on December 31, 2017, also yields $50,000 of dividends (the current E & P for 2017) and a $50,000 return of capital. ∎

13-3 PROPERTY DIVIDENDS

The previous discussion assumed that all distributions by a corporation to its shareholders are in the form of cash. Although most corporate distributions are paid in cash, a corporation may distribute a **property dividend** for various reasons. For example, the shareholders may want a particular property that is held by the corporation. Or a corporation that is strapped for cash may want to distribute a dividend to its shareholders.

Property distributions have the same tax impact as distributions of cash except for effects attributable to any difference between the basis and the fair market value of the distributed property. In most situations, distributed property is appreciated, so its sale would result in a gain to the corporation. Distributions of property with a basis that differs from fair market value raise several tax questions.

LO.4

Evaluate the tax effects of property dividends on the recipient shareholder and the corporation making the distribution.

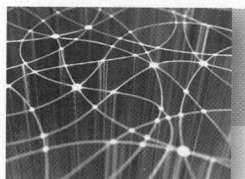

BRIDGE DISCIPLINE   Bridge to Investments

Most investors look to the stocks of utilities, real estate investment trusts, and tobacco companies as the source of steady dividend payments. This is a prudent decision on the investor's part, as the typical S&P 500 stock offers a dividend yield of about 2 percent. But an investor could put together an effective portfolio using only stocks and mutual funds that regularly produce higher dividend yields.

Dividends can be important to the investor because:

• They can be used in a tax-sheltered account, like a § 401(k) plan, such that the tax inefficiency of the dividends is not recognized immediately by the investor.

• Even today, about 40 percent of the total return from an investment can be traced to holding stocks that make regular distributions.

• Generally, a dividend-paying company is a profitable company, and corporate profits often are hard to come by.

• Earning and reinvesting dividends is an easy way to put into place an investment policy of dollar-cost averaging, a technique that forces the investor to buy more shares when prices are low and fewer shares when prices are high. Dollar-cost averaging often implements a contrarian investment strategy.

- For the shareholder:
  - What is the amount of the distribution?
  - What is the basis of the property in the shareholder's hands?
- For the corporation:
  - Is a gain or loss recognized as a result of the distribution?
  - What is the effect of the distribution on E & P?

13-3a Property Dividends—Effect on the Shareholder

When a corporation distributes property rather than cash to a shareholder, the amount distributed is measured by the fair market value of the property on the date of distribution.[12] As with a cash distribution, the portion of a property distribution covered by existing E & P is a dividend, and any excess is treated as a return of capital. If the fair market value of the property distributed exceeds the corporation's E & P and the shareholder's basis in the stock investment, a capital gain usually results.

The amount distributed is reduced by any liabilities to which the distributed property is subject immediately before and immediately after the distribution and by any liabilities of the corporation assumed by the shareholder. The basis in the distributed property to the shareholder is the fair market value of the property on the date of the distribution.

THE BIG PICTURE

Example 14

Return to the facts of *The Big Picture* on p. 13-1. Lime Corporation distributed property with a $300,000 fair market value and $20,000 adjusted basis to one of its shareholders, Gustavo. The property was subject to a $100,000 mortgage, which Gustavo assumed. As a result, Gustavo reports a distribution of $200,000 [$300,000 (fair market value) − $100,000 (liability)], which is taxed as a dividend. The basis of the property to Gustavo is $300,000, its fair market value.

Example 15

Red Corporation owns 10% of Tan Corporation. Tan has ample E & P to cover any distributions made during the year. One distribution made to Red consists of a vacant lot with a basis of $50,000 and a fair market value of $30,000. Red recognizes dividend income of $30,000 (before the dividends received deduction), and its basis in the lot becomes $30,000.

Distributing property that has depreciated in value as a property dividend may reflect poor income tax planning. Note what happens in Example 15. Basis of $20,000 disappears due to the loss (Tan's basis $50,000, fair market value $30,000). As an alternative, if Tan Corporation sells the lot, it can use the $20,000 loss to reduce its taxes. Then Tan can distribute the $30,000 cash proceeds to its shareholders.

13-3b Property Dividends—Effect on the Corporation

As noted earlier, the distribution of a property dividend raises two questions related to the corporation's tax position: Is a gain or loss recognized? What is the effect on E & P?

Recognition of Gain or Loss

All distributions of appreciated property generate gain to the distributing corporation.[13] In effect, a corporation that distributes appreciated property is treated as if it had sold the property to the shareholder for its fair market value. However, the distributing corporation does *not* recognize loss on distributions of property.

[12]§ 301.　　[13]§ 311.

Example 16

Return to the facts of *The Big Picture* on p. 13-1. Lime Corporation distributed property with a fair market value of $300,000 and an adjusted basis of $20,000 to Gustavo, one of its shareholders. As a result, Lime recognizes a $280,000 gain on the distribution.

Example 17

A corporation distributes land with a basis of $30,000 and a fair market value of $10,000. The corporation does not recognize a loss on the distribution.

If the distributed property is subject to a liability in excess of basis or the shareholder assumes such a liability, a special rule applies. For purposes of determining gain on the distribution, the fair market value of the property is treated as not being less than the amount of the liability.[14]

Example 18

Assume that the land in Example 17 is subject to a liability of $35,000, which is assumed by the shareholder who receives the land. The corporation recognizes gain of $5,000 on the distribution ($35,000 liability − $30,000 basis in the land).

Effect of Corporate Distributions on E & P

Corporate distributions reduce E & P by the amount of money distributed and by the greater of the fair market value or the adjusted basis of property distributed, less the amount of any liability on the property.[15] E & P is increased by gain recognized on appreciated property distributed as a property dividend.

Example 19

Crimson Corporation distributes property (basis $10,000 and fair market value $20,000) to Brenda, its shareholder. Crimson recognizes a $10,000 gain, which is added to its E & P. E & P then is reduced by $20,000, the fair market value of the distributed property. Brenda reports dividend income of $20,000 (presuming sufficient E & P).

Example 20

Assume the same facts as in Example 19, except that the property's adjusted basis in the hands of Crimson Corporation is $25,000. Crimson's E & P is reduced by $25,000, the property's adjusted basis. Brenda reports dividend income of $20,000 (the fair market value of the property received).

Example 21

Assume the same facts as in Example 20, except that the property is subject to a liability of $6,000, which Brenda assumes. E & P is now reduced by $19,000 [$25,000 (adjusted basis) − $6,000 (liability)]. Brenda records a dividend of $14,000 [$20,000 (amount of the distribution) − $6,000 (liability)], and her basis in the property is $20,000, its fair market value.

Under no circumstances can a distribution, whether cash or property, either generate a deficit in E & P or add to a deficit in E & P. Deficits can arise only through recognized corporate losses.

Example 22

Teal Corporation holds accumulated E & P of $10,000 at the beginning of the current tax year. During the year, it records current E & P of $15,000. At the end of the year, it distributes cash of $30,000 to its sole shareholder, Walter. Teal's E & P at the end of the year is zero. The accumulated E & P of $10,000 is increased by current E & P of $15,000 and reduced by the $25,000 dividend distribution. The remaining $5,000 of the distribution to Walter does not reduce E & P because a distribution cannot generate a deficit in E & P.

---

[14]§ 311(b)(2).

[15]§§ 312(a), (b), and (c).

BRIDGE DISCIPLINE   Bridge to Finance

The double tax on corporate income always has been controversial. Arguably, taxing dividends twice creates several undesirable economic distortions, including:

- An incentive to invest in noncorporate rather than corporate entities.
- An incentive for corporations to finance operations with debt rather than with equity because interest payments are deductible. Notably, this behavior increases the vulnerability of corporations in economic downturns because of higher leverage.
- An incentive for corporations to retain earnings and structure distributions of profits to avoid the double tax.

Collectively, these distortions raise the cost of capital for corporate investments. Eliminating the double corporate income tax would increase capital stock in the corporate sector by as much as $500 billion. In addition, elimination of the double tax would make the United States more competitive globally. Bear in mind that a majority of U.S. trading partners assess only one tax on corporate income.

While many support a reduced or zero tax rate on dividends, others contend that the double tax should remain in place because of the concentration of economic power held by publicly traded corporations. Furthermore, many of the distortions noted can be avoided through the use of deductible payments by C corporations (e.g., compensation, interest), and by utilizing other legal and tax forms of doing business (e.g., partnerships, limited liability entities, and S corporations). Those favoring retention of the double tax also note that the benefits of reduced tax rates on dividends flow disproportionately to the wealthy.

The United States continues to struggle to find the appropriate course to follow on the taxation of dividends. The reduced tax rate on **qualified dividends** for individuals reflects a compromise between the complete elimination of tax on dividends and the treatment of dividends as ordinary income.

Digging Deeper | In-depth coverage can be found on this book's companion website: **www.cengagebrain.com**

13-4 CONSTRUCTIVE DIVIDENDS

LO.5

Identify the nature and treatment of constructive dividends.

Any measurable economic benefit conveyed by a corporation to its shareholders can be treated as a dividend for Federal income tax purposes even though it is not formally declared or designated as a dividend. A so-called **constructive dividend** typically is not issued pro rata to all shareholders.[16] Nor must the distribution satisfy the legal requirements of a dividend as set forth by applicable state law.

Constructive dividends usually arise in the context of closely held corporations. Here the dealings between the parties are less structured, and frequently, formalities are not preserved. The constructive dividend might be seen as a substitute for actual distributions. Usually, it is intended to accomplish some tax objective not available through the use of direct dividends. The shareholders may be attempting to distribute corporate profits in a form deductible to the corporation, like compensation. Alternatively, the shareholders may be seeking benefits for themselves while avoiding the recognition of income. Some constructive dividends are, in reality, disguised dividends. But not all constructive dividends are deliberate attempts to avoid actual and formal dividends; many are inadvertent. Thus, an awareness of the various constructive dividend situations is essential to protect the parties from unanticipated, undesirable tax consequences.

---

[16]See *Lengsfield v. Comm.*, 57–1 USTC ¶9437, 50 AFTR 1683, 241 F.2d 508 (CA–5, 1957).

13-4a Types of Constructive Dividends

The most frequently encountered types of constructive dividends are summarized below and on the following pages.

Shareholder Use of Corporate-Owned Property

A constructive dividend can occur when a shareholder uses the corporation's property for personal purposes at no cost. Personal use of corporate-owned automobiles, airplanes, yachts, fishing camps, hunting lodges, and other entertainment facilities is commonplace in some closely held corporations. The shareholder has dividend income to the extent of the fair rental value of the property for the period of its personal use.[17]

Bargain Sale of Corporate Property to a Shareholder

Shareholders often purchase property from a corporation at a cost below the fair market value of the property. These bargain sales produce dividend income to the extent the property's fair market value on the date of sale differs from the amount the shareholder paid for the property.[18] These situations might be avoided by appraising the property on or about the date of the sale. The appraised value should become the price to be paid by the shareholder.

Bargain Rental of Corporate Property

A bargain rental of corporate property by a shareholder also produces dividend income. Here the measure of the constructive dividend is the excess of the property's fair rental value over the rent actually paid. Again, appraisal data should be used to avoid any questionable situations.

Payments for the Benefit of a Shareholder

If a corporation pays an obligation of a shareholder, the payment is treated as a constructive dividend. The obligation involved need not be legally binding on the shareholder; it may, in fact, be a moral obligation.[19] Forgiveness of shareholder indebtedness by the corporation creates an identical problem.[20] Excessive rentals paid by a corporation for the use of shareholder property also are treated as constructive dividends.

Unreasonable Compensation

A salary payment to a shareholder-employee that is deemed to be **unreasonable compensation** is frequently treated as a constructive dividend. As a consequence, it is not deductible by the corporation. In determining the reasonableness of salary payments, the following factors are considered.

- The employee's qualifications.
- A comparison of salaries with dividend distributions.
- The prevailing rates of compensation for comparable positions in comparable business concerns.
- The nature and scope of the employee's work.
- The size and complexity of the business.
- A comparison of salaries paid with both gross and net income.
- The taxpayer's salary policy toward all employees.
- For small corporations with a limited number of officers, the amount of compensation paid to the employee in question in previous years.
- For large corporations, whether a "reasonable investor" would have agreed to the level of compensation paid.[21]

[17]*Daniel L. Reeves*, 94 TCM 287, T.C.Memo. 2007–273.

[18]Reg. § 1.301–1(j).

[19]*Montgomery Engineering Co. v. U.S.*, 64–2 USTC ¶9618, 13 AFTR 2d 1747, 230 F.Supp. 838 (D.Ct. N.J., 1964), *aff'd* in 65–1 USTC ¶9368, 15 AFTR 2d 746, 344 F.2d 996 (CA–3, 1965).

[20]Reg. § 1.301–1(m).

[21]*Mayson Manufacturing Co. v. Comm.*, 49–2 USTC ¶9467, 38 AFTR 1028, 178 F.2d 115 (CA–6, 1949) and *Alpha Medical v. Comm.*, 99–1 USTC ¶50,461, 83 AFTR 2d 99–697, 172 F.3d 942 (CA–6, 1999).

Global Tax Issues

A Worldwide View of Dividends

From an international perspective, U.S. double taxation of dividends is unusual. Most developed countries have adopted a policy of corporate integration, which imposes a single tax on corporate profits. Corporate integration takes several forms. One popular approach is to impose a tax at the corporate level, but allow shareholders to claim a credit for corporate-level taxes paid when dividends are received. A second alternative is to allow a corporate-level deduction for dividends paid to shareholders. A third approach is to allow shareholders to exclude corporate dividends from income. A fourth alternative is the adoption of a "comprehensive business income tax," which excludes both dividend and interest income while disallowing deductions for interest expense.

Facing trade-offs between equity and the economic distortions introduced by the double tax and the prevalence of corporate integration throughout the world, the United States continues to struggle with the issue of how corporate distributions should be taxed.

Loans to Shareholders

Advances to shareholders that are not bona fide loans are constructive dividends. Whether an advance qualifies as a bona fide loan is a question of fact to be determined in light of the particular circumstances. Factors considered in determining whether the advance is a bona fide loan include the following.[22]

- Whether the advance is on open account or is evidenced by a written instrument.
- Whether the shareholder furnished collateral or other security for the advance.
- How long the advance has been outstanding.
- Whether any repayments have been made.
- The shareholder's ability to repay the advance.
- The shareholder's use of the funds (e.g., payment of routine bills versus non-recurring, extraordinary expenses).
- The regularity of the advances.
- The dividend-paying history of the corporation.

Even when a corporation makes a bona fide loan to a shareholder, a constructive dividend may be triggered, equal to the amount of any imputed (forgone) interest on the loan.[23] Imputed interest equals the amount of interest (using the rate the Federal government pays on new borrowings, compounded semiannually) that exceeds the interest charged on the loan. The corporation reports both interest income and a nondeductible dividend payment, and the shareholder records taxable dividend income and an interest payment.

Example 23

Mallard Corporation lends its principal shareholder, Henry, $100,000 on January 2 of the current year. The loan is interest-free and payable on demand. On December 31, the imputed interest rules are applied. Assuming that the Federal interest rate is 3%, compounded semiannually, the amount of imputed interest is $3,045. This amount is deemed paid by Henry to Mallard in the form of interest. Mallard is then deemed to return the amount to Henry as a constructive dividend.

Thus, Henry reports dividend income of $3,045, and perhaps a deduction for the interest deemed paid to Mallard. Mallard records interest income of $3,045 for the amount that it was deemed to have received, with no deduction for the dividend payment.

---

[22]*Fin Hay Realty Co. v. U.S.*, 68–2 USTC ¶9438, 22 AFTR 2d 5004, 398 F.2d 694 (CA–3, 1968).

[23]See § 7872. A more detailed discussion of imputed interest is found in Chapter 4.

TAX IN THE NEWS Hard Work Pays Off!

By 1985, William Rogers, a pharmacist with 25 years of experience in health care, had successfully developed and sold two businesses—a pharmacy chain and a medical supply company. In 1986, after turning down a $1 million offer to manage the home health care division of a large corporation, Rogers founded Alpha Medical, Inc., with a $1,000 contribution. Over the next four years, Rogers built Alpha Medical into a business with 60 employees, a taxable income of almost $7 million, and a 1990 return on equity of almost 100 percent. The business provided both financial management and medical consulting services to hospitals and home health care companies.

Rogers was the company's sole shareholder and president. He regularly worked 12 hours a day and was on call 24 hours a day. Rogers made all major decisions for Alpha Medical, acquired all of the company's clients, and personally negotiated all of the company's contracts. In addition, he personally developed many of the company's products and collaborated with programmers to develop proprietary software used by the company.

In 1986, Rogers received only $67,000 in compensation. The amount increased to $431,000 in 1988 and $928,000 in 1989. In 1990, Rogers was paid over $4.4 million, 64 percent of the company's taxable income, while the company paid only a $1,500 dividend.

During an audit of Alpha Medical, the IRS argued that only $400,000 of Rogers' compensation in 1990 was reasonable and that the remaining $4 million was not deductible. As a result, the IRS assessed a $1.3 million tax deficiency and an accuracy-related penalty.

The Tax Court split the difference between the IRS and the taxpayer, holding that $2.3 million of Rogers' pay was reasonable. On appeal, however, the Sixth Circuit Court of Appeals ruled that all $4.4 million of the compensation paid to Rogers was reasonable. In its decision, the Court of Appeals said that "in light of Rogers' record of accomplishment, risks he assumed, and amazing growth, reasonable shareholders would have gladly agreed to Rogers' level of compensation."

The Court of Appeals also explicitly noted that Rogers had been undercompensated in prior years and that he had incurred a substantial opportunity cost when he refused the $1 million job offer so that he could start Alpha Medical.

Loans to a Corporation by Shareholders

Shareholder loans to a corporation may be reclassified as equity if the debt has too many features of stock. Any interest and principal payments made by the corporation to the shareholder are then treated as constructive dividends. This topic was covered more thoroughly in the discussion of "thin capitalization" in Chapter 12.

13-4b Tax Treatment of Constructive Dividends

For tax purposes, constructive distributions are treated the same as actual distributions.[24] Thus, a corporate shareholder is entitled to the dividends received deduction (refer to Chapter 12). The constructive distribution is taxable as a dividend only to the extent of the corporation's current and accumulated E & P. The burden rests with the taxpayer to prove that the distribution constitutes a return of capital because of inadequate E & P.[25]

In-depth coverage can be found on this book's companion website: **www.cengagebrain.com**   2   Digging Deeper

When testing for reasonableness, the IRS looks at the total compensation package, including indirect compensation payments to a shareholder-employee. Thus, indirect payments must not be overlooked.

---

[24]*Simon v. Comm.*, 57–2 USTC ¶9989, 52 AFTR 698, 248 F.2d 869 (CA–8, 1957).

[25]*DiZenzo v. Comm.*, 65–2 USTC ¶9518, 16 AFTR 2d 5107, 348 F.2d 122 (CA–2, 1965).

Tax Planning Strategies	CONSTRUCTIVE DIVIDENDS

FRAMEWORK FOCUS: INCOME AND EXCLUSIONS

Strategy: Avoid Income Recognition.

Tax planning can be particularly effective in avoiding constructive dividend situations. Shareholders should try to structure their dealings with the corporation on an arm's length basis. For example, reasonable rent should be paid for the use of corporate property, and a fair price should be paid for its purchase. The parties should make every effort to support the amount involved with appraisal data or market information obtained from reliable sources at or near the time of the transaction.

Dealings between shareholders and a closely held corporation should be as formal as possible. In the case of loans to shareholders, for example, the parties should provide for an adequate rate of interest and written evidence of the debt. Shareholders also should establish and follow a realistic repayment schedule.

If shareholders want to distribute corporate profits in a form deductible to the corporation, a balanced mix of the possible alternatives lessens the risk of constructive dividend treatment. Rent for the use of shareholder property, interest on amounts borrowed from shareholders, or salaries for services rendered by shareholders are all feasible substitutes for dividend distributions. But overdoing any one approach may attract the attention of the IRS. Too much interest, for example, may mean that the corporation is thinly capitalized, and some of the debt may be reclassified as equity.

Much can be done to protect against the disallowance of unreasonable compensation. Example 24 is an illustration, all too common in a family corporation, of what *not* to do.

Example 24

Bob Cole wholly owns Eagle Corporation. Corporate employees and annual salaries include Rebecca, Bob's wife ($120,000); Sam, Bob's son ($80,000); Bob ($640,000); and Ed, an unrelated long-time friend ($320,000). The operation of Eagle is shared about equally between Bob and Ed. Rebecca performed significant services for Eagle during its formative years but now merely attends the annual meeting of the board of directors. Sam is a full-time student and occasionally signs papers for the corporation in his capacity as treasurer.

Eagle has not made a cash distribution for 10 years, although it has accumulated substantial E & P. Rebecca, Sam, and Bob run the risk of a finding of unreasonable compensation, based on the following factors.

- Rebecca's salary is vulnerable unless proof is available that some or all of her $120,000 annual salary is payment for services rendered to the corporation in prior years and that she was underpaid for those years.[26]
- Sam's salary also is vulnerable; he does not appear to earn the $80,000 paid to him by the corporation. Although neither Sam nor Rebecca is a shareholder, each one's relationship to Bob is enough of a tie-in to raise the unreasonable compensation issue.
- Bob's salary appears susceptible to challenge. Why is he receiving $320,000 more than Ed when it appears that they share equally in the operation of the corporation?
- The fact that Eagle has not distributed any cash over the past 10 years, even though it is capable of doing so, increases the likelihood of a constructive dividend. ■

What could have been done to improve the tax position of the parties in Example 24? Rebecca and Sam are not entitled to a salary, as neither seems to be performing any services for the corporation. Paying them a salary simply aggravates the problem. The IRS is more apt to consider *all* of the salaries to members of the family as being excessive under the circumstances. Bob probably should reduce his compensation to correspond to that paid to Ed. He then can attempt to distribute corporate earnings to himself in some other form.

Paying some dividends to Bob also would help alleviate the problems raised in Example 24. The IRS has been successful in denying a deduction for salary paid to a shareholder-employee, even when the payment was reasonable, in a situation where the corporation had not distributed any dividends.[27] Most courts, however, have not denied deductions for compensation solely because a dividend was not paid. A better approach is to compare an employee's compensation with the level of compensation prevalent in the particular industry.

The corporation can substitute *indirect* compensation for Bob by paying expenses that benefit him personally but are nevertheless deductible to the corporation. For example, premiums paid by the corporation for sickness, accident, and hospitalization insurance for Bob are deductible to the corporation and generally nontaxable to him.[28] Any payments under the policy are not taxable to Bob unless they exceed his medical expenses.[29]

The corporation also can pay for travel and entertainment expenses incurred by Bob on behalf of the corporation. If these expenditures are primarily for the benefit of the corporation, Bob recognizes no taxable income, and the corporation claims a deduction.[30] The tax treatment of these benefits is discussed in more detail in Chapter 11.

---

[26]See, for example, *R. J. Nicoll Co.*, 59 T.C. 37 (1972).

[27]*McCandless Tile Service v. U.S.*, 70–1 USTC ¶9284, 25 AFTR 2d 70–870, 422 F.2d 1336 (Ct.Cls., 1970). The court in *McCandless* concluded that a return on equity of 15% of net profits was reasonable.

[28]Reg. § 1.162–10.

[29]The medical reimbursement plan must meet certain nondiscrimination requirements. § 105(h)(2).

[30]Reg. § 1.62–2(c)(4).

FINANCIAL DISCLOSURE INSIGHTS Dividend Payments React to Tax Law Changes

Recurring dividend payments are rare, but U.S. C corporations can pay dividends when they want to. A decade ago, when the tax law allowed a one-time exclusion for 85 percent of dividends repatriated from overseas subsidiaries, suddenly large corporate taxpayers responded. About 1,000 U.S. C corporations increased their dividend payments for the year by more than $300 billion over their average annual payments to shareholders. As a result, attributable Federal corporate income tax revenues increased by about $16 billion.

Some politicians are calling for adoption of another *tax holiday* of this sort, as a means of increasing U.S. jobs and decreasing the country's budget deficits. Estimates are that Apple, Cisco, Google, and Microsoft alone have about $320 billion of cash overseas, and similar cash stockpiles can be found in the pharmaceutical, energy, and financial industries. Could a second tax holiday on dividends paid from offshore act as another economic stimulus and create thousands of new jobs, as some expect?

Some observers maintain that strings should be attached to the repatriated funds if the corporation is to enjoy the tax holiday. Oversight measures should be enacted, they say, to make certain the funds are not used for executive compensation or stock buybacks, as it appears was the case with the first tax holiday. The funds should be traceable to hiring, research, and infrastructure spending.

A second tax holiday might be more productive than the first, in terms of both tax revenues and job creation, if the law is written and administered properly.

Example 25

Cora, the president and sole shareholder of Willet Corporation, is paid an annual salary of $100,000 by the corporation. Cora would like to draw funds from the corporation but is concerned that additional salary payments might cause the IRS to contend that her salary is unreasonable.

Cora does not want Willet to pay any dividends. She also wants to donate $50,000 to her alma mater to establish scholarships for needy students. Willet Corporation could make the contribution on Cora's behalf. The payment clearly benefits Cora, but the amount of the contribution is not taxed to her.[31] Willet claims a charitable contribution deduction for the payment.

Example 26

Assume in Example 25 that Cora has made an individual pledge to the university to provide $50,000 for scholarships for needy students. Willet Corporation satisfies Cora's pledge by paying the $50,000 to the university. The $50,000 will be taxed to Cora. In this context, the $50,000 payment to the university may be treated as *indirect* compensation to Cora.[32]

In determining whether Cora's salary is unreasonable, both the *direct* payment of $100,000 and the *indirect* $50,000 payment are considered. Cora's total compensation package is $150,000. Cora may be eligible for a charitable contribution deduction of up to 50% of her adjusted gross income (see Chapter 10).

Certain activities can combine both business and personal dimensions (e.g., a business trip to Hawaii). A country club membership can generate both business and personal use. Such items can be attractive as forms of indirect compensation, but disentangling the business and personal use of business assets can be a challenge.

In fact, many companies have policies that allow for the "limited personal use" of certain corporate assets (such as computers, telephones, mobile devices, copy machines, conference rooms, and vehicles). This "limited personal use" exception is normally provided as long as the use is occasional, is not for outside employment, does not result in excessive costs, and does not interfere with work responsibilities. Ultimately, whether a constructive dividend exists when indirect compensation is

---

[31]*Henry J. Knott,* 67 T.C. 681 (1977).

[32]*Schalk Chemical Co. v. Comm.,* 62–1 USTC ¶9496, 9 AFTR 2d 1579, 304 F.2d 48 (CA–9, 1962).

used often depends on the employer's policies and related documentation substantiating some business justification for the usage.

13-5 STOCK DIVIDENDS

LO.6

Distinguish between taxable and nontaxable stock dividends.

On occasion, a C corporation issues a dividend in the form of its own stock (i.e., instead of using cash or other property). This may occur because the entity is short of cash or because it wants to dispose of some treasury stock that it holds. A **stock dividend** is triggered by a board directive. Stock dividends are rare events; about 2 percent of all C corporation distributions during a typical tax year involve the corporation's own shares.

As a general rule, stock dividends are excluded from income if they are pro rata distributions of stock or stock rights paid on common stock.[33] However, there are exceptions to this general rule.

Digging Deeper   3   In-depth coverage can be found on this book's companion website: **www.cengagebrain.com**

If a stock dividend is not taxable, the corporation's E & P is not reduced.[34] If a stock dividend is taxable, the distributing corporation treats the distribution in the same manner as any other taxable distribution.

If a stock dividend is taxable, the shareholder's basis of the newly received shares is fair market value and the holding period starts on the date of receipt. If a stock dividend is not taxable, the basis of the stock on which the dividend is distributed is reallocated.[35] If the dividend shares are identical to these formerly held shares, basis in the old stock is reallocated by dividing the taxpayer's cost in the old stock by the total number of shares. If the dividend stock is not identical to the underlying shares (e.g., a stock dividend of preferred on common), basis is determined by allocating the basis of the formerly held shares between the old and new stock according to the fair market value of each. The holding period includes the holding period of the previously held stock.[36]

Example 27	Gail bought 1,000 shares of common stock two years ago for $10,000. In the current tax year, Gail receives 10 shares of common stock as a nontaxable stock dividend. Gail's basis of $10,000 is divided by 1,010. Consequently, each share of stock has a basis of $9.90 instead of the pre-dividend $10 basis.

Example 28	Assume instead that Gail received a nontaxable preferred stock dividend of 100 shares. The preferred stock has a fair market value of $1,000, and the common stock, on which the preferred is distributed, has a fair market value of $19,000. After the receipt of the stock dividend, the basis of the common stock is $9,500, and the basis of the preferred is $500, computed as follows.

Fair market value of common	$19,000
Fair market value of preferred	1,000
	$20,000
Basis of common: $19/20 \times \$10,000$	$ 9,500
Basis of preferred: $1/20 \times \$10,000$	$ 500

---

[33]Companies often issue stock dividends or authorize stock splits to keep the stock price in an affordable range. Stock splits do not change the total value of an investment. For example, 100 shares at $100 will become 200 shares at $50 after the split. However, some studies show that a stock split often leads to an upward price trend over the year following the split.

[34]§ 312(d)(1).
[35]§ 307(a).
[36]§ 1223(5).

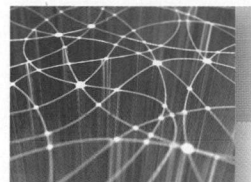

BRIDGE DISCIPLINE   Bridge to Finance

Stock buybacks are popular among U.S. corporations as a means to manipulate share prices. If a buyback is executed properly, all shareholders retain their respective levels of control over the entity, but because fewer shares now are available on the market, an artificial increase in share price occurs. Often, the market temporarily "overcorrects" for the buyback, probably because of the publicity the transaction attracts in the press, and the corporation's total capitalized value actually increases.

Most stock buybacks result in dividend income to the shareholders. Stock redemptions of this type generally do not qualify for capital gain/loss treatment under the tax law. Thus, parties must measure the costs associated with an effective distribution of retained earnings in this way. If dividend income is subject to a favorable tax rate or if the corporate owner of the redeemed shares qualifies for the dividends received deduction, there are few impediments to the plans for the buyback.

Some analysts see an increase in stock buyback activity as a sign of an increasingly healthy economy. A combination of large corporate cash balances and low market interest rates tends to accelerate the buyback market. Even Berkshire Hathaway began buyback activity recently, and the market may have seen that development alone as a sign that there would not be another recession in the near future.

© iStockphoto.com/enot-poloskun

In-depth coverage can be found on this book's companion website: **www.cengagebrain.com**    **4** | Digging Deeper

13-6 STOCK REDEMPTIONS

LO.7

Discuss the tax treatment of stock redemptions and corporate liquidations.

Many investors are tempted to use a "no dividends" strategy in working with a healthy corporation whose accumulated profits and market value continue to rise over time.

> **Example 29**
>
> Sally invests $100,000 in the new Cream Corporation. Cream is successful in generating operating profits, and it reinvests its accumulated profits in the business rather than paying dividends. Fifteen years later, Sally's shares are worth $300,000, and her share of Cream's E & P exceeds $1 million. Sally sells the shares for a $200,000 long-term capital gain, taxed at a rate of only 20%. By selling her stock to a third party, Sally can reduce the sales proceeds by her stock basis, resulting in a significant tax savings to her, at no detriment to Cream.

A similar strategy would seem to work where several shareholders can act in concert. Using a **stock redemption** to carry out this strategy, the corporation buys back shares from its shareholders in a market transaction. Stock redemptions occur for numerous reasons, including the following.

- To acquire the holdings of a retiring or deceased shareholder.
- To carry out a property settlement related to a divorce.
- To increase the per-share price of the stock as it trades in a market.
- To implement a business succession plan (e.g., using a buy-sell agreement to transfer shares from one generation of shareholders to a younger one).

> **Example 30**
>
> Mike and Cheryl are husband and wife, and each owns 100 shares in Mauve Corporation, the total of all of Mauve's outstanding stock. Mauve's operations have produced a sizable aggregated operating profit over the years, such that its E & P exceeds $5 million. Mike and Cheryl have realized appreciation of $600,000 on their original investment of $100,000 each, and they would like to enjoy some of the cash that Mauve has accumulated during their holding period. At Mike's request, instead of paying a dividend, Mauve buys back one-half of Mike's shares for $350,000. This seems to produce a $300,000 long-term capital gain [$350,000 (sales proceeds) − $50,000 (basis in 50 shares of Mauve stock)], rather than a $350,000 dividend for Mike.

Stock redemptions, however, generally result in dividend income for the shareholder whose stock is redeemed, rather than a sale or exchange, unless the shareholder surrenders significant control in the entity as a result of the redemption. Section 302 allows sale or exchange treatment where either:

- All of the shareholder's stock is redeemed.[37]
- After the redemption, the investor is a minority shareholder and owns less than 80 percent of the interest owned in the corporation before the redemption.[38]

Digging Deeper   5   In-depth coverage can be found on this book's companion website: **www.cengagebrain.com**

When the transaction is treated as a dividend, the investor's basis in the redeemed shares *does not disappear* but attaches to any remaining shares that he or she owns. Corporate E & P is reduced by the amount of any dividend.

Some redemptions can be structured so that shareholders recognize a capital gain, not a dividend.[39] In measuring the investor's stock holdings before and after the redemption, shares owned by related taxpayers also are counted.[40]

Digging Deeper   6   In-depth coverage can be found on this book's companion website: **www.cengagebrain.com**

Other tax consequences for the redeeming corporation are summarized as follows.

- If noncash property is used to acquire the redeemed shares, the corporation recognizes any realized gain (but not loss) on the distributed assets.[41]
- When the shareholder is taxed as having received a capital gain, E & P of the redeeming corporation *disappears* to the extent of the percentage of shares redeemed relative to the shares outstanding before the buyback.[42]

Thus, a dividend likely results in Example 30. The strategy illustrated in Example 29, though, can be effective in avoiding dividend income and converting it instead into a long-term capital gain.

Tax Planning Strategies   **STOCK REDEMPTIONS**

FRAMEWORK FOCUS: TAX RATES

Strategy: Control the Character of Income and Deductions.

Stock redemptions offer several possibilities for tax planning.

- Usually a stock redemption triggers dividend treatment. A preferential tax rate on dividend income reduces some of the adverse consequences of a nonqualified stock redemption for noncorporate shareholders.
- Dividend treatment for a stock redemption may be preferable to a redemption that produces a capital gain if the distributing corporation has little or no E & P, or where the distributee-shareholder is another C corporation. In the latter situation, dividend treatment may be preferred due to the availability of the dividends received deduction.

- Stock redemptions are particularly well suited for purchasing the interest of a retiring or deceased shareholder. Rather than the remaining shareholders buying the stock of the retiring or deceased shareholder, corporate funds are used to redeem the stock from the retiring shareholder or from the decedent shareholder's estate. A corporate buy-sell agreement can be used to effect a redemption of a retiring or deceased shareholder's stock. The ability to use the corporation's funds to buy out a shareholder's interest also can be advantageous in property settlements between divorcing taxpayers.

---

[37]§ 302(b)(3).

[38]§ 302(b)(2).

[39]For example, see §§ 302(b)(1), 302(b)(4), and 303.

[40]Section 318 is used for this purpose.

[41]§ 311.

[42]The E & P reduction cannot exceed the amount of the redemption proceeds. § 312(n)(7).

Non-U.S. Shareholders Prefer Capital Gain Treatment in Stock Redemptions

Global Tax Issues

© iStockphoto.com/Andrey Prokhorov

As a general rule, non-U.S. shareholders of U.S. corporations are subject to U.S. income tax on dividend income but not on capital gains. In some situations, a nonresident alien or business entity is taxed on a capital gain from the disposition of stock in a U.S. corporation, but only if the stock was effectively connected with the conduct of a U.S. trade or business of the individual.

Whether a stock redemption qualifies for capital gain treatment therefore takes on added significance for non-U.S. shareholders. If one of the qualifying stock redemption rules can be satisfied, the foreign shareholder typically will avoid U.S. income tax on the transaction. If, instead, dividend income is the result, a 30 percent withholding tax typically applies.

13-7 CORPORATE LIQUIDATIONS

When a corporation makes a nonliquidating distribution (e.g., a cash dividend or a stock redemption), the entity typically continues as a going concern. With a complete liquidation, however, corporate existence terminates, as does the shareholder's ownership interest. A complete liquidation, like a qualifying stock redemption, produces sale or exchange treatment to the *shareholder*. However, the tax effects of a liquidation to the *corporation* vary somewhat from those of a redemption. Gain/loss treatment is the general rule for the liquidating corporation, although some losses are disallowed.

13-7a The Liquidation Process

A **corporate liquidation** exists when a corporation ceases to be a going concern. The corporation continues solely to wind up its affairs, pay debts, and distribute any remaining assets to its shareholders. Legal dissolution under state law is not required for a liquidation to be complete for tax purposes. A liquidation can exist even if the corporation retains a nominal amount of assets to pay remaining debts and preserve legal status.[43]

Shareholders may decide to liquidate a corporation for one or more reasons, including the following.

- The corporate business has been unsuccessful.
- The shareholders want to acquire the corporation's assets.
- Another person or entity wants to purchase the corporation's assets. The purchaser may buy the shareholders' stock and then liquidate the corporation to acquire the assets. Alternatively, the purchaser may buy the assets directly from the corporation. After the assets are sold, the corporation distributes the sales proceeds to its shareholders and liquidates.

13-7b Liquidating and Nonliquidating Distributions Compared

As noted previously, a *nonliquidating* property distribution, whether in the form of a dividend or a stock redemption, triggers gain (but not loss) to the distributing

---

[43]Reg. § 1.332–2(c).

corporation. For the shareholder, the receipt of cash or property produces dividend income to the extent of the corporation's E & P or, in the case of a qualifying stock redemption, results in sale or exchange treatment.

Like a qualifying stock redemption, a complete *liquidation* produces sale or exchange treatment for the shareholders. E & P has no effect on the gain or loss to be recognized by the shareholder in either type of distribution.[44] However, a complete liquidation produces different tax consequences to the liquidating corporation. With certain exceptions, a liquidating corporation recognizes gain *and* loss upon the distribution of its assets.

Example 31

Goose Corporation, with an E & P balance of $40,000, makes a cash distribution of $50,000 to one of its shareholders. The shareholder's basis in the Goose stock is $24,000. If the distribution is not a qualifying stock redemption or in complete liquidation, the shareholder recognizes dividend income of $40,000 (the amount of Goose's E & P) and treats the remaining $10,000 of the distribution as a return of capital (i.e., stock basis is reduced to $14,000). If the distribution is a qualifying stock redemption or is pursuant to a complete liquidation, the shareholder recognizes a capital gain of $26,000 ($50,000 distribution − $24,000 stock basis). In the latter case, Goose's E & P is of no consequence to the tax result to the shareholder.

Digging Deeper 7 In-depth coverage can be found on this book's companion website: **www.cengagebrain.com**

Tax Planning Strategies CORPORATE LIQUIDATIONS

FRAMEWORK FOCUS: TAX RATES

Strategy: Avoid Double Taxation.

Usually, distributions in liquidation are taxed at both the corporate level and the shareholder level. When a corporation liquidates, it can, as a general rule, claim losses on assets that have depreciated in value. These assets should not be distributed in the form of a property dividend or stock redemption, because losses are not recognized on nonliquidating distributions.

Shareholders faced with large prospective gains in a liquidation may consider shifting part or all of that gain to other taxpayers. One approach is to donate the liquidating corporation's stock to charity. A charitable contribution of

the stock can produce a deduction equal to the stock's fair market value.

Alternatively, the stock may be transferred by gift to family members. Some or all of the later capital gain on liquidation could be taxed at a lower tax rate on long-term capital gains. However, possible gift tax issues on the stock transfer must be considered (see Chapter 1). Effective planning for stock transfers in the context of a liquidation therefore is crucial in arriving at the desired tax result.

13-8 RESTRICTIONS ON CORPORATE ACCUMULATIONS

Two provisions of the Code are designed to prevent corporations and their shareholders from avoiding the double tax on dividend distributions. Both provisions impose a penalty tax on undistributed income retained by the corporation. The rules underlying these provisions are complex and beyond the scope of this text. However, a brief description is provided as an introduction.

---

[44]§ 331.

TAX IN THE NEWS Closing a Chapter of a Good Book(store)

In 1971, two brothers, Tom and Louis Borders, opened a used bookstore in Ann Arbor, Michigan. By 2010, the Borders bookstore brand had expanded into a conglomerate (the Borders Group) that operated over 650 Borders and Waldenbooks bookstores and employed over 19,000 people. Unable to compete profitably in the digital era, where more and more consumers buy and read their books electronically, the Borders Group filed for bankruptcy in February 2011 and closed its stores for good in September 2011.

As is common with liquidations of large concerns, third-party liquidators handled the actual disposition of Borders' remaining assets (e.g., book and music inventory, fixtures, furniture, and equipment). A consortium of liquidators won the liquidation rights with a bid that was expected to pay Borders' creditors a minimum of $252 million. To generate a profit for their work, the liquidators would need to sell Borders' assets for an amount that exceeded any guaranteed minimum payout to those creditors. This fact probably was lost on customers who went to their neighborhood Borders during the liquidation sale in search of steep discounts on popular books and music.

The *accumulated earnings tax*[45] imposes a 20 percent tax on the current year's corporate earnings that have been accumulated without a reasonable business need. The burden of proving what constitutes a reasonable need is borne by the taxpayer. In determining the excessive accumulated income, most businesses are allowed a $250,000 minimum exemption. Thus, most corporations can accumulate $250,000 in earnings over a series of years without fear of an accumulated earnings tax. Beyond the exemption amount, a C corporation's earnings can be accumulated, without incurring the penalty tax, for:

- Working capital needs (to purchase inventory),
- Retirement of debt incurred in connection with the business,
- Investment or loans to suppliers or customers (if necessary to maintain the corporation's business), or
- Realistic business contingencies, including lawsuits or self-insurance.

The *personal holding company (PHC) tax*[46] was enacted to discourage the sheltering of certain kinds of passive income in corporations owned by individuals with high marginal tax rates. Historically, the tax was aimed at "incorporated pocketbooks" that were frequently found in the entertainment and construction industries. For example, a taxpayer could shelter income from securities in a corporation, which would pay no dividends, and allow the corporation's stock to increase in value.

Like the accumulated earnings tax, the PHC tax employs a 20 percent rate and is designed to force a corporation to distribute earnings to shareholders. However, in any single year, the IRS cannot impose both the PHC tax and the accumulated earnings tax. Generally, a company is considered a PHC and may be subject to the tax if:

- More than 50 percent of the value of the outstanding stock was owned by five or fewer individuals at any time during the last half of the year, and
- A substantial portion (60 percent or more) of the corporation's income is comprised of passive types of income, including dividends, interest, rents, royalties, or certain personal service income.

---

[45]§§ 531–537.

[46]§§ 541–547.

REFOCUS ON THE BIG PICTURE

TAXING CORPORATE DISTRIBUTIONS

A number of factors affect the tax treatment of Lime Corporation's distributions. The amount of current and accumulated E & P (which differs from the financial reporting concept of retained earnings) partially determines the tax effect on the shareholders. Given that Lime had a highly profitable year, it is possible that current E & P equals or exceeds the amount of the distributions. If so, they are dividends to the shareholders rather than a return of capital.

Orange Corporation receives $200,000 of dividend income that is mostly offset by the dividends received deduction. The amount of the offsetting deduction depends on the ownership percentage that Orange holds in Lime. In this situation, Orange likely would qualify for a dividends received deduction of $160,000 ($200,000 × 80%). Gustavo has $200,000 of dividend income (i.e., $300,000 value of the real estate less the $100,000 mortgage). Assuming that Lime is a domestic corporation and that Gustavo has held his stock for the entire year, the distribution is a qualified dividend. As a result, the dividend is subject to reduced income tax rates. Gustavo's basis in the real estate is its fair market value at distribution, or $300,000.

From Lime's perspective, the distribution of the appreciated property triggers a recognized gain, equal to $280,000 ($300,000 fair market value less $20,000 adjusted basis). While the gain increases Lime's E & P, the distributions to the shareholders reduce it by $200,000 for the cash and $200,000 for the real estate ($300,000 fair market value reduced by the $100,000 mortgage).

What If?

What if the balance of current E & P is less than the cash and real estate distributed to the shareholders? Current E & P is applied pro rata to the cash and the real estate. Because the amounts received by the two shareholders are equal ($200,000 each), the current E & P applied is taxed as a dividend and is treated as described above. To the extent the distributions are not paid from current E & P, accumulated E & P is applied in a pro rata fashion (both distributions were made on December 31). However, if Lime reports a deficit in accumulated E & P, the remaining amounts distributed to the two shareholders are first a tax-free recovery of stock basis, and any excess is taxed as a sale of the stock (probably classified as capital gain).

© Alexander Raths/Shutterstock.com

Suggested Readings

Julie Allen, et al., "The Forgotten Impact of Accounting Methods When Computing E & P," *Corporate Taxation*, September/October 2010.

Michelle A. Kassab, "$17.4 Million Bonus Was Reasonable," *Journal of Taxation*, December 2009.

Shawn Novak and Mark Persellin, "Redemption Costs: The Disallowance Provision of § 162(k)," *Corporate Taxation*, January/February 2008.

John C. Ramirez, "Reasonable Compensation for Corporate Owner/Employees," *Valuation Strategies*, July/August 2012.

Edward J. Schnee and W. Eugene Seago, "Constructive Dividends from Related Entities: The Distributing Corporation's Issues," *Journal of Taxation*, March 2010.

Key Terms

Accumulated E & P, 13-3

Constructive dividend, 13-14

Corporate liquidation, 13-23

Current E & P, 13-3

Dividend, 13-2

Earnings and profits, 13-2

Property dividend, 13-11

Qualified dividends, 13-14

Stock dividend, 13-20

Stock redemption, 13-21

Unreasonable compensation, 13-15

Problems

1. **LO.1, 3** At the start of the current year, Blue Corporation (a calendar year taxpayer) holds accumulated E & P of $100,000. Blue's current E & P is $60,000. At the end of the year, it distributes $200,000 ($100,000 each) to its equal shareholders, Pam and Jon. Their basis in the stock is $11,000 for Pam and $26,000 for Jon. How is the distribution treated for tax purposes?

2. **LO.2** Cardinal Corporation, a calendar year taxpayer, receives dividend income of $250,000 from a corporation in which it holds a 10% interest. Cardinal also receives interest income of $35,000 from municipal bonds. (The municipality used the proceeds from the bond issue to construct a public library.) Cardinal borrowed funds to purchase the municipal bonds and pays $20,000 of interest on the loan. Excluding these items, Cardinal's taxable income is $500,000.
   a. What is Cardinal's taxable income after these items are taken into account?
   b. What is Cardinal's accumulated E & P at the start of next year if its beginning balance this year is $150,000?

3. **LO.2** Compute current E & P for Sparrow Corporation (a calendar year, accrual basis taxpayer). Sparrow reported the following transactions during 2014, its second year of operation.

Taxable income	$330,000
Federal income tax liability paid	112,000
Tax-exempt interest income	5,000
Meals and entertainment expenses (total)	3,000
Premiums paid on key employee life insurance	3,500
Increase in cash surrender value attributable to life insurance premiums	700
Proceeds from key employee life insurance policy	130,000
Cash surrender value of life insurance policy at distribution	20,000
Excess of capital losses over capital gains	13,000
MACRS deduction	26,000
Straight-line depreciation using ADS lives	16,000
Section 179 expense elected during 2013	100,000
Dividends received from domestic corporations (less than 20% owned)	25,000

   • Sparrow uses the LIFO inventory method, and its LIFO recapture amount increased by $10,000 during 2014.
   • Sparrow sold some property on installments during 2013. The property was sold for $40,000 and had an adjusted basis then of $32,000. During 2014, Sparrow received a $15,000 payment on the installment sale.

4. **LO.1, 2, 3** On September 30, Silver Corporation, a calendar year taxpayer, sold a parcel of land (basis of $400,000) for a $1 million note. The note is payable in five installments, with the first payment due next year. Because Silver did not elect out of the installment method, none of the $600,000 gain is taxed this year.

Silver Corporation had a $300,000 deficit in accumulated E & P at the beginning of the year. Before considering the effect of the land sale, Silver had a deficit in current E & P of $50,000.

Sam, the sole shareholder of Silver, has a basis of $200,000 in his stock. If Silver distributes $900,000 to Sam on December 31, how much income must he report for tax purposes?

5. **LO.2** In determining Blue Corporation's current E & P for 2014, how should taxable income be adjusted as a result of the following transactions?
   a. A capital loss carryover from 2013, fully used in 2014.
   b. Nondeductible meal expenses in 2014.
   c. Interest on municipal bonds received in 2014.
   d. Nondeductible lobbying expenses in 2014.
   e. Loss on a sale between related parties in 2014.
   f. Federal income tax refund received in 2014.

6. **LO.I, 3** Sparrow Corporation is a calendar year taxpayer. At the beginning of the current year, Sparrow holds accumulated E & P of $33,000. The corporation incurs a deficit in current E & P of $46,000 that accrues ratably throughout the year. On June 30, Sparrow distributes $20,000 to its sole shareholder, Libby. If Libby's stock has a basis of $4,000, how is she taxed on the distribution?

7. **LO.I, 3** Complete the following schedule for each case. Unless otherwise indicated, assume that the shareholders have ample basis in the stock investment. All taxpayers use a calendar tax year.

	Accumulated E & P Beginning of Year	Current E & P	Cash Distributions (All on Last Day of Year)	Dividend Income	Return of Capital
a.	($200,000)	$ 70,000	$130,000	$_____	$_____
b.	150,000	(120,000)	210,000	_____	_____
c.	90,000	70,000	150,000	_____	_____
d.	120,000	(60,000)	130,000	_____	_____
e.	Same as (d), except that the distribution of $130,000 is made on June 30.			_____	_____

8. **LO.I, 3** Larry, the sole shareholder of Brown Corporation, sold his stock to Ed on July 30 for $270,000. Larry's basis in the stock was $200,000 at the beginning of the year. Brown had accumulated E & P of $120,000 on January 1 and current E & P of $240,000. During the year, Brown made the following distributions: $450,000 cash to Larry on July 1 and $150,000 cash to Ed on December 30. How will Larry and Ed be taxed on the distributions? How much gain will Larry recognize on the sale of his stock to Ed?

9. **LO.I, 2** In each of the following independent situations, indicate the effect on taxable income and E & P, stating the amount of any increase (or decrease) in each as a result of the transaction. Assume that E & P has already been increased by taxable income.

Transaction	Taxable Income Increase (Decrease)	E & P Increase (Decrease)
a. Realized gain of $80,000 on involuntary conversion of building ($10,000 of gain is recognized).	_____	_____
b. Mining exploration costs incurred on May 1 of current year; $24,000 is deductible from current-year taxable income.	_____	_____

Transaction	Taxable Income Increase (Decrease)	E & P Increase (Decrease)
c. Sale of equipment to unrelated third party for $240,000; basis is $120,000 (no election out of installment method; no payments are received in current year).	_____	_____
d. Dividends of $20,000 received from 5% owned corporation, together with dividends received deduction (assume that the taxable income limit does not apply).	_____	_____
e. Domestic production activities deduction of $45,000 claimed in current year.	_____	_____
f. Section 179 expense deduction of $100,000 in current year.	_____	_____
g. Continue with the facts of (f) for the next tax year.	_____	_____
h. MACRS depreciation of $80,000. ADS depreciation would have been $90,000.	_____	_____
i. Federal income taxes of $80,000 paid in current year.	_____	_____

10. **LO.2** Penguin Corporation (a cash basis, calendar year taxpayer) recorded the following income and expenses in the current year.

Income from services	$400,000
Salaries paid to employees	70,000
Tax-exempt interest income	24,000
Dividends from a corporation in which Penguin holds a 12% interest	40,000
Short-term capital loss on the sale of stock	17,000
Estimated Federal income taxes paid	110,000

Penguin purchased seven-year MACRS property in the current year for $80,000. No § 179 election was made. The property has a 10-year ADR midpoint life. Determine Penguin's taxable income and current E & P.

11. **LO.1, 3** At the beginning of the year, Teal Corporation held E & P of $225,000. On March 30, Teal sold an asset at a loss of $225,000. For the calendar year, Teal incurred a deficit in current E & P of $305,000, which includes the $225,000 loss on the sale of the asset. If Teal made a distribution of $50,000 to its sole shareholder on April 1, how is the shareholder taxed?

12. **LO.1, 3** Green Corporation (a calendar year taxpayer) had a deficit in accumulated E & P of $250,000 at the beginning of the current year. Its net profit for the period January 1 through July 30 was $300,000, but its E & P for the entire taxable year was only $40,000. If Green made a distribution of $60,000 to its sole shareholder on August 1, how will the shareholder be taxed?

13. **LO.1, 3** Black Corporation and Tom each own 50% of Tan Corporation's common stock. On January 1, Tan holds a deficit in accumulated E & P of $200,000. Its current E & P is $90,000. During the year, Tan makes cash distributions of $40,000 each to Black and Tom.
    a. How are the two shareholders taxed on the distribution?
    b. What is Tan's accumulated E & P at the end of the year?

14. **LO.1, 4** Heather, an individual, owns all of the outstanding stock in Silver Corporation. Heather purchased her stock in Silver nine years ago, and her basis is $56,000. At the beginning of this year, the corporation has $76,000 of accumulated E & P and no current E & P (before considering the effect of the distributions as noted below). What are the tax consequences to Heather (amount and type of income and basis in property received) and Silver Corporation (gain or loss and effect on E & P) in each of the following situations?

a. Silver distributes land to Heather. The land was held as an investment and has a fair market value of $54,000 and an adjusted basis of $42,000.

b. Assume that Silver has no current or accumulated E & P prior to the distribution. How would your answer to (a) change?

c. Assume that the land distributed in (a) is subject to a $46,000 mortgage (which Heather assumes). How would your answer change?

d. Assume that the land has a fair market value of $54,000 and an adjusted basis of $62,000 on the date of the distribution. How would your answer to (a) change?

15. **LO.I, 4** Lime Corporation, with E & P of $500,000, distributes land (worth $300,000, adjusted basis of $350,000) to Harry, its sole shareholder. The land is subject to a liability of $120,000, which Harry assumes. What are the tax consequences to Lime and to Harry?

Decision Making

16. **LO.4** Raven Corporation owns three machines that it uses in its business. It no longer needs two of these machines and is considering distributing them to its two shareholders as a property dividend. The machines have a fair market value of $20,000 each. The basis of each machine is as follows: A, $27,000; B, $20,000; and C, $12,000. Raven has asked you for advice. What do you recommend?

Issue ID

17. **LO.I, 2, 3, 4** Cerulean Corporation has two equal shareholders, Eloise and Olivia. Eloise acquired her Cerulean stock three years ago by transferring property worth $700,000, basis of $300,000, for 70 shares of the stock. Olivia acquired 70 shares in Cerulean Corporation two years ago by transferring property worth $660,000, basis of $110,000. Cerulean Corporation's accumulated E & P as of January 1 of the current year is $350,000.

On March 1 of the current year, the corporation distributed to Eloise property worth $120,000, basis to Cerulean of $50,000. It distributed cash of $220,000 to Olivia. On July 1 of the current year, Olivia sold her stock to Magnus for $820,000. On December 1 of the current year, Cerulean distributed cash of $90,000 each to Magnus and Eloise. What are the tax issues?

Decision Making

18. **LO.I, 2, 4** Petrel Corporation has accumulated E & P of $85,000 at the beginning of the year. Its current-year taxable income is $320,000. On December 31, Petrel distributed business property (worth $140,000, adjusted basis of $290,000) to Juan, its sole shareholder. Juan assumes a $70,000 liability on the property.

Included in the determination of Petrel's current taxable income is $16,000 of income recognized from an installment sale in a previous year. In addition, the corporation incurred a Federal income tax liability of $112,000, paid life insurance premiums of $4,500, and received term life insurance proceeds of $150,000 on the death of an officer.

a. What is Juan's gross income from the distribution?

b. What is Petrel's E & P after the property distribution?

c. What is Juan's tax basis in the property received?

d. How would your answers to (a) and (b) change if Petrel had sold the property at its fair market value, used $70,000 of the proceeds to pay off the liability, and distributed the remaining cash and any tax savings to Juan?

19. **LO.5** Parrot Corporation is a closely held company with accumulated E & P of $300,000 and current E & P of $350,000. Tom and Jerry are brothers; each owns a 50% share in Parrot, and they share management responsibilities equally. What are the tax consequences of each of the following independent transactions involving Parrot, Tom, and Jerry? How does each transaction affect Parrot's E & P?

a. Parrot sells an office building (adjusted basis of $350,000; fair market value of $300,000) to Tom for $275,000.

b. Parrot lends Jerry $250,000 on March 31 of this year. The loan is evidenced by a note that is payable on demand. No interest is charged on the loan (the current applicable Federal interest rate is 7%).

c. Parrot owns an airplane that it leases to others for a specified rental rate. Tom and Jerry also use the airplane for personal use and pay no rent. During the year, Tom used the airplane for 120 hours, and Jerry used it for 160 hours. The rental value of the airplane is $350 per hour, and its maintenance costs average $80 per hour.

d. Tom leases equipment to Parrot for $20,000 per year. The same equipment can be leased from another company for $9,000 per year.

20. **LO.5** Robin Corporation would like to transfer excess cash to its sole shareholder, Adam, who is also an employee. Adam is in the 28% tax bracket, and Robin is in the 34% bracket.

    Because Adam's contribution to Robin's profit is substantial, Robin believes that a $25,000 bonus in the current year is reasonable compensation and should be deductible in full. However, Robin is considering paying Adam a $25,000 dividend because Adam's tax rate on dividends is lower than his tax rate on compensation. Is Robin correct in believing that a dividend is the better choice? Why or why not?

    Decision Making

21. **LO.6** Your client, Raptor Corporation, declares a dividend permitting its common shareholders to elect to receive 9 shares of cumulative preferred stock or 3 additional shares of Raptor common stock for every 10 shares of common stock held. Raptor has only common stock outstanding (fair market value of $45 per share). One shareholder elects to receive preferred stock, while the remaining shareholders choose the common stock.

    Raptor asks you whether the shareholders recognize any taxable income on the receipt of the stock. Prepare a letter to Raptor or a memo for the tax research file regarding this matter. Raptor's address is 1812 S. Camino Seco, Tucson, AZ 85710.

    Communications

    Critical Thinking

22. **LO.6** Ken purchased 10,000 shares of Gold Corporation common stock six years ago for $160,000. In the current year, Ken received a preferred stock dividend of 800 shares, while the other holders of common stock received a common stock dividend. The preferred stock that Ken received is worth $80,000, and his common stock has a fair market value of $240,000. Assume that Gold holds ample E & P to cover any distributions made during the year. What is Ken's basis in the preferred and common stock after the dividend is received? When does his holding period commence for the preferred stock?

    Critical Thinking

23. **LO.6** Denim Corporation declares a nontaxable dividend payable in rights to subscribe to common stock. One right and $60 entitle the holder to subscribe to one share of stock. One right is issued for every two shares of stock owned. At the date of distribution of the rights, the market value of the stock is $110 per share, and the market value of the rights is $55 each. Lauren owns 300 shares of stock that she purchased two years ago for $9,000. Lauren receives 150 rights, of which she exercises 105 to purchase 105 additional shares. She sells the remaining 45 rights for $2,475. What are the tax consequences of this transaction to Lauren?

    Critical Thinking

24. **LO.6** Jacob Corcoran bought 10,000 shares of Grebe Corporation stock two years ago for $24,000. Last year, Jacob received a nontaxable stock dividend of 2,000 shares in Grebe. In the current tax year, Jacob sold all of the stock received as a dividend for $18,000. Prepare a letter to Jacob or a memo for the tax research file describing the tax consequences of the stock sale. Jacob's address is 925 Arapahoe Street, Boulder, CO 80304.

    Critical Thinking

    Communications

25. **LO.7** Joseph and Erica, husband and wife, jointly own all of the stock in Velvet Corporation. The two are currently involved in divorce proceedings, and pursuant to those negotiations, they have agreed that only one of them will remain a shareholder in Velvet after the divorce. Because Erica has been more involved in Velvet's management and operations over the years, the parties have agreed that Joseph's ownership should be acquired by either Erica or Velvet. What issues should be considered in determining whether Erica or Velvet should acquire Joseph's shares in the corporation?

    Issue ID

26. **LO.1, 7** Julio is in the 33% tax bracket. He acquired 2,000 shares of stock in Gray Corporation seven years ago at a cost of $50 per share. In the current year, Julio received a payment of $150,000 from Gray Corporation in exchange for 1,000 of his shares in Gray. Gray has E & P of $1 million. What tax liability would Julio incur on the payment in each of the following situations? Assume that Julio has no capital losses.
    a. The stock redemption qualifies for sale or exchange treatment.
    b. The stock redemption does not qualify for sale or exchange treatment.

27. **LO.1, 7** How would your answer to Problem 26 differ if Julio were a corporate shareholder (in the 34% tax bracket) rather than an individual shareholder and the stock ownership in Gray Corporation represented a 25% interest?

Decision Making

28. **LO.I, 7** Assume in Problem 26 that Julio has a capital loss carryover of $50,000 in the current tax year. Julio has no other capital gain transactions during the year. What amount of the capital loss may Julio deduct in the current year in the following situations?

a. The payment from Gray Corporation is a qualifying stock redemption for tax purposes (i.e., receives sale or exchange treatment).

b. The payment from Gray does not qualify as a stock redemption for tax purposes (i.e., does not receive sale or exchange treatment).

c. If Julio had the flexibility to structure the transaction as described in either (a) or (b), which form would he choose?

29. **LO.I, 7** How would your answer to parts (a) and (b) of Problem 28 differ if Julio were a corporate shareholder (in the 34% tax bracket) rather than an individual shareholder and the stock ownership in Gray Corporation represented a 25% interest?

Critical Thinking

30. **LO.7** Silver Corporation has 2,000 shares of common stock outstanding. Howard owns 600 shares, Howard's grandfather owns 300 shares, Howard's mother owns 300 shares, and Howard's son owns 100 shares. In addition, Maroon Corporation owns 500 shares. Howard owns 70% of the stock of Maroon.

a. Applying the stock attribution rules, how many shares does Howard own in Silver?

b. Assume that Howard owns only 40% of the stock in Maroon. How many shares does Howard own, directly and indirectly, in Silver?

c. Assume the same facts as in (a) above, but in addition, Howard owns a 25% interest in the Yellow Partnership. Yellow owns 200 shares in Silver. How many shares does Howard own, directly and indirectly, in Silver?

Critical Thinking

31. **LO.7** Shonda owns 1,000 of the 1,500 shares outstanding in Rook Corporation (E & P of $1 million). Shonda paid $50 per share for the stock seven years ago. The remaining stock in Rook is owned by unrelated individuals. What are the tax consequences to Shonda in the following independent situations?

a. Rook redeems 450 shares of Shonda's stock for $225,000.

b. Rook redeems 600 shares of Shonda's stock for $300,000.

Critical Thinking

32. **LO.7** Broadbill Corporation (E & P $650,000) has 1,000 shares of common stock outstanding. The shares are owned by the following individuals: Tammy, 300 shares; Yvette, 400 shares; and Jeremy, 300 shares. Each of the shareholders paid $50 per share for the Broadbill stock four years ago.

In the current year, Broadbill distributes $75,000 to Tammy in redemption of 150 of her shares. Determine the tax consequences of the redemption to Tammy and to Broadbill under the following independent circumstances.

a. Tammy and Jeremy are grandmother and grandson.

b. The three shareholders are siblings.

Critical Thinking

33. **LO.7** For the last eleven years, Lime Corporation has owned and operated four different trades or businesses. Lime also owns stock in several corporations that it purchased for investment purposes.

The stock of Lime is held equally by Sultan, an individual, and by Turquoise Corporation. Sultan and Turquoise each own 1,000 shares in Lime, purchased nine years ago at a cost of $200 per share.

Determine whether either of the following independent transactions qualify as partial liquidations under § 302(b)(4). In each transaction, determine the tax consequences to Lime, to Turquoise, and to Sultan. Lime holds E & P of $2.1 million on the date of the distribution. Lime redeems 250 shares from each shareholder.

a. Lime sells one of its business lines (basis $500,000, fair market value $700,000) and distributes the proceeds equally to Sultan and Turquoise.

b. Lime equally distributes stock (basis $425,000, fair market value $700,000) that it holds in other corporations to Sultan and Turquoise.

Critical Thinking

34. **LO.7** Compare the tax treatment of liquidating and redemption distributions in terms of the following.

a. Recognition of gain or loss by the shareholder.

b. Basis of property received by the shareholder.

35. **LO.7** Dove Corporation (E & P of $800,000) has 1,000 shares of stock outstanding. The shares are owned as follows: Julia, 600 shares; Maxine (Julia's sister), 300 shares; and Janine (Julia's daughter), 100 shares. Dove owns land (basis $300,000, fair market value $260,000) that it purchased as an investment seven years ago.

   Critical Thinking

   Dove distributes the land to Julia in exchange for all of her shares in the corporation. Julia had a basis of $275,000 in the shares. What are the tax consequences for both Dove and Julia if the distribution is:
   a. A qualifying stock redemption?
   b. A liquidating distribution?

36. **LO.5** Pink Corporation has several employees. Their names and salaries are listed below.

   Issue ID

Judy	$470,000
Holly (Judy's daughter)	100,000
Terry (Judy's son)	100,000
John (an unrelated third party)	320,000

   Holly and Terry are the only shareholders of Pink. Judy and John share equally in the management of the company's operations. Holly and Terry are both full-time college students at a university 200 miles away. Pink has substantial E & P and never has distributed a dividend. Discuss any income tax issues related to Pink's salary arrangement.

BRIDGE DISCIPLINE

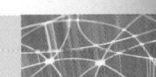

1. Find the audited financial statements of five major U.S. corporations, each in a different operating industry (e.g., manufacturing, energy, financial services, health care).
   a. Compute the total return on each corporation's stock for the past two years.
   b. Compute the dividend yield of the stock for the past two years.

2. Find a report involving the buyback of common stock by a publicly traded U.S. corporation. In no more than four PowerPoint slides, summarize the transaction, and discuss the tax and finance motivations for the redemption presented in the article.

   Communications

3. A dividend is declared by the corporation's board of directors, and it is paid to each shareholder in an equal fashion. Evaluate this statement from an accounting and Federal income tax standpoint. Summarize your position in no more than four PowerPoint slides in preparation for a presentation to your classmates in Business Law I.

   Communications

Research Problems

Note: Solutions to Research Problems can be prepared by using the **Checkpoint®** **Student Edition** online research product, which is available to accompany this text. It is also possible to prepare solutions to the Research Problems by using tax research materials found in a standard tax library.

THOMSON REUTERS
CHECKPOINT®

Research Problem 1. Kenny Merinoff and his son, John, own all of the outstanding stock of Flamingo Corporation. John and Kenny are officers in the corporation and, together with their uncle, Ira, comprise the entire board of directors. Flamingo uses the cash method of accounting and adopted a calendar year-end.

   Communications

   In late 2007, the board of directors adopted the following legally enforceable resolution (agreed to in writing by each of the officers).

   Salary payments made to an officer of the corporation that are disallowed in whole or in part as a deductible expense for Federal income tax purposes shall be reimbursed by such officer to the corporation to the full extent of the disallowance. It shall be the duty of the board of directors to enforce the collection of each such amount.

In 2012, Flamingo paid Kenny $800,000 in compensation. John received $650,000. As part of an audit in late 2013, the IRS found the compensation of both officers to be excessive. It disallowed deductions for $400,000 of the payment to Kenny and $350,000 of the payment to John. The IRS recharacterized the disallowed payments as constructive dividends. Complying with the resolution by the board of directors, both Kenny and John repaid the disallowed compensation to Flamingo Corporation in 2014.

John and Kenny have asked you to determine how their repayments are treated for Federal income tax purposes. John still is working as a highly compensated executive for Flamingo, while Kenny is retired and living off of his savings. Prepare a memo for your firm's tax research files describing the results of your review.

Partial list of research aids:
§ 1341.
Vincent E. Oswald, 49 T.C. 645 (1968).

Research Problem 2. Your client, White Corporation, has done well since its formation 20 years ago. This year, it recognized a $50 million capital gain from the sale of a subsidiary. White's CEO has contacted you to discuss a proposed transaction to reduce the tax on the capital gain. Under the proposal, White will purchase all of the common stock in Purple Corporation for $200 million. Purple is a profitable corporation that has $63 million in cash and marketable securities, $137 million in operating assets, and approximately $280 million in E & P.

After its acquisition, Purple will distribute $50 million in cash and marketable securities to White. Due to the 100% dividends received deduction, no taxable income results to White from the dividend. White then will resell Purple for $150 million.

The subsequent sale of Purple generates a $50 million capital loss [$150 million (sale price) − $200 million (stock basis)]. The loss from the stock sale can then be used to offset the preexisting $50 million capital gain. Will the proposed plan work? Why or why not?

Partial list of research aids:
§ 1059.

Communications

Research Problem 3. Emerald Corporation must change its method of accounting for Federal income tax purposes. The change will require that an adjustment to income be made over three tax periods. Jonas, the sole shareholder of Emerald, wants to better understand the implications of this adjustment for E & P purposes, as he anticipates a distribution from Emerald in the current year. Prepare a memo for your firm's files describing the results of your research.

Partial list of research aids:
§ 481(a).
Rev.Proc. 97–27, 1997–1 C.B. 680.

Internet Activity

Use the tax resources of the Internet to address the following questions. Do not restrict your search to the Web, but include a review of newsgroups and general reference materials, practitioner sites and resources, primary sources of the tax law, chat rooms and discussion groups, and other opportunities.

Research Problem 4. In July 2013, Windstream Corp. (Nasdaq: WIN), a Fortune 500 and S&P 500 company, made an announcement regarding the taxation of a recent distribution. It also made a projection regarding the anticipated tax consequences of future distributions.

Locate articles or press releases regarding Windstream's announcement and related distribution. What might have led Windstream to make the announcement? What implications might the information contained in the announcement have for investors' expectations regarding the company's future earnings? On what might the predictions regarding the taxation of future distributions be based?

Research Problem 5. Just how common are dividend distributions in today's economic climate? Are dividends concentrated in the companies traded on the New York Stock Exchange, or do closely held corporations pay dividends with the same frequency and at the same rates? Did dividends decrease during the financial downturn of 2008 and thereafter?

Financial institutions and observers are acutely interested in these issues. Search for comments on such questions at various commercial websites as well as one or two academic journals or blogs.

Research Problem 6. Investigate websites of for-profit investment managers, and summarize the information you find in a two-page discussion entitled "The Market in Stock Splits: How You Can Profit." Submit the summary to your professor.

Communications

Research Problem 7. Write an e-mail query to two tax consultants who practice in your state. Ask each for an example or two of a constructive dividend that a client recently paid. Give your instructor copies of your query and the responses you receive.

Communications

Research Problem 8. The requirements for effectively liquidating a corporate entity vary from state to state. Prepare an outline discussing how an entity incorporated in your home state is liquidated, including any reporting requirements associated with such liquidation. E-mail your outline to your tax professor.

Communications

Research Problem 9. Publicly traded corporations reacquire their own shares for various reasons. Through the use of a tender offer, a corporation can purchase a substantial percentage of the company's stock. Prepare an outline discussing (1) why publicly traded corporations reacquire their own shares and (2) how the tender offer process works for both corporations and shareholders. E-mail your outline to your tax professor.

Communications

Partnerships and Limited Liability Entities

LEARNING OBJECTIVES: *After completing Chapter 14, you should be able to:*

LO.1 **Identify governing principles and theories of partnership taxation.**

LO.2 **Apply the tax rules regarding the formation of a partnership with cash and property contributions.**

LO.3 **Determine the tax treatment of expenditures of a newly formed partnership and identify elections available to the partnership.**

LO.4 **Calculate partnership taxable income and describe how partnership items affect a partner's income tax return.**

LO.5 **Determine a partner's basis in the partnership interest.**

LO.6 **Apply the limitations on deducting partnership losses.**

LO.7 **Use the tax laws regarding transactions between a partner and the partnership.**

LO.8 **Apply partnership tax law provisions to limited liability companies (LLCs) and limited liability partnerships (LLPs).**

CHAPTER OUTLINE

TAX TALK *If you are truly serious about preparing your child for the future, don't teach him to subtract—teach him to deduct.* —FRAN LEBOWITZ

Dennis Flaherty/Photographer's Choice/Getty Images

THE BIG PICTURE   Tax Solutions for the Real World

THE TAX CONSEQUENCES OF PARTNERSHIP FORMATION AND OPERATIONS

For 15 years, Maria has owned and operated a seaside bakery and café called The Beachsider. Each morning, customers line up on the boardwalk in front of the building and enjoy fresh coffee and croissants while waiting for a table. "The building is too small," Maria commented to her landlord, Kyle. "Is there any way we can expand?" The Beachsider is one of several older buildings on 3 acres of a 10-acre parcel that Kyle inherited 30 years ago. The remaining 7 acres are undeveloped.

Kyle and Maria talked to Josh, a real estate developer, and he proposed an expansion to The Beachsider and upgrades to the other buildings. The improvements would preserve the character of the original retail center, and the remaining acreage would be available for future expansion. Kyle and Maria were impressed with Josh's vision and excited about the plans to upgrade the property and expand Maria's business.

The parties agreed to form a partnership to own and operate The Beachsider and to improve and lease the other buildings. Josh summarized the plan as follows: "Kyle and Maria will each contribute one-half of the capital we need. Kyle's real estate is valued at about $2 million. Maria's bakery equipment and the café furnishings are valued at about $500,000. The improvements will cost about $1.5 million, which Maria has agreed to contribute to the partnership."

Josh continued, "You have agreed that I do not need to contribute any capital to the partnership. I will oversee the construction, and when it is complete, I will vest in a 5 percent interest in the partnership's capital. On an ongoing basis, I will oversee the partnership's operations in exchange for a fixed salary and 20 percent of the partnership's ongoing profits. The construction is estimated to be completed in June of this year, and my capital interest is estimated to be valued at $200,000 at that time."

What are the tax consequences if the trio forms Beachside Properties as a limited liability company (LLC) to own and operate the retail center? What issues might arise later in the life of the entity?

Read the chapter and formulate your response.

Much of the new business in today's world of commerce is conducted in what the Internal Revenue Code would classify as *partnerships*. As evidence of their popularity, about 3 million partnership tax returns are filed with the IRS annually.

Whether termed a *joint venture, a working agreement, a shared operating arrangement,* or some other designation, a partnership is formed when individuals or separate business entities get together for the specific purpose of earning profits by jointly operating a trade or business. For example, a partnership likely exists when a U.S. business enters into a joint venture with a foreign distributor to gain access to an overseas consumer market. Or a number of businesses located in a blighted downtown area might work together to boost sales and customer traffic by forming a group that unifies and improves the appearance of the storefronts in the area, conducts joint advertising, and coordinates sales and coupon activities.

Partnerships allow a great degree of flexibility in the conduct of business: for example, a group can limit its goals to a specific list of agreed-to projects or to a given time period, or businesses can work together without altering any of their underlying capital structures. In many service professions, such as law, medicine, and accounting, state laws prohibit the owners from using a corporation to limit their liability to clients or patients; so the partnership form prevails.

14-1 OVERVIEW OF PARTNERSHIP TAXATION

LO.1

Identify governing principles and theories of partnership taxation.

There are several types of partnership entities, each suited for different situations. Partnerships are used in almost every imaginable industry, and their popularity among business owners continues to rise.

The tax law addressing the transactions of partners and partnerships is found in Subchapter K of the Internal Revenue Code. These provisions comprise only a few short pages in the Code, however. Most of the details of partnership tax law have evolved through extensive Regulations and a healthy number of court cases.

14-1a Forms of Doing Business—Federal Tax Consequences

This chapter and the next chapter analyze business forms that offer certain advantages over C corporations. These entities are partnerships and S corporations, which are called *flow-through* or *pass-through* entities because the owners of the trade or business elect to avoid treating the enterprise as a separate taxable entity. Instead, the owners are taxed on a proportionate share of the firm's taxable income at the end of each of its taxable years, regardless of the amount of cash or property distributions the owners receive during the year. The entity serves as an information provider to the IRS and its owners with respect to the proportionate income shares, and the tax falls directly upon the owners of those shares.

A partnership may be especially advantageous in many cases. A partnership's income is subject to only a single level of taxation, whereas C corporation income can be subject to *double taxation.* Corporate income is taxed at the entity level at rates up to 35 percent. Any after-tax income that is distributed to corporate owners is taxed again as a dividend at the owner level. Although partnership income may be subject to high individual rates, the resulting tax likely will be lower than a combined corporate-level tax and a second tax on dividends.

In addition, the entity offers certain planning opportunities not available to other entities. Both C and S corporations are subject to rigorous allocation and distribution requirements (generally, each allocation or distribution is proportionate to the ownership interest of the shareholder). A partnership, though, may adjust its allocations of income and cash flow among the partners each year according to their needs, as long as certain standards are met. Any previously unrealized income (such as appreciation of corporate assets) of a C corporation is recognized at the

TAX FACT Partnership Power

Partnerships and limited liability entities represent a sizable number of business enterprises, and they generate a significant part of the net income of the economy, especially in the investment sectors. The table at the right presents some statistics about the activities of these entities from the most recent year for which data are available.

Number of partnerships	3,100,000
Number of partners	20,650,000
Reported partnership net income—total	$410 billion
Number of limited partnerships	395,000
Number of limited liability entities	2,500,000

entity level when the corporation liquidates, but a partnership generally may liquidate tax-free. Finally, many states impose reporting and licensing requirements on corporate entities, including S corporations. These include franchise or capital stock tax returns that may require annual assessments and costly professional preparation assistance. Partnerships, on the other hand, often have no reporting requirements beyond Federal and state informational tax returns.

Although partnerships may avoid many of the income tax and reporting burdens faced by other entities, they are subject to all other taxes in the same manner as any other business. Thus, the partnership files returns and pays the outstanding amount of pertinent sales taxes, property taxes, and payroll taxes.

In summary, partnerships offer advantages to both large and small businesses. For smaller business operations, a partnership enables several owners to combine their resources at low cost. For larger business operations, a partnership offers a unique ability to raise capital with low filing and reporting costs (compared to corporate bond issuances, for example).

14-1b What Is a Partnership?

A partnership is an association of two or more persons formed to carry on a trade or business, with each contributing money, property, labor, or skill, and with all expecting to share in profits and losses. A "person" can be an individual, a corporation, or another partnership. For Federal income tax purposes, a partnership includes a syndicate, a group, a pool, a joint venture, or another unincorporated organization through which any business, financial operation, or venture is carried on. The entity must not be otherwise classified as a corporation, trust, or estate.[1]

An eligible noncorporate entity can "check the box" on the partnership tax return, indicating that the entity wants to be taxed as a partnership.[2] A partnership must have at least two owners, so a sole proprietor or one-owner limited liability entity cannot "check the box" and be taxed as a partnership.[3]

Businesses operating in several forms are taxed as partnerships. Provisions controlling these legal forms of doing business typically are dictated by the laws of the states in which the businesses operate.

- In a general partnership, the partners share profits and losses in some specified manner, as dictated by the partnership agreement. Creditors can reach the assets of the business and the personal assets of the general partners to satisfy any outstanding debts. A general partner can be bankrupted by a judgment against the entity, even though the partner did not cause the violation triggering the damages.
- In a limited partnership, profits and losses are shared as the partners agree, but ownership interests are either general (creditors can reach the personal assets of the partner) or limited (a partner's exposure to entity liabilities is limited to the partner's own capital contributions). Usually, the general

---

[1]§ 7701(a)(2).
[2]Reg. §§ 301.7701–1 to −3, as discussed in Chapter 12.
[3]§ 761(a).

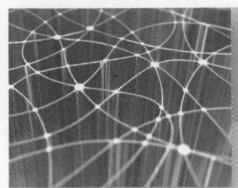

BRIDGE DISCIPLINE   Bridge to Finance

As movies have become more expensive to produce, many production studios have turned to limited partnerships or LLCs as a lucrative source of investment capital. For example, several well-known studios have sold limited partnership or LLC interests in entities formed to produce specific movies.

The sponsoring studio usually injects capital for a small (1–5 percent) general partnership interest, and the limited partners contribute the remaining capital—millions of dollars in most cases. The partnership agreement spells out the number and types of films the partnership intends to produce and provides a formula for allocating cash flows to the partners. The agreement includes various benefits for the general partner (studio), such as a preferred allocation of cash flows (the first $5 million per year, for example), distribution fees for marketing the movies, and/or reimbursement of specified amounts of corporate overhead. Any cash remaining after these expenses is allocated under a fixed formula between the general and limited partners (for example, the limited partners may receive 90 percent of remaining cash flows).

These film-financing partnerships are not necessarily private operations. A layperson with a well-connected tax or investment adviser can become a partner in the next Johnny Depp project, perhaps financed by Silver Screen Partners. Partnership shares sell for multiples of $100,000 or more, and in return, the investor can become part-owner in an entity that is certain to throw off operating losses for many years to come.

Especially interested in movie financing of this type can be non-U.S. investors. The use of partnerships and limited liability entities is a common way to attract cross-border investment, as many developed countries treat such joint ventures favorably under their tax laws, allowing deferral of income recognition and lower tax withholding on the income of these entities.

U.S. investors are attracted to joint venture financing of film projects in several countries, including Germany and Canada, and U.S. states, including Illinois and Louisiana, that offer generous tax credits for projects that are filmed and processed chiefly within their borders. The partnership tax regime can offer an immediate flow-through of these tax benefits.

Think about traditional bank financing of manufacturing or distribution activities in comparison, and you will see why the movie studio finds partnerships so appealing: How many banks would allow the general partner to receive reimbursements and allocations before debt principal and interest are paid?

This capital-raising technique has proved so advantageous to the studios that some related industries, such as movie lighting contractors and special effects companies, also use limited partnerships to raise capital. The next time you go to a movie, watch the credits and think about the large number of people who invested cash in the movie, all benefiting from the partnership tax laws!

© iStockphoto.com/enot-poloskun

partners conduct most of the partnership business, and they have a greater say in making decisions that affect the entity operations.
- The limited liability partnership (LLP) is used chiefly in the service professions, such as accounting and consulting. The primary difference between an LLP and a general partnership is that an LLP partner is not personally liable for acts of negligence, fraud, or malpractice committed by other partners.
- The limited liability company (LLC) is discussed in more detail later in this chapter. This entity is taxed as a partnership, but its capital structure resembles that of a corporation, with shares for sale and an owner's liability limited almost strictly to the extent of capital contributions. Most states allow LLCs to be owned solely by one person.

14-1c Partnership Taxation and Reporting

A partnership is not a taxable entity.[4] Rather, the taxable income or loss of the partnership flows through to the partners at the end of the entity's tax year.[5] Partners report their allocable share of the partnership's income or loss for the year on their tax returns. As a result, the partnership itself pays no Federal income tax on its income; instead, the partners' individual tax liabilities are affected by the activities of the entity.

[4]§ 701.   [5]§ 702.

Example 1

Adam is a 40% partner in the ABC Partnership. Both Adam's and the partnership's tax years end on December 31. This year, the partnership generates $200,000 of ordinary taxable income. However, because the partnership needs capital for expansion and debt reduction, Adam makes no cash withdrawals during the year. He meets his living expenses by reducing his investment portfolio. Adam is taxed on his $80,000 allocable share of the partnership's income ($200,000 × 40%), even though he received no distributions from the entity during the year. This allocated income is included in Adam's gross income.

Example 2

Assume the same facts as in Example 1, except that the partnership realizes a taxable loss of $100,000. Adam's $40,000 proportionate share of the loss flows through to him from the partnership, and he can deduct the loss. (Note: Loss limitation rules discussed later in the chapter may result in some or all of this loss being deducted by Adam in a later year.)

Separately Stated Items

Many items of partnership income, expense, gain, or loss retain their tax identity as they flow through to the partners. These separately stated items include those items that may affect any two partners' tax liability computations differently.[6] For example, the § 179 expense of a partnership is separately stated because one partner might be able to deduct his or her share of the expense completely, while another's deduction might be limited.

Separately stated items include recognized gains and losses from property transactions, dividend income, preferences and adjustments for the alternative minimum tax (see Chapter 17), foreign tax payments, and expenditures that individual partners would treat as itemized deductions (e.g., charitable contributions).

Items that are not separately stated, because all partners treat them the same on their income tax returns, are aggregated and form the *ordinary income* of the partnership. Thus, profits from product sales, advertising expenses, and depreciation recapture amounts are combined to form the entity's ordinary income. This amount then is allocated among the partners and flows through to their tax returns. The ordinary income that flows through to a general partner, as well as any salary-like guaranteed payments (discussed in a later section) received, usually is subject to self-employment tax, as well as Federal income tax.[7]

Example 3

Beth is a 25% partner in the BR Partnership. The cash basis entity collected sales income of $60,000 and incurred $15,000 in business expenses. In addition, it sold a corporate bond for a $9,000 long-term capital gain. Finally, the partnership made a $1,000 contribution to the local Performing Arts Fund. The fund is a qualifying charity. BR and all of its partners use a calendar tax year.

Beth is allocated ordinary taxable income of $11,250 [($60,000 − $15,000) × 25%] from the partnership. She also reports her allocated share of the entity's long-term capital gain ($2,250) and charitable contributions ($250). The ordinary income increases Beth's gross income, and the capital gain and charitable contribution are combined with her other similar activities for the year as though she had incurred them herself. These items could be treated differently on the tax returns of the various partners (e.g., because a partner may be subject to a percentage limitation on charitable contribution deductions), so they are not included in the computation of ordinary partnership income. Instead, the items flow through to the partners separately.

Tax Reporting Rules

Even though it is not a taxpaying entity, the partnership files an information tax return, Form 1065. This return is due by the fifteenth day of the fourth month following the end of the tax year. For a calendar year partnership, this deadline is April 15.

---

[6]§ 703(a)(1).　　　　　　　　　　　　　　[7]§ 1402(a).

TAX IN THE NEWS   The Extent of Partnership Usage

Partnerships come in all flavors and sizes! In about a decade, the number of U.S. partnerships has increased by 50 percent. More than 3 million entities are treated as partnerships; these entities own assets with a combined gross book value of more than $20 trillion.

Partnerships are used in almost every type of industry—from agriculture to health care to waste management.

Almost half of all partnerships are engaged in some sort of real estate business. Certain elements of the tax law make partnerships especially appealing for activities such as research and development, and oil and gas exploration and extraction. All kinds of service activities are operated through some sort of partnership (especially limited liability partnerships): partnerships are common in the accounting, law, education, and transportation services industries.

An automatic five-month extension is available (to September 15 for a calendar year partnership) for filing the Form 1065. As part of the Form 1065, the partnership prepares a Schedule K–1 for each partner that shows that partner's share of partnership items.

The partnership incurs a penalty if it fails to file a timely (by the extended due date) Form 1065. The penalty is $195 per month times the numbers of partners, up to a maximum of 12 months.

Look at Form 1065 in Appendix B, and refer to it during the following discussion. The ordinary income and expense items generated by the partnership's trade or business activities are netted to produce a single income or loss amount. The partnership reports this ordinary income or loss from its trade or business activities on Form 1065, page 1. Schedule K (page 4 of Form 1065) accumulates all items that must be separately reported to the partners, including net trade or business income or loss (from page 1). The amounts on Schedule K are allocated among and reported by the partners on each owner's Schedule K–1.

Example 4

The BR Partnership in Example 3 reports its $60,000 of sales income on Form 1065, page 1, line 1. The $15,000 of business expenses are reported in the appropriate amounts on page 1, line 2 or lines 9–20. Partnership ordinary income of $45,000 is shown on page 1, line 22, and on Schedule K, line 1. The $9,000 capital gain and the $1,000 charitable contribution are reported only on Schedule K, on lines 9a and 13a, respectively.

Beth receives a Schedule K–1 from the partnership that shows her shares of partnership ordinary income of $11,250, long-term capital gain of $2,250, and charitable contributions of $250 on lines 1, 9a, and 13 (Code A), respectively.

She combines these amounts with similar items from other sources on her personal tax return. For example, if she has a $5,000 long-term capital loss from a stock transaction during the year, her overall net capital loss is $2,750. She then evaluates this net amount to determine the amount she may deduct on her Form 1040.

Thus, one must look at both page 1 and Schedule K to get complete information regarding a partnership's operations for the year.

The partnership reconciles book income with its tax return data on Schedule M–1 or Schedule M–3. This reconciliation is similar to the book-tax reconciliation prepared by a C corporation.

Schedule M–3 generally is required in lieu of Schedule M–1 if the partnership owns $10 million or more in assets at the end of the year or it reports gross receipts of at least $35 million. The net taxable income calculated on the Analysis of Net Income (Loss) schedule should agree with the reconciled taxable income on Schedule M–1 or Schedule M–3. Schedule L shows an accounting-basis balance sheet, and Schedule M–2 reconciles partners' beginning and ending capital accounts.

BRIDGE DISCIPLINE   **Bridge to Financial Accounting**

The equivalent in financial accounting to the partner's basis in his or her partnership interest is the **capital account**. A partner's ending balance in the capital account is not required to be the same as his or her basis in the partnership interest. Just as the tax and accounting bases of a specific asset may differ, a partner's capital account and basis in the partnership interest usually are not equal.

Whereas contributions and most distributions from the partnership do not create financial accounting income, the capital account is "written up or down" to aggregate fair market value when the entity is formed. For most partnerships with simple financial transactions, *changes* to the capital account parallel closely the annual changes to the partner's basis in the partnership. Basis in one's partnership interest cannot be a negative number, but the capital account can become negative.

Oddly, the Schedules K–1 for the partners require an accounting for their capital accounts, but there is no required reconciliation for the partner's tax basis on the Schedule K–1. As a result, the tax adviser may find that a new partnership client has poor records with respect to the basis amounts of the partners, and a reconstruction must take place so that future computations will be correct. Sometimes, lacking adequate information with which to make this computation, the capital account is used because it is "close enough" and forms a good surrogate for the partner's basis in the partnership.

14-1d Partner's Ownership Interest in a Partnership

Each partner typically owns both a **capital interest** and a **profits (loss) interest** in the partnership. A capital interest is measured by a partner's **capital sharing ratio**, which is the partner's percentage ownership of the capital of the partnership. A partner's capital interest can be determined in several ways. The most widely accepted method measures the capital interest as the percentage of net asset value (asset value remaining after payment of all partnership liabilities) a partner would receive upon immediate liquidation of the partnership.

A profits (loss) interest relates to the partner's percentage allocation of current partnership operating results. **Profit and loss sharing ratios** usually are specified in the partnership agreement. They are used to determine each partner's allocation of partnership ordinary taxable income (loss) and separately stated items.[8] The partnership can change its profit and loss allocations at any time by amending the partnership agreement.

The partnership agreement may provide for a **special allocation** of certain items to specified partners, or it may allocate items in a different proportion from the general profit and loss sharing ratios. These items are reported separately to the partner receiving the allocation. For a special allocation to be recognized for tax purposes, it must produce nontax economic consequences to the partners receiving the allocation.[9]

Example 5

When the George-Helen Partnership was formed, George contributed cash and Helen contributed some City of Boise bonds that she had held for investment purposes. The partnership agreement allocates all of the tax-exempt interest income from the bonds ($15,000 this year) to Helen as an inducement for her to remain a partner.

This is an acceptable special allocation for income tax purposes; it reflects the differing economic circumstances that underlie the partners' contributions to the capital of the entity. Because Helen would have received the tax-exempt income if she had not joined the partnership, she can retain the tax-favored treatment via the special allocation.

---

[8]§ 704(a).   [9]§ 704(b).

Example 6	Assume the same facts as in Example 5. Three years after it was formed, the George-Helen Partnership purchased some City of Butte bonds. The municipal bond interest income of $15,000 flows through to the partners as a separately stated item, so it retains its tax-exempt status.
	The partnership agreement allocates all of this income to George because he is subject to a higher marginal income tax rate than is Helen. The partnership then allocates $15,000 more of the partnership's ordinary income to Helen than to George. These allocations are not effective for income tax purposes because they have no purpose other than a reduction of the partners' combined income tax liability.

A partner has a basis in the partnership interest, just as he or she would have a tax basis in any asset owned. When income flows through to a partner from the partnership, the partner's basis in the partnership interest increases accordingly. When a loss flows through to a partner, basis is reduced.[10] A partner's basis is important when determining the treatment of distributions from the partnership to the partner, establishing the deductibility of partnership losses, and calculating gain or loss on the disposition of the partnership interest.

Example 7	The Philly Clinic contributes $20,000 of cash to acquire a 30% capital and profits interest in the Red Robin LLC. In its first year of operations, the LLC earns ordinary income of $40,000 and makes no distributions to its members. The Clinic's initial basis is the $20,000 it paid for the interest. Philly recognizes ordinary income of $12,000 (30% interest × $40,000 ordinary income). Philly increases its basis in Red Robin by the same amount, to $32,000.

The Code provides for increases and decreases in a partner's basis so that the income or loss from partnership operations is taxed only once. In Example 7, if the Philly Clinic sold its interest at the end of the first year for $32,000, it would recognize no gain or loss. If the Code did not provide for an adjustment to the owner's basis for flow-through amounts, Philly's basis still would be $20,000. In that case, Philly would recognize a gain of $12,000 in addition to being taxed on its $12,000 share of the flow-through income from Red Robin.

Digging Deeper | In-depth coverage can be found on this book's companion website: **www.cengagebrain.com**

Concept Summary 14.1 reviews the general concepts of partnership taxation.

14-2 FORMATION OF A PARTNERSHIP: TAX EFFECTS

14-2a Gain or Loss on Contributions to the Partnership

LO.2

Apply the tax rules regarding the formation of a partnership with cash and property contributions.

When a taxpayer transfers property to an entity in exchange for valuable consideration, a taxable exchange usually results. Typically, both the taxpayer and the entity realize and recognize gain or loss on the exchange.[11] The gain or loss recognized by the transferor is the difference between the fair market value of the consideration received and the adjusted basis of the property transferred.[12]

In most situations, however, neither the partner nor the partnership recognizes the gain or loss that is realized when a partner contributes property to a partnership in exchange for a partnership interest. Instead, recognition of any realized gain or loss is deferred.[13]

---

[10]§§ 705, 722, and 723.
[11]§ 1001(c).

[12]§ 1001(a).
[13]§ 721.

CONCEPT SUMMARY 14.1

Overview of Partnership/LLC Taxation

1. Compared with a C corporation, a partnership may offer some advantages, including a single level of taxation, the availability of certain planning opportunities, and simplified administration and reporting.
2. Entities treated as a partnership for tax purposes include general partnerships, limited partnerships, limited liability companies (LLCs), and limited liability partnerships (LLPs).
3. Partnership income and losses flow through to the partners and are reported on the partners' tax returns.

The partnership reports ordinary income or loss as well as *separately stated items* to the partners. Under certain conditions, items may be *specially allocated* to specified partners.

4. The partnership files Form 1065 as an information return and prepares a Schedule K–1 to report each partner's share of income and deductions.

There are two reasons for this nonrecognition treatment. First, forming a partnership allows investors to combine their assets toward greater economic goals than could be achieved separately. Only the form of ownership, rather than the amount owned by each investor, has changed. Requiring that gain be recognized on such transfers would make the formation of some partnerships economically unfeasible. Second, because the partnership interest received is typically not a liquid asset, the partner may not be able to generate the cash with which to pay the tax. Thus, deferral of the gain recognizes the economic realities of the business world and follows the wherewithal to pay principle.

Alicia transfers two assets to the Wren LLC on the day the entity is created in exchange for a 60% profits and loss interest worth $60,000. She contributes cash of $40,000 and retail display equipment (basis to her as a sole proprietor, $8,000; fair market value, $20,000). Because an exchange has occurred between two parties, Alicia *realizes* a $12,000 gain on this transaction. The gain realized is the fair market value of the LLC interest of $60,000 less the basis of the assets that Alicia surrendered to the entity [$40,000 (cash) + $8,000 (equipment)]. Under § 721, Alicia *does not recognize* the $12,000 realized gain in the year of contribution. Alicia might not have had sufficient cash if she had been required to pay tax on the $12,000 gain. All that she received from the entity was an illiquid LLC interest; she received no cash with which to pay any resulting tax liability.	**Example 8**

Assume the same facts as in Example 8, except that the equipment Alicia contributes to the LLC has an adjusted basis of $25,000. She has incurred a $5,000 *realized* loss [$60,000 − ($40,000 + $25,000)], but she cannot deduct the loss. Realized losses, as well as realized gains, are deferred by § 721. Unless it was essential that the entity receive Alicia's display equipment rather than similar equipment purchased from an outside supplier, Alicia should have considered selling the equipment to a third party. This would have allowed her to deduct a $5,000 loss in the year of the sale. Alicia then could have contributed $60,000 of cash (including the proceeds from the sale) for her interest in the entity, and Wren would have had funds to purchase similar equipment.	**Example 9**

Five years after Wren (Examples 8 and 9) was created, Alicia contributes another piece of equipment to the entity. This property has a basis of $35,000 and a fair market value of $50,000. Alicia defers the recognition of the $15,000 realized gain. Section 721 is effective *whenever* an owner makes a contribution to the capital of the partnership or LLC, not just when the entity is formed.	**Example 10**

14-2b Exceptions to Nonrecognition

Contributions to the capital of a partnership or limited liability entity sometimes trigger recognized gain or loss. Realized gain or loss may be recognized when:

- The transaction is essentially a taxable exchange of properties,
- The transaction is the equivalent of a taxable sale of properties, or
- The partnership interest is received in exchange for services rendered to the partnership by the partner.[14]

Disguised Exchange

If a transaction is essentially a taxable exchange of properties, tax on the gain is not deferred under the nonrecognition provisions of § 721.[15]

Example 11

Sara owns land, and Bob owns stock. Sara would like to have Bob's stock, and Bob wants Sara's land. If Sara and Bob both contribute their property to newly formed SB Partnership in exchange for interests in the partnership, the tax on the transaction appears to be deferred under § 721. The tax on a subsequent distribution by the partnership of the land to Bob and the stock to Sara also appears to be deferred under partnership distribution rules.

Not so! Tax law disregards the passage of the properties through the partnership and holds, instead, that Sara and Bob exchanged the land and stock directly. Thus, the transaction is treated as any other taxable exchange.

Disguised Sale

A similar result (i.e., immediate recognition) occurs in a **disguised sale** of property or of a partnership interest. A disguised sale occurs when a partner contributes property to a partnership and soon thereafter receives a distribution from the partnership. This distribution could be viewed as a payment by the partnership for purchase of the property.[16]

Example 12

Kim transfers property to the existing KLM Partnership. The property has an adjusted basis of $10,000 and a fair market value of $30,000. Two weeks later, the partnership distributes $30,000 of cash to Kim. Lacking an exception under the distribution rules, the $30,000 of cash received would not be taxable to Kim if the basis for her partnership interest prior to the distribution was greater than the amount distributed.

However, the transaction appears to be a disguised purchase-sale transaction, rather than an asset contribution and distribution. Therefore, Kim recognizes gain of $20,000 on transfer of the property, and the partnership is deemed to have purchased the property for $30,000.

A disguised sale is presumed to exist when a contribution by one partner is followed within two years by a specified distribution to him or her from the partnership.

Services

Another exception to the nonrecognition provision of § 721 occurs when a partner receives a capital interest in the partnership as compensation for services rendered to the partnership. This is not a tax-deferred transaction because services are not treated as "property" that can be transferred to a partnership on a tax-free basis. Instead, the partner performing the services recognizes ordinary compensation income equal to the fair market value of the partnership interest received.[17]

The partnership may deduct the amount included in the *service partner's* income if the services are of a deductible nature. If the services are not deductible by the partnership, they are capitalized. For example, architectural plans created by a partner are capitalized into the basis of a structure built with those plans.

---

[14]§ 721(b). A few other exceptions to § 721 treatment also exist.
[15]Reg. § 1.731–1(c)(3).
[16]§ 707(a)(2)(B).
[17]§ 83(a).

Alternatively, day-to-day management services performed by a partner for the partnership usually are deductible by the partnership.

> **Example 13**
>
> Bill, Carol, and Dave form the BCD Partnership, with each receiving a one-third capital and profits interest in the entity. Dave receives his one-third interest as compensation for the accounting and tax planning services he rendered to the partnership. The value of a one-third capital interest in the partnership (for each of the parties) is $20,000.
>
> The partnership deducts $20,000 for Dave's services in computing ordinary income. Dave recognizes $20,000 of compensation income, and he takes a $20,000 basis in his partnership interest. The same result would occur if the partnership had paid Dave $20,000 for his services and he immediately contributed that amount to the entity for a one-third ownership interest.

In-depth coverage can be found on this book's companion website: **www.cengagebrain.com**  2 | Digging Deeper

14-2c Tax Issues Related to Contributed Property

When a partner makes a tax-deferred contribution of an asset to the capital of a partnership, the entity assigns a *carryover basis* to the property.[18] The partnership's basis in the asset (the asset's "inside basis") is equal to the basis the partner held in the property prior to its transfer to the partnership. The partner's basis in the new partnership interest (the owner's "outside basis") equals the prior basis in the contributed asset. The tax term for this basis concept is *substituted basis*. Thus, two assets are created out of one when a partnership is formed, namely, the property in the hands of the new entity and the new asset (the partnership interest) in the hands of the partner. Both assets are assigned a basis that is derived from the partner's basis in the contributed property.

The holding period of a partner's interest includes that of the contributed property when the property was a § 1231 asset or capital asset in the partner's hands. Otherwise, the holding period starts on the day the interest is acquired. The holding period of an interest acquired by a cash contribution starts at acquisition.

To understand the logic of these rules, consider what Congress was attempting to accomplish in this deferral transaction. For both parties, realized gain is deferred, under the wherewithal to pay concept, until the asset or ownership interest is subsequently disposed of in a taxable transaction. The deferral is accomplished through the use of a substituted basis by the partner and a carryover basis by the partnership. This treatment is similar to the treatment of assets transferred to a controlled corporation and the treatment of like-kind exchanges.[19]

> **Example 14**
>
> On June 1, José transfers property to the JKL LLC in exchange for a one-third interest in the entity. The property has an adjusted basis to José of $10,000 and a fair market value of $30,000. José incurs a $20,000 realized gain on the exchange ($30,000 − $10,000), but he does not recognize any of the gain. Jose's basis for his interest in JKL is the amount necessary to recognize the $20,000 deferred gain if his interest later is sold for its $30,000 fair market value. This amount, $10,000, is the substituted basis.
>
> The basis of the property contributed to JKL is the amount necessary to allow for the recognition of the $20,000 deferred gain if the property later is sold for its $30,000 fair market value. This amount, also $10,000, is the carryover basis.
>
> The holding period for the contributed asset also carries over to the entity. Thus, JKL's holding period for the asset includes the period during which José owned the asset individually.

---

[18]§ 723.

[19]§§ 351 and 1031.

Depreciation Method and Period

If depreciable property is contributed to the partnership, the partnership usually is required to use the same cost recovery method and life as had been used by the partner. The partnership merely "steps into the shoes" of the partner and continues the same cost recovery calculations.

Intangible Assets

If a partner contributes an existing "§ 197" intangible asset to the partnership, the partnership generally will "step into the shoes" of the partner in determining future amortization deductions. Section 197 intangible assets include purchased goodwill, going-concern value, information systems, customer- or supplier-related intangible assets, patents, licenses obtained from a governmental unit, franchises, trademarks, covenants not to compete, and other items.

Receivables, Inventory, and Losses

To prevent ordinary income from being converted into capital gain, gain or loss is treated as ordinary when the partnership disposes of either of the following.[20]

- Contributed receivables that were unrealized in the contributing partner's hands at the contribution date. Such receivables include the right to receive payment for goods or services.
- Contributed property that was inventory in the contributor's hands on the contribution date, if the partnership disposes of the property within *five years of the contribution*. For this purpose, inventory includes all tangible property except capital and real or depreciable business assets.

A similar rule is designed to prevent a capital loss from being converted into an ordinary loss. Under the rule, if contributed property is disposed of at a loss and the property had a "built-in" capital loss on the contribution date, the loss is treated as a capital loss if the partnership disposes of the property *within five years of the contribution*. The capital loss is limited to the "built-in" loss on the date of contribution.[21]

THE BIG PICTURE

Example 15

Return to the facts of *The Big Picture* on p. 14-1. Recall that Kyle, Maria, and Josh decide to structure their venture as an LLC. Assume that Kyle has a basis of $600,000 in the $2 million of real estate he contributed, and that Maria has a $0 basis in the bakery equipment and the café furnishings.

When Beachside Properties, LLC, is formed, no tax results for the LLC or for Kyle or Maria. Kyle does not recognize his $1.4 million realized gain, nor does Maria recognize her $500,000 realized gain.

Kyle takes a substituted basis of $600,000 for his interest, and Maria takes a substituted basis of $1.5 million ($1.5 million for contributed cash + $0 for contributed property). Beachside Properties assumes a carryover basis of $600,000 for the real estate contributed by Kyle and $0 for the property contributed by Maria. To the extent the buildings and other land improvements are depreciable, the LLC "steps into Kyle's shoes" in calculating depreciation deductions.

When Josh vests in his 5% capital interest in the LLC, the $200,000 value of the interest is taxable to him, because it is a capital interest received in exchange for services. Beachside Properties probably will capitalize this amount because it relates to construction activities. Josh's 20% share of the future profits of the LLC are taxed to him as they flow through from the LLC.

---

[20]§ 724. For this purpose, § 724(d)(2) waives the holding period requirement in defining § 1231 property.

[21]§ 724(c).

CONCEPT SUMMARY 14.2

Partnership Formation and Basis Computation

1. Generally, partners or partnerships do not recognize gain or loss when property is contributed in exchange for capital interests.
2. Partners contributing property in exchange for partnership interests take the contributed property's adjusted basis for their *outside basis* in their partnership interest. The partners are said to take a substituted basis in their partnership interest.
3. The partnership will continue to use the contributing partner's basis as the *inside basis* in property it

receives. The contributed property is said to take a carryover basis.
4. The partnership's holding period for contributed property may include the contributing partner's holding period.
5. Income or gain is recognized by a contributing partner when services are contributed or when the capital contribution is a disguised sale or exchange.
6. Special rules may apply when the partnership disposes of contributed receivables, inventory, or loss assets.

© iStockphoto.com/Andrey Prokhorov

14-2d Inside and Outside Bases

Reference has been made previously to the partnership's inside basis and the partners' outside basis. **Inside basis** refers to the adjusted basis of each partnership asset, as determined from the partnership's tax accounts. **Outside basis** represents each partner's basis in the partnership interest. Each partner "owns" a share of the partnership's inside basis for all of its assets, and all partners should maintain a record of their respective outside bases.

In many cases—especially on the date of the formation of the partnership—the total of all of the partners' outside bases equals the partnership's inside bases for all of its assets. Differences between inside and outside basis arise when a partner's interest is sold to another person for more or less than the selling partner's share of the inside basis of partnership assets. The buying partner's outside basis equals the price paid for the interest, but the buyer's share of the partnership's inside basis is the same amount as the seller's share of the inside basis.

Concept Summary 14.2 reviews the rules that apply to partnership asset contributions and the related basis computations.

14-2e Tax Accounting Elections

A newly formed partnership must make numerous tax accounting elections. These elections are formal decisions on how a particular transaction or tax attribute should be handled. Most of these elections must be made by the partnership rather than by the partners individually.[22] For example, the *partnership* makes the elections involving the following tax accounting items.

LO.3

Determine the tax treatment of expenditures of a newly formed partnership and identify elections available to the partnership.

- Inventory method.
- Cost or percentage depletion method, excluding oil and gas wells.
- Tax year and accounting method (cash, accrual, or hybrid).
- Cost recovery methods and assumptions.
- First-year cost recovery deductions for certain tangible personal property.
- Treatment (i.e., deduction or credit) of research and experimentation costs.
- Amortization of organizational costs and amortization period.
- Amortization of startup expenditures and amortization period.
- Nonrecognition treatment for gains from involuntary conversions.
- Cost allocation methods to compute the domestic production activities deduction.

Each partner is bound by the decisions made by the partnership relative to these elections. If the partnership fails to make an election, a partner cannot make the election individually.

---

[22]§ 703(b).

Although most elections are made by the partnership, each *partner* individually makes a specific election for the following relatively narrow tax accounting issues.

- Whether to take a deduction or a credit for taxes paid to foreign countries.
- Whether to claim the cost or percentage depletion method for oil and gas wells.
- Whether to reduce the basis of depreciable property first when excluding income from discharge of indebtedness.

14-2f Initial Costs of a Partnership

In its initial stages, a partnership incurs expenses relating to some or all of the following: forming the partnership (organizational costs), admitting partners to the partnership, marketing and selling partnership units to prospective partners (syndication costs), acquiring assets, starting business operations (startup costs), negotiating contracts, and dealing with other items.

Many of these expenditures are not currently deductible. However, the Code permits a deduction or ratable (straight-line) amortization of "organizational" and "startup" costs. Costs incurred to acquire tangible assets are included in the initial basis of the acquired assets, leading to depreciation deductions. "Syndication costs" may be neither amortized nor deducted.[23]

Organizational Costs

Organizational costs are incurred incident to the creation of the partnership and are capital in nature. Such costs include accounting and legal fees associated with the partnership formation.[24] Costs incurred for the following purposes are *not* organizational costs.

- Acquiring assets for the partnership.
- Transferring assets to the partnership.
- Admitting partners, other than at formation.
- Removing partners, other than at formation.
- Negotiating operating contracts.

A partnership may deduct up to $5,000 of organizational costs in the year in which it begins business. This amount is reduced, however, by these organizational costs that exceed $50,000. Any organizational costs that cannot be deducted under this provision are amortizable over 180 months beginning with the month in which the partnership begins business.

The election to deduct organizational costs is made by entering the proper amounts on the first partnership return. Lacking such a computation, no deduction or amortization of the organizational costs is allowed until the entity is liquidated.

| Example 16 | The Bluejay LLC, which was formed on March 1, incurs $52,000 in organizational costs. Bluejay uses a calendar tax year. On its first tax return for the period March–December, Bluejay can deduct $5,722 for these items. This deduction is the sum of:

- $5,000 reduced by the $2,000 ($52,000 − $50,000) amount by which the organizational costs exceed $50,000 = $3,000.
- $2,722 ($49,000 × 10/180) amortization of the remaining $49,000 ($52,000 − $3,000) of organizational costs for 10 months.

If Bluejay had failed to make a proper election to deduct or amortize the organizational costs, none of these costs would have been deductible until the entity liquidated.

Startup Costs

Operating costs that are incurred after the entity is formed but before it begins business are known as startup costs. Like organizational costs, startup costs are

[23]§ 709(a).   [24]§ 709(b)(2).

capitalized and may be immediately expensed and/or amortized.[25] Such costs include marketing surveys prior to conducting business, pre-operating advertising expenses, costs of establishing an accounting system, and salaries paid to executives and employees before the start of business.

A partnership may deduct up to $5,000 of startup costs in the year in which it begins business. This amount is reduced, however, by the startup costs that exceed $50,000.

Costs that are not deductible under this provision are amortizable over 180 months beginning with the month in which the partnership begins business. If the deduction for startup costs is not claimed, no deduction or amortization of the startup costs is allowed until the partnership is liquidated.

> In-depth coverage can be found on this book's companion website: **www.cengagebrain.com**   **3**   Digging Deeper

14-3 OPERATIONS OF THE PARTNERSHIP

A key consideration in the taxation of partnerships is that a variety of entities can be partners and each may be affected differently by the partnership's operations. In particular, any combination of individuals, corporations, trusts, estates, or other partnerships may be partners. Furthermore, at the end of each year, every partner receives a share of the partnership's income, deductions, credits, and alternative minimum tax (AMT) preferences and adjustments.[26]

These flow-through items ultimately may be reported and taxed on a wide variety of income tax returns [e.g., Forms 1040 (Individuals), 1041 (Fiduciaries), 1120 (C corporations), and 1120S (S corporations)], each facing different limitations and rules. Thus, the ultimate tax treatment of partnership operations is directly affected by how the partnership reports its operating results.

LO.4

Calculate partnership taxable income and describe how partnership items affect a partner's income tax return.

14-3a Reporting Operating Results

A partnership measures and reports two kinds of income: separately stated items and nonseparately stated ordinary (operating) income. A separately stated item is any item with tax attributes that could affect partners differently. Separately stated items are segregated and reported separately on the partnership's Schedule K and each partner's Schedule K–1. All other (nonseparately stated) income and expenses are reported on page 1 of the partnership's Form 1065 and then allocated to the partners on Schedules K and K–1. Items passed through separately include the following.[27]

- Net short-term and net long-term capital gains or losses.
- Section 1231 gains and losses.
- Charitable contributions.
- Portfolio income items (qualified and ordinary dividends, interest, and royalties).
- Expenses related to portfolio income.
- Immediately expensed tangible personal property (§ 179).
- Data used by partners to compute their deduction for domestic production activities.[28]
- AMT preference and adjustment items.
- Self-employment income.
- Passive activity items (e.g., rental real estate income or loss).
- Intangible drilling and development costs.
- Taxes paid to other countries.

A partnership is not allowed to claim the following deductions.

---

[25]§ 195.
[26]§ 702(a).

[27]§ 702(b).
[28]§ 199.

- Net operating loss (NOL).
- Dividends received deduction.
- Items that are allowed only to individuals, such as standard deductions or personal exemptions.

THE BIG PICTURE

Example 17

Return to the facts of *The Big Picture* on p. 14-1. In its second year of operations, Beachside Properties, LLC, reports income and expenses from operating the café as well as rent income and expenses from leasing the other buildings. Beachside's activities are summarized as follows.

Sales revenue	$2,000,000
Cost of sales	800,000
Salaries to employees	500,000
Cost recovery deductions	91,984
Utilities, supplies, and other expenses	128,016
Taxes and licenses (including payroll taxes)	60,000
Contribution to charity	6,000
Short-term capital gain	12,000
Net income from rental real estate	300,000
Qualified dividends received	4,000
Tax-exempt income (bond interest)	2,100
AMT adjustment (cost recovery)	18,224
Payment of medical expenses on behalf of partner Kyle	4,000
Net operating loss (NOL) from last year's operations	250,000
Cash distribution to Maria	20,000

Refer to Form 1065 in Appendix B. Beachside's ordinary income is determined and reported on the partnership return as follows.

Nonseparately Stated Items (Ordinary Income)	
Sales revenue	$2,000,000
Cost of sales	(800,000)
Salaries to employees	(500,000)
Cost recovery deductions	(91,984)
Utilities, supplies, and other expenses	(128,016)
Taxes and licenses (including payroll taxes)	(60,000)
Ordinary income [Form 1065, page 1, line 22, and Form 1065, page 4 (Schedule K), line 1]	$ 420,000

Beachside's separately stated income and deduction items are:

Separately Stated Income and Deductions (Schedule K)	
Net income from rental real estate (line 2)	$300,000
Qualified dividends received (line 6b)	4,000
Short-term capital gain (line 8)	12,000
Contribution to charity (line 13a)	(6,000)

Beachside is not allowed a deduction for last year's NOL—this item was passed through to the owners in the previous year. Moreover, the LLC is not allowed a deduction for payment of Kyle's medical expenses. This payment probably is handled as a distribution to Kyle, who may report it as a medical expense on his Form 1040, Schedule A in determining itemized deductions.

Maria's distribution is not deducted by Beachside. That amount instead reduces Maria's basis in her LLC interest.

The AMT adjustment is not a separate component of Beachside's ordinary income. It is reported by Beachside's members so that they can properly calculate any AMT liability of their own.

Beachside reports the following additional information the members may utilize in preparing their own income tax returns.

Additional Information (Schedule K)	
AMT adjustment—cost recovery (line 17a)	$18,224
Tax-exempt income—bond interest (line 18a)	2,100
Distributions (line 19a)	24,000
Investment income (line 20a)	4,000

The LLC members' pass-through income represents net earnings (loss) from self-employment and is reported on line 14a.

THE BIG PICTURE

Example 18

Continue with the facts in Example 17, but now consider the entity's book-tax reconciliation. Beachside Properties, LLC, must prepare the Analysis of Income (Loss) and Schedule M–1 on Form 1065, page 5. In preparing these schedules, the LLC combines the ordinary income of $420,000 and the four separately stated income and deduction amounts in Example 17 to arrive at "net income" of $730,000. This amount is shown on line 1 of the Analysis of Income (Loss) and is the amount to which book income is reconciled on Schedule M–1, line 9.

THE BIG PICTURE

Example 19

Assume the same facts as in Example 17, but now consider the effect of the LLC's operations on one of its members. Maria, a 40% owner, will receive a Schedule K–1 from Beachside Properties, on which she is allocated a 40% share of ordinary income and separately stated items. Thus, on her Form 1040, Maria includes $168,000 of ordinary income, a $2,400 charitable contribution, a $4,800 short-term capital gain, $120,000 of passive rent income, and $1,600 of qualified dividend income. Maria's Schedule K-1 also reports the $20,000 cash distribution received.

Maria discloses her $840 share of tax-exempt interest on the first page of Form 1040. In determining her AMT liability (if any), Maria will take into account a $7,290 positive adjustment.

Domestic Production Activities Deduction (§ 199)

As noted in Chapter 5, the conduct of certain businesses, usually manufacturing activities, can yield a domestic production activities deduction (DPAD). To determine the base for the deduction, domestic production gross receipts (DPGR) is computed. Then related cost of goods sold and direct and indirect expenses are subtracted to arrive at qualified production activities income (QPAI). The deduction (or DPAD) generally is 9 percent of the lesser of QPAI or taxable income.[29] When the taxpayer is not a corporation, modified AGI is substituted for taxable

---
[29]§ 199(a).

Global Tax Issues

© iStockphoto.com/Andrey Prokhorov

Withholding Procedures Apply to Foreign Partners

A U.S. partnership may have non-U.S. partners, and these owners are taxed on their share of the entity's U.S. income. Because it might be difficult for the IRS to collect the Federal income tax that is owed by such partners, several Code sections require the partnership to withhold and pay to the U.S. Treasury an amount relating to the non-U.S. partners.

If the partnership reports U.S. business income, withholding is required using the highest applicable Federal income tax rate. For instance, the withholding amount for a partner who is a non-U.S. individual is 39.6 percent of the owner's applicable share of the year's U.S. business income. The rate is 35 percent for a non-U.S. corporate partner.

Gross income that relates to dividends, interest, rents, or other "fixed and determinable annual or periodic payments (FDAP)" generally is subject to withholding at a 30 percent rate. If a partnership sells U.S. real estate, the entity typically withholds 20 percent of the gain allocated to any non-U.S. partner.

Tax treaties can reduce these withholding tax rates or provide exceptions as to whether withholding is required at all.

income. In no event, however, may the DPAD exceed 50 percent of the W–2 wages paid that are attributable to domestic production activities.[30]

When pass-through entities are involved (i.e., partnerships, S corporations, estates, and trusts), special rules apply.[31] Specifically, in the case of partnerships and limited liability entities, the following rules govern the DPAD computation and allowance.

- Whether an activity qualifies for the DPAD is determined at the entity level.
- Each partner is allocated its share of QPAI and W–2 wages related to domestic production activities. The appropriate amounts are listed on Schedule K–1 of Form 1065.
- The partner combines the partnership pass-through items with those from other sources (e.g., if the partner operates a separate factory).
- The deduction then is computed at the partner level.
- Guaranteed payments, discussed in detail in a later section, are not W–2 wages for DPAD purposes.[32]

Digging Deeper   4      In-depth coverage can be found on this book's companion website: **www.cengagebrain.com**

Distributions, Withdrawals

Asset distributions and withdrawals by partners during the year do not affect the partnership's income determination and reporting process.[33] These items usually are treated as distributions made on the last day of the partnership's tax year. Such distributions reduce the partner's outside basis by the amount of the cash received. The entity's inside basis in assets is similarly reduced.

Example 20

Bueno Company is a partner in the BB Partnership. The basis in Bueno's partnership interest is $10,000. The partnership distributes $3,000 of cash to Bueno at the end of the year. Bueno does not recognize any gain on the distribution and reduces its basis in BB by $3,000 (the amount of the distribution) to $7,000. Bueno's basis in the cash received is $3,000, and the partnership's inside basis for its assets is reduced by the $3,000 of cash distributed.

---

[30]§ 199(b).
[31]The rules applicable to pass-through entities are contained in § 199(d)(1) and Reg. § 1.199–5.
[32]Reg. § 1.199–5(b)(1)(i).
[33]§ 731(a).

© tuuliijumala/Shutterstock.com

CONCEPT SUMMARY 14.3

Tax Reporting of Partnership Activities

Item	Partnership Level (Form 1065)	Partner Level (Schedule K–1)
1. Compute partnership ordinary income.	Page 1, line 22. Schedule K, line 1.	Line 1. Each partner's share is passed through for separate reporting. Each partner's basis is increased.
2. Compute partnership ordinary loss.	Page 1, line 22. Schedule K, line 1.	Line 1. Each partner's share is passed through for separate reporting. Each partner's basis is decreased. The amount of a partner's loss deduction may be limited. Losses that may not be deducted are carried forward for use in future years.
3. Separately reported income and deduction items such as portfolio income, capital gain and loss, AMT and foreign tax items, and § 179 deductions.	Schedule K, various lines.	Various lines. Each partner's share of each item is passed through for separate reporting.
4. Net earnings from self-employment.	Schedule K, line 14a, Code A.	Line 14, Code A.

© iStockphoto.com/Andrey Prokhorov

The result in Example 20 arises whether or not a similar distribution is made to other partners. In a partnership, all partners need not receive a pro rata distribution at the same time, as long as capital account balances are maintained appropriately.

In-depth coverage can be found on this book's companion website: **www.cengagebrain.com**   **5**   Digging Deeper

14-3b Partnership Allocations

After ordinary income, separately stated items, and other related information are determined at the partnership level, those amounts are allocated among the partners and reported on their tax returns. Allocations are made as required by the partnership agreement, using the profit and loss sharing ratios agreed to by the owners.

Alternatively, two key special allocation rules also can affect a partner's Schedule K–1 results.[34]

Economic Effect

The partnership agreement can provide that any partner may share capital, profits, and losses in ratios that are tailored to their needs.[35] For example, a partner could have a 25 percent capital sharing ratio, yet be allocated 30 percent of the profits and 20 percent of the losses of the partnership, or, as in Examples 5 and 6, a partner could be allocated a specific amount or items of income, deduction, gain, or loss. Such special allocations are permissible if they meet the **economic effect test**.[36] The rules prevent partners from shifting income and loss items merely to reduce current taxes.

---

[34]The Code requires or allows certain other allocations not discussed here.
[35]§ 704(a).
[36]Reg. § 1.704–1(b).

Digging Deeper 6 In-depth coverage can be found on this book's companion website: **www.cengagebrain.com**

Precontribution Gain or Loss

Certain income, gain, loss, and deductions relative to contributed property may not be allocated under the economic effect rules.[37] Instead, **precontribution gain or loss** is allocated among the partners to take into account the variation between the basis of the property and its fair market value on the date of contribution.[38] For nondepreciable property, this means that *built-in* gain or loss on the date of contribution is allocated to the contributing partner when the property eventually is disposed of by the partnership in a taxable transaction.

THE BIG PICTURE

Example 21

Return to the facts of *The Big Picture* on p. 14-1. When Beachside Properties, LLC, was formed, among other items, Kyle contributed land (value of $800,000 and basis of $600,000) and buildings (value of $1,200,000 and basis of $0). Maria contributed equipment and furnishings (value of $500,000 and basis of $0).

For book purposes, Beachside records the land and other properties at their fair market values. For tax purposes, the LLC takes carryover bases in the properties. The LLC must keep track of the differences between the basis in each property and the value at the contribution date. If any of this property is sold, the gain is allocated to the contributing partner to the extent of any previously unrecognized built-in gain.

For example, if Beachside sells the land contributed by Kyle for $1.1 million, the gain is calculated and allocated as follows.

	Book	Tax
Amount realized	$1,100,000	$1,100,000
Less: Adjusted basis	(800,000)	(600,000)
Gain realized	$ 300,000	$ 500,000
Built-in gain allocated solely to Kyle	(–0–)	(200,000)
Remaining gain (allocated among members)	$ 300,000	$ 300,000

For tax purposes, Kyle recognizes $320,000 of the gain [($300,000 × 40%) + $200,000], Maria recognizes $120,000 ($300,000 × 40%), and Josh recognizes $60,000 ($300,000 × 20%).

14-3c Basis of a Partnership Interest

LO.5

Determine a partner's basis in the partnership interest.

A partner's basis in the partnership interest is important for determining the treatment of distributions from the partnership to the partner, establishing the deductibility of partnership losses, and calculating gain or loss on the partner's disposition of the partnership interest.

A partner's basis is not reflected anywhere on the Schedule K–1. Instead, each partner maintains a personal record of the basis in the partnership interest.

Initial Basis in the Partnership Interest

A partner's basis in a newly formed partnership usually equals (1) the adjusted basis in any property contributed to the partnership plus (2) the fair market value of any services the partner performed for the partnership (i.e., the amount of ordinary income reported by the partner for services rendered to the partnership).

---

[37]§ 704(b).   [38]§ 704(c)(1)(A).

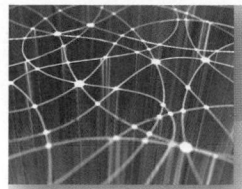

A partnership interest also can be acquired after the partnership has been formed. The method of acquisition controls how the partner's initial basis is computed. If the partnership interest is purchased from another partner, the purchasing partner's basis is the amount paid (cost basis) for the partnership interest. The basis of a partnership interest acquired by gift is the donor's basis for the interest plus, in certain cases, some or all of the transfer (gift) tax paid by the donor. The basis of a partnership interest acquired through inheritance generally is the fair market value of the interest on the date the partner dies.

Basis Adjustments Due to Entity Operations

After the partnership begins its activities, or after a new partner is admitted to the partnership, the partner's basis is adjusted for numerous items. The following operating results *increase* a partner's basis.

- The partner's proportionate share of partnership income (including capital gains and tax-exempt income).
- The partner's proportionate share of any increase in partnership liabilities.

The following operating results *decrease* the partner's basis in the partnership. A partner's basis in the partnership interest cannot be reduced below zero.

- The partner's proportionate share of partnership deductions and losses (including capital losses).
- The partner's proportionate share of nondeductible expenses.
- The partner's proportionate share of any reduction in partnership liabilities.[39]

Increasing the basis for the partner's share of partnership taxable income is logical, because the partner has already been taxed on the income. By increasing the partner's basis, the partner is not taxed again on the income when he or she sells the interest or receives a distribution from the partnership.

It also is logical that tax-exempt income should increase the partner's basis. If the income is tax-exempt in the current period, it should not contribute to the recognition of gain when the partner either sells the interest or receives a distribution from the partnership. Decreasing the basis for the partner's share of deductible losses, deductions, and noncapitalizable, nondeductible expenditures is done for the same reasons.

Example 22

Yuri is a one-third member in the XYZ LLC. His proportionate share of operations during the current year consists of $20,000 of ordinary taxable income and $10,000 of tax-exempt income. None of the income is distributed to Yuri.

The basis of Yuri's LLC interest before adjusting for his share of income is $35,000, and the fair market value of the interest before considering the income items is $50,000.

---

[39]§§ 705 and 752.

The unrealized gain inherent in Yuri's investment in XYZ is $15,000 ($50,000 − $35,000). Yuri's proportionate share of the income items should increase the fair market value of the interest to $80,000 ($50,000 + $20,000 + $10,000). When the basis of Yuri's interest is increased to $65,000 ($35,000 + $20,000 + $10,000), the unrealized gain inherent in Yuri's investment remains at $15,000.

Thus, $20,000 of ordinary taxable income is taxed to Yuri this year and should not be taxed again when Yuri either sells his interest or receives a distribution. Similarly, the tax-exempt income is exempt this year and should not increase Yuri's gain when he either sells his interest or receives a distribution from XYZ.

Partnership Liabilities

A partner's basis includes the partner's share of partnership debt.[40] Partnership debt includes most debt that is considered a liability under financial accounting rules. However, partnership debt for this purpose does *not* include the accounts payable of a cash basis partnership and certain contingent liabilities.

Partnership debt is classified as either recourse or nonrecourse.[41] For **recourse debt**, the partnership or at least one of the partners is personally liable. This liability can exist, for example, through the operation of state law or through personal guarantees that a partner makes to the creditor. If the entity defaults on the loan, the lender can pursue the other assets of the borrower, including personal-use property.

For **nonrecourse debt**, no partner is personally liable. Lenders of nonrecourse debt generally require that collateral be pledged against the loan. Upon default, the lender can claim only the collateral, not the partners' personal assets.

TAX FACT   What Do Partnerships Do?

Partnerships report over $20 trillion in assets on their Form 1065 balance sheets. The partnership form seems to be especially popular for businesses operating in the financial services and real estate industries. Manufacturing assets tend not to be found as frequently in these entities.

Assets of Partnerships, by Industry

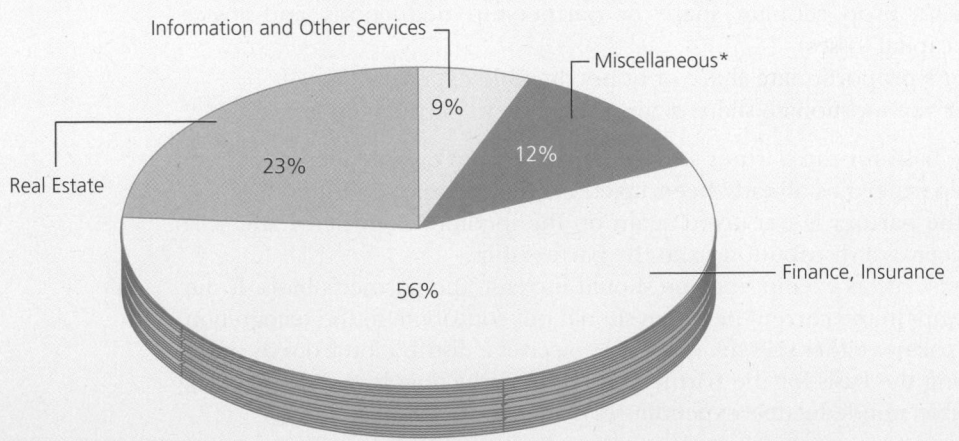

Information and Other Services — 9%
Miscellaneous* — 12%
Real Estate — 23%
Finance, Insurance
56%

*Includes aggregated amounts from the agriculture, health care, construction, manufacturing, wholesale and retail trade, education, and arts and entertainment sectors.

[40]§ 752.

[41]Reg. § 1.752–1(a). All of the debts of an LLC generally are treated as nonrecourse debt for its members, because it is the entity, and not the members, that is ultimately liable for repayment.

> **Example 23**
>
> The Bay Partnership financed its asset acquisitions with debt. If the partnership defaults on the debt, the lender can place a lien on the partners' salaries and personal assets. This constitutes recourse debt.

> **Example 24**
>
> The Tray LLC financed its asset acquisitions with debt. If the entity defaults on the debt, the lender can repossess the equipment purchased with the loan proceeds. This constitutes nonrecourse debt.

> **Example 25**
>
> When Ray bought into the Sleigh LLC, the entity was in the midst of settling litigation as to its liability to those who had purchased its products and were making warranty claims against the entity. Ray's basis in his Sleigh interest does not include his share of these contingent liabilities.

A partner's share of entity-level debt usually increases as a result of increases in outstanding partnership debt. This creates additional basis in the partnership for the partner, against which flow-through losses can be deducted.

> **Example 26**
>
> Jim and Becky contribute property to form the JB Partnership. Jim contributes cash of $30,000. Becky contributes land with an adjusted basis and fair market value of $45,000, subject to a liability of $15,000. The partnership borrows $50,000 to finance construction of a building on the contributed land. At the end of the first year, the accrual basis partnership owes $3,500 in trade accounts payable to various vendors. No other operating activities occurred. If Jim and Becky share equally in liabilities, the partners' bases in their partnership interests are determined as follows.
>
> | Jim's Basis | | Becky's Basis | |
> |---|---|---|---|
> | Contributed cash | $30,000 | Basis in contributed land | $ 45,000 |
> | | | Less: Debt assumed by partnership | (15,000) |
> | Share of debt on land (assumed by partnership) | 7,500 | Share of debt on land (assumed by partnership) | 7,500 |
> | Share of construction loan | 25,000 | Share of construction loan | 25,000 |
> | Share of trade accounts payable | 1,750 | Share of trade accounts payable | 1,750 |
> | Basis, end of year 1 | $64,250 | Basis, end of year 1 | $ 64,250 |

A decrease in a partner's share of partnership debt is treated as a cash distribution and decreases the partner's basis. This limits the partner's ability to deduct current-year flow-through losses.

In-depth coverage can be found on this book's companion website: **www.cengagebrain.com** **7**   Digging Deeper

14-3d Partner's Basis, Gain, and Loss

The partner's basis also is affected by (1) postacquisition contributions of cash or property to the partnership and (2) postacquisition distributions of cash or property from the partnership.

> **Example 27**
>
> Ed is a one-third member in ERM LLC. On January 1, Ed's basis in his interest was $50,000. The calendar year, accrual basis entity generated ordinary taxable income of $210,000. It also received $60,000 of tax-exempt interest income from City of Buffalo bonds. It paid $3,000 in nondeductible fines and penalties.
>
> On July 1, Ed contributed $20,000 cash and a computer (zero basis to him) to ERM. Ed's monthly cash draw from the LLC is $3,000; this is not a guaranteed payment. The only entity liabilities are trade accounts payable. On January 1, the trade accounts payable totaled $45,000; this account balance was $21,000 on December 31. Ed shares in one-third of the entity's liabilities for basis purposes.

Ed's basis in the LLC on December 31 is $115,000, computed as follows.

Beginning basis in the LLC interest	$ 50,000
Share of ordinary income	70,000
Share of tax-exempt income	20,000
Share of nondeductible fines and penalties	(1,000)
Ed's basis in noncash capital contribution (computer)	–0–
Additional cash contributions	20,000
Capital withdrawal ($3,000 per month)	(36,000)
Share of net decrease in ERM liabilities [$\frac{1}{3} \times$ ($45,000 − $21,000)]	(8,000)
Ending basis in the LLC interest	$115,000

If Ed withdraws cash of $115,000 from ERM the next year, the withdrawal is tax-free to him and reduces his basis to zero. The distribution is tax-free because Ed has recognized his share of net income throughout his association with the entity via the annual flow-through of his share of the ERM income and expense items to his personal tax return.

Note that the $20,000 cash withdrawal of his share of the municipal bond interest retains its nontaxable character in this distribution. Ed receives the $20,000 tax-free because his basis was increased when ERM received the interest income.

Property Distributions

When a distribution involves something other than cash, the recipient partner (1) reduces the basis in the partnership interest and (2) assigns a basis to the asset received, both by the amount of the inside basis of the distributed asset. When cash and another asset are distributed at the same time, the partner first accounts for the cash received. Loss never is recognized when a partnership makes a distribution other than possibly in its own liquidation. A partner recognizes gain only when receiving *cash* in an amount in excess of the basis in the partnership.

Example 28

Pert Corporation has a $100,000 basis in the PQR Partnership. Pert receives a distribution from PQR in the form of a plot of land (basis to PQR of $40,000, fair market value of $50,000). Pert recognizes no gain from the distribution. Pert's basis in the land is $40,000 (i.e., a carryover basis), and its basis in PQR now is $60,000 ($100,000 − $40,000).

Example 29

Pert Corporation has a $100,000 basis in the PQR Partnership. Pert receives a distribution from PQR in the form of a plot of land (basis to PQR of $40,000, fair market value of $50,000) and $75,000 of cash.

Pert recognizes no gain from the distribution because the cash received ($75,000) does not exceed Pert's partnership basis ($100,000). Pert's basis in the land is $25,000, the basis in PQR remaining after accounting for the cash ($100,000 partnership basis − $75,000 cash = $25,000 basis assigned to land). Pert's basis in the partnership now is zero ($25,000 basis after accounting for the cash − $25,000 assigned to the land).

Example 30

Pert Corporation has a $100,000 basis in the PQR Partnership. Pert receives a distribution from PQR in the form of a plot of land (basis to PQR of $40,000, fair market value of $50,000) and $125,000 of cash. Pert recognizes $25,000 of gain from the distribution ($125,000 cash received − $100,000 basis in PQR). Pert's basis in the land is $0, as there is no basis in PQR remaining after accounting for the cash. Pert's basis in the partnership also is zero.

Entity-level liabilities, and thus a partner's basis in the partnership, may change from day to day, but the partner's basis generally needs to be computed only once or twice a year. Figure 14.1 on p. 14-27 summarizes the rules for computing a partner's basis in a partnership interest.

Capital Changes

When a partnership interest is sold, exchanged, or retired, the partner must compute the basis as of the date the transaction occurs. The partner recognizes gain or loss on the disposition of the partnership interest, and this usually is a capital gain or loss. Income "bunching" may occur if the partner recognizes the pass-through of operating income in the same tax year during which the sale of the interest occurs. To the extent the partner is allocated a share of ordinary income items (i.e., "hot assets") that have yet to be recognized by the partnership, some of the capital gain is converted to ordinary income.[42]

When its basis in the TUV Partnership is $100,000, taking into account all earnings to date and the sale-date liabilities of the partnership, Kurt Corporation sells its interest in the entity to Gloria for $120,000. Kurt recognizes a $20,000 capital gain [$120,000 (amount realized) − $100,000 (basis in partnership interest)].	**Example 31**

When its basis in the TUV Partnership is $100,000, taking into account all earnings to date and the sale-date liabilities of the partnership, Kurt Corporation sells its interest in the entity to Gloria for $120,000. At the time of the sale, Kurt's share of the TUV hot assets is $8,000. Kurt recognizes $8,000 of ordinary income and $12,000 of capital gain (i.e., the total gain of $20,000 is comprised of $8,000 of ordinary income and $12,000 of capital gain).	**Example 32**

When its basis in the TUV Partnership is $100,000, taking into account all earnings to date and the sale-date liabilities of the partnership, Kurt Corporation sells its interest in the entity to Gloria for $120,000. At the time of the sale, Kurt's share of the TUV hot assets is $28,000. Kurt recognizes $28,000 of ordinary income and $8,000 of capital loss (i.e., the total gain of $20,000 is comprised of $28,000 of ordinary income and $8,000 of capital loss).	**Example 33**

14-3e Loss Limitations

Partnership losses flow through to the partners for use on their tax returns. However, the amount and nature of the partner's deductible losses may be limited. When limitations apply, all or some of the losses are suspended and carried forward until the rules allow them to be used. Only then can the losses decrease the partner's tax liability.

Three different limitations may apply to partnership losses that are passed through to a partner. The first allows the deduction of *losses* only to the extent the partner has a positive basis in the partnership interest. Losses that are deductible under this basis limitation may then be subject to the *at-risk* limitations. Losses are deductible under this provision only to the extent the partner is at risk for the partnership interest. Any losses that survive this second limitation may be subject to a third limitation, the *passive* loss rules. Only losses that make it through all three of these applicable limitations are eligible to be deducted on the partner's tax return.

LO.6

Apply the limitations on deducting partnership losses.

Meg is a 50% member in MQ Telecomm Services LLC. On January 1, Meg's basis in her LLC interest is $50,000, and her at-risk amount is $35,000. Her share of losses from MQ for the year is $60,000, all of which is passive. Meg owns another income-producing investment that generated $25,000 of passive income during the year. Meg can deduct $25,000 of the MQ losses on her Form 1040.	**Example 34**

Applicable Provision	Deductible Loss	Suspended Loss
Basis limitation	$50,000	$10,000
At-risk limitation	35,000	15,000
Passive loss limitation	25,000	10,000

---

[42]Partnership items that hold unrecognized ordinary income are known as *hot assets*. Hot assets include the unrealized receivables of a cash basis partnership and a broadly defined concept of inventory. §§ 751(a) and (d).

Meg can deduct only $50,000 under the basis limitation rule. Of this $50,000, only $35,000 is deductible under the at-risk limitation. Under the passive loss limitation, passive losses can only be deducted against passive income. Thus, Meg can deduct only $25,000 on her return. The remaining $35,000 of losses is suspended.

Basis Limitation

As just discussed, a partner may deduct losses and deductions flowing through from the partnership only to the extent of the partner's basis in the partnership.[43] Items that cannot be deducted because of this rule are suspended and carried forward (never back) for use against future increases in the partner's basis. Such increases might result from additional capital contributions, from sharing in additional partnership debts, or from future partnership income.

Example 35

Carol and Dan do business as the CD Partnership, sharing profits and losses equally. All parties use the calendar year. At the start of the current year, the basis of Carol's partnership interest is $25,000. The partnership sustains an operating loss of $80,000 in the current year. Only $25,000 of Carol's $40,000 allocable share of the partnership loss can be deducted under the basis limitation. As a result, the basis of Carol's partnership interest is zero as of January 1 of the following year, and Carol must carry forward the remaining $15,000 of partnership losses.

Now assume that CD earns a profit of $70,000 for the next calendar year. Carol reports net partnership income of $20,000 ($35,000 share of income − $15,000 carryforward loss). The basis of Carol's partnership interest becomes $20,000.

Tax Planning Strategies MAKE YOUR OWN TAX SHELTER

FRAMEWORK FOCUS: DEDUCTIONS

Strategy: Maximize Deductible Amounts.

In Example 35, Carol's entire $40,000 share of the current-year partnership loss could have been deducted under the basis limitation in the current year if she had contributed an additional $15,000 or more in capital by December 31 of the first tax year. Alternatively, if the partnership had incurred additional debt by the end of the first tax year, Carol's basis might have been increased to permit some or all of the loss to be deducted in that year.

Thus, if partnership losses are projected for a given year, careful tax planning can ensure their deductibility under the basis limitation. Note, however, that the effects of the at-risk and passive activity limitations as discussed below also must be considered.

Figure 14.1 shows that contributions to capital, partnership income items, and distributions from the partnership are taken into account before loss items. This *losses last* rule can produce some unusual results in taxation of partnership distributions and deductibility of losses.

Example 36

The Ellen-Glenn Partnership is owned equally by two partners: Ellen and the Glenn Hospital. At the beginning of the year, Ellen's basis in her partnership interest is $0. Her share of partnership income is $12,000 for the year, and she receives a $10,000 distribution from the partnership.

Under the basis adjustment ordering rules of Figure 14.1, Ellen's basis first is increased by the $12,000 of partnership income; then it is decreased by her $10,000 distribution. She reports her $12,000 share of partnership taxable income on her personal tax return. Her basis in the partnership at the end of the year is $2,000 ($0 beginning basis + $12,000 income − $10,000 distribution).

---

[43]§ 704(d).

FIGURE 14.1	Partner's Basis in Partnership Interest

Basis generally is adjusted in the following order.

Initial basis. Amount paid for partnership interest, or gift or inherited basis (including share of partnership debt).

+ Partner's subsequent asset contributions and allocable debt increases.
+ Since interest acquired, partner's share of the partnership's:
  - Income items.
  - Tax-exempt income items.
  - Excess of depletion deductions over adjusted basis of property subject to depletion.
− Partner's distributions and withdrawals and allocable debt decreases.
− Since interest acquired, partner's share of the partnership's:
  - Separately stated deductions.
  - Nondeductible items not chargeable to a capital account.
  - Special depletion deduction for oil and gas wells.
  - Loss items.

The basis of a partner's interest never can be negative.

Example 37

Assume the same facts as in Example 36, except that Ellen's share of partnership operating results is a $12,000 loss instead of $12,000 income. She again receives a $10,000 distribution.

A distribution of cash in excess of basis in the partnership interest results in a gain to the distributee partner to the extent of the excess. Ellen's distribution is considered before the deductibility of the loss is evaluated under the basis limitation.

Therefore, Ellen recognizes gain on the $10,000 distribution because she has a $0 basis in her partnership interest. Unfortunately for Ellen, the operating loss cannot be deducted under the basis limitation rule, because Ellen still holds a $0 basis in her partnership interest. The loss is suspended, and Ellen carries it forward to a future tax year.

At-Risk Limitation

Under the at-risk rules (see Chapter 6), a partner's deductions for certain pass-through losses are limited to amounts that are economically invested in the partnership. Invested amounts include the cash and the adjusted basis of property contributed by the partner and the partner's share of partnership earnings that has not been distributed.[44]

Losses that are not deductible under the at-risk rules are suspended. When a positive at-risk amount arises in a future tax year, the suspended loss is allowed.

When some or all of the partners are personally liable for partnership recourse debt, that debt is included in the basis of the partnership for those partners. Usually, those partners also include the debt in their amount at risk.

No partner, however, carries any financial risk on nonrecourse debt. Therefore, as a general rule, partners cannot include nonrecourse debt in their amount at risk even though that debt is included in the basis of their partnership interest. This rule has an important exception, however. Real estate nonrecourse financing provided by a bank, retirement plan, or similar party or by a Federal, state, or local government generally is deemed to be at risk.[45] Such debt is termed **qualified nonrecourse debt**.

Example 38

Kelly invests $5,000 in the Kelly Green Limited Partnership as a 5% general partner. Shortly thereafter, the partnership acquires the master recording of a well-known vocalist for $250,000 ($50,000 from the partnership and $200,000 secured from a local bank via *recourse* debt). Kelly's share of the recourse debt is $10,000, and her basis in the interest is $15,000 ($5,000 cash investment + $10,000 debt share).

---

[44]§ 465(a). [45]§ 465(b)(6).

Because the debt is recourse, Kelly's at-risk amount also is $15,000. Kelly's share of partnership losses in the first year of operations is $11,000. Kelly can deduct the full $11,000 of partnership losses under both the basis and the at-risk limitations because this amount is less than both her outside basis and at-risk amount.

Example 39

Assume the same facts as in Example 38, except that the bank loan is nonrecourse. Kelly's basis in the partnership interest still is $15,000, but she can deduct only $5,000 of the flow-through loss. The amount she has at risk in the partnership does not include the nonrecourse debt. (The debt does not relate to real estate, so it cannot be qualified nonrecourse debt.)

The $6,000 suspended loss ($11,000 loss pass-through − $5,000 deduction) is deducted in a future tax year when a positive at-risk amount exists. This might occur because the entity has generated an undistributed net profit, or due to a capital contribution by Kelly.

Passive Activity Rules

A partnership loss pass-through also may be disallowed under the passive activity rules. Recall from Chapter 6 that an activity is considered passive if the taxpayer (in this case, a partner) does not materially participate or if the activity is considered a rental activity.

Losses from passive partnership activities are aggregated by each partner with his or her other passive income and losses. Any net passive loss is suspended and carried forward to future years, unless the partner also has generated net passive income for the tax year. The passive activity limitation applies after the owner's basis and at-risk limitations.

14-4 TRANSACTIONS BETWEEN PARTNER AND PARTNERSHIP

LO.7

Use the tax laws regarding transactions between a partner and the partnership.

Many types of transactions occur between a partnership and its partners. A partner may contribute property to the partnership, perform services for the partnership, or receive distributions from the partnership. A partner may borrow money from or lend money to the partnership. Property may be bought and sold between a partner and the partnership. Several of these transactions were discussed earlier in the chapter. The remaining types of partner-partnership transactions are the focus of this section.

14-4a Guaranteed Payments

A **guaranteed payment** is a payment for services performed by the partner or for the use of the partner's capital. The payment is not determined by reference to partnership income. Guaranteed payments usually are expressed as a fixed-dollar amount or as a percentage of capital the partner has invested in the partnership. Whether the partnership deducts or capitalizes the guaranteed payment depends on the nature of the payment.

Example 40

Donna, Deepak, and Dale formed the accrual basis DDD Partnership. DDD and each of the partners are calendar year taxpayers. According to the partnership agreement, Donna is to manage the partnership and receive a $21,000 distribution from the entity every year, payable in 12 monthly installments. Deepak is to receive an amount that is equal to 18% of his capital account, as it is computed by the firm's accountant at the beginning of the year, payable in 12 monthly installments. Dale is DDD's advertising specialist. She withdraws 4% of the partnership's net income for personal use. Donna and Deepak receive guaranteed payments from the partnership, but Dale does not.

Guaranteed payments resemble the salary or interest payments of other businesses and receive somewhat similar income tax treatment.[46] In contrast to the

---
[46]§ 707(c).

provision that usually applies to withdrawals of assets by partners from their partnerships, guaranteed payments are deductible (or capitalized) by the entity. Deductible guaranteed payments, like any other deductible expenses of a partnership, can create an ordinary loss for the entity.

The partner's guaranteed payment is reported as a separately stated item on Schedules K and K–1. The partner uses this information (in lieu of a Form W–2 or 1099) to report the income on the partner's tax return. Partners receiving a guaranteed payment report ordinary income and treat it as paid on the last day of the entity's tax year.

Example 41

Continue with the situation introduced in Example 40. For calendar year 2014, Donna receives the $21,000 as provided by the partnership agreement, Deepak's guaranteed payment is $17,000, and Dale withdraws $20,000 under the personal expenditures clause. Before considering these amounts, the partnership's ordinary income for the year is $650,000.

DDD can deduct its payments to Donna and Deepak, so the final amount of its ordinary income is $612,000 ($650,000 − $21,000 − $17,000). Thus, each of the equal partners is allocated $204,000 of ordinary partnership income ($612,000 ÷ 3). In addition, Donna reports the $21,000 guaranteed payment as gross income, and Deepak includes the $17,000 guaranteed payment in his gross income.

Dale's partnership draw is a distribution from her interest basis and is not taxed separately to her.

Example 42

Assume the same facts as in Example 41, except that the partnership uses a "natural business" tax year that ends on March 31, 2015. Thus, even though Donna received 9 of her 12 payments for fiscal 2015 in the 2014 calendar year, all of Donna's guaranteed payments are taxable to her in 2015. Similarly, all of Deepak's guaranteed payments are taxable to him in 2015, rather than when they are received.

The deduction for, and the gross income from, guaranteed payments is allowed on the same date that all of the other income and expense items relative to the partnership are allocated to the partners (i.e., on the last day of the entity's tax year).

14-4b Other Transactions between a Partner and a Partnership

Many common transactions between a partner and the partnership are treated as if the partner were an outsider, dealing with the partnership at arm's length.[47] Loan transactions, rental payments, and sales of property between the partner and the partnership generally are treated in this manner.

Example 43

The Eastside Co-op, a one-third partner in the ABC Partnership, owns a tract of land the partnership wants to purchase. The land has a fair market value of $30,000 and an adjusted basis to Eastside of $17,000. If Eastside sells the land to ABC, Eastside recognizes a $13,000 gain on the sale, and ABC takes a $30,000 cost basis in the land. If the land has a fair market value of $10,000 on the sale date, Eastside recognizes a $7,000 loss.

In-depth coverage can be found on this book's companion website: **www.cengagebrain.com**   **8** | Digging Deeper

Sales of Property

No loss is recognized on a sale of property between a person and a partnership when the person owns, directly or indirectly, more than 50 percent of partnership capital or profits.[48] The disallowed loss may not vanish entirely, however. If the person later sells the property at a gain, the disallowed loss reduces the gain that would otherwise be recognized.[49]

---

[47]§ 707(a).
[48]§ 707(b).

[49]This is similar to treatment under § 267.

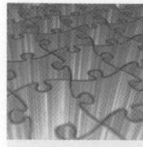

CONCEPT SUMMARY 14.4

Partner-Partnership Transactions

1. Partners can transact business with their partnerships in a nonpartner capacity. These transactions include the sale and exchange of property, rentals, and loans of funds.
2. A payment to a partner may be classified as a guaranteed payment if it is for services or use of the partner's capital and is not based on partnership income. A guaranteed payment usually is deductible by the partnership and is included in the partner's income on the last day of the partnership's tax year.
3. Losses are disallowed between a partner or related party and a partnership when the partner or related party owns more than a 50% interest in the partnership's capital or profits.
4. Income from a related-party sale is treated as ordinary income if the property is not a capital asset to both the transferor and the transferee.
5. Partners are not employees of their partnership, so the entity cannot deduct payments for partner fringe benefits, nor need it withhold or pay any payroll tax for payments to partners.
6. A partner may be subject to self-employment tax on guaranteed payments received and on a distributive share of flow-through income.

© iStockphoto.com/Andrey Prokhorov

Example 44

Barry sells land (adjusted basis, $30,000; fair market value, $45,000) to the BCD LLC, of which he controls a 60% capital interest. BCD pays him only $20,000 for the land. Barry cannot deduct his $10,000 realized loss. Barry and the LLC are related parties, and the loss is disallowed.

When BCD sells the land to an outsider at a later date, it receives a sales price of $44,000. The entity can offset the recognition of its $24,000 realized gain on the subsequent sale ($44,000 sales proceeds − $20,000 adjusted basis) by the amount of the $10,000 prior disallowed loss ($20,000 − $30,000). Thus, BCD recognizes a $14,000 gain on its sale of the land.

Using a similar rationale, any gain that is realized on a sale or exchange between a partner and a partnership in which the partner controls a capital or profits interest of more than 50 percent is recognized as ordinary income, unless the asset is a capital asset to both the seller and the purchaser.[50]

Example 45

The Kent School purchases some land (adjusted basis, $30,000; fair market value, $45,000) for $45,000 from the JJ Realty LLC, in which Kent controls a 90% profits interest. The land was a capital asset to JJ. If Kent holds the land as a capital asset, the LLC recognizes a $15,000 capital gain. However, if the school also is a land developer and the property is not a capital asset to it, JJ recognizes $15,000 of ordinary income from the sale, even though it held the property as a capital asset.

14-4c Partners as Employees

A partner usually does not qualify as an employee for tax purposes. For example, a partner receiving guaranteed payments is not regarded as an employee of the partnership for purposes of payroll taxes (e.g., FICA or FUTA). Moreover, because a partner is not an employee, the partnership cannot deduct its payments for the partner's fringe benefits. Nonetheless, a general partner's share of ordinary partnership income and guaranteed payments for services generally are classified as Federal self-employment (SE) income.[51]

The partner pays an SE tax in addition to the Federal income tax on pass-through items, and the combination of these tax obligations can become expensive. Tax liabilities on SE income of a partner include:

- A 12.4 percent tax on the first $117,000 (for 2014) of SE income, for the individual's account in the FICA retirement system.

[50]§ 707(b)(2).   [51]§ 1402(a).

- A 2.9 percent tax on all SE income, to support the Medicare system.
- An additional .9 percent tax to support the Medicare system, on the excess of SE income over $200,000 ($250,000 for a taxpayer filing a joint return).

With respect to pass-through items of investment income, another 3.8 percent Medicare tax applies to the extent that modified AGI exceeds $200,000 ($250,000 for a taxpayer filing a joint return).

In-depth coverage can be found on this book's companion website: **www.cengagebrain.com** **9** | Digging Deeper

---

| *Tax Planning Strategies* | TRANSACTIONS BETWEEN PARTNERS AND PARTNERSHIPS |

FRAMEWORK FOCUS: DEDUCTIONS

Strategy: **Maximize Deductible Amounts.**

To ensure that no negative tax results occur, partners should be careful when engaging in transactions with the partnership. A partner who owns a majority of the partnership generally should not sell property at a loss to the partnership because the loss is disallowed. Similarly, a majority partner should not sell a capital asset to the partnership at a gain if the asset is to be used by the partnership as other than a capital asset. The gain on this transaction is taxed as ordinary income to the selling partner rather than as capital gain.

As an alternative to selling property to a partnership, the partner may lease it to the partnership. The partner recognizes rent income, and the partnership has a rent expense. A partner who needs more cash immediately can sell the property to an outside third party; then the third party can lease the property to the partnership for a fair rental.

14-5 LIMITED LIABILITY ENTITIES

14-5a Limited Liability Companies

The *limited liability company (LLC)* combines partnership taxation with limited personal liability for all owners of the entity. All states and the District of Columbia have passed legislation permitting the establishment of LLCs.

LO.8

Apply partnership tax law provisions to limited liability companies (LLCs) and limited liability partnerships (LLPs).

Taxation of LLCs

A properly structured LLC is taxed as a partnership. Because LLC members are not personally liable for the debts of the entity, the LLC effectively is treated as a limited partnership with no general partners. This may result in an unusual application of partnership taxation rules. The IRS has not specifically ruled on most aspects of LLC taxation, so several of the following comments apply rules as to how a limited partner would be taxed.

- Formation of a new LLC is treated in the same manner as formation of a partnership. Generally, no gain or loss is recognized by the LLC member or the LLC, the member takes a substituted basis in the LLC interest, and the LLC takes a carryover basis in the assets it receives.
- An LLC's income and losses are allocated proportionately. Special allocations are permitted, as long as they are supported by a nontax economic effect.
- An LLC member contributing property with built-in gains can be subject to tax on certain distributions within seven years of the contribution.
- A loss must meet the basis, at-risk, and passive loss requirements to be currently deductible. Because debt of an LLC is considered nonrecourse to each of the members, it is not included in the at-risk limitation unless it is "qualified nonrecourse financing."

CONCEPT SUMMARY 14.5

Advantages and Disadvantages of the Partnership Form

The partnership form may be attractive when one or more of the following factors is present.

- The entity is generating net taxable losses and/or valuable tax credits, which will be of use to the owners.
- The owners want to avoid complex corporate administrative and filing requirements.
- The owners want to make special allocations of certain income or deduction items that are not possible under the C or S corporation forms.
- Other means of reducing the effects of the double taxation of corporate business income (e.g., compensation to owners, interest, and rental payments) have been exhausted.
- The entity does not generate material amounts of tax preference and adjustment items, which increase the AMT liabilities of its owners.
- The entity is generating net passive income, which its owners can use to claim immediate deductions for net passive losses they have generated from other sources.
- The owners hold adequate bases in their ownership interests to facilitate the deduction of flow-through losses and the assignment of an adequate basis to assets distributed in kind to the owners.

The partnership form may be less attractive when one or more of the following factors is present.

- The tax paid by the owners on the entity's income is greater than that payable by the entity as a C corporation, and the income is not expected to be distributed soon. (If distributed by a C corporation, double taxation would likely occur.)
- The entity is generating net taxable income without distributing any cash to the owners. The owners may not have sufficient cash with which to pay the tax on the entity's earnings.
- The type of income the entity is generating (e.g., business and portfolio income) is not as attractive to its owners as net passive income would be, because the owners could use net passive income to offset the net passive losses they have generated on their own.
- The entity is in a high-exposure business, and the owners want protection from personal liability. An LLC or LLP structure may be available, however, to limit personal liability.
- The owners want to avoid Federal self-employment tax.
- Partnership operations are complex (indicating that Form 1065 might not be filed until near the due date for the return), but partners with the same tax year need to file their returns as early as possible for personal reasons (e.g., to meet debt requirements or to receive a tax refund).

- The initial accounting period and accounting method elections are available to an LLC.
- Property takes a carryover or substituted basis when distributed from an LLC.

Advantages of an LLC

An LLC offers certain advantages over a limited partnership.

- Generally, none of the members of an LLC is personally liable for the entity's debts. In contrast, general partners in a limited partnership have personal liability for partnership recourse debts.
- Limited partners cannot participate in the management of a partnership. All owners of an LLC have the legal right to participate in the entity's management.

An LLC also offers certain advantages over an S corporation (see Chapter 15), including the following.

- An LLC can have an unlimited number of owners, while an S corporation is limited to 100 shareholders.
- Any taxpayers, including corporations, nonresident aliens, other partnerships, and trusts, can be owners of an LLC. S corporation shares can be held only by specified parties.
- The transfer of property to an LLC in exchange for an ownership interest in the entity is governed by partnership tax provisions rather than corporate tax

Partnerships around the World

Global Tax Issues

© iStockphoto.com/Andrey Prokhorov

Technology continues to act as a catalyst—and incentive—for the creation of joint ventures. From web kiosks at gas stations to global satellite networks, high-tech companies are forging alliances to bring technology to consumers.

Microsoft has teamed up with BP to provide news, weather, and other content for customers to watch while they fill up at the gas station. Time Warner and Radiant Systems, Inc., formed their own venture to offer programming at other gas stations, pizza parlors, and numerous other retail outlets. These ventures appear to be spurred by a desire to capture larger shares of the ever-expanding global market.

Meanwhile, various domestic communications companies are continuing to align themselves with partners in non-U.S. markets; each wants to have the widest possible service coverage area so it can offer efficient networking to business clients with a global presence.

provisions. Thus, the transfers need not satisfy the 80 percent control requirement needed for tax-free treatment under the corporate tax statutes (see Chapter 12).

- The S corporation taxes on built-in gains and passive income do not apply to LLCs.
- An owner's basis in an LLC includes the owner's share of almost all LLC liabilities under the law. Only certain entity liabilities are included in the S corporation shareholder's basis.
- An LLC may make special allocations, whereas S corporations must allocate income, loss, etc., only on a per-share/per-day basis.

Disadvantages of an LLC

Only a limited body of case law interprets the various state statutes, so the application of specific provisions in a specific state may be uncertain. An additional uncertainty for LLCs that operate in more than one jurisdiction pertains to which state's law will prevail and how it will be applied.

Among other factors, statutes differ from state to state as to the type of business an LLC can conduct—primarily the extent to which a service-providing firm can operate as an LLC. Special rules also may apply where the LLC has only one member.

Despite these uncertainties and limitations, LLCs are being formed at increasing rates, and the ranks of multistate LLCs also are rising quickly.

14-5b Limited Liability Partnerships

The difference between a general partnership and a limited liability partnership (LLP) is small, but very significant. General partners are jointly and severally liable for all partnership debts. Partners in an LLP are jointly and severally liable for commercial debt. They also are personally liable for their own malpractice or other torts. They are not, however, personally liable for the malpractice and torts of their partners. As a result, the exposure of their personal assets to lawsuits filed against other partners and the partnership is considerably reduced.

14-6 SUMMARY

Partnerships and LLCs are popular among business owners because formation of the entity is relatively simple and tax-free. The Code places very few restrictions on who can be a partner. Partnerships are especially attractive when operating losses are anticipated or when marginal rates that would apply to partnership income are less than those that would be paid by a C corporation. Partnerships do not offer the limited liability of a corporate entity, but the use of limited partnerships, LLCs, and LLPs can offer some protection to the owners.

Partnerships are tax-reporting, not taxpaying, entities. Distributive shares of ordinary income and separately stated items are taxed to the partners on the last day of the tax year. Special allocations and guaranteed payments are allowed and offer partners the ability to tailor the cash-flow and taxable amounts that are distributed by the entity to its owners. Deductions for flow-through losses may be limited by the related-party, passive activity, and at-risk rules, as well as by the partner's basis in the partnership. The flexibility of the partnership rules makes this form continually attractive to new businesses, especially in a global setting.

REFOCUS ON THE BIG PICTURE

THE TAX CONSEQUENCES OF PARTNERSHIP FORMATION AND OPERATIONS

After considering the various types of partnerships, Kyle, Maria, and Josh decided to form Beachside Properties as an LLC. Upon formation of the entity, there was no gain or loss recognized by the LLC or any of its members (see Example 15). Beachside Properties computes its income as shown in Example 17 and allocates the income as illustrated in Example 19. The LLC's income affects the members' bases and capital accounts. An important consideration for the LLC members is whether their distributive shares and guaranteed payments will be treated as self-employment income.

What If?

What happens in the future when the LLC members decide to expand or renovate Beachside's facilities? At that time, the existing members can contribute additional funds, the entity can receive capital from new members, or the entity can borrow money. A partnership or limited liability entity is not subject to the 80 percent control requirement applicable to the formation of a corporation and subsequent transfers to it. Therefore, new investors can contribute cash or other property in exchange for interests in the entity—and the transaction will qualify for tax-deferred treatment.

© Roderick Paul Walker/Alamy

Suggested Readings

J. Everett, W. Raabe, and C. Hennig, "Planning Considerations When Converting a C Corporation to an LLC," *The Tax Adviser*, February 2011.

Susan L. Megaard and Michael M. Megaard, "Reducing Self-Employment Taxes on Owners of LLPs and LLCs," *Business Entities*, March/April 2012.

W. E. Seago, K. Orbach, and E. Schnee, "Working with the Unearned Income Medicare Tax," *Journal of Taxation*, March 2013.

Patrick H. Smith, "Taxation by States of Single-Member LLCs," *Business Entities*, September/October 2007.

Key Terms

Basis in the partnership interest, 14-8

Capital account, 14-7

Capital interest, 14-7

Capital sharing ratio, 14-7

Disguised sale, 14-10

Economic effect test, 14-19

General partnership, 14-3

Guaranteed payment, 14-28

Inside basis, 14-13

Limited liability company (LLC), 14-4

Limited liability partnership (LLP), 14-4

Limited partnership, 14-3

Nonrecourse debt, 14-22

Organizational costs, 14-14

Outside basis, 14-13

Precontribution gain or loss, 14-20

Profit and loss sharing ratios, 14-7

Profits (loss) interest, 14-7

Qualified nonrecourse debt, 14-27

Recourse debt, 14-22

Separately stated items, 14-5

Special allocation, 14-7

Syndication costs, 14-14

Problems

1. **LO.2** Janda and Kelsey contributed $1 million each to the JKL LLC in exchange for 45% capital and profits interests in the entity. Lilli will contribute no cash, but has agreed to manage the LLC's business operations in exchange for an $80,000 annual salary and a 10% interest in the LLC's capital and profits (valued at $200,000). What are the consequences of the entity formation and Lilli's compensation arrangement to the LLC members? To the LLC itself?   Issue ID

2. **LO.2** Emma and Laine form the equal EL Partnership. Emma contributes cash of $100,000. Laine contributes property with an adjusted basis of $40,000 and a fair market value of $100,000.
   a. How much gain, if any, must Emma recognize on the transfer? Must Laine recognize any gain? If so, how much?
   b. What is Emma's basis in her partnership interest?
   c. What is Laine's basis in her partnership interest?
   d. What basis does the partnership take in the property transferred by Laine?

3. **LO.2** Kenisha and Shawna form the equal KS LLC with a cash contribution of $360,000 from Kenisha and a property contribution (adjusted basis of $380,000, fair market value of $360,000) from Shawna.   Decision Making
   a. How much gain or loss, if any, does Shawna realize on the transfer? Does Shawna recognize any gain or loss? If so, how much?
   b. What is Kenisha's basis in her LLC interest?
   c. What is Shawna's basis in her LLC interest?
   d. What basis does the LLC take in the property transferred by Shawna?
   e. Are there more effective ways to structure the formation? Explain.

4. **LO.2** Liz and John formed the equal LJ Partnership on January 1 of the current year. Liz contributed $80,000 of cash and land with a fair market value of $90,000 and an adjusted basis of $75,000. John contributed equipment with a fair market value of $170,000 and an adjusted basis of $20,000. John previously used the equipment in his sole proprietorship.
   a. How much gain or loss will Liz, John, and LJ realize?
   b. How much gain or loss will Liz, John, and LJ recognize?
   c. What bases will Liz and John take in their partnership interests?
   d. What bases will LJ take in the assets it receives?
   e. How will LJ depreciate any assets it receives from the partners?

5. **LO.2, 3** Skylark, Inc., a calendar year general contractor, and Teal, Inc., a development corporation with a March 31 year-end, formed the equal ST LLC on January 1 of the current year. Both LLC members are C corporations. The LLC was formed to construct and lease retail centers in Seattle.   Issue ID
   Skylark contributed cash of $1.2 million and equipment (basis and fair market value of $800,000). Teal contributed land (basis of $300,000, fair market value of $600,000) and cash of $1.4 million. The cash was used as follows.

Legal fees for drafting the LLC operating agreement	$ 10,000
Materials and labor costs for construction in progress on retail centers	2,500,000
Office expenses (utilities, rent, overhead, etc.)	90,000

What issues must the LLC address in preparing its initial tax return?

6. **LO.2, 5** Sam and Drew are equal members of the SD LLC, formed on June 1 of the current year. Sam contributed land that he inherited from his uncle in 2006. Sam's uncle purchased the land in 1981 for $30,000. The land was worth $100,000 when Sam's uncle died. The fair market value of the land was $200,000 at the date it was contributed to SD.

   Drew has significant experience developing real estate. After SD is formed, he will prepare a plan for developing the property and secure zoning approvals for the LLC. Drew normally would bill a third party $50,000 for these efforts. Drew will also contribute $150,000 of cash in exchange for his 50% interest in SD. The value of Drew's 50% interest is $200,000.

   a. How much gain or income does Sam recognize on his contribution of the land to SD? What is the character of any gain or income recognized?
   b. What basis does Sam take in his LLC interest?
   c. How much gain or income will Drew recognize on the formation of SD? What is the character of any gain or income recognized?
   d. What basis will Drew take in his LLC interest?

7. **LO.2** Continue with the facts presented in Problem 6. At the end of the first year, SD distributes $100,000 cash to Sam. No distribution is made to Drew.

   a. How does Sam treat the payment?
   b. How much income or gain would Sam recognize as a result of the payment?
   c. Under general tax rules, what basis would SD take in the land Sam contributed?

8. **LO.5** Describe the tax treatment of a proportionate nonliquidating distribution of cash, land, and inventory. How are the partner's basis in the property received and the partner's gain or loss on the distribution determined? What are the tax effects to the partnership?

Issue ID   9. **LO.5** The LizMack LLC distributes the following assets to its member, Liz.

   - $20,000 cash.
   - Inventory with a $20,000 value and a $10,000 basis to the entity.
   - A parcel of land with a $30,000 value and a $35,000 basis to the entity.

   What issues must be considered in determining the Federal income tax treatment of the distribution?

10. **LO.3** On July 1 of the current year, the R&R Partnership was formed to operate a bed-and-breakfast inn. The partnership paid $3,000 in legal fees for drafting the partnership agreement and $5,000 for accounting fees related to organizing the entity. It also paid $10,000 in syndication costs to locate and secure investments from limited partners.

   In addition, before opening the inn for business, the entity paid $15,500 for advertising and $36,000 in costs related to an open house just before the grand opening of the property. The partnership opened the inn for business on October 1.

   a. How are these expenses classified?
   b. How much may the partnership deduct in its initial year of operations?
   c. How are costs treated that are not deducted currently?

11. **LO.2, 4** Phoebe and Parker are equal members of Phoenix Investors LLC. They are real estate investors who formed the entity several years ago with equal cash contributions. Phoenix then purchased a parcel of land.

   On January 1 of the current year, to acquire a one-third interest in the entity, Reece contributed to Phoenix some land she had held for investment. Reece purchased the land five years ago for $75,000; its fair market value at the contribution date was $90,000. No special allocation agreements were in effect before or after Reece was admitted to the LLC. Phoenix holds all land for investment.

   Immediately before Reece's property contribution, the Phoenix balance sheet was as follows.

	Basis	FMV		Basis	FMV
Land	$30,000	$180,000	Phoebe, capital	$15,000	$ 90,000
			Parker, capital	15,000	90,000
	$30,000	$180,000		$30,000	$180,000

a. At the contribution date, what is Reece's basis in her interest in Phoenix?

b. When does the LLC's holding period begin for the contributed land?

c. On June 30 of the current year, the LLC sold the land contributed by Reece for $90,000. How much is the recognized gain or loss? How is it allocated among the LLC members?

d. Prepare a balance sheet reflecting basis and fair market value for the entity immediately after the land sale.

12. **LO.4** Assume the same facts as in Problem 11, with the following exceptions.

- Reece purchased the land five years ago for $120,000. Its fair market value was $90,000 when it was contributed to Phoenix.
- Phoenix sold the land contributed by Reece for $84,000.

a. How much is the recognized gain or loss? How is it allocated among the LLC members?

b. Prepare a balance sheet reflecting basis and fair market value for the LLC immediately after the land sale. Complete schedules that support the tax basis and fair market value of each LLC member's capital account.

13. **LO.4, 5** Amy and Mitchell are equal partners in the accrual basis AM Partnership. At the beginning of the current tax year, Amy's capital account has a balance of $300,000, and the partnership has recourse debts of $200,000 payable to unrelated parties. All partnership recourse debt is shared equally between the partners.

The following information about AM's operations for the current year is obtained from the partnership's records.

Ordinary income	$400,000
Interest income from P&G bond	4,000
Long-term capital loss	6,000
Short-term capital gain	12,000
Charitable contribution	4,000
Cash distribution to Amy	20,000

Year-end partnership debt payable to unrelated parties is $140,000. If all transactions are reflected in her beginning capital and basis in the same manner:

a. What is Amy's basis in the partnership interest at the beginning of the year?

b. What is Amy's basis in the partnership interest at the end of the current year?

14. **LO.4, 5** Assume the same facts as in Problem 13. What income, gains, losses, and deductions does Amy report on her income tax return? Based on the information provided, what other calculations is she required to make?

15. **LO.4, 5** Continue with the same facts of Problem 13. Consider Amy's capital account.

a. What is Amy's capital account at the beginning of the year?

b. What is Amy's capital account at the end of the year?

c. How do the capital account balances differ from her basis amounts in Problem 13?

16. **LO.3** Cerulean, Inc., Coral, Inc., and Crimson, Inc., form the Three Cs Partnership on January 1 of the current year. Cerulean is a 50% partner, and Crimson and Coral are 25% partners. For reporting purposes, Crimson uses a fiscal year with an October 31 year-end, Coral uses the calendar year, and Cerulean uses a fiscal year with a February 28/29 year-end. What is the required tax year for Three Cs under the least aggregate deferral method?

Critical Thinking

17. **LO.2, 4, 5** The JM Partnership was formed to acquire land and subdivide it as residential housing lots. On March 1, 2014, Jessica contributed land valued at $600,000 to the partnership in exchange for a 50% interest. She had purchased the land in 2006 for $420,000 and held it for investment purposes (capital asset). The partnership holds the land as inventory.

On the same date, Matt contributed land valued at $600,000 that he had purchased in 2004 for $720,000. He became a 50% owner. Matt is a real estate developer, but he held this land personally for investment purposes. The partnership holds this land as inventory.

In 2015, the partnership sells the land contributed by Jessica for $620,000. In 2016, the partnership sells the real estate contributed by Matt for $580,000.

a. What is each partner's initial basis in his or her partnership interest?

b. What is the amount of gain or loss recognized on the sale of the land contributed by Jessica? What is the character of this gain or loss?

c. What is the amount of gain or loss recognized on the sale of the land contributed by Matt? What is the character of this gain or loss?

d. How would your answer in (c) change if the property were sold in 2021?

18. **LO.2, 5** Lee, Brad, and Rick form the LBR Partnership on January 1 of the current year. In return for a 25% interest, Lee transfers property (basis of $15,000, fair market value of $17,500) subject to a nonrecourse liability of $10,000. The liability is assumed by the partnership. Brad transfers property (basis of $16,000, fair market value of $7,500) for a 25% interest, and Rick transfers cash of $15,000 for the remaining 50% interest.

a. How much gain must Lee recognize on the transfer?

b. What is Lee's basis in his interest in the partnership?

c. How much loss may Brad recognize on the transfer?

d. What is Brad's basis in his interest in the partnership?

e. What is Rick's basis in his interest in the partnership?

f. What basis does the LBR Partnership take in the property transferred by Lee?

g. What is the partnership's basis in the property transferred by Brad?

Critical Thinking

19. **LO.2, 5** Assume the same facts as in Problem 18, except that the property contributed by Lee has a fair market value of $27,500 and is subject to a nonrecourse mortgage of $20,000.

a. What is Lee's basis in his partnership interest?

b. How much gain must Lee recognize on the transfer?

c. What is Brad's basis in his partnership interest?

d. What is Rick's basis in his partnership interest?

e. What basis does the LBR Partnership take in the property transferred by Lee?

Issue ID

20. **LO.2, 4, 5** Sam has operated a microbrewery (sole proprietorship) in southern Oregon for the past 15 years. The business has been highly profitable lately, and demand for the product will soon exceed the amount Sam can produce with his present facilities. Marcie, a long-time fan of the brewery, has offered to invest $1,500,000 for equipment to expand production. The assets and goodwill of the brewery are currently worth $1,000,000 (tax basis is only $200,000). Sam will continue to manage the business. He is not willing to own less than 50% of whatever arrangement they arrive at. What issues should Sam and Marcie address and document before finalizing their venture?

Issue ID

Decision Making

21. **LO.5, 6** The BCD Partnership plans to distribute cash of $20,000 to partner Brad at the end of the tax year. The partnership reported a loss for the year, and Brad's share of the loss is $10,000. Brad has a basis of $15,000 in the partnership interest, including his share of partnership liabilities. The partnership expects to report substantial income in future years.

a. How does Brad calculate the ending basis in his partnership interest?

b. How much income or loss must Brad report for the tax year?

c. Will the deduction for any of the $10,000 loss be suspended? Why or why not?

d. Could any planning opportunities be used to minimize the tax ramifications of the distribution? Explain.

22. **LO.2, 3** The Pelican Partnership was formed on August 1 of the current year and admitted Morlan and Merriman as equal partners on that date. The partners both contributed $300,000 of cash to establish a children's clothing store in the local mall. The partners spent August and September buying inventory, equipment, supplies, and advertising for their "Grand Opening" on October 1. The partnership will use the accrual method of accounting. The following are some of the costs incurred during Pelican's first year of operations.

Legal fees to form partnership	$ 8,000
Advertising for "Grand Opening"	18,000
Advertising after opening	30,000
Consulting fees for establishing accounting system	20,000
Rent, at $2,000 per month	10,000
Utilities, at $1,000 per month	5,000
Salaries to salesclerks (beginning in October)	50,000
Payments to Morlan and Merriman for services ($6,000 per month each for three months)	36,000
Tax return preparation expense	12,000

In addition, on October 1, Pelican purchased all of the assets of Granny Newcombs, Inc. Of the total purchase price for these assets, $200,000 was allocated to the Granny Newcombs trade name and logo.

Determine how each of the listed costs is treated by Pelican, and identify the period over which the costs can be deducted, if any.

23. **LO.7** Four GRRLs Partnership is owned by four friends. Lacy holds a 40% interest; each of the others owns 20%. Lacy sells investment property to the partnership for its fair market value of $200,000. Her tax basis in the property was $250,000.
    a. How much loss, if any, may Lacy recognize?
    b. If Four GRRLs later sells the property for $260,000, how much gain must it recognize?
    c. How would your answers in (a) and (b) change if Lacy owned a 60% interest in the partnership?
    d. If Lacy's basis in the investment property was $120,000 instead of $250,000 and she was a 60% partner, how much, if any, gain would she recognize on the sale of the property to Four GRRLs? How is it characterized?

24. **LO.7** Burgundy, Inc., and Violet Gomez are equal partners in the calendar year BV LLC. Burgundy uses a fiscal year ending April 30, and Violet uses a calendar year. Burgundy receives an annual guaranteed payment of $100,000 for use of capital contributed by Burgundy. BV's taxable income (after deducting the payment to Burgundy) is $80,000 for 2014 and $90,000 for 2015.
    a. How much income from BV must Burgundy report for its tax year ending April 30, 2015?
    b. How much income from BV must Violet report for her tax year ending December 31, 2015?

25. **LO.7** Continue with the facts presented in Problem 24. Assume that Burgundy, Inc.'s annual guaranteed payment is increased to $120,000 starting on January 1, 2015, and the LLC's taxable income for 2014 and 2015 (after deducting Burgundy's guaranteed payment) is the same (i.e., $80,000 and $90,000, respectively). How much income from BV must Burgundy report for its tax year ending April 30, 2015?

26. **LO.6** Jasmine Gregory is a 20% member in Sparrow Properties LLC, which is a lessor of residential rental property. Her share of the LLC's losses for the current year is $100,000. Immediately before considering the deductibility of this loss, Jasmine's capital account (which, in this case, corresponds to her basis excluding liabilities) reflected a balance of $50,000. Jasmine has personally guaranteed a $10,000 debt of the LLC that is allocated to her as a recourse debt. Her share of the LLC's nonrecourse debt is $30,000. This debt cannot be treated as qualified nonrecourse debt. Jasmine spends several hundred hours a year working for Sparrow Properties.

    Jasmine also is a managing member of Starling Rentals LLC, which is engaged in long-term (more than 30 days) equipment rental activities. (This is considered a passive activity.) Jasmine's share of Starling's income is $36,000.

    Jasmine's modified adjusted gross income before considering the LLCs' activities is $300,000. Ignore the $25,000 "active participation" rental real estate deduction.

    Determine how much of Sparrow's $100,000 loss Jasmine can deduct on her current calendar year return. Draft a memo for the client's tax file describing the loss limitations. In the memo, identify the Code sections under which losses are suspended.

Communications

Critical Thinking

27. **LO.4, 7** Mona and Denise, mother and daughter, operate a local restaurant as an LLC. The MD LLC earned a profit of $200,000 in the current year. Denise's equal LLC interest was acquired by gift from Mona. Assume that capital is a material income-producing factor and that Mona manages the day-to-day operations of the restaurant without any help from Denise. Reasonable compensation for Mona's services is $50,000.
    a. How much of the MD income is allocated to Mona?
    b. What is the maximum amount of LLC income that can be allocated to Denise?
    c. Assuming that Denise is 15 years old, has no other income, and is claimed as a dependent by Mona, how is Denise's income from the restaurant taxed?

Critical Thinking

28. **LO.5** In each of the following independent cases in which the partnership owns no hot assets, indicate the following. All of the partners received proportionate distributions.

    • Whether the partner recognizes gain or loss.
    • Whether the partnership recognizes gain or loss.
    • The partner's adjusted basis for the property distributed.
    • The partner's outside basis in the partnership after the distribution.

    a. Kim receives $20,000 of cash in partial liquidation of her interest in the partnership. Kim's outside basis for her partnership interest immediately before the distribution is $3,000.
    b. Kourtni receives $40,000 of cash and land with a $30,000 inside basis to the partnership (value $50,000) in partial liquidation of her interest. Kourtni's outside basis for her partnership interest immediately before the distribution is $80,000.
    c. Assume the same facts as in (b), except that Kourtni's outside basis for her partnership interest immediately before the distribution is $60,000.
    d. Klois receives $50,000 of cash and inventory with a basis of $30,000 and a fair market value of $50,000 in partial liquidation of her partnership interest. Her basis was $90,000 before the distribution.

Critical Thinking

29. **LO.4, 5, 7** At the beginning of the tax year, Melodie's basis in the MIP LLC was $60,000, including Melodie's $40,000 share of the LLC's liabilities. At the end of the year, MIP distributed to Melodie cash of $10,000 and inventory (basis of $6,000, fair market value of $10,000). MIP repaid all of its liabilities by the end of the year.
    a. If this is a proportionate nonliquidating distribution, what is the tax effect of the distribution to Melodie and MIP? After the distribution, what is Melodie's basis in the inventory and in her MIP interest?
    b. Would your answers to (a) change if this had been a proportionate liquidating distribution? Explain.

Critical Thinking

30. **LO.2, 4, 5** Suzy contributed business-related assets valued at $360,000 (basis of $200,000) in exchange for her 40% interest in the Suz-Anna Partnership. Anna contributed land and a building valued at $640,000 (basis of $380,000) in exchange for the remaining 60% interest. Anna's property was encumbered by a qualified nonrecourse debt of $100,000, which was assumed by the partnership. The partnership reports the following income and expenses for the current tax year.

Sales	$560,000
Utilities, salaries, and other operating expenses	360,000
Short-term capital gain	10,000
Tax-exempt interest income	4,000
Charitable contributions	8,000
Distribution to Suzy	10,000
Distribution to Anna	20,000

    At the end of the year, Suz-Anna held recourse debt of $100,000 for partnership accounts payable and qualified nonrecourse debt of $200,000.
    a. What is Suzy's basis after formation of the partnership? Anna's basis?
    b. What income and separately stated items does Suz-Anna report on Suzy's Schedule K–1? What items does Suzy report on her tax return?
    c. All partnership debts are shared proportionately. At the end of the tax year, what are Suzy's basis and amount at risk in her partnership interest?

31. **LO.2, 4, 5, 8** Continue with the facts presented in Problem 30, except that Suz-Anna was formed as an LLC instead of a general partnership.

    a. What would be Suzy's share of the LLC's ending liabilities?

    b. How would Suzy's basis and amount at risk be different? Explain.

Critical Thinking

Issue ID

32. **LO.4** The Sparrow Partnership plans to distribute $200,000 cash to its partners at the end of the year. Marjorie is a 40 percent partner and would receive $80,000. Her basis in the partnership is only $10,000, however, so she would recognize a $70,000 gain if she receives the proposed cash distribution.

Ethics and Equity

Communications

Marjorie has asked Sparrow instead to purchase a parcel of land that she has found, on which she will build her retirement residence. The partnership then will distribute that land to her. Under the partnership distribution rules, Marjorie would take a $10,000 basis in the land worth $80,000. Her basis in the partnership would be reduced to $0, but recognition of the $70,000 gain is deferred.

Do you think this is an appropriate transaction? Explain your conclusion in an e-mail to your instructor.

Comprehensive Tax Return Problem

1. Ryan Ross (111-11-1111), Oscar Oleander (222-22-2222), Clark Carey (333-33-3333), and Kim Kardigan (444-44-4444) are equal members in ROCK the Ages LLC. ROCK serves as agent and manager for prominent musicians in the Los Angeles area. The LLC's Federal ID number is 55-5555555. It uses the cash basis and a calendar tax year, and it began operations on January 1, 2002. Its current address is 6102 Wilshire Boulevard, Suite 2100, Los Angeles, CA 90036. ROCK was the force behind such music icons as Rhiannon and Burgundy 5, and it has had a very profitable year. The following information was taken from the LLC's income statement for the current year.

Tax Return Problem

TAX SOFTWARE

Revenues

Fees and commissions	$4,800,000
Taxable interest income from bank deposits	1,600
Tax-exempt interest	3,200
Net gains on stock sales	4,000
Total revenues	$4,808,800

Expenses

Advertising and public relations	$ 380,000
Charitable contributions	28,000
Section 179 expense	20,000
Employee salaries and wages	1,000,000
Guaranteed payment, Ryan Ross, office manager	800,000
Guaranteed payment, other members	600,000
Entertainment, subject to 50% disallowance	200,000
Travel	320,000
Legal and accounting fees	132,000
Office rentals paid	80,000
Interest expense on line of credit for operations	10,000
Insurance premiums	52,000
Office expense	200,000
Payroll taxes	92,000
Utilities	54,800
Total expenses	$3,968,800

During the past few years, ROCK has taken advantage of bonus depreciation and § 179 deductions and fully remodeled the premises and upgraded its leasehold improvements. This year, ROCK wrapped up its remodeling with the purchase of $20,000 of office furniture, for which it will claim a § 179 deduction. ROCK uses the same cost recovery methods for both tax and financial purposes. There is no depreciation adjustment for alternative minimum tax purposes.

ROCK invests much of its excess cash in non-dividend-paying growth stocks and tax-exempt securities. During the year, the LLC sold two securities. On June 15, 2013, ROCK purchased 1,000 shares of Tech, Inc. stock for $100,000; it sold those shares on December 15, 2013, for $80,000. On March 15, 2012, ROCK purchased 2,000 shares of BioLabs, Inc. stock for $136,000; it sold those shares for $160,000 on December 15, 2013. These transactions were reported to the IRS on Forms 1099–B; ROCK's basis in these shares was reported on the form.

Net income per books is $840,000. The firm's activities do not constitute "qualified production activities" for purposes of the § 199 deduction. On January 1, 2013, the members' capital accounts equaled $200,000 each. No additional capital contributions were made in 2013. In addition to their guaranteed payments, each member withdrew $250,000 cash during the year.

ROCK's book balance sheet as of December 31, 2013, is as follows.

	Beginning	Ending
Cash	$ 444,000	$??
Tax-exempt securities	120,000	120,000
Marketable securities	436,000	300,000
Leasehold improvements, furniture, and equipment	960,000	980,000
Accumulated depreciation	(960,000)	(980,000)
Total assets	$1,000,000	$??
Line of credit for operations	$ 200,000	$ 160,000
Capital, Ross	200,000	??
Capital, Oleander	200,000	??
Capital, Carey	200,000	??
Capital, Kardigan	200,000	??
Total liabilities and capital	$1,000,000	$??

All debt is shared equally by the members. Each member has personally guaranteed the debt of the LLC.

The business code for "Agents and Managers for Artists, Athletes, Entertainers, and Other Public Figures" is 711410. The LLC's Form 1065 was prepared by Ryan Ross and sent to the Ogden, UT IRS Service Center. All of the owners are active in ROCK's operations.

a. Prepare pages 1, 4, and 5 of the Form 1065 for ROCK the Ages LLC.
b. If you are using tax return preparation software, prepare Form 4562 and Schedule D.
c. Prepare Schedule K-1 for Ryan Ross, 15520 W. Earlson Street, Pacific Palisades, CA 90272.

BRIDGE DISCIPLINE

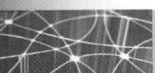

1. What is the function of a partner's capital account under the rules of generally accepted accounting principles (GAAP)? What is the partner's initial balance in the capital account? How and when does the capital account increase and decrease? What is the GAAP treatment of distributions to a partner?

2. Jim Dunn, Amy Lauersen, and Tony Packard have agreed to form a partnership. In return for a 30% capital interest, Dunn transferred machinery (basis $268,000, fair market value $400,000) subject to a liability of $100,000. The liability was assumed by the partnership. Lauersen transferred land (basis $450,000, fair market value $300,000) for a 30% capital interest. Packard transferred cash of $400,000 for the remaining 40% interest. Compute the initial values of Dunn's:
a. Basis in his partnership interest for tax purposes.
b. Capital account for financial reporting purposes.

3. To what extent are the personal assets of a general partner, limited partner, or member of an LLC subject to (a) contractual liability claims, such as trade accounts payable, and (b) malpractice claims against the entity? Answer the question for partners or members in a general partnership, an LLP, a nonprofessional LLC, and a limited partnership.

THOMSON REUTERS
CHECKPOINT®

Note: Solutions to Research Problems can be prepared by using the **Checkpoint®** **Student Edition** online research product, which is available to accompany this text. It is also possible to prepare solutions to the Research Problems by using tax research materials found in a standard tax library.

Research Problem 1. Fredstone Consolidated, Inc., a real estate developer, owns a 50% general partnership interest in Realty Partners, Ltd (Realty). The 50% limited partnership interests are owned by various individual taxpayers.

Fredstone and the limited partner group each contributed $15,000 to form the partnership. The partnership uses the $30,000 contributed by the partners and a recourse loan of $100,000 obtained from an unrelated third-party lender to acquire $130,000 of rental properties. (All amounts are in millions.)

The partners believe that they will generate extensive tax losses in the first year due to depreciation expense and initial cash-flow requirements. Fredstone and the limited partners agreed to share losses equally. To make sure that the losses can be allocated as intended, they included a provision in the partnership agreement requiring each partner to restore any deficit balance in their partnership capital account upon liquidation of the partnership.

Fredstone also was willing to include a provision that requires it to make up any deficit balance within 90 days of liquidation of the partnership. This provision does not apply to the limited partners; instead, they are required to restore any deficit balance in their capital accounts within two years of liquidation of the partnership. No interest accrues on the deferred restoration payment.

Can Realty allocate the $100,000 recourse debt equally to the two partner groups so that they can deduct their respective shares of partnership losses? Explain.

Research Problem 2. Barney Chang and Aldrin, Inc., a domestic C corporation, have decided to form BA LLC. The new entity will produce a product that Barney recently developed and patented. Barney and Aldrin each will own a 50% capital and profits interest in the LLC. Barney is a calendar year taxpayer, while Aldrin is taxed using a June 30 fiscal year end. BA does not have a "natural business year" and elects to be taxed as a partnership.
a. Determine the taxable year of the LLC under the Code and Regulations.
b. Two years after formation of BA, Barney sells half of his interest (25%) to Aldrin. Can BA retain the taxable year determined in part (a)? Why or why not?

Critical Thinking

Research Problem 3. Andy has operated his moving company as a sole proprietorship for several years. In 2014, he put into service $20,000 of property qualifying for immediate expensing under § 179. In 2014, Andy also joined with another local mover to form and operate a storage company, The Attic, organized as an LLC. Andy holds a 90% capital and profits interest in The Attic. In 2014, The Attic purchased and placed into service $215,000 of property qualifying for expensing under § 179. Andy has $150,000 of taxable income from his proprietorship and a $75,000 share of ordinary income from his 90% interest in The Attic, both before considering any § 179 expense. Assuming Andy wants to maximize his current deductions (without sacrificing future deductions), how much can he elect to deduct under § 179?

Use the tax resources of the Internet to address the following questions. Do not restrict your search to the Web, but include a review of newsgroups and general reference materials, practitioner sites and resources, primary sources of the tax law, chat rooms and discussion groups, and other opportunities.

Internet Activity

Communications

Research Problem 4. Find an article posted by a law firm that comments on pitfalls to avoid in drafting partnership agreements. Ideally, use the home page of a firm that has offices in your state. Summarize the posting in no more than four PowerPoint slides, and send your file to your instructor.

Research Problem 5. Find the statutes and regulations that control limited liability companies (LLCs) in your state. An LLC can and cannot conduct what types of business activities?

© iStockphoto.com/Alex Slobodkin

Communications   **Research Problem 6.** Find a blog that concentrates on the taxation of partners and partnerships. Post a message defining the terms *inside basis* and *outside basis* and illustrating why the distinction between them is important. Respond to any replies you receive. Print your message and one or two of the replies.

Communications   **Research Problem 7.** Determine the statutory tax treatment in your state of a one-member LLC. Write an e-mail to your professor, comparing this rule with Federal tax law.

Communications   **Research Problem 8.** Graph the increases in the numbers of LLCs and LLPs filing Federal tax returns for five-year periods beginning with 1970. Explain any trends in the data that you identify. Send your report as an e-mail to your instructor.

LEARNING OBJECTIVES: *After completing Chapter 15, you should be able to:*

LO.1 **Explain the tax effects associated with S corporation status.**

LO.2 **Identify corporations that qualify for the S election.**

LO.3 **Explain how to make and terminate an S election.**

LO.4 **Compute nonseparately stated income and allocate income, deductions, and credits to shareholders.**

LO.5 **Determine how distributions to S corporation shareholders are taxed.**

LO.6 **Calculate a shareholder's basis in S corporation stock.**

LO.7 **Explain the tax effects of losses on S shareholders.**

LO.8 **Compute the entity-level taxes on S corporations.**

CHAPTER OUTLINE

TAX TALK *In levying taxes and in shearing sheep it is well to stop when you get down to the skin.* —AUSTIN O'MALLEY

Dennis Flaherty/Photographer's Choice/Getty Images

Tax Solutions for the Real World   © Wavebreakmedia Ltd/Shutterstock.com

CONVERTING A C CORPORATION TO AN S CORPORATION

Fowle, Inc., has been operating as a C corporation for a number of years, earning taxable income of less than $100,000 per year. The company has accumulated its earnings for a variety of business needs and has not paid dividends to date. Thus, the corporation has been able to take advantage of lower C corporation tax rates and has avoided double taxation problems so far.

Fowle receives some tax-exempt income, generates a small domestic production activities deduction (DPAD), and holds about $200,000 of C corporation earnings and profits. The company's sole owner, David, currently draws a salary of $92,000. Fowle has issued two classes of stock, voting and nonvoting common.

The company now is facing increased competition as a result of cheaper imports from China. David expects very large operating losses for the next few years. David would like to know if he can deduct the anticipated losses.

Read the chapter and formulate your response.

An individual establishing a business has a number of choices as to the form of business entity under which to operate. Chapters 12 and 13 outline many of the rules, advantages, and disadvantages of operating as a regular C corporation. Chapter 14 discusses the partnership entity, as well as the limited liability company (LLC) and limited liability partnership (LLP) forms.

Another alternative, the **S corporation**, provides many of the benefits of partnership taxation and at the same time gives the owners limited liability protection from creditors. The S corporation rules, which are contained in **Subchapter S** of the Internal Revenue Code (§§ 1361–1379), were enacted to allow flexibility in the entity choice that businesspeople face. Thus, S status combines the legal environment of C corporations with taxation similar to that applying to partnerships. S corporation status is obtained through an election by a *qualifying* corporation with the consent of its shareholders.

S corporations are treated as corporations under state law. They are recognized as separate legal entities and generally provide shareholders with the same liability protection afforded by C corporations. Some states (such as Michigan) treat S corporations as C corporations for tax purposes, resulting in a state corporate income or franchise tax liability. For Federal income tax purposes, however, the taxation of S corporations resembles that of partnerships. As with partnerships, the income, deductions, and tax credits of an S corporation flow through to shareholders annually, regardless of whether distributions are made. Thus, income generally is taxed at the shareholder level and not at the corporate level. Distributions made to S shareholders by the corporation are tax-free to the extent the distributed earnings were previously taxed.

Although the tax treatment of S corporations and partnerships is similar, it is not identical. For example, liabilities affect an owner's basis differently, and S corporations may incur a tax liability at the corporate level. In addition, a variety of C corporation provisions apply to S corporations. For example, the liquidation of C and S corporations is taxed in the same way. As a rule, where the S corporation provisions are silent, C corporation rules apply.

The S corporation rules should be seen as supplementary to the Federal income tax rules for all C corporations (see Chapters 12 and 13) and to those for partnerships and limited liability entities (contained in Code Subchapter K; see Chapter 14). Some provisions apply only to electing S corporations (addressed throughout this chapter), but S corporations also must apply certain tax rules of Code Subchapters C and K.

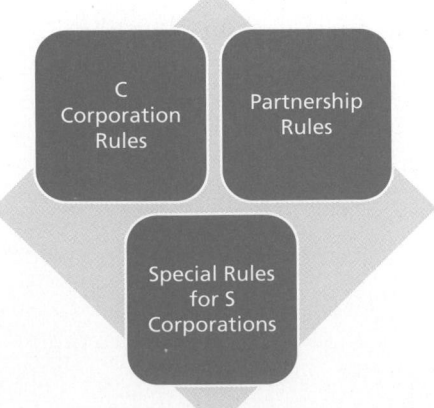

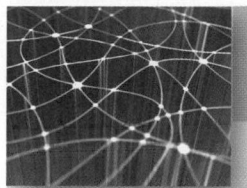

BRIDGE DISCIPLINE   Bridge to Business Law

An S corporation is a corporation for all purposes other than its Federal and state income tax law treatment. The entity registers as a corporation with the secretary of state of the state of its incorporation. It issues shares and may hold some treasury stock. Dealings in its own stock are not taxable to the S corporation.

The corporation itself is attractive as a form of business ownership because it offers limited liability to all shareholders from the claims of customers, employees, and others. This is not the case for any type of partnership, where there always is at least one general partner bearing the ultimate personal liability for the operations of the entity (except in the new limited liability limited partnership). Forming an entity as an S corporation facilitates the raising of capital for the business, as an infinite number of shares can be divided in any way imaginable, so as to pass income and deductions, gains, losses, and credits through to the owners, assuming that the fairly generous "type of shareholder" requirements continue to be met.

An S corporation must comply with all licensing and registration requirements of its home state under the rules applicable to corporate entities. Some states levy privilege taxes on the right to do business in the corporate form, and the S corporation typically is not exempted from this tax.

Because an S corporation is a separate legal entity from its owners, shareholders can be treated as employees and receive qualified retirement and fringe benefits under the Code, as well as unemployment and worker's compensation protection through the corporation. Some limitations apply to the deductibility of fringe benefits, though.

The tax fiction of the S corporation is attractive to investors, as well over one-half of all U.S. corporations have an S election in effect.

15-1 AN OVERVIEW OF S CORPORATIONS

Since the inception of S corporations in 1958, their popularity has waxed and waned with changes in the tax law. Before the Tax Reform Act of 1986, their ranks grew slowly. In contrast, in the two years following the 1986 law change, the number of S corporations increased by 52 percent. Now more than 4 million of the country's 5.8 million corporations have elected S status. The IRS projects that S corporations and limited liability companies (LLCs) will be the most-chosen forms of business entity for the next decade.

Example 1

An S corporation earns $300,000, and all after-tax income is distributed currently. The marginal individual tax rate applicable to the entity's shareholders is 39.6% for ordinary income and 20% for dividend income. The marginal corporate tax rate is 34%. The entity's available after-tax earnings, compared with those of a similar C corporation, are computed below.

	C Corporation	S Corporation
Earnings	$ 300,000	$ 300,000
Less: Corporate income tax	(102,000)	(−0−)
Amount available for distribution	$ 198,000	$ 300,000
Less: Income tax at owner level	(39,600)*	(118,800)**
Available after-tax earnings	$ 158,400	$ 181,200

* $198,000 × 20% dividend income tax rate.
** $300,000 × 39.6% ordinary income tax rate.

The S corporation generates an extra $22,800 of after-tax earnings ($181,200 − $158,400) when compared with a similar C corporation. The C corporation might be able to reduce this disadvantage, however, by paying out its earnings as compensation, rents, or interest to its owners. In addition, tax at the owner level is deferred or avoided by not distributing after-tax earnings.

S corporations file more than 4 million tax returns every year, concentrated in the service and financial industries.

S Corporation Returns Filed (%), 2010 Tax Year

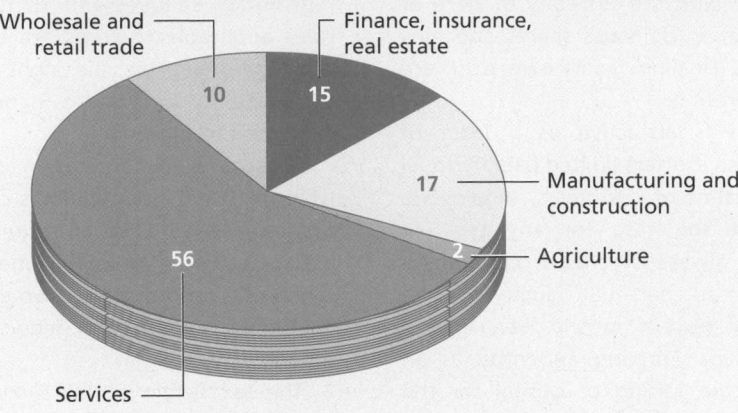

Example 2	A new corporation elects S status and incurs a net operating loss (NOL) of $300,000. The shareholders may use their proportionate shares of the NOL to offset other taxable income in the current year, providing an immediate tax savings. In contrast, a newly formed C corporation is required to carry the NOL forward for up to 20 years and receives no tax benefit in the current year. Hence, an S corporation can accelerate the use of NOL deductions and thereby provide a greater present value for the tax savings generated by the loss.

Limited liability companies can provide tax results similar to those of an S corporation, while avoiding some of the key restrictions that are imposed on S corporations and their shareholders.

15-2 QUALIFYING FOR S CORPORATION STATUS

LO.2

Identify corporations that qualify for the S election.

There are certain conditions that a corporation must meet before S corporation status is available.

15-2a Definition of a Small Business Corporation

To achieve S corporation status, a corporation *first* must qualify as a **small business corporation**. A small business corporation:

* Is a domestic corporation (incorporated and organized in the United States).
* Is eligible to elect S corporation status.
* Issues only one class of stock.
* Is limited to a maximum of 100 shareholders.
* Has only individuals, estates, and certain trusts and exempt organizations as shareholders.
* Has no nonresident alien shareholders.

Unlike other small business provisions in the tax law (e.g., § 1244), no maximum or minimum dollar sales or capitalization restrictions apply to S corporations.

Tax Planning Strategies   WHEN TO ELECT **S** CORPORATION STATUS

FRAMEWORK FOCUS: DEDUCTIONS

Strategy: Maximize Deductible Amounts.

FRAMEWORK FOCUS: TAX RATE

Strategy: Shift Net Income from High-Bracket Taxpayers to Low-Bracket Taxpayers.
Shift Net Income from High-Tax Jurisdictions to Low-Tax Jurisdictions.

A number of considerations will affect a decision to make an S election.

- Avoid the S election if shareholders have high marginal income tax rates relative to C corporation rates.
- If corporate losses are anticipated and there is unlikely to be corporate taxable income soon, S corporation status is advisable.
- If a C corporation holds an NOL carryover from prior years, the losses cannot be used in an S corporation year.

- There may be tax advantages to the S shareholder who receives a flow-through of passive income or the domestic production activities deduction.
- Some states treat S corporations as C corporations and apply a corporate income tax to them.
- Tax-exempt income at the S level does not lose its special tax treatment for shareholders.
- An S corporation avoids the corporate ACE adjustment, personal holding company tax, and accumulated earnings tax.

Ineligible Corporations

S status is not permitted for foreign corporations, certain banks, or insurance companies. S corporations are permitted to have wholly owned C and S corporation subsidiaries.[1]

One Class of Stock

A small business corporation may have only one class of stock issued and outstanding.[2] This restriction permits differences in voting rights, but not differences in distribution or liquidation rights.[3] Thus, two classes of common stock that are identical except that one class is voting and the other is nonvoting are treated as a single class of stock for S corporation purposes. In contrast, voting common stock and voting preferred stock (with a preference on dividends) are treated as two classes of stock. Authorized and unissued stock or treasury stock of another class does not disqualify the corporation. Likewise, unexercised stock options, phantom stock, stock appreciation rights, warrants, and convertible debentures usually do not constitute a second class of stock.[4]

In-depth coverage can be found on this book's companion website: **www.cengagebrain.com**   Digging Deeper

Although the one-class-of-stock requirement seems straightforward, it is possible for debt to be reclassified as stock, resulting in an unexpected loss of S corporation status.[5] To mitigate concern over possible reclassification of debt as a second class of stock, the law provides a set of *safe harbor* provisions. Neither straight debt[6] nor short-term advances[7] constitute a second class of stock.

---

[1]Other eligibility rules exist. § 1361(b).
[2]§ 1361(b)(1)(D).
[3]§ 1361(c)(4).
[4]Reg. § 1.1361–1(l)(2).

[5]Refer to the discussion of debt-versus-equity classification in Chapter 12.
[6]§ 1361(c)(5)(A).
[7]Reg. § 1.1361–1(l)(4).

TAX IN THE NEWS   S Corporation Audits

The IRS is studying S corporations' reporting compliance. Benson Goldstein, technical manager for the AICPA Tax Division, says that "recent research points to S corporations as a significant source of noncompliance, particularly among high-income individuals." But Tom Ochsenschlager, vice president of taxation for the AICPA, points out that "a lot of the errors made are errors, not malfeasance."

Form 1120S audits have increased by about 25 percent in recent years. In 2011, .4 percent of all S corporation returns were audited by the IRS.

Digging Deeper   2   In-depth coverage can be found on this book's companion website: **www.cengagebrain.com**

Number of Shareholders

A small business corporation is limited to 100 shareholders. If shares of stock are owned jointly by two individuals, they generally are treated as separate shareholders. However, family members (e.g., ancestors, descendants, spouses, and former spouses) of the investor can be counted as one shareholder for purposes of determining the number of shareholders.[8]

Example 3	Fred and Wilma (husband and wife) jointly own 10 shares in Oriole, Inc., an S corporation, with the remaining 90 shares outstanding owned by 99 other shareholders. Fred and Wilma are divorced. Both before and after the divorce, the 100-shareholder limit is met, and Oriole can qualify as a small business corporation.

Type of Shareholder Limitation

Small business corporation shareholders may be individuals, estates, or certain trusts and exempt organizations.[9] This limitation prevents partnerships, corporations, most LLCs, LLPs, and most IRAs from owning S corporation stock. Without this rule, partnerships and corporate shareholders could easily circumvent the 100-shareholder limitation.

Example 4	Paul and 200 other individuals want to form an S corporation. Paul reasons that if the group forms a partnership, the partnership can then form an S corporation and act as a single shareholder, thereby avoiding the 100-shareholder rule. Paul's plan will not work, because partnerships cannot own stock in an S corporation.

Nonresident Aliens

Nonresident aliens cannot own stock in a small business corporation.[10] Thus, individuals who are not U.S. citizens *must live in the United States* to own S corporation stock. Shareholders with nonresident alien spouses in community property states[11] cannot own S corporation stock because the nonresident alien spouse is treated as owning half of the stock.[12] Similarly, if a resident alien shareholder moves outside the United States, the S election is terminated.

---

[8]§§ 1361(c)(1)(A)(ii) and (B)(i). TD 9422, 2008–42 I.R.B. 898.

[9]§ 1361(b)(1)(B). A one-member LLC typically is an eligible S shareholder.

[10]§ 1362(b)(1)(C).

[11]Assets acquired by a married couple are generally considered community property in these states: Alaska (by election), Arizona, California, Idaho, Louisiana, Nevada, New Mexico, Texas, Washington, and Wisconsin.

[12]See *Ward v. U.S.*, 81–2 USTC ¶9674, 48 AFTR 2d 81–5942, 661 F.2d 226 (Ct.Cls., 1981), where the court found that the stock was owned as community property. Because the taxpayer-shareholder (a U.S. citizen) was married to a citizen and resident of Mexico, the nonresident alien prohibition was violated. If the taxpayer-shareholder had held the stock as separate property, the S election would have been valid.

> ### *Tax Planning Strategies*   BEATING THE 100-SHAREHOLDER LIMIT
>
> **FRAMEWORK FOCUS: TAX RATE**
>
> *Strategy:* Avoid Double Taxation.
>
> Although partnerships and corporations cannot own small business corporation stock, S corporations themselves can be partners in a partnership or shareholders in a corporation. In this way, the 100-shareholder requirement can be bypassed in a limited sense. For example, if two S corporations, each with 80 shareholders, form a partnership, the shareholders of both corporations can enjoy the limited liability conferred by S corporation status and a single level of tax on the resulting profits.

15-2b Making the Election

To become an S corporation, the entity must file a valid election with the IRS. The election is made on Form 2553. For the election to be valid, it should be filed on a timely basis and all shareholders must consent. For S corporation status to apply in the current tax year, the election must be filed either in the previous year or on or before the fifteenth day of the third month of the current year.[13]

LO.3

Explain how to make and terminate an S election.

> **THE BIG PICTURE**
>
> **Example 5**
>
> Return to the facts of *The Big Picture* on p. 15-1. Suppose that in 2014, David decides to elect that Fowle, Inc., become an S corporation beginning January 1, 2015. Fowle's S election can be made at any time in 2014 or by March 15, 2015. An election after March 15, 2015, will not be effective until the 2016 calendar tax year.

Even if the $2\frac{1}{2}$-month deadline is met, an S election is not valid unless the corporation qualifies as a small business corporation for the *entire* tax year. Otherwise, the election is effective for the following tax year. Late elections, filed after the $2\frac{1}{2}$-month deadline, may be considered timely if there is reasonable cause for the late filing.

A corporation that does not yet exist cannot make an S corporation election.[14] Thus, for new corporations, a premature election may not be effective. A new corporation's $2\frac{1}{2}$-month election period begins at the earliest occurrence of any of the following events.

- When the corporation has shareholders.
- When it acquires assets.
- When it begins doing business.[15]

15-2c Shareholder Consent

A qualifying election requires the consent of all of the corporation's shareholders.[16] Consent must be in writing, and it generally must be filed by the election deadline.

---

[13]§ 1362(b). Extensions of time to file Form 2553 may be possible in certain situations; see Rev.Proc. 2007–62, 2007–41 I.R.B. 786.

[14]See, for example, *T.H. Campbell & Bros., Inc.*, 34 TCM 695, T.C.Memo. 1975–149; Ltr.Rul. 8807070.

[15]Reg. § 1.1372–2(b)(1). Also see, for example, *Nick A. Artukovich*, 61 T.C. 100 (1973).

[16]§ 1362(a)(2).

Both husband and wife must consent if they own their stock jointly (as joint tenants, tenants in common, tenants by the entirety, or community property).[17] Although only limited authority exists for the entity to obtain an extension of time to file an S election (Form 2553), a shareholder may receive an extension of time to file a consent.

Example 6	Vern and Yvonne decide to convert their calendar year C corporation into an S corporation, effective for this year. At the end of February (before the election is filed), Yvonne travels to Ukraine and forgets to sign a consent to the election. Yvonne will not return to the United States until June and cannot be reached by fax or e-mail.
	Vern files the Form 2553 and requests an extension of time to file Yvonne's consent to the election. Vern indicates that there is a reasonable cause for the extension: a shareholder is out of the country.
	Because the government's interest is not jeopardized, the IRS probably will grant Yvonne an extension of time to file the consent. Vern must file the corporation's election on Form 2553 on or before March 15 for S status to be effective for the current calendar year.

Tax Planning Strategies   MAKING A PROPER ELECTION

FRAMEWORK FOCUS: TAX RATE

Strategy: Avoid Double Taxation.

- Because S corporation status is *elected*, strict compliance with the requirements is demanded by both the IRS and the courts. Any failure to meet a condition in the law may lead to loss of the S election and raise the specter of double tax.
- Make sure all shareholders consent. If any doubt exists concerning the shareholder status of an individual, it would be wise to request that he or she sign a consent

anyway.[18] Missing consents are fatal to the election; the same cannot be said for too many consents.
- Make sure the election is timely and properly filed. Either deliver the election to an IRS office in person or send it by certified or registered mail or via a major overnight delivery service. The date used to determine timeliness is the postmark date, not the date the IRS receives the election.

Digging Deeper   3   In-depth coverage can be found on this book's companion website: **www.cengagebrain.com**

15-2d Loss of the Election

An S election remains in force until it is revoked or lost. Election or consent forms are not required for future years. However, an S election can terminate if any of the following occurs.[19]

- Shareholders owning a majority of shares (voting and nonvoting) voluntarily revoke the election.
- A new shareholder owning more than one-half of the stock affirmatively refuses to consent to the election.
- The corporation no longer qualifies as a small business corporation.
- The corporation does not meet the passive investment income limitation.

---

[17]Rev.Rul. 60–183, 1960–1 C.B. 625; *William Pestcoe*, 40 T.C. 195 (1963); Reg. § 1.1362–6(b)(3)(iii). This rule likely also applies to all family members who are being treated as one shareholder.

[18]See *William B. Wilson*, 34 TCM 463, T.C.Memo. 1975–92.
[19]§ 1362(d).

Voluntary Revocation

A **voluntary revocation** of the S election requires the consent of shareholders owning a majority of shares on the day the revocation is to be made.[20] A revocation filed up to and including the fifteenth day of the third month of the tax year is effective for the entire tax year, unless a later date is specified. Similarly, unless an effective date is specified, a revocation made after the first $2\frac{1}{2}$ months of the current tax year is effective for the following tax year.

The shareholders of Petunia Corporation, a calendar year S corporation, voluntarily revoke the S election on January 5, 2014. They do not specify a future effective date in the revocation. If the revocation is properly executed and timely filed, Petunia will be a C corporation for the entire 2014 tax year. If the revocation is not made until June 2014, Petunia remains an S corporation in 2014 and becomes a C corporation at the beginning of 2015.

Example 7

A corporation can revoke its S status *prospectively* by specifying a future date when the revocation is to be effective. A revocation that designates a future effective date splits the corporation's tax year into a short S corporation year and a short C corporation year. The day on which the revocation occurs is treated as the first day of the C corporation year. The corporation allocates income or loss for the entire year on a pro rata basis using the number of days in each short year.

Assume the same facts as in the preceding example, except that Petunia designates July 1, 2014, as the revocation date. Accordingly, June 30, 2014, is the last day of the S corporation's tax year. The C corporation's tax year runs from July 1, 2014, to December 31, 2014. Income or loss for the 12-month period is allocated between the two short years (i.e., 184/365 to the C corporation year).

Example 8

Rather than allocating on a pro rata basis, the corporation can elect to compute the actual income or loss attributable to the two short years. This election requires the consent of everyone who was a shareholder at any time during the S corporation's short year and everyone who owns stock on the first day of the C corporation's year.[21]

Loss of Small Business Corporation Status

If an S corporation fails to qualify as a small business corporation at any time after the election has become effective, its status as an S corporation ends. The termination occurs on the day the corporation ceases to be a small business corporation.[22] Thus, if the corporation ever has more than 100 shareholders, a second class of stock, or a nonqualifying shareholder or it otherwise fails to meet the definition of a small business corporation, the S election is terminated immediately.

Peony Corporation has been a calendar year S corporation for three years. On August 13, one of its 100 shareholders sells *some* of her stock to an outsider. Peony now has 101 shareholders, and it ceases to be a small business corporation. Peony is an S corporation through August 12 and a C corporation from August 13 to December 31.

Example 9

---

[20]§ 1362(d)(1)(B).
[21]§ 1362(e)(3).

[22]§ 1362(d)(2)(B).

Passive Investment Income Limitation

The Code provides a **passive investment income (PII)** limitation for some S corporations that previously were C corporations, or for S corporations that have merged with C corporations. If an S corporation has C corporation earnings and profits (E & P) and passive income in excess of 25 percent of its gross receipts for three consecutive taxable years, the S election is terminated as of the beginning of the fourth year.[23]

Example 10

For 2013, 2014, and 2015, Chrysanthemum Corporation, a calendar year S corporation, derived passive investment income in excess of 25% of its gross receipts. If Chrysanthemum holds accumulated E & P from years in which it was a C corporation, its S election is terminated as of January 1, 2016.

PII includes dividends, interest, rents, gains and losses from sales of capital assets, and royalties net of investment deductions. Rents are not considered PII if the corporation renders significant personal services to the occupant.

Example 11

Violet Corporation owns and operates an apartment building. The corporation provides utilities for the building, maintains the lobby, and furnishes trash collection for tenants. These activities are not considered significant personal services, so any rent income earned by the corporation will be considered PII.

Alternatively, if Violet also provides maid services to its tenants (personal services beyond what normally would be expected from a landlord in an apartment building), the rent income would no longer be PII.

Reelection after Termination

After an S election has been terminated, the corporation must wait five years before reelecting S corporation status. The five-year waiting period is waived if:

* There is a more-than-50-percent change in ownership of the corporation after the first year for which the termination is applicable, or
* The event causing the termination was not reasonably within the control of the S corporation or its majority shareholders.

Tax Planning Strategies PRESERVING THE S ELECTION

FRAMEWORK FOCUS: TAX RATE

Strategy: Avoid Double Taxation.

Unexpected loss of S corporation status can be costly to a corporation and its shareholders. Given the complexity of the rules facing these entities, constant vigilance is necessary to preserve the S election.

* As a starting point, the corporation's management and shareholders should be made aware of the various transactions that can lead to the loss of an election.
* Prevent violations of the small business corporation limitations. Because most such violations result from

transfers of stock, the corporation and its shareholders should consider adopting a set of stock transfer restrictions.

A carefully designed set of restrictions could prevent sale of stock to nonqualifying entities or violation of the 100-shareholder rule. Similarly, stock could be repurchased by the corporation under a buy-sell agreement upon the death of a shareholder, thereby preventing nonqualifying trusts from becoming shareholders.[24]

---

[23]§ 1362(d)(3)(A)(ii).

[24]Most such agreements do not create a second class of stock. Rev.Rul. 85–161, 1985–2 C.B. 191; *Portage Plastics Co. v. U.S.*, 72–2 USTC ¶9567, 30 AFTR 2d 72–5229, 470 F.2d 308 (CA–7, 1973).

| FIGURE 15.1 | Flow-Through of Items of Income and Loss to S Corporation Shareholders |

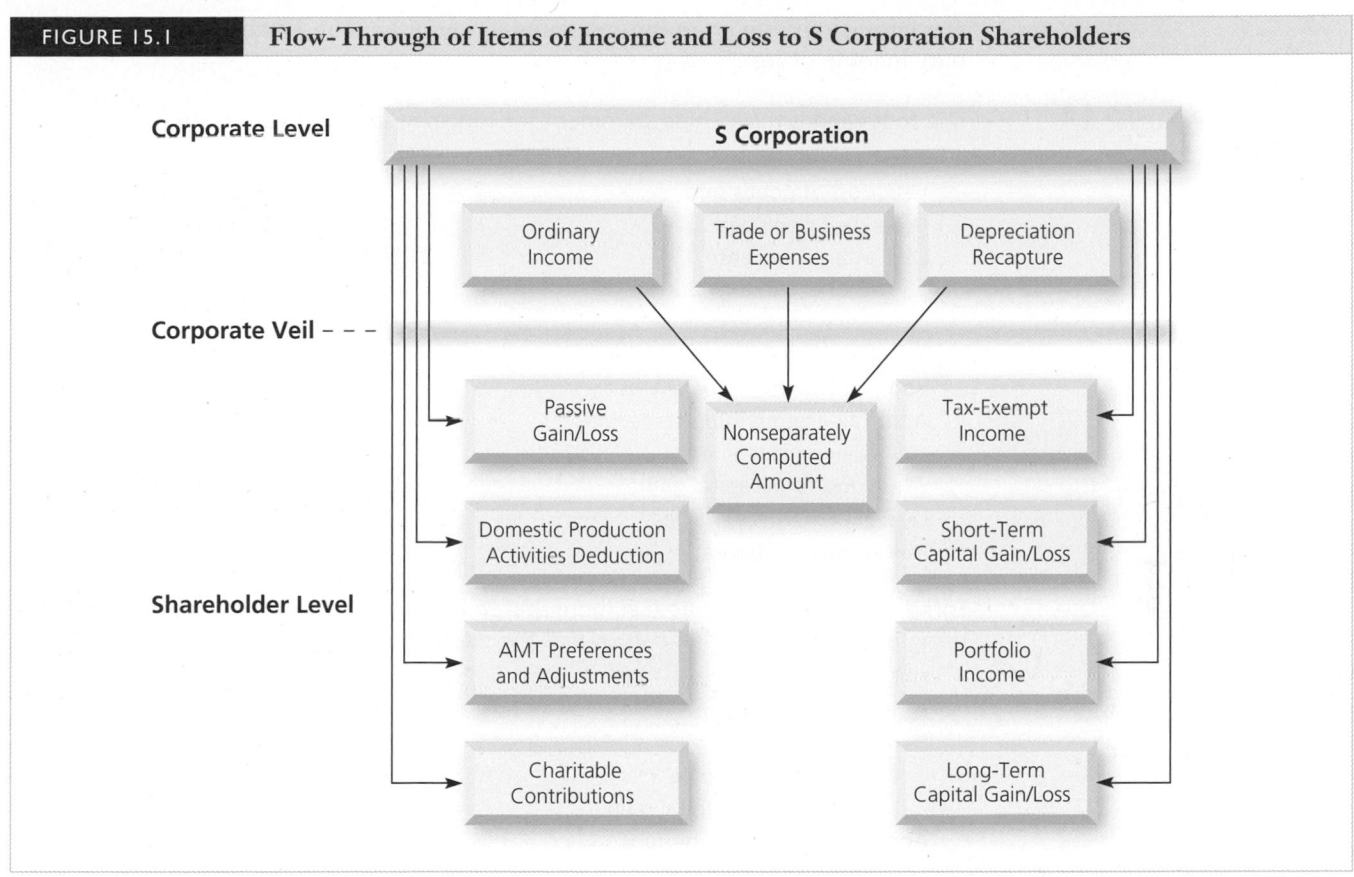

15-3 OPERATIONAL RULES

S corporations are treated much like partnerships for tax purposes. With a few exceptions, S corporations generally make tax accounting and other elections at the corporate level.[25] Each year, the S corporation determines nonseparately stated income or loss and separately stated income, deductions, and credits. These items are taxed only once, as they pass through to shareholders. All items are allocated to each shareholder based on average ownership of stock throughout the year.[26] The flow-through of each item of income, deduction, and credit from the corporation to the shareholder is illustrated in Figure 15.1.

LO.4

Compute nonseparately stated income and allocate income, deductions, and credits to shareholders.

15-3a Computation of Taxable Income

An S corporation's taxable income or loss is determined in a manner similar to the tax rules that apply to partnerships, except that S corporations recognize gains (but not losses) on distributions of appreciated property to shareholders.[27] Other special provisions affecting only the computation of C corporation income, such as the dividends received deduction, do not extend to S corporations.[28] Finally, as with partnerships, certain deductions of individuals are not permitted, including alimony payments, personal moving expenses, certain dependent care expenses, the personal exemption, and the standard deduction.

In general, S corporation items are divided into (1) nonseparately stated income or loss and (2) separately stated income, losses, deductions, and credits that could uniquely affect the tax liability of any shareholder. In essence, nonseparate items

---

[25]Certain elections are made at the shareholder level (e.g., the choice between a foreign tax deduction or credit).

[26]§§ 1366(a), (b), and (c).

[27]§ 1363(b).

[28]§ 703(a)(2).

are aggregated into an undifferentiated amount that constitutes Subchapter S ordinary income or loss.

Example 12	

The following is the income statement for Larkspur, Inc., an S corporation.

Sales		$ 40,000
Less: Cost of goods sold		(23,000)
Gross profit on sales		$ 17,000
Less: Interest expense	$1,200	
Charitable contributions	400	
Advertising expenses	1,500	
Other operating expenses	2,000	(5,100)
Book income from operations		$ 11,900
Add: Tax-exempt interest income	$ 300	
Dividend income	200	
Long-term capital gain	500	1,000
Less: Short-term capital loss		(150)
Net income per books		$ 12,750

Larkspur's ordinary income (i.e., nonseparately stated income) is calculated as follows, using net income for book purposes as the starting point.

Net income per books		$12,750
Separately stated items		
Deduct: Tax-exempt interest income	$300	
Dividend income	200	
Long-term capital gain	500	(1,000)
Add: Charitable contributions	$400	
Short-term capital loss	150	550
Ordinary income		$12,300

The $12,300 of Larkspur's nonseparately stated income, as well as each of the five separately stated items, is divided among the shareholders based upon their stock ownership.

An S corporation reports details as to the differences between book income and pass-through items on its Form 1120S, Schedule M–1 or M–3.

15-3b Allocation of Income and Loss

Each shareholder is allocated a pro rata portion of nonseparately stated income or loss and all separately stated items. The pro rata allocation method assigns an equal amount of each of the S items to each day of the year. If a shareholder's stock holding changes during the year, this allocation assigns the shareholder a pro rata share of each item for each day the stock is owned. On the date of transfer, the transferor (not the transferee) is considered to own the stock.[29]

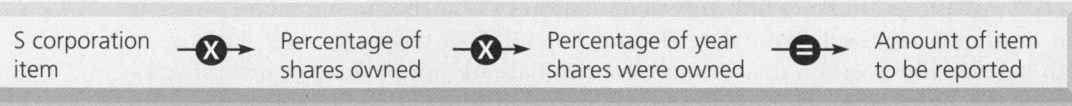

The per-day allocation must be used, unless the shareholder disposes of his or her entire interest in the entity.[30] In the case of a complete termination, a short year may result, as discussed in the next section. If a shareholder dies during the year, his or her share of the pro rata items up to and including the date of death is reported on the final individual income tax return.

---

[29]Reg. § 1.1377–1(a)(2)(ii).

[30]§§ 1366(a)(1) and 1377(a)(1).

TAX FACT A "Small" Business Corporation

The majority of S corporations have only one shareholder.

Returns Filed by Number of S Corporation Shareholders, 2010 Tax Year

4% 1%
5%
62%
28%

Shareholders: ☐ One ☐ Two ■ Three ☐ Four to Ten ■ More than Ten

© iStockphoto.com/Pali Rao

Example 13

Pat, a shareholder, owned 10% of Larkspur's stock (from Example 12) for 100 days and 12% for the remaining 265 days. Using the required per-day allocation method, Pat's share of the Subchapter S ordinary income is the total of $12,300 \times [10\% \times (100/365)]$ plus $12,300 \times [12\% \times (265/365)]$, or $1,409. All of Pat's Schedule K–1 totals flow through to the corresponding lines on his individual income tax return (Form 1040).

The Short-Year Election

If a shareholder's interest is completely terminated during the tax year by disposition or death, all shareholders owning stock during the year and the corporation may elect to treat the S taxable year as two taxable years. The first year ends on the date of the termination. Under this election, an interim closing of the books is undertaken, and the shareholders report their shares of the S corporation items as they occurred during the short tax year.[31]

The short-year election provides an opportunity to shift income, losses, and credits among shareholders. The election is desirable in circumstances where more loss can be allocated to taxpayers with higher marginal tax rates.

In-depth coverage can be found on this book's companion website: **www.cengagebrain.com**  4 Digging Deeper

Example 14

Alicia, the owner of all of the shares of an S corporation, transfers her stock to Cindy halfway through the tax year. There is a $100,000 NOL for the entire tax year, but $30,000 of the loss occurs during the first half of the year. Without a short-year election, $50,000 of the loss is allocated to Alicia and $50,000 is allocated to Cindy. If the corporation makes the short-year election, Cindy is allocated $70,000 of the loss. In this case, the sales price of the stock probably would be increased to recognize the tax benefits being transferred from Alicia to Cindy.

---

[31]§ 1377(a)(2).

Tax Planning Strategies	SALARY STRUCTURE

FRAMEWORK FOCUS: TAX RATE

Strategy: Shift Net Income from High-Bracket Taxpayers to Low-Bracket Taxpayers.
Avoid Double Taxation.

The amount of any salary paid to a shareholder-employee of an S corporation can have varying tax consequences and should be considered carefully. Larger amounts might be advantageous if the maximum contribution allowed under the employee's retirement plan has not been reached. Smaller amounts may be beneficial if the parties are trying to shift taxable income to lower-bracket shareholders, reduce payroll taxes, curtail a reduction of Social Security benefits, or restrict losses that do not pass through because of the basis limitation.

A strategy of decreasing compensation and correspondingly increasing distributions to shareholder-employees often results in substantial savings in employment taxes. However, a shareholder of an S corporation cannot always perform substantial services and arrange to receive distributions rather than compensation so that the corporation may avoid paying employment taxes. The shareholder may be deemed an employee, and any distributions will be recharacterized as wages subject to FICA and FUTA taxes.[32] For planning purposes, some level of compensation should be paid to all shareholder-employees to avoid any recharacterization of distributions as deductible salaries—especially in personal service corporations.

Use of S corporations as an income-shifting device within a family (e.g., through a gift of stock from a high-marginal-rate taxpayer to a low-marginal-rate taxpayer) may be ineffective. The IRS can ignore such transfers unless the stock is purchased at fair market value.[33] Effectively, the IRS can require that reasonable compensation be paid to family members who render services or provide capital to the S corporation.

15-3c Tax Treatment of Distributions to Shareholders

LO.5

Determine how distributions to S corporation shareholders are taxed.

S corporations do not generate E & P while the S election is in effect. Indeed, all profits are taxed in the year earned, as though they were distributed on a pro rata basis to the shareholders. Thus, distributions from S corporations do not constitute dividends in the traditional sense—there is no corporate E & P to distribute.

It is possible, however, for S corporations to have an accumulated E & P (AEP) account. This can occur when:

- The S corporation was previously a C corporation, or
- A C corporation with its own AEP merged into the S corporation.

Distributions from S corporations are measured as the cash received plus the fair market value of any other distributed property. The tax treatment of distributions differs, depending upon whether the S corporation has AEP.

S Corporation with No AEP

If the S corporation has no AEP, the distribution is a tax-free recovery of capital to the extent it does not exceed the basis of the shareholder's stock. When the amount of the distribution exceeds the stock basis, the excess is treated as a gain from the sale or exchange of property (capital gain in most cases). The vast majority of S corporations fall into this favorable category.

---

[32]Rev.Rul. 74–44, 1974–1 C.B. 287; *Spicer Accounting, Inc. v. U.S.*, 91–1 USTC ¶50,103, 66 AFTR 2d 90–5806, 918 F.2d 90 (CA–9, 1990); *Radtke v. U.S.*, 90–1 USTC ¶50,113, 65 AFTR 2d 90–1155, 895 F.2d 1196 (CA–7, 1990); *Joseph M. Grey Public Accountant, P.C.*, 119 T.C. 121 (2002); *David E. Watson, P.C. v. U.S.*, 2010–1 USTC ¶50,444, 105 AFTR 2d 2010-2624, 714

F. Supp.2d 954 (D.C. S.IA). The IRS uses salary surveys and other statistical methods to determine the appropriate compensation level. *McAlary Ltd.*, T.C. Summary Opinion 2013–62.
[33]§ 1366(e) and Reg. § 1.1373–1(a).

© iStockphoto.com/Andrey Prokhorov

TAX IN THE NEWS   Some Guidelines for S Corporation Shareholder-Employee Compensation

Shareholder compensation issues differ between C and S corporations. Usually, a C corporation guards against shareholder salaries being "too high," so as to avoid IRS charges of unreasonable compensation and the conversion of a salary into a nondeductible dividend distribution. An S corporation must make certain that its shareholder salaries are not "too low," to counter potential IRS assertions that the compensation structure was designed to avoid payroll tax liabilities.

An IRS fact sheet provides taxpayers with these factors to determine reasonable compensation for an S shareholder.

- Training, education, and experience.
- Duties and responsibilities.
- Time and effort devoted to business.
- Dividend history.
- Payments to nonshareholders-employees.
- Timing and manner of paying bonuses to key employees.
- What comparable businesses pay for similar services.
- Compensation agreements.
- Use of a formula to determine compensation.

Source: FS-2008-25, Wage Compensation for S Corporation Officers, August 2008.

Example 15

Hyacinth, Inc., a calendar year S corporation, has no AEP. During the year, Juan, an individual shareholder of the corporation, receives a cash distribution of $12,200 from Hyacinth. Juan's basis in his stock is $9,700. Juan recognizes a capital gain of $2,500, the excess of the distribution over the stock basis ($12,200 − $9,700). The remaining $9,700 is tax-free, but it reduces Juan's basis in his stock to zero.

S Corporation with AEP

For S corporations with AEP, a more complex set of rules applies. These rules blend the entity and conduit approaches to taxation, treating distributions of pre-election (C corporation) and postelection (S corporation) earnings differently. Distributions of AEP are taxed as dividends, while distributions of previously taxed S corporation earnings are tax-free to the extent of the shareholder's basis in the stock.

The treatment of distributions is determined by their order. Specifically, distributions are deemed to be first from previously taxed, undistributed earnings of the S corporation. Such distributions are tax-free and are determined by reference to a special account, the **accumulated adjustments account (AAA)**.[34] Next, AEP is distributed as taxable dividends (i.e., as payments from AEP). After AEP is depleted, tax-free distributions are made from the **other adjustments account (OAA)**, as discussed below. Remaining amounts of the distribution are received tax free until the shareholder's stock basis reaches zero,[35] with any excess being treated typically as capital gain.

Example 16

Short, a calendar year S corporation, distributes $1,300 of cash to its only shareholder, Otis, on December 31. Otis's basis in his stock is $1,400, AAA is $500, and Short holds $750 of AEP before the distribution.

The first $500 of the distribution is a tax-free recovery of basis from the AAA. The next $750 is a taxable dividend distribution from AEP. The remaining $50 of cash is a tax-free recovery of basis. Immediately after the distribution, Short records a zero balance in AAA and AEP. Otis's stock basis now is $850.

---

[34]For S corporations in existence prior to 1983, an account similar to the AAA was used. This account, called *previously taxed income* (PTI), can be distributed in cash tax free to shareholders after AAA has been distributed. See §§ 1368(c)(1) and (e)(1).

[35]§ 1368(c).

	Corporate AAA	Corporate AEP	Otis's Stock Basis
Beginning balance	$ 500	$ 750	$1,400
Distribution from AAA	(500)		(500)
Distribution from AEP		(750)	
Distribution from stock basis			(50)
Ending balance	$ –0–	$ –0–	$ ·850

Example 17

Assume the same facts as in the preceding example. The next year, Short's income totals zero. It distributes $1,000 to Otis. Of the distribution, $850 is a tax-free recovery of the stock basis, and $150 is taxed to Otis as a capital gain.

With the consent of all of its shareholders, an S corporation can elect to have a distribution treated as if it were made from AEP rather than from the AAA. This mechanism is known as an **AAA bypass election**. This election may be desirable when making distributions to move the entity to the no-AEP system of accounting for distributions, at a maximum tax cost of 20 percent of the AEP (i.e., the maximum income tax rate applied to dividends for most shareholders).

Example 18

Rotor, an S corporation, has $50 of AEP. An AAA bypass election for Rotor's next shareholder distribution would eliminate the need to track the AAA and would greatly simplify the accounting for future distributions. The cost for this simplification is the tax on $50 of dividend income.

Accumulated Adjustments Account

The AAA is the cumulative total of undistributed nonseparately and separately stated income and deduction items for S corporation years beginning after 1982. As noted, it provides a mechanism to ensure that earnings of an S corporation are taxed only once. Changes to the AAA are reported annually in Schedule M–2 on page 4 of the Form 1120S.

The initial AAA balance is zero when an S election is made. AAA then is computed at the end of each tax year rather than at the time of a distribution. First, add to the year's beginning balance any current nonseparately computed income and positive separately stated items (except tax-exempt income). Next, account for distributions *prior* to subtracting the negative items.

CONCEPT SUMMARY 15.1

Distributions from an S Corporation

Where Earnings and Profits Exist	Where No Earnings and Profits Exist
1. Distributions are tax-free to the extent of the AAA.*	
2. Next, the distribution constitutes dividend income to the extent of AEP.[†]	
3. Distributions are tax-free to the extent of the other adjustments account (OAA).*	
4. Any residual distribution is nontaxable to the extent of the shareholder's basis in stock.*	1. Distributions are nontaxable to the extent of shareholder's basis in stock.*
5. Excess is treated as gain from a sale or exchange of stock (capital gain in most cases).	2. Excess is treated as gain from a sale or exchange of stock (capital gain in most cases).

* The distribution reduces the shareholder's stock basis. A shareholder's stock basis serves as the upper limit on the amount that may be received tax free.
† The AAA bypass election is available to pay out AEP before reducing the AAA [§ 1368 (e) (3)].

EXHIBIT 15.1	Adjustments to the Corporate AAA

Increase by:

1. Schedule K income items other than tax-exempt income.
2. Nonseparately computed income.

Decrease by:

3. Distribution(s) from AAA (but not below zero).
4. Negative Schedule K items other than distributions (e.g., losses, deductions).

AAA is applied to the distributions made during the year on a pro rata basis (in a fashion similar to the application of current E & P, discussed in Chapter 13). The determination of AAA is summarized in Exhibit 15.1.

Although adjustments to AAA and stock basis adjustments are similar, there are some important differences between the two amounts. In particular,

- The AAA is not affected by tax-exempt income and related expenses.
- The AAA can have a negative balance. All losses decrease the AAA balance, even those in excess of the shareholder's basis. However, distributions may not make the AAA negative or increase a negative balance in the account.
- Every shareholder has a proportionate interest in the AAA, regardless of the amount of his or her stock basis.[36] In fact, AAA is a corporate account, so there is no connection between the amount and any specific shareholder.[37] Thus, the benefits of AAA can be shifted from one shareholder to another. For example, when an S corporation shareholder sells stock to another party, any AAA balance on the purchase date can be distributed tax free to the purchaser.

Other Adjustments Account

The OAA tracks the entity's net items that affect basis but not the AAA, such as tax-exempt income and any related nondeductible expenses. Distributions are made from the OAA after AEP and the AAA are reduced to zero. Distributions from this account are tax-free.

Schedule M–2

Page 4 of the Form 1120S includes Schedule M–2, a reconciliation of beginning and ending balances in the AAA and OAA accounts. Most tax professionals recommend that the Schedule M–2 be kept current even if the entity has retained no AEP so that if future events require the use of these amounts, they need not be reconstructed after the fact.

Example 19

Poinsettia, an S corporation, records the following items.

AAA, beginning of year	$ 8,500
OAA, beginning of year	–0–
Ordinary income	25,000
Tax-exempt interest income	4,000
Key employee life insurance proceeds received	5,000
Payroll penalty expense	2,000
Charitable contributions	3,000
Unreasonable compensation	5,000
Premiums on key employee life insurance	2,100
Distributions to shareholders	16,000

---

[36] § 1368(c).   [37] § 1368(e)(1)(A).

Poinsettia's Schedule M–2 appears as follows.

Schedule M-2	Analysis of Accumulated Adjustments Account, Other Adjustments Account, and Shareholders' Undistributed Taxable Income Previously Taxed (see instructions)		
		(a) Accumulated adjustments account	**(b)** Other adjustments account
1	Balance at beginning of tax year	8,500	0
2	Ordinary income from page 1, line 21 . . .	25,000	
3	Other additions		9,000**
4	Loss from page 1, line 21	( )	
5	Other reductions	(10,000*)	(2,100)
6	Combine lines 1 through 5	23,500	6,900
7	Distributions other than dividend distributions	16,000	
8	Balance at end of tax year. Subtract line 7 from line 6	7,500	6,900

**$2,000 (payroll penalty) + $3,000 (charitable contributions) + $5,000 (unreasonable compensation).*

***$4,000 (tax-exempt interest income) + $5,000 (life insurance proceeds).*

© www.irs.gov

Digging Deeper   5   In-depth coverage can be found on this book's companion website: **www.cengagebrain.com**

© tuuliujumala/Shutterstock.com

Effect of Terminating the S Election

Normally, distributions to shareholders from a C corporation are taxed as dividends to the extent of E & P. However, any distribution of *cash* by a C corporation to shareholders during a one-year period[38] following an S election termination receives special treatment. Such a distribution is treated as a tax-free recovery of stock basis to the extent that it does not exceed the AAA.[39] Because *only* cash distributions reduce the AAA during this *postelection termination period*, a corporation should not make property distributions during this time. Instead, the entity should sell property and distribute the proceeds to shareholders.

THE BIG PICTURE

Example 20

Return to the facts of *The Big Picture* on p. 15-1. Assume that Fowle has operated as an S corporation for many years and that the entity turned profitable once it mastered the pricing methods of its import markets. Then David decides to terminate the S election as of the end of 2014. On December 31, 2014, Fowle's AAA balance totals $1.3 million. David can receive a nontaxable distribution of cash during Fowle's 2015 post-termination period to the full extent of the entity's AAA balance. Any cash distributions so received reduce the basis of David's Fowle stock, but not below zero.

Tax Planning Strategies   THE ACCUMULATED ADJUSTMENTS ACCOUNT

FRAMEWORK FOCUS: TAX RATE

Strategy: Avoid Double Taxation.

The AAA is needed to determine the tax treatment of distributions from S corporations with AEP *and* distributions made during the post-termination election period. Therefore, it is important for all S corporations (even those with no AEP) to maintain a current AAA (and OAA) balance. Without an accurate AAA balance, distributions could needlessly be classified as taxable dividends. Alternatively,

it will be costly to reconstruct the AAA after the S election terminates.

Distributions should be made when AAA is positive. If future years bring operating losses, AAA is reduced and shareholder exposure to AEP and taxable dividends increases.

---

[38]§ 1377(b).

[39]§ 1371(e). Termination-period distributions from the OAA are not exempt.

15-3d Tax Treatment of Noncash Distributions by the Corporation

An S corporation recognizes a gain on any distribution of appreciated property as if the asset were sold to the shareholder at its fair market value.[40] The corporate gain is passed through to the shareholders. There is an important reason for this rule. Without it, property might be distributed tax free (other than for certain recapture items) and later sold without income recognition to the shareholder because the shareholder's basis equals the asset's fair market value. The character of the gain—capital gain or ordinary income—depends upon the type of asset being distributed.

The S corporation does not recognize a loss when distributing assets that are worth less than their basis. As with gain property, the shareholder's basis is equal to the asset's fair market value. Thus, the potential loss is postponed until the shareholder sells the stock of the S corporation. Because loss property receives a step-down in basis without any loss recognition by the S corporation, distributions of loss property should be avoided. See Concept Summary 15.2.

Yarrow, Inc., an S corporation for 12 years, distributes to one of its shareholders a tract of land held as an investment. The land was purchased for $22,000 many years ago and is currently worth $82,000. Yarrow recognizes a capital gain of $60,000, which increases the AAA by $60,000. The gain flows through proportionately to Yarrow's shareholders and is taxed to them. Then a tax-free property distribution reduces AAA and shareholder stock basis by $82,000 (fair market value). The tax consequences are the same for appreciated property whether (a) it is distributed to the shareholders and they dispose of it or (b) the corporation sells the property and distributes the proceeds to the shareholders.	**Example 21**

Continue with the facts of Example 21. If the land had been purchased for $82,000 and was currently worth $22,000, the shareholder would take a $22,000 basis in the land. The $60,000 realized loss is not recognized at the corporate level. The loss does not reduce Yarrow's AAA. Only when the S corporation sells the asset to an unrelated party does it recognize the loss and reduce AAA.	**Example 22**

Assume the same facts as in Examples 21 and 22, except that Yarrow is a C corporation (E & P balance of $1 million) or a partnership. Assume that the partner's basis in the partnership interest is $100,000, and ignore any corporate-level taxes. Compare the results.	**Example 23**

	Appreciated Property		
	S Corporation	C Corporation	Partnership
Entity gain/loss	$60,000	$60,000	$ –0–
Owner's gain/loss/dividend	60,000	82,000	–0–
Owner's basis in land	82,000	82,000	22,000

	Property That Has Declined in Value		
	S Corporation	C Corporation	Partnership
Entity gain/loss	$ –0–	$ –0–	$ –0–
Owner's gain/loss/dividend	–0–	22,000	–0–
Owner's basis in land	22,000	22,000	82,000

---

[40]§ 311(b).

CONCEPT SUMMARY 15.2

Consequences of Noncash Distributions

	Appreciated Property	Depreciated Property
S corporation	Realized gain is recognized by the corporation, which passes it through to the shareholders. Such gain increases a shareholder's stock basis, generating a basis in the property equal to FMV. On the distribution, the shareholder's stock basis is reduced by the FMV of the property (but not below zero).	Realized loss is not recognized. The shareholder takes an FMV basis in the property.
C corporation	Realized gain is recognized under § 311(b) and increases E & P (net of tax). The shareholder reports a taxable dividend to the extent of corporate E & P, equal to the property's FMV (reduced by any liabilities assumed). The shareholder takes a basis in the asset equal to its FMV.	Realized loss is not recognized. The shareholder takes an FMV basis in the property.
Partnership	No gain to the partnership or partner. The partner takes a carryover basis in the asset, but the asset basis is limited to the partner's basis in the partnership.	Realized loss is not recognized. The partner takes a carryover basis in the asset, but the asset basis is limited to the partner's basis in the partnership.

15-3e Shareholder's Basis in S Stock

LO.6

Calculate a shareholder's basis in S corporation stock.

The calculation of the initial tax basis of stock in an S corporation is similar to that for the basis of stock in a C corporation and depends upon the manner in which the shares are acquired (e.g., gift, inheritance, purchase, exchange under § 351). Once the initial tax basis is determined, various transactions during the life of the corporation affect the shareholder's basis in the stock. Although each shareholder is required to compute his or her own basis in the S shares, neither Form 1120S nor Schedule K–1 provides a place for tracking this amount.

A shareholder's basis is increased by stock purchases and capital contributions. Operations during the year cause the following additional upward adjustments to basis.[41]

- Nonseparately computed income.
- Separately stated income items (e.g., tax-exempt income).

Basis then is reduced by distributions not reported as income by the shareholder (e.g., an AAA distribution). Next, the following items reduce basis (but not below zero).

- Nondeductible expenses of the corporation (e.g., fines, penalties, and illegal kickbacks).
- Nonseparately computed loss.
- Separately stated loss and deduction items.

As under the partnership rules, basis first is increased by income items; then it is decreased by distributions and finally by losses.[42] In most cases, this *losses last* rule is advantageous to the S shareholder.

Example 24

In its first year of operation, Iris, Inc., a calendar year S corporation, earns income of $2,000. Before accounting for the entity's operating results, assume the stock basis of Iris's sole shareholder, Marty, is zero. Therefore, Marty's stock basis is increased to $2,000. On February 2 in its second year of operation, Iris distributes $2,000 to Marty. During the remainder of the second year, the corporation incurs a $2,000 loss.

---

[41]§ 1367(a).   [42]Reg. § 1.1367–1(f).

Under the S corporation ordering rules, the $2,000 distribution is tax-free AAA to Marty. The distribution is accounted for before the loss. The $2,000 loss is suspended until Marty generates additional stock basis (e.g., from capital contributions or future entity profits).

A shareholder's basis in S corporation stock never is reduced below zero. Once stock basis is zero, any additional basis reductions (losses or deductions, but *not* distributions) decrease (but not below zero) the shareholder's basis in loans made to the S corporation. Any excess of losses or deductions over both stock and loan bases is not deductible in the current year. Losses can be deducted only to the extent they offset stock or loan basis. Thus, until additional basis is created due to capital contributions or flow-through income, the loss deductions are suspended.

When there is a capital contribution or an item of flow-through income, basis first is restored to the shareholder loans, up to the original principal amount.[43] Then basis in the stock is restored.

Stacey, a sole shareholder, holds a $7,000 stock basis and a $2,000 basis in a loan that she made to Romulus, a calendar year S corporation with zero AEP. At the beginning of the year, the corporation's AAA and OAA balances are zero. Ordinary income for the year is $8,200. During the year, the corporation also received $2,000 of tax-exempt interest income.

Cash of $17,300 is distributed to Stacey on November 15. As a result, Stacey recognizes only a $100 capital gain.

Example 25

	Corporate AAA	Corporate OAA	Stacey's Stock Basis	Stacey's Loan Basis
Beginning balance	$ –0–	$ –0–	$ 7,000	$2,000
Ordinary income	8,200		8,200	
Tax-exempt income		2,000	2,000	
Subtotal	$ 8,200	$ 2,000	$17,200	$2,000
Distribution ($17,300)				
From AAA	(8,200)		(8,200)	
From OAA		(2,000)	(2,000)	
From stock basis			(7,000)	
Ending balance	$ –0–	$ –0–	$ –0–	$2,000
Distribution in excess of stock basis (capital gain)			$ 100	

Pass-through losses can reduce loan basis, but distributions do not. Stock basis cannot be reduced below zero, and the $100 excess distribution does not reduce Stacey's loan basis.

The basis rules for S corporation stock are similar to the rules for determining a partner's basis in a partnership interest. However, a partner's basis in the partnership interest includes the partner's direct investment plus a *ratable share* of partnership liabilities.[44] If a partnership borrows from a partner, the partner receives a basis increase as if the partnership had borrowed from an unrelated third party.[45] In contrast, corporate borrowing has no effect on the stock basis of an S corporation shareholder. Loans from a shareholder to the S corporation have a tax basis only for the shareholder making the loan.

If a loan's basis has been reduced and is not restored, income is recognized when the corporation repays the loan. If the corporation issued a note as evidence

---

[43]§ 1367(b)(2); Reg. § 1.1367–2(e).
[44]§ 752(a).

[45]Reg. § 1.752–1(e).

of the debt, repayment constitutes an amount received in exchange for a capital asset and the amount that exceeds the shareholder's basis is capital gain.[46] However, if the loan is made on open account, the repayment constitutes ordinary income to the extent it exceeds the shareholder's basis in the loan. Thus, a note should be given to ensure capital gain treatment for the income that results from a loan's repayment.

THE BIG PICTURE

Example 26

Return to the facts of *The Big Picture* on p. 15-1. Assume that Fowle has made an S election and that David, its sole shareholder, consented. At the beginning of 2014, David's basis in his Fowle stock was $90,000. During 2014, he made a $40,000 loan to the corporation, using a written debt instrument and market interest rates.

Fowle generated a $93,000 taxable loss for 2014. Thus, at the beginning of 2015, David's stock basis was zero, and the basis in his loan to Fowle was $37,000.

Fowle repaid the loan in full on March 1, 2015. David recognizes a $3,000 capital gain on the repayment.

Digging Deeper 6   In-depth coverage can be found on this book's companion website: **www.cengagebrain.com**

Tax Planning Strategies   WORKING WITH SUSPENDED LOSSES

FRAMEWORK FOCUS: INCOME AND EXCLUSION

Strategy: Avoid Income Recognition.

Distributions made to shareholders with suspended losses usually create capital gain income because there is no stock basis to offset. Usually, distributions should be deferred until the shareholder creates stock basis in some form. In this way, no gross income is recognized until the suspended losses are fully used.

THE BIG PICTURE

Example 27

Continue with the facts of Example 26, except that Fowle's loss cannot be deducted by David because of the lack of stock or loan basis. David purchases $5,000 of additional stock in Fowle. David gets an immediate deduction for his investment, due to his $93,000 in suspended losses. Alternatively, if Fowle shows a $5,000 profit for the year, David pays no tax on the flow-through income, as it is offset by the suspended losses.

However, if Fowle distributes $5,000 to David in 2015 without earning any profit for the year, and prior to any capital contribution by him, David recognizes a $5,000 capital gain, because the distribution exceeds the zero stock basis. ∎

15-3f Treatment of Losses

LO.7

Explain the tax effects of losses on S shareholders.

Net Operating Loss

One major advantage of an S election is the ability to pass through net operating losses (NOLs) of the corporation directly to the shareholders. A shareholder can deduct an NOL for the year in which the S corporation's tax year ends.

---

[46]*Joe M. Smith*, 48 T.C. 872 (1967), *aff'd* and *rev'd* in 70–1 USTC ¶9327, 25 AFTR 2d 70–936, 424 F.2d 219 (CA–9, 1970); Rev.Rul. 64–162, 1964–1 C.B. 304. An open account loan is treated as evidenced by a note if the shareholder's net payable at the end of the tax year exceeds $25,000. Reg. § 1.1367–2.

The corporation does not deduct the NOL. A shareholder's basis in the stock is reduced by any NOL pass-through, but not below zero. The entity's AAA is reduced by the same deductible amount.[47]

Deductions for an S corporation's pass-throughs (e.g., NOL, capital loss, and charitable contributions) cannot exceed a shareholder's stock basis *plus* the basis of any loans made by the shareholder to the corporation.[48] A shareholder is entitled to carry forward a loss pass-through to the extent the loss for the year exceeds basis. Any pass-through carried forward may be deducted *only* by the *same* shareholder if and when the basis in the stock of or loans to the corporation is restored.[49]

Example 28

Ginny owns 10% of the stock of Pilot, a calendar year S corporation. Her basis in the shares is $10,000 at the beginning of 2013. The indicated events are accounted for under the S corporation rules as follows.

Tax Year	Event	Tax Consequences
2013	Ginny's share of Pilot's operating loss is $15,000.	Ginny deducts $10,000. Her stock basis is reduced to zero. She holds a $5,000 suspended loss.
2014	Ginny's share of Pilot's operating loss is $4,000.	No current deduction allowed for the loss, as Ginny has no stock basis to offset. Her suspended loss is now $9,000.
2015	Ginny's share of Pilot's operating loss is $7,000. She purchases an additional $10,000 of stock from Pilot.	The purchase creates $10,000 of stock basis. Ginny deducts $10,000—the current $7,000 loss and $3,000 of the suspended loss. Stock basis again is zero, and the new suspended loss is $6,000.
2016	Ginny sells all of her Pilot shares to Christina on January 1.	The $6,000 suspended loss disappears—it cannot be transferred to Christina.

Tax Planning Strategies   LOSS CONSIDERATIONS

FRAMEWORK FOCUS: DEDUCTIONS

Strategy: Maximize Deductible Amounts.

A net loss in excess of tax basis may be carried forward and deducted only by the same shareholder in succeeding years. Thus, before disposing of the stock, a shareholder should increase stock/loan basis to flow through the loss. The next shareholder cannot acquire the loss carryover.

The NOL provisions create a need for sound tax planning during the last election year and the post-termination transition period. If it appears that the S corporation is going to sustain an NOL or use up any loss carryover, each shareholder's basis should be analyzed to determine whether it can absorb the owner's share of the loss. If basis is insufficient to absorb the loss, further investments should be considered before the end of the post-termination period. Such investments can be accomplished through additional stock purchases from the corporation or from other shareholders to increase basis.

Example 29

A calendar year C corporation records a $20,000 NOL in 2014. The corporation makes a valid S election in 2015 and incurs another $20,000 NOL in that year. At all times during 2015, the stock of the corporation was owned by the same 10 shareholders, each of whom owned 10% of the stock.

Tim, one of the shareholders, holds a stock basis of $1,800 at the beginning of 2015. None of the 2014 NOL may be carried forward into the S year. Although Tim's share of the 2015 NOL is $2,000, his deduction for the loss is limited to $1,800 in 2015 with a $200 carryover to 2016. ∎

---

[47]§§ 1368(a)(1)(A) and (e)(1)(A).

[48]See *Donald J. Sauvigne*, 30 TCM 123, T.C.Memo. 1971–30.

[49]§ 1366(d).

CONCEPT SUMMARY 15.3

Treatment of S Corporation Losses

Step 1. Allocate total loss to the shareholder on a daily basis, based upon stock ownership.

Step 2. If the shareholder's loss exceeds his or her stock basis, apply any excess to the basis of corporate indebtedness to the shareholder. Loss allocations do not reduce stock or loan basis below zero.

Step 3. Where a flow-through loss exceeds the stock and loan basis, any excess is suspended and carried over to succeeding tax years.

Step 4. In succeeding tax years, any net increase in basis restores the debt basis first, up to its original amount.

Step 5. Once debt basis is restored, any remaining net increase restores stock basis.

If the S election terminates, any suspended loss carryover may be deducted during the post-termination period to the extent of the stock basis at the end of this period. Any loss remaining at the end of this period is lost forever.

At-Risk Rules

As discussed in Chapters 6 and 14, S corporation shareholders, like partners, are limited in the amount of loss they may deduct by their "at-risk" amounts. The rules for determining at-risk amounts are similar, but not identical, to the partnership at-risk rules.

An amount at risk is determined separately for each shareholder. The amount of the corporate losses that are passed through and deductible by the shareholders is not affected by the amount the corporation has at risk. A shareholder usually is considered at risk with respect to an activity to the extent of cash and the adjusted basis of other property contributed to the electing corporation, any amount borrowed for use in the activity for which the taxpayer has personal liability for payment from personal assets, and the net fair market value of personal assets that secure nonrecourse borrowing.

Any losses that are suspended under the at-risk rules are carried forward and are available during the post-termination period. The S stock basis limitations and at-risk limitations are applied before the passive activity limitations (see below).

Example 30

Carl has a basis of $35,000 in his S corporation stock. He takes a $15,000 nonrecourse loan from a relative and lends the proceeds to the S corporation. Carl now has a stock basis of $35,000 and a loan basis of $15,000. However, due to the at-risk limitation, he can deduct only $35,000 of losses from the S corporation.

Passive Losses and Credits

Net passive losses and credits are not deductible when incurred and must be carried over to a year when there is passive income. Thus, one must be aware of three major classes of income, losses, and credits—active, portfolio, and passive. S corporations are not directly subject to the passive activity limits, but corporate rental activities are inherently passive, and other activities of an S corporation may be passive unless the shareholder(s) materially participate(s) in operating the business. An S corporation may engage in more than one such activity.

If the corporate activity involves rentals or the shareholders do not materially participate, any passive loss or credit that flows through is passive. The shareholders can apply such losses or credits only against income from other passive activities. An S shareholder's stock basis is reduced by passive losses that flow through to the shareholder, even though the shareholder may not be entitled to a current deduction due to the passive loss limitations.

15-3g Other Operational Rules

Several other points may be made about the possible effects of various Code provisions on S corporations.

- An S corporation must make estimated tax payments with respect to any recognized built-in gain and excess passive investment income tax (discussed next).
- An S corporation may own stock in another corporation, but an S corporation may not have a C corporation shareholder. An S corporation is *not* eligible for the dividends received deduction.
- An S corporation is *not* subject to the 10 percent of taxable income limitation applicable to charitable contributions made by a C corporation.
- Any family member who renders services or furnishes capital to an S corporation must be paid reasonable compensation. Otherwise, the IRS can make adjustments to reflect the value of the services or capital. This rule may make it more difficult for related parties to shift Subchapter S taxable income to children or other family members.
- The flow-through of S items to a shareholder is not self-employment income and is not subject to the self-employment tax.[50] Compensation for services rendered to an S corporation is, however, subject to FICA taxes. This treatment of earned income of S corporations is attractive compared to the treatment of a proprietorship or a partnership, whose income is taxed as self-employment income to the owners.
- A number of qualified fringe benefits, which typically are received by employees on a tax-free basis, are subject to tax when received by a more-than-2 percent shareholder-employee of an S corporation. Such benefits include the value of group term life insurance, medical insurance, and meals and lodging furnished for the convenience of the employer. These items are treated as wages and are subject to most payroll taxes. The employee can deduct medical insurance premiums on his or her Form 1040.
- An accrual basis S corporation uses the cash method of accounting for purposes of deducting business expenses and interest owed to a cash basis related party.[51] Thus, the timing of the shareholder's income and the corporate deduction must match.
- With respect to the domestic production activities deduction (DPAD), the S corporation passes through the various amounts needed, and the deduction is computed at the shareholder level. For instance, domestic production gross receipts (DPGR), the corresponding cost of goods sold, and attributable W–2 wages, among other items, are separately stated items reported to the shareholders on a pro rata basis.
- The S election is not recognized by the District of Columbia and several states, including Connecticut, Michigan, and Tennessee. Thus, some or all of the entity's income may be subject to a state-level income tax.
- An S corporation may issue § 1244 stock to its shareholders to obtain ordinary loss treatment.
- Loss deductions may be disallowed due to a lack of a profit motive. If the activities at the corporate level are not profit-motivated, the losses may be disallowed under the hobby loss rules (see Chapter 11).[52]

[50]Rev.Rul. 59–221, 1959–1 C.B. 225.
[51]§ 267(b).
[52]§183; *Michael J. Houston*, 69 TCM 2360, T.C.Memo. 1995–159; *Mario G. De Mendoza, III*, 68 TCM 42, T.C.Memo. 1994–314.

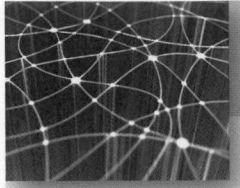

BRIDGE DISCIPLINE   Bridge to Public Finance

Proceeds from the Federal self-employment tax are used by the Federal government to fund retirement and health care entitlements. Any shortfalls in these funds mean that the following may occur.

- Citizens needing retirement annuities and/or health care services will receive less than is needed. This may not be a desirable result in a moral or ethical sense, as life will be more difficult than it otherwise might be for those of modest means.

- Retirement income and health care services must be funded from general revenues, meaning almost exclusively funds from the Federal income tax. This represents a mismatch of payor and payee, an income redistribution result that would not be attractive to some. In a zero-sum sense, benefits of this sort reduce funding for other budgetary needs of the Federal government (e.g., for defense, transportation, or research).

15-4 ENTITY-LEVEL TAXES

LO.8

Compute the entity-level taxes on S corporations.

15-4a Tax on Pre-Election Built-In Gain

Normally, an S corporation does *not* pay an income tax, because all items flow through to the shareholders. But an S corporation that was previously a C corporation may be required to pay a built-in gains tax, a LIFO recapture tax, a general business credit recapture, or a passive investment income tax.

Without the **built-in gains tax**, it would be possible to avoid the corporate double tax on a disposition of appreciated property by electing S corporation status.

> **Example 31**
>
> Zinnia, Inc., a C corporation, owns a single asset with a basis of $100,000 and a fair market value of $500,000. If Zinnia sells this asset and distributes the cash to its shareholders, there are two levels of tax, one at the corporate level and one at the shareholder level. Alternatively, if Zinnia distributes the asset to its shareholders as a dividend, a double tax still results.
>
> In an attempt to avoid the double tax, Zinnia elects S corporation status. It then sells the asset and distributes the proceeds to shareholders. Without the built-in gains tax, the gain would be taxed only once, at the shareholder level. The distribution of the sales proceeds would be a tax-free reduction of the stock basis and the AAA.

The built-in gains tax generally applies to C corporations converting to S status. It is a *corporate-level* tax on any built-in gain recognized when the S corporation disposes of an asset in a taxable disposition within 10 calendar years after the date on which the S election took effect. The 10-year holding period is reduced to 7 years for tax years beginning in 2009 and 2010, and to 5 years for 2011 through 2013.[53] The steps in computing the tax are summarized in Concept Summary 15.4.

---

[53]§ 1374(d)(7)(B). Not all of the states followed this temporary reduction of the recognition period. After 2013, the holding period returned to ten 12-month years.

CONCEPT SUMMARY 15.4

Calculation of the Built-In Gains Tax Liability

Step 1. Select the smaller of built-in gain or taxable income.*

Step 2. Deduct unexpired NOLs and capital losses from C corporation tax years.

Step 3. Multiply the tax base obtained in step 2 by the top corporate income tax rate.

Step 4. Deduct any business credit carryforwards and AMT credit carryforwards arising in a C corporation tax year from the amount obtained in step 3.

Step 5. The corporation pays any tax resulting in step 4.

*Any net recognized built-in gain in excess of taxable income is carried forward to the next year within the 5-, 7-, or 10-year recognition period.

© iStockphoto.com/Andrey Prokhorov

General Rules

The base for the built-in gains tax includes any unrealized gain on appreciated assets (e.g., real estate, cash basis receivables, goodwill) held by a corporation on the day it elects S status. The highest corporate tax rate (currently 35 percent) is applied to the unrealized gain when any of the assets are sold. Any gain from the sale (net of the built-in gains tax)[54] also passes through as a taxable gain to shareholders.

> **Example 32**
>
> Assume the same facts as in the preceding example. A corporate-level built-in gains tax must be paid by Zinnia if it sells the asset after electing S status. Upon sale of the asset, the corporation owes a tax of $140,000 ($400,000 × 35%). In addition, the shareholders report a $260,000 taxable flow-through gain ($400,000 − $140,000). Hence, the built-in gains tax effectively imposes a double tax on Zinnia and its shareholders, as would have been the case had Zinnia remained a C corporation.

In-depth coverage can be found on this book's companion website: **www.cengagebrain.com**   🔍 **7** Digging Deeper

The amount of built-in gain recognized in any year is limited to an *as if* taxable income for the year, computed as if the corporation were a C corporation. Any built-in gain that escapes taxation due to the taxable income limitation is carried forward and recognized in future tax years. Thus, a corporation can defer a built-in gain tax liability whenever it has a low or negative taxable income.

> **Example 33**
>
> Vinca's recognized built-in gain for 2015 is $400,000. If Vinca were a C corporation, its 2015 taxable income would be $300,000. The amount of built-in gain subject to tax in 2015 is $300,000. The excess built-in gain of $100,000 is carried forward and taxed in 2016 (assuming adequate C corporation taxable income in that year).
>
> There is no statutory limit on the carryforward period, but the gain would effectively expire at the end of the 5-, 7-, or 10-year recognition period applicable to all built-in gains.[55]

An S corporation can offset built-in gains with unexpired NOLs or capital losses from C corporation years.

---

[54]§ 1366(f)(2).

[55]§ 1374(d)(7); Notice 90–27, 1990–1 C.B. 336.

Example 34

Yowler, an S corporation, reports a built-in gain of $100,000 and taxable income of $90,000. Yowler's built-in gains tax liability is calculated as follows, applying the indicated loss carryforwards.

Lesser of taxable income or built-in gain	$ 90,000
Less: NOL carryforward from C year	(12,000)
Capital loss carryforward from C year	(8,000)
Tax base	$ 70,000
Highest corporate income tax rate	× .35
Tentative tax	$ 24,500
Less: Business credit carryforward from C year	(4,000)
Built-in gains tax liability	$ 20,500

The $10,000 realized (but not taxed) built-in gain in excess of taxable income is carried forward to the next year, as long as the next year is within the 5-, 7-, or 10-year recognition period.

LIFO Recapture Tax

When a C corporation uses the FIFO method for its last year before making the S election, any built-in gain is recognized and taxed as the inventory is sold. A LIFO-basis corporation would not recognize this gain unless the corporation invaded the LIFO layer during the built-in gains tax period. To preclude a deferral of gain recognition by a C corporation that is electing S status, any LIFO recapture amount at the time of the S election is subject to a corporate-level tax.

Tax Planning Strategies   MANAGING THE BUILT-IN GAINS TAX

FRAMEWORK FOCUS: INCOME AND EXCLUSION

Strategy: Avoid Income Recognition.
Postpone Recognition of Income to Achieve Tax Deferral.

Although limitations exist on contributions of loss property to the corporation before S status is elected, it still is possible for a corporation to minimize built-in gains and maximize built-in losses prior to the S election. A cash basis S corporation can accomplish this by reducing receivables, accelerating payables, and accruing compensation costs.

To further reduce or defer the tax, the corporation may take advantage of the taxable income limitation by shifting income and deductions to minimize taxable income in years when built-in gain is recognized. Although the postponed built-in gain is carried forward to future years, the time value of money makes the postponement beneficial. For example, paying compensation to shareholder-employees in place of a distribution creates a deduction that reduces taxable income and postpones the built-in gains tax.

before payment of salaries to its shareholders. If Tulip pays at least $120,000 in salaries to the shareholders (rather than making a distribution), its taxable income drops to zero and the built-in gains tax is postponed. Thus, Tulip may want to keep the salaries as high as possible to postpone the built-in gains tax in future years and reap a benefit from the time value of money. Of course, paying the salaries may increase the associated payroll tax liabilities. ∎

Giving built-in gain property to a charitable organization does not trigger the built-in gains tax.

Built-in *loss* property may be sold in the same year built-in gain property is sold to reduce or eliminate the built-in gains tax. Generally, the taxpayer should sell built-in loss property in a year when an equivalent amount of built-in gain property is sold. Otherwise, the built-in loss could be wasted.

Example 35

Tulip, Inc., an S corporation, holds a built-in gain of $110,000 and reports current taxable income of $120,000

The taxable LIFO recapture amount equals the excess of the inventory's value under FIFO over the LIFO value. The resulting tax is payable in four equal installments, with the first payment due on or before the due date for the corporate return for the last C corporation year (without regard to any extensions). The remaining three installments are paid on or before the due dates of the succeeding corporate returns. No interest is due if payments are made by the due dates, and no estimated taxes are due on the four tax installments. No refund is allowed if the LIFO value is higher than the FIFO value.

Example 36

Daffodil Corporation converts from a C corporation to an S corporation at the beginning of 2015. Daffodil used the LIFO inventory method in 2014 and had an ending LIFO inventory of $110,000 (FIFO value of $190,000).

Daffodil adds the $80,000 LIFO recapture amount to its 2014 taxable income, resulting in an increased tax liability of $28,000 ($80,000 × 35%). Daffodil pays one-fourth of the tax ($7,000) with its 2014 (final) C corporation tax return. The three succeeding installments of $7,000 each are paid with Daffodil's 2015–2017 S corporation tax returns.

15-4b Passive Investment Income Penalty Tax

A tax is imposed on the excess passive income of S corporations that possess AEP from C corporation years. The tax rate is the highest corporate income tax rate for the year. The rate is applied to excess net passive income (ENPI), which is determined using the following formula.

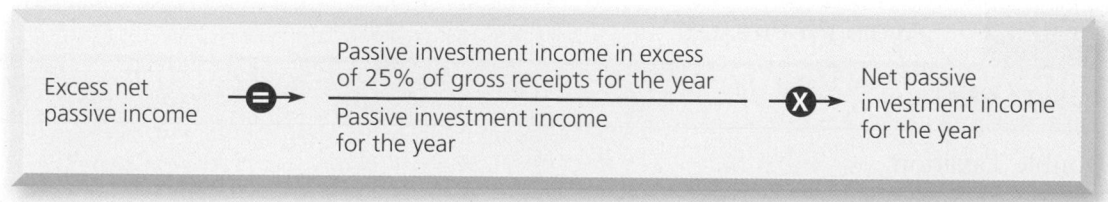

Passive investment income (PII) includes gross receipts derived from royalties, rents, dividends, interest, and annuities. Only the net gain from the disposition of capital assets is taken into account in computing PII gross receipts.[56] Net passive income is passive income reduced by any deductions directly connected with the production of that income. Any passive income tax reduces the amount the shareholders must take into income.

---

[56]§§ 1362(d)(3)(B) and (C).

TAX IN THE NEWS   The Self-Employment Income Advantage

A significant advantage of an S corporation involves the current definition of self-employment income. Although compensation for services rendered to an S corporation is subject to FICA taxes, a shareholder's share of income from an S corporation is not self-employment income. The rationale for this S corporation loophole is that the S shareholder does not personally carry on the entity's trade or business. In contrast, the earned income of a partnership or proprietorship is treated as self-employment income to the partner or proprietor.

The choice between a salary and pass-through income is not clear-cut, however.

- Although a salary is subject to payroll tax and pass-through income is not [*P.B. Ding v. Comm.*, 2000–1 USTC ¶50137, 84 AFTR 2d 99–7517, 200 F.3d 587 (CA–9, 1999)], this income does not accrue Social Security benefits for its recipient.
- S corporation income distributions do not count as compensation for computing an employee's contribution formula for a qualified retirement plan.
- The IRS and the courts require an S shareholder to take a reasonable salary (see footnote 32).
- If a partner or proprietor reports salary income from other sources and the aggregate salaries exceed the annual FICA ceiling, the partnership or proprietorship may provide tax savings compared to those of an S corporation.

© iStockphoto.com/Andrey Prokhorov

The excess net passive income cannot exceed a hypothetical C corporate taxable income for the year, before considering special C corporation deductions (e.g., the dividends received deduction) or an NOL carryover.[57]

Example 37

Lilac Corporation, an electing S corporation, has gross receipts totaling $264,000 (of which $110,000 is PII). Expenditures directly connected to the production of the PII total $30,000. Therefore, Lilac has net PII of $80,000 ($110,000 − $30,000), and its PII exceeds 25% of its gross receipts by $44,000 [$110,000 PII − (25% × $264,000)]. Excess net passive income (ENPI) is $32,000, calculated as follows.

$$\text{ENPI} = \frac{\$44,000}{\$110,000} \times \$80,000 = \$32,000$$

Lilac's PII tax is $11,200 ($32,000 × 35%).

Tax Planning Strategies   AVOID PII PITFALLS

FRAMEWORK FOCUS: TAX RATE

Strategy: Avoid Double Taxation.

Watch for a possible violation of the PII limitation. Avoid a consecutive third year with excess passive income when the corporation has accumulated E & P from C corporation years. In this connection, assets that produce passive income (e.g., stocks and bonds, certain rental assets) might be retained by the shareholders in their individual capacities and kept out of the corporation.

---

[57]§§ 1374(d)(4) and 1375(a) and (b).

TAX FACT   The S Corporation Economy

Total assets controlled by even the smallest S corporations make up a significant part of the economy. The 4.1 million S corporations that file Federal tax returns, representing over 7 million shareholders, employ $3.32 trillion in assets in their investments and operations.

Here are some more data about the S corporation sector.

- Trade or business income accounts for about 85 percent of all S corporation net income.
- About two-thirds of all S corporations report a positive amount of gross income.
- About 60 percent of all S corporations report business gross receipts of $250,000 or less.

© iStockphoto.com/Pali Rao

In-depth coverage can be found on this book's companion website: **www.cengagebrain.com**   **8**   Digging Deeper

15-5 SUMMARY

The S corporation rules are elective and can be used to benefit a number of owners of small businesses.

- When the business is profitable, the S corporation election removes the threat of double taxation on corporate profits.
- When the business is generating losses, deductions for allocable losses are immediately available to the shareholders.

More than two-thirds of all U.S. corporations operate under the S rules. Flow-through income is taxed to the shareholders, who increase basis in their corporate stock accordingly. In this manner, subsequent distributions to shareholders can be made tax free. Flow-through losses reduce stock and debt basis, but loss deductions are suspended when basis reaches zero. Flow-through items that could be treated differently by various shareholders are separately stated on Schedule K–1 of the Form 1120S.

Corporate-level taxes seldom are assessed on S corporations, but they guard against abuses of the S rules, such as shifting appreciated assets from higher C corporation rates to lower individual rates (the built-in gains tax) or doing the same with investment assets (the tax on excessive PII). The S corporation is liable for a penalty if it does not file its Form 1120S on a timely basis. The penalty is $195 per month times the number of S shareholders, for up to 12 months.[58]

The S rules are designed for the closely held business with a simple capital structure. Eligibility rules are not oppressive, and they do not include any limitations on the corporation's capitalization value, sales, number or distribution of employees, or other operating measures. Accounting for an S corporation's shareholder distributions can be complex, though, and maintenance of S status must be monitored on an ongoing basis.

---

[58]§ 6699. The penalty is waived if the entity can show reasonable cause for the failure to file.

© tuulijumala/Shutterstock.com

REFOCUS ON THE BIG PICTURE

CONVERTING A C CORPORATION TO AN S CORPORATION

As long as Fowle, Inc., is a C corporation, David cannot deduct on his individual tax return the losses the business incurs. However, the corporation can carry any net operating losses (NOLs) back and claim refunds for prior taxes paid and carry any remaining NOLs forward to reduce taxes paid if the company becomes profitable again.

If David wants to deduct the losses on his individual return, the corporation should make an S election or possibly become an LLC. Assuming that Fowle meets the one class of stock requirement, an S election may be appropriate. The election should be made before any losses are incurred because any regular corporate NOLs do not flow through to an S shareholder.

Fowle should make a timely election on Form 2553, and David must consent to the election in writing. For the S election to be effective this year, it should be made on or before the fifteenth day of the third month of the current year.

What If?

What if David expects the loss years to be followed by increased profitability as the company shifts some of its manufacturing to other countries with cheaper labor and material costs? In this case, David expects that the corporation will make significant distributions to him. How might this affect David's decision about whether the corporation should make an S election?

David should be aware of several rules that may result in income tax being paid by the S corporation or by him as the shareholder. First, distributions from an S corporation may be treated as taxable dividends to a shareholder to the extent the S corporation has earnings and profits dating to its years as a C corporation. While distributions are deemed to be made first from accumulated net S corporation earnings (i.e., the balance in AAA), distributions in excess of that amount may be treated as a taxable dividend, being paid from AEP (accumulated E & P).

The S corporation's DPAD computations flow through to David, as does Fowle's tax-exempt interest income. The entity may want to reconsider its salary and fringe benefits levels for David, so as to minimize the creation of a payroll tax burden, and to manage the restrictions on deductions for fringe benefits provided to an S shareholder. Fowle's tax-exempt interest can be distributed to David tax free only after all of the entity's AEP has been accounted for.

In addition, David should be aware that an S corporation that has been a C corporation in the past may be required to pay a built-in gains tax or LIFO recapture tax. The base for the built-in gains tax includes any unrealized gain on appreciated assets held by Fowle, Inc., on the day the company becomes an S corporation. The highest Federal corporate income tax rate is applied to the unrealized gains when any of the assets are sold within a specified number of years. If Fowle uses the LIFO inventory method, any LIFO recapture amount at the time of the S election also is subject to a corporate-level tax.

Suggested Readings

"Forming an S Corporation to Reduce Self-Employment Taxes," **www.mymoneyblog.com**.

Christopher W. Hesse, "Five-Year Built-In Gain Recognition Period," *The Tax Adviser*, December 2013.

Tony Nitti, "S Corporation Shareholder Compensation: How Much Is Enough?" *The Tax Adviser*, August 2011.

Ryan H. Pace, "Debunking the Notion That S Corporations Are Taxed 'Just Like' Partnerships," *Business Entities*, July/August 2007.

Jose M. Zambrano, "How Changes in Corporate Tax Rate Can Affect Choice of C vs. S Corporation," *The Tax Adviser*, October 2012.

Key Terms

AAA bypass election, 15-16

Accumulated adjustments account (AAA), 15-15

Built-in gains tax, 15-26

Other adjustments account (OAA), 15-15

Passive investment income (PII), 15-10

S corporation, 15-2

Small business corporation, 15-4

Subchapter S, 15-2

Voluntary revocation, 15-9

Problems

1. **LO.1** What are some Federal income tax differences between a partnership and an S corporation?

2. **LO.2** Which of the following can be a shareholder of an S corporation?
   a. Resident alien.
   b. Partnership.
   c. IRA.
   d. Estate.

3. **LO.2** Isaac and 121 of his close friends want to form an S corporation. Isaac reasons that if he and his friends form a partnership, the partnership then can establish an S corporation and act as a single shareholder, thereby avoiding the 100 shareholder rule. Will Isaac's plan work? Why or why not?

4. **LO.2** Joey lives in North Carolina, a common law state. He is a shareholder in an S corporation. If he marries a nonresident alien, will the S election terminate? Would your answer change if he lived in Louisiana? Explain.

5. **LO.3** On March 2, the two 50% shareholders of a calendar year corporation decide to elect S status. One of the shareholders, Terry, purchased her stock from a previous shareholder (a nonresident alien) on January 18 of the same year. Identify any potential problems for Terry or the corporation.

   Issue ID

6. **LO.5, 6** Scott Tyrney owns 21% of an S corporation. He is confused with respect to the amounts of the corporate AAA and his stock basis. Write a memo to the tax research file, identifying the key differences between AAA and an S shareholder's stock basis.

   Communications

7. **LO.6** For each of the following independent statements, indicate whether the transaction will increase (+), decrease (−), or have no effect (*NE*) on the basis of a shareholder's stock in an S corporation.
   a. Expenses related to tax-exempt income.
   b. Short-term capital gain.
   c. Nonseparately computed loss.

       d. Section 1231 gain.

       e. Depletion *not* in excess of basis.

       f. Separately computed income.

       g. Nontaxable return-of-capital distribution by the corporation.

       h. Advertising expenses.

       i. Business gifts in excess of $25.

       j. Depreciation recapture income.

       k. Dividends received by the S corporation from an investment in ExxonMobil stock.

       l. LIFO recapture tax paid.

       m. Recovery of a bad debt previously deducted.

       n. Long-term capital loss.

       o. Shareholder distribution out of AAA.

Issue ID   8. **LO.6, 7** Junie's share of her S corporation's net operating loss is $50,000, but her stock basis is only $30,000. Point out the Federal income tax consequences that Junie must face.

    9. **LO.5, 6** Mary is a shareholder in Sheets, Inc., a calendar year S corporation. At the beginning of the year, her stock basis is $10,000, her share of the AAA is $2,000, and her share of corporate AEP is $6,000. At the end of the year, Mary receives a $6,000 cash distribution from Sheets.

       Mary's share of S corporation items includes a $2,000 long-term capital gain and a $10,000 ordinary loss. Determine the effects of these events on Mary's share of Sheets's AAA, on Sheets's AEP, and on Mary's stock basis.

   10. **LO.4** The profit and loss statement of Kitsch Ltd., an S corporation, shows $100,000 book income. Kitsch is owned equally by four shareholders. From supplemental data, you obtain the following information about items that are included in book income.

Selling expenses	($21,200)
Tax-exempt interest income	3,000
Dividends received	9,000
§1231 gain	7,000
Depreciation recapture income	11,000
Recovery of bad debts previously deducted	5,000
Long-term capital loss	(6,000)
Salary paid to owners (each)	(12,000)
Cost of goods sold	(91,000)

       a. Compute Kitsch's nonseparately stated income or loss for the tax year.

       b. What would be the share of this year's income or loss items for James Billings, one of the Kitsch shareholders?

   11. **LO.4** Maul, Inc., a calendar year S corporation, incurred the following items.

Tax-exempt interest income	$ 7,000
Sales	140,000
Depreciation recapture income	12,000
Long-term capital gain	20,000
§1231 gain	7,000
Cost of goods sold	(42,000)
Administrative expenses	(15,000)
Depreciation expense (MACRS)	(17,000)
Charitable contributions	(7,000)

       a. Calculate Maul's nonseparately computed income or loss.

       b. If Carl is a 40% shareholder of Maul, what is Carl's share of Maul's long-term capital gain?

   12. **LO.4** Zebra, Inc., a calendar year S corporation, incurred the following items this year. Sammy is a 40% Zebra shareholder throughout the year.

Operating income	$100,000
Cost of goods sold	(40,000)
Depreciation expense (MACRS)	(10,000)

Administrative expenses	($ 5,000)
§1231 gain	21,000
Depreciation recapture income	25,000
Short-term capital loss from stock sale	(6,000)
Long-term capital loss from stock sale	(4,000)
Long-term capital gain from stock sale	15,000
Charitable contributions	(4,500)

a. Calculate Sammy's share of Zebra's nonseparately computed income or loss.
b. Calculate Sammy's share of any Zebra long-term capital gain.

13. **LO.4** On January 1, Bobby and Alicia own equally all of the stock of an electing S corporation called Prairie Dirt Delight. The company has a $60,000 loss for the year (not a leap year). On the 219th day of the year, Bobby sells his half of the stock to his son, Bubba. How much of the $60,000 loss, if any, is allocated to Bubba?

14. **LO.4, 5** McLin, Inc., a calendar year S corporation, holds $90,000 of AEP. Tobias, the sole McLin shareholder, has an $80,000 basis in his stock with a zero balance in the AAA.
a. Determine the tax aspects if a $90,000 salary is paid to Tobias.
b. Same as (a), except that Tobias receives a cash distribution of $90,000 from AEP.

Decision Making

15. **LO.4, 5** Tiger, Inc., a calendar year S corporation, is owned equally by four shareholders: Ann, Becky, Chris, and David. Tiger owns investment land that was purchased for $160,000 four years ago. On September 14, when the land is worth $240,000, it is distributed to David. Assuming that David's basis in his S corporation stock is $270,000 on the distribution date, discuss any Federal income tax ramifications.

16. **LO.4, 5, 6** Spence, Inc., a calendar year S corporation, generates an ordinary loss of $110,000 and makes a distribution of $140,000 to its sole shareholder, Storm Nelson. Nelson's stock basis at the beginning of the year is $200,000. Write a memo to your senior manager, Aaron McMullin, discussing the tax treatment of Spence's activities.

Communications

17. **LO.5** Polly has been the sole shareholder of a calendar year S corporation since its inception. Polly's stock basis is $15,500, and she receives a distribution of $19,000. Corporate-level accounts are as follows. How is Polly taxed on the distribution?

AAA .... $6,000   AEP $500

18. **LO.4, 7** A calendar year S corporation reports an ordinary loss of $80,000 and a capital loss of $20,000. Mei Freiberg owns 30% of the corporate stock and holds a $24,000 basis in the stock. Determine the amounts of the ordinary loss and capital loss, if any, that flow through to Freiberg. Prepare a memo for the tax research files explaining your computations.

Communications

19. **LO.5** Money, Inc., a calendar year S corporation, has two unrelated shareholders, each owning 50% of the stock. Both shareholders have a $400,000 stock basis as of January 1, and Money has AAA of $300,000 and AEP of $600,000. During the year, Money has operating income of $100,000. At the end of the year, Money distributes securities worth $1 million, with an adjusted basis of $800,000. Determine the tax effects of these transactions.

20. **LO.5** Assume the same facts as in Problem 19, except that the two shareholders consent to an AAA bypass election (i.e., to distribute AEP first).

Decision Making

21. **LO.4, 5, 6** Valence Corporation's Form 1120S shows ordinary income of $88,000 for the year. Daniel owns 40% of the Valence stock throughout the year. The following information is obtained from the corporate records.

Salary paid to Daniel	($40,000)
Tax-exempt interest income	5,000
Charitable contributions	(6,000)
Dividends received from a non-U.S. corporation	5,000
Long-term capital loss	(6,000)
Depreciation recapture income	11,000
Refund of prior-year state income taxes	5,000

Cost of goods sold	($ 80,000)
Short-term capital loss	(7,000)
Administrative expenses	(18,000)
Short-term capital gain	14,000
Selling expenses	(11,000)
Daniel's beginning stock basis	32,000
Daniel's additional stock purchases	9,000
Beginning AAA	45,000
Daniel's loan to corporation	20,000

a. Compute Valence's book income or loss.
b. Compute Daniel's ending stock basis.
c. Calculate ending corporate AAA.

22. **LO.4, 6, 7** Cloris owns 35% of the stock of Jacket, Inc., an S corporation, and she lends the corporation $7,000 during the year. Her stock basis in the Jacket stock at the end of the year is $25,000. If Jacket sustains a $110,000 operating loss during the year, what amount, if any, can Cloris deduct with respect to the pass-through loss?

Communications

23. **LO.4, 6, 7** Candy owns 40% of the stock of Park, Inc., an S corporation. Her stock basis is $25,000, and she loaned $10,000 to the corporation during the year. How much of Park's $100,000 operating loss can Candy deduct for this year? Show your computation of the tax consequences in spreadsheet form, and include them in a memo to your manager.

24. **LO.5** If the beginning balance in Swan, Inc.'s OAA is $6,700 and the following transactions occur, what is Swan's ending OAA balance?

Depreciation recapture income	$ 21,600
Payroll tax penalty	(4,200)
Tax-exempt interest income	4,012
Nontaxable life insurance proceeds	100,000
Life insurance premiums paid (nondeductible)	(3,007)

25. **LO.5, 6** Cougar, Inc., is a calendar year S corporation. Cougar's Form 1120S shows nonseparately stated ordinary income of $80,000 for the year. Johnny owns 40% of the Cougar stock throughout the year. The following information is obtained from Cougar's corporate records.

Tax-exempt interest income	$ 3,000
Salary paid to Johnny	(52,000)
Charitable contributions	(6,000)
Dividends received from a non-U.S. corporation	5,000
Short-term capital loss	(6,000)
Depreciation recapture income	11,000
Refund of prior state income taxes	5,000
Cost of goods sold	(72,000)
Long-term capital loss	(7,000)
Administrative expenses	(18,000)
Long-term capital gain	14,000
Selling expenses	(11,000)
Johnny's beginning stock basis	32,000
Johnny's additional stock purchases	9,000
Beginning AAA	31,000
Johnny's loan to corporation	20,000

a. Compute Cougar's book income or loss.
b. Compute Johnny's ending stock basis.
c. Calculate Cougar's ending AAA balance.

26. **LO.5, 6** Jeff, a 52% owner of an S corporation, has a stock basis of zero at the beginning of the year. Jeff's basis in a $10,000 loan made to the corporation and evidenced by a corporate note has been reduced to zero by pass-through losses. During the year, his net share of the corporate taxable income is $11,000. At the end of the year, Jeff receives a $15,000 cash distribution. Discuss the tax effects of the distribution.

27. **LO.6** Assume the same facts as in Problem 26, except that there is no cash distribution, but the corporation repays the loan principal to Jeff. Discuss the tax effects.

28. **LO.6** Assume the same facts as in Problem 26, except that Jeff's share of corporate taxable income is only $8,000 and there is no cash distribution. The corporation repays the $10,000 loan principal to Jeff. Discuss the tax effects. Assume that there was no corporate note (i.e., only an account payable). Does this change your answer? Explain.

29. **LO.6** Maple, Inc., is an S corporation with a single shareholder, Bob Maple. Bob believes that his stock basis in the entity is $50,000, but he has lost some of the records to substantiate this amount. Maple reports an ordinary loss for the year of $80,000. What are the Federal income tax aspects to consider?   **Issue ID**

30. **LO.7** Sheila Jackson is a 50% shareholder in Washington, Inc., an S corporation. This year, Jackson's share of the Washington operating loss is $100,000. Jackson has income from several other sources. Identify at least four tax issues related to the effects of the S corporation loss on Jackson's tax return.   **Issue ID**

31. **LO.4, 5, 6** Friedman, Inc., an S corporation, holds some highly appreciated land and inventory and some marketable securities that have declined in value. It anticipates a sale of these assets and a complete liquidation of the company over the next two years. Arnold Schwartz, the CFO, calls you, asking how to treat these transactions. Prepare a tax memo indicating what you told Arnold in the phone conversation.   **Issue ID**

    Communications

32. **LO.6, 7** Orange, Inc., a calendar year corporation in Clemson, South Carolina, elects S corporation status for 2014. The company generated a $74,000 NOL in 2013 and another NOL of $43,000 in 2014.   **Issue ID**

    At all times in 2013 and 2014, the stock of the corporation is owned by the same four shareholders, each owning 25% of the stock. Pete, one of the shareholders, holds a $6,020 basis in this Orange stock at the beginning of 2014. Identify the Federal income tax issues that Pete faces.

33. **LO.7** Samuel Reese sold 1,000 shares of his stock in Maroon, Inc., an S corporation. He sold the stock for $15,700 after he had owned it for six years. Samuel had paid $141,250 for the stock, which was issued under § 1244. Samuel is married and separately owns the 1,000 shares. Determine the appropriate Federal income tax treatment of any gain or loss on the stock sale.   **Critical Thinking**

34. **LO.7** Blue is the owner of all of the shares of an S corporation, and Blue is considering receiving a salary of $110,000 from the business. She will pay the 7.65% FICA taxes on the salary, and the S corporation will pay the same amount of FICA tax. If Blue reduces her salary to $50,000 and takes an additional $60,000 as a cash distribution from AAA, how would her Federal income tax liabilities change?   **Critical Thinking**

    Decision Making

35. **LO.1** One of your clients, Texas, Inc., is considering electing S status. Both of Texas's equal shareholders paid $30,000 for their stock. As of the beginning of 2013, Texas's Subchapter C NOL carryforward is $110,000. Its taxable income projections for the next few years are as follows. Will you counsel Texas to make the S election? Explain.   **Critical Thinking**

    Decision Making

2013	$40,000
2014	25,000
2015	25,000
2016	25,000

36. **LO.6, 7** C&C Properties is an S corporation that owns two rental real estate undertakings: Carrot Plaza and Cantaloupe Place. Both properties produce an annual $10,000 operating loss. C&C's Schedule K aggregates the results of the two locations into one number.   **Critical Thinking**

Dan and Marta, C&C's two equal shareholders, both hold a $7,000 stock basis in C&C as of the beginning of the year. Marta actively participates in the Cantaloupe location, but not at Carrot. Dan actively participates at neither location. Determine the amount of the available loss pass-throughs for both shareholders.

Comprehensive Tax Return Problem

Tax Return Problem

TAX SOFTWARE

1. John Parsons (123-45-6781) and George Smith (123-45-6782) are 70% and 30% owners, respectively, of Premium, Inc. (11-1111111), a candy company located at 1005 16th Street, Cut and Shoot, TX 77303. Premium's S election was made on January 15, 2008, its date of incorporation. The following information was taken from the 2013 income statement. Premium's book income for the year was $704,574.

Interest income	$ 100,000
Gross sales receipts	2,410,000
Beginning inventory	9,607
Direct labor	(203,102)
Direct materials purchased	(278,143)
Direct other costs	(249,356)
Ending inventory	3,467
Salaries and wages	(442,103)
Officers' salaries	(150,000)
Repairs	(206,106)
Depreciation expense	(15,254)
Interest expense	(35,222)
Rent expense (operating)	(40,000)
Taxes	(65,101)
Charitable contributions (cash)	(20,000)
Advertising expenses	(20,000)
Payroll penalties	(15,000)
Other deductions	(59,899)

A comparative balance sheet appears below.

	January 1, 2013	December 31, 2013
Cash	$ 47,840	$?
Accounts receivable	93,100	123,104
Inventories	9,607	3,467
Prepaid expenses	8,333	17,582
Building and equipment	138,203	185,348
Accumulated depreciation	(84,235)	(?)
Land	2,000	2,000
Total assets	$214,848	$844,422
Accounts payable	$ 42,500	$ 72,300
Notes payable (less than 1 year)	4,500	2,100
Notes payable (more than 1 year)	26,700	24,300
Capital stock	30,000	30,000
Retained earnings	111,148	?
Total liabilities and capital	$214,848	$844,422

Premium's accounting firm provides the following additional information.

Cash distributions to shareholders	$100,000
Beginning balance, accumulated adjustments account	$111,148

Using the preceding information, prepare a complete Form 1120S and Schedule K–1s for John Parsons and George Smith, both of whom live at 5607 20th Street, Cut and Shoot, TX 77303. If any information is missing, make realistic assumptions.

BRIDGE DISCIPLINE

1. Using an online research service, determine whether your state:
    a. Allows flow-through treatment for Federal S corporations.
    b. Requires any state-specific form to elect or elect out of S treatment at the state level.
    c. Places any additional withholding tax burdens on out-of-state U.S. shareholders or on non-U.S. shareholders of an S corporation.
    d. Requires any additional information disclosures or compliance deadlines for S corporations operating in the state *other than* to the revenue department (e.g., a report that must be filed with the secretary of state).
    e. Accepts "composite" or "block" income tax returns.

2. Using no more than five slides, at least two of which include a chart or graphic to illustrate your observations, prepare a presentation for your fellow students at the annual Pay It Forward conference at the university student union. In your talk, discuss the societal implications of the rule that excludes from the self-employment tax any flow-through income (other than salary and wages) that is assigned to a shareholder in an S corporation, while taxing that of the owners of a partnership or an LLC.

Communications

Research Problems

Note: Solutions to Research Problems can be prepared by using the **Checkpoint®** **Student Edition** online research product, which is available to accompany this text. It is also possible to prepare solutions to the Research Problems by using tax research materials found in a standard tax library.

THOMSON REUTERS
CHECKPOINT®

Decision Making

Research Problem 1. Eel Corporation, in Spivey Corners, North Carolina, has filed a Form 1120S for six years, and the local office of the IRS has sent the company a letter requesting an audit next month. Carrie, who is in charge of tax matters at Eel, cannot find a copy of the original S election, Form 2553.

The original shareholders and officers all agree that a local accountant filed the form, but he passed away last year. Several of the shareholders instruct Carrie to prepare a back-dated Form 2553, which they will sign. Carrie could then copy the form and tell the agent that this was a copy of the original Form 2553. What should Carrie do? She estimates that any proposed deficiency would be in the range of $625,000.

Partial list of research aids:
§§ 1362(b)(5) and (f).
Rev.Proc. 97–48, 1997–2 C.B. 521.
Ltr.Rul. 9748033.

Research Problem 2. Cher Holder owns all of the outstanding stock of two separate corporations, Common Corp and S.O. Teric, Inc. Common Corp is taxed under subchapter C of the Internal Revenue Code; S.O. is an S corporation. In 2014, Common and S.O. each put in service $150,000 of property qualifying for immediate expensing under § 179. Before considering any amount deductible under § 179, both Common and S.O. record over $100,000 of taxable income.

What is the greatest amount deductible under § 179 that will be available to Cher by virtue of her ownership of S.O.? (Assume that the aggregate amount of qualified property that may be immediately expensed under § 179 in 2014 is $25,000, with the amount subject to phaseout beginning when total qualifying property exceeds $200,000.)

Research Problem 3. Bushong, Inc., a calendar year S corporation, has a "tax cash-flow" provision in its shareholder agreement. Bushong must make annual distributions by the December 31 following a tax year in which there is an income pass-through. Each distribution must be in an amount sufficient to enable shareholders to pay their state and Federal income taxes on the pass-through.

The agreement also provides that if an audit adjustment is made to items reported on the Schedule K–1, Bushong can make a discretionary distribution to handle the increased taxes resulting from the adjustment.

The shareholders want to change the agreement. Under the proposal, if an audit adjustment is made and Bushong makes a discretionary payment, the payment would be in accordance with the shareholders' ownership shares during the tax year of the adjustment, rather than as of the distribution date.

Would the proposal create a second class of stock and terminate Bushong's S election? Explain.

Internet Activity

Communications

Use the tax resources of the Internet to address the following questions. Do not restrict your search to the Web, but include a review of newsgroups and general reference materials, practitioner sites and resources, primary sources of the tax law, chat rooms and discussion groups, and other opportunities.

Research Problem 4. Go to the website of a newspaper or business magazine, find a case study of how to start a small business, and choose the best tax entity (C corporation, S corporation, etc.). Summarize your findings in an e-mail to your instructor.

Communications

Research Problem 5. Use spreadsheet software to graph the growth in the number of S corporation returns filed. Obtain data for these years: 1975, 1980, 1985, 1990, 1995, 2000, and 2005. In a note to your instructor, explain the trends that you found in S returns filed.

Communications

Research Problem 6. Retrieve a copy of the S corporation Schedule M–3. Compare it to the partnership Schedule M–3. On one slide, list the four most important differences between the forms.

Communications

Research Problem 7. Summarize the trends in court decisions concerning salaries paid to shareholders of small S corporations. Title your essay "S Corporation Salaries: Too Much or Too Little?" Send your essay in an e-mail to your instructor.

Communications

Research Problem 8. Summarize in no more than five slides the purpose and provisions of the S Corporation Modernization Act of 2009.

part 6

SPECIAL BUSINESS TOPICS

Part 6 covers several topics that are relevant to all types of business entities. Business entities operate in both the international arena and state arenas. Therefore, multijurisdictional taxation is addressed from both a multinational business perspective and a multistate business perspective. A very important component of the basic tax model, tax credits, is presented next. This is followed by a discussion of the alternative tax system applicable to certain C corporations, that is, the AMT. Part 6 concludes with a comparative analysis of the different types of business entities previously discussed. This analysis recognizes the relevance of each of the three life cycle components in selecting a business entity form.

CHAPTER

16

Multijurisdictional Taxation

LEARNING OBJECTIVES: *After completing Chapter 16, you should be able to:*

LO.1 Discuss the computational and compliance issues that arise when a taxpayer operates in more than one taxing jurisdiction.

LO.2 Identify the sources of tax law applicable to a taxpayer operating in more than one country.

LO.3 Outline the U.S. tax effects related to the offshore operations of a U.S. taxpayer.

LO.4 Describe the tax effects related to the U.S. operations of a non-U.S. taxpayer.

LO.5 Identify the sources of tax law applicable to a taxpayer operating in more than one U.S. state.

LO.6 Apply computational principles designed for a taxpayer operating in more than one U.S. state.

LO.7 Synthesize the international and multistate tax systems and recognize common issues faced by both systems.

CHAPTER OUTLINE

TAX TALK *Don't tax you, don't tax me; tax the fellow behind the tree.* —RUSSELL B. LONG

Don't tax you, don't tax me; tax the companies across the sea. —DAN ROSTENKOWSKI

Dennis Flaherty/Photographer's Choice/Getty Images

THE BIG PICTURE   Tax Solutions for the Real World

GOING INTERNATIONAL

VoiceCo, a domestic corporation, designs, manufactures, and sells specialty microphones for use in theaters. All of its activities take place in Florida, although it ships products to customers all over the United States. When it receives inquiries about its products from foreign customers, VoiceCo decides to test the foreign market and places ads in foreign trade journals. Soon it is taking orders from foreign customers.

VoiceCo is concerned about its potential foreign income tax exposure. Although it has no assets or employees in the foreign jurisdictions, it now is involved in international commerce. Is VoiceCo subject to income taxes in foreign countries? Must it pay U.S. income taxes on the profits from its foreign sales? What if VoiceCo pays taxes to other countries? Does it receive any benefit from these payments on its U.S. tax return?

VoiceCo establishes a manufacturing plant in Ireland to meet the European demand for its products. VoiceCo incorporates the Irish operation as a controlled foreign corporation (CFC) named VoiceCo-Ireland. So long as VoiceCo-Ireland does not distribute profits to VoiceCo, will the profits escape U.S. taxation? What are the consequences to VoiceCo of being the owner of the CFC?

Read the chapter and formulate your response.

One of the tax planning principles that has been discussed throughout this text relates to the use of favorable tax jurisdictions—moving income into lower-taxed districts and deductions into higher-taxed ones. Many individuals dream of moving all of their income and wealth to a tax-friendly state or a proverbial island in the tropics, never to be taxed again. This chapter examines the temptations that attract taxpayers to this idea and various ways in which this goal can and cannot be accomplished.

16-1 THE MULTIJURISDICTIONAL TAXPAYER

LO.1

Discuss the computational and compliance issues that arise when a taxpayer operates in more than one taxing jurisdiction.

Companies large and small must deal with the consequences of earning income through activities in different jurisdictions. A small business may have its center of operations in a single city but have customers in many states and countries. Consider the typical U.S. multinational corporation. Its assets, employees, customers, suppliers, lenders, and owners are located in numerous locations, crossing city, county, state, national, and even "virtual" borders.

Example 1

RobotCo, a corporation created and organized in Delaware, produces and sells robotic manufacturing equipment. It holds its valuable patents and intangible property in Delaware and Bermuda. The company has manufacturing operations in Ireland, Singapore, Germany, Texas, and New Jersey. It has distribution centers in Canada, the United Kingdom, Germany, Hong Kong, Texas, New Jersey, Georgia, California, Illinois, and Arizona. RobotCo's sales force spends time in Europe, Asia, Mexico, Canada, and almost every state in the union. RobotCo's engineers likewise provide technical service to customers wherever they may be located. And in recent years, RobotCo has developed a substantial Web presence.

RobotCo must determine its potential exposure to tax in each of these jurisdictions. Such exposure usually is based on RobotCo's nexus (or economic connection) to the various locations. Unfortunately for all concerned, each of these taxing jurisdictions uses a different taxing system and methods, imposes taxes under differing structures, and even defines the tax base differently. How does RobotCo divide its income among the various jurisdictions that want a piece of the tax pie, determine its tax costs, mitigate any potential double taxation, and file the appropriate information returns with this diverse set of taxing authorities? Such questions and more must be addressed by modern-day businesses.

Thousands of state and local jurisdictions are involved in the taxation of interstate transactions through income, property, sales, or other taxes. State and local taxes make up over one-third of all taxes collected in the United States. Global trade also represents a major portion of the U.S. economy. In a recent year, U.S. exports of goods and services amounted to $2.2 trillion, with imports reaching $2.7 trillion. U.S. companies hold direct investments abroad exceeding $3 trillion, and foreign companies had invested over $2 trillion in U.S. businesses. Hundreds of countries and many more political subdivisions participated in the taxation of these transactions. These interstate and international trade flows, along with cross-state and cross-country investments, create significant Federal, state, and local tax consequences for both U.S. and foreign entities.

16-2 U.S. TAXATION OF MULTINATIONAL TRANSACTIONS

Cross-border transactions create the need for special tax considerations for both the United States and its trading partners. From a U.S. perspective, international tax laws should promote the global competitiveness of U.S. enterprises and at

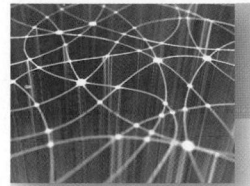

Many of the provisions of the U.S. tax law relating to international transactions are thinly disguised extensions of a principle of international law—the ability of sovereign countries to protect the safety and privacy of their citizens abroad.

For instance, U.S. tax auditors often have difficulty obtaining or reviewing the documentation supporting deductions claimed by U.S. taxpayers operating overseas. Banking, credit card, and other records that are available (in the course of business or forcibly by summons) for strictly U.S. transactions are not available once those same transactions cross national borders.

How could the U.S. tax base include rental and royalty income of a U.S. investor operating through a corporation in another country when property ownership and taxation records are not available for substantiation or audit outside the country of the investment? Perhaps this explains why the U.S. tax base typically excludes such items.

Conversely, when the taxing agencies of multiple countries are allowed by law to trade among themselves information about business operations and taxpayers, the fairness and completeness of the taxing process may improve. But such lengthening of the reach of the taxing authorities results from diplomatic negotiations among the countries, not from the passage of legislation.

the same time protect the tax revenue base of the United States. These two objectives sometimes conflict, however. The need to deal with both objectives contributes to the complexity of the rules governing the U.S. taxation of cross-border transactions.

> **Example 2**
>
> U.S. persons engage in activities outside the United States for many different reasons. Consider two U.S. corporations that have established sales subsidiaries in foreign countries. Dedalus, Inc., operates in Germany, a high-tax country, because customers demand local attention from sales agents. Mulligan, Inc., operates in the Cayman Islands, a tax haven country, simply to shift income outside the United States. U.S. tax law must fairly address both situations with the same law.

U.S. international tax provisions are concerned primarily with two types of potential taxpayers: U.S. persons earning income from outside the United States and non-U.S. persons earning income from inside the United States.[1] U.S. persons earning income only from inside the United States do not create any international tax issues and are taxed under the purely domestic provisions of the Internal Revenue Code. Non-U.S. persons earning income from outside the United States are not within the taxing jurisdiction of the United States (unless this income is somehow directly connected to U.S. operations).

The U.S. taxation of international transactions can be organized in terms of "outbound" and "inbound" taxation. **Outbound taxation** refers to the U.S. taxation of foreign-source income earned by U.S. taxpayers. **Inbound taxation** refers to the U.S. taxation of U.S.-source income earned by foreign taxpayers. Figure 16.1 summarizes these concepts.

U.S. taxpayers often "internationalize" gradually over time. A U.S. business may operate on a strictly domestic basis for several years, then explore offshore markets by exporting its products abroad, and later license its products to a foreign manufacturer or enter into a joint venture with a foreign partner. If its forays into non-U.S. markets are successful, the U.S. business may create a foreign subsidiary and move a portion of its operations abroad by establishing a sales or manufacturing facility.

---

[1] The term *person* includes an individual, corporation, partnership, trust, estate, or association. § 7701(a)(1). The terms *domestic* and *foreign* are defined in §§ 7701(a)(4) and (5).

FIGURE 16.1	**U.S. Taxation of Cross-Border Transactions**

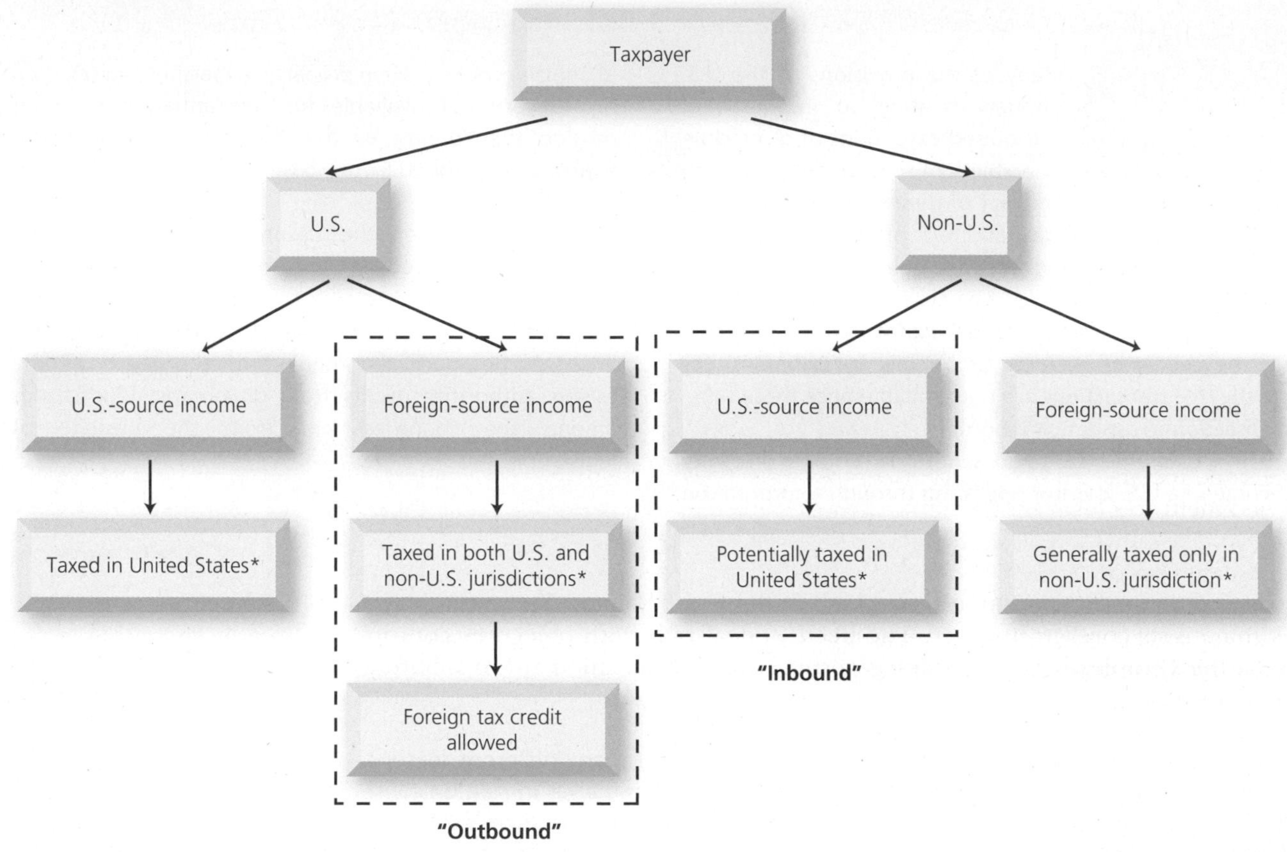

Taxpayer

U.S.   Non-U.S.

| U.S.-source income | Foreign-source income | U.S.-source income | Foreign-source income |

| Taxed in United States* | Taxed in both U.S. and non-U.S. jurisdictions* | Potentially taxed in United States* | Generally taxed only in non-U.S. jurisdiction* |

Foreign tax credit allowed

"Outbound"

"Inbound"

*Income may or may not be subject to tax in the non-U.S. jurisdiction, depending on local country tax law.
Some U.S.-source income is exempt from tax in the United States for both U.S. and non-U.S. persons.

A domestically controlled foreign corporation can have significant U.S. tax consequences for the U.S. owners, including potential deferrals of income recognition from offshore activities. Non-U.S. businesses likewise enter the U.S. market in stages. In either case, each step generates increasingly significant international tax consequences. Figure 16.2 shows a typical timeline for "going global."

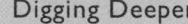

Digging Deeper | In-depth coverage can be found on this book's companion website: **www.cengagebrain.com**

16-2a Sources of Law

LO.2

Identify the sources of tax law applicable to a taxpayer operating in more than one country.

U.S. individuals and companies operating across national borders are subject to both U.S. law and the laws of the other jurisdictions in which they operate or invest. Accordingly, the source of law depends on the nature of a taxpayer's connection with a particular country. For U.S. persons, the Internal Revenue Code addresses the tax consequences of earning income anywhere in the world. However, U.S. persons also must comply with the local tax law of the other nations in which they operate. Taxpayers should attempt to resolve any conflicts between a treaty and local law. A common way of doing so is to apply the "later-in-time" rule, under which preference is given to whichever is newer, the treaty or the law.

For non-U.S. persons, U.S. statutory law is relevant to income they earn that is connected to U.S. income-producing activities, whether those activities involve a passive investment or an active trade or business. Whether non-U.S. persons also are subject to potential tax in their home countries on their U.S. income depends on their own local tax law.

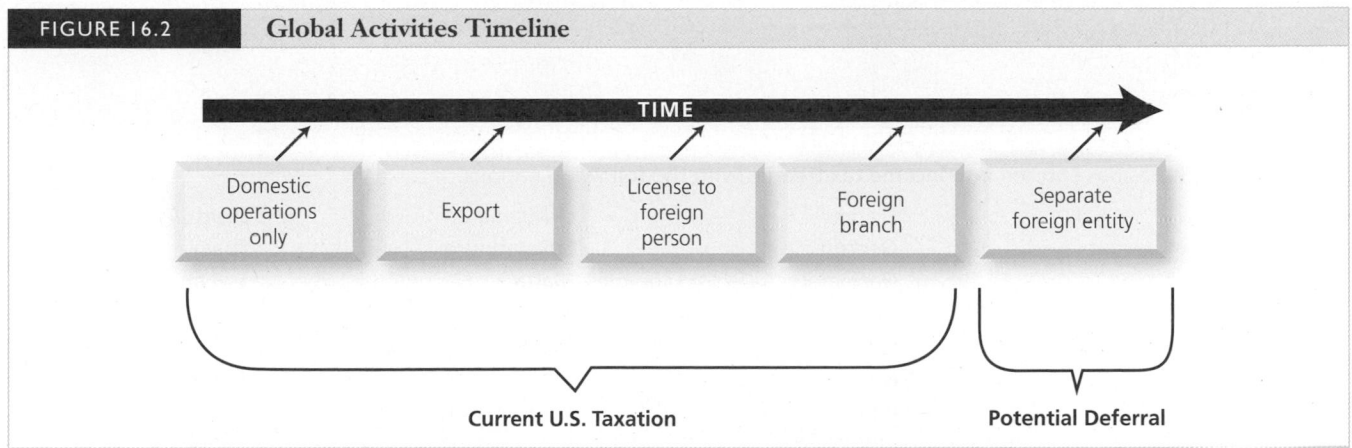

FIGURE 16.2   **Global Activities Timeline**

It is difficult for the United States (or any country) to craft local tax laws that equitably address all of the potential issues that arise when two countries attempt to tax the same income. Furthermore, any uncertainty as to tax consequences can be an impediment to global business investment. Consequently, countries enter into **income tax treaties** with each other to provide more certainty to taxpayers.

Tax treaties are the result of specific negotiations with each treaty partner, so each treaty is unique. Nevertheless, all tax treaties are organized in the same way and address similar issues. For example, all treaties include provisions regarding the taxation of investment income, business profits from a **permanent establishment (PE)**, personal service income, and exceptions for certain persons (e.g., athletes, entertainers, students, and teachers).

Permanent establishment (PE) is an important concept that is defined in all income tax treaties. A person has a PE within a country when its activities within that country rise beyond a minimal level. Tax treaties outline the activities that create a PE, including an office, plant, or other fixed place of business. Treaties also specify specific activities that do not create a PE (e.g., maintaining goods in a warehouse or a temporary construction project). Once a person has a PE within a country, the business profits associated with the PE become subject to tax in that country.

Example 3

Amelia, Inc., a U.S. corporation, sells boating supplies to customers in the United States and Canada. Amelia has no assets in Canada. All Canadian sales transactions are conducted via the Internet or telephone from Amelia's Florida office. Because Amelia does not have any assets in Canada or conduct any activities within Canada, it does not have a Canadian PE. Consequently, Canada does not impose an income tax on the profit associated with Amelia's Canadian sales. However, if Amelia opens a sales office in Canada, a PE will exist and Canada will tax the profits associated with the PE.

Although the United States has entered into almost 70 income tax treaties, many jurisdictions where U.S. taxpayers operate are not covered by a treaty. Where there is no tax treaty, the more subjective test of whether a person is "engaged in a trade or business" within a country replaces the PE determination. Both the PE concept and the engaged in a trade or business concept are closely related to the determination of whether a person has nexus within a jurisdiction for state and local tax purposes (discussed later in this chapter).

16-2b Tax Issues

Authority to Tax

The United States taxes the *worldwide* income of U.S. taxpayers.[2] The United States claims the right to tax all of a U.S. person's income because of the protection

LO.3

Outline the U.S. tax effects related to the offshore operations of a U.S. taxpayer.

---

[2]Gross income for a U.S. person includes all income from whatever source derived. "Source" in this context means not only type of income (e.g., wages or interest) but geographic source as well (e.g., the United States or Belgium). § 61.

TAX FACT   U.S. Income Tax Treaties in Force

The United States has entered into income tax treaties with the following nations.

Armenia	France	Lithuania	South Africa
Australia	Georgia	Luxembourg	Spain
Austria	Germany	Malta	Sri Lanka
Azerbaijan	Greece	Mexico	Sweden
Bangladesh	Hungary	Moldova	Switzerland
Barbados	Iceland	Morocco	Tajikistan
Belarus	India	Netherlands	Thailand
Belgium	Indonesia	New Zealand	Trinidad
Bulgaria	Ireland	Norway	Tunisia
Canada	Israel	Pakistan	Turkey
China	Italy	Philippines	Turkmenistan
Cyprus	Jamaica	Poland	Ukraine
Czech Republic	Japan	Portugal	United Kingdom
Denmark	Kazakhstan	Romania	Uzbekistan
Egypt	Korea	Russia	Venezuela
Estonia	Kyrgyzstan	Slovak Republic	
Finland	Latvia	Slovenia	

© iStockphoto.com/Pali Rao

of U.S. law provided to a person connected to the United States through citizenship, residency, or place of organization.

Because non-U.S. governments also may tax some of the U.S. person's income when it is earned within the other country's borders, U.S. taxpayers may be subjected to double taxation. There are two broad methods of mitigating this double taxation problem. Under the *territorial* approach, a country simply exempts from tax the income derived from sources outside its borders. Most European and Asian countries have adopted this approach.[3] The second approach, and the one adopted by the United States, is to tax the *worldwide* income of all domestic persons, and then provide a **foreign tax credit** (FTC) against home country taxes for taxes paid to other countries on the same income. The United States allows its taxpayers to reduce their U.S. tax liability by some or all of the foreign income taxes paid on income earned outside the United States.

Example 4

Gator Enterprises, Inc., a U.S. corporation, operates a manufacturing branch in Italy because of customer demand in Italy, local availability of raw materials, and the high cost of shipping finished goods. This branch income is taxed in the United States as part of Gator's worldwide income, but it is also taxed in Italy. Without the availability of a foreign tax credit to mitigate this double taxation, Gator Enterprises would suffer an excessive tax burden and could not compete with local Italian companies.

The United States does adopt the territorial approach in taxing non-U.S. persons. Such inbound taxpayers generally are subject to tax only on income earned within U.S. borders.

Example 5

Purdie, Ltd., a corporation based in the United Kingdom, operates in the United States. Although not a U.S. person, Purdie is taxed in the United States on its U.S.-source business income. If Purdie, Ltd., could operate free of U.S. tax, its U.S.-based competitors would face a serious disadvantage.

---

[3]In some cases, countries allow the territorial exemption from home country taxation only if the income has been subject to tax in another country. Other countries, however, exempt such income even if no source country tax is imposed.

FINANCIAL DISCLOSURE INSIGHTS Effective Tax Strategies Using Overseas Operations

In a global economy, publicly traded business entities can operate in many taxing jurisdictions. For instance, General Electric reports that it files current-year tax returns with more than 250 countries, amounting to over 7,000 income tax returns at the Federal and local levels worldwide. Note that this tax activity does not take into account the sales, value added, property, and other tax returns that are required by the U.S. states and localities.

The financial reports of profitable U.S. companies indicate that overseas operations can produce tax benefits of their own, not taking into account the effects of increased market share and financial stability. For instance, the trucking firm Ryder Systems recently reported current tax refunds of about $235,000 and deferred tax savings of about $500,000 on non-U.S. profits of about $11.5 million.

In a recent period, Eli Lilly reduced its effective tax rate by about one-third due to overseas operations. And General Electric recently reduced its effective tax rate to a negative amount because of various income deferrals related to overseas earnings. These deferral techniques are discussed later in the chapter.

© iStockphoto.com/Pali Rao

Income Sourcing

Determining the source of net income is a critical component in calculating the U.S. tax consequences to both U.S. and foreign persons. A number of specific provisions contained in §§ 861 through 865 address the income-sourcing rules for all types of income, including interest, dividends, rents, royalties, services, and sales of assets. Although sometimes complex and subject to various special exceptions, these sourcing rules generally assign income to a geographic source based on the location where the economic activity producing the income took place. In some cases, this relationship is clear, and in others, the connection is more obscure.

Wickless, Inc., a U.S. corporation, provides scuba diving lessons to customers in Florida and in the Bahamas. These services are sourced based on the place where the activity is performed. The services performed in Florida are U.S.-source income, and those performed in the Bahamas are foreign-source income. Because Wickless, Inc., is a U.S. person, all the income, U.S. and foreign, is subject to U.S. taxation. But the foreign-source portion is important in determining any available foreign tax credits for Wickless.	**Example 6**

Brown, Inc., a U.S. corporation, receives dividend income from Takeda Corporation, a Japanese corporation, based on its ownership of Takeda common stock. Brown purchased the stock in the United States and receives all payments in the United States. At first glance, it appears that all of the activities related to earning the dividend income take place in the United States. Nevertheless, the dividend income is treated as foreign source because it is paid by a foreign corporation.[4]	**Example 7**

In addition to sourcing income, the U.S. rules require taxpayers to assign deductions to U.S.- or foreign-source categories. Deductions that are directly related to an activity or property are first allocated to classes of income to which they directly relate. This is followed by an apportionment between the U.S. and foreign groupings using some reasonable basis (e.g., revenue, gross profit, assets, units sold, time spent). If a deduction is not definitely related to any class of gross income, the deduction is first assigned to all classes of gross income and then apportioned between U.S.- and foreign-source income.

---

[4]Section 861(a)(2) establishes that only dividends from domestic corporations are U.S.-source income.

TAX FACT   Where Do We Stand?

The drastic reductions in marginal tax rates brought about in the United States in 1981 and 1986 and the ongoing effort by Congress to make the Federal corporate income tax neutral as to the business decisions of U.S. entities operating in the global economy have rippled through the rest of the world. Even perpetually high-tax countries such as Sweden and the United Kingdom were forced to cut back marginal tax rate structures to remain competitive and often had to change the tax base to match the revisions of the U.S. tax law.

As a result of this dramatic evolution in international tax rates, the average marginal business income tax rate in developed countries now lies between 30 and 35 percent, down from perhaps 50 percent in the 1960s. This description does not take into account, though, the dependence of many U.S. trading partners on transaction taxes, such as the value added tax and wealth-based taxes, which make difficult an apples-to-apples comparison of rates alone. Further, each country treats payroll taxes and entitlements differently, and these are increasingly expensive components of the tax structure. After taking these other taxes into account, the United States may be closer to the worldwide average.

But U.S. corporate income tax law has not changed much since the 1980s, and the rest of the world appears to be continuing the rate-cutting the United States started. The United States may need another round of rate cuts to stay in the game. By one measure, at least, after significant rate cuts by Japan and the United Kingdom, the United States applies the highest corporate income tax rate in the developed world.

Top Statutory Corporate Income Tax Rates for Selected Countries	
Bermuda	0.0%
France	34.4%
Germany	15.8%
Ireland	12.5%
Japan	28.0%
United Kingdom	23.0%
United States	35.0%

Note: Additional taxes on corporate taxable income may be levied by states, cities, provinces, cantons, and other smaller jurisdictions.

THE BIG PICTURE

Example 8

Return to the facts of *The Big Picture* on p. 16-1. Assume that VoiceCo makes an overseas investment and generates $2 million of gross income and a $50,000 expense, all related to real estate sales and rental activities. The expense is allocated and apportioned using gross income as a basis.

	Gross Income			Apportionment	
	Foreign	U.S.	Allocation	Foreign	U.S.
Sales	$1,000,000	$500,000	$37,500*	$25,000	$12,500**
Rentals	400,000	100,000	12,500	10,000	2,500***
			$50,000	$35,000	$15,000

* $50,000 × ($1,500,000/$2,000,000) = $37,500.
** $37,500 × ($500,000/$1,500,000) = $12,500.
*** $12,500 × ($100,000/$500,000) = $2,500.

If VoiceCo could show that $45,000 of the expense was directly related to sales income, the $45,000 would be allocated directly to that class of gross income, with the remainder allocated and apportioned between U.S. and foreign source ratably based on gross income.

Many deductions may be allocated and apportioned based on any reasonable method the taxpayer chooses.[5] However, the U.S. tax rules impose a specific

---

[5]Reg. § 1.861–8.

Tax Planning Strategies — DEFERRAL AND REPATRIATION

FRAMEWORK FOCUS: TAX RATE

Strategy: Shift Net Income from High-Tax Jurisdictions to Low-Tax Jurisdictions.

FRAMEWORK FOCUS: INCOME

Strategy: Postpone Recognition of Income to Achieve Tax Deferral.

U.S. taxpayers with foreign operations have a choice as to how they structure such operations for U.S. tax purposes. If the U.S. taxpayer operates through an unincorporated foreign branch, the net profits from the foreign branch are subject to current taxation in the U.S. tax return of the U.S. taxpayer. If instead the U.S. taxpayer operates abroad through a separate wholly owned foreign corporation, the income from the foreign operation is deferred from U.S. taxation until the profits are repatriated back to the United States (via a dividend or similar distribution), or when they are treated as repatriated through the operation of the Subpart F deemed dividend provisions (as discussed later). This option can have a significant effect on a U.S. taxpayer's current-period tax burden, particularly if the foreign operations are in a lower-tax jurisdiction.

LeshCo, Inc., a domestic corporation, wants to establish a manufacturing operation in Ireland. The Irish operations are expected to produce 2 million euros in net profits each year, and the income tax rate in Ireland is 12.5 percent. Consider the difference between operating in Ireland as a branch versus using an Irish corporate subsidiary. If LeshCo operates as an unincorporated branch, it directly

pays 250,000 euros in Irish taxes (2 million × 12.5%). Assuming that $1 equals 1 euro for simplicity, this has the following effect on LeshCo's U.S. tax liability for the current year.

Irish branch profits	$2,000,000
U.S. tax at 35% (before FTC)	$ 700,000
FTC allowed	(250,000)
Residual U.S. tax	$ 450,000

With a branch operation, LeshCo pays a total tax of $700,000 on its $2 million of foreign income ($250,000 in Irish taxes and $450,000 in U.S. taxes).

If instead LeshCo operates in Ireland through a wholly owned Irish subsidiary and does not repatriate its profits back to the United States, LeshCo pays only the $250,000 in Irish taxes at this time. The potential $450,000 in U.S. taxes is deferred until LeshCo later repatriates its Irish profits. As discussed in Chapter 3, under ASC 740 (APB 23), this deferral of taxes also can reduce the financial statement tax expense if the Irish profits are indefinitely reinvested outside the United States.

method for certain types of deductions, including interest and research and experimentation expenses. Interest expense is allocated and apportioned based on the theory that money is fungible. For example, if a taxpayer borrows to support its manufacturing activity, this frees up other funds for use to support its investment activities. Accordingly, the tax rules require that interest expense be allocated and apportioned to all activities and property of the taxpayer, regardless of the specific purpose for incurring the debt on which interest is paid. Taxpayers must allocate and apportion interest expense on the basis of asset location, using either the fair market value or the tax book value of the assets.

THE BIG PICTURE

Example 9

Return to the facts of *The Big Picture* on p. 16-1. Assume that VoiceCo makes an overseas investment and generates both U.S.-source and foreign-source gross income for the current year. VoiceCo's assets (measured at tax book value) are as follows.

Assets generating U.S.-source income	$18,000,000
Assets generating foreign-source income	5,000,000
	$23,000,000

VoiceCo incurs interest expense of $800,000 for the current year. Using the tax book value method, interest expense is apportioned to foreign-source income as follows.

$$\frac{\$5,000,000 \text{ (foreign assets)}}{\$23,000,000 \text{ (total assets)}} \times \$800,000 \text{ (interest expense)} = \$173,913$$

TAX IN THE NEWS   The IRS Watches from Abroad

Taxpayers long have tried to shield information from the IRS about assets and income (e.g., in the proverbial Swiss bank account). Computing resources and cooperation among government taxing authorities make it more difficult to do so than ever before.

The IRS stations agents in Beijing, Hong Kong, Sydney, the British Virgin Islands, and other jurisdictions where it perceives that taxpayers are shifting financial resources with tax evasion motives. It often takes many years to put together a case to show the tax evasion activities of a U.S. person, but the wheels are starting to turn to accomplish just that. Typical IRS weapons include information-sharing agreements among governments and/or taxing agencies, whistleblower programs, and litigation.

The U.S. Foreign Account Tax Compliance Act (FATCA) requires that a bank (even one organized outside the United States) provide the IRS with certain identifying information about all U.S. persons with an account at the bank. Lacking such compliance information, the bank must pay a fine if it wants to hold assets in the United States.

FATCA, along with other efforts to disclose holdings in non-U.S. banks, can be an effective revenue-raiser for the United States. Recently, about 40,000 U.S. taxpayers took advantage of a tax amnesty program related to hidden assets, paying about $10 billion in understated income taxes. But as Switzerland starts to cooperate with other countries and discloses information about secret bank accounts, some investors are moving money to similar accounts in less cooperative countries, like Singapore and Hong Kong.

Tax Planning Strategies   SOURCING INCOME FROM SALES OF INVENTORY

FRAMEWORK FOCUS: TAX RATE

Strategy: Control the Character of Income and Deductions.

Generally, income from the sale of personal property is sourced according to the residence of the seller under § 865. Several important exceptions exist for inventory. Income from the sale of purchased inventory is sourced in the country in which the sale takes place under the "title passage" rule. This rule provides the taxpayer with flexibility with regard to sourcing and allows for the creation of zero-taxed foreign-source income.

USCo, a domestic corporation, purchases inventory for resale from unrelated parties and sells the inventory to customers in the United States and Brazil. If title on the Brazilian sales passes in the United States (i.e., risks of loss shift to the Brazilian customers at the shipping point), the inventory income is U.S. source. If title passes outside the United States (e.g., at the customer's warehouse in Brazil), the inventory income is foreign source.

Although the Code identifies the income item as foreign source, this income likely is not subject to any Brazilian tax because USCo has no employees, assets, or activities in Brazil. Although the income is subject to U.S. tax in either case (as it represents taxable income to USCo), in the latter case, USCo has generated foreign-source income with no corresponding foreign income tax. This will prove very useful in managing USCo's ability to use foreign tax credits, as discussed later in this chapter.

When a taxpayer both produces and sells inventory, the income is apportioned between the country of production and the country of sale. Taxpayers often elect a 50–50 allocation method as allowed by § 863(b), where 50 percent of the profits from the sale are automatically assigned to the location of the production assets and 50 percent of the profits are assigned to the location where title passes.

Assume that USCo manufactures inventory in its Texas plant and sells the inventory to customers in Mexico. Regardless of the actual economic profit relationship between the manufacturing and selling activities, 50 percent of the profit on the Mexican sales can be assigned to foreign-source income by simply passing title outside the United States.

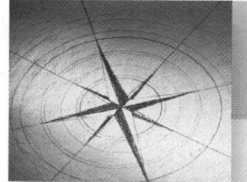

ETHICS & EQUITY When Is Cash Repatriated?

Much of the U.S. income tax on the profits of multinational entities is deferred until the profits are repatriated to the United States. One might picture, as part of this deferral technique, overseas bank accounts holding piles of cash for the multinational business, perhaps waiting for a tax holiday or a change in the tax law that would allow the funds to return to the United States.

Change that picture, please. More than half of the "unrepatriated" earnings of Google and Microsoft, generated and held by their non-U.S. subsidiaries, are in U.S. bank accounts or invested in U.S. government or corporate bonds.

Legally, such accounts are still "overseas"—at least until they are moved to a U.S. account of the subsidiary or into the parent corporation's control.

One might say that the United States benefits from these arrangements through the purchase of its government securities. And the entities probably would rather keep the funds in U.S. investments (or in U.S. bank accounts) to reduce risks associated with their portfolios.

Do you think that, when the profits physically are located in the United States, repatriation has occurred? Or should the legality of the owner of the investment accounts be respected? Is it fair to defer tax payments in this manner?

Foreign Tax Credit

As discussed earlier, the United States retains the right to tax its citizens and residents on their worldwide taxable income. This approach can result in double taxation, presenting a potential problem to U.S. persons who operate abroad. To reduce the possibility of double taxation, Congress created the foreign tax credit (FTC).

A qualified taxpayer is allowed a tax credit for foreign income taxes paid or accrued. All of the taxes paid by the taxpayer to various countries on its operations are combined to compute the FTC. The credit is a dollar-for-dollar reduction of U.S. income tax liability.

> **Example 10**
>
> Caulkin Tools, Inc., a U.S. corporation, operates a branch operation in Mexico from which it earns taxable income of $750,000 for the current year. Caulkin pays income tax of $150,000 on these earnings to the Mexican tax authorities. Caulkin also includes the $750,000 in gross income for U.S. tax purposes.
>
> Before considering the FTC, Caulkin owes $255,000 in U.S. income taxes on this foreign-source income. Thus, total taxes on the $750,000 could equal $405,000 ($150,000 + $255,000), a 54% effective rate.
>
> But Caulkin takes an FTC of $150,000 against its U.S. tax liability on the foreign-source income. Caulkin's total taxes on the $750,000 now are $255,000 ($150,000 + $105,000), a 34% effective rate.

> **Example 11**
>
> MettCo, Inc., a domestic corporation, receives a $5,000 dividend from DeanCo, Ltd., a foreign corporation owned less than 5% by MettCo. The foreign country imposes a 20% withholding tax on dividend payments to nonresidents. Accordingly, DeanCo withholds $1,000 ($5,000 × 20%) from the dividend and remits this tax to the local country tax authorities. DeanCo pays the remaining $4,000 to MettCo.
>
> Although MettCo did not directly pay the $1,000 in foreign tax, the entire amount is allowed as a direct tax to MettCo for FTC purposes. MettCo reports $5,000 in dividend income on its U.S. tax return (the gross amount of the dividend), but it receives an FTC against any U.S. tax for the $1,000 in foreign withholding tax.

The FTC is elective for the tax year. Lacking an election to take the FTC, a deduction is claimed for foreign taxes paid or incurred. One cannot take a credit and a deduction for the same foreign income taxes, and in most situations, the FTC is more valuable to the taxpayer.

FTC Limits The United States does not grant an FTC for all foreign taxes paid, and there are limits on the amount of foreign taxes that can be taken as a credit. First, only foreign *income* taxes are potentially creditable. Second, the FTC allowed in any

---

TAX FACT   Corporate Use of the Foreign Tax Credit

Information from recent Forms 1120 indicates that the foreign tax credit is used by a small number of corporate taxpayers, but that the credit spans a very large portion of the global economy.

Of foreign tax payments reported on Forms 1118 and 1120, almost 50 percent were paid to European countries, with the most going to the United Kingdom, Luxembourg, Norway, and the Netherlands. Tax payments to Canada accounted for 6.3 percent of the total. South Korea received less than 1 percent of total foreign tax payments, and all of Africa totaled only about 6 percent.

Tax returns claiming a foreign tax credit	6,900
Total assets of corporations claiming the credit	$32.9 trillion
Taxable income of corporations claiming the credit	$770 billion
U.S. income tax liability of corporations claiming the credit	$271 billion
Foreign tax credit claimed	$118 billion
Foreign income taxes available for the credit	$197 billion

© iStockphoto.com/Pali Rao

tax year is limited to the U.S. tax imposed on the foreign-source income included on the U.S. tax return.[6] Thus, taxpayers are allowed a credit for the lesser of the foreign income taxes paid or accrued, or the following limitation.

$$\text{FTC limit} = \frac{\text{Foreign-source taxable income}}{\text{Worldwide taxable income}} \times \text{U.S. tax liability before FTC}$$

Worldwide taxable income is the total taxable income reported on the taxpayer's U.S. tax return, not the total worldwide income of a group of related domestic and foreign entities. Any potential FTCs disallowed because of the FTC limitation may be carried back one year or forward 10 years, subject to the FTC limits in those tax years.

Example 12	Lassaline, Inc., a domestic corporation, invests in the bonds of non-U.S. corporations. Lassaline's worldwide taxable income for the tax year is $1.2 million, consisting of $1 million of profits from U.S. sales and $200,000 of interest income from foreign sources. Foreign taxes of $90,000 were withheld on these interest payments.
	Lassaline's U.S. tax before the FTC is $408,000. Its FTC is limited to $68,000 [($200,000/$1,200,000) × $408,000]. Thus, Lassaline's net U.S. tax liability is $340,000 after allowing the $68,000 FTC. The remaining $22,000 of FTCs ($90,000 − $68,000) may be carried back or forward.

Tax Planning Strategies   UTILIZING THE FOREIGN TAX CREDIT

FRAMEWORK FOCUS: TAX CREDITS

Strategy: **Maximize Tax Credits.**

The FTC limitation can prevent the total amount of foreign taxes paid in high-tax jurisdictions from being credited. Taxpayers can overcome this problem by generating additional foreign-source income that is subject to no or low foreign taxation.

A U.S. taxpayer's ability to use FTCs is directly related to its level of foreign-source income relative to its total taxable income. To the extent a U.S. taxpayer can keep the average tax rate on its foreign-source income at or below the U.S.

tax rate on such income, the foreign taxes will be fully creditable. Consequently, combining high- and low-tax foreign-source income is an important planning objective.

Compare the following scenarios where a U.S. corporation's FTC situations differ depending on its ability to mix high- and low-taxed income. In the first scenario, the corporation has only $500,000 of highly taxed foreign-source income. In the second scenario, the corporation also has $100,000 of low-taxed foreign-source passive income.

---

[6]Sections 901, 902, and 903 provide definitions of creditable foreign taxes. Section 904 contains the FTC limitation rules.

	Only Highly Taxed Income	With Low-Taxed Passive Income
Foreign-source income	$500,000	$600,000
Foreign taxes	275,000	280,000
U.S.-source income	700,000	700,000
U.S. taxes (34%)	408,000	442,000
FTC limitation	170,000*	204,000**

* ($500,000/$1,200,000) × $408,000 = $170,000.
** ($600,000/$1,300,000) × $442,000 = $204,000.

The corporation's actual foreign taxes increase by only $5,000 ($280,000 versus $275,000), but its FTC limitation increases by $34,000 (from $170,000 to $204,000). The ability to "cross-credit" high- and low-taxed foreign income is available, though, only when all of the foreign-source income is classified in the same income basket.

To limit the ability of U.S. taxpayers to cross-credit foreign taxes, the FTC rules provide for two **separate foreign tax credit income categories** (or baskets): passive and general. In any tax year, taxpayers are allowed to credit the lesser of foreign income taxes paid or accrued or the FTC limit *within each separate basket*. The separate FTC limitation categories for different types of income each use this same basic FTC limitation formula. The separate limitation categories affect the amount of FTC that can be taken by generally segregating income subject to a high level of foreign tax from lower-taxed foreign income.

THE BIG PICTURE
Example 13

Return to the facts of *The Big Picture* on p. 16-1. Assume that VoiceCo invests in the bonds of non-U.S. corporations. VoiceCo's worldwide taxable income for the tax year is $1,200,000, consisting of $1,000,000 of profits from U.S. sales and $200,000 of interest income from foreign sources. All of the foreign income is in the passive basket. Foreign taxes of $90,000 were withheld by tax authorities on these interest payments.

VoiceCo's U.S. tax before the FTC is $420,000 ($1,200,000 × 35%). Its FTC is limited to $70,000 [$420,000 × ($200,000/$1,200,000)]. Thus, VoiceCo's net U.S. tax liability on this income is $350,000 after allowing the $70,000 FTC. The remaining $20,000 ($90,000 foreign tax paid − $70,000 FTC claimed) of foreign taxes may be carried back one year or forward 10 years for use within the passive basket.

Example 14

BenCo, Inc., a U.S. corporation, operates a foreign branch in Germany that earns taxable income of $1.5 million from manufacturing operations and $600,000 from passive activities. BenCo pays foreign taxes of $600,000 (40%) and $100,000 ($16\frac{2}{3}$%), respectively, on this foreign-source income.

The corporation earns $4 million of U.S.-source taxable income, resulting in worldwide taxable income of $6.1 million. BenCo's U.S. taxes before the FTC are $2,074,000 (at 34%). The following table illustrates the effect of the separate limitation baskets on cross-crediting.

Separate Foreign Income Category	Net Taxable Amount	Foreign Taxes	U.S. Tax before FTC at 34%	FTC Allowed with Separate Limits
General	$1,500,000	$600,000	$510,000	$510,000
Passive	600,000	100,000	204,000	100,000
Total	$2,100,000	$700,000	$714,000	$610,000

Without the separate limitation provisions, the FTC would be the lesser of (1) $700,000 foreign taxes or (2) $714,000 share of U.S. tax [($2,100,000/$6,100,000) × $2,074,000]. The separate limitation provisions reduce the FTC by $90,000 ($700,000 versus $610,000). The effect of the separate limitation rules is that the foreign-source income taxed at the foreign tax rate of 40% cannot be aggregated with foreign-source income taxed at only $16\frac{2}{3}$%.

Direct and Indirect FTCs   U.S. taxpayers may claim FTCs for foreign taxes they pay directly or through withholding as so-called direct credits. In addition, U.S. corporate taxpayers may claim FTCs for foreign taxes paid indirectly. If a U.S. corporation operates in a foreign country through a branch, the direct credit is available for foreign taxes paid.

If, however, a U.S. corporation operates in a country through a foreign subsidiary, the direct credit is not available for foreign taxes paid by the foreign corporation. An indirect or **deemed-paid credit** is available to U.S. corporate taxpayers that receive actual or constructive dividends from foreign corporations that have paid foreign income taxes.[7] These foreign taxes are deemed paid by the corporate shareholders in the same proportion as the dividends actually or constructively received bear to the foreign corporation's undistributed E & P.

$$\text{Deemed-paid credit} = \frac{\text{Actual or constructive dividend}}{\text{Undistributed E \& P}} \times \text{Foreign taxes paid}$$

If a U.S. taxpayer claims a deemed-paid credit, § 78 requires the corporation to *gross up* (add to income) the dividend income by the amount of the deemed-paid credit.

Example 15	Wren, Inc., a domestic corporation, owns 50% of Finch, Inc., a foreign corporation. Wren receives a dividend of $120,000 from Finch. Finch paid foreign taxes of $500,000 on its E & P, which totals $1.2 million. Wren's deemed-paid foreign taxes for FTC purposes are $50,000.

Cash dividend from Finch	$120,000
Deemed-paid foreign taxes [($120,000/$1,200,000) × $500,000]	50,000
Gross income to Wren	$170,000

Wren includes $170,000 in gross income for the year. As a result of the dividend received, Wren can claim a credit for the $50,000 in deemed-paid foreign taxes.

Digging Deeper   2   In-depth coverage can be found on this book's companion website: **www.cengagebrain.com**

Controlled Foreign Corporations

Foreign corporations—even those controlled by U.S. shareholders—generally are not included in a U.S. consolidated income tax return. Consequently, in the absence of some other provision, the income of a foreign corporation is included on the U.S. shareholder's U.S. income tax return only when dividend income is received. To minimize current U.S. tax liability, taxpayers often attempt to defer the recognition of taxable income. One way to do this is to shift the income-generating activity to a foreign entity where the income earned will not be subject to U.S. tax until repatriated.

For example, a U.S. person can create a foreign holding company to own the stock of foreign operating affiliates or intangible assets, such as patents and trademarks. Thus, the income generated by these foreign holdings would escape current U.S. taxation. A non-U.S. corporation can also be used to accumulate income from sales or service activities by acting as an intermediary between the U.S. corporation and an offshore customer. The offshore subsidiary corporation would be used to purchase goods from the U.S. parent or domestic affiliates and then resell the goods to foreign customers or provide services on behalf of the U.S. parent or affiliates.

In some cases, the use of intermediate overseas subsidiaries is based on a substantive business purpose. In other cases, they are employed only to reduce tax costs. Because of this potential for abuse, Congress has enacted various provisions to limit the availability of deferral.

---

[7]U.S. corporations must meet certain minimum ownership requirements under § 902 to claim a deemed-paid credit. In the formula for the indirect credit, only foreign taxes paid and E & P generated after 1986 are used.

FINANCIAL DISCLOSURE INSIGHTS Overseas Operations and Book-Tax Differences

Non-U.S. operations account for a large portion of the permanent book-tax differences of U.S. business entities. These differences may relate to different tax bases, different tax rate structures, or special provisions concerning tax-based financing with the other country. For instance, lower tax rates applied by Ireland, Bermuda, and the Netherlands recently reduced Cisco's current-year tax liabilities by about $1 billion per year.

Tax planning strategies using non-U.S. operations also are found in the deferred tax asset and liability accounts. Tax deferrals allowed under current U.S. tax rules and carryforwards of the foreign tax credit can be substantial for some businesses. For example, IBM recently reported a deferred tax asset relating to delays in using its FTCs amounting to about $500 million. For the operating arm of General Electric, that amount was about $2 billion.

© iStockphoto.com/Pali Rao

The most important of these antideferral provisions are those affecting **controlled foreign corporations (CFCs)**. Subpart F of the Code provides that certain types of "tainted" income generated by CFCs are included in current-year gross income by the U.S. shareholders, without regard to actual distributions. U.S. shareholders must include in gross income their pro rata share of **Subpart F income**. This rule applies to U.S. shareholders who own stock in the corporation on the last day of the tax year or on the last day the foreign corporation is a CFC.

Example 16

Jordan, Ltd., a calendar year foreign corporation, is a CFC for the entire tax year. Taylor, Inc., a U.S. corporation, owns 60% of Jordan's one class of stock for the entire year. Jordan earned $100,000 of Subpart F income for the year and makes no actual distributions during the year. Taylor, a calendar year taxpayer, includes $60,000 in gross income as a constructive dividend for the tax year.

To the extent Jordan has paid any foreign income taxes, Taylor may claim a deemed-paid foreign tax credit for the portion of the foreign taxes related to the $60,000 constructive dividend.

What Is a CFC? A CFC is any non-U.S. corporation in which more than 50 percent of the total combined voting power of all classes of stock entitled to vote, or the total value of the stock of the corporation, is owned by U.S. shareholders on any day during the taxable year of the foreign corporation. The offshore subsidiaries of most multinational U.S. parent corporations are CFCs.

For purposes of determining whether a foreign corporation is a CFC, a **U.S. shareholder** is a U.S. person who owns, or is considered to own, 10 percent or more of the total combined voting power of all classes of voting stock of the foreign corporation. Stock owned directly, indirectly, and constructively is counted. Indirect ownership involves stock held through a foreign entity, such as a foreign corporation, foreign partnership, or foreign trust. This stock is considered to be actually owned proportionately by the shareholders, partners, or beneficiaries.

Constructive ownership rules, with certain modifications, apply in determining whether a U.S. person is a U.S. shareholder, in determining whether a foreign corporation is a CFC, and for certain related-party provisions of Subpart F.

Subpart F Income A U.S. shareholder of a CFC does not necessarily lose the ability to defer U.S. taxation of income earned by the CFC. Only certain income earned by the CFC triggers immediate U.S. taxation as a constructive dividend. This tainted income, referred to as Subpart F income, can be characterized as income that is easily shifted or has little or no economic connection with the CFC's country of incorporation. Examples include:

- Passive income such as interest, dividends, rents, and royalties.
- Sales income where neither the manufacturing activity nor the customer base is in the CFC's country and either the property supplier or the customer is related to the CFC.

- Service income where the CFC is providing services on behalf of its U.S. owners outside the CFC's country.

Example 17

Collins, Inc., a domestic corporation, sells $1 million of its products to customers in Europe. All manufacturing and sales activities take place in the United States. Collins has no employees, assets, or operations in Europe and thus is not subject to income tax in any European jurisdiction.

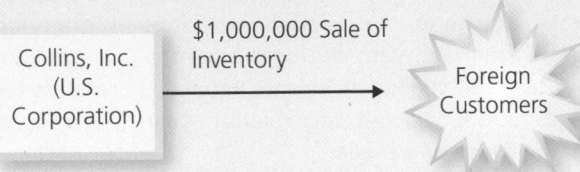

Collins reported the following tax consequences from these inventory sales.

Sales revenue	$1,000,000
Cost of goods sold	(600,000)
Net income	$ 400,000
U.S. tax at 35%	$ 140,000

Assume that Collins instead creates a wholly owned foreign subsidiary in the Cayman Islands, where no income taxes are imposed on corporate income. Collins then sells the inventory to the subsidiary at an intercompany transfer price of $700,000, and the subsidiary sells the inventory to the ultimate European customers for $1 million. The subsidiary does not further process the inventory and is only minimally involved in the sales function, as Collins's employees arrange the transactions with the ultimate customers. In essence, the sale to the subsidiary is simply a "paper" transaction.

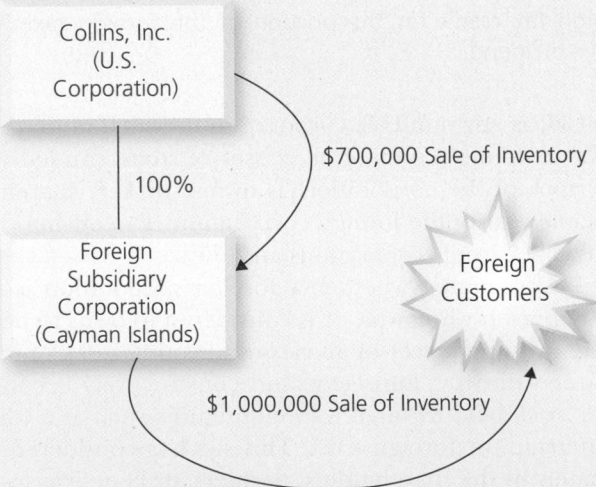

If there were no tax law restrictions, this structure would create the following tax consequences.

	Collins, Inc.	Foreign Subsidiary
Sales revenue	$ 700,000	$1,000,000
Cost of goods sold	(600,000)	(700,000)
Net income	$ 100,000	$ 300,000
U.S. tax at 35%	$ 35,000	
Foreign tax at 0%		$ –0–

Because the Cayman subsidiary is not engaged in a U.S. trade or business, it is not subject to any U.S. tax on its income. So long as the subsidiary's profits are kept outside the United States, Collins believes it can avoid any U.S. income tax on these profits (i.e., the deferral privilege). Thus, at first glance, it appears that using the foreign subsidiary significantly reduces Collins's current tax cost from $140,000 to $35,000.

However, Collins will find this strategy attacked by the U.S. taxing authorities on two fronts, either of which results in the loss of all or most of the tax savings.

First, the IRS may use the transfer pricing rules of § 482 to claim that the $700,000 intercompany transfer price between Collins and its subsidiary is not a correct arm's length price. The IRS may claim that the transfer price should be $1 million because the subsidiary does not add any value to the inventory through further processing or sales activities and all of the risks of the transaction are borne by Collins. With this transfer pricing adjustment, Collins will have a $400,000 profit from the sales and the same $140,000 tax cost as if it had not used the foreign subsidiary as an intermediary.

Determining a correct transfer price is a subjective exercise. Accordingly, Congress enacted the Subpart F provisions to create more certainty in the effort to prevent unwarranted tax benefits from accruing to U.S. taxpayers using offshore subsidiaries to shield profits from the reach of the U.S. tax authorities. Under the Subpart F rules, the subsidiary's $300,000 income creates a constructive dividend for Collins, thus producing a $105,000 tax cost ($300,000 × 35%). Combined with its original $35,000 tax, Collins's total tax cost for the sales is $140,000 ($35,000 + $105,000), and the use of the foreign subsidiary does not achieve any tax savings.

Example 18

Assume that in Example 17, Collins's foreign subsidiary instead was incorporated in Ireland, where the tax rate on such sales income is 12.5%. The subsidiary purchases raw materials from Collins and performs substantial manufacturing activity in Ireland before selling the inventory to customers in Hong Kong.

In this case, the sales income is not Subpart F income. Even without the manufacturing activity, sales to customers in Ireland would not produce Subpart F income. In both instances, there is economic substance to the non-U.S. subsidiary earning the income.

The fact that the Irish subsidiary pays a substantially lower tax rate than the U.S. parent does not by itself trigger a constructive dividend. However, Collins must still document the appropriateness of its intercompany transfer price on raw material sales to its Irish subsidiary.

Tax Planning Strategies | AVOIDING CONSTRUCTIVE DIVIDENDS

FRAMEWORK FOCUS: TAX CREDITS

Strategy: **Maximize Deductible Amounts.**

To defer U.S. taxes on foreign income, U.S. taxpayers often create separate foreign subsidiaries to hold their offshore operations. This approach is successful so long as the foreign subsidiaries do not pay dividends to the U.S. owners and do not earn Subpart F income that creates constructive dividends. U.S. companies often set up foreign holding companies in tax-favorable jurisdictions to hold the foreign operating subsidiaries.

For example, a U.S. parent might create a CFC holding company to hold its two operating subsidiaries. The subsidiaries both pay interest to the holding company on intercompany loans. The interest is deductible by the operating subsidiaries at a high tax rate (providing tax savings in those countries) and is taxed to the holding company at a relatively low tax rate. This approach provides a net tax savings to the foreign group. However, the interest payments to the holding company may constitute Subpart F income and trigger a constructive dividend back to the U.S. parent. If so, the tax savings related to the intercompany loans are offset by the U.S. taxes on the Subpart F income.

A mechanism exists that allows the holding company to avoid Subpart F treatment for the interest income. The check-the-box Regulations provide a great deal of flexibility for U.S.-based multinational corporations. For example, corporations are allowed to elect (i.e., check the box on a form) to treat certain foreign subsidiaries as unincorporated branches for U.S. purposes rather than separate legal entities. This election does not change the treatment of the entities under local tax law.

Using the check-the-box rules, the U.S. parent can elect to treat the foreign subsidiaries as branches for U.S. purposes. In this case, the two foreign subsidiaries are treated as mere divisions of the holding company. Accordingly, the intercompany loans do not exist from a U.S. perspective, and there is no interest income because the interest payments are treated as simply fund transfers within a single corporation. Without the interest income, there is no Subpart F income and thus no constructive dividends. However, the foreign tax savings still exist because the interest payments do exist from a foreign tax perspective and continue to provide interest deductions at the subsidiary level.

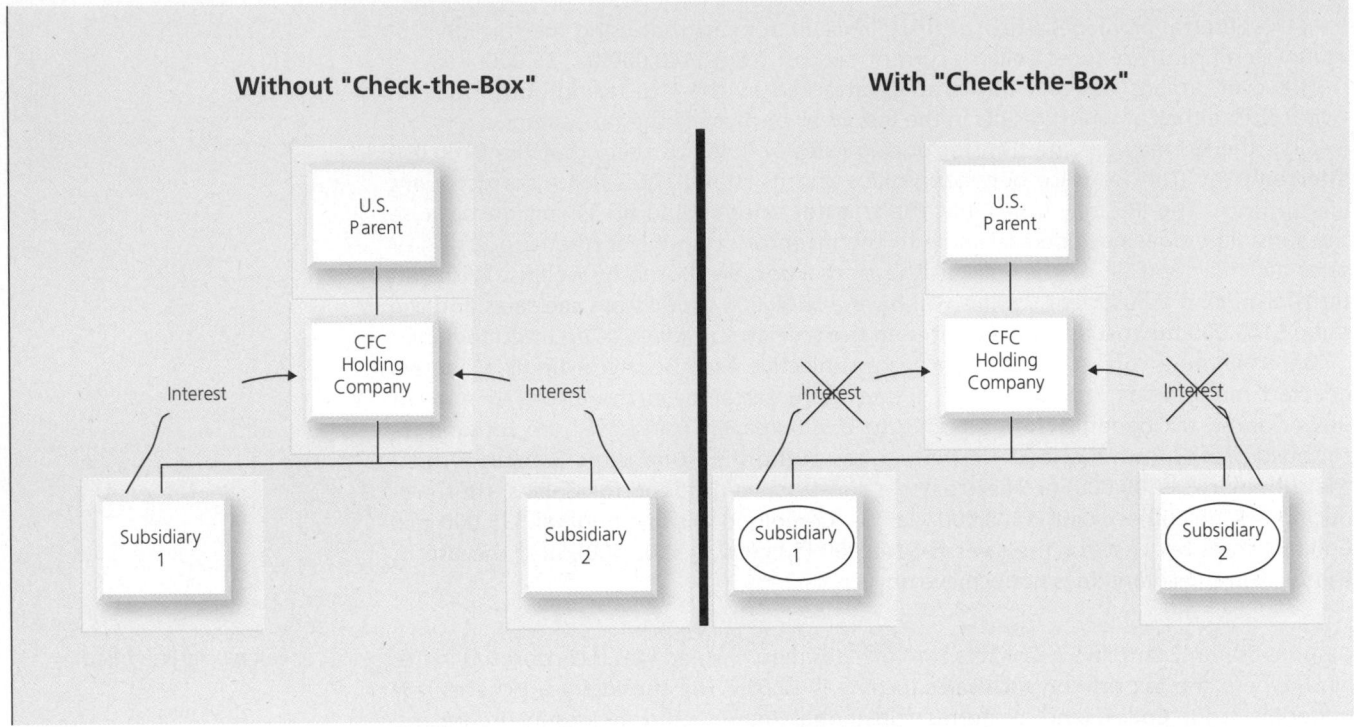

Subpart F Income—Summary The Subpart F provisions are quite complex and subject to numerous exceptions. Still, in general, any time a CFC earns income that has little economic connection to its local country, the income is potentially tainted income under Subpart F and generates a constructive dividend to the CFC's U.S. shareholders. Alternatively, if the CFC is actively generating the income, it likely is not Subpart F income. Unfortunately, the mechanistic application required by the Subpart F provisions sometimes catches active foreign corporations within the Subpart F web.

Example 19

Murphy, Inc., a U.S. corporation owns all of GreenCo, Ltd., an Irish manufacturing corporation, and SwissCo, a Swiss distribution corporation. Both GreenCo and SwissCo are CFCs. GreenCo sells its inventory production to SwissCo. SwissCo sells the inventory to unrelated customers located in Switzerland, Italy, and Germany.

Because SwissCo does not manufacture the inventory and acquires it from a related supplier, any sales to customers outside Switzerland will produce Subpart F income and a constructive dividend to Murphy, Inc. This is true even though SwissCo is engaged in an active business and is not merely a "paper" corporation. To avoid Subpart F treatment, Murphy, Inc., should create a distribution company within each country where it operates to sell to customers only within that country.

Inbound Issues

LO.4

Describe the tax effects related to the U.S. operations of a non-U.S. taxpayer.

Generally, only the U.S.-source income of nonresident alien individuals and foreign corporations is subject to U.S. taxation. This reflects the reach of the U.S. tax jurisdiction. This constraint, however, does not prevent the United States from also taxing the foreign-source income of nonresident alien individuals and foreign corporations when that income is effectively connected with the conduct of a U.S. trade or business.

A **nonresident alien (NRA)** is an individual who is not a citizen or resident of the United States. *Citizenship* is determined under the immigration and naturalization laws of the United States. A person is treated as a *resident* of the United States for income tax purposes if he or she meets either the green card test or the substantial presence test. If either of these tests is met for the calendar year, the individual is deemed a U.S. resident for the year.

Two important definitions determine the U.S. tax consequences to foreign persons with U.S.-source income: "the conduct of a U.S. trade or business" and "**effectively connected income.**" Specifically, for a foreign person's noninvestment

TAX IN THE NEWS Taxes Take a Smaller Bite Out of Apple

Apple, Inc., is a good case study for how effective tax planning can make a successful tech company even more profitable after taxes are considered. The company's business model produces plenty of free cash flow, but it operates in an industry that is based as much on intellectual property as physical plant and employee productivity. As the current tax laws largely were drafted to operate in a manufacturing and merchandising economy, Apple and other similar companies can exploit to their tax advantage a number of items that a more current tax code might address.

Apple's tax planning appears to follow the letter and the spirit of current tax law. Even though most of Apple's executives, engineers, and designers work in the United States, much of the company's profit is taxed elsewhere. Here are some highlights of how Apple uses current tax laws effectively.

- Over time, the company moves its physical plant to low-tax jurisdictions such as Nevada, Ireland, and the Netherlands.
- The company lobbies for and then uses tax incentives (e.g., for research and experimentation activities) that are offered by the Federal, state, and local governments.

- Apple uses tax planning arrangements that create subsidiaries in low-tax countries (e.g., in the British Virgin Islands). Using proper transfer pricing techniques, sales transactions are routed through the low-tax jurisdictions, and more profits are left after tax for corporate growth and development.
- Another tax-shifting strategy employs so-called commissionaires, who arrange sales of the company's goods but never take possession of any inventory. Thus, Apple's profit derived from the work distributors in high-tax countries is taxed in a low-tax country such as Singapore.

In response to criticism surrounding its tax planning, Apple counters that the company and its employees still pay billions of dollars in payroll, sales, property, and individual income taxes. And Apple's retail stores certainly draw customer traffic that benefits other tenants in shopping malls.

One downside of these tax-shifting strategies is that Apple can defer the Federal income tax on such profits only as long as the related cash remains overseas; a repatriation would trigger high-rate U.S. taxes. The U.S. Treasury might have a good argument if Apple's offshore cash was "idle," but surely most of it is used to grow the business as it operates in a global environment.

income to be subject to U.S. taxation, the non-U.S. person must be considered engaged in a U.S. trade or business and must earn income effectively connected with that business.

General criteria for determining whether a U.S. trade or business exists include the location of production activities, management, distribution activities, and other business functions. The Code does not explicitly define a U.S. trade or business, but case law has described the concept as activities carried on in the United States that are regular, substantial, and continuous.

Once a non-U.S. person is considered engaged in a U.S. trade or business, all U.S.-source income other than investment and capital gain income is considered effectively connected to that trade or business and is therefore subject to U.S. taxation. Effectively connected income is taxed at the same rates that apply to U.S. persons, and deductions for expenses attributable to that income are allowed.

TAX FACT The Inbound Sector

Inbound corporate operations produce a small but significant portion of U.S. income tax collections.

With an average U.S. income tax rate of about 28 percent on inbound commerce, perhaps some of the other countries in the world look at the United States as a high-tax jurisdiction.

Number of Forms 1120-F filed	15,000
Taxable income reported	$12 billion
Net tax liability	$3.3 billion

CONCEPT SUMMARY 16.1

U.S. Tax Treatment of a Non-U.S. Person's Income*

Type of Income	Tax Rate
U.S.-source fixed, determinable, annual, or periodic (FDAP) income (not effectively connected to a U.S. business)	Generally 30% withholding on gross amount (or lower treaty rate) with certain limited exceptions.
U.S.-source income effectively connected with a U.S. trade or business	Regular individual or corporate rates applied against net income (after deductions).
Gain on U.S. real property (direct or indirect interest)	Taxed as if effectively connected to a U.S. trade or business.
Capital gains (other than on U.S. real property) not effectively connected to a U.S. trade or business	Foreign corporation: Not subject to U.S. tax.
	Individual: Generally not taxed but may be subject to a 30% U.S. tax if taxpayer is physically present in the United States for 183 days or more in a taxable year.
Foreign-source business income	Generally not subject to U.S. taxation unless attributable to a U.S. office or fixed place of business.

*Subject to change under treaty provisions.

© iStockphoto.com/Andrey Prokhorov

Certain U.S.-source income that is *not* effectively connected with the conduct of a U.S. trade or business is subject to a flat 30 percent tax. This income includes dividends; certain interest; rents; royalties; certain compensation; premiums; annuities; and other income of this type from fixed, determinable, annual or periodic (**FDAP**) sources. This tax generally is levied by a withholding mechanism that requires the payors of the income to withhold 30 percent of gross amounts (or a lower rate as established by a treaty). This method improves the collectability of Federal taxes from nonresidents and non-U.S. corporations.

Example 20

Robert, a citizen and resident of New Zealand, produces wine for export. During the current year, Robert earns $500,000 from exporting wine to unrelated wholesalers in the United States. The title to the wine passes to the U.S. wholesalers in New York. Robert has no offices or employees in the United States. The income from the wine sales is U.S.-source income, but because Robert is not engaged in a U.S. trade or business, the income is not subject to taxation in the United States.

Robert begins operating a hot dog cart in New York City. This activity constitutes a U.S. trade or business. Consequently, all U.S.-source income other than FDAP or capital gain income is taxed in the United States as income effectively connected with a U.S. trade or business. Thus, both the hot dog cart profits and the $500,000 in wine income are taxed in the United States.

Several exceptions exempt non-U.S. persons from U.S. taxation on their U.S. investment income that is not connected with a U.S. business. For example, certain U.S.-sourced portfolio debt investments and capital gains (other than gains on U.S. real property investments) are exempt from U.S. tax for most non-U.S. investors. Gains from investments in U.S. real property (held directly or indirectly through other entities) are subject to U.S. taxation. Concept Summary 16.1 summarizes the U.S. taxation of non-U.S. persons.

Digging Deeper   3   In-depth coverage can be found on this book's companion website: **www.cengagebrain.com**

FINANCIAL DISCLOSURE INSIGHTS   Tax Rates in Non-U.S. Jurisdictions

When Congress changes the U.S. tax law, it seldom applies tax rate changes retroactively or prospectively— the rate changes usually are applicable on the date the tax bill is effective. Other countries do not always enact tax law changes in this way. Sometimes a country will adopt a schedule of tax rate increases or decreases to go into effect over a period of years.

Tax legislation of this sort can have an important effect on the U.S. taxpayer's effective tax rate as computed in the footnotes to the financial statements. When another country adopts prospective tax rate changes, an increase or decrease in the effective tax rate is reported with respect to the deferred tax accounts for GAAP purposes. Specifically, the effective tax rate decreases when a tax rate cut is scheduled in a country that does business with the U.S. party, and the rate increases when a tax rate increase is adopted for future tax years. In the last three decades, most developed countries have been cutting business income tax rates.

A recent effective tax rate computation for Berkshire Hathaway showed a decrease of about one percentage point due to scheduled tax rate cuts in Germany and the United Kingdom. Allied Healthcare Products showed a similar adjustment of about two percentage points. In contrast, the effective tax rate increased by about one percentage point for American Travellers Life Insurance Company.

16-3 CROSSING STATE LINES: STATE AND LOCAL INCOME TAXATION IN THE UNITED STATES

Very few taxpayers sell goods and services solely in the U.S. state in which they are based. Sales in other states are attractive for a variety of business reasons, including the expansion of market share and the achievement of economies of scale. By extending its operations into other states, a firm may be able to lower its labor and distribution costs, obtain additional sources of long-term debt and equity, and perhaps find a more favorable tax climate.

Many of the same issues discussed earlier in the chapter concerning international operations are encountered when a multistate operation is in place. Both international and multistate operations raise basic questions such as where did the transaction occur and who is liable for the collection of the tax.

However, as state and local income taxation has evolved in the United States, differences in terminology, definitions, and scope of the tax have arisen. Although prior knowledge of the U.S. international tax regime can be helpful in studying the state and local income tax structure, there still is much to learn. In addition, the sheer number of income taxing districts at the state and local level make an encounter with the state and local income tax laws of the United States a challenging experience.

16-3a Sources of Law

Think of how complicated a tax professional's work would be if there were several hundred different Internal Revenue Codes, each with its own Regulations, rulings, and court decisions. That description is hardly an exaggeration of the state and local income tax law faced by a taxpayer operating in more than one jurisdiction. Unless a firm's salable goods or services are designed, made, and sold strictly within one taxing jurisdiction, the multistate regime comes into effect.

Almost every U.S. state taxes the business income of proprietors, corporations, and other entities that have a presence in the state.[8] All of those states have

LO.5

Identify the sources of tax law applicable to a taxpayer operating in more than one U.S. state.

---

[8]Some states tax the investment income of individuals, but those taxes are not addressed in this chapter. Nevada, South Dakota, Washington, and Wyoming do not have a corporate income tax. Washington uses a business and occupation tax; several states impose a tax on the gross receipts (not on the net income) of a business.

TAX FACT   State Tax Revenue Sources

The corporate income tax accounts for only a small portion of total tax revenues of the states. For 2012, about $800 billion in taxes was collected by the states (i.e., about $2,500 per U.S. individual).

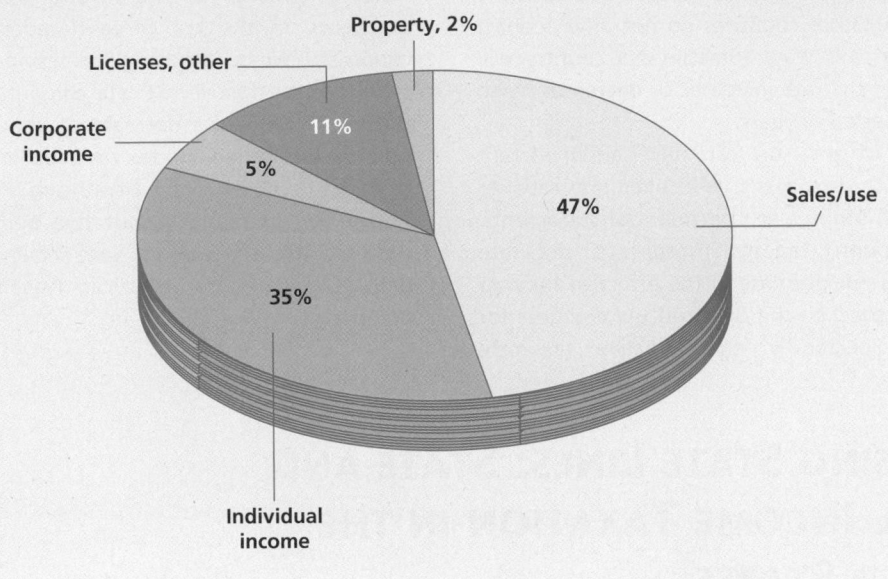

Property, 2%
Licenses, other
Corporate income
11%
5%
47%
Sales/use
35%
Individual income

© iStockphoto.com/Pali Rao

constitutional provisions allowing an income tax and aggregated legislation defining the tax base, specifying when the tax is due and from whom, and otherwise administering the tax. A separate revenue department interprets the law and administers the annual taxing process.

Every one of these systems is distinct and different in multiple ways—the name and location of the chief tax official, the definitions of what is taxable and deductible and what is not, the due dates and filing requirements applicable to the tax, and the taxpayer-friendliness of the audit and appeals system.

Despite the no-new-taxes pledge of many politicians on election day, income taxes are still popular in the United States. Income taxes are levied by states, cities, counties, villages, commuter districts, stadium boards, and numerous other bodies that have been granted taxing authority by their states. And politicians think that they can gain economic development advantages over their neighbors by granting special tax breaks—"Locate your assembly plant here, and we'll exempt one-half of your employees' wages from the state income tax"—so the laws are constantly changing. By one estimate, a business taxpayer might be exposed to almost 500 different income taxing jurisdictions in the United States.

The Federal government has stayed out of the fray and has not attempted to force states and localities to use a single common tax formula and administrative organization. Only in **Public Law 86–272** has Congress attempted to bring order to the multistate income tax process. This 1957 pro-interstate commerce provision exempts from state and local taxation a sale of tangible personal property where the only contact with the state was the **solicitation** activity of the taxpayer.

In the past 20 or 30 years, the states have taken some steps to coordinate their activities. Several groups of states exchange information as to the seller and purchase price for cross-border sales so that income and sales/use tax obligations can be computed and collected properly. A few states have reciprocity arrangements with their neighbors to straighten out the complications that can arise when an employee lives in one jurisdiction but works in another.

TAX IN THE NEWS   So Where Did You Work Today?

The dream of many intellectual-property employees is to work at home with the employer's computer and communications equipment. Not only is the dress code there targeted to the worker's comfort, but the employee can avoid the time and cost of commuting. The employer saves by not having to provide office space.

But what are the tax effects when the employee or independent contractor submits work to an employer located in a different state? The general rule has been that state income taxes fall in full in the state where the work is done. Is this still the rule, or must the employee apportion the hours of the day among the various states that receive the work product? If so, on what basis should such apportionment be made? Furthermore, how will the worker reduce any potential taxation of the same income by more than one state?

A few states and cities, most notably in New York, are aggressively trying to impose income taxes on the work of telecommuters that enters the state. In these situations, enough nexus purportedly exists to permit the levying of income taxes on telecommuters based in other states. The lost revenue to New York State relative to nonresident workers is at least $50 million per year.

The Federal government may end up as the referee in this issue. Under the proposed Mobile Workforce State Tax Simplification Act, only the state of the employee's residence could tax income from services, even if the services are performed elsewhere. This could make life easier for telecommuters and those who live close to a state border and commute to their jobs.

Example 21

Harry works at the Illinois plant of Big Corporation, but he lives in Iowa. His wages are subject to Iowa tax. If Illinois and Iowa had a reciprocity agreement in place, either (1) Big would collect and remit income tax at Iowa's rates and remit the tax to the Iowa revenue department, or (2) Big would collect Illinois tax, and that state would keep the withholdings paid, in full satisfaction of Harry's Iowa tax obligations for the year.

About half of the states are members of the **Multistate Tax Commission (MTC)**, a body that proposes legislation to the states and localities and issues its own regulations and informational materials. A majority of the non-MTC members follow the agency's rules virtually without exception. The Uniform Division of Income for Tax Purposes Act (UDITPA) is made available to states and localities interested in a coherent set of income assignment rules, and it forms the basis for the income tax statutes in most of the MTC member states.

The MTC, which provides very specific formulas and definitions to be used in computing state taxable income, is as close as the states have come so far to a multilateral tax treaty process. If all states and localities followed all of the MTC rules, taxpayers would be unable to gain any "border advantages" or disadvantages. But political concerns likely will keep this coordinated result from ever happening.

16-3b Tax Issues

The key issues facing a state or locality in drafting and implementing an income tax model are the same as those facing the international tax community. The results of the deliberative process, though, have produced somewhat different sets of rules and terminology.

Authority to Tax

A business is taxable in the state in which it is resident, organized, or incorporated. Tax liabilities also arise in other jurisdictions where **nexus** exists; that is, a sufficient presence in the other state has been established on an ongoing basis. Such presence might come about because the corporation was organized there, the proprietor lives there, an in-state customer made a purchase, or the business employed people or equipment within the borders of the state. The precise activities that

FIGURE 16.3 — Computing State Income Tax Liability

	Federal taxable income
±	State modification items
	State tax base
±	Nonbusiness income/loss (for allocation)
	Business income (for apportionment)
×	Apportionment percentage for the state
	Taxable income apportioned to the state
±	Taxable income/loss allocated to the state
	State taxable income/loss
	State tax, per tax table or rate schedule
−	State's tax credits
	Net state tax liability

create nexus vary from jurisdiction to jurisdiction, although most of the taxing states follow the broad rules of Public Law 86–272 and the regulations of the MTC.[9]

When a taxpayer operates in more than one state, total taxable income for the year is split among the jurisdictions in which the operations take place. Portions of the total income amount are assigned to each of the business locations, so several tax returns and payments will be due. For a taxpayer considering an expansion of operations, the tax adviser can make an important contribution in helping to decide with which state(s) nexus will be created.

The nexus rules of state/local taxation serve much the same function as do the permanent establishment provisions of international taxation. The PE standards are based in the language of the applicable tax treaty and interpretive court decisions. They look for real estate holdings and manufacturing equipment. Permanent establishment is found when an office in the host country participates significantly in the making of a sales or service contract.

Digging Deeper   4      In-depth coverage can be found on this book's companion website: **www.cengagebrain.com**

LO.6

Apply computational principles designed for a taxpayer operating in more than one U.S. state.

Income Sourcing

The multistate business, like its international counterpart, must divide the taxable income generated for the year among the states in which it operates. Then tax liability is computed for the states in which nexus has been established. The computational template illustrated in Figure 16.3 indicates how most states derive their shares of the entity's aggregate taxable income. Usually, the starting point for this computation is Federal taxable income.

State modification items come about because each state creates its own tax base in the legislative process, and some of the rules adopted may differ from those used in the Internal Revenue Code. The modification items reflect such differences in the tax base. For example, modifications might be created to reflect the following differences between state and Federal taxable income.

---

[9]Income and sales/use tax regimes use different nexus standards. Generally, it has been "easier" to establish nexus for sales/use tax purposes; most states have a separate set of rules to determine the taxability of income or a transaction. But recent U.S. Supreme Court cases apply a "physical presence" test for the sales/use tax, a somewhat stricter and smokestack-industry test than the income tax nexus rules of the MTC. This chapter concentrates on income tax nexus provisions.

Tax Planning Strategies	NEXUS: TO HAVE OR HAVE NOT

FRAMEWORK FOCUS: TAX RATE

Strategy: Shift Net Income from High-Tax Jurisdictions to Low-Tax Jurisdictions.

Most taxpayers try to avoid establishing nexus in a new state, for example, by providing a sales representative with a cash auto allowance rather than a company car, by restricting the situs of inventory to only a few states, or by limiting a salesperson's activities to those that are protected by the solicitation standard of Public Law 86–272. This effort to avoid nexus stems in part from the additional compliance burden that falls upon the taxpayer when a new set of income tax returns, information forms, and deadlines must be dealt with in the new state.

Another concern is that the marginal tax rate that applies to the net taxable income generated by the taxpayer may increase. Such a tax increase occurs, of course, only when the applicable tax rate in the new state is higher than the rate that would apply in the home state. If a business already is based in a tax-friendly state such as Florida or Texas or in a no-tax state such as Nevada, its aggregate tax liability is sure to increase.

Still, nexus is not necessarily a bad thing. Consider what happens if a business based in California, Maryland, Wisconsin, or another high-tax jurisdiction purposely creates nexus in a low- or no-tax state. If the new state applies a lower marginal rate than is available in the home state or offers special exemptions or exclusions that match the taxpayer's operations, the aggregate tax bill can decrease. Then the planning efforts include determining which activities will *create* nexus in the new jurisdiction and meeting or maintaining that standard.

For instance, an entertainer based in Manhattan is subject to the high income taxes of New York City and New York State. By establishing a permanent office in Tennessee, nexus will be created, and some portion of the taxpayer's income will be subject to taxation there, instead of New York. These are permanent savings, accruing immediately to after-tax income and the share price of the stock of the taxpayer.

- The state might allow a different cost recovery schedule.
- The state might tax interest income from its own bonds or from those of other states.
- The state might allow a deduction for Federal income taxes paid.
- The state might disallow a deduction for payment of its own income taxes.
- The state might allow a net operating loss (NOL) deduction only for losses generated in the state.
- The state's NOL deduction might reflect different carryover periods than Federal law allows.

State tax modifications are made even if the taxpayer operates only in its home state.

Allocation and Apportionment The next step in computing state taxable income is to **allocate** items of nonbusiness income and loss to the states in which such items are derived. For instance, a Kansas entity might recognize some net income from the rental of a Missouri office building to a tenant. The net rental amount is in Federal taxable income, but it must appear only and fully in Missouri taxable income. So by means of the modification process, the rents are removed from the taxable income for both states and then added back into Missouri taxable income. The allocation process is very much like the income-sourcing procedures employed in international taxation.

Example 22

HammerCo reports $400,000 in taxable income for the year from its sales operations based exclusively in Mississippi and Arkansas. HammerCo recognized net rent income of $60,000 from a building it owns in Mississippi. It earned $20,000 in interest income from Arkansas bonds. This amount is excluded from Federal taxable income, and it is taxed by Mississippi but not Arkansas. HammerCo also claimed a Federal NOL carryforward of $75,000 from a prior period. Mississippi follows Federal law for NOLs, but

Arkansas does not allow such carryovers. The modifications to the state tax base are as follows.

Mississippi		Arkansas	
Amount	**Modification**	**Amount**	**Modification**
− $60,000	Total nonbusiness income	− $60,000	Total nonbusiness income
+ $20,000	Municipal bond interest income	+ $75,000	Remove Federal NOL deduction
+ $60,000	Net rent income from Mississippi rentals		

The business income of the taxpayer is **apportioned** among the states in which it operates. The apportionment percentage for the state is multiplied times the business income of the taxpayer to measure the extent of the taxpayer's exposure to the state's income tax. The application of the apportionment percentage is illustrated in Figure 16.3.

Most states apply an apportionment procedure involving three factors, each meant to estimate the taxpayer's relative activities in the state.

- The **sales factor** = In-state sales/total sales.
- The **payroll factor** = In-state payroll/total payroll.
- The **property factor** = In-state property/total property.

The state's apportionment percentage is the average of these three factors. This three-factor apportionment can be traced to the earliest days of state income taxation. Today, most states add additional weight to the sales factor, believing it to be the most accurate and measurable reflection of the taxpayer's in-state activities. It is common to "double-weight" the sales factor. A few states use only the sales factor in the apportionment procedure.

TAX IN THE NEWS   State Deficits Change How Revenue Departments Work

The current crunch in state budget making has lasted for several years, and new sources of revenue and new attitudes toward enforcement are prime goals of state and local operations.

Much of this budget squeeze has been felt in the increased attention toward sales and use taxes, with many states now dedicating more resources toward those taxes than toward the individual and corporate income taxes. Collecting unpaid use taxes on Internet and mail-order sales and finding new taxpayers to add to the income and sales/use tax rolls are prime enforcement targets for many states.

But a sustained revenue shortfall tends to make some revenue departments more desperate or more creative. In either event, we can observe the use of new or recycled approaches to tax enforcement that can surprise the taxpayer who has not been paying attention. Some of the techniques observed lately include the following.

- Applying local business and occupation taxes, payroll taxes, and license fees to telecommuters and work-at-home entrepreneurs and creative workers.

- Increasing audit staff and travel resources, resulting in increased and better-targeted auditing of returns.
- Temporary increases in underpayment and nonfiling fines and penalties and reductions in grace periods for late filing or payment.
- Denial of other licenses and permits (such as hunting and boating permissions, driver's licenses, and professional certifications) where income and sales/use taxes are underpaid.
- Adding "unpaid use tax" lines to the income tax return. This does result in some revenue collected from taxpayers who have guilty consciences or high levels of integrity, but mainly it sets up the taxpayer for penalties on a later audit, when the sworn-to-be-complete income tax return shows a zero balance on the use tax line.
- Refusing legislatively to adopt certain Federal tax breaks, such as special cost recovery elections or the increases in deductible or tax-deferred retirement and education allowances.
- Increased use of private collection agencies to find delinquent taxpayers and produce dollars for the state treasury.

| **Tax Planning Strategies** | WHERE SHOULD MY INCOME GO? |

FRAMEWORK FOCUS: TAX RATE

Strategy: Shift Net Income from High-Tax Jurisdictions to Low-Tax Jurisdictions.

Every state defines its apportionment factors in a slightly different manner. The multistate taxpayer needs to keep track of these differences and place activities in the state that will serve them best.

Planning with the sales factor includes a detailed analysis of the destination point of the product shipments for the year, especially when the firm has customers in low- and no-tax states. The property factor should include only assets that are used in the taxpayer's trade or business, not the investment, leasing, or research functions. Permanently idle property is excluded from the property factor as well. The payroll factor can be manipulated by hiring independent contractors to carry out certain sales and distribution work or by relocating highly paid managers to low-tax states.

By setting up an investment holding company in a no- or low-tax state such as Delaware or Nevada and transferring income-producing securities and intangible assets to that entity, significant tax reductions can be obtained. When the net investment income is paid back to the parent corporation, the dividends received deduction eliminates the tax liability there.

The unitary system does not always result in a tax increase, although the additional record-keeping burden of operating in a unitary state cannot be understated. If the affiliates make available less profitable operations or a presence in low- or no-tax states or countries, the current tax liability may be reduced. The record-keeping burden can be reduced if the taxpayer makes a waters'-edge election, which allows it to include only affiliate data from within the boundaries of the United States.

Example 23

LinkCo, Inc., operates in two states. It reports the following results for the year. LinkCo's apportionment percentages for both states are computed as shown. Amounts are stated in millions of dollars.

	State A	State B	Totals
Sales	$30	$20	$50
Payroll	40	20	60
Property	45	5	50
Sales factor	$30/$50 = .6	$20/$50 = .4	
Payroll factor	$40/$60 = .67	$20/$60 = .33	
Property factor	$45/$50 = .9	$5/$50 = .1	
Apportionment percentage	(.6 + .67 + .9) ÷ 3 = .72	(.4 + .33 + .1) ÷ 3 = .28	

Note that 100% of the business income is apportioned between the two states: 72% to State A and 28% to State B.

Now assume that State A double-weights the sales factor. LinkCo's apportionment percentages are computed as follows.

	State A	State B	Totals
Sales	$30	$20	$50
Payroll	40	20	60
Property	45	5	50
Sales factor	$30/$50 = .6	$20/$50 = .4	
Payroll factor	$40/$60 = .67	$20/$60 = .33	
Property factor	$45/$50 = .9	$5/$50 = .1	
Apportionment percentage	(.6 + .6 + .67 + .9) ÷ 4 = .69	(.4 + .33 + .1) ÷ 3 = .28	

State B's apportionment computations are not affected by A's double-weighting of the sales factor. The percentages now do not total 100%. The effect of the special weighting is to reduce LinkCo's tax liability in A. This is likely LinkCo's "home state" given the location of its personnel and plant and equipment.

Finally, assume that State B uses a "sales-factor-only" weighting. The A apportionment percentage is .69, and the B percentage is .4. Now the apportionment percentages *exceed* 100%.

Most states follow the regulations of the MTC and the outline of the UDITPA in defining and applying the apportionment factors. But because the states do not follow identical rules in the makeup of the factors, the apportionment percentages seldom total precisely to 100 percent. Some other aspects of the three-factor approach include the following.

- Sales are assigned using the tax accounting methods of the taxpayer. Sales are assigned using the "ultimate destination" concept; that is, a sale is usually assigned to the state of the purchaser.
- If a sale is made into a state with no income tax or a state with which the taxpayer has not established nexus, tax is likely escaped. But over a third of the states apply a **throwback rule** that causes the sale to be sourced to the state of the seller (i.e., by overriding the "ultimate destination" rule).
- Payroll is assigned to the state in which the employee's services primarily are performed. Payroll includes wages, bonuses, commissions, and taxable fringe benefits. Some states exclude officer compensation because it can distort the computations. Some states exclude contributions to a § 401(k) plan.
- The property factor uses an average historical cost basis, net of accumulated depreciation. Idle property is ignored, but construction in progress is included. Property in transit is assigned to the state of its presumed destination.
- Property leased but not owned by the taxpayer is included in the property factor at eight times the annual rentals paid.

Many states use specialized apportionment percentages for industries whose sales and asset profile is not properly reflected in the traditional three-factor formula. For instance, the airline industry might divide its income based on passenger-miles beginning and ending in the state. Truckers might be able to divide taxable income among the states based on in-state vehicle-trips or tons-per-day. Communications companies might use the in-state miles of cable or number of wireless devices to make up an apportionment formula.

FINANCIAL DISCLOSURE INSIGHTS   State/Local Taxes and the Tax Expense

In applying GAAP principles for a business entity, state and local tax expenses are found in several places in the taxpayer's financial reports. In the tax footnote, the state/local tax costs often are reported in dollar and/or percentage terms, in both current and deferred components. The following are examples of state/local tax expenses that were reported in a recent year.

	Current State/Local Tax Expense ($ million)	Deferred State/Local Tax Expense ($ million)
Eli Lilly	$ 49	($ 1)
ExxonMobil	340	221
Ryder Systems	6	3
Ford Motor	7	(59)

Corporations also report permanent book-tax differences in determining the effective tax rate for the reporting period. In a recent year, Berkshire Hathaway reported that state/local permanent book-tax differences reduced its effective income tax rate by about 1.5 percentage points. Ford Motor reported a similar rate reduction, but Ryder Systems's effective tax rate increased by about 6 percentage points for the year due to such permanent book-tax differences.

CONCEPT SUMMARY 16.2

Corporate Multistate Income Taxation

1. A taxpayer is subject to income tax in the state in which it resides or is organized.
2. A taxpayer is subject to income tax in states where it has a business presence and enjoys the resources of the host state in conducting its operations.
3. A multistate taxpayer must divide its aggregate taxable income for the year among the states in which it conducts business.
4. Nonbusiness income is allocated to the state in which it is generated.
5. Business income is apportioned among the states in which the taxpayer has nexus.
6. Apportionment usually is conducted using a formula based on the relative sales, employment, and asset holdings in the various states.
7. The sales factor uses a destination test, while the payroll and property factors use a source test.
8. Most states weight the sales factor higher than the other apportionment factors.
9. Some states apply a special apportionment formula for certain industries when the traditional three-factor formula could distort the income division procedure in some way.
10. About 30 states employ the unitary theory in deriving the apportionment factors, using the data from a group of corporations to compute the apportionment formula. Other states allow or require a consolidated return from a conglomerate.

© iStockphoto.com/Andrey Prokhorov

In-depth coverage can be found on this book's companion website: **www.cengagebrain.com**   🔍 **5** | Digging Deeper |

The Unitary Theory About 30 states use a **unitary approach** in computing the apportionment factors. Conglomerates are required, or can elect, to base their computations on the data for all of their affiliated corporations, not just the legal entities that do business with the state. Affiliates included under the unitary theory share a majority ownership with a parent or group of shareholders. They also often share data processing, sales force, and marketing resources.

The *combined return* that the unitary business files includes much more data than might be expected on a separate-entity basis, but the taxing jurisdictions often believe that the unitary figures offer a more accurate reflection of the taxpayer's activity within the state and that, therefore, a more accurate tax liability can be derived.

Example 24

Kipp Industries is a holding company for three subsidiaries: GrapeCo operating in California, PotatoCo operating in Idaho, and BratCo operating in Germany. Only GrapeCo has nexus with California. But because California is a unitary state, the California apportionment percentage is computed also using PotatoCo and BratCo data.

Example 25

Return to the facts of Example 24. If Kipp Industries files a waters'-edge election, the unitary group that files a California income tax return can be limited to GrapeCo and PotatoCo.

In-depth coverage can be found on this book's companion website: **www.cengagebrain.com**   🔍 **6** | Digging Deeper |

Concept Summary 16.2 sets out some of the key issues in corporate multistate income taxation.

16-4 COMMON CHALLENGES

LO.7

Practical and policy issues facing the U.S. states, developed countries, and the taxpayers operating in all of them show a great degree of similarity between the multistate and international tax regimes. Terminology may differ, and the evolution of

Synthesize the international and multistate tax systems and recognize common issues faced by both systems.

© tuulijumala/Shutterstock.com

tax solutions may take radically different paths, but the key issues that face the multijurisdictional community are at once challenging and rewarding.

16-4a Authority to Tax

The old-economy orientation of the nexus and permanent establishment rules presents great difficulty in today's economy, as jurisdictions attempt to describe the income and sales/use tax base fairly. An electronic presence also exploits the resources of the host country and should trigger a tax in the visited jurisdiction. Mathematically, the apportionment and sourcing rules should result in only a modest tax liability in the host jurisdiction, but to maintain that no presence exists and no tax should be paid in the context of an 800 telephone number or Internet sale is improper.

But perhaps the notion of *presence* is becoming less important over time, and the level of resource usage in the host jurisdiction also is declining. For example, just-in-time manufacturing and purchasing strategies reduce the need for warehousing by some taxpayers. Human capital can be dispersed through telecommuting, video conferencing, and project rotation using work-group software that provides acceptable levels of data security. If the future is to a great degree wireless, perhaps the standard of presence will diminish, as the buyer and the seller are both "everywhere."

16-4b Division of Income

The multistate apportionment procedure could use an overhaul. The fact that a majority of states change the weighting of the sales factor indicates that some other income division method might better serve taxpayers and governments. Three-factor apportionment was designed for an age of traveling sales representatives and sales of built, grown, and manufactured goods. Sales reps were assigned territories they could drive through on short notice, so they usually lived close to their customer base. In that case, the sales and payroll factors could be highly redundant.

Today, with communication and distribution systems more highly developed, the sales factor appears incrementally to be the preferred income-sourcing device. Sales of goods and services should be assigned based on a destination test so that the transaction is assigned to the state of the purchaser.

The three-factor formula further breaks down for income derived from specialized industries, as evidenced by the special computational methods allowed by many states. Perhaps the economy is so specialized today that income simply cannot be assigned by the use of one simple formula. Nonetheless, more uniformity among the states as to definitions and computational rules for the factors would be welcome.

The U.S. Treasury has held hearings in the last decade concerning the adoption of an apportionment approach to the sourcing of international taxable income. Although a formulary apportionment would represent a more reliable and predictable method of dividing multinational income and deduction amounts, the data collection burden that such a system would create may be too much to expect from most of the trading partners in the short term. Moreover, the model treaties developed by the United States and the Organization for Economic Cooperation and Development (OECD) include language relating to the income-sourcing rules and transfer pricing at arm's length, not an apportionment approach.

16-4c Transfer Pricing

The transfer pricing system used in international trade requires the taxpayer to keep a database of comparable prices and transactions, even though often no such comparability exists. Especially when dealing with proprietary goods and design, it may be impossible to find comparable goods and, therefore, an acceptable transfer price for them. One solution to this situation would be to allow additional definitions of comparable goods, or of ranges of acceptable transfer prices, perhaps subjected to audit on a rotating five-year basis. The use of advance pricing agreements further allows a greater degree of control by the governments in data collection and analysis, ideally prior to the undertaking of the sales or manufacturing transactions.

Example 26

Consider the transaction depicted in the diagram below. A U.S. corporation manufactures and sells inventory to an unrelated foreign customer. The sales price for the inventory is $1,000, and the related cost of goods sold (COGS) is $600. All of the resulting profit of $400 is taxed to the U.S. corporation, resulting in a $140 U.S. income tax liability ($400 × 35%). If the U.S. corporation has no business presence in the foreign jurisdiction and merely is selling to a customer located there, the foreign government is unlikely to impose any local income tax on the U.S. corporation. Consequently, the total tax burden imposed on the inventory sale is $140.

Sale without Using Related Party

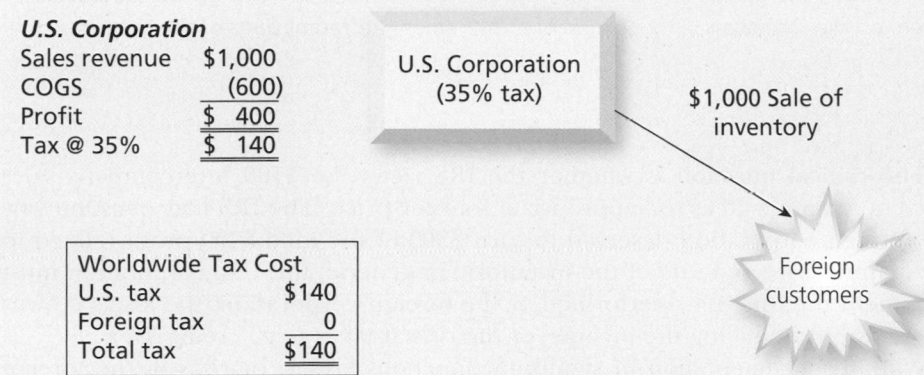

U.S. Corporation

Sales revenue	$1,000
COGS	(600)
Profit	$ 400
Tax @ 35%	$ 140

Worldwide Tax Cost	
U.S. tax	$140
Foreign tax	0
Total tax	$140

Suppose instead that the U.S. corporation attempts to reduce its total tax expense by channeling the inventory sale through a foreign subsidiary in the same country as the foreign customer. In this case, because the U.S. corporation controls the foreign subsidiary, it chooses an intercompany sales price (the transfer price) that moves a portion of the profits from the United States to the foreign country. By selling the inventory it manufactured to its 100%-owned foreign subsidiary for $700, the U.S. corporation reports only $100 of profits and an associated U.S. tax liability of $35. The foreign subsidiary then sells the inventory to the ultimate customer for $1,000, and with a $700 COGS, it earns a $300 profit. Now the foreign country imposes only a 10% tax on corporate profits, resulting in a foreign income tax of $30 ($300 × 10%). By using a related foreign entity in a lower-tax jurisdiction, the U.S. corporation has lowered its overall tax liability on the sale from $140 (all U.S.) to $65 ($35 U.S. and $30 foreign).

Sale Using Related Party

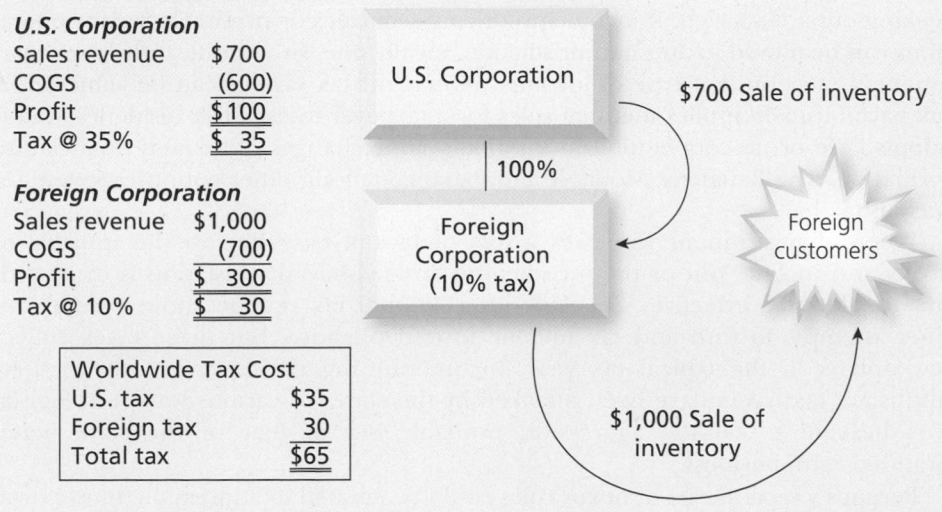

U.S. Corporation

Sales revenue	$700
COGS	(600)
Profit	$100
Tax @ 35%	$ 35

Foreign Corporation

Sales revenue	$1,000
COGS	(700)
Profit	$ 300
Tax @ 10%	$ 30

Worldwide Tax Cost	
U.S. tax	$35
Foreign tax	30
Total tax	$65

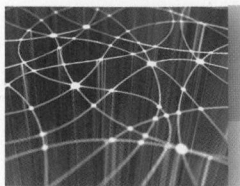

BRIDGE DISCIPLINE   Bridge to Cost Accounting and Executive Compensation

Multijurisdictional companies operate across state and country borders. As illustrated, the transfer price used by a company can have a significant effect on the amount of profits subject to taxation within a particular taxing jurisdiction. Companies face other concerns when establishing transfer pricing policies. For example, the internal determination of how a division of the company is performing may be based on transfer pricing between related entities within the global group. Furthermore, the compensation of the managers within those divisions may be tied directly to divisional performance.

If an intercompany price is set in a manner that optimizes the global tax position, a separate cost accounting policy may be required to determine an entity's profitability for purposes of compensating employees. Tax advisers often face resistance from operations managers when suggesting improved transfer pricing methods, because such improvements often change the traditional division of profits among different parts of the business.

© iStockphoto.com/enot-poloskun

The critical question is whether the IRS views the $700 intercompany sales price of Example 26 as the appropriate transfer price. The IRS may question why the foreign corporation deserved to earn $300 of the total $400 profit related to the manufacture and sale of the inventory. In general, the U.S. corporation must document the functions performed by the foreign corporation, the assets it owns that assist in producing the income, or the risks it takes (e.g., credit risk).

Without documentation of significant functions, assets, or risks of the foreign subsidiary, the IRS will not consider the $300 profit earned by the foreign corporation to be appropriate, and it will adjust the transfer price upward. If the IRS determines that the transfer price should have been $990, the U.S. corporation reports a $390 profit (with $136.50 U.S. income tax), and the foreign corporation earns a $10 profit (with $1 in foreign income tax).

With this change in transfer price, the U.S. corporation does not succeed in transferring a meaningful portion of its profits to the lower-tax jurisdiction and reduces its tax liability by only $2.50 [$140 − ($136.50 + $1)].

Digging Deeper   7      In-depth coverage can be found on this book's companion website: **www.cengagebrain.com**

16-4d Tax Havens

When taxpayers perceive effective tax rates as too high, planning usually includes seeking out a **tax haven**. If income-producing securities or profitable service operations can be moved to another jurisdiction, ideally one with significantly lower marginal tax rates on that type of income, permanent tax savings can be achieved. A tax haven usually applies minimal rules for a taxpayer to establish residency, and it adopts little or no cooperation in international exchanges of tax and financial information. The Bahamas, Monaco, and Panama, among other countries, often are seen as tax havens.

When a government witnesses a loss of its tax base due to the transfer of assets and income out of the jurisdiction, anti-tax-haven legislation is discussed, but it seldom is effective. The U.S. international tax regime shows several distinct attempts to find and tax income moved offshore, but those taxes collect few dollars in the typical tax year. Income-shifting devices currently used by multistate taxpayers have been attacked by the states in various ways, but legislators hesitate to be too aggressive, probably out of fear of the state being branded "anti-business."

Perhaps a separate set of nexus rules could be created to address the most portable types of income, such as that from interest and dividends. But this difficult

© tuulijumala/Shutterstock.com

FINANCIAL DISCLOSURE INSIGHTS Deferred Tax Assets Overseas

U.S. corporations are not the only entities that can have balance sheets with excessive deferred tax accounts. Restrictive regulatory rules as to how non-U.S. banks compute their capital amounts tend to create large deferred tax assets for them.

Deferred tax assets do not affect the entity's actual cash balances, but they can affect the stock price in the short term. Even professional equity analysts can have difficulty understanding announcements of tax adjustments to the balance sheet. Regulations limit the level of deferred tax assets that banks can hold in a given country, and political pressure to increase those limits is appearing as the proportion of shareholder equity that is made up of deferred tax assets has grown significantly in the last five years.

The following are estimates from JPMorgan Chase of the magnitude of deferred tax asset balances for selected banks overseas and banks in the United States.

	Percentage of Shareholder Equity Constituted by Deferred Tax Assets
Dexia	44%
Deutsche Bank	24
Monte dei Paschi	23
UBS	21
Credit Suisse	20
U.S. banks, average	11

© iStockphoto.com/Pali Rao

problem likely needs a multilateral solution, which is unlikely to be found in the short term among states and countries, each with unique revenue shortfalls and political profiles.

In-depth coverage can be found on this book's companion website: **www.cengagebrain.com** **8**   Digging Deeper

ETHICS & EQUITY Encouraging Economic Development through Tax Concessions

The tax professional occasionally is in a position to negotiate with a state or city taxing jurisdiction to garner tax relief for a client as an incentive to locate a plant or distribution center in that geographic area. In times when construction budgets are high and interstate competition is fierce to attract or retain businesses that are making location decisions, such tax concessions can be significant.

For instance, to encourage a business to build a large distribution center in the area, community leaders might be agreeable to:

- paying for roads, sewer, water, and other improvements through taxpayer bonds;
- reducing property taxes by 50 percent for the first 10 years of the center's operations; and
- permanently excluding any distribution-related vehicles and equipment from the personal property tax.

An incentive-granting community provides the concessions even though the influx of new workers will place a great strain on public school facilities and likely necessitate improvements in traffic patterns and other infrastructure.

Consider the position of a large employer that has been located in the area for more than 50 years. By how much should it be willing to absorb the tax increases that result when economic development concessions are used to attract new, perhaps temporary, businesses to the area? Should the employer challenge the constitutionality of the grant of such sizable tax breaks to some, but not all, business taxpayers in the jurisdiction? Should higher "impact fees" be assessed on new developments?

Does your analysis change if the new business competes with the longtime resident for sales? For employees? For political power?

© iStockphoto.com/LdF

16-4e Interjurisdictional Agreements

Treaties are documents that address many issues other than the taxable income computation. They involve several players within the governmental structure, and they take several years to draft and adopt. Treaties involving the United States tend to be only bilateral, meaning that it is difficult to anticipate and coordinate the interaction of several treaties as they apply to a single taxpayer.

At the multistate level, the Federal government has been slow to take up issues involving a synchronization of the income tax systems used by the states. Although this reluctance may be partly for strictly constitutional reasons, it is largely because of the difficulties presented by the lack of uniformity among the states' tax laws and enforcement efforts.

But the future must hold a greater degree of cooperation among various taxing jurisdictions, at least in the trading of information and the coordination of enforcement efforts. The United States must create additional treaties or information-sharing agreements with countries in South America and Africa. And the future of the European Union probably holds a series of highly developed agreements addressing tax issues with the United States.

Procedural developments may accomplish the same result. For instance, block filing by S corporations and their shareholders with various states accomplishes a number of income division and information-sharing goals. Applying the same approach to partnerships and limited liability entities, and perhaps C corporations with a small number of shareholders, would be an important step forward. Including the multinational activities of such flow-through and closely held entities would also allow for a more coordinated result.

Sharing data, while still respecting the confidentiality needs of the taxpayer and requirements of the governments, represents a technologically sound method of collecting taxes in today's multijurisdictional economy.

Digging Deeper   9   In-depth coverage can be found on this book's companion website: **www.cengagebrain.com**

© tuulijumala/Shutterstock.com

REFOCUS ON THE BIG PICTURE

GOING INTERNATIONAL

Simply selling into a foreign jurisdiction probably will not trigger any overseas income tax consequences. However, income earned from foreign sales is taxed currently to VoiceCo in the United States. When VoiceCo establishes a CFC in Ireland, it benefits from deferral. As long as the income is not distributed to VoiceCo and as long as the income is not "tainted" Subpart F income, VoiceCo can avoid taxes on the profits of VoiceCo-Ireland. If VoiceCo receives dividends from its foreign subsidiary, it can claim foreign tax credits, which help alleviate the double taxation that would otherwise result.

What If?

VoiceCo is considering building a new manufacturing facility in another state in the United States. How will VoiceCo's expansion decision be affected by state tax considerations? In making the decision to expand, VoiceCo should consider a variety of state tax issues including whether the state imposes a corporate income tax at all and, if so, whether the state requires unitary reporting. Other relevant issues affecting the tax calculation in the state include what apportionment formula is used by the state and whether the state has a throwback rule.

Suggested Readings

B. P. Ely, C. R. Grissom, and W. T. Thistle, "State Taxation of Pass-Through Entities and Their Owners," *Journal of Multistate Taxation and Incentives*, September 2012.

Albena Peters, "Controlled Foreign Corporation Rules in the United States, Canada, and Germany," *Corporate Taxation*, March/April 2012.

Michael S. Schadewald and William A. Raabe, "Present and Future Directions in Federal and State Taxation of Income from Cross Border Trade," *TAXES*, April 1997.

Jeffrey M. Tolin and Steven M. Danowitz, "States' Application of Code's Differing Treatment of U.S. and Foreign Taxpayers May Violate Commerce Clause," *Corporate Taxation*, November/December 2011.

Brett R. Wilkinson and Katherine Wilkinson, "The Creditability of Foreign Taxes," *The Tax Adviser*, January 2014.

Key Terms

Allocate, 16-25

Apportioned, 16-26

Arm's length price, 16-17

Check-the-box Regulations, 16-17

Controlled foreign corporations (CFCs), 16-15

Deemed-paid credit, 16-14

Effectively connected income, 16-18

FDAP, 16-20

Foreign tax credit, 16-6

Inbound taxation, 16-3

Income tax treaties, 16-5

Multistate Tax Commission (MTC), 16-23

Nexus, 16-23

Nonresident alien (NRA), 16-18

Outbound taxation, 16-3

Payroll factor, 16-26

Permanent establishment (PE), 16-5

Property factor, 16-26

Public Law 86–272, 16-22

Sales factor, 16-26

Separate foreign tax credit income categories, 16-13

Solicitation, 16-22

Subpart F income, 16-15

Tax haven, 16-32

Throwback rule, 16-28

Unitary approach, 16-29

U.S. shareholder, 16-15

Waters'-edge election, 16-27

Problems

1. **LO.2, 3** "U.S. persons are taxed on their worldwide income." Explain.

2. **LO.3** Liang, a U.S. citizen, owns 100% of ForCo, a foreign corporation not engaged in a U.S. trade or business. Is Liang subject to any U.S. income tax on her dealings with ForCo? Explain.

3. **LO.3** BlueCo, a domestic corporation, incorporates GreenCo, a new wholly owned entity in Germany. Under both German and U.S. legal principles, this entity is a corporation. BlueCo faces a 35% U.S. tax rate.

   GreenCo earns $1,500,000 in net profits from its German activities, and GreenCo makes no dividend distributions to BlueCo. How much Federal income tax will BlueCo pay for the current year as a result of GreenCo's earnings, assuming that there is no deemed dividend under Subpart F? Ignore any foreign tax credit (FTC) implications.

4. **LO.3** Evaluate this statement: It is unfair that the United States taxes its citizens and residents on their worldwide income.

5. **LO.2** Kelly, a U.S. citizen, earns interest income that is sourced in Germany. How could a U.S. tax treaty with Germany reduce Kelly's taxes on the interest?

6. **LO.3** Describe the different approaches used by countries to tax the earnings of their citizens and residents generated outside the borders of the country.

7. **LO.3** Determine the source (U.S. or foreign) of the following items of income.
   a. Interest income paid by a foreign corporation.
   b. Dividend income paid by a U.S. corporation that has no foreign operations.

c. Dividend income paid by a foreign corporation that has U.S. operations that historically produce 32% of the corporation's income.

d. Income from providing consulting services to clients with 27% of the services provided to clients on-site in Mexico.

Decision Making

8. **LO.3** Create, Inc., produces inventory in its foreign manufacturing plants for sale in the United States. Its foreign manufacturing assets have a tax book value of $5 million and a fair market value of $15 million. Its assets related to the sales activity have a tax book value of $2 million and a fair market value of $5 million. Create's interest expense totaled $400,000 for the current year.

a. What amount of interest expense is allocated and apportioned to foreign-source income using the tax book value method? What amount of Create's interest expense is allocated and apportioned to foreign-source income using the fair market value method?

b. If Create wants to maximize its FTC, which method should it use?

9. **LO.3** Chock, a U.S. corporation, purchases inventory for resale from distributors within the United States and resells this inventory at a $1 million profit to customers outside the United States. Title to the goods passes outside the United States. What is the source of Chock's inventory sales income?

10. **LO.3** Willa, a U.S. corporation, owns the rights to a patent related to a medical device. Willa licenses the rights to use the patent to IrishCo, which uses the patent in its manufacturing facility located in Ireland. What is the source of the $1 million royalty income received by Willa from IrishCo for the use of the patent?

11. **LO.3** USCo incurred $100,000 in interest expense for the current year. The tax book value of USCo's assets generating foreign-source income is $5 million. The tax book value of USCo's assets generating U.S.-source income is $45 million. How much of the interest expense is allocated and apportioned to foreign-source income?

12. **LO.3** QuinnCo could not claim all of the income taxes it paid to Japan as a foreign tax credit (FTC) this year. What computational limit probably kept QuinnCo from taking its full FTC? Explain.

13. **LO.3** FoldIt, a U.S. business, paid income taxes to Mexico relative to profitable sales of shipping boxes it made in that country. Can it claim a deduction for these taxes in computing U.S. taxable income? A tax credit? Both? Explain.

14. **LO.3** Klein, a domestic corporation, receives a $10,000 dividend from ForCo, a wholly owned foreign corporation. The deemed-paid (indirect) foreign tax credit associated with this dividend is $3,000. What is the total gross income included in Klein's tax return as a result of this dividend?

15. **LO.3** ABC, Inc., a domestic corporation, reports $50 million of taxable income, including $15 million of general limitation foreign-source taxable income, on which ABC paid $5 million in foreign income taxes. The U.S. tax rate is 35%. What is ABC's foreign tax credit?

16. **LO.3** Mary, a U.S. citizen, is the sole shareholder of CanCo, a Canadian corporation. During its first year of operations, CanCo earns $14 million of foreign-source taxable income, pays $6 million of Canadian income taxes, and distributes a $2 million dividend to Mary. Can Mary claim a deemed-paid (indirect) foreign tax credit on her Form 1040 with respect to receipt of a dividend distribution from CanCo? Why or why not?

17. **LO.3** ABC, Inc., a domestic corporation, owns 100% of HighTax, a foreign corporation. HighTax has $50 million of undistributed E & P, all of which is attributable to general limitation income, and $30 million of foreign income taxes paid. HighTax distributes a $5 million dividend to ABC. The dividend, which is subject to a 5% foreign withholding tax, is ABC's only item of income during the year. ABC's marginal U.S. tax rate is 35%. How much foreign tax credit and carryover is produced by the dividend?

18. **LO.3** USCo, a domestic corporation, reports worldwide taxable income of $1.5 million, including a $400,000 dividend from ForCo, a wholly owned foreign corporation. ForCo's undistributed E & P totals $16 million, and it has paid $10 million of foreign income taxes attributable to these earnings. All foreign income is in the general limitation basket. What is USCo's deemed-paid (indirect) foreign tax credit related to the dividend received (before consideration of any limitation)?

19. **LO.3** USCo, a domestic corporation, reports worldwide taxable income of $500,000, including a $300,000 dividend from ForCo, a wholly owned foreign corporation. ForCo's undistributed E & P totals $1 million, and it has paid $200,000 of foreign income taxes attributable to these earnings. All foreign income is in the general limitation basket. What is USCo's deemed-paid (indirect) foreign tax credit related to the dividend received (before consideration of any limitation)?

20. **LO.3** Fleming, Inc., a domestic corporation, operates in both Canada and the United States. This year, the business generated taxable income of $400,000 from foreign sources and $300,000 from U.S. sources. All of Fleming's foreign-source income is in the general limitation basket. Fleming's total worldwide taxable income is $700,000. Fleming pays Canadian taxes of $152,000. What is Fleming's allowed FTC for the tax year? Assume a 35% U.S. income tax rate.

21. **LO.3** Drake, Inc., a U.S. corporation, operates a branch sales office in Turkey. During the current year, Drake earned $500,000 in taxable income from U.S. sources and $100,000 in taxable income from sources in Turkey. Drake paid $40,000 in income taxes to Turkey. All of the income is characterized as general limitation income. Compute Drake's U.S. income tax liability after consideration of any foreign tax credit. Drake's U.S. tax rate is 35%.

22. **LO.3** Crank, Inc., a U.S. corporation, operates a branch sales office in Ghana. During the current year, Crank earned $200,000 in taxable income from U.S. sources and $50,000 in taxable income from sources in Ghana. Crank paid $5,000 in income taxes to Ghana. All of the income is characterized as general limitation income. Compute Crank's U.S. income tax liability after consideration of any foreign tax credit. Crank's U.S. tax rate is 35%.

23. **LO.3** Harold, Inc., a domestic corporation, earned $500,000 from foreign manufacturing activities on which it paid $150,000 of foreign income taxes. Harold's foreign sales income is taxed at a 45% foreign tax rate. Both sales and manufacturing income are assigned to the general limitation basket. What amount of foreign sales income can Harold earn without generating any excess FTCs for the current year? Assume a 35% U.S. rate.

Decision Making

24. **LO.3** Food, Inc., a domestic corporation, owns 70% of the stock of Drink, Inc., a foreign corporation. For the current year, Food receives a dividend of $20,000 from Drink. Drink's E & P (after taxes) and foreign taxes are $6 million and $800,000, respectively. What is Food's total gross income from receipt of this dividend if it elects to claim the FTC for deemed-paid foreign taxes?

25. **LO.3** Orion, Inc., a U.S. corporation, reports foreign-source income and pays foreign taxes for the tax year as follows.

	Income	Taxes
Passive category	$150,000	$ 13,000
General category	300,000	150,000

Orion's worldwide taxable income is $600,000, and U.S. taxes before the FTC are $210,000 (assume a 35% rate). What is Orion's U.S. tax liability after the FTC?

26. **LO.3** Discuss the policy reasons for the existence of the Subpart F rules. Give two examples of Subpart F income.

Issue ID

27. **LO.3** USCo owns 65% of the voting stock of LandCo, a Country X corporation. Terra, an unrelated Country Y corporation, owns the other 35% of LandCo. LandCo owns 100% of the voting stock of OceanCo, a Country Z corporation. Assuming that USCo is a U.S. shareholder, do LandCo and OceanCo meet the definition of a CFC? Explain.

28. **LO.3** Is a foreign corporation owned equally by 100 unrelated U.S. citizens considered to be a controlled foreign corporation (CFC)? Explain.

29. **LO.3** Hart Enterprises, a domestic corporation, owns 100% of OK, Ltd., an Irish corporation. OK's gross income for the year is $10 million. Determine whether any of the following transactions produce Subpart F gross income for the current year.

a. OK earned $600,000 from sales of products purchased from Hart and sold to customers outside Ireland.

b. OK earned $1 million from sales of products purchased from Hart and sold to customers in Ireland.

c. OK earned $400,000 from sales of products purchased from unrelated suppliers and sold to customers in Germany.

d. OK purchased raw materials from Hart, used these materials to manufacture finished goods, and sold these goods to customers in Italy. OK earned $300,000 from these sales.

e. OK earned $100,000 for the performance of warranty services on behalf of Hart. These services were performed in Japan for customers located in Japan.

f. OK earned $50,000 in dividend income from Canada and Mexico passive investments.

30. **LO.3** HiramCo, a U.S. entity, operates a manufacturing business in both Mexico and Costa Rica, and it holds its investment portfolio in Sweden. How many foreign tax credit computations must HiramCo make? Be specific, and use the term *basket* in your answer.

31. **LO.4** Give a simple answer to Andre's question: "If I move to the United States, how will the Federal government tax my widget sales and capital gains?" Andre will be living in New York City, where state and local taxes are very high. Ignore the effects of tax treaties in your answer.

32. **LO.3** Skills, Inc., a U.S. corporation, reports current foreign-source income classified in two different FTC income baskets. It earns $50,000 in passive foreign-source income, and it suffers a net loss of $30,000 in the general limitation basket. What is the numerator of Skills's FTC limitation formula for the passive basket in the current year? Explain.

Decision Making

33. **LO.3** Night, Inc., a domestic corporation, earned $300,000 from foreign manufacturing activities, on which it paid $90,000 of foreign income taxes. Night's foreign sales income is taxed at a 50% foreign tax rate. What amount of foreign sales income can Night earn without generating any excess FTCs for the current year? Assume a 34% U.S. tax rate.

34. **LO.4** Evaluate the following statement: Foreign persons never are subject to U.S. taxation on U.S.-source investment income so long as they are not engaged in a U.S. trade or business.

Critical Thinking

35. **LO.3** Lili, Inc., a domestic corporation, operates a branch in France. The earnings record of the branch is as follows.

Year	Taxable Income (Loss)	Foreign Taxes Paid
2012	($ 25,000)	$ –0–
2013	(40,000)	–0–
2014	(10,000)	–0–
2015	120,000	40,000

For 2012–2015, Lili, Inc., reports U.S.-source taxable income of $500,000 each year. What is the allowed FTC for 2015? Assume a 35% U.S. tax rate.

Communications

36. **LO.3, 4** Write a memo for the tax research file on the difference between "inbound" and "outbound" activities in the context of U.S. taxation of international income.

37. **LO.3** Warwick, Inc., a U.S. corporation, owns 100% of NewGrass, Ltd., a foreign corporation. NewGrass earns only general limitation income. During the current year, NewGrass paid Warwick a $10,000 dividend. The deemed-paid foreign tax credit associated with this dividend is $3,000. The foreign jurisdiction requires a withholding tax of 10%, so Warwick received only $9,000 in cash as a result of the dividend. What is Warwick's total U.S. gross income reported as a result of the cash dividend?

38. **LO.4** ForCo, a foreign corporation not engaged in a U.S. trade or business, received a $600,000 dividend from USCo, a domestic corporation. ForCo incurred $45,000 in expenses related to earning the dividend. All of USCo's income is from U.S. sources. ForCo is not eligible for any treaty benefits. What is the withholding tax on the dividend paid to ForCo?

39. **LO.5** Evaluate this statement: A state can tax only its resident individuals and the corporations and partnerships that are organized in-state.

40. **LO.5** What is the function of the Multistate Tax Commission? Why have some U.S. states not joined the MTC?

41. **LO.5** You are working with the top management of one of your clients in selecting the U.S. location for a new manufacturing operation. Craft a plan for the CEO to use in discussions with the economic development representatives of each of the top candidate states. In no more than two PowerPoint slides, list some of the tax incentives the CEO should request from a particular state during the bilateral negotiations between the parties. Your list should be both creative and aggressive in its requests.

Issue ID

Communications

42. **LO.5** Considering only the aggregate state income tax liability, how should a taxpayer who is a resident in State A selling widgets deploy its sales force? The states that entail the taxpayer's entire customer base use the following flat income tax rates.

Decision Making

State A	5%
State B	3
State C	6
State D	0

43. **LO.5** Continue to consider the case of the taxpayer in Problem 42. Is it acceptable to you if the taxpayer purposely shifts its sales force among the states to reduce its tax liabilities?

Ethics and Equity

44. **LO.6** Compute state taxable income for HippCo, Inc. Its Federal taxable income for the year is $1 million. Its operations are confined to Oregon and Montana. HippCo generates only business and interest income for the year.

- Federal cost recovery deductions totaled $200,000. Montana used this amount, but Oregon allowed only $120,000.
- Interest income of $25,000 from Oregon bonds was excluded from Federal taxable income. Oregon taxes all municipal bond income, while Montana taxes all such interest except that from its own bonds.
- Interest income from Treasury bonds that was recognized on the Federal return came to $11,000. Neither state taxes such income.

45. **LO.6** Continue with the facts of Problem 44. Using the format of Figure 16.3, compute state taxable income for HippCo, assuming also that the taxpayer recognized $225,000 of net rent income during the year from a warehouse building in Montana. Federal taxable income still is $1 million.

46. **LO.6** PinkCo, Inc., operates in two states. It reports the following results for the year. Compute the apportionment percentage for both states. Amounts are stated in millions of dollars.

	State A	State B	Totals
Sales	$25	$ 75	$100
Payroll	20	30	50
Property	0	100	100

47. **LO.6** Repeat the computations of Problem 46, but now assume that State B uses a double-weighted sales factor in its apportionment formula.

48. **LO.6** Repeat the computations of Problem 46, but now assume that State A is a sales-factor-only state and that State B uses the following weights: sales .70, payroll .15, and property .15.

49. **LO.6** State A enjoys a prosperous economy, with high real estate values and compensation levels. State B's economy has seen better days—property values are depressed, and unemployment is higher than in other states. Most consumer goods are priced at about 10% less in B as compared to prices in A. Both A and B apply unitary income taxation on businesses that operate in-state. Does unitary taxation distort the assignment of taxable income between A and B? Explain.

Issue ID

50. **LO.6** Hernandez, which has been an S corporation since inception, is subject to tax in States Y and Z. On Schedule K of its Federal Form 1120S, Hernandez reported ordinary income of $500,000 from its business, taxable interest income of $10,000, capital loss of $30,000, and $40,000 of dividend income from a corporation in which it owns 30%.

Critical Thinking

Communications

Both states apportion income by use of a three-factor formula that equally weights sales, payroll, and the average cost of property; both states treat interest and dividends as business income. In addition, both Y and Z follow Federal provisions with respect to the determination of corporate taxable income. Y recognizes S status, but Z does not.

Based on the following information, write a memo to the shareholders of Hernandez, detailing the amount of taxable income on which Hernandez will pay tax in Y and Z. Hernandez corporate offices are located at 5678 Alabaster Circle, Bowling Green, KY 42103.

	State Y	State Z
Sales	$1,000,000	$800,000
Property (average cost)	500,000	100,000
Payroll	800,000	200,000

Issue ID

Communications

51. **LO.6** Prepare a PowerPoint presentation (maximum of six slides) entitled "Planning Principles for Our Multistate Clients." The slides will be used to lead a 20-minute discussion with colleagues in the corporate tax department. Keep the outline general, but assume that your colleagues already work with clients operating in at least 15 states. Address only income tax issues.

Issue ID

Communications

52. **LO.3, 7** Miha Ohua is the CFO of a U.S. company that has operations in Europe and Asia. The company has several manufacturing subsidiaries in low-tax foreign countries where the tax rate averages 6%. These subsidiaries purchase raw materials used in the production process from related subsidiaries located in countries where the tax rate averages 33%.

Miha is considering establishing a transfer price for the raw materials so that the higher-tax subsidiaries charge a low price for the raw materials. In this way, little of the profit is left in these subsidiaries, and most of the profits end up in the low-tax subsidiaries. This approach might reduce the U.S. company's overall global tax rate. Write a memo to Miha outlining the issues with this plan.

BRIDGE DISCIPLINE

1. What type of information-sharing agreements does the IRS have with the revenue agency of the Bahamas? Canada? Germany? Israel? Argentina?

Communications

2. Write a paper of no more than two pages discussing the treatment of state and local taxes that is found in the text of U.S. income tax treaties with two other countries.

Communications

3. Several U.S. states finance their operations without the benefit of a corporate income tax. Prepare five to seven PowerPoint slides, and make a presentation to your school's Accounting Club. In your presentation, discuss the public economic and policy effects of using nontraditional revenue sources to fund state operating and infrastructure projects. Compare the taxing and expenditure process used in your state with at least two of these jurisdictions: Alaska; Hawaii; Michigan; Texas; Washington, D.C.; and Washington State.

4. The trend in state income taxation is to move from an equal three-factor apportionment formula to a formula that places extra weight on the sales factor. Several states now use sales-factor-only apportionment. Explain why this development is attractive to the taxing states.

Research Problems

THOMSON REUTERS
CHECKPOINT

Note: Solutions to Research Problems can be prepared by using the **Checkpoint®** **Student Edition** online research product, which is available to accompany this text. It is also possible to prepare solutions to the Research Problems by using tax research materials found in a standard tax library.

Communications

Research Problem 1. Jerry Jeff Keen, the CFO of Boots Unlimited, a Texas corporation, has come to you regarding a potential restructuring of business operations. Boots long has manufactured its western boots in plants in Texas and Oklahoma.

Recently, Boots has explored the possibility of setting up a manufacturing subsidiary in Ireland, where manufacturing profits are taxed at 10%. Jerry Jeff sees this as a great idea, given that the alternative is to continue all manufacturing in the United States, where profits are taxed at 34%. Boots plans to continue all of the cutting, sizing, and hand tooling of leather in its U.S. plants. This material will be shipped to Ireland for final assembly, with the finished product shipped to retail outlets all over Europe and Asia. Your initial concern is whether the income generated by the Irish subsidiary will be considered foreign base company income. Address this issue in a research memo, along with any planning suggestions.

Partial list of research aids:
§ 954(d).
Reg. § 1.954–3(a).
Bausch & Lomb, 71 TCM 2031, T.C.Memo. 1996–57.

Research Problem 2. Polly Ling is a successful professional golfer. She is a resident of a country that does not have a tax treaty with the United States. Ling plays matches around the world, about one-half of which are in the United States. Ling's reputation is without blemish; in fact, she is known as being exceedingly honest and upright, and many articles discuss how she is a role model for young golfers due to her tenacious and successful playing style and her favorable character traits. Every year, she reports the most penalty strokes on herself among the participants in womens' matches, and this is seen as reinforcing her image as an honest and respectful competitor.

This combination of quality play and laudable reputation has brought many riches to Ling. She comes to you with several Federal income tax questions. She knows that as a non-U.S. resident, any of her winnings from tournament play that occurs in the United States are subject to U.S. income taxation. But what about each of the following items? How does U.S. tax law affect Ling? Apply the sourcing rules in this regard, and determine whether the graduated U.S. Federal income tax rate schedules apply.

* Endorsement income from YourGolf, for wearing clothing during matches with its logo prominently displayed. Ling must play in at least 10 tournaments per year that are televised around the world. She also must participate in photo sessions and in blogs and tweets associated with the tournaments. Payment to Ling is structured as a flat fee, with bonuses paid if she finishes in the top five competitors for each match. This is known as an *on-court endorsement*.
* Endorsement income from GolfZone, for letting the company use her likeness in a video game that simulates golf tournaments among known golfers and other players that the (usually middle-aged men and women) gamers identify. In this way, the gamer seems to be playing against Ling on famous golf courses. Two-thirds of all dollar sales of the game licenses are to U.S. customers.
* Endorsement income from Eliteness, for appearing in print and Internet ads that feature Ling wearing the company's high-end watches. One-fifth of all dollar sales of the watches are to U.S. customers. The latter two items are known as *off-court endorsements*.

Research Problem 3. Supervise and Wager Company produces consumer goods that are distributed and sold primarily in North America, Europe, and Asia. The business includes a U.S. parent company, S&W, Inc., and separate operating subsidiaries in each region in which the company conducts significant business.

The company's board is considering a structural reorganization to reduce the global tax costs. Options include reorganizing the parent company in either Bermuda or Ireland. Under any option, current shareholders will contribute their stock in the U.S. parent company in return for an equivalent amount of stock in the new parent. The U.S. parent will be liquidated, and the new corporation then will be the sole shareholder of the operating subsidiaries.

a. What might S&W be trying to achieve with the proposed organizational restructuring?

b. What insight can you provide regarding the immediate and longer-term tax consequences of the reorganization?

Internet Activity

Use the tax resources of the Internet to address the following questions. Do not restrict your search to the Web, but include a review of newsgroups and general reference materials, practitioner sites and resources, primary sources of the tax law, chat rooms and discussion groups, and other opportunities.

Research Problem 4. Make a list of the countries with which the United States currently has an income tax treaty. Then make a list of the countries with which the United States currently is negotiating an income tax treaty. For the second list, include the date on which negotiations started and the current status of the negotiations. Finally, list five countries with which the United States does *not* have in force a bilateral income tax treaty.

Communications

Research Problem 5. For your analysis, choose 10 countries, one of which is the United States. Create a table showing whether each country applies a worldwide or territorial approach to international income taxation. Then list the country's top income tax rate on business profits. Send a copy of this table to your instructor.

Communications

Research Problem 6. In no more than five PowerPoint slides, summarize and diagram the tax-shifting behavior of a multinational corporation. Pick a specific product (e.g., the Kindle, the Surface, or iTunes), and describe how the corporation routes its profits through low-tax jurisdictions.

Communications

Research Problem 7. Locate data on the size of the international economy, including data on international trade, foreign direct investment of U.S. firms, and investments in the United States by foreign firms. Useful web locations include **www.census.gov** and **www.bea.gov**. Prepare an analysis of these data for a three-year period using spreadsheet and graphing software, and e-mail your findings to your instructor.

Research Problem 8. Determine for your state and two of its neighbors:
a. Whether a Federal affiliated group is allowed to file a consolidated return with the state.
b. What the return is called (i.e., a "combined," a "consolidated," or other type of return).
c. Whether any special rules apply to the use of consolidated returns in the state (e.g., a special election is required, a limitation on deductible losses applies, a specified term exists during which the election to consolidate is binding).

Communications

Research Problem 9. For your state and one of its neighbors, determine the following. Place your data in a chart and e-mail it to your professor.
a. To what extent do the states follow the rulings of the Multistate Tax Commission?
b. Does the state adopt pertinent changes to the Internal Revenue Code? If so, as of what date?
c. Does the state apply entity-level income taxes for S corporations, partnerships, and LLCs? If so, what are the terms of those taxes?
d. Does the state levy a "minimum tax" or "alternative minimum tax"? If so, what are the terms and rates for the tax?

Communications

Research Problem 10. Read the "tax footnote" of five publicly traded U.S. corporations. Find the effective state/local income tax rates of each. Create a PowerPoint presentation (maximum of five slides) for your instructor, summarizing the search and reporting your findings.

Communications

Research Problem 11. Find a state/local tax organization (e.g., the Council on State Taxation). Read its current newsletter. In an e-mail to your instructor, summarize a major article at the site. Look especially for articles on one of these topics.

- Application of nexus rules to tax profits from intangible assets.
- The positive or negative "business tax climate" of your state and its neighbors, as measured by two or more policy centers or think tanks, and any measurable trends in the climate over the last 20 years.
- Attempts by the legislatures of your state and its neighbors to add advertising services to the sales/use tax base.
- Limitations on the taxpayer's ability to carry back net operating losses in computing your state's corporate taxable income.
- Responses to the economic downturn (e.g., more aggressive enforcement, new taxes and fees, and installment options for the late payment of taxes and penalties).
- Development of nexus rules that apply to cloud computing services.

Research Problem 12. Identify three states considered to be in the same economic region as your own. For each of the three states, answer the following questions. Answers to most can be found at **www.taxadmin.org**.

- What is the overall tax burden per capita, and where does it rank among all states?
- What is the overall tax burden as a percentage of personal income, and where does it rank among all states?
- From what source(s) does it raise most of its revenues (e.g., sales/use tax, highway tolls)?
- What is the highest marginal tax rate on corporate income?
- What is its apportionment formula, including factors and weights?

What advice or insight might you provide to your state legislature regarding your state's tax system, based on your responses to the above?

Business Tax Credits and Corporate Alternative Minimum Tax

LEARNING OBJECTIVES: *After completing Chapter 17, you should be able to:*

LO.1 **Explain how tax credits are used as a tool of Federal tax policy.**

LO.2 **Work with various business-related tax credits.**

LO.3 **Explain the reason for the alternative minimum tax.**

LO.4 **Identify and calculate the tax preferences that are included in determining the AMT.**

LO.5 **Identify and calculate AMT adjustments.**

LO.6 **State and explain the function of adjusted current earnings (ACE).**

LO.7 **Compute the AMT liability for corporations and individuals.**

CHAPTER OUTLINE

TAX TALK *A government which robs Peter to pay Paul can always count on the support of Paul.* —George Bernard Shaw

Tax Solutions for the Real World

DEALING WITH TAX CREDITS AND THE AMT

Mike, the CEO of Progress Corporation, is committed to helping revitalize the crumbling downtown area in his hometown. The area has experienced high unemployment as companies have left for the suburbs, and Mike is considering expanding his business and purchasing an old office building in a historic section of downtown. The building will require substantial renovations, and Mike has heard that there are tax credits that might help reduce his costs. He would also like to hire inner-city workers and help working families by providing on-site child care for working families. He is interested in learning whether his company might take advantage of any other tax credits offered by the Federal government that might reduce his costs.

Read the chapter and formulate your response.

LO.1

Explain how tax credits are used as a tool of Federal tax policy.

Federal tax law often serves other purposes besides merely raising revenue for the government. Evidence of equity, social, and economic considerations, among others, is found throughout the tax law. These considerations also have considerable import in the area of tax credits. Congress has generally used tax credits to promote social or economic objectives or to work toward greater tax equity among different types of taxpayers. For example, the disabled access credit was enacted to accomplish a social objective: to encourage taxpayers to renovate older buildings so that they would be in compliance with the Americans with Disabilities Act. This Act requires businesses and institutions to make their facilities more accessible to persons with various types of disabilities. As another example, the foreign tax credit, which has been a part of the law for decades, has as its chief purpose the economic and equity objectives of mitigating the burden of multiple taxation on a single stream of income.

A tax credit should not be confused with an income tax deduction. Certain expenditures (e.g., business expenses) are permitted as deductions from gross income in arriving at taxable income. While the tax benefit received from a tax deduction depends on the tax rate, a tax credit is not affected by the tax rate of the taxpayer. All taxpayers can benefit equally when a tax credit is used.

Example 1	Assume that Congress wants to encourage a certain type of expenditure. One way to accomplish this objective is to allow a tax credit of 25% for such expenditures. Another way is to allow a deduction for the expenditures. Assume that Red Corporation's tax rate is 15%, while Blue Corporation's tax rate is 34%. The following tax benefits are available to each corporation for a $1,000 expenditure.

	Red	Blue
Tax benefit if a 25% credit is allowed	$250	$250
Tax benefit if a deduction is allowed	150	340

As these results indicate, tax credits can provide benefits on a more equitable basis than tax deductions often do.

In order to prevent a taxpayer from completely avoiding a Federal income tax liability, the alternative minimum tax (AMT) was introduced into the Code in 1969. To better achieve this objective, the statutory provisions have been amended on multiple occasions through the years. The AMT applicable to corporations is similar to the AMT applicable to individuals. Many of the adjustments and tax preference items necessary to arrive at alternative minimum taxable income (AMTI) are the same. The rates and exemptions are different, but the objective is identical—to force taxpayers that are more profitable than their taxable income reflects to pay additional income taxes.

17-1 BUSINESS-RELATED TAX CREDIT PROVISIONS

LO.2

Work with various business-related tax credits.

17-1a General Business Credit

As shown in Exhibit 17.1, the general business credit is comprised of a number of other credits, each of which is computed separately under its own set of rules. The general business credit combines these credits into one amount to limit the annual credit that can be used to offset a taxpayer's income tax liability. The idea behind combining the credits is to prevent a taxpayer from completely avoiding an income tax liability in any one year by offsetting it with several business credits that would otherwise be available.

Two special rules apply to the general business credit. First, any unused credit is carried back 1 year, then forward 20 years. Second, for any tax year, the

TAX FACT   Where Have All the Credits Gone?

The number of individual income tax returns claiming tax credits has fluctuated over the years, usually due to tax law changes, revenue needs, and political requirements.

Year	Returns Claiming Credits (in Millions)
1975	65.9
1985	21.0
1995	15.2
2000	37.7
2008	55.2
2011	49.6

Source: IRS Tax Statistics.

© iStockphoto.com/Pali Rao

EXHIBIT 17.1	**Principal Components of the General Business Credit**

The general business credit combines (but is not limited to) the following.

- Tax credit for rehabilitation expenditures
- Work opportunity tax credit
- Research activities credit
- Various energy credits
- Low-income housing credit
- Disabled access credit
- Credit for small employer pension plan startup costs
- Credit for employer-provided child care

---

general business credit is limited to the taxpayer's *net income tax* reduced by the greater of:[1]

- The *tentative minimum tax* [see the discussion of the alternative minimum tax (AMT) later in this chapter].
- 25 percent of *net regular tax liability* that exceeds $25,000.[2]

To understand these general business credit limitations, several terms need defining.

- *Net income tax* is the sum of the regular tax liability and the alternative minimum tax reduced by certain nonrefundable tax credits.
- *Tentative minimum tax* is reduced by any foreign tax credit allowed, as specified in Exhibit 17.2 later in this chapter.
- *Regular tax liability* is determined from the appropriate tax table or tax rate schedule based on taxable income. However, the regular tax liability does not include certain taxes (e.g., alternative minimum tax).
- *Net regular tax liability* is the regular tax liability reduced by certain nonrefundable credits (e.g., foreign tax credit).

Tanager Corporation's general business credit for the current year is $70,000. Tanager's net income tax is $150,000, tentative minimum tax is $130,000, and net regular tax liability is $150,000. Tanager has no other tax credits. The general business credit allowed for the tax year is computed as follows.

Example 2

---

[1]§ 38(c). This rule works to keep the general business credit from completely eliminating the tax liability for many taxpayers.

[2]§ 38(c)(3)(B). The $25,000 amount is apportioned among the members of a controlled group.

Net income tax	$ 150,000
Less: The greater of—	
• $130,000 (tentative minimum tax)	
• $31,250 [25% × ($150,000 − $25,000)]	(130,000)
Amount of general business credit allowed for tax year	$ 20,000

Tanager then has $50,000 ($70,000 − $20,000) of unused general business credits that may be carried back or forward.

Treatment of Unused General Business Credits

Unused general business credits are initially carried back one year and reduce the tax liability of that year. Thus, the taxpayer may receive a tax refund as a result of the carryback. Any remaining unused credits are then carried forward 20 years.[3]

A FIFO method is applied to the carryback, carryovers, and utilization of credits earned during a particular year. The oldest credits are used first in determining the amount of the general business credit. The FIFO method minimizes the potential for loss of a general business credit benefit due to the expiration of credit carryovers and generally works to the taxpayer's benefit.

Example 3

This example illustrates the use of general business credit carryovers for the taxpayer's 2014 tax year.

General business credit carryovers (unused in prior tax years)		
2011	$ 4,000	
2012	6,000	
2013	2,000	
Total carryovers	$12,000	
2014 general business credit		$ 40,000
Total credit allowed in 2014 (based on tax liability)	$50,000	
Less: Carryovers used		
2011	(4,000)	
2012	(6,000)	
2013	(2,000)	
Remaining credit allowed in 2014	$38,000	
2014 general business credit used		(38,000)
2014 unused amount carried forward to 2015		$ 2,000

TAX IN THE NEWS   Many Taxpayers Become "Nonpayers" Because of Tax Credits

One of the key domestic policy initiatives of recent administrations has been to reduce marginal tax rates and then retain a lower marginal rate structure than under prior law. Many opponents of this policy have argued that the main beneficiaries of the lower tax rates are upper-income taxpayers who are the most affluent individuals in our country. However, economists have estimated that these policies also have led to more Americans than ever before being relieved of any Federal income tax liability.

Since 2000, the number of "nonpayers" has grown by about 59 percent. In 2008, almost 52 million Americans filed a tax return and did not owe any taxes because of deductions and credits available to them. Thus, more than 36 percent of all filers were "nonpayers." That trend has continued. In 2011, almost 54 million returns were filed without taxes due (almost 37 percent of all filers).

Sources: Based on "Record Number of Tax Filers Paid No Federal Income Taxes in 2008," *Tax Foundation*, March 10, 2010, and Internal Revenue Service Statistics of Income Division data.

---

[3]§ 39(a)(1).

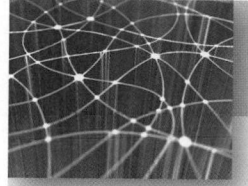

BRIDGE DISCIPLINE Bridge to Finance

When calculating the cash-flow benefit of particular tax attributes and making a decision based on this analysis, an inappropriate decision can be made unless present value analysis is incorporated into the calculation.

The general business credit and the related carryback and carryover provisions can be used to illustrate the cash-flow impact.

Blonde, Inc.'s general business credit for 2014 is $400,000. However, the amount that may be used to reduce the current-year tax liability is only $280,000. None can be used in 2013 (the carryback year), so the $120,000 is carried forward. The $120,000 of unused general business credit is expected to offset Blonde's future tax liability as follows.

2015	$20,000
2016	40,000
2017	60,000

It appears that the cash-flow benefit to Blonde is $400,000. In nominal dollars, this result is correct. However, when the present value concept is applied, the cash-flow benefit is only $376,280 (assuming that Blonde's discount rate is 4 percent).

2014	$280,000 × 1.000	=	$280,000
2015	20,000 × .9615	=	19,230
2016	40,000 × .9246	=	36,984
2017	60,000 × .8890	=	53,340
			$389,554

The carryforward period for the general business credit is 20 years. Using a 4 percent discount rate, one dollar in 20 years is worth about 46 cents ($1 × .4564) today. So taxpayers should use the general business credit to offset tax liability as rapidly as possible.

Most of the various credits that make up the general business credit are discussed in the following paragraphs.

17-1b Tax Credit for Rehabilitation Expenditures

Taxpayers are allowed a tax credit for expenditures incurred to rehabilitate older industrial and commercial buildings and certified historic structures. The **rehabilitation expenditures credit** is intended to discourage businesses from moving from economically distressed areas (e.g., an inner city) to outlying locations and to encourage the preservation of historic structures. The current operating features of this credit follow.[4]

Rate of the Credit for Rehabilitation Expenses	Nature of the Property
10%	Nonresidential buildings and residential rental property, other than certified historic structures, originally placed in service before 1936
20%	Nonresidential and residential certified historic structures

Taxpayers who claim the rehabilitation credit must reduce the basis of the rehabilitated building by the credit allowed.[5]

Return to the facts of *The Big Picture* on p. 17-1. Assume that Progress spends $60,000 to rehabilitate a building (adjusted basis of $40,000) that had been placed in service in 1932. Progress is allowed a credit of $6,000 (10% × $60,000) for rehabilitation expenditures. The corporation then increases the basis of the building by $54,000 [$60,000 (rehabilitation expenditures) − $6,000 (credit allowed)]. If the building were a historic structure, the credit allowed would be $12,000 (20% × $60,000) and the building's depreciable basis would increase by $48,000 [$60,000 (rehabilitation expenditures) − $12,000 (credit allowed)].

---

[4]§ 47.   [5]§ 50(c).

TABLE 17.1	Recapture Calculation for Rehabilitation Expenditures Credit

If the Property Is Held for	The Recapture Percentage Is
Less than 1 year	100
One year or more but less than 2 years	80
Two years or more but less than 3 years	60
Three years or more but less than 4 years	40
Four years or more but less than 5 years	20

To qualify for the credit, buildings must be substantially rehabilitated. A building has been *substantially rehabilitated* if qualified rehabilitation expenditures exceed the *greater of*:

- The adjusted basis of the property before the rehabilitation expenditures, or
- $5,000.

Qualified rehabilitation expenditures do not include the cost of acquiring a building, the cost of facilities related to a building (such as a parking lot), and the cost of enlarging an existing building. Stringent rules apply concerning the retention of the building's original internal and external walls.

Recapture of Tax Credit for Rehabilitation Expenditures

The rehabilitation credit taken is recaptured if the rehabilitated property is disposed of prematurely or if it ceases to be qualifying property. The **rehabilitation expenditures credit recapture** is added to the taxpayer's regular tax liability in the recapture year. The recapture amount also is *added* to the adjusted basis of the building.

The portion of the credit recaptured is a specified percentage of the credit that was taken by the taxpayer. This percentage is based on the period the property was held by the taxpayer, as shown in Table 17.1. If the property is held at least five years, no recapture can result.

Example 5	On March 15, 2011, Chickadee Corporation rehabilitated a building qualifying for the 10% credit. The company spent $30,000 in qualifying rehabilitation expenditures and claimed a $3,000 credit ($30,000 × 10%). The basis of the building was increased by $27,000 ($30,000 − $3,000). Chickadee sold the building on December 15, 2014. Chickadee recaptures a portion of the rehabilitation credit based on the schedule in Table 17.1. Because Chickadee held the rehabilitated property for more than three years but less than four, 40% of the credit, or $1,200, is added to the company's 2014 income tax liability. In addition, the adjusted basis of the building is increased by the $1,200 recapture amount.

17-1c Work Opportunity Tax Credit

The **work opportunity tax credit**[6] was enacted to encourage employers to hire individuals from a variety of targeted and economically disadvantaged groups. Examples of such targeted persons include qualified ex-felons, high-risk youths, food stamp recipients, veterans, summer youth employees, and long-term family assistance recipients.

---

[6]§ 51. The credit is available only if qualifying employees start work by December 31, 2013; Congress is expected to extend this credit and the examples and end-of-chapter materials that follow assume this is the case.

Computation of the Work Opportunity Tax Credit: General

The credit generally is equal to 40 percent of the first $6,000 of wages (per eligible employee) for the first 12 months of employment. The credit is not available for wages paid to an employee after the *first year* of employment. If the employee's first year overlaps two of the employer's tax years, however, the employer may take the credit over two tax years. If the credit is claimed, the employer's tax deduction for wages is reduced by the amount of the credit.

To qualify an employer for the 40 percent credit, the employee must (1) be certified by a designated local agency as being a member of one of the targeted groups and (2) have completed at least 400 hours of service to the employer. If an employee meets the first condition but not the second, the credit is reduced to 25 percent, provided the employee has completed a minimum of 120 hours of service to the employer.

In-depth coverage can be found on this book's companion website: **www.cengagebrain.com**    | Digging Deeper

THE BIG PICTURE
Example 6

Return to the facts of *The Big Picture* on p. 17-1. In January 2014, Progress Corporation hires four individuals who are certified to be members of a qualifying targeted group. Each employee works 1,000 hours and is paid wages of $8,000 during the year. Progress's work opportunity credit is $9,600 [($6,000 × 40%) × 4 employees]. If the tax credit is taken, Progress reduces its deduction for wages paid by $9,600. No credit is available for wages paid to these employees after their first year of employment.

Example 7

On June 1, 2014, Maria, a calendar year taxpayer, hires Joe, a member of a certified group, and obtains the required certification to qualify Maria for the work opportunity credit. During his seven months of work in 2014, Joe is paid $3,500 for 500 hours of work. Maria is allowed a credit of $1,400 ($3,500 × 40%) for 2014.

Joe continues to work for Maria in 2015 and is paid $7,000 through May 31, 2015. Because up to $6,000 of first year wages are eligible for the credit, Maria is also allowed a 40% credit on $2,500 [$6,000 − $3,500 (wages paid in 2014)] of 2015 wages paid, or $1,000 ($2,500 × 40%). None of Joe's wages paid after May 31, 2015, the end of the first year of employment, are eligible for the credit.

Computation of the Work Opportunity Tax Credit: Long-Term Family Assistance Recipient

The credit[7] is available to employers hiring individuals who have been long-term recipients of family assistance welfare benefits. In general, *long-term recipients* are those individuals who are certified by a designated local agency as being members of a family receiving assistance under a public aid program for the 18-month period ending on the hiring date. Unlike the work opportunity credit for other targeted groups, which applies only to first-year wages paid to qualified individuals, the credit is available for qualified wages paid in the first *two years* of employment if the employee is a long-term family assistance recipient. If an employee's first and second work years overlap two or more of the employer's tax years, the employer may take the credit during the applicable tax years.

The credit is equal to 40 percent of the first $10,000 of qualified wages paid to an employee in the first year of employment plus 50 percent of the first $10,000 of

---

[7]Prior to 2007, this component of the work opportunity tax credit was called the welfare-to-work credit, provided for under § 51A. Under current law, long-term family assistance recipients are a designated targeted group under the work opportunity tax credit, and the maximum credit is now slightly more generous than under prior law. § 51(d)(1)(I).

qualified wages in the second year of employment, resulting in a maximum credit per qualified employee of $9,000 [$4,000 (year 1) + $5,000 (year 2)]. The credit rate is higher for second-year wages to encourage employers to retain qualified individuals, thereby promoting the overall welfare-to-work goal.

Example 8	In April 2014, Blue hires three individuals who are certified as long-term family assistance recipients. Each employee is paid $12,000 during 2014. Two of the three individuals continue to work for Blue in 2015, earning $9,000 each during the year. Blue's work opportunity tax credit is $12,000 [(40% × $10,000) × 3 employees] for 2014 and $9,000 [(50% × $9,000) × 2 employees] for 2015. In each year, Blue must reduce its deduction for wages paid by the amount of the credit for that year.

17-1d Research Activities Credit

To encourage research and development (R & D) in the U.S. business community, a credit is allowed for certain qualifying expenditures paid or incurred by a taxpayer. The **research activities credit** is the *sum* of three components: (1) an incremental research activities credit, (2) a basic research credit, and (3) an energy research credit.[8]

Incremental Research Activities Credit

The incremental research activities credit applies at a 20 percent rate to the *excess* of qualified research expenses for the taxable year (the credit year) over a base amount.[9]

In general, *research expenditures* qualify if the research relates to discovering technological information that is intended for use in the development of a new or improved business component of the taxpayer. Such expenses qualify fully if the research is performed in-house (by the taxpayer or its employees). If the research is conducted by persons outside the taxpayer's business (under contract), only 65 percent of the amount paid qualifies for the credit.[10]

Example 9	Bobwhite Company incurs the following research expenditures: In-house wages, supplies, computer time ..... $50,000 Payment to Cutting Edge Scientific Foundation for research ..... 30,000 Bobwhite's qualified research expenditures are $69,500 [$50,000 + ($30,000 × 65%)].

Beyond the general guidelines described above, the Code does not give specific examples of qualifying research. However, the credit is *not* allowed for research that falls into certain categories, including the following.[11]

- Research conducted after the beginning of commercial production of the business component.
- Surveys and studies such as market research, testing, or routine data collection.
- Research conducted *outside* the United States (other than research undertaken in Puerto Rico or possessions of the United States).
- Research in the social sciences, arts, or humanities.

Determining the *base amount* involves a relatively complex series of computations meant to approximate recent historical levels of research activity by the taxpayer. Thus, the credit is allowed only for increases in research expenses.

---

[8]§ 41. Each component of the research credit is available only if qualifying expenditures are paid or incurred by December 31, 2013; Congress is expected to extend this credit and the examples and end-of-chapter materials that follow assume this is the case.

[9]In lieu of determining the incremental research credit as described here, a taxpayer may elect to calculate the credit using an alternative simplified credit procedure. See §§ 41(c)(4) and (5).

[10]§ 41(b)(3)(A). In the case of payments to a qualified research consortium, § 41(b)(3)(A) provides that 75% of the amount paid qualifies for the credit. In contrast, for amounts paid to an energy research consortium, § 41(b)(3)(D) allows the full amount to qualify for the credit.

[11]§ 41(d).

Hawk, Inc., a calendar year taxpayer, incurs qualifying research expenditures of $200,000 during the year. If the base amount is $100,000, the incremental research activities credit is $20,000 [($200,000 − $100,000) × 20%].	**Example 10**

Qualified research and experimentation expenditures not only are eligible for the 20 percent credit but also can be *expensed* in the year incurred. In this regard, a taxpayer has two choices.[12]

- Use the full credit and reduce the expense deduction for research expenses by 100 percent of the credit.
- Retain the full expense deduction and reduce the credit by the product of the full credit times the maximum corporate tax rate (35 percent).

As an alternative to the expense deduction, the taxpayer may *capitalize* the research expenses and *amortize* them over 60 months or more. In this case, the amount capitalized and subject to amortization is reduced by the full amount of the credit *only* if the credit exceeds the amount allowable as a deduction.

Assume the same facts as in Example 10, which shows that the potential incremental research activities credit is $20,000. In the current year, the amounts Hawk can deduct and the credit amount under each of the three choices are computed as follows.	**Example 11**

	Credit Amount	Deduction Amount
• Full credit and reduced deduction		
$20,000 − $0	$20,000	
$200,000 − $20,000		$180,000
• Reduced credit and full deduction		
$20,000 − [(100% × $20,000) × 35%]	13,000	
$200,000 − $0		200,000
• Full credit and capitalize and elect to amortize costs over 60 months		
$20,000 − $0	20,000	
($200,000/60) × 12		40,000

The value of the deduction depends on Hawk's marginal tax rates.

Basic Research Credit

Corporations (other than S corporations or personal service corporations) are allowed an additional 20 percent credit for basic research expenditures incurred, in *excess* of a base amount.[13] This credit is not available to individual taxpayers. *Basic research expenditures* are defined as amounts paid in cash to a qualified basic research organization, such as a college or university or a tax-exempt organization operated primarily to conduct scientific research.

Basic research is defined generally as any original investigation for the advancement of scientific knowledge not having a specific commercial objective. The definition excludes basic research conducted outside the United States and basic research in the social sciences, arts, or humanities.

Energy Research Credit

This component of the research credit is intended to stimulate additional energy research. The calculation of the credit is relatively straightforward; it is equal to 20 percent of the amounts paid or incurred by a taxpayer to an energy research consortium for energy research.

---

[12]§§ 174 and 280C(c). Recall the discussion of rules for deducting research and experimental expenditures in Chapter 5.

[13]§ 41(e).

17-1e Energy Credits

The Internal Revenue Code contains a variety of credits for businesses and individuals to encourage the conservation of natural resources and the development of energy sources other than oil and gas. The primary goals of the tax provisions are to improve energy-related infrastructure and encourage higher levels of energy conservation.

Some of the more widely applicable provisions include credits for:

- Builders who construct energy-efficient homes.
- Individuals who make energy-saving improvements to their residences.
- Manufacturers that make energy-efficient appliances.
- Businesses that buy fuel cell and microturbine power plants.
- Taxpayers who purchase alternative power motor vehicles and refueling property.

Like many other tax credits, the **energy credits** have been designed to modify taxpayer behavior. More specifically, in this case, Congress's intention is that these credits will lead to greater conservation and more efficient use of energy.

Digging Deeper   2   In-depth coverage can be found on this book's companion website: **www.cengagebrain.com**

17-1f Disabled Access Credit

The **disabled access credit** is designed to encourage small businesses to make their facilities more accessible to disabled individuals. The credit is available for any eligible access expenditures paid or incurred by an eligible small business. The credit is calculated at the rate of 50 percent of the eligible expenditures that exceed $250 but do not exceed $10,250. Thus, the maximum amount for the credit is $5,000 ($10,000 × 50%).[14]

An *eligible small business* is a business that during the previous year either had gross receipts of $1 million or less or had no more than 30 full-time employees. A sole proprietorship, a partnership, a regular corporation, or an S corporation can qualify as such an entity.

Eligible access expenditures generally include any reasonable and necessary amounts that are paid or incurred to make certain changes to facilities. These changes must involve the removal of architectural, communication, physical, or transportation barriers that would otherwise make a business inaccessible to disabled and handicapped individuals. Examples of qualifying projects include installing ramps, widening doorways, and adding raised markings on elevator control buttons. The improved facility must have been placed into service prior to November 5, 1990.

To the extent a disabled access credit is available, no deduction or credit is allowed under any other provision of the tax law. The asset's adjusted basis is reduced by the amount of the credit.

Example 12   This year, Red, Inc., an eligible business, makes $11,000 of capital improvements to business realty that had been placed in service in June 1990. The expenditures are intended to make Red's business more accessible to the disabled and are considered eligible expenditures for purposes of the disabled access credit. The amount of the credit is $5,000 [($10,250 maximum − $250 floor) × 50%]. The depreciable basis of the capital improvement is $6,000 [$11,000 (cost) − $5,000 (amount of the credit)].

17-1g Credit for Small Employer Pension Plan Startup Costs

Small businesses are entitled to a nonrefundable credit for administrative costs associated with establishing and maintaining certain qualified retirement plans.[15] While such costs (e.g., payroll system changes and consulting fees) generally are

---

[14]§ 44.   [15]§ 45E.

deductible as ordinary and necessary business expenses, the credit is intended to lower the after-tax cost of establishing a qualified retirement program and thereby to encourage qualifying businesses to offer retirement plans for their employees.

The **credit for small employer pension plan startup costs** is available for eligible employers at the rate of 50 percent of qualified startup costs. An eligible employer is one with fewer than 100 employees who have earned at least $5,000 of compensation. The maximum credit is $500 (based on a maximum $1,000 of qualifying expenses), and the deduction for the startup costs incurred is reduced by the amount of the credit. The credit can be claimed for qualifying costs incurred in each of the three years beginning with the tax year in which the retirement plan becomes effective (maximum total credit of $1,500).

Maple Company decides to establish a qualified retirement plan for its employees. In the process, it pays consulting fees of $1,200 to a firm that will provide educational seminars to Maple's employees and will assist the payroll department in making necessary changes to the payroll system. Maple may claim a credit for the pension plan startup costs of $500 ($1,200 of qualifying costs, limited to $1,000 × 50%), and its deduction for these expenses is reduced to $700 ($1,200 − $500).

Example 13

17-1h Credit for Employer-Provided Child Care

An employer can deduct expenditures incurred to provide for the care of children of employees as ordinary and necessary business expenses. Alternatively, employers may claim a credit for qualifying expenditures incurred while providing child care facilities to their employees during normal working hours.[16]

The **credit for employer-provided child care**, limited annually to $150,000, is composed of the aggregate of two components: 25 percent of qualified child care expenses and 10 percent of qualified child care resource and referral services. *Qualified child care expenses* include the costs of acquiring, constructing, rehabilitating, expanding, and operating a child care facility. *Child care resource and referral services* include amounts paid or incurred under a contract to provide child care resource and referral services to an employee.

Any qualifying expenses otherwise deductible by the taxpayer are reduced by the amount of the credit. In addition, the taxpayer's basis for any property acquired or constructed and used for qualifying purposes is reduced by the amount of the credit. If within 10 years of being placed in service a child care facility ceases to be used for a qualified use, the taxpayer recaptures a portion of the credit previously claimed.[17]

THE BIG PICTURE

Example 14

Return to the facts of *The Big Picture* on p. 17-1. During the year, Progress Corporation constructs a child care facility for $400,000 to be used by its employees who have pre-school-aged children in need of child care services while their parents are at work. In addition, Progress incurs salaries for child care workers and other administrative costs associated with the facility of $100,000 during the year. As a result, Progress's credit for employer-provided child care is $125,000 [($400,000 + $100,000) × 25%]. Correspondingly, the basis of the facility is reduced to $300,000 ($400,000 − $100,000), and the deduction for salaries and administrative costs is reduced to $75,000 ($100,000 − $25,000).

In-depth coverage can be found on this book's companion website: **www.cengagebrain.com**    **3**   Digging Deeper

---

[16]§ 45F.   [17]§ 45F(d).

Global Tax Issues

© iStockphoto.com/Andrey Prokhorov

Sourcing Income in Cyberspace—Getting It Right When Calculating the Foreign Tax Credit

The overall limitation on the foreign tax credit plays a critical role in restricting the amount of the credit available to a taxpayer. In the overall limitation formula, the taxpayer must characterize the year's taxable income as either earned (or sourced) inside or outside the United States. As a general rule, a relatively greater percentage of foreign-source income in the formula leads to a larger foreign tax credit. But classifying income as either foreign or U.S. source is not always a simple matter.

The existing income-sourcing rules were developed long before the existence of the Internet, and taxing authorities are finding it challenging to apply these rules to Internet transactions. Where does a sale take place when the web server is in Scotland, the seller is in India, and the customer is in Illinois? Where is a service performed when all activities take place over the Net? These questions and more must be answered by the United States and its trading partners as the Internet economy grows in size and importance.

17-1i Foreign Tax Credit

Both individual taxpayers and corporations may claim a credit for foreign income tax paid on income earned and subject to tax in another country or a U.S. possession.[18] The purpose of the **foreign tax credit (FTC)** is to reduce the possibility of double taxation of foreign income.

| **Example 15** | Ace Tools, Inc., a U.S. corporation, has a branch operation in Mexico, from which it earns taxable income of $750,000 for the current year. Ace pays income tax of $150,000 on these earnings to the Mexican tax authorities. Ace must also include the $750,000 in gross income for U.S. tax purposes.

Before considering the FTC, Ace owes $255,000 in U.S. income taxes on this foreign-source income. Thus, total taxes on the $750,000 could equal $405,000 ($150,000 + $255,000), a 54% effective rate. But Ace takes the FTC of $150,000 against its U.S. tax liability on the foreign-source income. Ace Tools' total taxes on the $750,000 now are $255,000 ($150,000 + $105,000), a 34% effective rate. |
|---|---|

The tax year's FTC equals the *lesser* of the foreign taxes imposed or the *overall limitation* determined according to the following formula. Thus, where applicable foreign tax rates exceed those of the United States, the credit offsets no more than the marginal U.S. tax on the double-taxed income.

$$\frac{\text{Foreign-source taxable income}}{\text{Worldwide taxable income}} \times \text{U.S. tax before FTC}$$

Foreign taxes paid but not allowed as a credit due to the overall limitation are carried back 1 tax year and then forward 10 years.[19]

| **Example 16** | Oriole, Inc., a U.S. corporation, conducts business in a foreign country. Oriole's worldwide taxable income for the tax year is $120,000, consisting of $100,000 in income from U.S. operations and $20,000 of income from the foreign source. Foreign tax of $6,000 was paid to foreign tax authorities on the $20,000. Before the FTC, Oriole's U.S. tax on the $120,000 is $30,050.

The corporation's FTC is $5,008 {lesser of $6,000 paid or $5,008 limitation [$30,050 × ($20,000/$120,000)]}. Oriole's net U.S. tax liability is $25,042 ($30,050 − $5,008). Thus, Oriole carries over (back 1 year and forward 10 years) a $992 FTC ($6,000 − $5,008) because of the overall limitation. |
|---|---|

---

[18]§ 27 provides for the credit, but the qualifications and calculation procedure for the credit are contained in §§ 901–908. Alternatively, the taxpayer can *deduct* the foreign taxes paid.

[19]§ 904(c).

CONCEPT SUMMARY 17.1

Tax Credits

Credit	Computation	Comments
General business (§ 38)	May not exceed net income tax minus the greater of tentative minimum tax or 25% of net regular tax liability that exceeds $25,000.	Components include tax credit for rehabilitation expenditures, work opportunity tax credit, research activities credit, low-income housing credit, disabled access credit, credit for small employer pension plan startup costs, and credit for employer-provided child care.
		Unused credit may be carried back 1 year and forward 20 years. FIFO method applies to carrybacks, carryovers, and credits earned during current year.
Rehabilitation expenditures (§ 47)	Qualifying investment times rehabilitation percentage, depending on type of property. Regular rehabilitation rate is 10%; rate for certified historic structures is 20%.	Part of general business credit and therefore subject to same carryback, carryover, and FIFO rules. Purpose is to discourage businesses from moving from economically distressed areas to new locations.
Work opportunity (§ 51)	Credit is limited to 40% of the first $6,000 of wages paid to each eligible employee. For long-term family assistance recipients, credit is limited to 40% of first $10,000 of wages paid to each eligible employee in first year of employment, plus 50% of first $10,000 of wages paid to same employee in second year of employment.	Part of the general business credit and therefore subject to the same carryback, carryover, and FIFO rules. Purpose is to encourage employment of members of economically disadvantaged groups.
Research activities (§ 41)	Incremental credit is 20% of excess of computation-year expenditures over a base amount. Basic research credit is allowed to certain corporations for 20% of cash payments to qualified organizations that exceed a specially calculated base amount. An energy research credit is allowed for 20% of qualifying payments made to an energy research consortium.	Part of general business credit and therefore subject to same carryback, carryover, and FIFO rules. Purpose is to encourage high-tech and energy research in the United States.
Low-income housing (§ 42)	Appropriate rate times eligible basis (portion of project attributable to low-income units).	Part of general business credit and therefore subject to same carryback, carryover, and FIFO rules. Recapture may apply. Purpose is to encourage construction of housing for low-income individuals. Credit is available each year for 10 years.
Energy credits	Various items to encourage individuals and businesses to "go green."	Part of general business credit and therefore subject to same carryback, carryover, and FIFO rules.
Disabled access (§ 44)	Credit is 50% of eligible access expenditures that exceed $250 but do not exceed $10,250. Maximum credit is $5,000.	Part of general business credit and therefore subject to same carryback, carryover, and FIFO rules. Purpose is to encourage small businesses to become more accessible to disabled individuals. Available only to eligible small businesses.

Tax Credits—Continued

Credit	Computation	Comments
Credit for small employer pension plan startup costs (§ 45E)	The credit equals 50% of qualified startup costs incurred by eligible employers. Maximum annual credit is $500. Deduction for related expenses is reduced by the amount of the credit.	Part of general business credit and therefore subject to same carryback, carryover, and FIFO rules. Purpose is to encourage small employers to establish qualified retirement plans for their employees.
Credit for employer-provided child care (§ 45F)	Credit is equal to 25% of qualified child care expenses plus 10% of qualified expenses for child care resource and referral services. Maximum credit is $150,000. Deduction for related expenses or basis must be reduced by the amount of the credit.	Part of general business credit and therefore subject to same carryback, carryover, and FIFO rules. Purpose is to encourage employers to provide child care for their employees' children during normal working hours.
Foreign tax (§ 27)	Foreign taxable income/total worldwide taxable income × U.S. tax = overall limitation. Lesser of foreign taxes imposed or overall limitation.	Unused credits may be carried back 1 year and forward 10 years. Purpose is to reduce double taxation of foreign income.

17-2 CORPORATE ALTERNATIVE MINIMUM TAX

LO.3

Explain the reason for the alternative minimum tax.

A perception that many large corporations were not paying their fair share of Federal income tax was especially widespread in the early 1980s. A study released in 1986 reported that 130 of the 250 largest corporations in the United States (e.g., Reynolds Metals, General Dynamics, Georgia Pacific, and Texas Commerce Bankshares) paid no Federal tax, or received refunds, in at least one year between 1981 and 1985. Political pressure subsequently led to the adoption of an **alternative minimum tax (AMT)** to ensure that corporations with substantial economic income pay at least a minimum amount of Federal taxes.

The AMT limits the tax savings for some taxpayers who are seen as gaining "too much" from exclusions, deductions, and credits available under the law. A separate tax system with a proportional tax rate is applied each year to a corporation's economic income. If the tentative AMT is greater than the regular corporate income tax, then the corporation must pay the regular tax plus this excess, the AMT.

Since its inception, the AMT has been vulnerable to criticisms that it is too complex. Smaller corporations especially find that the imposition of a second tax structure unduly increases their compliance burdens. Thus, under current rules, most smaller corporations are not subject to the AMT at all. A corporation is exempted from the AMT if it meets the following tests:

- It was treated as a small corporation exempt from the AMT for all prior years beginning after 1997.
- Its annual average gross receipts for the three-year period (or portion thereof during which the corporation was in existence) ending before its current tax year did not exceed $7.5 million ($5 million if the corporation had only one prior tax year).

This provision exempts up to 95 percent of all C corporations from the AMT. A corporation *automatically* is classified as a small corporation in the first tax year of existence. A corporation that fails these tests *never* (other than the first year exception) can be exempt from the AMT.

17-2a The AMT Formula

The AMT is imposed in addition to the regular corporate income tax, but is computed in a manner wholly separate and independent from it.[20] The AMT is a parallel income tax system that generally uses more conservative accounting methods than the regular income tax. Typically, more items are subject to tax under AMT rules, some gross income items are accelerated, and some deductions are deferred.

The formula for determining the AMT liability of corporate taxpayers appears in Exhibit 17.2 and follows the format of Form 4626 (Alternative Minimum Tax—Corporations).

The base for the AMT, alternative minimum taxable income (AMTI), begins with regular taxable income before any deductions for net operating losses (NOLs). A series of adjustments then is made. Most AMT adjustments relate to *timing differences* that arise because of separate regular income tax and AMT treatments. Adjustments that are caused by timing differences eventually reverse; that is, positive adjustments are offset by negative adjustments in the future, and vice versa.

The adjustments related to *circulation expenditures* illustrate this concept. Circulation expenditures include expenses incurred to establish, maintain, or increase the circulation of a newspaper, a magazine, or other periodical.

In computing *taxable income*, corporations that are personal holding companies are allowed to deduct circulation expenditures in the year incurred. In computing AMTI, however, these expenditures must be capitalized and amortized ratably over the three-year period beginning with the year in which the expenditures were made.

Example 17

Bobwhite, Inc., a personal holding company, incurred circulation expenditures of $30,000 in 2014. For regular income tax purposes, Bobwhite deducts $30,000 in 2014. For AMT purposes, the corporation is required to capitalize the expenditures and amortize them over a three-year period. Therefore, the deduction for AMT purposes is only $10,000. The AMT adjustment for 2014 is computed as follows.

Circulation expenditures deducted for regular income tax purposes	$ 30,000
Circulation expenditures deducted for AMT purposes	(10,000)
AMT adjustment (positive)	$ 20,000

EXHIBIT 17.2	AMT Formula for Corporations

Regular taxable income before NOL deduction		
Plus/minus:		AMT adjustments (except ACE adjustment)
Plus:		Tax preferences
	Equals:	AMTI before AMT NOL deduction and ACE adjustment
Plus/minus:		ACE adjustment
	Equals:	AMTI before AMT NOL deduction
Minus:		AMT NOL deduction (limited to 90%)
	Equals:	Alternative minimum taxable income (AMTI)
Minus:		Exemption
	Equals:	AMT base
Times:		20% rate
	Equals:	Tentative AMT before credits
Minus:		AMT foreign tax credit and other credits
	Equals:	Tentative minimum tax
Minus:		Regular income tax liability before credits minus regular foreign tax credit
	Equals:	Alternative minimum tax (AMT) if positive

---

[20]The AMT provisions are contained in §§ 55 through 59.

Example 18

Assume the same facts as in Example 17. The timing difference that gave rise to the positive adjustment in 2014 will reverse in the future. For AMT purposes, Bobwhite will deduct $10,000 in 2015 and $10,000 in 2016. The regular income tax deduction for circulation expenditures in each of those years will be $0, because the entire $30,000 expenditure was deducted in 2014. This results in a negative AMT adjustment of $10,000 each in 2015 and 2016. The AMT adjustments over the three-year period are summarized below.

Year	Regular Income Tax Deduction	AMT Deduction	AMT Adjustment
2014	$30,000	$10,000	$ 20,000
2015	–0–	10,000	(10,000)
2016	–0–	10,000	(10,000)
Totals	$30,000	$30,000	$ –0–

Timing differences eventually reverse. Thus, positive AMT adjustments can be offset later by negative adjustments.

17-2b Tax Preferences

LO.4

Identify and calculate the tax preferences that are included in determining the AMT.

AMTI includes designated **tax preference items**. In many cases, this part of the AMT formula has the effect of subjecting otherwise nontaxable income to the AMT. Tax preferences always increase AMTI. Some of the principal tax preferences are discussed on the following pages.

Percentage Depletion

Congress originally enacted the percentage depletion rules to provide taxpayers with incentives to invest in the development of specified natural resources. Percentage depletion is computed by multiplying a rate specified in the Code times the gross income from the property (refer to Chapter 5). The percentage rate is based on the type of mineral involved. The basis of the property is reduced by the amount of depletion taken until the basis reaches zero. However, once the basis of the property reaches zero, taxpayers are allowed to continue taking percentage depletion deductions. Thus, over the life of the property, depletion deductions may greatly exceed the cost of the property.

The percentage depletion preference is equal to the excess of the regular income tax deduction for percentage depletion over the adjusted basis of the property at the end of the taxable year.[21] Basis is determined without regard to the depletion deduction for the taxable year. This preference item is figured separately for each piece of property for which the taxpayer is claiming depletion.

Example 19

Finch, Inc., owns a mineral property that qualifies for a 22% depletion rate. The basis of the property at the beginning of the year is $10,000. Gross income from the property for the year is $100,000. For regular income tax purposes, Finch's percentage depletion deduction (assume that it is not limited by taxable income from the property) is $22,000. For AMT purposes, Finch has a tax preference of $12,000 ($22,000− $10,000).

Interest on Private Activity Bonds

Income from private activity bonds is not included in taxable income, and expenses related to carrying such bonds are not deductible for regular income

---

[21]§ 57(a)(1). Percentage depletion on oil and gas wells taken by independent producers and royalty owners does not create an AMT preference. See § 613A(c).

TAX IN THE NEWS   The AMT—Then and Now

The AMT was enacted to target wealthy individuals who, because of numerous legitimate tax minimization strategies, paid little or no Federal income tax. However, over time, more and more middle-class taxpayers were subject to the AMT. According to the Tax Policy Center, the number of taxpayers subject to the AMT grew from about 20,000 in 1970 to nearly 4 million in 2011. What explains the increased numbers of middle-class taxpayers subject to the AMT?

When enacted, the AMT exemption amount was not indexed to inflation. As a result, as incomes increased and the exemption amount stayed the same, more taxpayers were subject to the AMT. To try to limit the reach of the AMT to wealthy taxpayers, Congress had regularly increased the AMT exemption amount. Usually very near the end of the year and using what was often referred to as the AMT "patch," Congress would increase the individual exemption amount to prevent inflation from subjecting taxpayers to the AMT. As part of the tax legislation that emerged in 2012 to moderate the effects of the fiscal cliff, a patch will no longer be needed. Beginning in 2013, both the exemption amount and the dollar amount dividing the 26 and 28 percent tax rates are permanently indexed to inflation.

From a tax revenue perspective, indexing the exemption amount to inflation is not free. The Joint Committee on Taxation estimates that indexing the exemption to inflation will cost $1.8 billion over the next decade.

Sources: **www.taxpolicycenter.org/taxtopics/AMT.cfm**; The Joint Committee on Taxation Report: JCX-1-13.

© iStockphoto.com/Andrey Prokhorov

tax purposes. However, interest on private activity bonds usually is included as a preference in computing AMTI. Expenses incurred in carrying the bonds are offset against the interest income in computing the tax preference.[22] However, interest on private activity bonds that were issued in 2009 or 2010 is not a tax preference.

The Code contains a lengthy, complex definition of **private activity bonds**.[23] In general, such debt is issued by states or municipalities, but more than 10 percent of the proceeds are used to benefit private business. For example, a bond issued by a city whose proceeds are used to construct a factory that is leased to a private business at a favorable rate is a private activity bond.

The vast majority of tax-exempt bonds issued by states and municipalities are not classified as private activity bonds. Therefore, the interest income from such bonds is not a tax preference item.

In-depth coverage can be found on this book's companion website: **www.cengagebrain.com**   **4**   Digging Deeper

17-2c AMT Adjustments

As Exhibit 17.2 indicates, the starting point for computing AMTI is the taxable income of the corporation before any NOL deduction. Certain *adjustments* must be made to this amount. Unlike tax preference items, which always increase AMTI, the adjustments may be either increases or decreases to taxable income.

Although NOLs are listed separately in Exhibit 17.2, they are actually negative adjustments. They are listed separately in Exhibit 17.2 and on the AMT tax form because they may not exceed more than 90 percent of AMTI. Thus, such adjustments cannot be determined until all other adjustments and tax preference items are considered.

LO.5

Identify and calculate AMT adjustments.

---

[22]§ 57(a)(5).   [23]§ 141.

© tuuljumala/Shutterstock.com

TAX IN THE NEWS   The AMT: From 155 Individuals to Millions

Often, the tax law is changed to prevent or reduce certain perceived abuses. Such was the case when the AMT was enacted in 1969. The identifiable perceived abuse was that 155 individual taxpayers had zero Federal income tax liability despite having incomes in excess of $200,000.

Thus, the original idea behind the AMT was one of fairness, based on the premise that taxpayers with significant economic income should pay at least a minimum amount of tax. Although this idea has not changed, the tax is fast becoming anything but fair, according to most observers. That same concept of fairness later led Nina Olsen, the IRS's Taxpayer Advocate, to identify the expanding scope of the AMT as the number one problem facing taxpayers that needs to be legislatively addressed. The American Taxpayer Relief Act of 2012 addressed a portion of the concerns raised by increasing the individual AMT exemption amounts and adjusting them for inflation.

Yet, the AMT still applies to a large number of taxpayers—about 4 million in 2013. What has caused this shift in what is deemed fair? The idea that taxpayers with significant economic income should pay at least a minimum amount of tax has not changed. Thus, a tax that was perceived as fair when it affected only a "few" now is perceived as unfair because it affects "many."

Computing Adjustments

It is necessary to determine not only the amount of an adjustment but also whether the adjustment is positive or negative. Careful study of Examples 17 and 18 reveals the following pattern with regard to *deductions*.

- If the deduction allowed for regular income tax purposes exceeds the deduction allowed for AMT purposes, the difference is a positive adjustment.
- If the deduction allowed for AMT purposes exceeds the deduction allowed for regular income tax purposes, the difference is a negative adjustment.

Conversely, the direction of an adjustment attributable to an *income* item can be determined as follows.

- If the income reported for regular income tax purposes exceeds the income reported for AMT purposes, the difference is a negative adjustment.
- If the income reported for AMT purposes exceeds the income reported for regular income tax purposes, the difference is a positive adjustment.

The principal AMT adjustments are discussed next. The adjustment for circulation expenditures was discussed previously.

Depreciation of Post-1986 Real Property

Tax legislation enacted in 1997 eliminated the AMT depreciation adjustment for real property by providing that the MACRS recovery periods (see Table 5.3) used in calculating the regular income tax apply in calculating the AMT. Note, however, that this AMT recovery period conformity provision applies only to property placed in service after 1998.[24] Thus, the AMT depreciation adjustment discussed below applies only for real property placed in service before 1999.

For real property placed in service after 1986 (MACRS property) and before 1999, AMT depreciation is computed under the alternative depreciation system (ADS), which uses the straight-line method over a 40-year life. The depreciation lives for regular income tax purposes are 27.5 years for residential rental property and 39 years for all other real property.[25] The difference between AMT depreciation and regular income tax depreciation is treated as an adjustment in computing

---

[24]§ 56(a)(1)(A)(i).

[25]The 39-year life generally applies to nonresidential real property placed in service on or after May 13, 1993.

the AMT. The differences will be positive during the regular income tax life of the asset because the cost is written off over a shorter period for regular income tax purposes. For example, during the 27.5-year income tax life of residential real property, the regular income tax depreciation will exceed the AMT depreciation because AMT depreciation is computed over a 40-year period.

Table 5.3 is used to compute regular income tax depreciation on real property placed in service after 1986. For AMT purposes, depreciation on real property placed in service after 1986 and before 1999 is computed under the ADS (refer to Table 5.7).

Example 20

In January 1998, Robin Rentals placed in service a residential building that cost $100,000. Regular income tax depreciation, AMT depreciation, and the AMT adjustment are as follows.

Year	Depreciation		AMT Adjustment
	Regular Income Tax	AMT	
1998	$ 3,485[1]	$ 2,396[2]	$ 1,089
1999–2013	54,540[3]	37,500[4]	17,040
2014	3,636	2,500	1,136
Total	$61,661	$42,396	$19,265

[1] $100,000 cost × 3.485% (Table 5.3) = $3,485
[2] $100,000 cost × 2.396% (Table 5.7) = $2,396
[3] $100,000 cost × 3.636% (Table 5.3) = $3,636 for each year
[4] $100,000 cost × 2.500% (Table 5.7) = $2,500 for each year

If the building had been placed in service after 1998, there would have been no AMT depreciation adjustment for the tax year it was placed in service or for subsequent years. The depreciation for the tax year the building was placed in service for both regular income tax purposes and AMT purposes would have been $3,485 ($100,000 × 3.485%).

After real property placed in service before 1999 has been held for the entire depreciation period for regular income tax purposes, the asset is fully depreciated. However, the depreciation period under the ADS is 41 years due to application of the mid-month convention, so depreciation will continue for AMT purposes. This causes negative adjustments after the property has been fully depreciated for regular income tax purposes.

Example 21

Assume the same facts as in the previous example for the building placed in service in 1998. Regular income tax depreciation in the year 2027 (the thirtieth year of the asset's life) is zero (refer to Table 5.3). AMT depreciation is $2,500 ($100,000 cost × 2.500% from Table 5.7). Therefore, Robin has a negative AMT adjustment of $2,500 ($0 regular income tax depreciation – $2,500 AMT depreciation).

After real property is fully depreciated for both regular income tax and AMT purposes, the positive and negative adjustments that have been made for AMT purposes will net to zero.

Depreciation of Post-1986 Personal Property

For most personal property placed in service after 1986 (MACRS property), the MACRS deduction for regular income tax purposes is based on the 200 percent declining-balance method with a switch to straight-line when that method produces a larger depreciation deduction for the asset. Refer to Table 5.1 for computing regular income tax depreciation.

For AMT purposes, the taxpayer must use the ADS for such property placed in service before 1999. This method is based on the 150 percent declining-balance method with a similar switch to straight-line for all personal property.[26] Refer to Table 5.5 for percentages to be used in computing AMT depreciation.

The MACRS deduction for personal property is larger than the ADS deduction in the early years of an asset's life. However, the ADS deduction is larger in the later years. This is so because ADS lives are sometimes longer than MACRS lives and use less accelerated depreciation methods.[27] Over the ADS life of the asset, the same aggregate amount of depreciation is deducted for both regular income tax and AMT purposes. In the same manner as other timing adjustments, the AMT adjustments for depreciation will net to zero over the ADS life of the asset.

The taxpayer may elect to use the ADS for regular income tax purposes. If this election is made, no AMT adjustment is required because the depreciation deduction is the same for regular income tax and for the AMT. The election eliminates the burden of maintaining two sets of tax depreciation records at the cost of a higher regular tax liability.

For personal property placed in service after 1998, MACRS recovery periods are used in calculating AMT depreciation, but the 150 percent declining-balance method still is used. Thus, if the taxpayer elects to use the 150 percent declining-balance method for regular income tax purposes, there are no AMT adjustments. Conversely, if the taxpayer uses the 200 percent declining-balance method for regular income tax purposes, there is an AMT adjustment for depreciation.

Pollution Control Facilities

For regular income tax purposes, the cost of certified pollution control facilities may be amortized over a period of 60 months. For AMT purposes, the cost of these facilities placed in service after 1986 and before 1999 is depreciated under the ADS over the appropriate class life, determined as explained previously for depreciation of post-1986 property.[28] The required adjustment for AMTI is the difference between the amortization deduction allowed for regular income tax purposes and the depreciation deduction computed under the ADS. The adjustment may be positive or negative.

The AMT adjustment for pollution control facilities is reduced for property placed in service after 1998. This reduction is achieved by providing conformity in the recovery periods used for regular income tax purposes and AMT purposes (MACRS recovery periods).

Digging Deeper   5   In-depth coverage can be found on this book's companion website: **www.cengagebrain.com**

Use of Completed Contract Method of Accounting

For a long-term contract, taxpayers are required to use the percentage of completion method for AMT purposes.[29] However, in limited circumstances, taxpayers can use the

---

[26]§ 56(a)(1).

[27]Class lives and recovery periods are established for all assets in Rev.Proc. 87–56, 1987–2 C.B. 674.

[28]§ 56(a)(5).

[29]§ 56(a)(3).

completed contract method for regular income tax purposes.[30] The resulting AMT adjustment is equal to the difference between income reported under the percentage of completion method and the amount reported using the completed contract method.[31] The adjustment can be either positive or negative, depending on the amount of income recognized under the different methods.

A taxpayer can avoid an AMT adjustment on long-term contracts by using the percentage of completion method for regular income tax purposes rather than the completed contract method.

Adjusted Gain or Loss

When property is sold during the year or a casualty occurs to business or income-producing property, gain or loss reported for regular income tax may be different than gain or loss determined for the AMT. This difference occurs because the adjusted basis of the property for AMT purposes must reflect any current and prior AMT adjustments for the following.[32]

- Depreciation.
- Circulation expenditures.
- Amortization of certified pollution control facilities.

A negative gain or loss adjustment is required if:

- The gain for AMT purposes is less than the gain for regular income tax purposes,
- The loss for AMT purposes is more than the loss for regular income tax purposes, or
- A loss is computed for AMT purposes and a gain is computed for regular income tax purposes.

Otherwise, the AMT gain or loss adjustment is positive.

Example 22

In January 1998, Cardinal Corporation paid $100,000 for a duplex acquired for rental purposes. Regular income tax depreciation, AMT depreciation, and the AMT adjustment are as follows.

Year	Depreciation Regular Income Tax	AMT	AMT Adjustment
1998	$ 3,485[1]	$ 2,396[2]	$ 1,089
1999	3,636[3]	2,500[4]	1,136
2000–2012	47,268[5]	32,500[6]	14,768
2013	3,636	2,500	1,136

[1] $100,000 cost × 3.485% (Table 5.3) = $3,485
[2] $100,000 cost × 2.396% (Table 5.7) = $2,396
[3] $100,000 cost × 3.636% (Table 5.3) = $3,636
[4] $100,000 cost × 2.500% (Table 5.7) = $2,500
[5] $3,636 each year for 13 years (2000 through 2012)
[6] $2,500 each year for 13 years (2000 through 2012)

Cardinal then sold the duplex on December 20, 2014, for $105,000. Regular income tax depreciation for 2014 is $3,485 [($100,000 cost × 3.636% from Table 5.3) × ($11.5/12$)]. AMT depreciation for 2014 is $2,396 [($100,000 cost × 2.500% from Table 5.7) × ($11.5/12$)]. Cardinal's positive AMT adjustment for 2014 is $1,089 ($3,485 regular income tax depreciation − $2,396 AMT depreciation).

Because depreciation on the duplex differs for regular income tax and AMT purposes, Cardinal's adjusted basis for the property is different for regular income tax and AMT purposes. Consequently, the gain or loss on disposition of the duplex is different for regular income tax and AMT purposes.

---

[30] See Chapter 18 of *South-Western Federal Taxation: Individual Income Taxes* for a detailed discussion of the completed contract and percentage of completion methods of accounting.

[31] § 56(a)(3).

[32] § 56(a)(6).

The adjusted basis for Cardinal's duplex is $38,490 for regular income tax purposes and $57,708 for AMT purposes.

	Regular Income Tax	AMT
Cost	$100,000	$100,000
Depreciation:		
1998	(3,485)	(2,396)
1999	(3,636)	(2,500)
2000–2012	(47,268)	(32,500)
2013	(3,636)	(2,500)
2014	(3,485)	(2,396)
Adjusted basis	$ 38,490	$ 57,708

The regular income tax gain is $66,510, and the AMT gain is $47,292.

	Regular Income Tax	AMT
Amount realized	$105,000	$105,000
Adjusted basis	(38,490)	(57,708)
Recognized gain	$ 66,510	$ 47,292

Because the regular income tax and AMT gain on the sale of the duplex differ, Cardinal makes a negative AMT adjustment of $19,218 ($66,510 regular income tax gain − $47,292 AMT gain). The negative adjustment matches the $19,218 total of the 17 positive adjustments for depreciation ($1,089 in 1998 + $1,136 in 1999 + $14,768 from 2000 through 2012 + $1,136 in 2013 + $1,089 in 2014).

Passive Activity Losses

Net losses on passive activities are not deductible in computing either the regular income tax or the AMT for closely held C corporations (cannot offset portfolio income) and personal service corporations (cannot offset either active income or portfolio income).[33] This does not, however, eliminate the possibility of adjustments attributable to passive activities.

The rules for computing taxable income differ from the rules for computing AMTI. It follows, then, that the rules for computing a loss for regular income tax purposes differ from the AMT rules for computing a loss. Therefore, any *passive loss* computed for regular income tax purposes may differ from the passive loss computed for AMT purposes.

Example 23

Robin, Inc., a personal service corporation, acquired two passive activities in 2014. Robin received net passive income of $10,000 from Activity A and had no AMT adjustments or preferences in connection with the activity. Activity B had gross income of $27,000 and operating expenses (not affected by AMT adjustments or preferences) of $19,000. Robin claimed MACRS depreciation of $20,000 for Activity B; depreciation under the ADS would have been $15,000. In addition, Robin deducted $10,000 of percentage depletion in excess of basis. The following comparison illustrates the differences in the computation of the passive loss for regular income tax and AMT purposes for Activity B.

	Regular Income Tax	AMT
Gross income	$27,000	$27,000
Deductions:		
Operating expenses	($19,000)	($19,000)
Depreciation	(20,000)	(15,000)
Depletion	(10,000)	–0–
Total deductions	($49,000)	($34,000)
Passive loss	($22,000)	($ 7,000)

---

[33]§ 469(a).

Because the adjustment for depreciation ($5,000) applies and the preference for deple-tion ($10,000) is not taken into account in computing AMTI, the regular income tax passive activity loss of $22,000 for Activity B is reduced by these amounts, resulting in a passive activity loss of $7,000 for AMT purposes.

For regular income tax purposes, Robin would offset the $10,000 of net passive income from Activity A with $10,000 of the passive loss from Activity B. For AMT pur-poses, the corporation would offset the $10,000 of net passive income from Activity A with the $7,000 passive activity loss allowed from Activity B, resulting in passive activity income of $3,000. Thus, in computing AMTI, Robin makes a positive passive loss adjust-ment of $3,000 [$10,000 (passive activity loss allowed for regular income tax) − $7,000 (passive activity loss allowed for the AMT)].[34]

For regular income tax purposes, Robin, Inc., has a suspended passive loss of $12,000 [$22,000 (amount of loss) − $10,000 (used in 2014)]. This suspended passive loss can offset passive income in the future or can offset active or portfolio income when the corporation disposes of the loss activity (refer to Chapter 6). For AMT purposes, Robin's suspended passive loss is $0 [$7,000 (amount of loss) − $7,000 (amount used in 2014)].

Tax Planning Strategies — AVOIDING PREFERENCES AND ADJUSTMENTS

FRAMEWORK FOCUS: TAX RATE

Strategy: Control the Character of Income and Deductions.

Investments in state and local bonds are attractive for income tax purposes because the interest is not included in gross income. Some of these bonds (most private activity bonds) are issued to generate funds that are not used for an essential function of the government (e.g., to provide infrastructure for shopping malls or industrial parks or to build sports facilities). The interest on such bonds is a tax preference item (except for private activity bonds issued in 2009 and 2010) and could lead to the imposition of the AMT. When the AMT applies, an investment in regular tax-exempt bonds or even fully taxed private-sector bonds might yield a higher after-tax rate of return.

For a corporation anticipating AMT problems, capitalizing rather than expensing certain costs can avoid generating preferences and adjustments. The decision should be based on the present discounted value of after-tax cash flows under the available alternatives. Costs that may be capital-ized and amortized, rather than expensed, include circula-tion expenditures, mining exploration and development costs, and research and experimentation expenditures.

17-2d Adjusted Current Earnings (ACE)

The **adjusted current earnings (ACE)** rules make up a third, separate tax system, par-allel to both AMT and taxable income. S corporations, real estate investment trusts, regulated investment companies, and real estate mortgage investment conduits are not subject to the ACE provisions.

The purpose of the ACE adjustment is to ensure that the mismatching of finan-cial statement income and taxable income will not produce inequitable results. ACE represents another attempt by Congress to ensure that large corporations with significant financial accounting income pay a fair share of Federal corporate income tax.

The ACE adjustment is tax-based and can be negative or positive. AMTI is increased by 75 percent of the excess of ACE over unadjusted AMTI, or AMTI is reduced by 75 percent of the excess of unadjusted AMTI over ACE. Any negative ACE adjustment is limited to the aggregate of the positive adjustments under ACE for prior years reduced by the previously claimed negative adjustments (see Figure 17.1).[35] Any unused negative adjustment is lost forever.

LO.6

State and explain the function of adjusted current earnings (ACE).

---

[34]The depreciation adjustment and depletion preference are combined as part of the passive loss adjustment and are *not* reported separately.

[35]§§ 56(g)(1) and (2). *Unadjusted AMTI* is AMTI before the ACE adjust-ment and the AMT NOL deduction; the IRS refers to this item as "pre-adjustment AMTI."

| FIGURE 17.1 | **Determining the ACE Adjustment*** |

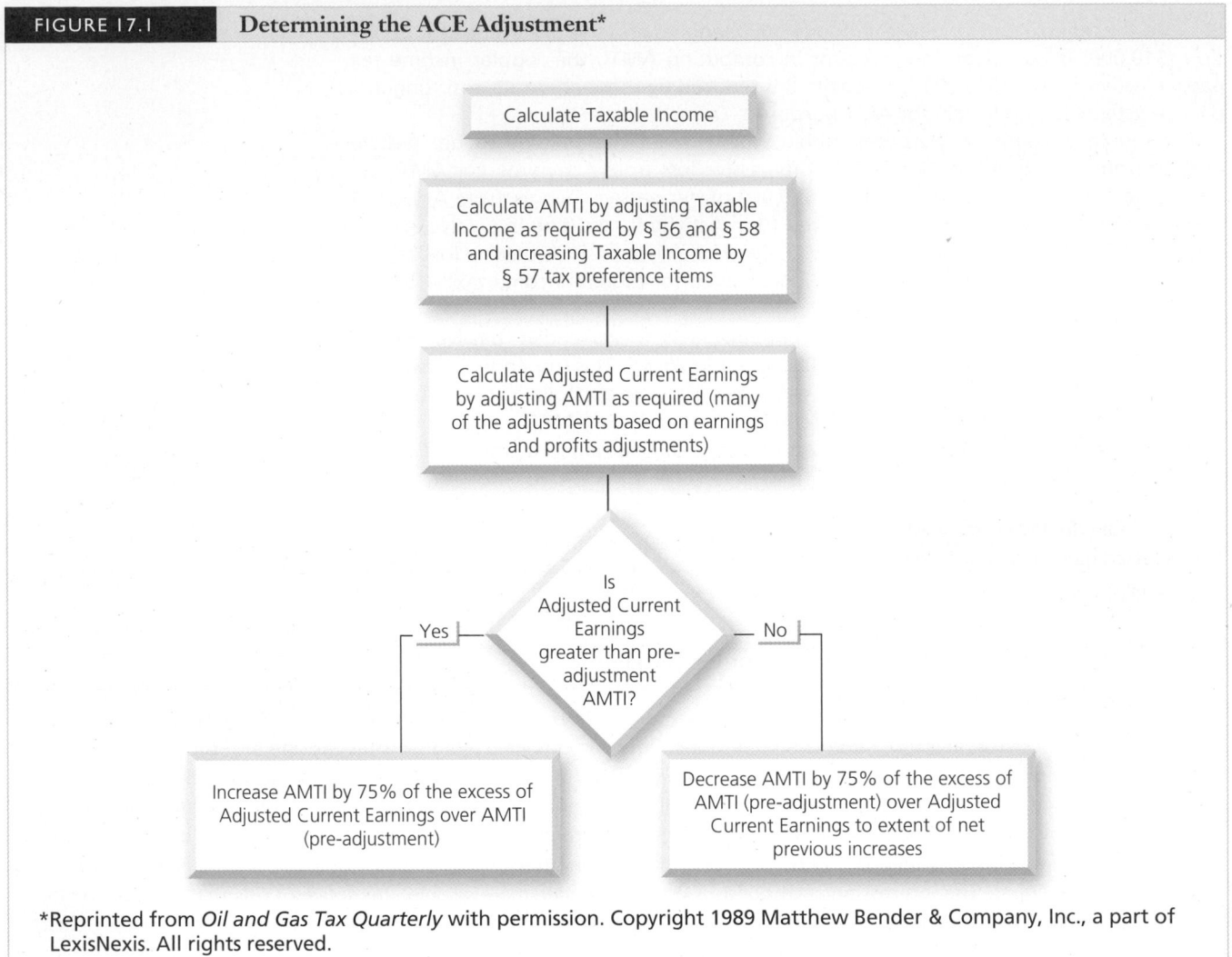

*Reprinted from *Oil and Gas Tax Quarterly* with permission. Copyright 1989 Matthew Bender & Company, Inc., a part of LexisNexis. All rights reserved.

Example 24

A calendar year corporation reports the following.

	2013	2014	2015
Unadjusted AMTI	$3,000,000	$3,000,000	$3,100,000
Adjusted current earnings	4,000,000	3,000,000	2,000,000

In 2013, because ACE exceeds unadjusted AMTI by $1 million, the positive ACE adjustment is $750,000 (75% × $1,000,000). No adjustment is necessary for 2014. Unadjusted AMTI exceeds ACE by $1,100,000 in 2015, so there is a potential negative ACE adjustment of $825,000. Because the total increases to AMTI for prior years equal $750,000 (and there are no negative adjustments), only $750,000 of the potential negative ACE adjustment reduces AMTI for 2015. Further, $75,000 of negative ACE is lost forever.

The starting point for computing ACE is AMTI, which is regular taxable income after AMT adjustments (other than the NOL and ACE adjustments) and tax preferences.[36] Pre-NOL AMTI is adjusted for certain items to determine ACE. See Concept Summary 17.2.

---

[36]§ 56(g)(3).

CONCEPT SUMMARY 17.2

How Various Transactions Affect ACE and E & P

	Effect on Unadjusted AMTI in Arriving at ACE	Effect on Taxable Income in Arriving at Corporate E & P
Tax-exempt income (net of expenses)	Add	Add
Federal income tax	No effect	Subtract
Dividends received deduction (80% and 100% rules)	No effect	Add
Dividends received deduction (70% rule)	Add	Add
Exemption amount ($40,000)	No effect	No effect
Excess charitable contribution	No effect	Subtract
Excess capital losses	No effect	Subtract
Disallowed meals and entertainment expenses	No effect	Subtract
Penalties and fines	No effect	Subtract
Intangible drilling costs deducted currently	Add	Add
Deferred gain on installment sales	Add	Add
Realized (not recognized) gain (e.g., involuntary conversion, like-kind exchanges)	No effect	No effect
Loss on sale between related parties	No effect	Subtract
Key employee insurance proceeds	Add	Add
Premiums paid on key employee life insurance	Subtract	Subtract
Cash surrender value increase on life insurance policy	Add	Add
Organization expense amortization	Add	Add

© iStockphoto.com/Andrey Prokhorov

In-depth coverage can be found on this book's companion website: **www.cengagebrain.com**   **6**   Digging Deeper

Crimson Corporation makes the ACE adjustment calculation as follows.   **Example 25**

AMTI		$ 5,780,000
Plus:		
Municipal bond interest	$210,000	
Installment gain	140,000	
70% dividends received deduction	300,000	
Income element in cash surrender life insurance	60,000	
Organization expense amortization	70,000	780,000
Subtotal		$ 6,560,000
Less:		
Life insurance premiums paid	$240,000	(240,000)
Adjusted current earnings		$ 6,320,000
AMTI		(5,780,000)
Base amount		$ 540,000
Times 75%		× .75
ACE adjustment (positive)		$ 405,000

© tuulijumala/Shutterstock.com

ACE should not be confused with current E & P. Many items are treated in the same manner, but certain items that are deductible in computing E & P (but are not deductible in calculating taxable income) generally are not deductible in computing ACE (e.g., Federal income taxes). Concept Summary 17.2 compares the effects that various transactions have on the determination of ACE and E & P.

17-2e Computing Alternative Minimum Taxable Income

LO.7

Compute the AMT liability for corporations and individuals.

The following example illustrates the effect of tax preferences and adjustments in arriving at AMTI.

Example 26

Tan Corporation (a calendar year company) recorded the following transactions.

Taxable income	$4,250,000
Income deferred by using completed contract method (versus percentage of completion method)	450,000
Percentage depletion claimed (the property has a zero adjusted basis)	1,575,000
Interest on City of Elmira (Michigan) 2007 private activity bonds	1,175,000

Tan Corporation's AMTI is determined as follows.

Taxable income		$4,250,000
Adjustments		
Income deferred by using completed contract method (versus percentage of completion method)		
Tax preferences		450,000
Excess depletion deduction	$1,575,000	
Interest on private activity municipal bonds	1,175,000	2,750,000
AMTI		$7,450,000

Optimum Use of the AMT and Regular Corporate Income Tax Rate Difference

Tax Planning Strategies

FRAMEWORK FOCUS: TAX RATE

Strategy: Shift Net Income from High-Bracket Years to Low-Bracket Years.

A corporation that cannot avoid the AMT in a particular year often can save taxes by taking advantage of the difference between the AMT and the regular income tax rates. In general, a corporation that expects to be subject to the AMT should consider accelerating income and deferring deductions for the remainder of the year. Because the difference between the regular income tax rate and the AMT rate may be as much as 14 or 15 percentage points, this strategy may result in the income being taxed at less than it would be if reported in the next year (a non-AMT year). If the same corporation expects to be subject to the AMT for the next year (or years) and is not subject to AMT this year, this technique should be reversed.

Example 27

Falcon Corporation expects to be in the 34% regular income tax bracket in 2015, but is subject to the AMT in 2014. In late 2014, Falcon is contemplating selling a tract of unimproved land (basis of $200,000 and fair market value of $1 million), which is classified as inventory. Under these circumstances, it may be preferable to sell the land in 2014. The gain of $800,000 ($1,000,000 − $200,000) generates a tax of $160,000 [$800,000 (recognized gain) × 20% (AMT rate)]. However, if the land is sold in 2015, the resulting tax is $272,000 [$800,000 (recognized gain) × 34% (regular corporate income tax rate)]. A nominal savings of $112,000 ($272,000 − $160,000) materializes by making the sale in 2014. ■

Whenever one accelerates income or defers deductions, a present value analysis should be conducted. This technique to accelerate gross income is attractive only if it reduces the present value of tax liabilities.

17-2f AMT Rate and Exemption

The AMT rate is 20 percent. The rate is applied to the *AMT base*, which is AMTI reduced by the *AMT exemption*. The exemption amount for a corporation is $40,000 reduced by 25 percent of the amount by which AMTI exceeds $150,000. The exemption phases out entirely when AMTI reaches $310,000.

| Tax Planning Strategies | CONTROLLING THE TIMING OF PREFERENCES AND ADJUSTMENTS |

FRAMEWORK FOCUS: TAX RATE

Strategy: Control the Character of Income and Deductions.

In many situations, corporations with modest levels of income may be able to avoid the AMT by making use of the exemption. To maximize the exemption, taxpayers should attempt to avoid bunching positive adjustments and tax preferences in any one year. Rather, net these items against negative adjustments to keep AMTI low. When the expenditure is largely within the control of the taxpayer, timing to avoid bunching is more easily accomplished.

Example 28

Beige Corporation has AMTI of $180,000. Because the exemption amount is reduced by $7,500 [25% × ($180,000 − $150,000)], the amount remaining is $32,500 ($40,000 − $7,500). Thus, Beige Corporation's alternative minimum tax base (refer to Exhibit 17.2) is $147,500 ($180,000 − $32,500).

17-2g Minimum Tax Credit

The **minimum tax credit** acts to make the AMT merely a *prepayment of tax* for corporations. Essentially, the AMT paid in one tax year may be carried forward indefinitely and used as a credit against the corporation's future *regular* tax liability that exceeds its tentative minimum tax. The minimum tax credit may not be carried back and may not be offset against any future AMT liability.

Example 29

Return to the facts of Example 26. As Tan Corporation's AMTI exceeds $310,000, there is no AMT exemption amount. The tentative minimum tax is $1,490,000 (20% of $7,450,000).

Tan's regular income tax liability is $1,445,000 ($4,250,000 × 34%). As a result, its AMT liability is $45,000 ($1,490,000 − $1,445,000). The minimum tax credit carried forward is $45,000, the current year's AMT. The credit can be used to reduce regular income tax liability in a future tax year (but not below the tentative minimum tax for that year).

17-2h Other Aspects of the AMT

In addition to paying their regular income tax liability, corporations must make estimated tax payments of the AMT liability. Even corporations that prepare quarterly financial statements may find that this requirement adds to compliance costs.

| Tax Planning Strategies | THE S CORPORATION OPTION |

FRAMEWORK FOCUS: TAX RATE

Strategy: Avoid Double Taxation.

Corporations that make the S election are not subject to the corporate AMT. As noted in Chapter 15, however, various AMT adjustments and preferences pass through to the individual shareholders. But one troublesome computation, the one involving the ACE adjustment, is avoided because it does not apply to individual taxpayers.

TAX IN THE NEWS   Is a New Version of the AMT Needed?

Nearly all of the discussion regarding the AMT relates to reducing the number of taxpayers projected to be subject to its reach in the future. A look at IRS statistics, however, suggests that perhaps the AMT needs to be revised to "catch" certain taxpayers.

In 2009, nearly 10,000 individual taxpayers with AGI of at least $200,000 paid no Federal income tax (i.e., neither the regular income tax nor the AMT). This is an interesting statistic, considering that the original AMT came about in 1969 because only 155 wealthy taxpayers had no tax liability.

© iStockphoto.com/Andrey Prokhorov

Certain small corporations can use specified tax credits to reduce the AMT liability. For all other corporations, only the foreign tax credit can be claimed in an AMT year.[37]

17-3 INDIVIDUAL ALTERNATIVE MINIMUM TAX

The AMT applicable to individuals is similar to the corporate AMT. Most of the adjustments and preferences discussed previously apply equally to individuals and corporations. However, there are several important differences.

- The individual AMT rate is slightly progressive, with rates at 26 percent on the first $182,500 ($91,250 for married, filing separately) of AMTI and at 28 percent on any additional AMTI.
- The alternative rate on net capital gain of 0, 15, or 20 percent applies.
- The AMT exemption and phaseout amounts are tied to the individual's filing status for the year. The exemption phases out at a rate of $1 for every $4 of AMTI.[38] The exemption amounts for 2014 are listed in the table below.

Filing Status	Exemption Amount	Phaseout Range Begins at	Phaseout Range Ends at
Married, joint	$82,100	$156,500	$484,900
Married, separate	41,050	78,250	242,450
Single or Head of household	52,800	117,300	328,500

- Individuals make no AMT adjustment for ACE.
- Some additional adjustments apply to individual taxpayers. Taxes and miscellaneous itemized deductions subject to the 2 percent-of-AGI floor are not allowed as deductions for AMTI. Medical expenses are allowed only to the extent they exceed 10 percent of AGI (instead of a 7.5 percent limitation for regular income tax purposes if at least age 65). Interest expense deductions are limited to qualified residence interest, interest on certain student loans, and investment interest (subject to limitations). The 3 percent phaseout of itemized deductions that applies to certain high-income taxpayers (refer to Chapter 9) does *not* apply in computing the individual AMT. Finally, the standard deduction and personal and dependency exemptions are not allowed as deductions when computing AMTI. Other individual-specific adjustments also exist, including an adjustment accelerating the taxation of incentive stock options.
- Determination of the minimum tax credit is more complex for individual taxpayers. The credit usually applies only to AMT generated as a result of *timing* differences.

---

[37]§ 38(c)(5)(A).

[38]AMT exemption amounts for 2013 were $80,800, $40,400, and $51,900, respectively.

In most years, 85 percent of the AMT revenue collected from individual taxpayers results because two regular-tax items are not allowed in computing AMT income—deductions for state and local taxes and for personal and dependency exemptions.

Although there are several computational differences, the individual AMT and the corporate AMT have the same objective: to force taxpayers who have more economic income than that reflected in taxable income to pay a fair share of Federal income tax.

REFOCUS ON THE BIG PICTURE

DEALING WITH TAX CREDITS AND THE AMT

© iStockphoto.com/monkeybusinessimages/Catherine Yeulet

Tax credits are used by the Federal government to promote certain social and economic objectives. Credits are dollar-for-dollar reductions in tax liability. While tax credits may have strict qualification requirements, taking advantage of available credits may significantly reduce a business's tax liability. Progress Corporation qualifies for a 10 percent tax credit for rehabilitating a building placed in service before 1936 (see Example 4). In addition, Progress hires workers from economically disadvantaged groups, so it qualifies for the work opportunity tax credit (see Example 6).

The company also qualifies for the credit for employer-provided child care, equal to 25 percent of qualified child care expenses (see Example 14). Mike and his CPA might also want to explore taking advantage of the disabled access credit, which is designed to encourage small businesses to make their facilities accessible to disabled individuals.

What If?

Mike has heard horror stories about the alternative minimum tax (AMT) and is concerned about its potential impact on his company. What if Mike's company is subject to the AMT?

If Progress Corporation is subject to the AMT, the company's general business credits (including the tax credit for rehabilitation expenditures, the work opportunity tax credit, the disabled access credit, and the credit for employer-provided child care) are limited to the taxpayer's regular income tax reduced by the greater of the company's tentative minimum tax or 25 percent of the regular income tax liability exceeding $25,000. Accordingly, much of the tax benefit may be lost or require a carryback or carryover to another tax year. However, small corporations with average gross receipts under certain thresholds may be exempt from the AMT. Before Mike proceeds with his plans, his exposure to the AMT should be determined.

Suggested Readings

Beth Henricks, "Enlist Human Resources to Screen for Employment Tax Credits," *Practical Tax Strategies*, April 2008.

Thomas Horan and Margaret Horan, "Strategies for Reducing the Alternative Minimum Tax Liability," *The CPA Journal*, March 2013.

Kreig D. Mitchell, "The R&D Tax Credit for Start-Up Companies," *Practical Tax Strategies*, February 2012.

Tom Prieto, "AMT Planning with Listed Options," *Practical Tax Strategies*, October 2010.

William R. Swindle, "Recent Cases Provide Relief for Substantiating Research Tax Credit Claims," *Practical Tax Strategies*, June 2010.

Dean Zerbe, Benjamin Yaker, and David Ji, "New Law Opens Door for Businesses to Take R&D Tax Credit," *Practical Tax Strategies*, April 2011.

Key Terms

Adjusted current earnings (ACE), 17-23

Alternative minimum tax (AMT), 17-14

Alternative minimum taxable income (AMTI), 17-15

Credit for employer-provided child care, 17-11

Credit for small employer pension plan startup costs, 17-11

Disabled access credit, 17-10

Energy credits, 17-10

Foreign tax credit (FTC), 17-12

General business credit, 17-2

Minimum tax credit, 17-27

Private activity bonds, 17-17

Rehabilitation expenditures credit, 17-5

Rehabilitation expenditures credit recapture, 17-6

Research activities credit, 17-8

Tax credits, 17-2

Tax preference items, 17-16

Work opportunity tax credit, 17-6

Problems

1. **LO.2** Charles has a tentative general business credit of $42,000 for the current year. His net regular tax liability before the general business credit is $107,000, and his tentative minimum tax is $88,000. Compute Charles's allowable general business credit for the year.

2. **LO.2** Oak Corporation holds the following general business credit carryovers.

2010	$ 5,000
2011	15,000
2012	6,000
2013	19,000
Total carryovers	$45,000

   If the general business credit generated by activities during 2014 equals $36,000 and the total credit allowed during the current year is $60,000 (based on tax liability), what amounts of the current general business credit and carryovers are utilized against the 2014 income tax liability? What is the amount of the unused credit carried forward to 2015?

Issue ID

3. **LO.2** Clint, a self-employed engineering consultant, is contemplating purchasing an old building for renovation. After the work is completed, Clint plans to rent out two-thirds of the floor space to businesses; he would live and work in the remaining portion. Identify the relevant tax issues for Clint.

4. **LO.2** In January 2013, Iris Corporation purchased and placed into service a 1933 building that houses retail businesses. The cost was $300,000, of which $25,000 applied to the land. In modernizing the facility, Iris Corporation incurred $312,000 of renovation costs of the type that qualify for the rehabilitation credit. These improvements were placed into service in October 2014.
   a. Compute Iris Corporation's rehabilitation tax credit for 2014.
   b. Calculate the cost recovery deductions for the building and the renovation costs for 2014.

Decision Making

Communications

5. **LO.2** In the current year, Paul Chaing (4522 Fargo Street, Geneva, IL 60134) acquires a qualifying historic structure for $350,000 (excluding the cost of the land) and plans to substantially rehabilitate the structure. He is planning to spend either $320,000 or $380,000 on rehabilitation expenditures. Write a letter to Paul and a memo for the tax files explaining, for the two alternative expenditures, (1) the computation that determines the rehabilitation expenditures tax credit available to Paul, (2) the effect of the credit on Paul's adjusted basis in the property, and (3) the cash-flow differences as a result of the tax consequences related to his expenditure choice.

6. **LO.2** The tax credit for rehabilitation expenditures is available to help offset the costs related to substantially rehabilitating certain buildings. The credit is calculated on the rehabilitation expenditures incurred and not on the acquisition cost of the building itself.

   You are a developer who buys, sells, and does construction work on real estate in the inner city of your metropolitan area. A potential customer approaches you about acquiring one of your buildings that easily could qualify for the 20% rehabilitation credit on historic structures. The stated sales price of the structure is $100,000 (based on appraisals ranging from $80,000 to $120,000), and the rehabilitation expenditures, if the job is done correctly, would be about $150,000.

   Your business has been slow recently due to the sluggish real estate market in your area, and the potential customer makes the following proposal: if you reduce the sales price of the building to $75,000, he will pay you $175,000 to perform the rehabilitation work. Although the buyer's total expenditures would be the same, he would benefit from this approach by obtaining a larger tax credit ($25,000 increased rehabilitation costs × 20% = $5,000).

   It has been a long time since you have sold any of your real estate. How will you respond?

Ethics and Equity

7. **LO.2** Green Corporation hires six individuals on January 4, 2014, all of whom qualify for the work opportunity credit. Three of these individuals receive wages of $8,500 during 2014, and each individual works more than 400 hours during the year. The other three individuals each work 300 hours and receive wages of $5,000 during the year.
   a. Calculate the amount of Green's work opportunity credit for 2014.
   b. If Green pays total wages of $140,000 to its employees during the year, how much of this amount is deductible in 2014 assuming that the work opportunity credit is taken?

8. **LO.2** In March 2014, Sparrow Corporation hired three individuals—Austin, Adam, and Angela—all of whom are certified as long-term family assistance recipients. Each of these individuals earned $11,000 during 2014. Only Adam continued to work for Sparrow in 2015, and he earned $13,500 then. In March 2015, Sparrow hired Sam, who also is certified as a long-term family assistance recipient. During 2015, Sam earned $12,000.
   a. Compute Sparrow Corporation's work opportunity credit for 2014 and 2015.
   b. If Sparrow pays total wages to its employees of $325,000 in 2014 and $342,000 in 2015, what is its wage deduction in each of those years?

9. **LO.2** Tom, a calendar year taxpayer, informs you that during the year, he incurs expenditures of $40,000 that qualify for the incremental research activities credit. In addition, it is determined that his research-credit base amount for the year is $32,800.
   a. Determine Tom's incremental research activities credit for the year.
   b. Tom is in the 25% tax bracket. Determine which approach to the research expenditures and the research activities credit (other than capitalization and subsequent amortization) would provide the greater tax benefit to Tom.

Decision Making

10. **LO.2** Ahmed Zinna (16 Southside Drive, Charlotte, NC 28204), one of your clients, owns two retail establishments in downtown Charlotte and has come to you seeking advice concerning the tax consequences of complying with the Americans with Disabilities Act. He understands that he needs to install various features at his stores (e.g., ramps, doorways, and restrooms that are handicapped-accessible) to make them more accessible to disabled individuals.

    Ahmed asks whether any tax credits will be available to help offset the cost of the necessary changes. He estimates the cost of the planned changes to his facilities as follows.

Communications

Location	Projected Cost
Calvin Street	$22,000
Stowe Avenue	8,500

Ahmed reminds you that the Calvin Street store was constructed in 2004, while the Stowe Avenue store is in a building that was constructed in 1947. Ahmed operates his business as a sole proprietorship and has approximately eight employees at each location. Write a letter to Ahmed in which you summarize your conclusions concerning the tax consequences of the proposed capital improvements.

11. **LO.2** Blue Horizons, Inc., a U.S. corporation, is a manufacturing concern that sells most of its products in the United States. It also does some business in the European Union through various branches. During the current year, Blue Horizons has taxable income of $700,000, of which $500,000 is U.S.-sourced and $200,000 is foreign-sourced. Foreign income taxes paid amounted to $45,000. Blue Horizons's U.S. income tax liability is $238,000. What is its U.S. income tax liability net of the allowable foreign tax credit?

12. **LO.3** Aqua, Inc., a calendar year corporation, has the following gross receipts and taxable income for 2011–2014:

Year	Gross Receipts	Taxable Income
2011	$6,000,000	$1,400,000
2012	7,000,000	1,312,000
2013	7,500,000	985,000
2014	7,200,000	1,002,000

Aqua's first year of operations was 2011.
a. When is Aqua first exempt from the AMT as a small corporation?
b. Is Aqua subject to the AMT for 2014? Explain.

13. **LO.4** Falcon, Inc., owns a silver mine that it purchased several years ago for $925,000. The adjusted basis at the beginning of the year is $400,000. For the year, Falcon deducts depletion of $700,000 (greater of cost depletion of $290,000 or percentage depletion of $700,000) for regular income tax purposes.
a. Calculate Falcon's AMT preference.
b. Calculate Falcon's adjusted basis for regular income tax purposes.
c. Calculate Falcon's adjusted basis for AMT purposes.

Decision Making

Communications

14. **LO.5** In March 2014, Grackle, Inc., acquired used equipment for its business at a cost of $300,000. The equipment is five-year class property for regular income tax purposes and for AMT purposes. Grackle does not claim any available additional first-year depreciation.
a. If Grackle depreciates the equipment using the method that will produce the greatest deduction for 2014 for regular income tax purposes, what is the amount of the AMT adjustment? Grackle does not elect §179 limited expensing.
b. How can Grackle reduce the AMT adjustment to $0? What circumstances would motivate Grackle to do so?
c. Draft a letter to Helen Carlon, Grackle's controller, regarding the choice of depreciation methods. Helen's address is 500 Monticello Avenue, Glendale, AZ 85306.

15. **LO.5** Rust Company is a real estate construction business with average annual gross receipts of $3 million. Rust uses the completed contract method on a particular contract that requires 16 months to complete. The contract is for $500,000, with estimated costs of $300,000. At the end of 2014, $180,000 of costs had been incurred. The contract is completed in 2015, with the total cost being $295,000. Determine the amount of adjustments for AMT purposes for 2014 and 2015.

Ethics and Equity

16. **LO.5** Allie, who was an accounting major in college, is the controller of a medium-size construction corporation. She prepares the corporate tax return each year. Due to reporting a home construction contract using the completed contract method, the corporation is subject to the AMT in 2014. Allie files the 2014 corporate tax return in early February 2015. The total tax liability is $58,000 ($53,000 regular income tax liability + $5,000 AMT).

In early March, Allie reads an article on minimizing income taxes. Based on this article, she decides that it would be beneficial for the corporation to report the home construction contract using the percentage of completion method on its 2014 return. Although this will increase the corporation's 2014 income tax liability, it will minimize the total income tax liability over the two-year construction period. Therefore, Allie files an amended return on March 14, 2015. Evaluate Allie's actions from both a tax avoidance and an ethical perspective.

17. **LO.5** Buford sells an apartment building for $720,000. His adjusted basis is $500,000 for regular income tax purposes and $550,000 for AMT purposes. Calculate Buford's:
    a. Gain for regular income tax purposes.
    b. Gain for AMT purposes.
    c. AMT adjustment, if any.

18. **LO.5** Pheasant, Inc., is going to be subject to the AMT in 2014. The corporation owns an investment building and is considering disposing of it and investing in other realty. Based on an appraisal of the building's value, the realized gain would be $85,000. Ed has offered to purchase the building from Pheasant with a December 29, 2014 closing date.   Issue ID

    Ed wants to close the transaction in 2014 because he will receive certain beneficial tax consequences only if the transaction is closed prior to 2015. Abby has offered to purchase the building with a January 2, 2015 closing date. The adjusted basis of the building is $95,000 greater for AMT purposes than for the regular income tax. Pheasant expects to be in the 34% regular income tax bracket.

    What are the relevant Federal income tax issues that Pheasant faces in making its decision?

19. **LO.5** Flicker, Inc., a closely held corporation, acquired a passive activity this year. Gross income from operations of the activity was $160,000. Operating expenses, not including depreciation, were $122,000. Regular income tax depreciation of $49,750 was computed under MACRS. AMT depreciation, computed using the ADS, was $41,000. Compute Flicker's passive loss deduction and passive loss suspended for regular income tax purposes. Then determine the same amounts for AMT purposes.

20. **LO.6** Maize Corporation (a calendar year corporation) reports the following information for the years listed.

	2013	2014	2015
Adjusted current earnings	$5,000,000	$5,000,000	$7,000,000
Unadjusted AMTI	8,000,000	5,000,000	3,000,000

Compute the ACE adjustment for each year.

21. **LO.6** Based on the following facts, calculate adjusted current earnings (ACE).

Alternative minimum taxable income (AMTI before ACE adjustment)	$5,120,000
Municipal bond interest	630,000
Expenses related to municipal bonds	50,000
Key employee life insurance proceeds in excess of cash surrender value	2,000,000
Organization expense amortization	100,000
Cost of goods sold	6,220,000
Advertising expenses	760,000
Loss between related parties	260,000
Life insurance premiums paid	300,000

22. **LO.6** Purple Corporation, a calendar year taxpayer, began operations in 2012. It reported the following amounts for its first four tax years. Calculate Purple's positive and negative ACE adjustments for each year.

	Unadjusted AMTI	ACE
2012	$85,000,000	$70,000,000
2013	70,000,000	90,000,000
2014	54,000,000	40,000,000
2015	60,000,000	20,000,000

23. **LO.4, 5, 6** Determine whether each of the following transactions is a preference (P), is an adjustment (A), or is not applicable (NA) for purposes of the corporate AMT.
    a. Depletion in excess of basis taken by Giant Oil Company.
    b. Accelerated depreciation on property.
    c. Charitable contributions of cash.
    d. Adjusted current earnings.
    e. Untaxed appreciation on property donated to charity.
    f. Dividends received deduction.

24. **LO.7** In each of the following *independent* situations, determine the tentative minimum tax. Assume that the company is not in small corporation status.

	AMTI (before the Exemption Amount)
Quincy Corporation	$150,000
Redland Corporation	160,000
Tanzen Corporation	320,000

25. **LO.7** Peach Corporation (a calendar year company) recorded the following transactions.

Taxable income	$5,000,000
Regular tax depreciation on realty in excess of ADS (placed in service in 1991)	1,700,000
Amortization of certified pollution control facilities (in excess of ADS amortization)	200,000
Tax-exempt interest on private activity bonds issued in 2006	300,000
Percentage depletion in excess of the property's adjusted basis	700,000

   a. Determine Peach Corporation's AMTI.
   b. Determine the alternative minimum tax base (refer to Exhibit 17.2).
   c. Determine the tentative minimum tax.
   d. What is the amount of the AMT?

26. **LO.7** Included in Alice's regular taxable income and in her AMT base is a $300,000 capital gain on the sale of stock she owned for three years. Alice is in the 35% tax bracket for regular income tax purposes. In calculating her regular income tax liability, she uses the appropriate alternative tax rate on net capital gain of 15%.
    a. What rate should Alice use in calculating her tentative AMT?
    b. What is Alice's AMT adjustment?
    c. How would your answers in (a) and (b) change if the taxpayer were a C corporation in the 34% tax bracket for regular income tax purposes?

Critical Thinking

27. **LO.7** Calculate the AMT for the following cases in 2014. The individual taxpayer reports regular taxable income of $450,000 and no tax credits.

	Tentative Minimum Tax	
Filing Status	Case 1	Case 2
Single	$200,000	$190,000
Married, filing jointly	200,000	190,000

Critical Thinking

28. **LO.4, 5** Grayson, who is single with no dependents and does not itemize, provides you with the following information for 2014.

Short-term capital loss	$ 4,000
Long-term capital gain	19,000
Municipal bond interest received on private activity bonds acquired in 1997	17,000
Dividends from IBM	6,500
Excess of FMV over exercise price for incentive stock options (no restrictions apply to the stock received as a result of the options exercised)	40,000
Charitable contributions	10,000
Qualified residence interest	9,000

What are Grayson's tax preference items and AMT adjustments for 2014?

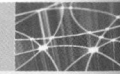

BRIDGE DISCIPLINE

1. Balm, Inc., has a general business credit for 2014 of $90,000. Balm's regular income tax liability before credits is $140,000, and its tentative AMT is $132,000.
   a. Calculate the amount of general business credit Balm can use in 2014, and calculate its general business credit carryback and carryforward, if any.
   b. Balm projects a $140,000 regular 2015 income tax liability. Its tentative AMT will be $132,000. Balm is considering making an investment early in 2015 that annually will produce $45,000 of tax-exempt income. Balm is trying to decide between two alternatives. The first alternative is a tax-exempt bond that is a 2004 private activity bond. The second alternative is a tax-exempt bond that is not a private activity bond. Advise Balm on the preferable investment.

2. Cooper Partnership, a calendar year partnership, made qualifying rehabilitation expenditures to a building that it has used in its business for eight years. These improvements were placed in service on January 5, 2013. The amount of the rehabilitation expenditures credit was $40,000.

   Cooper is negotiating to sell the building in either December 2014 or January 2015. The sales price will be $600,000, and the recognized gain will be $100,000. Provide support for the CFO's position that Cooper should delay the sale until 2015.

3. For many years, Saul's sole proprietorship and his related Form 1040 have had a number of AMT tax preferences and AMT adjustments. He has made the AMT calculation each year, but the calculated amount always has been $0. Saul's regular taxable income and the AMT adjustments and preferences for 2014 are the same as for last year. Yet, he must pay AMT this year. Explain how this could happen.

Research Problems

Note: Solutions to Research Problems can be prepared by using the **Checkpoint®** **Student Edition** online research product, which is available to accompany this text. It is also possible to prepare solutions to the Research Problems by using tax research materials found in a standard tax library.

THOMSON REUTERS
CHECKPOINT®

Research Problem 1. During a recent Sunday afternoon excursion, Miriam, an admirer of early twentieth-century architecture, discovers a 1920s-era house in the countryside outside Mobile, Alabama, during a recent Sunday excursion. She wants not only to purchase and renovate this particular house but also to move the structure into Mobile so that her community can enjoy its architectural features.

Being aware of the availability of the tax credit for rehabilitation expenditures, she wants to maximize her use of the provision, if it is available in this case, once the renovation work begins in Mobile. However, Miriam also informs you that she will pursue the purchase, relocation, and renovation of the house only if the tax credit is available.

Comment on Miriam's decision and on whether any renovation expenditures incurred will qualify for the tax credit for rehabilitation expenditures.

Partial list of research aids:
George S. Nalle III v. Comm., 72 AFTR 2d 93–5705, 997 F.2d 1134, 93–2 USTC ¶50,468 (CA–5, 1993).

Research Problem 2. Oriole Corporation is a large wholesaler of office products. To remain successful in a fiercely competitive industry, Oriole has automated and computerized many of its business operations. Specifically, the corporation has developed several new software programs to:

Communications

- Maintain files of customer histories.
- Create a paperless invoicing system.
- Develop a computer-to-computer order entry system.
- Monitor inventory levels more closely.

Oriole estimates that it spent more than $1 million to develop and test the new software programs that are used throughout the business. To date, Oriole has not sold the software to the public, but it is contemplating doing so. Oriole has claimed a research and experimentation deduction for the costs associated with developing the software. The corporation also wants to claim the research activities credit relating to the software development. Can Oriole do so? Write a memo to the tax research file summarizing your conclusions.

Communications

Research Problem 3. Your ophthalmologist, Dr. Hunter Francis (55 Wheatland Drive, Hampton, CT 06247), has been very pleased with the growth of his practice in the 15 years he has been in business. This growth has resulted, at least in part, because he has aggressively marketed his services and tried to accommodate clients with various needs. This year, Dr. Francis purchased a sophisticated piece of equipment that enables him to diagnose persons with mental handicaps, hearing impairments, and physical disabilities without having to go through a series of questions. In addition, he can treat his patients who are not disabled more accurately and efficiently by using this equipment.

Since purchasing the machine this year for $9,500, Dr. Francis has used it on many occasions. Unfortunately, he has not been able to attract any patients with disabilities, even though previously he referred such people to other ophthalmologists who owned the necessary equipment. Therefore, the primary purpose for acquiring the equipment (i.e., to attract patients with disabilities) has not been realized, but he has put it to good use in treating other patients. Write a letter to Dr. Francis explaining whether he may claim the disabled access credit for this acquisition.

Research Problem 4. Stuart is a columnist for a metropolitan newspaper. He has a degree in journalism from a major midwestern university.

For the past 10 years, Stuart has prepared his own income tax returns. He finds doing so to be challenging and stimulating and believes that he pays lower taxes than he would if he hired a tax return preparer.

His 2012 return is audited. Although it included an AMT form (Form 6251), Stuart had not prepared it properly. Data from his Form 1040 were transferred to the wrong line in several places. In other cases, positive adjustments were not included because Stuart had failed to calculate them (e.g., he did not recalculate itemized deductions for AMT purposes and did not have a positive adjustment for the personal exemption). Based on the IRS's calculation, a deficiency of $3,000 was assessed. Stuart's response to the IRS is that Form 6251 is ambiguous and misleading and, therefore, he should not be liable for the AMT. Evaluate Stuart's argument.

Partial list of research aids:
William M. Christine, 66 TCM 1025, T.C.Memo. 1993–473.

Research Problem 5. Teal, Inc., owns two warehouses that were placed in service before 1987. This year, accelerated depreciation on Warehouse A is $36,000 (straight-line depreciation would have been $30,000). On Warehouse B, accelerated depreciation was $16,000 (straight-line depreciation would have been $20,000). What is the amount of Teal's AMT tax preference for excess depreciation?

Internet Activity

Use the tax resources of the Internet to address the following questions. Do not restrict your search to the Web, but include a review of newsgroups and general reference materials, practitioner sites and resources, primary sources of the tax law, chat rooms and discussion groups, and other opportunities.

Research Problem 6. The foreign tax credit is especially valuable when a U.S. business earns income in a country whose income tax rates exceed those of the United States. List five countries whose tax rates on business income exceed those of the United States and five where the corresponding U.S. rates are higher.

Research Problem 7. Some parties believe that many corporations are paying little, if any, corporate income tax and blame the AMT for being ineffective. Examine both government and press sites on the Internet, and summarize these complaints.

Research Problem 8. Ascertain whether your state's income tax has an AMT component. If your state does not levy an income tax, choose a contiguous state that does. List the AMT tax rate for corporations, and describe if or how the AMT tax base follows Federal AMTI.

Comparative Forms of Doing Business

LEARNING OBJECTIVES: *After completing Chapter 18, you should be able to:*

LO.1 Identify the principal legal and tax forms for conducting a business.

LO.2 Include nontax factors in business decisions.

LO.3 Distinguish between the forms for conducting a business according to whether they are subject to single taxation or double taxation.

LO.4 Identify techniques for avoiding double taxation.

LO.5 State and apply the conduit and entity concepts as they affect operations, capital changes, and distributions.

LO.6 Analyze the effects of the disposition of a business on the owners and the entity for each of the forms for conducting a business.

LO.7 Compare the tax consequences of the most common legal forms of doing business.

TAX TALK *[My firm] had a rule—at least it seemed to be a rule—that everybody that came had to spend at least a year working on taxes. The general rationale for the rule as I could understand it was that taxes were so important to everything that you do, whatever the kind of case you are handling, you have to know something about the tax consequences of things.* —CHARLES A. HORSKY

Dennis Flaherty/Photographer's Choice/Getty Images

THE BIG PICTURE   Tax Solutions for the Real World

CHOOSING A BUSINESS FORM AND OTHER INVESTMENTS

Bill and George are going to start a new business and have come to you for advice on the most appropriate form for the business. They have narrowed the choice to a C corporation, an S corporation, or an LLC but would like you to advise them as to the primary advantages and disadvantages of the different forms. They have an adequate amount in savings to finance the business initially. Limited liability is a significant concern as is limiting the amount of taxes paid. Bill and George anticipate that the company will lose money in the first two years of operation. After that, however, they expect to earn $200,000 in before-tax profit and distribute any after-tax profit to the owners. Bill and George are both single, and both are subject to a 28 percent marginal tax rate.

George also is considering investing $10,000 in a limited partnership. He provides you with information on projected partnership profits and losses. See Example 2.

As a way of leveraging the risks and rewards associated with his investments, Bill earlier had acquired a 30 percent interest in a boutique retail coffee franchise outlet. Bill now is considering selling this investment, which has experienced rapid appreciation. Because he is considering selling this investment and cashing out the gain, he needs to know the adjusted basis of his ownership interest. See Example 13.

Read the chapter and formulate your response.

A variety of factors, both tax and nontax, can affect the choice of the form of business entity. The form that is appropriate at one point in the life of an entity and its owners may not be appropriate at a different time.

Example 1

Eva is a tax practitioner in Kentwood, the Dairy Center of the South. Many of her clients are dairy farmers. She recently had tax planning discussions with two of them: Jesse, a Line Creek dairy farmer, and Larry, a Spring Creek dairy farmer.

Jesse recently purchased his dairy farm. He is 52 years old and just retired after 30 years of service as a chemical engineer at an oil refinery in Baton Rouge. Eva recommended that he incorporate his dairy farm and elect S corporation status for Federal income tax purposes.

Larry has owned his dairy farm since 2008. He inherited it from his father. At that time, Larry retired after 20 years of service in the U.S. Air Force. He has a master's degree in Agricultural Economics from LSU. His farm is incorporated, and shortly after the date of incorporation, Eva advised him to elect S corporation status. She now advises him to revoke the S election.

Example 1 raises a number of interesting questions. Does Eva advise all of her dairy farmer clients to elect S corporation status initially? Why has she advised Larry to revoke his S election? Will she advise Jesse to revoke his S election at some time in the future? Will she advise Larry to make another S election at some time in the future? Why did she not advise Larry to dissolve his corporation outright? Could Larry and Jesse have achieved the same tax consequences for their dairy farms if they had operated the farms as limited liability entities or partnerships instead of using a corporation? Does the way the farm is acquired (e.g., purchase versus inheritance) affect the choice of business entity for tax purposes?

This chapter provides the basis for comparing and analyzing the tax consequences of business decisions for various types of tax entities (sole proprietorship, partnership, corporation, limited liability entity, and S corporation). Understanding the comparative tax consequences for the different types of entities and being able to apply them effectively to specific fact patterns will facilitate effective tax planning. As the following discussion illustrates, a variety of potential answers may exist for each of the questions raised by Eva's advice.

18-1 FORMS OF DOING BUSINESS

18-1a Principal Forms

LO.1

Identify the principal legal and tax forms for conducting a business.

The principal *legal* forms for conducting a business entity are the sole proprietorship, partnership, limited liability entity, and corporation.[1] From a *Federal income tax* perspective, these same forms are available, but the corporate form can be taxed in either of two ways (S corporation and C or regular corporation). In most instances, the legal form and the tax form are the same.

The taxpayer generally is bound for tax purposes by the legal form that is selected. A major statutory exception to this is the ability of an S corporation to receive tax treatment similar to that of a partnership.[2] In addition, taxpayers sometimes can control which set of tax rules will apply to their business operations. The "check-the-box" Regulations provide an elective procedure that enables certain entities to be classified as partnerships for Federal income tax purposes even though they have corporate characteristics.[3] These Regulations have greatly

---

[1] A business entity can also be conducted in the form of a trust or an estate.
[2] §§ 1361 and 1362. See Chapter 15.

[3] Reg. §§ 301.7701–1 through –4, and –6. Note that if the business has only one owner, the elective procedure enables the entity to be classified as a sole proprietorship.

TAX IN THE NEWS Should You Check That Box?

The check-the-box rules have been evolving since their introduction into the Regulations in late 1996. They are designed to remove tax considerations from the owners' choice of the legal form in which to conduct business. These provisions act to reduce the owners' exposure to the double taxation of taxable business profits. But taxpayers considering the use of these rules have run into several complications.

- Changing tax entity classifications from year to year comes at a cost. Changing the business form from a corporation to a partnership might trigger taxes for both the entity and its owners, defeating the purpose of the entity change.
- State income tax laws do not always match those of the Code. Several states have been slow to adopt the check-the-box rules, and others have modified the rules in some way. For instance, in several states a one-member limited liability company does not receive the expected tax treatment as a partnership; it is reclassified as a corporation or sole proprietorship. Uncertainty as to the state income tax treatment of a check-the-box selection alone may keep the owners from exercising their supposed freedom of choice of tax entity.

simplified the determination of entity classification. See Chapter 12 for a more detailed discussion of the check-the-box provisions.

An individual conducting a sole proprietorship files Schedule C of Form 1040. If more than one trade or business is conducted, a separate Schedule C is filed for each trade or business. A partnership files Form 1065. A corporation files Form 1120, and an S corporation files Form 1120S. An LLC that has elected to be taxed as a partnership files Form 1065.

About 7 million corporations file U.S. income tax returns every year, and about 4.4 million of these use S corporation status. About 3.4 million partnership returns are filed every year, and more than 21 million individual returns report sole proprietorship activities on Schedule C in a typical tax year. The business entity forms that are growing in number the fastest are the sole proprietorship (twice as many as 15 years ago) and the partnership (perhaps due to the popularity of limited liability entities).

18-1b Limited Liability Companies

A **limited liability company (LLC)** is a hybrid business form that combines the corporate characteristic of limited liability for the owners with the tax characteristics of a partnership.[4] All of the states now permit this legal form for conducting a business.

The most frequently cited nontax benefit of an LLC is the limited liability of the owners. Compared to the other forms of ownership, LLCs offer additional benefits over other forms of business, including the following.

Advantages over S corporations
- Greater flexibility in terms of the number of owners, types of owners, special allocation opportunities, and capital structure.
- Inclusion of entity debt in the owner's basis for an ownership interest.
- More liberal deferral of gain recognition on contributions of appreciated property by an owner (determined under § 721 rather than § 351).
- For securities law purposes, an ownership interest in an LLC is not necessarily a security.

---

[4]Depending on state law, an LLC may be organized as a limited liability corporation or a limited liability partnership.

TAX IN THE NEWS Professional Service Firms and Organizational Form

Many professional service firms (e.g., accountants, architects, attorneys) have chosen to become limited liability partnerships. In the accounting profession, this includes all of the Big 4 (i.e., Deloitte, EY, KPMG, and PwC) and most regional and local accounting firms.

An LLP helps to provide protection for the purely personal assets of the partners. Under the LLP organizational structure, the only partners whose personal assets are at risk to pay a judgment are those actually involved in the negligence or wrongdoing at issue. Note, however, that the entity is still responsible for the full judgment. Thus, the capital of the entity is still at risk.

Advantages over C corporations
- Ability to pass tax attributes through to the owners.
- Absence of double taxation.

Advantages over limited partnerships
- Right of all owners to participate in the management of the business.
- Ability of all owners to have limited liability (no need for a general partner).
- For securities law purposes, an ownership interest in an LLC is not necessarily a security (the interest of a limited partner normally is classified as a security).

Advantages over general partnerships
- Limited liability for owners.
- Greater continuity of life.
- Limitation on an owner's ability to withdraw from the business.

Among the disadvantages associated with LLCs are the following.

- Requirement in most states that there be at least two owners.
- Inability to qualify for § 1244 ordinary loss treatment.
- Absence of a developed body of case law on LLCs.

18-2 NONTAX FACTORS

LO.2

Include nontax factors in business decisions.

Taxes are only one of many factors to consider when making a business decision. Above all, any business decision should make economic sense.

THE BIG PICTURE

Example 2

Return to the facts of *The Big Picture* on p. 18-1. George is considering investing $10,000 in a limited partnership. He projects that he will be able to deduct the $10,000 capital contribution within the next two years (as his share of partnership losses). Because George's marginal tax rate is 28%, the deductions will produce a positive cash-flow effect of $2,800 ($10,000 × 28%). However, there is a substantial risk that he will not recover any of his original investment. If this occurs, his negative cash flow from the investment in the limited partnership is $7,200 ($10,000 − $2,800). George must decide whether the investment makes economic sense.

18-2a Capital Formation

The ability of an entity to raise capital is a factor that must be considered by the original owners of the business. A sole proprietorship has the narrowest capital base.

TAX FACT Revenue Relevance of Corporate versus Individual Taxpayers

Federal income taxes (FIT) provide over half of the Federal budget receipts. As indicated in the table to the right, the portion provided by individual taxpayers (which includes the effect of flow-through entities) far exceeds that provided by corporate taxpayers.

	2013	2014
% of budget receipts from FIT	59%	57%
% of FIT from individual taxpayers	80%	81%
% of FIT from corporate taxpayers	20%	19%

Source: Federal Budget of the United States.

Compared to the sole proprietorship, the partnership has a greater opportunity to raise funds through the pooling of owner resources.

> Adam and Beth decide to form a partnership, AB. Adam contributes cash of $200,000, and Beth contributes land with an adjusted basis of $60,000 and a fair market value of $200,000. The partnership is going to construct an apartment building at a cost of $800,000. AB pledges the land and the building to secure a loan of $700,000.

Example 3

The limited partnership offers even greater potential than the general partnership form because a limited partnership can secure funds from investors (i.e., future limited partners).

> Carol and Dave form a limited partnership, CD. Carol contributes cash of $200,000, and Dave contributes land with an adjusted basis of $60,000 and a fair market value of $200,000. The partnership is going to construct a shopping center at a cost of $5 million. Included in this cost is the purchase price of $800,000 for land adjacent to that contributed by Dave. Thirty limited partnership interests are sold for $100,000 each to raise $3 million. CD then pledges the shopping center (including the land) and obtains nonrecourse creditor financing of another $2 million.

Example 4

Both the at-risk limitations and the passive activity loss provisions reduce the tax attractiveness of investments in real estate, particularly in the limited partnership form. In effect, the tax rules themselves place a severe curb on the economic consequences. Chapter 6 presents these loss rules and their critical interaction.

Of the different business entities, the corporate form offers the greatest ease and potential for obtaining owner financing because it can issue additional shares of stock. The ultimate examples of this form are the large public companies that are listed on the stock exchanges.

18-2b Limited Liability

A corporation offers its owners limited liability under state law. This absence of personal liability on the part of the owners is the most frequently cited advantage of the corporate form.

> Ed, Fran, and Gabriella each invest $25,000 for all of the shares of stock of Brown Corporation. Brown obtains creditor financing of $100,000. Brown is the defendant in a personal injury suit resulting from an accident involving one of its delivery trucks. The court awards a judgment of $2.5 million to the plaintiff. The award exceeds Brown's insurance coverage by $1.5 million. Even though the judgment probably will result in Brown's bankruptcy, the shareholders will have no personal liability for the unpaid corporate debts.

Example 5

FIGURE 18.1   Limited Partnership with a Corporate General Partner

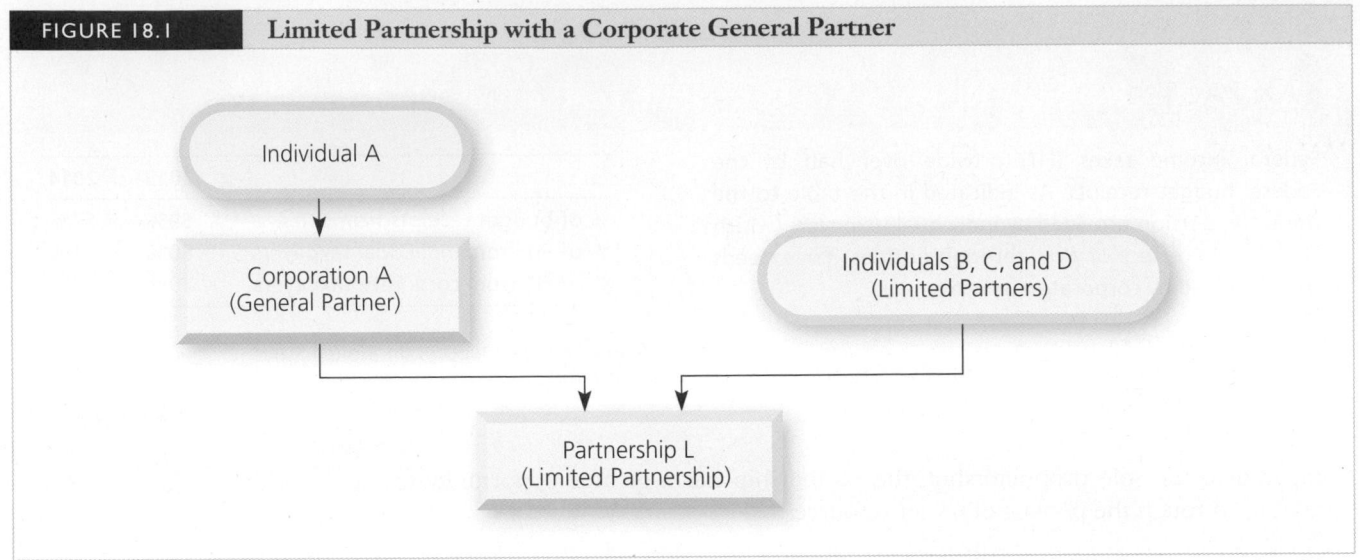

Limited liability is not available to all corporations. For many years, state laws did not permit professional individuals (e.g., accountants, attorneys, architects, and physicians) to incorporate. Even though professionals now are allowed to incorporate, the statutes do not provide limited liability for the performance of professional services.

Even if state law provides for limited liability, the shareholders of small corporations may forgo this benefit. Quite often, a corporation may be unable to obtain external financing (e.g., a bank loan) at reasonable interest rates unless the shareholders guarantee the loan.

The limited partnership form provides limited liability to the limited partners. Their liability is limited to the amount invested plus any additional amount they agree to invest. In contrast, a general partner has unlimited liability.

Example 6	Hazel, the general partner, invests $250,000 in HIJ, a limited partnership. Iris and Jane, the limited partners, each invest $50,000. While the potential loss for Iris and Jane is limited to $50,000 each, Hazel's liability is unlimited.

Indirectly, it may be possible to provide the general partner with limited liability by establishing a corporation as the general partner (see Figure 18.1). When a venture is structured this way, the general partner (the corporation) has limited its liability under the corporate statutes. In the figure, individual A is protected from personal liability by being merely the shareholder of Corporation A.

18-2c Other Factors

Other nontax factors may be significant in selecting an organization form, such as:

* Estimated life of the business.
* Number of owners and their roles in the management of the business.
* Freedom of choice in transferring ownership interests.
* Organizational formality, including the related cost and extent of government regulation.

LO.3

Distinguish between the forms for conducting a business according to whether they are subject to single taxation or double taxation.

18-3 SINGLE VERSUS DOUBLE TAXATION

18-3a Overall Effect on Entity and Owners

The sole proprietorship, limited liability entity, and partnership are subject to a *single* level of Federal income taxation. This result occurs because the owner(s) and

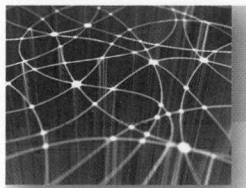

BRIDGE DISCIPLINE Bridge to Business Law and Financial Accounting

When a business entity is created and assets are transferred to the business entity by the owners, the tax balance sheet and the financial accounting balance sheet generally show different amounts for the assets. The balance sheet amounts reflect the extent to which the *conduit theory* or *entity theory* is applied.

Conduit theory, also referred to as aggregate theory or proprietary theory, assumes that the business entity is merely an extension of the owners. Therefore, the transfer of the assets by the owners to the entity is not a taxable event. The owners' basis for their ownership interests is a carryover basis. The business entity's basis for its assets is a carryover basis.

Entity theory assumes that the business entity is separate and apart from the owners. Therefore, the transfer of assets by the owners to the entity is a taxable event. The owners' basis for their ownership interests is a new basis (i.e., fair market value). The business entity's basis for its assets is a new basis (i.e., fair market value).

Financial accounting uses a form of the entity theory. Thus, the critical value is the fair market value of each asset contributed by an owner to the business entity. Tax law generally applies the conduit theory. Thus, the critical value for income tax computations is the owner's adjusted basis for the contributed assets.

the business generally are not considered separate entities for tax purposes. The tax liability is levied at the owner level rather than at the entity level.

In contrast, a corporation and its owners can be subject to *double* taxation. This is frequently cited as the major tax disadvantage of the corporate form. The entity is taxed on the earnings of the corporation, and the owners are taxed on distributions to the extent they are made from corporate earnings.[5]

The S corporation provides a way to avoid double taxation and possibly subject corporate earnings to a lower tax rate (the individual tax rate may be lower than the corporate tax rate). However, the ownership structure of an S corporation is restricted in both the number and type of shareholders. In addition, statutory exceptions subject the entity to taxation in certain circumstances.[6] To the extent these corporate-level taxes apply, double taxation results. Finally, the distribution policy of the S corporation may create difficulties under the *wherewithal to pay* concept.

Example 7

Hawk Corporation has been operating as an S corporation since it began its business two years ago. For both of the prior years, Hawk incurred a tax loss. Hawk has taxable income of $75,000 this year and expects that its earnings will increase each year in the foreseeable future. Part of this earnings increase results from Hawk's expansion into other communities in the state. Because most of this expansion will be financed internally, no dividend distributions will be made to Hawk's shareholders.

Assuming that all of Hawk's shareholders are in the 33% tax bracket, their tax liability on corporate earnings will be $24,750 ($75,000 × 33%). Even though Hawk will not distribute any cash to the shareholders, they still will be required to pay the tax liability. This creates a wherewithal to pay problem. In addition, the corporate tax liability would have been less if Hawk had not been an S corporation [(15% × $50,000) + (25% × $25,000) = $13,750].

The shareholders' wherewithal to pay problem could be resolved by terminating the S corporation election. The tax liability would then be imposed at the corporate level. Because Hawk does not intend to make any dividend distributions, double taxation at the present time would be avoided. Terminating the election also reduces the overall tax liability by $11,000 ($24,750 − $13,750).[7]

In making the decision about the form of business entity, Hawk's shareholders should consider more than the current taxable year. If the S election is terminated,

---

[5]If the corporation is a personal service corporation (see Chapter 12), the corporation is subject to a flat tax rate of 35%.

[6]Recall the Chapter 15 discussions of the taxes on an S corporation's built-in gains, LIFO recapture, and investment income.

[7]The absence of distributions to shareholders could create an accumulated earnings tax (AET) problem under § 531. However, as long as earnings are used to finance expansion, the "reasonable needs" provision will be satisfied, and the corporation will avoid any AET. Refer to the discussion of the AET in Chapter 13.

another election might not be available for five years. Thus, the decision to revoke the election should be made using at least a five-year planning horizon. Perhaps a better solution would be to retain the election and distribute enough dividends to the S corporation shareholders to enable them to pay the shareholder tax liability.

Two other variables that relate to the adverse effect of double taxation are the timing and form of corporate distributions. If no distributions are made, then only single taxation occurs in the short run.[8]

First, to the extent that double taxation does occur in the future, the cash-flow effect should be discounted to its present value. Second, when the distribution is made, is it in the form of a dividend or a return of capital?[9] The owners likely would prefer to receive long-term capital gain (subject to lower tax rates) instead of ordinary income. Proper structuring of the distribution can accomplish this result. Note that for distributions made in 2003 and thereafter, the availability of the beneficial rate for qualified dividends reduces the potential negative impact of double taxation (see Chapter 4).

Tax Planning Strategies   SELLING STOCK VERSUS SELLING CORPORATE ASSETS

FRAMEWORK FOCUS: TAX RATE

Strategy: Avoid Double Taxation.

Molly owns all of the stock of Peach, Inc., a C corporation that she wants to sell. Since she started the business, the fair market value of the corporate assets and the value of her stock investment have appreciated by about $7 million. The C corporation's marginal tax rate is 34 percent. Unfortunately, the buyer of the corporation is interested only in purchasing its assets and does not want to buy the stock.

Molly's objective is to avoid double taxation, and she is considering the following alternatives.

• Sell the C corporation stock for its fair market value to her wholly owned S corporation. The S corporation then will liquidate the C corporation. As the value of the assets received will equal the purchase price of the

stock, no gain will result, and only the C corporation is subject to tax.
• Have the C corporation elect S corporation status and then liquidate.
• Liquidate the C corporation (i.e., sell off all of the assets). Because the sale of the assets produces the same results as a sale of the stock, she accounts for the liquidation as a stock sale.
• Offer the buyer a $500,000 reduction in the purchase price if he will agree to purchase the stock rather than the corporate assets.

Evaluate these four alternatives in terms of achieving Molly's objective.

18-3b Alternative Minimum Tax

All of the forms of business are directly or indirectly subject to the alternative minimum tax (AMT).[10] For the sole proprietorship and the C corporation, the effect is direct (the AMT liability calculation is attached to the tax form that reports the entity's taxable income—Form 1040 or Form 1120). For the partnership, limited liability entity, and S corporation, the effect is indirect; the tax preferences and adjustments pass through from the entity to the owners, and the AMT liability calculation is *not* assessed on the tax form that reports the entity's taxable income— Form 1065 or Form 1120S.

When compared to other entities, the C corporation appears to have a slight advantage. The corporate AMT rate of 20 percent is less than the individual AMT rates of 26 and 28 percent.

---

[8]This assumes that there is no accumulated earnings tax problem. See especially Example 10 in the subsequent discussion of distributions in Minimizing Double Taxation.

[9]Redemptions of stock and corporate liquidations may be taxed as a sale of stock to shareholders (i.e., as capital gain or loss). See § 302 and Chapter 13.

[10]§ 55.

Do Corporations Pay Taxes?

Global Tax Issues

© iStockphoto.com/Andrey Prokhorov

A disadvantage of being a C corporation is the potential for double taxation. This potential disappears, however, if the taxable income of the corporation is zero or negative.

A Government Accountability Office (GAO) study indicates that for the period 1996–2000, more than 60 percent of U.S. corporations did not owe or pay any Federal income taxes. Neither did 70 percent of foreign-owned corporations doing business in the United States. By 2003, corporate tax receipts had fallen to 7.4 percent of overall Federal receipts, the lowest percentage since 1983.

Another GAO study released in early 2009 found that 83 of the largest publicly traded corporations maintain subsidiaries in 50 tax havens. Senator Carl Levin (who requested the GAO study) along with Senator Byron Dorgan (now retired), both Democrats, concluded that "too many corporations are finagling ways to dodge paying Uncle Sam, despite the benefits they receive from doing business in this country."

An even better perspective is provided by comparing the maximum AMT rate with the maximum regular rate for both the individual and the corporation. For the individual, the AMT rate is 71 percent (28%/39.6%) of the maximum regular rate. The AMT rate for the corporation is 57 percent (20%/35%) of the maximum regular rate. Therefore, on the basis of comparative rates, the C corporation appears to offer lower AMT tax burdens. In addition, as discussed below, under certain circumstances, a C corporation is exempt from the AMT.

The apparent corporate AMT rate advantage may be more than offset by the ACE adjustment, which applies only to C corporations.[11] If the ACE adjustment continually causes the C corporation to be subject to the AMT, the owners should consider electing S corporation status (if eligibility requirements can be satisfied). Because the S corporation does not compute an ACE adjustment, it may be possible to reduce the tax liability.

The AMT does not apply to modest-sized C corporations. To be exempt from the tax, the corporation must meet both of the following tests.

- Average annual gross receipts of not more than $5 million for the three tax years after 1993.
- Average annual gross receipts of not more than $7.5 million for every subsequent three-tax-year period.

A corporation automatically is classified as a small corporation in the first year of existence. About 95 percent of all C corporations are likely to meet these tests and be exempt from the AMT in the future.

Tax Planning Strategies   PLANNING FOR THE AMT

FRAMEWORK FOCUS: TAX RATE

Strategy: Shift Net Income from High-Bracket Years to Low-Bracket Years.

If the AMT will apply in the current year, the entity should consider accelerating income and delaying deductions, so that current-year taxable income is taxed at the lower AMT rate.

For a C corporation, the potential rate differential is 15 percentage points (20 percent AMT rate versus 35 percent top regular tax rate). For an individual (i.e., as a sole proprietor, as a partner, or as an S corporation shareholder), the potential tax rate differential is 11.6 percentage points (28 percent highest AMT rate versus 39.6 percent top regular tax rate).

A present value analysis should be used to make such decisions about any income acceleration and deduction deferrals.

---

[11]§§ 56(c)(1) and (f). Refer to the discussion of the corporate AMT in Chapter 17.

TAX IN THE NEWS   Who Pays Corporate AMT?

One of the issues often raised in debates over tax legislation is whether the corporate AMT should be repealed. Among the topics discussed are the revenue generated, the related compliance costs, and the number of corporations subject to the AMT.

According to the IRS, nearly 6 million corporate tax returns were filed in 2003. Of these returns, under 15,000 included any AMT.

Proponents of the corporate AMT argue that these statistics show that the AMT is being paid by corporations targeted by the law (i.e., large corporations). Opponents argue that the same statistics show that the compliance costs borne by the mass of corporations do not justify the continuation of this tax system.

The exemption from the AMT for small corporations may be providing the needed solution. Large corporations must make minimal Federal income tax payments when the AMT applies. Most C corporations no longer need to compute the tax.

———————

Source: IRS *Tax Stats.*

18-3c State Taxation

In selecting a form for doing business, the determination of the tax consequences should not be limited to Federal income taxes. Consideration also should be given to state income taxes and, if applicable, local income taxes.

The S corporation provides a good illustration of this point. Suppose that the forms of business being considered are a limited partnership and a corporation. An operating loss is projected for the next several years. The owners decide to operate the business in the corporate form. The principal nontax criterion for the decision is the limited liability attribute of the corporation. The owners consent to an S corporation election so that the corporate losses can be passed through to the shareholders to deduct on their individual tax returns. However, assume that state law does not permit the S corporation election. Thus, the owners will not receive the tax benefits of the loss deductions that would have been available on their state income tax returns if they had chosen the limited partnership form. As a result of providing limited liability to the owner who would have been the general partner for the limited partnership, the loss deduction at the state level is forgone.

18-4 MINIMIZING DOUBLE TAXATION

LO.4

Identify techniques for avoiding double taxation.

Only the corporate form is potentially subject to double taxation. Several techniques are available for eliminating or at least reducing the second layer of taxation.

- Making distributions to the shareholders that are deductible to the corporation.
- Not making distributions to the shareholders.
- Making distributions that qualify for return of capital treatment at the shareholder level.
- Making the S corporation election.

18-4a Making Deductible Distributions

Corporations often distribute net profits to their owners in a form that results in a deduction to the corporation. Examples of such deductible distributions include:

- Salary payments to shareholder-employees.
- Lease or rental payments to shareholder-lessors.
- Interest payments to shareholder-creditors.

Recognizing the potential for abuse, the IRS scrutinizes these types of distributions carefully. All three forms are evaluated in terms of *reasonableness.*[12] In addition, interest payments to shareholders may lead to reclassification of some or all of the debt as equity.[13] IRS success with either approach raises the specter of double taxation.

Example 8

Donna owns all the stock of Green Corporation and is the chief executive officer. Green's taxable income before salary payments to Donna is as follows.

2012	2013	2014
$80,000	$50,000	$250,000

During the year, Donna receives a monthly salary of $3,000. In December of each year, Donna reviews the operations for the year and determines the year-end bonus she is to receive. Donna's yearly bonuses are as follows.

2012	2013	2014
$44,000	$14,000	$214,000

The apparent purpose of Green's bonus program is to reduce the corporate taxable income to zero and thereby avoid double taxation. An examination of Green's tax return by the IRS would likely result in a deduction disallowance for **unreasonable compensation.**

Example 9

Tom and Vicki each contribute $20,000 to TV Corporation for all of its stock. In addition, they each lend $80,000 to TV. The loan is documented by formal notes, the interest rate is 8%, and the maturity date is 10 years from the date of the loan.

The notes provide the opportunity for the corporation to make payments of $6,400 each year to both Tom and Vicki and for the payments not to be subject to double taxation. This happens because the interest payments are includible in the gross income of Tom and Vicki, but are deductible by TV in calculating its taxable income. At the time of repayment in 10 years, neither Tom nor Vicki recognizes gross income from the repayment; the $80,000 amount realized is equal to the basis for the note of $80,000.

If the IRS succeeded in reclassifying the notes as equity, Tom and Vicki still would have gross income of $6,400, but the interest would be reclassified as dividend income (which may be taxed at the 15% rate). Because dividend payments are not deductible by TV, the corporation's taxable income would increase by $12,800 ($6,400 × 2). To make matters worse, the repayment of the notes in 10 years would not qualify as a recovery of capital, resulting in additional dividend income for Tom and Vicki.

18-4b Not Making Distributions

Double taxation will not occur unless the corporation makes (actual or deemed) distributions to the shareholders. A closely held C corporation that does not make distributions may eventually encounter an accumulated earnings tax problem unless the reasonable needs requirement is satisfied. When making distribution decisions each year, the board of directors should be apprised of any potential accumulated earnings tax problem and take the appropriate steps to eliminate it. The accumulated earnings tax rate of 20 percent in 2014 is higher than the 15 percent rate for qualified dividends that applies to most individual investors.[14] It equals the top 20 percent tax rate for qualified dividends that applies to certain high-income taxpayers.

---

[12]§ 162(a)(1). *Mayson Manufacturing Co. v. Comm.,* 49–2 USTC ¶9467, 38 AFTR 1028, 178 F.2d 115 (CA–6, 1949); *Harolds Club v. Comm.,* 65–1 USTC ¶9198, 15 AFTR 2d 241, 340 F.2d 861 (CA–9, 1965).

[13]§ 385; Rev.Rul. 83–98, 1983–2 C.B. 40; *Bauer v. Comm.,* 84–2 USTC ¶9996, 55 AFTR 2d 85–433, 748 F.2d 1365 (CA–9, 1984).

[14]§ 531. Refer to the discussion of the accumulated earnings tax in Chapter 13.

TAX IN THE NEWS   Changing the Tax Treatment of Debt

Interest payments made by a business on entity debt are deductible. Dividend payments made by a business on entity equity are not deductible. The same tax results as to these payments could be achieved by either of the following changes.

- Make the dividend payments deductible.
- Make the interest payments nondeductible.

Although only at the embryonic stage, serious analysis is under way with respect to the latter approach. A 2010 proposal by the panel appointed by President Obama considered the change in the current tax treatment of debt among one of the main aspects of a corporate tax overhaul.

Congress and legislative advisers have requested a study on the issue by the Joint Committee on Taxation. Among the factors supporting such an analysis are the following.

- Curtailing the interest deductions would generate revenue.
- Limiting such interest deductions could help discourage another buildup of leverage by financial firms, which many people believe contributed to the 2008 U.S. financial meltdown.
- The present advantage of debt financing when compared with equity financing would disappear.
- The problems arising from thin capitalizations would be eliminated.

Of course, with any change in the tax law, there are winners and losers. Perceived losers would include Wall Street, big manufacturers, and small businesses that do not have access to equity markets.

_____

Source: Based on John D. McKinnon, "Potential Tax Change Is Red Flag for Some Firms," *Wall Street Journal,* April 4, 2011, p. A2.

FINANCIAL DISCLOSURE INSIGHTS   Who Pays the Corporate Federal Income Tax and Why It Is Decreasing

C corporations and their shareholders potentially are subject to double taxation. Tax legislation enacted in 2003 substantially reduced the combined burden by making qualified dividends eligible for beneficial tax rates (i.e., 15%/5%/0%). Another option considered at that time, but rejected by the administration and Congress, was to eliminate taxation at the C corporation level and have corporate profits taxed at the shareholder level.

A question that frequently arises in this continuing debate is just how heavy the corporate Federal income tax burden is. An analysis by the Government Accountability Office shows that larger companies (assets of more than $250 million or gross receipts over $50 million) are more likely to pay income taxes than are smaller ones. In 2000,

55 percent of larger companies paid Federal income taxes whereas fewer than 50 percent did so in 2002. The authors of the report believe that many larger companies could bring their tax burden down to $0 if they chose to do so. To do so, however, would create "unwanted attention."

One of the reasons for the falling corporate tax burden is that larger portions of corporate earnings are being generated in countries that impose lower tax rates. General Electric is an example of this trend. GE paid income tax on earnings at a rate of 21.7 percent in 2003 compared with 28.3 percent in 2001. GE's annual report for 2003 attributed this decline in its tax burden to "the increasing share of earnings from lower taxed international operations." For 2010, General Electric paid $0 Federal income tax.

Example 10

According to an internal calculation made by Dolphin Corporation, its accumulated taxable income is $400,000. The board of directors would prefer not to declare any dividends, but is considering a dividend declaration of $400,000 to avoid the accumulated earnings tax. All of the shareholders are in the 35% bracket.

If a dividend of $400,000 is declared, the tax cost to the shareholders is $60,000 ($400,000 × 15%, assuming that the dividends are qualified dividends). If a dividend is not declared and the IRS assesses the accumulated earnings tax, the tax cost to the corporation for the accumulated earnings tax is $80,000 ($400,000 × 20%).

To make matters worse, Dolphin will have incurred the accumulated earnings tax cost without getting any funds out of the corporation to the shareholders. If the unwise decision were now made to distribute the remaining $320,000 ($400,000 − $80,000) to the shareholders, the additional tax cost at the shareholder level is $48,000 ($320,000 × 15%). Therefore, the combined shareholder-corporation tax cost is $128,000 ($80,000 + $48,000). This is 160% ($128,000/$80,000) of the tax cost that would have resulted from an initial dividend distribution of $400,000.

Assuming that the accumulated earnings tax can be avoided (e.g., a growth company whose reasonable needs justify its failure to pay dividends), a policy of no distributions to shareholders can avoid the second layer of taxation on corporate earnings. The retained earnings will drive the value of the shares upward, equal to the accumulated after-tax cash. As a result of the step-up in basis rules for inherited property, the basis of the stock for the beneficiaries will be the fair market value at the date of the decedent's death rather than the decedent's basis.

18-4c Return of Capital Distributions

The exposure to double taxation can be reduced if the corporate distributions to the shareholders can qualify for return of capital rather than dividend treatment. This can occur when the corporation's earnings and profits (E & P) are low or negative in amount. Review Example 1 in Chapter 13. In some cases, the stock redemption provisions offer an opportunity to avoid dividend treatment altogether. Under these rules, the distribution may be treated as a sale of the shareholder's stock, resulting in a tax-free recovery of basis and then recognition of low-tax long-term capital gain.

18-4d Electing S Corporation Status

Electing S corporation status generally eliminates double taxation. Several factors, listed below, should be considered when making this election.

- Are all of the shareholders willing to consent to the election?
- Can the qualification requirements under § 1361 be satisfied at the time of the election?

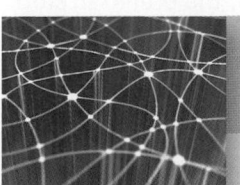

BRIDGE DISCIPLINE Bridge to Economics

Corporations such as Coca-Cola, IBM, Microsoft, Walmart, and Exxon-Mobil are major players not only in their industries, but also in the world economy. However, some people also are attracted to "mom-and-pop stores," which cumulatively play a major role in the economy.

In recognition of the important role of small businesses and their size competitive disadvantage at times, Congress has provided small businesses with beneficial tax treatment that is not available to major business entities. Included among such beneficial treatments are the following.

- § 11 beneficial tax rates.
- § 44 disabled access credit.

- § 55(e) exemption from the AMT for small corporations.
- § 179 limited expensing for tangible personal property.
- § 1045 deferral of gain for qualified small business stock.
- § 1202 for partial exclusion of gain for certain small business stock.
- § 1244 ordinary loss treatment.

Each of these provisions defines "small" in a different way. Sometimes, however, when beneficial tax treatment is provided for a business entity, *small* may be used inappropriately. The classic example is the small business corporation of Subchapter S. Some S corporations hold billions of dollars of assets. They are "small" only in the sense that the number of shareholders cannot exceed 100 unrelated shareholders.

TAX FACT Income Tax Returns Filed

Type of Taxpayer	Tax Returns Filed (millions)			
	1980	1990	2000	2012
Individual	93.1	112.3	126.9	146.2
Partnership	1.4	1.8	2.1	3.3
C corporation	2.1	2.3	2.2	2.3
S corporation	.5	1.5	2.8	4.1

The number of S corporation returns has increased dramatically since 1980. LLCs usually file using the Federal income tax partnership rules, and the popularity of this entity form has led to a notable increase in the number of partnership returns filed.

Source: IRS *Tax Stats.*

- Can the S corporation requirements continue to be satisfied?
- For what period will the conditions that make the election beneficial continue to prevail?
- Will the corporate distribution policy create wherewithal to pay problems at the shareholder level?

Example 11

Emerald Corporation commenced business in January 2014. The two shareholders, Diego and Jaime, are both in the 28% tax bracket. The following operating results are projected for the first five years of operations.

2014	2015	2016	2017	2018
($50,000)	$400,000	$600,000	$800,000	$1,000,000

The corporation plans to expand rapidly. Therefore, no distributions will be made to shareholders. In addition, beginning in 2015, preferred stock will be offered to a substantial number of investors to help finance the expansion.

If the S corporation election is made for 2014, the $50,000 loss can be passed through to Diego and Jaime. The loss will generate a positive cash-flow effect of $14,000 ($50,000 × 28%). Assume that the election is either revoked or involuntarily terminated at the beginning of 2015 as a result of the issuance of the preferred stock. The corporate tax liability for 2015 is $136,000 ($400,000 × 34%).

If the S corporation election is not made for 2014, the $50,000 loss is a net operating loss. The amount can be carried forward to reduce the 2015 corporate taxable income to $350,000 ($400,000 − $50,000). The resultant tax liability is $119,000 ($350,000 × 34%).

Should the S corporation election be made for just the one-year period? The answer is unclear. With an assumed after-tax rate of return to Diego and Jaime of 10%, the value of the $14,000 one year hence is $15,400 ($14,000 × 110%). Even considering the time value of money, the combined corporation-shareholder negative cash-flow effect of $120,600 ($136,000 − $15,400) in the case of an S election is not significantly different from the $119,000 corporate tax liability that would result for a C corporation.

Another benefit of electing S corporation status is that the corporation is not subject to the accumulated earnings or personal holding company taxes.

18-5 Conduit versus Entity Treatment

Under the **conduit concept**, the entity is viewed as merely an extension of the owners. Under the **entity concept**, the entity is regarded as being separate and distinct from its owners. The effects of the conduit and entity concepts extend to a variety of tax rules, including the following.

- Recognition at time of contribution to the entity.
- Basis of ownership interest.
- Results of operations.
- Recognition at time of distribution.
- Passive activity losses.
- At-risk rules.
- Special allocations.

LO.5

State and apply the conduit and entity concepts as they affect operations, capital changes, and distributions.

The sole proprietorship is not analyzed separately because the owner and the business are the same tax entity. In one circumstance, however, a tax difference can result. Income recognition does not occur when an owner contributes an asset to a sole proprietorship. Thus, the business generally takes a carryover basis. However, if the asset is a personal-use asset, the sole proprietorship's basis is the *lower of* the adjusted basis or the fair market value at the date of contribution. If a personal-use asset is contributed to a partnership or corporation, this same *lower-of* rule applies.

18-5a Effect on Recognition at Time of Contribution to the Entity

Because the conduit approach applies to partnerships, § 721 provides for no recognition on the contribution of property to a partnership in exchange for a partnership interest. Section 721 protects both a contribution associated with the formation of the partnership and later contributions. The partnership takes a carryover basis in the contributed property, and the partners have a carryover basis in their partnership interests.[15]

Because the entity approach applies to corporations, the transfer of property to a corporation in exchange for its stock is a taxable event. However, if the § 351 control requirement (80 percent) is satisfied, no gain or loss is recognized. In this case, both the corporate property and the shareholders' stock have a carryover basis.[16] This control requirement makes it possible for shareholders who contribute appreciated property to the corporation *after* its formation to recognize gain.

To the extent that the fair market value of property contributed to the entity at the time of formation is not equal to the property's adjusted basis, the entity might want to make a special allocation associated with the subsequent sale of the contributed property. With a special allocation, the owner contributing the property receives the tax benefit or detriment for any recognized gain or loss that subsequently results because of the initial difference between the adjusted basis and the fair market value. For the partnership, this special allocation treatment is mandatory. No such allocation is available for a C corporation because the gain or loss is recognized at the corporation level rather than at the shareholder level. As with a C corporation, no such allocation is available for an S corporation. The recognized gain or loss is reported on the shareholders' tax returns according to their stock ownership.

Example 12

Khalid contributes land with an adjusted basis of $10,000 and a fair market value of $50,000 for a 50% ownership interest. At the same time, Tracy contributes cash of $50,000 for the remaining 50% ownership interest. Because the entity is unable to obtain the desired zoning, it subsequently sells the land for $50,000.

---

[15]Refer to the pertinent discussion in Chapter 14. [16]Refer to the pertinent discussion in Chapter 12.

If the entity is a C corporation, Khalid has a realized gain of $40,000 ($50,000 − $10,000) and a recognized gain of $0 resulting from the contribution. His basis in the stock is $10,000, and the corporation has a basis in the land of $10,000. The corporation realizes and recognizes a gain of $40,000 ($50,000 − $10,000) when it sells the land. Thus, what should have been Khalid's recognized gain is now the corporation's taxable gain. There is no way by which the corporation can allocate the recognized gain directly to Khalid. The corporation could distribute the land to Khalid and let him sell it, but such a distribution is likely to be taxable to Khalid as a dividend, and gain on the distribution is also recognized at the corporate level.

If the entity is a partnership or limited liability entity, the tax consequences are the same as for the C corporation, except for the $40,000 recognized gain on the sale of the land. The partnership realizes and recognizes a gain of $40,000 ($50,000 − $10,000). However, even though Khalid's share of profits and losses is only 50%, all of the $40,000 recognized gain is allocated to him. If the entity is an S corporation, the tax consequences are the same as for the C corporation, except that Khalid reports $20,000 of the recognized gain on his tax return and Tracy also reports $20,000.

Not all contributions of assets to corporations are made by shareholders. States and local governments continue to lure businesses to locate in a particular state or locality with promises of tax breaks and grants.

18-5b Effect on Basis of Ownership Interest

In the case of a partnership or an LLC, the contribution of property to the entity in exchange for an ownership interest is not a taxable event under § 721. Therefore, the owner's basis for the ownership interest is a carryover basis. For C and S corporations, the nontaxable and related carryover basis results are appropriate only if the 80 percent control requirement of § 351 is satisfied. If the control requirement is not satisfied, any realized gain or loss on the transaction is recognized, and the stock basis is equal to the fair market value of the contributed property.

In a partnership or a limited liability entity, because the owner is the taxpayer, profits and losses of the partnership affect the owner's basis in the entity interest. Likewise, the owner's basis is increased by the share of entity liability increases and is decreased by the share of liability decreases. Accordingly, ownership basis changes frequently.[17]

Because a C corporation is a taxpaying entity, the shareholder's basis for the stock is not affected by corporate profits and losses or corporate liability changes.

The treatment of an S corporation shareholder falls between that of the partner and the C corporation shareholder. The S corporation shareholder's stock basis is increased by the share of profits and decreased by the share of losses, but it usually is not affected by corporate liability increases or decreases.[18]

THE BIG PICTURE

Example 13

Return to the facts of *The Big Picture* on p. 18-1. Bill contributed cash of $100,000 to an entity for a 30% ownership interest in the franchise. The entity borrows $50,000 and repays $20,000 of this amount by the end of the taxable year. The profits for the year are $90,000.

If the entity is a partnership or limited liability entity, Bill's basis at the end of the period is $136,000 ($100,000 investment + $9,000 share of net liability increase + $27,000 share of profits). If Bill is a C corporation shareholder instead, his stock basis is $100,000 ($100,000 original investment). If the corporation is an S corporation, Bill's stock basis is $127,000 ($100,000 + $27,000).

---

[17]§§ 705 and 752.

[18]Recall from Chapter 15 that pass-through S corporation losses can reduce a *shareholder's* basis in loans to the entity.

18-5c Effect on Results of Operations

The entity concept is responsible for producing potential double taxation for the C corporation if the corporation is taxed on its earnings, and the shareholders are taxed on the distribution of earnings. Thus, from the perspective of taxing the results of operations, the entity concept appears to provide a disadvantage to C corporations. However, whether the entity concept actually produces disadvantageous results depends on the following.

- Whether the corporation generates positive taxable income.
- Which tax rates apply to the corporation and to the shareholders.
- What is the distribution policy of the corporation.

As discussed previously, techniques exist for getting cash out of the corporation to the shareholders without incurring double taxation (e.g., compensation payments to shareholder-employees, lease payments to shareholder-lessors, and interest payments to shareholder-creditors). Because these payments are deductible to the corporation, they reduce corporate taxable income. If the payments can be used to reduce corporate taxable income to zero, the corporation will have no tax liability.

The maximum individual tax rate (39.6 percent) exceeds the maximum C corporation tax rate (35 percent). However, for a specific shareholder, the corporate tax rate that applies may be greater than or less than the applicable individual tax rate.

Double taxation occurs only if distributions (actual or constructive) are made to the shareholders. Thus, if no distributions (actual or constructive) are made and if the entity can avoid the accumulated earnings tax (e.g., based on the statutory credit or the reasonable needs adjustment) and the personal holding company tax (e.g., the corporation primarily generates active income), only one current level of taxation will occur. If the distribution can qualify for return of capital rather than dividend treatment, the shareholder tax liability is decreased. Finally, taxation of the earnings at the shareholder level can be avoided permanently if the stock passes through the decedent shareholder's estate.[19]

Application of the entity concept causes income and deductions to lose any unique tax characteristics when they are passed through to shareholders in the form of dividends. This may produce a negative result for capital gains. Because capital gains lose their identity when passed through in the form of dividends, they cannot be used to offset capital losses at the shareholder level. An even more negative result is produced when dividends are paid out of tax-exempt income. Tax-exempt income is excludible in calculating corporate taxable income, but is included in calculating current earnings and profits. Thus, exclusions from income may be taxed because of the entity concept.

Partnerships, limited liability entities, and S corporations use the conduit concept in reporting the results of operations. Any item that is subject to special treatment on the taxpayer-owner's tax return is reported separately to the owner. Other items are aggregated and reported as taxable income. Thus, taxable income merely represents the sum of income and deductions that are not subject to special treatment.[20]

Many of the problems the entity concept may produce for the C corporation form are not present in pass-through entities. In particular, pass-through entities are not subjected to double taxation, problems with the reasonableness requirement, or loss of identity of the income or expense item at the owner level.

Only partnerships and limited liability entities completely apply the conduit concept when reporting the results of operations. In several circumstances, the S corporation is subject to taxation at the corporate level, including the tax on built-in gains. This limited application of the entity concept necessitates additional planning to attempt to avoid taxation at the corporate level.

---

[19]Recall Chapter 7's analysis of the basis step-up rules for property acquired from a decedent.

[20]§§ 701, 702, 1363, and 1366.

Section 311(b) of the Internal Revenue Code, which is applicable to C corporations and S corporations, provides that realized gain on the distribution of appreciated property to a shareholder results in recognized gain to the corporation. There is no similar statutory provision for the distribution of appreciated property made by a partnership to a partner.

However, the IRS has held that in one limited circumstance a distribution of appreciated property made by a partnership to a partner results in recognized gain to the partnership. If the appreciated property is distributed to the partner in satisfaction of a guaranteed payment under §707(c), the distribution is treated as a sale or exchange under § 1001 rather than a distribution under §731.

18-5d Effect on Recognition at Time of Distribution

The application of the conduit concept results in distributions not being taxed to the owners. The application of the entity concept produces the opposite result. Therefore, tax-free distributions can be made to owners of flow-through entities, whereas distributions to C corporation shareholders may be taxable.

A combination entity/conduit concept applies to property distributions from S corporations. The conduit concept applies with respect to the shareholder. However, if the distributed property has appreciated in value, any realized gain is recognized at the corporate level.[21] This is the same treatment received by C corporations. Thus, corporate-level gain recognition is an application of the entity concept, whereas the pass-through of the gain to shareholders is an application of the conduit concept.

Example 14

Tan, an S corporation, is equally owned by Leif and Matt. Tan distributes two parcels of land to Leif and Matt. Tan has a basis of $10,000 for each parcel. Each parcel has a fair market value of $15,000. The distribution results in a $10,000 ($30,000 − $20,000) recognized gain for Tan. Leif and Matt each report $5,000 of the gain on their individual income tax returns.

Stock redemptions and complete liquidations receive identical treatment whether a C or S corporation is involved.[22]

18-5e Effect on Passive Activity Losses

The passive activity loss rules apply to flow-through entities, personal service corporations, and closely held C corporations. A *closely held C corporation* exists when more than 50 percent of the value of the outstanding stock at any time during the last half of the taxable year is owned by or for not more than five individuals. A corporation is classified as a *personal service corporation* if the following requirements are satisfied.[23]

- The principal activity of the corporation is the performance of personal services.
- The services are substantially performed by owner-employees.
- Owner-employees own more than 10 percent in value of the stock of the corporation.

The general passive loss rules apply to personal service corporations. Therefore, passive activity losses can be offset only against passive activity income. For closely held corporations, the application of the passive activity rules is less harsh. Passive activity losses can be offset against both active and passive income.

Because the conduit concept applies to partnerships, S corporations, and limited liability entities, the passive activity results are separately stated at the entity level and are passed through to the owners with their passive character maintained.

---

[21]§ 311(b).
[22]§§ 302, 331, and 336.

[23]§ 469, derived from the definition in § 269A.

A major shareholder of a closely held S corporation leased an airplane to the corporation at a fair rental. As part of the lease agreement, the owner provided a pilot and crew. The lease also required that a replacement airplane be made available when repairs were needed for the leased aircraft. If the deductions associated with the airplane exceed the rent income, is any such loss active or passive? According to a recent Revenue Ruling, significant services are being provided. Thus, the lease activity is classified as active rather than passive, and the loss is not subject to the § 469 passive activity limits.

18-5f Effect of At-Risk Rules

The at-risk rules apply to all flow-through entities and to closely held C corporations. The rules produce a harsher result for partnerships and limited liability entities than for S corporations. This occurs because of the way liabilities affect partners' basis.

Example 15

Walt is the general partner, and Ira and Vera are the limited partners in the WIV limited partnership. Walt contributes land with an adjusted basis of $40,000 and a fair market value of $50,000 for his partnership interest, and Ira and Vera each contribute cash of $100,000 for their partnership interests. They agree to share profits and losses equally. To finance construction of an apartment building, the partnership obtains $600,000 of nonrecourse financing [not qualified nonrecourse financing under § 465(b)(6)] using the land and the building as the pledged assets. Each partner's basis for the partnership interest is as follows.

	Walt	Ira	Vera
Contribution	$ 40,000	$100,000	$100,000
Share of nonrecourse debt	200,000	200,000	200,000
Basis	$240,000	$300,000	$300,000

Without the at-risk rules, Ira and Vera could pass through losses up to $300,000 each even though they invested only $100,000 and have no personal liability for the nonrecourse debt. However, the at-risk rules limit the loss pass-through to the at-risk basis, which is $100,000 for Ira and $100,000 for Vera.

The at-risk rules also affect the general partner. Because Walt is not at risk for the nonrecourse debt, his at-risk basis is $40,000. If the mortgage were recourse debt, his at-risk basis would be $640,000 ($40,000 + $600,000).

If, instead, the entity were an S corporation and Walt received 20% of the stock and Ira and Vera each received 40%, the basis for their stock would be as follows.

Walt	Ira	Vera
$40,000	$100,000	$100,000

In S corporations, nonrecourse debt does not affect the calculation of stock basis. The stock basis for each shareholder would remain the same even if the debt were recourse debt. Only direct loans by the shareholders increase the ceiling on loss pass-through.

18-5g Effect of Special Allocations

An advantage of the conduit concept over the entity concept is the ability to make special allocations. Special allocations are not permitted in C corporations. Indirectly, however, the corporate form may be able to achieve results similar to those produced by special allocations through payments to owners (e.g., salary payments,

TAX FACT   Profitability of Partnerships

Since 1980, the number of partnership income tax returns has more than doubled (i.e., from 1.4 million returns to 3.4 million returns). The beneficial tax treatment of LLCs is expected to cause this trend to continue. While the partnership provides a tax shelter opportunity by passing losses through to the partner, a majority of partnerships are profitable.

	1985	1990	1995	2000	2010	2011
% of returns with profits	53%	56%	63%	60%	47%	48%
% of returns with losses	47%	44%	37%	40%	53%	52%

Source: IRS *Tax Stats.*

lease rental payments, and interest payments) and through different classes of stock (e.g., preferred and common). However, even in these cases, the breadth of the treatment and the related flexibility are far less than that achievable under the conduit concept.

Although S corporations generally operate as conduits, they are treated more like C corporations than partnerships with respect to special allocations. This treatment results from the application of the per-share and per-day allocation rule in § 1377(a). Although S corporations are limited to one class of stock, they still can use salary, interest, and rental payments to owners to shift income to the desired recipient. However, the IRS can reallocate income among members of a family if fair returns are not provided for services rendered or capital invested.[24]

Example 16

The stock of an S corporation is owned by Debra (50%), Helen (25%), and Joyce (25%). Helen and Joyce are Debra's adult children. Debra is subject to a 35% marginal tax rate, and Helen and Joyce have a 15% marginal tax rate. Only Debra is an employee of the corporation. She is paid an annual salary of $20,000, whereas employees with similar responsibilities in other corporations earn $100,000. The corporation generates earnings of approximately $200,000 each year.

It appears that the reason Debra is paid a low salary is to enable more of the earnings of the S corporation to be taxed to Helen and Joyce, who are in lower tax brackets. Thus, the IRS could use its statutory authority to allocate a larger salary to Debra.

Partnerships and limited liability entities have many opportunities to use special allocations, including the following (refer to Chapter 14).

* The ability to share profits and losses differently from the share in capital.
* The ability to share profits and losses differently.
* A required special allocation for the difference between the adjusted basis and the fair market value of contributed property.
* The special allocation of some items if a substantial economic effect rule is satisfied.

18-6 DISPOSITION OF A BUSINESS OR AN OWNERSHIP INTEREST

LO.6

Analyze the effects of the disposition of a business on the owners and the entity for each of the forms for conducting a business.

A key factor in evaluating the tax consequences of a business disposition is whether the disposition is viewed as the sale of an ownership interest or as a sale of assets. Generally, the tax consequences are more favorable to the seller if the transaction is treated as a sale of the ownership interest.

[24]§ 1366(e).

18-6a Sole Proprietorships

Regardless of the form of the transaction, the sale of a sole proprietorship is treated as the sale of individual assets. Thus, gains and losses must be calculated separately for each asset. Classification as capital gain or ordinary income depends on the nature and holding period of the individual assets. Ordinary income property such as inventory will result in ordinary gains and losses. Section 1231 property such as land, buildings, and machinery used in the business will produce § 1231 gains and losses (subject to depreciation recapture under §§ 1245 and 1250). Capital assets such as investment land and stocks qualify for capital gain or loss treatment.

If the amount realized exceeds the fair market value of the identifiable assets, the excess is allocated to goodwill, which generates capital gain for the seller. If instead the excess payment is allocated to a covenant not to compete, the related gain is classified as ordinary income rather than capital gain. Both goodwill and covenants are amortized over a 15-year statutory period.[25]

Seth, who is in the 35% tax bracket, sells his sole proprietorship to Wilma for $600,000. The identifiable assets are as follows.

	Adjusted Basis	Fair Market Value
Inventory	$ 20,000	$ 25,000
Accounts receivable	40,000	40,000
Machinery and equipment*	125,000	150,000
Buildings**	175,000	250,000
Land	40,000	100,000
	$400,000	$565,000

*Potential § 1245 recapture of $50,000.
**Potential § 1250 recapture of $20,000.

The sale produces the following results for Seth.

	Gain (Loss)	Ordinary Income	§ 1231 Gain	Capital Gain
Inventory	$ 5,000	$ 5,000		
Accounts receivable	–0–			
Machinery and equipment	25,000	25,000		
Buildings	75,000	20,000	$ 55,000	
Land	60,000		60,000	
Goodwill	35,000			$35,000
	$200,000	$50,000	$115,000	$35,000

Example 17

If the sale is structured this way, Wilma can deduct the $35,000 paid for goodwill over a 15-year period. If instead Wilma paid the $35,000 to Seth for a covenant not to compete for a period of seven years, she still would amortize the $35,000 over a 15-year period. However, Seth's $35,000 capital gain would now be taxed to him as ordinary income. If the covenant has no legal relevance to Wilma, in exchange for treating the payment as a goodwill payment, she should negotiate for a price reduction that reflects Seth's benefit from the lower capital gains tax.

18-6b Partnerships and Limited Liability Entities

The sale of a partnership or limited liability entity can be structured as the sale of assets or as the sale of an ownership interest. If the transaction takes the form of an asset sale, it is treated the same as for a sole proprietorship (described previously). The sale of an ownership interest is treated as the sale of a capital asset, although

---

[25]§ 197.

TAX IN THE NEWS A One-Way Street for Partners

Janel paid $800,000 for Waldo's partnership interest in the DWT Partnership. Waldo's outside basis was $600,000, which equaled his share of the partnership's inside basis for the partnership assets. Unless the partnership makes a § 754 election, Janel eventually will pay income taxes on the $200,000 difference between her outside basis of $800,000 and her share of the inside basis of $600,000. A § 754 election will activate § 743 and provide her with a special basis adjustment of $200,000. But does she recognize the need for making the § 754 election, and will the other partners cooperate?

Suppose the amounts are reversed (i.e., Janel paid $600,000 for an inside basis of $800,000). In this situation, Janel would prefer to avoid making the § 754 election. But the tax law limits the partners' ability to make this choice. An automatic downward basis adjustment is required if the partnership has a "substantial built-in loss" at the time of the transfer.

This § 743 treatment applies only to losses. For built-in gains, an affirmative § 754 election is necessary to trigger an upward § 743 basis adjustment.

ordinary income potential exists for unrealized receivables and substantially appreciated inventory. Thus, if capital gain treatment can produce beneficial results for the taxpayer (e.g., he or she has capital losses to offset or has beneficially treated net capital gain), the sale of an ownership interest is preferable.

From a buyer's perspective, tax consequences are not affected by the form of the transaction. If the transaction is an asset purchase, the basis for the assets equals the amount paid. If a buyer intends to continue to operate as an LLC or a partnership, the assets can be contributed to the entity under § 721. Therefore, the owner's basis in the entity interest is equal to the purchase price for the assets. Likewise, if ownership interests are purchased, the owner's basis is the purchase price paid. The partnership's basis for the assets is the purchase price because the original partnership was terminated.[26]

When the inside and outside bases of a partner's ownership interest differ (see Chapter 14), an election can be made to step up the partner's share of the entity's asset bases.[27] This tax-free basis step-up applies to all such exchanges by all of the partners as long as the election is in effect. The election allows asset basis to reflect increases in fair market value and the goodwill that a new partner has purchased.

Example 18

Roz buys a one-third interest in the RST Partnership for $50,000 (outside basis). All of the entity's assets are depreciable, and their basis to the partnership (inside basis) is $90,000. If a § 754 election is in effect, the partnership can step up the basis of its depreciable assets by $20,000, the difference between Roz's outside and inside basis amounts [$50,000 − (1/3 × $90,000)]. All of the "new" asset basis is allocated to Roz.

18-6c C Corporations

The sale of a business held by a C corporation can be structured as either an asset sale or a stock sale. The stock sale has the dual advantage to the seller of being less complex both as a legal transaction and as a tax transaction. It also has the advantage of providing a way to avoid double taxation. Finally, any gain or loss on the sale of the stock is treated as a capital gain or loss to the shareholder.

Example 19

Jane and Zina each own 50% of the stock of Purple Corporation. They have owned the business for 10 years. Jane's basis in her stock is $40,000, and Zina's basis in her stock is $60,000. They agree to sell the stock to Rex for $300,000. Jane recognizes a long-term capital gain of $110,000 ($150,000 − $40,000), and Zina recognizes a long-term capital gain of $90,000 ($150,000 − $60,000). Rex has a basis in his stock of $300,000. Purple's basis in its assets does not change as a result of the stock sale.

[26]§ 708(b)(1)(B).   [27]§§ 743 and 754.

| *Tax Planning Strategies* | SELLING STOCK OR ASSETS |

FRAMEWORK FOCUS: TAX RATE

Strategy: Avoid Double Taxation.

Structuring the transfer of the business as a stock sale may produce detrimental tax results for the purchaser. As Example 19 illustrates, the basis of the corporation's assets is not affected by the stock sale. If the fair market value of the stock exceeds the corporation's adjusted basis for its assets, the purchaser is denied the opportunity to step up the basis of the assets to reflect the amount in effect paid for them through the stock acquisition—no § 754 election is available to C corporations.

If an asset sale is used, the seller of the business can be either the corporation or its shareholders. If the seller is the corporation, the corporation sells the business (the assets), pays any debts not transferred, and makes a liquidating distribution to the shareholders. If the sellers are the shareholders, the corporation pays any debts that will not be transferred and makes a liquidating distribution to the shareholders; then the shareholders sell the business.

Regardless of the approach used for an asset sale, double taxation occurs. The corporation is taxed on the actual sale of the assets, and it is taxed as if it had sold the assets when it makes the liquidating distribution to the shareholders. The shareholders are taxed when they receive cash or assets distributed in kind by the corporation.

An asset sale resolves the purchaser's problem of not being able to step up the basis of the assets to their fair market value. The basis for each asset is its purchase price. Then the purchaser needs to transfer the property to a corporation in a § 351 transaction.

From the perspective of the seller, the ideal form of the transaction is a stock sale. Conversely, from the purchaser's perspective, the ideal form is an asset purchase. Thus, a conflict exists between the buyer's and the seller's objectives regarding the form of the transaction. Therefore, the bargaining ability of the seller and the purchaser to structure the sale as a stock sale or an asset sale, respectively, is critical.

Rather than selling off all of the assets of the business, an owner may sell his or her ownership interest. Because the form of this transaction is a stock sale, a capital gain or loss typically results.

18-6d S Corporations

Because the S corporation is a corporation, it is subject to the provisions for a C corporation discussed previously. Either an asset sale at the corporate level or a liquidating distribution of assets produces recognition at the corporate level. However, under the conduit concept applicable to the S corporation, the recognized amount is taxed at the shareholder level. Therefore, double taxation is avoided directly (only the shareholder is involved) for a stock sale and indirectly (the conduit concept ignores the involvement of the corporation) for an asset sale.

Double taxation might seem to be avoided by making an S corporation election prior to the liquidation of a C corporation, but the built-in gains tax closes this loophole; taxation occurs at the corporate level, and double taxation results.

Concept Summary 18.1 reviews the tax consequences of business dispositions.

18-7 CONVERTING TO OTHER ENTITY TYPES

Rather than disposing of a business, the owners may decide to convert the tax entity form to a different tax entity form. This raises three primary issues.

- Does the conversion result in the recognition of gain or loss?
- What is the basis for the ownership interest in the new entity form?
- What is the basis of the assets of the new entity form?

CONCEPT SUMMARY 18.1

Tax Treatment of Disposition of a Business

Form of Entity	Form of Transaction	Tax Consequences	
		Seller	Buyer
Sole proprietorship	Sale of individual assets.	Gain or loss is calculated separately for the individual assets. Classification as capital or ordinary depends on the nature and holding period of the individual assets. If amount realized exceeds the fair market value of the identifiable assets, the excess is allocated to goodwill (except to the extent identified with a covenant not to compete), which is a capital asset.	Basis for individual assets is the allocated cost. Prefers that any excess of purchase price over the fair market value of identifiable assets be identified with a covenant not to compete. Otherwise, the buyer is neutral, because both goodwill and covenants are amortized over a 15-year statutory period.
	Sale of the business.	Treated as a sale of the individual assets (as above).	Treated as a purchase of the individual assets (as above).
Partnership and limited liability entity	Sale of individual assets.	Treatment is the same as for the sole proprietorship.	Treatment is the same as for the sole proprietorship. If the intent is to operate in partnership form, the assets can be contributed to a partnership under § 721.
	Sale of ownership interest.	Entity interest is treated as the sale of a capital asset under § 741 (subject to ordinary income potential under § 751 for unrealized receivables and substantially appreciated inventory).	Basis for new owner's ownership interest is the cost. The new entity's basis for the assets is also the pertinent cost (i.e., contributed to the entity under § 721), because the original entity will have terminated.
C corporation	Sale of corporate assets by corporation (i.e., corporation sells assets, pays debts, and makes liquidating distribution to the shareholders).	Double taxation occurs. Corporation is taxed on the sale of the assets with the gain or loss determination and the classification as capital or ordinary treated the same as for the sole proprietorship. Shareholders calculate gain or loss as the difference between the stock basis and the amount received from the corporation in the liquidating distribution. Capital gain or loss usually results, because stock typically is a capital asset.	Basis for individual assets is the allocated cost. If the intent is to operate in corporate form, the assets can be contributed to a corporation under § 351.
	Sale of corporate assets by the shareholders (i.e., corporation pays debts and makes liquidating distribution to the shareholders).	Double taxation occurs. At the time of the liquidating distribution to the shareholders, the corporation is taxed as if it had sold the assets. Shareholders calculate gain or loss as the difference between the stock basis and the fair market value of the assets received from the corporation in the liquidating distribution. Capital gain or loss usually results, because stock typically is a capital asset.	Same as corporate asset sale.

Tax Treatment of Disposition of a Business—Continued

Form of Entity	Form of Transaction	Tax Consequences	
		Seller	Buyer
	Sale of corporate stock.	Enables double taxation to be avoided. Because the corporation is not a party to the transaction, there are no tax consequences at the corporate level. Shareholders calculate gain or loss as the difference between the stock basis and the amount received for the stock. Capital gain or loss usually results, because stock typically is a capital asset.	Basis for the stock is its cost. The basis for the corporate assets is not affected by the stock purchase.
S corporation	Sale of corporate assets by corporation.	Recognition occurs at the corporate level on the sale of the assets, with the gain or loss determination and the classification as capital or ordinary treated the same as for the sole proprietorship. Conduit concept applicable to the S corporation results in the recognized amount being taxed at the shareholder level. Double taxation associated with the asset sale is avoided, because the shareholder's stock basis is increased by the amount of gain recognition and decreased by the amount of loss recognition. Shareholders calculate gain or loss as the difference between the stock basis and the amount received from the corporation in the liquidating distribution. Capital gain or loss usually results, because stock typically is a capital asset.	Basis for individual assets is the allocated cost. If the intent is to operate in corporate form (i.e., as an S corporation), the assets can be contributed to a corporation under § 351.
	Sale of corporate assets by the shareholders.	At the time of the liquidating distribution to the shareholders, recognition occurs at the corporation level as if the corporation had sold the assets. The resultant tax consequences for the shareholders and the corporation are the same as for the sale of corporate assets by the S corporation.	Same as corporate asset sale by the corporation.
	Sale of corporate stock.	Same as the treatment for the sale of stock of a C corporation.	Same as the treatment for the purchase of stock of a C corporation.

18-7a Sole Proprietorship

The conversion of a sole proprietorship into another entity form can be achieved without any recognition of gain or loss at the entity level or at the owner level. This result occurs regardless of the choice of the new entity form. If the proprietorship is converted into a partnership or an LLC, nonrecognition can be achieved.[28] If the business is converted into either an S corporation or a C corporation, nonrecognition also is available.[29]

---

[28]§ 721(a).   [29]§ 351(a).

If the proprietorship converts into a partnership or LLC, the basis of an ownership interest of the partner or LLC member is a carryover basis.[30] If the proprietorship converts into a corporation, the shareholder's basis for the stock received is a carryover basis.[31]

After a conversion, the partnership or LLC takes a carryover basis for its assets.[32] Similarly, a corporation takes a carryover basis for its assets.[33]

18-7b C Corporation

A C corporation can convert into any of the following entity forms, all of which permit having multiple owners.

- Partnership or LLC.
- S corporation.

Converting to the S corporation tax entity form merely requires the election of S status.[34] As discussed in Chapter 15, the S election can be made only if all shareholders consent to the election and if the S corporation qualification requirements are satisfied.[35] These qualification requirements become maintenance requirements that must be met to retain the S election.

Therefore, the election of S status produces the following tax consequences.

- No recognition of gain or loss.
- Carryover basis for the shareholders' stock.
- Carryover basis for the assets of the corporation.

If a C corporation converts into a partnership or LLC, the corporation must be liquidated. This produces the following tax consequences.

- Recognition of gain or loss at the corporate level.[36]
- Recognition of gain or loss at the shareholder level.[37]
- Fair market value basis for the assets distributed in liquidation.[38]

After liquidation, the C corporation contributes its assets to the new partnership or LLC. The tax consequences to the owners and to the entity are the same as those for a sole proprietorship that converts to a partnership or an LLC.

18-7c Partnership

A partnership can convert into either of the following entity forms, both of which permit having multiple owners.

- C corporation.
- S corporation.

The partners can transfer their partnership interests to the C corporation or S corporation in exchange for the stock of the entity. Because the transfer likely satisfies the § 351 requirements, any realized gain or loss is not recognized.[39] If, however, the 80 percent control requirement is not satisfied, the realized gain or loss is recognized by the partners.[40]

Assuming that the § 351 requirements for nonrecognition are satisfied, the following tax results occur.

- The basis of the stock to the shareholders is a carryover basis.[41]
- The basis of the assets to the corporation is a carryover basis.[42]

[30]§ 722.
[31]§ 358(a).
[32]§ 723.
[33]§ 362(a).
[34]§ 1362(a).
[35]§§ 1361(a), 1361(b), and 1362(a)(2).
[36]§ 336(a).

[37]§ 331(a).
[38]§ 334(a).
[39]§ 351(a).
[40]§ 368(c).
[41]§ 358(a).
[42]§ 362(a).

18-8 OVERALL COMPARISON OF FORMS OF DOING BUSINESS

LO.7

Compare the tax consequences of the most common legal forms of doing business.

Concept Summary 18.2 provides a detailed comparison of the tax consequences of the various forms of doing business.

CONCEPT SUMMARY 18.2

Tax Attributes of Different Forms of Doing Business (Assume That Partners and Shareholders Are All Individuals)

	Sole Proprietorship	Partnership/Limited Liability Entity	S Corporation	C Corporation
Restrictions on type or number of owners	One owner. The owner must be an individual.	Must have at least 2 owners.	Only individuals, estates, certain trusts, and certain tax-exempt entities can be owners. Maximum number of shareholders limited to 100.*	None, except some states require a minimum of 2 shareholders.
Incidence of tax	Sole proprietorship's income and deductions are reported on Schedule C of the individual's Form 1040. A separate Schedule C is prepared for each business.	Entity not subject to tax. Owners in their separate capacity subject to tax on their distributive share of income. Entity files Form 1065.	Except for certain built-in gains and passive investment income when earnings and profits are present from C corporation tax years, entity not subject to Federal income tax. S corporation files Form 1120S. Shareholders are subject to tax on income attributable to their stock ownership.	Income subject to double taxation. Entity subject to tax, and shareholder subject to tax on any corporate dividends received. Corporation files Form 1120.
Highest tax rate	39.6% at individual level.	39.6% at owner level.	39.6% at shareholder level.	35% at corporate level plus 20%/15%/0% on any corporate dividends at shareholder level (if qualified dividends; otherwise 39.6%).
Choice of tax year	Same tax year as owner.	Selection generally restricted to coincide with tax year of majority owners or principal owners, or to tax year determined under the least aggregate deferral method.	Restricted to a calendar year unless IRS approves a different year for business purposes or other exceptions apply.	Unrestricted selection allowed at time of filing first tax return.

*Spouses and family members can be treated as 1 shareholder.

Tax Attributes of Different Forms of Doing Business—Continued

	Sole Proprietorship	Partnership/Limited Liability Entity	S Corporation	C Corporation
Timing of taxation	Based on owner's tax year.	Owners report their share of income in their tax year within which the entity's tax year ends. Owners in their separate capacities are subject to payment of estimated taxes.	Shareholders report their shares of income in their tax year within which the corporation's tax year ends. Shareholders may be subject to payment of estimated taxes.	Corporation subject to tax at close of its tax year. May be subject to payment of estimated taxes. Dividends are subject to tax at the shareholder level in the tax year received.
Basis for allocating income to owners	Not applicable (only one owner).	Profit and loss sharing agreement. Cash basis items of cash basis entities are allocated on a daily basis. Other entity items are allocated after considering varying interests of owners.	Pro rata share based on stock ownership. Shareholder's pro rata share is determined on a daily basis, according to the number of shares of stock held on each day of the corporation's tax year.	Not applicable.
Contribution of property to the entity	Not a taxable transaction.	Generally not a taxable transaction.	Is a taxable transaction unless the § 351 requirements are satisfied.	Is a taxable transaction unless the § 351 requirements are satisfied.
Character of income taxed to owners	Retains source characteristics.	Conduit—retains source characteristics.	Conduit—retains source characteristics.	All source characteristics are lost when income is distributed to owners.
Basis for allocating a net operating loss to owners	Not applicable (only one owner).	Profit and loss sharing agreement. Cash basis items of cash basis entities are allocated on a daily basis. Other entity items are allocated after considering varying interests of owners.	Prorated among shareholders on a daily basis.	Not applicable.
Limitation on losses deductible by owners	Investment plus liabilities.	Owner's investment plus share of liabilities.	Shareholder's investment plus loans made by shareholder to corporation.	Not applicable.
Subject to at-risk rules?	Yes, at the owner level. Indefinite carryover of excess loss.	Yes, at the owner level. Indefinite carryover of excess loss.	Yes, at the shareholder level. Indefinite carryover of excess loss.	Yes, for closely held corporations. Indefinite carryover of excess loss.
Subject to passive activity loss rules?	Yes, at the owner level. Indefinite carryover of excess loss.	Yes, at the owner level. Indefinite carryover of excess loss.	Yes, at the shareholder level. Indefinite carryover of excess loss.	Yes, for closely held corporations and personal service corporations. Indefinite carryover of excess loss.

Tax Attributes of Different Forms of Doing Business—Continued

	Sole Proprietorship	Partnership/Limited Liability Entity	S Corporation	C Corporation
Tax consequences of earnings retained by entity	Taxed to owner when earned and increases his or her investment in the sole proprietorship.	Taxed to owners when earned and increases their respective interest bases in the entity.	Taxed to shareholders when earned and increases their respective interest bases in stock.	Taxed to corporation when earned and may be subject to penalty tax if accumulated unreasonably.
Nonliquidating distributions to owners	Not taxable.	Not taxable unless money received exceeds recipient owner's basis in entity interest. Existence of § 751 assets may cause recognition of ordinary income.	Generally not taxable unless the distribution exceeds the shareholder's AAA or stock basis. Existence of accumulated earnings and profits could cause some distributions to be dividends.	Taxable in year of receipt to extent of earnings and profits or if exceeds basis in stock.
Capital gains	Taxed at owner level using maximum rate of 0%, 15%, 20%, 25%, or 28%.	Conduit—owners must account for their respective shares. Taxed at owner level.	Conduit, with certain exceptions (a possible penalty tax)—shareholders must account for their respective shares. Tax treatment determined at shareholder level.	Taxed at corporate level with a maximum 35% rate. No other benefits.
Capital losses	Only $3,000 of capital losses can be offset each tax year against ordinary income. Indefinite carryover.	Conduit—owners must account for their respective shares. Tax treatment determined at owner level.	Conduit—shareholders must account for their respective shares. Tax treatment determined at shareholder level.	Carried back three years and carried forward five years. Deductible only to the extent of capital gains.
§ 1231 gains and losses	Taxable or deductible at owner level. Five-year lookback rule for § 1231 losses.	Conduit—owners must account for their respective shares. Tax treatment determined at owner level.	Conduit—shareholders must account for their respective shares. Tax treatment determined at shareholder level.	Taxable or deductible at corporate level only. Five-year lookback rule for § 1231 losses.
Foreign tax credits	Available at owner level.	Conduit—tax payments passed through to owners.	Generally conduit—tax payments passed through to shareholders.	Available at corporate level only.
§ 1244 treatment of loss on sale of interest	Not applicable.	Not applicable.	Available.	Available.
Basis treatment of entity liabilities	Not applicable.	Includible in interest basis.	Not includible in stock basis.	Not includible in stock basis.
Built-in gains	Not applicable.	Not applicable.	Possible corporate tax.	Not applicable.
Special allocations to owners	Not applicable (only one owner).	Available if supported by substantial economic effect.	Not available.	Not applicable.
Availability of fringe benefits to owners	None.	None.	None unless a 2% or less shareholder.	Available within antidiscrimination rules.

Tax Attributes of Different Forms of Doing Business—Continued

	Sole Proprietorship	Partnership/Limited Liability Entity	S Corporation	C Corporation
Effect of liquidation/ redemption/ reorganization on basis of entity assets	Not applicable.	Usually carried over from entity to owner.	Taxable step-up to fair market value.	Taxable step-up to fair market value.
Sale of ownership interest	Treated as the sale of individual assets. Classification of recognized gain or loss depends on the nature of the individual assets.	Treated as the sale of an entity interest. Recognized gain or loss is classified as capital, although appreciated inventory and receivables are subject to ordinary income treatment.	Treated as the sale of corporate stock. Recognized gain is classified as capital gain. Recognized loss is classified as capital loss, subject to ordinary loss treatment under § 1244.	Treated as the sale of corporate stock. Recognized gain is classified as capital gain. Recognized loss is classified as capital loss, subject to ordinary loss treatment under § 1244.
Distribution of appreciated property	Not taxable.	No recognition at the entity level.	Recognition at the corporate level to the extent of the appreciation. Conduit—amount of recognized gain is passed through to shareholders.	Taxable at the corporate level to the extent of the appreciation.
Splitting of income among family members	Not applicable (only one owner).	Difficult—IRS will not recognize a family member as an owner unless certain requirements are met.	Rather easy—gift of stock will transfer tax on a pro rata share of income to the donee. However, IRS can make adjustments to reflect adequate compensation for services.	Same as an S corporation, except that donees will be subject to tax only on earnings actually or constructively distributed to them. Other than unreasonable compensation, IRS generally cannot make adjustments to reflect adequate compensation for services and capital.
Organizational costs	Startup expenditures are eligible for $5,000 limited expensing (subject to phaseout) and amortizing balance over 180 months.	Organizational costs are eligible for $5,000 limited expensing (subject to phaseout) and amortizing balance over 180 months.	Same as partnership.	Same as partnership.
Charitable contributions	Limitations apply at owner level.	Conduit—owners are subject to deduction limitations in their own capacities.	Conduit—shareholders are subject to deduction limitations in their own capacities.	Limited to 10% of taxable income before certain deductions.

Tax Attributes of Different Forms of Doing Business—Continued

	Sole Proprietorship	Partnership/Limited Liability Entity	S Corporation	C Corporation
Alternative minimum tax	Applies at owner level. AMT rates are 26% and 28%.	Applies at the owner level rather than at the entity level. AMT preferences and adjustments are passed through from the entity to the owners.	Applies at the shareholder level rather than at the corporate level. AMT preferences and adjustments are passed through from the S corporation to the shareholders.	Applies at the corporate level. AMT rate is 20%. Modest-sized C corporations are exempt.
ACE adjustment	Does not apply.	Does not apply.	Does not apply.	The adjustment is made in calculating AMTI. The adjustment is 75% of the excess of adjusted current earnings over unadjusted AMTI. If the unadjusted AMTI exceeds adjusted current earnings, the adjustment may be negative.

Tax Planning Strategies | CHOOSING A BUSINESS FORM: CASE STUDY

FRAMEWORK FOCUS: TAX RATE

Strategy: Avoid Double Taxation.
Shift Net Income from High-Bracket Taxpayers to Low-Bracket Taxpayers.

Example 1 illustrated the relationship between tax planning and the choice of business form; it also raised a variety of questions about the advice given by the tax practitioner. By this time, one should be able to develop various scenarios supporting the tax advice given. The actual fact situations that produced the tax adviser's recommendations were as follows.

- Jesse's experience in the dairy industry consists of raising a few heifers during the final five years of his employment. Eva anticipates that Jesse will generate tax losses for the indeterminate future. In addition, Jesse indicated that he and his wife must have limited liability associated with the dairy farm.
- Larry was born and raised on his father's dairy farm. Both his education and his Air Force managerial experience provide him with useful tools for managing his business. However, Larry inherited his farm when milk prices were at a low for the modern era. Because none of her dairy farm clients were profitable, Eva anticipated that Larry would operate his dairy farm at a loss. Larry, like Jesse, thought that limited liability was imperative. Thus, he incorporated the dairy farm and made the S election.
- For the first two years, Larry's dairy farm produced tax losses. Since then, the dairy farm has produced tax

profits large enough to absorb the losses. Larry anticipates that his profits will remain relatively stable in the $50,000 to $75,000 range in the future. Because Larry is subject to a 28 percent marginal tax rate and anticipates that no dividend distributions will be made, his tax liability associated with the dairy farm will be reduced if he terminates the S corporation election.

As Jesse and Larry's example illustrates, selection of the proper business form can result in both nontax and tax advantages. Both of these factors should be considered in making the selection decision. Furthermore, this choice should be reviewed periodically, because a proper business form at one point in time may not be the proper form at a different time. Note that another business form Eva could have considered for Jesse is the limited liability entity.

In looking at the tax attributes, consideration should be given to the tax consequences of the following.

- Contribution of assets to the entity by the owners at the time the entity is created and at later dates.
- Taxation of the results of operations.
- Distributions to owners.
- Disposition of an ownership interest.
- Termination of the entity.

REFOCUS ON THE BIG PICTURE

CHOOSING A BUSINESS FORM AND OTHER INVESTMENTS

Conducting their business as a C corporation, an S corporation, or an LLC would meet Bill and George's objectives of providing limited liability. From a tax perspective, both the S corporation and the LLC would allow the early-year losses to be passed through to the owners. This cannot be achieved with a C corporation, in which the losses are trapped until future years when the company is profitable. Once the entity turns profitable, the tax consequences are as follows.

- As a C corporation, the entity would pay income tax of $61,250 on taxable earnings of $200,000. If the remaining after-tax earnings of $138,750 are distributed equally to Bill and George (each owner would receive a taxable dividend of $69,375), each shareholder pays an additional income tax of $10,406 ($69,375 × 15%). The combined entity/owner tax liability is $82,062, resulting in after-tax cash flows of $117,938.

- If the entity is operated as an S corporation or an LLC, no tax is paid at the entity level. However, the entire $200,000 is taxed as ordinary income at the owner level, resulting in each owner paying $28,000 ($100,000 × 28%) income tax. The combined entity/owner tax liability is $56,000, resulting in after-tax cash flows of $144,000.

It appears that either the S corporation or the LLC meets Bill and George's objectives of having limited liability and minimizing tax liability. The LLC form offers an additional advantage in that an LLC need not satisfy the numerous statutory qualification requirements to elect and maintain S corporation status. However, based on the facts in this situation, it is unlikely that satisfying the requirements would create any difficulty for Bill and George.

The results of George's investing in a limited partnership appear in Example 2. While beneficial tax results are expected to occur, George needs to be aware of the economic risk of losing his $10,000 investment.

For Bill, the recognized gain on the sale of his investment in the retail coffee franchise outlet is dependent on the entity form. If Bill uses a pass-through entity, the recognized gain differs from that if the entity were a C corporation: entity profits increase the owner's interest basis in a pass-through entity, whereas entity profits have no effect on a shareholder's basis in C corporation stock.

What If?

What if Bill and George decide to expand the business and reinvest the annual $200,000 before-tax earnings instead of paying out dividends to the owners? If the business is organized as a C corporation, it can accumulate the earnings—as long as the company has reasonable business needs—and avoid the additional tax that is paid by Bill and George when the company makes taxable dividend distributions. Although the entity-level tax of $61,250 must still be paid, after-tax cash flows increase to $138,750. While the S corporation or LLC with after-tax cash flows of $144,000 still would be preferred in this situation, the double tax problem of the C corporation can be minimized with effective planning.

© Fuse/Jupiter Images

Suggested Readings

John O. Everett, Cherie J. Hennig, and William A. Raabe, "Converting a C Corporation into an LLC: Quantifying the Tax Costs and Benefits," *Journal of Taxation*, August 2010.

Janel Grieman and Thomas J. Nash, "Did Averting Fiscal Cliff Allow C Corporations to Overtake Passthroughs?" *Practical Tax Strategies*, August 2013.

"Payments to a Taxpayer for the Sale of Business Were Ordinary Income," *Practical Tax Strategies*, November 2010.

Joseph Pozzuolo, Jeffrey H. Smith, and Jeffrey S. Pozzuolo, "Structure a Buy-Sell Agreement for Maximum Utility," *Practical Tax Strategies*, October 2009.

W. Eugene Seago and Edward J. Schnee, "Double Deductions Resulting from Transfers to Controlled Corporations" *Journal of Taxation*, March 2011.

Jay A. Soled, Leonard Goodman, and Anthony Pochesci, "Unlocking the Mystery of C Corporations Paying Zero Tax," *Practical Tax Strategies*, November 2012.

Key Terms

Conduit concept, 18-15

Entity concept, 18-15

Limited liability company (LLC), 18-3

Unreasonable compensation, 18-11

Problems

1. **LO.2, 3, 4, 5, 6, 7** Using the legend provided, indicate which form of business entity each of the following characteristics describes. Some of the characteristics may apply to more than one form of business entity.

Legend
SP = Applies to sole proprietorship
P = Applies to partnership and LLC
S = Applies to S corporation
C = Applies to C corporation
N = Applies to none

a. Has limited liability.
b. Greatest ability to raise capital.
c. Subject to double taxation.
d. Subject to accumulated earnings tax.
e. Limit on types and number of shareholders.
f. Has unlimited liability.
g. Sale of the business can be subject to double taxation.
h. Contribution of property to the entity in exchange for an ownership interest can result in the nonrecognition of realized gain.
i. Profits and losses affect the basis for an ownership interest.
j. Entity liabilities affect the basis for an ownership interest.
k. Distributions of earnings are taxed as dividend income to the owners.
l. Total invested capital cannot exceed $1 million.
m. AAA is an account that relates to this entity.

2. **LO.5** Using the legend provided, indicate which form of business entity each of the following characteristics describes. Some of the characteristics may apply to more than one form of business entity.

Legend
P = Applies to partnership and LLC
S = Applies to S corporation
C = Applies to C corporation

a. Basis for an ownership interest is increased by an investment by the owner.
b. Basis for an ownership interest is decreased by a distribution to the owner.
c. Basis for an ownership interest is increased by entity profits.

d. Basis for an ownership interest is decreased by entity losses.

e. Basis for an ownership interest is increased as the entity's liabilities increase.

f. Basis for an ownership interest is decreased as the entity's liabilities decrease.

3. **LO.2** Sea Green Enterprises reports the following assets and liabilities on its balance sheet.

	Net Book Value	Fair Market Value
Assets	$600,000	$925,000
Liabilities	200,000	200,000

Sea Green has just lost a product liability suit with damages of $10 million being awarded to the plaintiff. Although Sea Green will appeal the judgment, legal counsel indicates that the judgment is highly unlikely to be overturned by the appellate court. The product liability insurance carried by Sea Green includes a payout ceiling of $6 million. What is the amount of liability of the entity and its owners if Sea Green is:

a. A sole proprietorship?

b. A partnership or an LLC?

c. A C corporation?

d. An S corporation?

Ethics and Equity

4. **LO.3, 4** Bryan operates his business as a C corporation. He is the only shareholder. The accumulated E & P is $800,000. Starting next year, he plans on distributing $200,000. In future years, he intends to distribute all of the annual earnings. Recognizing that the distribution would be taxed as dividend income, he has developed the following tax strategy.

• Sell the corporate assets to himself for the fair market value.

• Have the corporation invest the sales proceeds in a mutual fund.

• Contribute the assets to an LLC and operate his business in this legal form.

Evaluate Bryan's proposal to avoid double taxation.

5. **LO.3** Red, White, Blue, and Orange report taxable income as follows.

Corporation	Taxable Income
Red	$ 99,000
White	330,000
Blue	900,000
Orange	40,000,000

a. Calculate the marginal tax rate and the effective tax rate for each of the C corporations.

b. Explain why the marginal tax rate for a C corporation can exceed 35% but the effective tax rate cannot.

Decision Making
Communications

6. **LO.1, 2, 3** Amy and Jeff Barnes are going to operate their florist shop as a partnership or as an S corporation. Their mailing address is 5700 Richmond Highway, Alexandria, VA 22301. After paying salaries of $100,000 to each of the owners, the shop's annual earnings are projected to be about $150,000. The earnings are to be invested in the growth of the business. Write a letter to Amy and Jeff advising them of which of the two entity forms they should select.

Decision Making

7. **LO.3** Gerald is an entrepreneur who likes to be actively involved in his business ventures. He is going to invest $500,000 in a business that he projects will produce a tax loss of approximately $125,000 per year in the short run. However, once consumers become aware of the new product being sold by the business and the quality of the service it provides, he is confident the business will generate a profit of at least $200,000 per year. Gerald has substantial other income (from both business ventures and investment activities) each year. Advise Gerald on the business form he should select for the short run. He will be the sole owner.

Decision Making

8. **LO.2, 3** Coleman, a married taxpayer, is going to establish a manufacturing business. He anticipates that the business will be profitable immediately due to a patent he holds. He anticipates that profits for the first year will be about $300,000 and will increase at a

rate of about 20% per year for the foreseeable future. He will be the sole owner of the business. Advise Coleman on the form of business entity he should select. Coleman and his wife will be in the 39.6% Federal income tax bracket.

9. **LO.3** Plum Corporation will begin operations on January 1. Earnings for the next five years are projected to be relatively stable at about $80,000 per year. The shareholders of Plum are in the 33% tax bracket.

    a. Plum will reinvest its after-tax earnings in the growth of the company. Should Plum operate as a C corporation or as an S corporation?

    b. Plum will distribute its after-tax earnings each year to its shareholders. Should Plum operate as a C corporation or as an S corporation?

Decision Making

10. **LO.3** Mabel and Alan, who are in the 35% tax bracket, recently acquired a fast-food franchise. Both of them will work in the business and receive a salary of $175,000. They anticipate that the annual profits of the business, after deducting salaries, will be approximately $450,000. The entity will distribute enough cash each year to Mabel and Alan to cover their Federal income taxes associated with any flow-through income from the franchise.

    a. What amount will the entity distribute if the franchise operates as a C corporation?

    b. What amount will the entity distribute if the franchise operates as an S corporation?

    c. What will be the amount of the combined entity/owner tax liability in (a) and (b)?

11. **LO.3** Owl is a closely held corporation owned by eight shareholders (each has 12.5% of the stock). Selected financial information provided by Owl follows.

Taxable income	$6,250,000
Positive AMT adjustments (excluding ACE adjustment)	600,000
Negative AMT adjustments	(30,000)
Tax preferences	5,000,000
Retained earnings	900,000
Accumulated E & P	2,000,000
ACE adjustment	750,000

    a. Calculate Owl's regular Federal income tax liability and AMT if it is a C corporation.

    b. Calculate Owl's regular Federal income tax liability and AMT if it is an S corporation.

    c. How would your answers in (a) and (b) change if Owl was not closely held (e.g., 5,000 shareholders with no shareholder owning more than 2% of the stock)?

12. **LO.3** Falcon Corporation, a calendar year taxpayer, is a deepwater offshore drilling company that is planning to sell drilling equipment that it no longer needs. The drilling equipment has an adjusted basis of $400,000 ($700,000 − $300,000 depreciation) and a fair market value of $500,000. The AMT adjusted basis of the equipment is $425,000.

Decision Making

    The buyer of the drilling equipment would like to close the transaction prior to the end of the calendar year. Falcon is uncertain whether the tax consequences would be better if the sale took place this year or next year and is considering the following options.

- $500,000 in cash payable on December 31, 2014.
- The sale is closed on December 31, 2014; the consideration is a $500,000 note issued by the buyer. The maturity date of the note is January 2, 2015, with the equipment pledged as security.

    Falcon projects that its taxable income for 2014 and 2015 will be $400,000 (gross receipts of about $9.5 million) without the sale. Falcon has other AMT adjustments and tax preferences of $425,000 in 2014, which will not recur in 2015. Determine the tax consequences to Falcon under both options, and recommend the option that is preferable.

13. **LO.4** Heron Corporation has been in operation for 10 years. Since Heron's creation, all of the stock has been owned by Andy, who initially invested $200,000 in the corporation. Heron has been successful far beyond Andy's expectations, and the current fair market value of the stock is $10 million. While he has been paid a salary of $200,000 per year by the corporation, all of Heron's earnings have been reinvested in the growth of the corporation.

Ethics and Equity

Heron is currently being audited by the IRS. One of the issues raised by the IRS agent is the possibility of the assessment of the accumulated earnings tax. Andy is not concerned about this issue because he believes Heron can easily justify the accumulations based on its past rapid expansion by opening new outlets. The expansion program is fully documented in the minutes of Heron's board of directors. Andy has provided this information to the IRS agent.

Two years ago, Andy decided that he would curtail any further expansion into new markets by Heron. In his opinion, further expansion would exceed his ability to manage the corporation effectively. Because the tax year under audit is three years in the past, Andy sees no reason to provide the IRS agent with this information.

Heron will continue its policy of no dividend payments into the foreseeable future. Andy believes that if the accumulated earnings issue is satisfactorily resolved on this audit, it probably will not be raised again on any subsequent audits. Thus, double taxation in the form of the tax on dividends at the shareholder level or the accumulated earnings tax at the corporate level can be avoided.

What is Heron's responsibility to disclose to the IRS agent the expected change in its growth strategy? Are Andy's beliefs regarding future accumulated earnings tax issues realistic? Explain.

Critical Thinking

14. **LO.4** Two sisters and their brother, all unmarried, own and operate a dairy farm. They live on the farm and take their meals there for the "convenience of the employer." The fair market value of their lodging is $45,000, and the fair market value of their meals is $18,000. The meals are prepared by the farm cook, who provides their meals along with those of the eight other farm employees.
   a. Determine the tax consequences of the meals and lodging to the sisters and their brother if the farm is incorporated.
   b. Determine the tax consequences of the meals and lodging to the sisters and their brother if the farm is not incorporated.

Critical Thinking

15. **LO.4** A business entity has four equal owners. Its taxable income before the cost of certain fringe benefits paid to owners and other employees is $400,000. The amounts paid for these fringe benefits are reported as follows.

	Owners	Other Employees
Group term life insurance	$20,000	$40,000
Meals and lodging incurred for the convenience of the employer	50,000	75,000
Qualified retirement plan	30,000	90,000

   a. Calculate the Federal taxable income of the entity, assuming that it is a(n):
   • Partnership.
   • C corporation.
   • S corporation.
   b. Determine the Federal income effects on the owners, assuming the use of each of the three business forms.

16. **LO.4** Turtle, a C corporation, has taxable income of $300,000 before paying salaries to the three equal shareholder-employees, Britney, Shania, and Alan. Turtle follows a policy of distributing all after-tax earnings to the shareholders.
   a. Determine the tax consequences for Turtle, Britney, Shania, and Alan if the corporation pays salaries to Britney, Shania, and Alan as follows.

Option 1		Option 2	
Britney	$135,000	Britney	$67,500
Shania	90,000	Shania	45,000
Alan	75,000	Alan	37,500

   b. Is Turtle likely to encounter any tax problems associated with either option? Explain.

17. **LO.4** Parrott, Inc., a C corporation, is owned by Abner (60%) and Deanna (40%). Abner is the president, and Deanna is the vice president for sales. Parrott, Abner, and Deanna are cash basis taxpayers. Late in the year, Parrott encounters working capital difficulties. Therefore, Abner loans the corporation $810,000 and Deanna loans the

corporation $540,000. Each loan uses a 5% note that is due in five years with interest payable annually.

a. Determine the tax consequences to Parrott, Abner, and Deanna if the notes are classified as debt.

b. Determine the tax consequences to Parrott, Abner, and Deanna if the notes are classified as equity.

18. **LO.4** Laurie Gladin owns land and a building that she has been using in her sole proprietorship. She is going to incorporate her sole proprietorship as a C corporation. Laurie must decide whether to contribute the land and building to the corporation or to lease them to the corporation. The net income of the sole proprietorship for the past five years has averaged $250,000. Advise Laurie on the tax consequences. Summarize your analysis in a memo for the tax file.

Decision Making

Communications

19. **LO.4** Marci and Jennifer each own 50% of the stock of Lavender, a C corporation. After each of them is paid a "reasonable" salary of $150,000, the taxable income of Lavender is normally around $800,000.

Decision Making

The corporation is about to purchase a $2 million shopping mall ($1,500,000 allocated to the building and $500,000 allocated to the land). The mall will be rented to tenants at a net rental rate (including rental commissions, depreciation, etc.) of $600,000 annually. Marci and Jennifer will contribute $1 million each to the corporation to provide the cash required for the acquisition.

Their CPA has suggested that Marci and Jennifer purchase the shopping mall as individuals and lease it to Lavender for a fair rental of $400,000. Both Marci and Jennifer are in the 35% tax bracket. The acquisition will occur on January 2, 2015. Determine whether the shopping mall should be acquired by Lavender or by Marci and Jennifer in accordance with their CPA's recommendation. Depreciation on the shopping mall for 2015 is $37,000.

20. **LO.3, 4** Flower, Inc., a C corporation, reports taxable income of $800,000 for 2014. Flower has been in business for many years and long ago used up its accumulated earnings credit. Flower has no additional "reasonable needs of the business" for the current tax year.

a. Determine Flower's total potential tax liability if it declares no dividends.

b. Determine Flower's total potential tax liability if it declares and pays dividends equal to the entity's after-tax earnings.

c. Determine Flower's total potential tax liability in (a) and (b) if it is an S corporation.

21. **LO.4** Since Garnet Corporation was formed five years ago, its stock has been held as follows: 525 shares by Frank and 175 shares by Grace. Their basis in the stock is $350,000 for Frank and $150,000 for Grace. As part of a stock redemption, Garnet redeems 125 of Frank's shares for $175,000 and 125 of Grace's shares for $175,000.

Decision Making

a. What are the tax consequences of the stock redemption to Frank and Grace?

b. How would the tax consequences to Frank and Grace be different if, instead of the redemption, they each sell 125 shares to Chuck (an unrelated party)?

c. What factors should influence their decision on whether to redeem or sell the 250 shares of stock?

22. **LO.4** Oscar created Lavender Corporation four years ago. The C corporation has paid Oscar as president a salary of $200,000 each year. Annual earnings after taxes approximate $700,000 each year. Lavender has not paid any dividends, nor does it intend to do so in the future. Instead, Oscar wants his heirs to receive the stock with a step-up in stock basis when he dies. Identify the relevant tax issues.

Issue ID

23. **LO.4** Tammy and Willy own 40% of the stock of Roadrunner, an S corporation. The other 60% is owned by 99 other shareholders, all of whom are single and unrelated. Tammy and Willy have agreed to a divorce and are in the process of negotiating a property settlement. Identify the relevant tax issues for Tammy and Willy.

Issue ID

24. **LO.4** Clay Corporation has been an S corporation since its incorporation 10 years ago. During the first three years of operations, it incurred total losses of $250,000. Since then, Clay has generated earnings of approximately $180,000 each year. None of the earnings have been distributed to the three equal shareholders, Claire, Lynn, and Todd, because the corporation has been in an expansion mode.

Decision Making

At the beginning of this year, Claire sells her stock to Nell for $400,000. Nell has reservations about the utility of the S election. Therefore, Lynn, Todd, and Nell are discussing whether the election should be continued. They expect the earnings to remain at approximately $180,000 each year. However, because they perceive that the company's expansion period is over and Clay has adequate working capital, they may start distributing the earnings to the shareholders. All of the shareholders are in the 33% tax bracket.

Advise the three shareholders as to whether Clay's S election should be maintained.

Decision Making   25. **LO.5** Phillip and Evans form a business entity. Each contributes the following property.

	Phillip	Evans
Cash	$600,000	
Land		$600,000*

*Fair market value. Evans's adjusted basis is $200,000.

Three months later, the entity sells the land for $652,000 because of unexpected zoning problems. The proceeds are to be applied toward the purchase of another parcel of land, to be used for real estate development. Determine the Federal income tax consequences to the entity and to the owners upon both the formation and the later sale of the land. Perform your analysis assuming that the entity is:
a. A partnership.
b. An S corporation.
c. A C corporation.

How could the parties structure the transaction so as to defer any recognized tax gain? Be specific.

26. **LO.5** Agnes, Becky, and Carol form a business entity with each contributing the following.

	Adjusted Basis	Fair Market Value
Agnes: Cash	$100,000	$100,000
Becky: Land	60,000	120,000
Carol: Services		50,000

Their ownership percentages will be as follows.

Agnes	40%
Becky	40%
Carol	20%

Becky's land has a $20,000 mortgage that is assumed by the entity. Carol is an attorney who receives her ownership interest in exchange for legal services. Determine the recognized gain to the owners, the basis for their ownership interests, and the entity's basis for its assets if the entity is organized as:
a. A partnership.
b. A C corporation.
c. An S corporation.

27. **LO.5** Eloise contributes $40,000 to MeldCo in exchange for a 30% ownership interest. During the first year of operations, MeldCo earns a profit of $200,000. At the end of that year, MeldCo holds liabilities of $75,000.
a. Calculate Eloise's basis for her stock if MeldCo is a C corporation.
b. Calculate Eloise's basis for her stock if MeldCo is an S corporation.
c. Calculate Eloise's basis for her partnership interest if MeldCo is a partnership.

28. **LO.5** ListCo reports the following income for the current tax year.

Operations	$92,000
Tax-exempt interest income	19,000
Long-term capital gain	60,000

ListCo holds earnings and profits (AAA for an S corporation) of $900,000 at the beginning of the year. Then ListCo distributes $200,000 in total to the owners.

a. Calculate the taxable income if ListCo is (1) a C corporation and (2) an S corporation.

b. Determine the effect of the distribution on the shareholders if ListCo is (1) a C corporation and (2) an S corporation.

29. **LO.5** For many years, Sophie has owned and operated several apartment buildings. In 2001 and upon the advice of her attorney, Sophie transferred the apartment buildings to a newly created corporation. Her main reason for incorporating the business was to achieve the legal protection of limited liability.

   Ethics and Equity

   Every year since 2001, Sophie has prepared and filed a Form 1120 for the corporation. No corporate income tax has been paid because, after the deduction of various expenses (including Sophie's "management fee"), the corporation reports zero taxable income.

   This year, Sophie decides that filing Form 1120 is a waste of time and serves no useful purpose. Instead, she plans to report all of the financial activities of the apartment business on her own individual Form 1040.

   Comment on the propriety of what Sophie plans to do.

30. **LO.5** The Coffee Company engages in the following transactions during the taxable year.

   - Sells stock held for three years as an investment for $30,000 (adjusted basis of $20,000).
   - Sells land used in the business for $65,000. The land has been used as a parking lot and originally cost $40,000.
   - Receives tax-exempt interest on municipal bonds of $5,000.
   - Receives dividends on IBM stock of $80,000.

   Describe the effect of these transactions on the entity and its owners if the entity is organized as:
   a. A partnership.
   b. A C corporation.
   c. An S corporation.

31. **LO.5** Swift Corporation distributes land (basis of $55,000 and fair market value of $120,000) to Sam and cash ($240,000) to Allison in exchange for part of their stock. Other shareholders do not redeem any of their stock. Sam surrenders shares of stock that have a basis of $25,000. Prior to the stock redemption, Sam owned 20% of the Swift stock, and after the redemption, he owns 15%.

   At the same time, Swift distributes cash to Allison, and she surrenders shares of stock with a basis of $40,000. Prior to the stock redemption, Allison owned 70% of the Swift stock, and after the redemption, she owns 60%.

   Determine the tax consequences to Swift, Sam, and Allison if Swift is:
   a. A C corporation.
   b. An S corporation.

32. **LO.5** Indigo, Inc., a personal service corporation, has the following types of income and losses.

Active income	$325,000
Portfolio income	49,000
Passive activity loss	333,000

   a. Calculate Indigo's taxable income.
   b. Assume that instead of being a personal service corporation, Indigo is a closely held corporation. Calculate Indigo's taxable income.
   c. Would the answer in (b) change if the passive loss was $320,000 rather than $333,000? Explain.

33. **LO.5** Rosa contributes $50,000 to FlipCo in exchange for a 10% ownership interest. Rosa materially participates in FlipCo's business.

   FlipCo incurs a loss of $900,000 for 2014. Entity liabilities at the end of 2014 are $700,000. Of this amount, $150,000 is for recourse debt, and $550,000 is for nonrecourse debt.

a. Assume that FlipCo is a partnership. How much of Rosa's share of the loss can she deduct on her 2014 individual tax return? What is Rosa's basis for her partnership interest at the end of 2014?

b. Assume that FlipCo is a C corporation. How much of Rosa's share of the loss can she deduct on her 2014 individual tax return? What is Rosa's basis for her stock at the end of 2014?

34. **LO.5** Bishop contributes undeveloped land to a business entity in January for a 40% ownership interest. Bishop's basis for the land is $140,000, and the fair market value is $600,000. The business entity was formed three years ago by Petula and Rene, who have equal ownership. The entity is successful in getting the land rezoned from agricultural to residential use, but decides to sell it so that the entity can invest in another project. In August, the land is sold for $650,000. Determine the tax consequences of the sale of the undeveloped land for the business entity and the three owners if the entity is organized as:

a. A C corporation.

b. An S corporation.

c. A partnership.

d. An LLC.

35. **LO.5** Jo and Velma are equal owners of the JV Partnership. Jo invests $500,000 cash in the partnership. Velma contributes land and a building (basis to her of $125,000, fair market value of $500,000). The entity then borrows $250,000 cash using recourse financing and $100,000 using nonrecourse financing.

a. Compute the outside basis in the partnership interest for Jo and Velma.

b. Compute the at-risk amount for Jo and Velma.

36. **LO.5** Megan owns 55% and Vern owns 45% of a business entity. The owners would like to use the entity to share profits (55% for Megan and 45% for Vern) and to share losses (80% for Vern and 20% for Megan). Determine the tax consequences for 2014 if the entity has a tax loss of $160,000 and is organized as:

a. A partnership.

b. A C corporation.

c. An S corporation.

37. **LO.5** Sanjay contributes land to a business entity in January 2014 for a 30% ownership interest. Sanjay's basis for the land is $60,000, and the fair market value is $100,000. The business entity was formed three years ago by Polly and Rita, who have equal ownership. The entity is unsuccessful in getting the land rezoned from agricultural to residential. In October 2014, the land is sold for $110,000.

Determine the tax consequences of the sale of the land for the entity and its owners if the entity is organized as:

a. A C corporation.

b. An S corporation.

c. A partnership.

38. **LO.7** Emily and Freda are negotiating with George to purchase the business he operates as Pelican, Inc. The assets of Pelican, Inc., a C corporation, are as follows.

Asset	Basis	FMV
Cash	$ 20,000	$ 20,000
Accounts receivable	50,000	50,000
Inventory	100,000	110,000
Furniture and fixtures	150,000	170,000*
Building	200,000	250,000**
Land	40,000	150,000

*Potential depreciation recapture is $45,000.
**The straight-line method was used to depreciate the building. Accumulated depreciation is $340,000.

George's basis for the Pelican stock is $560,000. George is subject to a 35% marginal tax rate, and Pelican faces a 34% marginal tax rate.

a. Emily and Freda purchase the *stock* of Pelican from George for $908,000. Determine the tax consequences to Emily and Freda; Pelican; and George.

b. Emily and Freda purchase the *assets* from Pelican for $908,000. Determine the tax consequences to Emily and Freda; Pelican; and George.

c. The purchase price is $550,000 because the fair market value of the building is $150,000, and the fair market value of the land is $50,000. No amount is assigned to goodwill. Emily and Freda purchase the *stock* of Pelican from George. Determine the tax consequences to Emily and Freda; Pelican; and George.

39. **LO.7** Linda is the owner of a sole proprietorship. The entity has the following assets.   *Decision Making*

Asset	Basis	FMV
Cash	$10,000	$10,000
Accounts receivable	–0–	25,000
Office furniture and fixtures*	15,000	17,000
Building**	75,000	90,000
Land	60,000	80,000

*Potential depreciation recapture is $5,000.
**The straight-line method has been used to depreciate the building.

Linda sells the business for $260,000 to Juan.

a. Determine the tax consequences to Linda, including the classification of any recognized gain or loss.

b. Determine the tax consequences to Juan.

c. Advise Juan on how the purchase agreement could be modified to produce more beneficial tax consequences for him.

40. **LO.7** Gail and Harry own the GH Partnership. They have conducted the business as a partnership for 10 years. The bases for their partnership interests are as follows.   *Decision Making*

Gail	Harry
$100,000	$150,000

GH Partnership holds the following assets.

Asset	Basis	FMV
Cash	$ 10,000	$ 10,000
Accounts receivable	30,000	28,000
Inventory	25,000	26,000
Building*	100,000	150,000
Land	250,000	400,000

*The straight-line method has been used to depreciate the building. Accumulated depreciation is $70,000.

Gail and Harry sell their partnership interests to Keith and Liz for $307,000 each.

a. Determine the tax consequences of the sale to Gail, Harry, and GH Partnership.

b. From a tax perspective, should it matter to Keith and Liz whether they purchase Gail and Harry's partnership interests or the partnership assets from GH Partnership? Explain.

41. **LO.7** Hector and Walt are purchasing the Copper Partnership from Jan and Gail for $700,000; Hector and Walt will be equal partners. During the negotiations, Jan and Gail succeeded in having the transaction structured as the purchase of the partnership rather than as a purchase of the individual assets. The adjusted basis of the individual assets of Copper is $580,000.   *Decision Making*

a. What are Hector's and Walt's bases for their partnership interests (i.e., outside bases)?

b. What is Copper's adjusted basis for its assets after the transaction? Would an optional adjustment-to-basis election be helpful? Why or why not?

42. **LO.7** Vladimir owns all of the stock of Ruby Corporation. The fair market value of the stock (and Ruby's assets) is about four times his adjusted basis for the stock. Vladimir is negotiating with an investor group for the sale of the corporation. Identify the relevant tax issues for Vladimir.   *Issue ID*

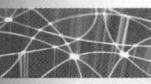

Decision Making

Communications

43. **LO.7** Maurice Allred is going to purchase either the stock or the assets of Jewel Corporation. All of the Jewel stock is owned by Charley. Maurice and Charley agree that Jewel is worth $700,000. The tax basis for Jewel's assets is $500,000.

Write a letter to Maurice advising him on whether he should negotiate to purchase the stock or the assets. Prepare a memo for the tax research file on this matter. Maurice's address is 100 Aspen Green, Chattanooga, TN 37403.

BRIDGE DISCIPLINE

1. Parchment, Inc., is created with the following asset and liability contributions. Jake and Fran each receive 100 shares of Parchment common stock.

Shareholder	Assets	Basis	Fair Market Value
Jake	Cash	$100,000	$100,000
Fran	Land	40,000	120,000*

*The land is subject to a mortgage of $20,000 that Parchment assumes.

   a. Prepare a financial accounting balance sheet for Parchment. Discuss the relevance of conduit theory and entity theory in the creation of Parchment.
   b. Prepare a tax balance sheet for Parchment. Discuss the relevance of conduit theory and entity theory in the creation of Parchment.
   c. Assume that Parchment sells the land for $150,000 four months after Parchment was created. Discuss the effect of the sale on the financial accounting balance sheet and the tax balance sheet.

2. Assume that Parchment in (1) elects S corporation status at the time of its creation. Respond to (a), (b), and (c).

3. Assume that Parchment in (1) is a general partnership rather than a corporation. Respond to (a), (b), and (c). Would your answer change if Parchment were an LLC that "checked the box" to be taxed as a partnership? Explain.

4. Teal, Inc., owns total assets of $100 million, and it reports annual revenues of $700 million. Lavender, Inc., owns total assets of $12 million, and it reports annual revenues of $900,000. Both corporations have been in existence for three years.
   a. Explain why neither Teal nor Lavender computes an AMT liability for its first tax year.
   b. Explain why, in later years, Teal computes an AMT liability and Lavender is not required to do so.
   c. Do you think that this different tax treatment for Teal and Lavender is equitable? Explain your position.

Research Problems

THOMSON REUTERS
CHECKPOINT®

Note: Solutions to Research Problems can be prepared by using the **Checkpoint®** **Student Edition** online research product, which is available to accompany this text. It is also possible to prepare solutions to the Research Problems by using tax research materials found in a standard tax library.

Research Problem 1. The Turnaround LLC was formed several years ago. It incurred losses for several years, reducing many of its members' bases in their interests to zero. However, the business recently obtained some new and promising contracts, and there is an expectation of profits in the coming years.

Turnaround then admitted several new members, who each made capital contributions for their interests. The new owners anticipate that it will be necessary to reinvest any profits back into the business for some time. As there no longer will be losses to pass through, and any double taxation of profits will be delayed for some time, the owners of Turnaround are considering converting the business to a C corporation.

The business controls the following assets. There is no § 754 election in effect.

	Fair Market Value	Adjusted Basis
Cash	$ 500,000	$500,000
PP&E	500,000	500,000
Customer contracts	1,000,000	0

The original owners of Turnaround now hold a 50% capital and profits interest. They have come to you for advice regarding the potential tax consequences of the conversion for them, as well as for the new corporation.

Partial list of research aids:
Rev.Rul. 70-239, 1970-1 C.B. 74.
Rev.Rul. 84-111, 1984-2 C.B. 88.
Rev.Rul. 2004–59, 2004-24 I.R.B 1050.
Treas. Reg. § 301.7701–3(g)(i).

Research Problem 2. Crane is a partner in the Cardinal Partnership. A dispute arose with the partnership regarding Crane's share of current earnings. The partnership contends that the amount is $75,000, while Crane believes his share is $100,000.

Crane ceased being a partner on November 1. As a result of the dispute, the partnership distributed only $75,000 to Crane. It placed the disputed $25,000 in escrow. However, Crane's Schedule K–1 from the partnership included the full $100,000. Crane believes that the K–1 should include only the $75,000 that is not in dispute. Is Crane correct? Explain.

Use the tax resources of the Internet to address the following questions. Do not restrict your search to the Web, but include a review of newsgroups and general reference materials, practitioner sites and resources, primary sources of the tax law, chat rooms and discussion groups, and other opportunities.

Internet Activity

Research Problem 3. Find an article about a state that contributed assets to a private business as a location inducement and later recovered some or all of the assets under a "clawback" provision. What are the tax consequences to the business when it returns these assets to the state? Do states always enforce the clawback provisions? Summarize your findings in no more than five PowerPoint slides, to present to your school's accounting club.

Communications

Research Problem 4. When did your state adopt LLC legislation? When did it receive IRS approval to apply partnership tax law to the entities? Provide the pertinent dates, and give full citations for the resulting documents.

Research Problem 5. Find an article or a blog posting describing how a specific business put together its employee fringe benefit package in light of the limitations presented by the tax law and the business's form of operation.

Research Problem 6. Find a blog posting or discussion thread with comments from tax professionals about Federal income tax consequences that occur when a business converts from an LLC to an S corporation, or when a C corporation converts to a pass-through entity. Summarize the comments and suggestions that you find in these discussions in a one-page memo to your instructor.

Communications

Research Problem 7. For your state, list the forms that are required to be filed when a pass-through entity incorporates, or when a corporation converts to a pass-through entity. Give statutory citations for the conversion rules, due dates for any required forms, and addresses for where the forms are to be sent. Attach a copy of one of the forms to a memo summarizing your findings, and send the documents to your instructor.

Communications

Research Problem 8. Summarize the marketing campaign used by a company that works with clients to identify investment properties that are producing passive activity income.

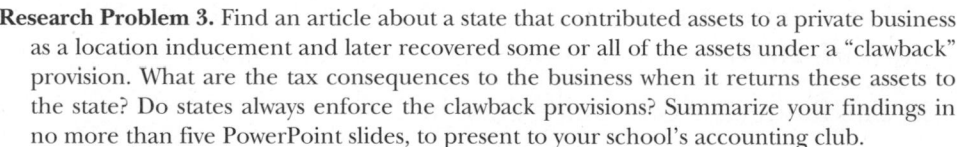

Tax Rate Schedules and Tables

(The 2014 Tax Tables and 2014 Sales Tax Tables can be accessed at the IRS website [**www.irs.gov**] when released.)

2013 Tax Rate Schedules

Single—Schedule X

If taxable income is: Over—	But not over—	The tax is:	of the amount over—
$ 0	$ 8,925	.........10%	$ 0
8,925	36,250	$ 892.50 + 15%	8,925
36,250	87,850	4,991.25 + 25%	36,250
87,850	183,250	17,891.25 + 28%	87,850
183,250	398,350	44,603.25 + 33%	183,250
398,350	400,000	115,586.25 + 35%	398,350
400,000	....	116,163.75 + 39.6%	400,000

Head of household—Schedule Z

If taxable income is: Over—	But not over—	The tax is:	of the amount over—
$ 0	$ 12,750	.........10%	$ 0
12,750	48,600	$ 1,275.00 + 15%	12,750
48,600	125,450	6,652.50 + 25%	48,600
125,450	203,150	25,865.00 + 28%	125,450
203,150	398,350	47,621.00 + 33%	203,150
398,350	425,000	112,037.00 + 35%	398,350
425,000	....	121,364.50 + 39.6%	425,000

Married filing jointly or Qualifying widow(er)—Schedule Y–1

If taxable income is: Over—	But not over—	The tax is:	of the amount over—
$ 0	$ 17,850	.........10%	$ 0
17,850	72,500	$ 1,785.00 + 15%	17,850
72,500	146,400	9,982.50 + 25%	72,500
146,400	223,050	28,457.50 + 28%	146,400
223,050	398,350	49,919.50 + 33%	223,050
398,350	450,000	107,768.50 + 35%	398,350
450,000	....	125,846.00 + 39.6%	450,000

Married filing separately—Schedule Y–2

If taxable income is: Over—	But not over—	The tax is:	of the amount over—
$ 0	$ 8,925	.........10%	$ 0
8,925	36,250	$ 892.50 + 15%	8,925
36,250	73,200	4,991.25 + 25%	36,250
73,200	111,525	14,228.75 + 28%	73,200
111,525	199,175	24,959.75 + 33%	111,525
199,175	225,000	53,884.25 + 35%	199,175
225,000	....	62,923.00 + 39.6%	225,000

2014 Tax Rate Schedules

Single—Schedule X

If taxable income is: Over—	But not over—	The tax is:	of the amount over—
$ 0	$ 9,075	.........10%	$ 0
9,075	36,900	$ 907.50 + 15%	9,075
36,900	89,350	5,081.25 + 25%	36,900
89,350	186,350	18,193.75 + 28%	89,350
186,350	405,100	45,353.75 + 33%	186,350
405,100	406,750	117,541.25 + 35%	405,100
406,750	....	118,118.75 + 39.6%	406,750

Head of household—Schedule Z

If taxable income is: Over—	But not over—	The tax is:	of the amount over—
$ 0	$ 12,950	.........10%	$ 0
12,950	49,400	$ 1,295.00 + 15%	12,950
49,400	127,550	6,762.50 + 25%	49,400
127,550	206,600	26,300.00 + 28%	127,550
206,600	405,100	48,434.00 + 33%	206,600
405,100	432,200	113,939.00 + 35%	405,100
432,200	....	123,424.00 + 39.6%	432,200

Married filing jointly or Qualifying widow(er)—Schedule Y–1

If taxable income is: Over—	But not over—	The tax is:	of the amount over—
$ 0	$ 18,150	.........10%	$ 0
18,150	73,800	$ 1,815.00 + 15%	18,150
73,800	148,850	10,162.50 + 25%	73,800
148,850	226,850	28,925.00 + 28%	148,850
226,850	405,100	50,765.00 + 33%	226,850
405,100	457,600	109,587.50 + 35%	405,100
457,600	....	127,962.50 + 39.6%	457,600

Married filing separately—Schedule Y–2

If taxable income is: Over—	But not over—	The tax is:	of the amount over—
$ 0	$ 9,075	.........10%	$ 0
9,075	36,900	$ 907.50 + 15%	9,075
36,900	74,425	5,081.25 + 25%	36,900
74,425	113,425	14,462.50 + 28%	74,425
113,425	202,550	25,382.50 + 33%	113,425
202,550	228,800	54,793.75 + 35%	202,550
228,800	....	63,981.25 + 39.6%	228,800

2013 Tax Table

See the instructions for line 44 to see if you must use the Tax Table below to figure your tax.

Example. Mr. and Mrs. Brown are filing a joint return. Their taxable income on Form 1040, line 43, is $25,300. First, they find the $25,300-25,350 taxable income line. Next, they find the column for married filing jointly and read down the column. The amount shown where the taxable income line and filing status column meet is $2,906. This is the tax amount they should enter on Form 1040, line 44.

Sample Table

At Least	But Less Than	Single	Married filing jointly *	Married filing separately	Head of a household
			Your tax is—		
25,200	25,250	3,338	2,891	3,338	3,146
25,250	25,300	3,345	2,899	3,345	3,154
25,300	25,350	3,353	(2,906)	3,353	3,161
25,350	25,400	3,360	2,914	3,360	3,169

If line 43 (taxable income) is— At least	But less than	And you are— Single	Married filing jointly *	Married filing separately	Head of a house-hold
			Your tax is—		
0	5	0	0	0	0
5	15	1	1	1	1
15	25	2	2	2	2
25	50	4	4	4	4
50	75	6	6	6	6
75	100	9	9	9	9
100	125	11	11	11	11
125	150	14	14	14	14
150	175	16	16	16	16
175	200	19	19	19	19
200	225	21	21	21	21
225	250	24	24	24	24
250	275	26	26	26	26
275	300	29	29	29	29
300	325	31	31	31	31
325	350	34	34	34	34
350	375	36	36	36	36
375	400	39	39	39	39
400	425	41	41	41	41
425	450	44	44	44	44
450	475	46	46	46	46
475	500	49	49	49	49
500	525	51	51	51	51
525	550	54	54	54	54
550	575	56	56	56	56
575	600	59	59	59	59
600	625	61	61	61	61
625	650	64	64	64	64
650	675	66	66	66	66
675	700	69	69	69	69
700	725	71	71	71	71
725	750	74	74	74	74
750	775	76	76	76	76
775	800	79	79	79	79
800	825	81	81	81	81
825	850	84	84	84	84
850	875	86	86	86	86
875	900	89	89	89	89
900	925	91	91	91	91
925	950	94	94	94	94
950	975	96	96	96	96
975	1,000	99	99	99	99

1,000

If line 43 (taxable income) is— At least	But less than	And you are— Single	Married filing jointly *	Married filing separately	Head of a house-hold
1,000	1,025	101	101	101	101
1,025	1,050	104	104	104	104
1,050	1,075	106	106	106	106
1,075	1,100	109	109	109	109
1,100	1,125	111	111	111	111
1,125	1,150	114	114	114	114
1,150	1,175	116	116	116	116
1,175	1,200	119	119	119	119
1,200	1,225	121	121	121	121
1,225	1,250	124	124	124	124
1,250	1,275	126	126	126	126
1,275	1,300	129	129	129	129
1,300	1,325	131	131	131	131
1,325	1,350	134	134	134	134
1,350	1,375	136	136	136	136
1,375	1,400	139	139	139	139
1,400	1,425	141	141	141	141
1,425	1,450	144	144	144	144
1,450	1,475	146	146	146	146
1,475	1,500	149	149	149	149
1,500	1,525	151	151	151	151
1,525	1,550	154	154	154	154
1,550	1,575	156	156	156	156
1,575	1,600	159	159	159	159
1,600	1,625	161	161	161	161
1,625	1,650	164	164	164	164
1,650	1,675	166	166	166	166
1,675	1,700	169	169	169	169
1,700	1,725	171	171	171	171
1,725	1,750	174	174	174	174
1,750	1,775	176	176	176	176
1,775	1,800	179	179	179	179
1,800	1,825	181	181	181	181
1,825	1,850	184	184	184	184
1,850	1,875	186	186	186	186
1,875	1,900	189	189	189	189
1,900	1,925	191	191	191	191
1,925	1,950	194	194	194	194
1,950	1,975	196	196	196	196
1,975	2,000	199	199	199	199

2,000

If line 43 (taxable income) is— At least	But less than	And you are— Single	Married filing jointly *	Married filing separately	Head of a house-hold
2,000	2,025	201	201	201	201
2,025	2,050	204	204	204	204
2,050	2,075	206	206	206	206
2,075	2,100	209	209	209	209
2,100	2,125	211	211	211	211
2,125	2,150	214	214	214	214
2,150	2,175	216	216	216	216
2,175	2,200	219	219	219	219
2,200	2,225	221	221	221	221
2,225	2,250	224	224	224	224
2,250	2,275	226	226	226	226
2,275	2,300	229	229	229	229
2,300	2,325	231	231	231	231
2,325	2,350	234	234	234	234
2,350	2,375	236	236	236	236
2,375	2,400	239	239	239	239
2,400	2,425	241	241	241	241
2,425	2,450	244	244	244	244
2,450	2,475	246	246	246	246
2,475	2,500	249	249	249	249
2,500	2,525	251	251	251	251
2,525	2,550	254	254	254	254
2,550	2,575	256	256	256	256
2,575	2,600	259	259	259	259
2,600	2,625	261	261	261	261
2,625	2,650	264	264	264	264
2,650	2,675	266	266	266	266
2,675	2,700	269	269	269	269
2,700	2,725	271	271	271	271
2,725	2,750	274	274	274	274
2,750	2,775	276	276	276	276
2,775	2,800	279	279	279	279
2,800	2,825	281	281	281	281
2,825	2,850	284	284	284	284
2,850	2,875	286	286	286	286
2,875	2,900	289	289	289	289
2,900	2,925	291	291	291	291
2,925	2,950	294	294	294	294
2,950	2,975	296	296	296	296
2,975	3,000	299	299	299	299

* This column must also be used by a qualifying widow(er).

(Continued)

2013 Tax Table—*Continued*

If line 43 (taxable income) is—		And you are—				If line 43 (taxable income) is—		And you are—				If line 43 (taxable income) is—		And you are—			
At least	But less than	Single	Married filing jointly *	Married filing separately	Head of a household	At least	But less than	Single	Married filing jointly *	Married filing separately	Head of a household	At least	But less than	Single	Married filing jointly *	Married filing separately	Head of a household
		Your tax is—						Your tax is—						Your tax is—			
3,000						**6,000**						**9,000**					
3,000	3,050	303	303	303	303	6,000	6,050	603	603	603	603	9,000	9,050	908	903	908	903
3,050	3,100	308	308	308	308	6,050	6,100	608	608	608	608	9,050	9,100	915	908	915	908
3,100	3,150	313	313	313	313	6,100	6,150	613	613	613	613	9,100	9,150	923	913	923	913
3,150	3,200	318	318	318	318	6,150	6,200	618	618	618	618	9,150	9,200	930	918	930	918
3,200	3,250	323	323	323	323	6,200	6,250	623	623	623	623	9,200	9,250	938	923	938	923
3,250	3,300	328	328	328	328	6,250	6,300	628	628	628	628	9,250	9,300	945	928	945	928
3,300	3,350	333	333	333	333	6,300	6,350	633	633	633	633	9,300	9,350	953	933	953	933
3,350	3,400	338	338	338	338	6,350	6,400	638	638	638	638	9,350	9,400	960	938	960	938
3,400	3,450	343	343	343	343	6,400	6,450	643	643	643	643	9,400	9,450	968	943	968	943
3,450	3,500	348	348	348	348	6,450	6,500	648	648	648	648	9,450	9,500	975	948	975	948
3,500	3,550	353	353	353	353	6,500	6,550	653	653	653	653	9,500	9,550	983	953	983	953
3,550	3,600	358	358	358	358	6,550	6,600	658	658	658	658	9,550	9,600	990	958	990	958
3,600	3,650	363	363	363	363	6,600	6,650	663	663	663	663	9,600	9,650	998	963	998	963
3,650	3,700	368	368	368	368	6,650	6,700	668	668	668	668	9,650	9,700	1,005	968	1,005	968
3,700	3,750	373	373	373	373	6,700	6,750	673	673	673	673	9,700	9,750	1,013	973	1,013	973
3,750	3,800	378	378	378	378	6,750	6,800	678	678	678	678	9,750	9,800	1,020	978	1,020	978
3,800	3,850	383	383	383	383	6,800	6,850	683	683	683	683	9,800	9,850	1,028	983	1,028	983
3,850	3,900	388	388	388	388	6,850	6,900	688	688	688	688	9,850	9,900	1,035	988	1,035	988
3,900	3,950	393	393	393	393	6,900	6,950	693	693	693	693	9,900	9,950	1,043	993	1,043	993
3,950	4,000	398	398	398	398	6,950	7,000	698	698	698	698	9,950	10,000	1,050	998	1,050	998
4,000						**7,000**						**10,000**					
4,000	4,050	403	403	403	403	7,000	7,050	703	703	703	703	10,000	10,050	1,058	1,003	1,058	1,003
4,050	4,100	408	408	408	408	7,050	7,100	708	708	708	708	10,050	10,100	1,065	1,008	1,065	1,008
4,100	4,150	413	413	413	413	7,100	7,150	713	713	713	713	10,100	10,150	1,073	1,013	1,073	1,013
4,150	4,200	418	418	418	418	7,150	7,200	718	718	718	718	10,150	10,200	1,080	1,018	1,080	1,018
4,200	4,250	423	423	423	423	7,200	7,250	723	723	723	723	10,200	10,250	1,088	1,023	1,088	1,023
4,250	4,300	428	428	428	428	7,250	7,300	728	728	728	728	10,250	10,300	1,095	1,028	1,095	1,028
4,300	4,350	433	433	433	433	7,300	7,350	733	733	733	733	10,300	10,350	1,103	1,033	1,103	1,033
4,350	4,400	438	438	438	438	7,350	7,400	738	738	738	738	10,350	10,400	1,110	1,038	1,110	1,038
4,400	4,450	443	443	443	443	7,400	7,450	743	743	743	743	10,400	10,450	1,118	1,043	1,118	1,043
4,450	4,500	448	448	448	448	7,450	7,500	748	748	748	748	10,450	10,500	1,125	1,048	1,125	1,048
4,500	4,550	453	453	453	453	7,500	7,550	753	753	753	753	10,500	10,550	1,133	1,053	1,133	1,053
4,550	4,600	458	458	458	458	7,550	7,600	758	758	758	758	10,550	10,600	1,140	1,058	1,140	1,058
4,600	4,650	463	463	463	463	7,600	7,650	763	763	763	763	10,600	10,650	1,148	1,063	1,148	1,063
4,650	4,700	468	468	468	468	7,650	7,700	768	768	768	768	10,650	10,700	1,155	1,068	1,155	1,068
4,700	4,750	473	473	473	473	7,700	7,750	773	773	773	773	10,700	10,750	1,163	1,073	1,163	1,073
4,750	4,800	478	478	478	478	7,750	7,800	778	778	778	778	10,750	10,800	1,170	1,078	1,170	1,078
4,800	4,850	483	483	483	483	7,800	7,850	783	783	783	783	10,800	10,050	1,178	1,083	1,178	1,083
4,850	4,900	488	488	488	488	7,850	7,900	788	788	788	788	10,850	10,900	1,185	1,088	1,185	1,088
4,900	4,950	493	493	493	493	7,900	7,950	793	793	793	793	10,900	10,950	1,193	1,093	1,193	1,093
4,950	5,000	498	498	498	498	7,950	8,000	798	798	798	798	10,950	11,000	1,200	1,098	1,200	1,098
5,000						**8,000**						**11,000**					
5,000	5,050	503	503	503	503	8,000	8,050	803	803	803	803	11,000	11,050	1,208	1,103	1,208	1,103
5,050	5,100	508	508	508	508	8,050	8,100	808	808	808	808	11,050	11,100	1,215	1,108	1,215	1,108
5,100	5,150	513	513	513	513	8,100	8,150	813	813	813	813	11,100	11,150	1,223	1,113	1,223	1,113
5,150	5,200	518	518	518	518	8,150	8,200	818	818	818	818	11,150	11,200	1,230	1,118	1,230	1,118
5,200	5,250	523	523	523	523	8,200	8,250	823	823	823	823	11,200	11,250	1,238	1,123	1,238	1,123
5,250	5,300	528	528	528	528	8,250	8,300	828	828	828	828	11,250	11,300	1,245	1,128	1,245	1,128
5,300	5,350	533	533	533	533	8,300	8,350	833	833	833	833	11,300	11,350	1,253	1,133	1,253	1,133
5,350	5,400	538	538	538	538	8,350	8,400	838	838	838	838	11,350	11,400	1,260	1,138	1,260	1,138
5,400	5,450	543	543	543	543	8,400	8,450	843	843	843	843	11,400	11,450	1,268	1,143	1,268	1,143
5,450	5,500	548	548	548	548	8,450	8,500	848	848	848	848	11,450	11,500	1,275	1,148	1,275	1,148
5,500	5,550	553	553	553	553	8,500	8,550	853	853	853	853	11,500	11,550	1,283	1,153	1,283	1,153
5,550	5,600	558	558	558	558	8,550	8,600	858	858	858	858	11,550	11,600	1,290	1,158	1,290	1,158
5,600	5,650	563	563	563	563	8,600	8,650	863	863	863	863	11,600	11,650	1,298	1,163	1,298	1,163
5,650	5,700	568	568	568	568	8,650	8,700	868	868	868	868	11,650	11,700	1,305	1,168	1,305	1,168
5,700	5,750	573	573	573	573	8,700	8,750	873	873	873	873	11,700	11,750	1,313	1,173	1,313	1,173
5,750	5,800	578	578	578	578	8,750	8,800	878	878	878	878	11,750	11,800	1,320	1,178	1,320	1,178
5,800	5,850	583	583	583	583	8,800	8,850	883	883	883	883	11,800	11,850	1,328	1,183	1,328	1,183
5,850	5,900	588	588	588	588	8,850	8,900	888	888	888	888	11,850	11,900	1,335	1,188	1,335	1,188
5,900	5,950	593	593	593	593	8,900	8,950	893	893	893	893	11,900	11,950	1,343	1,193	1,343	1,193
5,950	6,000	598	598	598	598	8,950	9,000	900	898	900	898	11,950	12,000	1,350	1,198	1,350	1,198

* This column must also be used by a qualifying widow(er).

(Continued)

2013 Tax Table—Continued

If line 43 (taxable income) is—		And you are—			
At least	But less than	Single	Married filing jointly *	Married filing separately	Head of a household
		Your tax is—			

12,000

At least	But less than	Single	Married filing jointly *	Married filing separately	Head of a household
12,000	12,050	1,358	1,203	1,358	1,203
12,050	12,100	1,365	1,208	1,365	1,208
12,100	12,150	1,373	1,213	1,373	1,213
12,150	12,200	1,380	1,218	1,380	1,218
12,200	12,250	1,388	1,223	1,388	1,223
12,250	12,300	1,395	1,228	1,395	1,228
12,300	12,350	1,403	1,233	1,403	1,233
12,350	12,400	1,410	1,238	1,410	1,238
12,400	12,450	1,418	1,243	1,418	1,243
12,450	12,500	1,425	1,248	1,425	1,248
12,500	12,550	1,433	1,253	1,433	1,253
12,550	12,600	1,440	1,258	1,440	1,258
12,600	12,650	1,448	1,263	1,448	1,263
12,650	12,700	1,455	1,268	1,455	1,268
12,700	12,750	1,463	1,273	1,463	1,273
12,750	12,800	1,470	1,278	1,470	1,279
12,800	12,850	1,478	1,283	1,478	1,286
12,850	12,900	1,485	1,288	1,485	1,294
12,900	12,950	1,493	1,293	1,493	1,301
12,950	13,000	1,500	1,298	1,500	1,309

13,000

At least	But less than	Single	Married filing jointly *	Married filing separately	Head of a household
13,000	13,050	1,508	1,303	1,508	1,316
13,050	13,100	1,515	1,308	1,515	1,324
13,100	13,150	1,523	1,313	1,523	1,331
13,150	13,200	1,530	1,318	1,530	1,339
13,200	13,250	1,538	1,323	1,538	1,346
13,250	13,300	1,545	1,328	1,545	1,354
13,300	13,350	1,553	1,333	1,553	1,361
13,350	13,400	1,560	1,338	1,560	1,369
13,400	13,450	1,568	1,343	1,568	1,376
13,450	13,500	1,575	1,348	1,575	1,384
13,500	13,550	1,583	1,353	1,583	1,391
13,550	13,600	1,590	1,358	1,590	1,399
13,600	13,650	1,598	1,363	1,598	1,406
13,650	13,700	1,605	1,368	1,605	1,414
13,700	13,750	1,613	1,373	1,613	1,421
13,750	13,800	1,620	1,378	1,620	1,429
13,800	13,850	1,628	1,383	1,628	1,436
13,850	13,900	1,635	1,388	1,635	1,444
13,900	13,950	1,643	1,393	1,643	1,451
13,950	14,000	1,650	1,398	1,650	1,459

14,000

At least	But less than	Single	Married filing jointly *	Married filing separately	Head of a household
14,000	14,050	1,658	1,403	1,658	1,466
14,050	14,100	1,665	1,408	1,665	1,474
14,100	14,150	1,673	1,413	1,673	1,481
14,150	14,200	1,680	1,418	1,680	1,489
14,200	14,250	1,688	1,423	1,688	1,496
14,250	14,300	1,695	1,428	1,695	1,504
14,300	14,350	1,703	1,433	1,703	1,511
14,350	14,400	1,710	1,438	1,710	1,519
14,400	14,450	1,718	1,443	1,718	1,526
14,450	14,500	1,725	1,448	1,725	1,534
14,500	14,550	1,733	1,453	1,733	1,541
14,550	14,600	1,740	1,458	1,740	1,549
14,600	14,650	1,748	1,463	1,748	1,556
14,650	14,700	1,755	1,468	1,755	1,564
14,700	14,750	1,763	1,473	1,763	1,571
14,750	14,800	1,770	1,478	1,770	1,579
14,800	14,850	1,778	1,483	1,778	1,586
14,850	14,900	1,785	1,488	1,785	1,594
14,900	14,950	1,793	1,493	1,793	1,601
14,950	15,000	1,800	1,498	1,800	1,609

15,000

At least	But less than	Single	Married filing jointly *	Married filing separately	Head of a household
15,000	15,050	1,808	1,503	1,808	1,616
15,050	15,100	1,815	1,508	1,815	1,624
15,100	15,150	1,823	1,513	1,823	1,631
15,150	15,200	1,830	1,518	1,830	1,639
15,200	15,250	1,838	1,523	1,838	1,646
15,250	15,300	1,845	1,528	1,845	1,654
15,300	15,350	1,853	1,533	1,853	1,661
15,350	15,400	1,860	1,538	1,860	1,669
15,400	15,450	1,868	1,543	1,868	1,676
15,450	15,500	1,875	1,548	1,875	1,684
15,500	15,550	1,883	1,553	1,883	1,691
15,550	15,600	1,890	1,558	1,890	1,699
15,600	15,650	1,898	1,563	1,898	1,706
15,650	15,700	1,905	1,568	1,905	1,714
15,700	15,750	1,913	1,573	1,913	1,721
15,750	15,800	1,920	1,578	1,920	1,729
15,800	15,850	1,928	1,583	1,928	1,736
15,850	15,900	1,935	1,588	1,935	1,744
15,900	15,950	1,943	1,593	1,943	1,751
15,950	16,000	1,950	1,598	1,950	1,759

16,000

At least	But less than	Single	Married filing jointly *	Married filing separately	Head of a household
16,000	16,050	1,958	1,603	1,958	1,766
16,050	16,100	1,965	1,608	1,965	1,774
16,100	16,150	1,973	1,613	1,973	1,781
16,150	16,200	1,980	1,618	1,980	1,789
16,200	16,250	1,988	1,623	1,988	1,796
16,250	16,300	1,995	1,628	1,995	1,804
16,300	16,350	2,003	1,633	2,003	1,811
16,350	16,400	2,010	1,638	2,010	1,819
16,400	16,450	2,018	1,643	2,018	1,826
16,450	16,500	2,025	1,648	2,025	1,834
16,500	16,550	2,033	1,653	2,033	1,841
16,550	16,600	2,040	1,658	2,040	1,849
16,600	16,650	2,048	1,663	2,048	1,856
16,650	16,700	2,055	1,668	2,055	1,864
16,700	16,750	2,063	1,673	2,063	1,871
16,750	16,800	2,070	1,678	2,070	1,879
16,800	16,850	2,078	1,683	2,078	1,886
16,850	16,900	2,085	1,688	2,085	1,894
16,900	16,950	2,093	1,693	2,093	1,901
16,950	17,000	2,100	1,698	2,100	1,909

17,000

At least	But less than	Single	Married filing jointly *	Married filing separately	Head of a household
17,000	17,050	2,108	1,703	2,108	1,916
17,050	17,100	2,115	1,708	2,115	1,924
17,100	17,150	2,123	1,713	2,123	1,931
17,150	17,200	2,130	1,718	2,130	1,939
17,200	17,250	2,138	1,723	2,138	1,946
17,250	17,300	2,145	1,728	2,145	1,954
17,300	17,350	2,153	1,733	2,153	1,961
17,350	17,400	2,160	1,738	2,160	1,969
17,400	17,450	2,168	1,743	2,168	1,976
17,450	17,500	2,175	1,748	2,175	1,984
17,500	17,550	2,183	1,753	2,183	1,991
17,550	17,600	2,190	1,758	2,190	1,999
17,600	17,650	2,198	1,763	2,198	2,006
17,650	17,700	2,205	1,768	2,205	2,014
17,700	17,750	2,213	1,773	2,213	2,021
17,750	17,800	2,220	1,778	2,220	2,029
17,800	17,850	2,228	1,783	2,228	2,036
17,850	17,900	2,235	1,789	2,235	2,044
17,900	17,950	2,243	1,796	2,243	2,051
17,950	18,000	2,250	1,804	2,250	2,059

18,000

At least	But less than	Single	Married filing jointly *	Married filing separately	Head of a household
18,000	18,050	2,258	1,811	2,258	2,066
18,050	18,100	2,265	1,819	2,265	2,074
18,100	18,150	2,273	1,826	2,273	2,081
18,150	18,200	2,280	1,834	2,280	2,089
18,200	18,250	2,288	1,841	2,288	2,096
18,250	18,300	2,295	1,849	2,295	2,104
18,300	18,350	2,303	1,856	2,303	2,111
18,350	18,400	2,310	1,864	2,310	2,119
18,400	18,450	2,318	1,871	2,318	2,126
18,450	18,500	2,325	1,879	2,325	2,134
18,500	18,550	2,333	1,886	2,333	2,141
18,550	18,600	2,340	1,894	2,340	2,149
18,600	18,650	2,348	1,901	2,348	2,156
18,650	18,700	2,355	1,909	2,355	2,164
18,700	18,750	2,363	1,916	2,363	2,171
18,750	18,800	2,370	1,924	2,370	2,179
18,800	18,850	2,378	1,931	2,378	2,186
18,850	18,900	2,385	1,939	2,385	2,194
18,900	18,950	2,393	1,946	2,393	2,201
18,950	19,000	2,400	1,954	2,400	2,209

19,000

At least	But less than	Single	Married filing jointly *	Married filing separately	Head of a household
19,000	19,050	2,408	1,961	2,408	2,216
19,050	19,100	2,415	1,969	2,415	2,224
19,100	19,150	2,423	1,976	2,423	2,231
19,150	19,200	2,430	1,984	2,430	2,239
19,200	19,250	2,438	1,991	2,438	2,246
19,250	19,300	2,445	1,999	2,445	2,254
19,300	19,350	2,453	2,006	2,453	2,261
19,350	19,400	2,460	2,014	2,460	2,269
19,400	19,450	2,468	2,021	2,468	2,276
19,450	19,500	2,475	2,029	2,475	2,284
19,500	19,550	2,483	2,036	2,483	2,291
19,550	19,600	2,490	2,044	2,490	2,299
19,600	19,650	2,498	2,051	2,498	2,306
19,650	19,700	2,505	2,059	2,505	2,314
19,700	19,750	2,513	2,066	2,513	2,321
19,750	19,800	2,520	2,074	2,520	2,329
19,800	19,850	2,528	2,081	2,528	2,336
19,850	19,900	2,535	2,089	2,535	2,344
19,900	19,950	2,543	2,096	2,543	2,351
19,950	20,000	2,550	2,104	2,550	2,359

20,000

At least	But less than	Single	Married filing jointly *	Married filing separately	Head of a household
20,000	20,050	2,558	2,111	2,558	2,366
20,050	20,100	2,565	2,119	2,565	2,374
20,100	20,150	2,573	2,126	2,573	2,381
20,150	20,200	2,580	2,134	2,580	2,389
20,200	20,250	2,588	2,141	2,588	2,396
20,250	20,300	2,595	2,149	2,595	2,404
20,300	20,350	2,603	2,156	2,603	2,411
20,350	20,400	2,610	2,164	2,610	2,419
20,400	20,450	2,618	2,171	2,618	2,426
20,450	20,500	2,625	2,179	2,625	2,434
20,500	20,550	2,633	2,186	2,633	2,441
20,550	20,600	2,640	2,194	2,640	2,449
20,600	20,650	2,648	2,201	2,648	2,456
20,650	20,700	2,655	2,209	2,655	2,464
20,700	20,750	2,663	2,216	2,663	2,471
20,750	20,800	2,670	2,224	2,670	2,479
20,800	20,850	2,678	2,231	2,678	2,486
20,850	20,900	2,685	2,239	2,685	2,494
20,900	20,950	2,693	2,246	2,693	2,501
20,950	21,000	2,700	2,254	2,700	2,509

* This column must also be used by a qualifying widow(er).

(Continued)

2013 Tax Table—*Continued*

If line 43 (taxable income) is— At least	But less than	Single	Married filing jointly *	Married filing separately	Head of a household
21,000					
21,000	21,050	2,708	2,261	2,708	2,516
21,050	21,100	2,715	2,269	2,715	2,524
21,100	21,150	2,723	2,276	2,723	2,531
21,150	21,200	2,730	2,284	2,730	2,539
21,200	21,250	2,738	2,291	2,738	2,546
21,250	21,300	2,745	2,299	2,745	2,554
21,300	21,350	2,753	2,306	2,753	2,561
21,350	21,400	2,760	2,314	2,760	2,569
21,400	21,450	2,768	2,321	2,768	2,576
21,450	21,500	2,775	2,329	2,775	2,584
21,500	21,550	2,783	2,336	2,783	2,591
21,550	21,600	2,790	2,344	2,790	2,599
21,600	21,650	2,798	2,351	2,798	2,606
21,650	21,700	2,805	2,359	2,805	2,614
21,700	21,750	2,813	2,366	2,813	2,621
21,750	21,800	2,820	2,374	2,820	2,629
21,800	21,850	2,828	2,381	2,828	2,636
21,850	21,900	2,835	2,389	2,835	2,644
21,900	21,950	2,843	2,396	2,843	2,651
21,950	22,000	2,850	2,404	2,850	2,659
22,000					
22,000	22,050	2,858	2,411	2,858	2,666
22,050	22,100	2,865	2,419	2,865	2,674
22,100	22,150	2,873	2,426	2,873	2,681
22,150	22,200	2,880	2,434	2,880	2,689
22,200	22,250	2,888	2,441	2,888	2,696
22,250	22,300	2,895	2,449	2,895	2,704
22,300	22,350	2,903	2,456	2,903	2,711
22,350	22,400	2,910	2,464	2,910	2,719
22,400	22,450	2,918	2,471	2,918	2,726
22,450	22,500	2,925	2,479	2,925	2,734
22,500	22,550	2,933	2,486	2,933	2,741
22,550	22,600	2,940	2,494	2,940	2,749
22,600	22,650	2,948	2,501	2,948	2,756
22,650	22,700	2,955	2,509	2,955	2,764
22,700	22,750	2,963	2,516	2,963	2,771
22,750	22,800	2,970	2,524	2,970	2,779
22,800	22,850	2,978	2,531	2,978	2,786
22,850	22,900	2,985	2,539	2,985	2,794
22,900	22,950	2,993	2,546	2,993	2,801
22,950	23,000	3,000	2,554	3,000	2,809
23,000					
23,000	23,050	3,008	2,561	3,008	2,816
23,050	23,100	3,015	2,569	3,015	2,824
23,100	23,150	3,023	2,576	3,023	2,831
23,150	23,200	3,030	2,584	3,030	2,839
23,200	23,250	3,038	2,591	3,038	2,846
23,250	23,300	3,045	2,599	3,045	2,854
23,300	23,350	3,053	2,606	3,053	2,861
23,350	23,400	3,060	2,614	3,060	2,869
23,400	23,450	3,068	2,621	3,068	2,876
23,450	23,500	3,075	2,629	3,075	2,884
23,500	23,550	3,083	2,636	3,083	2,891
23,550	23,600	3,090	2,644	3,090	2,899
23,600	23,650	3,098	2,651	3,098	2,906
23,650	23,700	3,105	2,659	3,105	2,914
23,700	23,750	3,113	2,666	3,113	2,921
23,750	23,800	3,120	2,674	3,120	2,929
23,800	23,850	3,128	2,681	3,128	2,936
23,850	23,900	3,135	2,689	3,135	2,944
23,900	23,950	3,143	2,696	3,143	2,951
23,950	24,000	3,150	2,704	3,150	2,959
24,000					
24,000	24,050	3,158	2,711	3,158	2,966
24,050	24,100	3,165	2,719	3,165	2,974
24,100	24,150	3,173	2,726	3,173	2,981
24,150	24,200	3,180	2,734	3,180	2,989
24,200	24,250	3,188	2,741	3,188	2,996
24,250	24,300	3,195	2,749	3,195	3,004
24,300	24,350	3,203	2,756	3,203	3,011
24,350	24,400	3,210	2,764	3,210	3,019
24,400	24,450	3,218	2,771	3,218	3,026
24,450	24,500	3,225	2,779	3,225	3,034
24,500	24,550	3,233	2,786	3,233	3,041
24,550	24,600	3,240	2,794	3,240	3,049
24,600	24,650	3,248	2,801	3,248	3,056
24,650	24,700	3,255	2,809	3,255	3,064
24,700	24,750	3,263	2,816	3,263	3,071
24,750	24,800	3,270	2,824	3,270	3,079
24,800	24,850	3,278	2,831	3,278	3,086
24,850	24,900	3,285	2,839	3,285	3,094
24,900	24,950	3,293	2,846	3,293	3,101
24,950	25,000	3,300	2,854	3,300	3,109
25,000					
25,000	25,050	3,308	2,861	3,308	3,116
25,050	25,100	3,315	2,869	3,315	3,124
25,100	25,150	3,323	2,876	3,323	3,131
25,150	25,200	3,330	2,884	3,330	3,139
25,200	25,250	3,338	2,891	3,338	3,146
25,250	25,300	3,345	2,899	3,345	3,154
25,300	25,350	3,353	2,906	3,353	3,161
25,350	25,400	3,360	2,914	3,360	3,169
25,400	25,450	3,368	2,921	3,368	3,176
25,450	25,500	3,375	2,929	3,375	3,184
25,500	25,550	3,383	2,936	3,383	3,191
25,550	25,600	3,390	2,944	3,390	3,199
25,600	25,650	3,398	2,951	3,398	3,206
25,650	25,700	3,405	2,959	3,405	3,214
25,700	25,750	3,413	2,966	3,413	3,221
25,750	25,800	3,420	2,974	3,420	3,229
25,800	25,850	3,428	2,981	3,428	3,236
25,850	25,900	3,435	2,989	3,435	3,244
25,900	25,950	3,443	2,996	3,443	3,251
25,950	26,000	3,450	3,004	3,450	3,259
26,000					
26,000	26,050	3,458	3,011	3,458	3,266
26,050	26,100	3,465	3,019	3,465	3,274
26,100	26,150	3,473	3,026	3,473	3,281
26,150	26,200	3,480	3,034	3,480	3,289
26,200	26,250	3,488	3,041	3,488	3,296
26,250	26,300	3,495	3,049	3,495	3,304
26,300	26,350	3,503	3,056	3,503	3,311
26,350	26,400	3,510	3,064	3,510	3,319
26,400	26,450	3,518	3,071	3,518	3,326
26,450	26,500	3,525	3,079	3,525	3,334
26,500	26,550	3,533	3,086	3,533	3,341
26,550	26,600	3,540	3,094	3,540	3,349
26,600	26,650	3,548	3,101	3,548	3,356
26,650	26,700	3,555	3,109	3,555	3,364
26,700	26,750	3,563	3,116	3,563	3,371
26,750	26,800	3,570	3,124	3,570	3,379
26,800	26,850	3,578	3,131	3,578	3,386
26,850	26,900	3,585	3,139	3,585	3,394
26,900	26,950	3,593	3,146	3,593	3,401
26,950	27,000	3,600	3,154	3,600	3,409
27,000					
27,000	27,050	3,608	3,161	3,608	3,416
27,050	27,100	3,615	3,169	3,615	3,424
27,100	27,150	3,623	3,176	3,623	3,431
27,150	27,200	3,630	3,184	3,630	3,439
27,200	27,250	3,638	3,191	3,638	3,446
27,250	27,300	3,645	3,199	3,645	3,454
27,300	27,350	3,653	3,206	3,653	3,461
27,350	27,400	3,660	3,214	3,660	3,469
27,400	27,450	3,668	3,221	3,668	3,476
27,450	27,500	3,675	3,229	3,675	3,484
27,500	27,550	3,683	3,236	3,683	3,491
27,550	27,600	3,690	3,244	3,690	3,499
27,600	27,650	3,698	3,251	3,698	3,506
27,650	27,700	3,705	3,259	3,705	3,514
27,700	27,750	3,713	3,266	3,713	3,521
27,750	27,800	3,720	3,274	3,720	3,529
27,800	27,850	3,728	3,281	3,728	3,536
27,850	27,900	3,735	3,289	3,735	3,544
27,900	27,950	3,743	3,296	3,743	3,551
27,950	28,000	3,750	3,304	3,750	3,559
28,000					
28,000	28,050	3,758	3,311	3,758	3,566
28,050	28,100	3,765	3,319	3,765	3,574
28,100	28,150	3,773	3,326	3,773	3,581
28,150	28,200	3,780	3,334	3,780	3,589
28,200	28,250	3,788	3,341	3,788	3,596
28,250	28,300	3,795	3,349	3,795	3,604
28,300	28,350	3,803	3,356	3,803	3,611
28,350	28,400	3,810	3,364	3,810	3,619
28,400	28,450	3,818	3,371	3,818	3,626
28,450	28,500	3,825	3,379	3,825	3,634
28,500	28,550	3,833	3,386	3,833	3,641
28,550	28,600	3,840	3,394	3,840	3,649
28,600	28,650	3,848	3,401	3,848	3,656
28,650	28,700	3,855	3,409	3,855	3,664
28,700	28,750	3,863	3,416	3,863	3,671
28,750	28,800	3,870	3,424	3,870	3,679
28,800	28,850	3,878	3,431	3,878	3,686
28,850	28,900	3,885	3,439	3,885	3,694
28,900	28,950	3,893	3,446	3,893	3,701
28,950	29,000	3,900	3,454	3,900	3,709
29,000					
29,000	29,050	3,908	3,461	3,908	3,716
29,050	29,100	3,915	3,469	3,915	3,724
29,100	29,150	3,923	3,476	3,923	3,731
29,150	29,200	3,930	3,484	3,930	3,739
29,200	29,250	3,938	3,491	3,938	3,746
29,250	29,300	3,945	3,499	3,945	3,754
29,300	29,350	3,953	3,506	3,953	3,761
29,350	29,400	3,960	3,514	3,960	3,769
29,400	29,450	3,968	3,521	3,968	3,776
29,450	29,500	3,975	3,529	3,975	3,784
29,500	29,550	3,983	3,536	3,983	3,791
29,550	29,600	3,990	3,544	3,990	3,799
29,600	29,650	3,998	3,551	3,998	3,806
29,650	29,700	4,005	3,559	4,005	3,814
29,700	29,750	4,013	3,566	4,013	3,821
29,750	29,800	4,020	3,574	4,020	3,829
29,800	29,850	4,028	3,581	4,028	3,836
29,850	29,900	4,035	3,589	4,035	3,844
29,900	29,950	4,043	3,596	4,043	3,851
29,950	30,000	4,050	3,604	4,050	3,859

* This column must also be used by a qualifying widow(er).

(Continued)

2013 Tax Table—Continued

30,000 – 33,000 – 36,000

If line 43 (taxable income) is— At least	But less than	And you are— Single	Married filing jointly *	Married filing separately	Head of a house-hold
30,000					
30,000	30,050	4,058	3,611	4,058	3,866
30,050	30,100	4,065	3,619	4,065	3,874
30,100	30,150	4,073	3,626	4,073	3,881
30,150	30,200	4,080	3,634	4,080	3,889
30,200	30,250	4,088	3,641	4,088	3,896
30,250	30,300	4,095	3,649	4,095	3,904
30,300	30,350	4,103	3,656	4,103	3,911
30,350	30,400	4,110	3,664	4,110	3,919
30,400	30,450	4,118	3,671	4,118	3,926
30,450	30,500	4,125	3,679	4,125	3,934
30,500	30,550	4,133	3,686	4,133	3,941
30,550	30,600	4,140	3,694	4,140	3,949
30,600	30,650	4,148	3,701	4,148	3,956
30,650	30,700	4,155	3,709	4,155	3,964
30,700	30,750	4,163	3,716	4,163	3,971
30,750	30,800	4,170	3,724	4,170	3,979
30,800	30,850	4,178	3,731	4,178	3,986
30,850	30,900	4,185	3,739	4,185	3,994
30,900	30,950	4,193	3,746	4,193	4,001
30,950	31,000	4,200	3,754	4,200	4,009
31,000					
31,000	31,050	4,208	3,761	4,208	4,016
31,050	31,100	4,215	3,769	4,215	4,024
31,100	31,150	4,223	3,776	4,223	4,031
31,150	31,200	4,230	3,784	4,230	4,039
31,200	31,250	4,238	3,791	4,238	4,046
31,250	31,300	4,245	3,799	4,245	4,054
31,300	31,350	4,253	3,806	4,253	4,061
31,350	31,400	4,260	3,814	4,260	4,069
31,400	31,450	4,268	3,821	4,268	4,076
31,450	31,500	4,275	3,829	4,275	4,084
31,500	31,550	4,283	3,836	4,283	4,091
31,550	31,600	4,290	3,844	4,290	4,099
31,600	31,650	4,298	3,851	4,298	4,106
31,650	31,700	4,305	3,859	4,305	4,114
31,700	31,750	4,313	3,866	4,313	4,121
31,750	31,800	4,320	3,874	4,320	4,129
31,800	31,850	4,328	3,881	4,328	4,136
31,850	31,900	4,335	3,889	4,335	4,144
31,900	31,950	4,343	3,896	4,343	4,151
31,950	32,000	4,350	3,904	4,350	4,159
32,000					
32,000	32,050	4,358	3,911	4,358	4,166
32,050	32,100	4,365	3,919	4,365	4,174
32,100	32,150	4,373	3,926	4,373	4,181
32,150	32,200	4,380	3,934	4,380	4,189
32,200	32,250	4,388	3,941	4,388	4,196
32,250	32,300	4,395	3,949	4,395	4,204
32,300	32,350	4,403	3,956	4,403	4,211
32,350	32,400	4,410	3,964	4,410	4,219
32,400	32,450	4,418	3,971	4,418	4,226
32,450	32,500	4,425	3,979	4,425	4,234
32,500	32,550	4,433	3,986	4,433	4,241
32,550	32,600	4,440	3,994	4,440	4,249
32,600	32,650	4,448	4,001	4,448	4,256
32,650	32,700	4,455	4,009	4,455	4,264
32,700	32,750	4,463	4,016	4,463	4,271
32,750	32,800	4,470	4,024	4,470	4,279
32,800	32,850	4,478	4,031	4,478	4,286
32,850	32,900	4,485	4,039	4,485	4,294
32,900	32,950	4,493	4,046	4,493	4,301
32,950	33,000	4,500	4,054	4,500	4,309
33,000					
33,000	33,050	4,508	4,061	4,508	4,316
33,050	33,100	4,515	4,069	4,515	4,324
33,100	33,150	4,523	4,076	4,523	4,331
33,150	33,200	4,530	4,084	4,530	4,339
33,200	33,250	4,538	4,091	4,538	4,346
33,250	33,300	4,545	4,099	4,545	4,354
33,300	33,350	4,553	4,106	4,553	4,361
33,350	33,400	4,560	4,114	4,560	4,369
33,400	33,450	4,568	4,121	4,568	4,376
33,450	33,500	4,575	4,129	4,575	4,384
33,500	33,550	4,583	4,136	4,583	4,391
33,550	33,600	4,590	4,144	4,590	4,399
33,600	33,650	4,598	4,151	4,598	4,406
33,650	33,700	4,605	4,159	4,605	4,414
33,700	33,750	4,613	4,166	4,613	4,421
33,750	33,800	4,620	4,174	4,620	4,429
33,800	33,850	4,628	4,181	4,628	4,436
33,850	33,900	4,635	4,189	4,635	4,444
33,900	33,950	4,643	4,196	4,643	4,451
33,950	34,000	4,650	4,204	4,650	4,459
34,000					
34,000	34,050	4,658	4,211	4,658	4,466
34,050	34,100	4,665	4,219	4,665	4,474
34,100	34,150	4,673	4,226	4,673	4,481
34,150	34,200	4,680	4,234	4,680	4,489
34,200	34,250	4,688	4,241	4,688	4,496
34,250	34,300	4,695	4,249	4,695	4,504
34,300	34,350	4,703	4,256	4,703	4,511
34,350	34,400	4,710	4,264	4,710	4,519
34,400	34,450	4,718	4,271	4,718	4,526
34,450	34,500	4,725	4,279	4,725	4,534
34,500	34,550	4,733	4,286	4,733	4,541
34,550	34,600	4,740	4,294	4,740	4,549
34,600	34,650	4,748	4,301	4,748	4,556
34,650	34,700	4,755	4,309	4,755	4,564
34,700	34,750	4,763	4,316	4,763	4,571
34,750	34,800	4,770	4,324	4,770	4,579
34,800	34,850	4,778	4,331	4,778	4,586
34,850	34,900	4,785	4,339	4,785	4,594
34,900	34,950	4,793	4,346	4,793	4,601
34,950	35,000	4,800	4,354	4,800	4,609
35,000					
35,000	35,050	4,808	4,361	4,808	4,616
35,050	35,100	4,815	4,369	4,815	4,624
35,100	35,150	4,823	4,376	4,823	4,631
35,150	35,200	4,830	4,384	4,830	4,639
35,200	35,250	4,838	4,391	4,838	4,646
35,250	35,300	4,845	4,399	4,845	4,654
35,300	35,350	4,853	4,406	4,853	4,661
35,350	35,400	4,860	4,414	4,860	4,669
35,400	35,450	4,868	4,421	4,868	4,676
35,450	35,500	4,875	4,429	4,875	4,684
35,500	35,550	4,883	4,436	4,883	4,691
35,550	35,600	4,890	4,444	4,890	4,699
35,600	35,650	4,898	4,451	4,898	4,706
35,650	35,700	4,905	4,459	4,905	4,714
35,700	35,750	4,913	4,466	4,913	4,721
35,750	35,800	4,920	4,474	4,920	4,729
35,800	35,850	4,928	4,481	4,928	4,736
35,850	35,900	4,935	4,489	4,935	4,744
35,900	35,950	4,943	4,496	4,943	4,751
35,950	36,000	4,950	4,504	4,950	4,759
36,000					
36,000	36,050	4,958	4,511	4,958	4,766
36,050	36,100	4,965	4,519	4,965	4,774
36,100	36,150	4,973	4,526	4,973	4,781
36,150	36,200	4,980	4,534	4,980	4,789
36,200	36,250	4,988	4,541	4,988	4,796
36,250	36,300	4,998	4,549	4,998	4,804
36,300	36,350	5,010	4,556	5,010	4,811
36,350	36,400	5,023	4,564	5,023	4,819
36,400	36,450	5,035	4,571	5,035	4,826
36,450	36,500	5,048	4,579	5,048	4,834
36,500	36,550	5,060	4,586	5,060	4,841
36,550	36,600	5,073	4,594	5,073	4,849
36,600	36,650	5,085	4,601	5,085	4,856
36,650	36,700	5,098	4,609	5,098	4,864
36,700	36,750	5,110	4,616	5,110	4,871
36,750	36,800	5,123	4,624	5,123	4,879
36,800	36,850	5,135	4,631	5,135	4,886
36,850	36,900	5,148	4,639	5,148	4,894
36,900	36,950	5,160	4,646	5,160	4,901
36,950	37,000	5,173	4,654	5,173	4,909
37,000					
37,000	37,050	5,185	4,661	5,185	4,916
37,050	37,100	5,198	4,669	5,198	4,924
37,100	37,150	5,210	4,676	5,210	4,931
37,150	37,200	5,223	4,684	5,223	4,939
37,200	37,250	5,235	4,691	5,235	4,946
37,250	37,300	5,248	4,699	5,248	4,954
37,300	37,350	5,260	4,706	5,260	4,961
37,350	37,400	5,273	4,714	5,273	4,969
37,400	37,450	5,285	4,721	5,285	4,976
37,450	37,500	5,298	4,729	5,298	4,984
37,500	37,550	5,310	4,736	5,310	4,991
37,550	37,600	5,323	4,744	5,323	4,999
37,600	37,650	5,335	4,751	5,335	5,006
37,650	37,700	5,348	4,759	5,348	5,014
37,700	37,750	5,360	4,766	5,360	5,021
37,750	37,800	5,373	4,774	5,373	5,029
37,800	37,850	5,385	4,781	5,385	5,036
37,850	37,900	5,398	4,789	5,398	5,044
37,900	37,950	5,410	4,796	5,410	5,051
37,950	38,000	5,423	4,804	5,423	5,059
38,000					
38,000	38,050	5,435	4,811	5,435	5,066
38,050	38,100	5,448	4,819	5,448	5,074
38,100	38,150	5,460	4,826	5,460	5,081
38,150	38,200	5,473	4,834	5,473	5,089
38,200	38,250	5,485	4,841	5,485	5,096
38,250	38,300	5,498	4,849	5,498	5,104
38,300	38,350	5,510	4,856	5,510	5,111
38,350	38,400	5,523	4,864	5,523	5,119
38,400	38,450	5,535	4,871	5,535	5,126
38,450	38,500	5,548	4,879	5,548	5,134
38,500	38,550	5,560	4,886	5,560	5,141
38,550	38,600	5,573	4,894	5,573	5,149
38,600	38,650	5,585	4,901	5,585	5,156
38,650	38,700	5,598	4,909	5,598	5,164
38,700	38,750	5,610	4,916	5,610	5,171
38,750	38,800	5,623	4,924	5,623	5,179
38,800	38,850	5,635	4,931	5,635	5,186
38,850	38,900	5,648	4,939	5,648	5,194
38,900	38,950	5,660	4,946	5,660	5,201
38,950	39,000	5,673	4,954	5,673	5,209

* This column must also be used by a qualifying widow(er).

(Continued)

2013 Tax Table—*Continued*

If line 43 (taxable income) is—		And you are—			
At least	But less than	Single	Married filing jointly *	Married filing separately	Head of a house-hold
		Your tax is—			

39,000

At least	But less than	Single	MFJ *	MFS	HoH
39,000	39,050	5,685	4,961	5,685	5,216
39,050	39,100	5,698	4,969	5,698	5,224
39,100	39,150	5,710	4,976	5,710	5,231
39,150	39,200	5,723	4,984	5,723	5,239
39,200	39,250	5,735	4,991	5,735	5,246
39,250	39,300	5,748	4,999	5,748	5,254
39,300	39,350	5,760	5,006	5,760	5,261
39,350	39,400	5,773	5,014	5,773	5,269
39,400	39,450	5,785	5,021	5,785	5,276
39,450	39,500	5,798	5,029	5,798	5,284
39,500	39,550	5,810	5,036	5,810	5,291
39,550	39,600	5,823	5,044	5,823	5,299
39,600	39,650	5,835	5,051	5,835	5,306
39,650	39,700	5,848	5,059	5,848	5,314
39,700	39,750	5,860	5,066	5,860	5,321
39,750	39,800	5,873	5,074	5,873	5,329
39,800	39,850	5,885	5,081	5,885	5,336
39,850	39,900	5,898	5,089	5,898	5,344
39,900	39,950	5,910	5,096	5,910	5,351
39,950	40,000	5,923	5,104	5,923	5,359

40,000

At least	But less than	Single	MFJ *	MFS	HoH
40,000	40,050	5,935	5,111	5,935	5,366
40,050	40,100	5,948	5,119	5,948	5,374
40,100	40,150	5,960	5,126	5,960	5,381
40,150	40,200	5,973	5,134	5,973	5,389
40,200	40,250	5,985	5,141	5,985	5,396
40,250	40,300	5,998	5,149	5,998	5,404
40,300	40,350	6,010	5,156	6,010	5,411
40,350	40,400	6,023	5,164	6,023	5,419
40,400	40,450	6,035	5,171	6,035	5,426
40,450	40,500	6,048	5,179	6,048	5,434
40,500	40,550	6,060	5,186	6,060	5,441
40,550	40,600	6,073	5,194	6,073	5,449
40,600	40,650	6,085	5,201	6,085	5,456
40,650	40,700	6,098	5,209	6,098	5,464
40,700	40,750	6,110	5,216	6,110	5,471
40,750	40,800	6,123	5,224	6,123	5,479
40,800	40,850	6,135	5,231	6,135	5,486
40,850	40,900	6,148	5,239	6,148	5,494
40,900	40,950	6,160	5,246	6,160	5,501
40,950	41,000	6,173	5,254	6,173	5,509

41,000

At least	But less than	Single	MFJ *	MFS	HoH
41,000	41,050	6,185	5,261	6,185	5,516
41,050	41,100	6,198	5,269	6,198	5,524
41,100	41,150	6,210	5,276	6,210	5,531
41,150	41,200	6,223	5,284	6,223	5,539
41,200	41,250	6,235	5,291	6,235	5,546
41,250	41,300	6,248	5,299	6,248	5,554
41,300	41,350	6,260	5,306	6,260	5,561
41,350	41,400	6,273	5,314	6,273	5,569
41,400	41,450	6,285	5,321	6,285	5,576
41,450	41,500	6,298	5,329	6,298	5,584
41,500	41,550	6,310	5,336	6,310	5,591
41,550	41,600	6,323	5,344	6,323	5,599
41,600	41,650	6,335	5,351	6,335	5,606
41,650	41,700	6,348	5,359	6,348	5,614
41,700	41,750	6,360	5,366	6,360	5,621
41,750	41,800	6,373	5,374	6,373	5,629
41,800	41,850	6,385	5,381	6,385	5,636
41,850	41,900	6,398	5,389	6,398	5,644
41,900	41,950	6,410	5,396	6,410	5,651
41,950	42,000	6,423	5,404	6,423	5,659

42,000

At least	But less than	Single	MFJ *	MFS	HoH
42,000	42,050	6,435	5,411	6,435	5,666
42,050	42,100	6,448	5,419	6,448	5,674
42,100	42,150	6,460	5,426	6,460	5,681
42,150	42,200	6,473	5,434	6,473	5,689
42,200	42,250	6,485	5,441	6,485	5,696
42,250	42,300	6,498	5,449	6,498	5,704
42,300	42,350	6,510	5,456	6,510	5,711
42,350	42,400	6,523	5,464	6,523	5,719
42,400	42,450	6,535	5,471	6,535	5,726
42,450	42,500	6,548	5,479	6,548	5,734
42,500	42,550	6,560	5,486	6,560	5,741
42,550	42,600	6,573	5,494	6,573	5,749
42,600	42,650	6,585	5,501	6,585	5,756
42,650	42,700	6,598	5,509	6,598	5,764
42,700	42,750	6,610	5,516	6,610	5,771
42,750	42,800	6,623	5,524	6,623	5,779
42,800	42,850	6,635	5,531	6,635	5,786
42,850	42,900	6,648	5,539	6,648	5,794
42,900	42,950	6,660	5,546	6,660	5,801
42,950	43,000	6,673	5,554	6,673	5,809

43,000

At least	But less than	Single	MFJ *	MFS	HoH
43,000	43,050	6,685	5,561	6,685	5,816
43,050	43,100	6,698	5,569	6,698	5,824
43,100	43,150	6,710	5,576	6,710	5,831
43,150	43,200	6,723	5,584	6,723	5,839
43,200	43,250	6,735	5,591	6,735	5,846
43,250	43,300	6,748	5,599	6,748	5,854
43,300	43,350	6,760	5,606	6,760	5,861
43,350	43,400	6,773	5,614	6,773	5,869
43,400	43,450	6,785	5,621	6,785	5,876
43,450	43,500	6,798	5,629	6,798	5,884
43,500	43,550	6,810	5,636	6,810	5,891
43,550	43,600	6,823	5,644	6,823	5,899
43,600	43,650	6,835	5,651	6,835	5,906
43,650	43,700	6,848	5,659	6,848	5,914
43,700	43,750	6,860	5,666	6,860	5,921
43,750	43,800	6,873	5,674	6,873	5,929
43,800	43,850	6,885	5,681	6,885	5,936
43,850	43,900	6,898	5,689	6,898	5,944
43,900	43,950	6,910	5,696	6,910	5,951
43,950	44,000	6,923	5,704	6,923	5,959

44,000

At least	But less than	Single	MFJ *	MFS	HoH
44,000	44,050	6,935	5,711	6,935	5,966
44,050	44,100	6,948	5,719	6,948	5,974
44,100	44,150	6,960	5,726	6,960	5,981
44,150	44,200	6,973	5,734	6,973	5,989
44,200	44,250	6,985	5,741	6,985	5,996
44,250	44,300	6,998	5,749	6,998	6,004
44,300	44,350	7,010	5,756	7,010	6,011
44,350	44,400	7,023	5,764	7,023	6,019
44,400	44,450	7,035	5,771	7,035	6,026
44,450	44,500	7,048	5,779	7,048	6,034
44,500	44,550	7,060	5,786	7,060	6,041
44,550	44,600	7,073	5,794	7,073	6,049
44,600	44,650	7,085	5,801	7,085	6,056
44,650	44,700	7,098	5,809	7,098	6,064
44,700	44,750	7,110	5,816	7,110	6,071
44,750	44,800	7,123	5,824	7,123	6,079
44,800	44,850	7,135	5,831	7,135	6,086
44,850	44,900	7,148	5,839	7,148	6,094
44,900	44,950	7,160	5,846	7,160	6,101
44,950	45,000	7,173	5,854	7,173	6,109

45,000

At least	But less than	Single	MFJ *	MFS	HoH
45,000	45,050	7,185	5,861	7,185	6,116
45,050	45,100	7,198	5,869	7,198	6,124
45,100	45,150	7,210	5,876	7,210	6,131
45,150	45,200	7,223	5,884	7,223	6,139
45,200	45,250	7,235	5,891	7,235	6,146
45,250	45,300	7,248	5,899	7,248	6,154
45,300	45,350	7,260	5,906	7,260	6,161
45,350	45,400	7,273	5,914	7,273	6,169
45,400	45,450	7,285	5,921	7,285	6,176
45,450	45,500	7,298	5,929	7,298	6,184
45,500	45,550	7,310	5,936	7,310	6,191
45,550	45,600	7,323	5,944	7,323	6,199
45,600	45,650	7,335	5,951	7,335	6,206
45,650	45,700	7,348	5,959	7,348	6,214
45,700	45,750	7,360	5,966	7,360	6,221
45,750	45,800	7,373	5,974	7,373	6,229
45,800	45,850	7,385	5,981	7,385	6,236
45,850	45,900	7,398	5,989	7,398	6,244
45,900	45,950	7,410	5,996	7,410	6,251
45,950	46,000	7,423	6,004	7,423	6,259

46,000

At least	But less than	Single	MFJ *	MFS	HoH
46,000	46,050	7,435	6,011	7,435	6,266
46,050	46,100	7,448	6,019	7,448	6,274
46,100	46,150	7,460	6,026	7,460	6,281
46,150	46,200	7,473	6,034	7,473	6,289
46,200	46,250	7,485	6,041	7,485	6,296
46,250	46,300	7,498	6,049	7,498	6,304
46,300	46,350	7,510	6,056	7,510	6,311
46,350	46,400	7,523	6,064	7,523	6,319
46,400	46,450	7,535	6,071	7,535	6,326
46,450	46,500	7,548	6,079	7,548	6,334
46,500	46,550	7,560	6,086	7,560	6,341
46,550	46,600	7,573	6,094	7,573	6,349
46,600	46,650	7,585	6,101	7,585	6,356
46,650	46,700	7,598	6,109	7,598	6,364
46,700	46,750	7,610	6,116	7,610	6,371
46,750	46,800	7,623	6,124	7,623	6,379
46,800	46,850	7,635	6,131	7,635	6,386
46,850	46,900	7,648	6,139	7,648	6,394
46,900	46,950	7,660	6,146	7,660	6,401
46,950	47,000	7,673	6,154	7,673	6,409

47,000

At least	But less than	Single	MFJ *	MFS	HoH
47,000	47,050	7,685	6,161	7,685	6,416
47,050	47,100	7,698	6,169	7,698	6,424
47,100	47,150	7,710	6,176	7,710	6,431
47,150	47,200	7,723	6,184	7,723	6,439
47,200	47,250	7,735	6,191	7,735	6,446
47,250	47,300	7,748	6,199	7,748	6,454
47,300	47,350	7,760	6,206	7,760	6,461
47,350	47,400	7,773	6,214	7,773	6,469
47,400	47,450	7,785	6,221	7,785	6,476
47,450	47,500	7,798	6,229	7,798	6,484
47,500	47,550	7,810	6,236	7,810	6,491
47,550	47,600	7,823	6,244	7,823	6,499
47,600	47,650	7,835	6,251	7,835	6,506
47,650	47,700	7,848	6,259	7,848	6,514
47,700	47,750	7,860	6,266	7,860	6,521
47,750	47,800	7,873	6,274	7,873	6,529
47,800	47,850	7,885	6,281	7,885	6,536
47,850	47,900	7,898	6,289	7,898	6,544
47,900	47,950	7,910	6,296	7,910	6,551
47,950	48,000	7,923	6,304	7,923	6,559

* This column must also be used by a qualifying widow(er).

(Continued)

2013 Tax Table—*Continued*

48,000 / 49,000 / 50,000

If line 43 (taxable income) is— At least	But less than	Single	Married filing jointly *	Married filing separately	Head of a household
48,000					
48,000	48,050	7,935	6,311	7,935	6,566
48,050	48,100	7,948	6,319	7,948	6,574
48,100	48,150	7,960	6,326	7,960	6,581
48,150	48,200	7,973	6,334	7,973	6,589
48,200	48,250	7,985	6,341	7,985	6,596
48,250	48,300	7,998	6,349	7,998	6,604
48,300	48,350	8,010	6,356	8,010	6,611
48,350	48,400	8,023	6,364	8,023	6,619
48,400	48,450	8,035	6,371	8,035	6,626
48,450	48,500	8,048	6,379	8,048	6,634
48,500	48,550	8,060	6,386	8,060	6,641
48,550	48,600	8,073	6,394	8,073	6,649
48,600	48,650	8,085	6,401	8,085	6,659
48,650	48,700	8,098	6,409	8,098	6,671
48,700	48,750	8,110	6,416	8,110	6,684
48,750	48,800	8,123	6,424	8,123	6,696
48,800	48,850	8,135	6,431	8,135	6,709
48,850	48,900	8,148	6,439	8,148	6,721
48,900	48,950	8,160	6,446	8,160	6,734
48,950	49,000	8,173	6,454	8,173	6,746
49,000					
49,000	49,050	8,185	6,461	8,185	6,759
49,050	49,100	8,198	6,469	8,198	6,771
49,100	49,150	8,210	6,476	8,210	6,784
49,150	49,200	8,223	6,484	8,223	6,796
49,200	49,250	8,235	6,491	8,235	6,809
49,250	49,300	8,248	6,499	8,248	6,821
49,300	49,350	8,260	6,506	8,260	6,834
49,350	49,400	8,273	6,514	8,273	6,846
49,400	49,450	8,285	6,521	8,285	6,859
49,450	49,500	8,298	6,529	8,298	6,871
49,500	49,550	8,310	6,536	8,310	6,884
49,550	49,600	8,323	6,544	8,323	6,896
49,600	49,650	8,335	6,551	8,335	6,909
49,650	49,700	8,348	6,559	8,348	6,921
49,700	49,750	8,360	6,566	8,360	6,934
49,750	49,800	8,373	6,574	8,373	6,946
49,800	49,850	8,385	6,581	8,385	6,959
49,850	49,900	8,398	6,589	8,398	6,971
49,900	49,950	8,410	6,596	8,410	6,984
49,950	50,000	8,423	6,604	8,423	6,996
50,000					
50,000	50,050	8,435	6,611	8,435	7,009
50,050	50,100	8,448	6,619	8,448	7,021
50,100	50,150	8,460	6,626	8,460	7,034
50,150	50,200	8,473	6,634	8,473	7,046
50,200	50,250	8,485	6,641	8,485	7,059
50,250	50,300	8,498	6,649	8,498	7,071
50,300	50,350	8,510	6,656	8,510	7,084
50,350	50,400	8,523	6,664	8,523	7,096
50,400	50,450	8,535	6,671	8,535	7,109
50,450	50,500	8,548	6,679	8,548	7,121
50,500	50,550	8,560	6,686	8,560	7,134
50,550	50,600	8,573	6,694	8,573	7,146
50,600	50,650	8,585	6,701	8,585	7,159
50,650	50,700	8,598	6,709	8,598	7,171
50,700	50,750	8,610	6,716	8,610	7,184
50,750	50,800	8,623	6,724	8,623	7,196
50,800	50,850	8,635	6,731	8,635	7,209
50,850	50,900	8,648	6,739	8,648	7,221
50,900	50,950	8,660	6,746	8,660	7,234
50,950	51,000	8,673	6,754	8,673	7,246

51,000 / 52,000 / 53,000

If line 43 (taxable income) is— At least	But less than	Single	Married filing jointly *	Married filing separately	Head of a household
51,000					
51,000	51,050	8,685	6,761	8,685	7,259
51,050	51,100	8,698	6,769	8,698	7,271
51,100	51,150	8,710	6,776	8,710	7,284
51,150	51,200	8,723	6,784	8,723	7,296
51,200	51,250	8,735	6,791	8,735	7,309
51,250	51,300	8,748	6,799	8,748	7,321
51,300	51,350	8,760	6,806	8,760	7,334
51,350	51,400	8,773	6,814	8,773	7,346
51,400	51,450	8,785	6,821	8,785	7,359
51,450	51,500	8,798	6,829	8,798	7,371
51,500	51,550	8,810	6,836	8,810	7,384
51,550	51,600	8,823	6,844	8,823	7,396
51,600	51,650	8,835	6,851	8,835	7,409
51,650	51,700	8,848	6,859	8,848	7,421
51,700	51,750	8,860	6,866	8,860	7,434
51,750	51,800	8,873	6,874	8,873	7,446
51,800	51,850	8,885	6,881	8,885	7,459
51,850	51,900	8,898	6,889	8,898	7,471
51,900	51,950	8,910	6,896	8,910	7,484
51,950	52,000	8,923	6,904	8,923	7,496
52,000					
52,000	52,050	8,935	6,911	8,935	7,509
52,050	52,100	8,948	6,919	8,948	7,521
52,100	52,150	8,960	6,926	8,960	7,534
52,150	52,200	8,973	6,934	8,973	7,546
52,200	52,250	8,985	6,941	8,985	7,559
52,250	52,300	8,998	6,949	8,998	7,571
52,300	52,350	9,010	6,956	9,010	7,584
52,350	52,400	9,023	6,964	9,023	7,596
52,400	52,450	9,035	6,971	9,035	7,609
52,450	52,500	9,048	6,979	9,048	7,621
52,500	52,550	9,060	6,986	9,060	7,634
52,550	52,600	9,073	6,994	9,073	7,646
52,600	52,650	9,085	7,001	9,085	7,659
52,650	52,700	9,098	7,009	9,098	7,671
52,700	52,750	9,110	7,016	9,110	7,684
52,750	52,800	9,123	7,024	9,123	7,696
52,800	52,850	9,135	7,031	9,135	7,709
52,850	52,900	9,148	7,039	9,148	7,721
52,900	52,950	9,160	7,046	9,160	7,734
52,950	53,000	9,173	7,054	9,173	7,746
53,000					
53,000	53,050	9,185	7,061	9,185	7,759
53,050	53,100	9,198	7,069	9,198	7,771
53,100	53,150	9,210	7,076	9,210	7,784
53,150	53,200	9,223	7,084	9,223	7,796
53,200	53,250	9,235	7,091	9,235	7,809
53,250	53,300	9,248	7,099	9,248	7,821
53,300	53,350	9,260	7,106	9,260	7,834
53,350	53,400	9,273	7,114	9,273	7,846
53,400	53,450	9,285	7,121	9,285	7,859
53,450	53,500	9,298	7,129	9,298	7,871
53,500	53,550	9,310	7,136	9,310	7,884
53,550	53,600	9,323	7,144	9,323	7,896
53,600	53,650	9,335	7,151	9,335	7,909
53,650	53,700	9,348	7,159	9,348	7,921
53,700	53,750	9,360	7,166	9,360	7,934
53,750	53,800	9,373	7,174	9,373	7,946
53,800	53,850	9,385	7,181	9,385	7,959
53,850	53,900	9,398	7,189	9,398	7,971
53,900	53,950	9,410	7,196	9,410	7,984
53,950	54,000	9,423	7,204	9,423	7,996

54,000 / 55,000 / 56,000

If line 43 (taxable income) is— At least	But less than	Single	Married filing jointly *	Married filing separately	Head of a household
54,000					
54,000	54,050	9,435	7,211	9,435	8,009
54,050	54,100	9,448	7,219	9,448	8,021
54,100	54,150	9,460	7,226	9,460	8,034
54,150	54,200	9,473	7,234	9,473	8,046
54,200	54,250	9,485	7,241	9,485	8,059
54,250	54,300	9,498	7,249	9,498	8,071
54,300	54,350	9,510	7,256	9,510	8,084
54,350	54,400	9,523	7,264	9,523	8,096
54,400	54,450	9,535	7,271	9,535	8,109
54,450	54,500	9,548	7,279	9,548	8,121
54,500	54,550	9,560	7,286	9,560	8,134
54,550	54,600	9,573	7,294	9,573	8,146
54,600	54,650	9,585	7,301	9,585	8,159
54,650	54,700	9,598	7,309	9,598	8,171
54,700	54,750	9,610	7,316	9,610	8,184
54,750	54,800	9,623	7,324	9,623	8,196
54,800	54,850	9,635	7,331	9,635	8,209
54,850	54,900	9,648	7,339	9,648	8,221
54,900	54,950	9,660	7,346	9,660	8,234
54,950	55,000	9,673	7,354	9,673	8,246
55,000					
55,000	55,050	9,685	7,361	9,685	8,259
55,050	55,100	9,698	7,369	9,698	8,271
55,100	55,150	9,710	7,376	9,710	8,284
55,150	55,200	9,723	7,384	9,723	8,296
55,200	55,250	9,735	7,391	9,735	8,309
55,250	55,300	9,748	7,399	9,748	8,321
55,300	55,350	9,760	7,406	9,760	8,334
55,350	55,400	9,773	7,414	9,773	8,346
55,400	55,450	9,785	7,421	9,785	8,359
55,450	55,500	9,798	7,429	9,798	8,371
55,500	55,550	9,810	7,436	9,810	8,384
55,550	55,600	9,823	7,444	9,823	8,396
55,600	55,650	9,835	7,451	9,835	8,409
55,650	55,700	9,848	7,459	9,848	8,421
55,700	55,750	9,860	7,466	9,860	8,434
55,750	55,800	9,873	7,474	9,873	8,446
55,800	55,850	9,885	7,481	9,885	8,459
55,850	55,900	9,898	7,489	9,898	8,471
55,900	55,950	9,910	7,496	9,910	8,484
55,950	56,000	9,923	7,504	9,923	8,496
56,000					
56,000	56,050	9,935	7,511	9,935	8,509
56,050	56,100	9,948	7,519	9,948	8,521
56,100	56,150	9,960	7,526	9,960	8,534
56,150	56,200	9,973	7,534	9,973	8,546
56,200	56,250	9,985	7,541	9,985	8,559
56,250	56,300	9,998	7,549	9,998	8,571
56,300	56,350	10,010	7,556	10,010	8,584
56,350	56,400	10,023	7,564	10,023	8,596
56,400	56,450	10,035	7,571	10,035	8,609
56,450	56,500	10,048	7,579	10,048	8,621
56,500	56,550	10,060	7,586	10,060	8,634
56,550	56,600	10,073	7,594	10,073	8,646
56,600	56,650	10,085	7,601	10,085	8,659
56,650	56,700	10,098	7,609	10,098	8,671
56,700	56,750	10,110	7,616	10,110	8,684
56,750	56,800	10,123	7,624	10,123	8,696
56,800	56,850	10,135	7,631	10,135	8,709
56,850	56,900	10,148	7,639	10,148	8,721
56,900	56,950	10,160	7,646	10,160	8,734
56,950	57,000	10,173	7,654	10,173	8,746

* This column must also be used by a qualifying widow(er).

(Continued)

2013 Tax Table—*Continued*

If line 43 (taxable income) is—		And you are—			
At least	But less than	Single	Married filing jointly *	Married filing separately	Head of a household
		Your tax is—			

57,000

At least	But less than	Single	Married filing jointly *	Married filing separately	Head of a household
57,000	57,050	10,185	7,661	10,185	8,759
57,050	57,100	10,198	7,669	10,198	8,771
57,100	57,150	10,210	7,676	10,210	8,784
57,150	57,200	10,223	7,684	10,223	8,796
57,200	57,250	10,235	7,691	10,235	8,809
57,250	57,300	10,248	7,699	10,248	8,821
57,300	57,350	10,260	7,706	10,260	8,834
57,350	57,400	10,273	7,714	10,273	8,846
57,400	57,450	10,285	7,721	10,285	8,859
57,450	57,500	10,298	7,729	10,298	8,871
57,500	57,550	10,310	7,736	10,310	8,884
57,550	57,600	10,323	7,744	10,323	8,896
57,600	57,650	10,335	7,751	10,335	8,909
57,650	57,700	10,348	7,759	10,348	8,921
57,700	57,750	10,360	7,766	10,360	8,934
57,750	57,800	10,373	7,774	10,373	8,946
57,800	57,850	10,385	7,781	10,385	8,959
57,850	57,900	10,398	7,789	10,398	8,971
57,900	57,950	10,410	7,796	10,410	8,984
57,950	58,000	10,423	7,804	10,423	8,996

58,000

At least	But less than	Single	Married filing jointly *	Married filing separately	Head of a household
58,000	58,050	10,435	7,811	10,435	9,009
58,050	58,100	10,448	7,819	10,448	9,021
58,100	58,150	10,460	7,826	10,460	9,034
58,150	58,200	10,473	7,834	10,473	9,046
58,200	58,250	10,485	7,841	10,485	9,059
58,250	58,300	10,498	7,849	10,498	9,071
58,300	58,350	10,510	7,856	10,510	9,084
58,350	58,400	10,523	7,864	10,523	9,096
58,400	58,450	10,535	7,871	10,535	9,109
58,450	58,500	10,548	7,879	10,548	9,121
58,500	58,550	10,560	7,886	10,560	9,134
58,550	58,600	10,573	7,894	10,573	9,146
58,600	58,650	10,585	7,901	10,585	9,159
58,650	58,700	10,598	7,909	10,598	9,171
58,700	58,750	10,610	7,916	10,610	9,184
58,750	58,800	10,623	7,924	10,623	9,196
58,800	58,850	10,635	7,931	10,635	9,209
58,850	58,900	10,648	7,939	10,648	9,221
58,900	58,950	10,660	7,946	10,660	9,234
58,950	59,000	10,673	7,954	10,673	9,246

59,000

At least	But less than	Single	Married filing jointly *	Married filing separately	Head of a household
59,000	59,050	10,685	7,961	10,685	9,259
59,050	59,100	10,698	7,969	10,698	9,271
59,100	59,150	10,710	7,976	10,710	9,284
59,150	59,200	10,723	7,984	10,723	9,296
59,200	59,250	10,735	7,991	10,735	9,309
59,250	59,300	10,748	7,999	10,748	9,321
59,300	59,350	10,760	8,006	10,760	9,334
59,350	59,400	10,773	8,014	10,773	9,346
59,400	59,450	10,785	8,021	10,785	9,359
59,450	59,500	10,798	8,029	10,798	9,371
59,500	59,550	10,810	8,036	10,810	9,384
59,550	59,600	10,823	8,044	10,823	9,396
59,600	59,650	10,835	8,051	10,835	9,409
59,650	59,700	10,848	8,059	10,848	9,421
59,700	59,750	10,860	8,066	10,860	9,434
59,750	59,800	10,873	8,074	10,873	9,446
59,800	59,850	10,885	8,081	10,885	9,459
59,850	59,900	10,898	8,089	10,898	9,471
59,900	59,950	10,910	8,096	10,910	9,484
59,950	60,000	10,923	8,104	10,923	9,496

60,000

At least	But less than	Single	Married filing jointly *	Married filing separately	Head of a household
60,000	60,050	10,935	8,111	10,935	9,509
60,050	60,100	10,948	8,119	10,948	9,521
60,100	60,150	10,960	8,126	10,960	9,534
60,150	60,200	10,973	8,134	10,973	9,546
60,200	60,250	10,985	8,141	10,985	9,559
60,250	60,300	10,998	8,149	10,998	9,571
60,300	60,350	11,010	8,156	11,010	9,584
60,350	60,400	11,023	8,164	11,023	9,596
60,400	60,450	11,035	8,171	11,035	9,609
60,450	60,500	11,048	8,179	11,048	9,621
60,500	60,550	11,060	8,186	11,060	9,634
60,550	60,600	11,073	8,194	11,073	9,646
60,600	60,650	11,085	8,201	11,085	9,659
60,650	60,700	11,098	8,209	11,098	9,671
60,700	60,750	11,110	8,216	11,110	9,684
60,750	60,800	11,123	8,224	11,123	9,696
60,800	60,850	11,135	8,231	11,135	9,709
60,850	60,900	11,148	8,239	11,148	9,721
60,900	60,950	11,160	8,246	11,160	9,734
60,950	61,000	11,173	8,254	11,173	9,746

61,000

At least	But less than	Single	Married filing jointly *	Married filing separately	Head of a household
61,000	61,050	11,185	8,261	11,185	9,759
61,050	61,100	11,198	8,269	11,198	9,771
61,100	61,150	11,210	8,276	11,210	9,784
61,150	61,200	11,223	8,284	11,223	9,796
61,200	61,250	11,235	8,291	11,235	9,809
61,250	61,300	11,248	8,299	11,248	9,821
61,300	61,350	11,260	8,306	11,260	9,834
61,350	61,400	11,273	8,314	11,273	9,846
61,400	61,450	11,285	8,321	11,285	9,859
61,450	61,500	11,298	8,329	11,298	9,871
61,500	61,550	11,310	8,336	11,310	9,884
61,550	61,600	11,323	8,344	11,323	9,896
61,600	61,650	11,335	8,351	11,335	9,909
61,650	61,700	11,348	8,359	11,348	9,921
61,700	61,750	11,360	8,366	11,360	9,934
61,750	61,800	11,373	8,374	11,373	9,946
61,800	61,850	11,385	8,381	11,385	9,959
61,850	61,900	11,398	8,389	11,398	9,971
61,900	61,950	11,410	8,396	11,410	9,984
61,950	62,000	11,423	8,404	11,423	9,996

62,000

At least	But less than	Single	Married filing jointly *	Married filing separately	Head of a household
62,000	62,050	11,435	8,411	11,435	10,009
62,050	62,100	11,448	8,419	11,448	10,021
62,100	62,150	11,460	8,426	11,460	10,034
62,150	62,200	11,473	8,434	11,473	10,046
62,200	62,250	11,485	8,441	11,485	10,059
62,250	62,300	11,498	8,449	11,498	10,071
62,300	62,350	11,510	8,456	11,510	10,084
62,350	62,400	11,523	8,464	11,523	10,096
62,400	62,450	11,535	8,471	11,535	10,109
62,450	62,500	11,548	8,479	11,548	10,121
62,500	62,550	11,560	8,486	11,560	10,134
62,550	62,600	11,573	8,494	11,573	10,146
62,600	62,650	11,585	8,501	11,585	10,159
62,650	62,700	11,598	8,509	11,598	10,171
62,700	62,750	11,610	8,516	11,610	10,184
62,750	62,800	11,623	8,524	11,623	10,196
62,800	62,850	11,635	8,531	11,635	10,209
62,850	62,900	11,648	8,539	11,648	10,221
62,900	62,950	11,660	8,546	11,660	10,234
62,950	63,000	11,673	8,554	11,673	10,246

63,000

At least	But less than	Single	Married filing jointly *	Married filing separately	Head of a household
63,000	63,050	11,685	8,561	11,685	10,259
63,050	63,100	11,698	8,569	11,698	10,271
63,100	63,150	11,710	8,576	11,710	10,284
63,150	63,200	11,723	8,584	11,723	10,296
63,200	63,250	11,735	8,591	11,735	10,309
63,250	63,300	11,748	8,599	11,748	10,321
63,300	63,350	11,760	8,606	11,760	10,334
63,350	63,400	11,773	8,614	11,773	10,346
63,400	63,450	11,785	8,621	11,785	10,359
63,450	63,500	11,798	8,629	11,798	10,371
63,500	63,550	11,810	8,636	11,810	10,384
63,550	63,600	11,823	8,644	11,823	10,396
63,600	63,650	11,835	8,651	11,835	10,409
63,650	63,700	11,848	8,659	11,848	10,421
63,700	63,750	11,860	8,666	11,860	10,434
63,750	63,800	11,873	8,674	11,873	10,446
63,800	63,850	11,885	8,681	11,885	10,459
63,850	63,900	11,898	8,689	11,898	10,471
63,900	63,950	11,910	8,696	11,910	10,484
63,950	64,000	11,923	8,704	11,923	10,496

64,000

At least	But less than	Single	Married filing jointly *	Married filing separately	Head of a household
64,000	64,050	11,935	8,711	11,935	10,509
64,050	64,100	11,948	8,719	11,948	10,521
64,100	64,150	11,960	8,726	11,960	10,534
64,150	64,200	11,973	8,734	11,973	10,546
64,200	64,250	11,985	8,741	11,985	10,559
64,250	64,300	11,998	8,749	11,998	10,571
64,300	64,350	12,010	8,756	12,010	10,584
64,350	64,400	12,023	8,764	12,023	10,596
64,400	64,450	12,035	8,771	12,035	10,609
64,450	64,500	12,048	8,779	12,048	10,621
64,500	64,550	12,060	8,786	12,060	10,634
64,550	64,600	12,073	8,794	12,073	10,646
64,600	64,650	12,085	8,801	12,085	10,659
64,650	64,700	12,098	8,809	12,098	10,671
64,700	64,750	12,110	8,816	12,110	10,684
64,750	64,800	12,123	8,824	12,123	10,696
64,800	64,850	12,135	8,831	12,135	10,709
64,850	64,900	12,148	8,839	12,148	10,721
64,900	64,950	12,160	8,846	12,160	10,734
64,950	65,000	12,173	8,854	12,173	10,746

65,000

At least	But less than	Single	Married filing jointly *	Married filing separately	Head of a household
65,000	65,050	12,185	8,861	12,185	10,759
65,050	65,100	12,198	8,869	12,198	10,771
65,100	65,150	12,210	8,876	12,210	10,784
65,150	65,200	12,223	8,884	12,223	10,796
65,200	65,250	12,235	8,891	12,235	10,809
65,250	65,300	12,248	8,899	12,248	10,821
65,300	65,350	12,260	8,906	12,260	10,834
65,350	65,400	12,273	8,914	12,273	10,846
65,400	65,450	12,285	8,921	12,285	10,859
65,450	65,500	12,298	8,929	12,298	10,871
65,500	65,550	12,310	8,936	12,310	10,884
65,550	65,600	12,323	8,944	12,323	10,896
65,600	65,650	12,335	8,951	12,335	10,909
65,650	65,700	12,348	8,959	12,348	10,921
65,700	65,750	12,360	8,966	12,360	10,934
65,750	65,800	12,373	8,974	12,373	10,946
65,800	65,850	12,385	8,981	12,385	10,959
65,850	65,900	12,398	8,989	12,398	10,971
65,900	65,950	12,410	8,996	12,410	10,984
65,950	66,000	12,423	9,004	12,423	10,996

* This column must also be used by a qualifying widow(er).

(Continued)

2013 Tax Table—*Continued*

If line 43 (taxable income) is— At least	But less than	Single	Married filing jointly *	Married filing separately	Head of a household
66,000					
66,000	66,050	12,435	9,011	12,435	11,009
66,050	66,100	12,448	9,019	12,448	11,021
66,100	66,150	12,460	9,026	12,460	11,034
66,150	66,200	12,473	9,034	12,473	11,046
66,200	66,250	12,485	9,041	12,485	11,059
66,250	66,300	12,498	9,049	12,498	11,071
66,300	66,350	12,510	9,056	12,510	11,084
66,350	66,400	12,523	9,064	12,523	11,096
66,400	66,450	12,535	9,071	12,535	11,109
66,450	66,500	12,548	9,079	12,548	11,121
66,500	66,550	12,560	9,086	12,560	11,134
66,550	66,600	12,573	9,094	12,573	11,146
66,600	66,650	12,585	9,101	12,585	11,159
66,650	66,700	12,598	9,109	12,598	11,171
66,700	66,750	12,610	9,116	12,610	11,184
66,750	66,800	12,623	9,124	12,623	11,196
66,800	66,850	12,635	9,131	12,635	11,209
66,850	66,900	12,648	9,139	12,648	11,221
66,900	66,950	12,660	9,146	12,660	11,234
66,950	67,000	12,673	9,154	12,673	11,246
67,000					
67,000	67,050	12,685	9,161	12,685	11,259
67,050	67,100	12,698	9,169	12,698	11,271
67,100	67,150	12,710	9,176	12,710	11,284
67,150	67,200	12,723	9,184	12,723	11,296
67,200	67,250	12,735	9,191	12,735	11,309
67,250	67,300	12,748	9,199	12,748	11,321
67,300	67,350	12,760	9,206	12,760	11,334
67,350	67,400	12,773	9,214	12,773	11,346
67,400	67,450	12,785	9,221	12,785	11,359
67,450	67,500	12,798	9,229	12,798	11,371
67,500	67,550	12,810	9,236	12,810	11,384
67,550	67,600	12,823	9,244	12,823	11,396
67,600	67,650	12,835	9,251	12,835	11,409
67,650	67,700	12,848	9,259	12,848	11,421
67,700	67,750	12,860	9,266	12,860	11,434
67,750	67,800	12,873	9,274	12,873	11,446
67,800	67,850	12,885	9,281	12,885	11,459
67,850	67,900	12,898	9,289	12,898	11,471
67,900	67,950	12,910	9,296	12,910	11,484
67,950	68,000	12,923	9,304	12,923	11,496
68,000					
68,000	68,050	12,935	9,311	12,935	11,509
68,050	68,100	12,948	9,319	12,948	11,521
68,100	68,150	12,960	9,326	12,960	11,534
68,150	68,200	12,973	9,334	12,973	11,546
68,200	68,250	12,985	9,341	12,985	11,559
68,250	68,300	12,998	9,349	12,998	11,571
68,300	68,350	13,010	9,356	13,010	11,584
68,350	68,400	13,023	9,364	13,023	11,596
68,400	68,450	13,035	9,371	13,035	11,609
68,450	68,500	13,048	9,379	13,048	11,621
68,500	68,550	13,060	9,386	13,060	11,634
68,550	68,600	13,073	9,394	13,073	11,646
68,600	68,650	13,085	9,401	13,085	11,659
68,650	68,700	13,098	9,409	13,098	11,671
68,700	68,750	13,110	9,416	13,110	11,684
68,750	68,800	13,123	9,424	13,123	11,696
68,800	68,850	13,135	9,431	13,135	11,709
68,850	68,900	13,148	9,439	13,148	11,721
68,900	68,950	13,160	9,446	13,160	11,734
68,950	69,000	13,173	9,454	13,173	11,746

If line 43 (taxable income) is— At least	But less than	Single	Married filing jointly *	Married filing separately	Head of a household
69,000					
69,000	69,050	13,185	9,461	13,185	11,759
69,050	69,100	13,198	9,469	13,198	11,771
69,100	69,150	13,210	9,476	13,210	11,784
69,150	69,200	13,223	9,484	13,223	11,796
69,200	69,250	13,235	9,491	13,235	11,809
69,250	69,300	13,248	9,499	13,248	11,821
69,300	69,350	13,260	9,506	13,260	11,834
69,350	69,400	13,273	9,514	13,273	11,846
69,400	69,450	13,285	9,521	13,285	11,859
69,450	69,500	13,298	9,529	13,298	11,871
69,500	69,550	13,310	9,536	13,310	11,884
69,550	69,600	13,323	9,544	13,323	11,896
69,600	69,650	13,335	9,551	13,335	11,909
69,650	69,700	13,348	9,559	13,348	11,921
69,700	69,750	13,360	9,566	13,360	11,934
69,750	69,800	13,373	9,574	13,373	11,946
69,800	69,850	13,385	9,581	13,385	11,959
69,850	69,900	13,398	9,589	13,398	11,971
69,900	69,950	13,410	9,596	13,410	11,984
69,950	70,000	13,423	9,604	13,423	11,996
70,000					
70,000	70,050	13,435	9,611	13,435	12,009
70,050	70,100	13,448	9,619	13,448	12,021
70,100	70,150	13,460	9,626	13,460	12,034
70,150	70,200	13,473	9,634	13,473	12,046
70,200	70,250	13,485	9,641	13,485	12,059
70,250	70,300	13,498	9,649	13,498	12,071
70,300	70,350	13,510	9,656	13,510	12,084
70,350	70,400	13,523	9,664	13,523	12,096
70,400	70,450	13,535	9,671	13,535	12,109
70,450	70,500	13,548	9,679	13,548	12,121
70,500	70,550	13,560	9,686	13,560	12,134
70,550	70,600	13,573	9,694	13,573	12,146
70,600	70,650	13,585	9,701	13,585	12,159
70,650	70,700	13,598	9,709	13,598	12,171
70,700	70,750	13,610	9,716	13,610	12,184
70,750	70,800	13,623	9,724	13,623	12,196
70,800	70,850	13,635	9,731	13,635	12,209
70,850	70,900	13,648	9,739	13,648	12,221
70,900	70,950	13,660	9,746	13,660	12,234
70,950	71,000	13,673	9,754	13,673	12,246
71,000					
71,000	71,050	13,685	9,761	13,685	12,259
71,050	71,100	13,698	9,769	13,698	12,271
71,100	71,150	13,710	9,776	13,710	12,284
71,150	71,200	13,723	9,784	13,723	12,296
71,200	71,250	13,735	9,791	13,735	12,309
71,250	71,300	13,748	9,799	13,748	12,321
71,300	71,350	13,760	9,806	13,760	12,334
71,350	71,400	13,773	9,814	13,773	12,346
71,400	71,450	13,785	9,821	13,785	12,359
71,450	71,500	13,798	9,829	13,798	12,371
71,500	71,550	13,810	9,836	13,810	12,384
71,550	71,600	13,823	9,844	13,823	12,396
71,600	71,650	13,835	9,851	13,835	12,409
71,650	71,700	13,848	9,859	13,848	12,421
71,700	71,750	13,860	9,866	13,860	12,434
71,750	71,800	13,873	9,874	13,873	12,446
71,800	71,850	13,885	9,881	13,885	12,459
71,850	71,900	13,898	9,889	13,898	12,471
71,900	71,950	13,910	9,896	13,910	12,484
71,950	72,000	13,923	9,904	13,923	12,496

If line 43 (taxable income) is— At least	But less than	Single	Married filing jointly *	Married filing separately	Head of a household
72,000					
72,000	72,050	13,935	9,911	13,935	12,509
72,050	72,100	13,948	9,919	13,948	12,521
72,100	72,150	13,960	9,926	13,960	12,534
72,150	72,200	13,973	9,934	13,973	12,546
72,200	72,250	13,985	9,941	13,985	12,559
72,250	72,300	13,998	9,949	13,998	12,571
72,300	72,350	14,010	9,956	14,010	12,584
72,350	72,400	14,023	9,964	14,023	12,596
72,400	72,450	14,035	9,971	14,035	12,609
72,450	72,500	14,048	9,979	14,048	12,621
72,500	72,550	14,060	9,989	14,060	12,634
72,550	72,600	14,073	10,001	14,073	12,646
72,600	72,650	14,085	10,014	14,085	12,659
72,650	72,700	14,098	10,026	14,098	12,671
72,700	72,750	14,110	10,039	14,110	12,684
72,750	72,800	14,123	10,051	14,123	12,696
72,800	72,850	14,135	10,064	14,135	12,709
72,850	72,900	14,148	10,076	14,148	12,721
72,900	72,950	14,160	10,089	14,160	12,734
72,950	73,000	14,173	10,101	14,173	12,746
73,000					
73,000	73,050	14,185	10,114	14,185	12,759
73,050	73,100	14,198	10,126	14,198	12,771
73,100	73,150	14,210	10,139	14,210	12,784
73,150	73,200	14,223	10,151	14,223	12,796
73,200	73,250	14,235	10,164	14,236	12,809
73,250	73,300	14,248	10,176	14,250	12,821
73,300	73,350	14,260	10,189	14,264	12,834
73,350	73,400	14,273	10,201	14,278	12,846
73,400	73,450	14,285	10,214	14,292	12,859
73,450	73,500	14,298	10,226	14,306	12,871
73,500	73,550	14,310	10,239	14,320	12,884
73,550	73,600	14,323	10,251	14,334	12,896
73,600	73,650	14,335	10,264	14,348	12,909
73,650	73,700	14,348	10,276	14,362	12,921
73,700	73,750	14,360	10,289	14,376	12,934
73,750	73,800	14,373	10,301	14,390	12,946
73,800	73,850	14,385	10,314	14,404	12,959
73,850	73,900	14,398	10,326	14,418	12,971
73,900	73,950	14,410	10,339	14,432	12,984
73,950	74,000	14,423	10,351	14,446	12,996
74,000					
74,000	74,050	14,435	10,364	14,460	13,009
74,050	74,100	14,448	10,376	14,474	13,021
74,100	74,150	14,460	10,389	14,488	13,034
74,150	74,200	14,473	10,401	14,502	13,046
74,200	74,250	14,485	10,414	14,516	13,059
74,250	74,300	14,498	10,426	14,530	13,071
74,300	74,350	14,510	10,439	14,544	13,084
74,350	74,400	14,523	10,451	14,558	13,096
74,400	74,450	14,535	10,464	14,572	13,109
74,450	74,500	14,548	10,476	14,586	13,121
74,500	74,550	14,560	10,489	14,600	13,134
74,550	74,600	14,573	10,501	14,614	13,146
74,600	74,650	14,585	10,514	14,628	13,159
74,650	74,700	14,598	10,526	14,642	13,171
74,700	74,750	14,610	10,539	14,656	13,184
74,750	74,800	14,623	10,551	14,670	13,196
74,800	74,850	14,635	10,564	14,684	13,209
74,850	74,900	14,648	10,576	14,698	13,221
74,900	74,950	14,660	10,589	14,712	13,234
74,950	75,000	14,673	10,601	14,726	13,246

* This column must also be used by a qualifying widow(er).

(Continued)

2013 Tax Table—*Continued*

If line 43 (taxable income) is—		And you are—			
At least	But less than	Single	Married filing jointly *	Married filing separately	Head of a household
		Your tax is—			

75,000

At least	But less than	Single	MFJ *	MFS	HoH
75,000	75,050	14,685	10,614	14,740	13,259
75,050	75,100	14,698	10,626	14,754	13,271
75,100	75,150	14,710	10,639	14,768	13,284
75,150	75,200	14,723	10,651	14,782	13,296
75,200	75,250	14,735	10,664	14,796	13,309
75,250	75,300	14,748	10,676	14,810	13,321
75,300	75,350	14,760	10,689	14,824	13,334
75,350	75,400	14,773	10,701	14,838	13,346
75,400	75,450	14,785	10,714	14,852	13,359
75,450	75,500	14,798	10,726	14,866	13,371
75,500	75,550	14,810	10,739	14,880	13,384
75,550	75,600	14,823	10,751	14,894	13,396
75,600	75,650	14,835	10,764	14,908	13,409
75,650	75,700	14,848	10,776	14,922	13,421
75,700	75,750	14,860	10,789	14,936	13,434
75,750	75,800	14,873	10,801	14,950	13,446
75,800	75,850	14,885	10,814	14,964	13,459
75,850	75,900	14,898	10,826	14,978	13,471
75,900	75,950	14,910	10,839	14,992	13,484
75,950	76,000	14,923	10,851	15,006	13,496

76,000

At least	But less than	Single	MFJ *	MFS	HoH
76,000	76,050	14,935	10,864	15,020	13,509
76,050	76,100	14,948	10,876	15,034	13,521
76,100	76,150	14,960	10,889	15,048	13,534
76,150	76,200	14,973	10,901	15,062	13,546
76,200	76,250	14,985	10,914	15,076	13,559
76,250	76,300	14,998	10,926	15,090	13,571
76,300	76,350	15,010	10,939	15,104	13,584
76,350	76,400	15,023	10,951	15,118	13,596
76,400	76,450	15,035	10,964	15,132	13,609
76,450	76,500	15,048	10,976	15,146	13,621
76,500	76,550	15,060	10,989	15,160	13,634
76,550	76,600	15,073	11,001	15,174	13,646
76,600	76,650	15,085	11,014	15,188	13,659
76,650	76,700	15,098	11,026	15,202	13,671
76,700	76,750	15,110	11,039	15,216	13,684
76,750	76,800	15,123	11,051	15,230	13,696
76,800	76,850	15,135	11,064	15,244	13,709
76,850	76,900	15,148	11,076	15,258	13,721
76,900	76,950	15,160	11,089	15,272	13,734
76,950	77,000	15,173	11,101	15,286	13,746

77,000

At least	But less than	Single	MFJ *	MFS	HoH
77,000	77,050	15,185	11,114	15,300	13,759
77,050	77,100	15,198	11,126	15,314	13,771
77,100	77,150	15,210	11,139	15,328	13,784
77,150	77,200	15,223	11,151	15,342	13,796
77,200	77,250	15,235	11,164	15,356	13,809
77,250	77,300	15,248	11,176	15,370	13,821
77,300	77,350	15,260	11,189	15,384	13,834
77,350	77,400	15,273	11,201	15,398	13,846
77,400	77,450	15,285	11,214	15,412	13,859
77,450	77,500	15,298	11,226	15,426	13,871
77,500	77,550	15,310	11,239	15,440	13,884
77,550	77,600	15,323	11,251	15,454	13,896
77,600	77,650	15,335	11,264	15,468	13,909
77,650	77,700	15,348	11,276	15,482	13,921
77,700	77,750	15,360	11,289	15,496	13,934
77,750	77,800	15,373	11,301	15,510	13,946
77,800	77,850	15,385	11,314	15,524	13,959
77,850	77,900	15,398	11,326	15,538	13,971
77,900	77,950	15,410	11,339	15,552	13,984
77,950	78,000	15,423	11,351	15,566	13,996

78,000

At least	But less than	Single	MFJ *	MFS	HoH
78,000	78,050	15,435	11,364	15,580	14,009
78,050	78,100	15,448	11,376	15,594	14,021
78,100	78,150	15,460	11,389	15,608	14,034
78,150	78,200	15,473	11,401	15,622	14,046
78,200	78,250	15,485	11,414	15,636	14,059
78,250	78,300	15,498	11,426	15,650	14,071
78,300	78,350	15,510	11,439	15,664	14,084
78,350	78,400	15,523	11,451	15,678	14,096
78,400	78,450	15,535	11,464	15,692	14,109
78,450	78,500	15,548	11,476	15,706	14,121
78,500	78,550	15,560	11,489	15,720	14,134
78,550	78,600	15,573	11,501	15,734	14,146
78,600	78,650	15,585	11,514	15,748	14,159
78,650	78,700	15,598	11,526	15,762	14,171
78,700	78,750	15,610	11,539	15,776	14,184
78,750	78,800	15,623	11,551	15,790	14,196
78,800	78,850	15,635	11,564	15,804	14,209
78,850	78,900	15,648	11,576	15,818	14,221
78,900	78,950	15,660	11,589	15,832	14,234
78,950	79,000	15,673	11,601	15,846	14,246

79,000

At least	But less than	Single	MFJ *	MFS	HoH
79,000	79,050	15,685	11,614	15,860	14,259
79,050	79,100	15,698	11,626	15,874	14,271
79,100	79,150	15,710	11,639	15,888	14,284
79,150	79,200	15,723	11,651	15,902	14,296
79,200	79,250	15,735	11,664	15,916	14,309
79,250	79,300	15,748	11,676	15,930	14,321
79,300	79,350	15,760	11,689	15,944	14,334
79,350	79,400	15,773	11,701	15,958	14,346
79,400	79,450	15,785	11,714	15,972	14,359
79,450	79,500	15,798	11,726	15,986	14,371
79,500	79,550	15,810	11,739	16,000	14,384
79,550	79,600	15,823	11,751	16,014	14,396
79,600	79,650	15,835	11,764	16,028	14,409
79,650	79,700	15,848	11,776	16,042	14,421
79,700	79,750	15,860	11,789	16,056	14,434
79,750	79,800	15,873	11,801	16,070	14,446
79,800	79,850	15,885	11,814	16,084	14,459
79,850	79,900	15,898	11,826	16,098	14,471
79,900	79,950	15,910	11,839	16,112	14,484
79,950	80,000	15,923	11,851	16,126	14,496

80,000

At least	But less than	Single	MFJ *	MFS	HoH
80,000	80,050	15,935	11,864	16,140	14,509
80,050	80,100	15,948	11,876	16,154	14,521
80,100	80,150	15,960	11,889	16,168	14,534
80,150	80,200	15,973	11,901	16,182	14,546
80,200	80,250	15,985	11,914	16,196	14,559
80,250	80,300	15,998	11,926	16,210	14,571
80,300	80,350	16,010	11,939	16,224	14,584
80,350	80,400	16,023	11,951	16,238	14,596
80,400	80,450	16,035	11,964	16,252	14,609
80,450	80,500	16,048	11,976	16,266	14,621
80,500	80,550	16,060	11,989	16,280	14,634
80,550	80,600	16,073	12,001	16,294	14,646
80,600	80,650	16,085	12,014	16,308	14,659
80,650	80,700	16,098	12,026	16,322	14,671
80,700	80,750	16,110	12,039	16,336	14,684
80,750	80,800	16,123	12,051	16,350	14,696
80,800	80,850	16,135	12,064	16,364	14,709
80,850	80,900	16,148	12,076	16,378	14,721
80,900	80,950	16,160	12,089	16,392	14,734
80,950	81,000	16,173	12,101	16,406	14,746

81,000

At least	But less than	Single	MFJ *	MFS	HoH
81,000	81,050	16,185	12,114	16,420	14,759
81,050	81,100	16,198	12,126	16,434	14,771
81,100	81,150	16,210	12,139	16,448	14,784
81,150	81,200	16,223	12,151	16,462	14,796
81,200	81,250	16,235	12,164	16,476	14,809
81,250	81,300	16,248	12,176	16,490	14,821
81,300	81,350	16,260	12,189	16,504	14,834
81,350	81,400	16,273	12,201	16,518	14,846
81,400	81,450	16,285	12,214	16,532	14,859
81,450	81,500	16,298	12,226	16,546	14,871
81,500	81,550	16,310	12,239	16,560	14,884
81,550	81,600	16,323	12,251	16,574	14,896
81,600	81,650	16,335	12,264	16,588	14,909
81,650	81,700	16,348	12,276	16,602	14,921
81,700	81,750	16,360	12,289	16,616	14,934
81,750	81,800	16,373	12,301	16,630	14,946
81,800	81,850	16,385	12,314	16,644	14,959
81,850	81,900	16,398	12,326	16,658	14,971
81,900	81,950	16,410	12,339	16,672	14,984
81,950	82,000	16,423	12,351	16,686	14,996

82,000

At least	But less than	Single	MFJ *	MFS	HoH
82,000	82,050	16,435	12,364	16,700	15,009
82,050	82,100	16,448	12,376	16,714	15,021
82,100	82,150	16,460	12,389	16,728	15,034
82,150	82,200	16,473	12,401	16,742	15,046
82,200	82,250	16,485	12,414	16,756	15,059
82,250	82,300	16,498	12,426	16,770	15,071
82,300	82,350	16,510	12,439	16,784	15,084
82,350	82,400	16,523	12,451	16,798	15,096
82,400	82,450	16,535	12,464	16,812	15,109
82,450	82,500	16,548	12,476	16,826	15,121
82,500	82,550	16,560	12,489	16,840	15,134
82,550	82,600	16,573	12,501	16,854	15,146
82,600	82,650	16,585	12,514	16,868	15,159
82,650	82,700	16,598	12,526	16,882	15,171
82,700	82,750	16,610	12,539	16,896	15,184
82,750	82,800	16,623	12,551	16,910	15,196
82,800	82,850	16,635	12,564	16,924	15,209
82,850	82,900	16,648	12,576	16,938	15,221
82,900	82,950	16,660	12,589	16,952	15,234
82,950	83,000	16,673	12,601	16,966	15,246

83,000

At least	But less than	Single	MFJ *	MFS	HoH
83,000	83,050	16,685	12,614	16,980	15,259
83,050	83,100	16,698	12,626	16,994	15,271
83,100	83,150	16,710	12,639	17,008	15,284
83,150	83,200	16,723	12,651	17,022	15,296
83,200	83,250	16,735	12,664	17,036	15,309
83,250	83,300	16,748	12,676	17,050	15,321
83,300	83,350	16,760	12,689	17,064	15,334
83,350	83,400	16,773	12,701	17,078	15,346
83,400	83,450	16,785	12,714	17,092	15,359
83,450	83,500	16,798	12,726	17,106	15,371
83,500	83,550	16,810	12,739	17,120	15,384
83,550	83,600	16,823	12,751	17,134	15,396
83,600	83,650	16,835	12,764	17,148	15,409
83,650	83,700	16,848	12,776	17,162	15,421
83,700	83,750	16,860	12,789	17,176	15,434
83,750	83,800	16,873	12,801	17,190	15,446
83,800	83,850	16,885	12,814	17,204	15,459
83,850	83,900	16,898	12,826	17,218	15,471
83,900	83,950	16,910	12,839	17,232	15,484
83,950	84,000	16,923	12,851	17,246	15,496

* This column must also be used by a qualifying widow(er).

(Continued)

2013 Tax Table—Continued

If line 43 (taxable income) is—		And you are—			
At least	But less than	Single	Married filing jointly *	Married filing separately	Head of a household
		Your tax is—			

84,000

At least	But less than	Single	MFJ *	MFS	HoH
84,000	84,050	16,935	12,864	17,260	15,509
84,050	84,100	16,948	12,876	17,274	15,521
84,100	84,150	16,960	12,889	17,288	15,534
84,150	84,200	16,973	12,901	17,302	15,546
84,200	84,250	16,985	12,914	17,316	15,559
84,250	84,300	16,998	12,926	17,330	15,571
84,300	84,350	17,010	12,939	17,344	15,584
84,350	84,400	17,023	12,951	17,358	15,596
84,400	84,450	17,035	12,964	17,372	15,609
84,450	84,500	17,048	12,976	17,386	15,621
84,500	84,550	17,060	12,989	17,400	15,634
84,550	84,600	17,073	13,001	17,414	15,646
84,600	84,650	17,085	13,014	17,428	15,659
84,650	84,700	17,098	13,026	17,442	15,671
84,700	84,750	17,110	13,039	17,456	15,684
84,750	84,800	17,123	13,051	17,470	15,696
84,800	84,850	17,135	13,064	17,484	15,709
84,850	84,900	17,148	13,076	17,498	15,721
84,900	84,950	17,160	13,089	17,512	15,734
84,950	85,000	17,173	13,101	17,526	15,746

85,000

At least	But less than	Single	MFJ *	MFS	HoH
85,000	85,050	17,185	13,114	17,540	15,759
85,050	85,100	17,198	13,126	17,554	15,771
85,100	85,150	17,210	13,139	17,568	15,784
85,150	85,200	17,223	13,151	17,582	15,796
85,200	85,250	17,235	13,164	17,596	15,809
85,250	85,300	17,248	13,176	17,610	15,821
85,300	85,350	17,260	13,189	17,624	15,834
85,350	85,400	17,273	13,201	17,638	15,846
85,400	85,450	17,285	13,214	17,652	15,859
85,450	85,500	17,298	13,226	17,666	15,871
85,500	85,550	17,310	13,239	17,680	15,884
85,550	85,600	17,323	13,251	17,694	15,896
85,600	85,650	17,335	13,264	17,708	15,909
85,650	85,700	17,348	13,276	17,722	15,921
85,700	85,750	17,360	13,289	17,736	15,934
85,750	85,800	17,373	13,301	17,750	15,946
85,800	85,850	17,385	13,314	17,764	15,959
85,850	85,900	17,398	13,326	17,778	15,971
85,900	85,950	17,410	13,339	17,792	15,984
85,950	86,000	17,423	13,351	17,806	15,996

86,000

At least	But less than	Single	MFJ *	MFS	HoH
86,000	86,050	17,435	13,364	17,820	16,009
86,050	86,100	17,448	13,376	17,834	16,021
86,100	86,150	17,460	13,389	17,848	16,034
86,150	86,200	17,473	13,401	17,862	16,046
86,200	86,250	17,485	13,414	17,876	16,059
86,250	86,300	17,498	13,426	17,890	16,071
86,300	86,350	17,510	13,439	17,904	16,084
86,350	86,400	17,523	13,451	17,918	16,096
86,400	86,450	17,535	13,464	17,932	16,109
86,450	86,500	17,548	13,476	17,946	16,121
86,500	86,550	17,560	13,489	17,960	16,134
86,550	86,600	17,573	13,501	17,974	16,146
86,600	86,650	17,585	13,514	17,988	16,159
86,650	86,700	17,598	13,526	18,002	16,171
86,700	86,750	17,610	13,539	18,016	16,184
86,750	86,800	17,623	13,551	18,030	16,196
86,800	86,850	17,635	13,564	18,044	16,209
86,850	86,900	17,648	13,576	18,058	16,221
86,900	86,950	17,660	13,589	18,072	16,234
86,950	87,000	17,673	13,601	18,086	16,246

87,000

At least	But less than	Single	MFJ *	MFS	HoH
87,000	87,050	17,685	13,614	18,100	16,259
87,050	87,100	17,698	13,626	18,114	16,271
87,100	87,150	17,710	13,639	18,128	16,284
87,150	87,200	17,723	13,651	18,142	16,296
87,200	87,250	17,735	13,664	18,156	16,309
87,250	87,300	17,748	13,676	18,170	16,321
87,300	87,350	17,760	13,689	18,184	16,334
87,350	87,400	17,773	13,701	18,198	16,346
87,400	87,450	17,785	13,714	18,212	16,359
87,450	87,500	17,798	13,726	18,226	16,371
87,500	87,550	17,810	13,739	18,240	16,384
87,550	87,600	17,823	13,751	18,254	16,396
87,600	87,650	17,835	13,764	18,268	16,409
87,650	87,700	17,848	13,776	18,282	16,421
87,700	87,750	17,860	13,789	18,296	16,434
87,750	87,800	17,873	13,801	18,310	16,446
87,800	87,850	17,885	13,814	18,324	16,459
87,850	87,900	17,898	13,826	18,338	16,471
87,900	87,950	17,912	13,839	18,352	16,484
87,950	88,000	17,926	13,851	18,366	16,496

88,000

At least	But less than	Single	MFJ *	MFS	HoH
88,000	88,050	17,940	13,864	18,380	16,509
88,050	88,100	17,954	13,876	18,394	16,521
88,100	88,150	17,968	13,889	18,408	16,534
88,150	88,200	17,982	13,901	18,422	16,546
88,200	88,250	17,996	13,914	18,436	16,559
88,250	88,300	18,010	13,926	18,450	16,571
88,300	88,350	18,024	13,939	18,464	16,584
88,350	88,400	18,038	13,951	18,478	16,596
88,400	88,450	18,052	13,964	18,492	16,609
88,450	88,500	18,066	13,976	18,506	16,621
88,500	88,550	18,080	13,989	18,520	16,634
88,550	88,600	18,094	14,001	18,534	16,646
88,600	88,650	18,108	14,014	18,548	16,659
88,650	88,700	18,122	14,026	18,562	16,671
88,700	88,750	18,136	14,039	18,576	16,684
88,750	88,800	18,150	14,051	18,590	16,696
88,800	88,850	18,164	14,064	18,604	16,709
88,850	88,900	18,178	14,076	18,618	16,721
88,900	88,950	18,192	14,089	18,632	16,734
88,950	89,000	18,206	14,101	18,646	16,746

89,000

At least	But less than	Single	MFJ *	MFS	HoH
89,000	89,050	18,220	14,114	18,660	16,759
89,050	89,100	18,234	14,126	18,674	16,771
89,100	89,150	18,248	14,139	18,688	16,784
89,150	89,200	18,262	14,151	18,702	16,796
89,200	89,250	18,276	14,164	18,716	16,809
89,250	89,300	18,290	14,176	18,730	16,821
89,300	89,350	18,304	14,189	18,744	16,834
89,350	89,400	18,318	14,201	18,758	16,846
89,400	89,450	18,332	14,214	18,772	16,859
89,450	89,500	18,346	14,226	18,786	16,871
89,500	89,550	18,360	14,239	18,800	16,884
89,550	89,600	18,374	14,251	18,814	16,896
89,600	89,650	18,388	14,264	18,828	16,909
89,650	89,700	18,402	14,276	18,842	16,921
89,700	89,750	18,416	14,289	18,856	16,934
89,750	89,800	18,430	14,301	18,870	16,946
89,800	89,850	18,444	14,314	18,884	16,959
89,850	89,900	18,458	14,326	18,898	16,971
89,900	89,950	18,472	14,339	18,912	16,984
89,950	90,000	18,486	14,351	18,926	16,996

90,000

At least	But less than	Single	MFJ *	MFS	HoH
90,000	90,050	18,500	14,364	18,940	17,009
90,050	90,100	18,514	14,376	18,954	17,021
90,100	90,150	18,528	14,389	18,968	17,034
90,150	90,200	18,542	14,401	18,982	17,046
90,200	90,250	18,556	14,414	18,996	17,059
90,250	90,300	18,570	14,426	19,010	17,071
90,300	90,350	18,584	14,439	19,024	17,084
90,350	90,400	18,598	14,451	19,038	17,096
90,400	90,450	18,612	14,464	19,052	17,109
90,450	90,500	18,626	14,476	19,066	17,121
90,500	90,550	18,640	14,489	19,080	17,134
90,550	90,600	18,654	14,501	19,094	17,146
90,600	90,650	18,668	14,514	19,108	17,159
90,650	90,700	18,682	14,526	19,122	17,171
90,700	90,750	18,696	14,539	19,136	17,184
90,750	90,800	18,710	14,551	19,150	17,196
90,800	90,850	18,724	14,564	19,164	17,209
90,850	90,900	18,738	14,576	19,178	17,221
90,900	90,950	18,752	14,589	19,192	17,234
90,950	91,000	18,766	14,601	19,206	17,246

91,000

At least	But less than	Single	MFJ *	MFS	HoH
91,000	91,050	18,780	14,614	19,220	17,259
91,050	91,100	18,794	14,626	19,234	17,271
91,100	91,150	18,808	14,639	19,248	17,284
91,150	91,200	18,822	14,651	19,262	17,296
91,200	91,250	18,836	14,664	19,276	17,309
91,250	91,300	18,850	14,676	19,290	17,321
91,300	91,350	18,864	14,689	19,304	17,334
91,350	91,400	18,878	14,701	19,318	17,346
91,400	91,450	18,892	14,714	19,332	17,359
91,450	91,500	18,906	14,726	19,346	17,371
91,500	91,550	18,920	14,739	19,360	17,384
91,550	91,600	18,934	14,751	19,374	17,396
91,600	91,650	18,948	14,764	19,388	17,409
91,650	91,700	18,962	14,776	19,402	17,421
91,700	91,750	18,976	14,789	19,416	17,434
91,750	91,800	18,990	14,801	19,430	17,446
91,800	91,850	19,004	14,814	19,444	17,459
91,850	91,900	19,018	14,826	19,458	17,471
91,900	91,950	19,032	14,839	19,472	17,484
91,950	92,000	19,046	14,851	19,486	17,496

92,000

At least	But less than	Single	MFJ *	MFS	HoH
92,000	92,050	19,060	14,864	19,500	17,509
92,050	92,100	19,074	14,876	19,514	17,521
92,100	92,150	19,088	14,889	19,528	17,534
92,150	92,200	19,102	14,901	19,542	17,546
92,200	92,250	19,116	14,914	19,556	17,559
92,250	92,300	19,130	14,926	19,570	17,571
92,300	92,350	19,144	14,939	19,584	17,584
92,350	92,400	19,158	14,951	19,598	17,596
92,400	92,450	19,172	14,964	19,612	17,609
92,450	92,500	19,186	14,976	19,626	17,621
92,500	92,550	19,200	14,989	19,640	17,634
92,550	92,600	19,214	15,001	19,654	17,646
92,600	92,650	19,228	15,014	19,668	17,659
92,650	92,700	19,242	15,026	19,682	17,671
92,700	92,750	19,256	15,039	19,696	17,684
92,750	92,800	19,270	15,051	19,710	17,696
92,800	92,850	19,284	15,064	19,724	17,709
92,850	92,900	19,298	15,076	19,738	17,721
92,900	92,950	19,312	15,089	19,752	17,734
92,950	93,000	19,326	15,101	19,766	17,746

* This column must also be used by a qualifying widow(er).

(Continued)

2013 Tax Table—*Continued*

If line 43 (taxable income) is—		And you are—			
At least	But less than	Single	Married filing jointly *	Married filing separately	Head of a house-hold
		Your tax is—			

93,000

At least	But less than	Single	MFJ	MFS	HoH
93,000	93,050	19,340	15,114	19,780	17,759
93,050	93,100	19,354	15,126	19,794	17,771
93,100	93,150	19,368	15,139	19,808	17,784
93,150	93,200	19,382	15,151	19,822	17,796
93,200	93,250	19,396	15,164	19,836	17,809
93,250	93,300	19,410	15,176	19,850	17,821
93,300	93,350	19,424	15,189	19,864	17,834
93,350	93,400	19,438	15,201	19,878	17,846
93,400	93,450	19,452	15,214	19,892	17,859
93,450	93,500	19,466	15,226	19,906	17,871
93,500	93,550	19,480	15,239	19,920	17,884
93,550	93,600	19,494	15,251	19,934	17,896
93,600	93,650	19,508	15,264	19,948	17,909
93,650	93,700	19,522	15,276	19,962	17,921
93,700	93,750	19,536	15,289	19,976	17,934
93,750	93,800	19,550	15,301	19,990	17,946
93,800	93,850	19,564	15,314	20,004	17,959
93,850	93,900	19,578	15,326	20,018	17,971
93,900	93,950	19,592	15,339	20,032	17,984
93,950	94,000	19,606	15,351	20,046	17,996

94,000

At least	But less than	Single	MFJ	MFS	HoH
94,000	94,050	19,620	15,364	20,060	18,009
94,050	94,100	19,634	15,376	20,074	18,021
94,100	94,150	19,648	15,389	20,088	18,034
94,150	94,200	19,662	15,401	20,102	18,046
94,200	94,250	19,676	15,414	20,116	18,059
94,250	94,300	19,690	15,426	20,130	18,071
94,300	94,350	19,704	15,439	20,144	18,084
94,350	94,400	19,718	15,451	20,158	18,096
94,400	94,450	19,732	15,464	20,172	18,109
94,450	94,500	19,746	15,476	20,186	18,121
94,500	94,550	19,760	15,489	20,200	18,134
94,550	94,600	19,774	15,501	20,214	18,146
94,600	94,650	19,788	15,514	20,228	18,159
94,650	94,700	19,802	15,526	20,242	18,171
94,700	94,750	19,816	15,539	20,256	18,184
94,750	94,800	19,830	15,551	20,270	18,196
94,800	94,850	19,844	15,564	20,284	18,209
94,850	94,900	19,858	15,576	20,298	18,221
94,900	94,950	19,872	15,589	20,312	18,234
94,950	95,000	19,886	15,601	20,326	18,246

95,000

At least	But less than	Single	MFJ	MFS	HoH
95,000	95,050	19,900	15,614	20,340	18,259
95,050	95,100	19,914	15,626	20,354	18,271
95,100	95,150	19,928	15,639	20,368	18,284
95,150	95,200	19,942	15,651	20,382	18,296
95,200	95,250	19,956	15,664	20,396	18,309
95,250	95,300	19,970	15,676	20,410	18,321
95,300	95,350	19,984	15,689	20,424	18,334
95,350	95,400	19,998	15,701	20,438	18,346
95,400	95,450	20,012	15,714	20,452	18,359
95,450	95,500	20,026	15,726	20,466	18,371
95,500	95,550	20,040	15,739	20,480	18,384
95,550	95,600	20,054	15,751	20,494	18,396
95,600	95,650	20,068	15,764	20,508	18,409
95,650	95,700	20,082	15,776	20,522	18,421
95,700	95,750	20,096	15,789	20,536	18,434
95,750	95,800	20,110	15,801	20,550	18,446
95,800	95,850	20,124	15,814	20,564	18,459
95,850	95,900	20,138	15,826	20,578	18,471
95,900	95,950	20,152	15,839	20,592	18,484
95,950	96,000	20,166	15,851	20,606	18,496

96,000

At least	But less than	Single	MFJ	MFS	HoH
96,000	96,050	20,180	15,864	20,620	18,509
96,050	96,100	20,194	15,876	20,634	18,521
96,100	96,150	20,208	15,889	20,648	18,534
96,150	96,200	20,222	15,901	20,662	18,546
96,200	96,250	20,236	15,914	20,676	18,559
96,250	96,300	20,250	15,926	20,690	18,571
96,300	96,350	20,264	15,939	20,704	18,584
96,350	96,400	20,278	15,951	20,718	18,596
96,400	96,450	20,292	15,964	20,732	18,609
96,450	96,500	20,306	15,976	20,746	18,621
96,500	96,550	20,320	15,989	20,760	18,634
96,550	96,600	20,334	16,001	20,774	18,646
96,600	96,650	20,348	16,014	20,788	18,659
96,650	96,700	20,362	16,026	20,802	18,671
96,700	96,750	20,376	16,039	20,816	18,684
96,750	96,800	20,390	16,051	20,830	18,696
96,800	96,850	20,404	16,064	20,844	18,709
96,850	96,900	20,418	16,076	20,858	18,721
96,900	96,950	20,432	16,089	20,872	18,734
96,950	97,000	20,446	16,101	20,886	18,746

97,000

At least	But less than	Single	MFJ	MFS	HoH
97,000	97,050	20,460	16,114	20,900	18,759
97,050	97,100	20,474	16,126	20,914	18,771
97,100	97,150	20,488	16,139	20,928	18,784
97,150	97,200	20,502	16,151	20,942	18,796
97,200	97,250	20,516	16,164	20,956	18,809
97,250	97,300	20,530	16,176	20,970	18,821
97,300	97,350	20,544	16,189	20,984	18,834
97,350	97,400	20,558	16,201	20,998	18,846
97,400	97,450	20,572	16,214	21,012	18,859
97,450	97,500	20,586	16,226	21,026	18,871
97,500	97,550	20,600	16,239	21,040	18,884
97,550	97,600	20,614	16,251	21,054	18,896
97,600	97,650	20,628	16,264	21,068	18,909
97,650	97,700	20,642	16,276	21,082	18,921
97,700	97,750	20,656	16,289	21,096	18,934
97,750	97,800	20,670	16,301	21,110	18,946
97,800	97,850	20,684	16,314	21,124	10,959
97,850	97,900	20,698	16,326	21,138	18,971
97,900	97,950	20,712	16,339	21,152	18,984
97,950	98,000	20,726	16,351	21,166	18,996

98,000

At least	But less than	Single	MFJ	MFS	HoH
98,000	98,050	20,740	16,364	21,180	19,009
98,050	98,100	20,754	16,376	21,194	19,021
98,100	98,150	20,768	16,389	21,208	19,034
98,150	98,200	20,782	16,401	21,222	19,046
98,200	98,250	20,796	16,414	21,236	19,059
98,250	98,300	20,810	16,426	21,250	19,071
98,300	98,350	20,824	16,439	21,264	19,084
98,350	98,400	20,838	16,451	21,278	19,096
98,400	98,450	20,852	16,464	21,292	19,109
98,450	98,500	20,866	16,476	21,306	19,121
98,500	98,550	20,880	16,489	21,320	19,134
98,550	98,600	20,894	16,501	21,334	19,146
98,600	98,650	20,908	16,514	21,348	19,159
98,650	98,700	20,922	16,526	21,362	19,171
98,700	98,750	20,936	16,539	21,376	19,184
98,750	98,800	20,950	16,551	21,390	19,196
98,800	98,850	20,964	16,564	21,404	19,209
98,850	98,900	20,978	16,576	21,418	19,221
98,900	98,950	20,992	16,589	21,432	19,234
98,950	99,000	21,006	16,601	21,446	19,246

99,000

At least	But less than	Single	MFJ	MFS	HoH
99,000	99,050	21,020	16,614	21,460	19,259
99,050	99,100	21,034	16,626	21,474	19,271
99,100	99,150	21,048	16,639	21,488	19,284
99,150	99,200	21,062	16,651	21,502	19,296
99,200	99,250	21,076	16,664	21,516	19,309
99,250	99,300	21,090	16,676	21,530	19,321
99,300	99,350	21,104	16,689	21,544	19,334
99,350	99,400	21,118	16,701	21,558	19,346
99,400	99,450	21,132	16,714	21,572	19,359
99,450	99,500	21,146	16,726	21,586	19,371
99,500	99,550	21,160	16,739	21,600	19,384
99,550	99,600	21,174	16,751	21,614	19,396
99,600	99,650	21,188	16,764	21,628	19,409
99,650	99,700	21,202	16,776	21,642	19,421
99,700	99,750	21,216	16,789	21,656	19,434
99,750	99,800	21,230	16,801	21,670	19,446
99,800	99,850	21,244	16,814	21,684	19,459
99,850	99,900	21,258	16,826	21,698	19,471
99,900	99,950	21,272	16,839	21,712	19,484
99,950	100,000	21,286	16,851	21,726	19,496

$100,000 or over use the Tax Rate Schedules on p. A-2

* This column must also be used by a qualifying widow(er).

Income Tax Rates—Estates and Trusts

Tax Year 2013

| Taxable Income | | The Tax Is: | Of the Amount |
Over—	But not Over—		Over—
$ 0	$ 2,450	15%	$ 0
2,450	5,700	$ 367.50 + 25%	2,450
5,700	8,750	1,180.00 + 28%	5,700
8,750	11,950	2,034.00 + 33%	8,750
11,950	....	3,090.00 + 39.6%	11,950

Tax Year 2014

| Taxable Income | | The Tax Is: | Of the Amount |
Over—	But not Over—		Over—
$ 0	$ 2,500	15%	$ 0
2,500	5,800	$ 375.00 + 25%	2,500
5,800	8,900	1,200.00 + 28%	5,800
8,900	12,150	2,068.00 + 33%	8,900
12,150	....	3,140.50 + 39.6%	12,150

Income Tax Rates—Corporations

| Taxable Income | | The Tax Is: | Of the Amount |
Over—	But not Over—		Over—
$ 0	$ 50,000	15%	$ 0
50,000	75,000	$ 7,500 + 25%	50,000
75,000	100,000	13,750 + 34%	75,000
100,000	335,000	22,250 + 39%	100,000
335,000	10,000,000	113,900 + 34%	335,000
10,000,000	15,000,000	3,400,000 + 35%	10,000,000
15,000,000	18,333,333	5,150,000 + 38%	15,000,000
18,333,333	....	35%	0

Unified Transfer Tax Rates

For Gifts Made and for Deaths in 2007–2009

If the Amount with Respect to Which the Tentative Tax to Be Computed Is:	The Tentative Tax Is:
Not over $10,000	18 percent of such amount.
Over $10,000 but not over $20,000	$1,800, plus 20 percent of the excess of such amount over $10,000.
Over $20,000 but not over $40,000	$3,800, plus 22 percent of the excess of such amount over $20,000.
Over $40,000 but not over $60,000	$8,200, plus 24 percent of the excess of such amount over $40,000.
Over $60,000 but not over $80,000	$13,000, plus 26 percent of the excess of such amount over $60,000.
Over $80,000 but not over $100,000	$18,200, plus 28 percent of the excess of such amount over $80,000.
Over $100,000 but not over $150,000	$23,800, plus 30 percent of the excess of such amount over $100,000.
Over $150,000 but not over $250,000	$38,800, plus 32 percent of the excess of such amount over $150,000.
Over $250,000 but not over $500,000	$70,800, plus 34 percent of the excess of such amount over $250,000.
Over $500,000 but not over $750,000	$155,800, plus 37 percent of the excess of such amount over $500,000.
Over $750,000 but not over $1,000,000	$248,300, plus 39 percent of the excess of such amount over $750,000.
Over $1,000,000 but not over $1,250,000	$345,800, plus 41 percent of the excess of such amount over $1,000,000.
Over $1,250,000 but not over $1,500,000	$448,300, plus 43 percent of the excess of such amount over $1,250,000.
Over $1,500,000	$555,800, plus 45 percent of the excess of such amount over $1,500,000.

Gift Tax Rates

For Gifts Made Only in 2010

If the Amount with Respect to Which the Tentative Tax to Be Computed Is:	The Tentative Tax Is:
Not over $10,000	18 percent of such amount.
Over $10,000 but not over $20,000	$1,800, plus 20 percent of the excess of such amount over $10,000.
Over $20,000 but not over $40,000	$3,800, plus 22 percent of the excess of such amount over $20,000.
Over $40,000 but not over $60,000	$8,200, plus 24 percent of the excess of such amount over $40,000.
Over $60,000 but not over $80,000	$13,000, plus 26 percent of the excess of such amount over $60,000.
Over $80,000 but not over $100,000	$18,200, plus 28 percent of the excess of such amount over $80,000.
Over $100,000 but not over $150,000	$23,800, plus 30 percent of the excess of such amount over $100,000.
Over $150,000 but not over $250,000	$38,800, plus 32 percent of the excess of such amount over $150,000.
Over $250,000 but not over $500,000	$70,800, plus 34 percent of the excess of such amount over $250,000.
Over $500,000	$155,800, plus 35 percent of the excess of such amount over $500,000.

Unified Transfer Tax Rates

For Gifts Made and for Deaths in 2011–2012

If the Amount with Respect to Which the Tentative Tax to Be Computed Is:	The Tentative Tax Is:
Not over $10,000	18 percent of such amount.
Over $10,000 but not over $20,000	$1,800, plus 20 percent of the excess of such amount over $10,000.
Over $20,000 but not over $40,000	$3,800, plus 22 percent of the excess of such amount over $20,000.
Over $40,000 but not over $60,000	$8,200, plus 24 percent of the excess of such amount over $40,000.
Over $60,000 but not over $80,000	$13,000, plus 26 percent of the excess of such amount over $60,000.
Over $80,000 but not over $100,000	$18,200, plus 28 percent of the excess of such amount over $80,000.
Over $100,000 but not over $150,000	$23,800, plus 30 percent of the excess of such amount over $100,000.
Over $150,000 but not over $250,000	$38,800, plus 32 percent of the excess of such amount over $150,000.
Over $250,000 but not over $500,000	$70,800, plus 34 percent of the excess of such amount over $250,000.
Over $500,000	$155,800, plus 35 percent of the excess of such amount over $500,000.

Unified Transfer Tax Rates

For Gifts Made and for Deaths after 2012

If the Amount with Respect to Which the Tentative Tax to Be Computed Is:	The Tentative Tax Is:
Not over $10,000	18 percent of such amount.
Over $10,000 but not over $20,000	$1,800, plus 20 percent of the excess of such amount over $10,000.
Over $20,000 but not over $40,000	$3,800, plus 22 percent of the excess of such amount over $20,000.
Over $40,000 but not over $60,000	$8,200, plus 24 percent of the excess of such amount over $40,000.
Over $60,000 but not over $80,000	$13,000, plus 26 percent of the excess of such amount over $60,000.
Over $80,000 but not over $100,000	$18,200, plus 28 percent of the excess of such amount over $80,000.
Over $100,000 but not over $150,000	$23,800, plus 30 percent of the excess of such amount over $100,000.
Over $150,000 but not over $250,000	$38,800, plus 32 percent of the excess of such amount over $150,000.
Over $250,000 but not over $500,000	$70,800, plus 34 percent of the excess of such amount over $250,000.
Over $500,000 but not over $750,000	$155,800, plus 37 percent of the excess of such amount over $500,000.
Over $750,000 but not over $1,000,000	$248,300, plus 39 percent of the excess of such amount over $750,000.
Over $1,000,000	$345,800, plus 40 percent of the excess of such amount over $1,000,000.

2013 OPTIONAL SALES TAX TABLES

When Used

The election to deduct state and local general sales taxes requires that the taxpayer forgo any deduction for state and local income taxes. Whether this is advisable or not depends on a comparison of the amounts involved. In making the choice, however, the outcome could be influenced by the additional sales tax incurred due to certain "big ticket" purchases that were made. For example, a taxpayer who chose to deduct state and local income taxes for 2012 might well prefer the sales tax deduction in 2013 if a new boat was purchased or home improvements were made during the year. To make the sales tax election, the taxpayer must enter the amount on Schedule A, line 5, and check box b. Unless extended by Congress, the sales tax deduction will expire as to tax years after 2013.

If the sales tax election is made, the amount of the deduction can be determined by use of the *actual expense method* or the *optional sales tax tables* issued by the IRS. The actual expense method can be used only when the taxpayer has actual receipts to support the deduction claimed. In the absence of receipts, the usual case with most taxpayers, resorting to the optional sales tax tables is necessary. Under neither method, however, is the purchase of items used in a taxpayer's trade or business to be considered.

Adjustments Necessary

The optional sales tax tables are based on a number of assumptions that require adjustments to be made. As the starting point for the use of the tables is AGI, nontaxable receipts have not been included. Examples of receipts that should be added include: tax-exempt interest, veterans' benefits, nontaxable combat pay, public assistance payments, workers' compensation, nontaxable Social Security, and other retirement benefits. They do not include any large nontaxable items that are not likely to be spent. For example, a $100,000 inheritance should not be added if it was invested in a certificate of deposit.

The tables represent the sales tax on the average (and recurring) expenditures based on level of income by family size and do not include exceptional purchases. Therefore, add to the table amount any sales taxes on major purchases (such as motor vehicles, aircraft, boats, and home building materials, etc.).

When the optional sales tax tables are utilized, special adjustments may be needed when a taxpayer has lived in more than one taxing jurisdiction (e.g., state, county, city) during the year. The adjustments involve apportionment of taxes based on days involved and are illustrated in Instructions for Schedule A (Form 1040), pages A-3 to A-6.

Local Sales Taxes

Local sales taxes (i.e., those imposed by counties, cities, transit authorities) may or may not require a separate determination. In those states where they are not imposed, no further computations are necessary. This is also the case where the local taxes are uniform and are incorporated into the state sales tax table. In other situations, another step is necessary to arrive at the optional sales tax table deduction. Depending on where the taxpayer lives, one of two procedures needs to be used. In one procedure, the local sales tax is arrived at by using the **state table** amount—see the Example 1 worksheet. In the other procedure, special **local tables** issued by the IRS for enumerated state and local jurisdictions are modified (if necessary) and used—see the Example 2 worksheet.

Use Illustrated

EXAMPLE 1 The Archers file a joint return for 2013 reflecting AGI of $88,000 and claiming three exemptions. They have tax-exempt interest of $3,000, and during the year they incurred sales tax of $1,650 on the purchase of an automobile for their dependent teenage son. They live in Bellaire, Texas, where the general sales tax rates are 6.25% for state and 2% for local. Since the IRS *has not issued* optional local sales tax tables for Texas, use the Worksheet below to arrive at the Archers' general sales tax deduction of $3,085.

Sales Tax Deduction Worksheet
(To be used when *no* IRS Optional Local Sales Tax Table Available)

Adjusted Gross Income (AGI) as listed on line 38 of Form 1040		$88,000
Add nontaxable items		3,000
Table income to be used for purposes of line 1 below		$91,000
1. Use table income to determine table amount—go to state of residence and find applicable range of table income and exemption column* for *state* sales tax		$ 1,087
2a. Enter local general sales tax rate	2.0	
2b. Enter state general sales tax rate	6.25	
2c. Divide 2a by 2b	0.32	
2d. Multiply line 1 by line 2c for the local sales tax		348
3. Enter general sales tax on large purchases		1,650
4. Deduction for general sales tax (add lines 1 + 2d + 3) and report on line 5 of Schedule A of Form 1040		$ 3,085

*Use total of personal and dependency exemptions as reported in item 6d of Form 1040.

EXAMPLE 2 The Hardys file a joint return for 2013, reporting AGI of $40,000 and claiming four exemptions (two personal and two dependency). They received $30,000 in nontaxable pension benefits. Although the Hardys do not keep sales tax receipts, they can prove that they paid $4,800 in sales tax on the purchase of a new boat in 2013. The Hardys are residents of Georgia and live in a jurisdiction that imposes a 2% local sales tax. Since the IRS *has issued* optional local sales tax tables for Georgia, use the Worksheet below to arrive at the Hardys' general sales tax deduction of $5,679.

Sales Tax Deduction Worksheet
[To be used for Alaska, Arizona, Arkansas, Colorado, Georgia, Illinois, Louisiana, Missouri, New York, North Carolina, South Carolina, Tennessee, Utah, Virginia, and West Virginia]

Adjusted Gross Income (AGI) as listed on line 38 of Form 1040		$40,000
Add nontaxable income		30,000
Table income to be used for purposes of line 1 below		$70,000
1. Use the table income to determine *state* sales tax amount—go to table for state of residence and find applicable income range and exemption column*		$ 539
2a. Enter local general sales tax rate	2.0	
2b. Enter IRS *local* sales tax table amount (based on 1%)	$170	
2c. Multiply line 2b by 2a for the local sales tax		340
3. Enter general sales tax on large purchases		4,800
4. Deduction for general sales tax (add lines 1 + 2c + 3) and report on line 5 of Schedule A of Form 1040		$ 5,679

*Use total of personal and dependency exemptions as reported in item 6d of Form 1040.

2013 Optional State Sales Tax Tables (State Sales Tax Rate Shown Next to State Name)

Income At least	Income But less than	Alabama[1] 4.0000% Exemptions 1	2	3	4	5	Over 5
$0	$20,000	217	256	282	302	319	343
20,000	30,000	329	387	426	456	482	517
30,000	40,000	384	451	497	532	561	602
40,000	50,000	431	506	556	596	628	674
50,000	60,000	472	554	609	652	687	737
60,000	70,000	509	597	656	702	741	794
70,000	80,000	544	638	701	750	790	848
80,000	90,000	576	675	741	793	836	897
90,000	100,000	606	710	780	834	879	942
100,000	120,000	646	755	830	887	935	1002
120,000	140,000	699	818	897	960	1011	1084
140,000	160,000	746	871	956	1022	1077	1154
160,000	180,000	792	924	1014	1084	1142	1223
180,000	200,000	833	972	1066	1139	1200	1285
200,000	or more	1034	1204	1319	1409	1483	1588

Income At least	Income But less than	Arizona[2] 6.0137% Exemptions 1	2	3	4	5	Over 5
$0	$20,000	206	228	242	253	261	273
20,000	30,000	364	403	428	447	462	483
30,000	40,000	449	497	528	552	570	596
40,000	50,000	524	581	617	644	666	697
50,000	60,000	593	657	698	729	754	789
60,000	70,000	657	728	774	808	836	874
70,000	80,000	719	796	846	884	914	956
80,000	90,000	776	860	914	954	987	1032
90,000	100,000	831	921	979	1022	1058	1106
100,000	120,000	905	1002	1065	1113	1151	1204
120,000	140,000	1007	1116	1186	1239	1282	1340
140,000	160,000	1097	1216	1293	1350	1397	1461
160,000	180,000	1188	1317	1400	1463	1514	1583
180,000	200,000	1271	1410	1499	1566	1620	1694
200,000	or more	1697	1882	2001	2091	2164	2264

Income At least	Income But less than	Arkansas[2] 6.2521% Exemptions 1	2	3	4	5	Over 5
$0	$20,000	273	304	324	339	351	367
20,000	30,000	461	513	547	572	593	621
30,000	40,000	559	623	664	695	720	754
40,000	50,000	644	718	766	801	830	870
50,000	60,000	722	805	858	898	931	976
60,000	70,000	793	885	943	987	1023	1072
70,000	80,000	861	960	1024	1072	1111	1164
80,000	90,000	924	1031	1099	1151	1193	1250
90,000	100,000	985	1098	1171	1226	1271	1332
100,000	120,000	1064	1187	1266	1326	1374	1441
120,000	140,000	1174	1310	1398	1464	1517	1590
140,000	160,000	1271	1419	1513	1585	1643	1722
160,000	180,000	1368	1527	1629	1706	1769	1854
180,000	200,000	1456	1625	1734	1816	1883	1974
200,000	or more	1900	2122	2264	2372	2459	2579

Income At least	Income But less than	California[3] 7.5000% Exemptions 1	2	3	4	5	Over 5
$0	$20,000	257	282	298	309	319	331
20,000	30,000	446	489	516	536	553	575
30,000	40,000	547	599	632	657	677	705
40,000	50,000	635	696	735	764	787	819
50,000	60,000	716	785	828	861	887	923
60,000	70,000	791	866	915	951	980	1019
70,000	80,000	862	944	997	1036	1068	1111
80,000	90,000	928	1017	1074	1116	1151	1197
90,000	100,000	992	1087	1148	1193	1230	1280
100,000	120,000	1076	1180	1246	1295	1335	1389
120,000	140,000	1194	1308	1381	1436	1480	1540
140,000	160,000	1297	1422	1501	1561	1609	1674
160,000	180,000	1401	1536	1622	1686	1738	1809
180,000	200,000	1496	1640	1732	1800	1856	1931
200,000	or more	1978	2168	2290	2381	2454	2554

Income At least	Income But less than	Colorado[2] 2.9000% Exemptions 1	2	3	4	5	Over 5
$0	$20,000	108	121	129	135	140	147
20,000	30,000	174	194	207	217	225	236
30,000	40,000	208	232	247	259	269	282
40,000	50,000	237	264	282	295	306	321
50,000	60,000	263	293	313	327	339	356
60,000	70,000	287	320	341	357	370	388
70,000	80,000	310	345	367	385	399	418
80,000	90,000	330	368	392	410	425	446
90,000	100,000	350	390	415	435	450	472
100,000	120,000	376	418	446	467	484	507
120,000	140,000	412	458	488	511	529	554
140,000	160,000	443	492	525	549	569	596
160,000	180,000	474	527	561	587	608	637
180,000	200,000	501	558	594	621	644	674
200,000	or more	640	711	757	792	821	859

Income At least	Income But less than	Connecticut[4] 6.3500% Exemptions 1	2	3	4	5	Over 5
$0	$20,000	254	279	295	306	316	329
20,000	30,000	432	475	503	523	539	562
30,000	40,000	527	579	613	637	658	685
40,000	50,000	609	670	709	738	761	793
50,000	60,000	684	753	796	829	855	891
60,000	70,000	754	829	877	913	942	981
70,000	80,000	819	902	954	993	1025	1068
80,000	90,000	881	969	1026	1068	1102	1148
90,000	100,000	940	1034	1094	1139	1176	1225
100,000	120,000	1017	1120	1185	1234	1273	1327
120,000	140,000	1125	1239	1311	1365	1409	1468
140,000	160,000	1220	1343	1422	1481	1528	1593
160,000	180,000	1315	1449	1533	1597	1648	1718
180,000	200,000	1402	1544	1634	1702	1757	1831
200,000	or more	1840	2028	2147	2236	2309	2407

Income At least	Income But less than	District of Columbia[4] 5.9370% Exemptions 1	2	3	4	5	Over 5
$0	$20,000	162	174	182	188	193	200
20,000	30,000	285	307	322	333	342	353
30,000	40,000	351	379	397	411	422	437
40,000	50,000	410	443	464	480	493	510
50,000	60,000	463	501	526	544	558	578
60,000	70,000	513	556	583	603	619	641
70,000	80,000	561	608	637	659	677	701
80,000	90,000	606	658	688	712	732	758
90,000	100,000	649	703	737	763	784	812
100,000	120,000	706	765	803	831	854	884
120,000	140,000	786	852	894	925	951	985
140,000	160,000	857	929	975	1009	1037	1074
160,000	180,000	928	1007	1056	1094	1124	1165
180,000	200,000	993	1077	1131	1171	1203	1247
200,000	or more	1327	1440	1513	1567	1610	1670

Income At least	Income But less than	Florida[1] 6.0000% Exemptions 1	2	3	4	5	Over 5
$0	$20,000	230	252	267	277	286	298
20,000	30,000	396	435	459	478	493	514
30,000	40,000	484	532	562	585	603	629
40,000	50,000	562	617	652	678	700	729
50,000	60,000	632	694	734	764	788	821
60,000	70,000	697	766	810	843	869	906
70,000	80,000	759	834	882	918	947	987
80,000	90,000	817	898	949	988	1020	1063
90,000	100,000	872	958	1014	1055	1089	1135
100,000	120,000	946	1039	1099	1144	1181	1231
120,000	140,000	1047	1151	1218	1268	1308	1364
140,000	160,000	1137	1250	1323	1377	1421	1481
160,000	180,000	1227	1350	1428	1487	1534	1599
180,000	200,000	1309	1440	1523	1586	1637	1707
200,000	or more	1726	1898	2009	2092	2160	2252

Income At least	Income But less than	Georgia[2] 4.0000% Exemptions 1	2	3	4	5	Over 5
$0	$20,000	146	163	173	181	188	196
20,000	30,000	241	267	285	298	308	323
30,000	40,000	290	321	342	358	370	388
40,000	50,000	332	368	392	410	424	444
50,000	60,000	370	410	436	456	472	494
60,000	70,000	404	449	477	499	517	541
70,000	80,000	437	485	516	539	558	584
80,000	90,000	468	519	552	577	597	625
90,000	100,000	497	551	586	613	634	663
100,000	120,000	535	593	631	660	683	714
120,000	140,000	587	652	693	724	749	784
140,000	160,000	634	703	747	781	808	845
160,000	180,000	679	753	801	837	866	906
180,000	200,000	721	799	850	888	919	962
200,000	or more	929	1029	1094	1143	1183	1237

Income At least	Income But less than	Hawaii[1,7] 4.0000% Exemptions 1	2	3	4	5	Over 5
$0	$20,000	212	247	269	287	302	322
20,000	30,000	356	414	453	483	507	542
30,000	40,000	431	502	549	585	615	657
40,000	50,000	497	578	632	674	709	757
50,000	60,000	556	647	708	755	794	848
60,000	70,000	610	711	778	829	872	932
70,000	80,000	662	771	844	900	946	1011
80,000	90,000	710	827	905	965	1015	1085
90,000	100,000	756	880	964	1028	1081	1155
100,000	120,000	817	951	1041	1111	1168	1248
120,000	140,000	900	1049	1148	1225	1288	1377
140,000	160,000	974	1134	1242	1325	1394	1490
160,000	180,000	1047	1220	1336	1426	1500	1603
180,000	200,000	1114	1298	1421	1517	1595	1705
200,000	or more	1449	1690	1851	1976	2078	2222

Income At least	Income But less than	Idaho[1] 6.0000% Exemptions 1	2	3	4	5	Over 5
$0	$20,000	327	385	424	454	480	515
20,000	30,000	501	588	647	693	731	784
30,000	40,000	587	688	757	810	854	916
40,000	50,000	660	773	850	909	959	1028
50,000	60,000	724	848	932	997	1051	1127
60,000	70,000	782	916	1006	1076	1134	1216
70,000	80,000	837	979	1075	1150	1212	1299
80,000	90,000	887	1037	1139	1218	1283	1375
90,000	100,000	934	1092	1199	1282	1351	1447
100,000	120,000	996	1164	1278	1366	1439	1541
120,000	140,000	1080	1262	1384	1479	1558	1669
140,000	160,000	1153	1346	1477	1578	1662	1780
160,000	180,000	1225	1430	1568	1675	1764	1889
180,000	200,000	1290	1505	1650	1762	1856	1987
200,000	or more	1607	1871	2050	2189	2301	2466

Income At least	Income But less than	Illinois[2] 6.2500% Exemptions 1	2	3	4	5	Over 5
$0	$20,000	244	273	292	307	319	335
20,000	30,000	389	435	465	488	507	533
30,000	40,000	462	516	552	579	602	633
40,000	50,000	525	586	627	657	683	718
50,000	60,000	582	649	693	727	755	794
60,000	70,000	633	706	754	791	821	863
70,000	80,000	681	759	811	851	883	928
80,000	90,000	725	809	864	906	941	989
90,000	100,000	768	856	914	958	995	1045
100,000	120,000	823	917	979	1027	1066	1120
120,000	140,000	899	1001	1069	1121	1163	1222
140,000	160,000	965	1075	1147	1202	1248	1311
160,000	180,000	1031	1147	1225	1284	1332	1399
180,000	200,000	1090	1213	1294	1357	1408	1479
200,000	or more	1383	1538	1640	1718	1783	1872

Income At least	Income But less than	Indiana[4] 7.0000% Exemptions 1	2	3	4	5	Over 5
$0	$20,000	279	312	333	349	361	379
20,000	30,000	448	500	534	559	579	607
30,000	40,000	534	596	635	665	690	723
40,000	50,000	607	677	723	757	784	822
50,000	60,000	673	751	801	838	869	911
60,000	70,000	733	817	872	913	946	992
70,000	80,000	789	880	939	983	1019	1068
80,000	90,000	841	938	1001	1048	1086	1138
90,000	100,000	890	993	1059	1109	1149	1205
100,000	120,000	955	1065	1136	1190	1233	1293
120,000	140,000	1044	1164	1242	1300	1347	1412
140,000	160,000	1121	1250	1333	1396	1447	1517
160,000	180,000	1198	1336	1425	1492	1546	1621
180,000	200,000	1267	1413	1507	1578	1635	1714
200,000	or more	1610	1796	1915	2005	2078	2178

Income At least	Income But less than	Iowa[1] 6.0000% Exemptions 1	2	3	4	5	Over 5
$0	$20,000	237	264	281	293	304	318
20,000	30,000	408	454	484	506	524	549
30,000	40,000	498	555	592	619	642	672
40,000	50,000	578	644	687	719	745	781
50,000	60,000	651	725	773	810	839	879
60,000	70,000	718	800	853	893	926	971
70,000	80,000	781	872	930	974	1009	1058
80,000	90,000	841	939	1001	1048	1087	1139
90,000	100,000	898	1002	1069	1120	1161	1217
100,000	120,000	974	1087	1160	1215	1260	1321
120,000	140,000	1079	1205	1286	1347	1397	1465
140,000	160,000	1172	1309	1397	1464	1518	1592
160,000	180,000	1266	1414	1509	1581	1639	1719
180,000	200,000	1351	1509	1611	1687	1750	1835
200,000	or more	1783	1993	2128	2230	2313	2427

Income At least	Income But less than	Kansas[1] 6.2244% Exemptions 1	2	3	4	5	Over 5
$0	$20,000	343	401	439	469	494	528
20,000	30,000	546	637	699	746	785	840
30,000	40,000	649	757	830	886	932	997
40,000	50,000	736	859	941	1005	1058	1132
50,000	60,000	815	950	1041	1112	1170	1252
60,000	70,000	886	1033	1132	1209	1272	1361
70,000	80,000	953	1111	1218	1300	1368	1464
80,000	90,000	1015	1183	1297	1384	1457	1559
90,000	100,000	1073	1252	1371	1464	1541	1648
100,000	120,000	1150	1341	1469	1569	1651	1766
120,000	140,000	1255	1463	1603	1712	1801	1927
140,000	160,000	1346	1570	1720	1836	1932	2067
160,000	180,000	1437	1676	1836	1960	2062	2206
180,000	200,000	1518	1771	1940	2071	2179	2331
200,000	or more	1922	2241	2455	2621	2758	2950

Income At least	Income But less than	Kentucky[4] 6.0000% Exemptions 1	2	3	4	5	Over 5
$0	$20,000	227	253	270	283	294	308
20,000	30,000	371	414	442	462	479	503
30,000	40,000	445	496	530	554	575	603
40,000	50,000	509	568	605	634	657	689
50,000	60,000	567	632	673	705	731	766
60,000	70,000	619	690	736	770	798	837
70,000	80,000	669	745	794	832	862	904
80,000	90,000	715	797	849	889	921	966
90,000	100,000	759	845	901	943	977	1024
100,000	120,000	817	909	969	1014	1051	1102
120,000	140,000	896	997	1063	1112	1153	1208
140,000	160,000	965	1074	1145	1198	1241	1301
160,000	180,000	1034	1151	1226	1284	1330	1394
180,000	200,000	1097	1220	1300	1361	1410	1477
200,000	or more	1409	1566	1668	1746	1808	1895

Income At least	Income But less than	Louisiana[2] 4.0000% Exemptions 1	2	3	4	5	Over 5
$0	$20,000	155	169	178	184	189	197
20,000	30,000	267	291	306	318	327	340
30,000	40,000	327	356	375	389	400	416
40,000	50,000	379	413	435	451	465	482
50,000	60,000	427	465	490	508	523	543
60,000	70,000	471	514	541	561	577	600
70,000	80,000	513	559	589	611	629	653
80,000	90,000	552	602	634	658	677	703
90,000	100,000	590	643	677	703	723	751
100,000	120,000	639	698	735	762	785	815
120,000	140,000	708	773	814	845	870	903
140,000	160,000	769	840	884	918	945	981
160,000	180,000	830	906	955	991	1020	1060
180,000	200,000	886	967	1019	1057	1089	1131
200,000	or more	1168	1276	1344	1396	1437	1493

Income At least	Income But less than	Maine[4] 5.1260% Exemptions 1	2	3	4	5	Over 5
$0	$20,000	141	153	161	166	171	177
20,000	30,000	246	267	281	291	299	311
30,000	40,000	302	329	346	358	368	382
40,000	50,000	352	383	403	417	429	445
50,000	60,000	398	433	455	471	485	503
60,000	70,000	440	478	503	521	536	556
70,000	80,000	480	522	549	569	585	607
80,000	90,000	518	563	592	614	631	655
90,000	100,000	554	603	634	657	676	701
100,000	120,000	602	655	689	714	734	762
120,000	140,000	668	728	765	793	816	846
140,000	160,000	727	792	833	863	888	921
160,000	180,000	787	857	901	934	961	997
180,000	200,000	841	916	963	998	1027	1065
200,000	or more	1117	1216	1279	1326	1364	1416

Income At least	Income But less than	Maryland[4] 6.0000% Exemptions 1	2	3	4	5	Over 5
$0	$20,000	200	221	235	246	254	266
20,000	30,000	344	380	404	422	437	458
30,000	40,000	420	464	494	516	534	560
40,000	50,000	486	538	572	598	619	649
50,000	60,000	547	605	644	673	697	730
60,000	70,000	603	667	710	742	768	805
70,000	80,000	656	726	773	808	837	876
80,000	90,000	706	782	831	869	900	943
90,000	100,000	753	834	887	928	961	1007
100,000	120,000	816	904	962	1006	1042	1092
120,000	140,000	903	1001	1065	1114	1154	1209
140,000	160,000	980	1086	1156	1209	1252	1312
160,000	180,000	1058	1172	1247	1305	1351	1416
180,000	200,000	1128	1250	1330	1391	1441	1511
200,000	or more	1484	1645	1751	1832	1898	1989

Income At least	Income But less than	Massachusetts[4] 6.2500% Exemptions 1	2	3	4	5	Over 5
$0	$20,000	195	212	223	231	238	247
20,000	30,000	317	345	363	376	387	402
30,000	40,000	380	413	435	451	464	481
40,000	50,000	434	472	496	515	530	550
50,000	60,000	482	525	552	572	589	611
60,000	70,000	527	573	603	625	643	667
70,000	80,000	568	619	650	674	693	720
80,000	90,000	607	661	695	720	741	769
90,000	100,000	644	701	737	764	785	815
100,000	120,000	693	753	792	821	844	876
120,000	140,000	759	826	868	900	925	960
140,000	160,000	817	889	934	969	996	1034
160,000	180,000	875	952	1001	1037	1067	1107
180,000	200,000	928	1009	1060	1099	1130	1173
200,000	or more	1189	1292	1358	1407	1447	1501

Income At least	Income But less than	Michigan[4] 6.0000% Exemptions 1	2	3	4	5	Over 5
$0	$20,000	219	243	258	269	279	291
20,000	30,000	357	395	419	438	453	473
30,000	40,000	427	473	502	524	542	567
40,000	50,000	488	540	573	598	619	647
50,000	60,000	543	600	637	665	688	719
60,000	70,000	593	655	696	726	751	785
70,000	80,000	640	708	751	784	810	847
80,000	90,000	684	756	802	837	865	904
90,000	100,000	725	802	851	888	918	959
100,000	120,000	780	862	915	954	987	1031
120,000	140,000	855	945	1003	1046	1081	1130
140,000	160,000	921	1017	1079	1126	1164	1216
160,000	180,000	986	1089	1156	1206	1246	1302
180,000	200,000	1045	1154	1225	1278	1320	1379
200,000	or more	1340	1479	1569	1636	1691	1766

Income At least	Income But less than	Minnesota[1] 6.8750% Exemptions 1	2	3	4	5	Over 5
$0	$20,000	226	244	256	264	271	280
20,000	30,000	394	426	446	461	473	490
30,000	40,000	483	523	548	567	582	602
40,000	50,000	563	609	639	660	678	702
50,000	60,000	635	688	721	746	766	793
60,000	70,000	702	761	798	825	847	877
70,000	80,000	766	830	871	901	925	957
80,000	90,000	826	896	939	972	998	1033
90,000	100,000	884	958	1005	1040	1068	1105
100,000	120,000	960	1041	1092	1130	1161	1202
120,000	140,000	1066	1157	1214	1256	1290	1336
140,000	160,000	1161	1259	1321	1367	1404	1455
160,000	180,000	1255	1362	1429	1479	1520	1574
180,000	200,000	1342	1456	1528	1582	1625	1683
200,000	or more	1783	1936	2033	2105	2162	2241

Income At least	Income But less than	Mississippi[1] 7.0000% Exemptions 1	2	3	4	5	Over 5
$0	$20,000	401	462	502	533	559	594
20,000	30,000	642	739	804	853	894	951
30,000	40,000	764	880	957	1016	1064	1131
40,000	50,000	869	1000	1087	1154	1209	1286
50,000	60,000	962	1108	1204	1279	1340	1424
60,000	70,000	1047	1206	1311	1392	1458	1550
70,000	80,000	1127	1298	1411	1498	1569	1669
80,000	90,000	1201	1383	1504	1596	1672	1778
90,000	100,000	1271	1464	1592	1689	1770	1882
100,000	120,000	1363	1570	1707	1812	1898	2018
120,000	140,000	1489	1715	1864	1979	2073	2205
140,000	160,000	1599	1841	2002	2125	2226	2367
160,000	180,000	1708	1967	2138	2270	2378	2529
180,000	200,000	1807	2080	2261	2400	2515	2674
200,000	or more	2293	2641	2871	3047	3192	3394

Income At least	Income But less than	Missouri[2] 4.2250% Exemptions 1	2	3	4	5	Over 5
$0	$20,000	166	189	205	216	226	239
20,000	30,000	272	309	334	353	369	390
30,000	40,000	326	371	400	423	442	468
40,000	50,000	373	424	458	484	505	534
50,000	60,000	415	472	509	538	562	594
60,000	70,000	453	515	556	588	614	649
70,000	80,000	490	557	601	635	663	701
80,000	90,000	523	595	642	678	708	749
90,000	100,000	555	631	681	720	751	795
100,000	120,000	598	679	733	774	808	855
120,000	140,000	656	745	804	849	886	937
140,000	160,000	706	802	866	914	954	1009
160,000	180,000	757	860	928	980	1022	1081
180,000	200,000	803	912	983	1038	1083	1146
200,000	or more	1031	1170	1262	1332	1390	1470

Income At least	Income But less than	Nebraska[1] 5.5000% Exemptions 1	2	3	4	5	Over 5
$0	$20,000	216	238	252	263	272	284
20,000	30,000	371	411	436	455	470	491
30,000	40,000	454	503	534	557	576	602
40,000	50,000	527	584	620	647	669	699
50,000	60,000	594	658	699	729	754	788
60,000	70,000	655	726	771	805	833	870
70,000	80,000	714	791	841	878	908	949
80,000	90,000	769	852	905	945	978	1022
90,000	100,000	821	910	967	1010	1045	1092
100,000	120,000	891	988	1050	1097	1134	1186
120,000	140,000	988	1095	1164	1216	1258	1315
140,000	160,000	1073	1190	1265	1322	1367	1430
160,000	180,000	1159	1286	1367	1428	1477	1545
180,000	200,000	1237	1373	1460	1525	1578	1650
200,000	or more	1635	1815	1931	2018	2088	2184

(Continued)

2013 Optional State Sales Tax Tables *(Continued)*

Income		Nevada[5] 6.8500%						New Jersey[4,6] 7.0000%						New Mexico[1] 5.1250%						New York[2] 4.0000%						North Carolina[2] 4.7500%					
At least	But less than	1	2	3	4	5	Over 5	1	2	3	4	5	Over 5	1	2	3	4	5	Over 5	1	2	3	4	5	Over 5	1	2	3	4	5	Over 5
$0	$20,000	257	284	301	315	325	340	239	257	268	276	283	292	188	209	222	232	240	252	139	149	155	160	164	169	213	242	261	276	288	304
20,000	30,000	412	455	483	504	520	544	413	444	463	478	490	505	337	376	401	420	435	456	239	257	268	276	283	292	350	398	429	453	472	499
30,000	40,000	491	542	575	599	620	647	505	544	568	586	600	620	420	468	499	523	542	568	292	314	328	338	347	358	421	478	515	544	567	599
40,000	50,000	558	616	654	682	704	736	587	631	659	680	697	720	493	550	587	615	638	669	339	364	381	393	402	416	481	547	590	622	649	686
50,000	60,000	619	683	724	755	780	815	661	711	743	767	786	812	561	626	669	700	726	762	381	410	429	442	453	468	536	609	657	693	723	764
60,000	70,000	674	744	789	822	850	887	729	785	820	847	868	896	624	697	744	780	809	849	421	453	473	488	500	517	586	666	718	758	790	835
70,000	80,000	726	801	849	885	915	955	795	856	894	923	946	977	685	765	818	857	889	933	458	493	516	532	545	563	633	720	776	819	854	902
80,000	90,000	774	854	905	944	975	1018	856	922	963	994	1019	1053	742	830	887	929	964	1012	493	531	555	573	587	607	677	769	830	876	913	965
90,000	100,000	820	904	958	999	1032	1077	914	985	1029	1063	1089	1126	797	892	953	999	1036	1088	527	567	593	612	628	648	719	817	881	930	969	1024
100,000	120,000	880	970	1028	1072	1107	1156	992	1069	1117	1153	1182	1222	871	975	1042	1092	1133	1190	571	616	643	664	681	704	774	879	948	1001	1044	1103
120,000	140,000	962	1061	1124	1171	1210	1263	1100	1185	1239	1279	1312	1355	975	1091	1166	1223	1269	1333	633	682	713	736	755	780	849	965	1041	1098	1145	1210
140,000	160,000	1034	1140	1207	1258	1300	1356	1195	1288	1347	1391	1426	1474	1067	1195	1277	1340	1390	1460	688	741	775	800	820	848	915	1040	1122	1184	1234	1305
160,000	180,000	1105	1218	1290	1345	1389	1449	1291	1391	1455	1503	1541	1592	1160	1300	1390	1458	1513	1589	742	800	837	864	886	916	981	1115	1202	1269	1323	1399
180,000	200,000	1169	1289	1365	1422	1469	1533	1378	1486	1554	1604	1645	1701	1246	1396	1493	1566	1626	1708	792	854	893	923	946	978	1041	1183	1275	1346	1404	1483
200,000	or more	1489	1639	1736	1808	1867	1948	1821	1965	2056	2123	2178	2251	1689	1895	2028	2129	2210	2323	1046	1128	1180	1219	1250	1293	1338	1520	1640	1731	1805	1908

Income		North Dakota[1] 5.0000%						Ohio[1] 5.5836%						Oklahoma[1] 4.5000%						Pennsylvania[1] 6.0000%						Rhode Island[4] 7.0000%					
At least	But less than	1	2	3	4	5	Over 5	1	2	3	4	5	Over 5	1	2	3	4	5	Over 5	1	2	3	4	5	Over 5	1	2	3	4	5	Over 5
$0	$20,000	182	204	218	229	238	251	217	237	249	259	266	276	235	270	294	312	327	348	187	203	213	220	226	234	247	270	284	294	303	315
20,000	30,000	295	330	353	371	385	406	371	405	426	442	455	473	379	435	473	502	526	560	319	346	363	376	387	401	397	433	455	472	486	504
30,000	40,000	353	394	422	443	460	485	453	494	520	539	555	577	452	519	564	599	628	668	389	422	443	459	472	489	473	515	542	562	579	601
40,000	50,000	402	450	481	505	525	552	524	571	602	624	643	668	515	592	643	682	715	761	450	488	513	531	546	566	538	586	617	640	658	683
50,000	60,000	447	499	534	561	583	613	589	642	676	702	722	750	572	656	713	757	793	843	505	548	576	597	614	636	596	649	683	709	729	757
60,000	70,000	487	545	583	612	635	669	648	707	745	773	796	827	623	715	777	824	864	919	556	604	634	657	676	701	649	707	744	772	794	824
70,000	80,000	526	587	628	659	685	721	705	769	810	841	866	899	672	771	837	888	931	990	604	657	690	715	735	763	698	761	801	831	855	888
80,000	90,000	561	627	671	704	731	769	758	827	871	904	931	967	717	822	893	948	993	1056	650	706	742	769	791	821	745	812	854	886	911	946
90,000	100,000	595	665	711	746	775	815	809	883	930	965	993	1032	759	871	946	1004	1051	1118	693	753	792	820	844	876	788	859	904	938	965	1002
100,000	120,000	639	714	763	801	832	876	876	956	1007	1045	1076	1118	815	935	1015	1077	1128	1200	750	816	857	889	914	948	846	922	970	1006	1035	1075
120,000	140,000	700	782	836	877	911	958	968	1057	1114	1156	1190	1237	892	1023	1110	1178	1234	1312	830	902	948	983	1011	1049	924	1007	1060	1099	1131	1174
140,000	160,000	753	841	899	943	980	1031	1050	1147	1208	1254	1291	1342	959	1099	1193	1266	1326	1410	900	978	1029	1066	1097	1139	992	1082	1138	1181	1215	1261
160,000	180,000	806	900	962	1009	1048	1103	1132	1237	1303	1352	1392	1447	1025	1175	1276	1354	1418	1508	970	1055	1109	1150	1183	1228	1061	1156	1216	1262	1298	1348
180,000	200,000	854	953	1018	1069	1110	1167	1207	1318	1389	1441	1484	1542	1085	1244	1350	1433	1501	1595	1033	1124	1182	1226	1261	1309	1122	1223	1287	1334	1373	1425
200,000	or more	1092	1217	1301	1364	1417	1490	1584	1731	1824	1893	1950	2026	1384	1585	1720	1825	1911	2031	1356	1476	1553	1611	1657	1721	1426	1554	1635	1696	1745	1811

Income		South Carolina[2] 6.0000%						South Dakota[1] 4.0000%						Tennessee[2] 7.0000%						Texas[1] 6.2500%						Utah[2] 4.7000%					
At least	But less than	1	2	3	4	5	Over 5	1	2	3	4	5	Over 5	1	2	3	4	5	Over 5	1	2	3	4	5	Over 5	1	2	3	4	5	Over 5
$0	$20,000	225	248	263	274	283	295	228	263	286	305	319	340	354	403	436	460	481	509	246	273	291	304	315	330	228	259	279	294	307	324
20,000	30,000	386	426	451	470	485	505	367	424	462	491	515	548	579	659	711	752	785	831	419	467	497	521	539	565	376	426	459	484	505	533
30,000	40,000	471	520	550	573	592	617	437	505	551	585	614	654	694	790	853	902	941	996	511	569	607	635	658	690	452	512	552	582	607	641
40,000	50,000	546	602	638	664	686	715	498	576	627	667	699	745	794	903	975	1031	1076	1139	591	659	703	736	763	799	518	587	632	667	695	734
50,000	60,000	613	677	717	747	772	805	553	639	696	740	776	826	884	1005	1085	1147	1197	1267	664	741	790	827	857	899	578	654	705	743	775	818
60,000	70,000	676	746	790	824	850	887	602	696	758	806	845	900	965	1098	1185	1253	1308	1384	732	816	871	912	945	991	632	716	771	813	847	895
70,000	80,000	736	812	860	896	926	966	649	750	817	868	911	970	1043	1186	1280	1353	1412	1494	796	888	947	992	1028	1078	683	774	833	879	916	968
80,000	90,000	791	873	926	965	996	1039	692	800	871	926	972	1035	1114	1267	1368	1445	1509	1597	856	955	1019	1067	1106	1160	731	828	892	940	980	1035
90,000	100,000	845	932	988	1030	1063	1109	733	847	923	981	1029	1096	1182	1345	1452	1534	1601	1694	913	1019	1087	1139	1181	1238	776	879	947	998	1041	1099
100,000	120,000	915	1010	1071	1116	1152	1202	787	909	991	1053	1105	1177	1272	1446	1562	1650	1722	1822	989	1104	1178	1234	1279	1342	836	947	1020	1075	1121	1184
120,000	140,000	1013	1118	1185	1235	1276	1331	861	995	1084	1152	1208	1287	1395	1586	1712	1809	1888	1998	1094	1222	1304	1366	1416	1485	918	1040	1120	1181	1231	1300
140,000	160,000	1099	1213	1286	1341	1385	1445	925	1069	1165	1238	1299	1383	1503	1709	1844	1948	2034	2152	1187	1325	1415	1482	1537	1612	990	1121	1208	1273	1327	1402
160,000	180,000	1185	1309	1388	1447	1494	1559	989	1143	1245	1324	1389	1479	1610	1830	1976	2087	2179	2306	1280	1430	1526	1599	1658	1739	1062	1203	1295	1366	1423	1503
180,000	200,000	1264	1396	1480	1543	1593	1663	1047	1210	1318	1401	1470	1565	1707	1940	2095	2213	2310	2444	1365	1524	1627	1705	1768	1855	1127	1276	1374	1449	1510	1595
200,000	or more	1663	1837	1948	2031	2098	2189	1333	1541	1679	1785	1872	1994	2190	2490	2687	2838	2962	3135	1793	2004	2141	2243	2327	2442	1452	1643	1770	1866	1945	2054

Income		Vermont[1] 6.0000%						Virginia[2] 4.1512%						Washington[1] 6.5000%						West Virginia[2] 6.0000%						Wisconsin[1] 5.0000%					
At least	But less than	1	2	3	4	5	Over 5	1	2	3	4	5	Over 5	1	2	3	4	5	Over 5	1	2	3	4	5	Over 5	1	2	3	4	5	Over 5
$0	$20,000	158	168	175	180	184	189	173	196	212	224	233	247	251	277	293	306	316	329	241	269	287	301	312	327	204	225	239	249	257	268
20,000	30,000	253	270	281	288	295	303	274	310	334	353	368	389	432	476	505	526	544	567	413	461	493	516	535	562	347	383	405	423	436	455
30,000	40,000	302	322	334	343	351	361	324	367	396	417	435	460	528	582	617	643	665	694	504	564	602	631	655	687	422	466	494	514	531	554
40,000	50,000	343	366	380	391	399	410	368	416	448	473	493	520	612	675	716	746	771	805	584	653	698	732	759	797	488	538	571	595	614	641
50,000	60,000	380	405	421	433	442	455	406	460	495	522	544	575	688	759	805	840	868	906	657	735	785	823	854	897	547	604	640	668	690	720
60,000	70,000	414	441	459	471	481	495	441	499	538	567	591	624	759	837	888	926	957	1000	724	810	866	908	942	989	602	665	705	735	759	792
70,000	80,000	446	475	494	507	518	533	474	537	578	609	634	670	826	912	967	1009	1042	1089	788	882	943	989	1026	1077	654	722	766	799	825	861
80,000	90,000	475	507	526	541	552	568	505	571	615	648	675	712	889	981	1041	1086	1122	1172	848	949	1015	1064	1104	1160	703	776	823	859	887	926
90,000	100,000	503	536	557	573	585	601	534	604	649	684	713	753	949	1048	1111	1159	1198	1252	905	1014	1083	1136	1179	1238	749	828	878	915	946	987
100,000	120,000	540	575	598	614	627	645	572	646	695	733	763	806	1029	1136	1205	1257	1299	1357	981	1099	1175	1232	1279	1343	811	896	950	991	1024	1069
120,000	140,000	590	629	653	671	686	705	624	705	758	798	832	878	1139	1258	1335	1393	1439	1504	1086	1217	1301	1365	1417	1488	896	990	1050	1095	1132	1182
140,000	160,000	633	675	702	721	736	757	669	755	812	856	891	940	1237	1366	1449	1512	1563	1633	1179	1321	1413	1482	1538	1616	971	1073	1139	1187	1227	1281
160,000	180,000	677	722	750	770	787	809	713	806	866	912	950	1003	1334	1474	1564	1632	1687	1762	1272	1426	1525	1600	1661	1744	1046	1157	1227	1280	1322	1381
180,000	200,000	716	763	793	815	832	856	754	851	915	964	1003	1059	1423	1573	1669	1741	1800	1880	1357	1521	1627	1707	1772	1861	1114	1232	1307	1364	1409	1471
200,000	or more	910	970	1008	1035	1058	1087	953	1075	1155	1216	1266	1335	1875	2072	2199	2295	2373	2479	1787	2004	2144	2251	2337	2456	1460	1615	1714	1788	1848	1929

Income		Wyoming[1] 4.0000%					
At least	But less than	1	2	3	4	5	Over 5
$0	$20,000	155	169	178	184	190	197
20,000	30,000	266	290	305	317	326	339
30,000	40,000	325	354	373	387	399	414
40,000	50,000	376	411	433	449	462	480
50,000	60,000	423	462	487	505	520	541
60,000	70,000	466	509	537	557	574	596
70,000	80,000	508	554	584	606	624	649
80,000	90,000	546	597	629	653	672	698
90,000	100,000	583	637	671	697	717	746
100,000	120,000	632	690	727	755	778	808
120,000	140,000	699	764	805	836	861	895
140,000	160,000	759	829	874	908	935	972
160,000	180,000	819	895	943	979	1009	1049
180,000	200,000	873	954	1006	1045	1076	1118
200,000	or more	1149	1256	1325	1376	1417	1473

Note. Residents of **Alaska** do not have a state sales tax, but should follow the instructions on the next page to determine their local sales tax amount.

1 Use the Ratio Method to determine your local sales tax deduction, then add that to the appropriate amount in the state table. Your state sales tax rate is provided next to the state name.

2 Follow the instructions on the next page to determine your local sales tax deduction, then add that to the appropriate amount in the state table.

3 The California table includes the 1.25% uniform local sales tax rate in addition to the 6.25% state sales tax rate for a total of 7.50%. Some California localities impose a larger local sales tax. Taxpayers who reside in those jurisdictions should use the Ratio Method to determine their local sales tax deduction, then add that to the appropriate amount in the state table. The denominator of the correct ratio is 7.50%, and the numerator is the total sales tax rate minus 7.50%.

4 This state does not have a local general sales tax, so the amount in the state table is the only amount to be deducted.

5 The Nevada table includes the 2.25% uniform local sales tax rate in addition to the 4.6000% state sales tax rate for a total of 6.85%. Some Nevada localities impose a larger local sales tax. Taxpayers who reside in those jurisdictions should use the Ratio Method to determine their local sales tax deduction, then add that to the appropriate amount in the state table. The denominator of the correct ratio is 6.85%, and the numerator is the total sales tax rate minus 6.85%.

6 Residents of Salem County, New Jersey should deduct only half of the amount in the state table.

7 The 4.0% rate for Hawaii is actually an excise tax but is treated as a sales tax for purpose of this deduction.

Which Optional Local Sales Tax Table Should I Use?

IF you live in the state of...	AND you live in...	THEN use Local Table...
Alaska	Any locality	C
Arizona	Glendale, Mesa or Tucson	A
	Chandler, Gilbert, Peoria, Phoenix, Scottsdale, Tempe, Yuma, or any other locality	B
Arkansas	Any locality	B
Colorado	Adams County, Arapahoe County, Boulder County, Centennial, Colorado Springs, Denver City/Denver County, El Paso County, Jefferson County, Larimer County, Pueblo County, or any other locality	A
	Aurora, Lakewood, or Longmont	B
	Arvada, Boulder, Fort Collins, Greeley, Thornton, or Westminster	C
Georgia	Any locality	B
Illinois	Any locality	A
Louisiana	Ascension Parish, Bossier Parish, Caddo Parish, Calcasieu Parish, East Baton Rouge Parish, Iberia Parish, Jefferson Parish, Lafayette Parish, Lafourche Parish, Livingston Parish, Orleans Parish, Ouachita Parish, Rapides Parish, St. Bernard Parish, St. Landry Parish, St. Tammany Parish, Tangipahoa Parish, or Terrebonne Parish	C
	Any other locality	B
Missouri	Any locality	B
New York	Chautauqua County, Chenango County, Columbia County, Delaware County, Greene County, Hamilton County, Tioga County, Wayne County, New York City, or Norwich City	A
	Counties: Albany, Allegany, Broome, Cattaraugus, Cayuga, Chemung, Clinton, Cortland, Dutchess, Erie, Essex, Franklin, Fulton, Genesee, Herkimer, Jefferson, Lewis, Livingston, Madison, Monroe, Montgomery, Nassau, Niagara, Oneida, Onondaga, Ontario, Orange, Orleans, Oswego, Otsego, Putnam, Rensselaer, Rockland, St. Lawrence, Saratoga, Schenectady, Schoharie, Schuyler, Seneca, Steuben, Suffolk, Sullivan, Tompkins, Ulster, Warren, Washington, Westchester, Wyoming, or Yates	B
	Any other locality	D*
North Carolina	Any locality	A
South Carolina	Aiken County, Cherokee County, Chesterfield County, Darlington County, Dillon County, Horry County, Jasper County, Lexington County, Marlboro County, Newberry County, Orangeburg County, York County, or Myrtle Beach	A
	Bamberg County, Charleston County, Hampton County, Lee County, Marion County, or any other locality	B
Tennessee	Any locality	B
Utah	Any locality	A
Virginia	Any locality	C
West Virginia	Any locality	C

2013 Optional Local Sales Tax Tables for Certain Local Jurisdictions
(Based on a local sales tax rate of 1 percent)

Income		Exemptions						Exemptions						Exemptions						Exemptions					
At least	But less than	1	2	3	4	5	Over 5	1	2	3	4	5	Over 5	1	2	3	4	5	Over 5	1	2	3	4	5	Over 5
		Local Table A						Local Table B						Local Table C						Local Table D*					
$0	$20,000	37	42	45	47	49	51	47	55	60	64	67	71	53	61	66	70	73	78	35	37	39	40	41	42
20,000	30,000	60	67	72	75	78	82	74	86	93	99	104	111	85	97	105	112	117	124	60	64	67	69	71	73
30,000	40,000	72	80	85	89	93	97	87	101	110	117	123	131	101	116	126	133	139	148	73	79	82	85	87	90
40,000	50,000	82	91	97	102	106	111	99	114	125	133	139	148	115	132	143	151	158	168	85	91	95	98	101	104
50,000	60,000	91	101	108	113	117	123	109	126	137	146	153	164	127	146	158	168	175	186	95	103	107	111	113	117
60,000	70,000	99	110	117	123	127	134	118	137	149	159	166	177	139	159	172	183	191	203	105	113	118	122	125	129
70,000	80,000	106	119	126	132	137	144	127	147	160	170	179	190	149	171	186	197	206	218	115	123	129	133	136	141
80,000	90,000	114	126	135	141	146	154	135	156	170	181	190	202	159	182	198	210	219	233	123	133	139	143	147	152
90,000	100,000	120	134	143	149	155	163	143	165	179	191	200	213	169	193	209	222	232	246	132	142	148	153	157	162
100,000	120,000	129	144	153	160	166	174	153	176	192	204	214	228	181	207	225	238	249	264	143	154	161	166	170	176
120,000	140,000	141	157	167	175	182	191	166	192	209	222	233	248	198	226	245	260	272	289	158	171	178	184	189	195
140,000	160,000	152	169	180	188	195	205	178	205	224	238	249	266	212	243	264	279	292	310	172	185	194	200	205	212
160,000	180,000	162	180	192	201	209	219	190	219	238	253	266	283	227	260	282	298	312	331	186	200	209	216	222	229
180,000	200,000	172	191	203	213	221	231	200	231	251	267	280	298	240	275	298	315	330	350	198	214	223	231	237	245
200,000	or more	219	243	259	271	281	294	252	290	316	336	352	375	305	349	378	401	419	445	262	282	295	305	313	323

*Note. Local Table D is just 25% of the NY State table.

Appendix B

Tax Forms

(Tax forms can be obtained from the IRS website: **www.irs.gov**)

Form **1040** Department of the Treasury—Internal Revenue Service (99) **2013**
U.S. Individual Income Tax Return OMB No. 1545-0074 IRS Use Only—Do not write or staple in this space.

For the year Jan. 1–Dec. 31, 2013, or other tax year beginning _____, 2013, ending _____, 20___   See separate instructions.

Your first name and initial	Last name	Your social security number

If a joint return, spouse's first name and initial	Last name	Spouse's social security number

Home address (number and street). If you have a P.O. box, see instructions. Apt. no.

▲ Make sure the SSN(s) above and on line 6c are correct.

City, town or post office, state, and ZIP code. If you have a foreign address, also complete spaces below (see instructions).

Presidential Election Campaign
Check here if you, or your spouse if filing jointly, want $3 to go to this fund. Checking a box below will not change your tax or refund. ☐ You ☐ Spouse

Foreign country name	Foreign province/state/county	Foreign postal code

Filing Status
Check only one box.

1 ☐ Single
2 ☐ Married filing jointly (even if only one had income)
3 ☐ Married filing separately. Enter spouse's SSN above and full name here. ▶
4 ☐ Head of household (with qualifying person). (See instructions.) If the qualifying person is a child but not your dependent, enter this child's name here. ▶
5 ☐ Qualifying widow(er) with dependent child

Exemptions

6a ☐ **Yourself.** If someone can claim you as a dependent, **do not** check box 6a . . . . . .
 b ☐ **Spouse** . . . .
 c **Dependents:**

(1) First name Last name	(2) Dependent's social security number	(3) Dependent's relationship to you	(4) ✓ if child under age 17 qualifying for child tax credit (see instructions)
			☐
			☐
			☐
			☐

If more than four dependents, see instructions and check here ▶ ☐

Boxes checked on 6a and 6b ___
No. of children on 6c who:
• lived with you ___
• did not live with you due to divorce or separation (see instructions) ___
Dependents on 6c not entered above ___
Add numbers on lines above ▶ ___

 d Total number of exemptions claimed . . . .

Income

Attach Form(s) W-2 here. Also attach Forms W-2G and 1099-R if tax was withheld.

If you did not get a W-2, see instructions.

7	Wages, salaries, tips, etc. Attach Form(s) W-2	7	
8a	**Taxable** interest. Attach Schedule B if required	8a	
b	**Tax-exempt** interest. **Do not** include on line 8a **8b**		
9a	Ordinary dividends. Attach Schedule B if required	9a	
b	Qualified dividends **9b**		
10	Taxable refunds, credits, or offsets of state and local income taxes	10	
11	Alimony received	11	
12	Business income or (loss). Attach Schedule C or C-EZ	12	
13	Capital gain or (loss). Attach Schedule D if required. If not required, check here ▶ ☐	13	
14	Other gains or (losses). Attach Form 4797	14	
15a	IRA distributions **15a** b Taxable amount	15b	
16a	Pensions and annuities **16a** b Taxable amount	16b	
17	Rental real estate, royalties, partnerships, S corporations, trusts, etc. Attach Schedule E	17	
18	Farm income or (loss). Attach Schedule F	18	
19	Unemployment compensation	19	
20a	Social security benefits **20a** b Taxable amount	20b	
21	Other income. List type and amount	21	
22	Combine the amounts in the far right column for lines 7 through 21. This is your **total income** ▶	22	

Adjusted Gross Income

23	Educator expenses **23**	
24	Certain business expenses of reservists, performing artists, and fee-basis government officials. Attach Form 2106 or 2106-EZ **24**	
25	Health savings account deduction. Attach Form 8889 **25**	
26	Moving expenses. Attach Form 3903 **26**	
27	Deductible part of self-employment tax. Attach Schedule SE **27**	
28	Self-employed SEP, SIMPLE, and qualified plans **28**	
29	Self-employed health insurance deduction **29**	
30	Penalty on early withdrawal of savings **30**	
31a	Alimony paid b Recipient's SSN ▶ **31a**	
32	IRA deduction **32**	
33	Student loan interest deduction **33**	
34	Tuition and fees. Attach Form 8917 **34**	
35	Domestic production activities deduction. Attach Form 8903 **35**	
36	Add lines 23 through 35	36	
37	Subtract line 36 from line 22. This is your **adjusted gross income** ▶	37	

For Disclosure, Privacy Act, and Paperwork Reduction Act Notice, see separate instructions. Cat. No. 11320B Form **1040** (2013)

Form 1040 (2013)   Page **2**

Tax and Credits	38	Amount from line 37 (adjusted gross income)		38	
	39a	Check if: ☐ **You** were born before January 2, 1949, ☐ Blind. ☐ **Spouse** was born before January 2, 1949, ☐ Blind. } Total boxes checked ▶ 39a			
Standard Deduction for—	b	If your spouse itemizes on a separate return or you were a dual-status alien, check here▶ 39b☐			
• People who check any box on line 39a or 39b **or** who can be claimed as a dependent, see instructions.	40	**Itemized deductions** (from Schedule A) **or** your **standard deduction** (see left margin) . .		40	
	41	Subtract line 40 from line 38		41	
	42	**Exemptions.** If line 38 is $150,000 or less, multiply $3,900 by the number on line 6d. Otherwise, see instructions		42	
	43	**Taxable income.** Subtract line 42 from line 41. If line 42 is more than line 41, enter -0-		43	
• All others: Single or Married filing separately, $6,100	44	**Tax** (see instructions). Check if any from: **a** ☐ Form(s) 8814 **b** ☐ Form 4972 **c** ☐ _____		44	
	45	**Alternative minimum tax** (see instructions). Attach Form 6251		45	
Married filing jointly or Qualifying widow(er), $12,200	46	Add lines 44 and 45 . . . . ▶		46	
	47	Foreign tax credit. Attach Form 1116 if required	47		
	48	Credit for child and dependent care expenses. Attach Form 2441	48		
Head of household, $8,950	49	Education credits from Form 8863, line 19	49		
	50	Retirement savings contributions credit. Attach Form 8880	50		
	51	Child tax credit. Attach Schedule 8812, if required . . .	51		
	52	Residential energy credits. Attach Form 5695	52		
	53	Other credits from Form: **a** ☐ 3800 **b** ☐ 8801 **c** ☐ _____	53		
	54	Add lines 47 through 53. These are your **total credits**		54	
	55	Subtract line 54 from line 46. If line 54 is more than line 46, enter -0- . . . . . ▶		55	
Other Taxes	56	Self-employment tax. Attach Schedule SE		56	
	57	Unreported social security and Medicare tax from Form: **a** ☐ 4137 **b** ☐ 8919 . .		57	
	58	Additional tax on IRAs, other qualified retirement plans, etc. Attach Form 5329 if required . .		58	
	59a	Household employment taxes from Schedule H		59a	
	b	First-time homebuyer credit repayment. Attach Form 5405 if required		59b	
	60	Taxes from: **a** ☐ Form 8959 **b** ☐ Form 8960 **c** ☐ Instructions; enter code(s) _____		60	
	61	Add lines 55 through 60. This is your **total tax** . . . . ▶		61	
Payments	62	Federal income tax withheld from Forms W-2 and 1099 . .	62		
	63	2013 estimated tax payments and amount applied from 2012 return	63		
If you have a qualifying child, attach Schedule EIC.	64a	**Earned income credit (EIC)**	64a		
	b	Nontaxable combat pay election 64b _____			
	65	Additional child tax credit. Attach Schedule 8812 . . .	65		
	66	American opportunity credit from Form 8863, line 8 . . .	66		
	67	Reserved	67		
	68	Amount paid with request for extension to file	68		
	69	Excess social security and tier 1 RRTA tax withheld . . .	69		
	70	Credit for federal tax on fuels. Attach Form 4136 . . .	70		
	71	Credits from Form: **a** ☐ 2439 **b** ☐ Reserved **c** ☐ 8885 **d** ☐	71		
	72	Add lines 62, 63, 64a, and 65 through 71. These are your **total payments** . . . . . . ▶		72	
Refund	73	If line 72 is more than line 61, subtract line 61 from line 72. This is the amount you **overpaid**		73	
	74a	Amount of line 73 you want **refunded to you.** If Form 8888 is attached, check here . ▶ ☐		74a	
Direct deposit? ▶ See instructions.	b	Routing number _____ ▶ c Type: ☐ Checking ☐ Savings			
	d	Account number _____			
	75	Amount of line 73 you want **applied to your 2014 estimated tax** ▶ 75 _____			
Amount You Owe	76	**Amount you owe.** Subtract line 72 from line 61. For details on how to pay, see instructions ▶		76	
	77	Estimated tax penalty (see instructions) . . . . 77 _____			

Third Party Designee

Do you want to allow another person to discuss this return with the IRS (see instructions)? ☐ **Yes.** Complete below.   ☐ **No**

Designee's name ▶	Phone no. ▶	Personal identification number (PIN) ▶

Sign Here

Under penalties of perjury, I declare that I have examined this return and accompanying schedules and statements, and to the best of my knowledge and belief, they are true, correct, and complete. Declaration of preparer (other than taxpayer) is based on all information of which preparer has any knowledge.

Joint return? See instructions. Keep a copy for your records.

Your signature	Date	Your occupation	Daytime phone number
Spouse's signature. If a joint return, **both** must sign.	Date	Spouse's occupation	If the IRS sent you an Identity Protection PIN, enter it here (see inst.)

Paid Preparer Use Only

Print/Type preparer's name	Preparer's signature	Date	Check ☐ if self-employed	PTIN
Firm's name ▶			Firm's EIN ▶	
Firm's address ▶			Phone no.	

Form **1040** (2013)

SCHEDULE C
(Form 1040)

Department of the Treasury
Internal Revenue Service (99)

Profit or Loss From Business
(Sole Proprietorship)

▶ For information on Schedule C and its instructions, go to *www.irs.gov/schedulec.*
▶ Attach to Form 1040, 1040NR, or 1041; partnerships generally must file Form 1065.

OMB No. 1545-0074

2013

Attachment
Sequence No. **09**

Name of proprietor

Social security number (SSN)

A Principal business or profession, including product or service (see instructions)

B Enter code from instructions
▶

C Business name. If no separate business name, leave blank.

D Employer ID number (EIN), (see instr.)

E Business address (including suite or room no.) ▶
City, town or post office, state, and ZIP code

F Accounting method: **(1)** ☐ Cash   **(2)** ☐ Accrual   **(3)** ☐ Other (specify) ▶

G Did you "materially participate" in the operation of this business during 2013? If "No," see instructions for limit on losses   . ☐ Yes ☐ No

H If you started or acquired this business during 2013, check here   . . . . ▶ ☐

I Did you make any payments in 2013 that would require you to file Form(s) 1099? (see instructions)   . . . . ☐ Yes ☐ No

J If "Yes," did you or will you file required Forms 1099?   . . . . ☐ Yes ☐ No

Part I   Income

1	Gross receipts or sales. See instructions for line 1 and check the box if this income was reported to you on Form W-2 and the "Statutory employee" box on that form was checked . . . . . ▶ ☐	**1**	
2	Returns and allowances	**2**	
3	Subtract line 2 from line 1 . . .	**3**	
4	Cost of goods sold (from line 42) . . .	**4**	
5	**Gross profit.** Subtract line 4 from line 3 . .	**5**	
6	Other income, including federal and state gasoline or fuel tax credit or refund (see instructions) . . .	**6**	
7	**Gross income.** Add lines 5 and 6 . . . . ▶	**7**	

Part II   Expenses   Enter expenses for business use of your home only on line 30.

8	Advertising	**8**		**18**	Office expense (see instructions)	**18**
9	Car and truck expenses (see instructions)	**9**		**19**	Pension and profit-sharing plans .	**19**
10	Commissions and fees .	**10**		**20**	Rent or lease (see instructions):	
11	Contract labor (see instructions)	**11**		**a**	Vehicles, machinery, and equipment	**20a**
12	Depletion	**12**		**b**	Other business property . . .	**20b**
13	Depreciation and section 179 expense deduction (not included in Part III) (see instructions)	**13**		**21**	Repairs and maintenance . . .	**21**
				22	Supplies (not included in Part III) .	**22**
				23	Taxes and licenses	**23**
				24	Travel, meals, and entertainment:	
14	Employee benefit programs (other than on line 19) . .	**14**		**a**	Travel	**24a**
15	Insurance (other than health)	**15**		**b**	Deductible meals and entertainment (see instructions) .	**24b**
16	Interest:			**25**	Utilities	**25**
a	Mortgage (paid to banks, etc.)	**16a**		**26**	Wages (less employment credits) .	**26**
b	Other	**16b**		**27a**	Other expenses (from line 48) . .	**27a**
17	Legal and professional services	**17**		**b**	**Reserved for future use** . . .	**27b**

28	**Total expenses** before expenses for business use of home. Add lines 8 through 27a . . . . . ▶	**28**	
29	Tentative profit or (loss). Subtract line 28 from line 7	**29**	
30	Expenses for business use of your home. Do not report these expenses elsewhere. Attach Form 8829 unless using the simplified method (see instructions). **Simplified method filers only:** enter the total square footage of: (a) your home: _____ and (b) the part of your home used for business: _____ . Use the Simplified Method Worksheet in the instructions to figure the amount to enter on line 30	**30**	
31	**Net profit or (loss).** Subtract line 30 from line 29. • If a profit, enter on both **Form 1040, line 12** (or **Form 1040NR, line 13**) and on **Schedule SE, line 2.** (If you checked the box on line 1, see instructions). Estates and trusts, enter on **Form 1041, line 3.** • If a loss, you **must** go to line 32.	**31**	
32	If you have a loss, check the box that describes your investment in this activity (see instructions). • If you checked 32a, enter the loss on both **Form 1040, line 12,** (or **Form 1040NR, line 13**) and on **Schedule SE, line 2.** (If you checked the box on line 1, see the line 31 instructions). Estates and trusts, enter on **Form 1041, line 3.** • If you checked 32b, you **must** attach **Form 6198.** Your loss may be limited.	**32a** ☐ All investment is at risk. **32b** ☐ Some investment is not at risk.	

For Paperwork Reduction Act Notice, see the separate instructions.   Cat. No. 11334P   Schedule C (Form 1040) 2013

| Part III | Cost of Goods Sold (see instructions) |

33 Method(s) used to
value closing inventory: **a** ☐ Cost   **b** ☐ Lower of cost or market   **c** ☐ Other (attach explanation)

34 Was there any change in determining quantities, costs, or valuations between opening and closing inventory?
If "Yes," attach explanation . . . .   ☐ Yes   ☐ No

35 Inventory at beginning of year. If different from last year's closing inventory, attach explanation . . .	**35**	
36 Purchases less cost of items withdrawn for personal use	**36**	
37 Cost of labor. Do not include any amounts paid to yourself	**37**	
38 Materials and supplies	**38**	
39 Other costs	**39**	
40 Add lines 35 through 39	**40**	
41 Inventory at end of year	**41**	
42 **Cost of goods sold.** Subtract line 41 from line 40. Enter the result here and on line 4	**42**	

| Part IV | Information on Your Vehicle. Complete this part **only** if you are claiming car or truck expenses on line 9 and are not required to file Form 4562 for this business. See the instructions for line 13 to find out if you must file Form 4562. |

43 When did you place your vehicle in service for business purposes? (month, day, year)   ▶ _____ / _____ / _____

44 Of the total number of miles you drove your vehicle during 2013, enter the number of miles you used your vehicle for:

a Business _____   **b** Commuting (see instructions) _____   **c** Other _____

45 Was your vehicle available for personal use during off-duty hours? . . . .   ☐ Yes   ☐ No

46 Do you (or your spouse) have another vehicle available for personal use?. . . . .   ☐ Yes   ☐ No

47a Do you have evidence to support your deduction? . . . .   ☐ Yes   ☐ No

b If "Yes," is the evidence written? . . . .   ☐ Yes   ☐ No

| Part V | Other Expenses. List below business expenses not included on lines 8–26 or line 30. |

--------------------------		
48 **Total other expenses.** Enter here and on line 27a	**48**	

Capital Gains and Losses

SCHEDULE D
(Form 1040)

Department of the Treasury
Internal Revenue Service (99)

▶ Attach to Form 1040 or Form 1040NR.
▶ **Information about Schedule D and its separate instructions is at** *www.irs.gov/scheduled*.
▶ **Use Form 8949 to list your transactions for lines 1b, 2, 3, 8b, 9, and 10.**

OMB No. 1545-0074

20**13**

Attachment
Sequence No. **12**

Name(s) shown on return

Your social security number

Part I   Short-Term Capital Gains and Losses—Assets Held One Year or Less

See instructions for how to figure the amounts to enter on the lines below. This form may be easier to complete if you round off cents to whole dollars.	**(d)** Proceeds (sales price)	**(e)** Cost (or other basis)	**(g)** Adjustments to gain or loss from Form(s) 8949, Part I, line 2, column (g)	**(h) Gain or (loss)** Subtract column (e) from column (d) and combine the result with column (g)
1a Totals for all short-term transactions reported on Form 1099-B for which basis was reported to the IRS and for which you have no adjustments (see instructions). However, if you choose to report all these transactions on Form 8949, leave this line blank and go to line 1b .				
1b Totals for all transactions reported on Form(s) 8949 with **Box A** checked				
2 Totals for all transactions reported on Form(s) 8949 with **Box B** checked				
3 Totals for all transactions reported on Form(s) 8949 with **Box C** checked				

4 Short-term gain from Form 6252 and short-term gain or (loss) from Forms 4684, 6781, and 8824 .	**4**	
5 Net short-term gain or (loss) from partnerships, S corporations, estates, and trusts from Schedule(s) K-1	**5**	
6 Short-term capital loss carryover. Enter the amount, if any, from line 8 of your **Capital Loss Carryover Worksheet** in the instructions	**6**	( )
7 **Net short-term capital gain or (loss).** Combine lines 1a through 6 in column (h). If you have any long-term capital gains or losses, go to Part II below. Otherwise, go to Part III on the back	**7**	

Part II   Long-Term Capital Gains and Losses—Assets Held More Than One Year

See instructions for how to figure the amounts to enter on the lines below. This form may be easier to complete if you round off cents to whole dollars.	**(d)** Proceeds (sales price)	**(e)** Cost (or other basis)	**(g)** Adjustments to gain or loss from Form(s) 8949, Part II, line 2, column (g)	**(h) Gain or (loss)** Subtract column (e) from column (d) and combine the result with column (g)
8a Totals for all long-term transactions reported on Form 1099-B for which basis was reported to the IRS and for which you have no adjustments (see instructions). However, if you choose to report all these transactions on Form 8949, leave this line blank and go to line 8b .				
8b Totals for all transactions reported on Form(s) 8949 with **Box D** checked				
9 Totals for all transactions reported on Form(s) 8949 with **Box E** checked				
10 Totals for all transactions reported on Form(s) 8949 with **Box F** checked.				

11 Gain from Form 4797, Part I; long-term gain from Forms 2439 and 6252; and long-term gain or (loss) from Forms 4684, 6781, and 8824	**11**	
12 Net long-term gain or (loss) from partnerships, S corporations, estates, and trusts from Schedule(s) K-1	**12**	
13 Capital gain distributions. See the instructions	**13**	
14 Long-term capital loss carryover. Enter the amount, if any, from line 13 of your **Capital Loss Carryover Worksheet** in the instructions	**14**	( )
15 **Net long-term capital gain or (loss).** Combine lines 8a through 14 in column (h). Then go to Part III on the back	**15**	

For Paperwork Reduction Act Notice, see your tax return instructions.   Cat. No. 11338H   Schedule D (Form 1040) 2013

Part III   **Summary**

16   Combine lines 7 and 15 and enter the result **16**

          • If line 16 is a **gain,** enter the amount from line 16 on Form 1040, line 13, or Form 1040NR, line 14. Then go to line 17 below.
          • If line 16 is a **loss,** skip lines 17 through 20 below. Then go to line 21. Also be sure to complete line 22.
          • If line 16 is zero, skip lines 17 through 21 below and enter -0- on Form 1040, line 13, or Form 1040NR, line 14. Then go to line 22.

17   Are lines 15 and 16 **both** gains?
      ☐ **Yes.** Go to line 18.
      ☐ **No.** Skip lines 18 through 21, and go to line 22.

18   Enter the amount, if any, from line 7 of the **28% Rate Gain Worksheet** in the instructions . . ▶   **18**

19   Enter the amount, if any, from line 18 of the **Unrecaptured Section 1250 Gain Worksheet** in the instructions . . . . ▶   **19**

20   Are lines 18 and 19 **both** zero or blank?
      ☐ **Yes.** Complete the **Qualified Dividends and Capital Gain Tax Worksheet** in the instructions for Form 1040, line 44 (or in the instructions for Form 1040NR, line 42). **Do not** complete lines 21 and 22 below.

      ☐ **No.** Complete the **Schedule D Tax Worksheet** in the instructions. **Do not** complete lines 21 and 22 below.

21   If line 16 is a loss, enter here and on Form 1040, line 13, or Form 1040NR, line 14, the **smaller** of:

          • The loss on line 16 or ⎫
          • ($3,000), or if married filing separately, ($1,500) ⎬ . . . .   **21** (   )
                                    ⎭

    Note. When figuring which amount is smaller, treat both amounts as positive numbers.

22   Do you have qualified dividends on Form 1040, line 9b, or Form 1040NR, line 10b?

      ☐ **Yes.** Complete the **Qualified Dividends and Capital Gain Tax Worksheet** in the instructions for Form 1040, line 44 (or in the instructions for Form 1040NR, line 42).

      ☐ **No.** Complete the rest of Form 1040 or Form 1040NR.

Form **1065**

Department of the Treasury
Internal Revenue Service

U.S. Return of Partnership Income

For calendar year 2013, or tax year beginning _____ , 2013, ending _____ , 20 _____ .

▶ Information about Form 1065 and its separate instructions is at *www.irs.gov/form1065*.

OMB No. 1545-0099

2013

A Principal business activity	Name of partnership	**D** Employer identification number
B Principal product or service	**Type or Print** — Number, street, and room or suite no. If a P.O. box, see the instructions.	**E** Date business started
C Business code number	City or town, state or province, country, and ZIP or foreign postal code	**F** Total assets (see the instructions) $

G Check applicable boxes: **(1)** ☐ Initial return **(2)** ☐ Final return **(3)** ☐ Name change **(4)** ☐ Address change **(5)** ☐ Amended return
  (6) ☐ Technical termination - also check (1) or (2)

H Check accounting method: **(1)** ☐ Cash **(2)** ☐ Accrual **(3)** ☐ Other (specify) ▶ _____

I Number of Schedules K-1. Attach one for each person who was a partner at any time during the tax year ▶ _____

J Check if Schedules C and M-3 are attached . . . . ☐

Caution. *Include* **only** *trade or business income and expenses on lines 1a through 22 below. See the instructions for more information.*

Income

1a	Gross receipts or sales	**1a**	
b	Returns and allowances	**1b**	
c	Balance. Subtract line 1b from line 1a	**1c**	
2	Cost of goods sold (attach Form 1125-A)	**2**	
3	Gross profit. Subtract line 2 from line 1c	**3**	
4	Ordinary income (loss) from other partnerships, estates, and trusts (attach statement) . .	**4**	
5	Net farm profit (loss) (attach Schedule F (Form 1040))	**5**	
6	Net gain (loss) from Form 4797, Part II, line 17 (attach Form 4797)	**6**	
7	Other income (loss) (attach statement)	**7**	
8	**Total income (loss).** Combine lines 3 through 7	**8**	

Deductions (see the instructions for limitations)

9	Salaries and wages (other than to partners) (less employment credits)	**9**	
10	Guaranteed payments to partners	**10**	
11	Repairs and maintenance	**11**	
12	Bad debts	**12**	
13	Rent	**13**	
14	Taxes and licenses	**14**	
15	Interest	**15**	
16a	Depreciation (if required, attach Form 4562)	**16a**	
b	Less depreciation reported on Form 1125-A and elsewhere on return	**16b**	**16c**
17	Depletion **(Do not deduct oil and gas depletion.)**	**17**	
18	Retirement plans, etc.	**18**	
19	Employee benefit programs	**19**	
20	Other deductions (attach statement)	**20**	
21	**Total deductions.** Add the amounts shown in the far right column for lines 9 through 20 .	**21**	
22	**Ordinary business income (loss).** Subtract line 21 from line 8	**22**	

Sign Here

Under penalties of perjury, I declare that I have examined this return, including accompanying schedules and statements, and to the best of my knowledge and belief, it is true, correct, and complete. Declaration of preparer (other than general partner or limited liability company member manager) is based on all information of which preparer has any knowledge.

May the IRS discuss this return with the preparer shown below (see instructions)? ☐ **Yes** ☐ **No**

▶ _____   ▶ _____
Signature of general partner or limited liability company member manager   Date

Paid Preparer Use Only

Print/Type preparer's name	Preparer's signature	Date	Check ☐ if self-employed	PTIN
Firm's name ▶			Firm's EIN ▶	
Firm's address ▶			Phone no.	

For Paperwork Reduction Act Notice, see separate instructions.   Cat. No. 11390Z   Form **1065** (2013)

Form 1065 (2013)   Page **2**

Schedule B	**Other Information**		Yes	No

1 What type of entity is filing this return? Check the applicable box:

a ☐ Domestic general partnership   **b** ☐ Domestic limited partnership

c ☐ Domestic limited liability company   **d** ☐ Domestic limited liability partnership

e ☐ Foreign partnership   **f** ☐ Other ▶

2 At any time during the tax year, was any partner in the partnership a disregarded entity, a partnership (including an entity treated as a partnership), a trust, an S corporation, an estate (other than an estate of a deceased partner), or a nominee or similar person? . . . .

3 At the end of the tax year:

a Did any foreign or domestic corporation, partnership (including any entity treated as a partnership), trust, or tax-exempt organization, or any foreign government own, directly or indirectly, an interest of 50% or more in the profit, loss, or capital of the partnership? For rules of constructive ownership, see instructions. If "Yes," attach Schedule B-1, Information on Partners Owning 50% or More of the Partnership . . . .

b Did any individual or estate own, directly or indirectly, an interest of 50% or more in the profit, loss, or capital of the partnership? For rules of constructive ownership, see instructions. If "Yes," attach Schedule B-1, Information on Partners Owning 50% or More of the Partnership . . . .

4 At the end of the tax year, did the partnership:

a Own directly 20% or more, or own, directly or indirectly, 50% or more of the total voting power of all classes of stock entitled to vote of any foreign or domestic corporation? For rules of constructive ownership, see instructions. If "Yes," complete (i) through (iv) below . . . .

(i) Name of Corporation	**(ii)** Employer Identification Number (if any)	**(iii)** Country of Incorporation	**(iv)** Percentage Owned in Voting Stock

b Own directly an interest of 20% or more, or own, directly or indirectly, an interest of 50% or more in the profit, loss, or capital in any foreign or domestic partnership (including an entity treated as a partnership) or in the beneficial interest of a trust? For rules of constructive ownership, see instructions. If "Yes," complete (i) through (v) below . .

(i) Name of Entity	**(ii)** Employer Identification Number (if any)	**(iii)** Type of Entity	**(iv)** Country of Organization	**(v)** Maximum Percentage Owned in Profit, Loss, or Capital

		Yes	No

5 Did the partnership file Form 8893, Election of Partnership Level Tax Treatment, or an election statement under section 6231(a)(1)(B)(ii) for partnership-level tax treatment, that is in effect for this tax year? See Form 8893 for more details . . . .

6 Does the partnership satisfy **all four** of the following conditions?

a The partnership's total receipts for the tax year were less than $250,000.

b The partnership's total assets at the end of the tax year were less than $1 million.

c Schedules K-1 are filed with the return and furnished to the partners on or before the due date (including extensions) for the partnership return.

d The partnership is not filing and is not required to file Schedule M-3 . . . .
If "Yes," the partnership is not required to complete Schedules L, M-1, and M-2; Item F on page 1 of Form 1065; or Item L on Schedule K-1.

7 Is this partnership a publicly traded partnership as defined in section 469(k)(2)? . . . .

8 During the tax year, did the partnership have any debt that was cancelled, was forgiven, or had the terms modified so as to reduce the principal amount of the debt? . . . .

9 Has this partnership filed, or is it required to file, Form 8918, Material Advisor Disclosure Statement, to provide information on any reportable transaction? . . . .

10 At any time during calendar year 2013, did the partnership have an interest in or a signature or other authority over a financial account in a foreign country (such as a bank account, securities account, or other financial account)? See the instructions for exceptions and filing requirements for FinCEN Form 114, Report of Foreign Bank and Financial Accounts (FBAR) (formerly TD F 90-22.1). If "Yes," enter the name of the foreign country. ▶

Form **1065** (2013)

Form 1065 (2013)   Page **3**

Schedule B	**Other Information** *(continued)*		

		Yes	No
11	At any time during the tax year, did the partnership receive a distribution from, or was it the grantor of, or transferor to, a foreign trust? If "Yes," the partnership may have to file Form 3520, Annual Return To Report Transactions With Foreign Trusts and Receipt of Certain Foreign Gifts. See instructions		
12a	Is the partnership making, or had it previously made (and not revoked), a section 754 election? . . . . . . See instructions for details regarding a section 754 election.		
b	Did the partnership make for this tax year an optional basis adjustment under section 743(b) or 734(b)? If "Yes," attach a statement showing the computation and allocation of the basis adjustment. See instructions		
c	Is the partnership required to adjust the basis of partnership assets under section 743(b) or 734(b) because of a substantial built-in loss (as defined under section 743(d)) or substantial basis reduction (as defined under section 734(d))? If "Yes," attach a statement showing the computation and allocation of the basis adjustment. See instructions		
13	Check this box if, during the current or prior tax year, the partnership distributed any property received in a like-kind exchange or contributed such property to another entity (other than disregarded entities wholly-owned by the partnership throughout the tax year) . . . . ▶ ☐		
14	At any time during the tax year, did the partnership distribute to any partner a tenancy-in-common or other undivided interest in partnership property?		
15	If the partnership is required to file Form 8858, Information Return of U.S. Persons With Respect To Foreign Disregarded Entities, enter the number of Forms 8858 attached. See instructions ▶		
16	Does the partnership have any foreign partners? If "Yes," enter the number of Forms 8805, Foreign Partner's Information Statement of Section 1446 Withholding Tax, filed for this partnership. ▶		
17	Enter the number of Forms 8865, Return of U.S. Persons With Respect to Certain Foreign Partnerships, attached to this return. ▶		
18a	Did you make any payments in 2013 that would require you to file Form(s) 1099? See instructions		
b	If "Yes," did you or will you file required Form(s) 1099?		
19	Enter the number of Form(s) 5471, Information Return of U.S. Persons With Respect To Certain Foreign Corporations, attached to this return. ▶		
20	Enter the number of partners that are foreign governments under section 892. ▶		

Designation of Tax Matters Partner (see instructions)

Enter below the general partner or member-manager designated as the tax matters partner (TMP) for the tax year of this return:

Name of designated TMP ▶		Identifying number of TMP ▶	
If the TMP is an entity, name of TMP representative ▶		Phone number of TMP ▶	
Address of designated TMP ▶			

Form **1065** (2013)

Form 1065 (2013)   Page **4**

Schedule K	Partners' Distributive Share Items		Total amount
Income (Loss)	**1** Ordinary business income (loss) (page 1, line 22)	**1**	
	2 Net rental real estate income (loss) (attach Form 8825)	**2**	
	3a Other gross rental income (loss) **3a**		
	b Expenses from other rental activities (attach statement) **3b**		
	c Other net rental income (loss). Subtract line 3b from line 3a	**3c**	
	4 Guaranteed payments	**4**	
	5 Interest income	**5**	
	6 Dividends: **a** Ordinary dividends	**6a**	
	b Qualified dividends **6b**		
	7 Royalties	**7**	
	8 Net short-term capital gain (loss) (attach Schedule D (Form 1065))	**8**	
	9a Net long-term capital gain (loss) (attach Schedule D (Form 1065))	**9a**	
	b Collectibles (28%) gain (loss) **9b**		
	c Unrecaptured section 1250 gain (attach statement) . . **9c**		
	10 Net section 1231 gain (loss) (attach Form 4797)	**10**	
	11 Other income (loss) (see instructions) Type ▶	**11**	
Deductions	**12** Section 179 deduction (attach Form 4562)	**12**	
	13a Contributions	**13a**	
	b Investment interest expense	**13b**	
	c Section 59(e)(2) expenditures: **(1)** Type ▶ _____ **(2)** Amount ▶	**13c(2)**	
	d Other deductions (see instructions) Type ▶	**13d**	
Self-Employment	**14a** Net earnings (loss) from self-employment	**14a**	
	b Gross farming or fishing income	**14b**	
	c Gross nonfarm income	**14c**	
Credits	**15a** Low-income housing credit (section 42(j)(5))	**15a**	
	b Low-income housing credit (other)	**15b**	
	c Qualified rehabilitation expenditures (rental real estate) (attach Form 3468)	**15c**	
	d Other rental real estate credits (see instructions) Type ▶ _____	**15d**	
	e Other rental credits (see instructions) Type ▶ _____	**15e**	
	f Other credits (see instructions) Type ▶ _____	**15f**	
Foreign Transactions	**16a** Name of country or U.S. possession ▶ _____		
	b Gross income from all sources	**16b**	
	c Gross income sourced at partner level	**16c**	
	Foreign gross income sourced at partnership level		
	d Passive category ▶ _____ **e** General category ▶ _____ **f** Other ▶	**16f**	
	Deductions allocated and apportioned at partner level		
	g Interest expense ▶ _____ **h** Other . . . . ▶	**16h**	
	Deductions allocated and apportioned at partnership level to foreign source income		
	i Passive category ▶ _____ **j** General category ▶ _____ **k** Other ▶	**16k**	
	l Total foreign taxes (check one): ▶ Paid ☐ Accrued ☐	**16l**	
	m Reduction in taxes available for credit (attach statement)	**16m**	
	n Other foreign tax information (attach statement)		
Alternative Minimum Tax (AMT) Items	**17a** Post-1986 depreciation adjustment	**17a**	
	b Adjusted gain or loss	**17b**	
	c Depletion (other than oil and gas)	**17c**	
	d Oil, gas, and geothermal properties—gross income	**17d**	
	e Oil, gas, and geothermal properties—deductions	**17e**	
	f Other AMT items (attach statement)	**17f**	
Other Information	**18a** Tax-exempt interest income	**18a**	
	b Other tax-exempt income	**18b**	
	c Nondeductible expenses	**18c**	
	19a Distributions of cash and marketable securities	**19a**	
	b Distributions of other property	**19b**	
	20a Investment income	**20a**	
	b Investment expenses	**20b**	
	c Other items and amounts (attach statement)		

Form **1065** (2013)

Form 1065 (2013)   Page **5**

Analysis of Net Income (Loss)

1	Net income (loss). Combine Schedule K, lines 1 through 11. From the result, subtract the sum of Schedule K, lines 12 through 13d, and 16l					**1**	

2	Analysis by partner type:	**(i)** Corporate	**(ii)** Individual (active)	**(iii)** Individual (passive)	**(iv)** Partnership	**(v)** Exempt Organization	**(vi)** Nominee/Other
a	General partners						
b	Limited partners						

Schedule L   Balance Sheets per Books

	Assets	Beginning of tax year		End of tax year	
		(a)	**(b)**	**(c)**	**(d)**
1	Cash				
2a	Trade notes and accounts receivable . . .				
b	Less allowance for bad debts				
3	Inventories				
4	U.S. government obligations				
5	Tax-exempt securities				
6	Other current assets (attach statement) . .				
7a	Loans to partners (or persons related to partners)				
b	Mortgage and real estate loans . . .				
8	Other investments (attach statement) . . .				
9a	Buildings and other depreciable assets . .				
b	Less accumulated depreciation				
10a	Depletable assets				
b	Less accumulated depletion				
11	Land (net of any amortization)				
12a	Intangible assets (amortizable only) . . .				
b	Less accumulated amortization				
13	Other assets (attach statement)				
14	Total assets				
	Liabilities and Capital				
15	Accounts payable				
16	Mortgages, notes, bonds payable in less than 1 year				
17	Other current liabilities (attach statement) .				
18	All nonrecourse loans				
19a	Loans from partners (or persons related to partners)				
b	Mortgages, notes, bonds payable in 1 year or more				
20	Other liabilities (attach statement)				
21	Partners' capital accounts				
22	Total liabilities and capital				

Schedule M-1   Reconciliation of Income (Loss) per Books With Income (Loss) per Return
Note. Schedule M-3 may be required instead of Schedule M-1 (see instructions).

1	Net income (loss) per books		**6**	Income recorded on books this year not included on Schedule K, lines 1 through 11 (itemize):	
2	Income included on Schedule K, lines 1, 2, 3c, 5, 6a, 7, 8, 9a, 10, and 11, not recorded on books this year (itemize): _____		**a**	Tax-exempt interest $ _____	
3	Guaranteed payments (other than health insurance)		**7**	Deductions included on Schedule K, lines 1 through 13d, and 16l, not charged against book income this year (itemize):	
4	Expenses recorded on books this year not included on Schedule K, lines 1 through 13d, and 16l (itemize):		**a**	Depreciation $ _____	
a	Depreciation $ _____		**8**	Add lines 6 and 7	
b	Travel and entertainment $ _____		**9**	Income (loss) (Analysis of Net Income (Loss), line 1). Subtract line 8 from line 5 .	
5	Add lines 1 through 4				

Schedule M-2   Analysis of Partners' Capital Accounts

1	Balance at beginning of year . . .		**6**	Distributions: **a** Cash	
2	Capital contributed: **a** Cash . . .			**b** Property	
	b Property . .		**7**	Other decreases (itemize): _____	
3	Net income (loss) per books				
4	Other increases (itemize): _____		**8**	Add lines 6 and 7	
5	Add lines 1 through 4		**9**	Balance at end of year. Subtract line 8 from line 5	

651113

☐ Final K-1   ☐ Amended K-1   OMB No. 1545-0099

Schedule K-1
(Form 1065)

2013

Department of the Treasury
Internal Revenue Service

For calendar year 2013, or tax
year beginning _____, 2013
ending _____, 20 _____

Partner's Share of Income, Deductions,
Credits, etc.   ▶ See back of form and separate instructions.

Part I	**Information About the Partnership**

A   Partnership's employer identification number

B   Partnership's name, address, city, state, and ZIP code

C   IRS Center where partnership filed return

D   ☐ Check if this is a publicly traded partnership (PTP)

Part II	**Information About the Partner**

E   Partner's identifying number

F   Partner's name, address, city, state, and ZIP code

G   ☐ General partner or LLC member-manager   ☐ Limited partner or other LLC member

H   ☐ Domestic partner   ☐ Foreign partner

I1   What type of entity is this partner? _____

I2   If this partner is a retirement plan (IRA/SEP/Keogh/etc.), check here (see instructions) . . . . ☐

J   Partner's share of profit, loss, and capital (see instructions):

	Beginning	Ending
Profit	%	%
Loss	%	%
Capital	%	%

K   Partner's share of liabilities at year end:

Nonrecourse . . . . . . $ _____
Qualified nonrecourse financing . $ _____
Recourse . . . . . . $ _____

L   Partner's capital account analysis:

Beginning capital account . . . $ _____
Capital contributed during the year $ _____
Current year increase (decrease) . $ _____
Withdrawals & distributions . . $ (_____)
Ending capital account . . . . $ _____

☐ Tax basis   ☐ GAAP   ☐ Section 704(b) book
☐ Other (explain)

M   Did the partner contribute property with a built-in gain or loss?
☐ Yes   ☐ No
If "Yes," attach statement (see instructions)

Part III	**Partner's Share of Current Year Income, Deductions, Credits, and Other Items**

1	Ordinary business income (loss)	15	Credits
2	Net rental real estate income (loss)		
3	Other net rental income (loss)	16	Foreign transactions
4	Guaranteed payments		
5	Interest income		
6a	Ordinary dividends		
6b	Qualified dividends		
7	Royalties		
8	Net short-term capital gain (loss)		
9a	Net long-term capital gain (loss)	17	Alternative minimum tax (AMT) items
9b	Collectibles (28%) gain (loss)		
9c	Unrecaptured section 1250 gain		
10	Net section 1231 gain (loss)	18	Tax-exempt income and nondeductible expenses
11	Other income (loss)		
		19	Distributions
12	Section 179 deduction		
13	Other deductions	20	Other information
14	Self-employment earnings (loss)		

*See attached statement for additional information.

For IRS Use Only

Form **1120**
Department of the Treasury
Internal Revenue Service

U.S. Corporation Income Tax Return

For calendar year 2013 or tax year beginning _____ , 2013, ending _____ , 20 _____

▶ Information about Form 1120 and its separate instructions is at *www.irs.gov/form1120*.

OMB No. 1545-0123

2013

A Check if:
1a Consolidated return (attach Form 851) ☐
 b Life/nonlife consolidated return . ☐
2 Personal holding co. (attach Sch. PH) . ☐
3 Personal service corp. (see instructions) . ☐
4 Schedule M-3 attached ☐

TYPE OR PRINT

Name

Number, street, and room or suite no. If a P.O. box, see instructions.

City or town, state, or province, country and ZIP or foreign postal code

B Employer identification number

C Date incorporated

D Total assets (see instructions)
$

E Check if: **(1)** ☐ Initial return **(2)** ☐ Final return **(3)** ☐ Name change **(4)** ☐ Address change

Income

1a	Gross receipts or sales	1a	
b	Returns and allowances	1b	
c	Balance. Subtract line 1b from line 1a	1c	
2	Cost of goods sold (attach Form 1125-A)	2	
3	Gross profit. Subtract line 2 from line 1c	3	
4	Dividends (Schedule C, line 19)	4	
5	Interest	5	
6	Gross rents	6	
7	Gross royalties	7	
8	Capital gain net income (attach Schedule D (Form 1120))	8	
9	Net gain or (loss) from Form 4797, Part II, line 17 (attach Form 4797)	9	
10	Other income (see instructions—attach statement)	10	
11	**Total income.** Add lines 3 through 10 . . . . ▶	11	

Deductions (See instructions for limitations on deductions.)

12	Compensation of officers (see instructions—attach Form 1125-E) . . . . . . ▶	12	
13	Salaries and wages (less employment credits)	13	
14	Repairs and maintenance	14	
15	Bad debts	15	
16	Rents	16	
17	Taxes and licenses	17	
18	Interest	18	
19	Charitable contributions	19	
20	Depreciation from Form 4562 not claimed on Form 1125-A or elsewhere on return (attach Form 4562) . .	20	
21	Depletion	21	
22	Advertising	22	
23	Pension, profit-sharing, etc., plans	23	
24	Employee benefit programs	24	
25	Domestic production activities deduction (attach Form 8903)	25	
26	Other deductions (attach statement)	26	
27	**Total deductions.** Add lines 12 through 26 . . . . ▶	27	
28	Taxable income before net operating loss deduction and special deductions. Subtract line 27 from line 11.	28	
29a	Net operating loss deduction (see instructions)	29a	
b	Special deductions (Schedule C, line 20)	29b	
c	Add lines 29a and 29b	29c	

Tax, Refundable Credits, and Payments

30	**Taxable income.** Subtract line 29c from line 28 (see instructions)	30	
31	Total tax (Schedule J, Part I, line 11)	31	
32	Total payments and refundable credits (Schedule J, Part II, line 21)	32	
33	Estimated tax penalty (see instructions). Check if Form 2220 is attached . . . . . . ▶ ☐	33	
34	**Amount owed.** If line 32 is smaller than the total of lines 31 and 33, enter amount owed	34	
35	**Overpayment.** If line 32 is larger than the total of lines 31 and 33, enter amount overpaid	35	
36	Enter amount from line 35 you want: **Credited to 2014 estimated tax** ▶ Refunded ▶	36	

Sign Here

Under penalties of perjury, I declare that I have examined this return, including accompanying schedules and statements, and to the best of my knowledge and belief, it is true, correct, and complete. Declaration of preparer (other than taxpayer) is based on all information of which preparer has any knowledge.

▶ _____   ▶ _____
Signature of officer   Date   Title

May the IRS discuss this return with the preparer shown below (see instructions)? ☐ Yes ☐ No

Paid Preparer Use Only

Print/Type preparer's name	Preparer's signature	Date	Check ☐ if self-employed	PTIN

Firm's name ▶   Firm's EIN ▶
Firm's address ▶   Phone no.

For Paperwork Reduction Act Notice, see separate instructions.   Cat. No. 11450Q   Form **1120** (2013)

Form 1120 (2013)   Page **2**

Schedule C	Dividends and Special Deductions (see instructions)	(a) Dividends received	(b) %	(c) Special deductions (a) × (b)
1	Dividends from less-than-20%-owned domestic corporations (other than debt-financed stock)		70	
2	Dividends from 20%-or-more-owned domestic corporations (other than debt-financed stock)		80	
3	Dividends on debt-financed stock of domestic and foreign corporations		see instructions	
4	Dividends on certain preferred stock of less-than-20%-owned public utilities . . .		42	
5	Dividends on certain preferred stock of 20%-or-more-owned public utilities		48	
6	Dividends from less-than-20%-owned foreign corporations and certain FSCs . . .		70	
7	Dividends from 20%-or-more-owned foreign corporations and certain FSCs . . .		80	
8	Dividends from wholly owned foreign subsidiaries		100	
9	**Total.** Add lines 1 through 8. See instructions for limitation			
10	Dividends from domestic corporations received by a small business investment company operating under the Small Business Investment Act of 1958		100	
11	Dividends from affiliated group members		100	
12	Dividends from certain FSCs		100	
13	Dividends from foreign corporations not included on lines 3, 6, 7, 8, 11, or 12 . . .			
14	Income from controlled foreign corporations under subpart F (attach Form(s) 5471) .			
15	Foreign dividend gross-up			
16	IC-DISC and former DISC dividends not included on lines 1, 2, or 3			
17	Other dividends			
18	Deduction for dividends paid on certain preferred stock of public utilities			
19	**Total dividends.** Add lines 1 through 17. Enter here and on page 1, line 4 . . . ▶			
20	**Total special deductions.** Add lines 9, 10, 11, 12, and 18. Enter here and on page 1, line 29b . . . . ▶			

Form **1120** (2013)

Form 1120 (2013) Page **3**

| **Schedule J** | **Tax Computation and Payment** (see instructions) | | | | |

Part I—Tax Computation

1	Check if the corporation is a member of a controlled group (attach Schedule O (Form 1120)) . . . . . ▶ ☐				
2	Income tax. Check if a qualified personal service corporation (see instructions) . . . . ▶ ☐		2		
3	Alternative minimum tax (attach Form 4626)		3		
4	Add lines 2 and 3		4		
5a	Foreign tax credit (attach Form 1118)	5a				
b	Credit from Form 8834 (see instructions)	5b				
c	General business credit (attach Form 3800)	5c				
d	Credit for prior year minimum tax (attach Form 8827)	5d				
e	Bond credits from Form 8912	5e				
6	**Total credits.** Add lines 5a through 5e		6		
7	Subtract line 6 from line 4		7		
8	Personal holding company tax (attach Schedule PH (Form 1120))		8		
9a	Recapture of investment credit (attach Form 4255)	9a				
b	Recapture of low-income housing credit (attach Form 8611)	9b				
c	Interest due under the look-back method—completed long-term contracts (attach Form 8697)	9c				
d	Interest due under the look-back method—Income forecast method (attach Form 8866)	9d				
e	Alternative tax on qualifying shipping activities (attach Form 8902)	9e				
f	Other (see instructions—attach statement)	9f				
10	**Total.** Add lines 9a through 9f		10		
11	**Total tax.** Add lines 7, 8, and 10. Enter here and on page 1, line 31		11		

Part II—Payments and Refundable Credits

12	2012 overpayment credited to 2013		12		
13	2013 estimated tax payments		13		
14	2013 refund applied for on Form 4466		14 (		)
15	Combine lines 12, 13, and 14		15		
16	Tax deposited with Form 7004		16		
17	Withholding (see Instructions)		17		
18	**Total payments.** Add lines 15, 16, and 17		18		
19	Refundable credits from:				
a	Form 2439	19a				
b	Form 4136	19b				
c	Form 8827, line 8c	19c				
d	Other (attach statement—see instructions). . . .	19d				
20	**Total credits.** Add lines 19a through 19d		20		
21	**Total payments and credits.** Add lines 18 and 20. Enter here and on page 1, line 32		21		

| **Schedule K** | **Other Information** (see instructions) | | | Yes | No |

1	Check accounting method: **a** ☐ Cash **b** ☐ Accrual **c** ☐ Other (specify) ▶ _____			
2	See the instructions and enter the:			
a	Business activity code no. ▶ _____			
b	Business activity ▶ _____			
c	Product or service ▶ _____			
3	Is the corporation a subsidiary in an affiliated group or a parent-subsidiary controlled group? . . . . If "Yes," enter name and EIN of the parent corporation ▶ _____			
4	At the end of the tax year:			
a	Did any foreign or domestic corporation, partnership (including any entity treated as a partnership), trust, or tax-exempt organization own directly 20% or more, or own, directly or indirectly, 50% or more of the total voting power of all classes of the corporation's stock entitled to vote? If "Yes," complete Part I of Schedule G (Form 1120) (attach Schedule G)			
b	Did any individual or estate own directly 20% or more, or own, directly or indirectly, 50% or more of the total voting power of all classes of the corporation's stock entitled to vote? If "Yes," complete Part II of Schedule G (Form 1120) (attach Schedule G) .			

Form **1120** (2013)

Form 1120 (2013)   Page **4**

Schedule K	**Other Information** *continued* (see instructions)		Yes	No

5 At the end of the tax year, did the corporation:

a Own directly 20% or more, or own, directly or indirectly, 50% or more of the total voting power of all classes of stock entitled to vote of any foreign or domestic corporation not included on **Form 851,** Affiliations Schedule? For rules of constructive ownership, see instructions. If "Yes," complete (i) through (iv) below.

(i) Name of Corporation	**(ii)** Employer Identification Number (if any)	**(iii)** Country of Incorporation	**(iv)** Percentage Owned in Voting Stock

b Own directly an interest of 20% or more, or own, directly or indirectly, an interest of 50% or more in any foreign or domestic partnership (including an entity treated as a partnership) or in the beneficial interest of a trust? For rules of constructive ownership, see instructions. If "Yes," complete (i) through (iv) below.

(i) Name of Entity	**(ii)** Employer Identification Number (if any)	**(iii)** Country of Organization	**(iv)** Maximum Percentage Owned in Profit, Loss, or Capital

6 During this tax year, did the corporation pay dividends (other than stock dividends and distributions in exchange for stock) in excess of the corporation's current and accumulated earnings and profits? (See sections 301 and 316.) . . . .

If "Yes," file **Form 5452,** Corporate Report of Nondividend Distributions.

If this is a consolidated return, answer here for the parent corporation and on Form 851 for each subsidiary.

7 At any time during the tax year, did one foreign person own, directly or indirectly, at least 25% of **(a)** the total voting power of all classes of the corporation's stock entitled to vote or **(b)** the total value of all classes of the corporation's stock? . . . .

For rules of attribution, see section 318. If "Yes," enter:

(i) Percentage owned ▶ _____ and **(ii)** Owner's country ▶ _____

(c) The corporation may have to file **Form 5472,** Information Return of a 25% Foreign-Owned U.S. Corporation or a Foreign Corporation Engaged in a U.S. Trade or Business. Enter the number of Forms 5472 attached ▶ _____

8 Check this box if the corporation issued publicly offered debt instruments with original issue discount . . . . . . ▶ ☐

If checked, the corporation may have to file **Form 8281,** Information Return for Publicly Offered Original Issue Discount Instruments.

9 Enter the amount of tax-exempt interest received or accrued during the tax year ▶ $ _____

10 Enter the number of shareholders at the end of the tax year (if 100 or fewer) ▶ _____

11 If the corporation has an NOL for the tax year and is electing to forego the carryback period, check here . . . . . ▶ ☐

If the corporation is filing a consolidated return, the statement required by Regulations section 1.1502-21(b)(3) must be attached or the election will not be valid.

12 Enter the available NOL carryover from prior tax years (do not reduce it by any deduction on line 29a.) ▶ $ _____

13 Are the corporation's total receipts (page 1, line 1a, plus lines 4 through 10) for the tax year **and** its total assets at the end of the tax year less than $250,000? . . . .

If "Yes," the corporation is not required to complete Schedules L, M-1, and M-2. Instead, enter the total amount of cash distributions and the book value of property distributions (other than cash) made during the tax year ▶ $ _____

14 Is the corporation required to file Schedule UTP (Form 1120), Uncertain Tax Position Statement (see instructions)? . . . .

If "Yes," complete and attach Schedule UTP.

15a Did the corporation make any payments in 2013 that would require it to file Form(s) 1099? . . . .

b If "Yes," did or will the corporation file required Forms 1099? . . . .

16 During this tax year, did the corporation have an 80% or more change in ownership, including a change due to redemption of its own stock? . . . .

17 During or subsequent to this tax year, but before the filing of this return, did the corporation dispose of more than 65% (by value) of its assets in a taxable, non-taxable, or tax deferred transaction? . . . .

18 Did the corporation receive assets in a section 351 transfer in which any of the transferred assets had a fair market basis or fair market value of more than $1 million? . . . .

Form **1120** (2013)

Form 1120 (2013)   Page **5**

Schedule L   Balance Sheets per Books

	Assets	Beginning of tax year		End of tax year	
		(a)	(b)	(c)	(d)
1	Cash				
2a	Trade notes and accounts receivable				
b	Less allowance for bad debts	( )		( )	
3	Inventories				
4	U.S. government obligations				
5	Tax-exempt securities (see instructions)				
6	Other current assets (attach statement)				
7	Loans to shareholders				
8	Mortgage and real estate loans				
9	Other investments (attach statement)				
10a	Buildings and other depreciable assets				
b	Less accumulated depreciation	( )		( )	
11a	Depletable assets				
b	Less accumulated depletion	( )		( )	
12	Land (net of any amortization)				
13a	Intangible assets (amortizable only)				
b	Less accumulated amortization	( )		( )	
14	Other assets (attach statement)				
15	Total assets				
	Liabilities and Shareholders' Equity				
16	Accounts payable				
17	Mortgages, notes, bonds payable in less than 1 year				
18	Other current liabilities (attach statement)				
19	Loans from shareholders				
20	Mortgages, notes, bonds payable in 1 year or more				
21	Other liabilities (attach statement)				
22	Capital stock: a Preferred stock				
	b Common stock				
23	Additional paid-in capital				
24	Retained earnings—Appropriated (attach statement)				
25	Retained earnings—Unappropriated				
26	Adjustments to shareholders' equity (attach statement)				
27	Less cost of treasury stock		( )		( )
28	Total liabilities and shareholders' equity				

Schedule M-1   Reconciliation of Income (Loss) per Books With Income per Return

Note: Schedule M-3 required instead of Schedule M-1 if total assets are $10 million or more—see instructions

1	Net income (loss) per books		7	Income recorded on books this year not included on this return (itemize):	
2	Federal income tax per books				
3	Excess of capital losses over capital gains			Tax-exempt interest $ _____	
4	Income subject to tax not recorded on books this year (itemize): _____				
			8	Deductions on this return not charged against book income this year (itemize):	
5	Expenses recorded on books this year not deducted on this return (itemize):		a	Depreciation . . $ _____	
a	Depreciation . . . . $ _____		b	Charitable contributions $ _____	
b	Charitable contributions . $ _____				
c	Travel and entertainment . $ _____		9	Add lines 7 and 8	
6	Add lines 1 through 5		10	Income (page 1, line 28)—line 6 less line 9	

Schedule M-2   Analysis of Unappropriated Retained Earnings per Books (Line 25, Schedule L)

1	Balance at beginning of year		5	Distributions: a Cash	
2	Net income (loss) per books			b Stock	
3	Other increases (itemize): _____			c Property	
			6	Other decreases (itemize): _____	
			7	Add lines 5 and 6	
4	Add lines 1, 2, and 3		8	Balance at end of year (line 4 less line 7)	

Form **1120** (2013)

SCHEDULE M-3 (Form 1120)	Net Income (Loss) Reconciliation for Corporations With Total Assets of $10 Million or More	OMB No. 1545-0123
Department of the Treasury Internal Revenue Service	▶ Attach to Form 1120 or 1120-C. ▶ Information about Schedule M-3 (Form 1120) and its separate instructions is available at *www.irs.gov/form1120.*	2013

Name of corporation (common parent, if consolidated return)	Employer identification number

Check applicable box(es): (1) ☐ Non-consolidated return (2) ☐ Consolidated return (Form 1120 only)

(3) ☐ Mixed 1120/L/PC group (4) ☐ Dormant subsidiaries schedule attached

Part I **Financial Information and Net Income (Loss) Reconciliation** (see instructions)

1a Did the corporation file SEC Form 10-K for its income statement period ending with or within this tax year?
   ☐ **Yes.** Skip lines 1b and 1c and complete lines 2a through 11 with respect to that SEC Form 10-K.
   ☐ **No.** Go to line 1b. See instructions if multiple non-tax-basis income statements are prepared.
 b Did the corporation prepare a certified audited non-tax-basis income statement for that period?
   ☐ **Yes.** Skip line 1c and complete lines 2a through 11 with respect to that income statement.
   ☐ **No.** Go to line 1c.
 c Did the corporation prepare a non-tax-basis income statement for that period?
   ☐ **Yes.** Complete lines 2a through 11 with respect to that income statement.
   ☐ **No.** Skip lines 2a through 3c and enter the corporation's net income (loss) per its books and records on line 4a.
2a Enter the income statement period: Beginning ___MM/DD/YYYY___ Ending ___MM/DD/YYYY___
 b Has the corporation's income statement been restated for the income statement period on line 2a?
   ☐ **Yes.** (If "Yes," attach an explanation and the amount of each item restated.)
   ☐ **No.**
 c Has the corporation's income statement been restated for any of the five income statement periods preceding the period on line 2a?
   ☐ **Yes.** (If "Yes," attach an explanation and the amount of each item restated.)
   ☐ **No.**
3a Is any of the corporation's voting common stock publicly traded?
   ☐ **Yes.**
   ☐ **No.** If "No," go to line 4a.
 b Enter the symbol of the corporation's primary U.S. publicly traded voting common stock . . . .
 c Enter the nine-digit CUSIP number of the corporation's primary publicly traded voting common stock . . . .

4a	Worldwide consolidated net income (loss) from income statement source identified in Part I, line 1 .	**4a**
b	Indicate accounting standard used for line 4a (see instructions): (1) ☐ GAAP (2) ☐ IFRS (3) ☐ Statutory (4) ☐ Tax-basis (5) ☐ Other (specify) _____	
5a	Net income from nonincludible foreign entities (attach statement)	**5a** ( )
b	Net loss from nonincludible foreign entities (attach statement and enter as a positive amount) . . .	**5b**
6a	Net income from nonincludible U.S. entities (attach statement)	**6a** ( )
b	Net loss from nonincludible U.S. entities (attach statement and enter as a positive amount)	**6b**
7a	Net income (loss) of other includible foreign disregarded entities (attach statement)	**7a**
b	Net income (loss) of other includible U.S. disregarded entities (attach statement)	**7b**
c	Net income (loss) of other includible entities (attach statement)	**7c**
8	Adjustment to eliminations of transactions between includible entities and nonincludible entities (attach statement)	**8**
9	Adjustment to reconcile income statement period to tax year (attach statement)	**9**
10a	Intercompany dividend adjustments to reconcile to line 11 (attach statement)	**10a**
b	Other statutory accounting adjustments to reconcile to line 11 (attach statement)	**10b**
c	Other adjustments to reconcile to amount on line 11 (attach statement)	**10c**
11	**Net income (loss) per income statement of includible corporations.** Combine lines 4 through 10 .	**11**

Note. Part I, line 11, must equal the amount on Part II, line 30, column (a), and Schedule M-2, line 2.

12 Enter the total amount (not just the corporation's share) of the assets and liabilities of all entities included or removed on the following lines.

	Total Assets	Total Liabilities
a Included on Part I, line 4 . . . . ▶		
b Removed on Part I, line 5 . . . . ▶		
c Removed on Part I, line 6 . . . . ▶		
d Included on Part I, line 7 . . . . ▶		

For Paperwork Reduction Act Notice, see the Instructions for Form 1120.   Cat. No. 37961C   Schedule M-3 (Form 1120) 2013

Schedule M-3 (Form 1120) 2013   Page **2**

Name of corporation (common parent, if consolidated return)	Employer identification number

Check applicable box(es): **(1)** ☐ Consolidated group **(2)** ☐ Parent corp **(3)** ☐ Consolidated eliminations **(4)** ☐ Subsidiary corp **(5)** ☐ Mixed 1120/L/PC group

Check if a sub-consolidated: **(6)** ☐ 1120 group **(7)** ☐ 1120 eliminations

Name of subsidiary (if consolidated return)	Employer identification number

Part II Reconciliation of Net Income (Loss) per Income Statement of Includible Corporations With Taxable Income per Return (see instructions)

Income (Loss) Items (Attach statements for lines 1 through 11)	(a) Income (Loss) per Income Statement	(b) Temporary Difference	(c) Permanent Difference	(d) Income (Loss) per Tax Return
1 Income (loss) from equity method foreign corporations				
2 Gross foreign dividends not previously taxed . . .				
3 Subpart F, QEF, and similar income inclusions . .				
4 Section 78 gross-up				
5 Gross foreign distributions previously taxed . . .				
6 Income (loss) from equity method U.S. corporations				
7 U.S. dividends not eliminated in tax consolidation				
8 Minority interest for includible corporations . . .				
9 Income (loss) from U.S. partnerships				
10 Income (loss) from foreign partnerships				
11 Income (loss) from other pass-through entities . .				
12 Items relating to reportable transactions (attach statement)				
13 Interest income (attach Form 8916-A)				
14 Total accrual to cash adjustment				
15 Hedging transactions				
16 Mark-to-market income (loss)				
17 Cost of goods sold (attach Form 8916-A)	( )			( )
18 Sale versus lease (for sellers and/or lessors) . . .				
19 Section 481(a) adjustments				
20 Unearned/deferred revenue				
21 Income recognition from long-term contracts . .				
22 Original issue discount and other imputed interest .				
23a Income statement gain/loss on sale, exchange, abandonment, worthlessness, or other disposition of assets other than inventory and pass-through entities				
b Gross capital gains from Schedule D, excluding amounts from pass-through entities				
c Gross capital losses from Schedule D, excluding amounts from pass-through entities, abandonment losses, and worthless stock losses				
d Net gain/loss reported on Form 4797, line 17, excluding amounts from pass-through entities, abandonment losses, and worthless stock losses				
e Abandonment losses				
f Worthless stock losses (attach statement)				
g Other gain/loss on disposition of assets other than inventory				
24 Capital loss limitation and carryforward used . . .				
25 Other income (loss) items with differences (attach statement)				
26 **Total income (loss) items.** Combine lines 1 through 25				
27 **Total expense/deduction items** (from Part III, line 38)				
28 Other items with no differences				
29a Mixed groups, see instructions. All others, combine lines 26 through 28				
b PC insurance subgroup reconciliation totals . . .				
c Life insurance subgroup reconciliation totals . . .				
30 **Reconciliation totals.** Combine lines 29a through 29c				

Note. Line 30, column (a), must equal the amount on Part I, line 11, and column (d) must equal Form 1120, page 1, line 28.

Schedule M-3 (Form 1120) 2013

Schedule M-3 (Form 1120) 2013   Page **3**

Name of corporation (common parent, if consolidated return)	Employer identification number

Check applicable box(es): **(1)** ☐ Consolidated group **(2)** ☐ Parent corp **(3)** ☐ Consolidated eliminations **(4)** ☐ Subsidiary corp **(5)** ☐ Mixed 1120/L/PC group

Check if a sub-consolidated: **(6)** ☐ 1120 group **(7)** ☐ 1120 eliminations

Name of subsidiary (if consolidated return)	Employer identification number

Part III **Reconciliation of Net Income (Loss) per Income Statement of Includible Corporations With Taxable Income per Return—Expense/Deduction Items** (see instructions)

Expense/Deduction Items	(a) Expense per Income Statement	(b) Temporary Difference	(c) Permanent Difference	(d) Deduction per Tax Return
1 U.S. current income tax expense				
2 U.S. deferred income tax expense				
3 State and local current income tax expense . . .				
4 State and local deferred income tax expense . . .				
5 Foreign current income tax expense (other than foreign withholding taxes)				
6 Foreign deferred income tax expense				
7 Foreign withholding taxes				
8 Interest expense (attach Form 8916-A)				
9 Stock option expense				
10 Other equity-based compensation				
11 Meals and entertainment				
12 Fines and penalties				
13 Judgments, damages, awards, and similar costs .				
14 Parachute payments				
15 Compensation with section 162(m) limitation . . .				
16 Pension and profit-sharing				
17 Other post-retirement benefits				
18 Deferred compensation				
19 Charitable contribution of cash and tangible property				
20 Charitable contribution of intangible property . .				
21 Charitable contribution limitation/carryforward . .				
22 Domestic production activities deduction				
23 Current year acquisition or reorganization investment banking fees				
24 Current year acquisition or reorganization legal and accounting fees				
25 Current year acquisition/reorganization other costs .				
26 Amortization/impairment of goodwill				
27 Amortization of acquisition, reorganization, and start-up costs				
28 Other amortization or impairment write-offs . . .				
29 Reserved				
30 Depletion				
31 Depreciation				
32 Bad debt expense				
33 Corporate owned life insurance premiums . . .				
34 Purchase versus lease (for purchasers and/or lessees)				
35 Research and development costs				
36 Section 118 exclusion (attach statement)				
37 Other expense/deduction items with differences (attach statement)				
38 **Total expense/deduction items.** Combine lines 1 through 37. Enter here and on Part II, line 27, reporting positive amounts as negative and negative amounts as positive				

Form **1120S**

Department of the Treasury
Internal Revenue Service

U.S. Income Tax Return for an S Corporation

▶ Do not file this form unless the corporation has filed or is
attaching Form 2553 to elect to be an S corporation.
▶ Information about Form 1120S and its separate instructions is at *www.irs.gov/form1120s.*

OMB No. 1545-0130

2013

For calendar year 2013 or tax year beginning , 2013, ending , 20

A S election effective date	**TYPE OR PRINT**	Name
B Business activity code number (see instructions)		Number, street, and room or suite no. If a P.O. box, see instructions.
C Check if Sch. M-3 attached ☐		City or town, state or province, country, and ZIP or foreign postal code

D Employer identification number

E Date incorporated

F Total assets (see instructions)
$

G Is the corporation electing to be an S corporation beginning with this tax year? ☐ Yes ☐ No If "Yes," attach Form 2553 if not already filed

H Check if: **(1)** ☐ Final return **(2)** ☐ Name change **(3)** ☐ Address change **(4)** ☐ Amended return **(5)** ☐ S election termination or revocation

I Enter the number of shareholders who were shareholders during any part of the tax year . . . . ▶

Caution. Include **only** trade or business income and expenses on lines 1a through 21. See the instructions for more information.

Income

1a	Gross receipts or sales	**1a**		
b	Returns and allowances	**1b**		
c	Balance. Subtract line 1b from line 1a		**1c**	
2	Cost of goods sold (attach Form 1125-A)		**2**	
3	Gross profit. Subtract line 2 from line 1c		**3**	
4	Net gain (loss) from Form 4797, line 17 (attach Form 4797)		**4**	
5	Other income (loss) (see instructions—attach statement)		**5**	
6	**Total income (loss).** Add lines 3 through 5 . . . . ▶		**6**	

Deductions (see instructions for limitations)

7	Compensation of officers (see instructions—attach Form 1125-E)	**7**	
8	Salaries and wages (less employment credits)	**8**	
9	Repairs and maintenance	**9**	
10	Bad debts	**10**	
11	Rents	**11**	
12	Taxes and licenses	**12**	
13	Interest	**13**	
14	Depreciation not claimed on Form 1125-A or elsewhere on return (attach Form 4562)	**14**	
15	Depletion **(Do not deduct oil and gas depletion.)**	**15**	
16	Advertising	**16**	
17	Pension, profit-sharing, etc., plans	**17**	
18	Employee benefit programs	**18**	
19	Other deductions (attach statement)	**19**	
20	**Total deductions.** Add lines 7 through 19 . . . . ▶	**20**	
21	**Ordinary business income (loss).** Subtract line 20 from line 6	**21**	

Tax and Payments

22a	Excess net passive income or LIFO recapture tax (see instructions) . .	**22a**		
b	Tax from Schedule D (Form 1120S)	**22b**		
c	Add lines 22a and 22b (see instructions for additional taxes)		**22c**	
23a	2013 estimated tax payments and 2012 overpayment credited to 2013	**23a**		
b	Tax deposited with Form 7004	**23b**		
c	Credit for federal tax paid on fuels (attach Form 4136)	**23c**		
d	Add lines 23a through 23c		**23d**	
24	Estimated tax penalty (see instructions). Check if Form 2220 is attached . . . . . . ▶ ☐		**24**	
25	**Amount owed.** If line 23d is smaller than the total of lines 22c and 24, enter amount owed . .		**25**	
26	**Overpayment.** If line 23d is larger than the total of lines 22c and 24, enter amount overpaid . .		**26**	
27	Enter amount from line 26 **Credited to 2014 estimated tax** ▶ **Refunded** ▶		**27**	

Sign Here

Under penalties of perjury, I declare that I have examined this return, including accompanying schedules and statements, and to the best of my knowledge and belief, it is true, correct, and complete. Declaration of preparer (other than taxpayer) is based on all information of which preparer has any knowledge.

▶ Signature of officer   Date

▶ Title

May the IRS discuss this return with the preparer shown below (see instructions)? ☐ Yes ☐ No

Paid Preparer Use Only

Print/Type preparer's name	Preparer's signature	Date	Check ☐ if self-employed	PTIN
Firm's name ▶			Firm's EIN ▶	
Firm's address ▶			Phone no.	

For Paperwork Reduction Act Notice, see separate instructions.   Cat. No. 11510H   Form **1120S** (2013)

Form 1120S (2013)   Page **2**

Schedule B	**Other Information** (see instructions)	Yes	No

1 Check accounting method: **a** ☐ Cash **b** ☐ Accrual

                    c ☐ Other (specify) ▶ --

2 See the instructions and enter the:

  a Business activity ▶ ---------------------------------- **b** Product or service ▶ ----------------------------------

3 At any time during the tax year, was any shareholder of the corporation a disregarded entity, a trust, an estate, or a nominee or similar person? If "Yes," attach Schedule B-1, Information on Certain Shareholders of an S Corporation . .

4 At the end of the tax year, did the corporation:

a Own directly 20% or more, or own, directly or indirectly, 50% or more of the total stock issued and outstanding of any foreign or domestic corporation? For rules of constructive ownership, see instructions. If "Yes," complete (i) through (v) below . . . .

(i) Name of Corporation	**(ii)** Employer Identification Number (if any)	**(iii)** Country of Incorporation	**(iv)** Percentage of Stock Owned	**(v)** If Percentage in (iv) is 100%, Enter the Date (if any) a Qualified Subchapter S Subsidiary Election Was Made

b Own directly an interest of 20% or more, or own, directly or indirectly, an interest of 50% or more in the profit, loss, or capital in any foreign or domestic partnership (including an entity treated as a partnership) or in the beneficial interest of a trust? For rules of constructive ownership, see instructions. If "Yes," complete (i) through (v) below . . . .

(i) Name of Entity	**(ii)** Employer Identification Number (if any)	**(iii)** Type of Entity	**(iv)** Country of Organization	**(v)** Maximum Percentage Owned in Profit, Loss, or Capital

5 a At the end of the tax year, did the corporation have any outstanding shares of restricted stock? . . . .

    If "Yes," complete lines (i) and (ii) below.

    (i)   Total shares of restricted stock . . . . ▶ ----------------------------

    (ii)   Total shares of non-restricted stock . . . . ▶ ----------------------------

b At the end of the tax year, did the corporation have any outstanding stock options, warrants, or similar instruments? .

    If "Yes," complete lines (i) and (ii) below.

    (i)   Total shares of stock outstanding at the end of the tax year ▶ ----------------------------

    (ii)   Total shares of stock outstanding if all instruments were executed ▶ ----------------------------

6 Has this corporation filed, or is it required to file, **Form 8918,** Material Advisor Disclosure Statement, to provide information on any reportable transaction? . . . .

7 Check this box if the corporation issued publicly offered debt instruments with original issue discount . . . . ▶ ☐

    If checked, the corporation may have to file **Form 8281,** Information Return for Publicly Offered Original Issue Discount Instruments.

8 If the corporation: **(a)** was a C corporation before it elected to be an S corporation **or** the corporation acquired an asset with a basis determined by reference to the basis of the asset (or the basis of any other property) in the hands of a C corporation **and (b)** has net unrealized built-in gain in excess of the net recognized built-in gain from prior years, enter the net unrealized built-in gain reduced by net recognized built-in gain from prior years (see instructions) . . . . ▶ $ --------------------------------

9 Enter the accumulated earnings and profits of the corporation at the end of the tax year. $ --------------------------

10 Does the corporation satisfy **both** of the following conditions?

  a The corporation's total receipts (see instructions) for the tax year were less than $250,000 . . . .

  b The corporation's total assets at the end of the tax year were less than $250,000 . . . .

    If "Yes," the corporation is not required to complete Schedules L and M-1.

11 During the tax year, did the corporation have any non-shareholder debt that was canceled, was forgiven, or had the terms modified so as to reduce the principal amount of the debt? . . . .

    If "Yes," enter the amount of principal reduction $ ----------------------------

12 During the tax year, was a qualified subchapter S subsidiary election terminated or revoked? If "Yes," see instructions .

13 a Did the corporation make any payments in 2013 that would require it to file Form(s) 1099? . . . .

  b If "Yes," did the corporation file or will it file required Forms 1099? . . . .

Form 1120S (2013)   Page **3**

		Schedule K	Shareholders' Pro Rata Share Items		Total amount	

					Total amount	
Income (Loss)	**1**	Ordinary business income (loss) (page 1, line 21)		**1**		
	2	Net rental real estate income (loss) (attach Form 8825)		**2**		
	3a	Other gross rental income (loss)	**3a**			
	b	Expenses from other rental activities (attach statement) . .	**3b**			
	c	Other net rental income (loss). Subtract line 3b from line 3a		**3c**		
	4	Interest income		**4**		
	5	Dividends: **a** Ordinary dividends		**5a**		
		b Qualified dividends	**5b**			
	6	Royalties		**6**		
	7	Net short-term capital gain (loss) (attach Schedule D (Form 1120S)) . . .		**7**		
	8a	Net long-term capital gain (loss) (attach Schedule D (Form 1120S))		**8a**		
	b	Collectibles (28%) gain (loss)	**8b**			
	c	Unrecaptured section 1250 gain (attach statement) . . .	**8c**			
	9	Net section 1231 gain (loss) (attach Form 4797)		**9**		
	10	Other income (loss) (see instructions) . . Type ▶		**10**		
Deductions	**11**	Section 179 deduction (attach Form 4562)		**11**		
	12a	Charitable contributions		**12a**		
	b	Investment interest expense		**12b**		
	c	Section 59(e)(2) expenditures **(1)** Type ▶ _____ **(2)** Amount ▶		**12c(2)**		
	d	Other deductions (see instructions) . . . Type ▶		**12d**		
Credits	**13a**	Low-income housing credit (section 42(j)(5))		**13a**		
	b	Low-income housing credit (other)		**13b**		
	c	Qualified rehabilitation expenditures (rental real estate) (attach Form 3468) . . .		**13c**		
	d	Other rental real estate credits (see instructions) Type ▶ _____		**13d**		
	e	Other rental credits (see instructions) . . . Type ▶ _____		**13e**		
	f	Biofuel producer credit (attach Form 6478)		**13f**		
	g	Other credits (see instructions) . . . . . Type ▶		**13g**		
Foreign Transactions	**14a**	Name of country or U.S. possession ▶ _____				
	b	Gross income from all sources		**14b**		
	c	Gross income sourced at shareholder level		**14c**		
		Foreign gross income sourced at corporate level				
	d	Passive category		**14d**		
	e	General category		**14e**		
	f	Other (attach statement)		**14f**		
		Deductions allocated and apportioned at shareholder level				
	g	Interest expense		**14g**		
	h	Other		**14h**		
		Deductions allocated and apportioned at corporate level to foreign source income				
	i	Passive category		**14i**		
	j	General category		**14j**		
	k	Other (attach statement)		**14k**		
		Other information				
	l	Total foreign taxes (check one): ▶ ☐ Paid ☐ Accrued		**14l**		
	m	Reduction in taxes available for credit (attach statement)		**14m**		
	n	Other foreign tax information (attach statement)				
Alternative Minimum Tax (AMT) Items	**15a**	Post-1986 depreciation adjustment		**15a**		
	b	Adjusted gain or loss		**15b**		
	c	Depletion (other than oil and gas)		**15c**		
	d	Oil, gas, and geothermal properties—gross income		**15d**		
	e	Oil, gas, and geothermal properties—deductions		**15e**		
	f	Other AMT items (attach statement)		**15f**		
Items Affecting Shareholder Basis	**16a**	Tax-exempt interest income		**16a**		
	b	Other tax-exempt income		**16b**		
	c	Nondeductible expenses		**16c**		
	d	Distributions (attach statement if required) (see instructions)		**16d**		
	e	Repayment of loans from shareholders		**16e**		

Form **1120S** (2013)

Form 1120S (2013)   Page **4**

Schedule K	Shareholders' Pro Rata Share Items (continued)		Total amount	

Other Information

	17a	Investment income	17a	
	b	Investment expenses	17b	
	c	Dividend distributions paid from accumulated earnings and profits	17c	
	d	Other items and amounts (attach statement)		

Reconciliation

| | 18 | **Income/loss reconciliation.** Combine the amounts on lines 1 through 10 in the far right column. From the result, subtract the sum of the amounts on lines 11 through 12d and 14l | 18 | |

Schedule L	Balance Sheets per Books	Beginning of tax year		End of tax year	
	Assets	(a)	(b)	(c)	(d)
1	Cash				
2a	Trade notes and accounts receivable				
b	Less allowance for bad debts	( )		( )	
3	Inventories				
4	U.S. government obligations				
5	Tax-exempt securities (see instructions)				
6	Other current assets (attach statement)				
7	Loans to shareholders				
8	Mortgage and real estate loans				
9	Other investments (attach statement)				
10a	Buildings and other depreciable assets				
b	Less accumulated depreciation	( )		( )	
11a	Depletable assets				
b	Less accumulated depletion	( )		( )	
12	Land (net of any amortization)				
13a	Intangible assets (amortizable only)				
b	Less accumulated amortization	( )		( )	
14	Other assets (attach statement)				
15	Total assets				
	Liabilities and Shareholders' Equity				
16	Accounts payable				
17	Mortgages, notes, bonds payable in less than 1 year				
18	Other current liabilities (attach statement)				
19	Loans from shareholders				
20	Mortgages, notes, bonds payable in 1 year or more				
21	Other liabilities (attach statement)				
22	Capital stock				
23	Additional paid-in capital				
24	Retained earnings				
25	Adjustments to shareholders' equity (attach statement)				
26	Less cost of treasury stock		( )		( )
27	Total liabilities and shareholders' equity				

Form **1120S** (2013)

Form 1120S (2013)   Page **5**

Schedule M-1	**Reconciliation of Income (Loss) per Books With Income (Loss) per Return**

Note. Schedule M-3 required instead of Schedule M-1 if total assets are $10 million or more—see instructions

1	Net income (loss) per books		5	Income recorded on books this year not included on Schedule K, lines 1 through 10 (itemize):	
2	Income included on Schedule K, lines 1, 2, 3c, 4, 5a, 6, 7, 8a, 9, and 10, not recorded on books this year (itemize) _____		a	Tax-exempt interest $ _____	
3	Expenses recorded on books this year not included on Schedule K, lines 1 through 12 and 14l (itemize):		6	Deductions included on Schedule K, lines 1 through 12 and 14l, not charged against book income this year (itemize):	
a	Depreciation $ _____		a	Depreciation $ _____	
b	Travel and entertainment $ _____			_____	
	_____		7	Add lines 5 and 6	
4	Add lines 1 through 3		8	Income (loss) (Schedule K, line 18). Line 4 less line 7	

Schedule M-2	**Analysis of Accumulated Adjustments Account, Other Adjustments Account, and Shareholders' Undistributed Taxable Income Previously Taxed** (see instructions)

		(a) Accumulated adjustments account	(b) Other adjustments account	(c) Shareholders' undistributed taxable income previously taxed
1	Balance at beginning of tax year			
2	Ordinary income from page 1, line 21 . . .			
3	Other additions			
4	Loss from page 1, line 21	( )		
5	Other reductions	( )	( )	
6	Combine lines 1 through 5			
7	Distributions other than dividend distributions			
8	Balance at end of tax year. Subtract line 7 from line 6			

Form **1120S** (2013)

671113

☐ Final K-1	☐ Amended K-1		OMB No. 1545-0130

Schedule K-1
(Form 1120S)

Department of the Treasury
Internal Revenue Service

20**13**

For calendar year 2013, or tax
year beginning _____ , 2013
ending _____ , 20 _____

Shareholder's Share of Income, Deductions, Credits, etc.
▶ See back of form and separate instructions.

Part I	Information About the Corporation

A Corporation's employer identification number

B Corporation's name, address, city, state, and ZIP code

C IRS Center where corporation filed return

Part II	Information About the Shareholder

D Shareholder's identifying number

E Shareholder's name, address, city, state, and ZIP code

F Shareholder's percentage of stock
ownership for tax year . . . . _____ %

For IRS Use Only

Part III	Shareholder's Share of Current Year Income, Deductions, Credits, and Other Items

1	Ordinary business income (loss)	13	Credits
2	Net rental real estate income (loss)		
3	Other net rental income (loss)		
4	Interest income		
5a	Ordinary dividends		
5b	Qualified dividends	14	Foreign transactions
6	Royalties		
7	Net short-term capital gain (loss)		
8a	Net long-term capital gain (loss)		
8b	Collectibles (28%) gain (loss)		
8c	Unrecaptured section 1250 gain		
9	Net section 1231 gain (loss)		
10	Other income (loss)	15	Alternative minimum tax (AMT) items
11	Section 179 deduction	16	Items affecting shareholder basis
12	Other deductions		
		17	Other information

* See attached statement for additional information.

For Paperwork Reduction Act Notice, see Instructions for Form 1120S.   IRS.gov/form1120s   Cat. No. 11520D   **Schedule K-1 (Form 1120S) 2013**

Form **2553**

(Rev. December 2013)

Department of the Treasury
Internal Revenue Service

Election by a Small Business Corporation
(Under section 1362 of the Internal Revenue Code)

▶ See Parts II and III on page 3.
▶ **You can fax this form to the IRS (see separate instructions).**
▶ **Information about Form 2553 and its separate instructions is at** *www.irs.gov/form2553.*

OMB No. 1545-0123

Note. This election to be an S corporation can be accepted only if all the tests are met under *Who May Elect* in the instructions, all shareholders have signed the consent statement, an officer has signed below, and the exact name and address of the corporation (entity) and other required form information have been provided.

Part I Election Information

Type or Print

Name (see instructions)

Number, street, and room or suite no. (If a P.O. box, see instructions.)

City or town, state, and ZIP code

A Employer identification number

B Date incorporated

C State of incorporation

D Check the applicable box(es) if the corporation (entity), after applying for the EIN shown in **A** above, changed its ☐ name or ☐ address

E Election is to be effective for tax year beginning (month, day, year) (see instructions) . . . . . . ▶

Caution. A corporation (entity) making the election for its first tax year in existence will usually enter the beginning date of a short tax year that begins on a date other than January 1.

F Selected tax year:
(1) ☐ Calendar year
(2) ☐ Fiscal year ending (month and day) ▶
(3) ☐ 52-53-week year ending with reference to the month of December
(4) ☐ 52-53-week year ending with reference to the month of ▶
If box (2) or (4) is checked, complete Part II.

G If more than 100 shareholders are listed for item J (see page 2), check this box if treating members of a family as one shareholder results in no more than 100 shareholders (see test 2 under *Who May Elect* in the instructions) ▶ ☐

H Name and title of officer or legal representative who the IRS may call for more information

I Telephone number of officer or legal representative

If this S corporation election is being filed late, I declare that I had reasonable cause for not filing Form 2553 timely, and if this late election is being made by an entity eligible to elect to be treated as a corporation, I declare that I also had reasonable cause for not filing an entity classification election timely and that the representations listed in Part IV are true. See below for my explanation of the reasons the election or elections were not made on time and a description of my diligent actions to correct the mistake upon its discovery (see instructions).

Sign Here

Under penalties of perjury, I declare that I have examined this election, including accompanying documents, and, to the best of my knowledge and belief, the election contains all the relevant facts relating to the election, and such facts are true, correct, and complete.

▶ _____ _____ _____
Signature of officer   Title   Date

For Paperwork Reduction Act Notice, see separate instructions.   Cat. No. 18629R   Form **2553** (Rev. 12-2013)

Form 2553 (Rev. 12-2013)

| Part I | Election Information (continued) | Note. If you need more rows, use additional copies of page 2. |

J Name and address of each shareholder or former shareholder required to consent to the election. (see instructions)	K Shareholder's Consent Statement Under penalties of perjury, I declare that I consent to the election of the above-named corporation (entity) to be an S corporation under section 1362(a) and that I have examined this consent statement, including accompanying documents, and, to the best of my knowledge and belief, the election contains all the relevant facts relating to the election, and such facts are true, correct, and complete. I understand my consent is binding and may not be withdrawn after the corporation (entity) has made a valid election. If seeking relief for a late filed election, I also declare under penalties of perjury that I have reported my income on all affected returns consistent with the S corporation election for the year for which the election should have been filed (see beginning date entered on line E) and for all subsequent years.		L Stock owned or percentage of ownership (see instructions)		M Social security number or employer identification number (see instructions)	N Shareholder's tax year ends (month and day)
	Signature	Date	Number of shares or percentage of ownership	Date(s) acquired		

Form **2553** (Rev. 12-2013)

Form **4562**	**Depreciation and Amortization** (Including Information on Listed Property)	OMB No. 1545-0172
Department of the Treasury Internal Revenue Service (99)	▶ See separate instructions. ▶ Attach to your tax return.	20**13** Attachment Sequence No. **179**

Name(s) shown on return	Business or activity to which this form relates	Identifying number

Part I   Election To Expense Certain Property Under Section 179
Note: *If you have any listed property, complete Part V before you complete Part I.*

1	Maximum amount (see instructions)	1
2	Total cost of section 179 property placed in service (see instructions)	2
3	Threshold cost of section 179 property before reduction in limitation (see instructions)	3
4	Reduction in limitation. Subtract line 3 from line 2. If zero or less, enter -0-	4
5	Dollar limitation for tax year. Subtract line 4 from line 1. If zero or less, enter -0-. If married filing separately, see instructions	5

6	(a) Description of property	(b) Cost (business use only)	(c) Elected cost	

7	Listed property. Enter the amount from line 29 . . . . **7**	
8	Total elected cost of section 179 property. Add amounts in column (c), lines 6 and 7	8
9	Tentative deduction. Enter the **smaller** of line 5 or line 8	9
10	Carryover of disallowed deduction from line 13 of your 2012 Form 4562	10
11	Business income limitation. Enter the smaller of business income (not less than zero) or line 5 (see instructions)	11
12	Section 179 expense deduction. Add lines 9 and 10, but do not enter more than line 11	12
13	Carryover of disallowed deduction to 2014. Add lines 9 and 10, less line 12 ▶ **13**	

Note: *Do not use Part II or Part III below for listed property. Instead, use Part V.*

Part II   Special Depreciation Allowance and Other Depreciation (Do not include listed property.**)** (See instructions.)

14	Special depreciation allowance for qualified property (other than listed property) placed in service during the tax year (see instructions)	14
15	Property subject to section 168(f)(1) election	15
16	Other depreciation (including ACRS)	16

Part III   MACRS Depreciation (Do not include listed property.**)** (See instructions.)

Section A

17	MACRS deductions for assets placed in service in tax years beginning before 2013	17
18	If you are electing to group any assets placed in service during the tax year into one or more general asset accounts, check here . . . . ▶ ☐	

Section B—Assets Placed in Service During 2013 Tax Year Using the General Depreciation System

(a) Classification of property	(b) Month and year placed in service	(c) Basis for depreciation (business/investment use only—see instructions)	(d) Recovery period	(e) Convention	(f) Method	(g) Depreciation deduction
19a 3-year property						
b 5-year property						
c 7-year property						
d 10-year property						
e 15-year property						
f 20-year property						
g 25-year property			25 yrs.		S/L	
h Residential rental property			27.5 yrs.	MM	S/L	
			27.5 yrs.	MM	S/L	
i Nonresidential real property			39 yrs.	MM	S/L	
				MM	S/L	

Section C—Assets Placed in Service During 2013 Tax Year Using the Alternative Depreciation System

20a Class life					S/L	
b 12-year			12 yrs.		S/L	
c 40-year			40 yrs.	MM	S/L	

Part IV   Summary (See instructions.)

21	Listed property. Enter amount from line 28	21
22	**Total.** Add amounts from line 12, lines 14 through 17, lines 19 and 20 in column (g), and line 21. Enter here and on the appropriate lines of your return. Partnerships and S corporations—see instructions .	22
23	For assets shown above and placed in service during the current year, enter the portion of the basis attributable to section 263A costs **23**	

For Paperwork Reduction Act Notice, see separate instructions.   Cat. No. 12906N   Form **4562** (2013)

Form 4562 (2013)

Part V Listed Property (Include automobiles, certain other vehicles, certain computers, and property used for entertainment, recreation, or amusement.)

Note: *For any vehicle for which you are using the standard mileage rate or deducting lease expense, complete **only** 24a, 24b, columns (a) through (c) of Section A, all of Section B, and Section C if applicable.*

Section A—Depreciation and Other Information (Caution: *See the instructions for limits for passenger automobiles.*)

24a Do you have evidence to support the business/investment use claimed? ☐ Yes ☐ No   **24b** If "Yes," is the evidence written? ☐ Yes ☐ No

(a) Type of property (list vehicles first)	(b) Date placed in service	(c) Business/ investment use percentage	(d) Cost or other basis	(e) Basis for depreciation (business/investment use only)	(f) Recovery period	(g) Method/ Convention	(h) Depreciation deduction	(i) Elected section 179 cost
25 Special depreciation allowance for qualified listed property placed in service during the tax year and used more than 50% in a qualified business use (see instructions) . **25**								
26 Property used more than 50% in a qualified business use:								
		%						
		%						
		%						
27 Property used 50% or less in a qualified business use:								
		%			S/L –			
		%			S/L –			
		%			S/L –			

28 Add amounts in column (h), lines 25 through 27. Enter here and on line 21, page 1 . **28**

29 Add amounts in column (i), line 26. Enter here and on line 7, page 1 . . . . **29**

Section B—Information on Use of Vehicles

Complete this section for vehicles used by a sole proprietor, partner, or other "more than 5% owner," or related person. If you provided vehicles to your employees, first answer the questions in Section C to see if you meet an exception to completing this section for those vehicles.

	(a) Vehicle 1		(b) Vehicle 2		(c) Vehicle 3		(d) Vehicle 4		(e) Vehicle 5		(f) Vehicle 6	
30 Total business/investment miles driven during the year (**do not** include commuting miles) .												
31 Total commuting miles driven during the year												
32 Total other personal (noncommuting) miles driven												
33 Total miles driven during the year. Add lines 30 through 32												
34 Was the vehicle available for personal use during off-duty hours?	Yes	No	Yes	No	Yes	No	Yes	No	Yes	No	Yes	No
35 Was the vehicle used primarily by a more than 5% owner or related person? . .												
36 Is another vehicle available for personal use?												

Section C—Questions for Employers Who Provide Vehicles for Use by Their Employees

Answer these questions to determine if you meet an exception to completing Section B for vehicles used by employees who **are not** more than 5% owners or related persons (see instructions).

		Yes	No
37	Do you maintain a written policy statement that prohibits all personal use of vehicles, including commuting, by your employees? . . .		
38	Do you maintain a written policy statement that prohibits personal use of vehicles, except commuting, by your employees? See the instructions for vehicles used by corporate officers, directors, or 1% or more owners . .		
39	Do you treat all use of vehicles by employees as personal use?		
40	Do you provide more than five vehicles to your employees, obtain information from your employees about the use of the vehicles, and retain the information received?		
41	Do you meet the requirements concerning qualified automobile demonstration use? (See instructions.) . . .		

Note: *If your answer to 37, 38, 39, 40, or 41 is "Yes," do not complete Section B for the covered vehicles.*

Part VI Amortization

(a) Description of costs	(b) Date amortization begins	(c) Amortizable amount	(d) Code section	(e) Amortization period or percentage	(f) Amortization for this year
42 Amortization of costs that begins during your 2013 tax year (see instructions):					

43 Amortization of costs that began before your 2013 tax year **43**

44 **Total.** Add amounts in column (f). See the instructions for where to report **44**

Form **4562** (2013)

Form **4626**

Department of the Treasury
Internal Revenue Service

Alternative Minimum Tax—Corporations

▶ Attach to the corporation's tax return.
▶ Information about Form 4626 and its separate instructions is at *www.irs.gov/form4626.*

OMB No. 1545-0175

20**13**

Name

Employer identification number

Note: *See the instructions to find out if the corporation is a small corporation exempt from the alternative minimum tax (AMT) under section 55(e).*

1	Taxable income or (loss) before net operating loss deduction	**1**
2	**Adjustments and preferences:**	
a	Depreciation of post-1986 property	**2a**
b	Amortization of certified pollution control facilities.	**2b**
c	Amortization of mining exploration and development costs	**2c**
d	Amortization of circulation expenditures (personal holding companies only) . .	**2d**
e	Adjusted gain or loss	**2e**
f	Long-term contracts	**2f**
g	Merchant marine capital construction funds.	**2g**
h	Section 833(b) deduction (Blue Cross, Blue Shield, and similar type organizations only) . .	**2h**
i	Tax shelter farm activities (personal service corporations only)	**2i**
j	Passive activities (closely held corporations and personal service corporations only) . .	**2j**
k	Loss limitations	**2k**
l	Depletion	**2l**
m	Tax-exempt interest income from specified private activity bonds	**2m**
n	Intangible drilling costs	**2n**
o	Other adjustments and preferences	**2o**
3	Pre-adjustment alternative minimum taxable income (AMTI). Combine lines 1 through 2o. . . .	**3**

4   **Adjusted current earnings (ACE) adjustment:**

a	ACE from line 10 of the ACE worksheet in the instructions	**4a**	
b	Subtract line 3 from line 4a. If line 3 exceeds line 4a, enter the difference as a negative amount (see instructions)	**4b**	
c	Multiply line 4b by 75% (.75). Enter the result as a positive amount	**4c**	
d	Enter the excess, if any, of the corporation's total increases in AMTI from prior year ACE adjustments over its total reductions in AMTI from prior year ACE adjustments (see instructions). **Note:** *You **must** enter an amount on line 4d (even if line 4b is positive).*	**4d**	
e	ACE adjustment.		

• If line 4b is zero or more, enter the amount from line 4c
• If line 4b is less than zero, enter the **smaller** of line 4c or line 4d as a negative amount   } . . . **4e**

5	Combine lines 3 and 4e. If zero or less, stop here; the corporation does not owe any AMT	**5**
6	Alternative tax net operating loss deduction (see instructions).	**6**
7	**Alternative minimum taxable income.** Subtract line 6 from line 5. If the corporation held a residual interest in a REMIC, see instructions	**7**
8	**Exemption phase-out** (if line 7 is $310,000 or more, skip lines 8a and 8b and enter -0- on line 8c):	

a	Subtract $150,000 from line 7 (if completing this line for a member of a controlled group, see instructions). If zero or less, enter -0-	**8a**	
b	Multiply line 8a by 25% (.25).	**8b**	
c	Exemption. Subtract line 8b from $40,000 (if completing this line for a member of a controlled group, see instructions). If zero or less, enter -0-		**8c**

9	Subtract line 8c from line 7. If zero or less, enter -0-	**9**
10	Multiply line 9 by 20% (.20)	**10**
11	Alternative minimum tax foreign tax credit (AMTFTC) (see instructions)	**11**
12	Tentative minimum tax. Subtract line 11 from line 10	**12**
13	Regular tax liability before applying all credits except the foreign tax credit	**13**
14	**Alternative minimum tax.** Subtract line 13 from line 12. If zero or less, enter -0-. Enter here and on Form 1120, Schedule J, line 3, or the appropriate line of the corporation's income tax return . . .	**14**

For Paperwork Reduction Act Notice, see separate instructions.   Cat. No. 12955I   Form **4626** (2013)

Form **4797**	**Sales of Business Property** (Also Involuntary Conversions and Recapture Amounts Under Sections 179 and 280F(b)(2)) ▶ Attach to your tax return. ▶ Information about Form 4797 and its separate instructions is at *www.irs.gov/form4797*.	OMB No. 1545-0184 **2013** Attachment Sequence No. **27**

Department of the Treasury
Internal Revenue Service

Name(s) shown on return	Identifying number

1 Enter the gross proceeds from sales or exchanges reported to you for 2013 on Form(s) 1099-B or 1099-S (or substitute statement) that you are including on line 2, 10, or 20 (see instructions) . . . . | **1** |

Part I — Sales or Exchanges of Property Used in a Trade or Business and Involuntary Conversions From Other Than Casualty or Theft—Most Property Held More Than 1 Year (see instructions)

2	(a) Description of property	(b) Date acquired (mo., day, yr.)	(c) Date sold (mo., day, yr.)	(d) Gross sales price	(e) Depreciation allowed or allowable since acquisition	(f) Cost or other basis, plus improvements and expense of sale	(g) Gain or (loss) Subtract (f) from the sum of (d) and (e)

3 Gain, if any, from Form 4684, line 39	**3**	
4 Section 1231 gain from installment sales from Form 6252, line 26 or 37	**4**	
5 Section 1231 gain or (loss) from like-kind exchanges from Form 8824	**5**	
6 Gain, if any, from line 32, from other than casualty or theft.	**6**	
7 Combine lines 2 through 6. Enter the gain or (loss) here and on the appropriate line as follows:	**7**	

Partnerships (except electing large partnerships) and S corporations. Report the gain or (loss) following the instructions for Form 1065, Schedule K, line 10, or Form 1120S, Schedule K, line 9. Skip lines 8, 9, 11, and 12 below.

Individuals, partners, S corporation shareholders, and all others. If line 7 is zero or a loss, enter the amount from line 7 on line 11 below and skip lines 8 and 9. If line 7 is a gain and you did not have any prior year section 1231 losses, or they were recaptured in an earlier year, enter the gain from line 7 as a long-term capital gain on the Schedule D filed with your return and skip lines 8, 9, 11, and 12 below.

8 Nonrecaptured net section 1231 losses from prior years (see instructions)	**8**	
9 Subtract line 8 from line 7. If zero or less, enter -0-. If line 9 is zero, enter the gain from line 7 on line 12 below. If line 9 is more than zero, enter the amount from line 8 on line 12 below and enter the gain from line 9 as a long-term capital gain on the Schedule D filed with your return (see instructions)	**9**	

Part II — Ordinary Gains and Losses (see instructions)

10 Ordinary gains and losses not included on lines 11 through 16 (include property held 1 year or less):

11 Loss, if any, from line 7	**11** ( )
12 Gain, if any, from line 7 or amount from line 8, if applicable	**12**	
13 Gain, if any, from line 31	**13**	
14 Net gain or (loss) from Form 4684, lines 31 and 38a	**14**	
15 Ordinary gain from installment sales from Form 6252, line 25 or 36	**15**	
16 Ordinary gain or (loss) from like-kind exchanges from Form 8824.	**16**	
17 Combine lines 10 through 16	**17**	

18 For all except individual returns, enter the amount from line 17 on the appropriate line of your return and skip lines a and b below. For individual returns, complete lines a and b below:

a If the loss on line 11 includes a loss from Form 4684, line 35, column (b)(ii), enter that part of the loss here. Enter the part of the loss from income-producing property on Schedule A (Form 1040), line 28, and the part of the loss from property used as an employee on Schedule A (Form 1040), line 23. Identify as from "Form 4797, line 18a." See instructions . . | **18a** |

b Redetermine the gain or (loss) on line 17 excluding the loss, if any, on line 18a. Enter here and on Form 1040, line 14 | **18b** |

For Paperwork Reduction Act Notice, see separate instructions.   Cat. No. 13086I   Form **4797** (2013)

Form 4797 (2013)

Page **2**

Part III Gain From Disposition of Property Under Sections 1245, 1250, 1252, 1254, and 1255
(see instructions)

19	(a) Description of section 1245, 1250, 1252, 1254, or 1255 property:	(b) Date acquired (mo., day, yr.)	(c) Date sold (mo., day, yr.)
A			
B			
C			
D			

	These columns relate to the properties on lines 19A through 19D. ▶		Property A	Property B	Property C	Property D
20	Gross sales price (**Note:** *See line 1 before completing.*) .	20				
21	Cost or other basis plus expense of sale	21				
22	Depreciation (or depletion) allowed or allowable. . . .	22				
23	Adjusted basis. Subtract line 22 from line 21.	23				
24	Total gain. Subtract line 23 from line 20	24				
25	**If section 1245 property:**					
a	Depreciation allowed or allowable from line 22	25a				
b	Enter the **smaller** of line 24 or 25a	25b				
26	**If section 1250 property:** If straight line depreciation was used, enter -0- on line 26g, except for a corporation subject to section 291.					
a	Additional depreciation after 1975 (see instructions) .	26a				
b	Applicable percentage multiplied by the **smaller** of line 24 or line 26a (see instructions)	26b				
c	Subtract line 26a from line 24. If residential rental property **or** line 24 is not more than line 26a, skip lines 26d and 26e	26c				
d	Additional depreciation after 1969 and before 1976. .	26d				
e	Enter the **smaller** of line 26c or 26d	26e				
f	Section 291 amount (corporations only)	26f				
g	Add lines 26b, 26e, and 26f.	26g				
27	**If section 1252 property:** Skip this section if you did not dispose of farmland or if this form is being completed for a partnership (other than an electing large partnership).					
a	Soil, water, and land clearing expenses	27a				
b	Line 27a multiplied by applicable percentage (see instructions)	27b				
c	Enter the **smaller** of line 24 or 27b	27c				
28	**If section 1254 property:**					
a	Intangible drilling and development costs, expenditures for development of mines and other natural deposits, mining exploration costs, and depletion (see instructions)	28a				
b	Enter the **smaller** of line 24 or 28a	28b				
29	**If section 1255 property:**					
a	Applicable percentage of payments excluded from income under section 126 (see instructions)	29a				
b	Enter the **smaller** of line 24 or 29a (see instructions) .	29b				

Summary of Part III Gains. Complete property columns A through D through line 29b before going to line 30.

30	Total gains for all properties. Add property columns A through D, line 24	30	
31	Add property columns A through D, lines 25b, 26g, 27c, 28b, and 29b. Enter here and on line 13	31	
32	Subtract line 31 from line 30. Enter the portion from casualty or theft on Form 4684, line 33. Enter the portion from other than casualty or theft on Form 4797, line 6	32	

Part IV Recapture Amounts Under Sections 179 and 280F(b)(2) When Business Use Drops to 50% or Less
(see instructions)

			(a) Section 179	(b) Section 280F(b)(2)
33	Section 179 expense deduction or depreciation allowable in prior years.	33		
34	Recomputed depreciation (see instructions)	34		
35	Recapture amount. Subtract line 34 from line 33. See the instructions for where to report . . .	35		

Form **4797** (2013)

Form **6251**	**Alternative Minimum Tax—Individuals**	OMB No. 1545-0074
Department of the Treasury Internal Revenue Service (99)	▶ Information about Form 6251 and its separate instructions is at *www.irs.gov/form6251*. ▶ Attach to Form 1040 or Form 1040NR.	20**13** Attachment Sequence No. **32**

Name(s) shown on Form 1040 or Form 1040NR | Your social security number

Part I   Alternative Minimum Taxable Income (See instructions for how to complete each line.)

1	If filing Schedule A (Form 1040), enter the amount from Form 1040, line 41, and go to line 2. Otherwise, enter the amount from Form 1040, line 38, and go to line 7. (If less than zero, enter as a negative amount.)	1
2	Medical and dental. If you or your spouse was 65 or older, enter the **smaller** of Schedule A (Form 1040), line 4, **or** 2.5% (.025) of Form 1040, line 38. If zero or less, enter -0-	2
3	Taxes from Schedule A (Form 1040), line 9	3
4	Enter the home mortgage interest adjustment, if any, from line 6 of the worksheet in the instructions for this line	4
5	Miscellaneous deductions from Schedule A (Form 1040), line 27.	5
6	If Form 1040, line 38, is $150,000 or less, enter -0-. Otherwise, see instructions	6 ( )
7	Tax refund from Form 1040, line 10 or line 21	7 ( )
8	Investment interest expense (difference between regular tax and AMT).	8
9	Depletion (difference between regular tax and AMT)	9
10	Net operating loss deduction from Form 1040, line 21. Enter as a positive amount	10
11	Alternative tax net operating loss deduction	11 ( )
12	Interest from specified private activity bonds exempt from the regular tax	12
13	Qualified small business stock (7% of gain excluded under section 1202)	13
14	Exercise of incentive stock options (excess of AMT income over regular tax income)	14
15	Estates and trusts (amount from Schedule K-1 (Form 1041), box 12, code A)	15
16	Electing large partnerships (amount from Schedule K-1 (Form 1065-B), box 6)	16
17	Disposition of property (difference between AMT and regular tax gain or loss)	17
18	Depreciation on assets placed in service after 1986 (difference between regular tax and AMT) . .	18
19	Passive activities (difference between AMT and regular tax income or loss)	19
20	Loss limitations (difference between AMT and regular tax income or loss)	20
21	Circulation costs (difference between regular tax and AMT)	21
22	Long-term contracts (difference between AMT and regular tax income)	22
23	Mining costs (difference between regular tax and AMT)	23
24	Research and experimental costs (difference between regular tax and AMT)	24
25	Income from certain installment sales before January 1, 1987	25 ( )
26	Intangible drilling costs preference	26
27	Other adjustments, including income-based related adjustments	27
28	**Alternative minimum taxable income.** Combine lines 1 through 27. (If married filing separately and line 28 is more than $238,550, see instructions.)	28

Part II   Alternative Minimum Tax (AMT)

29 Exemption. (If you were under age 24 at the end of 2013, see instructions.)

IF your filing status is . . .	**AND line 28 is not over . . .**	**THEN enter on line 29 . . .**	
Single or head of household	$115,400	$51,900	
Married filing jointly or qualifying widow(er)	153,900	80,800	
Married filing separately.	76,950	40,400	29

If line 28 is **over** the amount shown above for your filing status, see instructions.

30	Subtract line 29 from line 28. If more than zero, go to line 31. If zero or less, enter -0- here and on lines 31, 33, and 35, and go to line 34	30
31	• If you are filing Form 2555 or 2555-EZ, see instructions for the amount to enter. • If you reported capital gain distributions directly on Form 1040, line 13; you reported qualified dividends on Form 1040, line 9b; **or** you had a gain on both lines 15 and 16 of Schedule D (Form 1040) (as refigured for the AMT, if necessary), complete Part III on the back and enter the amount from line 60 here. • **All others:** If line 30 is $179,500 or less ($89,750 or less if married filing separately), multiply line 30 by 26% (.26). Otherwise, multiply line 30 by 28% (.28) and subtract $3,590 ($1,795 if married filing separately) from the result.	31
32	Alternative minimum tax foreign tax credit (see instructions)	32
33	Tentative minimum tax. Subtract line 32 from line 31	33
34	Tax from Form 1040, line 44 (minus any tax from Form 4972 and any foreign tax credit from Form 1040, line 47). If you used Schedule J to figure your tax, the amount from line 44 of Form 1040 must be refigured without using Schedule J (see instructions)	34
35	**AMT.** Subtract line 34 from line 33. If zero or less, enter -0-. Enter here and on Form 1040, line 45	35

For Paperwork Reduction Act Notice, see your tax return instructions.   Cat. No. 13600G   Form **6251** (2013)

Form 6251 (2013)   Page **2**

Part III Tax Computation Using Maximum Capital Gains Rates

Complete Part III only if you are required to do so by line 31 or by the Foreign Earned Income Tax Worksheet in the instructions.

36 Enter the amount from Form 6251, line 30. If you are filing Form 2555 or 2555-EZ, enter the amount from line 3 of the worksheet in the instructions for line 31 . . . . **36**

37 Enter the amount from line 6 of the Qualified Dividends and Capital Gain Tax Worksheet in the instructions for Form 1040, line 44, or the amount from line 13 of the Schedule D Tax Worksheet in the instructions for Schedule D (Form 1040), whichever applies (as refigured for the AMT, if necessary) (see instructions). If you are filing Form 2555 or 2555-EZ, see instructions for the amount to enter **37**

38 Enter the amount from Schedule D (Form 1040), line 19 (as refigured for the AMT, if necessary) (see instructions). If you are filing Form 2555 or 2555-EZ, see instructions for the amount to enter **38**

39 If you did not complete a Schedule D Tax Worksheet for the regular tax or the AMT, enter the amount from line 37. Otherwise, add lines 37 and 38, and enter the **smaller** of that result or the amount from line 10 of the Schedule D Tax Worksheet (as refigured for the AMT, if necessary). If you are filing Form 2555 or 2555-EZ, see instructions for the amount to enter **39**

40 Enter the **smaller** of line 36 or line 39 . . . . **40**

41 Subtract line 40 from line 36 . . . . **41**

42 If line 41 is $179,500 or less ($89,750 or less if married filing separately), multiply line 41 by 26% (.26). Otherwise, multiply line 41 by 28% (.28) and subtract $3,590 ($1,795 if married filing separately) from the result . . . ▶ **42**

43 Enter:
 • $72,500 if married filing jointly or qualifying widow(er),
 • $36,250 if single or married filing separately, or **43**
 • $48,600 if head of household.

44 Enter the amount from line 7 of the Qualified Dividends and Capital Gain Tax Worksheet in the instructions for Form 1040, line 44, or the amount from line 14 of the Schedule D Tax Worksheet in the instructions for Schedule D (Form 1040), whichever applies (as figured for the regular tax). If you did not complete either worksheet for the regular tax, enter the amount from Form 1040, line 43; but do not enter less than -0- **44**

45 Subtract line 44 from line 43. If zero or less, enter -0- **45**

46 Enter the **smaller** of line 36 or line 37 . . . . **46**

47 Enter the **smaller** of line 45 or line 46. This amount is taxed at 0% **47**

48 Subtract line 47 from line 46 . . . . **48**

49 Enter the amount from the Line 49 Worksheet in the instructions **49**

50 Enter the smaller of line 48 or line 49 . . . . **50**

51 Multiply line 50 by 15% (.15) . . . . ▶ **51**

52 Add lines 47 and 50 . . . . **52**

If lines 52 and 36 are the same, skip lines 53 through 57 and go to line 58. Otherwise, go to line 53.

53 Subtract line 52 from line 46 . . . . **53**

54 Multiply line 53 by 20% (.20) . . . . ▶ **54**

If line 38 is zero or blank, skip lines 55 through 57 and go to line 58. Otherwise, go to line 55.

55 Add lines 41, 52, and 53 . . . . **55**

56 Subtract line 55 from line 36 . . . . **56**

57 Multiply line 56 by 25% (.25) . . . . ▶ **57**

58 Add lines 42, 51, 54, and 57 . . . . **58**

59 If line 36 is $179,500 or less ($89,750 or less if married filing separately), multiply line 36 by 26% (.26). Otherwise, multiply line 36 by 28% (.28) and subtract $3,590 ($1,795 if married filing separately) from the result **59**

60 Enter the **smaller** of line 58 or line 59 here and on line 31. If you are filing Form 2555 or 2555-EZ, do not enter this amount on line 31. Instead, enter it on line 4 of the worksheet in the instructions for line 31 . . **60**

Form **6251** (2013)

Form **8949**

Department of the Treasury
Internal Revenue Service

Sales and Other Dispositions of Capital Assets

▶ Information about Form 8949 and its separate instructions is at *www.irs.gov/form8949.*
▶ File with your Schedule D to list your transactions for lines 1b, 2, 3, 8b, 9, and 10 of Schedule D.

OMB No. 1545-0074

2013

Attachment
Sequence No. **12A**

Name(s) shown on return	Social security number or taxpayer identification number

Most brokers issue their own substitute statement instead of using Form 1099-B. They also may provide basis information (usually your cost) to you on the statement even if it is not reported to the IRS. Before you check Box A, B, or C below, determine whether you received any statement(s) and, if so, the transactions for which basis was reported to the IRS. Brokers are required to report basis to the IRS for most stock you bought in 2011 or later.

Part I   **Short-Term.** Transactions involving capital assets you held one year or less are short term. For long-term transactions, see page 2.

Note. You may aggregate all short-term transactions reported on Form(s) 1099-B showing basis was reported to the IRS and for which no adjustments or codes are required. Enter the total directly on Schedule D, line 1a; you are not required to report these transactions on Form 8949 (see instructions).

You *must* check Box A, B, *or* C below. Check only one box. If more than one box applies for your short-term transactions, complete a separate Form 8949, page 1, for each applicable box. If you have more short-term transactions than will fit on this page for one or more of the boxes, complete as many forms with the same box checked as you need.

☐ **(A)** Short-term transactions reported on Form(s) 1099-B showing basis was reported to the IRS (see **Note** above)
☐ **(B)** Short-term transactions reported on Form(s) 1099-B showing basis was **not** reported to the IRS
☐ **(C)** Short-term transactions not reported to you on Form 1099-B

1 (a) Description of property (Example: 100 sh. XYZ Co.)	(b) Date acquired (Mo., day, yr.)	(c) Date sold or disposed (Mo., day, yr.)	(d) Proceeds (sales price) (see instructions)	(e) Cost or other basis. See the **Note** below and see *Column (e)* in the separate instructions	Adjustment, if any, to gain or loss. If you enter an amount in column (g), enter a code in column (f). **See the separate instructions.**		(h) Gain or (loss). Subtract column (e) from column (d) and combine the result with column (g)
					(f) Code(s) from instructions	(g) Amount of adjustment	

2 Totals. Add the amounts in columns (d), (e), (g), and (h) (subtract negative amounts). Enter each total here and include on your Schedule D, **line 1b** (if **Box A** above is checked), **line 2** (if **Box B** above is checked), or **line 3** (if **Box C** above is checked) ▶

Note. If you checked Box A above but the basis reported to the IRS was incorrect, enter in column (e) the basis as reported to the IRS, and enter an adjustment in column (g) to correct the basis. See *Column (g)* in the separate instructions for how to figure the amount of the adjustment.

For Paperwork Reduction Act Notice, see your tax return instructions.   Cat. No. 37768Z   Form **8949** (2013)

Form 8949 (2013)   Attachment Sequence No. **12A**   Page **2**

Name(s) shown on return. (Name and SSN or taxpayer identification no. not required if shown on other side.)	Social security number or taxpayer identification number

Most brokers issue their own substitute statement instead of using Form 1099-B. They also may provide basis information (usually your cost) to you on the statement even if it is not reported to the IRS. Before you check Box D, E, or F below, determine whether you received any statement(s) and, if so, the transactions for which basis was reported to the IRS. Brokers are required to report basis to the IRS for most stock you bought in 2011 or later.

Part II   **Long-Term.** Transactions involving capital assets you held more than one year are long term. For short-term transactions, see page 1.

Note. You may aggregate all long-term transactions reported on Form(s) 1099-B showing basis was reported to the IRS and for which no adjustments or codes are required. Enter the total directly on Schedule D, line 8a; you are not required to report these transactions on Form 8949 (see instructions).

You *must* check Box D, E, *or* F below. Check only one box. If more than one box applies for your long-term transactions, complete a separate Form 8949, page 2, for each applicable box. If you have more long-term transactions than will fit on this page for one or more of the boxes, complete as many forms with the same box checked as you need.

☐ **(D)** Long-term transactions reported on Form(s) 1099-B showing basis was reported to the IRS (see **Note** above)

☐ **(E)** Long-term transactions reported on Form(s) 1099-B showing basis was **not** reported to the IRS

☐ **(F)** Long-term transactions not reported to you on Form 1099-B

1 (a) Description of property (Example: 100 sh. XYZ Co.)	(b) Date acquired (Mo., day, yr.)	(c) Date sold or disposed (Mo., day, yr.)	(d) Proceeds (sales price) (see instructions)	(e) Cost or other basis. See the **Note** below and see *Column (e)* in the separate instructions	Adjustment, if any, to gain or loss. If you enter an amount in column (g), enter a code in column (f). See the separate instructions. (f) Code(s) from instructions	(g) Amount of adjustment	(h) Gain or (loss). Subtract column (e) from column (d) and combine the result with column (g)

2 Totals. Add the amounts in columns (d), (e), (g), and (h) (subtract negative amounts). Enter each total here and include on your Schedule D, **line 8b** (if **Box D** above is checked), **line 9** (if **Box E** above is checked), or **line 10** (if **Box F** above is checked) ▶

Note. If you checked Box D above but the basis reported to the IRS was incorrect, enter in column (e) the basis as reported to the IRS, and enter an adjustment in column (g) to correct the basis. See *Column (g)* in the separate instructions for how to figure the amount of the adjustment.

Form **8949** (2013)

Glossary

The key terms in this glossary have been defined to reflect their conventional use in the field of taxation. The definitions may therefore be incomplete for other purposes.

A

AAA bypass election. In the context of a distribution by an S corporation, an election made by the entity to designate that the distribution is first from accumulated earnings and profits (AEP) and only then from the accumulated adjustments account (AAA).

Accelerated cost recovery system (ACRS). A method in which the cost of tangible property is recovered over a prescribed period of time. The approach disregards salvage value, imposes a period of cost recovery that depends upon the classification of the asset into one of various recovery periods, and prescribes the applicable percentage of cost that can be deducted each year. § 168.

Accident and health insurance benefits. Employee fringe benefits provided by employers through the payment of health and accident insurance premiums or the establishment of employer-funded medical reimbursement plans. Employers generally are entitled to a deduction for such payments, whereas employees generally exclude such fringe benefits from gross income. §§ 105 and 106.

Accountable plan. A type of expense reimbursement plan that requires an employee to render an adequate accounting to the employer and return any excess reimbursement or allowance. If the expense qualifies, it will be treated as a deduction *for* AGI.

Accounting income. The accountant's concept of income is generally based upon the realization principle. Financial accounting income may differ from taxable income (e.g., accelerated depreciation might be used for Federal income tax and straight-line depreciation for financial accounting purposes). Differences are included in a reconciliation of taxable and accounting income on Schedule M–1 or Schedule M–3 of Form 1120 for corporations.

Accounting method. The method under which income and expenses are determined for tax purposes. Important accounting methods include the cash basis and the accrual basis. Special methods are available for the reporting of gain on installment sales, recognition of income on construction projects (the completed contract and percentage of completion methods), and the valuation of inventories (last-in, first-out and first-in, first-out). §§ 446–474.

Accounting period. The period of time, usually a year, used by a taxpayer for the determination of tax liability. Unless a fiscal year is chosen, taxpayers must determine and pay their income tax liability by using the calendar year (January 1 through December 31) as the period of measurement. An example of a fiscal year is July 1 through June 30. A change in accounting period (e.g., from a calendar year to a fiscal year) generally requires the consent of the IRS. Some new taxpayers, such as a newly formed corporation, are free to select either an initial calendar or a fiscal year without the consent of the IRS. §§ 441–444.

Accrual method. A method of accounting that reflects expenses incurred and income earned for any one tax year. In contrast to the cash basis of accounting, expenses need not be paid to be deductible, nor need income be received to be taxable. Unearned income (e.g., prepaid interest and rent) generally is taxed in the year of receipt regardless of the method of accounting used by the taxpayer. § 446(c)(2).

Accumulated adjustments account (AAA). An account that aggregates an S corporation's post-1982 income, loss, and deductions for the tax year (including nontaxable income and nondeductible losses and expenses). After the year-end income and expense adjustments are made, the account is reduced by distributions made during the tax year. § 1368(e)(1).

Accumulated earnings and profits. Net undistributed tax-basis earnings of a corporation aggregated from March 1, 1913, to the end of the prior tax year. Used to determine the amount of dividend income associated with a distribution to shareholders. § 316 and Reg. § 1.316–2.

Acquiescence. Agreement by the IRS on the results reached in certain judicial decisions; sometimes abbreviated *Acq.* or *A.*

Acquisition indebtedness. Debt incurred in acquiring, constructing, or substantially improving a qualified residence of the taxpayer. The interest on such loans is deductible as qualified residence interest. However, interest on such debt is deductible only on the portion of the indebtedness that does not exceed $1,000,000 ($500,000 for married persons filing separate returns). § 163(h)(3).

Active income. Income that includes wages, salary, commissions, bonuses, profits from a trade or business in which the taxpayer is a material participant; gain on the sale or other disposition of assets used in an active trade or business; and income from intangible property if the taxpayer's personal efforts significantly contributed to the creation of the property. The passive activity loss rules require classification of income and losses into three categories with active income being one of them. § 465.

Ad valorem tax. A tax imposed on the value of property. The most common ad valorem tax is that imposed by states, counties, and cities on real estate. Ad valorem taxes can be imposed on personal property as well.

Additional depreciation. The excess of the amount of depreciation actually deducted over the amount that would have been deducted had the straight-line method been used. § 1250(b).

Additional first-year depreciation. See *fifty percent additional first-year depreciation* and *one hundred percent additional first-year depreciation.*

Adjusted basis. The cost or other basis of property reduced by depreciation allowed or allowable and increased by capital improvements. Other special adjustments are provided in § 1016 and the related Regulations.

Adjusted current earnings (ACE). An adjustment in computing corporate alternative minimum taxable income (AMTI), computed at 75 percent of the excess of adjusted current earnings (ACE) over unadjusted AMTI. ACE computations reflect longer and slower cost recovery deductions and other restrictions on the timing of certain recognition events. Exempt interest, life insurance proceeds, and other receipts that are included in earnings and profits but not in taxable income also increase the ACE adjustment. If unadjusted AMTI exceeds ACE, the ACE adjustment is negative. The negative adjustment is limited to the aggregate of the positive adjustments under ACE for prior years, reduced by any previously claimed negative adjustments. § 56(g).

Adoption expenses credit. A provision intended to assist taxpayers who incur nonrecurring costs directly associated with the adoption process, such as legal costs, social service review costs, and transportation costs. Up to $13,190 ($13,190 for a child with special needs regardless of the actual adoption expenses) of costs incurred to adopt an eligible child qualify for the credit. A taxpayer may claim the credit in the year qualifying expenses are paid or incurred if the expenses are paid during or after the year in which the adoption is finalized. For qualifying expenses paid or incurred in a tax year prior to the year the adoption is finalized, the credit must be claimed in the tax year following the tax year during which the expenses are paid or incurred. § 23.

Alimony and separate maintenance payments. Alimony deductions result from the payment of a legal obligation arising from the termination of a marital relationship. Payments designated as alimony generally are included in the gross income of the recipient and are deductible *for* AGI by the payer. §§ 62(a)(10), 71, and 215.

Allocate. The assignment of income for various tax purposes. A multistate corporation's nonbusiness income usually is allocated to the state where the nonbusiness assets are located; it is not apportioned with the rest of the entity's income. International taxpayers allocate certain expenses in computing the taxable income from specific activities. Partnerships can allocate specific items of income, deduction, and credit if certain requirements are met.

Alternative depreciation system (ADS). A cost recovery system that produces a smaller deduction than would be calculated under ACRS or MACRS. The alternative system must be used in certain instances and can be elected in other instances. § 168(g).

Alternative minimum tax (AMT). The AMT is a fixed percentage of alternative minimum taxable income (AMTI). AMTI generally starts with the taxpayer's adjusted gross income (for individuals) or taxable income (for other taxpayers). To this amount, the taxpayer (1) adds designated preference items (e.g., tax-exempt interest income on private activity bonds), (2) makes other specified adjustments (e.g., to reflect a longer straight-line cost recovery deduction), (3) subtracts certain AMT itemized deductions for individuals (e.g., interest incurred on housing but not taxes paid), and (4) subtracts an exemption amount (e.g., $40,000 on a C corporation's return). The taxpayer must pay the greater of the resulting AMT (reduced by only the foreign tax credit) or the regular income tax (reduced by all allowable tax credits). The AMT does not apply to certain small C corporations. AMT preferences and adjustments are assigned to partners and S corporation shareholders. §§ 55–59.

Alternative minimum tax credit. The AMT can result from timing differences that give rise to positive adjustments in calculating the AMT base. To provide equity for the taxpayer when these timing differences reverse, the regular tax liability may be reduced by a tax credit for a prior year's minimum tax liability attributable to timing differences. § 53.

Alternative minimum taxable income (AMTI). The base (prior to deducting the exemption amount) for computing a taxpayer's alternative minimum tax. This consists of the taxable income for the year modified for AMT adjustments and AMT preferences. § 55(b)(2).

Alternative tax. An option that is allowed in computing the tax on net capital gain. For the corporate taxpayer, the rate is 35 percent (the same as the highest regular corporate tax rate). Thus, for corporate taxpayers, the alternative tax does not produce a beneficial result. For noncorporate taxpayers, the rate is usually 15 percent (but it is 25 percent for unrecaptured § 1250 gain and 28 percent for collectibles and § 1202 gain). However, if the noncorporate taxpayer is in either the 10 percent or the 15 percent tax bracket, the alternative tax rate is 0 percent in 2008, 2009, 2010, 2011, 2012, 2013, and 2014 and 5 percent in 2007 and prior years (rather than 15 percent). Certain high-income taxpayers (i.e., in the 39.6 percent tax bracket) have an alternative tax rate of 20 percent. §§ 1(h) and 1201. See also *collectibles, net capital gain,* and *unrecaptured § 1250 gain (25 percent gain).*

American Opportunity credit. This credit replaces the HOPE scholarship credit for 2009, 2010, 2011, 2012, 2013, and 2014 and applies for qualifying expenses for the first four years of postsecondary education. Qualified expenses include tuition and related expenses and books and other course materials. Room and board are ineligible for the credit. The maximum credit available per student is $2,500 (100 percent of the first $2,000 of qualified expenses and 25 percent of the next $2,000 of qualified expenses). Eligible students include the taxpayer, taxpayer's spouse, and taxpayer's dependents. To qualify for the credit, a student must take at least one-half of the full-time course load for at least one academic term at a qualifying educational institution. The credit is phased out for higher income taxpayers. § 25A. See also *HOPE scholarship credit* and *lifetime learning credit.*

Amortization. The tax deduction for the cost or other basis of an intangible asset over the asset's estimated useful life. Examples of amortizable intangibles include patents, copyrights, and leasehold interests. The intangible goodwill can be amortized for income tax purposes over a 15-year period. § 197.

Amount realized. The amount received by a taxpayer upon the sale or exchange of property. Amount realized is the sum of the cash and the fair market value of any property or services received by the taxpayer plus any related debt assumed by the buyer. Determining the amount realized is the starting point for arriving at realized gain or loss. § 1001(b).

Apportion. The assignment of the business income of a multistate corporation to specific states for income taxation. Usually, the apportionment procedure accounts for the property, payroll, and sales activity levels of the various states, and a proportionate assignment of the entity's total income is made using a three-factor apportionment formula. Some states exclude nonbusiness income from the apportionment procedure; they allocate nonbusiness income to the states where the nonbusiness assets are located.

Arm's length concept. The standard under which unrelated parties would carry out a transaction. Suppose Bint Corporation sells property to its sole shareholder for $10,000. In determining whether $10,000 is an arm's length price, one would ascertain the amount for which the corporation could have sold the property to a disinterested third party.

Arm's length price. See *arm's length concept.*

ASC 450 (SFAS 5). Under Generally Accepted Accounting Principles, the rules for the financial reporting of contingent liabilities, including deferred taxes.

ASC 740 (SFAS 109). Under Generally Accepted Accounting Principles, the rules for the financial reporting of the tax expense of an enterprise. *Permanent differences* affect the enterprise's effective tax rate. *Temporary differences* create a deferred tax asset or a deferred tax liability on the balance sheet.

ASC 740-10 (FIN 48). Under Generally Accepted Accounting Principles, an interpretation of *ASC 740 (SFAS 109)* relating to when a tax benefit should be reported in an enterprise's financial statements. A tax benefit should be recorded for book purposes only if it is more likely than not that the taxpayer's filing position will be sustained after an audit, an administrative appeal, and the highest applicable judicial review.

ASC 740-30 (APB 23). Under Generally Accepted Accounting Principles, the rules for the financial reporting of the tax expense relative to a U.S. corporation's non-U.S. subsidiary. If the parent documents that it is *permanently reinvesting* the non-U.S. earning of a non-U.S. subsidiary, the parent does not record as an expense any U.S. income tax the parent might pay on such earnings [i.e., the book tax expense is deferred until such earnings are (if ever) repatriated to the United States].

Assignment of income. A procedure whereby a taxpayer attempts to avoid the recognition of income by assigning to another the property that generates the income. Such a procedure will not avoid the recognition of income by the taxpayer making the assignment if it can be said that the income was earned at the point of the transfer. In this case, usually referred to as an anticipatory assignment of income, the income will be taxed to the person who earns it.

Assumption of liabilities. In a corporate formation, a corporate takeover, or an asset purchase, the new owner often takes assets and agrees to assume preexisting debt. Such actions do not create boot received on the transaction for the new shareholder unless there is no *bona fide* business purpose for the exchange or the principal purpose of the debt assumption is the avoidance of tax liabilities. Gain is recognized to the extent liabilities assumed exceed the aggregated bases of the transferred assets. § 357.

At-risk limitation. Generally, a taxpayer can deduct losses related to a trade or business, an S corporation, a partnership, or an investment asset only to the extent of the at-risk amount.

Automatic mileage method. Automobile expenses are generally deductible only to the extent the automobile is used in business or for the production of income. Personal commuting expenses are not deductible. The taxpayer may deduct actual expenses (including depreciation and insurance), or the standard (automatic) mileage rate may be used (56.5 cents per mile for 2013 and 56.0 cents for 2014). Automobile expenses incurred for medical purposes or in connection with job-related moving expenses are deductible to the extent of actual out-of-pocket expenses or at the rate of 24 cents per mile for 2013 and 23.5 cents per mile for 2014. For charitable activities, the rate is 14 cents per mile. See also *transportation expenses.*

B

Bad debts. A deduction is permitted if a business account receivable subsequently becomes partially or completely worthless, providing the income arising from the debt previously was included in income. Available methods are the specific charge-off method and the reserve method. However, except for certain financial institutions, TRA of 1986 repealed the use of the reserve method for 1987 and thereafter. If the reserve method is used, partially or totally worthless accounts are charged to the reserve. A nonbusiness bad debt deduction is allowed as a short-term capital loss if the loan did not arise in connection with the creditor's trade or business activities. Loans between related parties (family members) generally are classified as nonbusiness. § 166.

Balance sheet approach. The process under *ASC 740 (SFAS 109)* by which an entity's *deferred tax expense* or *deferred tax benefit* is determined as a result of the reporting period's changes in the balance sheet's deferred tax asset and deferred tax liability accounts.

Basis in the partnership interest. The acquisition cost of the partner's ownership interest in the partnership. Includes purchase price and associated debt acquired from other partners and in the course of the entity's trade or business. § 705.

Benchmarking. The tax professional's use of two or more entities' effective tax rates and deferred tax balance sheet accounts. Used chiefly to compare the effectiveness of the entities' tax planning techniques and to suggest future tax-motivated courses of action.

Boot. Cash or property of a type not included in the definition of a nontaxable exchange. The receipt of boot causes an otherwise nontaxable transfer to become taxable to the extent of the lesser of the fair market value of the boot or the realized gain on the transfer. For example, see transfers to controlled corporations under § 351(b) and like-kind exchanges under § 1031(b).

Brother-sister controlled group. More than one corporation owned by the same shareholders. If, for example, Chris and Pat each own one-half of the stock in Wren Corporation and Redbird Corporation, Wren and Redbird form a brother-sister controlled group. § 1563(a)(2).

Built-in gains tax. A penalty tax designed to discourage a shift of the incidence of taxation on unrealized gains from a C corporation to its shareholders via an S election. Under this provision, any recognized gain during the first 10 years of S status generates a corporate-level tax on a base not to exceed the aggregate untaxed built-in gains brought into the S corporation upon its election from C corporation taxable years. § 1374.

Built-in loss property. Property contributed to a corporation under § 351 or as a contribution to capital that has a basis in excess of its fair market value. An adjustment is necessary to step down the basis of the property to its fair market value. The adjustment prevents the corporation and the contributing shareholder from obtaining a double tax benefit. The corporation allocates the adjustment proportionately among the assets with the built-in loss. As an alternative to the corporate adjustment, the shareholder may elect to reduce the basis in the stock.

Business bad debt. A tax deduction allowed for obligations obtained in connection with a trade or business that have become either partially or completely worthless. In contrast to nonbusiness bad debts, business bad debts are deductible as business expenses. § 166.

Buy-sell agreement. An arrangement, particularly appropriate in the case of a closely held corporation or a partnership, whereby the surviving owners (shareholders or partners) or the entity agrees to purchase the interest of a withdrawing owner. The buy-sell agreement provides for an orderly disposition of an interest in a business and may aid in setting the value of the interest for estate tax purposes.

C

C corporation. A separate taxable entity subject to the rules of Subchapter C of the Code. This business form may create a double taxation effect relative to its shareholders. The entity is subject to the regular corporate tax and a number of penalty taxes at the Federal level.

Cafeteria plan. An employee benefit plan under which an employee is allowed to select from among a variety of employer-provided fringe benefits. Some of the benefits may be taxable, and some may be statutory nontaxable benefits (e.g., health and accident insurance and group term life insurance). The employee is taxed only on the taxable benefits selected. A cafeteria benefit plan is also referred to as a flexible benefit plan. § 125.

Capital account. The financial accounting analog of a partner's tax basis in the entity.

Capital asset. Broadly speaking, all assets are capital except those specifically excluded by the Code. Major categories of noncapital assets include property held for resale in the normal course of business (inventory), trade accounts and notes receivable, and depreciable property and real estate used in a trade or business (§ 1231 assets). § 1221.

Capital contribution. Various means by which a shareholder makes additional funds available to the corporation (placed at the risk of the business), sometimes without the receipt of additional stock. If no stock is received, the contributions are added to the basis of the shareholder's existing stock investment and do not generate gross income to the corporation. § 118.

Capital gain. The gain from the sale or exchange of a capital asset.

Capital gain property. Property contributed to a charitable organization that if sold rather than contributed, would have resulted in long-term capital gain to the donor.

Capital interest. Usually, the percentage of the entity's net assets that a partner would receive upon liquidation. Typically determined by the partner's capital sharing ratio.

Capital loss. The loss from the sale or exchange of a capital asset.

Capital sharing ratio. A partner's percentage ownership of the entity's capital.

Cash receipts method. A method of accounting that reflects deductions as paid and income as received in any one tax year. However, deductions for prepaid expenses that benefit more than one tax year (e.g., prepaid rent and prepaid interest) usually must be spread over the period benefited rather than deducted in the year paid. For fixed assets, the cash basis taxpayer claims deductions through depreciation or amortization in the same manner as an accrual basis taxpayer. § 446(c)(1).

Casualty loss. A casualty is defined as "the complete or partial destruction of property resulting from an identifiable event of a sudden, unexpected or unusual nature" (e.g., floods, storms, fires, auto accidents). Individuals may deduct a casualty loss only if the loss is incurred in a trade or business or in a transaction entered into for profit or arises from fire, storm, shipwreck, or other casualty or from theft. Individuals usually deduct personal casualty losses as itemized deductions subject to a $100 ($500 for 2009) nondeductible amount and to an annual floor equal to 10 percent of adjusted gross income that applies after the $100 ($500 for 2009) per casualty floor has been applied. Special rules are provided for the netting of certain casualty gains and losses. § 165(c)(3).

Charitable contributions. Contributions are deductible (subject to various restrictions and ceiling limitations) if made to qualified nonprofit charitable organizations. A cash basis taxpayer is entitled to a deduction solely in the year of payment. Accrual basis corporations may accrue contributions at year-end if payment is properly authorized before the end of the year and payment is made within two and one-half months after the end of the year. § 170.

Check-the-box Regulation. A business entity can elect to be taxed as a partnership, an S corporation, or a C corporation by indicating its preference on the tax return. Legal structure and operations are irrelevant in this regard. Thus, by using the check-the-box rules prudently, an entity can select the most attractive tax results offered by the Code, without being bound by legal forms. Not available if the entity is incorporated under state law.

Child tax credit. A tax credit based solely on the number of qualifying children under age 17. The maximum credit available is $1,000 per child through 2014. A qualifying child must be claimed as a dependent on a parent's tax return to qualify for the credit. Taxpayers who qualify for the child tax credit may also qualify for a supplemental credit. The supplemental credit is treated as a component of the earned income credit and is therefore refundable. The credit is phased out for higher-income taxpayers. § 24.

Circuit Court of Appeals. Any of 13 Federal courts that consider tax matters appealed from the U.S. Tax Court, a U.S. District Court, or the U.S. Court of Federal Claims. Appeal from a U.S. Court of Appeals is to the U.S. Supreme Court by *Certiorari*.

Citator. A tax research resource that presents the judicial history of a court case and traces the subsequent references to the case. When these references include the citing cases' evaluations of the cited case's precedents, the research can obtain some measure of the efficacy and reliability of the original holding.

Claim of right doctrine. A judicially imposed doctrine applicable to both cash and accrual basis taxpayers that holds that an amount is includible in income upon actual or constructive receipt if the taxpayer has an unrestricted claim to the payment. For the tax treatment of amounts repaid when previously included in income under the claim of right doctrine, see § 1341.

Closely held C corporation. A regular corporation (i.e., the S election is not in effect) for which more than 50 percent of the value of its outstanding stock is owned, directly or indirectly, by five or fewer individuals at any time during the tax year. The term is relevant in identifying C corporations that are subject to the passive activity loss provisions. § 469.

Collectibles. A special type of capital asset, the gain from which is taxed at a maximum rate of 28 percent if the holding period is more than one year. Examples include art, rugs, antiques, gems, metals, stamps, some coins and bullion, and alcoholic beverages held for investment. § 1(h).

Compensatory damages. Damages received or paid by the taxpayer can be classified as compensatory damages or as punitive damages. Compensatory damages are paid to compensate one for harm caused by another. Compensatory damages are excludible from the recipient's gross income. § 104(a)(2).

Conduit concept. An approach assumed by the tax law in the treatment of certain entities and their owners. Specific tax characteristics pass through the entity without losing their identity. For example, items of income and expense, capital gains and losses, tax credits, etc., realized by a part-

nership pass through the partnership (a conduit) and are subject to taxation at the partner level. Also, in an S corporation, certain items pass through and are reported on the returns of the shareholders.

Conservatism principle. The theory behind much of Generally Accepted Accounting Principles, under which assurance is provided that an entity's balance sheet assets are not overstated, nor liabilities understated. For instance, under *ASC 740 (SFAS 109)*, a deferred tax asset is not recorded until it is more likely than not that the future tax benefit will be realized.

Constructive dividend. A taxable benefit derived by a shareholder from his or her corporation that is not actually called a dividend. Examples include unreasonable compensation, excessive rent payments, bargain purchases of corporate property, and shareholder use of corporate property. Constructive dividends generally are found in closely held corporations.

Constructive receipt. If income is unqualifiedly available although not physically in the taxpayer's possession, it is subject to the income tax. An example is accrued interest on a savings account. Under the constructive receipt of income concept, the interest is taxed to a depositor in the year available, rather than the year actually withdrawn. The fact that the depositor uses the cash basis of accounting for tax purposes is irrelevant. See Reg. § 1.451–2.

Control. Holding a specified level of stock ownership in a corporation. For § 351, the new shareholder(s) must hold at least 80 percent of the total combined voting power of all voting classes of stock and at least 80 percent of the shares of all nonvoting classes. Other tax provisions require different levels of control to bring about desired effects, such as 50 or 100 percent.

Controlled foreign corporation (CFC). A non-U.S. corporation in which more than 50 percent of the total combined voting power of all classes of stock entitled to vote or the total value of the stock of the corporation is owned by "U.S. shareholders" on any day during the taxable year of the foreign corporation. For purposes of this definition, a U.S. shareholder is any U.S. person who owns, or is considered to own, 10 percent or more of the total combined voting power of all classes of voting stock of the foreign corporation. Stock owned directly, indirectly, and constructively is used in this measure. Certain Subpart F income of the CFC is taxed to the U.S. shareholders when it is earned, not when it is later repatriated.

Controlled group. A group of corporations that is required to share the lower-level corporate tax rates and various other tax benefits among the members of the group. A controlled group may be either a brother-sister or a parent-subsidiary group. §§ 1561 and 1563.

Corporate liquidation. Occurs when a corporation distributes its net assets to its shareholders and ceases to be a going concern. Generally, a shareholder recognizes capital gain or loss upon the liquidation of the entity, regardless of the corporation's balance in its earnings and profits account. The liquidating corporation recognizes gain and loss on assets that it sells during the liquidation period and on assets that it distributes to shareholders in kind.

Cost depletion. Depletion that is calculated based on the adjusted basis of the asset. The adjusted basis is divided by the expected recoverable units to determine the depletion per unit. The depletion per unit is multiplied by the units sold during the tax year to calculate cost depletion. § 612.

Cost recovery system. The system that provides for the write-off of the cost of an asset under ACRS or MACRS. The cost recovery system replaced the depreciation system as the method of writing off the cost of an asset for most capitalized assets placed in service after 1980 (after 1986 for MACRS). See also *alternative depreciation system, fifty percent additional first-year depreciation*, and *one hundred percent additional first-year depreciation*. § 168.

Court of Federal Claims. A trial court (court of original jurisdiction) that decides litigation involving Federal tax matters. Appeal from this court is to the Court of Appeals for the Federal Circuit.

Court of original jurisdiction. The Federal courts are divided into courts of original jurisdiction and appellate courts. A dispute between a taxpayer and the IRS is first considered by a court of original jurisdiction (i.e., a trial court). The four Federal courts of original jurisdiction are the U.S. Tax Court, the U.S. District Court, the Court of Federal Claims, and the Small Cases Division of the U.S. Tax Court.

Coverdell Education Savings Account (CESA). A savings account established to pay for qualified education expenses (i.e., tuition, fees, books, supplies, related equipment, and room and board if the student's course load is at least one-half of the full-time course load). The maximum annual contribution to the savings account of a beneficiary is $2,000. The maximum annual contribution is subject to phaseout beginning at $95,000 for single taxpayers and $190,000 for married couples who file a joint return. Contributions are not deductible and cannot be made to a savings account once the beneficiary attains age 18. Distributions used to pay for qualified education expenses for a designated beneficiary are tax-free. § 530.

Credit for child and dependent care expenses. A tax credit ranging from 20 percent to 35 percent of employment-related expenses (child and dependent care expenses) for amounts of up to $6,000 is available to individuals who are employed (or deemed to be employed) and maintain a household for a dependent child under age 13, disabled spouse, or disabled dependent. § 21.

Credit for employer-provided child care. A nonrefundable credit is available to employers who provided child care facilities to their employees during normal working hours. The credit, limited to $150,000, is comprised of two components. The portion of the credit for qualified child care expenses is equal to 25 percent of these expenses, while the portion of the credit for qualified child care resources and referral services is equal to 10 percent of these expenses. Any qualifying expenses otherwise deductible by the taxpayer must be reduced by the amount of the credit. In addition, the taxpayer's basis for any property used for qualifying purposes is reduced by the amount of the credit. § 45F.

Credit for small employer pension plan startup costs. A nonrefundable credit available to small businesses based on administrative costs associated with establishing and maintaining certain qualified plans. While such qualifying costs generally are deductible as ordinary and necessary business expense, the availability of the credit is intended to lower the costs of starting a qualified retirement program and therefore encourage qualifying businesses to establish retirement plans for their employees. The credit is available for eligible employers at the rate of 50 percent of qualified startup costs. The maximum credit is $500 (based on a maximum of $1,000 of qualifying expenses). § 45E.

Current earnings and profits. Net tax-basis earnings of a corporation aggregated during the current tax year. A corporate distribution is deemed to be first from the entity's current earnings and profits and then from accumulated earnings and profits. Shareholders recognize dividend income to the extent of the earnings and profits of the corporation. A dividend results to the extent of current earnings and profits, even if there is a larger negative balance in accumulated earnings and profits.

Current tax expense. Under *ASC 740* (*SFAS 109*), the book tax expense that relates to the current reporting period's net income and is actually payable (or creditable) to the appropriate governmental agencies for the current period. Also known as "cash tax" or "tax payable."

D

***De minimis* fringe benefits.** Benefits provided to employees that are too insignificant to warrant the time and effort required to account for the benefits received by each employee and the value of those benefits. Such amounts are excludible from the employee's gross income. § 132.

Death tax. See *estate tax*.

Deduction for qualified tuition and related expenses. Taxpayers are allowed a deduction of up to $4,000 for higher-education expenses. Certain taxpayers are not eligible for the deduction: those whose AGI exceeds a specified amount and those who can be claimed as a dependent by another taxpayer. These expenses are classified as a deduction *for* AGI and they need not be employment-related. § 222.

Deemed-paid credit. A foreign tax credit allowed to a U.S. taxpayer that has received an actual or constructive dividend from a non-U.S. corporation that has paid foreign income taxes. The credit is computed using the proportion of foreign income taxes paid by the payor corporation to its post-1986 undistributed earnings. Under § 78, the U.S. taxpayer claiming a deemed-paid credit includes the same amount in gross income for the tax year.

Deferred tax asset. Under *ASC 740* (*SFAS 109*), an item created on an enterprise's balance sheet by a temporary book-tax difference, such that a tax benefit is not recognized until a later date, although it already has been reported in the financial statements (e.g., the carryforward of a disallowed deduction).

Deferred tax benefit. Under *ASC 740* (*SFAS 109*), a reduction in the book tax expense that relates to the current reporting period's net income but will not be realized until a future reporting period. Creates or adds to the entity's deferred tax asset balance sheet account. For instance, the carryforward of a *net operating loss* is a deferred tax benefit.

Deferred tax expense. Under *ASC 740* (*SFAS 109*), a book tax expense that relates to the current reporting period's net income but will not be realized until a future reporting period. Creates or adds to the entity's deferred tax liability balance sheet account. For instance, a deferred tax expense is created when tax depreciation deductions for the period are "accelerated" and exceed the corresponding book depreciation expense.

Deferred tax liability. As determined under the rules of *ASC 740* (*SFAS 109*), an item created on an enterprise's balance sheet by a temporary book-tax difference, such that a tax benefit is recognized earlier for tax purposes than it is in the financial accounting records (e.g., the use of an accelerated cost recovery deduction).

Dependency exemption. The tax law provides an exemption for each individual taxpayer and an additional exemption for the taxpayer's spouse if a joint return is filed. An individual may also claim a dependency exemption for each dependent, provided certain tests are met. The amount of the personal and dependency exemptions is $3,950 in 2014 ($3,900 in 2013). The exemption was subject to phaseout once adjusted gross income exceeded certain statutory threshold amounts. This phaseout provision was subject to partial phaseout beginning in 2006. For 2009, two-thirds of the reduction in the exemption amount is phased out, and for 2010, all of the reduction is phased out. Under the sunset provision, the phaseout of personal and dependency exemptions was scheduled to be reinstated in 2011. The Tax Relief Act (TRA) of 2010 put off the reinstatement for two years (i.e., 2011 and 2012). For 2013 and 2014, the American Taxpayer Relief Act of 2012 restored the phaseout of personal and dependency exemptions. §§ 151 and 152.

Depletion. The process by which the cost or other basis of a natural resource (e.g., an oil or gas interest) is recovered upon extraction and sale of the resource. The two ways to determine the depletion allowance are the cost and percentage (or statutory) methods. Under cost depletion, each unit of production sold is assigned a portion of the cost or other basis of the interest. This is determined by dividing the cost or other basis by the total units expected to be recovered. Under percentage (or statutory) depletion, the tax law provides a special percentage factor for different types of minerals and other natural resources. This percentage is multiplied by the gross income from the interest to arrive at the depletion allowance. §§ 611–613 and 613A.

Depreciation rules. The depreciation system that existed prior to the enactment of the Accelerated Cost Recovery System (ACRS). This system applies to depreciable assets placed in service prior to January 1, 1981, and to certain post-1980 assets that do not qualify for ACRS. § 167.

Determination letter. Upon the request of a taxpayer, an IRS Area Director will comment on the tax status of a completed transaction. Determination letters frequently are used to clarify employee status, determine whether a retirement or profit sharing plan qualifies under the Code, and determine the tax-exempt status of certain nonprofit organizations.

Disabled access credit. A tax credit designed to encourage small businesses to make their facilities more accessible to disabled individuals. The credit is equal to 50 percent of the eligible expenditures that exceed $250 but do not exceed $10,250. Thus, the maximum amount for the credit is $5,000. The adjusted basis for depreciation is reduced by the amount of the credit. To qualify, the facility must have been placed in service before November 6, 1990. § 44.

Disaster area loss. A casualty sustained in an area designated as a disaster area by the President of the United States. In such an event, the disaster loss may be treated as having occurred in the taxable year immediately preceding the year in which the disaster actually occurred. Thus, immediate tax benefits are provided to victims of a disaster. § 165(i).

Disguised sale. When a partner contributes property to the entity and soon thereafter receives a distribution from the partnership, the transactions are collapsed and the distribution is seen as a purchase of the asset by the partnership. § 707(a)(2)(B).

Disregarded entity. The Federal income tax treatment of business income usually follows the legal form of the taxpayer (i.e., an individual's sole proprietorship is reported on the Form 1040); a C corporation's taxable income is computed on Form 1120. The check-the-box regulations are used if the unincorporated taxpayer wants to use a different tax regime. Under these rules, a disregarded entity is taxed as an individual or a corporate division; other tax regimes are not available. For instance, a one-member limited liability company is a disregarded entity.

District Court. A Federal District Court is a trial court for purposes of litigating (among others) Federal tax matters. It is the only trial court where a jury trial can be obtained.

Dividend. A nondeductible distribution by a corporation to a shareholder. A dividend constitutes gross income to the recipient if it is from the current or accumulated earnings and profits of the corporation.

Dividends received deduction. A deduction allowed a shareholder that is a corporation for dividends received from a domestic corporation. The deduction usually is 70 percent of the dividends received, but it could be 80 or 100 percent depending upon the ownership percentage held by the recipient corporation. §§ 243–246.

Domestic production activities deduction (DPAD). See *production activities deduction (PAD)*.

Domestic production gross receipts (DPGR). A key component in computing the domestic production activities deduction (DPAD). Includes receipts from the sale and other disposition of qualified production property produced in significant part within the United States. DPGR is defined in § 199(c)(4). See also *production activities deduction (PAD)*.

E

Earned income credit. A tax credit designed to provide assistance to certain low-income individuals who generally have a qualifying child. This is a refundable credit. To receive the most beneficial treatment, the taxpayer must have qualifying children. However, it is possible to qualify for the credit without having a child. To calculate the credit for a taxpayer with one or more children for 2013, a statutory rate of 34 percent for one child (40 percent for two children and 45 percent for three or more children) is multiplied by the earned income (subject to a statutory maximum of $9,720 with one qualifying child or $13,650 with two qualifying children, and $13,650 for three or more qualifying children). Once the earned income exceeds certain thresholds, the credit is phased out using a 15.98 percent rate for one qualifying child and a 21.06 percent rate for two or more qualifying children. For the qualifying taxpayer without children, the credit is calculated on a maximum earned income of $6,480 applying a 7.65 percent rate with the phaseout beginning later applying the same rate. § 32.

Earnings and profits (E & P). Measures the economic capacity of a corporation to make a distribution to shareholders that is not a return of capital. Such a distribution results in dividend income to the shareholders to the extent of the corporation's current and accumulated earnings and profits. §§ 312 and 316.

Economic effect test. Requirements that must be met before a special allocation may be used by a partnership. The premise behind the test is that each partner who receives an allocation of income or loss from a partnership bears the economic benefit or burden of the allocation.

Economic income. The change in the taxpayer's net worth, as measured in terms of market values, plus the value of the assets the taxpayer consumed during the year. Because of the impracticality of this income model, it is not used for tax purposes.

Education expenses. Employees may deduct education expenses that are incurred either (1) to maintain or improve existing job-related skills or (2) to meet the express requirements of the employer or the requirements imposed by law to retain employment status. The expenses are not deductible if the education is required to meet the minimum educational standards for the taxpayer's job or if the education qualifies the individual for a new trade or business. Reg. § 1.162–5.

Educational savings bonds. U.S. Series EE bonds whose proceeds are used for qualified higher educational expenses for the taxpayer, the taxpayer's spouse, or a dependent. The interest may be excluded from gross income, provided the taxpayer's adjusted gross income does not exceed certain amounts. § 135.

Effective tax rate. The financial statements for an entity include several footnotes, one of which reconciles the expected (statutory) income tax rate (e.g., 35 percent for a C corporation) with the effective tax rate (i.e., total tax expense as a percentage of book income). The reconciliation often is done in dollar and/or percentage terms.

Effectively connected income. Income of a nonresident alien or non-U.S. corporation that is attributable to a trade or business operating in the United States. Income effectively connected to a U.S. trade or business usually is subject to U.S. income taxation, after deductions and allowing other credits, using the appropriate progressive tax rate schedule.

E-file. The electronic filing of a tax return. The filing is either direct or indirect. As to direct, the taxpayer goes online using a computer and tax return preparation software. Indirect filing occurs when a taxpayer utilizes an authorized IRS e-file provider. The provider often is the tax return preparer.

Employment taxes. Taxes that an employer must pay on account of its employees. Employment taxes include FICA (Federal Insurance Contributions Act) and FUTA (Federal Unemployment Tax Act) taxes. Employment taxes are paid to the IRS in addition to income tax withholdings at specified intervals. Such taxes can be levied on the employees, the employer, or both. §§ 1401 and 1402.

Energy credits. Various tax credits are available to those who invest in certain energy property. The purpose of the credit is to create incentives for conservation and to develop alternative energy sources.

Entertainment expenses. Expenses that are deductible only if they are directly related to or associated with a trade or business. Various restrictions and documentation requirements have been imposed upon the deductibility of entertainment expenses to prevent abuses by taxpayers. See, for example, the provision contained in § 274(n) that disallows 50 percent of entertainment expenses. § 274.

Entity concept. The theory of partnership taxation under which a partnership is treated as a separate and distinct entity from the partners and has its own tax attributes.

Equity method. Under Generally Accepted Accounting Principles, the method of financial reporting for the operations of a subsidiary when the parent corporation owns between 20 and 50 percent of the subsidiary's stock. Creates a book-tax difference, as the two entities' operating results are combined for book purposes, but a Federal income tax consolidated return cannot be filed.

Estate tax. A tax imposed on the right to transfer property by death. Thus, an estate tax is levied on the decedent's estate and not on the heir receiving the property. §§ 2001–2058.

Estimated tax. The amount of tax (including alternative minimum tax and self-employment tax) a taxpayer expects to owe for the year after subtracting tax credits and income tax withheld. The estimated tax must be paid in installments at designated intervals (e.g., for the individual taxpayer, by April 15, June 15, September 15, and January 15 of the following year). § 6654.

Excise tax. A tax on the manufacture, sale, or use of goods; on the carrying on of an occupation or activity; or on the transfer of property. Thus, the Federal estate and gift taxes are, theoretically, excise taxes.

F

Fair market value. The amount at which property would change hands between a willing buyer and a willing seller, neither being under any compulsion to buy or to sell and both having reasonable knowledge of the relevant facts. Reg. §§ 1.1001–1(a) and 20.2031–1(b).

FDAP. Income of a nonresident alien or non-U.S. corporation that is received in the form of dividends, interest, rents, royalties, certain compensation, premiums, annuities, and other "fixed, determinable, annual, or periodic" forms. FDAP income usually is subject to U.S. income taxation at a flat 30 percent tax rate.

FICA tax. An abbreviation that stands for Federal Insurance Contributions Act, commonly referred to as the Social Security tax. The FICA tax is comprised of the Social Security tax (old age, survivors, and disability insurance) and the Medicare tax (hospital insurance) and is imposed on both employers and employees. The employer is responsible for withholding from the employee's wages the Social Security tax at a rate of 6.2 percent on a maximum wage base of $106,800 (for 2011) and the Medicare tax at a rate of 1.45 percent (no maximum wage base). The employer is required to match the employee's contribution. For 2011 and 2012, the employee rate is reduced to 4.2 percent for the Social Security tax. The employer's contribution is at the 6.2 percent rate for 2011 and 2012. The maximum wage base for 2013 is $113,700 and for 2014 is $117,000. § 3101.

Fifty percent additional first-year depreciation. This provision, which was effective for property acquired after December 31, 2007, and placed in service before January 1, 2009, provided for an additional cost recovery deduction of 50 percent in the tax year the qualified property was placed in service. Qualified property included most types of new property other than buildings. The taxpayer can elect to forgo this bonus depreciation. The American Recovery and Reinvestment Tax Act of 2009 extended the additional first-year depreciation provision for an additional year. The Small Business Jobs Creation Act of 2010 extended the additional first-year depreciation for an additional year. The American Taxpayer Relief Act of 2012 reinstated bonus depreciation for 2013 using a 50 percent rate. See also *cost recovery system* and *one hundred percent additional first-year depreciation.*

Final Regulation. The U.S. Treasury Department Regulations (abbreviated Reg.) represent the position of the IRS as to how the Internal Revenue Code is to be interpreted. Their purpose is to provide taxpayers and IRS personnel with rules of general and specific application to the various provisions of the tax law. Regulations are published in the *Federal Register* and in all tax services.

Financial Accounting Standards Board (FASB). See *Generally accepted accounting principles (GAAP).*

Flexible spending plan. An employee benefit plan that allows the employee to take a reduction in salary in exchange for the employer paying benefits that can be provided by the employer without the employee being required to recognize income (e.g., medical and child care benefits).

Flow-through entity. The entity is a tax reporter rather than a taxpayer. The owners are subject to tax. Examples are partnerships, S corporations, and limited liability companies.

Foreign earned income exclusion. The foreign earned income exclusion is a relief provision that applies to U.S. citizens working in a foreign country. To qualify for the exclusion, the taxpayer must be either a bona fide resident of the foreign country or present in the foreign country for 330 days during any 12 consecutive months. The exclusion is limited to $99,200 per year for 2014 ($97,600 in 2013). § 911.

Foreign tax credit (FTC). A U.S. citizen or resident who incurs or pays income taxes to a foreign country on income subject to U.S. tax may be able to claim some or all of these taxes as a credit against the U.S. income tax. §§ 27 and 901–905.

Franchise. An agreement that gives the transferee the right to distribute, sell, or provide goods, services, or facilities within a specified area. The cost of obtaining a franchise may be amortized over a statutory period of 15 years. In general, the franchisor's gain on the sale of franchise rights is an ordinary gain because the franchisor retains a significant power, right, or continuing interest in the subject of the franchise. §§ 197 and 1253.

Franchise tax. A tax levied on the right to do business in a state as a corporation. Although income considerations may come into play, the tax usually is based on the capitalization of the corporation.

Fruit and tree metaphor. The courts have held that an individual who earns income from property or services cannot assign that income to another. For example, a father cannot assign his earnings from commissions to his child and escape income tax on those amounts.

FUTA tax. An employment tax levied on employers. Jointly administered by the Federal and state governments, the tax provides funding for unemployment benefits. FUTA applies at a rate of 6.0 percent on the first $7,000 of covered wages paid during the year for each employee in 2014. The Federal government allows a credit for FUTA paid (or allowed under a merit rating system) to the state. The credit cannot exceed 5.4 percent of the covered wages. § 3301.

G

General business credit. The summation of various nonrefundable business credits, including the tax credit for rehabilitation expenditures, business energy credit, work opportunity credit, research activities credit, low-income housing credit, disabled access credit, credit for small employer pension plan startup costs, and credit for employer-provided child care. The amount of general business credit that can be used to reduce the tax liability is limited to the taxpayer's net income tax reduced by the greater of (1) the tentative minimum tax or (2) 25 percent of the net regular tax liability that exceeds $25,000. Unused general business credits can be carried back 1 year and forward 20 years. § 38.

General partnership. A partnership that is owned by one or more general partners. Creditors of a general partnership can collect amounts owed them from both the partnership assets and the assets of the partners individually.

Generally accepted accounting principles (GAAP). Guidelines relating to how to construct the financial statements of enterprises doing business in the United States. Promulgated chiefly by the *Financial Accounting Standards Board (FASB).*

Gift. A transfer of property for less than adequate consideration. Gifts usually occur in a personal setting (such as between members of the same family). They are excluded from the income tax base but may be subject to a transfer tax.

Gift tax. A tax imposed on the transfer of property by gift. The tax is imposed upon the donor of a gift and is based on the fair market value of the property on the date of the gift. §§ 2501–2524.

Goodwill. The reputation and built-up business of a company. For accounting purposes, goodwill has no basis unless it is purchased. In the purchase of a business, goodwill generally is the difference between the purchase price and the fair market value of the assets acquired. Because acquired goodwill is a § 197 intangible asset, it is amortized for tax purposes over a 15-year period. Reg. § 1.167(a)–3.

Gross income. Income subject to the Federal income tax. Gross income does not include all economic income. That is, certain exclusions are allowed (e.g., interest on municipal bonds). For a manufacturing or merchandising business, gross income usually means gross profit (gross sales or gross receipts less cost of goods sold). § 61 and Reg. § 1.61–3(a).

Guaranteed payments. Payments made by a partnership to a partner for services rendered or for the use of capital to the extent the payments are determined without regard to the income of the partnership. The payments are treated as though they were made to a nonpartner and thus are usually deductible by the entity. § 707(c).

H

Half-year convention. A cost recovery convention that assumes that all property is placed in service at mid-year and thus provides for a half-year's cost recovery for that year.

Head of household. An unmarried individual who maintains a household for another and satisfies certain conditions set forth in § 2(b). This status enables the taxpayer to use a set of income tax rates that are lower than those applicable to other unmarried individuals but higher than those applicable to surviving spouses and married persons filing a joint return.

Health Savings Account (HSA). A medical savings account created in legislation enacted in December 2003 that is designed to replace and expand Archer Medical Savings Accounts. See also *medical savings account.*

Holding period. The period of time during which property has been held for income tax purposes. The holding period is significant in determining whether gain or loss from the sale or exchange of a capital asset is long-term or short-term. § 1223.

Home equity loans. Loans that utilize the personal residence of the taxpayer as security. The interest on such loans is deductible as qualified residence interest. However, interest is deductible only on the portion of the loan that does not exceed the lesser of (1) the fair market value of the residence, reduced by the acquisition indebtedness, or (2) $100,000 ($50,000 for married persons filing separate returns). A major benefit of a home equity loan is that there are no tracing rules regarding the use of the loan proceeds. § 163(h)(3).

HOPE scholarship credit. A tax credit for qualifying expenses paid for the first two years of postsecondary education. Room, board, and book costs are ineligible for the credit. The maximum credit available is $1,800 per year per student, computed as 100 percent of the first $1,200 of qualifying expenses, plus 50 percent of the second $1,200 of qualifying expenses. Eligible students include the taxpayer, taxpayer's spouse, and taxpayer's dependents. To qualify for the credit, a student must take at least one-half of the full-time course load for at least one academic term at a qualifying educational institution. The credit is phased out for higher-income taxpayers. For 2009, 2010, 2011, 2012, 2013, and 2014, the HOPE scholarship credit is replaced with the American Opportunity credit. See also *American Opportunity credit* and *lifetime learning credit.* § 25A.

Hybrid method. A combination of the accrual and cash methods of accounting. That is, the taxpayer may account for some items of income on the accrual method (e.g., sales and cost of goods sold) and other items (e.g., interest income) on the cash method.

I

Implicit tax. A tax that is paid through higher prices or lower returns on tax-favored investments rather than being paid directly to the government (i.e., an explicit tax). The value added tax is an example of an implicit tax.

Inbound taxation. U.S. tax effects when a non-U.S. person undertakes an investment or business activity in the United States.

Income. For tax purposes, an increase in wealth that has been realized.

Income tax provision. Under *ASC 740* (*SFAS 109*), a synonym for the book tax expense of an entity for the financial reporting period. Following the "matching principle," all book tax expense that relates to the net income for the reporting period is reported on that period's financial statements, including not only the *current tax expense* but also any *deferred tax expense* and *deferred tax benefit.*

Income tax treaties. An agreement between the U.S. State Department and another country designed to alleviate potential double taxation and to share administrative information useful to tax agencies in both countries, relative to taxpayers with investment or business activities in both countries.

Independent contractor. A self-employed person as distinguished from one who is employed as an employee.

Indexation. A procedure whereby adjustments are made by the IRS to key tax components (e.g., standard deduction, tax brackets, personal and dependency exemptions) to reflect inflation. The adjustments usually are made annually and are based on the change in the consumer price index.

Individual Retirement Account (IRA). A type of retirement plan to which an individual with earned income can contribute a maximum of $3,000 ($3,000 each in the case of a married couple with a spousal IRA) per tax year for 2002–2004. The maximum amount increases to $4,000 in 2005 and $5,000 in 2008. The amount remains at $5,000 for 2009, 2010, 2011, and 2012. For 2013 and 2014, the amount is $5,500. IRAs can be classified as traditional IRAs or Roth IRAs. With a traditional IRA, an individual can contribute and deduct a maximum of $5,500 per tax year in 2014. The deduction is a deduction *for* AGI. However, if the individual is an active participant in another qualified retirement plan, the deduction is phased out proportionally between certain AGI ranges. (Note that the phaseout limits the amount of the deduction and not the amount of the contribution.) With a Roth IRA, an individual can contribute a maximum of $5,500 per tax year in 2014. No deduction is permitted. However, if a five-year holding period requirement is satisfied and if the distribution is a qualified distribution, the taxpayer can make tax-free withdrawals from a Roth IRA. The maximum annual contribution is phased out proportionally between certain AGI ranges. §§ 219 and 408A.

Inheritance tax. A tax imposed on the right to receive property from a decedent. Thus, theoretically, an inheritance tax is imposed on the heir. The Federal estate tax is imposed on the estate.

Inside basis. A partnership's basis in the assets it owns.

Intangible drilling and development costs (IDC). Taxpayers may elect to expense or capitalize (subject to amortization) intangible drilling and development costs. However, ordinary income recapture provisions apply to oil and gas properties on a sale or other disposition if the expense method is elected. §§ 263(c) and 1254(a).

International Accounting Standards Board (IASB). The body that promulgates *International Financial Reporting Standards (IFRS)*. Based in London, representing accounting standard setting bodies in over 100 countries, the IASB develops accounting standards that can serve as the basis for harmonizing conflicting reporting standards among nations.

International Financial Reporting Standards (IFRS). Produced by the *International Accounting Standards Board (IASB)*, guidelines developed since 2001 as to revenue recognition, accounting for business combinations, and a conceptual framework for financial reporting. IFRS provisions are designed so that they can be used by all entities, regardless of where they are based or conduct business. IFRS have gained widespread acceptance throughout the world, and the SEC is considering how to require U.S. entities to use IFRS in addition to, or in lieu of, the accounting rules of the *Financial Accounting Standards Board*.

Interpretive Regulation. A Regulation issued by the Treasury Department that purports to explain the meaning of a particular Code Section. An interpretive Regulation is given less deference than a legislative Regulation.

Investment interest. Payment for the use of funds used to acquire assets that produce investment income. The deduction for investment interest is limited to net investment income for the tax year.

Involuntary conversion. The loss or destruction of property through theft, casualty, or condemnation. Any gain realized on an involuntary conversion can, at the taxpayer's election, be deferred for Federal income tax purposes if the owner reinvests the proceeds within a prescribed period of time in property that is similar or related in service or use. § 1033.

Itemized deductions. Personal and employee expenditures allowed by the Code as deductions from adjusted gross income. Examples include certain medical expenses, interest on home mortgages, state income taxes, and charitable contributions. Itemized deductions are reported on Schedule A of Form 1040. Certain miscellaneous itemized deductions are reduced by 2 percent of the taxpayer's adjusted gross income. In addition, a taxpayer whose adjusted gross income exceeds a certain level (indexed annually) must reduce the itemized deductions by 3 percent of the excess of adjusted gross income over that level. Medical, casualty and theft, and investment interest deductions are not subject to the 3 percent reduction. The 3 percent reduction may not reduce itemized deductions that are subject to the reduction to below 20 percent of their initial amount. Beginning in 2006, this reduction is subject to partial phaseout. For 2009, two-thirds of the reduction is phased out, and for 2010, all of the reduction is phased out. Under the sunset provision, the phaseout of itemized deductions was scheduled to be reinstated beginning in 2011. The Tax Relief Act (TRA) of 2010 put off the reinstatement for two years (i.e., 2011 and 2012). For 2013 and 2014, the American Taxpayer Relief Act of 2012 restored the phaseout for itemized deductions. §§ 63(d), 67, and 68.

K

Keogh plan. A retirement plan that is available to self-employed taxpayers; also referred to as an H.R. 10 plan. Under such plans, in 2014, a taxpayer may deduct each year up to 100 percent of net earnings from self-employment or $52,000, whichever is less. If the plan is a profit sharing plan, the percentage is 25 percent.

Kiddie tax. Passive income, such as interest and dividends, that is recognized by a child under age 19 (under age 24 if a full-time student) is taxed to him or her at the rates that would have applied had the income been incurred by the child's parents, generally to the extent the income exceeds $2,000. The additional tax is assessed regardless of the source of the income or the income's underlying property. If the child's parents are divorced, the custodial parent's rates are used. The parents' rates reflect any applicable alternative minimum tax and the phaseouts of lower tax brackets and other deductions. § 1(g).

L

Legislative Regulation. Some Code Sections give the Secretary of the Treasury or his delegate the authority to prescribe Regulations to carry out the details of administration or to otherwise complete the operating rules. Regulations issued pursuant to this type of authority truly possess the force and effect of law. In effect, Congress is almost delegating its legislative powers to the Treasury Department.

Lessee. One who rents property from another. In the case of real estate, the lessee is also known as the tenant.

Lessor. One who rents property to another. In the case of real estate, the lessor is also known as the landlord.

Letter ruling. The written response of the IRS to a taxpayer's request for interpretation of the revenue laws with respect to a proposed transaction (e.g., concerning the tax-free status of a reorganization). Not to be relied on as precedent by other than the party who requested the ruling.

Life insurance proceeds. A specified sum (the face value or maturity value of the policy) paid to the designated beneficiary of the policy by the life insurance company upon the death of the insured.

Lifetime learning credit. A tax credit for qualifying expenses for taxpayers pursuing education beyond the first two years of postsecondary education. Individuals who are completing their last two years of undergraduate studies, pursuing graduate or professional degrees, or otherwise seeking new job skills or maintaining existing job skills are all eligible for the credit. Eligible individuals include the taxpayer, taxpayer's spouse, and taxpayer's dependents. The maximum credit is 20 percent of the first $10,000 of qualifying expenses and is computed per taxpayer. The credit is phased out for higher-income taxpayers. § 25A.

Like-kind exchange. An exchange of property held for productive use in a trade or business or for investment (except inventory and stocks and bonds) for other investment or trade or business property. Unless non-like-kind property (boot) is received, the exchange is fully nontaxable. § 1031.

Limited liability company (LLC). A form of entity allowed by all of the states. The entity is taxed as a partnership in which all members or owners of the LLC are treated much like limited partners. There are no restrictions on ownership, all members may participate in management, and none has personal liability for the entity's debts.

Limited liability partnership (LLP). A form of entity allowed by many of the states, where a general partnership registers with the state as an LLP. Owners are general partners, but a partner is not liable for any malpractice committed by other partners. The personal assets of the partners are at risk for the entity's contractual liabilities, such as accounts payable. The personal assets of a specific partner are at risk for his or her own professional malpractice and tort liability and for malpractice and torts committed by those whom he or she supervises.

Limited partnership. A partnership in which some of the partners are limited partners. At least one of the partners in a limited partnership must be a general partner.

Listed property. Property that includes (1) any passenger automobile; (2) any other property used as a means of transportation; (3) any property of a type generally used for purposes of entertainment, recreation, or amusement; (4) any computer or peripheral equipment (with an exception for exclusive business use); (5) any cellular telephone (or other similar telecommunications equipment); and (6) any other property of a type specified in the Regulations. If listed property is predominantly used for business, the taxpayer is allowed to use the statutory percentage method of cost recovery. Otherwise, the straight-line cost recovery method must be used. § 280F.

Long-term nonpersonal-use capital assets. Includes investment property with a long-term holding period. Such property disposed of by casualty or theft may receive § 1231 treatment.

M

Marriage penalty. The additional tax liability that results for a married couple when compared with what their tax liability would be if they were not married and filed separate returns.

Material participation. If an individual taxpayer materially participates in a nonrental trade or business activity, any loss from that activity is treated as an active loss that can be offset against active income. Material participation is achieved by meeting any one of seven tests provided in the Regulations. § 469(h).

Medical expenses. Medical expenses of an individual, a spouse, and dependents are allowed as an itemized deduction to the extent such amounts (less insurance reimbursements) exceed 10 percent (or 7.5 percent if at least age 65) of adjusted gross income. § 213.

Medical savings account (MSA). A plan available to employees of small firms (50 or fewer employees) with high-deductible health insurance. The employee can place money in the fund and then deduct the contributions (within limits) from gross income. If the employer contributes to the fund, the employee can exclude the contribution from gross income. Income earned from the fund and withdrawals for medical care are not subject to tax. See also *Health Savings Account (HSA)*. §§ 106(b) and 220.

Mid-month convention. A cost recovery convention that assumes that property is placed in service in the middle of the month that it is actually placed in service.

Mid-quarter convention. A cost recovery convention that assumes that property placed in service during the year is placed in service at the middle of the quarter in which it is actually placed in service. The mid-quarter convention applies if more than 40 percent of the value of property (other than eligible real estate) is placed in service during the last quarter of the year.

Minimum tax credit (AMT). When a corporation pays an alternative minimum tax (AMT), a minimum tax credit is created on a dollar-for-dollar basis to be applied against regular tax liabilities incurred in future years. The credit is carried forward indefinitely, but it is not carried back. The effect of the credit for corporate taxpayers alternating between the AMT and regular tax models is to make the AMT liabilities a prepayment of regular taxes. Noncorporate AMT taxpayers are allowed the credit only with respect to the elements of the AMT that reflect timing differences between the two tax models. § 53.

Miscellaneous itemized deductions. A special category of itemized deductions that includes expenses such as professional dues, tax return preparation fees, job-hunting costs, unreimbursed employee business expenses, and certain investment expenses. Such expenses are deductible only to the extent they exceed 2 percent of adjusted gross income. § 67.

Modified accelerated cost recovery system (MACRS). A method in which the cost of tangible property is recovered over a prescribed period of time. Enacted by the Economic Recovery Tax Act (ERTA) of 1981 and substantially modified by the Tax Reform Act (TRA) of 1986 (the modified system is referred to as MACRS), the approach disregards salvage value, imposes a period of cost recovery that depends upon the classification of the asset into one of various recovery periods, and prescribes the applicable percentage of cost that can be deducted each year. § 168.

Modified adjusted gross income. A key determinant in computing the domestic production activities deduction (DPAD). The deduction is limited to a percentage of the *lesser of* qualified production activities income (QPAI) or modified adjusted gross income. Aside from limited changes required by § 199(d)(2)(A), modified adjusted gross income is AGI as usually determined but without any domestic production activities deduction (DPAD). See also *production activities deduction (PAD)*.

Moving expenses. A deduction *for* AGI is permitted to employees and self-employed individuals provided certain tests are met. The taxpayer's new job must be at least 50 miles farther from the old residence than the old residence was from the former place of work. In addition, an employee must be employed on a full-time basis at the new location for 39 weeks in the 12-month period following the move. Deductible moving expenses include the cost of moving the household and personal effects, transportation, and lodging expenses during the move. The cost of meals during the move is not deductible. Qualified moving expenses that are paid (or reimbursed) by the employer can be excluded from the employee's gross income. In this case, the related deduction by the employee is not permitted. §§ 62(a)(15), 132(a)(6), and 217.

Multiple support agreement. To qualify for a dependency exemption, the support test must be satisfied. This requires that over 50 percent of the support of the potential dependent be provided by the taxpayer. Where no one person provides more than 50 percent of the support, a multiple support agreement enables a taxpayer to still qualify for the dependency exemption. Any person who contributed more than 10 percent of the support is entitled to claim the exemption if each person in the group who contributed more than 10 percent files a written consent (Form 2120). Each person who is a party to the multiple support agreement must meet all of the other requirements for claiming the dependency exemption. § 152(c).

Multistate corporation. A corporation that has operations in more than one of the states of the United States. Issues arise relative to the assignment of appropriate amounts of the entity's taxable income to the states in which it has a presence. See also *allocate, apportion,* and *nexus.*

Multistate Tax Commission (MTC). A regulatory body of which about half of the U.S. states are members. The MTC develops operating rules and regulations to compute and assign the total taxable income of a multistate taxpayer to specific states.

N

Net capital gain. The excess of the net long-term capital gain for the tax year over the net short-term capital loss. The net capital gain of an individual taxpayer is eligible for the alternative tax. § 1222(11).

Net capital loss. The excess of the losses from sales or exchanges of capital assets over the gains from sales or exchanges of such assets. Up to $3,000 per year of the net capital loss may be deductible by noncorporate taxpayers against ordinary income. The excess net capital loss carries over to future tax years. For corporate taxpayers, the net capital loss cannot be offset against ordinary income, but it can be carried back three years and forward five years to offset net capital gains. §§ 1211, 1212, and 1221(10).

Net investment income. The excess of investment income over investment expenses. Investment expenses are those deductible expenses directly connected with the production of investment income. Investment expenses do not include investment interest. The deduction for investment interest for the tax year is limited to net investment income. § 163(d).

Net operating loss (NOL). To mitigate the effect of the annual accounting period concept, § 172 allows taxpayers to use an excess loss of one year as a deduction for certain past or future years. In this regard, a carryback period of 2 years and a carryforward period of 20 years currently are allowed.

Nexus. A multistate taxpayer's taxable income can be apportioned to a specific state only if the taxpayer has established a sufficient presence, or nexus, with that state. State law, which often follows the UDITPA, specifies various activities that lead to nexus in various states.

No-additional-cost services. Services the employer may provide the employee at no additional cost to the employer. Generally, the benefit is the ability to utilize the employer's excess capacity (e.g., vacant seats on an airliner). Such amounts are excludible from the recipient's gross income. § 132(b).

Nonaccountable plan. An expense reimbursement plan that does not have an accountability feature. The result is that employee expenses must be claimed as deductions *from* AGI. An exception is moving expenses that are deductions *for* AGI.

Nonacquiescence. Disagreement by the IRS on the result reached in certain judicial decisions. *Nonacq.* or *NA.*

Nonbusiness bad debt. A bad debt loss that is not incurred in connection with a creditor's trade or business. The loss is classified as a short-term capital loss and is allowed only in the year the debt becomes entirely worthless. In addition to family loans, many investor losses are nonbusiness bad debts. § 166(d).

Nonrecourse debt. Debt secured by the property it is used to purchase. The purchaser of the property is not personally liable for the debt upon default. Rather, the creditor's recourse is to repossess the related property. Nonrecourse debt generally does not increase the purchaser's at-risk amount.

Nonresident alien (NRA). An individual who is neither a citizen nor a resident of the United States. Citizenship is determined under the immigration and naturalization laws of the United States. Residency is determined under § 7701(b) of the Internal Revenue Code. Certain activities of the nonresident alien are subject to U.S. taxation.

Nontaxable exchange. A transaction in which realized gains or losses are not recognized. The recognition of gain or loss is postponed (deferred) until the property received in the nontaxable exchange is subsequently disposed of in a taxable transaction. Examples are § 1031 like-kind exchanges and § 1033 involuntary conversions.

O

Occupational tax. A tax imposed on various trades or businesses. A license fee that enables a taxpayer to engage in a particular occupation.

Office in the home expenses. Employment and business-related expenses attributable to the use of a residence (e.g., den or office) are allowed only if the portion of the residence is exclusively used on a regular basis as a principal place of business of the taxpayer or as a place of business that is used by patients, clients, or customers. If the expenses are incurred by an employee, the use must be for the convenience of the employer as opposed to being merely appropriate and helpful. § 280A.

One hundred percent additional first-year depreciation. The Tax Relief Act of 2010 provides for a cost recovery deduction of 100 percent in the tax year qualified property is placed in service. Qualified property includes most types of new property other than buildings. This provision is effective for property acquired after December 31, 2010, and placed in service before January 1, 2012. See also *cost recovery system* and *fifty percent additional first-year depreciation.*

Options. The sale or exchange of an option to buy or sell property results in capital gain or loss if the property is a capital asset. Generally, the closing of an option transaction results in short-term capital gain or loss to the writer of the call and the purchaser of the call option. § 1234.

Ordinary and necessary. An ordinary expense is common and accepted in the general industry or type of activity in which the taxpayer is engaged. It comprises one of the tests for the deductibility of expenses incurred or paid in connection with a trade or business; for the production or collection of income; for the management, conservation, or maintenance of property held for the production of income; or in connection with the determination, collection, or refund of any tax. §§ 162(a) and 212. A necessary expense is appropriate and helpful in furthering the taxpayer's business or income-producing activity. §§ 162(a) and 212.

Ordinary income property. Property contributed to a charitable organization that, if sold rather than contributed, would have resulted in other than long-term capital gain to the donor (i.e., ordinary income property and short-term capital gain property). Examples are inventory and capital assets held for less than the long-term holding period.

Organizational expenditures (costs). Items incurred early in the life of a corporate entity, qualifying for a special treatment under Federal tax law. A corporation can elect to immediately expense the first $5,000 (subject to phaseout) of organizational expenditures and generally amortize the balance over a period of 180 months. Amortizable expenditures exclude those incurred to obtain capital (underwriting fees) or assets (subject to cost recovery). Typically, amortizable expenditures include legal and accounting fees and state incorporation payments. Such items must be incurred by the end of the entity's first tax year. § 248.

Original issue discount. The difference between the issue price of a debt obligation (e.g., a corporate bond) and the maturity value of the obligation when the issue price is *less than* the maturity value. OID represents interest and must be amortized over the life of the debt obligation using the effective interest method. The difference is not considered to be original issue discount for tax purposes when it is less than one-fourth of 1 percent of the redemption price at maturity multiplied by the number of years to maturity. §§ 1272 and 1273(a)(3).

Other adjustments account (OAA). Used in the context of a distribution from an S corporation. The net accumulation of the entity's exempt income (e.g., municipal bond interest).

Outbound taxation. U.S. tax effects when a U.S. person undertakes an investment or a business activity outside the United States.

Outside basis. A partner's basis in his or her partnership interest.

P

Parent-subsidiary controlled group. A controlled or affiliated group of corporations where at least one corporation is at least 80 percent owned by one or more of the others. The affiliated group definition is more difficult to meet.

Passive investment holding company. A means by which a multistate taxpayer can reduce its overall effective tax rate by isolating investment income in a no- or low-tax state.

Passive investment income (PII). Gross receipts from royalties, certain rents, dividends, interest, annuities, and gains from the sale or exchange of stock and securities. With certain exceptions, if the passive investment income of an S corporation exceeds 25 percent of the corporation's gross receipts for three consecutive years, S status is lost. In another circumstance, if the S corporation has excessive passive income, a penalty tax is imposed on the S corporation. §§ 1362(d)(3) and 1375.

Passive loss. Any loss from (1) activities in which the taxpayer does not materially participate or (2) rental activities (subject to certain exceptions). Net passive losses cannot be used to offset income from nonpassive sources. Rather, they are suspended until the taxpayer either generates net passive income (and a deduction of such losses is allowed) or disposes of the underlying property (at which time the loss deductions are allowed in full). One relief provision allows landlords who actively participate in the rental activities to deduct up to $25,000 of passive losses annually. However, a phaseout of the $25,000 amount commences when the landlord's AGI exceeds $100,000. Another relief provision applies for material participation in a real estate trade or business. § 469.

Patent. An intangible asset that may be amortized over a statutory 15-year period as a § 197 intangible. The sale of a patent usually results in favorable long-term capital gain treatment. §§ 197 and 1235.

Payroll factor. The proportion of a multistate corporation's total payroll that is traceable to a specific state. Used in determining the taxable income that is to be apportioned to that state.

Percentage depletion. Depletion based on a statutory percentage applied to the gross income from the property. The taxpayer deducts the greater of cost depletion or percentage depletion. § 613.

Permanent differences. Under *ASC 740 (SFAS 109)*, tax-related items that appear in the entity's financial statements or its tax return, but not both. For instance, interest income from a municipal bond is a permanent book-tax difference.

Permanent establishment (PE). A level of business activity, as defined under an income tax treaty, that subjects the taxpayer to taxation in a country other than that in which the taxpayer is based. Often evidenced by the presence of a plant, an office, or other fixed place of business. Inventory storage and temporary activities do not rise to the level of a PE. PE is the treaty's equivalent to nexus.

Permanently reinvesting. Under *ASC 740-30 (APB 23)* of Generally Accepted Accounting Principles, a special rule that relates to the book tax expense of non-U.S. subsidiaries. If a parent corporation documents that it is *permanently reinvesting* the non-U.S. earnings of a non-U.S. subsidiary, the parent does not record as an expense any U.S. income tax the parent might pay on such earnings [i.e., the book tax expense is deferred until such earnings are (if ever) repatriated to the United States].

Personal and dependency exemptions. The tax law provides an exemption for each individual taxpayer and an additional exemption for the taxpayer's spouse if a joint return is filed. An individual may also claim a dependency exemption for each dependent, provided certain tests are met. The amount of the personal and dependency exemptions is $3,950 in 2014 and $3,900 in 2013. The amount is indexed for inflation. The exemption was subject to phaseout once adjusted gross income exceeded certain statutory threshold amounts. This phaseout provision is subject to partial phaseout beginning in 2006. For 2009, two-thirds of the reduction in the exemption amount is phased out, and in 2010 all of the reduction is phased out. Under the sunset provision, the phaseout of itemized deductions was scheduled to be reinstated in 2011. The Tax Relief Act (TRA) of 2010 put off the reinstatement for two years (i.e., 2011 and 2012). For 2013 and 2014, the American Taxpayer Relief Act of 2012 restored the phaseout of personal and dependency exemptions. §§ 151 and 152.

Personal service corporation (PSC). A corporation whose principal activity is the performance of personal services (e.g., health, law, engineering, architecture, accounting, actuarial science, performing arts, or consulting) where such services are substantially performed by the employee-owners. The 35 percent statutory income tax rate applies to PSCs.

Personalty. All property that is not attached to real estate (realty) and is movable. Examples of personalty are machinery, automobiles, clothing, household furnishings, inventory, and personal effects.

Points. Loan origination fees that may be deductible as interest by a buyer of property. A seller of property who pays points reduces the selling price by the amount of the points paid for the buyer. While the seller is not permitted to deduct this amount as interest, the buyer may do so. § 461(g).

Portfolio income. Income from interest, dividends, certain rentals, royalties, capital gains, or other investment sources. Net passive losses cannot be used to offset net portfolio income. § 469.

Precedent. A previously decided court decision that is recognized as authority for the disposition of future decisions.

Precontribution gain or loss. Partnerships allow for a variety of special allocations of gain or loss among the partners, but gain or loss that is "built in" on an asset contributed to the partnership is assigned specifically to the contributing partner. § 704(c)(1)(A).

Private activity bond. Interest on state and local bonds is excludible from gross income. § 103. Certain such bonds are labeled private activity bonds. Although the interest on such bonds is excludible for regular income tax purposes, it generally is treated as a tax preference in calculating the AMT.

Procedural Regulation. A Regulation issued by the Treasury Department that is a housekeeping-type instruction indicating information taxpayers should provide the IRS as well as information about the internal management and conduct of the IRS itself.

Production activities deduction (PAD). A deduction based on 3 percent of the lesser of qualified production activities income (QPAI) or modified adjusted gross income but not to exceed 50 percent of the W–2 production wages paid. In the case of a corporate taxpayer, taxable income

is substituted for modified AGI. The deduction rate increased to 6 percent for 2007 to 2009 and increased to 9 percent for 2010 and thereafter. § 199. See also *qualified production activities income (QPAI)*.

Profit and loss sharing ratios. Specified in the partnership agreement and used to determine each partner's allocation of ordinary taxable income and separately stated items. Profits and losses can be shared in different ratios. The ratios can be changed by amending the partnership agreement. § 704(a).

Profits (loss) interest. A partner's percentage allocation of partnership operating results determined by the profit and loss sharing ratios.

Property. Assets defined in the broadest legal sense. Property includes the unrealized receivables of a cash basis taxpayer, but not services rendered. § 351.

Property dividend. Generally treated in the same manner as a cash distribution, measured by the fair market value of the property on the date of distribution. The portion of the distribution representing E & P is a dividend; any excess is treated as a return of capital. Distribution of appreciated property causes the distributing corporation to recognize gain. The distributing corporation does not recognize loss on property that has depreciated in value. §§ 301 and 311.

Property factor. The proportion of a multistate corporation's total property that is traceable to a specific state. Used in determining the taxable income that is to be apportioned to that state.

Proposed Regulation. A Regulation issued by the Treasury Department in proposed, rather than final, form. The interval between the proposal of a Regulation and its finalization permits taxpayers and other interested parties to comment on the propriety of the proposal.

Proprietorship. A business entity for which there is a single owner. The net profit of the entity is reported on the owner's Federal income tax return (Schedule C of Form 1040).

Public Law 86–272. A congressional limit on the ability of the state to force a multistate taxpayer to assign income to that state. Under P.L. 86–272, where orders for tangible personal property are both filled and delivered outside the state, the entity must establish that more than the mere solicitation of such orders took place in-state before any income can be apportioned to the state.

Punitive damages. Damages received or paid by the taxpayer can be classified as compensatory damages or as punitive damages. Punitive damages are awarded to punish the defendant for gross negligence or the intentional infliction of harm. Such damages are includible in gross income. § 104(a)(2).

 Q

Qualified dividends. Distributions made by domestic (and certain non-U.S.) corporations to noncorporate shareholders that are subject to tax at the same rates as those applicable to net long-term capital gains (i.e., 0 percent, 15 percent, or 20 percent). The 20 percent rate applies to certain high-income taxpayers (i.e., whose tax bracket is 39.6 percent), beginning in 2013. The dividend must be paid out of earnings and profits, and the shareholders must meet certain holding period requirements as to the stock. §§ 1(h)(1) and (11).

Qualified employee discounts. Discounts offered employees on merchandise or services the employer ordinarily sells or provides to customers. The discounts must be generally available to all employees. In the case of property, the discount cannot exceed the employer's gross profit (the sales price cannot be less than the employer's cost). In the case of services, the discounts cannot exceed 20 percent of the normal sales price. § 132.

Qualified nonrecourse debt. Debt issued on realty by a bank, retirement plan, or governmental agency. Included in the at-risk amount by the investor. § 465(b)(6).

Qualified production activities income (QPAI). A key determinant in computing the domestic production activities deduction (DPAD). It consists of domestic production gross receipts (DPGR) reduced by cost of goods sold and other assignable expenses. Thus, QPAI represents the profit derived from production activities. § 199. See also *domestic production gross receipts (DPGR)* and *production activities deduction (PAD)*.

Qualified real property business indebtedness. Indebtedness that was incurred or assumed by the taxpayer in connection with real property used in a trade or business and is secured by such real property. The taxpayer must not be a C corporation. For qualified real property business indebtedness, the taxpayer may elect to exclude some or all of the income realized from cancellation of debt on qualified real property. If the election is made, the basis of the property must be reduced by the amount excluded. The amount excluded cannot be greater than the excess of the principal amount of the outstanding debt over the fair market value (net of any other debt outstanding on the property) of the property securing the debt. § 108(c).

Qualified residence interest. A term relevant in determining the amount of interest expense the individual taxpayer may deduct as an itemized deduction for what otherwise would be disallowed as a component of personal interest (consumer interest). Qualified residence interest consists of interest paid on qualified residences (principal residence and one other residence) of the taxpayer. Debt that qualifies as qualified residence interest is limited to $1 million of debt to acquire, construct, or substantially improve qualified residences (acquisition indebtedness) plus $100,000 of other debt secured by qualified residences (home equity indebtedness). The home equity indebtedness may not exceed the fair market value of a qualified residence reduced by the acquisition indebtedness for that residence. § 163(h)(3).

Qualified small business stock. Stock in a qualified small business corporation, purchased as part of an original issue after August 10, 1993. The shareholder may exclude from gross income 50 percent (75 percent for 2009 and 2010) of the realized gain on the sale of the stock if he or she held the stock for more than five years. § 1202.

Qualified transportation fringes. Transportation benefits provided by the employer to the employee. Such benefits include (1) transportation in a commuter highway vehicle between the employee's residence and the place of employment, (2) a transit pass, and (3) qualified parking. Qualified transportation fringes are excludible from the employee's gross income to the extent categories (1) and (2) above do not exceed $130 per month in 2014 ($125 in 2013) and category (3) does not exceed $250 per month in 2014 ($245 in 2013). These amounts are indexed annually for inflation. § 132(f).

Qualifying child. An individual who, as to the taxpayer, satisfies the relationship, abode, and age tests. To be claimed as a dependent, such individual must also meet the citizenship and joint return tests and not be self-supporting. §§ 152(a)(1) and (c). See also *personal and dependency exemptions.*

Qualifying relative. An individual who, as to the taxpayer, satisfies the relationship, gross income, support, citizenship, and joint return tests. Such an individual can be claimed as a dependent of the taxpayer. §§ 152(a)(2) and (d). See also *personal and dependency exemptions.*

R

Rate reconciliation. Under Generally Accepted Accounting Principles, a footnote to the financial statements often includes a table that accounts for differences in the statutory income tax rate that applies to the entity (say, 35 percent) and the higher or lower effective tax rate the entity realized for the reporting period. The rate reconciliation includes only *permanent differences* between the book tax expense and the entity's *income tax provision*. The rate reconciliation table often is expressed in dollar and/or percentage terms.

Realized gain or loss. The difference between the amount realized upon the sale or other disposition of property and the adjusted basis of the property. § 1001.

Realty. Real estate.

Reasonableness requirement. The Code includes a reasonableness requirement with respect to the deduction of salaries and other compensation for services. What constitutes reasonableness is a question of fact. If an expense is unreasonable, the amount that is classified as unreasonable is not allowed as a deduction. The question of reasonableness generally arises with respect to closely held corporations where there is no separation of ownership and management. § 162(a)(1).

Recognized gain or loss. The portion of realized gain or loss subject to income taxation.

Recourse debt. Debt for which the lender may both foreclose on the property and assess a guarantor for any payments due under the loan. A lender may also make a claim against the assets of any general partner in a partnership to which debt is issued, without regard to whether the partner has guaranteed the debt.

Recovery of capital doctrine. When a taxable sale or exchange occurs, the seller may be permitted to recover his or her investment (or other adjusted basis) in the property before gain or loss is recognized.

Regular corporation. See *C corporation.*

Rehabilitation expenditures credit. A credit that is based on expenditures incurred to rehabilitate industrial and commercial buildings and certified historic structures. The credit is intended to discourage businesses from moving from older, economically distressed areas to newer locations and to encourage the preservation of historic structures. § 47.

Rehabilitation expenditures credit recapture. When property that qualifies for the rehabilitation expenditures credit is disposed of or ceases to be used in the trade or business of the taxpayer, some or all of the tax credit claimed on the property may be recaptured as additional tax liability. The amount of the recapture is the difference between the amount of the credit claimed originally and what should have been claimed in light of the length of time the property was actually held or used for qualifying purposes. § 50.

Related corporation. See *controlled group.*

Related-party transactions. Various Code Sections define related parties and often include a variety of persons within this (usually detrimental) category. Generally, related parties are accorded different tax treatment from that applicable to other taxpayers who enter into similar transactions. For instance, realized losses that are generated between related parties are not recognized in the year of the loss (§ 267). However, these deferred losses can be used to offset recognized gains that occur upon the subsequent sale of the asset to a nonrelated party. Other uses of a related-party definition include the conversion of gain upon the sale of a depreciable asset into all ordinary income (§ 1239) and the identification of constructive ownership of stock relative to corporate distributions, redemptions, liquidations, reorganizations, and compensation.

Rental activity. Any activity where payments are received principally for the use of tangible property is a rental activity. Temporary Regulations provide that in certain circumstances, activities involving rentals of real and personal property are not to be *treated* as rental activities. The Temporary Regulations list six exceptions.

Research activities credit. A tax credit whose purpose is to encourage research and development. It consists of three components: the incremental research activities credit, the basic research credit, and the energy credit. The incremental research activities credit is equal to 20 percent of the excess qualified research expenditures over the base amount. The basic research credit is equal to 20 percent of the excess of basic research payments over the base amount. § 41.

Research and experimental expenditures. The Code provides three alternatives for the tax treatment of research and experimental expenditures. They may be expensed in the year paid or incurred, deferred subject to amortization, or capitalized. If the taxpayer does not elect to expense such costs or to defer them subject to amortization (over 60 months), the expenditures must be capitalized. § 174. Three types of research activities credits are available: the basic research credit, the incremental research activities credit, and the energy credit. The rate for each type is 20 percent. § 41.

Reserve method. A method of accounting whereby an allowance is permitted for estimated uncollectible accounts. Actual write-offs are charged to the reserve, and recoveries of amounts previously written off are credited to the reserve. The Code permits only certain financial institutions to use the reserve method. § 166.

Residential rental real estate. Buildings for which at least 80 percent of the gross rents are from dwelling units (e.g., an apartment building). This type of building is distinguished from nonresidential (commercial or industrial) buildings in applying the recapture of depreciation provisions. The term also is relevant in distinguishing between buildings that are eligible for a 27.5-year life versus a 39-year life for MACRS purposes. Generally, residential buildings receive preferential treatment. § 168(e)(2)(A).

Revenue Procedure. A matter of procedural importance to both taxpayers and the IRS concerning the administration of the tax laws is issued as a Revenue Procedure (abbreviated Rev.Proc.). A Revenue Procedure is first published in an *Internal Revenue Bulletin* (I.R.B.) and later transferred to the appropriate *Cumulative Bulletin* (C.B.). Both the *Internal Revenue Bulletins* and the *Cumulative Bulletins* are published by the U.S. Government Printing Office.

Revenue Ruling. A Revenue Ruling (abbreviated Rev.Rul.) is issued by the National Office of the IRS to express an official interpretation of the tax law as applied to specific transactions. It is more limited in application than a Regulation. A Revenue Ruling is first published in an *Internal Revenue Bulletin* (I.R.B.) and later transferred to the appropriate *Cumulative Bulletin* (C.B.). Both the *Internal Revenue Bulletins* and the *Cumulative Bulletins* are published by the U.S. Government Printing Office.

S

S corporation. The designation for a small business corporation. See also *Subchapter S.*

Sale or exchange. A requirement for the recognition of capital gain or loss. Generally, the seller of property must receive money or relief from debt to have sold the property. An exchange involves the transfer of property for other property. Thus, collection of a debt is neither a sale nor an exchange. The term *sale or exchange* is not defined by the Code.

Sales factor. The proportion of a multistate corporation's total sales that is traceable to a specific state. Used in determining the taxable income that is to be apportioned to that state.

Sales tax. A state- or local-level tax on the retail sale of specified property. Generally, the purchaser pays the tax, but the seller collects it as an agent for the government. Various taxing jurisdictions allow exemptions for purchases of specific items, including certain food, services, and manufacturing equipment. If the purchaser and seller are in different states, a use tax usually applies.

Schedule M–1. On the Form 1120, a reconciliation of book net income with Federal taxable income. Accounts for timing and permanent differences in the two computations, such as depreciation differences, exempt income, and nondeductible items. On Forms 1120S and 1065, the Schedule M–1 reconciles book income with owners' aggregate ordinary taxable income.

Schedule M–3. An *expanded* reconciliation of book net income with Federal taxable income (see *Schedule M–1*). Applies to corporations with total assets of $10 million or more. For tax years ending December 31, 2014, and later, an exception exists for entities with total assets of $10 million to $50 million.

Scholarships. Scholarships are generally excluded from the gross income of the recipient unless the payments are a disguised form of compensation for services rendered. However, the Code imposes restrictions on the exclusion. The recipient must be a degree candidate. The excluded amount is limited to amounts used for tuition, fees, books, supplies, and equipment required for courses of instruction. Amounts received for room and board are not eligible for the exclusion. § 117.

Section 179 expensing election. The ability to deduct a capital expenditure in the year an asset is placed in service rather than over the asset's useful life or cost recovery period. The annual ceiling on the deduction is $25,000 for 2014 ($500,000 for 2013). However, the deduction is reduced dollar for dollar when § 179 property placed in service during the taxable year exceeds $200,000 in 2014 ($2 million in 2013). In addition, the amount expensed under § 179 cannot exceed the aggregate amount of taxable income derived from the conduct of any trade or business by the taxpayer.

Section 1231 gains and losses. If the combined gains and losses from the taxable dispositions of § 1231 assets plus the net gain from business involuntary conversions (of both § 1231 assets and long-term capital assets) is a gain, the gains and losses are treated as long-term capital gains and losses. In arriving at § 1231 gains, however, the depreciation recapture provisions (e.g., §§ 1245 and 1250) are first applied to produce ordinary income. If the net result of the combination is a loss, the gains and losses from § 1231 assets are treated as ordinary gains and losses. § 1231(a).

Section 1231 lookback. For gain to be classified as § 1231 gain, the gain must survive the § 1231 lookback. To the extent of nonrecaptured § 1231 losses for the five prior tax years, the gain is classified as ordinary income. § 1231(c).

Section 1231 property. Depreciable assets and real estate used in trade or business and held for the required long-term holding period. Under certain circumstances, the classification also includes timber, coal, domestic iron ore, livestock (held for draft, breeding, dairy, or sporting purposes), and unharvested crops. § 1231(b).

Section 1245 property. Property that is subject to the recapture of depreciation under § 1245. For a definition of § 1245 property, see § 1245(a)(3).

Section 1245 recapture. Upon a taxable disposition of § 1245 property, all depreciation claimed on the property is recaptured as ordinary income (but not to exceed recognized gain from the disposition).

Section 1250 property. Real estate that is subject to the recapture of depreciation under § 1250. For a definition of § 1250 property, see § 1250(c).

Section 1250 recapture. Upon a taxable disposition of § 1250 property, some of the depreciation or cost recovery claimed on the property may be recaptured as ordinary income.

Securities. Generally, stock, debt, and other financial assets. To the extent securities other than the stock of the transferee corporation are received in a § 351 exchange, the new shareholder realizes a gain.

Self-employment tax. In 2011 and 2012, a tax of 10.4 percent is levied on individuals with net earnings from self-employment (up to $106,800 in 2011 and $110,100 in 2012) to provide Social Security benefits (i.e., the old age, survivors, and disability insurance portion) for such individuals. For 2010, 2013, and 2014, the rate is 12.4 percent. In addition, in 2014 (and 2010, 2011, 2012, and 2013), a tax of 2.9 percent is levied on individuals with net earnings from self-employment (with no statutory ceiling) to provide Medicare benefits (i.e., the hospital insurance portion) for such individuals. If a self-employed individual also receives wages from an employer that are subject to FICA, the self-employment tax will be reduced if total income subject to Social Security is more than $117,000 in 2014. A partial deduction is allowed in calculating the self-employment tax. Individuals with net earnings of $400 or more from self-employment are subject to this tax. §§ 1401 and 1402.

Separate foreign tax credit limitation category. The foreign tax credit of a taxpayer is computed for each of several types of income sources, as specified by the Code to limit the results of tax planning. FTC income "baskets" include general and passive. The FTC for the year is the sum of the credits as computed within all of the taxpayer's separate FTC baskets used for the tax year.

Separately stated item. Any item of a partnership or an S corporation that might be taxed differently to any two owners of the entity. These amounts are not included in ordinary income of the entity, but are instead reported separately to the owners; tax consequences are determined at the owner level. §§ 702(a) and 1366(a)(1).

Short sale. A sale that occurs when a taxpayer sells borrowed property (usually stock) and repays the lender with substantially identical property either held on the date of the short sale or purchased after the sale. No gain or loss is recognized until the short sale is closed, and such gain or loss is generally short-term. § 1233.

Significant participation activity. There are seven tests to determine whether an individual has achieved material participation in an activity, one of which is based on more than 500 hours of participation in significant participation activities. A significant participation activity is an activity in which the individual's participation exceeds 100 hours during the year. Temp.Reg. § 1.469–5T.

Small business corporation. A corporation that satisfies the definition of § 1361(b), § 1244(c), or both. Satisfaction of § 1361(b) permits an S election, and satisfaction of § 1244 enables the shareholders of the corporation to claim an ordinary loss on the worthlessness of stock.

Small business stock. See *small business corporation*.

Small Cases Division of the U.S. Tax Court. Jurisdiction is limited to claims of $50,000 or less. There is no appeal from this court.

Solicitation. A level of activity brought about by the taxpayer within a specific state. Under Public Law 86-272, certain types of solicitation activities do not create nexus with the state. Exceeding mere solicitation, though, creates nexus.

Special allocation. Any amount for which an agreement exists among the partners of a partnership outlining the method used for spreading the item among the partners.

Specific charge-off method. A method of accounting for bad debts in which a deduction is permitted only when an account becomes partially or completely worthless.

Standard deduction. The individual taxpayer can either itemize deductions or take the standard deduction. The amount of the standard deduction depends on the taxpayer's filing status (single, head of household, married filing jointly, surviving spouse, or married filing separately). For 2014, the amount of the standard deduction ranges from $6,200 (for married, filing separately or unmarried) to $12,400 (for married, filing jointly). Additional standard deductions of either $1,200 (for married taxpayers) or $1,550 (for single taxpayers) are available if the taxpayer is blind or age 65 or over. Limitations exist on the amount of the standard deduction of a taxpayer who is another taxpayer's dependent. The standard deduction amounts are adjusted for inflation each year. § 63(c).

Stock dividend. Not taxable if pro rata distributions of stock or stock rights on common stock. Section 305 governs the taxability of stock dividends and sets out five exceptions to the general rule that stock dividends are nontaxable.

Stock redemption. A corporation buys back its own stock from a specified shareholder. Typically, the corporation recognizes any realized gain on the noncash assets that it uses to effect a redemption, and the shareholder obtains a capital gain or loss upon receipt of the purchase price. §§ 301 and 302.

Subchapter S. Sections 1361–1379 of the Internal Revenue Code. An elective provision permitting certain small business corporations (§ 1361) and their shareholders (§ 1362) to elect to be treated for income tax purposes in accordance with the operating rules of §§ 1363–1379. S corporations usually avoid the corporate income tax, and corporate losses can be claimed by the shareholders.

Subpart F income. Certain income earned by a controlled foreign corporation. Usually, Subpart F income is included in the gross income of a U.S. shareholder of the CFC when the income is earned, not when it is later repatriated.

Sunset provision. A provision attached to new tax legislation that will cause such legislation to expire at a specified date. Sunset provisions are attached to tax cut bills for long-term budgetary reasons in order to make their effect temporary. Once the sunset provision comes into play, the tax cut is rescinded and former law is reinstated. An example of a sunset provision is the one contained in the Tax Relief Reconciliation Act of 2001, which relates to the estate tax. After the estate tax was phased out by 2010, a sunset provision reinstated the estate tax as of January 1, 2011.

Supreme Court. The highest appellate court or the court of last resort in the Federal court system and in most states. Only a small number of tax decisions of the U.S. Courts of Appeal are reviewed by the U.S. Supreme Court under its certiorari procedure. The Supreme Court usually grants certiorari when a conflict among the Courts of Appeal must be resolved (e.g., two or more appellate courts have assumed opposing positions on a particular issue) or when the tax issue is extremely important (e.g., size of the revenue loss to the Federal government).

Surviving spouse. When a husband or wife predeceases the other spouse, the survivor is known as a surviving spouse. Under certain conditions, a surviving spouse may be entitled to use the income tax rates in § 1(a) (those applicable to married persons filing a joint return) for the two years after the year of death of his or her spouse. § 2.

Syndication costs. Incurred in promoting and marketing partnership interests for sale to investors. Examples include legal and accounting fees, printing costs for prospectus and placement documents, and state registration fees. These items are capitalized by the partnership as incurred, with no amortization thereof allowed.

T

Tax avoidance. The minimization of one's tax liability by taking advantage of legally available tax planning opportunities. Tax avoidance can be contrasted with tax evasion, which entails the reduction of tax liability by illegal means.

Tax benefit rule. A provision that limits the recognition of income from the recovery of an expense or a loss properly deducted in a prior tax year to the amount of the deduction that generated a tax saving. Assume that last year, Gary, age 67, had medical expenses of $3,000 and adjusted gross income of $30,000. Because of the 7.5 percent limitation, Gary could deduct only $750 of these expenses [$3,000 − (7.5% × $30,000)]. If this year Gary is reimbursed by his insurance company for $900 of these expenses, the tax benefit rule limits the amount of income from the reimbursement to $750 (the amount previously deducted with a tax saving). § 111.

Tax Court. The U.S. Tax Court is one of four trial courts of original jurisdiction that decides litigation involving Federal income, death, or gift taxes. It is the only trial court where the taxpayer must not first pay the deficiency assessed by the IRS. The Tax Court will not have jurisdiction over a case unless a statutory notice of deficiency (90-day letter) has been issued by the IRS and the taxpayer files the petition for hearing within the time prescribed.

Tax credits. Amounts that directly reduce a taxpayer's tax liability. The tax benefit received from a tax credit is not dependent on the taxpayer's marginal tax rate, whereas the benefit of a tax deduction or exclusion is dependent on the taxpayer's tax bracket.

Tax evasion. The reduction of the taxpayer's tax liability through the use of illegal means. Tax evasion can be contrasted with tax avoidance, which entails the reduction of tax liability through the use of legal means.

Tax haven. A country in which either locally sourced income or residents of the country are subject to a low rate of taxation.

Tax preference items. Various items that may result in the imposition of the alternative minimum tax. §§ 55–58.

Tax rate schedules. Rate schedules that are used by upper-income taxpayers and those not permitted to use the tax table. Separate rate schedules are provided for married individuals filing jointly, head of household, single taxpayers, estates and trusts, and married individuals filing separate returns. § 1.

Tax shelters. The typical tax shelter generated large losses in the early years of the activity. Investors would offset these losses against other types of income and, therefore, avoid paying income taxes on this income. These tax shelter investments could then be sold after a few years and produce capital gain income, which is taxed at a lower rate than that of ordinary income. The passive activity loss rules and the at-risk rules now limit tax shelter deductions.

Tax table. A tax table that is provided for taxpayers with less than $100,000 of taxable income. Separate columns are provided for single taxpayers, married taxpayers filing jointly, head of household, and married taxpayers filing separately. § 3.

Taxable year. The annual period over which income is measured for income tax purposes. Most individuals use a calendar year, but many businesses use a fiscal year based on the natural business year.

Technical advice memoranda (TAMs). TAMs are issued by the National Office of the IRS in response to questions raised by IRS field personnel during audits. They deal with completed rather than proposed transactions and are often requested for questions related to exempt organizations and employee plans.

Temporary differences. Under *ASC 740 (SFAS 109)*, tax-related items that appear in the entity's financial statements and its tax return, but in different time periods. For instance, doubtful accounts receivable often create a temporary book-tax difference, as a bad debt reserve is used to compute an expense for financial reporting purposes, but a bad debt often is deductible only under the specific write-off rule for tax purposes, and the difference observed for the current period creates a temporary difference.

Temporary Regulation. A Regulation issued by the Treasury Department in temporary form. When speed is critical, the Treasury Department issues Temporary Regulations that take effect immediately. These Regulations have the same authoritative value as Final Regulations and may be cited as precedent for three years. Temporary Regulations are also issued as proposed Regulations.

Theft loss. A loss from larceny, embezzlement, or robbery. It does not include misplacement of items.

Thin capitalization. When debt owed by a corporation to the shareholders becomes too large in relation to the corporation's capital structure (i.e., stock and shareholder equity), the IRS may contend that the corporation is thinly capitalized. In effect, this means that some or all of the debt is reclassified as equity. The immediate result is to disallow any interest deduction to the corporation on the reclassified debt. To the extent of the corporation's earnings and profits, interest payments and loan repayments on the reclassified debt are treated as dividends to the shareholders. § 385.

Throwback rule. If there is no income tax in the state to which a sale otherwise would be apportioned, the sale essentially is exempt from state income tax, even though the seller is domiciled in a state that levies an income tax. Nonetheless, if the seller's state has adopted a throwback rule, the sale is attributed to the seller's state and the transaction is subjected to a state-level tax.

Transportation expenses. Transportation expenses for an employee include only the cost of transportation (e.g., taxi fares, automobile expenses, etc.) in the course of employment when the employee is not away from home in travel status. Commuting expenses are not deductible. See also *automatic mileage method*.

Travel expenses. Expenses that include meals (generally subject to a 50 percent disallowance) and lodging and transportation expenses while away from home in the pursuit of a trade or business (including that of an employee).

U

Unearned income. Income received but not yet earned. Normally, such income is taxed when received, even for accrual basis taxpayers. In certain cases involving advance payments for goods and services, income may be deferred. See Revenue Procedure 2004–34 (2004–1 C.B. 991) and Reg. § 1.451–5.

Unitary approach. Sales, property, and payroll of related corporations are combined for nexus and apportionment purposes, and the worldwide income of the unitary entity is apportioned to the state. Subsidiaries and other affiliated corporations found to be part of the corporation's unitary business (because they are subject to overlapping ownership, operations, or management) are included in the apportionment procedure. This approach can be limited if a waters' edge election is in effect.

Unreasonable compensation. A deduction is allowed for "reasonable" salaries or other compensation for personal services actually rendered. To the extent compensation is "excessive" ("unreasonable"), no deduction is allowed. The problem of unreasonable compensation usually is limited to closely held corporations, where the motivation is to pay out profits in some form that is deductible to the corporation. Deductible compensation therefore becomes an attractive substitute for nondeductible dividends when the shareholders also are employed by the corporation. § 162(a)(1).

Unrecaptured § 1250 gain (25 percent gain). Gain from the sale of depreciable real estate held more than one year. The gain is equal to or less than the depreciation taken on such property and is reduced by § 1245 and § 1250 gain.

U.S. shareholder. For purposes of classification of an entity as a controlled foreign corporation, a U.S. person who owns, or is considered to own, 10 percent or more of the total combined voting power of all classes of voting stock of a foreign corporation. Stock owned directly, indirectly, and constructively is counted for this purpose. The U.S. shareholder may be currently taxed on a proportionate share of Subpart F income.

U.S. trade or business. A set of activities that is carried on in a regular, continuous, and substantial manner. A non-U.S. taxpayer is subject to U.S. tax on the taxable income that is effectively connected with a U.S. trade or business.

Use tax. A sales tax that is collectible by the seller where the purchaser is domiciled in a different state.

V

Valuation allowance. Under *ASC 740 (SFAS 109)*, a tax-related item is reported for book purposes only when it is more likely than not that the item actually will be realized. When the "more likely than not" test is failed, a contra-asset account is created to offset some or all of the related *deferred tax asset*. For instance, if the entity projects that it will not be able to use all of its *net operating loss* carryforward due to a lack of future taxable income, a valuation allowance is created to reduce the net *deferred tax asset* that corresponds to the carryforward. If income projections later change and it appears that the carryforward will be used, the valuation allowance is reversed or "released." Creation of a valuation allowance usually increases the *current tax expense* and thereby reduces current book income, and its release often increases book income in the later reporting period.

Value added tax (VAT). A national sales tax that taxes the increment in value as goods move through the production process. A VAT is much used in other countries but has not yet been incorporated as part of the U.S. Federal tax structure.

Voluntary revocation. The owners of a majority of shares in an S corporation elect to terminate the S status of the entity, as of a specified date. The day on which the revocation is effective is the first day of the corporation's C tax year.

W

W–2 wages. The domestic production activities deduction (DPAD) cannot exceed 50 percent of the W–2 wages paid for any particular year. Prop.Reg. § 199–2(f)(2) provides several methods for calculating the W–2 wages, but the payments must involve common law employees. To qualify, the employees need to be involved in the production process. § 199. See also *production activities deduction (PAD)*.

Wash sale. A loss from the sale of stock or securities that is disallowed because the taxpayer, within 30 days before or after the sale, has acquired stock or securities substantially identical to those sold. § 1091.

Waters' edge election. A limitation on the worldwide scope of the unitary approach to computing state taxable income. If a waters' edge election is in effect, the state can consider only the activities that occur within the boundaries of the United States in the apportionment procedure.

Welfare-to-work credit. A tax credit available to employers hiring individuals who have been long-term recipients of family assistance welfare benefits. In general, long-term recipients are those individuals who are certified by a designated local agency as being members of a family receiving assistance under a public aid program for at least an 18-month period ending on the hiring date. The welfare-to-work credit is available for qualified wages paid in the first two years of employment. The maximum credit is equal to $9,000 per qualified employee, computed as 40 percent of the first $10,000 of qualified wages paid in the first year of employment plus 50 percent of the first $10,000 of qualified wages paid in the second year of employment. Starting in 2007, the welfare-to-work credit became part of the work opportunity tax credit. § 51(e). See also *work opportunity tax credit*.

Wherewithal to pay. This concept recognizes the inequity of taxing a transaction when the taxpayer lacks the means with which to pay the tax. Under it, there is a correlation between the imposition of the tax and the ability to pay the tax. It is particularly suited to situations in which the taxpayer's economic position has not changed significantly as a result of the transaction.

Work opportunity tax credit. Employers are allowed a tax credit equal to 40 percent of the first $6,000 of wages (per eligible employee) for the first year of employment. Eligible employees include certain hard-to-employ individuals (e.g., qualified ex-felons, high-risk youth, food stamp recipients, and veterans). The employer's deduction for wages is reduced by the amount of the credit taken. For qualified summer youth employees, the 40 percent rate is applied to the first $3,000 of qualified wages. See the *welfare-to-work credit* for the calculation for long-term recipients of family assistance welfare benefits. §§ 51 and 52.

Working condition fringe. A type of fringe benefit received by the employee that is excludible from the employee's gross income. It consists of property or services provided (paid or reimbursed) by the employer for which the employee could take a tax deduction if the employee had paid for them. § 132(d).

Worthless securities. A loss (usually capital) is allowed for a security that becomes worthless during the year. The loss is deemed to have occurred on the last day of the year. Special rules apply to securities of affiliated companies and small business stock. § 165.

Writ of Certiorari. Appeal from a U.S. Court of Appeals to the U.S. Supreme Court is by Writ of Certiorari. The Supreme Court need not accept the appeal, and it usually does not (*cert. den.*) unless a conflict exists among the lower courts that must be resolved or a constitutional issue is involved.

Appendix D-1

Table of Code Sections Cited

[See Title 26 U.S.C.A.]

Table of Regulations Cited

Table of Revenue Procedures and Revenue Rulings Cited

Revenue Procedures

Rev. Proc.	This Work Page
77–37	12-13
87–56	5-25, 13-5, 17-20
87–57	7-21
92–71	5-13
97–27	13-34
97–48	15-39
2004–34	4-12
2007–62	15-7
2014–1	2-9

Revenue Rulings

Rev. Rul.	This Work Page
54–96	12-12
56–60	7-14
56–406	7-15
57–418	5-11
59–44	2-25, 2-27
59–86	7-12
59–221	15-25
60–183	15-8
61	4-5
62–217	12-21
63–221	7-26
63–232	6-8
64–56	12-9
64–162	15-22
66–7	8-13
68–55	12-8
68–662	5-7
69–188	10-20

Revenue Rulings

Rev. Rul.	This Work Page
69–292	11-26
70–466	7-27
71–190	10-16
71–564	12-9
72–312	4-14
72–592	6-7
74–44	15-14
74–78	11-27
74–503	12-21
75–14	11-49
75–168	11-21
75–448	10-8
77–318	10-44
78–39	5-4
79–379	4-17
80	11-7
80–52	4-10
80–335	5-4
81–180	7-26
81–181	7-26
82–74	7-25
82–196	11-5
82–202	4-26
82–208	10-16
83–98	18-11
85–161	15-10
87–22	10-20
99–7	11-63
2008–18	2-37
2009–19	4-14
2009–34	2-35
2012–15	2-33
2014–3	2-9

Appendix E

Table of Cases Cited

Appendix F

Present Value and Future Value Tables

Present Value of $1

N/R	4%	5%	6%	7%	8%	9%	10%	11%	12%	13%	14%
1	0.9615	0.9524	0.9434	0.9346	0.9259	0.9174	0.9091	0.9009	0.8929	0.8850	0.8772
2	0.9246	0.9070	0.8900	0.8734	0.8573	0.8417	0.8264	0.8116	0.7972	0.7831	0.7695
3	0.8890	0.8638	0.8396	0.8163	0.7938	0.7722	0.7513	0.7312	0.7118	0.6931	0.6750
4	0.8548	0.8227	0.7921	0.7629	0.7350	0.7084	0.6830	0.6587	0.6355	0.6133	0.5921
5	0.8219	0.7835	0.7473	0.7130	0.6806	0.6499	0.6209	0.5935	0.5674	0.5428	0.5194
6	0.7903	0.7462	0.7050	0.6663	0.6302	0.5963	0.5645	0.5346	0.5066	0.4803	0.4556
7	0.7599	0.7107	0.6651	0.6227	0.5835	0.5470	0.5132	0.4817	0.4523	0.4251	0.3996
8	0.7307	0.6768	0.6274	0.5820	0.5403	0.5019	0.4665	0.4339	0.4039	0.3762	0.3506
9	0.7026	0.6446	0.5919	0.5439	0.5002	0.4604	0.4241	0.3909	0.3606	0.3329	0.3075
10	0.6756	0.6139	0.5584	0.5083	0.4632	0.4224	0.3855	0.3522	0.3220	0.2946	0.2697
11	0.6496	0.5847	0.5268	0.4751	0.4289	0.3875	0.3505	0.3173	0.2875	0.2607	0.2366
12	0.6246	0.5568	0.4970	0.4440	0.3971	0.3555	0.3186	0.2858	0.2567	0.2307	0.2076
13	0.6006	0.5303	0.4688	0.4150	0.3677	0.3262	0.2897	0.2575	0.2292	0.2042	0.1821
14	0.5775	0.5051	0.4423	0.3878	0.3405	0.2992	0.2633	0.2320	0.2046	0.1807	0.1597
15	0.5553	0.4810	0.4173	0.3624	0.3152	0.2745	0.2394	0.2090	0.1827	0.1599	0.1401
16	0.5339	0.4581	0.3936	0.3387	0.2919	0.2519	0.2176	0.1883	0.1631	0.1415	0.1229
17	0.5134	0.4363	0.3714	0.3166	0.2703	0.2311	0.1978	0.1696	0.1456	0.1252	0.1078
18	0.4936	0.4155	0.3503	0.2959	0.2502	0.2120	0.1799	0.1528	0.1300	0.1108	0.0946
19	0.4746	0.3957	0.3305	0.2765	0.2317	0.1945	0.1635	0.1377	0.1161	0.0981	0.0829
20	0.4564	0.3769	0.3118	0.2584	0.2145	0.1784	0.1486	0.1240	0.1037	0.0868	0.0728

Present Value of an Ordinary Annuity of $1

N/R	4%	5%	6%	7%	8%	9%	10%	11%	12%	13%	14%
1	0.9615	0.9524	0.9434	0.9346	0.9259	0.9174	0.9091	0.9009	0.8929	0.8850	0.8772
2	1.8861	1.8594	1.8334	1.8080	1.7833	1.7591	1.7355	1.7125	1.6901	1.6681	1.6467
3	2.7751	2.7232	2.6730	2.6243	2.5771	2.5313	2.4869	2.4437	2.4018	2.3612	2.3216
4	3.6299	3.5460	3.4651	3.3872	3.3121	3.2397	3.1699	3.1024	3.0373	2.9745	2.9137
5	4.4518	4.3295	4.2124	4.1002	3.9927	3.8897	3.7908	3.6959	3.6048	3.5172	3.4331
6	5.2421	5.0757	4.9173	4.7665	4.6229	4.4859	4.3553	4.2305	4.1114	3.9975	3.8887
7	6.0021	5.7864	5.5824	5.3893	5.2064	5.0330	4.8684	4.7122	4.5638	4.4226	4.2883
8	6.7327	6.4632	6.2098	5.9713	5.7466	5.5348	5.3349	5.1461	4.9676	4.7988	4.6389
9	7.4353	7.1078	6.8017	6.5152	6.2469	5.9952	5.7590	5.5370	5.3282	5.1317	4.9464
10	8.1109	7.7217	7.3601	7.0236	6.7101	6.4177	6.1446	5.8892	5.6502	5.4262	5.2161
11	8.7605	8.3064	7.8869	7.4987	7.1390	6.8052	6.4951	6.2065	5.9377	5.6869	5.4527
12	9.3851	8.8633	8.3838	7.9427	7.5361	7.1607	6.8137	6.4924	6.1944	5.9176	5.6603
13	9.9856	9.3936	8.8527	8.3577	7.9038	7.4869	7.1034	6.7499	6.4235	6.1218	5.8424
14	10.5631	9.8986	9.2950	8.7455	8.2442	7.7862	7.3667	6.9819	6.6282	6.3025	6.0021
15	11.1184	10.3797	9.7122	9.1079	8.5595	8.0607	7.6061	7.1909	6.8109	6.4624	6.1422
16	11.6523	10.8378	10.1059	9.4466	8.8514	8.3126	7.8237	7.3792	6.9740	6.6039	6.2651
17	12.1657	11.2741	10.4773	9.7632	9.1216	8.5436	8.0216	7.5488	7.1196	6.7291	6.3729
18	12.6593	11.6896	10.8276	10.0591	9.3719	8.7556	8.2014	7.7016	7.2497	6.8399	6.4674
19	13.1339	12.0853	11.1581	10.3356	9.6036	8.9501	8.3649	7.8393	7.3658	6.9380	6.5504
20	13.5903	12.4622	11.4699	10.5940	9.8181	9.1285	8.5136	7.9633	7.4694	7.0248	6.6231

Future Value of $1

N/R	4%	5%	6%	7%	8%	9%	10%	11%	12%	13%	14%
1	1.0400	1.0500	1.0600	1.0700	1.0800	1.0900	1.1000	1.1100	1.1200	1.1300	1.1400
2	1.0816	1.1025	1.1236	1.1449	1.1664	1.1881	1.2100	1.2321	1.2544	1.2769	1.2996
3	1.1249	1.1576	1.1910	1.2250	1.2597	1.2950	1.3310	1.3676	1.4049	1.4429	1.4815
4	1.1699	1.2155	1.2625	1.3108	1.3605	1.4116	1.4641	1.5181	1.5735	1.6305	1.6890
5	1.2167	1.2763	1.3382	1.4026	1.4693	1.5386	1.6105	1.6851	1.7623	1.8424	1.9254
6	1.2653	1.3401	1.4185	1.5007	1.5869	1.6771	1.7716	1.8704	1.9738	2.0820	2.1950
7	1.3159	1.4071	1.5036	1.6058	1.7138	1.8280	1.9487	2.0762	2.2107	2.3526	2.5023
8	1.3686	1.4775	1.5938	1.7182	1.8509	1.9926	2.1436	2.3045	2.4760	2.6584	2.8526
9	1.4233	1.5513	1.6895	1.8385	1.9990	2.1719	2.3579	2.5580	2.7731	3.0040	3.2519
10	1.4802	1.6289	1.7908	1.9672	2.1589	2.3674	2.5937	2.8394	3.1058	3.3946	3.7072
11	1.5395	1.7103	1.8983	2.1049	2.3316	2.5804	2.8531	3.1518	3.4785	3.8359	4.2262
12	1.6010	1.7959	2.0122	2.2522	2.5182	2.8127	3.1384	3.4985	3.8960	4.3345	4.8179
13	1.6651	1.8856	2.1329	2.4098	2.7196	3.0658	3.4523	3.8833	4.3635	4.8980	5.4924
14	1.7317	1.9799	2.2609	2.5785	2.9372	3.3417	3.7975	4.3104	4.8871	5.5348	6.2613
15	1.8009	2.0789	2.3966	2.7590	3.1722	3.6425	4.1772	4.7846	5.4736	6.2543	7.1379
16	1.8730	2.1829	2.5404	2.9522	3.4259	3.9703	4.5950	5.3109	6.1304	7.0673	8.1372
17	1.9479	2.2920	2.6928	3.1588	3.7000	4.3276	5.0545	5.8951	6.8660	7.9861	9.2765
18	2.0258	2.4066	2.8543	3.3799	3.9960	4.7171	5.5599	6.5436	7.6900	9.0243	10.5752
19	2.1068	2.5270	3.0256	3.6165	4.3157	5.1417	6.1159	7.2633	8.6128	10.1974	12.0557
20	2.1911	2.6533	3.2071	3.8697	4.6610	5.6044	6.7275	8.0623	9.6463	11.5231	13.7435

Future Value of an Ordinary Annuity of $1

N/R	4%	5%	6%	7%	8%	9%	10%	11%	12%	13%	14%
1	1.0000	1.0000	1.0000	1.0000	1.0000	1.0000	1.0000	1.0000	1.0000	1.0000	1.0000
2	2.0400	2.0500	2.0600	2.0700	2.0800	2.0900	2.1000	2.1100	2.1200	2.1300	2.1400
3	3.1216	3.1525	3.1836	3.2149	3.2464	3.2781	3.3100	3.3421	3.3744	3.4069	3.4396
4	4.2465	4.3101	4.3746	4.4399	4.5061	4.5731	4.6410	4.7097	4.7793	4.8498	4.9211
5	5.4163	5.5256	5.6371	5.7507	5.8666	5.9847	6.1051	6.2278	6.3528	6.4803	6.6101
6	6.6330	6.8019	6.9753	7.1533	7.3359	7.5233	7.7156	7.9129	8.1152	8.3227	8.5355
7	7.8983	8.1420	8.3938	8.6540	8.9228	9.2004	9.4872	9.7833	10.0890	10.4047	10.7305
8	9.2142	9.5491	9.8975	10.2598	10.6366	11.0285	11.4359	11.8594	12.2997	12.7573	13.2328
9	10.5828	11.0266	11.4913	11.9780	12.4876	13.0210	13.5795	14.1640	14.7757	15.4157	16.0853
10	12.0061	12.5779	13.1808	13.8164	14.4866	15.1929	15.9374	16.7220	17.5487	18.4197	19.3373
11	13.4864	14.2068	14.9716	15.7836	16.6455	17.5603	18.5312	19.5614	20.6546	21.8143	23.0445
12	15.0258	15.9171	16.8699	17.8885	18.9771	20.1407	21.3843	22.7132	24.1331	25.6502	27.2707
13	16.6268	17.7130	18.8821	20.1406	21.4953	22.9534	24.5227	26.2116	28.0291	29.9847	32.0887
14	18.2919	19.5986	21.0151	22.5505	24.2149	26.0192	27.9750	30.0949	32.3926	34.8827	35.5811
15	20.0236	21.5786	23.2760	25.1290	27.1521	29.3609	31.7725	34.4054	37.2797	40.4175	43.8424
16	21.8245	23.6575	25.6725	27.8881	30.3243	33.0034	35.9497	39.1899	42.7533	46.6717	50.9804
17	23.6975	25.8404	28.2129	30.8402	33.7502	36.9737	40.5447	44.5008	48.8837	53.7391	59.1176
18	25.6454	28.1324	30.9057	33.9990	37.4502	41.3013	45.5992	50.3959	55.7497	61.7251	68.3941
19	27.6712	30.5390	33.7600	37.3790	41.4463	46.0185	51.1591	56.9395	63.4397	70.7494	78.9692
20	29.7781	33.0660	36.7856	40.9955	45.7620	51.1601	57.2750	64.2028	72.0524	80.9468	91.0249

Index